Songs in Collections: An Index

Songs in Collections
An Index

Desiree de Charms & Paul F. Breed

INFORMATION SERVICE INCORPORATED

Information Service Incorporated
1435-37 Randolph
Detroit, Michigan 48226

ACKNOWLEDGMENTS

We wish to acknowledge and thank the many people and institutions who helped this index become a reality. First among them is Kurtz Myers who purchased for the Detroit Public Library all the collections we wished to index. Also we wish to thank the many librarians who answered our questionnaire and the staff members of the Detroit Public Library, the New York Public Library, and the Free Library of Philadelphia whose comments helped us decide which collections should be indexed and how the index should be organized to be of the greatest value to them. The compilation of preliminary lists of collections done by Betty Buyck Stack helped us greatly. Finally for their suggestions, criticisms and general support we wish to thank Bruno Nettl and Florence Kretzschmar.

TABLE OF CONTENTS

INTRODUCTION

An index must have definite limits and conform to specific ideas and standards. Qualitative and quantitative limits must be determined and these are, by and large, determined by the ideas and standards of the compilers. In the compilers' opinion an index of solo songs with piano accompaniment was the primary need. Among the vast quantities of collections available for this medium, collections of art songs and operatic arias were considered the most important for inclusion in this index. An effort was made to index all collections that were published between 1940 and 1957 and a few published before 1940 but not previously indexed. Also a selected group of folk song anthologies was included. Finally, because of the demand felt in libraries, a few collections containing Christmas carols, sacred songs, and community songs were indexed, although some of these were not entirely solo songs with piano accompaniment. Thus, included in the index are a few piano solos, unaccompanied songs, songs primarily for choral groups, and duets. Collections solely of this type of material were excluded. Also excluded were certain types of anthologies: collections of songs by a single composer, hymnals, children's songs, and collections devoted entirely to songs with texts in untransliterated Cyrillic, Greek or Oriental characters.

These qualitative standards, i.e. the restriction to classical, folk, sacred and some popular songs with piano accompaniment, did, in fact, limit the number of collections indexed to four hundred eleven volumes. An alphabetical list of these collections may be found beginning p xi.

In determining how the 9493 songs in these four hundred eleven collections should be indexed the compilers decided to depart quite radically from the practice of previous song indexes. Since the two largest categories consisted of composed songs and anonymous or folk songs, it seemed best to use an alphabetical arrangement by composer's name for the former and a geographical arrangement for the latter. These two parts are followed by separate sections for sea songs and carols. A complete alphabetical title and first line index, and a separate index listing authors form the final sections of the book.

Although the delineations regarding scope and format were ultimately the choice of the compilers, many factors, including the opinions of other librarians, the nature and availability of material, and the use of the index dictated these decisions. The opinions of other librarians as to scope and format were sought through the use of a questionnaire. This questionnaire was sent to over one hundred and fifty public and academic libraries requesting suggestions regarding the kinds of collections and specific titles to be included. The compilers also searched standard bibliographic sources for additional titles suitable for indexing. Included were the subject indexes of the Library of Congress Catalogs and the U.S. Copyright Catalogs, the Cumulated Book Index, publishers' catalogs, lists and reviews in periodicals, bibliographies of song literature and various other sources. The holdings of three large public libraries were examined to discover other titles.

The need felt by librarians for supplemental information other than composer, title and first line to identify the song led the compilers to add as much identifying information as was feasible. The composer's full name with dates was used whenever it could be determined in bibliographic sources. Library of Congress Catalog entries were preferred. Songs or arias forming parts of larger works were entered under the name of the larger work. Original titles, opus numbers, and special numberings such as Köchel, Schmeider, and Deutsch numbers, etc. were added to the entries. First lines of recitatives as well as arias, if they differed from the title of the aria, were also indexed. An attempt was made to determine that a particular song was, in fact, the work of a particular composer.

Supplemental identifying information concerning anonymous songs, folksongs, carols and sea songs is difficult to find so no attempt was made to verify these songs. They were entered alphabetically under geographical origin of these songs, so the country of origin should be used only as a rough guide. However, an attempt was made to enter the same tunes under a single title no matter what text accompanied the tune. This was done by translating and transposing all melodies into letters in the key of C major and interfiling them alphabetically. This is not, in the case of folksongs, a completely reliable method but it did help to discover some songs with different texts but the same melody. Folksongs with the same or very similar texts were entered under the best known title. Variant melodies with the same or similar text were entered under the same index number but with a different letter symbol (A, B, C, etc.) to show that the tune differed significantly from the previous one of the same title. The criteria used to decide whether the tune should be considered different were rather difficult to determine. Many tunes have minor differences in melodic line, minor rhythmic variations, different time signatures, and, of course, widely varying accompaniments. It was finally decided to designate a tune as different only if the melodic line was markedly different. Because variant tunes are entered under alphabetical subheadings with only one marginal reference number, the number of entries, 9493, is not completely accurate in determining the number of different songs indexed. An attempt was made to enter all textual variants under the same title but in case of doubt they were entered under their particular title. Many of the textual variants are so markedly different that their classification under one entry would be misleading to the general user.

The authors of the texts of both anonymous songs and songs by known composers were added to the entries if they were given in the collection indexed. If the composer of the music also wrote the text this was not mentioned. No attempt was made to verify or discover the author of the text if it was not given, nor were birth or death dates given. Librettists of operas were added and verified when possible.

In giving the language of the text for each song, the compilers make no claim to be experts in all the languages indexed. It may be used as a rough guide. We are grateful for the assistance given us by Willem Adriansz in the identifications of the various languages of the Netherlands and to Dragon Plamenac for his help with the Serbo-Croatian languages.

1   ADLER, KURT, 1907-   comp.
     Operatic anthology; celebrated arias selected from operas by old and modern composers in five volumes. Vol. 1
     Soprano. N.Y., G. Schirmer, c1903, 1955. 334p Pl no 16361 (43 arias in original language and English)

2   ADLER, KURT, 1907-   comp.
     Operatic anthology; celebrated arias selected from operas by old and modern composers in five volumes. Vol. 2
     Mezzo-soprano and alto. N.Y., G. Schirmer, c1903, 1954. 277p Pl no 16362

3   ADLER, KURT, 1907-   comp.
     Operatic anthology; celebrated arias selected from operas by old and modern composers in five volumes. Vol. 3
     Tenor. N.Y., G. Schirmer, c1904, 1954. 241p Pl no 16363 (41 songs)

4   ADLER, KURT, 1907-   comp.
     Operatic anthology; celebrated arias selected from operas by old and modern composers in five volumes. Vol. 4
     Baritone. N.Y., G. Schirmer, c1904, 1953. 278p Pl no 16364 (37 songs)

5   ADLER, KURT, 1907-   comp.
     Operatic anthology; celebrated arias selected from operas by old and modern composers in five volumes. Vol. 5
     Bass. N.Y., G. Schirmer, c1904, 1956. 267p Pl no 16365 (41 songs)

6   ADLER, KURT, 1907-   ed.
     The prima donna's album. 42 celebrated arias from famous operas. Newly revised. N.Y., G. Schirmer, c1946.
     298p Pl no 12727 (Text in the original language and English)

7   ADLER, KURT, 1907-   ed. and arr.
     Songs of many wars from the sixteenth to the twentieth century. N.Y., Howell, Soskin, 1943. 221p (65 songs;
     English words with music, original language words printed after each song)

8   ALBUM of eight sacred songs: high voice, low voice. Boston, Boston Music Co., N.Y., G. Schirmer, 1912. 42p
     Pl no B.M.Co.4284/2841

9   ANDRÉ, JULIE, ed.
     Songs from south of the border; with original Spanish text; English adaptation by Albert Gamse; supervised by
     Enric Madriguera. N.Y., E. B. Marks Music Corp., 1946. 64p Pl no 12376-56 (20 songs)

10   ARNOLD, JAY, ed.
     Songs for Americans. N.Y., Manhattan Pubs., 1940. 64p (51 songs)

11   ATTAWAY, WILLIAM
     Calypso song book; ed. and comp. by L. K. Engle, illustrations by William Charmatz. N.Y., McGraw-Hill,
     c1957. 64p (25 songs)

12   BAL Y GAY, JESÚS, comp. and arr.
     Romances y villancicos españoles del siglo XVI; dispuestos en edición moderna para canto y piano. Primera
     serie. n. p. La Casa de España en Mexico, 1939. 47p (15 songs)

13   BANTOCK, SIR GRANVILLE, 1868-1946, ed.
     Songs of England. Book 1. London, W. Paxton, 1940. 32p Pl no Paxton 15588 (23 songs)

14   BANTOCK, SIR GRANVILLE, 1868-1946, ed.
     Songs of England. Book 2. London, W. Paxton, 1943. 32p Pl no Paxton 15619 (19 songs)

15   BANTOCK, SIR GRANVILLE, 1868-1946, ed.
     Songs of Ireland. Book 1. London, W. Paxton, 1940. 32p Pl no 15590 (17 songs)

16   BANTOCK, SIR GRANVILLE, 1868-1946, ed.
     Songs of Ireland. (2nd collection). London, W. Paxton, 1945. 32p Pl no 15638 (16 songs)

17   BANTOCK, SIR GRANVILLE, 1868-1946, ed.
     Songs of Scotland. 1st collection. London, W. Paxton, 1940. 32p Pl no 15589 (21 songs)

18   BANTOCK, SIR GRANVILLE, 1868-1946, ed.
         Songs of Scotland. 2nd collection. London, W. Paxton, 1945. 32p Pl no 15639 (17 songs)

19   BANTOCK, SIR GRANVILLE, 1868-1946, ed.
         Songs of Wales. (1st collection). London, W. Paxton, 1942. 31p Pl no 15591 (15 songs)

20   BANTOCK, SIR GRANVILLE, 1868-1946, ed.
         Songs of Wales. (2nd collection). London, W. Paxton, 1946. 32p Pl no 15647 (16 songs)

21   BARBEAU, CHARLES MARIUS, 1883-   ed.
         Dansons à la ronde; danses et jeux populaires recueillis au Canada et en Nouvelle-Angleterre; accompagnements
         de piano Maurice Blackburn; interpretetes en anglais par Joy Tranter; illustrations de Marjorie Borden; couverture
         de Grace Melvin. Ottawa, Ministere du Nord canadien et des Ressources nationales, 1958. 104p. Musée National
         du Canada, Bulletin no. 151, No. 41 de la serie anthropologique. (21 songs; two arrangements of each song are
         given, the first of which is simplified)

22   BARTÓK, BÉLA, 1881-1945
         Eight Hungarian folksongs. Acht ungarische Volkslieder (1907-17). Voice and piano, Gesang und Klavier.
         London, Hawkes & Son, c1939, c1955. 19p Pl no B.&H. 18065 (Words in Hungarian, English and German;
         English version by Nancy Bush)

23   BARTÓK, BÉLA, 1881-1945
         Magyar Népdalok; énekhangra zongorakísérettel... Ungarische volkslieder mit Ungarischem text für gesang
         mit klavier; Hungarian folksongs with Hungarian words for song with piano. Budapest, Zeneműkiado Vallalat,
         1906. 26p Z. 1175 (20 songs)

24   BARTÓK, BÉLA, 1881-1945
         Zwanzig ungarische Volkslieder. Twenty Hungarian folksongs. I. Lieder der Trauer. Gesang und Klavier.
         London, Hawkes & Son, c1932. 15p Pl no B.&H. 17651 (4 songs in Hungarian and German)

25   BARTÓK, BÉLA, 1881-1945
         Zwanzig ungarische Volkslieder. Twenty Hungarian folksongs. II. Tanzlieder. Gesang und Klavier. London,
         Hawkes & Son, c1939. 21p Pl no B.&H. 17652 (4 songs in Hungarian and German)

26   BARTÓK, BÉLA, 1881-1945
         Zwanzig ungarische Volkslieder. Twenty Hungarian folksongs. III Diverse Lieder. Gesang und Klavier. London,
         Hawkes & Son, c1939. 25p Pl no B.&H. 17653 (7 songs in Hungarian and German)

27   BARTOK, BELA, 1881-1945
         Zwanzig ungarische Volkslieder. Twenty Hungarian folksongs. IV. Lieder der Jugend. Gesang und Klavier.
         London, Hawkes & Son, c1939. 12p Pl no B.&H. 17654 (5 songs in Hungarian and German)

28   BEATTIE, JOHN W.
         The new blue book of favorite songs, the golden book of favorite songs and the grey book of favorite songs
         combined with an enlarged supplement. 341 selections. Chicago, Hall & McCreary, c1941. 286p

29   BENNELL, RAYMOND, 1910-   arr.
         The Shell book of sea chanties; editor, Hereward King; book designed by G. E. Evans; musical editor, Gordon
         Hitchcock. London, Shell Petroleum Co., sole distributors: E. H. Freeman Co., c1952. 63p (25 songs)

30   BINDER, ABRAHAM WOLF, ed. and arr.
         Pioneer songs of Israel (Shire' Chalutzim); English adaptations by Olga Paul. N.Y., E. B. Marks, 1942. 44p
         Pl no 11722-40 (20 songs)

31   BÖHME, ERDMANN WERNER, arr.
         Deutsche Lieder, Singsang und Klingklang. Weisen aus dem Allgemeinen deutschen Kommersbuch. [Bearbeitet
         von Erdmann Werner Böhme in Verbindung mit Walther Haas.] Lahr in Baden, Moritz Schauenburg, 1956. 417p
         (288 songs)

32   BONI, MARGARET BRADFORD, 1893-   ed.
         Favorite American songs. Arranged for the piano by Norman Lloyd; illustrated by Aurelius Battaglia, with a
         foreword by Carl Van Doren. N.Y., Simon & Schuster, c1956. 128p (46 songs selected from the Fireside Book
         of Favorite American songs)

33 BONI, MARGARET BRADFORD, 1893-   ed.
    Favorite Christmas carols; fifty-nine Yuletide songs both old and new. Arranged for the piano by Norman Lloyd; illustrated by Peter Spier. N.Y., Simon & Schuster, c1957. 128p (for voice and piano)

34 BONI, MARGARET BRADFORD, 1893-   ed.
    The fireside book of favorite American songs. Arranged for the piano by Norman Lloyd; illustrated by Aurelius Battaglia, introduction by Anne Brooks, with a foreword by Carl Van Doren. N.Y., Simon & Schuster, c1952. 359p (132 songs)

35 BONI, MARGARET BRADFORD, 1893-   ed.
    Fireside book of folk songs. Arranged for the piano by Norman Lloyd; illustrated by Alice and Martin Provensen. N.Y., Simon & Schuster, c1947. 323p (147 songs)

36 BONI, MARGARET BRADFORD, 1893-   ed.
    Fireside book of love songs. Arranged for the piano by Norman Lloyd. N.Y., Simon & Schuster, 1954. 324p (111 folksongs, popular songs and art songs in English and in some cases the original language)

37 BOTSFORD, FLORENCE HUDSON (TOPPING), comp.
    The universal folk songster for home, school and community. N.Y., G. Schirmer, 1937. 154p (125 songs; many part songs included)

38 BOZYAN, HAGOP FRANK, 1899-   and LOVETT, SIDNEY, eds.
    The Yale carol book. London, Humphrey Milford, Oxford Univ. Press, Yale Univ. Press, 1944. 58p (35 songs)

39 BOZYAN, HAGOP FRANK, 1899-   and LOVETT, SIDNEY, eds.
    The Yale carol book, Rev. ed. London, Geoffrey Cumberlege, Oxford Univ. Press, Yale Univ. Press, 1950. not paged (40 songs, including 5 songs not in the 1944 edition)

40 BRADDICK, G. M. and MARE, M. L., eds.
    Stimmen des deutschen Volkes. Vol. 1: Um den Christbaum und in der Schule. London, Methuen, 1952. (47 songs)

41 BRADDICK, G. M. and MARE, M. L., eds.
    Stimmen des deutschens Volkes. Vol 2: Aus allen deutschen Gauen. London, Methuen, 1952. (40 songs)

42 BRADDICK, G. M. and MARE, M. L., eds.
    Stimmen des deutschen Volkes. Vol. 3: Was wir alle singen. London, Methuen, 1954. (41 songs)

43 BRADDICK, G. M. and MARE, M. L., eds.
    Stimmen des deutschen Volkes. Vol. 4: Bei Soldaten und Studenten. London, Methuen, 1954. 24p (38 songs)

44 BRAND, OSCAR, comp.
    Singing holidays; the calendar in folk song. Musical arrangements by Douglas Townsend. Illustrated by Roberta Moynihan. N.Y., Knopf, c1957. 258p (90 songs)

45 BREACH, WILLIAM, ed.
    Art-song argosy; a collection for use in class voice instruction, medium high voice [and] medium low voice. N.Y., G. Schirmer, 1937. 2 vols. 74p, 74p Pl no 37421; Pl no 37614 (25 songs)

46 BRITTEN, BENJAMIN, 1913-   arr.
    Benjamin Britten folk-song arrangements. Vol. 1, British Isles (for medium voice). N.Y., Boosey & Hawkes, 1943. 22p (7 songs)

47 BRITTEN, BENJAMIN, 1913-   arr.
    Benjamin Britten folk-song arrangements. Vol. 2, France. N.Y., Boosey & Hawkes, 1946. 40p Pl no H15754 (2 parts, high and medium voice, with the same songs in each part; 8 songs)

48 BRITTEN, BENJAMIN, 1913-   arr.
    Benjamin Britten folk-song arrangements. Vol. 3, British Isles. N.Y., Boosey & Hawkes, 1947. 28p (2 parts; high voice, Pl no B.&H. 16189; medium voice, Pl no B.&H. 16412; 7 songs, the same in each part)

49 BRUDER singer. Lieder unseres Volkes. Klavierausgabe. Kassel und Basel, Bärenreiter, 1956. 141p (282 songs)

50 BUNJES, PAUL, ed.
    Wedding blessings, a collection of sacred solos and a duet for church weddings. St. Louis, Mo., Concordia, 1952? 35p (12 songs)

51 BURKHART, FRANZ
    Bella Italia! Zwanzig italienische volkslieder für Gesang und Klavier neu gesetzt; deutsche nachdichtungen von
    Fritz Koselka. Wien, Universal, c1933. 47p Pl no U.E.10581

52 BURLEIGH, HARRY THACKER, 1866-   arr.
    Album of Negro spirituals, arranged for solo voice. N.Y., G. Ricordi, 1928. (2 parts: part 1, high voice, Pl no
    1432; part 2, low voice, Pl no 1433; 48p in each part). (12 songs, the same in each part)

53 BUXÓ, T., ed.
    Veinticinco cañciones populares catalanas navideñas. Cuaderno 1. Madrid, Unión Musical Española, 1950. 17p
    Pl no 18520-1 (7 songs)

54 BUXÓ, T., ed.
    Veinticinco cañciones populares catalanas navideñas. Cuaderno 2. Madrid, Unión Musical Española, 1951. 13p
    Pl no 18520-2 (6 songs)

55 BUXÓ, T., ed.
    Veinticinco cañciones populares catalanas navideñas. Cuaderno 3. Madrid, Unión Musical Española, 1951. 13p
    Pl no 18520-3 (6 songs)

56 BUXÓ, T., ed.
    Veinticinco cañciones populares catalanas navideñas. Cuaderno 4. Madrid, Unión Musical Española, 1951. 17p
    Pl no 18520-4 (6 songs)

57 CANÇÕES populares Portuguesas. Lisbon, Edicões do Gabinete de Estudos Musicais da Emissora Nacional de Radio-
    difusão, 1944. 64p (Álbums de Musica Portuguesa, Vol. 1). (24 songs)

58 CANÇÕES populares Portuguesas. Lisbon, Edicões do Gabinete de Estudos Musicais da Emissora Nacional de Radio-
    difusão, 1948. 64p (Álbums de Musica Portuguesa, Vol. 2). (23 songs)

59 CANTELOUBE, JOSEPH, 1879-   ed.
    Airs tendres des XVIIe et XVIIIe siècles. Paris, Heugel, c1949. 19p Pl no H.31270 (5 songs)

60 CANTELOUBE, JOSEPH, 1879-   ed.
    Chansons galantes du XVIIIme siècle pour voix seule avec accompagnement de piano (ou clavecin). Paris,
    Heugel, c1934. 10p Pl no H.30,748-H.30,751 (4 songs)

61 CANTELOUBE, JOSEPH, 1879-   ed.
    Chansons galantes du XVIIIme siècle (2me série) pour voix seule avec accompagnement de piano (ou clavecin).
    Paris, Heugel, c1946. 13p Pl no H.31067-H.31071 (5 songs)

62 CANTELOUBE, JOSEPH, 1879-   ed.
    Chants d'Auvergne. 1re Serie. Paris, Heugel, 1924. 24p Pl no D'Auvergne-Series 1-28 (5 songs)

63 CANTELOUBE, JOSEPH, 1879-   ed.
    Chants d'Auvergne. 2me Serie. Paris, Heugel, 1924. 25p Pl no H.28,797 (6 songs)

64 CANTELOUBE, JOSEPH, 1879-   ed.
    Chants d'Auvergne. 3me Serie. Paris, Heugel, 1927. 22p Pl no H.29,796 (5 songs)

65 CANTELOUBE, JOSEPH, 1879-   ed.
    Chants d'Auvergne. 4me Serie. Paris, Heugel, 1930. 36p Pl no H.30,377 (6 songs)

66 CANTELOUBE, JOSEPH, 1879-   ed.
    Chants d'Auvergne. 5me Serie. Paris, Heugel, 1955. 37p Pl no H.31683 (8 songs)

67 CANTELOUBE, JOSEPH, 1879-   ed.
    Chants de France. 1st series. Paris, Durand, 1948. 31p Pl no D.& F.13,317 (6 songs)

68 CANTELOUBE, JOSEPH, 1879-   ed.
    Chants de France. 2nd series. Paris, Durand, 1948. 33p Pl no D.& F 13,318 (6 songs)

69 CANTELOUBE, JOSEPH, 1879-   ed.
    Noëls populaires français de Roussillon Guyenne, Auvergne, Languedoc, Flandre et Bourgogne harmonisés.
    Paris, Heugel, c1949. 20p Pl no H.31271 (7 songs)

70 CASTAGNETTA, GRACE, 1912- and VAN LOON, HENDRIK WILLEM, 1882-1944, eds.
   Folk songs of many lands. N.Y., Simon & Schuster, 1938. 96p (24 songs)

71 CATHOLIC solo hymns; fifteen compositions with English texts for medium voice and organ. Boston, McLaughlin &
   Reilly, 1951. Vol. 1. 39p Pl no M&R Co.1568.171417-2(1568) and others

72 CAZDEN, NORMAN, 1914- ed.
   The Abelard folk song book. More than 101 ballads to sing, arranged for piano and guitar; illustrated by Abner
   Graboff. N.Y., and London, Abelard Schuman, 1958. 255p (102 songs)

73 CERÓN, JOSÉ DOLORES, comp.
   Canciones Dominicanas antiguas; compiladas, transcriptas y arregladas para voz y piano. Editora Montalvo,
   Ciudad Trujillo, Republica Dominicana, 1947. 143p (48 songs)

73a ČESKÁ moderní píseň; album písní českých moderních skladatelů. Das moderne tschechische Lied, Liederalbum
   der modernen tschechischen Komponisten. Vol. 1. Praha, Hudební matice umělecké besedy, Leipzig, Breitkopf
   & Härtel, 1925. 41p Pl no H.M.188 (361/I) (11 songs)

74 ČESKÁ moderní píseň; album písní českých moderních skladatelů. Das moderne tschechische Lied, Liederalbum
   der modernen tschechischen Komponisten. Vol. 2. Praha, Hudební matice umělecké besedy, Leipzig, Breitkopf
   & Härtel, 1925. 41p Pl no H.M.45 (361/II) (9 songs)

75 CHAMBERS, HERBERT ARTHUR, 1880- ed.
   A Shakespeare song book. London, Blandford, 1957. 62p Pl no B.P.105 (16 songs from Morley to Sullivan set
   to Shakespeare texts)

76 CHAMBERS, HERBERT ARTHUR, 1880- ed.
   The treasury of Negro spirituals. London, Blandford, 1953. 125p (42 songs)

77 CLARK, ROGIE, comp. and arr.
   Copper sun, a collection of Negro folk songs for voice and piano. Bryn Mawr, Pa., Theodore Presser, c1957.
   45p Pl no 411-41007-44 (16 songs)

78 CLARK, ROGIE, comp. and arr.
   Negro art songs; album by contemporary composers for voice and piano. N.Y., E. B. Marks, c1946. 72p
   Pl no 12297-5Ph/12229 5-5 (18 songs)

79 COLEMAN, SATIS NARRONA (BARTON), 1878-
   Christmas carols from many countries, a collection of old favorites, familiar carols with new settings, carols in
   original foreign languages and newly translated carols arranged for unchanged voices. N.Y., G. Schirmer, c1934.
   101p Pl no 36381 (83 songs)

80 COLEMAN, SATIS NARRONA (BARTON), 1878- and BREGMAN, ADOLPH
   Songs of American folks. N.Y., John Day, c1942. 128p (47 American folksongs)

81 COMBS, JOSIAH HENRY, 1886- ed.
   Folksongs from the Kentucky Highlands; with piano accompaniments by Keith Mixson. N.Y., G. Schirmer,
   c1939. 40p Pl no 38296 (Schirmer's American Folk-Song Series, Set 1). (16 songs)

82 CONNISTON, RUTH MUZZY
   Chantons un peu; a collection of French songs, with games, dances, and costumes, grammar drill and vocabulary.
   N.Y., Doubleday, Doran, 1929. 148p (56 songs)

83 COPLAND, AARON, 1900- arr.
   Old American songs (newly arranged) first set. N.Y., Boosey & Hawkes, c1950. 24p Pl no U.S. Bk.229 (5 songs)

84 COPLAND, AARON, 1900- arr.
   Old American songs, second set. N.Y., Boosey & Hawkes, c1954. 28p Pl no B.&H. 17485 (5 songs)

85 COS COB song volume, ten songs by American composers; Bowles, Blitzstein, Chanler, Citkowitz, Copland, Heilner,
   Ives, Lipsky, Sessions, Thomson. N.Y., Cos Cob, c1935. 32p

86 COWELL, HENRY, 1897- ed.
   United Nations; songs of the people. English adaptations by Robert Sour. N.Y., Broadcast Music, 1945. 101p
   (96 songs arranged in simple four-part harmony)

87   DANISH national music; national songs, morning and evening songs; folk songs and the most popular Danish music to operas and plays; English translations by Evelyn Heepe and Charles Bratli. Dansk Nationalmusik; Faedrelands-sange Morgen-og Aftensange - Folkeviser og den mest populaere danske dramatiske Musik. Copenhagen, Wilhelm Hansen, 1939. 51p Pl no 24975 (36 songs)

88   DAVIES, (SIR) HENRY WALFORD, 1869-   arr.
French songs. Selected by L. Lamport-Smith. London, Macmillan, 1938. 141p (70 songs)

89   DAVIS, KATHERINE KENNICOTT, 1892-   and LORING, NANCY, eds. and arr.
Sing unto the Lord; twenty sacred solos for medium voice and piano or organ. With original, paraphrased and adapted texts by K. K. Davis. N.Y., Carl Fischer, 1948. Vol. 1. 43p Pl no 30239-39N1292

90   DAVIS, KATHERINE KENNICOTT, 1892-   and LORING, NANCY, eds. and arr.
Sing unto the Lord; twenty sacred solos for medium voice and piano or organ. With original, paraphrased and adapted texts by K. K. Davis. N.Y., Carl Fischer, 1948. Vol. 2. 43p Pl no 30302-39N1293

91   DELOUP, RENÉ, ed. and arr.
Vieilles chansons et rondes francaises. Paris, Max Eschig, London, Schott, 1939. 95p Pl no B.S.S 35814 (86 songs)

92   DEMÉNY, DESIDERIUS, ed.
50 Magyar Nóta; 50 Hungarian songs; 50 Ungarische Lieder. English translations by E. M. Lockwood; deutsche Übersetzungen von Adalbert Heidelberg. Milano, Suvini Zerboni, 1952. 52p Pl no S.4761 Z

93   DE SEGUROLA, ANDRES, 1875-   ed.
Deanna Durbin's favorite songs and arias; new English lyrics by Ann Ronell. N.Y., G. Schirmer, 1939. 61p Pl no 38589 (10 songs)

94   DEUTSCH, LEONHARD, 1887-   comp. and arr.
Slovensky si Spievaj; a treasury of Slovak folk songs under general editorship of J. J. Lach; introductions by M. K. Mlynarovich and A. P. Lesinsky; explanatory notes and editing of Slovak lyrics by Francis Hrušofský; English verses by W. R. Trask; illustrations by Joseph Cincik. N.Y., Crown c1950. 127p (96 songs in English and literary Slovak)

95   DEUTSCH, LEONHARD, 1887-   comp. and arr.
A treasury of the world's finest folk song; with explanatory text by Claude Simpson, lyrics versified by W. R. Trask. N.Y., Howell, Soskin, c1942. 430p (171 songs; English only)

96   DAS DEUTSCHE Kunstlied; eine Auswahl von Liedern für eine Singstimme und Klavier für den Musikunterricht an höheren Lehranstalten. Herausgegeben vom "Verband der Lehrer für Musik an den höheren-Lehranstalten in Bayern." Heft 1, Edition Schott 4265. Mainz, B. Schott, c1951. 39p Pl no B.S.S 37750 (20 songs)

97   DAS DEUTSCHE Kunstlied; eine Auswahl von Liedern für eine Singstimme und Klavier für den Musikunterricht an höheren Lehranstalten. Herausgegeben vom "Verband der Lehrer für Musik an den höheren-Lehranstalten in Bayern." Heft 2, Edition Schott 4266. Mainz, B. Schott, c1951. 39p Pl no B.S.S 37751 (16 songs)

98   DAS DEUTSCHE Kunstlied; eine Auswahl von Liedern für eine Singstimme und Klavier für den Musikunterricht an höheren Lehranstalten. Herausgegeben vom "Verband der Lehrer für Musik an den höheren-Lehranstalten in Bayern." Heft 3, Edition Schott 4267. Mainz, B. Schott, c1951. 39p Pl no B.S.S 37752 (19 songs)

99   DEUTSCHER Liederschatz, die schoensten Weisen der alten Sammlung Ludwig Erks neu bearbeitet und durch hundert Lieder vermehrt. Leipzig, C. F. Peters, 1956? 254p Edition Peters nr. 395. Pl no 10613 (215 songs)

100   DIACK, JOHN MICHAEL, 1869-   ed.
The Scottish Orpheus; adopted by the Scottish National Song Society and the St. Andrew Society as an authoritative collection of the songs of Scotland. Piano accompaniments by J. M. Diack. Vol. 1. London, Paterson's Pubs., c1949 (posthumous pub) 159p (100 songs)

101   DIACK, JOHN MICHAEL, 1869-   ed.
The new Scottish Orpheus; adopted by the Scottish National Song Society as an authoritative collection of the songs of Scotland. Piano accompaniments by J. M. Diack. Vol. 2. London, Paterson's Pubs., c1924. 152p (82 songs)

102   DIACK, JOHN MICHAEL, 1869-   ed. and arr.
A selection of Scottish songs from the three volumes of the New Scottish Orpheus; baritone album. London, Paterson's Pubs., 1922. 80p (44 songs)

103   DIACK, JOHN MICHAEL, 1869-   ed. and arr.
        A selection of Scottish songs from the three volumes of the New Scottish Orpheus; contralto album. London, Paterson's Pubs., 1939. 80p (48 songs)

104   DIACK, JOHN MICHAEL, 1869-   ed. and arr.
        A selection of Scottish songs from the three volumes of the New Scottish Orpheus; soprano album. London, Paterson's Pubs., 1939. 80p (54 songs)

105   DIACK, JOHN MICHAEL, 1869-   ed. and arr.
        A selection of Scottish songs from the three volumes of the New Scottish Orpheus; tenor album. London, Paterson's Pubs., 1939. 80p (48 songs)

106   DOLMETSCH, ARNOLD, ed.
        Select English songs and dialogues of the 16th and 17th centuries. Book 1. London, Boosey, 1898. 36p Pl no H 2281 (9 solo songs, 3 duets; no titles given for the songs)

107   DOLMETSCH, ARNOLD, ed.
        Select English songs and dialogues of the 16th and 17th centuries. Book 2. London, Boosey, 1912. 34p Pl no H 7544 (11 songs, 1 duet)

108   DOLMETSCH, ARNOLD, ed.
        Select French songs from the 12th to the 18th century. London, Boosey, 1938. 37p Pl no H 14833 (14 songs)

109   DOWNES OLIN, 1886-   and SIEGMEISTER, ELIE, 1909-
        A treasury of American song. N.Y., Howell, Soskin, c1940. 351p (143 songs; a few songs from this collection were not included in the second edition, 1943)

110   DOWNES, OLIN, 1886-   and SIEGMEISTER, ELIE, 1909-
        A treasury of American song. Music arranged by E. Siegmeister. 2nd ed. rev. and enl. N.Y., Knopf, 1943. 408p (191 songs)

111   DYER-BENNETT, RICHARD
        Richard Dyer-Bennett, the 20th century minstrel; a collection of 20 songs and ballads with guitar and piano accompaniment; piano settings by John Ward. N.Y., Leeds Music, 1946. 48p

112   EASTON, FLORENCE
        Fifty selected songs, by Schubert, Schumann, Brahms, Wolf, and Strauss; original texts with English versions. N.Y., G. Schirmer, c1951. 2v. (Schirmer's library of musical classics, vols. 1754 and 1755; vol. 1754, high voice, 212p; vol. 1755, low voice, 212p) (German and English words)

113   ESPINEL, LUISA, comp.
        Canciones de mi padre, Spanish folksongs from southern Arizona collected by Luisa Espinel from her father Don Federico Ronstadt y Redondo. Tuscon, c1946. 56p (University of Arizona Bulletin, General Bulletin no. 10) (16 songs)

114   EVERYBODY'S favorite songs of the gay nineties. N.Y., Amsco Music, c1934? 191p (87 songs)

115   EWEN, DAVID, 1907-   ed.
        Songs of America; a cavalcade of popular songs. Arrangements by Mischa and Wesley Portnoff. Chicago, Ziff-Davis, 1947. 246p (58 songs)

116   FELLOWES, EDMUND HORACE, 1870-1951, ed. and arr.
        Forty Elizabethan songs; with the original accompaniments. Book 1. London, Stainer & Bell, n.d. 23p Pl no S.&B. 3999

117   FELLOWES, EDMUND HORACE, 1870-1951, ed. and arr.
        Forty Elizabethan songs; with the original accompaniments. Book 2. London, Stainer & Bell, n.d. 19p Pl no S.&B. 4000

118   FELLOWES, EDMUND HORACE, 1870-1951, ed. and arr.
        Forty Elizabethan songs; with the original accompaniments. Book 3. London, Stainer & Bell, n.d. 18p Pl no S.&B. 4001 (for low voice)

119   FELLOWES, EDMUND HORACE, 1870-1951, ed. and arr.
        Forty Elizabethan songs; with the original accompaniments. Book 4. London, Stainer & Bell, n.d. 20p Pl no S.&B. 4002 (for low voice)

120   FELTON, HAROLD W., 1902-   comp.
        Cowboy jamboree; western songs and lore. Musical arrangements by E. S. Breck. N.Y., Knopf, c1951. 107p
        (20 songs)

121   FIFTY art songs from the modern repertoire. N.Y., G. Schirmer, c1939. 214p Pl no 38818

122   FIFTY-SIX songs you like to sing. N.Y., G. Schirmer, c1937. 200p Pl no 37700

123   FIFTY-TWO sacred songs you like to sing. N.Y., G. Schirmer, c1939. 233p Pl no 38640

124   FINLAND sings; Finland in music and pictures. Suomi laulaa, Suomi sävelin ja kuvin. Helsinki, Fazer, c1952.
        96p Pl no F.M. 3125 (50 songs in Finnish and English)

125   THE J. FISCHER & BRO. collection of Christmas carols for choir, chorus or community singing. N.Y., J. Fischer,
        1945. 27p Pl no J.F.&B. 8149-26 (25 carols)

126   FLANDERS, HELEN (HARTNESS), 1891-   comp.
        Country songs of Vermont; with piano accompaniments by Helen Norfleet. N.Y., G. Schirmer, c1937. 49p
        Pl no 36594 (24 songs)

127   FOSS, HUBERT JAMES, 1899-   arr.
        A book of French songs; selected by E. M. Stephan; arranged with pianoforte accompaniment by H. J. Foss.
        London, Oxford Univ. Press, 1939. 73p (54 songs)

128   FREY, HUGO, ed. and arr.
        Fifty famous favorites and fifty other favorites. N.Y., Robbins Music, c1942. 95p

129   FREY, HUGO, ed.
        Robbins mammoth collection of American songs. N.Y., Robbins Music, c1941. 256p (Mammoth series no.11)
        (229 songs)

130   FREY, HUGO, ed.
        Robbins mammoth collection of American songs. N.Y., Robbins Music, c1941. 192p (Mammoth series no.11)
        (180 songs; this collection is different from the preceding only in arrangement of title page, number of songs,
        and number of pages; all songs in this collection are also in the preceding collection; 49 songs in the preceding
        collection are not in this collection)

131   FREY, HUGO, ed.
        Robbins mammoth collection of songs of the gay nineties. N.Y., Robbins Music, c1942. 256p (Mammoth
        series no.17) (122 songs)

132   FREY, HUGO, ed.
        Robbins mammoth collection of world famous songs. N.Y., Robbins Music, 1939. 256p (Mammoth series
        no.2) (224 songs)

133   FRIEL, REDMOND, ed. and arr.
        The Paterson Irish song book. London, Paterson's Pubs., 1957. 32p (21 songs; some titles in Gaelic and English -
        only English titles are indexed)

134   FUCHS, ALBERT, 1858-1910, ed.
        Italian songs of the late 18th century for voice and piano. English translation by Waldo Lyman. Medium.
        N.Y., International Music, c1954. 85p (20 songs in Italian and English)

135   GANSCHOW, THEODORE F., comp. and arr.
        Memories of Sweden; a collection of its best loved melodies with English and the original Swedish text; English
        lyrics by Olga Paul. N.Y., E. B. Marks, c1937. 48p Pl no 10804-47 (29 songs)

136   GLENN, MABELLE, 1881-   and SPOUSE, ALFRED, eds.
        Art songs for school and studio (for medium high voice). Vol.2. Phila., Oliver Ditson, 1930. 64p Pl no
        76112-3/ML-97-3 (25 songs)

137   GLENN, MABELLE, 1881-   and SPOUSE, ALFRED, eds.
        Art songs for school and studio (for medium low voice). Vol.2. Boston, Oliver Ditson, 1930. 64p (23 songs)

138   GLENN, MABELLE, 1881-   and TAYLOR, BERNARD U., eds.
          Classic Italian songs for school and studio; issued for medium high [and] medium low [voice]. Vol. 1 Bryn
          Mawr, Pa., Oliver Ditson, 1936. 64p (In 2 parts: medium high, Pl no ML-3041-4,3033-5 and others; medium
          low ML-3031-4,3073-5 and others) (18 songs, the same in each part)

139   GLENN, MABELLE, 1881-   and TAYLOR, BERNARD U., eds.
          Classic Italian songs for school and studio; issued for medium high [and] medium low [voice]. Vol. 2 Bryn
          Mawr, Pa., Theodore Presser, Oliver Ditson, 1949. 64p (In 2 parts: medium low, Pl no ML-3071-3,3156-5
          and others; medium high, Pl no ML-3031-31,3116-5 and others) (15 songs, the same in each part)

140   GLENN, MABELLE, 1881-   and TAYLOR, BERNARD U., eds.
          French art songs for school and studio. Issued for medium high [and] medium low [voice]. Phila., Oliver
          Ditson, 1937. 64p (In 2 parts: medium high, Pl no 77983-1, ML-528-3 and others; medium low, Pl no
          5-128-71057-1, ML-752-3 and others) (20 songs, the same in each part)

141   GOLDE, WALTER, 1887-   ed.
          Easy German classic songs. English translations by Constance Wardle. Bryn Mawr, Pa., Oliver Ditson, 1952.
          58p Pl no 431-41002-58 (29 songs)

142   GOYA, MANUEL, ed.
          Mexican and Spanish songs; the English texts by F. H. Martens and others; new and enl. ed. Philadelphia,
          Oliver Ditson, 1938. 51p Pl no 76149-3 and others (14 songs for high voice)

143   GRAND opera arias; with the original and English text; soprano. N.Y., G. Ricordi, 1928 (32 songs)

144   GREENBERG, NOAH, ed.
          An Elizabethan song book, lute songs, madrigals and rounds. Music edited by Noah Greenberg; text edited by
          W. H. Auden and Chester Kallman. Garden City, N.Y., Doubleday, 1956. 240p (84 songs; 12 part songs
          included)

145   GRENELL, HORACE, ed. and arr.
          Young people's records folk song book compiled. Illustrated by Ajay. N.Y., Young People's Records, 1949.
          48p (39 songs with very simple accompaniments)

146   GROVLEZ, GABRIEL, ed.
          Les plus beaux airs de l'opéra françois; transcrits et mis en recueils. English version by Percy Pinkerton. Baritone
          and bass, Vol. 1. London, J. & W. Chester, 1924. 24p Pl no 38891-38897 (7 songs)

147   GROVLEZ, GABRIEL, ed.
          Les plus beaux airs de l'opéra françois; transcrits et mis en recueils. English version by Percy Pinkerton. Baritone
          and bass, Vol. 2. London, J. & W. Chester, 1924. 27p Pl no 38898-388912 (5 songs)

148   GROVLEZ, GABRIEL, ed.
          Les plus beaux airs de l'opéra françois; transcrits et mis en recueils. English version by Percy Pinkerton. Mezzo-
          soprano and contralto, Vol. 1. London, J. & W. Chester, 1924. 24p Pl no J.W.C. 38871-38876 (6 songs)

149   GROVLEZ, GABRIEL, ed.
          Les plus beaux airs de l'opéra françois; transcrits et mis en recueils. English version by Percy Pinkerton. Mezzo-
          soprano and contralto, Vol. 2. London, J. & W. Chester, 1924. 22p (25-46) Pl no J.W.C. 38877-388712
          (6 songs)

150   GROVLEZ, GABRIEL, ed.
          Les plus beaux airs de l'opéra françois; transcrits et mis en recueils. English version by Percy Pinkerton.
          Soprano, Vol. 1. London, J. & W. Chester, c1924. 28p Pl no J.C.W. 38861-38866 (6 songs)

151   GROVLEZ, GABRIEL, ed.
          Les plus beaux airs de l'opéra françois; transcrits et mis en recueils. English version by Percy Pinkerton.
          Soprano, Vol. 2. London, J. & W. Chester, 1924. 32p (29-61) Pl no 38867-388612 (6 songs)

152   GROVLEZ, GABRIEL, ed.
          Les plus beaux airs de l'opéra françois; transcrits et mis en recueils. English version by Percy Pinkerton. Tenor,
          Vol. 1. London, J. & W. Chester, 1924. 32p Pl no J.W.C. 38881-38888 (8 songs)

153   GROVLEZ, GABRIEL, ed.
          Les plus beaux airs de l'opéra françois; transcrits et mis en recueils. English version by Percy Pinkerton. Tenor,
          Vol. 2. London, J. & W. Chester, 1924. 21p (33-63) Pl no 38889-388812 (4 songs)

154   GUENTHER, FELIX, 1886-1951
       Round-the-world Christmas album; a collection of Christmas carols and songs from many nations; compiled and
       arranged by Felix Guenther; English adaptations by Olga Paul. N.Y., E. B. Marks, 1943. 64p Pl no 12005-61
       (41 songs)

155   GUND, ROBERT, ed.
       Schweizer Volkslieder; chansons populaires de la Suisse romande; mit Klavierbegleitung, herausgegeben von
       Robert Gund; accompagnement par Robert Gund. Leipzig, Universal, 1922. 20p Pl no U.E. Nr.5815 (Cover
       title: Chansons populaires de la Suisse Romande et Italienne) (12 songs)

156   GUND, ROBERT, ed.
       Schweizer Volkslieder; chansons populaires de la Suisse romande; mit Klavierbegleitung, herausgegeben von
       Robert Gund; accompagnement par Robert Gund. Heft 1. Leipzig, Universal, 1918,1922. 18p Pl no U.E.
       5814a (12 songs)

157   GUND, ROBERT, ed.
       Schweizer Volkslieder; chansons populaires de la Suisse romande; mit Klavierbegleitung herausgegeben von
       Robert Gund; accompagnement par Robert Gund. Heft 2. Wien, N.Y., Universal, 1918,1922. 16p Pl no
       U.E. Nr.5814b (10 songs)

158   GUND, ROBERT, ed.
       Schweizer Volkslieder; chansons populaires de la Suisse romande; mit Klavierbegleitung herausgegeben von
       Robert Gund; accompagnement par Robert Gund. Heft 3. Wien, Leipzig, Universal, 1918,1922. 15p Pl no
       U.E. 5814c (10 songs)

159   HARASOWSKI, ADAM, ed.
       Złota Księga Pieśni Polskiej; album najbardziej znanych pieśni (130 na fortepian do spiewu i 20 na chór
       męski) z przedmowa D-ra Zygmunta Nowakowskiego. The golden book of Polish songs; a collection of
       best known Polish songs (130 for voice and piano and 20 for 4 part choir); English translations by A. Hara-
       sowski, J. Sliwinski and Joanna Davies; foreword by Zygmunt Nowakowski. London, Nakładem Ksiegarni
       Polkiej, Alma Book Co., 1955. 191p

160   HARRELL, MACK, 1909-   comp. and arr.
       The sacred hour of song; a collection of sacred solos suitable for Christian Science services, for high or medium
       voice. N.Y., Carl Fischer, c1939-1940. 67p Pl no 28912-62 (high voice); 28754-62 (low voice)

161   HARWELL, RICHARD BARKSDALE, ed.
       Songs of the Confederacy. N.Y., Broadcast Music, 1951. 112p (38 songs)

162   HAYWOOD, CHARLES, 1904-   ed.
       Art song of Soviet Russia; a panorama of Soviet life in song, with the original text; literal text translations by
       C. Haywood; English adaptations by Olga Paul. N.Y., E. B. Marks, 1947. 64p Pl no 12423-61 (18 songs;
       Russian text in Cyrillic characters omitted)

163   HAYWOOD, ERNEST, ed. and arr.
       Vocal gems of Scotland; 31 songs. London, Keith Prowse, 1938. 61p Pl no K.P. & Co.Ltd. 5786

164   HEIDELBERG, ALBERT HETÉNYI
       Hungarian folk-songs. English text by Béla Szilasi. Music transcription by A. H. Heidelberg. Budapest,
       George Vajna, c1933. 102p (102 songs)

165   HELLER, RUTH, 1920-   comp. and arr.
       Christmas; its carols, customs and legends. Minneapolis, Hall & McCreary, 1948. 112p (117 songs)

166   IRELAND in song; a collection of over 200 all-time favorites, from the Old and the New Sod, including many
       copyrights not found in any similar compilation. N.Y., Remick, c1955. 128p (103 songs)

167   ISORI, IDA
       Ida Isori-album; Altitalienische Arien aus dem 16., 17. und 18. Jahrhundert für eine Singstimme mit
       Klavierbegleitung. Neu bearbeitet und ausgewählt von Ida Isori; Deutsche Übersetzung der Gesangstexte von
       Richard Batka. Vol. 1. Wien, Universal, 1912. 50p Pl no U.E. 3630 (12 songs)

168   ISORI, IDA
       Ida Isori-album; Altitalienische Arien aus dem 16., 17. und 18. Jahrhundert für eine Singstimme mit
       Klavierbegleitung. Neu bearbeitet und ausgewählt von Ida Isori; Deutsche Übersetzung der Gesangstexte von
       Richard Batka. Vol. 2. Wien, Universal, 1913. 45p Pl no U. E. 3631 (12 songs)

169   IVES, BURL, 1909-   comp. and arr.
        The wayfarin' stranger; Burl Ives folio of folksongs and ballads; a collection of 13 recorded favorites with
        guitar, ukulele, and piano accompaniment. N.Y., Southern Music, 1952. 32p

170   IVES, BURL, 1909-   arr.
        Favorite folk ballads of Burl Ives. N.Y., Leeds Music, 1949. 35p (17 songs)

171   IVES, BURL, 1909-   arr.
        At home with Burl Ives; a collection of 20 folk songs and ballads with symbols for guitar and diagrams for
        ukulele. N.Y., Leeds Music, 1947. 40p Pl no L1510-2-L1529

172   IVES, BURL, 1909-
        Burl Ives Irish songs; edited with new piano accompaniments by Michael Bowles. N.Y., Duell, Sloan and
        Pearce, 1955. 126p (50 songs)

173   IVES, BURL, 1909-
        Burl Ives song book; American song in historical perspective. Song version by Burl Ives, text by Albert Hague,
        illustrations by Lamartine Le Goullon and R. J. Lee. N.Y., Ballantine, 1953. 303p (129 songs)

174   IVIMEY, ELLA
        9 French songs of the 17th and 18th centuries collected and translated by Gertrude Rutherford. The piano
        accompaniments by Ella Ivimey. London, Augener, c1934. 28p Pl no 17414

175   IVIMEY, ELLA
        10 French songs of the 17th and 18th centuries collected and translated by Gertrude Rutherford. The piano
        accompaniments by Ella Ivimey. London, Augener, c1930. 25p Pl no 17054

176   JEANETTE MacDonald's favorite operatic airs and concert songs. N.Y., G. Schirmer, 1940. 83p Pl no 38829
        (14 songs)

177   JELÍNEK, HANUŠ, 1878-   comp. and tr.
        Chansons populaires tchécoslovaques; choises et traduites pan Hanuš Jelínek, harmonisées par Jaroslav Křička;
        préface de Hanuš Jelínek. Geneva, Henn, 1922. 26p Pl no A.446H (16 songs)

178   JELÍNEK, HANUŠ, 1878-   comp. and tr.
        Chansons populaires tchécoslovaques; choises et traduites par Hanuš Jelínek; harmonisées par Jaroslav Křička.
        Nouvelle série. Geneva, Henn, (No.482), c1951. 24p Pl no A.482H (16 songs)

179   JEPPESEN, KNUD, 1892-   ed.
        La flora arie &c. antice italiane raccolte et edite per cura di Knud Jeppesen. Copenaghen, Wilhelm Hansen,
        1949. Vol. 1. 149p Pl no 26556 (45 songs with texts in Italian; English and German translations in text at
        beginning (not indexed))

180   JEPPESEN, KNUD, 1892-   ed.
        La flora arie &c. antiche italiane raccolte ed edite per cura di Knud Jeppesen. Copenaghen, Wilhelm Hansen,
        1949. Vol. 2. 135p Pl no 26572 (45 songs with texts in Italian; English and German translations in text at
        beginning (not indexed))

181   JEPPESEN, KNUD, 1892-   ed.
        La flora arie &c. antiche italiane raccolte ed edite per cura di Knud Jeppesen. Copenaghen, Wilhelm Hansen,
        1949. Vol. 3. 133p Pl no 26584 (45 songs including 19 duets in Italian; English and German translations in
        the text at beginning (not indexed))

182   JOHNSON, HALL, 1888-   ed. and arr.
        Thirty Negro spirituals; arranged for voice and piano. N.Y., G. Schirmer, c1949. 82p Pl no 41855

183   JOHNSON, JOHN ROSAMOND, 1873-   ed. and arr.
        Radio City edition album of Negro spirituals. N.Y., E. B. Marks, c1940. 56p Pl no 11197-2/11,213-3
        (26 songs)

184   JOHNSON, JOHN ROSAMOND, 1873-   ed. and arr.
        Rolling along in song. A chronological survey of American Negro music with eighty-seven arrangements of
        Negro songs, including ring shouts, spirituals, work songs, plantation ballads, chain-gang, jail-house, and
        minstrel songs, street cries, and blues. N.Y., Viking, 1937. 224p

185 JOHNSON, MARGARET (BASSETT), 1907-   ed.
Early American songs from the repertoire of the "Song-Spinners" arranged and edited with piano accompaniments and historical notes by Margaret and Travis Johnson. N.Y., Associated Music Pubs., c1943. 72p (64 songs)

186 JOHNSTON, RICHARD, 1917-   ed.
Folksongs of Canada. E. F. Fowke, literary editor, Richard Johnston, music editor. Illustrated by E. W. Hoey. 1st ed. Waterloo, Ontario, Waterloo Music, 1954. 198p (77 songs; words in English, or English and French)

187 JOHNSTON, RICHARD, 1917-   arr.
Folk songs of Quebec. (Chansons de Québec). Notes and translations by E. F. Fowke. Waterloo, Ontario, Waterloo Music, 1957. 93p (44 songs)

188 JONSSON, JOSEF, 1887-   arr.
Sweden sings; ballads, folk-songs and dances; photographs and text by K. W. Gullers; trans. by Noel Wirén and L. B. Eyre. Stockholm, Nordiska Musikförlaget, c1955. 103p Pl no N.M.S. 3550 (54 songs; Swedish and English words, for voice and piano; in part for piano only)

189 JORDAN, PHILIP DILLON, 1903-   comp.
Songs of yesterday; a song anthology of American life. Garden City, N.Y., Doubleday, Doran, 1941. 392p (96 songs; some SATB, others just chorus SATB)

190 KAGEN, SERGIUS, ed.
40 French songs for voice and piano. Vol. 1. (High) N.Y., International Music, 1951. 97p Pl no 1121 (English translations printed at the beginning of the volume)

191 KAGEN, SERGIUS, ed.
40 French songs for voice and piano. Vol. 2. (High) N.Y., International Music, 1951. 90p Pl no 1122 (English translations printed at the beginning of the volume)

192 KAGEN, SERGIUS, ed.
40 French songs for voice and piano. Vol. 1. (Low) N.Y., International Music, c1952. 92p Pl no 1125 (English translations of original language printed at beginning of the volume)

193 KAGEN, SERGIUS, ed.
40 French songs for voice and piano. Vol. 2. (Low) N.Y., International Music, c1952. 86p Pl no 1126 (English translations of original language printed at beginning of the volume)

194 KAGEN, SERGIUS, ed.
40 French songs for voice and piano. Vol. 1, Medium. N.Y., International Music, c1952. 93p Pl no 1123 (English translations of original language printed at beginning of the volume)

195 KAGEN, SERGIUS, ed.
40 French songs for voice and piano. Vol. 2, Medium. N.Y., International Music, c1952. 88p Pl no 1124 (English translations of original language printed at beginning of the volume)

196 KEEL, FREDERICK, ed. and arr.
Elizabethan love-songs, first set; edited and arranged with pianoforte accompaniments composed, or adapted from the lute tablature. London, Boosey, 1909. 113p Pl no H.10387 (high); Pl no H.6259 (low). (30 songs; first set issued for high voice, and low voice in 2 parts, with identical songs in each part)

197 KEEL, FREDERICK, ed. and arr.
Elizabethan love-songs, second set; edited and arranged with pianoforte accompaniments composed, or adapted from the lute tablature. London, Boosey, 1913. 114p Pl no H.7770 (high); Pl no H.7769 (low). (In 2 parts, one for high voice and one for low voice, with identical songs in each part; 30 songs)

198 KIDSON, FRANK, 1855-   ed.
A garland of English folk-songs; being a collection of sixty folk-songs; with pianoforte accompaniments by Alfred Moffat. London, Ascherberg, Hopwood & Crew, 1926. 121p Pl no A.H.&C. Ltd. 10969

199 KINLEY, ETHEL A., ed.
A song book. Toronto, Clarke, Irwin, Ltd., 1940. 251p (102 songs)

200 KIRBY, WALTER, comp.
Seventeen sacred songs; for church and general use, also suitable for Christian Science services. N.Y., G. Schirmer, 1937. 2 parts, Pl no 41854 (high) 90p; Pl no 41853 (low) 90p

201 KLERK, ALBERT DE, comp. and arr.
   Ons volkslied nederlandsche liederen uit noord en zuid om te zingen en te spelen verzameld door Albert de
   Klerk, Jan Mul en Herman Strategier met versieringen van Frans Mandos Tzn. Vol. 1. Heemstede, De Toorts,
   1945. 64p (43 songs; sources of tunes and texts given in notes)

202 KLERK, ALBERT DE, comp. and arr.
   Ons volkslied nederlandsche liederen uit noord en zuid om te zingen en te spelen verzameld door Albert de
   Klerk, Jan Mul en Herman Strategier met versieringen van Frans Mandos Tzn. Vol. 2. Heemstede, De Toorts,
   1945. p66-127 (53 songs; sources of tunes and texts given in notes)

203 KLERK, ALBERT DE, comp. and arr.
   Ons volkslied nederlandsche liederen uit noord en zuid om te zingen en te spelen verzameld door Albert de
   Klerk, Jan Mul en Herman Strategier met versieringen vans Franz Mandos Tzn. Vol. 3. Heemstede, De Toorts,
   1945. p128-192 (59 songs; sources of tunes and texts given in notes)

204 KRAMER, ALEXANDER MILTON, 1893-   ed.
   Beatrice Kay songs of the naughty 90's; arranged by Matt Ray. N.Y., Leeds Music, c1945. 64p (26 songs)

205 KRAMER, ALEXANDER MILTON, 1893-   comp. and arr.
   Salty sea songs and chanteys; 74 songs of the sea. Piano arrangements by A. M. Kramer and Harold Potter.
   Revised lyrics by Steve Graham. Compiled by A. M. Kramer. N.Y., Leeds Music, 1943. 96p

206 KVAMME, TORSTEIN O.
   The Christmas carolers' book in song and story. Chicago, Hall & McCreary, c1935. 80p (74 songs)

207 LABASTILLE, IRMA, comp. and arr.
   Recuerdo Latino-Americano (Memories of Latin-America). Album of folk songs for voice and piano, with
   original Spanish text and English adaptations. N.Y., E. B. Marks, 1953. 64p Pl no 11911-58 (19 songs,
   2 piano pieces)

208 LA FORGE, FRANK, 1879-   ed.
   Lily Pons song album. Selected songs from the repertoire of Lily Pons. N.Y., Carl Fischer, 1943. 79p Pl no
   29471-64 (18 songs; some songs in original language and English)

209 LA FORGE, FRANK, 1879-   and EARHART, WILL, eds.
   Pathways of songs; compiled, arranged, translated and edited by Frank LaForge and Will Earhart. Vol. 1, High
   voice. N.Y., Witmark Educational Pubs., 1934. 62p Pl no M.W. & Sons 19427-54 (23 songs)

210 LA FORGE, FRANK, 1879-   and EARHART, WILL, eds.
   Pathways of song; compiled, arranged, translated and edited by Will Earhart and Frank LaForge. Vol. 2, Low
   voice. N.Y., Witmark Educational Pubs., 1934. 64p Pl no M.W. & Sons 19438-56 (23 songs)

211 LA FORGE, FRANK, 1879-   ed.
   The second Lily Pons song album. N.Y., Carl Fischer, c1948. 87p Pl no 30378-53 N1414 (16 songs in the
   original language and English)

212 LAIR, JOHN, ed.
   Songs Lincoln loved; with an introduction by W. H. Townsend. N.Y., Duell, Sloan and Pearce; Boston, Little,
   Brown, 1954. 85p

213 LAMPE, J. BODEWALT, comp. and arr.
   Songs of Ireland, 100 most popular Irish songs. N.Y., Remick, 1916. 119p

214 LANDECK, BEATRICE, comp.
   More songs to grow on; a new collection of folk songs for children. Drawings by D. S. Martin, arrangements by
   Florence White. N.Y., E. B. Marks, c1954. 128p (62 songs)

215 LANDECK, BEATRICE, comp.
   Songs my true love sings; piano settings by Charity Bailey. N.Y., E. B. Marks, 1953. 64p Pl no 12377-56
   (32 songs)

216 LANDECK, BEATRICE, comp.
   Songs to grow on; a collection of American folk songs for children assembled with explanatory text and rhythm
   band arrangements. Piano settings by Florence White; designed and illustrated by D. S. Martin. N.Y., E. B.
   Marks; N.Y., William Sloane, 1950. 125p (59 songs)

217   LANDSHOFF, LUDWIG, 1874-1941, ed.
Alte Meister des bel Canto, eine Sammlung von Arien aus Opern und Kantaten, von Kanzonen, Kanzonetten, Opern- und Kammerduetten für den praktischen Gebrauch. Vol. 1. Frankfurt, C. P. Peters, n.d. 106p Pl no 9689 (29 songs with Italian text and German translation)

218   LANDSHOFF, LUDWIG, 1874-1941, ed.
Alte Meister des bel Canto, eine Sammlung von Arien aus Opern und Kantaten, von Kanzonen, Kanzonetten, Opern- und Kammerduetten für den praktischen Gebrauch. Vol. 2. Frankfurt, C. P. Peters, n.d. 121p Pl no 9689 (21 songs with Italian text and German translation)

219   THE LATIN-American song book. A varied and comprehensive collection of Latin-American songs...complete with piano accompaniment published in co-operation with the Music Division of the Pan American Union. Boston, N.Y., Ginn, 1942. 128p (72 songs)

220   LEHMANN, LOTTE, ed.
Lotte Lehmann album, favorite songs from her repertoire. N.Y., Boosey & Hawkes, c1945. 85p Pl no U.S. Bk. 125 (16 songs)

221   LIEBLING, ESTELLE, 1884-
Fifteen arias for coloratura soprano. N.Y., c1902, c1944. 142p Pl no 40448 (In original language, one other and English in most cases)

222   DAS LIEBSTE Lied; eine Sammlung von volkstümlichen Liedern für Klavier mit Singstimme und vollständigen Texten. Band 1. Edition Schott, 3799. Mainz, B. Schott, 1935. 45p Pl no B.S S. 36281 (19 songs)

223   DAS LIEBSTE Lied; eine Sammlung von volkstümlichen Liedern für Klavier mit Singstimme und vollständigen Texten. Band 2. Edition Schott, 4000. Mainz, B. Schott, 1935. 39p Pl no B.S.S. 37720 (16 songs)

224   LIEDER-ALBUM lettischer Komponisten; Album de chansons de compositeurs lettons. Für eine Singstimme und Klavier pour une voix et piano. Wien, Universal, c1940. 40p Pl no U.E. 11173 (14 songs; text in German and French)

225   LOESSER, ARTHUR, 1894-   ed.
Humor in American song. Arrangements by Alfred Kugel. N.Y., Howell, Soskin, 1942. 315p (98 songs)

226   LOHMANN, PAUL, comp.
Das Lied im Unterricht; 61 Lieder für eine Singstimme mit Klavierbegleitung ausgewählt und bezeichnet von Paul Lohmann. Mainz, B. Schott, [19--], n.d. Pl no B.S.S. 36245 2 parts High voice (Hohe Stimme) Edition Schott 2907, 94p; Medium voice (Mittlere oder tiefe Stimme) Edition Schott 2908, 94p

227   LOMAX, JOHN AVERY, 1872-1948 and LOMAX, ALAN, 1915-   comps.
The 111 best American ballads, folk song U.S.A. collected, adapted, and arranged by J. A. Lomax and Alan Lomax; Alan Lomax, editor; Charles Seeger and R. C. Seeger, music editors. N.Y., Duell, Sloan and Pearce, 1947. 407p

228   LONDON. POLISH CULTURAL INSTITUTE
Folk songs of Poland. London, Polish Cultural Institute, 1954. 31p (10 songs)

229   LOSSE, PAUL, 1890-   ed.
Unterrichtslieder; eine Sammlung von 60 beliebten Liedern mit Klavierbegleitung für den Unterricht im Einzelgesang und zum Gebrauch in Schule und Haus. Leipzig, C. F. Peters, 1949. 87p Pl no 8512 (for high voice, soprano or tenor and piano)

230   LUND, ENGEL
Engel Lund's book of folk-songs; with pianoforte accompaniments by Ferdinand Rauter. London, Oxford Univ. Press, 1936. 54p (25 songs; English texts by Eileen MacLeod)

231   LUND, ENGEL
A second book of folk-songs; with pianoforte accompaniments by Ferdinand Rauter. English translations by Ursula Wood. London, Oxford Univ. Press, 1947. 51p (24 songs; in English and original language)

232   McCOURT, TOM M., 1905-   ed. and arr.
The Robert Burns song book. London, Paterson's Pubs., 1955. (3 parts, for high, medium and low voices with the same songs in each part; 44p) (21 poems set to tunes originally selected by Burns)

233   MacLEAN, DOUGLAS, pseud., comp. and arr. (FRANK CAMPBELL-WATSON, 1899-   )
Song session, a community song book. N.Y., Remick, c1953. 128p (164 songs)

234   MACMAHON, DESMOND, ed. and arr.
The new national and folk song book...being a collection of well-known national and folk songs arranged for use in schools. Vol. 1. London, Thomas Nelson, 1938. 157p (81 songs; descants added to many of the songs)

235   MACMAHON, DESMOND, ed. and arr.
The new national and folk song book...being a collection of well-known national and folk songs arranged for use in schools. Vol. 2. London, Thomas Nelson, 1938. 212p (100 songs, 19 rounds; descants added to many of the songs)

236   MADDY, JOSEPH EDGAR, 1891-   and MIESSNER, W. O., eds.
All-American song book; a community song book, for schools, homes, clubs and community singing. N.Y., Robbins Music, c1942. 144p

237   MAGIC melodies from the world of song. A compilation of carefully chosen song classics representing the most outstanding titles from the classic era to the present day. N.Y., Remick, 1943. 239p (65 songs)

238   MALATESTA, LUIGI
Canti della montagna trascritti per canto a pianoforte e per cori. Disegni di nisa. Milano, Suvini Zerboni, c1939. 49p Pl no S.3726 Z. (23 songs; each song is also arranged SATB or TTBB)

239   MARAIS, JOSEF, 1905-   ed.
Songs from the veld, fourteen songs from South Africa by Josef Marais. N.Y., G. Schirmer, c1942. 32p (in English and Afrikaans)

240   MASON, MARTIN, ed.
Bass songs. Bryn Mawr, Pa., Oliver Ditson, 1936. 94p Pl no 4-28-60884-5, 4-76-63239-6 and others (21 songs)

241   MASON, MARTIN, ed.
Singable songs for studio and recital; thirty songs. Philadelphia, Oliver Ditson, 1936. (2 vols. with identical songs - one for high voice; one for medium voice) 94p each (30 songs)

242   MATTESON, MAURICE, ed. and arr.
American folk songs for young singers; arranged for chorus. N.Y., G. Schirmer, 1947. 102p Pl no 41376 (Schirmer's American folk-song series, set 25). (49 songs; 10 3-part, 15-2 part, 24 unison)

243   MATTESON, MAURICE, ed. and arr.
Beech mountain folk-songs and ballads; provided with piano accompaniments. Texts edited and foreword written by M. E. Henry. N.Y., G. Schirmer, c1936. 58p Pl no 37113 (Schirmer's American folk-song series, set 15) (29 songs)

244   MAUS, CYNTHIA PEARL, 1880-   and FIELDING, EVELYN LYSLE, eds.
The world's great Madonnas; an anthology of pictures, poetry, music and stories centering in the life of the Madonna and her Son. -------- -----. Music section, by C. P. Maus and E. L. Fielding, music collaborator. N.Y., Harper, 1947. 90p (62 songs)

245   MEMORIES of Spain, an album of Spanish songs with original Spanish lyrics and English adaptations. N.Y., E. B. Marks, 1941. 64p new rev. ed. Pl no 11618 to 10766-3 and others. (15 songs)

246   MEMORIES of the gay nineties; an inviting collection of some of the nostalgic song successes that helped to make the gay nineties gayer. N.Y., E. B. Marks, 1942. 64p (20 songs)

247   MENDOZA, VICENTE, T., 1894-   ed.
Canciones Mexicanas (Mexican folk songs); seleccionadas y armonizadas por V. T. Mendoza. N.Y., Hispanic Institute in the U.S., 1948. 126p (58 songs)

248   MEXICAN fiesta album, a collection of selected favorite Mexican melodies. N.Y., E. B. Marks, c1938. 54p Pl no 10930-3 and others. (16 songs)

249   MILLER, ALBERT, 1914-   comp.
Folksongs for young folk, edited by Alan Mills (pseud.)., musical arrangements by Arthur Morrow, illus. by Ted Graham. rev. ed. Toronto, Canadian Music Sales, c1957. 72p (44 songs)

250   MOSER, HANS JOACHIM, 1889-
        Das deutsche Sololied und die Ballade. Köln, Arno, c1957. 140p (56 songs; early songs with basso continuo
        realized)

251   MOTTINGER, ALVINA H., comp.
        Christmas carols, their authors and composers; a collection of favorite carols with biographical and historical
        annotations. N.Y., G. Schirmer, c1948. 95p Pl no 41920 (48 carols; some solo, most SATB)

252   MURRAY, TOM, ed. and arr.
        Folk songs of Jamaica. London, Oxford Univ. Press, 1952. 59p (30 songs; all songs in dialect, with transla-
        tions of some words and phrases appended to each song)

253   NEGRI BRYKES, VITTORIO, 1923-   ed.
        10 arie Italiane del sei e Settecento per canto e pianoforte. Milano, Ricordi, c1955. 35p

254   DAS NEUE Operetten Buch, die schönsten Melodien aus den Operetten von Lehár, Künneke, Strauss, Lincke,
        Kálmán, Suppé, Dostal, Raymond, Fall und anderen in ungekürzten Originalausgaben für Klavier mit Gesang-
        stimme und vollständigen Texten. Band 1, Edition Schott 2525. Mainz, B. Schott, c1935. 62p (20 songs)

255   DAS NEUE Operetten Buch, die schönsten Melodien aus den Operetten von Lehár, Stolz, Lincke, Raymond, Dostal,
        Strauss, Künneke, Suppé and anderen in ungekürzten Originalausgaben für Klavier mit Gesangstimme und voll-
        ständigen Texten. Band 2, Edition Schott 2850. Mainz, B. Schott, 1937. 63p (20 songs)

256   DAS NEUE Operetten Buch, die schönsten Melodien aus den Operetten von Lehár, Künneke, Strauss, Lincke, Kál-
        mán, Suppé, Dostal, Raymond, Fall und anderen in ungekürzten Originalsusgaben für Klavier mit gesangstimme
        und vollständigen Texten. Band 3, Edition Schott 3700. Mainz, B. Schott, c1940. 47p Pl no B.S.S.37334
        (16 songs)

257   DAS NEUE Operetten Buch, die schönsten Melodien aus den Operetten von Lehár, Künneke, Strauss, Lincke, Kál-
        mán, Suppé, Dostal, Raymond, Fall und anderen in ungekürsten Originalausgaben für Klavier mit Gesangstimme
        und vollständigen Texten. Band 4, Edition Schott 4300. Mainz, B. Schott, c1941. 47p Pl no B.S.S. 37822
        (17 songs)

258   DAS NEUE Operetten Buch, die schönsten Melodien aus den Operetten von Lehár, Künneke, Strauss, Lincke, Kál-
        mán, Suppé, Dostal, Raymond, Fall und anderen in ungekürzten originalausgaben für Klavier mit Gesangstimme
        und vollständigen Texten. Band 5, Edition Schott 4500. Mainz, B. Schott, c1951. 45p (20 songs)

259   A NEW anthology of American song; 25 songs by native American composers. N.Y., G. Schirmer, 1942. 105p
        Pl no 39640

260   NILES, JOHN JACOB, 1892-   comp. and arr.
        The Anglo-American ballad study book containing eight ballads in current tradition in the United States of
        America. N.Y., G. Schirmer, 1945. 38p (Schirmer's American folk-song series, set 24)

261   NILES, JOHN JACOB, 1892-   comp. and arr.
        The Anglo-American carol study book containing English carols in their early traditional form and surviving
        versions traditional in the United States. N.Y., G. Schirmer, c1948. 44p Pl no 42027 (Schirmer's American
        folk-song series, set 26) (8 carols; tunes with accompaniment given only for the ballad surviving in the U.S.;
        words only of the English ballads are given and are not indexed)

262   NILES, JOHN JACOB, 1892-   comp. and arr.
        Ballads, carols, and tragic legends from the Appalachian Mountains simply arranged with piano accompaniment.
        N.Y., G. Schirmer, 1937. 20p Pl no 37417 (Schirmer's American folk-song series, set 18) (10 songs)

263   NILES, JOHN JACOB, 1892-   comp. and arr.
        Ballads, love-songs, and tragic legends from the Southern Appalachian Mountains simply arranged with piano
        accompaniment. N.Y., G. Schirmer, 1938. 20p Pl no 37939 (Schirmer's American folk-song series, set 20)
        (10 songs)

264   NILES, JOHN JACOB, 1892-   comp. and arr.
        More songs of the hill-folk. Ten ballads and tragic legends from Kentucky, Virginia, Tennessee, North Carolina
        and Georgia; simply arranged with accompaniment for piano. N.Y., G. Schirmer, 1936. 20p Pl no 37112
        (Schirmer's American folk-song series, set 17)

265   NILES, JOHN JACOB, 1892-   comp. and arr.
       Seven Kentucky mountain songs as sung by Marion Kerby and J. J. Niles. N.Y., G. Schirmer, c1929. 13p
       Pl no 34690 (Schirmer's American folk-song series, set 8)

266   NILES, JOHN JACOB, 1892-   comp. and arr.
       Seven Negro exaltations as sung by Marion Kerby and J. J. Niles. N.Y., G. Schirmer, c1929. 15p Pl no 34689

267   NILES, JOHN JACOB, 1892-   comp. and arr.
       Songs of the hill-folk; twelve ballads from Kentucky, Virginia, and North Carolina. N.Y., G. Schirmer, 1934.
       25p Pl no 36361 (Schirmer's American folk-song series, set 14)

268   NILES, JOHN JACOB, 1892-   comp. and arr.
       Ten Christmas carols from the southern Appalachian mountains; simply arranged with accompaniment for piano.
       N.Y., G. Schirmer, c1935. 22p Pl no 36672 (Schirmer's American folk-song series, set 16)

269   NIN, JOAQUIN, ed. and arr.
       Classiques espagnols du chant; quatorze airs anciens d'auteurs espagnols; premier recueil; sept chants lyriques.
       Paris, Max Eschig, 1926. 33p Pl no M.E.1642(1)-M.E.1642(7)

270   NIN, JOAQUIN, ed. and arr.
       Classiques espagnols du chant; quatorze airs anciens d'auteurs espagnols; deuxieme recueil; sept chansons
       picaresques. Paris, Max Eschig, c192?. 25p Pl no M.E.1645(1)-M.E.1645(7)

271   NOBLE, THOMAS TERTIUS, 1867-   arr.
       A round of carols, illustrated by Helen Sewell. London, N.Y., Toronto, Oxford Univ. Press, 1935. 72p (34
       carols)

272   NORTHCOTE, SYDNEY, 1897-   ed. and arr.
       Baritone songs. new imperial ed. London, N.Y., Boosey, 1951. 122p Pl no B.&H. 17021 (30 songs by
       various composers from John Dowland to Ivor Gurney)

273   NORTHCOTE, SYDNEY, 1897-   ed. and arr.
       Bass songs. new imperial ed. London, N.Y., Boosey, 1950. 100p Pl no B.&H. 16735 (30 songs from Hume
       to Head)

274   NORTHCOTE, SYDNEY, 1897-   ed. and arr.
       Contralto songs. new imperial ed. London, N.Y., Boosey, 1950. 109p Pl no B.&H. 16893 (30 songs from
       Campian to Britten)

275   NORTHCOTE, SYDNEY, 1897-   ed. and arr.
       Mezzo-soprano songs. new imperial ed. London, N.Y., Boosey, 1952. 102p Pl no B.&H. 17130 (30 songs
       from Arne to Howells)

276   NORTHCOTE, SYDNEY, 1897-   ed. and arr.
       Soprano songs. new imperial ed. London, N.Y., Boosey, 1952. 124p Pl no B.&H. 17876 (30 songs)

277   NORTHCOTE, SYDNEY, 1897-   ed. and arr.
       Tenor songs. new imperial ed. London, N.Y., Boosey, 1953. 95p Pl no B.&H. 17129 (30 songs)

278   NOSKE, FRITS, ed.
       Das ausserdeutsche Sololied, 1500-1900. Köln, Arno, 1958. 84p (Das Musikwerk; eine Beispielsammlung zur
       Musikgeschichte Herausgegeben von Karl Gustav Fellerer) (30 songs)

279   OBERNDORFER, MARX, 1876-   comp.
       The new American song book (A century of progress in American song); Pan-American edition, comp. and ed.
       by A. F. Oberndorfer... and M. E. Oberndorfer with special arrangements by A. O. Andersen. Chicago, Hall &
       McCreary, c1933-1941. 190p (265 songs; issued in earlier printings with names of compilers reversed)

280   O'NEILL, NORMAN, ed. and arr.
       Echoes of Erin (Macalla as Eirinn); twelve Irish songs; the words by Harold Boulton; Irish translation by Douglas
       Hyde. London, Boosey, 1926. 59p Pl no H.11999

281   ONIS Y SÁNCHEZ, FEDERICO DE, ed.
       Canciones Españolas (Spanish folk songs); Seleccion 1; editadas por Federico de Onís y Emilio de Torre. N.Y.,
       Hispanic Institute in the U.S., 1931. 38p (6 songs)

282 ONÍS Y SÁNCHEZ, FEDERICO DE, ed.
Canciones Españolas (Spanish folk songs); Seleccion 2; editadas por Federico de Onís y Emilio de Torre. N.Y., Hispanic Institute in the U.S., 1946. 38p (12 songs)

283 ONÍS Y SANCHEZ, FEDERICO DE, ed.
Canciones Españolas (Spanish folk songs); selecciones 3 y 4; editadas por Federico de Onís y Emilio de Torre. N.Y., Hispanic Institute in the U.S., 1954. 75p (22 songs)

284 PAN AMERICAN UNION
Cancionero popular Americano, 75 canciones de las 21 republicas Americanas. Washington, D.C., Union Panamericana, 1950. 127p (no English translations)

285 PASTI, BARBARA, comp.
Memories of Hungary (Magyarország Legszebb Dalai) album; a collection of its best-loved songs with original Hungarian words and English lyrics by Olga Paul. N.Y., E. B. Marks, c1947. 63p Pl no 12387-59 (29 songs)

286 PATTERSON, MASSIE
Calypso songs of the West Indies by Massie Patterson and Lionel Belasco; free transcriptions by Maurice Baron. English version by Olga Paul. N.Y., M. Baron, c1943. 25p Pl no Calypso-24 (12 songs; in English, French and dialects)

287 PAUL, OLGA and BRONSKY, G., comps. and arr.
Songs of New Russia, an album of its most popular melodies for voice and piano, with English lyrics. N.Y., E. B. Marks, 1939. 47p Pl no 11039-3 - 11055-2 (17 songs; Russian text in Cyrillic alphabet omitted from index)

288 PAUL, OLGA and BRONSKY, G., comps. and arr.
Songs of new Russia, an album of the most popular melodies of the USSR for voice and piano with the original Russian text and with English lyrics. Rev. enl. ed. N.Y., E. B. Marks, c1942. 63p Pl no 11794-2/11046-2 (22 songs; Russian text in Cyrillic alphabet omitted from index)

289 PAULINI, BÉLA, 1881- comp.
The pearly bouquet (Gyöngyösbokréta). Budapest, George Vajna, c1937. 64p (The original folk songs were collected by Béla Bartók, Zoltán Kodaly, Ladislas Lajtha, Stephen Volly) (17 songs)

290 PAYNE, JOHN, 1872- arr.
Negro spirituals for low voice with piano accompaniment. N.Y., G. Schirmer, c1939,1942. 18p Pl no 40342 (5 songs)

291 PEDREIRA, JOSÉ ENRIQUE, 1904- comp. and arr.
Puerto Rico sings; an album of its best-loved songs with English and the original Spanish text; English lyrics by Olga Paul. N.Y., E. B. Marks, c1957. 47p Pl no 13582-41 (11 songs)

292 PELLETIER, WILFRED, ed.
Opera repertoire for coloratura soprano. Bryn Mawr, Pa., Theodore Presser, c1951. 203p (28 selections from 25 operas)

293 HILLE, WALDEMAR, 1908- ed.
The people's song book. Foreword by Alan Lomax. Preface by B. A. Botkin. N.Y., Boni and Gaer, c1948. 128p (102 songs)

294 PIGGOTT, HARRY EDWARD, ed.
Songs that made history. London, J.M. Dent, c1937. 77p (22 songs; words to the songs printed separately, usually in the original language)

295 POLANI CLUB
Treasured Polish songs with English translations. Selected and edited by J. K. Contoski [and others]. Original Marya Werten illustrations arranged and adapted by Lucille Jasinski; other illustrations by Stanley Legun, Judith Cieslak and Lucille Jasinski. Minneapolis, Minn., Polanie Club, c1953. 352p (227 songs)

296 PREUSS, THEODORE, comp. and arr.
Christmas in song, a treasury of traditional songs, favorite hymns, and choice carols from all ages and from many lands, selected for your singing Christmas for mixed voices (SATB) or unisonal singing. Chicago, Rubank, c1947. 80p (108 songs)

297 QUILTER, ROGER, 1877-1953, arr.
The Arnold book of old songs. London, Boosey & Hawkes, 1947. 68p Pl no B.&H. 15992-B.&H. 16007
(16 songs)

298 RACCOLTE di celebri arie d'opera per canto e pianoforte. Milano, G. Ricordi, 1946. 56p Pl no 127536 (12
arias for baritone)

299 RACCOLTE di celebri arie d'opera per canto e pianoforte. Milano, G. Ricordi, 1946. 59p Pl no 127537 (12
arias for basso)

300 RACCOLTE di celebri arie d'opera per canto e pianoforte. Milano, G. Ricordi, 1946. 63p Pl no 127534 (12
arias for mezzo-soprano and contralto)

301 RACCOLTE di celebri arie d'opera per canto e pianoforte. Milano, G. Ricordi, 1946. 55p Pl no 127533 (12
arias for soprano)

302 RACCOLTE di celebri arie d'opera per canto e pianoforte. Milano, G. Ricordi, 1946. 93p Pl no 127532 (12
arias for soprano leggero)

303 RAMIREZ-PERALTA, JOSE G., comp.
National music of the Dominican Republic; compiled in commemoration of the 100th anniversary of the
Dominican independence; with an historical preface by Julius Mattfeld. N.Y., Alpha Music, 1944. 45p
(16 songs)

304 RED BOOK of famous Latin solos; simplified arrangements for medium solo voice and organ of sacred songs with
Catholic Latin texts. Accompaniments simplified and texts adjusted by J. A. Reilly, Ludwig Bonvin, H. L.
Harts, or Charles Renard. Edition number 1566. Boston, McLaughlin & Reilly, 1951. 47p Pl no M.&R. Co.
1532, 323, 327 M-3(1566), 502, 329, 347, and others) (15 songs)

305 REED, WILL, ed.
The golden book of carols illustrated by Treyer Evans. London, Blandford, 1948. 40p (19 carols)

306 REED, WILL, ed.
Music of Britain. London, Blandford, 1953. 86p Pl no B.P. 104 (18 songs; 4 choral and 5 piano pieces)

307 REED, WILL, ed.
The treasury of Christmas music. London, Blandford, 1950. 150p Pl no B.P. 103 (76 songs and 4 instrumental
pieces; includes some carols other than Christmas carols, many SATB and composed Christmas songs and anthems)

308 REICHERT, ERNST, 1901-   ed.
Klingende Lyrik; seltene Meistergesänge aus drei Jahrhunderten, für hohe Stimme. Wien, Wiesbaden, Doblinger,
1957. 40p Pl no D. 9585 (19 songs)

309 REIN, WALTER, 1893-   and LANG, HANS, 1897-   , eds.
Der Wundergarten; deutsche Volkslieder für Gesang und Klavier. Edition Schott 4501/03; Melodie-Ausgabe
(ein- und zweistimmig) Edition Schott 4375. Mainz, B. Schott, 1953. 158p Pl no B.S.S. 38423-38425 (184
songs; notes concerning origin of the text and melody and first published editions of each song)

310 RICORDI'S Tito Gobbi album of baritone songs and arias in the original keys, favorite songs and arias with the
original text and English translation. London, G. Ricordi, 1958. 40p Pl no L.D. 411 (8 songs)

311 RIEGER, ERWIN, ed.
Sopran-Album aus dem Repertoire Irmgard Seefried; 19 Arien und Lieder. Wien, Doblinger, 1949. II Auflage.
80p Pl no D. 8170

312 RITCHIE, JEAN, ed.
A garland of mountain song; songs from the repertoire of the Ritchie Family of Viper, Kentucky; with piano
accompaniment by H. W. Gordon. Produced under the supervision of Milton Retterberg. N.Y., Broadcast
Music, 1953. 69p (24 American songs)

313 RITCHIE, JEAN
The swapping song book. Photos by George Pickow, piano accompaniments by A. K. Fossner and Edward Tripp.
N.Y., Oxford Univ. Press, 1952. 91p (21 American songs)

314   ROBB, JOHN DONALD, 1892-   ed. and arr.
        Hispanic folk songs of New Mexico; with selected songs for voice and piano. Alburquerque, New Mexico, New Mexico Univ. Press, 1954. 83p (University of New Mexico Publications in the Fine Arts, No. 1) (7 Christmas and 8 secular songs)

315   RODEHEAVER, HOMER ALVAN, 1880-   comp.
        Favorite Christmas carols. Winona Lake, Indiana, The Rodeheaver, Hall-Mack, c1949. unpaged (32 songs; mostly SATB arrangements)

316   ROEDER, ANN E., comp. and arr.
        Folksongs and games of Holland. Cover by Hans van Weeren-Griek. N.Y., G. Schirmer, 1956. 48p Pl no 43685 (25 songs; words in English and Dutch)

317   ROYAL SCHOOL OF CHURCH MUSIC
        The Saint Nicholas carol book. Addington Palace, Croydon Surrey, Royal School of Church Music, 1939. (Reprint 1957). 16p (12 carols, all SATB)

318   RUBIN, RUTH, ed.
        A treasury of Jewish folksong. Piano settings, Ruth Post; drawings, T. H. Rome; poetry adaptations, Isaac Schwartz, Jacob Sloane and the editor. N.Y., Schocken Books, 1950. 224p (110 songs)

319   RUSSELL, LESLIE, 1901-   comp. and arr.
        The Kingsway carol book (sacred and secular) collected (1925-1945). Harmonized ed. London, Evans Brothers, n.d. 71p (49 carols; unison or 4-part harmony)

320   SAMPSON, JOHN, ed.
        The seven seas shanty book containing 42 sea chanties and songs; arranged for piano by S. T. Harris, with a foreword by John Masefield. London, Boosey, 1927. 69p Pl no H.12082

321   SANDBURG, CARL, 1878-   ed.
        New American songbag. N.Y., Broadcast Music, 1950. 107p (59 songs)

322   SANDOVAL, MIGUEL, 1903-   arr.
        25 favorite Latin-American songs. Arranged for voice and piano with English versions by L. N. Finley. N.Y., G. Schirmer, 1949. 130p Pl no 41941

323   SAUNDERS, MAX and EVANS, HAL, eds.
        The Edric Connor collection of West Indian spirituals and folk tunes; arranged for voice and piano. London, Boosey, 1945. 32p Pl no H.15753 (8 songs)

324   SCHIMMERLING, HANNS ALDO, comp. and arr.
        Memories of Czechoslovakia. English lyrics by Olga Paul. N.Y., E. B. Marks, c1945. 56p Pl no 12132 (22 songs)

325   SCHINELLI, ACHILLE, 1892-   ed.
        35 canti populari italiani; transcritti e armonizzati con facile accompagnamento di pianoforte. Milano, Suvini Zerboni, 1952. 60p Pl no 4745 Z. (35 songs)

326   SCHNEIDER, WILLY, ed.
        Deutsche Weisen; die beliebtesten Volkslieder für Klavier. Stuttgart, Lausch & Zweigle, 1958. 320p (352 songs)

327   DIE SCHÖNSTEN deutschen Lieder; zum Singen und zum Spielen. Vol. 1. N.Y., Friedrich Krause, 1944. 48p (21 songs)

328   DIE SCHÖNSTEN deutschen Lieder; zum Singen und zum Spielen. Vol. 2. N.Y., Friedrich Krause, 1945. 48p (18 songs)

329   SCHUMANN, E. M., ed.
        Everybody's favorite selected songs. N.Y., Amsco Music, 1941. 191p (Everybody's favorite series, No.45) (56 songs)

330   SCHUMANN, ELIZABETH, comp.
        Elisabeth Schumann Liederbuch. Favorite songs. Wien, Universal, pref.1928. 98p Pl no U.E. 9559/ (30 songs)

331   SCOTT, THOMAS JEFFERSON, 1912-   comp. and arr.
      Sing of America; folk tunes. Text by Joy Scott-Wood, engravings by Bernard Brussel-Smith. N.Y., Thomas Crowell, c1947. 82p (35 American songs)

332   SEEGER, RUTH PORTER (CRAWFORD), 1901-
      American folk songs for Christmas; illustrated by Barbara Cooney. Garden City, N.Y., Doubleday, 1953. 80p (56 songs)

333   SHAW, GEOFFREY TURTON, 1879-   arr.
      Twice 33 carols for home and church use arranged by Geoffrey Shaw. London, Boosey & Hawkes, c1942. 59p Pl no H.15393

334   SHAW, MARTIN FALLAS, 1875-   ed.
      The English carol book; music edited by Martin Shaw; words edited by Percy Dearmer. London, A.R. Mowbray, 1938. 108p (54 songs)

335   SIEGMEISTER, ELIE, 1909-   ed. and arr.
      Work & sing; a collection of the songs that built America; with commentary, annotations and a critical bibliography. Illustrated by Julian Brazelton. N.Y., W. R. Scott, 1944. 96p (31 songs)

336   SILVERMAN, JERRY, ed. and arr.
      Folk blues; one hundred and ten American folk blues for voice, piano, and guitar, with a chart of basic guitar chord fingering patterns and a full bibliography and discography. N.Y., Macmillan, c1958. 297p

337   SIMON, HENRY WILLIAM, 1901-   ed.
      A treasury of Christmas songs and carols, with illustrations by Rafaello Busoni and new piano arrangements by the editor and Randolph Fellner. Boston, Houghton Mifflin, 1955. 243p (112 songs)

338   SINIGAGLIA, LEONE, 1868-   ed.
      24 vecchie canzoni popolari del Piemonte; 2ª serie (postuma); revisione di Luigi Rognoni. Milano, G Ricordi, 1956. 114p Pl no 129037 (24 songs)

339   SIRMAY, ALBERT, arr.
      Ten new songs the Soviets sing; English lyrics by H. J. Rome. N.Y., Am-Rus Music, 1943. 35p (10 songs)

340   SLONIMSKY, NICOLAS, 1894-   ed.
      50 Russian art songs from Glinka to Shostakovich. Introduction and translations by Nicolas Slonimsky. For voice and piano; English and Russian texts. Vol. 1. N.Y., Leeds, 1949. 64p (Am-Rus vocal series) (English text only indexed)

341   SLONIMSKY, NICOLAS, 1894-   ed.
      50 Russian art songs from Glinka to Shostakovich. Introduction and translations by Nicolas Slonimsky. For voice and piano; English and Russian texts. Vol. 2. N.Y., Leeds, 1951. 56p (Am-Rus vocal series) (English text only indexed)

342   SLONIMSKY, NICOLAS, 1894-   ed.
      50 Russian art songs from Glinka to Shostakovich. Introduction and translations by Nicolas Slonimsky. For voice and piano; English and Russian texts. Vol. 3. N.Y., Leeds, 1951. 86p (Am-Rus vocal series) (English text only indexed)

343   SMITH, FOWLER, ed. and arr.
      Songs we sing, including complete piano accompaniments...produced under the direction of Fowler Smith, H. R. Wilson, G. H. Woods. 2nd ed. Minneapolis, Hall & McCreary, c1940-41. 144p (120 songs)

344   SOCIETY OF ENGLISH SINGERS
      Fifty modern English songs. Selected by and published for the Society of English Singers. London, Boosey, 1923? 206p Pl no H.10910 (51 songs)

345   SONG hits of the roaring twenties. N.Y., Remick, c1952. 80p (27 songs)

346   SONGS of devotion with piano and organ accompaniment. [Arr. and ed. by Joseph Wood] N.Y., Broadcast Music, 1949. 115p (35 songs)

347   [PERRY, ROB ROY, 1900-   comp.]
      Songs of worship, a collection of sacred songs for the church soloist. For high voice. Bryn Mawr, Pa., Theodore Presser, c1949. 43p ------- ------. For low voice...Bryn Mawr, etc. 43p (12 songs in each part - the same songs)

348   SPAETH, SIGMUND GOTTFRIED, 1885-   and THOMPSON, CARL O., eds. and arr.
       55 art songs. New and original translations by Sigmund Spaeth. A book for unison choral singing, for class or
       individual teaching, and amateur and professional singers, at home or on the concert stage. Boston, C. C.
       Birchard, c1943. 121p

349   STANFORD, CHARLES VILLIERS and SHAW, GEOFFREY, eds.
       The new national song book; with new accompaniments by Sydney Northcote and Herbert Wiseman. London,
       Boosey & Hawkes, 1958. 242p Pl no B.&H. 18260 (202 songs)

350   STEVENS, DAVID KILBURN, 1860-   ed.
       Latin American songs for unison and two part singing with piano accompaniments. Boston, C. C. Birchard,
       c1941. 42p (28 songs)

351   STILL, WILLIAM GRANT, 1895-   arr.
       Twelve Negro spirituals; arranged for solo voice; illustrations by Albert Barbelle; edited by Wellington Adams.
       Vol. 1. N.Y., Handy Brothers, c1937. 61 + 3p (Vol. 1 has special title page: Six of the twelve Negro
       spirituals...)

352   STONE, GREGORY, and KIRILLOFF, ALEXANDER, eds., and arr.
       Album Russe; Russian, Gypsy, Ukrainian, Caucasian, Siberian, and regimental songs for voice and piano.
       English words by Carol Raven. N.Y., E. B. Marks, 1936. 41p Pl no 10459-3-10470-4 (12 songs; Russian
       words in Cyrillic characters omitted)

353   STRECKER, LUDWIG, 1883-   ed.
       Mein Heimatland; die schönsten Volks-, Wander-, Trink- und Scherzlieder; herausgegeben von Ludwig Andersen
       (pseud.); neu- Ausgabe mit Vollständigem Text. Klavier, Sätze von W. Lutz, Ed.2222. Mainz, B. Schott,
       [19-]. 91p Pl no B.S.S. 33064 (203 songs; for piano with superlinear words)

354   STRUBE, ADOLF, ed.
       Europäische Weihnachtslieder am Klavier zu singen. Berlin, Carl Merseburger, c1954. 55p (59 songs)

355   SVENSK sånglyrik. Stockholm, Nordiska Musikförlaget, 1951. Band 1. 64p Pl no N.M.S. 3500a (20 songs)

356   SVENSK sånglyrik. Stockholm, Nordiska Musikförlaget, 1951. Band 2. 66p Pl no N.M.S. 3500b (25 songs)

357   SWARTHOUT, GLADYS, 1904-   comp.
       Gladys Swarthout album of concert songs and arias. N.Y., G. Schirmer, c1946. 72p Pl no 41283 (16 songs)

358   TAYLOR, BERNARD UNDERHILL, 1896-   ed.
       Contemporary songs in English; songs by American and English composers for recital, concert and studio use.
       Medium high voice. N.Y., Carl Fischer, c1956. 79p Pl no N 2109 (16 songs)

359   TAYLOR, BERNARD UNDERHILL, 1896-   ed.
       German art songs for school and studio. Bryn Mawr, Pa., Oliver Ditson, 1947. 64p Pl no ML-579-5 and others
       (med. high); ML-629-5 and others (med. low) (16 songs; in 2 vols., medium high and medium low voice,
       with identical songs in each vol.)

360   TERRY, SIR RICHARD RUNCIMAN, 1865-1938
       A medieval carol book, the melodies chiefly from MSS. in the Bodleian Library, Oxford, and in the Library of
       Trinity College, Cambridge. London, Burns Oates & Washbourne, [pref.] 1931. 66p (35 songs)

361   TERRY, SIR RICHARD RUNCIMAN, 1865-1938
       Two hundred folk carols. London, Burns Oates & Washbourne, 1933. 11 parts in 1v. var. p., 395p (total)
       (Many SATB, but most can be sung by solo or unison choir)

362   TEYTE, MAGGIE
       Maggie Teyte album of French song. N.Y., G. Schirmer, 1946. 105p (19 art songs)

363   THIRTY-ONE traditional carols. London, Novello, 1951? 31p (31 songs; mostly SATB, many with descants)

364   THOMAS, JOHN CHARLES, 1891-1960
       John Charles Thomas album of favorite songs and arias. N.Y., G. Schirmer, 1946. 112p Pl no 41377 (20 songs)

365   THORNTON, ROBERT D., ed. and arr.
       The tun ful flame: songs of Robert Burns as he sang them. Lawrence, Kansas Univ. Press, 1957. 74p (25 songs
       in English)

366   SONGS we love to sing, songs for every purpose and occasion for home, school and assembly use. Chicago, Hall & McCreary, c1938. 256p

367   TOMELLERI, LUCIANO, ed.
Belcanto; 10 arie antiche italiane per canto e pianoforte. (Testo italiano-English text). Milano, G. Ricordi, c1956. 70p Pl no 129029 (text of songs in original language only)

368   HODGES, LESTER, comp.
Twenty-four Italian songs and arias of the seventeenth and eighteenth centuries. (English versions principally by Theodore Baker]. For medium high voice. N.Y., G. Schirmer, c1948. 100p (Schirmer's library of musical classics, Library vol. 1722)

369   UNIVERSITY carol book; a collection of Basque,French, Dutch, German, English folk-carols, lullabies and noëls. Book 1. Brighton, E. H. Freeman, 1952. 8p Pl no E.H.F. 2032-2039 (8 songs)

370   UNIVERSITY carol book; a collection of Basque, French, Dutch, German, English folk-carols, lullabies and noëls. Book 2. Brighton, E. H. Freeman, 1952. 8p Pl no E.H.F. 2040-2046 (7 songs)

371   UNIVERSITY carol book; a collection of Basque, French, Dutch, German, English folk-carols, lullabies and noëls. Book 3. Brighton, E. H. Freeman, 1953. 8p Pl no E.H.F. 2049-2056

372   UNIVERSITY carol book; a collection of Basque, French, Dutch, German, English folk-carols, lullabies and noëls. Book 4. Brighton, E. H. Freeman, 1953. 8p Pl no E.H.F. 2071-2077 (7 songs)

373   UNIVERSITY carol book; a collection of Basque, French, Dutch, German, English folk-carols, lullabies and noëls. Book 5. Brighton, E. H. Freeman, 1953. 8p Pl no E.H.F. 2078-2084 (7 songs)

374   UNIVERSITY carol book; a collection of Basque, French, Dutch, German, English folk-carols, lullabies and noëls. Book 6. Brighton, E.H. Freeman, 1954. 8p Pl no E.H.F. 2085-2091 (7 songs)

375   UNIVERSITY carol book; a collection of Basque, French, Dutch, German, English folk-carols, lullabies and noëls. Book 7. Brighton, E.H. Freeman, 1954. 8p Pl no E.H.F. 2092-2097 (6 songs)

376   UNIVERSITY carol book; a collection of Basque, French, Dutch, German, English folk-carols, lullabies and noëls. Book 8. Brighton, E. H.Freeman, 1954. 8p Pl no E.H.F. 2281-2288 (8 songs)

377   UNIVERSITY carol book; a collection of Basque, French, Dutch, German, English folk-carols, lullabies and noëls. Book 9. Brighton, E. H. Freeman, 1954. 8p Pl no E.H.F. 2099, 2311-2316 (7 songs)

378   UNIVERSITY carol book; a collection of Basque, French, Dutch, German, English folk-carols, lullabies and noëls. Book 10. Brighton, E. H. Freeman, c1955. 8p Pl no E.H.F. 2317-2322 (7 songs)

379   UNIVERSITY carol book; a collection of Basque, French, Dutch, German, English folk-carols, lullabies and noëls. Book 11. Brighton, E. H. Freeman, c1955. 8p Pl no E.H.F. 2323-2329 (7 songs)

380   UNIVERSITY carol book; a collection of Basque, French, Dutch, German, English folk-carols, lullabies and noëls. Book 12. Brighton, E. H. Freeman, c1955. 8p Pl no E.H.F. 2330-2335 (6 songs)

381   VAN WEY, ADELAIDE and MOORE, DONALD LEE, comps. and arr.
Smoky Mountain ballads; for voice and piano with guitar, banjo, ukulele and zither symbols. N.Y., Omega Music, 1946. 15p (10 songs)

382   VENÉ, RUGGERO, comp.
Catholic wedding folio for solo voice and organ or harmonium accompaniment. N.Y., G. Ricordi, c1957. 27p Pl no N.Y. 1838 (10 songs, including 3 piano pieces prelude, processional and recessional)

383   VIGNERAS, MARCEL, ed.
Chansons de France; transcrites avec accompagnement de piano, notes historiques et explicatives, et guide de pronunciation. Boston, D.C. Heath, 1941. 52p (44 songs)

384   VRANKEN, JOSEPH, 1870- comp. and arr.
Neerland zingt, hondert twee en veertig bekende liederen, samengesteld en bewerkt voor piano of harmonium. Illustrates en bandontwerp Piet Gertenaar. Amsterdam, Muziekuitgeverij ixijzet, 1947. 158p Pl no X.Y.X. 307 (Cover title: "Zo zingt Nederland een verzameling van 142 bekende liederen voor zang en piano of harmonium)

385   WARD, ARTHUR EDWARD, 1893-   ed.
     The singing road, an active repertory for artists and students, selected classical and modern songs. N.Y.,
     Carl Fischer, c1939. 2 vols. Vol 1, medium-high, 95p Pl no N.142-93; Vol. 1, medium-low, 95p Pl no
     N.143-92 (92 songs; includes 11 exercises by Vaccaj, not indexed)

386   WARD, ARTHUR EDWARD, 1893-
     The singing road, an active repertory for artists and students, selected classical and modern songs. N.Y.,
     Carl Fischer, c1950. 2 vols. Vol. 2, medium-high, 47p Pl no 1395; vol. 2, medium-low, 47p Pl no 1396
     (9 songs; includes 3 exercises by Marchesi, 1 by Vaccaj not indexed)

387   WARD, ARTHUR EDWARD, 1893-
     The singing road, an active repertory for artists and students, selected classical and modern songs. N.Y.,
     Carl Fischer, c1950. 2 parts; medium high, 47p Pl no N1556; medium low, 47p Pl no N1557 (9 songs;
     4 exercises by Marchesi not indexed)

388   WASNER, FRANZ, comp. and arr.
     The Trapp-family book of Christmas songs; illustrated by Agathe Trapp. N.Y., Pantheon Books, c1950. 128p
     (56 songs)

389   THE WEAVERS sing. Folk songs of America and other lands. N.Y., Folkways Music, 1951. 48p (32 songs)

390   WERBA, ERIK
     Bariton-Bass-Album; 17 Arien, Lieder und Monologe aus Opernwerken von Mozart, Beethoven, Wagner, Verdi,
     Rossini, Lortzing, Nicolai, Flotow, Offenbach. Wien, Wiesbaden, Doblinger, 1953. II Auffage. 64p Pl no
     D.8632

391   WERBA, ERIK, ed.
     Tenor-Album aus dem Repertoire von Julius Patzak, 16 Vokalwerke. Wien, Doblinger, c1951. 72p (2 songs
     and 14 operatic arias in the original language with German translations)

392   WETMORE, SUSANNAH and BARTHOLOMEW, MARSHALL, comps.
     Mountain songs of North Carolina arranged with pianoforte accompaniment by Marshall Bartholomew. N.Y.,
     G. Schirmer, c1926. 43p Pl no 32566 (14 songs)

393   WHEELER, MARY, 1892-   comp.
     Kentucky mountain folk-songs, the words and melodies collected by Mary Wheeler, the pianoforte accompani-
     ments by C. G. Bridge, with an introduction by Edgar Stillman-Kelley. Boston, Boston Music, c1937. 100p
     Pl no B.M.Co. 9273 (14 songs)

394   WHITEHILL, MICHAEL, ed.
     Everybody's favorite sacred songs. N.Y., Amsco Music, c1940. 192p (Everybody's favorite series, no.36)
     (50 songs)

395   WHITLOCK, JEAN, 1913-   and JAMES, LEONORE, 1914-   comps. and trs.
     A treasury of art songs. A collection of song classics for young singers. Piano arrangements by Joseph Honti.
     Boston, Boston Music, 1952. 65p Pl no B.M. Co. 11513 (14 songs; in English only)

396   WIEN, Wien, nur du allein; das Album der Schönsten Wiener Lieder. Mainz, B. Schott, 1936? 56p Pl no B.S.S.
     35065 (24 songs)

397   WILLAN, HEALEY, 1880-   arr.
     Songs of the British Isles. Boston, Boston Music, London, Oakville, Ontario, Frederick Harris, c1928. 89p
     (35 songs)

398   WILMANS, WILMAN, ed.
     Choice sacred songs. Bryn Mawr, Pa., Oliver Ditson, c1936. 125p 2 vols.; high and low voice (26 songs)

399   WOLFE, JACQUES, arr.
     Jacques Wolfe's American songster; 17 American folk-songs in arrangements for medium voice and piano. N.Y.,
     Carl Fischer, 1947. 35p

400   WOOD, JOSEPH, ed.
     Easter songs. N.Y., Broadcast Music, 1950. 64p (17 songs, English text only)

401   WOOD, JOSEPH, arr.
      Songs of the sea; for solo voice with piano accompaniment. N.Y., Broadcast Music, 1950. 23p (11 songs)

402   WOODGATE, LESLIE, comp.
      The Penguin song book. Harmondsworth, Middlesex, Penguin Books, 1951. 180p (114 songs)

403   WOODSIDE, JAMES, 1895-   ed. and arr.
      Seven centuries of solo-song (13th to 20th centuries); an educational song collection in six volumes with an
      historical treatise on the evolution of the art song. Vol. 1, high voice. Boston, Boston Music, 1942. 35p
      Pl no B.M. 10054 (10 songs)

404   WOODSIDE, JAMES, 1895-   ed. and arr.
      Seven centuries of solo-song (13th to 20th centuries) with an historical treatise on the evolution of the art song.
      Vol. 2, high voice. Boston, Boston Music, 1942. 35p Pl no B.M. Co. 10056 (10 songs)

405   WOODSIDE, JAMES, 1895-   ed. and arr.
      Seven centuries of solo-song (13th to 20th centuries) with an historical treatise on the evolution of the art song.
      Vol. 3, high voice. Boston, Boston Music, 1943. 39p (9 songs)

406   WOODSIDE, JAMES, 1895-   ed. and arr.
      Seven centuries of solo-song (13th to 20th centuries) with an historical treatise on the evolution of the art song.
      Vol. 4, high voice. Boston, Boston Music, 1943. 32p (13 songs)

407   WOODSIDE, JAMES, 1895-   ed. and arr.
      Seven centuries of solo-song (13th to 20th centuries) with an historical treatise on the evolution of the art song.
      Vol. 5, high voice. Boston, Boston Music, 1943. 39p Pl no B.M. Co. 10062 (10 songs)

408   WOODSIDE, JAMES, 1895-   ed. and arr.
      Seven centuries of solo-song (13th to 20th centuries) with an historical treatise on the evolution of the art song.
      Vol. 6, high voice. Boston, Boston Music, c1943. 40p Pl no B.M. Co. 10064 (13 songs)

409   WORK, JOHN WESLEY, 1901-   ed.
      American Negro songs; a comprehensive collection of 230 folk songs, religious and secular. N.Y., Howell,
      Soskin, c1940. 259p (unaccompanied)

410   YOUNG, PERCY MARSHALL, 1912-   comp. and arr.
      Carols for the twelve days of Christmas. London, Dennis Dobson, 1953. 140p (50 carols principally for voice
      and piano; some SATB)

411   ZANON, MAFFEO, ed.
      12 melodie Francesi; dei secoli XVII e XVIII per canto e pianoforte; testi italiani di Adelia Zanon; testo italiano,
      texte français. Milan, G. Ricordi, 1953. 40p Pl no E.R. 2433

This book is organized in two main sections, each of which is further subdivided. The following practices apply to all song entries in parts one and two of the book: a. Titles are in capital letters, b. First lines and refrains are in lower case letters within quotation marks, c. If the title and first line are identical, quotation marks enclose the title, d. Brackets around a title indicate that the title has been supplied.

PART I

Each song is fully described, each entry citing composer, all titles, first lines, languages of texts and author of texts

Section A

Composed songs are arranged alphabetically by composer and by title within each composer. Each song is assigned a marginal reference number and the following information is provided in this order:

1   Composer's name
2   Title of large work from which the song is taken or title in the original language in brackets
3   Title of the individual song and opus number in the original language if given in the collection indexed
4   First line of the song in the original language if given in the collection indexed
5   First line of the song in English and any other languages given in collection indexed
6   Abbreviations indicating the languages given in the collection indexed (See Table of Abbreviations and Symbols, beginning page xxxix)
7   Reference number of collection in which the song is found (See Collections Indexed, beginning page xi)
8   Author of text
9   Marginal reference number which is used in the Index to All Titles and First Lines, and Index of Authors

Section B

Anonymous songs and folksongs are arranged alphabetically by title within geographical subdivisions. Each song is assigned a marginal reference number and the following information is provided in this order:

1   Title of song
2   Tune title if it differs from title of song
3   First line of text
4   Refrain of text (if well known)
5   Abbreviations for language of text (See Table of Abbreviations and Symbols beginning page xxxix)
6   Reference number of collection in which song is found (See Collections Indexed beginning page xi)
7   Different title of the same tune
8   Different first line to the same tune

Section B (Continued)
- 9   Different refrain line to the same tune
- 10   Abbreviations for language of this text
- 11   Reference number of collection in which this version appears (Note that if items 7, 8, 9, 10 are the same as items 1, 2, 3, 4, they are not repeated but understood to be the same)
- 12   Author of text
- 13   Marginal reference number. The letter following the marginal reference indicates that the tune of the song is significantly different from the tunes with related or the same text with the same marginal reference number

Section C

Anonymous carols are arranged alphabetically by title within geographical subdivisions. Each song is assigned a marginal reference number. The same information is provided as outlined under Section B

Section D

Anonymous sea songs are arranged alphabetically by title. Each song has a marginal reference number. The same information is provided as outlined under Section B

PART II

Section A

Index of all titles, first lines, refrains and cross references in alphabetical order. A.L.A. rules for filing are generally applicable. In all instances, except see references, the marginal reference numbers are given. In most instances, except see references and tune names, the number in parenthesis representing the collection in which the item may be found is also given

Section B

Index of Authors. In the index of authors of song texts only marginal reference number are given. If the composer and the author are the same, the name does not appear in the author index. Authors are listed for texts of composed songs, folksongs, carols and sea songs when they are supplied in the collections indexed

TABLE OF ABBREVIATIONS AND SYMBOLS

ʿa	Arabic	lat	Latin
af	Africaans spelling	n	Norwegian
bret	Breton	nd	No date
c	Czechoslovakian	np	No place
ca	Catalonian	p	Polish
ch	Chinese	po	Portuguese
ch(tr)	Chinese transliterated	r	Russian
cr	Serbo-Croatian	r(tr)	Russian transliterated
d	Dutch	s	Spanish
D	Deutsch, Otto Erich. Schubert; thematic catalog of all his works in chronological order. London, Dent, 1951	S	Schmieder, Wolfgang. Thematisch-systematisches Verzeichnis der musikalischen Werke von Johann Sebastian Bach. Leipzig, Breitkopf & Härtel, 1950
da	Danish		
e	English	sc	Scottish
f	French	sl	Slovene
f(a)	Auvergne	sw	Swedish
fi	Finnish	t	Tagalog
fl	Flemish	w	Welsh
g	German	WoO	Werke ohne Opuszahl (from) Kinsky, Georg. Das Werke Beethovens, thematisch-bibliographisches Verzeichnis seiner sämtlichen vollendeten Kompositionen. München, G. Henle, 1955
gr	Greek		
gr(tr)	Greek transliterated		
h	Hebrew		
h(tr)	Hebrew transliterated		
ha	Hawaiian		
Ho	Hoboken, Anthony. Joseph Haydn; thematisch-bibliographisches Werkverzeichnis. Mainz, B. Schott's Söhne, 1957-	y	Yiddish
		[ ]	Used with titles to indicate conventional, or generally recognized titles
hu	Hungarian	( )	Used with numbers to indicate collections indexed. These are listed in the front of the book numbered 1 through 411
i	Italian		
ic	Icelandic		
ir	Irish	*	Used with reference numbers to insert additional songs in alphabetical sequence
K	Köchel, Ludwig Ritter von. Chronologisch-thematisches Verzeichnis sämtlicher Tonwerke Wolfgang Amadé Mozarts... Wiesbaden, Breitkopf & Härtel, 1964	A,B,C, etc.	Used with folksongs to indicate significantly different tunes when titles are the same

COMPOSED SONGS

A BECKET, THOMAS. See BECKET, THOMAS A.
AARONS, SAUL
>THE HORSE WITH A UNION LABEL; OLD PAINT; "My Daddy was a cowboy and I follow in his foot-   1
>steps" e 293 words by M. Stratton and S. Aarons
>PICKET LINE PRISCILLA; "Oh, picket line Priscilla, picket line Priscilla, had a line"; e 293 words   2
>by M. Stratton
ABBATINI, ANTONIO MARIA, ca1595-1677
>[LA COMICA DEL CIELO, opera; words by Rospigliosi] ARIE DER BALTASARA;   3
>"Quanto è bello il mio diletto"; "Wie schön ist mein Geliebter" g, i 217
ABRAHAM, PAUL, 1892-1950
>[DIE BLUME VON HAWAII, operetta; words by A. Grünwald and F. Löhner]   4
>BLUME VON HAWAII; "Das blaue Meer rauscht sehnsuchtsschwer" g 258
>[Ibid] DU TRAUMSCHÖNE PERLE DER SÜDSEE; "Sonnenreich, märchengleich liegst du im Meer   5
>wie ein Traum" g 258
>[VIKTORIA UND IHR HUSAR, operetta; words by A. Grünwald and F. Löhner]   6
>JA, SO EIN MÄDEL, UNGARISCHES MÄDEL; "Fahr' in das Landel nur hinunter" g 258
>[Ibid] REICH MIR ZUM ABSCHIED NOCH EINMAL DIE HÄNDE; GOOD NIGHT! "Einmal, da schlägt   7
>für uns die Stunde" g 258
ABT, FRANZ, 1819-1885
>AM GRENZWALL; "Ein Römer stand in finstrer Nacht am deutschen Grenzwall Posten" g 31 words by   8
>J. V. Scheffel
>AVE MARIA; "Ave Maria gratia plena"; "Hail Mary full of grace" e, lat 304   9
>GUTE NACHT, DU MEIN HERZIGES KIND; "All' Abend, bevor ich zur Ruhe geh'" g 328   10
>HERBST; "Wenn im Purpurschein blinkt der wilde Wein" g 31 words by R. Baumbach   11
>DAS HILDEBRANDLIED; "Hildebrand und sein Sohn Hadubrand" g 31 words by J. V. Scheffel   12
>KATHLEEN AROON; "Why should we parted be, Kathleen Aroon" e 36 words by Mrs. Crawford   13
>DIE LINDENWIRTIN; "Keinen Tropfen im Becher mehr" g 31, 99, 327; "KEINEN TROPFEN IM   14
>BECHER MEHR" g 43, 353, 326 words by R. Baumbach
>NIGHT; "The sunset glows in splendor" e 28, 366 words by M. K. Cherryman   15
>NOT A SPARROW FALLETH; "Not a sparrow falleth, but its God doth know" e 394 words by W. S.   16
>Passmore
>O SCHWARZWALD, O HEIMAT; "O Schwarzwald, o Heimat, wie bist du so schön!" Op. 465, no. 2,   17
>g 31, 326
>WALDANDACHT; "Frühmorgens, wenn die Hähne krähn" g 327   18
>WEIN HER!; "Merkt auf, ich weiss ein neu Gedicht"; "Die Welt ist rund und muss sich drehn" (ref)   19
>g 31 words by R. Baumbach
>[WENN DIE SCHWALBEN HEIMWÄRTS ZIEHN]; "WHEN THE SWALLOWS HOMEWARD   20
>FLY" e 28, 114, 132, 366
ACKLEY, ALFRED HENRY
>SLEEP, CHILD DIVINE; "Jesus, the meek and mild, came as a little child" e 315   21
>THE STORY THAT NEVER GROWS OLD; "O list to the story that never grows old" e 315   22
>WHEN THE LORD OF LOVE WAS BORN; "With shepherds watching lambs and sheep" e 315   23
>words by H. T. Kerr
ACQUA, EVA DELL', 1856-?
>CHANSON PROVENCALE; "Par les nuits sans rivales, les belles nuits d'été"; COUNTRY SONG; "Above   24
>the country thickets, the summer moon is bright" e, f 93
>VILLANELLE; "J'ai vu passer l'hirondelle dans le ciel pur du matin"; "Oft-times I look at the swallow   25
>fly thro' the clear morning air" e, f 237 words by F. van der Elst
ADAM, ADOLPHE CHARLES, 1803-1856
>CANTIQUE DE NOËL; "Minuit Chretien, c'est l'heure solemne"; CHRISTMAS SONG; "O holy night,   26
>the stars are brightly shining" e, f 123, 154; O HOLY NIGHT, e, f 337, 394, e 28, 125, 206, 244,
>251, 296, 315, 366 words by C. de Roquemaure
>[LE POSTILLON DE LONGJUMEAU, opera; words by A. de Leuven and L. L.   27
>Brunswick] [Mes amis, ecoutez l'histoire] "FREUNDE, VERNEHMET DIE GESCHICHTE" g 391
ADAM DE LA HALLE, ca1235-ca1288
>"D'AMOUROUS CUER VOEL CANTER"; "WITH AMOROUS HEART I SING THIS REFRAIN" e, f 403   28
>[LE JEU DE ROBIN ET MARION, opera] ROBIN M'AIME; ROBIN LOVES ME; "Robin   29
>loves me, Robin mine" e 35
ADAMS, BOB
>MOTHER PIN A ROSE ON ME. See 2125
ADAMS, STEPHEN, pseud. See MAYBRICK, MICHAEL, 1844-1913
AGER, MILTON, 1893-
>"EVERYTHING IS PEACHES DOWN IN GEORGIA" e 129, 130 joint composer G. W. Meyer,   30
>words by G. Clarke
AHLE, GEORG
>DIE GÜLDENE SONNE; "Die güldne Sonne bringt Leben und Wonne" g 326 words by P. von Zesen   31

1

ARNOLD, SAMUEL, 1740-1802
    AMO, AMAS. See 4538
    THE WAY-WORN TRAVELLER; "Faint and wearily the way-worn traveller plods unhurriedly afraid to   90
        stop" e 279 words by G. Coleman

ARREDONDO, ENRIQUE MEJÍA
    "AL SON DE LA MANGULINA" s 284   91

ARZONIA, JOE
    THE PREACHER AND THE BEAR; "A preacher went out a hunting"; "Oh Lord, didn't you deliver   92
        Daniel from the Lion's den?" (ref) e 114,131,246

ASCHER, JOSEPH, 1829-1869
    ALICE, WHERE ART THOU?; "The birds sleeping gently" e 132   joint composer J. L. Molloy, words   93
        by W. Guernsey

ASTOL, FELIX
    LA BORINQUEÑA; "La tierra de Borinquen donde he nacido yo"; "Island of rarest splendor, my Puerto   94
        Rican land" e, s 291 words by M. F. Juncos

ASTORGA, EMANUELE GIOACCHINO CESARE RINCON, 1680-1757
    FIORE INGRATO; "Fiore ingrato, ingrato fiore, perche t'armi di rigore" e 180   95
    IN QUESTO CORE; "In questo core più va crescendo" i 180   96
    [VO CERCANDO, cantata] KAMMERDUETT; "Vo cercando, fra le ombre sospirando";   97
        "Ich schweife umher, zu suchen" g, i 218

ATTEY, JOHN, d ca1640
    ON A TIME; "On a time the amorous Silvy said to her shepheard" e 196; "ON A TIME THE   98
        AMOROUS SILVY" e 119
    SWEET WAS THE SONG; "Sweet was the song the Virgin sung" e 144; "Sweet was the song the   99
        Virgin sang" e 197

ATUROV
    SONG OF THE FAR EASTERN PARTISANS; "Over mountain and through woodland" e, r 7; THROUGH   100
        THE HILLS AND VALES; "A battalion its way was wending" e, r 288 words by S. Alymov

AUBER, DANIEL FRANÇOIS ESPRIT, 1782-1871
    [LA MUETTE DE PORTICI, opera; words by A. E. Scribe and G. Dela-   101
        vigne] DU PAUVRE SEUL AMI, Act IV; "Du pauvre seul ami fidèle"; SLUMBER SONG;
        "Thou only comfort of the lowly" e, f 3

AUDRAN, EDMOND, 1842-1901
    [LES NOCHES D'OLIVETTE, opera; words by H. B. Farnie] THE TORPEDO   102
        AND THE WHALE; "In the North Sea lived a whale" e 205
    [Ibid] THE YACHT AND THE BRIG; "You shall be a clipper built yacht" e 205   103

AUGUSTO, B.
    BLESS'D LAND OF LOVE AND LIBERTY; "I've wander'd o'er the desert wide" e 189   104

AVISON, CHARLES, ca1710-1770
    SHOUT THE GLAD TIDINGS; "Shout the glad tidings, exultingly sing" e 337 words by W. A.   105
        Muhlenberg
    SOUND THE LOUD TIMBREL; "Sound the loud timbrel o'er Egypt's dark sea" e 28   106

AXMAN, EMIL, 1887-1949
    "LOS DRUHDY VLAST MNĚ KRÁSNOU PŘÁL"; "EINST HATTE ICH EIN VATERLAND" c, g 73a   107

AYER, NAT D.
    OH! YOU BEAUTIFUL DOLL; "Oh! you beautiful doll, you great big beautiful doll" e 233 words   108
        by A. S. Brown

BACH, CARL PHILIPP EMANUEL, 1714-1788
    BITTEN; "Gott, deine Güte reicht so weit" g 229,250 words by C. F. Gellert   109

BACH, JOHANN CHRISTIAN, 1735-1782
    [CARATTACO, opera] "NON È VER, CHE ASSISE IN TRONO"; "ES IST NICHT WAHR, DASS   110
        AUF DEM THRON" g, i 218

BACH, JOHANN ERNST, 1722-1777
    DER CANARIENVOGEL; "Philinden ward von ferner Künste" g 250 words by C. F. Gellert   111

BACH, JOHANN SEBASTIAN, 1685-1750
    [ACH WAS SOLL ICH SÜNDER MACHEN? S.259] "HUSH, MY DEAR, LIE STILL   112
        AND SLUMBER" e 337 words by I. Watts
    [ALLE MENSCHEN MÜSSEN STERBEN, S.262] "WATCHMAN, TELL US OF THE   113
        NIGHT" e 337 tune by J. Hintze, words by Sir J. Bowring
    [ALSO HAT GOTT DIE WELT GELIEBT, S.68] MEIN GLÄUBIGES HERZE, FROH-   114
        LOCKE; "Mein gläubiges Herze, frohlocke, sing scherze"; MY HEART EVER FAITHFUL; "My
        heart ever faithful sing praises, be joyful" e, g 329,394; MY HEART EVER FAITHFUL SING
        PRAISES. e. g 122,123; "Mein gläubiges Herze, frohlokke, sing' scherze" g 311

BACH, JOHANN SEBASTIAN, 1685-1750 (Continued)

[ARIA DI GIOVANNI, S.518] "WILLST DU DEIN HERZ MIR SCHENKEN" g 311,313; 115
"IF THOU THY HEART WILT GIVE ME" e 385

BIST DU BEI MIR, S.508; "Bist du bei mir, geh ich mit Freuden" g 98,226; IF THOU ART NEAR; 116
"If thou art near, I will with gladness" e, g 330, e 348; IF THOU BE NEAR; "If thou be near,
go I with gladness" e, g 210; IF YOU ARE NEAR; "If you are near if you are with me" e, g
357; STAY THOU NEAR BY; "Stay thou near by, then go I gladly" e, g 405; BE THOU WITH
ME; "Be thou with me, dear Lord and Father" e 160

"GEDENKE DOCH, MEIN GEIST, ZURÜCKE," S.509, g 308 117

"DIE GULDNE SONNE VOLL FREUD UND WONNE," S.451, g 226 words by P. Gerhardt 118

[DER HERR DENKET AN UNS, S.196] "DER HERR SEGNE EUCH"; "THE LORD BLESS 119
YOU" e, g 50

[HERZ UND MUND UND TAT UND LEBEN. WOHL MIR, DASS ICH JESUM 120
HABE, S.147] "JESU, JOY OF MAN'S DESIRING" e 394; "JESUS, JOY OF MAN'S DESIR-
ING" e 50; GOD AND MAN; "These words spake Jesus" (recit); "Holy Father, we Thy children"
(aria) e 89 recit by K. K. Davis

[ICH HALTE TREULICH STILL, S.466] "O LOVE THAT CASTS OUT FEAR" e 50 121
words by H. Bonar

[ICH STEH AN DEINER KRIPPE HIER, S.469] ZU WEIHNACHTEN; "Ich steh an deiner 122
Krippe hier"; CHRISTMAS SONG; "I stand beside Thy cradle here" e, g 388 words by P.
Gerhardt

KOMM, SÜSSER TOD, S.478; "Komm, süsser Tod, komm sel'ge Ruh!" g 99,226; COME, SWEETEST 123
DEATH; "Come, sweetest Death! Come, blessed rest!" e 346,400; COME SWEET REPOSE; "Come
thou, sweet rest, come sweet repose!" e 386

KOMMT, SEELEN, DIESER TAG, S.479; PFINGSLIED; "Kommt, Seelen, dieser Tag muss heilig sein 124
besungen" g 99; COME PRAISE THE LORD; "Come, praise, come, praise the Lord" e 160; WE
THANK THEE, GOD; "We thank Thee God, that they who in Thy faith abided" e 199

[LASSET UNS MIT JESU ZIEHEN, S.481] "LET US STRIVE TO BE LIKE OUR SAVIOR" 125
e 160 words by M. Harrell

[LOBT GOTT, IHR CHRISTEN ALLZUGLEICH, S.376] WHILE SHEPHERDS 126
WATCHED; "While shepherds watch'd their flocks by night" e 319 tune by N. Hermann, words
by N. Tate

THE LORD'S PRAYER; "Our Father which art in heaven" e 89 127

[MATTHAÜSPASSION] AUS LIEBE, WILL MEIN HEILAND STERBEN; "Aus Liebe, aus Liebe, 128
aus Liebe will mein Heiland sterben" g 311

[Ibid] SACRAMENT; [Da sie aber assen]; "And as they were eating, Jesus took bread and 129
blessed it" e 160

[O JESULEIN SÜSS, S.493] O JESULEIN ZART; "O Jesulein zart, dein Kripplein ist hart" 130
g 412; O LITTLE ONE; "O Little One sweet, O Little One mild" e 39,271; O SAVIOR SWEET;
"O Savior sweet, O Savior kind" e 160 tune by S. Scheidt

[SEHET, WIR GEH'N HINAUF GEN JERUSALEM, S.159] "ES IST VOLLBRACHT"; 131
"IT IS FULFILLED" e, g 330

"VERGISS MEIN NICHT" S.505 g 97,229 132

[WACHET AUF, RUFT UNS DIE STIMME. GLORIA SEI DIR GESUNGEN] 133
WACHET AUF; "Wachet auf, ruft uns die Stimme"; "WAKE, AWAKE FOR NIGHT IS FLYING"
e, g 337; Sleepers, wake (tune) e 38,39 words and tune by P. Nicolai. See also NICOLAI,
PHILIPP - "WACHET AUF, RUFT UNS DIE STIMME"

[WAS MIR BEHAGT, IST NUR DIE MUNTRE JAGD; SCHAFE KÖNNEN SICHER 134
WEIDEN, S.208] "JESUS, SHEPHERD, BE THOU NEAR ME" e 50

[WEIHNACHTS-ORATORIUM] "BRICH AN, DU SCHÖNES MORGENLICHT"; BREAK FORTH, 135
O BEAUTEOUS HEAVENLY LIGHT" e, g 337, e 307,319 tune by J. Schop, words by J. Rist

[Ibid] "ICH STEH AN DEINER KRIPPE HIER"; "BESIDE THY CRADLE HERE I STAND" e, g 337, 136
e 307; BESIDE THY CRADLE e 319,410 tune by J. Klug, words by P. Gerhardt, English words
by J. Troutbeck

[Ibid] ICH WILL DICH MIT FLEISS BEWAHREN; "ALL THE SKIES TONIGHT SING O'ER US" 137
e 361 words by J. O'Connor; THEE WITH TENDER CARE; "Thee with tender care I'll cherish"
e 319 tune by J. G. Ebeling, words by J. Troutbeck

[Ibid] SEID FROH, DIEWEIL; WIR CHRISTENLEUT; "Wir Christenleut, wir Christenleut sing 138
jetzt voll Freud'" g 412

[Ibid] SYMPHONY FROM THE CHRISTMAS ORATORIO piano 307; VORSPIEL piano 412 139

[Ibid] "WIE SOLL ICH DICH EMPFANGEN?"; "HOW SHALL I FITLY MEET THEE?" e, g 337 140
tune by H. L. Hassler, words by Picander

5

7

BEETHOVEN, LUDWIG VAN, 1770-1827 (Continued)

are telling Jehovah's glory" e, g 274; THE WORSHIP OF GOD IN NATURE; "The heav'ns are telling of the Lord's endless glory" e, g 123   words by C. F. Gellert

[FIDELIO, opera; words by J. Sonnleithner]   "ABSCHEULICHER! WO EILST DU HIN?"   229
Act I, no.10 (recit); "Komm, Hoffnung, lass den letzten Stern" (aria); "Thou monstrous fiend, whither dost haste" (recit); "Oh, Hope, thou wilt not let the star" (aria) e, g 1

[Ibid]   ARIE DER MARZELLINE, Act I, no.3 (erster Aufführung); "O wär' ich schon mit dir vereint   230
und dürfte Mann dich nennen!" g 311

[Ibid]   "GOTT! WELCH DUNKEL HIER!" Act II, no.13 (recit); "In des Lebens Frühlingstagen"   231
(aria) g 391

[Ibid]   HA, WELCH EIN AUGENBLICK, Act I, no.8; "Ha! Ha! Ha! welch ein Augenblick" g 390;   232
"Ha! Ha! Ha! it is not too late" e, g 4

[Ibid]   "HAT MAN NICHT AUCH GOLD DANEBEN," Act I, no.5; "IF YOU HAVE NO GOLD,   233
WITHAL" e, g 5

GRANT US, O LORD; "Grant us, O Lord, a joyous Christmas-tide" e 206   234

HYMNE AN DIE NACHT; "Heilge Nacht, o giesse du Himmelsfrieden in dies Herz" g 326   words by   235
C. F. Gellert

[ICH BITT' DICH, SCHREIB' MIR DIE ES-SCALA AUF, WoO 172]   THE SCALE   236
OF D FLAT; "I pray you, I pray you, sing me the scale of D flat" 3 pt round e 199

IN QUESTO TOMBA, WoO 133; "In questa tomba oscura"; "IN THIS DARK TOMB" e, i 405   words   237
by G. Carpani

DER KUSS, op.128; "Ich war bei Chloen ganz allein"; THE KISS; "I pled with Chloe, maid supreme"   238
e, g 405   words by C. F. Weisse

MAILIED, op.52, no.4; MAIGESANG; "Wie herrlich leuchtet mir die Natur" g 97   words by J. W.   239
von Goethe

[MARMOTTE, op.52, no.7]   LIED DES MARMOTTENBUBEN; "Ich komme schon durch mánche   240
Land" f (in part), g 229   words by J. W. von Goethe

[MIGNON, op.75, no.1]   KENNST DU DAS LAND; "Kennst du das Land, wo die Citronen   241
blüh'n"; KNOW'ST THOU THE LAND; "Know'st thou the land where citrons sweetly bloom"
e, g 275   words by J. W. von Goethe

MIT EINEM GEMALTEN BAND, op.83, no.3; "Kleine Blumen, kleine Blätter"; WITH A PAINTED   242
RIBBON; "Tiny leaflets, tiny flowers" e, g 330

OPFERLIED, WoO 126; "Die Flamme lodert, milder Schein'" g 99   words by F. von Matthisson   243

[SEHNSUCHT, WoO 134, no.4]   "NUR WER DIE SEHNSUCHT-KENNT" g 226   words by J.   244
W. von Goethe

[SIGNOR ABATE, WoO 178]   SIGNOR ABBATE; "Signor Abbate, io sono, io sono"; "Herr   245
Abt, ich fühle mich" g, i 42

[SONATA, piano, op.27, no.2; C minor, Adagio sostenuto, arr]   COME TO   246
ME; "Come to me, come to me, all ye that need rest" e 123

THE SONG OF THE FLEA, op.75, no.3; "Es war einmal ein König"; "There was a mighty King once"   247
e, g 273   words by J. W. von Goethe

[SYMPHONY, no.9, op.125, D minor.   Presto, arr]   AN DIE FREUDE; "Freude,   248
schöner Götterfunken, Tochter aus Elysium" g 99   words by F. Schiller

WONNE DER WEHMUT, op.83, no.1; "Trocknet nicht, trocknet nicht"; THE RAPTURE OF SORROW;   249
"Grieve you not, grieve you not" e, g 220, g 250   words by J. W. von Goethe

[ZÄRTLICHE LIEBE, WoO 123]   ICH LIEBE DICH; "Ich liebe dich, so wie du mich" g 99,   250
229; I LOVE THEE; "I love thee as thou lovest me" e, g 387; "I love but thee as thou dost me"
e, g 210; I LOVE YOU; "As you love me, so I love you" e, g 122; "I love you, dear, as you love
me" e, g 141; "As I love thee, so you love me" e, g 36   words by Herrossee

BEHREND, A. H.

DADDY; "Take my head on your shoulder"; "I'm sometimes afraid to think" (ref) e 129, 130   words   251
by M. M. Lemon

BELLINI, VINCENZO, 1801-1835

ARIETTA, NO.2; "Vanne o rosa fortunata a posar di Nice" i 278   252

[I CAPULETI E I MONTECCHI, opera; words by F. Romani]   "DEH! TU, BELL'   253
ANIMA" pt 4 i 300

[NORMA, opera; words by F. Romani]   CASTA DIVA, CHE INARGENTI, CAVATINA,   254
Act I; "Casta Diva, casta Diva, che inargenti"; "Goddess fairest, goddess fairest, so brightly
gleaming" e, i 6

[I PURITANI DI SCOZIA, opera; words by C. Pepoli]   QUI LA VOCE, Act II;   255
"O rendetemi la speme" (recit); "Qui la voce sua soave mi chiamava e poi spari" (aria); "O
return again beloved" (recit); "Here he swore to love me, ever, spoke his love and went away"
(aria) e, i 292

[Ibid]   SON VERGIN VEZZOSA, Act I; "Son vergin vezzosa in veste di sposa" i 302   256

[Ibid]   VIEN DILETTO; "Vien, diletto, è in ciel la luna"; "See, my dearest the moon of heaven"   257
e, i 292

9

BLUME, KARL
    JA GRÜN IST DIE HEIDE; "Als ich gestern einsam ging auf der grünen, grünen Heid" g 326   words   343
       by H. Löns
BLUMENTHAL, JACOB, 1849-1916
    THE BEND OF THE RIVER; "There's a bend of the river" e 205 words by F. E. Weatherly   344
Blumenthal, Jacques. See BLUMENTHAL, JACOB, 1849-1916
BOCHMANN, WERNER, 1900-
    "GUTE NACHT, MUTTER!" g 222 words by E. Lehnow   345
    LIEBESTRAUM; "Du warst für mich der schönste Liebestraum" g 223 words by E. Hübner   346
BODROGI, ZSIGMOND
    SZÉP, TAVASZI ÁLMOK; "Szép, tavaszi álmok, emlekek, virágok"; LOVELY DREAMS OF SPRING-   347
      TIME; "Lovely dreams of springtime, visions full of flowers" e, hu 285
BÖHEIM, JOSEF
    ALT-PRAG; "Heil dir, du selige holde Stolzprangende Königsbraut" g 31 words by W. Kosch   348
BÖHME, ERDMANN WERNER, 1906-
    BURSCHENHEIMAT; "Ich fahre von hinnen auf meine Weis" g 31 words by W. Haas   349
BÖHMER, KARL HERMANN EHRFRIED, 1799-1884
    KAISER WENZEL; "Was schiert mich Reich" g 31 words by F. G. Drimhorn   350
BOËSSET, ANTOINE, SIEUR DE VILLEDIEU, ca1585-1643
    AIR DE COUR; "Ie vouldrois bien, ô Cloris que j'adore"; "Knowe my deare Idoll Cloris that all   351
      zealous" e, f 278
BOHM, KARL, 1844-1920
    STILL WIE DIE NACHT, op.326, no.27; "Still wie die Nacht tief wie das Meer" g 327; CALM AS   352
      THE NIGHT; "Calm as the night, deep as the sea" e, g 122, e 28; "Still as the night, deep as
      the sea" e 237; STILL AS THE NIGHT; "Still as the night, deep as the sea" e, g 36,136,348;
      "Still as the night, true constantly" e 132
BOHNENBLUST, GOTTFRIED, 1883-
    "ANNELI, WO BIST GESTER GSI?" g 156   353
Boisset, Antoine. See BOËSSET, ANTOINE, SIEUR DE VILLEDIEU, ca1585-1643
BOITO, ARRIGO, 1842-1918
    [MEFISTOFELE, opera] "L'ALTRA NOTTE IN FONDO AL MARE," Act III i 301; LAST   354
      NIGHT IN THE DEEP SEA; "Last night in the deep, deep sea" e, i 143
    [Ibid] "SON LO SPIRITO CHE NEGA," Act I i 299   355
    [NERONE, opera] A NOTTE CUPA, Act I; "A notte cupa, quando negli antri del fulnereo suol";   356
      WHEN NIGHT HAS FALLEN; "When night has fallen, when in the caverns deep below the earth"
      e, i 143
    [Ibid] INVAN MI DANNI!, Act II; "Invan mi danni! ah, non moriro!"; THY SENTENCE IS USE-   357
      LESS!; "Thy sentence is useless! That will not make me die!" e, i 143
BOLAÑO, FRANCISCO
    SANTA MARTA; "Santa Marta, Santa Marta tiene tren" s 284   358
Boleyn, Ann. See ANNE BOLEYN, QUEEN CONSORT OF HENRY VIII, 1507-1536
BONE, GENE, 1915-
    DEBORAH; "Deborah danced, when she was two, as buttercups and daffodils do" e 358 joint composer   359
      H. Fenton, words by A. Kilmer
BONONCINI, GIOVANNI BATTISTA, 1670-ca1750
    [ASTARTÈ, opera] "L'ESPERTO NOCCHIERO"; "THE WISE SAILOR STEERING" e, i 139   360
    [ECCO, DORINDA, IL GIORNO, cantata] LUNGI DA TE; "Lungi da te, ben mio";   361
      "Away from you, my beloved" e, i 134
    [ERMINIA, opera] MENUETT FÜR 2 SOPRANE; "Sol per te le pene senze spene di mercè";   362
      "Wenn ich schon die einzig für dich erduldeten Leiden liebte" (duet) g, i 217
    [GRISELDA, opera] "PER LA GLORIA D'ADORARVI"; "FOR THE LOVE MY HEART DOTH   363
      PRIZE" e, i 368
    [MARIO FUGGITIVO, opera] ARIE DER DALINDA; "Più non ti voglio credere"; "Ich will   364
      dir nicht mehr Glauben schenken" g, i 217
    PIÙ VAGA E VEZZOSETTA; "Più vaga e vezzosetta sarai"; "More desirable and pretty you will be"   365
      e, i 134
    SI TI PIACE; "Da te, che pasci orgnora di sdegno l'alma" (recit); "Se te piace di farmi morire" (aria);   366
      "From you, who filled your soul with scorn" (recit); "If it pleases you to let me die" (aria) e, i 134
    "LA SPERANZA I CORI AFFIDA"; "Hope sustains the heart" e, i 134   367
BONONCINI, MARC ANTONIO, 1677-1726
    DATTI PUR PACE; "Datti pur pace e vivi lieto"; BE CONTENT; "Be content, live happily";   368
      BERUHIGE DICH; "Beruhige Dich und lebe fröhlich" e, g, i 253
    [IL TRIONFO DI CAMILLA, opera] PUPILLE NERE; "Pupille nere, se voi guardate";   369
      "LOVE LEADS TO BATTLE" e, i 273

13

BORODIN, ALEKSANDR PORFIR'EVICH, 1833-1887

 ARABIAN MELODY; "Leave me not, my beloved" e 407   370

 A DISSONANCE; ROMANCE; "Thy lips say, 'I love thee'" e 122   371

 THE SLEEPING PRINCESS; "Hush! Hush! with lovely eyes" e 121; DIE SCHLAFENDE PRINZESSIN;   372
  "Dans le bois ténébreux, la princesse aux si doux yeux" f, r 278

 YOUR NATIVE LAND; "Your native land, your distant nation" e, r 340   words by A. S. Pushkin   373

BORTNIÂNSKII, DMITRIĬ STEPANOVICH, 1751-1825

 "ICH BETE AN DIE MACHT DER LIEBE" g 326   words by G. Tersteegen   374

BOSCOVICH, ALEXANDER URIJAH, 1908-

 SHIR LA-NEGEV; "Hashamata eych ba-Negev"; "Have you heard how in the Negev" e, h 318   words   375
  A. Shlonsky

BOTSFORD, FLORENCE HUDSON

 PAUL SAID TO THE CORINTHIANS; "Love is very patient, very kind" e 37   words from Bible   376

BOUGHTON, RUTLAND, 1878-

 BEN JONSON'S CAROL; "I sing the birth was born tonight" e 334   words by B. Jonson   377

BOURGEOIS, LOUIS THOMAS, 1676-1750

 [LES AMOURS DÉGUISÉS, opera] AIR DE PARIS; "Paisible nuit, suspendez votre cours";   378
  "Oh! tranquil night, why haste away so soon?" e, f 152

 OLD HUNDREDTH; "Praise God from Whom all blessings flow" e 35; DOXOLOGY e 233; "PRAISE   379
  GOD FROM WHOM ALL BLESSINGS FLOW" e 28,279,366; OLD HUNDREDTH; "Shout to Jehovah,
  all the earth" e 32,34; OLD HUNDRED; "All people that on earth do dwell" e 173; "From all
  that dwell below the skies" e 132; THE ABOLITIONIST HYMN; "We ask not that the slave should
  lie" e 109,110,173

 PILGRIM'S MELODY; TOULON (tune); "Our Israel may say and that truly" e 34   380

BOUSSET, JEAN-BAPTISTE DROUART DE, 1662-1725

 AIR A BOIRE; "Je ne refuse point d'aimer" f 278   381

BOUVARD, FRANÇOIS, ca1670-1757

 LA BELLE CUISINIÈRE; "De l'aimable Catherine je veux chanter les talents" f 174   382

 [CASSANDRE, opera; words by F. Lagrange-Chancel] AIR D'ORESTE; "Ruisseau   383
  dont le bruit charmant"; "Thy music, Oh! gentle stream" e, f 152   joint composer T. B. de la
  Doue

BOWEN, E. E.

 FORTY YEARS ON, HARROW SCHOOL SONG; "Forty years on, when afar and a-sunder" e 402   joint   384
  composer J. Farmer

BOWLES, PAUL FREDERIC, 1911-

 [SCÈNES D'ANABASE, song cycle] "AINSI PARFOIS NOS SEUILS" f 85   words by J. Perse   385

BOWMAN

 GOOD MORNING, CARRIE! See 3519

BOYCE, WILLIAM, 1710-1779

 [HARLEQUIN'S INVASION, opera; words by D. Garrick] HEART OF OAK; "Come   386
  cheer up, my lads, 'tis to glory we steer" e 14,173,235,349; IN FREEDOM WE'RE BORN; "Come,
  join hand in hand, brave Americans all" e 44; THE LIBERTY SONG, e 34, 109,110; "Come swallow
  your bumpers, ye tories" e 115   words by J. Dickinson

BOYLE, RICHARD

 THE BOLD VOLUNTEER; "Here's to the Squire that goes on parade" e 44   387

BRADBURY, WILLIAM BATCHELDER, 1816-1868

 JESUS LOVES ME; "Jesus loves me! this I know" e 28   words by A. B. Warner   388

 "RALLY ROUND THE FLAG, BOYS" e 129,130   389

BRAGA, GAETANO, 1829-1907

 LA SERENATA; "O quali mi risvegliano Dolcissimi concenti"; ANGEL'S SERENADE; "What sounds are   390
  those that waken me" e, i 329,394

BRAHAM, DAVID

 ARE YOU THERE, MO-RI-AR-I-TY?; "Whin first I kem to Dublin town"; "I'm a well-known bobby of   391
  the stalwart squad" (ref) e 172

 THE MULLIGAN GUARDS; "We crave your condescension, we'll tell you what we know; "We shoul-   392
  dered guns and marched and marched away" (ref) e 225; THE MULLIGAN GUARD; "We shoulder'd
  guns and march'd and march'd away" (ref only) e 115

 OVER THE HILL TO THE POOR HOUSE; "What no! it can't be that they've driven their father, so help-   393
  less and old"; "For I'm old, and I'm helpless and feeble" (ref) e 114,129,130,131   words by G. L.
  Catlin

BRAHAM, JOHN, 1774-1856

 THE ANCHOR'S WEIGHED; "The tear fell gently from her eye" e 205   words by S. J. Arnold   394

BRAHAM, PHILIP

 LIMEHOUSE BLUES; "In Limehouse where yellow chinkies love to play"; "Oh! Limehouse kid, oh!   395
  oh! oh! Limehouse kid" (ref) e 345   words by D. Furber

BRAHMS, JOHANNES, 1833-1897

AUF DEM KIRCHHOFE, op.105, no.4; "Der Tag ging regenschwer und sturmbewegt" g 97,250; IN   396
   THE CHURCHYARD; "The day was cold with rain" e, g 112   words by D. von Liliencron

BOTSCHAFT, op.47, no.1; "Wehe, Lüftchen, lind und lieblich"; THE MESSAGE; "Blow O breezes,   397
   mild and lovely" e, g 112; "Haste away, ye lovely breezes" e, g 272   words by G. F. Daumer

ES IST EIN' ROS' ENTSPRUNGEN, op.122   piano 307   398

"FEINSLIEBCHEN, DU SOLLST MIR NICHT BARFUSS GEHN." See 4149

FELDEINSAMKEIT, op.86, no.2; "Ich ruhe still in hohen grünen Gras" g 98; EARTH AND SKY; "The   399
   sun far off, the waving grasses near" e, g 273; IN SUMMER FIELDS; "In summer fields I lie 'mid
   deep green grass" e, g 137; "I LIE QUITE STILL IN GRASS SO GREEN" e 348   words by H. Almers

DER FRÜHLING, op.6, no.2; "Es lockt und säuselt um den Baum"; SPRING'S SECRET; "A whisper stirs   400
   the slum'ring tree" e, g 275   words by J. B. Rousseau

IN STILLER NACHT; "In stiller Nacht, zur ersten Wächt" g 41,99, e 226   401

IN WALDESEINSAMKEIT, op.85, no.6; "Ich sass zu dienen Füssen"; FOREST SOLITUDE; "Within   402
   the woods' deep shadows" e, g 112   words by K. Lemcke

KLAGE, op.105, no.3; "Feins Liebchen, trau du nicht" g 229   403

DIE KRÄNZE, op.46, no.1; "Hier ob dem Eingang seid befestiget"; THE GARLAND; "Here at the   404
   portal shall my garland" e, g 272   words by G. F. Daumer

DAS MÄDCHEN SPRICHT, op.107, no.3; "Schwalbe sag' mir an, ist's dein alter Mann"; THE   405
   MAIDEN SPEAKS; "Swallow, tell me, pray Is't thine old mate, say" e, g 330   words by Gruppe

MÄDCHENLIED, op.107, no.5; "Auf die Nacht in der Spinnstub'n, da singen die Mädchen" g 226   406
   words by P. Heyse

DIE MAINACHT, op.43, no.2; "Wann der silberne Mond"; A NIGHT IN MAY; "When the silvery   407
   moon gleams" e, g 274   words by L. Hölty

"MEINE LIEBE IST GRÜN," op.63, no.5; MY LOVE IS GREEN; "O my love like the lilac is fresh   408
   and green" e, g 112; MY HEART IS IN BLOOM; "Oh, my heart is in bloom" e, g 359   words by
   F. Schumann

MEINE LIEDER, op.106, no.4; "Wenn mein Herz beginnt zu klingen und den Tönen löst die Schwingen";   409
   MY SONGS; "When my heart begins a-rhyming, to the music of its chiming" e 45   words by A. Frey

MINNELIED, op.71, no.5; "Holder klingt der Vogelsang"; LOVE SONG; "When she takes her way"   410
   e, g 277; "Sweeter sounds the song of birds" e, g 137   words by H. Hölty

"NICHT MEHR ZU DIR ZU GEHEN," op.32, no.2; "I SAID 'I WILL FORGET THEE'" e, g 273 words   411
   by G. F. Daumer

"O KOMME, HOLDE SOMMERNACHT," op.58, no.4; "O COME, DELIGHTFUL SUMMER NIGHT"   412
   e, g 112   words by M. Grohe

O KÜHLER WALD, op.72, no.3; "O kühler Wald, wo rauschest du"; OH FOREST COOL; "Where dost   413
   thou wave, oh forest cool" e, g 330   words by C. Brentano

O LIEBLICHE WANGEN, op.47, no.4; "O liebliche Wangen, ihr macht mir Verlangen"; YOUR   414
   CHEEKS SOFT AND LOVELY; "Your cheeks soft and lovely, I long for you only" e, g 220; SWEET
   CHEEKS TO ME TURNING; "Sweet cheeks to me turning, you fill me with yearning" e, g 364
   words by P. Flemming

"O WÜSST' ICH DOCH DEN WEG ZURÜCK," op.63, no.8 g 98; "OH, THAT I MIGHT RETRACE THE   415
   WAY" e, g 359   words by K. Groth

[QUINTET, VIOLINS, VIOLAS & VIOLONCELLO, NO.1, OP.88, F MAJOR.   416
   ALLEGRO NON TROPPO MA CON BRIO] WHAT SWEETER MUSIC; "What sweeter music
   can we bring" e 337   words by R. Herrick

[ROMANZEN AUS L. TIECK'S MAGELONE, OP.33, song cycle; words by L.   417
   Tieck] MUSS ES EINE TRENNUNG, no.12; "Muss es eine Trennung geben"; PARTING; "Wilt
   thou then indeed forsake me" e, g 275

[Ibid] "SIND ES SCHMERZEN, SIND ES FREUDEN"; no.3, "IS IT BLISS OR IS IT SORROW?" e, g   418
   277

[Ibid] "SO WILLST DU DES ARMEN"; no.5, AT LAST; "Thou'rt mine, then, at last" e, g 276   419

ROTE ABENDWOLKEN ZIEH'N, op.103, no.11; "Rote Abendwolken zieh'n am Firmament"; ROSEATE   420
   CLOUDS OF EVENING DRIFT; "Roseate clouds of evening drift across the sky" e, g 45

SALAMANDER, op.107, no.2; "Es sass ein Salamander" g 250   words by K. Lemcke   421

SAPPHISCHE ODE, op.94, no.4; "Rosen brach ich Nachts mir am dunklen Hage" g 99; SAPPHIC   422
   ODE; "Roses red I gathered beneath the moon's pale ray" e, g 387; "Roses culled at night from
   the dark'ning hedgerows" e, g 137; "Roses I at night from the hedge did sever" e, g 122; "Roses
   picked at twilight from off the hedgerows gray" e, g 329; "Roses that I picked in the dusk of
   ev'ning" e, g 274   words by H. Schmidt

DER SCHMIED, op.19, no.4; "Ich hör' meinen Schatz"; THE BLACKSMITH; "My true love is there"   423
   e, g 275; THE BLACKSMITH'S SWEETHEART; "That's George that I hear" e 199   words by L. Uhland

SEHNSUCHT, op.14, no.8; "Mein Schatz ist nicht da, ist weit überm See" g 229   424

SONNTAG, op.47, no.3; "So hab' ich doch die ganze Woche mein feines Liebchen nicht geseh'n"   425
   g 229; SUNDAY MORNING; "And here's a week I haven't seen her the little maid I'm looking for!"
   e, g 272

15

BRAHMS, JOHANNES, 1833-1897 (Continued)

STÄNDCHEN, op.106, no.1; "Der Mond steht über dem Berge"; SERENADE; "The moon hangs over   426
    the hill" e, g 112; "The moon shines over the mountain" e, g 407 words by F. Kugler

"DER TOD, DAS IST DIE KÜHLE NACHT," op.96, no.1; "OH, DEATH IS LIKE THE COOLING   427
    NIGHT" e, g 359; "OH, DEATH IS STILL AND COOL AS NIGHT" e, g 112 words by H. Heine

ÜBER DIE SEE, op.69, no.7; "Über die See, fern über die See ist mein Schatz gezogen"; OVER THE   428
    SEA; "Over the sea, far over the sea went my love a-sailing" e, g 141 words by K. Lemcke

"UNBEWEGTE LAUE LUFT," op.57, no.8; "ALL IS STILL WHILE NATURE SLEEPS" e, g 220   429

VERGEBLICHES STÄNDCHEN, op.84, no.4; "Guten Abend mein Schatz, guten Abend mein Kind"   430
    g 97; THE DISAPPOINTED SERENADER; "Ah, good evening, fair maiden, good evening my dear"
    e, g 359; THE VAIN SUIT; "Good evening my treasure" e, g 276; "Pleasant evening my sweet"
    e, g 112 words by A. W. Zuccalmaglio

VERRAT, op.105, no.5; "Ich stand in einer lauen Nacht" g 250 words by K. Lemcke   431

VON EWIGER LIEBE, op.43, no.1; "Dunkel wie dunkel in Wald und in Feld"; OF ETERNAL LOVE;   432
    "Darkness, what darkness in forest and dale" e, g 112; LOVE TRIUMPHANT; "Darkness hath fallen
    on forest and stream" e, g 274 words by J. Wentzig

VORSCHNELLER SCHWUR, op.95, no.5; "Schwor ein junges Mädchen: Blumen nie zu tragen' g 308   433

[WALTZ, PIANO, OP.39, NO.15] DREAM SONG; "Sleep, O wee one, sleep and drift   434
    on silent moonbeams" e 343

"WIE BIST DU, MEINE KÖNIGIN," op.32, bk.II, no.9; "HOW ART THOU, O MY GRACIOUS QUEEN"   435
    e, g 220; "REIGN HERE A QUEEN WITHIN THE HEART" e, g 277 words by G. F. Daumer

WIEGENLIED, op.49, no.4; "Guten Abend, gut' Nacht, mit Rosen bedacht" g 96,99,226,229,327;   436
    CRADLE SONG; "Go to bed and good night, with roses bedight" e, g 136,329, e 28,241,366;
    "Dear goodnight, yes goodnight, Mister Sandman is calling" e, g 132; "Lullaby, to the rest in
    rose-covered nest" e, g 210; "So good-night now once more, with roses roof'd o'er" e, g 122;
    LULLABY; "Lullaby and good night, with roses sleep tight" e, g 385; "Little baby, good night,
    'mid lilies of white" e, g 276; "Sleep my darling, good night, soft grey is the light" e, g 141;
    GUTEN ABEND, GUT NACHT g 42,326,353; ON THAT CHRISTMAS DAY MORN; "On that
    Christmas Day morn, when a new world was born" e 307

WIE MELODIEN ZIEHT ES MIR, op.105, no.1; "Wie Melodien zieht es mir leise durch den Sinn";   437
    MY THOUGHTS LIKE HAUNTING MUSIC; "My thoughts like haunting music drift through my mind
    today" e, g 112 words by K. Groth

WIR WANDELTEN, op.96, no.2; "Wir wandelten, wir zwei zusammen"; WE WANDERED; "We   438
    wandered, we two together" e, g 36 words by F. Baumer

BRAINE, ROBERT, 1896-1940

BROWN MEN; "On sultry days by river front" e 240 words by M. S. Burt   439

BRAND, OSCAR

THE AIR FORCE; "When the Navy floats its battle-boats to rule the rolling sea"; "The Air Force, the   440
    Air Force, that's the force for me" (ref) e 44

BRATTON, JOHN W., 1867-1947

THE SUNSHINE OF PARADISE ALLEY; "There's a little side street"; "Ev'ry Sunday down to her home   441
    we go" (ref) e 114,131; (ref only) e 128,132 words by W. H. Ford

BRAUN, JOHANN

AVE MARIA ZART; "Ave Maria zart, du edler Rosengart" g 326   442

BRENNAN, JAMES A., 1885-

ROSE OF NO MAN'S LAND. See 510

BREUER, ERNEST, 1886-

CHEER UP, MOLLY; "Cheer up, Molly, it's you that should be jolly" e 120,130 words by W. Tracy   443

BRIDGE, FRANK, 1879-1941

E'EN AS A LOVELY FLOWER; "E'en as a lovely flower, so fair, so pure thou art" e 277 words by K.   444
    Kroeker

BRIESEWITZ, AUGUST WILHELM ROBERT, 1810-1876

FIDUCIT; "Es hatten drei Gesellen ein Kein Kollegium" g 31,99 words by E. Salomon   445

BROADHURST, CECIL, 1908-

COWBOY CAROL; "There'll be a new world beginnin' from t'night!" e 305,307   446

BROCKWAY, W. H.

JOCKEY HAT AND FEATHER; "As I was walking out one day thinking of the weather"; "Oh! I said   447
    it's gay and pretty too" (ref) e 189 words by F. Wilson

BROOK, HARRY, 1893-

DREAM CRADLE SONG; "From groves of spice, o'er fields of rice" e 199 words by S. Naidu   448

"HUSH A BA, BIRDIE, CROON, CROON" e 199   449

THE MILLER'S SONG; "Full many a night in the clear moonlight" e 199 words by P. Tennant   450

THE SHEPHERD; "How sweet is the shepherd's sweet lot!" e 199 words by W. Blake   451

BROOKS, SHELTON, 1886-

THE DARKTOWN STRUTTERS' BALL; "I'll be down to get you in a taxie, honey" e 236   452

16

BUXTEHUDE, DIETRICH, 1634-1707 (Continued)
    [WAS MICH AUF DIESER WELT BETRÜBT, cantata] "O FATHER, ALL CREATING!"   485
    e 50
BUZZI-PECCIA, ARTURO, 1854-1943
    MARIOLINA; "Mariolina, bella Mariolina Come sole risplendente dell' april"; A LOVE CALL;   486
    "Mariolina, dearest Mariolina, charming as a lovely flower of the spring" e, i 237
BUZZOLENI, GIOVANNI, ca1680
    SÌ CHE MORTE; "Sì che morte, sì che morte e lontananza" i 179   487
    [SOGNO] NON FUGGIRAI; "Non fuggirai, no, no, sogno o vaneggio" i 180   488
    [SUPLICA AMOROSA] VOLGIMI, O CARA FILLI; "Volgimi, o cara Filli, pietosa un guardo   489
    almeno" i 179
BYELIJ, V.
    SHOULDER TO SHOULDER; "Brothers, the dark clouds are breaking"; "Brüder, zur Sonne, zur Freiheit"   490
    e, g 7
BYLES, BLANCHE DOUGLAS
    "WOOD OF THE CROSS" e 347 words by V. A. Storey   491
BYRD, WILLIAM, 1542 or 3-1621
    THE EARL OF SALISBURY'S PAVEN keyboard 306   492
    "HEY, HO! TO THE GREENWOOD" 3 pt round e 37,144,235 att to D. Melvill   493
    MY SWEET LITTLE DARLING; "My sweet little darling, my comfort and joy" e 319   494
    NON NOBIS DOMINE; "Non nobis Domine non nobis sed nomini" 3 pt round lat 402   495
    O MISTRESS MINE; "O Mistress mine, where are you roaming?" e 13,75,215,235 words by W.   496
    Shakespeare
    SING WE, THEN, MERRILY; "Jesus so meek, Jesus so mild" e 378   497

CACCINI, FRANCESCA, 1588-ca1640
    [LA LIBERAZIONE DI RUGGIERO DALL' ISOLA D'ALCINA, opera; words by   498
    F. Saracinelli] LIED EINES HIRTEN; "Per la più vaga e bella"; "Für den reizendsten und
    schönsten" g, i 217
CACCINI, GIULIO, d 1618
    AL FONTE, AL PRATO; "Al fonte, al prato, al bosco, al' ombra" i 181   499
    AMARILLI; "Amarilli, mia bella!" i 179; "Amarilli, my fairest" e, i 36; AMARYLLIS;   500
    "Amaryllis, my fair one" e, i 138; "Amaryllis, beloved" e, i 277; "AMARILLI, MIA BELLA";
    "AMARILLI, MY FAIR ONE" e, i 368; CANZONE; "Magst du mir's, Amarillis" g, i 168 words
    by G. B. Guarini
    AMOR, CH'ATTENDI; "Amor, ch'attendi, Amor, che fai?" i 181   501
    AUR' AMOROSA; "Aur' amorosa, che dolcemente spiri al bel matin" i 181   502
    DEH, DOVE SON FUGGITI; "Deh, deh, dove son fuggiti" i 179   503
    FERE SELVAGGIE; "Fere selvaggie, che per monti errate" i 179 words by F. Cini   504
    [LE NUOVE MUSICHE] ODI, EUTERPE, IL DOLCE CANTO; "Odi, Odi, Euterpe, il dolce   505
    canto che a lo stil"; LIST, O EUTERPE, TO THE SWEET SONG i 367
    O, CHE FELICE GIORNO; "O, che felice giorno! O, che lieto ritorno" i 181   506
    OCCH' INMORTALI; "Occh' inmortali, d'Amor gloria e splendore" i 179; OCCHI IMMORTALE;   507
    "Occhi immortali, d'amor gloria e splendore"; IMMORTAL EYES; "Immortal eyes, resplendent,
    glorious thou art" e, i 403 words by O. Rinuccini
    PERFIDISSIMO VOLTO; "Perfidissimo volto ben l'usata bellezza in te se vede"; MOST TREACHER-   508
    OUS FACE; "So beautiful, but so unfaithful"; TREULOSES ANGESICH; "Treuloses Angesich wohl
    man dir" e, g, i 253
    UDITE AMANTI; "Udite, udite, amanti, udite, o fere erranti" i 179 words by O. Rinuccini   509
CADDIGAN, JACK J., 1879-
    ROSE OF NO MAN'S LAND; "There's a rose that grows on 'No Man's Land'" e 129 joint composer   510
    J. A. Brennan
CADMAN, CHARLES WAKEFIELD, 1881-1946
    THE LITTLE ROAD TO KERRY; "When youth was at the spring-time" e 136,241 words by C. O. Roos   511
    A MOONLIGHT SONG, op.42, no.2; "The moonlight shimmers thro' the vine" e 259 words by J. P.   512
    Mills
CALBREATH, MARY EVELENE
    MY LOVE RODE BY; "My love rode by my window" e 136 words by G. R. Ross   513
CALDARA, ANTONIO, 1670-1736
    ARIE; "Mirti, faggi, tronchi e fronde"; "Myrten, Buchen, Bäume und Sträucher" g, i 218   514
    ARIE; "Vaghe luci, è troppo crudo"; "Ihr schönen Augen, zu grausam ist" g, i 218   515
    COME RAGGIO DI SOL; "Come raggio di sol mite e sereno"; AS A SUNBEAM AT MORN; "As a sun-   516
    beam at morn falleth serenely" e, i 274; AS ON THE SWELLING WAVE; "As on the swelling wave in
    idle motion" e, i 368; LIKE THE SUN'S GOLDEN RAY; "Like the sun's golden ray softly reposing"

CALDARA, ANTONIO, 1670-1736 (Continued)

e, i 139; ARIA; "Gleich wie der Sonne Strahl, heiter und selig" g, i 168

[LA COSTANZA IN AMOR VINCE L'INGANNO, pastorale] ALMA DEL CORE;   517
"Alma del core, Spirto dell' alma"; FAIREST ADORED; "Fairest adored, Spirit of beauty" e, i 368;
HEART OF MY OWN HEART; "Heart of my own heart, Breath of my spirit" e, i 139; ARIE; "Seele
meines Herzens, Abgott miner Seele" g, i 218

[Ibid] SEBBEN, CRUDELE; "Sebben, crudele mi failanguir"; CANZONETTA; THO' NOT DESERV-   518
ING; "Tho not deserving thy cruel scorn" e, i 368; ARIETTA; "Ob du auch grausam schmachten
mich lässt" g, i 167

SI T'INTENDO; "Si t'intendo, ecco t'intendo"; "I understand you, indeed I understand you well" e, i   519
134

CALESTANI, VINCENZIO, ca1600

ACCORTA LUSINGHIERA; "Accorta lusinghiera già m'annodasti il cor" i 179   520

FERMA, DORINDA MIA; "Ferma, Dorinda mia, deh ferma il piede" i 181   521

Caletti-Bruni, Pier Francesco. See CAVALLI, PIER FRANCESCO, 1602-1676

CALHOUN, JOHN, 1848-1939

PETER AMBERLEY; "My name is Peter Amberley" e 186   522

CALKIN, JOHN BAPTISTE, 1827-

"FLING OUT THE BANNER! LET IT FLOAT" e 28 words by G. W. Doane   523

"I HEARD THE BELLS ON CHRISTMAS DAY"; Waltham (tune) e 28,206,236,296,366 words by H.   524
W. Longfellow

CALLCOTT, JOHN WALL, 1766-1821

YE MARINERS OF ENGLAND; "Ye mariners of England, that guard our native seas" e 349,397 words   525
by Campbell

CALLEJA, RAFAEL, 1874-

EMIGRANTES. See 186

Calletto-Bruno, Pier Francesco. See CAVALLI, PIER FRANCESCO, 1602-1676

CAMPANA, FABIO, 1819-1882

OUR CREW; "Our good ship was bound for the west" e 205 words by M. M. Lemon   526

CAMPBELL, FRANK

"SHOO, FLY, DON'T BOTHER ME"; "I feel, I feel, I feel, I feel like a mornin' star" (verse) e 184;   527
"I feel, I feel, I feel, I feel like a morning star" (verse) e 32,34; "I feel, I feel, I feel like a
morning star" (verse) e 216; "I think I hear the angels sing"; "Shoo fly, don't bother me!" (ref)
e 129,130,131,185,225,399

CAMPBELL, JIMMY

GOOD NIGHT SWEETHEART. See 2666

CAMPBELL, PAUL

COME ON AND JOIN INTO THE GAME; JOIN INTO THE GAME; "Let ev'ryone clap hands like me"   528
e 389

FOLLOW THE DRINKIN' GOURD; "When the sun comes back and the first quail calls" e 389   529

CAMPBELL-TIPTON, LOUIS, 1877-1921

[SEA LYRICS, song cycle] THE CRYING OF WATER; "O water, voice of my heart"; LE CRI   530
DES EAUX; "Voix des eaux, voix de mon coeur" e, f 259 words by A. Symons

CAMPENHOUT, FRANÇOIS VAN, 1779-1848

LA BRABANÇONNE; "Qui l'aurait dit de l'arbitraire"; "Who would believe this arbitrary deed" e, f 7;   531
"The Belgians may exult again" e 279,366

CAMPION, THOMAS, 1567-1620

"ALL LOOKES BE PALE" e 144   532

AYRE; "It fell on a summers day, while sweet Bessy sleeping lay" e 278   533

"BEAUTY IS BUT A PAINTED HELL" e 197   534

"BREAKE NOW, MY HEART, AND DIE" e 197; "BREAKE NOW MY HEART AND DYE" e 144   535

"COME, YOU PRETTY FALSE-EYED WANTON" e 197   536

"THE CYPRESS CURTAIN OF THE NIGHT" e 118   537

"EV'RY DAME AFFECTS GOOD FAME" e 197   538

"FAIR, IF YOU EXPECT ADMIRING" e 119; "FAIRE, IF YOU EXPECT ADMIRING" e 144   539

FIRE, FIRE; "Fire, fire, fire, fire, loe here I burne" e 144   540

FOLLOW YOUR SAINT; "Follow your saint, follow with accents sweet" e 117,144   541

"FOLLOWE THY FAIRE SUNNE"; e 144; "FOLLOW THY FAIR SUN" e 119   542

HARKE AL YOU LADIES; "Harke al you ladies that do sleep" e 112   543

HER ROSIE CHEEKES; "Her rosie cheekes, her ever smiling eyes" e 197   544

"HERE SHE HER SACRED BOWER ADORNES" e 196   545

"I CARE NOT FOR THESE LADIES" e 144   546

"IF THOU LONGST SO MUCH TO LEARNE" e 144   547

JACK AND JOAN; "Jack and Joan they think no ill" e 118; JACKE AND JONE; "Jacke and Jone they   548
thinke no iil" e 144

"KINDE ARE HER ANSWERES" e 144   549

19

CARISSIMI, GIOVANNI GIACOMO, d 1674

ARIA; "Piangete ohimè! piangete, piangete ohimè!"; "O weint Ach und Weh! Ja weinet! O weint   585
Ach und Weh!" g, i 168

COME SETE IMPORTUNI; "Come sete importuni, come sete importuni, amorosi pensieri!" i 179   586
words by D. Benigni

DEH, CONTENTATEVI; "Deh, deh, contentatevi"; PRAY, LET ME SUFFERING; "Pray, pray, let me,   587
suffering" e, i 139

FRAGMENT EINER SOLO-KANTATE; "Così volete, così sarà"; "So wollt ihr es haben, so soll es sein"   588
g, i 217

[FUGGI, O MIO CORE] MA, NO, NON FUGGIR; "Ma no! Ma no! Non fuggir" i 179   589

[JUDICIUM SALOMONIS, oratorio] CANTO DELLA MADRE; "Congratula mini mihi   590
omnes"; THE MOTHER'S SONG lat 367

KANZONE; "Soccorretemi, soccorretemi, ch'io moro!"; "Eilt zu Hilfe mir, der ich sterbe" g, i 217   591

KANZONETTE; "La mia fede altrui giurata"; "Meine Treue, einer anderen geschworen" g, i 217   592

"NO, NO, NON SI SPERI!"; "NO, NO, HOPE HAS PERISHED!" e, i 138; KANZONE; "Nein, nein,   593
lasst alle Hoffnung fahren" g, i 217

NON POSSO VIVERE; "Non posso vivere, non posso vivere senza il mio ben, no, no" i 179   594

[PANOSA RIMEMBRANZA] FUGGITE, FUGGITE; "Fuggite, fuggite, pensieri guerrieri" i 179   595
words by C. Teodoli

RIMANTI IN PACE; "Rimanti in pace homai, rimanti in pace homai" (duet) i 181   words by C.   596
della Luna

SVENTURA, CUOR MIO; "Sventura, sventura, cuor mio" i 179   words by D. Benigni   597

VITTORIA, VITTORIA!; "Vittoria, vittoria! Vittoria, vittoria, mio cuore!" i 179; "Vittoria!   598
Vittoria! Vittoria! Vittoria, mio core"; I TRIUMPH! I TRIUMPH!; "I triumph! I triumph! I
triumph! The last word is spoken" e, i 273; VITTORIA, MIO CORE!; VICTORIOUS, MY HEART!;
"Victorious, victorious, victorious my heart! thou hast spoken" e, i 138; VICTORIOUS MY
HEART IS!; "Victorious, Victorious, Victorious, Victorious my heart is!" e, i 368

CARLETON

JOLLY IRISHMEN; "I am a jolly Irishman"; "Hurroo! boys, here we are again!" (ref) e 189   599

CARLETON, ROBERT LOUIS, 1896-

JA-DA; "Ja-da, Ja-da, Ja-da, Ja-da, Jing, Jing, Jing" e 129,130; JA DA, JA DA, JING, JING,   600
JING! e 236

CARPENTER, JOHN ALDEN, 1876-

[GITANJALI, song cycle; words by R. Tagore] "THE SLEEP THAT FLITS ON BABY'S   601
EYES," no.3 e 121

LOOKING-GLASS RIVER; "Smooth it slides upon its travel" e 259   words by R. L. Stevenson   602

"MAY, THE MAIDEN" e 241   words by S. Lanier   603

"TREAT ME NICE" e 45   words by P. L. Dunbar   604

CARR, LEROY

HOW LONG; "Baby, how long, baby, how long has that evening train been gone" e 336   605

CARREÑO, ALCIDES

QUISIERA; "Quisiera reir, llorar y cantar" s 284   606

CARROLL, HARRY, 1892-

I'M ALWAYS CHASING RAINBOWS; "I'm always chasing rainbows, watching clouds drifting by"   607
e 128,132,236 words by J. McCarthy

CARSTE, HANS

[LUMP MIT HERZ, operetta] SCHÖN IST DIESE ABENDSTUNDE; "Wenn der Tag zu Ende   608
geht" g 258

CARSTEN, BERT

NÄR BRÖLLOPSKLOCKOR RINGA; "Fran flydda dar jag än har kvar"; LET'S HONEYMOON AGAIN;   609
"Just hear those bells, those wedding bells" e, sw 135 words by S. O. Sandberg

CARTER, STANLEY

SHE WAS BRED IN OLD KENTUCKY; "When a lad, I stood one day" e 34   words by H. Braisted   610

CARVELHO, JOUBERT DE

MARINGA; "Foi numa léva que a cabocla Maringá" s 284   611

CASEY, KENNETH, 1899-

SWEET GEORGIA BROWN. See 293

CASEY, THOMAS S., att to

DRILL, YE TARRIERS, DRILL; "Every morning at seven o'clock"; "And drill, ye tarriers, drill" (ref)   612
e 145,335; "Ev'ry morning at seven o-clock"; "Drill, ye tarriers, drill!" (ref) e 35; TARRIER'S
SONG e 293; DRILL, YE TARRIERS, DRILL; "Oh, ev'ry morning at seven o'clock"; "Then drill,
ye tarriers, drill" (ref) e 115,246

CATALANI, ALFREDO, 1854-1893

[LA WALLY, opera; words by L. Illica] "EBBEN, N'ANDRO LONTANA" i 301;   613
"EBBEN? NE ANDRO LONTANA"; FAREWELL TO MY HOME; "'Tis well! my way lies yonder!"
e, i 143

21

CATEL, CHARLES-SIMON, 1773-1830
  [SÉMIRAMIS, opera; words by P. Desriaux] RECIT ET AIR DE SÉMIRAMIS; "J'avais   614
    cru ces Dieux, justement offensés" (recit); "Sous l'effort d'un bras invisible vois-tu la terre s'entr'
    ouvrir?" (aria); "I believe that the gods, being justly incensed" (recit); "All at once, by powers
    infernal, the earth is cleft before mine eyes" (aria) e, f 151
CAVALIERI, EMILIO DE', 1550(ca)-1602
  [RAPPRESENTAZIONE DI ANIMA E DI CORPO, opera; words by A. Manni]   615
    MONOLOGO DEL TEMPO; MONOLOG OF TIME; "Il tempo, il tempo fugge" i 367
Cavalli, Francesco. See CAVALLI, PIER FRANCESCO, 1602-1676
CAVALLI, PIER FRANCESCO, 1602-1676
  DONZELLE, FUGGITE; "Donzelle, fuggite procace beltà"; OH, HASTEN, YE MAIDENS; "Oh, hasten   616
    ye maidens from beauty to flee!" e, i 138
  [ELENA RAPITA DA TESEO, opera, words by N. Minato] MIO DILETTO; "Mio   617
    diletto, in te vivo, in te respiro" (duet) i 181
  [Ibid] SOSPIRI DI FOCO; "Sospiri di foco, che l'aure infiammate" i 181   618
  [L'ERISMENA, opera; words by A. Aureli] SPERANZE; "Speranze, speranze, voi, voi,   619
    che siete avvezze a lusingar" i 181
  [Ibid] VAGHE STELLE; "Vaghe stelle, luci belle, non dormite" i 181   620
  [GIASONE, opera; words by G. A. Cicognini] O, MIO CORE; "O mio core! Ardi tu?"   621
    (duet) i 181
  SON ANCOR PARGOLETTA; "Son ancor pargoletta, son ancor pargoletta e amor non provo" i 179   622
CAVANAUGH, JESSIE
  THE ROVING KIND; "She had a dark and a roving eye" e 389   joint composer A. Stanton   623
CAVENDISH, MICHAEL, 1565(ca)-1628
  "DOWN IN A VALLEY" e 144   624
  "EVERIE BUSH NEW SPRINGING" e 144   625
  FINETTA FAIR AND FEAT; "Finetta, Finetta, fair and feat" e 119   626
  "WANDRING IN THIS PLACE" e 144   627
CESARINI, CARLO FRANCESCO, 1664-1715
  [LA GELOSIA, cantata] REZITATIV UND ARIE; "Filli, Filli, nol niego" (recit); "Compat-   628
    itemi, sono infermo" (aria); "Phyllis, ich leugne es nicht" (recit); "Habt Mitleid mit mir, ich bin
    krank" (aria) g, i 218
CESTI, MARCANTONIO, 1623-1669
  [ORONTEA, opera; words by G. A. Cicognini] REZITATIV UND ARIE DER SILANDRA;   629
    "Addio Corindo, addio!" (recit); "Vieni, Alidoro, vieni, consola, chi si more!" (aria); "Leb wohl
    Corindo, lebe wohl!" (recit); "Komm, Alidoro, komm, Tröste, die (vor Sehnsucht) stirbt" (aria)
    g, i 217
  [IL POMO D'ORO, opera; words by W. F. Sbarra] AH! QUANTO È VERO; "Ah!   630
    quanto è vero, che il nundo arciero"; CUPID CAN NEVER; Cupid can never without our endeavor"
    e, i 139
  [Ibid] "E DOVE T'AGGIRI"; "OH, WHITHER ART ROAMING" e, i 139   631
CHABRIER, EMMANUEL, 1841-1894
  BALLADE DES GROS DINDONS; "Les gros dindons, à travers champs"; BALLAD OF THE FAT TURKEYS;   632
    "The fat turkeys across the fields" e, f 190,192,194   words by E. Rostand
  LES CIGALES; "Le soleil est droit sur la sente"; THE CRICKETS; "The sun is straight above the path"   633
    e, f 190,192,194   words by R. Gérard
  VILLANELLE DES PETITS CANARDS; "Ils vont, les petits canards"; SERENADE OF THE LITTLE DUCKS;   634
    "They go, little quacking ducks" e, f 208; A PASTORALE SONG OF THE LITTLE DUCKS; "They
    walk, the little ducks" e, f 190,192,194   words by R. Gérard
CHAĬKOVSKIĬ, PETR IL'ICH, 1840-1893
  AT THE BALL, op.38, no.3; "I know not how lovely your face is" e 121; "In the midst of the dancing   635
    entrancing" e 348; "BY CHANCE, IN THE BALLROOM" e, r 341   words by A. Tolstoi
  [CONCERTO, PIANO, NO.1, OP.23, B FLAT MAJOR. ALLEGRO NON TROPPO   636
    E MOLTO MAESTOSO] NO GREATER LOVE; "No greater love can I feel than I am feeling"
    e 263
  DON JUAN'S SERENADE, op.38, no.1; "All Grenada lieth sleeping"; SÉRÉNADE DE DON JUAN; "Tout   637
    sommeille dans Grenade"; STÄNDCHEN DES DON JUAN; "Alpuchariens gold'ne Streifen" e, f, g
    240; "Veiled in purple gloom of midnight" e 272   words by A. Tolstoi
  ER LIEBT MICH SO SEHR!, op.28, no.4; "Nein, nimmer liebte ich!" g 308   words by Apukhtin   638
  [EUGENE ONIÉGIN, opera; words by M. I. Chaĭkovskiĭ] GREMIN'S ARIA; "Lyubvi   639
    vse vozrasty pokorny"; "All men should once with love grow tender" e, r(tr) 5
  [Ibid] LENSKI'S ARIA, Act II, no.17; "Kuda, kuda, kuda vy udalilis"; "How far, how far, how far   640
    ye seem behind me" e, r(tr) 3
  [Ibid] ONEGIN'S ARIA; "Kogda by zhizn' domashnim krugom"; "If in this world a kindly fortune"   641
    e, r(tr) 4
  [Ibid] TATIANA'S LETTER SCENE; "Puskaĭ pogibnu ya"; "Though I should die for it"; e, r(tr) 1   642

22

CHAĬKOVSKIĬ, PETR IL'ICH, 1840-1893 (Continued)

JEANNE D'ARC. See 644

THE MAID OF ORLEANS. See 644

NUR WER DIE SEHNSUCHT KENNT, op.6, no.6; "Nur wer die Sehnsucht kennt, weiss, was ich leide!";   643
   NAY, THOUGH MY HEART SHOULD BREAK; "Nay, though my heart should break, I still would
   leave you" e, g 274; NO, ONLY THOSE WHO KNOW; "No only those who know love's burning
   passion" e, r 341; NONE BUT A LOVER KNOWS; "None but a lover knows my lonely yearning"
   e, g 36; NONE BUT THE LONELY HEART; "None but the lonely heart can know my anguish" e, g
   329; "None but the lonely heart can know my sadness" e, g 137, e 132; "None but the lonely
   heart knows of my sorrow" e, g 237; ONE WHO HAS YEARNED ALONE; "One who has yearned
   alone can know my anguish" e, g 122 words by J. W. von Goethe

[ORLEANSKAYA DYEVA, opera] ADIEU, FORÊTS; "Oui, Dieu le veut!" (recit); "Adieu,   644
   forêts, adieu, prés leuris, champs d'or" (aria); "So, will the Lord!" (recit); "Farewell, ye mountains, ye beloved meadows!" (aria) e, f 2

[PIKOVAĬA DAMA, opera; words by M. I. Chaĭkovskiĭ] PAULINE'S ARIA; "Da!   645
   vspomnila! Podrugi milyya"; "Ah! now I know! Dear friends for whom I sing" e, r(tr) 2; PAULINE'S
   ROMANCE; "My tender playmates, my sweet companions now hasten to the woodlands" e, r 357

[Ibid] SCENE AND ARIOSO OF LISA, Act III; "'Twill soon be midnight now" (recit); "Ah, I am   646
   worn with my sorrow" (aria) e 6

[PILGRIM'S SONG] TO THE FOREST, op.47, no.5; "Thrice blessed forest! with the town   647
   aweary" e 273

PIQUE DAME. See 645

SO SOON FORGOTTEN; "So soon forgotten, I and you, the only happiness we knew" e, r 341 words   648
   by A. Apukhtin

[SONGS FOR YOUNG PEOPLE, OP.54] LEGEND, no.5; THE CROWN OF ROSES; "When   649
   Jesus Christ was yet a child" e 334; "WHEN JESUS CHRIST WAS YET A CHILD" e 319; LEGEND;
   "Child Jesus in his garden"; LEGENDE; "L'enfant Jesus dans son jardin" e, f 121

[SYMPHONY, NO.5, OP.64, E MINOR. ANDANTE CANTABILE; arr] THE   650
   LORD IS MY SHEPHERD; "The Lord is my shepherd; I shall not want" e 123 words from Psalm XXIII

'TWAS APRIL, op.38, no.2; "Oh, once when lovely spring was young" e 277; WHEN SPRING WAS IN   651
   THE AIR; "It was when spring was in the air" e, r 341 words by A. Tolstoi

CHAMINADE, CÉCILE LOUISE STÉPHANIE, 1861-1944

TU ME DIRAIS; "Tu me dirais que l'on entend le souffle"; "IF THOU SHOULDST TELL ME' e, f 140   652
   words by R. Gerard

CHANLER, THEODORE WARD, 1902-

THESE, MY OPHELIA; "These, my Ophelia stars are not now" e 85 words by A. MacLeish   653

CHARLES, ERNEST, 1895-

AND SO, GOODBYE; "And so, goodbye, go now; no, do not say a word" e 259   654

CHARPENTIER, MARC ANTOINE, 1634-1704

[MÉDÉE, opera; words by P. Corneille] AIR DE MÉDÉE; "Quel prix de mon amour?";   655
   "Ah! what a price I pay" e, f 148

[Ibid] RÉCIT ET AIR DE MÉDÉE; "Que d'horreurs! que de maux suivront sa trahison" (recit); "Ne   656
   les épargons pas" (aria); "How I shrink! how I quail! yet must the deed be done!" (recit); "Yes,
   they shall not be spared" (aria) e, f 148

CHAUSSON, ERNEST, 1855-1899

LES PAPILLONS, op.2, no.3; "Les papillons couleur de neige"; THE BUTTERFLIES; "The butterflies   657
   rapidly winging" e, f 211 words by T. Gautier

[POÈME DE L'AMOUR ET DE LA MER, OP.19] LE TEMPS DES LILAS; "Le temps des   658
   lilas et le temps des roses"; LOVELY LILAC TIME; "Lovely lilac time and the time of roses" e, f
   357 words by M. Bouchor

CHENETTE, EDWARD STEPHEN

HEY, HEY, HO; "Hey, hey, ho, the north winds blow" e 296 words by M. L. Hohman   659

CHEREPNIN, ALEKSANDR NIKOLAEVICH, 1899-

"I WOULD KISS YOU," op.21, no.4 e, r 341 words by A. Maikov   660

CHERRY, J. W.

THERE'S A DEAR LITTLE PLANT; THE DEAR LITTLE SHAMROCK; "There's a dear little plant that   661
   grows in our Isle" e 166,213; THE DEAR LITTLE SHAMROCK e 15; THE GREEN LITTLE SHAM-
   ROCK e 172 words by A. Cherry

CHERUBINI, LUIGI, 1760-1842

AVE MARIA; "Ave, ave, Maria gratia plena"; "Hail, Mary, full of grace" e, lat 304   662

COME TO THE WATERS; "Come ye, come to the waters" e 89 words from Bible   663

SOLFA-ING; Doh doh' soh lah me fah soh!" 3 pt round e 199   664

VENI JESU; "Veni, Jesu, amormi"; "Come, Jesus, my love" e, lat 304   665

CHEVALIER, ALBERT

THE FUTURE MRS. 'AWKINS; "I knows a little stunner" (ref); "Oh Lizer! Sweet Lizer!" e 204,   666
   (ref only) e 128

CHIARA, VINCENZO DI

LA SPAGNOLA; THE SPANISH DANCER; "Leaving old Spain's haughty towers" e 142   667

CHOPIN, FRYDERYK FRANCISZEK, 1810-1840
    HULANKA, op.74, no.4; "Szynkareczko szafareczko"; REVELRY; "Pretty barmaid, laughing barmaid"; 668
        e, p 295; "Pretty barmaid, merry barmaid" e 86 words by S. Witwicki
    MOJA PIESZCZOTKA, op.74, no.12; "Moja pieszczotka gdy w wesołej chwili"; MAID OF MY DE- 669
        LIGHT; "In happy moments my love with smiles beaming" e, p 295 words by A. Mickiewicz
    PIERŚCIEŃ, op.74, no.14; "Smutno nianki ci śpiewały"; THE SILVER RING; "Lullabies were hummed 670
        in your ear" e, p 295 words by S. Witwickiego
    PIOSNKA LITEWSKA, op.74, no.16; "Bardzo raniuchno wschodziło słoneczko"; LITHUANIAN SONG; 670*
        "Early one morning as sunlight rose glist'ning" e, p 295 words by St. Witwicki
    PIOSNKA ZEGARMISTRZA; "Dzeń, dzeń, dzeń, dzeń"; CLOCKMAKER'S SONG; "Tick, tock, tick 671
        tock" e, p 295
    [PRELUDE, PIANO, OP.28, NO.7, A MAJOR] MARZENIE; "Czemu sercu smutno"; 671*
        REVERIE; "Why is my heart lonely" e, p 295
    [PRELUDE, PIANO, OP.28, NO.20, C MINOR] CHRIST BE WITH ME!; "Christ be with 672
        me, Christ within me" e 123 arr by C. Deia, words att to St. Patrick
    ŚLICZNY CHŁOPIEC, op.74, no.8; "Wzniosły, smukły i młody"; HANDSOME LADDIE; "Sturdy, 672*
        youthful, and handsome" e, p 295 words by B. Zaleski
    [SONATA, PIANO, NO.2, OP.35, B FLAT MAJOR. MARCHE FUNÉBRE] 673
        MARCHE FUNÉBRE; "Na wieczny sen odchodzisz już"; "For your last sleep you leave us now" e, p
        295
    WOJAK, op.74, no.10; "Rży mój gniady, ziemie grzebie, puśćcie czas juz czas"; THE WARRIOR; 673*
        "Cease your neighing, pawing, my steed" e, p 295 words by St. Witwicki
    ŻYCZENIE, op.74, no.1; "Gdybym ja był słoneczkiem na niebie"; THE MAIDEN'S WISH; "Were 674
        I the sunlight in the heavens beaming" e, p 295; "Were I the sun so high in heaven beaming" e 37
CHORINSKY-HARDEGG, A. M.
    WALZERMELODIE'N SIND EIN GRUSS AUS WIEN; WALZERLIED; "In jeder Stadt gibt es Freude und 674*
        Schmerz" g 396
CHRÉTIEN, HEDWIGE, 1859-
    QUE JE T'OUBLIE?; "Comment veux-tu que je t'oublie"; COULD I FORGET?; "Canst thou believe I 675
        could forget" e, f 140 words by L. Marcel
CHRISTIE, EDWIN
    MY HEART'S O'ER THE DEEP BLUE SEA; "The scenes that are 'round me are fair"; "Oh, still fly my 675*
        thoughts o'er the foam" (ref) e 205 words by G. Cooper
CHWATAL, FRANZ XAVER, 1808-1879
    LOVELY NIGHT; "Lovely night! O lovely night! Spreading over hill and meadow" e 28,366 676
CIAMPI, LEGRENZIO VINCENZO, att to
    TRE GIORNI SON CHE NINA. See 2769
CIFRA, ANTONIO, 1584-1629
    DEL MIO SOL; "Del mio sol ricciutegli i capegli" (duet) i 181 676*
    LA VIOLETTA; "La violetta ch'en su l'herbetta apre al matin novella" i 181 677
CIMARA, PIETRO, 1887-
    FIOCCA LA NEVE; "Lenta neve fiocca"; SNOW; "Slowly the starry flakes of snow" e, s 121 words 677*
        by G. Pascoli
CIMAROSA, DOMENICO, 1749-1801
    "BEL NUME CHE ADORO"; "Gott Amor, Verehrter" g, i 168 678
    [GLI ORAZI E I CURIAZI, opera; words by A. S. Sografi] "SI PIETA NEL COR 678*
        SERBATE"; "IF IN YOUR HEART LIES PITY" e, i 367
    [LA VIRGINE DEL SOLE, opera; words by F. Moretti] ARIE; "Ah tornar la belle 679
        aurora"; "Ach, die Wiederkehr der schönen Morgenröte" g, i 218
CITKOWITZ, ISRAEL, 1909-
    GENTLE LADY; "Gentle lady, do not sing" e 85 words by J. Joyce 679*
CLAIBORNE, BOB
    IT'S MY UNION; "When the papers run by Tories" e 293 680
Claribel, pseud. See BARNARD, CHARLOTTE (ALINGTON) 1830-1869
CLARK, EDGAR ROGIE, 1813-
    IMPRESSION; LE RÉVEILLON; "The sky is laced with fitful red" e 78 words by O. Wilde 680*
    NORTHBOUN; "O' de wurl' ain't flat an' de wurl' ain't roun'" e 78 words by L. A. Williams 681
CLARK, JAMES·G.
    HO FOR THE KANSAS PLAINS; "Huzza for the prairies wide and free" e 189 681*
CLARKE, WILLIAM A.
    A HANDFUL OF EARTH; "Its a sailin' I am at the dawn"; "Och Erin Machree" (ref) e 114 682
CLAUDIUS, MATTHIAS, 1740-1815
    DAS BAUERNLIED; "Wir pflügen, und wir streuen den Samen auf das Land"; "Alle gute Gabe kommt 682*
        oben her von Gott" (ref) g 49
CLAY, FREDERIC, 1838-1889
    GYPSY JOHN; "The Gipsy fires are burning" e 237 words by G. J. W. Melville 683

CLAY, FREDERIC, 1830-1889 (Continued)
    [LALLA ROUKH, opera; words by H. Lucas and M. Carré] "I'LL SING THEE SONGS   683*
       OF ARABY" e 128,132,237
CLAYTON, ARNOLD
    PITY THE DOWNTRODDEN LANDLORD; "Please open your hearts and your purses" e 293   words by B.   684
       Woolf
CLAYTON, WILLIAM
    "COME, COME, YE SAINTS" (Mormon hymn) e 34   684*
Clemens, Jacobus non Papa. See CLEMENT, JACQUES, 16th c
CLEMENT, JACQUES, 16th c
    CHANSON AU LUTH; "Aymer est ma vie, Aymer est ma vie" f 278   685
CLESI, N. J.
    I'M SORRY I MADE YOU CRY; "Dear little girl have I made you sad?" e 131   685*
CLIFTON, HARRY
    PADDLE YOUR OWN CANOE; "I've traveled about a bit in my time"; "Then love your neighbor as   686
       yourself" (ref) e 129,130,131
CLOKEY, JOSEPH WADDELL, 1890-
    THE ROSE; "This morning when I came awake" e 136,241   words by K. Howard   686*
COARD, HENRY A.
    THE GYPSY'S WARNING; "Do not trust him, gentle lady" e 129,130   687
COCKRAM, E. PURCELL, d 1932
    PASSING BY; "There is a lady sweet and kind" e 36,122,132,236,348; "There is a ladye sweet and   687*
       kind" e 136,209
CODINA, H. GENARO
    ZACATECAS; MEXICAN MARCH piano 248   688
COENEN, WILLEM, 1837-1918
    COME UNTO ME; "Come unto me, all ye that labour and are heavy laden" e 200   words from Bible   688*
COFFEY, CHARLES, 1746-?
    [THE BEGGAR'S WEDDING, ballad opera] THE JOVIAL BEGGAR; "There was a jovial   689
       beggar" e 234
COHAN, GEORGE MICHAEL, 1878-1942
    I GUESS I'LL HAVE TO TELEGRAPH MY BABY; "A darky left his happy home"; "Well, I guess I'll have   689*
       to telegraph my baby" (ref) e 114; "A man he left his happy home to go upon the stage" e 204;
       "Sam Johnson he left his happy home" e 131, (ref only) e 128
    OVER THERE; "Over there, over there, send the word" e 129   690
    THEN I'D BE SATISFIED WITH LIFE; "How seldom will you meet a man" e 114   691
COHEN, CECIL
    EPITAPH FOR A POET; "I have wrapped my dreams in a silken cloth" e 78   words by C. Cullen   692
    FOUR WINDS; "Four winds blowing through the sky" e 78   words by S. Teasdale   693
COLES, GEORGE
    "FROM EVERY SPIRE ON CHRISTMAS EVE" e 28,296,366   words by E. A. Hunter   694
COLLAN, KARL, 1828-1871
    SUKSIMIESTEN LAULU; "Ylös Suomen pojat nuoret"; SONG OF THE SKIERS; "Rise, ye Finnish youth   695
       together" e, fi 124   words by Suonio
COLLASSE, PASCAL, 1649-1709
    [LES SAISONS, opera; words by J. Pic] "ME PLAINDRAI-JE TOUJOURS"; "E SARÒ   696
       DUNQUE OGNOR" f, i 411
    [Ibid] "TOUT CÈDE À VOS DOUX APPAS"; TO THY FAIR CHARM; "To thy fair charm all yield"   697
       e, f 209
    [THÉTIS ET PELÉE, opera; words by B. de Fontenelle] AIR DE THÉTIS; "Tristes   698
       honneurs, Gloire cruelle"; "Honour and pomp, splendour and glory" e, f 148
COLONNA, GIOVANNI PAOLO, 1637-1695
    PARTO, O BELLA; "Parto, o bella, parto, o bella, crudo ciel mi vuol lontano" (recit); "Partirò, sì,   699
       sì, mio bene" (aria), (duet) i 181
COMPTON, L.
    MY GRANDFATHER HAD SOME VERY FINE DUCKS; "My grandfather had a very fine farm" e 189   700
CONNELLY, REG
    GOOD NIGHT SWEETHEART. See 2666
CONNOLLY, CHARLES
    DRILL, YE TARRIERS DRILL. See 612
Conrad, Con, pseud, 1891-1938. See DOBER, CONRAD K., 1891-1938
CONRADI, AUGUST, 1821-1873
    "HERZLIEBCHEN MEIN UNTERM REBENDACH" g 326,327   words by H. Wilken   701
CONSTANCE, ARTHUR F. M.
    THE FLAG OF OUR UNION FOREVER; "A song for our banner" e 129,130   words by G. P. Morris   702

25

CRÜGER, JOHANN, 1598-1662
    JESUS, MEINE ZUVERSICHT; "Jesus, meine Zuversicht und mein Heiland" g 326   735
    "NUN DANKET ALL UND BRINGET HER" g 326 words by P. Gerhardt   736
    "NUN DANKET ALLE GOTT" g 49,326; "NOW THANK WE ALL OUR GOD" e 28,366 words by M.   737
        Rinckart
CRUSELL, BERNHARD HENRIK, 1775-1838
    OI TERVE POHJOLA; "Oi terve, Pohjola, i säimme onnela!"; ALL HAIL! OH NORTHERN STRAND!;   738
        "All hail! Oh Northern Strand! Our fathers' joyous land!" e, fi 124 words by F. B. Cöster
CUI, CÉSAR, 1835-1918
    THE STATUE AT CZASKOE-SELO; "There stands the maiden of stone" e, r 357; THE STATUE OF   739
        TSARSKOYE SELO; "Fetching a water fill'd jar" e, r 340 words by A. S. Pushkin
CURRAN, PEARL GILDERSLEEVE, 1875-1941
    HOLD THOU MY HAND; "Dear God, hold Thou my hand" e 123   740
    NOCTURNE; "It is night and the stars are brightly shining" e 364   741
    THE RESURRECTION; "The first day of the week, cometh Mary Magdalene" e 200 words from Bible   742
    SONNY BOY; "Come you dear little sonny boy, come close your sleepy blue eyes" e 241   743
CURRY, JAMES B.
    "GOOD NIGHT, SWEET JESUS" e 71   744
CURTIS, ERNESTO DE, 1875-1937
    TORNA A SURRIENTO; "Guarda il mare com' e bello!"; "E tu di'ci 'lo parto, adio!" (ref); COME   745
        BACK TO SORRENTO; "O'er the sea the sunlight dancing"; "Now you say good-bye I'm leaving"
        (ref) e, i 132; COME BACK TO SORRENTO; "Playing gently o'er the water"; "For you said goodbye
        we parted" (ref) e 233; ERINNERUNG AN SORRENTO; "Mit der Laute bringt der Traute"; "Dein
        gedenk ich, Herzgeliebte!" (ref) g 222
CUTLER, HENRY STEPHEN, 1824-1902
    O STARRY FLAG; All saints (tune); "O banner bright with stars and stripes" e 343; "O starry flag of   746
        red and white" e 28
CZERWIŃSKI, W., 1837-1893
    MARSZ SOKOŁÓW; "Ospały, gnuśny, zgrzybiały ten świat"; MARCH OF THE FALCONS; "So drowsy   747
        and lazy, decrepit, this world" e, p 295; OSPAŁY I GNUŚNY; "Ospały i gnusny, zgrzybiały ten
        swiat" e, p 159 words by J. Lam
CZIBULKA, ALPHONS, 1842-1874
    AMONG THE LILIES; "Among the lilies stray'd they twain forgetting" e 132 words by H. B. Farnie   748

DACRE, HARRY
    DAISY BELL; A BICYCLE BUILT FOR TWO; "There is a flower within my heart"; "Daisy, Daisy, give   749
        me your answer, do"; (ref) e 32,34,114,131; (ref only) e 115,128,129,130,132,233,236
DAHL, VIKING, 1895-1945
    SAANG OM EN BLIND FLICKA, op.5, no.1; "En morgon kom i örtagaarden en blind flicka" sw 355   750
DAHLGREEN,
    DE SISTA SEPTEMBERDAGARNE; "Hösten är kommen, hör stormarnes gny!"; "AUTUMN HAS COME   751
        WITH A STORM IN ITS HEART" e, sw 135
DAILEY, J. ANTON
    DREAMING; "Out in the still summer's evening"; "Dreaming, dreaming, of you sweetheart I am   752
        dreaming" (ref) e 114,131; (ref only) e 128,236 words by L. W. Heiser
DALAYRAC, NICOLAS, 1753-1809
    "CE CHER ENFANT SUR MES GENOUX"; "IL BEL PICCIN QUA SUL MIO COR"; BERCEUSE f, i 411   753
    [GULISTAN, opera; words by C. G. Étienne and A. La Chabeaussiere] AIR DE   754
        GULISTAN; "Cent esclaves ornaient ce superbe festin"; "A hundred lovely slaves did the festival
        grace" e, f 153
    JEUNE FILLETTE; "Jeune fillette, profitez du temps"; MAIDENS, REMEMBER; "Maidens, remember,   755
        time is on the wing!" e, f 140
DANICAN-PHILADOR, FRANÇOIS ANDRÉ, 1736-1795
    [ERNELINDE, PRINCESSE DE NORVEGE, opera; words by A. A. H. Poinsinet]   756
        AIR DE RICIMER; "Né dans un camp parmi les armes"; "A soldier born, 'mid campfires gleaming"
        e, f 147
    [Ibid] "CHER OBJET D'UNE TENDRE FLAMME"; "A TE SOL TUTTO VA IL MIO ARDORE" f, i 411   757
DANIEL, JOHN, ca1565-ca1630
    TYME CRUELL TYME; "Tyme cruell tyme canst thou subdue that brow" e 144 words by S. Daniel   758
DANIEL, PETER
    FREIHEIT; "Spaniens Himmel breitet seine Sterne"; "Spanish heavens spread their brilliant starlight"   759
        e, g 293; SALUTE TO FREEDOM e 35; FAR OFF IS OUR LAND e, g 7 words by K. Ernst,
        att to P. David

DANIELS, CHARLES NEIL MORET, 1879-1943
>YOU TELL ME YOUR DREAM, I'LL TELL YOU MINE; "Two little children one morning, after their 760
breakfast was o'er"; "You had a dream, well, I had one too" (ref) e 131,246; "You had a dream,
dear, I had one too" (ref) e 233 words by A. H. Brown and S. Rice
DANKS, HART PEASE, 1834-1903
>AMBER TRESSES TIED IN BLUE; "Far away in sunny meadows"; "She was fairer than the fairest" (ref) 761
e 129,130,132 words by S. M. Mitchell
>SILVER THREADS AMONG THE GOLD; "Darling, I am growing old" e 10,32,34,129,130,131,132,233, 762
236,343 words by E. E. Rexford
DAQUIN, LOUIS CLAUDE, 1695-1772
>"COME NOW, SHEPHERDS, COME AWAY" e 33 763
DARÁZS, MILALY
>ÉRIK A, ÉRIK A; RIPE IS THE CORN; "Ripe is the corn and the harvest is due" e 164 764
DARGOMYZHSKIĬ, ALEKSANDR SERGEEVICH, 1813-1869
>"I WILL TELL NO ONE" e, r 340 words by Koltzov 765
>"LOOK DARLING GIRL" e, r 340 766
>[RUSALKA, opera] THE MILLER'S SONG, Act I; "Okh, toto vse vy, devki molodyye"; "Alas! 767
all you young girls are truly stupid" e, r 5
DĀRZIŅŠ, EMILS
>MUTTERSEELE; "Leise tret' ich an dein Bette her"; Âme de la mère; "A ton lit viendrai veiller, mon 768
petit" f, g 224
>"WENN DIE TRÄNEN AUSGEWEINT SIND"; QUAND LES LARMES SONT TARIES; "Tout passera le peine, 769
les larmes" f, g 224
DAUVERGNE, ANTOINE, 1713-1797
>[LES TROQUEURS, opera; words by J. J. Vadé] AIR DE MARGOT; "D'un amant 770
inconstant, l'amour se revenge"; "For a lover's caprice, love will be revenged" e, f 151; D'UN
AMANT INCONSTANT, L'INCONSTANTE IN AMOR; "L'inconstant in amor punisce Amore" f, i 411
>[Ibid] ARIETTE DE LUBIN; "J'ai cru faire un bon coup en changeant de future" (recit); "Sa 771
nonchalance serait mon tourment" (aria); "'Twas for luck, as I thought, that I chang'd my betrothed"
(recit); "Her placid manner I could never stand" (aria) e, f 147
DAVID, FÉLICIEN CESAR, 1810-1876
>[LA PERLE DU BRÉSIL, opera; words by J. J. Gabriel and S. Saint-Etienne] 772
CHARMANT OISEAU; COUPLETS DU MYSOLI; "Quel ravissant sejour!" (recit); "Charmant oiseau,
qui sous l'ombrage Étale à nos yeux éblouis" (aria); "O what a lovely day!" (recit); "O charming
bird, that swings so lightly upon the branches there" (aria) e, f 292
>TRISTESSE DE L'ODALISQUE; "Dans un soupir, l'onde au rivage" f 278 words by T. Gautier 773
DAVIDENKO, ALEKSANDR ALEKSANDROVICH, 1899-1934
>MY MOTHER; "Would that I could see those days of winter in Siberia many years ago" e, r 162 774
words by J. Utkin
DAVIES, HENRY WALFORD, 1869-1941
>CHRISTMAS IS COMING; "Christmas is coming, the geese are getting fat" e 307 775
>"O LITTLE TOWN OF BETHLEHEM" e 307,376 words by P. Brooks 776
>SOLEMN MELODY, piano 306 777
DAVIES, LAURENCE H.
>THE BETHLEHEM STAR; "Moonless darkness stands between, past, O past, no more be seen!" e 376 778
words by G. M. Hopkins
DAVIS, GUSSIE L.
>HE CARVED HIS MOTHER'S NAME UPON THE TREE; "'Twas an orphan boy one day"; "Oh, the little 779
orphan boy, while the tear stood in his eye" (ref) e 131 words by H. V. Neal
>IN THE BAGGAGE COACH AHEAD; "On a dark stormy night, as the train rattled on"; "While the train 780
rolled onward, a husband sat in tears" (ref) e 246
>SING AGAIN THAT SWEET REFRAIN; "The music hall was crowded"; "Sing again that sweet refrain" 781
(ref) e 114,131; (ref only) e 129,130
DAVIS, KATHERINE KENNICOTT, 1892-
>THE MIGHTY GOD HAS SPOKEN; "The mighty God, even the Lord, hath spoken"; "God, our help in 782
ages past" e 89
DAVIS, THOMAS
>A NATION ONCE AGAIN; "When boyhood's fire was in my blood" e 172 783
DAVISON, ALPHENS
>SLEEP, SOLDIER, SLEEP; "Sleep, soldier, sleep, sleep, comrade, 'neath the heav'ns blue" e 28,366 784
words by M. K. Cherryman
DAVY, JOHN, 1763-1824
>THE BAY OF BISCAY; "Loud roar'd the dreadful thunder" e 234,366; IN THE BAY OF BISCAY e 14 785
words by A. Cherry
DEBUSSY, CLAUDE ACHILLE, 1862-1918
>[ARIETTES OUBLIÉES, song cycle; words by P. Verlaine] "C'EST L'EXTASE 786

28

DEBUSSY, CLAUDE ACHILLE, 1862-1918 (Continued)

LANGOUREUSE" no.1; "'TIS THE ECSTASY OF LANGOUR" e, f 121

[Ibid] CHEVAUX DE BOIS, no.4; "Tournez, tournez, bons chevaux de bois"; MERRY-GO-ROUND;   787
"O turn, turn around, merry wooden steeds" e, f 362

[Ibid] "IL PLEURE DANS MON COEUR," no.2; "THERE'S WEEPING IN MY HEART" e, f 121   788

[Ibid] SPLEEN, no.6; "Les roses étaient toutes rouges" f 278   789

BEAU SOIR: "Lorsque au soleil couchant les rivières sont roses"; BEAUTIFUL EVENING; "See how   790
the setting sun tints the rivers like roses" e, f 408; AT EVENING; "When 'neath the setting sun"
e, f 237; EVENING FAIR; "When in the setting sun" e, f 122; PEACEFUL EVENING; "Under the
setting sun waters blush like roses" e 348 words by P. Bourget

[CHANSONS DE BILITIS, song cycle; words by P. Loüys] LA CHEVELURE, no.2;   791
"Il m'a dit: 'Cette nuit, j'ai rêvé'; HER WONDROUS HAIR; "Thus he spoke, 'Twas last night that
I dreamed'" e, f 362

[Ibid] LA FLÛTE DE PAN, no.1; "Pour le jour des Hyacinthies"; THE FLUTE OF PAN; "Hyacinthia,   792
festival time" e, f 362 words by P. Loüys

LES CLOCHES; "Les feuilles s'ouvraient sur le bord des branches"; THE BELLS; "The leaves on the   793
green boughs gently are swinging" e, f 140 words by P. Bourget

[FÊTES GALANTES, SERIES I, song cycle; words by P. Verlaine] CLAIR DE   794
LUNE, no.3; "Votre âme est un paysage choisi"; MOONLIGHT; "Your soul resembles a vision so
fair" e, f 211

[Ibid] FANTOCHES, no.2; "Scaramouche et Pulcinella qu'un mauvias dessein rassembla"; PUPPETS;   795
"Scaramouche and Polichinelle dark malicious plots do unite" e, f 211

MANDOLINE; "Les donneurs de sérénades et les belles écouteuses"; MANDOLIN; "Serenaders gaily   796
singing to enchanted maidens" e, f 208 words by P. Verlaine

[PROSES LYRIQUES, song cycle] DE FLEURS, no.3; "Dans l'ennui si désolément vert";   797
OF FLOWERS; "Weariness, so tormentingly green" e, f 362

[REVERIE, piano] MY REVERIE; "Listen to my reverie" e 236 arr by L. Clinton   798

ROMANCE; "L'âme évaporee et souffrante"; "Soul not of this world, soul tormented"; e, f 237;   799
"Soul of lightest breath, softly sailing" e, f 140 words by P. Bourget

VOICI QUE LE PRINTEMPS; "Voici que le printemps, ce fils léger d'Avril"; BEHOLD THE SPRING;   800
"Behold the lovely spring in courtly grace appears" e, f 211 words by P. Bourget

DE CAMPO, M. VENADO

LAS CASITA; "Que de a dón de amiga ven go"; MY DWELLING; "There's a pretty little dwelling"   801
e, s 248 words by F. Llera

CHIAPANECAS; "Risas por doquier, llenas de placer"; THE MEXICAN HAND-CLAPPING SONG;   802
"When the night is fair, music fills the air" e, s 9 words by J. Hernandez-Ribera; "Un clavel
corte por la sierra fui"; WHILE THERE'S MUSIC THERE'S ROMANCE; "While there's music sweet,
with rhythmic beat" e, s 248 words by E. de Torre

LAS CUATRO MILPAS. See 1781

MORIR SOÑANDO; "El recuerdo de tu amor vive en mi"; WHEN EYES ARE GLEAMING, MEXICAN   803
WALTZ; "Dearest, are we really waltzing alone?" e, s 248 words by L. DeCaen

DEDEKIND, CONTANTIN CHRISTIAN, 1628-1715

DER WAHREN TUGEND GEGENSTREIT RÜHRT VON DER ERDEN EITELKEIT; "O Eitelkeit, du rechte   804
Pest der Jugend" g 250 words by J. Rist

DEDEKIND, HENNING

TRINK ICH WEIN, SO VERDERB ICH. See 5567

DEGEYTER, PIERRE, d 1915

L'INTERNATIONALE; "Debout! les damnés de la terre!" f 294   805

DEIS, CARL, 1883-

A LOVER'S LAMENT; "To kiss my Celia's fairer breast" e 259 words by W. M. Johnson   806

WAITING; "I thought my heart would break" e 121 words by C. H. Towne   807

DEKOVEN, REGINALD, 1861-1920

[ROBIN HOOD, operetta; words by H. B. Smith] OH PROMISE ME; "Oh promise   808
me that some day you and I" e 32,34

De la Barre, Michel. See LA BARRE, MICHEL DE, ca1670-ca1744

DE LACHAU, COUNTESS ADA

LI'L LIZA JANE. See 7779A

Delibes, Clément Philibert Léo. See DELIBES, LÉO, 1836-1891

DELIBES, LÉO, 1836-1891

LES FILLES DE CADIX; "Nous venions de voir le taureau"; THE GIRLS OF CADIZ; "We have just   809
seen the bullfight" e, f 191,193,195; "The girls of old Cadiz, we know" e, f 93; THE MAIDS
OF CADIZ; "Returning from the fiesta" e, f 208

[LAKMÉ, opera; words by P. E. J. Gondinet and P. E. F. Gille] BERCEUSE,   810
Act III; "Sous le ciel tout étoile"; "Stars in heav'n are shining bright" e, f 292

[Ibid] FANTAISIE AUX DIVINS MENSONGES, Act I; "Prendre le dessin d'un bijou" (recit);   811
"Fantaisie aux divins mensonges" (aria); "Can it be so awfully bad" (recit); "Wanton fancy, so
divine in seeming" (aria) e, f 3

DIAZ CHAVEZ, A.
    ADIOS; "Adios, adios! la mano del destino"; DEAR LOVE, FAREWELL; "Dear love, farewell, now is   833
        the hour of parting" e, s 142   words by A. Guzman Aguilera
DIBDIN, CHARLES, 1745-1814
    HIGH BARBAREE. See 9447A
    [THE ODDITIES, opera] TOM BOWLING; "Here, a sheer hulk, lies poor Tom Bowling"
        e 205, 235, 349, 402   834
    THE LASS THAT LOVES A SAILOR; "The moon on the ocean was dimm'd by a ripple" e 205
    [THE SERAGLIO, opera] BLOW HIGH, BLOW LOW; "Blow high, blow low! let tempest tear the   835
        mainmast by the board" e 348   836
    [THE WATERMAN, ballad opera;] THE BAY OF BISCAY. See 785
    [YO YEA, OR THE FRIENDLY TARS, ballad opera] YO, YEA; "I sail'd in the good   837
        ship, the Kitty" e 235
DICHMONT, WILLIAM
    SUCH A LI'L' FELLOW; "He's such a li'l' fellow" e 136   words by F. Lowell   838
DIEHL, LOUIS
    MY LASS; "Now, my lads, 'tis time to go" e 205   words by F. E. Weatherly   839
DIETRICH, FRITZ, 1905-
    "BRUDER, ICH GEH AUCH MIT DIR" g 49   840
    "EH ICH MICH NIEDERLEGE" g 49   words by H. Claudius   841
DILLEA, HERBERT
    ABSENCE MAKES THE HEART GROW FONDER; "Sweetheart, I have grown so lonely"; "Absence   842
        makes the heart grow fonder" (ref) e 114, 131 (ref only) e 128   words by A. Gillespie
DIRNER, GUSTÁV
    HA ÉN PIROS ROZSA LENNÉK; IF I WERE A CRIMSON ROSE; "If I were a crimson rose and in full   843
        blossom" e 164
    NEM NAGY ESET; IT'S NOTHING NEW; "It's nothing new still it is true" e 164   844
DITON, CARL, 1886-
    ENTREATY; "Dearest, when I am dead, sing one last song for me" e 78   words by W. Henley   845
DJERJINSKY, I.
    FROM BORDER UNTO BORDER; "On ev'ry front and border" e, r 288   846
DOBER, CONRAD K., 1891-1938
    MEMORY LANE. See 3541
DOCHE, JOSEF DENIS, 1766-1825
    "DENKST DU DARAN?" g 31   847
DÓCZY, JÓZSEF
    "A KANYARGÓ TISZA PARTJÁN OTT SZÜLETTEM"; BORN THERE WHERE THE WINDING TISZA;   848
        "Born there where the winding Tisza still is flowing" e, hu 285
    "SZERETÖT KERESEK"; "I MUST HAVE A SWEETHEART" e, hu 285   849
    "VETT A RÓZSÁM PIROS SELYEM VIGANÓT"; "I RECEIVED A DRESS" e, hu 285   850
DODGE, GILBERT
    PEGGY O'NEIL. See 2757
DODGE, OSSIAN E.
    HO! WESTWARD HO!; "The Star of Empire poets say, Ho! westward ho!" e 189   851
DÖRFLINGER, KURT
    GANZ LEIS' ERKLINGT MUSIK; "Der Tag ist nun vorbei" g 223   words by E. Wallnau and K. Feltz   852
DONALDSON, WALTER, 1893-1947
    CAROLINA IN THE MORNING; "Wishing is good time wasted"; "Nothing could be finer than to be in   853
        Carolina in the morning" (ref) e 345   words by G. Kahn
    THE DAUGHTER OF ROSIE O'GRADY; "Yesterday while out a-walkin', I met a dear little girl"; "She's   854
        the daughter of Rosie O'Grady" (ref) e 166 (ref only) e 233   words by M. C. Brice
    MY BLUE HEAVEN; "When whippoorwills call and ev'ning is nigh" e 236   words by G. Whiting   855
    MY BUDDY; "Nights are long since you went away" e 233   words by G. Kahn   856
DONIZETTI, GAETANO, 1797-1848
    [DON PASQUALE, opera; words by G. D. Ruffini] "AH, UN FOCO INSOLITO,"   857
        Act I; CAVATINA; "Ah, wild thoughts come throngingly" e, i 5
    [Ibid] "BELLA SICCOME UN ANGELO," Act I i 298; ROMANZA; "Fair as an angel from above"   858
        e, i 4
    [Ibid] COM' È GENTIL, Act III; "Com' è gentil la notte a mezzo april"; SERENADE; "Thou   859
        wand'ring moon, whose soothing light" e, i 3
    [Ibid] SO ANCH'IO LA VIRTU MAGICA, Act I; "Quel guardo il cavaliere" (recit), "So anch'io   860
        la virtu magica" (aria) i 302; "Thus did her look transfix him" (recit); "I feel I also know the
        knack" (aria) e, i 6; CAVATINA; "Her cavalier was captured" (recit); "It may be true, but I
        know too" (aria) e, i 292

DONIZETTI, GAETANO, 1797-1848 (Continued)

[DON SEBASTIEN, ROI DE PORTUGAL, opera; words by A. E. Scribe] O   861
LISBONA, ALFIN TI MIRO; "Gioco di rea fortuna" (recit); "O Lisbona, alfin ti miro" (aria) i 298

[L'ELISIR D'AMORE, opera; words by F. Romani] UNA FURTIVA LAGRIMA, Act II;   862
"Una furtiva lagrima negl' occhi suoi spunto"; ROMANZA; "Shyly and slow a tear arose" e, i 3;
HEIMLICH AUS IHREM AUGE; "Heimlich aus ihrem Auge sich eine Träne stahl" g, i 391

[LA FAVORITE, opera; words by A. Royer, G. van Nieuwenhuysen and A. E.   863
Scribe] A TANTO AMOR, Act III; "Fernando, ei del suo cor la bravma" (recit); "A tanto amor,
Leonora" (aria); CAVATINA; "Fernando with all his heart doth love thee" (recit); "To such a love,
Leonora" (aria) e, i 5

[Ibid] O MIO FERNANDO, Act III; "Fia dunque vero oh ciel" (recit); "O mio Fernando! della terra   864
il trono" (aria) i 300; "It is the truth, then! O heav'n!" (recit); "O my Fernando! Earth's enchantments of pleasure" (aria) e, i 2

[Ibid] SPIRTO GENTIL; "Spirto gentil, ne' sogni miei Brillasti un dì ma ti perdei!"; ROMANZA;   865
"Angel of light, whom once I cherished fondly in dreams ever perished" e, i 3

[LA FILLE DU RÉGIMENT, opera; words by J. H. Vernoy de Saint-Georges   866
and J. F. A. Bayard] CHACUN LE SAIT, Act I; "Ah! Chacun le sait"; ALL ARE AWARE;
"Ah! All are aware"; CIASCUN LO DICE; "Ah! Ciascun lo dice" e, f, i 221; "Ah! That's what
they say" e, f 292; "Ah! None can gainsay it" e, i 6

[Ibid] IL FAUT PARTIR, Act I; "Il faut partir mes bons compagnons d'armes"; "Goodbye my dear   867
companions in arms" e, f 292

[Ibid] PAR LE RANG ET PAR L'OPULENCE, Act II; "C'en est donc fait et mon coeur va changer"   868
(recit); "Par le rang et par l'opulence" (aria); "Now is the time and my heart is afraid" (recit);
"They have sought me and won me with treasure" (aria) e, f 292

Der Liebestrank. See L'ELISIR D'AMORE

[LINDA DI CHAMOUNIX, opera; words by G. Rossi] "CARI LUOGHI OV'IO PASSAI"   869
Act I i 300

[Ibid] O LUCE DI QUEST' ANIMA, Act I; "Ah, tardai troppo" (recit); "O luce di quest' anima"   870
(aria); "Ah, 'tis too late" (recit); "My soul's delight and treasure" (aria) e, i 6; "Ah, so belated"
(recit); "O light of all my being" (aria) e, i 292

[LUCIA DI LAMMERMOOR, opera; words by S. Cammarano] ARDON GL'INCENSI,   871
Act III; THE MAD SCENE; "Il dolce suono mi colpì di sua voce!" (recit); "Ardon gl'incensi
splendon le sacre faci...Spargi d'amaro pianto" (aria) i 302; "It was his accents that so sweet to
me sounded!"; "The incense rises, the holy lamps are shining" (aria, pt 1 Ardon gl'incensi, and recit
only) e, i 221

[Ibid] [CHI ME FRENA IN TAL MOMENTO] Act II; SEXTETTE; "What from vengeance yet restrain   872
me" e 132

[Ibid] "CRUDA, FUNESTA SMANIA," Act I; CAVATINA; "Torments of hate and vengeance"   873
e, i 4

[Ibid] DALLE STANZE, OVE LUCIA, Act III; "Cesi, ah cesi quel contento!" (recit); "Dalle   874
stanze, ove Lucia tratta a vea col suo consorte" (aria); "Cease ye, oh cease these sounds of gladness!" (recit); "From the chamber, where sad and silent, to her Lord I Lucy guided" (aria) e, i 5

[Ibid] FRA POCO A ME RICOVERÒ, Act III; "Tombe degl' avi miei" (recit); "Fra poco a me   875
ricoverò" (aria); "Tomb of my sainted fathers" (recit); "To earth I bid a last fare-well" (aria)
e, i 3

[Ibid] REGNAVA NEL SILENZIO, Act I; "Regnava nel silenzio alta la notte e bruna" i 302; "Silent   876
the sombre wings of night darkness around were spreading"; e, i 6; "Silently all lay sleeping" e, i
292

DORSEY, THOMAS A. 1899-

TAKE MY HAND, PRECIOUS LORD; "Precious Lord, take my hand, lead me on, let me stand" e 394   877
WHEN I'VE DONE MY BEST; "When I've done the best I can, if my friends don't understand" e 394   878

DOSTAL, NICO, 1895-

[CLIVIA, operetta; words by C. Amberg] AM MANZANARES; "Kleines, sag' mir   879
eines" g 256

[Ibid] ICH BIN VERLIEBT, ICH WEISS NICHT WIE MIR GESCHAH; "Warum trieb das Schicksal   880
mich hieher?" g 254

[Ibid] WUNDERBAR, WIE NIE EIN WUNDER WAR; "Heisses Verlangen durch-pulst mir das Blut"   881
g 255

[DIE FLUCHT INS GLÜCK, operetta; words by H. Hermecke] DAS SOLL DER   882
SCHÖNSTE WALZER SEIN!; "Plaudern Sie, doch heit're Sachen nur" g 257

[Ibid] MEINES HERZENS BRENNENDE SEHNSUCHT; "Des Glückes ungemess'ne Stunden hab' ich im   883
Leben oft gesucht" g 257

"HEUT' MACHT DIE WELT SONNTAG FÜR MICH" g 396   884

[MONIKA, operetta; words by H. Hermecke] HEIMATLIED; "Heimatland, Heimatland,   885
dein gedenk' ich immerdar" g 255

DOSTAL, NICO, 1895- (Continued)

[PRINZESSIN NOFRETETE, operetta; words by R. Köller] FATA MORGANA; "Das   886
    Glück, das uns im Wachen nicht gegeben" g 257

[DIE UNGARISCHE HOCHZEIT, operetta; words by H. Hermecke]   887
    MÄRCHENTRAUM DER LIEBE; "Nun ging sie von mir, zu meinem Schmerz" g 258

[DIE VIELGELIEBTE, operetta] DU NUR BIST DAS GLÜCK MEINES LEBENS; "So stolz was   888
    ich, so unbeschwert und Liebe war" g 255

DOUGLAS, SALLIE HUME

FOLLOW THE GLEAM; Garden of paradise (tune); "To the knights in the days of old" e 343   889

DOWLAND, JOHN, 1563-1626

"AWAKE, SWEET LOVE, THOU ART RETURNED" e 118; AWAKE SWEET LOVE e 403   890

"AWAY WITH THESE SELFE LOVING LADS" e 144; "AWAY WITH THESE SELF-LOVING LADS" e 197   891
    words by F. Greville

"CAN SHEE EXCUSE MY WRONGS" e 144   892

COME AGAIN, SWEET LOVE; "Come again, sweet love doth now invite" e 272, 348; "COME   893
    AGAIN, SWEET LOVE DOTH NOW INVITE" e 117; COME AGAIN; "Come again, sweete love
    doth now invite" e 36, 196

"COME AWAY, COME SWEET LOVE" e 144; COME AWAY e 197   894

COME HEAVY SLEEPE; "Come heavy sleepe, the image of true death" e 144   895

"DEARE, IF YOU CHANGE" e 144, 196   896

"FAREWELL, UNKIND, FAREWELL" e 197   897

FINE KNACKS FOR LADIES; "Fine knacks for ladies, cheape choise brave and new" e 144; "Fine   898
    knacks for ladies, cheap, choice, brave and new!" e 119; PEDDLER'S SONG e 196

FLOW MY TEARES; LACRIME; "Flow my teares fall from your springs" e 144; FLOW, MY TEARS;   899
    "Flow my tears, fall from your springs" e 116; THE LACHRYMAE PAVAN; "Flow teares from your
    springs" e 107

"FLOW NOT SO FAST YE FOUNTAINES" e 196   900

GO CHRISTALL TEARES; "Go christall teares; like to the morning showers" e 144   901

"HIS GOLDEN LOCKS TIME HATH TO SILVER TURNDE" e 144 words by G. Peele   902

"I SAW MY LADY WEEPE" e 144; "I SAW MY LADY WEEP" e 119; AYRE; "I saw my lady weep"   903
    e 278

IF MY COMPLAINTS; "If my complaints could passions moove" e 144; "IF MY COMPLAINTS   904
    COULD PASSIONS MOVE" e 118

"IN DARKNESSE LET MEE DWELL" e 144   905

"THE LOWEST TREES HAVE TOPS" e 144 words att to E. Dyer   906

A LUTE LULLABY; "Lullay my babe, lie still and sleep" e 380   907

"NOW, O NOW, I NEEDS MUST PART" e 197   908

O SWEET WOODS; "O sweet woods the delight of solitarinesse" e 144 words by P. Sidney   909

"SAY LOVE, IF EVER THOU DIDST FIND" e 116   910

"SHALL I SUE, SHALL I SEEKE FOR GRACE?" e 197   911

"A SHEPHERD IN A SHADE" e 196   912

SLEEP, WAYWARD THOUGHTS; "Sleep, wayward thoughts, and rest you with my love" e 117   913

SORROW, STAY; "Sorrow, sorrow, stay!" e 117; "SORROW, SORROW, STAY" e 197   914

"STAY TIME, AWHILE, THY FLYING" e 197   915

"WEEP YOU NO MORE, SAD FOUNTAINES" e 118, 144, 197   916

"WHAT IF I NEVER SPEEDE?" e 197   917

"WHO EVER THINKS OR HOPES" e 144; "WHO EVER THINKS OR HOPES OF LOVE" e 275 words by   918
    F. Greville, Lord Brooke

"WOEFUL HEART WITH GRIEFE OPPRESSED" e 196   919

DRECHSLER, JOSEF, 1782-1852

BRÜDERLEIN FEIN; "Brüderlein fein, Brüderlein fein musst mir ja nicht böse sein!" g 99, 326, 353   920
    words by F. Raimund

DRESE, ADAM

JESU, GEH VORAN; "Jesu, geh voran auf der Lebensbahn!" g 326 words by N. L. von Zinzendorf   921

DRESSEL, GUSTAV

"MEI MUTTER MAG MI NET" g 326   922

DRESSER, PAUL, 1858-1906

JUST TELL THEM THAT YOU SAW ME; "While strolling down the street one eve"; "Just tell them   923
    that you saw me" (ref) e 114, 131; (ref only) e 129, 130, 132

THE LETTER THAT NEVER CAME; "A letter here for me?" "Was it from a gray-haired mother" (ref)   924
    e 114

DRIGO, RICCARDO, 1846-1930

[I MILIONI D'ARLECCHINO, ballet] SERENADE; "Under a tree in Paree ev'ry night you'll   925
    see a harlequin" e 132 words by H. Johnson

DRIZO, L.
    LOUDER, OH LET ME SING MY SONG; "The city skies are clouded" e, r 287,288   926
Drouet, Louis Francois Philippe, 1792-1873, supposed composer
    PARTANT POUR LA SYRIE. See HORTENSE, CONSORT OF LOUIS, KING OF HOLLAND, 1783-1837, supposed composer
Drourt, Jean-Baptiste de. See BOUSSET, JEAN BAPTISTE DE, 1662-1725
DU BUISSON, (17th century)
    PLAINTE SUR LA MORT DE MONSIEUR LAMBERT; "Ô mort! ô mort, affreuse mort! quelle est ta   927
    barbarie?" f 278
DUFRESNY, c 1700
    LE DÉPIT; "A mille soinsjaloux, Tircis abandonné" f 108   928
DUKE, JOHN, 1899-
    BELLS IN THE RAIN; "Sleep falls, with limpid drops of rain, upon the steep cliffs of the town" e 358   929
    words by E. Wylie
    LUKE HAVERGAL; "Go to the western gate, Luke Havergal" e 358 words by E. A. Robinson   930
DUNAEVSKIĬ, ISAAK OSIPOVICH, 1900-1955
    CAPTAIN BOLD; "Oh a captain bold was he" e, r 287,288 words by V. Lebedev-Kumach   931
    HEART IN MY BREAST; "What is the passion that holds me today" e, r 287,288   932
    IF THE VOLGA OVERFLOWS; "Full of suff'ring, full of sorrow" e, r 287,288 words by   933
    V. Lebedev-Kumach
    LET'S KEEP IN TRIM; "While the sun is brightly gleaming" e, r 288 words by V. Lebedev-Kumach   934
    LOVING; "Of all the many pretty maidens" e, r 287,288 words by V. Lebedev-Kumach   935
    "OH, IT IS A JOY" e, r 287,288 words by Schmidthoff   936
    OH, RETURN TO ME, MY DARLING; "I am weary, for you've left me here" e, r 287,288 words by   937
    Volzhenin
    SONG OF OUR COUNTRY; "We have forests, many fields and rivers" e, r 287,288   938
DUNIECKI, STANISLAW, 1839-1871
    "CO TAM MARZYC O KOCHANIU"; "NOT FOR US IS LOVE AND ROSES" e, p 159 words by M.   939
    Romanowski
DUNSTABLE, JOHN, ca1370-1453
    WHAT TIDINGS BRINGEST THOU, MESSENGER? See 9006
DUPARC, HENRI, 1848-1933
    CHANSON TRISTE; "Dans ton coeur dort un clair de lune"; A SONG OF SORROW; "Moonlight fullness   940
    thy heart illuming" e, f 362 words by J. Lahor
    EXTASE; "Sur un lys pâle mon coeur dort"; ECSTACY; "On a pale lily is my rest" e, f 140; "On a   941
    pale blossom my heart sleeps" e, f 121; "O'er a pale flow'ret broods my heart" e, f 237 words
    by J. Lahor
    L'INVITATION AU VOYAGE; "Mon enfant, ma soeur"; DREAM WORLD; "Come, my comrade fair"   942
    e, f 121 words by C. Baudelaire
    LAMENTO; "Connaissez-vous la blanche tombe"; LAMENT; "Do you know a pallid marble grave-   943
    stone" e, f 408 words by T. Gautier
    LE MANOIR DE ROSEMONDE; "De sa dent soudaine et vorace"; ROSAMOND'S MANOR; "With its   944
    fang so sharp and voracious" e, f 140 words by R. de Bonnières
    PHIDYLÉ; "L'herbe est molle au sommeil"; "Over mosses and grass" e, f 362,364 words by L. de   945
    Lisle
DUPONT, GABRIEL EDOUARD XAVIER, 1878-1914
    MANDOLINE; "Les donneurs de sérénades et les belles écouteuses"; MANDOLIN; "Gay, romantic   946
    serenaders greet their charming loves with playing" e, f 357; "The serenading swains and the
    lovely ladies listing" e, f 190,192,194 words by P. Verlaine
DURANTE, FRANCESCO, 1684-1755
    DANZA, DANZA, FANCIULLA GENTILE; "Danza, danza, fanciulla, al mio cantar"; "DANCE, O   947
    DANCE, GENTLE MAIDEN" e, i 139; "DANCE, O DANCE, MAIDEN GAY" e, i 368; "DANZA,
    DANZA, DANZA FANCIULLA"; "TANZE, TANZE, TANZE, MEIN MADCHEN" g, i 168
    FIERO, ACERBO DESTIN; "Fiero, acerbo destin dell' alma mia" (duet) i 181   948
    SON IO, BARBARA DONNA; "Son io, son io, barbara donna" (duet) i 181   949
    "VERGIN, TUTTA AMOR"; "VIRGIN, FULL OF GRACE" e, i 138; PRAYER; PREGHIERA; "VIRGIN,   950
    FOUNT OF LOVE" e, i 368
DURHAM, M. T.
    STAR OF COLUMBIA; "Columbia, Columbia, to glory arise" e 109,110 words by Dwight   951
DURHAM, MISS
    THE PROMISED LAND. See 7940
DURÓN, SEBASTIÁN, 1645?-1716?
    CLORIS HERMOSA; "Graciosa moda esa que han dado en usar"; BELLE CHLORIS; "O mode infâme de   952
    tant de femmes en ce jour" f, s 269
DURRANT, F. T.
    THE VIRGIN'S CRADLE HYMN; "Sleep, sweet Babe! my cares beguiling" e 307 words by S. T.   953
    Coleridge

DVOŘÁK, ANTONÍN, 1841-1904
    [BIBLICKÉ PÍSNĚ, song cycle] "GOD IS MY SHEPHERD," no.4 e 89 words from Bible   954
    [Ibid] "I WILL LIFT UP MINE EYES," no.9 e 90 words from Psalm CXXI:1-4   955
    HUMORESQUE, piano, op.101, no. 7; arr "Humoresque my heart's at rest" e 329; "Strains of   956
        Humoresque divine you thrill and fill this heart of mine" e 132
    THE LARK, op.7, no.4; "While the maiden weeds the hempfield" e 121   957
    [SYMPHONY, NO.5, OP.95. LARGO; arr] HYMN OF LOVE; "From the cloud, from   958
        the tree, from all things above" e 343; DOWN DE ROAD; "Down de road, down de road, on my
        way to home" e 132
    UKOLÉBAVKA; "Spi, mé dítě, spi, zamkni očka svý!"; WIEGENLIED; "Schlaf, mein Kind in Ruh,   959
        schliess die Äuglein zu!" c, g 74
    [ZIGEUNERMELODIEN, song cycle, OP.55] ALS DIE ALTE MUTTER, no.4; "Als die   960
        alte Mutter mich moch lehrte singen"; SONGS MY MOTHER TAUGHT ME, GIPSY MELODY; "Songs
        my mother taught me in the days long vanish'd" e, g 122,237,329; "When our dear old mother's
        voice train'd us all in singing" e 348; SONGS THAT MY MOTHER TAUGHT; "Songs that my
        Mother taught me in the days long vanished" e 132
DYER-BENNETT, RICHARD
    MY FATHER'S COOK; "When I was a young lad we had a fine cook" e 111   961
    PASSIVE RESISTANCE; "This is a story of passive resistance" e 111   962
    THE REAPER'S GHOST; "Oh do not cross the hayfield" e 111   963
    THE UNFORTUNATE TROUBADOUR; "In the coldest, darkest hour of night" e 111   964
DYKES, JOHN BACCHUS, 1823-1876
    "CALM ON THE LISTENING EAR OF NIGHT"; ST. AGNES (tune) e 315,337 words by E. H. Sears   965
    "ETERNAL FATHER, STRONG TO SAVE' e 346 words by W. Whiting   966
    HARK! TEN THOUSAND VOICES; St. Oswald (tune); "Hark! ten thousand voices sounding" e 28,366   967
        words by T. Kelly
    HOLY, HOLY, HOLY; "Holy, holy, holy, Lord God Almighty" e 28,233,236,346,366 words by R.   968
        Heber
    LEAD KINDLY LIGHT; "Lead kindly light, amid th' encircling gloom" e 28,132,233,236,279,366,394   969
        words by J. H. Newman
    SLEEP, HOLY BABE!; "Sleep, Holy Babe! upon Thy Mother's breast" e 251,296 words by E. Caswall   970

E.T.P.A., pseud. See MARIA ANTONIA WALPURGIS, Electress of Saxony, 1724-1780
Eastburn, pseud. See WINNER, JOSEPH E.
EAYRS, M. P.
    "SALVE REGINA"; "HAIL, HOLY QUEEN" e, lat 304   971
EBEL, E.
    LEISE RIESELT DER SCHNEE; "Leise rieselt der Schnee, still und starr ruht der See" g 326   972
EBELING, JOHANN GEORG, 1637-1676
    "ALL MY HEART THIS NIGHT REJOICES" e 317; ALL MY HEART THIS NIGHT e 271   973
    DIE GÜLDNE SONNE; "Die güldne Sonne voll Freud und Wonne" g 49,326 words by P. Gerhardt   974
EBERLE, F.
    UNTER DEM LINDENBAUM, op.7; "Ein Vöglein sang im Lindenbaum in lauer Sommernacht" g 327   975
EBERWEIN, TRAUGOTT MAXIMILIAN, 1775-1831
    ERGO BIBAMUS; "Hier sind wir versammelt zu löblichem Tun" g 31,99; "HIER SIND WIR   976
        VERSAMMELT" g 43,353 words by J. W. von Goethe
ECKERT, KARL ANTON FLORIAN, 1820-1879
    ER LIEBT NUR MICH ALLEIN; "Mein einz'ger Schatz ist fern, so fern"; IL N'AIME QUE MOI!; "Mon   977
        bien-aimé, mon seul espoir"; NONE HE LOVES BUT ME; SWISS ECHO SONG; "My dearest love is
        far away" e, f, g 221
EDMUNDS, JOHN, 1913-
    THE LONELY; "Lone and forgotten, through a long sleeping, in the heart of age a child woke weeping"   978
        e 358 words by G. W. Russell
EDWARDS, CLARA, 1887-
    INTO THE NIGHT; "Silently into the night I go" e 357   979
    LADY MOON; "Lady, swingin' in de sky" e 241 words by T. Hollingsworth   980
    WHEN JESUS WALKED ON GALILEE; "There comes a stillness in the heart" e 123   981
EDWARDS, GUS, 1879-1945
    "BY THE LIGHT OF THE SILVERY MOON" e 233 words by E. Madden   982
    IN MY MERRY OLDSMOBILE; "Come away with me Lucile in my merry Oldsmobile" e 233 words by   983
        V. Bryan
EDWARDS, JEHILA (Pat)
    I WALKED THE ROAD AGAIN; "I am a poor unlucky chap, I'm very fond of rum" e 72   984

EDWARDS, JULIAN
        MY OWN UNITED STATES; "I love ev'ry inch of her prairie land" e 233 words by S. Stange   985
EGERTON, FRANK
        "WE NEVER SPEAK AS WE PASS BY" e 204   986
EHLERS, WILHELM
        DAS MÜHLRAD. See 5263B
EHRSTRÖM, FREDRIK AUGUST, 1801-1850
        JOUTSEN; "Halk' illan ruskon auermaan käy lento joutsenen"; THE SWAN; "From purple tinted   987
        cloudlets sank the swan one eve in June" e, fi 124 words by J. L. Runeberg
EICHBERG, JULIUS, 1824-1893
        TO THEE, O COUNTRY!; "To thee O country great and free" e 28 words by Mrs. J. Lane   988
EISEMANN, MIHALY
        SZERET-E MÉG?; "Ragyogott a holdfény"; DO YOU LOVE ME?; "Over all the island" e, hu 285   989
EISENSTEIN, JUDITH (KAPLAN)
        THE BUS DRIVER'S SONG; "Travel in an Egged bus. No trouble no fuss" e 190   990
EISLER, HANNS
        UNITED FRONT; "And just because he's human" e 293 words by B. Brecht   991
ELGAR, SIR EDWARD WILLIAM, 1857-1934
        "IS SHE NOT PASSING FAIR" e 277 words by Charles, Duke of Orleans   992
        [SEA PICTURES, song cycle, OP.37] WHERE CORALS LIE, op.37, no.4; "The deeps   993
        have music soft and low" e 274 words by R. Garnett
        [VARIATIONS ON AN ORIGINAL THEME, ORCHESTRA. NIMROD] NIMROD   994
        piano 306
ELLERBROCK, CHARLES W. A.
        "GOD SAVE THE SOUTH" e 161 words by E. Halphin   995
ELLIOTT, ALONZO, 1891-
        THERE'S A LONG, LONG TRAIL; "There's a long, long trail a-winding" e 233 words by S. King   996
Elliott, Zo. See ELLIOTT, ALONZO
ELLIS, CECIL
        SEEK YE THE TRUTH; "Truth, that roll'd away the stone" e 398 words by T. King   997
ELVEY, GEORGE JOB, 1816-1893
        COME, YE THANKFUL PEOPLE; St. George's Windsor (tune); "Come, ye thankful people, come, raise 998
        the song of harvest home" e 28, 279, 343, 366 words by H. Alford
EMERSON, IDA
        HELLO! MA BABY. See 1712
EMMET, JOSEPH K.
        GO TO SLEEP, LENA DARLING; EMMET'S LULLABY; "Close your eyes, Lena, my darling" e 28, 129, 999
        130, 131, 233, 366; EMMET'S LULLABY e 114; EMMETT'S LULLABY e 132
EMMETT, DANIEL DECATUR
        THE BLUE TAIL FLY. See FOLKSONGS, UNITED STATES
        THE BOATMEN'S DANCE. See FOLKSONGS, UNITED STATES
        DIXIE; "I wish I was in the land of cotton" e 109, 110, 115, 284; "I wish I was in de land ob cotton" 1000
        e7, 28, 35, 212, 233, 343, 366; DIXIE LAND e 10, 236, 294; "I wish I was in the land of cotton"
        e 129, 130; A-WAY DOWN SOUTH IN DIXIE; "I wish I was in de land ob cotton" e 184; DIXIE'S
        LAND e 161; DIXIE LAND; "I wish I was in de land of cotton" e 279
        GREEN-BACKS; "How are you Green-backs ten or twenty!"; "Look to the East, look to the West" (ref) 1001
        e 189
        OLD DAN TUCKER; "Ah come to town de udder night" e 80; "Come to town the other night" e 185 1002
        "I came to town de udder night" e 34; "I come to town de udder night" e 109, 110, 115, 212; OLE
        DAN TUCKER e 28, 279, 366; OLD DAN TUCKER; "Ol' Dan Tucker's a fine ol' man" e 227;
        "Went to town the other night" e 173; OL' DAN TUCKER; "Hey! Get out the way, Ol' Dan Tucker"
        e 170
ENGEL, CARL, 1883-1944
        THE SEA SHELL; "Seashell, seashell, sing me a song, oh! Please!" e 121, 364 words by A. Lowell 1003
ENGEL, JOEL, 1868-1927
        SHABES BEYN HASHMOSHES; "Es geyt shoyn avek zich der heyliger"; "The Sabbath will soon be over 1004
        and gone" e, y 318 words by B. Kovner
        SHIR ERES; "Numi, numi, yaldati"; "Aba halach la-avoda" (verse); "Sleep, sleep, my baby girl"; 1005
        "Daddy has gone off to work" (verse) e, h 318 words by I. Halpern
ENRIQUEZ DE VALDERRABANO, ENRIQUE, 16th c
        "DE DÓNDE VENÍS, AMORE?" s 12   1006
ERIKSSON, JOSEF, 1872-
        "DU KUNDE JU EJ VETA" op.33, no.5 sw 355 words by V. Ekelund   1007
        NU FALLER NATT ÖFVER HAFVET, op.9, no.1; "Dofter af taang och af sälta" sw 355 words by 1008
        H. Johnsson

ERLEBACH, PHILIPP HEINRICH, 1657-1714
    WEM GELIEBET WEIN UND BIER DER GESELLE SICH ZU MIR; "Freut, ihr Brüder, freut euch jtzt"   1009
    g 250
ERNELINDA TALEA PASTORELLA ARCADA, pseud. See MARIA ANTONIA WALPURGIS,
    Electress of Saxony, 1724-1780
ESCARPENTER, JOSÉ
    GUAJIRITA MIA; "Al subir de la pendiente"; MY GUAJIRITA; "Imagine a Cuban flower" e, s 9   1010
ESPINOSA
    SONG OF THE INTERNATIONAL BRIGADE; "Volunteers for freedom we are fighting" e 7 words by   1011
    E. Weinert
ESPINOSA, J. J.
    LAS ALTEÑITAS; "Vamos a Tepa tierra soñada"; A GAY RANCHERO; "A gay ranchero de los   1012
    maizales" e, s 248
ESTERL, J. P.
    TIROL, TIROL, DU BIST MEIN HEIMATLAND; "Tirol, Tirol, Tirol, du bist mein Heimatland" g 326   1013
    joint composer A. Zweigle
ESTEVE, PABLO, ca1730-1794
    ALMA, SINTAMOS; "Alma, sintamos!; Ojos, llorar!"; SOUFFREZ, MON ÂME; "Mon coeur,   1014
    souffrez! Mes yeux, pleurez!" f, s 269
    [LOS PASAGES DE VERANO, tonadilla] A LA JOTA; "A la Jota que hay muchas   1015
    palomas"; "A la Jota il est des colombes" f, s 270
EVANS, EVERETT J.
    A ROSE WITH A BROKEN STEM; "At a gay masquerade in a ball room grand"; "She's just like a rose   1016
    with a broken stem" (ref) e 131 words by C. Fleming
EVANS, GEORGE
    I'LL BE TRUE TO MY HONEY BOY; "There's a charming little yallar gal, yallar gal she nearly drives   1017
    me wild"; "I'll be true to my baby" (ref) e 246
    IN THE GOOD OLD SUMMERTIME; "There's a time in each year that we always hold dear" e 32,34   1018
    words by R. Shields
EVANS, J. G.
    BELLE OB BALTIMORE; "I've been thro' Carolina"; "Oh, boys, Belle's a beauty" e 28,366   1019
EXAUDET, JOSEPH, 1710-1762
    MENUET D'EXAUDET; "Cet étang qui s'étend dans la plaine" f 383 words by C. Favart   1020
EZRACHI, Y.
    AYN CHAROD; "Tiyalti baemek b'makel nod"; "Walking in the Emek with my staff I trod" e 30   1021
    "YESH BANU KAOCH"; "OUR STRENGTH WITHIN US" e 30   1022

FÁBREGA, RICARDO
    GUARARE; "Viajando por Guararé" s 284   1023
FAGAN, BARNEY
    MY GAL IS A HIGH BORN LADY; "Thar' is gwine to be a festival this evenin'"; "My gal is a high   1024
    born lady" (ref) e 114,115,131; (ref only) e 128
Fagen, Barney. See FAGAN, BARNEY
FALCONIERI, ANDREA, 17th c
    BELLA FANCIULLA; "Bella fanciulla del viso rosato" i 181   1025
    "BELLA PORTA DI RUBINI" i 181   1026
    DONN' INGRATA; "Donn' ingrata, senza amore" i 180   1027
    "O BELLISSIMI CAPELLI"; "LOCKS SO BEAUTIFUL" e, i 139   1028
    "OCCHIETTI AMATI CHE M'INCENDETE"; "ÄUGLEIN, IHR LIEBEN, DIE MICH ENTZÜNDEN"   1029
    g, i 168; OCCHIETTI AMATI i 181; BELOVED EYES; "Beloved eyes, you so brightly burn me"
    e, i 36
FALL, LEO, 1873-1925
    [DIE DOLLARPRINZESSIN, operetta; words by A. M. Willner and F. Grün-   1030
    baum] WIR TANZEN RINGELREIHN; "Im Verkehr nur Bruder, Schwester" g 256
    [DIE FIDELE BAUER, operetta; words by V. Léon] JEDER TRAGT SEI PINKERL;   1031
    "Ja, ich trag a Zipfelhauben" g 256
FALLA, MANUEL DE, 1876-1946
    SÉGUIDILLE; "Un jupon serré sur les hanches"; SEGUIDILLA; "A tight skirt around her hips" e, f   1032
    190,192,194 words by T. Gautier
    TUS OJILLOS NEGROS; "Yo no sé qué tienen tus ojillos negros"; YOUR DARK EYES; "In your dark   1033
    eyes lies a magic that sustains me" e, s 121 words by C. de Castro
Falla y Matheu, Manuel de. See FALLA, MANUEL DE, 1876-1946
FARJEON, ELEANOR, 1881-
    FLY AWAY, CROW; "Here come the crows to steal the corn" e 199   1034

FARKAS, IMRE
    "MEGÁLLOK A KERESZTÚTNÁL"; "IN THE SUMMER AT THESE CROSSROADS" e, hu 285   1035
FARMER, J.
    OCTOBER; "The months are met with their crownlets on" e 28 words by E. E. Bowen   1036
FARMER, JOHN
    FORTY YEARS ON. See 384
FARNIE, H. B., att to
    UP IN A BALLOON; "I am, as you know a Madison belle"; "Up in a balloon, boys" (ref) e 189;   1037
        (ref only) e 214
FARRELL, BOB
    OLD ZIP COON. See 7893
FARWELL, ARTHUR GEORGE, 1872-1952
    ON A FADED VIOLET, op.43, no.2; "The odour from the flow'r is gone" e 259 words by P. B.   1038
        Shelley
FASOLO, GIOVANNI BATTISTA
    CANZONE; "Lungi lungi è amor da me"; "Fern, ach fern liegt mir Liebe schon" g, i 167   1039
FASTALSKY, S.
    LAYLAH FELEH; "Elef laylah v'od laylah tati shaylah"; NIGHT OF GLORY; "To my land a thousand   1040
        nights I've gladly given" e, h 30
FAURÉ, GABRIEL URBAIN, 1845-1924
    APRÈS UN RÊVE, op.7, no.1; "Dans un sommeil que charmait ton image"; AFTER A DREAM;   1041
        "Dreaming, to thee my heart I surrender" e, f 121; "After a dream when your likeness was charm-
        ing" e 348
    L'AURORE; "L'Aurore s'allume, l'ombre epaisse fuit" f 278 words by V. Hugo   1042
    AURORE, op.39, no.1; "Des jardins de la nuit"; AURORA; "From the gardens of night" e, f 121   1043
        words by A. Silvestre
    LES BERCEAUX, op.23, no.1; "Le long du quai, les grands vaisseaux"; THE CRADLES; "Moored by   1044
        the wharf, the vessels tall" e, f 210; "The stately ships along the quay" e, f 140 words by
        S. Prudhomme
    DANS LES RUINES D'UNE ABBAYE, op.2, no.1; "Seuls, tous deux, ravis, chantants"; IN THE RUINS   1045
        OF AN ABBEY; "Both entranced, the two alone sing of love" e, f 362 words by V. Hugo
    EN PRIÈRE; "Si la voix d'un enfant"; IN PRAYER; "If the voice of a child" e, f 121; PRAYER;   1046
        "Our Father in heaven, before Thee we come" e 89 words by S. Bordèse
    ICI-BAS, op.8, no.3; "Ici-bas tous les lilas meurent"; HERE BELOW; "Here below, lilacs die   1047
        and never is bird song more than a short refrain" e, f 362 words by S. Prudhomme
    LYDIA, op.4, no.2; "Lydia, sur tes roses joues"; "Lydia, on your cheeks so glowing" e, f 362   1048
        words by L. de Lisle
    LA RONDE DES MOISSONNEURS; "Dans la plaine immense"; SONG OF THE HARVESTERS; "'Cross   1049
        the fields all golden" e, f 408 words by P. de Chazot
    LES ROSES D'ISPAHAN; "Les roses d'Ispahan dans leur gaine de mousse"; THE ROSES OF ISPAHAN;   1050
        "The roses of Ispahan sheathed in soft verdant mosses" e, f 208 words by L. de Lisle
FAURE, JEAN BAPTISTE, 1830-1914
    CRUCIFIXUS; "Vous qui pleurez, venez à ce Dieu; car il pleure"; "Come unto Him, all ye who   1051
        weep; for He too weepeth" e, f 123; "Come ye that weep, to Him bow down, who sin forgiveth"
        e, f 394; CRUCIFIX, O COME TO HIM; "All ye that grieve, O come to Him relief he giveth"
        e 400
    LES RAMEUX; "Sur nos chemins les rameaux et les fleurs"; THE PSALMS; "O'er all the way green   1052
        palms and blossoms gay" e, f 123; e 400; "Crown ye with palms the Saviour's onward way" e, f
        394; "Blossoms and palms in varied beauty vie" e 329; "On this joyous day we wear the palms"
        e 132
FAX, MARK, 1911-
    LONGING; "Come to me in my dreams and then by day I shall be well again" e 78 words by M.   1053
        Arnold
    MAY DAY SONG; "Lovely elf of noble birth newly come to rule the earth" e 78   1054
FEAUTRIER, E.
    LA PAIMPOLAISE; "Quittant ses genets et sa lande" f 88 words by T. Botrel   1055
FEDELLI, RUGGIERO,
    IL MIO CORE; "Il mio core non è con me"; "My heart is no longer mine" e, i 134   1056
FEDERER,
    LES PROMESSES DU PRINTEMPS; "De la saison printanière" f 88   1057
FEIST, LEO
    DOES TRUE LOVE EVER RUN SMOOTH?; "Laura and May, loving sisters were they"; "Oh! how I   1058
        love him, if he but knew" (ref) e 131
FELTON, WILLIAM, 1715-1769
    FELTON'S GAVOTTE; FAREWELL MANCHESTER; "Farewell, Manchester! noble town, farewell!"   1059
        e 294,349

FENTON, HOWARD
    DEBORAH. See 359

FERGUS, JOHN
    O BOTHWELL BANK; "O Bothwell bank, thou bloomest fair" e 103,104   words by J. Pinkerton   1060

FERNSTRÖM, JOHN AXEL, 1897-
    [EXOTISK BUKETT, song cycle, OP.3] JAPANSKT, no.1; "Du fjärilsmö av rosigt   1061
      Yoshiwara" sw 355   words by H. Sköld

FERRABOSCO, ALFONSO, ca1575-1628
    COME MY CELIA; "Come my Celia, let us prove" e 144   words by B. Jonson   1062
    "SO BEAUTIE ON THE WATERS STOOD" e 144   words by B. Jonson   1063
    "SO, SO, LEAVE OFF THIS LAST LAMENTING KISS" e 144   words by J. Donne   1064

FERRARI, GUSTAVE, 1872-1948
    LE MIROIR; "L'odeur de vous flottait dans l'air silencieux"; THE MIRROR; "Your fragrance   1065
      floated in the silent air" e, f 191,193,195; "Your scent it seems to haunt and fill the very
      air" e, f 237   words by E. Haraucourt

FERRER, GUILLERMO, 1730?-1790?
    [EL REMEDO DEL GATO, tonadilla] TIRANA; "El día que se casare el tío Manga   1066
      ligera"; "Si jamais un jour se marie Le bon père La Folie" f, s 270

FESCA, FRIEDRICH ERNST, 1789-1826
    RUDELSBURG; Heute scheid ich (tune); "An der Saale hellem Strande stehen Burgen stolz und   1067
      kühn" g 31; AN DER SAALE HELLEM STRANDE g 42,326,353   words by F. Kugler; SOLDATEN-
      ABSCHIED; "Heute scheid ich, morgen wandr ich" g 99   words by M. F. Müller

FESCH, WILLEM de, 1687-1757?
    CANZONETTA; "Tu fai la superbetta, dorilla io so perchè" e 278   1068

FIBICH, ZDENĚK, 1850-1900
    [ŠÁRKA, opera; words by A. Schulzová] JAK BY LUNY ÚSVIT; "Jak by luny úsvit   1069
      zíral z temna mraků tich a něm"; WIE DER MOND; "Wie der Mond sich leuchtend dränget
      durch den dunklen Wolkenflor" c, g 73a
    [MY MOONLIGHT MADONNA] YOU'RE MY POEM OF LOVE; "Night and day, you are my   1070
      poem of love dear" e 132   words by H. Johnson; THE SEARCH; "Moon of old, striding alone thru
      the heavens" e 343   words by C. Quimby

FICHTHORN, CLAUDE LESLIE
    A PRAYER OF SUPPLICATION; "In all our trials, Lord" e 347   1071
    TRUSTING IN THEE; "In deep distress, O God, I cry to Thee" e 123   1072

FIELDING, EVELYN LYSLE
    THE MADONNA MUSES; "The star shines above Thee" e 244   1073

FILIBERTO, JUAN DE DIOS
    CAMINITO; "Caminito que el tiempo ha borrado" s 284   words by G. Corio Peñalosa   1074

FINN, F.
    "MOTHER ALL BEAUTIFUL" e 71   words by M. S. Pine   1075

FIORITO, TED, 1900-
    LAUGH! CLOWN! LAUGH!; "Life is a play and we all play a part"; "Even tho' you're only make   1076
      believing, laugh! clown! laugh!" (ref) e 345   words by S. M. Lewis and J. Young

FISCHER, LUDWIG, 1745-1825
    IM TIEFEN KELLER; "Im tiefen Keller sitz ich hier" g 353; "Im kühlen Keller sitz ich hier" g 31;   1077
      DER TRINKER g 99; "IM TIEFEN KELLER SITZ ICH HIER" g 43; "IM KÜHLEN KELLER SITZ' ICH
      HIER"; "DOWN DEEP WITHIN THE CELLAR"; "MY LODGING IS THE CELLAR HERE"; JUST SING-
      ING; "I've tried a hundred diff'rent ways" e, g 240; DRINKING; "My lodging is the cellar here"
      e 273   words by C. Müchler

FISCHER-KREFELD, ALFRED
    "TAUSEND KÜNSTE KANN DER TEUFEL" g 326   words by W. Vesper   1078

FISHER, WILLIAM ARMS, 1861-1948
    "I HEARD A CRY," op.18, no.1 e 137,241   words by S. Teasdale   1079
    SEEK YE FIRST THE KINGDOM OF GOD, op.16, no.2; "Is not the life more than meat and the   1080
      body than raiment?" e 398   words from Bible
    UNDER THE ROSE, op.8, no.4; "She wears a rose in her hair" e 136   words by R. H. Stoddard   1081

FLÉGIER, ANGE, 1846-1927
    LE COR; "J'aime le son du cor"; THE HORN; "Sweet sounds the woodland horn" e, f 240; "I   1082
      love the sound of the horn" e, f 193   words by A. de Vigny

FLEMMING, FRIEDRICH FERDINAND, 1778-1813
    INTEGER VITAE; "Integer vitae scelerisque purpus"; FREUNDSCHAFT UND LIEBE; "Hier in des   1083
      abends traulich ernster Stille" g, lat 99; "He who is noble, kind in thought and action" e, lat 28;
      "HIER IN DES ABENDS TRAULICH ERNSTER STILLE" g 326; PRAISE FOR PEACE; "Father in Heaven
      in Thy love abounding" e 28,36   words by Q. H. Flaccus

FLETCHER, JOHN

[WHEN I SAW SWEET NELLY HOME] THE QUILTING PARTY; "In the sky the bright stars   1084
glittered"; "I was seeing Nellie home" (ref) e 28, 32, 34, 129, 130, 233, 236, 279, 366; SEEING
NELLIE HOME e 10 joint composer F. Kyle

FLIES, BERNHARD

WIEGENLIED, K. Anh. 284f (350); "Schlafe, mein Prinzchen, schlaf' ein" g 326, 328; CRADLE   1085
SONG; "Sleep, oh my darling, oh sleep" e, g 209; "Schlafe, mein Prinzchen es ruhn" g 99, 229;
LULLABY; "Sleep, little dream prince of mine" e 348; "Sleep little darling and rest" e 385;
NINNA-NANNA; "Lulla, lullaby, all things now sleep 'neath the sky" e 199 words by F. W.
Gotter, att to W. A. Mozart

FLORENCE, W. J.

BOBBIN' AROUND; "In August last on one fine day" e 189, 242   1086

FLORENTINE, SISTER

"MARY IMMACULATE, QUEEN OF OUR LAND" e 71 words by J. F. Noll   1087

FLORES, JOSÉ ASUNCIÓN, 1904-

INDIA; "India bella mezcla de diosa" s 284 words by M. Ortiz Guerrero   1088

FLOTOW, FRIEDRICH VON, 1812-1883

[MARTHA, opera; words by W. F. Riese] ACH! SO FROMM, Act III; "Ach! so   1089
fromm, ach! so traut" g 391; "M'APPARI TUTT' AMOR"; AH! SO PURE; "Ah! so pure, Ah!
so bright" e, i 329; "None so rare, none so fair" e, i 3; M'APPARI, LIKE A DREAM; "Like a
dream bright and fair" e, i 237

[Ibid] "ESSER MESTO IL MIO COR NON SAPRIA", Act III i 300   1090

[Ibid] LASST MICH EUCH FRAGEN, Act III; "Lasst mich euch fragen, könnt ihr mir sagen";   1091
"Search the world over, can you discover" e, g 5, 390

[Ibid] THE LAST ROSE OF SUMMER. See 5921

FLYNN, CLEMENT

OBLATION; "There breathes no charming flow'r so fair that cannot fairer be" e 71   1092

FLYNN, JOSEPH

DOWN WENT McGINTY; "Sunday morning just at nine"; "Down went McGinty to the bottom of   1093
the wall" (ref) e 114, 131, 225; (ref only) e 128

FOERSTER, JOSEF BOHUSLAV, 1859-1951

MODLITBA, op.109b, no.3; "Když život Tebe zraní, nech lkání trp tiše!"; GEBET; "Lass dich   1094
nur nichts nicht dauern mit Trauern, sei stille!" c, g 73a words by P. Flemming

FONT, MANUEL

LA CRUZ DE MAYO; "El mosito paróse tras la cansela"; THE CROSS OF MAY; "I saw gay, festive   1095
dancing within my dwelling" e, s 245 words by S. Valverde

FONTENAILLES, H. de

OBSTINATION; "Vous aurez beau faire et beau dire!"; A RESOLVE; "It is all in vain to implore me"   1096
e, f 122, 237, 385

FORD, THOMAS, ca1580-1648

"COME, PHYLLIS, COME INTO THESE BOWERS" e 119; COME PHILLIS; "Come, Phillis, come into   1097
these bowers" e 196

FAIRE, SWEET CRUELL; "Faire, sweet, cruell, why dost thou flie me?" e 196; FAIR SWEET CRUEL;   1098
"Fair sweet cruel, why dost thou fly me?" e 117

"NOT FULL TWELVE YEARS" e 119   1099

"NOW I SEE THY LOOKS WERE FEIGNED" e 118 words by T. Lodge   1100

"SINCE FIRST I SAW YOUR FACE" e 144, 199, 297, 349   1101

THERE IS A LADIE SWEET AND KIND; "There was a ladie sweet and kind was never face so pleasde   1102
my mind" e 144

"WHAT THEN IS LOVE" e 144; "WHAT THEN IS LOVE, SINGS CORYDON" e 116   1103

FORSYTH, JOSEPHINE, 1889-1940

THE LORD'S PRAYER; "Our Father, which art in heaven" e 123 words from Bible   1104

FORTNER, WOLFGANG, 1907-

DER TOTENGRÄBER; "Als ich jung war, war ich verliebt"; "In youth when I did love" e, g 250   1105
words by W. Shakespeare

FOSTER, STEPHEN COLLINS, 1826-1864

ANGELINA BAKER; "Away down on de old plantation" e 129, 130   1106

BEAUTIFUL DREAMER; "Beautiful dreamer, wake unto me" e 10, 28, 36, 129, 130, 132, 329, 343, 385   1107

DE CAMPTOWN RACES; "De Camptown ladies sing dis song, doodah!" e 10, 35, 115, 129, 130, 132,   1108
184, 225, 233, 236, 343, 403; "De Camptown ladies sing dis song, dooda, dooda!" e 109

"COME, WHERE MY LOVE LIES DREAMING" e 28, 129, 130, 132   1109

COMRADES, FILL NO GLASS FOR ME; "Oh! comrades fill no glass for me" e 129, 132   1110

DOWN AMONG THE CANE BRAKES; "Once I could laugh and play" e 129   1111

ELLEN BAYNE; "Soft be thy slumbers, rude cares depart"; "Gentle slumbers o'er thee glide" (ref)   1112
e 129, 132

FOSTER, STEPHEN COLLINS, 1826-1864 (Continued)

FAIRY-BELLE; "The pride of the village, the fairest in the dell" e 28,279,366   1113

GENTLE ANNIE; "Thou wilt come no more, gentle Annie"; "Shall we never more behold thee" (ref) e 28,36,129,130,212,279,366   1114

HARD TIMES COME AGAIN NO MORE; "Let us pause in life's pleasures and count its many tears" e 28,236,279,366   1115

JEANIE WITH THE LIGHT BROWN HAIR; "I dream of Jeanie with the light brown hair" e 10,28,35, 37,109,110,114,129,130,131,233,236,329,343   1116

MARY LOVES THE FLOWERS; "Mary loves the flowers! Ah! how happy they!" e 129   1117

MASSA'S IN DE COLD GROUND; "'Round de meadows am a-ringing"; "Down in de cornfield hear dat mournful sound" (ref) e 28,128,129,130,132,279,366; MASSA'S IN DE COLD, COLD GROUND e 233   1118

MR. AND MRS. BROWN; "So Mister Brown you've come at last" e 189   words by G. Cooper   1119

MY OLD KENTUCKY HOME; "The sun shines bright in the old Kentucky home"; "Weep no more, my lady" (ref) e 10,28,32,34,109,110,122,129,130,184,233,279,343,366; MY OLD KENTUCKY HOME, GOOD NIGHT e 236   1120

NELLIE WAS A LADY; "Down on de Mississippi" e 129,130,132   1121

NELLY BLY; "Nelly Bly, Nelly Bly, Bring de broom along"; "Heigh! Nelly, Ho! Nelly, listen, lub to me" (ref) e 129,185; (ref only) e 34   1122

NO HOME, NO HOME; "No home! no home on my weary way I seek" e 189   1123

OH! BOYS, CARRY ME 'LONG; "Oh, carry me 'long, dere's no more trouble for me" e 129   1124

OH! LEMUEL! GO DOWN TO DE COTTON FIELD; "Oh! Lemuel, my lark" e 129   1125

OH! SUSANNA!; "I came from Alabama wid my banjo on my knee" e 10,28,109,110,128,129, 130,225,236,366; "I came to Alabama, wid my banjo on my knee" e 184,279; "I come from Alabama with my banjo on my knee" e 35,233   1126

OLD BLACK JOE; "Gone are the days"; "I'm coming, I'm coming, for my head is bending low" (ref) e 28,129,130,132,233,236,279,366   1127

OLD DOG TRAY; "The morn of life is past" e 28,129,278,366   1128

OLD FOLKS AT HOME; "'Way down upon the Swanee River"; "All the world is sad and dreary" (ref) e 284,35,115; "All de world is sad and dreary" e 132; "'Way down upon de Swanee River" e 129,130,236; "All de world am sad and dreary" (ref) e 28,70,279,343,366; "'Way down upon de Swanee Ribber" e 10,128,184,199,233,402   1129

OLD UNCLE NED; "Dere was an old Nigga, dey call'd him Uncle Ned"; "Den lay down de shubble and de hoe-o-o" e 129; UNCLE NED; "There was an old darkey and his name was Uncle Ned"; "Then lay down the shovel and the hoe" (ref) e 28,279,366   1130

"OPEN THY LATTICE LOVE' e 348   words by G. P. Morris   1131

OUR BRIGHT SUMMER DAYS ARE GONE; "I remember the days of our youth and love"; "Never-more will come those happy, happy hours" (ref) e 129   1132

RING, RING DE BANJO; "De time is nebber dreary" e 184; RING, RING THE BANJO; "The time is never dreary" e 28,279,366; RING DE BANJO; "De time is never dreary" e 129,132,236   1133

SOME FOLKS; "Some folks like to sigh"; "Long live the merry merry heart" (ref) e 129,343,366   1134

THE SONG OF ALL SONGS; "As you've walked through the town on a fine summer's day"; "Old songs! New songs! Ev'ry kind of song" (ref) e 189   1135

THERE'S A GOOD TIME COMING; "There's a good time coming, boys, a good time coming" e 129   1136

FOUSER, CHARLES E., 1889-1946

MERRY CHRISTMAS; "Merry Christmas ev'ryone! Christmas joy and Christmas fun!" 3 pt round e 337   words by S. C. Fouser   1137

FOX, OSCAR J., 1879-

I'LL NEVER ASK YOU TO TELL; "Come with the night and loneliness" e 385   words by C. Straub   1138

"MY HEART IS A SILENT VIOLIN" e 387   words by E. von der Goltz   1139

FRANCK, CÉSAR AUGUSTE, 1822-1890

LIED; "Pour moi sa main cueillait des roses"; "For me her hand, the heart disclosing" e, f 210; THE GATHERED ROSE; "Her gentle hand for me did sever" e, f 140   words by L. Paté   1140

[MESSE SOLONNELLE, OP. 12] PANIS ANGELICUS; "Panis Angelicus fit panis hominum" lat 382; "The bread of angels becomes the bread of men" e, lat 304; HEAVENLY MANNA; "Heavenly manna granted to mortals" e, lat 209; O LORD, MOST HOLY; "O Lord, most holy, O Lord, most mighty" e, lat 8,407; e 346; O LORD OF MERCY; "O Lord of mercy, O Lord of justice" e 394   1141

NOCTURNE; "O fraîche nuit, nuit transparente"; "Oh, cool night, transparent night" e, f 190,192, 194   words by L. de Fourcaud   1142

LA PROCESSION; "Dieu s'avance à travers les champs"; THE PROCESSION; "The Lord draws neigh across the fields" e, f 190,192,194; "BLESS THE LORD, O MY SOUL" e 90   words by C. Brizeux   1143

FRANCK, JOHANN WOLFGANG, 17th c

DER TOD IST MIR EIN WEG IM LEBEN DAS HAT MIR JESU TOD GEGEBEN; "Jesu neigt sein Haupt und stirbt!" g 250   words by H. Elmenhorst   1144

FRANCKENSTEIN, CLEMENS, FREIHERR VON UND ZU, 1875-1942

ÜBER DEN WILLEN; "Neckst du mich kleiner Schelm"; O'ER THE BILLOWS; "Tauntest me, tiny   1145
sprite?" e, g 330   words by A. Wildgans

FRANGEUL, FERNAND

M'AP RESODOU; "Tout ça pas existé cheri"; "TO THINK I THOUGHT SO MUCH OF YOU" e, f 9   1146

FRANKLIN, NORMAN

SONG OF THE PENNIES; "The pennies of the nation spoke one day" e 293   words by H. Foner   1147

FRANZ, ROBERT, 1815-1892

ABENDS, op.16, no.4; "Abendlich schon rauscht der Wald"; EVENING; "Evening comes with rust-   1148
ling leaves" e 45   words by J. von Eichendorff

AM LEUCHTENDEN SOMMERMORGEN, op.11, no.2; "Am leuchtenden Sommermorgen geh' ich im   1149
Garten herum"; I WANDER THIS SUMMER MORNING; "I wander this summer morning here in my
garden alone" e, g 137   words by H. Heine

AUS MEINEN GROSSEN SCHMERZEN, op.5, no.1; "Aus meinen grossen Schmerzen mach' ich die   1150
kleinen Lieder" g 98, 250; OUT OF MY SOUL'S GREAT SADNESS; "Out of my soul's great sadness
my little songs come winging" e, g 136; "Out of my soul's great sadness my little songs I'm singing" e, g 36   words by H. Heine

BITTE, op.9, no.3; "Weil' auf mir, du dunkles Auge"; PLEA; "Do not leave me, eyes of velvet"   1151
e, g 141; REQUEST; "Eyes so dark upon me gazing" e, g 210; "Turn to me, dark eye so tender"
e, g 137,210   words by N. Lenau

"DA DIE STUNDE KAM," op.7, no.3 g 229   words by W. Osterwald   1152

ER IST GEKOMMEN, op.4, no.7; "Er ist gekommen in Sturm und Regen"; HIS COMING; "Wild was   1153
the day when he came with greeting" e, g 137   words by F. Rückert

"ES HAT DIE ROSE SICH BEKLAGT," op.42, no.5 g 98,99; "ONE DAY THE LOVELY ROSE COM-   1154
PLAINED" e, g 36; THE ROSE COMPLAINED; "The rose complain'd with hanging head" e, g 136
words by F. Rückert

FÜR MUSIK, op.10, no.1; "Nun die Schatten dunkeln, Stern an Stern erwacht" g 226; FOR MUSIC;   1155
"Now the shadows darken, star on stars alight" e, g 136; "Now the shadows falling, stars are all
alight" e, g 209   words by E. Geibel

GUTE NACHT! op.5, no.7; "Die Höh'n und Wälder schon steigen"; FAREWELL!; "On hill and wood-   1156
land is falling" e, g 210; g 226,229   words by J. von Eichendorff

LIEBER SCHATZ, SEI WIEDER GUT MIR, op.26, no.2; "In dem Dornbusch blüht ein Röslein" g 99,   1157
229   words by W. Osterwald

LIEBESFEIER, op.21, no.4; "An ihren bunten Liedern klettert"; FEAST OF LOVE; "Upon her song's   1158
bright colored pinions" e, g 209   words by N. Lenau

[MARIE, OP.18, NO.1] THE LORD OF LOVE; "The Lord of love my shepherd is" e 90   1159
words from Psalm XXIII

"STERNE MIT DEN GOLD'NEN FÜSSCHEN," op.30, no.1; STARS WITH TINY FEET; "Stars with   1160
tiny feet so golden" e, g 407   words by H. Heine

STILLE SICHERHEIT, op.10, no.2; "Horch, wie still es wird im dunkeln Hain"; LOVE'S SANCTUARY;   1161
"Hark! how still the grove! soft breezes moan" e, g 330   words by N. Lenau

EIN STÜNDLEIN WOHL VOR TAG, op.28, no.2; "Derweil ich schlafend lag ein Stündlein wohl vor   1162
Tag" g 226   words by E. Mörike

WALDFAHRT, op.14, no.3; "Im Wald, im Wald ist's frisch und grün"; A WOODLAND JOURNEY;   1163
"The woods, the woods are fresh and green" e, g 209   words by T. Körner

WIDMUNG, op.14, no.1; "O danke nicht für diese Lieder"; DEDICATION; "Nay, thank me not   1164
that songs I sing thee" e, g 122; "Oh, thank me not for songs I bring thee" e 348; "O thank me
not for songs I render" e, g 385; "O thank me not for songs I tender" e, g 210; "Oh, thank me not
for what I sing thee" e, g 136,241,343,364; "Praise thou me not, I do not sing thee songs" e, g
329; "O THANK ME NOT FOR SONGS I SING THEE" e, g 36; THE WISDOM OF GOD; "O holy
Word of truth and wisdom" e 90   words by W. Müller

FRASER, GEORGE MACALPINE, 1905-

CALLING THE HEART; "Sweep of the coolins rolling to the sea" e 306   words by J. Morrison   1165

FRÁTER, LORÁND

"ELMEGYEK ABLAKOD ELŐTT"; WHEN I PASS BEFORE YOUR WINDOW; "When I pass before your   1166
window I must turn 'way from it" e, hu 285

SZÁZ SZÁL GYERTYÁT SZÁZ ITCE BORT; "Hull az eső sürü cseppje"; HUNDRED CANDLES,   1167
HUNDRED BOTTLES; "From the dark, low-clouded heavens" e, hu 285

FREED, ISADORE, 1900-

CHARTLESS; "I never saw a moor, I never saw the sea" e 358   words by E. Dickinson   1168

Freire, Osman Perez. See PEREZ FREIRE, OSMAN

FRENCH, FRANK

IDAHO; "They say there is a land where crystal waters flow" e 189   1169

FRESCOBALDI, GIROLAMO ALESSANDRO, 1583-1643

BEGLI OCCHI; "Begli occhi, io non provo fierezza o dolore" (duet) i 181   1170

SE L'AURA SPIRA; "Se l'aura spira tutta vezzosa" i 179; WHEN SOFT THE BREEZES; "When soft the   1171
breezes sweetly are blowing" e, i 138

FRIEND, CLIFF, 1893-
  GIVE ME A NIGHT IN JUNE; "I'm happy so happy sweetheart it's true" e 345   1172
FRIML, RUDOLF, 1881-
  [ROSE MARIE, operetta] INDIAN LOVE CALL; ÜBER DIE PRÄRIE; "Der Missouri rauscht"   1173
   g 223
FRÖHLICH, FRIEDRICH THEODOR, 1803-1836
  REISESEGEN; "Wem Gott will rechte Gunst erweisen" g 31; "WEM GOTT WILL RECHTE GUNST   1174
   ERWEISEN" g 326,353; DER FROHE WANDERSMANN g 99 words by J. F. von Eichendorff
FRUMERIE, GUNNAR DE, 1908-
  "DET ÄR VACKRAST NÄR DET SKYMMER" sw 355 words by P. Lagerkvist   1175
  DU ÄR MIN AFRODITE; "Du är min Afrodite, den ur havet född a" sw 355 words by P. Lagerkvist   1176
  DET KOM ETT BREV; "Det kom ett brev om sommarsäd" sw 355 words by P. Lagerkvist   1177
FRYER, HERBERT
  THE VIRGIN'S CRADLE-HYMN, op. 20, no. 1; "Holy Infant in Thy cradle"; "Dormi Jesu, mater   1178
   ridet" e, lat 344 words by A. Charlton
FRYKLÖF, HARALD LEONARD, 1882-1919
  "I DRÖMMER TRÄDEN STAA" sw 355 words by V. Ekelund   1179
  JAG HAR VARIT; "Jag har varit som ett som farit öfver haarda vägars smuts och damm" sw 355   1180
   words by S. Lidman
FUCHS, FRITZ
  AUSZUG AUS PRAG 1409; "Aus winkligen Gassen"; "Vorwärts Scholaren Barette gezogen" (ref) g 31   1181
Fuentes, Eduardo Sánchez de. See SÁNCHEZ DE FUENTES Y PELÁEZ, EDUARDO
FULMER, H. T.
  "WAIT TILL THE CLOUDS ROLL BY" e 129,130,131,132 words by J. T. Wood   1182
Fyles, Philip. See PHILE, PHILIP, 1734-1793

GABLER, CHRIST. AUG.
  MAILIED; "Wie herrlich leuchtet mir die Natur!" g 229 words by J. W. von Goethe   1183
GABRIEL, CHARLES HUTCHINSON, 1856-1932
  DEAR LITTLE STRANGER; "Low in a manger, dear little Stranger" e 315   1184
  HIS EYE IS ON THE SPARROW; "Why should we be discouraged?" e 398 words by Mrs. C. D. Martin 1185
GADE, NIELS WILHELM, 1813-1890
  "CHILD JESUS CAME TO EARTH THIS DAY" e 296 words by H. C. Andersen   1186
  [ET FOLKESAGN, ballet] BRUDE-VALS; BRIDE'S-WALTZ piano 87   1187
GAGLIANO, GIOVANBATISTA, ca1580-1643
  PUPILLE ANCIERE; "Pupille anciere, pupille nere, regio albergo d'Amore" i 180   1188
  SE TU SEI BELLA; "Se tu sei bella più d'Amarillide" (duet) i 181   1189
GAGLIANO, MARCO DA, ca1575-1642
  "ALMA MIA, DOVE TEN' VAI" (duet) i 181   1190
  FANCIULLETTA RITROSETTA; "Fanciulletta ritrosetta, che d'amor ti burlie ridi" (duet) i 181   1191
  [LA FLORA, opera; words by A. Salvadori] SZENE AUS DEM FESTSPIEL LA FLORA;   1192
   "O sia quest' aura o sia vostro soave canto" (recit); "Ist es diese Schwüle oder euer lieblicher
   Gesang" (recit) g, i 217
  IN UN LIMPIDO RIO; "In un limpido rio la mia dolce nemica un dì s'affisse" (duet) i 181   1193
  MIE SPERANZE; "Mie speranze lusinghiere desiate in van piacere" i 180   1194
  VALLI PROFONDE; "Valli profonde, al solnemiche" i 179   1195
GAIRDNER, I. A.
  NEW YORK, OR, OH! WHAT A CHARMING CITY; "The ardent, romantic, the charming god of   1196
   song" e 189,329
GAJDA, W.
  "JAK DŁUGO W SERCU NASZEM"; "AS LONG AS IN OUR BODIES" e, p 159   1197
GALBRAITH, J. LAMONT
  I SOUGHT THE LORD; "I sought the Lord, but afterwards I knew" e 8   1198
GALL, JAN KAROL, 1856-1912
  "DZIEWCZĘ Z BUZIĄ JAK MALINĄ," op. 1, no. 3; "LASS WITH LIPS LIKE RIPE RED BERRIES"   1199
   e, p 295 words by M. Gawalewicz
  "RUM TADERA RŻNIJ GRAJKU"; RAT-RATA-PLAN ('IN THE INN'); "Rat-rata-plan, play fiddler"   1200
   e, p 159
GALLARDO, LINO, att to
  LA PERICA; "Cuando la perica quiere que el perico" s 284   1201
GANNE, LOUIS GASTON, 1862-1923
  [LES SALTIMBANQUES, operetta; words by J. Tony and O. Pradels] MARCHE   1202
   LORRAINE; "Come on you lads of old Lorraine" e 35

GANSSER, HANS
    FREIHEIT; "Noch ist der Freiheit nicht verloren" g 31   words by R. Prutz   1203
GANZ, RUDOLPH, 1877-
    A MEMORY; "Somehow I feel that thou art near" e 121   words by M. K. Breid   1204
GARAT, PIERRE JEAN, 1762-1823
    "DANS LE PRINTEMPS DE MES ANNÉES"; "IN SULL' APRILE DI MIA VITA" f, i 411   1205
GARCIA, JUAN F.
    QUISQUEYANA piano 303   1206
    SERENATA piano 303   1207
    YO ME ENCELERÉ piano 303   1208
GARDINER, HENRY BALFOUR, 1877-1950
    CARGOES; "Quinquereme of Ninevah" e 306   words by J. Masefield   1209
GARNET, HORATIO, fl 1789
    [ODE FOR AMERICAN INDEPENDENCE] ODE TO THE FOURTH OF JULY; "'Tis done, the   1210
        edict past, by Heaven decreed" e 109,110   words by D. George
Garnett, Horatio. See GARNET, HORATIO, fl 1789
GARTON, TED
    MY BELGIAN ROSE. See 280
GASPARINI, FRANCESCO, 1668-1727
    ARIA; "Lasciar d'amarti per non penar"; "Verlassen dich, um zu enden Schmerz" g, i 168   1211
    [CANTATA DA CAMERA A VOCE SOLA, OP.1] ARIETTA; "Caro laccio, dolce nodo";   1212
        "Teures Bändchen, süsse Schlinge" g, i 167
    "DEH, LASCIATEMI IL NEMICO"; GRANT ME AN ENEMY; "Oh, friendly stars"; "LASST MIR DEN   1213
        FEIND" e, g, i 253
GASTOLDI, GIOVANNI GIACOMO, ca1566-1622
    ALS WIJ SOLDATEN; "Als wij soldaten 't saam te velde gaan" d 201   1214
GATTY, ALFRED SCOTT
    LIGHTS FAR OUT AT SEA; "The sunset gates were open'd wide" e 205   1215
    ON THE ROCKS BY ABERDEEN; "On the rocks of Aberdeen" e 205   words by J. Ingelow   1216
GAUL, ALFRED ROBERT, 1837-1913
    [THE HOLY CITY, cantata] COME YE BLESSED, no.12a; "Then shall the King say, Come   1217
        come, come ye blessed" e 394
    [Ibid] "EYE HATH NOT SEEN" e 123,200,394,398   1218
    [Ibid] "MY SOUL IS ATHIRST FOR GOD" e 123,394   1219
    [Ibid] A NEW HEAVEN AND A NEW EARTH; "Thus saith the Lord, Behold, I create new heav'ns   1220
        and a new earth" e 200
    [Ibid] THESE ARE THEY WHICH CAME; "These are they, these are they which came out of great   1221
        tribulation" (recit); "These are they which came out of great tribulation" (aria) e 123,394
GAUL, HARVEY BARTLETT, 1881-1945
    A SONG OF FELLOWSHIP; "Some men sing of petticoats" e 240   words by M. Wellings   1222
    "THOU ART THE NIGHT WIND" e 241   1223
GAUNT, PERCY
    THE BOWERY; A TRIP TO CHINATOWN; "Oh! the night that I struck New York"; "The Bow'ry, the   1224
        Bow'ry they say such things and they do strange things" (ref) e 131; (ref only) e 114,128,129,130,
        132,233   words by C. H. Hoyt
GAUNTLETT, HENRY JOHN, 1805-1876
    "ONCE IN ROYAL DAVID'S CITY"; Irby (tune) e 38,39,251,307,315,319,333,337,369,410   words   1225
        by C. F. Alexander
GAY, BYRON
    THE NAVY GOAT; "With a Navy goat hitched to our little boat" e 129,130   1226
GEBAUER, JOHAN CHRISTIAN, 1808-1884
    "I ALLE DE RIGER OG LANDE"; "IN EACH OF THE KINGDOMS AND COUNTRIES" da, e 87   words by   1227
        B. S. Ingemann
GEBHARDI, LUDWIG ERNST, 1787-1862
    "EHRE SEI GOTT IN DER HÖHE!" g 326; EHRE SEI GOTT; GLORY TO GOD; "Glory to God in the   1228
        highest" 4 pt round e, g 337
GEBIRTIG, MORDECAI, 1877-1942
    YANKELE; "Shlofzhe mir shoyn, Yankele"; "Sleep, Yankele, my darling little baby" e, y 318   1229
GEHRICKE, F. L.
    IM WALD UND AUF DER HEIDE. See 5408
GEIBEL, ADAM, 1855-1933
    KENTUCKY BABE; "Skeeters am a-hummin' on de honey suckle vine" e 233   words by R. H. Buck   1230
    SLEEP, MY LITTLE JESUS; "Sleep, my little Jesus, on Thy bed of hay" e 244,337   words by W. C.   1231
        Gannett
Geifer, George L. See GIEFER, GEORGE L.

45

GIRSCHNER, KARL FRIEDRICH, 1794-1860
    "ICH MÖCHTE DIR SO GERNE SAGEN" g 31   1256

GISELA, MARY
    "O MAGNIFY THE LORD" e 71   1257

GLÄSER, KARL LUDWIG TRAUGOTT, 1747-1797
    FLAMME EMPOR!; "Flamme empor! Flamme empor!; Steige mit lodern dem Scheine" g 31, 326   1258
    words by C. Nonne

GLAZUNOV, ALEKSANDR KONSTANTINOVICH, 1865-1936
    ORIENTAL ROMANCE, op. 27, no. 2; "My blood is fired with flames of passion" e, r 341   words by   1259
    A. Pushkin

GLIÈRE, REINHOLD MORITSEVICH, 1875-
    "SWEETLY SANG A GENTLE NIGHTINGALE," op. 36, no. 1 e, r 341   words by A. Merzliakov   1260

GLIK, HIRSH
    PARTIZANER LID; "Shtil di nacht iz oysgeshternt"; "Silence, and a starry night" e, y 318   words by   1261
    H. Glik

GLINKA, MIKHAIL IVANOVICH, 1804-1857
    DOUBT; "Be silent, my turbulent passions" e, r 340   words by A. Kukolnik   1262
    "SO CLEARLY I REMEMBER SEEING" e, r 340   words by A. S. Pushkin   1263
    TRAVELER'S SONG; "Puffing smoke, the locomotive chugs along!" e, r 340   words by A. Kukolnik   1264

GLOVER, CHARLES WILLIAM, 1806-1863
    THE ROSE OF TRALEE; "The pale moon was rising above the green mountain" e 15, 36, 132, 166, 329,   1265
    343, 402   words by C. M. Spencer

GLOVER, WILLIAM HOWARD, 1819-1875
    IN THE STARLIGHT; "In the starlight, in the starlight let us wander gay and free" e 279, 366   words   1266
    by Carpenter

GLUCK, CHRISTOPH WILLIBALD RITTER VON, 1714-1787
    [ALCESTE, opera; words by R. de' Calzabigi] DIVINITÉS DU STYX, Act I; "Divinités   1267
    du Styx, divinités du Styx, manistres de la mort"; "Ye gods of endless night, ye gods of endless
    nights that wait on death below" e, f 1
    [Ibid] NON! CE N'EST PAS UN SACRIFICE!; "Ou suis-je?" (recit); "Non! ce n'est pas un sacrifice!"   1268
    (aria); "Where am I?" (recit); "NO, 'TIS NO SACRIFICE I OFFER!" (aria) e, f 362
    [ARMIDE, opera; words by P. Quinault] "NOW THE WEATHER GROWS LESS WAYWARD";   1269
    SPRING SONG e 199
    DEIN LEBEN SIE BEGLUCKT; "TURN, TURN, MY BUSY WHEEL" e 199   words by A. G. Latham   1270
    DIE FRÜHEN GRÄBER; "Willkommen, o silberner Mond" g 250   words by M. Klopstock   1271
    [IPHIGÉNIE EN TAURIDE, opera; words by N. F. Guillard] DE NOIRS PRES-   1272
    SENTIMENTS; "Le ciel, par d'éclatants miracles" (recit); "De noirs pressentiments mon âme
    intimidée" (aria); "The gods have foreshewn me the future" (recit); "Foreboding fears of ill my
    wonted courage vanquish" (aria) e, f 5
    [DIE MAIENKÖNIGIN, words by M. Kalbeck] ARIETTE DER HELENE; "Gernbeim   1273
    Morgenscheine wandl' ich durch die Haine" g 308
    [ORFEO ED EURIDICE, opera; words by R. de' Calzabigi] "CHE FARÒ SENZA   1274
    EURIDICE?" (aria) i 300; "Ahimè! dove trascorsi" (recit); "Che farò senza Euridice?" (aria);
    "Alas! why hast thou left me" (recit); "Live without my dear Euridice!" (aria) e, i 2
    [Ibid] [Dance of the blessed spirits] O SAVIOUR HEAR ME!; "O Saviour hear me, I   1275
    implore thee" e 123
    [PARIDE ED ELENA, opera; words by R. de' Calzabigi] O DEL MIO DOLCE ARDOR;   1276
    "O del mio dolce ardor bramato oggetto"; AUTHOR OF ALL MY JOYS; "Author of all my joys, their
    crown and splendor" e, i 274; O THOU BELOV'D; "O thou belov'd, whom long my heart desireth"
    e, i 368; THOU ART, MY DEAR BELOVED; "Thou art, my dear beloved of all the most desir'd"
    e, i 404
    [LE RENCONTRE IMPRÉVUE, opera; words by L. H. Dancourt] EINEM BACH,   1277
    DER FLIESST; "Einem Bach, der fliesst und sich ergiesst" g 99, 229; HOLDE FRÜHLINGSZEIT;
    "Holde Frühlingszeit scheuch alles Leid!" (original text) g 229
    [SEMIRAMIDE, opera; words by P. Metastasio] "VIENI, CHE POI SERENO"; "COME,   1278
    FOR THY LOVE IS WAITING" e, i 357
    DIE SOMMERNACHT; "Wenn der Schimmer von dem Monde nun herab in die Wälder sich ergiesst"   1279
    g 99, 226   words by F. G. Klopstock
    [IL TRIONFO DI CLELIA, opera; words by P. Metastasio] ARIE DER LARISSA; "Ah,   1280
    ritorna, età dell' oro"; "Ach, kehre zurück, goldenes Zeitalter" g, i 218

GLÜCK, FRIEDRICH
    IN EINEM KÜHLEN GRUNDE; "In einem kühlen Grunde, da geht ein Mühlenrad" g 42, 309, 326, 353;   1281
    DAS ZERBROCHENE RINGLEIN g 99   words by J. von Eichendorff; DORT UNTEN IN DER MÜHLE;
    "Dort unten in der Mühle sass ich in süsser Ruh" g 326   words by J. Kerner

GNEIST, WERNER, 1898-
    "ES TAGT, DER SONNE MORGENSTRAHL" g 49   1282

GNEIST, WERNER, 1898- (Continued)

GRUSS; "Zuvor so lasst uns grüssen von Herzen" g 49; ZUVOR SO LASST UNS GRÜSSEN g 326 ... 1283

DIE HARMONIE DER STERNE; "Wie die hohen Sterne kreisen" g 49 ... 1284

"HOLDER MOND, DU SILBERN SCHIFFLEIN" g 49 ... 1285

IHR KLEINEN VÖGELEIN; "Ihr kleinen Vögelein, ihr Waldergötzerlein" g 49 words by A. Silesius ... 1286

WANDERLIED; "Wacht auf, schon will es tagen" g 49 ... 1287

ZU FRÜHER FAHRT; "Nichts kann mich mehr erfreuen" g 49 ... 1288

GODARD, BENJAMIN LOUIS PAUL, 1849-1895

CHANSON DE FLORIAN; "Ah! s'il est dans votre village"; FLORIAN'S SONG; "If there's a shepherd in ... 1289
your parish" e, f 136; "Oh, have you seen among the village lads" e 348; "Oh have you in your
village seen him" e, f 237 words by J. P. Claris de Florian

[JOCELYN, opera; words by P. S. Silvestre and V. Capoul] OH! NE T'ÉVEILLE ... 1290
PAS; "Cachés dans cet asile où Dieu nous a conduits" (recit); "Oh! ne t'éveille pas encore" (aria);
BERCEUSE; "Concealed in this retreat where-to we have been led" (recit); "Oh! wake not yet from
out thy dream" (aria) e, f 3; LULLABY e, f 122; "To this asylum led, by some protecting pow'r"
(recit); "Oh! let sweet sleep my child enfold" e, f 237; BERCEUSE e, f 329; LULLABY; "Together
here we are where the Lord has lit our way" (recit); "Rest gently rest in slumber's arms" (aria) e 132

TE SOUVIENS-TU?, op. 19, no. 6; "Te souviens-tu ta promesse?; REMEMBRANCE; "Dost thou recall ... 1291
thy wistful promise?" e, f 140

GOECKEL, GEORG, 1873-1945

BURSCH IN JENA; "Frisch als Fuchs fuhr ich ins Leben" g 31 words by K. Vogt ... 1292

GÖRNER, JOHANN VALENTIN, 1702-1762

DIE ALSTER; "Beförderer vieler Lustbarkeiten" g 250 words by F. von Hagedorn ... 1293

DIE ROSE; "Siehst du jene Rose blühen, Schönste!" g 308 words by F. von Hagedorn ... 1294

GOETZE, KARL, 1836-1887

O SCHÖNE ZEIT, op. 160; "Es war ein Sonntag hell und klar"; O HAPPY DAY!; "Twas on a Sunday ... 1295
bright and clear" e, g 385; "ES WAR EIN SONNTAG, HELL UND KLAR" g 353; O SCHÖNE ZEIT,
O SELGE ZEIT g 326 words by A. Freudenthal

GOLDFADEN, ABRAHAM, 1840-1908

"HAYNT IZ PURIM, BRIDER"; "Today is Purim, brothers" e 318 words by M. Rivesman ... 1296

GOMES, CARLOS, 1836-1896

[SALVATOR ROSA, opera; words by A. Ghislanzoni] "DI SPOSO DI PADRE LE ... 1297
GIOIE SERENE," Act II, (aria); "E'il foglio io segnerò?" (recit) i 299

GÓMEZ CALLEJA, RAFAEL, 1874-1938

ALMA ANDALUZA; "Yo soy el mejor torero Naciodo en Andalucia"; SOUL OF ANDALUSIA; "My ... 1298
Andalusia spirit is guiding my soul forever" e, s 245

GOOCH, WILLIAM

REUBEN AND RACHEL; "Reuben, I have long been thinking" e 225; "Reuben, Reuben, I've been think- ... 1299
ing" e 28, 114, 233, 236, 279, 366; THE ROOKIE; "I ain't been long in this here army" e 225 words
by H. Birch

GOODELL, WALTER, 1884-

AMERICA, MY COUNTRY; "America, my country, great nation of the world" e 28, 366 words by ... 1300
N. H. Hall

MULES; "On mules we find two legs behind" 4 pt round e 28, 366 ... 1301

GOODHART, ARTHUR MURRAY, 1866-

THE BELLS OF CLERMONT TOWN; AUVERGNAT; "There was a man was half a clown" e 344 words ... 1302
by H. Belloc

GORDIGIANI, LUIGI, 1806-1860

SANTA LUCIA; "Sul mare luccica l'astro d'argento"; NEAPOLITAN BARCAROLLE; "Silver the distant ... 1303
shore, moonlight is gleaming" e, i 310; "Now 'neath the silver moon ocean is glowing" e 28, 35,
233, 236, 279, 343, 366; HERE IN THE TWILIGHT; "Twilight is drawing near, bright stars will soon
appear" e 132; "Schon glänzt das Mondenlicht am Himmelsbogen" g 326; SCHON GLÄNZT DAS
MONDENLICHT g 353

GORDON, A.

"CHRIST THE LORD IS RISEN TODAY" e 371 words by C. Weslsy, 1707-1788 ... 1304

GORDON, HERMANN ALBERT VON

ARGONNERWALD; "Argonnerwald! Um Mitternacht ein Pionier stand auf der Wacht" g 43 ... 1305

GORMAN, LARRY

THE OXEN SONG. See 7911

GOSS, SIR JOHN, 1800-1880

"SEE AMID THE WINTER'S SNOW" e 305, 307, 333, 410 words by E. Caswall ... 1306

GOSSEC, FRANÇOIS JOSEPH, 1734-1829

[ROSINE, opera; words by N. Gersin] AIR DE ROSINE; "Dors mon enfant, clos ta ... 1307
paupière"; "Sleep, baby mine, rest on my bosom" e, f 149

GOTTSCHALK, LOUIS MOREAU, 1829-1869

"HOLY GHOST! WITH LIGHT DIVINE" e 28, 366 words by A. Reed ... 1308

47

GOULD, JOHN EDGAR, 1822-1875

"JESUS, SAVIOUR, PILOT ME"; Pilot (tune) e 35   words by E. Hopper   1309

GOUNOD, CHARLES FRANÇOIS, 1818-1893

AVE MARIA; "Ave Maria, gratia plena"; "Ave Maria, Thou virgin pure, divine" e, lat 329; "Ave   1310
Maria, Thou highly favored" e, lat 394; "Ave Maria, Thou happy mother" e 132; "Hail Mary,
full of grace" e, lat 304; "Mighty yet lowly, pure and most holy" e 346 (set to Bach's Prelude
No. 1 from the Well-tempered Klavier)

AVE MARIA; "Ave Maria gratia plena"; THE CROSS OF CALVARY; "Come all ye weary, cease from   1311
your sighing" e, lat 394; GOD IS SPIRIT; "Hark to the scriptures; thus it is written" e 90

BETHLEHEM; "Cradled all lowly, behold the Saviour Child" e 376   1312

LE CALVAIRE; "Il est au loin une colline"; "THERE IS A GREEN HILL FAR AWAY" e, f 123,394   1313

CE QUE JE SUIS SANS TOI; "Ce qu'est le lierre sans l'ormeau"; WITHOUT THEE!; "As droops the   1314
ivy, rudely torn" e, f 276   words by L. de Peyre

[LE CIEL A VISITÉ LA TERRE] ADORE AND BE STILL; "High heav'n hath stoop'd to earth so   1315
lowly" e 394

ENTREAT ME NOT TO LEAVE THEE; "And Ruth said: Entreat me not to leave thee" e 394   words from   1316
Bible

[FAUST, opera; words by J. Barbier and M. Carré] [Air des bijoux, Act   1317
III] SCENE ET AIR DES BIJOUX; "Les grands seigneurs ont seuls des airs si résolus" (recit); "Ah! Je
ris de me voir si belle en ce miroir" (aria); JEWEL SONG; "Nobles alone can bear them with so bold
a mien" (recit); "Ah! the joy past compare, these jewels bright to wear!" (aria); ARIA DI
MARGHERITA; "I gran signori sol han quell' altero andar" (recit); "Ah! E strano poter il viso suo
veder" (aria) e, f, i 221; JEWEL SONG e, f 1,6

[Ibid] "AVANT DE QUITTER CE LIEUX," Act II; "Even bravest heart may swell" e, f 4;   1318
DIO POSSENTE; "Dio possente, Dio d'amor"; CAVATINA e, i 237

[Ibid] FAITES-LUI MES AVEUX, Act III; "Faites-lui mes aveux portez mes voeux?"; "Lovely flowers   1319
I pray my love betray" e 132; "Gentle flow'rs in the dew, bear love from me!" e, f 2; LIED DES
SIEBEL; "Blümlein traut, sprecht für mich recht inniglich" g 311

[Ibid] THE KING OF THULÉ, Act III; "Je voudrais bien savoir quel était ce jeune homme" (recit);   1320
"Il était un roi de Thulé" (aria); "I wish I could but know who was he that addressed me" (recit);
"Reigned a King in Thulé" (aria) e, f 6 (aria only) e, f 1

[Ibid] SALUT! DEMEURE CHASTE ET PURE, Act III; "Quel trouble inconnu me pénètre" (recit);   1321
"Salut! demeure chaste et pure" (aria); "Whence comes this unwonted oppression?" (recit); "All
hail, thou dwelling pure and lowly" (aria) e, f 3

[Ibid] LE VEAU D'OR, Act II; "Le veau d'or est toujours debout!"; SONG OF THE GOLDEN CALF;   1322
"Clear the way for the Calf of Gold!" e, f 5

[Ibid] "VOUS QUI FAITES L'ENDORMIE"; SERENADE; "Catarina, while you sham a-sleep" e, f 5   1323

THE KING OF LOVE MY SHEPHERD IS; "The King of love my Shepherd is, whose goodness faileth never"   1324
e 200,394   words by H. W. Baker

MIGHTY LAND, WONDROUS LAND; "Mighty land, wondrous land, land of peace and plenty" e 28,343   1325

[MIREILLE, opera; words by M. Carré] "O LÉGÈRE HIRONDELLE," Act I; "Swallow,   1326
flying so high" e, f 292

NAZARETH; "Nascendo in un presepio"; "Though poor be the chamber" e, lat 346,394   1327

O COME TO ME; "These words spake Jesus: O come to Me" e 89   words from Bible   1328

Ô MA BELLE REBELLE; "Ô ma belle rebelle, Las! que tu m'es cruelle" f 278   words by A. de Baïf   1329

PARCE DOMINE; "Parce, parce Domine, parce populo tuo"; REPENTIR; "Ah! ne repousse pas mon   1330
âme pécheresse!"; O DIVINE REDEEMER!; "Ah! turn me not away, receive me, tho' unworthy"
e, f, lat 123,394

PRAISE YE THE FATHER; "Praise ye the Father! Let ev'ry heart give thanks to Him!" e 28   1331

QUAND TU CHANTES; "Quand tu chantes bercée le soir entre mes bras"; SERENADE; "When thou'rt   1332
cradled at eve on my breast, breathing forth song" e, f 274; SING, SMILE, SLUMBER; SERENADE;
"Sweetly sing when the hour of daylight fades away" e, f 237; "When thou singest when nestling at
eve close by my side" e 348   words by V. Hugo

[THE REDEMPTION, oratorio] LOVELY APPEAR; "Lovely appear over the mountains" e 28   1333

[Ibid] UNFOLD, YE PORTALS; "Unfold, unfold, unfold ye portals everlasting" e 28   1334

RING OUT, WILD BELLS; "Ring out, wild bells, to the wild sky" e 123,394   words by A. Tennyson   1335

[ROMÉO ET JULIETTE, opera; words by J. Barbier and M. Carré] AH! JE   1336
VEUX VIVRE; "Ah! je veux vivre dans ce rêve"; AH! I WOULD LINGER; "Ah! I would linger in
this daydream"; AH! NELLA CALMA; "Ah! nella calma d'un bel sogno" e, f, i 221; "Ah! wake
me never, dreaming ever" e, f 292; JULIET'S WALTZ SONG; "Ah! In my fairy dream" e, f 6;
DAYDREAMS; "Ah! I wish I could live in daydreams" e, f 93

[Ibid] AH, LÈVE-TOI, SOLEIL!, Act II; CAVATINA; "L'amour! l'amour! oui, son ardeur a troublé   1337
tout mon être" (recit); "Ah! lève-toi, soleil!" (aria); "On love! On love! Ay, for my heart in his
bondage is aching" (recit); "Star of the morn, arise" (aria) e, f 3

[Ibid] QUE FAIS-TU, BLANCHE TOURTERELLE, Act III; "Depuis hier je cherche en vain mon maître"   1338
(recit); "Que fais-tu, blanche tourterelle" (aria); "Since yesterday I vainly seek my master" (recit);
"Dainty dove, wherefore art thou lying" (aria) e, f 2

48

GOUNOD, CHARLES FRANÇOIS, 1818-1893 (Continued)

SEND OUT THY LIGHT; "Send out Thy light, send out Thy light! Send out Thy light and Thy truth, 1339
let them lead me" e 28

LE VALLON; "Mon coeur lasse de tout"; THE VALLEY; "Alas, poor lonely heart" e, f 273   words by 1340
Lamartine

VENISE; "Dans Venise la rouge Pas un bateau qui bouge"; VENICE; "In glowing Venice no boat is 1341
stirring" e, f 190,192,194   words by A. de Musset

GOW, NATHANIEL, 1763-1831

CALLER HERRIN'; "Wha'll buy caller herrin'?" e 17,100,163,349; "Wha'll buy my caller herrin'?" 1342
e 235   words att to N. Gow and Lady Baronese Nairne

GOW, NIEL, JR., c 1795-1823

CAM' YE BY ATHOL?; "Cam' ye by Athol lad wi' the philabeg?" e 100,103   words by J. Hogg 1343

GRAFTON, GERALD

BREAKFAST IN MY BED ON SUNDAY MORNIN'; "I never, never worry"; "To beautiful Sunday! I wish 1344
it would never come Monday!" (ref) e 131   joint composer H. Lauder

GRAHAM, CHARLES W.

MY DAD'S THE ENGINEER; "We were none of us thinking of danger" e 114 1345

THE PICTURE THAT IS TURNED TOWARD THE WALL; "Far away beyond the glamor of the city and its 1346
strife"; "There's a name that's never spoken" (ref) e 114,204

GRANADOS Y CAMPIÑA, ENRIQUE, 1867-1916

EL MAJO DISCRETO; "Dican que mi majoes feo"; MY DISCREET SWEETHEART; "They tell me, my 1347
sweetheart has no looks" e, s 245   words by F. Periquet

GRANICHSTAEDTEN, BRUNO, 1879-

[IM WEISSEN RÖSS, singspeil] ZUSCHAU'N KANN ICH NICHT!"; "Für ein Lächeln von ihr" 1348
g 257   words by R. Gilbert

GRANIER, JULES

HOSANNA!; "Une homme est mort, il va renaître"; EASTER SONG; "A man is dead he will arise 1349
again" e, f 123; "A man is dead yet is He living" e 398; "A man is dead yet he shall rise again"
346,400   words by J. Didiée

GRANNIS, S. M.

"DO THEY MISS ME AT HOME?" e 129,130 1350

YOUR MISSION; "If you can not on the ocean sail among the swiftest fleet" e 212 1351

GRANOM, LEWIS CHRISTIAN AUSTIN, fl 1750

THE MORNING AIR; "Would you taste the morning air" e 278 1352

GRANT-SCHAEFER, GEORGE ALFRED, 1872-1939

THE WIND SPEAKS; "When I blow from the frozen north" e 136   words by W. H. Hayne 1353

GRAUN, KARL HEINRICH, 1704-1759

[PORCIA, cantata] REZITATIV UND ARIE; "Disperata Porcia al veder spirar lo sposo" (recit); 1354
"Quanto dolce, o caro sposo" (aria); "Porzia, verzweifelt belm Anblick des sterbenden Gatten"
(recit); "Wie süss, o teurer Gatte" (aria) e, i 218

DAS TÖCHTERCHEN - DAS SÖHNCHEN; "Als mich heut Mama" g 250   words by W. Hagedorn and 1355
Hiller

GRAY, HAMILTON

A DREAM OF PARADISE; "Once in the ev'ning twilight, I dreamt a happy dream" e 394   words by 1356
C. Lyttleton

GRAY, WILLIAM B.

SHE IS MORE TO BE PITIED THAN CENSURED; "At the old concert hall on the Bow'ry" e 114,131,204 1357

GREAVES, THOMAS, fl 1604

"SHADED WITH OLIVE TREES" e 196 1358

"WHAT IS BEAUTY BUT A BREATH" e 144 1359

GRECHANINOV, ALEKSANDR TIKHONOVICH, 1864-1956

BERCEUSE, op.1, no.5; "Dors, mignon, près de ta mère"; SLUMBER SONG; "Rest thee now in 1360
mother's keeping" e 237; "Sleep, my baby, close to mother" e, f 241; "Sleep, my baby, softly
dreaming" e 348; "Sleep, my pretty one, close to mother" e 121; e, f 136

MY NATIVE LAND, op.1, no.4; "Native land, salute to you!" e, r 341; LAND OF MINE; "Land of 1361
mine, dear native land!" e 408   words by A. Tolstoy

GREENSPAN, P.

SPIN, SEVIVON; "Spin, spin, spin, spin, sevivon" e 33 1362

GREGORIO CABRERA, H.

HE VENIDO A DESPEDIRME; "No te extrañes, mi amada" s 284 1363

GRENET, ELISEO

AY! MAMA INES; "Aquíestan todos los negros" s 284 1364

GRÉTRY, ANDRÉ ERNEST MODESTE, 1741-1813

[ANACRÉON CHEZ POLYCRATE, opera; words by J. H. Guy] AIR D'ANAÏS; "Eprise 1365
d'un feu téméraire"; "A prey to my passion o'er-whelming" e, f 151; "Imprison'd by love by love
o'er pow'ring" e, f 292

GRÉTRY, ANDRÉ ERNEST MODESTE, 1741-1813 (Continued)

    [Ibid] AIR DE POLYCRATE; "Ô fortune ennemie! Eh quoi! toujours le Ciel"; "Oh! malevolent   1366
    Fortune! Alas! relentless Fate" e, f 147

    [LES DEUX AVARES, opera; words by C. G. F. de Falbaire] "PLUS DE DÉPIT,   1367
    PLUS DE TRISTESSE"; NO MORE SHALL SORROW; "No more shall sorrow displease or vex me"
    e, f 211

    [LE JUGEMENT DE MIDAS, opera; words by T. d'Hèle] AIR D'APOLLON; "Certain   1368
    coucou certain hibou au rossignol dans un bocage"; "The cuckoo bird, the owl as well, the nightin-
    gale once sought to rival" e, f 153

    [RICHARD COEUR-DE-LION, opera; words by J. M. Sedaine] "JE CRAINS DE LUI   1369
    PARLER LA NUIT"; "A NOTTE S'EI MI VUOL PARLAR" f, i 411; ARIETTE FROM RICHARD THE
    LION-HEARTED; "I fear the magic of the night" e, f 211

    [LE TABLEAU PARLANT, opera; words by L. Anseaume] "VOUS ÉTIEZ CE QUE VOUS   1370
    N'ÊTES PLUS"; "YOU WERE ONCE THAT WHICH YOU ARE NO MORE" e, f 362

    [ZÉMIRE ET AZOR, opera; words by J. F. Marmontel] ARIETTE FROM ZÉMIRE AND   1371
    AZOR; "Rose chérie, aimable fleur"; "Rose sweet and tender, oh lovely flower!" e, f 211

GRETSCHER, KONRAD, 1856-1929

    OKTOBERLIED; "Der Nebel steigt, es fällt das Laub" g 31 words by T. Storm   1372

GRETSCHER, PHILIPP, 1859-1937

    AN DAS VATERLAND; "Du bist das Land wo von den Hängen der Freiheit Rosengarten lacht" g 31   1373
    words by A. Frey

    GOLIARDENLIED; "Ecce gratum et optatum" lat 31 words from Carmina Burana   1374

    THÜRINGERLAND; "Rauscht ihr noch, ihr alten Wälder" g 31 words by F. Landheinrich   1375

    VATERLAND, HEILIG LAND!; "Vaterland, heilig Land! Brausender Meeresstrand, Täler und Höhn!"   1376
    g 31 words by P. Warncke

    WILDROSEN; "Wär' ich ein Knab geboren" g 31 words by A. Frey   1377

GREVER, MARIA

    GITANERIAS; "Gitano soy, el destino me ha privao de sus favores"; THE GYPSY; "Only a Gypsy, I'm   1378
    knowing, fate bids my love vainly languish" e, s 176

    JÚRAME; "Todos dicen que es mentira que to quiero"; PROMISE LOVE, SPANISH TANGO; "They all   1379
    say my love for you is just pretending" e, s 122

    RATAPLAN; "Rataplan! Rataplan! Rataplan! Monotono sonido, me hiere el alma al pensar"; "Rataplan!   1380
    Rataplan! Rataplan! Oh, roll of drums foreboding, Relentless, merciless fate" e, s 121

GRIEG, EDVARD HAGERUP, 1843-1907

    [HUN ER SAA HVID, OP.18, V.I, NO.2] WENN EINST SIE LAG; "Wenn einst sie lag   1381
    an meiner Brust" g 229

    [JEG ELSKER DIG, OP.5, NO.3] ICH LIEBE DICH; "Du mein Gedanke, du mein Sein und   1382
    Werden"; I LOVE YOU; "You are my thoughts, my end and my beginning" e, g 36; I LOVE THEE;
    "My thought of thoughts, my very inmost being" e, g 241; "Thou art my thoughts, my present and
    my future" e, g 122,176; JE T'AIME; "O toi, doux ange, à mes pensers si cher"; "Light of my life,
    whose image my heart holdeth!" e, f, g 132,237,329; "My waking thoughts to thee are ever turn-
    ing" e 387

    [LANGS EI AA, OP.33, NO.5] BY THE BROOK; "Thou wood, low bending there, apart"   1383
    e 121

    [LIDEN KIRSTEN, OP.60, NO.1] PRETTY MARGARET; "Pretty Margaret sat in the evening   1384
    glow" e 208 words by V. Krag

    [MED EN PRIMULA VERIS, OP.26, NO.4] MIT EINER PRIMULA VERIS; "Mag dir, du   1385
    zartes Frühlingskind"; THE FIRST PRIMROSE; "May thou, O tender child of spring" e, g 209

    [MENS JEG VENTER] IM KAHNE, op.60, no.3; BOAT SONG; "Sea gulls, sea gulls in white   1386
    clouds" e 348; IN THE BOAT; "Sea gulls, sea gulls in great white masses" e 395; "Seagulls,
    seagulls with white wings gleaming" e 208 words by V. Krag

    [MODERSONG, OP.15, NO.4] A MOTHER'S SORROW; "Have you seen my bonny boy" e 208   1387
    words by C. Richardt

    MY NATIVE LAND; "Oh, native land, how fair you seem" e 28,366   1388

    [PEER GYNT, incidental music, op.23] SOLVEJGS LIED; "Der Winter mag scheiden,   1389
    der Frühling vergeh'n"; SOLVEJG'S SONG; "Let winter be gone and the spring follow too" e, g
    329; "The winter may go, and the spring may die" e, g 122; "The winter may wane and the
    springtime go by" e, g 137; "Cold winter may go and gay springtime depart" e 395; SOLVEIG'S
    SONG; "The winter may pass and the spring fade away" e 276

    [PRINSESSEN] THE PRINCESS; "The golden haired princess sat high in her tow'r" e 395   1390

    [EN SVANA, OP.25, NO.2] EIN SCHWAN; "Mein Schwan, mein stiller mit weissem   1391
    Gefieder"; A SWAN; "My swan, my treasure, with snowy white feather" e, g 137; "My swan, so
    silent with white snowy pinions" e, g 237

    [TIL EN I] HVORFOR SVÖMMER DIT OGE?; "Hvorfor svömmer dit öge tidt i en taareglans?"; WHY   1392
    WITH TEARS SOFTLY SHIMM'RING?; "Why with tears softly shimm'ring greet your beloved one?"
    e, n 407

GRIEG, EDVARD HAGERUP, 1843-1907 (Continued)

[TIL NORGE, OP.58, NO.2] AN DAS VATERLAND; "O Mutter du ich liebe dich" g 229　　1393

[TO BRUNE ÖJNE, OP.5, NO.1] ZWEI BRAUNE AUGEN; "Hab' jüngst gesehen zwei Augen　1394
braun"; TWO BROWN EYES; "Two eyes of brown I've seen today!" e, g 45,229

[TURISTEN, OP.58, NO.4] THE DAIRYMAID; "The fragrance of pine boughs perfumes all　1395
the air" e 208

GRIFFES, CHARLES TOMLINSON, 1884-1920

"AUF GEHEIMEM WALDESPFADE"; "BY A LONELY FOREST PATHWAY"; e, g 121　words by N. Lenau　1396

THE LAMENT OF IAN THE PROUD, op.11, no.1; "What is this crying" e 259　words by F. MacLeod　1397

"WE'LL TO THE WOODS AND GATHER MAY", op.3, no.3 e 408　words by W. E. Henley　1398

GRIMES, G.

"A BABE IS BORN ALL OF A MAID" e 372　　1399

CRADLE SONG; "Hush! my dear, lie still and slumber" e 374　words by I. Watts　1400

ON CHRISTMAS NIGHT; "The snow lay on the ground" e 376　　1401

GROOS, CARL, 1798-1861

FREIHEIT; "Freiheit, die ich meine" g 99; "FREIHEIT, DIE ICH MEINE" g 31,49,326　　1402

GROTHE, FRANZ JOHANNES AUGUST, 1908-

"AN DER DONAU, WENN DER WEIN BLÜHT" g 396　joint composer A. Melichar; words by H. Dekner　1403

FRÜHLING IN WIEN; "Frühling in Wien! Frühling in Wien! Drum ist der Himmel so blau!" g 223　1404

LIED DER NACHTIGALL; ZAUBERLIED DER NACHT; "Nachtigall! Nachtigall!" g 223　words by　1405
W. Dehmel

POSTILLION-LIED; "Mein Schatz, der ist Postillion" g 223　words by W. Dehmel　1406

GRUBER, EDMUND L.

THE CAISSONS GO ROLLING ALONG; "Over hill, over dale when we hit the dusty trail" e 233;　1407
"Over hill, over dale, we have hit the dusty trail" e 236

GRUBER, FRANZ XAVIER, 1787-1863

STILLE NACHT, HEILIGE NACHT; "Stille Nacht, heilige Nacht! Alles schläft, einsam wacht"　1408
g 326,353,354; "Silent night, holy night! All asleep, watch doth keep" e, g 402; SILENT
NIGHT; "Silent night! Holy night! all is calm, all is bright" e, g 28,35,125,154,165,233,
236,271,279,296,315,343,366,410; STILLE NACHE g 401,412; e, g 79,337; e 206; WEIH-
NACHTSLIED e, g 388; SILENT NIGHT, HOLY NIGHT e 33,38,39,251,305,307; HOLY NIGHT,
PEACEFUL NIGHT e 394; HOLY NIGHT, SILENT NIGHT e 377; PEACEFUL NIGHT, HOLY
NIGHT; "Peaceful night!; Holy night! All around is calm delight" e 333; DIE HEILIGE NACHT
g 99; SAINTE NUIT; "Sainte nuit! a minuit, le hameau dort sans bruit" f 383; "Douce nuit,
Sainte nuit dans le ciel tout reluit" f 88; NOCHE DE PAZ, NOCHE DE AMOR!; "Noche de paz,
noche de amor! Todo duerme en derredor" e, s 244　words by J. Mohr

GRUBER, LUDWIG

MEI' MUATTERL WAR A WIENERIN, op.1000; WIENERLIED; "'s ist mir heut' noch in Errinn'rung"　1409
g 396

'S WIRD SCHÖNE MADERLIN GEB'N, op.394; ES WIRD A WEIN SEIN; "Weil wir heut so lusti　1410
beinander g'rad san" g 396　words by J. Hornig

GRUWE, STEFAN, 1834-1901

PERKÊO; "Das was der Zwerg Perkeo im Heidelberger Schloss" g 31　words by J. Scheffel　1411

GÜNTHER, ANTON

"DE SONN STEIGT HINNERN WALD," op.30; FEIEROMD g 353　　1412

GUILLAUME DE MACHAUT, d 1377

"C'EST FORCE, FAIRE LE WEIL"; VIRELAI; THE GALLANT; "Lady, prithee hear me bowing above　1413
thy hand" e, f 403

"DOUCE DAME JOLIE"; "LADY FAIR AND GENTLE" e, f 36　　1414

GUION, DAVID WENDEL FENTRESS, 1895-

"ALL DAY ON THE PRAIRIE" e 45　　1415

MARY ALONE; "Mother of Christ, this path you've trod" e 259　words by L. I. Stall　1416

GURNEY, IVOR, 1890-1937

THE BONNIE EARL OF MURRAY; "Ye Hielands and ye Lawlands, o whare hae ye been?" e 272　1417

CAROL OF THE SKIDDAW YOWES; "The shepherds on the fellside" e 344　words by E. Casson　1418

"I WILL GO WITH MY FATHER A-PLOUGHING" e 344　words by S. MacCathmhaoil　1419

SLEEP; "Come, Sleep and with thy sweet deceiving" e 277　words by J. Fletcher　1420

GUSTAV ADOLF VI, KING OF SWEDEN, 1882-

GLAD SAASOM FAGELN; "Glad saasom faageln i morgonstunden"; GAY AS A BIRD; "Gay as a　1421
bird in the dew of the morning" e, sw 188　words by H. Sätherberg

"SJUNG OM STUDENTENS LYCKLIGA DAG"; SING TO THE STUDENT'S HAPPIEST DAY!; "Sing　1422
of the student's happiest day" e, sw 188　words by H. Sätherberg

GUTH, EDUARD, 1820-1890

DIE PFÄNDUNG; "Und wieder sass beim Weine" g 31　words by J. V. Scheffel　1423

GUTHOERL, CYRIL

MEMORARE; "Remember, O most gracious Virgin Mary" e 71　　1424

GUTHRIE, WOODY, 1912-

DUST PNEUMONIA BLUES; "I got the dust pneumonee, pneumonee in my lung" e 336   1425

THE FARMER-LABOR TRAIN; "From the high Canadian Rockies to that land of Mexico" e 293   1426

HARD TRAVELIN'; "I been a-havin' some hard travelin'" e 293   1427

JIG ALONG HOME; "I went to the dance and the animals come" e 389   1428

NEW YORK TOWN; "Standin' down in New York Town one day" e 336   1429

SIXTY-SIX HIGHWAY BLUES; "There is a road from the coast to the coast" e 336   joint composer P. Seeger   1430

SO LONG IT'S BEEN GOOD TO KNOW YUH; "I've sung this song, but I'll sing it again" e 293, 389   1431

YOU GOTTA GO DOWN; "You gotta go down and join the union" e 293   1432

H. R.

TO THE WEST; "To the west! to the land of the free" e 189   words by C. M.   1433

HAAKANSON, KNUT ALGOT, 1887-1929

BUDBÄRERSKAN, op.41; "Ditt huvud är saa heligt skönt" sw 355   words by E. Lindorm   1434

SLOTTSTAPPNING, op.40, no.2; "Paa terassen blommar den sköna" sw 355   words by E. A. Karlfeldt   1435

HAAS, JOSEPH, 1879-

"LASST AUS DIESEM ENGEN HAUS", op.68, no.1 g 98   words by J. Kneip   1436

HADDEN, RICHARD M.

OL' MAN DEVIL GOTTA GO SOME; "Brokenhearted world, brokenhearted children" e 76   words by C. Broadhurst   1437

ROLL AWAY THAT STONE; "Roll away that stone, brother, and let Lord Jesus out!" e 76   1438

HADLEY, HENRY KIMBALL, 1871-1937

"IL PLEUT DES PÉTALES DE FLEURS," op.49, no.2; "THE ROSE LEAVES ARE FALLING LIKE RAIN" e, f 259   words by A. Samain   1439

HÄNDEL, GEORG FRIEDRICH, 1685-1759

[ACIS AND GALATEA, masque; words by J. Gay] "Would you gain the tender creature" e 277   1440

[ADMETO, opera; words by N. F. Haym] CANGIO D'ASPETTO; "Cangiò d'aspetto il crudo fato"; HOW CHANGED THE VISION; "How changed the vision now dawning o'er me" e, i 274   1441

[ALCINA, opera; words by A. Marchi] AMA, SOSPIRA; "Ama, sospira, ma no ti offende" i 181   1442

[Ibid] UN MOMENTO DI CONTENTO; "Un momento di contento dolce rende a un fido" i 181   1443

[Ibid] QUESTO E IL CIELO; BEAUTY LATELY; "Beauty lately dropped her sandal" e 199   1444

[Ibid] VERDI PRATI; "Verdi prati e selve amene" i 179; VERDANT MEADOWS; "Verdant meadows forests blooming" e, i 274; "Verdant meadows, woods beloved" e, i 209   1445

[ALESSANDRO, opera; words by P. A. Rolli] LUSINGHE PIÙ CARE; "Lusinghe più care, d'amor veri dardi"; CARESSES AND GLANCES; "Caresses and glances and love's ardent passion" e, i 211   1446

[ALEXANDER BALUS, oratorio; words by T. Morell] "HERE AMID THE SHADY WOODS" e 275   1447

[Ibid] "THRICE HAPPY THE MONARCH" e 272   1448

[ALEXANDER'S FEAST, ode; words by A. Pope] REVENGE! TIMOTHEUS CRIES; "'Revenge, revenge, revenge' Timotheus cries" e 272   1449

[L'ALLEGRO, IL PENSEROSO ED IL MODERATO; words by J. Milton] COME AND TRIP IT; "Come and trip it as you go" e 404   1450

[Ibid] LET ME WANDER NOT UNSEEN; "Let me wander not unseen by hedgerow elms, on hillocks green" e 276   1451

ALLELUJA AMEN; "Amen, amen, amen, amen, amen e 308   1452

[ATLANTA, opera] CARE SELVE; "Care Selve, care, care Selve"; COME BELOVED; "Come, my beloved! Through the sylvan gloom" e, i 276   1453

[Ibid] THE FAIRY FOLK; NOW THE MOON; "Now the moon with silver glamour" e 199   1454

AWAKE, MY SOUL; "Awake, my soul, stretch ev'ry nerve" e 366   1455

[BERENICE, opera; words by A. Salvi] "COME, SEE WHERE GOLDEN-HEARTED SPRING" e 199   1456

[Ibid] SI, TRA I CEPPI; "Si, tra i ceppi le ri torte"; "LOVE THAT'S TRUE WILL LIVE FOR EVER" e, i 273   1457

[DANK SEI DIR HERR] PRAISE BE TO THEE; "Praise be to Thee, Lord God of Hosts!" e 160   att to G. F. Händel, really by S. Ochs, words by M. Harrell   1458

[ESTHER, oratorio; words by A. Pope] HOW ART THOU FALL'N; "How art thou fall'n from thy height" e 272   1459

[EZIO, opera; words by P. Metastasio] [Se un bell' ardire] DROOP NOT, YOUNG LOVER; "Droop not, young lover; pine not in sadness" e 273   1460

[IL FLORIDANTE, opera; words by P. A. Rolli] ALMA MIA; "Alma mia, sì, sol tu sei"; MY BELOVED; "My beloved, thou art to me" e, i 211   1461

[JUDAS MACCABAEUS, oratorio; words by T. Morell] ARM, ARM, YE BRAVE; "I feel, I feel the Deity within" e 123   1462

[Ibid] [See, the conqu'ring hero comes] TOCHTER ZION, FREUE DICH; "Tochter Zion, freue dich, jauchze laut, Jerusalem!" g 326   1463

[THE MESSIAH, oratorio; words by C. Jennens] AND THE GLORY OF THE LORD; "And the glory, the glory of the Lord" e 28   1464

[Ibid] COMFORT YE MY PEOPLE; "Comfort ye, comfort ye, my people" e 89   1465

[Ibid] HE SHALL FEED HIS FLOCK; "Then shall the eyes of the blind be opened" (recit); "He shall feed His flock like a shepherd" (aria) e 123, 200, (aria only) e 337; COME UNTO HIM (aria only) e 394; COME UNTO HIM; "Come unto Him, all ye that labor" e 200   1466

[Ibid] "HOW BEAUTIFUL ARE THE FEET" e 90   1467

[Ibid] "I KNOW THAT MY REDEEMER LIVETH" e 123, 346, 394, 400   1468

[Ibid] PASTORAL SYMPHONY piano 307; HIRTENSYMPHONIE piano 412   1469

[RINALDO, opera; words by G. Rossi] CARA SPOSA; "Cara sposa! amante cara"; DEAREST CONSORT; "Dearest Consort! hope now doth falter" e, i 274; "CARA SPOSA AMANTE CARA"; "Wife beloved, thou whom I cherish" e, i 2   1470

[Ibid] LASCIA CH'IO PIANGA; "Armida, dispietata!" (recit); "Lascia ch'io pianga mia cruda sorte" (aria); LEAVE ME IN SORROW; "Armida, without pity" (recit); "Leave me in sorrow that knows no morrow" (aria) e, i 210 (aria only) i 179; LASS MICH MIT TRANEN; "Lass mich mit Tränen mein Los beklagen" (aria only) g 99   1471

[Ibid] "PAROLETTE, VEZZI E SGUARDI" i 179   1472

[Ibid] SCORTA REA; "Scorta rea de cieco Amore" i 181   1473

[Ibid] SORGE NEL PETTO; "Sorge nel petto certo diletto che bella calma promette al cor" i 181   1474

[RODELINDA, opera; words by A. Salvi] ART THOU TROUBLED?; "Art thou troubled? Music will calm thee" e 357   1475

[SAMSON, oratorio; words by N. Hamilton] HONOR AND ARMS; "Honor and arms scorn such a foe" e 123   1476

[SEMELE, opera; words by W. Congreve] ENDLESS PLEASURE, ENDLESS LOVE; "Endless pleasure, endless pleasure" e 276   1477

[Ibid] O SLEEP WHY DOST THOU LEAVE ME; "O sleep, O sleep, O sleep, why dost thou leave me" e 386   1478

[Ibid] WHERE'ER YOU WALK; "Where'er you walk, cool gales shall fan the glade" e 36, 122, 277, 329, 385   1479

[SERSE, opera; words by N. Minato] CARO VOI SIETE; "Caro voi siete all' alma" i 180   1480

[Ibid] "DI TACERE E DI SCHERNIRMI" i 179   1481

[Ibid] INGANNATA ROMILDA; "Ingannata Romilda! Ecco, leggete, dite poi" (duet) i 181   1482

[Ibid] NÉ MEN CON L'OMBRE; "Né men con l'ombre d'infedeltà" i 180   1483

[Ibid] "NON SO SE SIA LA SPEME" i 180   1484

[Ibid] OMBRA MAI FÙ; "Frondi tenere e belle del mio platano amato" (recit); "Ombrai mai fu di vegetabile" (aria); NE'ER SHADE SO DEAR; "Boughs so delicate and tender of my tree well beloved" (recit); "Ne'er shade so dear, made of such tender green" (aria) e, i 210; "Clad in verdure green thy branches as once more, friend, I great thee" (recit); "Thy blossoms fair, shedding rare radiance" (aria) e, i 2; (aria only) i 179; GOD SO LOVED THE WORLD; "Jesus lifted up His eyes to heaven and prayed for His disciples" (recit); "God so loved the world, God so loved the world" (aria) e 90; LARGO; "Father in heav'n, Thy children hear" (aria) e 28; LOVE YE THE LORD; LARGO; "Love ye the Lord, love ye the Lord for his great mercy" (aria) e 394   1485

[Ibid] QUELLA CHE TUTTA FÉ; "Quella che tutta fé per me languia d'amore" i 180   1486

[Ibid] VOI MI DITE; "Voi mi dite che non l'ami" i 180   1487

[SIROE, opera; words by P. Metastasio] [Non vi piacque; arr] "WHILE SHEPHERDS WATCHED THEIR FLOCKS" e 28, 38, 39, 296, 366; WHILE SHEPHERDS WATCHED e 315; "WHILE SHEPHERDS WATCHED THEIR FLOCKS BY NIGHT" e 251, 337 words by N. Tate; "RING OUT, O BELLS, YOUR JOYOUS SONG!" e 206 words by T. O. Kvamme; "SONGS OF PRAISE THE ANGELS SANG" e 206 words by J. Montgomery   1488

[SOSARME, opera; words by M. Noris] "REND' IL SERENO AL CIGLIO"; "GRACE THY FAIR BROW" e, i 209   1489

[SUSANNA, oratorio] FRAG' OB DIE ROSE; "Frag' ob die Rose süss von Duft"; "ASK IF YON DAMASK ROSE BE SWEET" e, g 36   1490

[Ibid] YE VERDANT HILLS; "Ye verdant hills, ye balmy vales" e 277   1491

[TAMERLANO, opera; words by A. Piovene] DAMMI PACE; "Dammi pace, oh volto amato" i 181   1492

[Ibid] DEH! LASCIATEMI; "Deh! lasciatemi il nemico, se toglieste a me l'amante" i 181   1493

HÄNDEL, GEORG FRIEDRICH, 1685-1759 (Continued)

[Ibid] FIGLIA MIA, NON PIANGER; "Figlia mia, non pianger, no, no," i 181   1494

[Ibid] IL TARTARO AMA ASTERIA; "Il Tartaro ama Asteria; ed io ne fui cagion?" (recit); "Bella   1495
Asteria, bella Asteria, il tuo cor me difenda" (aria) i 180

[THEODORA, oratorio; words by T. Morell] "ANGELS, EVER BRIGHT AND FAIR"   1496
(aria); "O worse than death indeed" (recit) e 275,394

[TRIUMPH OF TIME AND TRUTH, oratorio; words by T. Morell] DRYADS,   1497
SYLVANS; "Dryads, Sylvans with fair Flora" e 275

[WATER MUSIC] HORNPIPE FROM WATER MUSIC piano 306   1498

HAGEMAN, RICHARD, 1882-

AT THE WELL; "When the two sisters go to fetch water" e 91,93,121 words by R. Tagore   1499

"DO NOT GO, MY LOVE" e 93,122,176 words by R. Tagore   1500

HAGUE, ALBERT

TELEPHONE BOOK; "A Phone-book full of names" e 321 words by W. Cuney   1501

TELL IRENE HELLO; "If you go to Birmingham" e 321 words by W. Cuney   1502

HAHN, REYNALDO, 1875-1947

[CHANSONS GRISES, song cycle] L'HEURE EXQUISE, no.5; "La lune blanche luit dans   1503
les bois"; EXQUISITE HOUR; "The white moon shines in the forest" e, f 191,193,195; "The
moonlight blanches on trees around" e 348; THE PERFECT HOUR; "The silv'ry moonlight streams
on the wood" e, f 140,241; THE HOUR OF DREAMING; "The moon-beams whiten boughs all
around" e, f 121; ENCHANTED HOUR; "The tender moon beam bathes in the wood" e, f 237
words by P. Verlaine

OFFRANDE; "Voici des fruits, des fleurs, des feuilles et des branches"; THE OFFERING; "Here are   1504
fruit, flowers, leaves, and branches" e, f 191,193,195; "O here are flow'rs and fruit" e, f 362
words by P. Verlaine

SI MES VERS AVAIENT DES AILES!; "Mes vers fuiraient, doux et frêles"; COULD MY SONGS THEIR   1505
WAY BE WINGING; "My songs to thee would be bringing" e, f 140; IF MY VERSES HAD WINGS;
"My verses would flee, sweet and frail" e, f 191,193,195; MY SONG ON WINGS; "This song of
mine all unaided" e, f 329; WERE MY SONG WITH WINGS PROVIDED; "My song would fly, all
unaided" e, f 122; IF MY SONG HAD WINGS; "My song to thee would be hieing" e, f 237
words by V. Hugo

HALÉVY, JACQUES FRANCOIS FROMENTAL ÉLIE, 1799-1862

[L'ÉCLAIR, opera; words by J. H. Vernoy de Saint-Georges and F. A. E. de   1506
Planard] [Quand de la nuit] CALL ME THINE OWN; "Call me 'thine own', name fond,
endearing" e 132

[LA JUIVE, opera; words by A. E. Scribe] RACHEL, QUAND DU SEIGNEUR, Act IV;   1507
"Va prononcer ma mort" (recit); "Rachel! quand du Seigneur la grâce tutélaire" (aria); "Though
you pronounce my death" (recit); "When God entrusted you, dear Rachel, to my keeping" (aria)
e, f 3

[Ibid] SI LA RIGUEUR, Act I; "Si la rigueur ou la vengeance leur font hair"; CAVATINA; "Should   1508
hot revenge or persecution" e, f 5; "SE OPRESSI OGNOR DA RIA SENTENZA" i 299

HALEY, ED

WHILE STROLLING THROUGH THE PARK ONE DAY; "While strolling thro' the park one day" e 115;   1509
WHILE STROLLING THROUGH THE PARK e 36; "WHILE STROLLING THRU' THE PARK ONE DAY";
IN THE MERRY MONTH OF MAY e 128,129,130,131,132,236; "WHILE STROLLING IN THE PARK
ONE DAY"; THE FOUNTAIN THE PARK e 114

HALL, FOLEY

[EVER OF THEE I'M DREAMING] "EVER OF THEE I AM FONDLY DREAMING"; "Ah!   1510
never 'Till life and mem'ry perish" (ref) e 132 words by G. Linley

HALL, FREDERICK DOUGLAS, 1896-

DAWN; "An angel robed in spotless white" e 78 words by P. L. Dunbar   1511

MANDY LOU; "Come away to dreamin' town, Mandy Lou" e 78 words by P. L. Dunbar   1512

HAMILTON, CLARENCE GRANT, 1865-1935

"THE KINGS OF THE EAST ARE RIDING" e 251 words by L. Bates   1513

HAMMERSCHMIDT, ANDREAS, 1611 or 12-1675

SCHLEISISCHER BAUER GRÄTE; "Gorga, mustu denn och klinsaln" g 250   1514

HANBY, BENJAMIN RUSSEL, 1833-1867

DARLING NELLY GRAY; "There's a low green valley on the old Kentucky shore"; "Oh, my poor Nelly   1515
Gray, they have taken you away" (ref) e 10,28,32,34,109,110,129,130,132,184,233,236,279,366

OLE SHADY; "Oh! yah! darkies laugh wid me"; "Den away, away, for I can't wait any longer" (ref)   1516
e 279,366

UP ON THE HOUSE-TOP; "Up on the house-top reindeer pause" e 28,206,366   1517

HANDY, WILLIAM CHRISTOPHER, 1873-1958

FRIENDLESS BLUES; "Feel so lowdown an' sad" e 109,110 words by M. Gilbert   1518

ST. LOUIS BLUES; "I hate to see de ev'nin' sun go down" e 34   1519

HANITSCH, GEORG FRIEDRICH, 1790-1865
    "SIND WIE VEREINT ZUR GUTEN STUNDE" g 31 words by E. M. Arndt   1520
HANN, SIDNEY, 1868-1921
    "LOVE CAME DOWN AT CHRISTMAS" e 307 words by C. Rossetti   1521
HAQUINIUS, ALGOT
    HJÄRTATS SAANGER; "Glömma, glömma bara glömma allt som var ditt liv" sw 355 words by   1522
      P. Lagerkvist
    MAANLJUSET; "Jag vet ej, varför jag vaken sitter" sw 355 words by W. von Heidenstam   1523
    SKAERGAARDSØ; "Nu glider Baaden mod Skaergaards-Ø-en" sw 355   1524
HARDING, JAMES P.
    "BRIGHTEST AND BEST OF THE SONS OF THE MORNING"; Morning star (tune) e 38,39 words by   1525
      R. Heber
HARINGTON, HENRY, 1727-1816
    GAPING CATCH; "'Tis humdrum, 'tis mum" 3 pt round e 349   1526
    LOOK, NEIGHBORS, LOOK!; "Look, neighbors, look! Here lies poor Thomas Day" 3 pt round e 235   1527
HARRINGTON, C. S.
    HOMEWARD BOUND; "Out on the ocean all boundless we ride" e 205 words by W. F. Warren   1528
HARRINGTON, KARL POMEROY, 1861-
    "LONG YEARS AGO O'ER BETHLEHEM'S HILLS" e 251 words by L. R. Brewer   1529
    "THERE'S A SONG IN THE AIR!" e 251,315 words by J. G. Holland   1530
HARRIS, CHARLES KASSELL, 1865-1930
    AFTER THE BALL; "A little maiden climbed an old man's knee"; "After the ball is over" (ref) e 32,   1531
      34,115 (ref only) e 233
    BREAK THE NEWS TO MOTHER; "While the shot and shell were screaming upon the battlefield";   1532
      "Just break the news to mother" (ref) e 32,34
    HELLO CENTRAL, GIVE ME HEAVEN; "Papa, I'm so sad and lonely"; "Hello Central, give me   1533
      heaven" (ref) e 114,131,246 (ref only) e 128
    "I'VE A LONGING IN MY HEART FOR YOU, LOUISE" e 114   1534
HARRIS, ROY, 1898-
    FOG; "The fog comes on little cat feet" e 358 words by C. Sandburg   1535
HARRISON, ANNIE FORTESCUE, d 1944
    IN THE GLOAMING; "In the gloaming, O my darling!" e 28,36,128,129,130,132,233,236,237,279,   1536
      343,364,366 words by M. Orred
HARRISS, CHARLES ALBERT EDWIN, 1862-1929
    "I HEARD THE VOICE OF JESUS SAY" e 123   1537
HART, HENRY
    GOOD SWEET HAM; "You may talk about good eating" e 225   1538
HARTMANN, JOHAN PETER EMILIUS, 1805-1900
    FLYV, FUGL, FLYV; "Flyv, Fugl, flyv over Furesøens Vove"; FLY, BIRDIE, FLY; "Fly, birdie,   1539
      fly! o'er Fura's waters flowing" da, e 87 words by C. Winther
    LIDEN KIRSTEN; HØR, UNGERSVEND, SIIG IKKE NEI; "Hør Ungersvend siig ikke nei, leeg   1540
      Tavlebord med mig!"; LIST, YOUTH TO ME; "List, youth to me, and say not nay, but play
      at dice with me!" da, e 87 words by H. C. Andersen
HARTY, SIR HAMILTON, 1879-1941
    A LULLABY; "I'll set you aswing" e 276 words by C. O'Byrne   1541
    MY LAGEN LOVE; "Where Lagan stream sings lullaby" e 273 words by S. MacCathmhaoil   1542
    THE OULD LAD; "I mind meself a wee boy wi' no plain talk" e 344 words by M. O'Neill   1543
    SCYTHE SONG; "She wakened in the early morn of June" e 344 words by R. Stephens   1544
    SEA WRACK; "The wrack was dark an' shiny" e 274 words by M. O'Neill   1545
    [SIX SONGS OF IRELAND, song cycle; OP.18] GRACE FOR LIGHT; "When we were   1546
      little childer we had a quare wee house" e 344 words by M. O'Neill
HASSE, GUSTAV, 1834-1889
    DIE VESPER-HYMNE, op.6, no.8; "Horch! Die Vesperhymne wallet"; THE VESPER-HYMN; "Hark!   1547
      the Vesper hymn is stealing" e, g 240 words by T. Moore
HASSE, JOHANN ADOLF, 1699-1783
    [EURISTEO, opera; words by A. Zeno] ARIE DE ISMENE; "La tua virtù mi dice";   1548
      "Deine Tugend sagt mir" g, i 218
    VOI CHE CREDETE; "Voi che credete ai pianti"; "You who believe in the tears" e, i 134   1549
HASSLER, HANS LEO, 1564-1612
    [HERLICH THUT MICH VERLANGEN] BEFIEHL DU DEINE WEGE; "Befiehl du deine   1550
      Wege und was dein Herze kränkt" g 326 words by P. Gerhardt; THE WHOLE WIDE WORLD
      AROUND; "Because all men are brothers" e 293 words by T. Glazer
HASTINGS, THOMAS, 1784-1872
    ROCK OF AGES; "Rock of ages, cleft for me" e 35,236,346 words by A. M. Toplady   1551
HATTON, JOHN LIPTROTT, 1809-1886
    THE ENCHANTRESS; "By the lore of ages far" e 274 words by H. F. Chorley   1552

HATTON, JOHN LIPTROTT, 1809-1886 (Continued)

    GOODBYE SWEETHEART, GOODBYE; "The bright stars fade, the morn is breaking" e 132   1553

    "O GOD, BENEATH THY GUIDING HAND" e 28,236,279,366 words by L. Bacon   1554

    TO ANTHEA; "Bid me to live, and I will live thy protestant to be" e 272 words by R. Herrick   1555

HAUSER, SAMUEL

    OLD SHIP OF ZION. See 7883A

HAUSMAN, RUTH L.

    SUFFER THE LITTLE CHILDREN; "And they brought young children to him" e 123 words from Mark   1556
        X:13-16

HAWEIS, THOMAS

    HARK THE GLAD SOUND; "Hark the glad sound! The Savior comes" e 296 words by P. Doddridge   1557

HAWES, BALDWIN

    ARTHRITIS BLUES; "Well, I went to the doctor"; "All kinds of trouble will find you some day" (ref)   1558
    e 336

Hawthorne, Alice, pseud. See WINNER, SEPTIMUS, 1827-1902

HAYDN, JOSEPH, 1732-1809

    AN DIE FREUNDSCHAFT; "In stiller Wehmuth"; TO FRIENDSHIP; "In pensive musing" e, g 210   1559

    "BIND' AUF DEIN HAAR"; "MY MOTHER BIDS ME BIND MY HAIR" e, g 122,275,329,386   1560

    DER GLEICHSINN; "Sollt ich voller Sorg und Pein um ein schönes Mädchen sein?" g 226 words by   1561
        J. J. Eschenburg

    GLORIA IN EXCELSIS; "Gloria, gloria in excelsis" 3 pt round e 343   1562

    GOTT ERHALTE FRANZ DEN KAISER; THE EMPEROR'S HYMN, no words setting in Kaiser quartet,   1563
        op.76, no.3 g 294; DEUTSCHLAND ÜBER ALLES; "Deutschland, Deutschland, über alles" g 294;
        "DEUTSCHLAND, DEUTSCHLAND ÜBER ALLES" g 42,326,353; DAS DEUTSCHLANDLIED e 49;
        DAS LIED ALLER DEUTSCHEN words by H. A. H. von Fallersleben g 31; "PRAISE THE LORD! YE
        HEAVENS ADORE HIM" e 199

    HARK! WHAT I TELL TO THEE; THE SPIRIT'S SONG; "Hark! Hark! what I tell to thee" e 274   1564

    DIE LANDLUST; "Entfernt von Gram und Sorgen erwach ich jeden Morgen" g 96,229; IN THE   1565
        COUNTRY; "Away from care and sorrow, I gladly greet the morrow" e, g 209

    DAS LEBEN IST EIN TRAUM; "Das Leben, das Leben, ist ein Traum!" g 226 words by J. W. L. Gleim   1566

    "DIE LIEBE MAIENZEIT HAT TANZ UND SPIEL BEREIT" 4 pt round g 326   1567

    "LIEBES MÄDCHEN, HÖR' MIR ZU" g 226; LOVELY MAIDEN, HEAR ME, LO; "Lovely maiden,   1568
        softly, lo" e, g 36; SERENADE; "Dearest maiden, hear me now" e, g 210

    LOB DER FAULHEIT; "Faulheit, endlich muss ich dir auch ein kleines Loblied singen" g 250 words   1569
        by G. E. Lessing

    [NIGHTINGALE CANON] CHRISTMAS EVE CANON; "All good children now are sleeping"   1570
        3 pt round e 337

    NOW THE DANCING SUNBEAMS PLAY; THE MERMAID'S SONG; "Now the dancing sunbeams play   1571
        on the green and grassy sea" e 275

    O WORSHIP THE KING; "O worship the King all glorious above" e 28,366 words by R. Grant   1572

    [OB ICH MORGEN LEBEN WERDE] "WILL I GET A CHRISTMAS PRESENT?" 4 pt round   1573
        e 337

    [DIE SCHÖPFUNG, oratorio] IN THE BEGINNING, no.1; "In the beginning God created   1574
        the heav'n and the earth" e 160

    [Ibid] REZITATIV UND ARIE DES GABRIEL, no.7; "Und Gott sprach: Es bringe die Erde Gras   1575
        hervor" (recit); "Nun beut die Flur das frische Grün dem Auge zur Ergötzung dar" (aria) g 311

    [Ibid] "THE SPACIOUS FIRMAMENT ON HIGH", no.13 e 28,343 words by J. Addison;   1576
        OH REALM OF LIGHT; "Oh realm of light! whose morning star" e 28 words by E. H. Miller

    EIN SEHR GEWÖHNLICHE GESCHICHTE; "Philint stand jüngst vor"; A VERY COMMONPLACE STORY;   1577
        "To Babet's door, Philint came near" e, g 405 words by C. F. Weisse

    "SHE NEVER TOLD HER LOVE" e 348 words by W. Shakespeare, Twelfth Night   1578

    SINGING IN THE RAIN; "Where the elm-tree branches" e 28 words by E. A. Allen   1579

    [TOBIAS HEIMKEHR, oratorio] REZITATIV UND ARIE DER SARA; "Lasst tiefsten Dank   1580
        dir sagen, ewiger, güt'ger Gott!" (recit); "Wohl aufgenommen im Haus des Gatten" (aria) g 308

    TOD IST EIN LANGER SCHLAF] LULLY, LULLAY; "Lully, lullay, lullay. O sisters too,   1581
        how may we do" 4 pt round e 337 words by R. Croo

HAYDN, MICHAEL, 1737-1806

    DIE SELIGKEIT DER LIEBE; "Beglückt durch dich, beglückt durch mich" g 308 words by Herrosee   1582

HAYES, DR.

    'TIS CHRISTMAS TIME; "'Tis Christmas time, the gladsome chime" 3 pt round e 319   1583

HAYES, PHILIP, 1738-1797

    GENTLY FLOW; "Gently flow, o lovely stream" 3 pt round e 199 words by F. B. Wood   1584

HAYES, WILLIAM, 1705-1777

    CHAIRS TO MEND; "Chairs to mend, old chairs to mend" 3 pt round e 235,343,349; LONDON CRIES   1585
        e 402

    THE ROSE'S AGE "The rose's age is but a day" 4 pt round e 235   1586

HAYES, WILLIAM, 1705-1777 (Continued)

THE SPRING; "The spring is come, I hear the birds that sing from bush to bush" 3 pt round e 28,279,   1587
366

WIND, GENTLE EVERGREEN; "Wind, gentle evergreen, to form a shade" 3 pt round e 235,349   1588

HAYS, LEE

LONESOME TRAVELER; "Trav'lin', trav'lin', I've been a-travelin' on"; "I am a lonely and a   1589
lonesome traveler" (ref) e 389

LOUSY DIME; "Well, I went down to the bank" e 389   1590

HAYS, WILLIAM SHAKESPEARE, 1837-1907

KEEP IN DE MIDDLE OF DE ROAD; "I hear dem angels callin' loud" e 185; KEEP IN DE MIDDLE   1591
OB DE ROAD; "I hear dem angels a callin' loud" e 10; KEEP IN THE MIDDLE OF THE ROAD;
"I hear them angels a-calling loud" e 343

MOLLIE DARLING; "Won't you tell me, Mollie darling"; "Mollie, fairest, sweetest, dearest" (ref)   1592
e 129,130

MY BOY ACROSS THE SEA; "'Twas a sad, sad hour of parting"; "Oh! I know he dreams of loved   1593
ones" (ref) e 205

SUSAN JANE; "I went to see my Susan" e 185   1594

THE TURNPIKE GATE; "O! I think of the days, when but a little child"; "O! the turnpike gate,   1595
'Tis the pride of my heart" (ref) e 189

"WE PARTED BY THE RIVER SIDE"; "Tell me that you love me yet" (ref) e 129,130,205   1596

HEAD, MICHAEL DEWAR, 1900-

A GREEN CORNFIELD; "The earth was green, the sky was blue" e 344 words by C. Rossetti   1597

MONEY, O!; "When I had money, money, O!" e 273 words by W. H. Davies   1598

THE SINGER; "I met a singer on the hill" e 276 words by B. Taylor   1599

HEANEY, PATRICK

THE SOLDIER'S SONG; "We'll sing a song, a soldier's song" e 172,294 words by P. Kearney   1600

HEATH, L.

THE SNOW STORM; "The cold wind swept the mountain's height" e 189 words by S. Smith   1601

HECKER, JOHANN MATTHIAS

O AKADEMIA; "Ich zog, ich zog zur Munsenstadt" g 31   1602

HEDWIG, JOHANN, 1802-1849

SIEGENBÜRGISCHE VOLKSHYMNE; "Siebenbürgen, Land des Segens" g 31 words by M. Moltke   1603

HEFFERMAN, I.

WATCHMAN'S SONG; "Hark! ye neighbors, and hear me tell" e 210   1604

HEILNER, IRWIN, 1908-

THE TIDE RISES; "The tide rises, the tide falls" e 85 words by H. W. Longfellow   1605

HEINRICH, ANTON PHILIPP, 1781-1861

THE MUSICAL BACHELOR; "I would not wed the finest lass that ever sway'd on beauty's throne"   1606
e 129

HEINZE, RICHARD

"A TROTZIGES DIRNDEL," op.164 g 353   1607

HEISE, PETER ARNOLD, 1830-1879

[DROT OG MARSK, opera] MENUET; MINUET piano 87   1608

HUSKER DU I HOEST; "Husker du i Hoest, da vi hjemad fra Marken gik"; LITTLE KAREN; "D'you   1609
recall, in autumn, when home from the fair we went" da, e 36

JYLLAND; "Jylland mellem tvende Have"; JUTLAND; "Jutland 'twixt two oceans stoutly" da, e 87   1610
words by H. C. Andersen

HEISER, WILHELM, 1816-1897

"ICH WAND'RE IN DIE WEITE WELT," op.409; GRÜSST MIR DAS BLONDE KIND AM RHEIN g 353   1611
words by H. Mertens

HELDER, BARTHOLOMÄUS, 1585-1635

[DER HER IST MEIN GETREUER HIRT] "THE LORD MY SHEPHERD IS" e 50 words from   1612
Psalm XXIII, setting by P. Bunjes

Helf, Fred J. See HELF, J. FRED

HELF, J. FRED

AIN'T YOU COMING BACK TO OLD NEW HAMPSHIRE, MOLLY; "I am writing to you, Molly while   1613
the fair moon softly shines" e 246 words by R. F. Roden

A PICTURE NO ARTIST CAN PAINT; "A quaint New England homestead where a gray haired couple   1614
dwell"; "Picture a home in New England town" (ref) e 130,131 (ref only) e 129

HELM, EVERETT BURTON, 1913-

PRAIRIE WATERS BY NIGHT; "Chatter of birds two by two raises a night song joining a litany of   1615
running water" e 358 words by C. Sandburg

HEMBERGER, THEO

WEINET NICHT ÜBER MICH, WEINET ÜBER EUCH, op.33; "Weint nicht über Jesu Schmerzen";   1616
WEEP NOT FOR ME, BUT WEEP FOR YOURSELVES; "Wherefore weep we over Jesus" e, g 8
words by C. J. P. Spitta and R. Massie

HEMPEL, LUDWIG
 FEUERLIED; "Aus Feuer ist der Geist geschaffen" g 99 words by E. M. Arndt 1617
HEMY, HENRI FREDERICK, 1818-1888
 "FAITH OF OUR FATHERS"; St. Catherine (tune) e 28,236,279,346,366 words by F. W. Faber 1618
HENDERSON, RAY, 1896-
 BLACK BOTTOM; "Oh, the black bottom of the Swanee River"; "They call it Black Bottom a new 1619
  twister" (ref) e 345 words by B. G. de Sylva and L. Brown
 "I'M SITTING ON TOP OF THE WORLD" e 129,130 words by S. M. Lewis and J. Young 1620
 JUST A MEMORY; "You are gone and all is gone, and through each weary day"; "Days I knew with 1621
  you, are just a memory" (ref) e 345 words by B. G. de Sylva and L. Brown
 LUCKY DAY; "Night time, day time I used to be blue"; "Oh, boy! I'm lucky! I'll say, I'm lucky!" 1622
  (ref) e 345 words by B. G. de Sylva and L. Brown
HENDRICKSON, W. D.
 THE SPANISH CAVALIER; "The Spanish cavalier stood in his retreat"; "On, say, darling, say when 1623
  I'm far away" (ref) e 28,129,130,131,132,233,366
HENRIQUES, FINI
 CANTA; DAGEN ER OMME; "Dagen er omme, Klokkerne ringe den synkende Sol i Ro"; DAY NOW 1624
  IS OVER; "Day now is over, church bells are ringing and sunset and peace bless our earth anew"
  da, e 87 words by C. Ewald
HENRY VIII, KING OF ENGLAND, 1491-1547
 GREEN GROW'TH THE HOLLY. See 8937
HENSCHEL, SIR GEORGE, 1850-1934
 KEIN FEUER, KEINE KOHLE, op.4, no.1; "Kein Feuer, keine Kohle kann brennen so heiss"; NO 1625
  EMBERS, NOR A FIRE BRAND; "No embers, nor a firebrand so fiercely can glow" e, g 137
 THE LORD'S PRAYER; "And he said unto them: When ye pray" e 160 words from Bible 1626
 MORNING HYMN, op.46, no.1; "Soon night will pass, through field and grass" e 346 words by 1627
  R. Reinick
 SPRING; "Spring, sweet spring is the year's pleasant King" e 276 words by T. Nashe 1628
HENSEL, WALTHER, pseud., 1887-1956
 "GEH AUS, MEIN HERZ" g 49 words by P. Gerhardt 1629
 "JETZT GEHT ES IN DIE WELT" g 49 1630
HERBERT, J. B.
 LUTHER'S CRADLE HYMN; AWAY IN A MANGER; "Away in a manger, no crib for His bed" e 28,366 1631
HERIG, C. G.
 MORGEN, KINDER, WIRDS WAS GEBEN. See 9171A
HERING, KARL FRIEDRICH AUGUST, 1819-1889
 KURFÜRST FRIEDRICH; "Wütend wälzt sich einst im Bette Kurfürst Friedrich von der Pfalz" g 31 1632
  words by A. Schuster 1860-
 RODENSTEINS AUSZUG; "Es regt sich was im Oderwald" g 31 words by J. V. Scheffel 1633
HERING, KARL GOTTLIEB, 1765-1853
 C-A-F-F-E-E; "C-a-f-f-e-e trink nicht so viel" 3 pt round g 42 1634
 DAS STECKENPFERD; "Hopp, hopp, hopp! Pferdchen, lauf Galopp" g 99 words by C. Hahn; HOP, 1635
  HOP, HOP!; "Hop, hop, hop! nimble as a top" e 28,366
HERMANN, NIKOLAUS, 1480-1561
 "LOBT GOTT, IHR CHRISTEN, ALLE GLEICH"; g 49; JOY TO THE WORLD; "Joy to the world, the 1636
  Lord is come" e 361 words by J. Sylvester
HERNÁNDEZ, JULIO ALBERTO, 1900-
 CAMINITO DE TU CASA; "Le pido a Dios que me diga" s 284,303 1637
 POR TI SOLA; "Por ti muero de amor, Por ti sola suspiro" s 303 1638
HERRERO, R. J.
 THE GAL WITH THE BALMORAL; "As I was walking down the street, I met my charming Kate" e 225 1639
  words by F. Wilson
HESELTINE, PHILIP, 1894-1930
 AS EVER I SAW; "She is gentle and also wise" e 277 1640
 BALULALOW; A CRADLE SONG; "O my deir hert, young Jesus sweit" e 307 1641
 WALKING THE WOODS; "I would I were Actaeon whom Diana did disguise" e 272 1642
HESS, CHARLES
 "LITTLE CHARLEY WENT A FISHING" e 189 1643
HEWITT, JOHN HILL, 1801-1890
 ALL QUIET ON THE POTOMAC; "All quiet along the Potomac tonight" e 109,110; ALL QUIET 1644
  ALONG THE POTOMAC e 161 words by L. Fontaine
 THE ATTACHE; "Oh! where is my lover, tell me I pray?" e 189 1645
 AUNT HARRIETT BECHA STOWE; "I went to New York City a month or two ago" e 189 1646
 THE KNIGHT OF THE RAVEN BLACK PLUME; "A lady sat mute in her bow'r" e 129 1647
 ROCK ME TO SLEEP, MOTHER!; "Backward, still backward, oh time, in your flight" e 212; 1648
  "Backward, turn backward, Oh! time in your flight" e 161 words by E. A. C. A. Allen

HEWITT, JOHN HILL, 1801-1890 (Continued)
    SOMEBODY'S DARLING; "Into the ward of the clean white wash'd halls" e 161   words by M. R.   1649
      de la Coste
    "YOU ARE GOING TO THE WARS, WILLIE BOY" e 161   1650
    THE YOUNG VOLUNTEER; "Our flag is unfurl'd, and our arms flash bright" e 161   1651
HILDACH, EUGEN, 1849-1924
    LENZ; "Die Finken schlagen, der Lenz ist da" g 328   1652
HILL, MILDRED
    "GOOD MORNING TO YOU" e 28   words by P. S. Hill   1653
HILL, WILHELM, 1838-1902
    DAS HERZ AM RHEIN; "Es liegt eine Krone im grünen Rhein" g 31,327   words by H. Dippel   1654
HILL, WILLIAM H.
    "THERE IS A TAVERN IN THE TOWN" e 36,236,366   1655
HILLER, FERDINAND, 1811-1885
    GEBET, op.46, no.1; "Herr! den ich tief im Herzen trage"; BE NEAR ME STILL; "Lord! in my   1656
      heart's love deep I hide Thee" e, g 123
HILTON, JOHN, 1599-1657
    AS FLORA SLEPT; "As Flora slept, and I lay waking, I smil'd" e 196   1657
    COME FOLLOW ME; "Come, follow, follow, follow, follow" 3 pt round e 235,349   1658
    "COME, LET US ALL A-MAYING GO" 3 pt round e 235   1659
HIMMEL, FRIEDRICH HEINRICH, 1765-1814
    DER BETTELVOGT; "Ich war noch so jung und was doch schon arm" g 31   1660
    EWIGER WECHSEL; "Es kann ja nicht immer so bleiben" g 99   words by A. von Kotzebue   1661
    GEBET WÄHREND DER SCHLACHT; "Vater, ich rufe dich" g 43   1662
    MIGNON; "Connais-tu le pays où fleur-it l'oranger?" f 88   1663
    DER ROSE SENDUNG; "An Alexis send ich dich" g 99   words by C. A. Tiedge   1664
HINDEMITH, PAUL, 1895-
    "AUF DER TREPPE SITZEN MEINE ÖHRCHEN," op.18, no.4 g 250   words by C. Morgenstern   1665
    [DAS MARIENLEBEN, song cycle; words by R. M. Rilke] STILLUNG MARIÄ   1666
      MIT DEM AUFERSTANDENEN; "Was sie damals empfanden" g 98
HIRSH, A. M.
    YALE BOOLA; "Away, way down on the old Swanee"; "Boola, boola, boola, boola" (ref) e 128;   1667
      (ref only) e 236
HOBBS, JOHN WILLIAM, 1779-1877
    "PHYLLIS IS MY ONLY JOY" e 397   words by C. Sedley   1668
HÖCHLE, E.
    VON DER TRUNKENEN ROTT; "Frisch frölich wend wir singen" g 156   words by R. Manuel   1669
HOFFMEISTER, LEON ABBOTT
    ARISE, O LORD; "Arise, O Lord, let not man prevail" e 123   words from Bible   1670
    BECAUSE OF THY GREAT BOUNTY; "Because I have been given much" e 123   words by G. N.   1671
      Crowell
    BEHOLD, THE TABERNACLE OF GOD; "And I heard a great voice" e 200   1672
HOFMAN, E.
    "GLÜCKLICH BLÜHE UNSER LAND" 4 pt round g 326   1673
HOFMANN, OSKAR
    DIE STADT DER LIEDER; "Jedem Wiener glänzt das Auge" g 396   1674
HOFTON, SCHILHERS
    DAS MURTENLIED DES MATTIAS ZOLLER; "Gott Vater in der Ewigkeit, gelobet sigst in der Gottheit"   1675
      g 157
HOGREBE, KARL, 1877-1953
    IN DER SCHENKE; "Nicht auf den Schülerbänken" g 31   words by H. Leuthold   1676
HOGUE, PAUL
    BE STILL AND LISTEN; "Sometimes I feel so lonely" e 76   1677
    RESTITUTION; "Oh, Restitution, Restitution, it's a great, great doctrine like the Constitution"   1678
      e 76
HOLDEN, ALBERT JUNOS
    O SALUTARIS HOSTIA; "O salutaris hostia. Quae caeli pandis ostium"; SOUL OF MY SAVIOR; "Soul   1679
      of my Savior sanctify my breast" e, lat 304
HOLDEN, OLIVER, 1765-1844
    OLD CORONATION; "All hail the power of Jesus' name; e 35   words by E. Perronet   1680
HOLDER, J. W.
    "O GIN I WERE A BARON'S HEIR" e 100   1681
HOLLAND, FRED
    OH, JOY UPON THE EARTH; "Oh, joy upon this earth to live and see the day" 3 pt round e 293   1682
      words by C. Sands

HOLLOWAY, JOHN
    WOOD UP QUICK STEP, piano 212   1683
HOLMES, HENRY J. E., 1839-1905
    "GOD OF THE EARTH, THE SKY, THE SEA"; Pater omnium (tune); "We give thee thanks, thy name   1684
        we sing" (ref) e 28,366   words by H. W. Longfellow
HOLST, GUSTAV, 1874-1934
    IN THE BLEAK MID-WINTER; "In the bleak mid-winter frosty wind made moan" e 305,307 words by 1685
        C. Rossetti
    INDRA; "Noblest of songs for the noblest of gods!" e 358 words from Hymn from the Rig Veda   1686
    LULLAY MY LIKING; "Lullay my liking, my dear son, my sweeting" e 307   1687
    [THE PLANETS. JUPITER] I VOW TO THEE, MY COUNTRY; "I vow to thee, my country,   1688
        all earthly things above" e 306 words by C. Spring-Rice
HOMER, SIDNEY, 1864-1953
    DOWN BYE STREET; "Down Bye Street, in a little Shropshire town" e 259 words by J. Masefield   1689
    REQUIEM, Op. 15, no. 2; "Under the wide and starry sky" e 45 words by R. L. Stevenson   1690
HOOK, JAMES, 1746-1827
    DOUN THE BURN; "When trees did bud, and fields were green"; "Gang doun the burn Davie, lad"   1691
        (ref) e 100,103 words by R. Crawford
    THE LASS OF RICHMOND HILL; "On Richmond Hill there lives a lass" e 14,234,349,402 words by   1692
        L. MacNally
    "'TWAS WITHIN A MILE O' EDINBURGH TOWN" e 163   1693
HOPKINS, A. A.
    SILVER BELL WALTZ, piano 212   1694
HOPKINS, JOHN HENRY, 1820-1891
    "GATHER AROUND THE CHRISTMAS TREE" e 79,296   1695
    "WE THREE KINGS OF ORIENT ARE" e 28,33,38,39,79,125,165,206,251,296,305,307,315,333   1696
        337,366,388; KINGS OF ORIENT e 271,334; THREE KINGS OF ORIENT e 349,410; WE THREE
        KINGS e 34
HOPKINSON, FRANCIS, 1737-1791
    "BENEATH A WEEPING WILLOW'S SHADE" e 279,348   1697
    ENRAPTURED I GAZE; "Enraptured I gaze, when my Delia, is by" e 34,129,130,279   1698
    THE GARLAND; "The pride of ev'ry grove" e 36   1699
    "MY DAYS HAVE BEEN SO WONDROUS FREE" e 109,110,129,130,145,173,279,405   1700
    "MY LOVE IS GONE TO SEA" e 36   1701
HORN, CHARLES EDWARD, 1786-1849
    CHERRY RIPE; "Cherry ripe, cherry ripe, ripe I cry" e 215,349,385   1702
    "I'VE BEEN ROAMING" e 348 words by G. Soane   1703
HORNEMAN, CHRISTIAN FREDERIK EMIL, 1840-1906
    KONGERNES KONGE; "Kongernes Konge! ene du kan"; KING OF ALL RULERS; "King of all rulers   1704
        Thy mighty hand" da, e 87 words by A. Recke
HORNIG, ALEX
    VOGERL, FLIAGST IN D'WELT HINAUS!; "'s arme Mutterl grämt sich hamlich ab" g 396 words by   1705
        J. Hornig
HORROCKS, AMY ELISE
    THE BIRD AND THE ROSE; "A rose that bloom'd in a desert land" e 385 words by S. Hichens   1706
HORSMAN, EDWARD, 1873-1918
    BIRD OF THE WILDERNESS; "My heart, the bird of the wilderness" e 259 words by R. Tagore   1707
HORTENSE, CONSORT OF LOUIS, KING OF HOLLAND, 1783-1837, supposed composer
    "PARTANT POUR LA SYRIE" f 88; THE SOLDIER'S FAREWELL, OR THE SOUTH SHALL YET BE FREE;   1708
        "The bugle sounds upon the plain" adapted by J. H. Hewitt e 161
HOSCHNA, KARL, 1877-1911
    [MADAME SHERRY, opera; words by O. A. Hauerbach] THE BIRTH OF PASSION;   1709
        "He kissed, he kissed, he kissed her!" e 237
HOSMER, ELMER SAMUEL, 1862-1945
    "OH! GIVE ME A HOME BY THE SEA" e 205   1710
HOWARD, FRANK, 1833-?
    WHEN THE ROBINS NEST AGAIN; "I will return he said to me"; "When the robins nest again" (ref)   1711
        e 114,204 (ref only) e 129,130,131,132
HOWARD, JOSEPH EDGAR, 1878-
    HELLO! MA BABY; "I'se got a little baby but she's out of sight"; "Hello! Ma baby, Hello! ma honey"   1712
        (ref) e 131 (ref only) e 128,129,130 joint composer I. Emerson
    I WONDER WHO'S KISSING HER NOW? "You have loved lots of girls" e 34 words by W. M. Hough   1713
        and F. R. Adams
    ON A SATURDAY NIGHT; "There's a time when we all feel gay"; "On a Saturday night" (ref)   1714
        e 114,131,204 (ref only) e 128,129,130

HOWARD, ROWLAND
  YOU NEVER MISS THE WATER TILL THE WELL RUNS DRY; "When a child I lived at Lindoln with my   1715
    parents at the farm"; "Waste not want not is the maxim I would teach" (ref) e 114,131,204 words
    by H. Linn
HOWE, MARY CARLISLE, 1882-
  LET US WALK IN THE WHITE SNOW; VELVET SHOES; "Let us walk in the white snow in a soundless   1716
    space" e 358 words by E. Wylie
HOWELL, CHARLES T.
  BY THE WATERS OF BABYLON; "By the waters of Babylon we sat down and wept" e 398   1717
HOWELLS, HERBERT NORMAN, 1892-
  GIRLS' SONG; "I saw three black pigs riding" e 275 words by W. W. Gibson   1718
  "HERE IS THE LITTLE DOOR" e 307 words by F. Chesterton   1719
  O, MY DEIR HERT; CRADLE SONG; "O, my deir hert, young Jesus sweit" e 274   1720
  A SPOTLESS ROSE; "A spotless Rose is blowing" e 307   1721
HSÜCH-AN, LIO
  SONG OF THE GREAT WALL; "Great Wall, stretching mile on mile" e 35   1722
HUBAY, JENÖ, 1858-1937
  MINEK TURBÉKOLTOK; "Minek turbékoltok, búgó vadgalambok?"; TELL ME WHY YOU'RE AL-   1723
    WAYS COOING; "Tell me why you're always cooing pretty white dove" e, hu 285
HUBBARD, JAMES M.
  ['TWAS OFF THE BLUE CANARIES, OR MY LAST CIGAR, attr to J. Payne]   1724
    MY LAST CIGAR; "'Twas off the blue Canary Isles"; "It was my last cigar" (ref) e 205,279,366
HUBER, FERDINAND FÜRCHTEGOTT, 1791-1863
  FEUERLIED; "Vaterland, höre! Wir rufen's hinaus in die Welt" e 31 words by P. Kaiser   1725
HÜE, GEORGES-ADOLPHE, 1858-1948
  À DES OISEAUX; "Bonjour, bonjour, les fauvettes"; TO THE BIRDS; "Good morning, good morning,   1726
    warblers" e, f 191; "Fair good morning, pretty warblers" e 211 words by E. Adenis
  "LES CLOCHETTES DES MUGUETS"; "THE LITTLE BELLS OF THE LILIES OF THE VALLEY" e 191,   1727
    193,195 words by J. Bénédict
  "J'AI PLEURÉ EN RÊVE"; "I WEPT, BELOVED, AS I DREAMED" e, f 121; I HAVE WEPT IN MY   1728
    DREAM; "I wept in my dream" e, f 191,193,195 words by G. de Nerval
HUERTER, CHARLES, 1885-
  PIRATE DREAMS; "The old rocking chair is baby's boat" e 241 words, 2nd verse by L. A. Garnett   1729
HUGHES, HERBERT, 1882-1937
  [SONGS FROM CONNACHT, song cycle] "O MEN FROM THE FIELDS"; A CRADLE   1730
    SONG e 344 words by P. Colum
HUHN, BRUNO, 1871-1950
  "THE LORD IS MY STRENGTH" e 200 words from Bible   1731
HULLAH, JOHN PYKE, 1812-1884
  "THREE FISHERS WENT SAILING" e 205 words by C. Kingsley   1732
HUME, ALEXANDER, 1811-1859
  FLOW GENTLY, SWEET AFTON; "Flow gently, sweet Afton, among thy green braes" e 35,132,336;   1733
    "Flow gently, sweet Afton, amang thy green braes" e 28,233,279,366 words by R. Burns; AWAY
    IN A MANGER; LUTHER'S CAROL; "Away in a manger, no crib for His bed" e 38,39,125 att to
    J. E. Spilman
HUME, TOBIAS, d 1645
  "FAIN WOULD I CHANGE THAT NOTE" e 118,144,196   1734
  TOBACCO; "Tobacco, tobacco, sing sweetly for tobacco"; e 273 TOBACCO IS LIKE LOVE e 144   1735
HUMPERDINCK, ENGELBERT, 1854-1921
  [HÄNSEL UND GRETEL, opera; words by A. Wette] ABENDSEGEN; "Abends, will   1736
    ich schlafen gehn" g 96,328; EVENING PRAYER; "While tonight I fall asleep" e 346; "When at
    night I go to sleep" e, g 236,237
HUNT, G. W.
  UP IN A BALOON. See 1037
HUNTLEY, W. A.
  "SOME DAY I'LL WANDER BACK AGAIN"; "I'll wander back" (ref) e 114   1737
HURLEBUSCH, KONRAD FRIEDRICH, 1696-1765
  LOB DER UNEMPFINDLICHKEIT; "Bemüht euch immer, wie ihr wollt" g 250 words by Hofmann-   1738
    swaldau
HUTCHINSON, A. B., 1823-1884
  LITTLE TOPSY'S SONG; "Topsy neber was born, neber had a moder" e 189 words by E. Cook   1739
HUTCHINSON, JUDSON, fl 1865
  GO CALL THE DOCTOR, & BE QUICK, OR ANTI-CALOMEL; "Physicians of the highest rank" e 189   1740
HUTCHINSON, W. M.
  DREAM FACES; "The shadows lie across the dim old room"; "Sweet, dreamland faces, passing to and   1741
    fro" (ref) e 129,130,132

HUTCHINSON FAMILY
        EXCELSIOR; "The shades of night were falling fast" e 189   words by H. W. Longfellow   1742
HUYGENS, CONSTANTIJN, HERR VAN ZUILICHEM, 1596-1687
        ARIA; "Quel neo, quel vago neo, Che fa d'aurate fila ombra vezzosa" i 278   words by G. Marino   1743

IGNACIO, RAFAEL, 1897-
        VIRONAY; ASI ES COMO SE BAILA; "Pongan atención senõres a lo que voy a explicár"; "Your   1744
           attention, please, senõres listen well while I explain" e, s 303
ILSLEY, E. CLARKE
        THE SOLDIERS SUIT OF GREY!; "I've seen some handsome uniforms" e 161   words by C. B. Sinclair 1745
INDIA, SIGISMONDO, D', fl 1600-1627
        MADRIGALE IN STILE RECITATIVO; "Forse vien fuor l'aurora, e queste dolci note e questi accenti" 1746
           i 278
INDY, VINCENT D', 1851-1931
        LIED MARITIME, op.43; "Au loin, dans la mer, s'éteint le soleil"; SONG OF THE SEA; "Far away, 1747
           into the sea, the sun goes down" e, f 191,193,195
        MADRIGAL, op.4; "Qui jamais fut de plus charmant visage"; "No one had ever lovelier features" 1748
           e, f 191,193,195   words by R. de Bonnières
INGLE, CHARLES
        MY OLD DUTCH; "I've got a pal, A reg'lar out an' outer"; "We've been together now for forty years" 1749
           (ref) e 131,132 (ref only) e 128
IPER,
        SINGENDE WANDERSCHAFT; "Gar fröhlich tret ich in die Welt" g 31   words by T. Körner   1750
IPPOLITOV-IVANOV, MIKHAIL MIKHAĬLOVICH, 1859-1935
        WHITE RUSSIAN LEGEND, op.66; "Feather-like the grass that profusely grows on the Steppes" e 162 1751
IRELAND, JOHN, 1879-
        THE HOLY BOY; "Lowly laid in a manger" e 337   words by H. S. Brown   1752
        I HAVE TWELVE OXEN; "I have twelve oxen that be fair and brown" e 276   1753
        NEW PRINCE, NEW POMP; "Nowell, Nowell, Nowell, sing we with mirth!" e 334   words by R.   1754
           Southwell
IRMISCHER, KARL, 1830-1880
        "MEIN HERZ IST IM HOCHLAND" g 31,326,353   words after R. Burns   1755
ISAAC, HEINRICH, 1450(ca)-1517
        "INNSBRUCK, ICH MUSS DICH LASSEN" g 31,41,49,326   words by Kaiser Maximilian?   1756
ISOUARD, NICOLO, 1775-1818
        "WE HAVE LIVED AND LOVED TOGETHER" e 129,130   words by C. Jeffery   1757
IVES, BURL, 1909-
        OLD MOBY DICK; "As I was a -walking down by the sea" e 171   1758
        PUEBLO GIRL; "In Pueblo City there lived a maid" e 171   1759
IVES, CHARLES EDWARD, 1874-1954
        WHERE THE EAGLE; "Where the eagle cannot see" e 85   words by M. P. Turnbull   1760

JACOBSON, MYRON
        CHANSON DE MARIE ANTOINETTE; "On dit que le plus fier c'est moi"; MARIE ANTOINETTE'S   1761
           SONG; "A gard'ner to the King am I" e, f 208
JACKSON, WILLIAM, 1730-1803
        STAR OF THE EAST; "Star of the East! whose beacon light" e 410   1762
JADASSOHN, SALOMON, 1831-1902
        GOD HATH MADE US ALL; "Now know ye, now know that the Lord is God" e 90   words from Bible 1763
JADIN, LOUIS EMMANUEL, 1768-1853
        LA MORT DE WERTHER; "Seul au milieu de la Nature, je veille hélas, lorsque tout dort" f 278 1764
JÄGER, WALTER
        ICH HAB' HEIMWEH NACH WIEN; "Gibt's a schönres Platzerl weit und breit" g 222   1765
JÄRNEFELT, ARMAS, 1869-
        KEHTOLAULU; "Uinu, uinu, lapsi armainen!"; BERCEUSE; "Bye-low, baby, go to sleep, my dear!" 1766
           e, fi 124   words by I. Koskimies
JAMES, JAMES
        HEN WLAD FY NHADAU; "Mae hen wlad fy nhadau yn annwyl imi"; LAND OF MY FATHERS; "Dear 1767
           land of my fathers, whose glories were told" e, w 19; "O land of my fathers, O land of my love"
           e, w 347; "Oh, land of my fathers, the land of the free" e, w 294; e 234   words by E. James
Janiczek, Julius, 1887-1956. See HENSEL, WALTHER, pseud., 1887-1956

62

JANSON, OTTO, 1868-1955
    ALT-MARBURG, WIE BIN ICH DIR GUT; "Ich habe in deutschen Gauen" g 31   1768

JAQUES-DALCROZE, ÉMILE, 1865-1950
    L'OISEAU BLEU; "Il est un tout petit oiseau qui toujours vole"; THE BLUEBIRD; "Ah, 'tis a tiny   1769
    bird which never ceases flying" e, f 208 words by A. L. Hettisch

JARNO, GEORG, 1868-1920
    [DIE FÖRSTERCHRISTEL, operetta] ICH TU NUR BÖS, BIN SONST FIDEL; "Nach meinem   1770
    Reh zu jagen, dem Herrn werd ich was sagen" g 256

JARY, MICHAEL
    "SING', NACHTIGALL, SING'" g 223 words by B. Balz   1771

JENKINS, JOHN, 1592-1678
    A BOAT, A BOAT; "A boat, a boat, haste to the ferry" 3 pt round e 235,349   1772
    "WHY SIGH'ST THOU SHEPHERD?" e 106 words by T. Randolph   1773

JENKO, DAVORIN, 1835-1914
    JUGOSLAV NATIONAL ANTHEM; "Bože pravde tišto spase"; "God of justice ever with us" e, sl 7;   1774
    combination of national hymns of Serbia, Croatia, and Slovenia words by J. Djordjevic, A.
    Mihanovic, and S. Jenko

JENSEN, ADOLF, 1837-1879
    "LEHN' DEINE WANG' AN MEINE WANG'"; "O press your cheek upon my own" e, g 36; PRESS THY   1775
    CHEEK AGAINST MINE OWN; "Oh, press thy cheek against mine own" e 137 words by H. Heine
    LETZTER WUNSCH, op. 14, no. 1; "Mein Schatz will Hochzeit halten, ich liege auf den Tod" g 226   1776
    words by W. Hertz

JENTES, HARRY
    KNIT, GIRLS, KNIT!; "Knit, girls, knit! with your needles and your cotton" e 129,130 words by   1777
    H. Johnson and H. Pease
    "PUT ON A BONNET WITH A RED CROSS ON IT" e 129,130 words by H. Johnson and H. Pease   1778

JEREMIÁŠ, JAROSLAV, 1889-1919
    PÍSEŇ NA SLOVA SHAKESPEAROVA; "Pojd'smrti, pojd'již ke mně"; LIED VON SHAKESPEARE;   1779
    "Komm, Tod, schliess' meine Lider!" c, g 73

JEROME, BEN M.
    LAM', LAM', LAM'; "A darkey heard the praises sung"; "Cow meat am good and sweet" (ref) e 114;   1780
    "A coon who heard the praises sung" e 131

JESÚS GARCIA, BELISARIO DE
    LAS CUATRO MILPAS; "Cuatro milpas ten sólo han quedado de aquel rancho que era mío, ay!" s 284;   1781
    FOUR CORN FIELDS; "These four corn fields, so lonely, remind me of the ranch I left behind me,
    Ah!" e, s 248 words by J. F. Elizondo, (att to M. Venado de Campo in collection 248); "Cuatro
    milpas tan solo ha que dado del ranchito que era mio, Ay!"; "Only four of my cornfields are left
    me of the ranch that was my glory, Ay!" e, s 322

JEWELL, LUCINA, 1874-
    IN MY FATHER'S HOUSE ARE MANY MANSIONS; "And Jesus said: Let not your heart be troubled" e   1782
    398 words from Bible

JEŽEK, JAROSLAV, 1906-1941
    AGAINST THE STORM; "Za větrem plesnivět nechcem" (verse); "Když nás pójdou milliony" (ref);   1783
    "Bowing before the storm" (verse); "We'll be marching millions of us" (ref) c, e 7 words by Vos-
    kovec and Werich
    HEY, MR. HACHA; "Bereme na potaz učené bakaláře"; "Let's ask the brilliant baccalaureates for   1784
    example" c, e 7
    V SONG; "Na vrata na zdi na veze, ha Kominy"; "In every city on wall and smoke-stack" c, e 7   1785
    words by Voskovec and Werich

JEZIORSKI, WL.
    PIEŚŃ KOŚCIUSZKI; "Tam w Szwajcarów wolnej ziemi"; SONG OF KOŚCIUSZKO; "There among   1786
    the Swiss free people" e 295 words by M. Konopnicka

JIMENEZ, MANUEL "CANARIO"
    CANTO A LA MADRE; "Le lo lai le lo"; "Yo quie ro mucho a la luna" (verse); SONG TO THE   1787
    MOTHER; "Oh I love the gleaming starlight" (verse) e, s 291
    EN TU SANTO; "Por ser hoy día de tu santo"; HAPPY BIRTHDAY; "I wish you joy on your birthday"   1788
    e 291
    MI CAMPESINA; "Las jíbaras de mi tierra esas"; MY DARLING; "The girls of my native country"   1789
    e, s 291
    LA ROCA DE LA LAGUNA; "Empieza con le lo le"; THE ROCK IN THE LAKE; "We start with a lay   1790
    lo lay" e, s 291

JIRÁK, KAREL BOLESLAV, 1891-
    CHANSON D'AMOUR, op. 11e; "Když hoch se loučil s ní"; "Als ihr Geliebter schied" c, g 73a   1791

JÖDE, FRITZ, 1887-
    "AUF DER LÜNEBURGER HAIDE"; "Valleri, vallera, und juchheirassassa" (ref) g 31 words by H.   1792
    Löns

JÖDE, FRITZ, 1887- (Continued)
    "ES STEHN DREI BIRKEN AUF DER HEIDE" g 31 words by H. Löns   1793
    ROSE-MARIE; "Rose-Marie, Rose-Marie, sieben Jahre mein Herz nach dir schrie" g 353 words by   1794
        H. Löns
    VERLOREN; "Rosmarienhaide zur Maienzeit blüht" g 31 words by H. Löns   1795
JOHNS, AL, 1878-1928
    GO 'WAY BACK AND SIT DOWN; "Old man Sam Jones he runs and owns a cafe on easy street"   1796
        e 204 words by E. Bowman
JOHNSON, HERBERT
    I'M A PILGRIM; "I'm a pilgrim, and I'm a stranger" e 123,394 words by M. S. B. Dana   1797
JOHNSON, HOWARD E., 1887-1917
    THE BEST THINGS IN LIFE ARE FREE; "You don't have to pay for a beautiful day" e 129,130 words   1798
        by W. G. Tracy
JOHNSON, JAMES P., 1894-
    CHARLESTON; "Carolina, Carolina, at last they're got you on the map"; "Charleston! Charleston!   1799
        Made in Carolina" (ref) e 345 words by C. Mack
    IF I COULD BE WITH YOU; ONE HOUR TONIGHT; "I'm so blue I don't know what to do"; "If I   1800
        could be with you I'd love you strong (ref) e 345 words by H. Creamer
JOHNSON, JOHN ROSAMOND, 1873-1954
    DE CHAIN GANG; "Gwine down dat lonesome road" e 184   1801
    FLORIDA CAKEWALK, piano 184   1802
    LAZY MOON; "Lazy moon come out soon!" e 34 words by B. Cole   1803
    LIFT EVERY VOICE AND SING; NEGRO NATIONAL ANTHEM; "Lift ev'ry voice and sing" e 293   1804
        words by J. W. Johnson
    LI'L GAL; "Oh, de weathah it is balmy" e 78,184 words by P. L. Dunbar   1805
    "MY BABY'S IN MEMPHIS, LAYIN' AROUN'" e 184   1806
    THEM LONESOME MOANIN' BLUES; "I don't know why I cry" e 184   1807
    UNDER THE BAMBOO TREE; "Down in the jungles lived a maid"; "If you lak-a-me, lak I lak-a-   1808
        you" (ref) e 32,34 words by B. Cole
JOHNSON, ROBERT, 1569-1633
    "AS I WALKT FORTH ONE SUMMER'S DAY" e 106   1809
JOMMELI, NICOLÒ, 1714-1774
    ARIETTA; LA CALANDRINA; "Chi vuol comprar la bella calandrina"; "Wer will die schöne Lerche   1810
        hier erstehen?" g, i 167
JONES, ISHAM, 1894-
    IT HAD TO BE YOU; "Why do I do just as you say" e 345 words by G. Kahn   1811
JONES, JESSE H.
    EIGHT HOURS; "We mean to make things over"; "Eight hours for work, eight hours for rest, eight   1812
        hours for what we will" (ref) e 34 words by I. G. Blanchard
JONES, RICHARD M., 1892-
    TROUBLE IN MIND; "Trouble in mind, I'm blue, but I won't be blue always" e 336   1813
JONES, ROBERT, ca1575-1617
    BEAUTY SATE BATHING; "Beauty sate bathing by a spring" e 144 words by A. Munday   1814
    DREAMES AND IMAGINATIONS; "Dreames and imaginations are all the recreations abscence can   1815
        gaine me" e 144
    "GOE TO BED SWEETE MUZE" e 144; "GO TO BED, SWEET MUSE" e 196   1816
    "IN SHERWOOD LIVED STOUT ROBIN HOOD" e 116; "IN SHERWOOD LIVDE STOUT ROBIN HOOD" 1817
        e 144
    "ITE CALDI SOSPIRI"; "What mean tears to the heartless" e, i 144   1818
    LOVE IS A BABLE; "Love, love, love, love, love is a bable" e 118,144   1819
    "LOVE'S GOD IS A BOY" e 119   1820
    NOW WHAT IS LOVE; "Now what is love I pray thee, tell?" e 117,144 words att to W. Raleigh 1821
    "SWEET IF YOU LIKE AND LOVE ME STIL" e 144 words by F. Davison   1822
    SWEET KATE; "Sweet Kate of late ran away and left me 'plaining" e 196,199; SWEETE KATE;   1823
        "Sweete Kate of late ran away and left me playning" e 144
    "THERE WAS A WYLY LADDE" e 144   1824
    "WHAT IF I SEEK FOR LOVE" e 196   1825
    WHAT IF I SPEEDE?; "What if I speede where I least expected" e 197; WHAT IF I SPED; "What if   1826
        I sped where I least expected" e 144
    "WHEN LOVE ON TIME AND MEASURE MAKES HIS GROUND" e 144 words att to J. Lilliatt   1827
    "WILL SAIDE TO HIS MAMMY" e 144   1828
JONES, SIDNEY, 1869-
    [DIE GEISHA, operetta; words by O. Hall and H. Greenbank] DER VERLIEBTE   1829
        GOLDFISH; "Fräulein Goldfisch schwamm in dem Goldfischglas wohl über den weissen Sand" g 255
JONES, WALTER HOWE
    ILLINOIS; "By thy rivers gently flowing Illinois, Illinois" e 28 words by C. H. Chamberlain   1830

JONSSON, JOSEF, 1887-
    BISP THOMAS' FRIHETSSAANG; "Frihet är det bästa ting"; "FREEDOM IS THE THING MOST DEAR"   1831
      e, sw 188
    "SOM ETT SILVERSMYCKE," op.26, no.2 sw 355   words by J. Hemmer   1832
    VID LÄGERELD, op.47, no.4; "Spejare, upp för att spana!" sw 355 words by P. Lagerkvist   1833
JUBITZ, FR. W.
    "DROBEN STEHET DIE KAPELLE" g 326   1834
JUDD, PERCY, 1892-
    THE SWING; "How do you like to go up in a swing" e 199 words by R. L. Stevenson   1835
JUDE, WILLIAM, HERBERT, 1851-1922
    "COME! YE LOFTY, COME! YE LOWLY" e 315   1836
    THE SKIPPER; "A skipper, am I, no danger can" e 240 words by F. J. Dennet   1837
JÜRGENS, FRITZ, 1888-1915
    DRAUSS IST ALLES SO PRÄCHTIG; "Drauss ist alles so prächtig und es ist mir so wohl" g 31 words   1838
      by F. Richter, 1811-1865
JUREK, WILHILM AUGUST
    DEUTSCHMEISTER-REGIMENTS-MARSCH, op.6 piano, 396   1839
    GEH' MACH DIE FENSTERL AUF; "Weil Alle gern a G'schicht woll'n hörn" g 396   1840

KABALEVSKIĬ, DMITRIĬ BORISOVICH, 1904-
    CAMPFIRE SONG; "Now the day is slowly ending" e, r 287,288 words by N. Shestalov   1841
    THE GIRL THAT WAITS FOR ME; "I see her face in the flames of the camp-fire" e 339 words by   1842
      E. Dolmatovsky
    SONG OF THE SEA; "Near the Soviet shore as the winds rush and roar" e 339 words by H. Nagaev   1843
    SPEED!; "In this new era, time moves with speed, speed, speed" e, r 162 words by S. Kirsanoff   1844
    TO HER SON; "With earnestness and dignity his mother said: 'High time, my son!'" e, r 342 words   1845
      by A. Bolaev-Kubatiev
Kabalevsky, D. See KABALEVSKIĬ, DMITRIĬ BORISOVICH, 1904-
KADAS, GYÖRGY
    "HOGYHA OLYKOR ÉJFÉLTAJBAN"; IF AT NIGHT A BAND OF GYPSIES; "I'd be happy if my music"   1846
      e, hu 285
KAHN, GRADE (LE BOY), 1891-
    I WISH I HAD A GIRL; "These days ev'ry fellow has a sweetheart"; "Gee, I wish that I had a girl like   1847
      the other fellows had" (ref) e131 (ref only) e 128,129,130,236 words by G. Kahn
Kaillmark, E. See KIALLMARK, GEORGE, 1781-1835
KAIN, JOHANN, 1820-1894
    DER SINNIERENDE NARR; "I woās nit, wie mir is, i woās nit, wie mir is" g 99   1848
KAIPER, NANCY LOU, 1911-
    CHRISTMAS HYMN; "Ring out, ring out, beneath the stars" e 251 words by D. Kaiper   1849
    OH, COME TO US, SWEET VIRGIN SAINT; "They heard the bleating of the sheep" e 251 words by   1850
      D. Kaiper
KALLSTENIUS, EDWIN, 1881-
    GUNHILD, op.15, no.3; "Du vita blom, som snöar ner paa"; "O Blütenschnee, sanft fällst du mir auf   1851
      meines Gartenweges Sand!" g, sw 355
    LUISE HENSELS BARNAFTONBÖN, op.9, no.3; "Sömnig är jag, mycket trött"; "MÜDE BIN ICH, GEH   1852
      ZUR RUH" g, sw 355
Kálmán, Emmerich. See KÁLMÁN, IMRE, 1882-1953
KÁLMÁN, IMRE, 1882-1953
    [GRÄFIN MARIZA, operetta; words by H. B. Smith] GRÜSS MIR MEIN WIEN;   1853
      "Wenn es Abend wird"; "Grüss mir die süssen" (ref) g 256
    [Ibid] KOMM, ZIGÁNY; "Auch ich war einst ein reicher Csárdáskavalier"; "Komm, Zigány,   1854
      komm Zigány, spiel mir was vor" (ref) g 256
    [DIE ZIRKUSPRINZESSIN, operetta] ZWEI MÄRCHENAUGEN; "Wieder hinaus ins strah-   1855
      lende Licht"; "Wenn man das Leben durchs Champagnerglas betrachtet" (verse) g 256
KALNIŅŠ, ALFREDS, 1879-
    AM REGENABEND; "Regne, regen, immerzu!"; UN SOIR, LORSQU'IL PLEUVAIT; "Tombe, oh,   1856
      tombe, pluie, encore" f, g 224
    IN DER HEIMAT; "Hebt sich die Sonne am Feldesrain"; DANS LE PAYS NATAL; "Brille le soleil   1857
      et les champs effleure" f, g 224
    KINDERZEIT; "Meiner Kinderzeit lichte Stunden im Nebel verlöscht und verschwunden"; LES MATINS   1858
      DE L'ENFANCE; "Le matin de l'enfance heureuse s'éteint dans lumière nebuleuse" f, g 224
KAMM, FERDINAND, 1845-1897
    HEIMKEHR, op.4, no.1; "Es war ein Knabe gezogen"; "Sommerzeit, wenn am Walle die Rosen   1859
      blühn" (ref) g 31 words by O. Roquette

KANKAROVICH, ANATOLIĬ
    IT'S SPRING!; "With straining backs, the workers wield their hammers as they sing" e, r 162   1860
        words by M. Samobitnik
KAREL, RUDOLF, 1880-1945
    CHRYSIS, op.24, no.3; "Knebesuum ráda se díváš, bĕloloktá Chrysis"; "Träumerisch schaust du   1861
        zum Himmel, o du weissarmige Chrysis" c, g 74 words by J. S. Machar
KARG-ELERT, SIGFRID, 1879-1933
    [PRAE-UND POSTLUDIEN, ORGAN, OP.78. ANTIPHONI MACH'S MIT MIR,   1862
        GOTT] "COME, FOLLOW ME, THE SAVIOUR SPAKE"; MACH'S MIT MIR, GOTT e 50
KARLOWICZ, MIECZYSLAW, 1876-1909
    "PAMIĘTAM CICHE, JASNE, ZŁOTE DNIE"; CHILDHOOD DAYS; "Oh, I recall those peaceful, golden 1863
        hours" e, p 295 words by K. Przerwa-Tetmajer
KARTZEV, ALEXANDER ALEXEYEVITCH, 1883-
    THE PARTISAN; "In the woods, the gray, old beard seems to grow a little whiter" e, r 162 words by 1864
        J. Utkin
KATSCHER, ROBERT, 1894-1942
    WHEN DAY IS DONE; "Since you've gone away one thing is clear to me"; "When day is done and   1865
        shadows fall" (ref) e 345 words by B. G. De Sylva
KATTNIGG, RUDOLF, 1895-1955
    [BALKANLIEBE, operetta; words by E. Kahr and B. Hardt-Warden] "HEIMAT,   1866
        MIT DER SEELE GRÜSS ICH DICH" g 256
    [Ibid] "LEISE ERKLINGEN GLOCKEN VON CAMPANILE" g 257   1867
    [KAISERIN KATHARINA, operetta; words by P. Berger and H. F. Beck-   1868
        mann] "EINE KAISERIN DARF KEINE LIEBE KENNEN" g 255
    [DER PRINZ VON THULE, operetta; words by O. Walleck and E. Kahr]   1869
        JUBLE, MEIN HERZ!; "Juble, mein Herz, juble mein Herz! Erfüllt ist mein glühend Verlangen"
        g 257
KATZ, FRED
    BELOVED COMRADE; "To you, beloved comrade" e 293 words by L. Allan   1870
KAY, F. L.
    "THE WISE MAY BRING THEIR LEARNING" e 378   1871
KAYSER, PHILIPP CHRISTIAN, 1755-1832
    WANDRERS NACHTLIED; "Der du von dem Himmel bist" g 42 words by J. W. von Goethe   1872
KAZURO, STANISLAW
    DALEKO, DALEKO; "Daleko, daleko, Za dworem, za borem"; FAR YONDER; "Far yonder, out   1873
        yonder, From forest's green bower" e, p 295; "DALEKO, DALEKO, ZA GÓRA, ZA RZEKĄ";
        FROM FAR AWAY COMING; "From far away coming, o'er streams and hills roaming" e, p 159
KEALOHA, YLAN K.
    ALOHA; TO THEE FOREVER; "A rainbow spans the somber sky" e 37   1874
KEATING, WILLIAM
    DOWN, DOWN, DOWN; "With your kind attention a song I will trill" e 227   1875
KEEL, FREDERICK
    "SIGH NO MORE, LADIES" e 344 words by W. Shakespeare   1876
KEISER, ROBERT A.
    HAS YOUR MOTHER ANY MORE LIKE YOU; "There is one for whom I'm sighing" e 131   1877
    THE MUSKET OR THE SWORD; "Along a city pavement while the crowd was surging by"; "One   1878
        bore a common musket" (ref) e 131 words by C. Fleming
KELLÉR, DEZSÖ
    "SZAGOS MÁLYVA, GYÖNGYVIRÁG"; "FRAGRANT MALVA, PRETTY FLOW'R" e, hu 285   1879
KELLER, LUDWIG, 1847-1930
    BIN EIN FAHRENDER GESELL; "Bin ein fahrender Gesell, kenne keine Sorgen" g 31 words by R.   1880
        Baumbach
KELLER, MATTHIAS, 1813-1875
    THE AMERICAN HYMN; "Speed our republic, O Father on high!" e 129,130,236; KELLER'S   1881
        AMERICAN HYMN e 28,279,366
KELLER, OTTO
    "I, WENN I GELD GNAUG HÄTT" g 326   1882
KELLEY, EDGAR STILLMAN, 1857-1944
    ELDORADO, op.8, no.1; "Gaily bedight, a gallant knight" e 259 words by E. A. Poe   1883
Kelley, John W. See KELLY, JOHN W.
KELLY, JOHN W.
    THROW HIM DOWN, McCLOSKEY; "'Twas down at Dan McDevitt's at the corner of this street"   1884
        e 114,115,131
KENNEDY, HARRY
    "SAY 'AU REVOIR' BUT NOT 'GOOD-BYE'" e 36,114,128,129,130,131,132,246   1885

KENT, WILLYS PECK, 1877-1957
    "WE WISH YOU A MERRY CHRISTMAS" 3 pt round e 337   1886
KEYL, HANNS, 1890-
    "MIR GLÄNZT DER TAG" g 31 words by R. Haas   1887
KHACHATURIÂN, ARAM IL'ICH, 1904-
    I'M CONSUMED BY A FLAME; "As a nut that's picked while yet its branch is green" e, r 162 words   1888
        by D. Ussov
    NINA'S SONG; "When tears becloud your eyes with sadness" e, r 342 words by M. Lermontov   1889
KHRENNIKOV, TIKHON NĂKOLAEVICH, 1913-
    SONG OF FAREWELL; "Go now, my own, my sweet, good-bye!" e 339 words by F. Kravchenko   1890
KIALLMARK, GEORGE, 1781-1835
    [ARABY'S DAUGHTER] THE OLD OAKEN BUCKET; "How dear to my heart are the scenes   1891
        of my childhood" e 28,32,34,279,366; "How dear to the heart are the scenes of my childhood"
        e 129,130,132; "How dear to this heart are the scenes of my childhood" e 233 words by S.
        Woodworth
KIENLEN, JOHANN CHRISTOPH, 1784-1830
    HEIDENRÖSLEIN; "Sah ein knab ein Röslein stehn" g 229 words by F. W. von Goethe   1892
KILLINEN, K.
    "METSÄN PUITA TUULI TUUDITTAA"; "FOREST TREES ARE SWAYING" e, fi 124   1893
KILPINEN, YRJÖ, 1892-
    [FJELDLIEDER, song cycle; op.52] LAULULLE, no.3; "Kuin tunturilla puro hiljaa"; TO   1894
        SONG; "As from the fells the brook so gently" e, fi 124 words by V. E. Törmänen
KING, CHARLES, 1687-1748
    O ABSALOM; "O Absalom, my son, my son" e 235,349; OH, ABSALOM, MY SON 3 pt round e 173   1895
KING, CHARLES M., fl 1835-1841
    "A YANKEE SHIP, AND A YANKEE CREW" e 205 words by J. S. Jones   1896
KINGSFORD, CHARLES, 1907-
    WALL-PAPER FOR A LITTLE GIRL'S ROOM; "Little fat ducks and geese" e 259 words by R. Kresensky   1897
KINKEL, JOHANNA (MOCKEL), 1810-1858
    THE SOLDIER'S FAREWELL; "Ah, love, how can I leave thee?" e 28,279,366   1898
KIRCHL, ADOLF, 1858-1936
    BANATER SCHWAGENLIED; "Es brennt ein Weh, wie Kinder tränen brennen" g 31 words by A.   1899
        Müller-Guttenbrunn
KIRKPATRICK, WILLIAM JAMES, 1838-1921
    AWAY IN A MANGER; "Away in a manger, no crib for a bed" e 305,307,410; IM STALL IN DER   1900
        KRIPPE; "Im Stall in der Krippe eine Wiege auf Streu" e, g 354
KISCO, CHARLES W., 1896-
    THE DAUGHTER OF PEGGY O'NEIL; "Ten fingers, ten toesies, as sweet as the posies" e 128 words   1901
        by H. Pease and H. Tobias
KITTEL, CASPAR, ca1610-ca1670
    "EIN JEGLICH DING HAT SEINE ZEIT" duet g 250   1902
KITTEL, JOHANN CHRISTIAN, 1732-1809
    "O FATHER, SON, AND HOLY GHOST" e 50 words by G. Anderson   1903
KITTREDGE, WALTER, 1834-1905
    TENTING ON THE OLD CAMP GROUND; "We are tenting on the old Camp Ground"; "Many are the   1904
        hearts that are weary tonight" (ref) e 10; "We're tenting tonight on the old Camp Ground" e 28,
        279,366; TENTING TONIGHT e 32,34,109,110; WE'RE TENTING TO-NIGHT e 129,130
KJERULF, HALFDAN, 1815-1868
    "LAST NIGHT THE NIGHTINGALE WOKE ME" e 28,366; LAST NIGHT e 132,236,348,385 words   1905
        by C. Winther
KLAUER, GUSTAV, 1827-1854
    MORGENWANDERUNG; "Wer recht in Freuden wandern will" g 31; "WER RECHT IN WANDERN WILL"   1906
        g 326,353 words by E. Geibel
KLEIN, BERNHARD, 1793-1832
    MEIN VATERLAND; "Treue Liebe bis zum Grabe" g 31 words by H. H. von Fallersleben   1907
KLEINE, WERNER
    PETERLE; "Peterle, du liebes Peterle" g 223   1908
KLEINMAN, LOUIS
    THE UNION MAN; "She works selling girdles and panties" e 293   1909
KLEMETTI, HEIKKI, 1876-
    "OI KALLIS SUOMENMAA," op.41, no.3; "OH, BLESSED FATHERLAND" e, fi 124   1910
KLEMM, GUSTAV, 1897-1947
    SOUNDS; "I heard a sound in the night" e 241 words by H. J. Pearl   1911
KNAB, ARMIN, 1881-1951
    "DA JESUS CHRIST GEBOREN WARD" g 250 words by H. von Themar   1912
    VERKÜNDIGUNG; "Du tatest mir die Tür auf" g 98 words by R. Dehmel   1913

Knapp, Mrs. Joesph F. See KNAPP, PHOEBE (PALMER)
KNAPP, PHOEBE (PALMER)
      OPEN THE GATES OF THE TEMPLE; "Open, open, open the gates of the Temple" e 346,400   words   1914
         by F. Crosby
KNAUFF, GEORGE P.
      WAIT FOR THE WAGON. See 465
KNEASS, NELSON
      BEN BOLT; "Oh, don't you remember sweet Alice, Ben Bolt" e 129,130,132,173,279,366; SWEET   1915
         ALICE e 114; SWEET ALICE, BEN BOLT e 36; BEN BOLT OR OH! DON'T YOU REMEMBER e 212;
         THE SHADY OLD CAMP; "Oh don't you remember the shady old camp" e 173
KNEBELSBERGER, LEOPOLD, 1814-1869
      ANDREAS HOFER; "Zu Mantua un Banden der treue Hofer war" g 31; "In Mantua's dark prison cell,   1916
         Andreas Hofer lay" e, g 7   words by J. Mosen
KNECHT, JUSTIN HEINRICH, 1752-1817
      "WIE GROSS IST DES ALLMÄCHTGEN GÜTE" g 326   words by C. F. Gellert   1917
KNEIP, GUSTAV, 1905-
      SCHWALBENLIED; "Auf und ab, kreuz und quer"; "MUTTERL, UNTERM DACH IST EIN NESTERL   1918
         GEBAUT" g 222   words by T. Rausch
KNIGHT, JOSEPH PHILIP, 1812-1887
      "ROCKED IN THE CRADLE OF THE DEEP" e 28,129,130,205,279,346,366,394   words by E. Willard   1919
      "SAY, WHAT SHALL MY SONG BE TONIGHT?" e 129,130   1920
KNIGHT, LAUNCE
      ROSALIE; "I'm Pierre de Bonton de Paris, de Paris"; "But I care not what others may say" (ref) e 28,   1921
         366
KNIPPER, LEV KONSTANTINOVICH, 1898-
      CAVALRY OF THE STEPPES; "Onward, ride onward!" e 7   1922
      MEADOWLANDS; "Heroes are threading through meadowlands" e, r 288; "Meadowlands, meadow-   1923
         lands, through you heroes now are treading" e 35; SONG OF THE MEADOW LAND; "Daylight is
         fading, as the Cossacks start parading" e 237   words by V. Gussev; MEADOWLAND; "Meadow-
         land, meadowland, meadows green and fields in blossom" e 293
KNORR, ERNST-LOTHAR VON, 1896-
      ANBETUNG DES KINDES; "Als ein behutsam Licht stiegst" g 49   words by J. Weinheber   1924
      "DER APFEL IST NICHT GLEICH AM BAUM" g 49   words by H. Claudius   1925
      AUF DER OFENBANK; "Auf der Ofenbank in der Abendzeit" g 49   words by F. Bischoff   1926
      DIE ENTSCHWUNDENE; "Es war ein heitres goldnes Jahr" g 49   words by G. Keller   1927
      "IM WALD, IM HELLEN SONNENSCHEIN" g 49,326   words by E. Geibel   1928
      NACHHALL; "Sieh den Abendstern erblinken" g 49   words by G. Keller   1929
      REGEN-SOMMER; "Nasser Staub auf allen Wegen!" g 49   words by G. Keller   1930
      TROST DES SOMMERS; "Hingestreckt im hohen Gras" g 49   words by A. von Hatzfeld   1931
      "WAS EINER IST, WAS EINER WAR" g 49   words by H. Carossa   1932
      WIR GEHN DAHIN; "Wir gehn dahin und wissen nicht wie bald" g 49   words by H. Frank   1933
Koch, Erland von. See KOCH, SIGURD CHRISTIAN ERLAND VON, 1910-
KOCH, OTTO
      ROTE HUSAREN; "HEISS IST DIE LIEBE" g 326   words by H. Löns   1934
KOCH, RICHERT SIGURD VALDEMAR VON, 1879-1919
      PAA TEFÄLTET;"Jag ser vid horisonten silhouetten"; AM TEEFELD; "Ich seh am Horizont die   1935
         Silhouette" g, sw 355   words by Schei-Min
      DE VILDA SVANARNA; "Ack, ännu synes icke morgonljuset"; DIE WILDEN SCHWÄNE; "Noch ist   1936
         der Glanz der Frühe nicht erschienen" g, sw 355   words by Ly-Y-Han
Koch, Sigurd. See KOCH, RICHERT SIGURD VALDEMAR VON, 1879-1919
KOCH, SIGURD CHRISTIAN ERLAND VON, 1910-
      KLAR SOM GULD; "Klar som guld staar horisontens rand"; REIN WIE GOLD; "Rein wie Gold des   1937
         Horizontes Rand" g, sw 356
KOCHER, KONRAD, 1786-1872
      "AS WITH GLADNESS MEN OF OLD"; Dix (tune) e 206,233,251,296,307,315   words by W. C.   1938
         Dix; "FOR THE BEAUTY OF THE EARTH" e 28,233,343   words by F. S. Pierpont
KOECHLIN, CHARLES, 1867-1950
      L'HIVER; "Au bois de Boulogne, l'hiver"; THE WINTER; "In winter, in the Bois de Boulogne"   1939
         e, f 192,194   words by T. de Banville
      SI TU LE VEUX; "Si tu le veux, ô mon amour"; IF YOU WISH IT; "If you wish it, oh my love"   1940
         e, f 190,192,194   words by M. de Marsan
      LE THÉ; "Miss Ellen, versez moi le thé"; THE TEA; "Miss Ellen, pour the tea for me" e, f 190,   1941
         192,194   words by T. de Banville
KÖHLER, EMMY
      "NU TÄNDAS TUSEN JULELJUS"; "A THOUSAND CHRISTMAS CANDLES NOW" e, sw 188   1942

KÖHLER, SIEGFRIED
  AN DIE FREUNDE; "Wieder einmal ausgeflogen" g 49 words by T. Storm 1943
  "EINEN BRIEF SOLL ICH SCHREIBEN" g 49 words by T. Storm 1944
  DU BIST MÍN; "Du bist mín ich bin dín" g 49 1945
  HERBSTLIED; "Der Wind, der Wind, der weht!" g 49 1946
  MORGENLIED; "Nun bricht der Morgen aus der Nacht" g 49 1947
  "NUN SCHLAFEN AUCH DIE WÄLDER WEIT" g 49 1948
KOLLO, WALTER
  [MARIETTA, operetta] WAS EINE FRAU IM FRÜHLING TRÄUMT; "Einmal kommt ein Tag 1949
   für alle Frauen voll von Frühlingsfarben" g 256
KOMOROWSKI, IGNACY
  KALINA; "Rosła kalina z liściem szerokiem"; THE BARBERRY; "Pretty barberry, her wide leaves 1950
   nodding" e, p 295
  NOWA MIŁOŚĆ; "Serce, serce, skąd to bicie"; NEW LOVE; "Tell me, my heart, why this beating?" 1951
   e, p 295
Komorowski, J. See KOMOROWSKI, IGNACY
KOMPANEETS, ZINOVII
  SOVIET SEAMEN; "The churning, foaming ocean waves are rolling towards the shore" e, r 162 words 1952
   by S. Bolotin
KORCHMAREV, KLIMENTII ARKAD'EVICH, 1899-
  LULLABY; "Sleep my little son, my love" e, r 162 words by G. P. Liubimov 1953
  MATRENA AND THE DEACON; "Going in the early evening to the deacon's house" e, r 162 words 1954
   by A. Lyubovsky
Korchmaryov, Kliment. See KORCHMAREV, KLIMENTII ARKAD'EVICH, 1899-
KORNGOLD, ERIC WOLFGANG
  DAS LIED DER LIEBE. See 3613
KOSCHAT, THOMAS, 1845-1914
  FORSAKEN; "Forsaken, forsaken, forsaken am I" e 132,279 1955
  "THE LORD IS MY SHEPHERD" e 28,366 words by J. Montgomery 1956
KOTARBIŃSKI, M., 1849-1928
  W CICHY WIECZÓR, NOC MAJOWĄ; "W cichy wieczór, w noc majową"; A NIGHT IN MAY; 1957
   "Evening song is softly winging" e, p 159; NOC MAJOWĄ; "In the stillness of a May night"
   e, p 295
KOTCHETOFF, NIKOLAI RASUMNIKOWITSCH, 1864-
  TELL, O TELL HER, op.16, no.4; "Tell, O tell her, forget the compulsion of fate" e 121 1958
KOVAL, MARIAN VICTOROVITCH, 1907-
  BLIND EXISTENCE; "Blind existence, dark persistence who gave me the breath of life" e, r 342 1959
   words by A. Pushkin
  RED RICE; "Oh, oh, oh! Run to the ford with the load" e, r 162 words by A. Romm 1960
  TIMES HAVE CHANGED; "Once we sowed seeds with a plough" e, r 162 words by H. Asseev 1961
KOVANOVSKI, DAVID
  SCHLOF MAYN KIND SCHLOF KESEYDER; "Schlof mayn kind mayn treyst mayn sheyner"; "Sleep 1962
   my child, my consolation" e, y 318 words by S. Aleichem
KOWALSKI, ADAM, d 1947
  "O PANIE, KTÓRYŚ JEST NA NIEBIE"; HEAR US O LORD; "Hear us, o Lord whose love we cherish" 1963
   e, p 159
KOZAR-SLOBODZ,
  BIAŁE RÓŻE; "Rozkwitały pąki białych róż"; WHITE ROSES; "Roses white are blooming once again" 1964
   e, p 295
KRAMER, A. WALTER, 1890-
  "I HAVE SEEN DAWN," op.48, no.1 e 259 words by J. Masefield 1965
KRASEV, M.
  SONG OF THE TARTAR MAIDEN; "With sweet hot sunlight in my veins, my name is Shamsinor" 1966
   e, r 162 words by M. Klokov
KRATZER, KAZIMIERZ
  DUMKA, LUDZIE MÓWIĄ; "Ludzie mówią, żem szczęśliwy"; LAMENT; "People say that I am 1967
   happy" e, p 295
KRATZL, KARL
  DAS GLÜCK IS A VOGERL, op.501; "Die Menschen sie zanken und streiten" g 396 words by A. von 1968
   Biczo
KREIN, ALEKSANDR ABRAMOVICH, 1883-1951
  WHY?; "My woe I cannot tell, I love you far too well" e, r 342 words by M. Lermontov 1969
KREIPL, JOSEPH, 1805-1866
  "WENN'S MAILÜFTERL WEHT" g 353 words by A. von Klesheim 1970

KREISLER, FRITZ, 1875-
    VIENNESE REFRAIN; "An old refrain is always haunting me" e 132,236; FAIR HILLS AND VALLEYS;   1971
       "Fair hills and valleys of my native home" e 343
KRESS, CHRISTIAN, 1767-1812
    PORIN MARSSI; "Pojat kansan urhokkaan"; THE PORI MARCH; "Children of a fold that bled" e, fi   1972
       124 words by J. L. Runeberg
KREUDER, PETER
    SERENADE; SCHÖN WAR DIE ZEIT; "Dein Herz ging auf die Reise" g 222 words by H. F. Beckmann 1973
KREUTZER, CONRADIN, 1780-1849
    [DAS NACHTLAGER VON GRANADA, opera; words by K. J. Braun von Braunthal] 1974
       "SCHON DIE ABENDGLOCKEN KLANGEN" Act I, no.11 g 326
    SCHÄFERS SONNTAGSLIED; "Das ist der Tag des Herrn! Das ist der Tag des Herrn!" g 326 words by 1975
       L. Uhland
    [DER VERSCHWENDER, opera; words by F. Raimund] DA STREITEN SICH DIE   1976
       LEUT HERUM; HOBELLIED; "Da streiten sich die Leut herum wohl um den Wert des Glücks"
       326,353; HOBELLIED; "Da streiten sich die Leut herum oft um den Wert des Glücks" g 99
KŘIČKA, JAROSLAV, 1882-
    SYSEL A KRTEK, op.29, no.3; "Jaro spěchá ke vsi. A sysel ještě spí"; DIE ZIESELMAUS UND DER   1977
       MAULWURF; "Frühling naht dem Dorfe. Noch schläft die Zieselmaus" c, g 74
KRIEGER, ADAM, 1634-1666
    ER IST VERMUNDT DURCH IHREN MUND; "Ich bin vermundt" g 250   1978
    "NUN SICH DER TAG GEENDET HAT" g 96,226   1979
KRIEGER, JOHANN, 1682-1755
    "WER DIE MUSIK IN EHREN HÄLT" g 226 words by C. Weisse   1980
KRØYER, HANS ERNST, 1798-1879
    "DER ER ET YNDIGT LAND"; PATRIOTIC SONG; "I know a lovely land" d, e 87 words by   1981
       Oehlenschläger
KROMER, CARL
    GRÜSSE AN DIE HEIMAT; "Nach der Heimat möcht ich wieder, nach dem teuren Vaterort" g 328   1982
KRUTCHININE, V.
    OUR BOY; "Where the houses stand, row on row" e 339 words by J. Schwartz   1983
    THE SHY SWEETHEART; "As the moon shone down in splendor there they stood to say farewell"   1984
       e 339 words by V. Alekhine
KUDELL, REINHOLD
    "WIE KÖNNT ICH DEIN VERGESSEN" g 31 words by H. H. von Fallersleben   1985
KÜCKEN, FRIEDRICH WILHELM, 1810-1882
    ROBIN REDBREAST; "Good-bye, good-bye to summer, For summer's nearly done"; "O Robin, Robin   1986
       Redbreast, O Robin, Robin dear" (ref) e 28 words by Allingham
    TREUE LIEBE; "Ach, wie ist's möglich dann"; g 99; "How can it ever be" e, g 402; "ACH, WIE   1987
       ISTS MÖGLICH DANN" g 42,326,353; "HOW CAN I LEAVE THEE" e 28,128,132,279,366;
       SOLDIER'S FAREWELL e 233 words by H. von Chezy
KÜNNEKE, EDUARD, 1885-1953
    [GLÜCKLICHE REISE, operetta; words by M. Bertuch and K. Schwabach]   1988
       AM AMAZONAS; "Kinder, seid ihr gespannt?" g 258
    [Ibid] GLÜCKLICHE REISE; "Auf nach drüben, alles ist gut disponiert!" g 254   1989
    [DIE GRÖSSE SUNDERIN, operetta] IMMERZU SINGT MEIN HERZ DEINEM HERZEN ZU;   1990
       "Komm mit mir vom Tanze, vom festlichen Glanze hinaus in die heimliche Nacht" g 256
    [HOCHZEIT IN SAMARKAND, operetta; words by R. Kessler] HEUT' HAB'   1991
       ICH DAS GLÜCK GEFUNDEN!; LANGSAMER WALZER; "Du hast mir gehört, du warst mein Weib"
       g 222
    [DIE LOCKENDE FLAMME; singspiel] "ICH TRÄUME MIT OFFENEN AUGEN" g 255   1992
    [DER VETTER AUS DINGSDA, operetta; words by H. Heller and Ride-   1993
       mus] "ICH BIN NUR EIN ARMER WANDERGESELL" g 254
    [Ibid] STRAHLENDER MOND; "Strahlender Mond, der am Himmels-zelt thront" g 255   1994
KUHLAU, FRIEDRICH, 1786-1832
    ELVERHØJ; MINUET; FAIRY HILL piano 87   1995
    HERLIGT EN SOMMERNAT; "Herligt en Sommernat drage til Elverkrat"; GLORIOUS SUMMER   1996
       NIGHT; "Glorious summer night, cool springs in elfin light" da, e 87 words by J. L. Heiberg
KUNC, JAN, 1883-
    JAKO V POHÁDCE, op.2, no.4; "Vše bylo jako v pohadce"; WIE IM MÄRCHEN; "Es war wie auf   1997
       des Märchens Flur" c, g 74 words by J. Kvapil
KURPIŃSKI, KAROL KAZIMIERZ, 1785-1857
    BOŻE, COŚ POLSKĘ; "Boże, coś Polskę, przez tak liczne wieki"; GOD, WHO HELD POLAND; "God,   1998
       who held Poland for so many ages"; SERDECZNA MATKO; "Serdeczna Matko, opiekunko ludzi";
       BELOVED MOTHER; "Beloved Mother, guardian of the nation" e, p 295 words by K. A. Felinzki;
       GOD, THOU KEPT'ST POLAND; "God, Thou kept'st Poland always in Thy power" e, p 159 att to
       Kaszewski

KURPIŃSKI, KAROL KAZIMIERZ, 1785-1857 (Continued)

    "GDY ZŁEK TANIEC POLSKI STANIE"; THE NOBLEMAN'S POLONAISE; "When our Polish dance's   1999
measure" e, p 159 words by J. N. Kaminski

    [KRAKOWIACY I GÓRALE, comic opera] "KIEDY NA ŚWIAT RZUCĘ OKIEM"; YOUR   2000
FORTUNE; "When I cast an eye on this world" e, p 295

    "OTO DZIŚ DZIEŃ KRWI I CHWAŁY"; THE SONG OF WARSAW; "Day of fame and blood is breaking"   2001
e, p 159; WARSZAWIANKA; "Comes the day of blood and glory" e, p 295 words by K. Sienkiewicz

KURUCZ, JÁNOS

    "BAKONY ERDÖN SIR A GERLE"; "THERE'S A DOVE WITHIN THE FOREST" e, hu 285   2002

    HA ELÉR HOZZÁD; "Ha elér hozzád néha egy dalom"; IF, WHEN YOU HEAR MY SONG; "If, when   2003
you hear my song you are amused" e, hu 285

    VALAHOL; "Valahol a Duna partján"; SOMEWHERE; "Somewhere near the Duna River" e, hu 285   2004

KUTSCHERA, ALOIS

    SCHÖNAU, MEIN PARADIES, op.62; "Ich suchte einst ein stilles Plätzchen" g 396   2005

KVAPIL, JAROSLAV, 1892-

    DÉŠŤ V SAMOTĚ; "Déšť drobný šelestí na listech osik"; REGEN IN DER EINSAMKEIT; "Lang in das   2006
Birkenlaub rinnt schon der Regen" c, g 73a words by A. Sova

KYLE, FRANCES

    WHEN I SAW SWEET NELLY HOME. See 1084

LA BARRE, MICHEL DE, ca1670-ca1744
    "ELOIGNÉ DE CE QU'ON AYME" f 108   2007

LACHMANN, WACLAW, 1882-

    EJ, UŚNIJ-ŻE MI, UŚNIJ; "Ej, uśnij-że mi Jędruś"; LULLABY FROM THE TATRA MOUNTAINS;   2008
"Sleep Andrew, my wee laddie" e, p 159

    GRZMIĄ, HUCZNE DZWONY; "Grzmią huczne dzwony ze Kremla szczytów"; POLISH BANNERS   2009
ON THE KREMLIN; "Bells at the Kremlin are tolling loudly" e, p 159

LACHNER, VINCENZ, 1811-1893

    KANON; "Trinke nie ein Glas zu wenig" g 31 words by F. Hornfeck and A. Pichler   2010

    MAILIED; "Es kommt ein wundersamer Knab" g 31 words by J. V. Scheffel   2011

    RÜCKKEHR DES ALTEN STUDENTEN; "Reicht mir das alte Burschenband" g 31 words by F. Weber   2012

    SANKT FLORIAN HILF; "Weil der Huberbauer Florian sich nennt" g 31 words by R. Baumbach   2013

LA FORGE, FRANK, 1879-

    RETREAT; "I flee from pleasures"; SCHLUPFWINKEL; "Ich flüchte mich in meine Klause" e, g 259   2014
words by Princess Gabriele Wrede

    SONG OF THE OPEN; "To your soul is it wine" e 241 words by J. H. Lowell   2015

LA HACHE, THEODORE VON

    THE CONQUERED BANNER; "Furl that banner! for 'tis weary" e 161 words by A. J. Ryan   2016

LAHUSEN, CHRISTIAN, 1886-

    "ES LAGEN IM FELDE DIE HIRTEN BEI NACHT" e 49 words by R. A. Schröder   2017

    "ICH HATT NIN MEI TRUTSCHEL" g 49   2018

    JAHR, DEIN HAUPT NEIG!; "Jahr, dein Haupt neig! Still abwärts steig!" g 49 words by M. Mell   2019

    KLEIN-MAREI; "Lass uns auf die Wiese gehn, Klein-Marei" g 49   2020

    KOMM, TROST DER WELT; "Komm, Trost der Welt du stille Nacht!" g 49 words by J. von Eichen-   2021
dorf

    NOCH HINTER BERGES RANDE; "Noch hinter Berges Rande steht braun der Abendschein" g 49 words   2022
by R. A. Schröder

    "TRITT EIN ZU DIESER SCHWELLE" g 49 words by L. Uhland   2023

    "WER RECHT IN FREUDEN WANDERN WILL" g 49 words by T. Geibel   2024

    "WIR DANKEN, HERR, FÜR BROT UND KLEID" g 49 words by J. Bauer   2025

LAJTAI, LAJOS

    ÉN NEM SZERETEK MAST CSAK TÉGED; "Ragyog egy pár kis csillag"; I LOVE NOBODY ELSE BUT   2026
YOU, DEAR; "In your eyes, stars are beaming" e, hu 285

LALO, ÉDOUARD VICTOR ANTOINE, 1823-1892

    L'ESCLAVE; "Captive, et peut-être oubliée"; THE BONDMAID; "A captive, and perchance   2027
unremember'd" e, f 21; THE CAPTIVE; "A captive, and forgotten" e, f 140; THE SLAVE;
"A captive slave with no friends" e 348 words by T. Gautier

    [LE ROI D'YS, opera; words by E. Blau] VAINEMENT, MA BIEN-AIMÉE, Act III;   2028
"Puisqu'on ne peut fléchir ces jalouses gardiennes" (recit); "Vainement ma bien-aimée, On croit
me désespérer" (aria); "Thy everwatchful guardians no ruse can vanquish" (recit); "My beloved
nothing can shake me, whatever thou try, is vain" (aria) e, f 3

Lambert, Louis, pseud. See GILMORE, PATRICK SARSFIELD, 1829-1892

LAMBERT, MICHEL, 1610-1696
 AIR: "Que faites-vous, Silvie dans ce charmant se jour?" f 278   2029
LANCELOT, SIR
 WALK IN PEACE; "Ev'ry one who's been to school" e 293   2030
LANE, GERALD M.
 WHEN THE LIGHTS ARE LOW; "When twilight falls on the dim old walls"; "Just when the day is over" 2031
  (ref) e 132
LANEARE, NICHOLAS
 "I PRETHEE KEEP MY SHEEP FOR ME" e 106   2032
LANGE-MÜLLER, PETER ERASMUS, 1850-1926
 DER VAR ENGANG; ONCE UPON A TIME; TAFFELMUSIK OG PRINSENS ANKOMST; DINNER MUSIC   2033
  AND THE PRINCE'S ARRIVAL piano 87
 VI ELSKE VORT LAND; "Vi elske vort Land, naar den signede Jul"; WE LOVE OUR LAND; "We love   2034
  our land when the blessed Yuletide" da, e 188
LANGER, G.
 GROSSMÜTTERCHEN; "Grossmütterchen, Grossmütterchen sitzt am Fenster und sie Lächelt leis'"   2035
  g 327
LARA, AUGUSTIN
 MARIMBA; "O ye la marimba"; "Sing your song Marimba" e, s 248   2036
LARA, MARIA TERESA
 MI RIVAL; "Rival de me carino el viento que te besa"; "Mi Rival es mi propio corazon por traicione 2037
  ro" (ref); MY RIVAL; "I'm jealous of a stranger who seems to admire you"; "For the sunshine that
  kisses your beautiful lips is my rival" (ref) e, s 248
 PIENSA EN MI; "Si tienes un hondo pesar piensa en mi"; "Piensa en mi cuando beses" (ref); TIME   2038
  HAS WINGS; "Whenever we happen to meet, time has wings"; "Time has wings when you're near
  me" (ref) e, s 248
LARA, PANCHO
 EL CARBONERO; "Soy carbonero que vengo de las cumbres" s 284   2039
LARDNER, WILLIAM
 OLD IRONSIDES; "Ay, tear her tattered ensign down!" e 129,130 words by O. W. Holmes   2040
 THE WATCHER; "The night was dark and fearful" e 189   2041
LASERNA, BLAS DE, 1751-1816
 [LOS AMANTES CHASQUEADOS, tonadilla] "EL JILGUERITO CON PICO DE ORA";   2042
  LE CHARDONNERET AU BEC D'OR; "Au bois chardonneret lance d'un bec doré" f, s 269
 [EL DESEO DE LA PULPILLO, tonadilla] LAS MAJAS DE PARIS; "Para ver si acaso logro   2043
  complacer á mis polacos"; LES BELLES DE PARIS; "Pour savoir si je puis plaire à leurs seigneuries
  du parterre" f, s 270
 [Ibid] LAS MAJAS MADRILEÑAS; "La majas madrileñas son de tal casta"; LES BELLES MADRI-   2044
  LÈNES; "Les belles madrilènes ont de la race" f, s 270
 TIRANA; "Del Trípili la tirana es la que más gusto da"; "Du Tripili la 'tirane' est notre danse   2045
  profane" f, s 270
 [LA VIDE CORTESANA Y ALDEANA, tonadilla] "POR COLACIÓN SEIS ABATES";   2046
  "POUR COLLATION SIX ABBÉS RÉUNIS" f, s 270
LASSEN, EDUARD, 1830-1904
 ALLERSEELEN; "Stell' auf den Tisch die duftenden Reseden" g 327   2047
 [ICH HATTE EINST EIN SCHÖNES VATERLAND] IT WAS A DREAM; "I saw the native   2048
  land I lov'd and knew"; e 348; AH, 'TIS A DREAM; "My native land, again it meets my eye" e
  28,366
 [MIT DEINEN BLAUEN AUGEN] THINE EYES SO BLUE; "Thine eyes so soft and tender"   2049
  e 387; "THINE EYES SO BLUE AND TENDER" e 132
LATHAM, W. H.
 BROADWAY SIGHTS; "In New York when the weathers fair" e 189   2050
LAUDER, HARRY

 BREAKFAST IN MY BED ON SUNDAY MORNIN'. See 1344
 ROAMIN' IN THE GLOAMIN'; "Roamin' in the gloamin' on the bonnie banks o' Clyde" e 233   2051
LAUE, ADOLF, 1831-1893
 AM RHEIN; "Wie glüht er im Glase" g 31 words by F. Schanz   2052
LAUFER, CALVIN W.
 "A KING MIGHT MISS THE GUIDING STAR" e 244 words by L. F. Benson   2053
LAVALLÉE, CALIXA
 O CANADA; "O Canada! Our home and native land!" "O Canada! Terre de nos aïeux" e, f 294;   2054
  e 199, 279 words by A. B. Routhier and R. S. Weir
LAVOTTA, RUDOLF
 HONNAN JÖ A FÉNY; "Honnan jö a fény, honnan a homály"; WHENCE COMES ALL OUR LIGHT;   2055
  "Whence comes all our light, whence the falling dusk" e, hu 285

LAVOTTA, RUDOLF, (Continued)
  MEZEI BOKRÉTA; "Bokrétát kötöttem mezei virágból"; I HAVE MADE A FINE BOUQUET; "I have   2056
    made a fine bouquet of meadow flowers" e, hu 285
LAW, ANDREW, 1749-1821
  BUNKER HILL; THE AMERICAN HERO; "Why should vain mortals tremble at the sight of death and   2057
    destruction in the field of battle" e 109,110 words by N. Niles
LAWES,
  TURN NOT; "Turn not from sad sorrow" 4 pt round e 235   2058
LAWES, HENRY, 1596-1662
  "ABOUT THE SWEET BAG OF A BEE" e 106 words by R. Herrick   2059
  "AMIDST THE MIRTLES AS I WALKE" e 106 words by R. Herrick   2060
  BID ME TO LIVE; "Bid me to live and I will live thy protestant to be" e 348; "Bid me but live and   2061
    I will live thy votary to be" e 106 words by R. Herrick
  THE HIGHER THE PLUM-TREE; "The higher the plum-tree, the riper the plum" 4 pt round e 235   2062
  "I AM CONFIRM'D A WOMAN CAN, LOVE THIS OR THAT OR ANY MAN" e 106 words by J. Suckling 2063
  "I PRETHEE, SEND ME BACK MY HEART" e 36 words by H. Hughes   2064
  I PRETHEE SWEET; "I prethee sweet to me be kind" e 107   2065
  THE LARK; "Swift through the yielding air I glide" e 107   2066
  "MAN'S LIFE IS BUT VAIN" e 106 words by I. Walton   2067
  THE NIGHTINGALE; "Hark how the nightingale displays the latest pleasures of her throat" e 404   2068
  O LET ME GROAN; "O let me groan one word into thine ear" e 278 words by W. Herbert, Earl of   2069
    Pembroke
  THE PRIMROSE; "Aske me why I send you here" e 107 words by R. Herrick   2070
LAWES, WILLIAM, 1602-1645
  GATHER YE ROSEBUDS; "Gather ye rosebuds while you may" e 36,234; "Gather your rosebuds   2071
    while you may" e 106 words by R. Herrick
  O MY CLARISSA; "O my Clarissa thou cruell fair" e 107   2072
  SHE WEEPETH SORE; "She weepeth sore in the night" 4 pt round e 349   2073
LAWLER, CHARLES B., 1852-1925
  THE IRISH JUBILEE; "Oh, a short time ago boys, an Irishman named Doherty" e 114,166,246   2074
    words by J. Thornton
Leadbelly. See LEDBETTER, HUDDIE, 1885?-1949
LECLAIR, JEAN MARIE, 1697-1764
  [SCYLLA ET GLAUCUS, opera; words by d'Albaret] AIR DE BLAUCUS; "Chantez   2075
    chantez l'amour"; "Oh! sing the praise of love" e, f 152
  [Ibid] AIR DE SCYLLA; "Serments trompeurs, tendre langage"; "Oh! faithless vows, never shall   2076
    ye beguile me!" e, f 149
Lecuona, Ernesto. See LECUONA Y CASADO, ERNESTO, 1895-
LECUONA Y CASADO, ERNESTO, 1895-
  LA COMPARSA; "Escucha el rumor escucha el sonar"; CUBAN PROCESSIONAL; "A scene I recall,   2077
    'twas down Cuba way" e, s 9
LEDBETTER, HUDDIE, 1885?-1949
  BOURGEOIS BLUES; "Me and my wife run all over town"; "Lord, it's a bourgeois town" (ref) e 336   2078
  DE KALB BLUES; "De Kalb blues, Lord, make me feel so bad" e 336   2079
  GOOD MORNING, BLUES; "Good morning, Blues, Blues, how do you do?"; SANTA CLAUS BLUES   2080
    e 336
  GOODNIGHT, IRENE; "Irene goodnight, Irene goodnight" e 389   2081
  LEAVIN' BLUES; "I'm leavin' in the morning, mama, and I don't know where to go" e 336   2082
  RED CROSS STORE; "I told her, 'no, Baby, you know I don't wanna go" e 336   2083
  TITANIC; "It was midnight on the sea, band playin' 'Nearer, my God, to Thee'" e 336   2084
LEE, ALFRED
  CHAMPAGNE CHARLIE; "Of gaiety I've seen a deal throughout my boisterous life" e 225 words by   2085
    H. J. Whymark
LEE, G. A.
  THE MACGREGOR'S GATHERING; "The moon's on the lake" e 101 words by W. Scott   2086
LEEVES, WILLIAM, 1748-1828
  AULD ROBIN GRAY; "Young Jamie lo'ed me weel, and socht me for his bride" e 100,103 words   2087
    by A. Lindsay
LEFÈVRE, JACQUES, fl 17th c
  AIME-MOI, BERGÈRE; "Aime-moi, bergère, et je t'aimerai" f 383; JOLI MOI DE MAI; PRETTY   2088
    MONTH OF MAY; "Will you love me, pretty one as I love thee?" e, f 297
LEGRENZI, GIOVANNI, ca1625-1690
  [ETEOCLE E POLINICE, opera] CHE FIERO COSTUME; "Che fiero costume d'aligero nume";   2089
    HOW VOID OF COMPASSION; "How void of compassion is Cupid his fashion" e, i 368; ARIETTA;
    "Gott Amor, verwogen, mit Flügeln und Bogen" g, i 167; WHAT STRANGE WHIM PURSUING;
    "What strange whim pursuing, when for our undoing" e, i 139

LEGRENZI, GIOVANNI, ca1625-1690   (Continued)

    KANZONE; "Non mi dir di palesar"; "Heisse mich nicht, zu offenbaren" g, i 217   2090

LEHÁR, FERENC, 1870-1948

    [FRIEDERIKE, singspiel; words by L. Herzer and F. Löhner] O MÄDCHEN,   2091
    MEIN MÄDCHEN, Act II; "O Mädchen, mein Mädchen, wie lieb ich dich!" g 254

    [Ibid] SAH EIN KNAB' EIN RÖSLEIN STEHN, Act I; "Heimlich klingt in meine Seele eine süsse   2092
    Melodei" g 255

    [GIUDITTA, operetta; words by P. Knepler and F. Löhner] "FREUNDE, DAS   2093
    LEBEN IST LEBENSWERT!" g 222

    [DAS LAND DES LÄCHELNS, operetta; words by V. Léon, L. Herzer and F.   2094
    Löhner] "DEIN IST MEIN GANZES HERZ," Act II g 255

    [Ibid] IMMER NUR LÄCHELN, Act I; "Ich trete ins Zimmer, von Sehnsucht durchbebt" g 254   2095

    [DIE LUSTIGE WITWE, operetta; words by V. Hirschfeld and L. Rosenstein]   2096
    KOM IN DEN KLEINEN PAVILLON; "Wie eine Rosenknospe im Maienlicht erblüht" g 256

    [Ibid] [Lippen Schweigen, 'sflütern Geigen] MERRY WIDOW WALTZ, Act III; "Hold   2097
    me tightly, waltz me lightly" (ref) e 329; LOVE REMAINED; "Long ago a belle and beau with
    hearts in tune" (ref) e 132; "Through the night I'm softly calling, 'I love you'" (ref) e 246;
    "Lovers often hum this soft and sweet refrain" (ref) e 128,236

    [Ibid] VILJA-LIED; "Es lebt' eine Vilja, ein Waldmägdelein"; "Vilja, o Vilja, du Waldmägdelein"   2098
    (ref) g 254; VILIA; "One Morning a huntsman all gallant and gay"; "Vilia, fair dryad, you rule
    in the wood" (ref) e 28 (ref only) e 343; "Vilia, dear Vilia, my whole heart is thine" (ref only)
    e 132,236

    [PAGANINI, operetta; words by P. Knepler and B. Jenbach] "GERN HAB' ICH   2099
    DIE FRAU'N GEKÜSST" g 254

    [Ibid] LIEBE, DU HIMMEL AUF ERDEN; "Ich kann es nicht fassen, nicht glauben" g 254   2100

    [Ibid] NIEMAND LIEBT DICH SO WIE ICH; "Sag' mir, wieviel süsse rote Lippen hast du schon   2101
    geküsst" g 257

    [DER RASTELBINDER, operetta] WENN ZWEI SICH LIEBEN, Act I; "Denk'ich zurück, drei   2102
    Jahre sind's g'rad" g 255

    [SCHÖN IST DIE WELT!, operetta] SCHÖN IST DIE WELT!; "Bruder Leichtsinn, so werd'   2103
    ich gennant" g 255

    [DER ZAREWITSCH, operetta; words by B. Jenbach and H. Reichert] EINER   2104
    WIRD KOMMEN; "Einer wird kommen, der wird mich begehren" g 254

    [Ibid] WOLGALIED; "Allein! Wieder allein!" (recit); "Es steht ein Soldat am Wolgastrand (aria)   2105
    g 254

LEHMANN, ALFRED

    NACH DEM EXAMEN; "Nun sollt ich mich wohl freuen" g 31   words by E. Heyck   2106

LEIGH, F. W.

    A LITTLE BIT OFF THE TOP; "Brown's a very old friend of mine"; "Carve a little bit off the top for   2107
    me, for me!" (ref) e 204

LE JEUNE, GEORGE FITZ CURWOOD, 1841-1904

    JERUSALEM THE GOLDEN; Urbs beata (tune); "Jerusalem the golden! with milk and honey blest"   2108
    e 28,366   words by Bernard of Cluny

LEMAIRE, CHARLES

    CHANSON À MANGER; "Quoi! toujours des chansons à boire?"; IN PRAISE OF FOOD; "Drinking songs,   2109
    what an old, old, story!" e, f 364

LEMARE, EDWIN HENRY, 1865-1934

    ANDANTINO; STARLIGHT AND SUNSHINE; "Starlight and sunshine will always remind me of you"   2110
    e 132   words by H. Johnson

LENNOX, LINSAY

    LOVE'S GOLDEN DREAM; "I hear tonight the old bells chime" e 129,130   2111

LEO, LEONARDO ORONZO SALVATORE DE, 1694-1744

    [OLIMPIADE, opera; words by P. Metastasio] REZITATIV UND ARIE DES MEGACLES;   2112
    "Io vado deh pensa ad Aristea!" (recit); "Ich scheide beschütze de Aristea!" (recit); "Se cerca, de
    dice: l'amico dove' è?" (aria); "Wenn sie mich sucht, wenn sie fragt: wo ist mein Freund?" (aria)
    g, i 218

LEONARD, EDDIE, 1875-1941

    IDA, SWEET AS APPLE CIDER; "In the region where the roses always bloom" e 34 words by E. Munson   2113

LEONCAVALLO, RUGGIERO, 1858-1919

    [I PAGLIACCI, opera] SI PUÒ; PROLOGUE; "Si può? Si può? Signore! Signori!"; "I may? So   2114
    please you! My ladies and gentlemen!" e, i 4

    [Ibid] STRIDONO LASSÙ; "Qual fiamma avea nel guardo" (recit); "Stridono lassù, liberamente   2115
    lanciati a vol" (aria); BALLATELLA; "His eyes with fire were flamming" (recit); "There on high
    they cry, in freedom flying" (aria) e, i 1, 176

LEONCAVALLO, RUGGIERO, 1858-1919 (Continued)
    [Ibid] VESTI LA GIUBBA, Act II; "Recitar! Mentre preso dal delirio" (recit); "Vesti la giubba   2116
        e la faccia in farina" (aria); "To go on! When my head's whirling with madness" (recit); "Put
        on your smock now, smear your face with powder" (aria) e, i 3; ARIOSO; "I must clown to get
        rid of my unhappiness" (recit); "Clown in a costume and my face masked with makeup" (aria)
        e, i 132

LEONTOVICH, M.
    RING, CHRISTMAS BELLS; UKRAINIAN CAROL; "Ring, Christmas bells, merrily ring" e 296   2117

LESLIE, ERNEST
    ROCK ME TO SLEEP, MOTHER; "Backward, turn backward, oh, time in your flight"; "Clasped to   2118
        your heart in a loving embrace" (ref) e 129,131 words by Mrs. E.A.C.A. Allen

LE SUEUR, JEAN FRANÇOIS, 1760-1837
    [OSSIAN, opera; words by Dercy and J. M. Deschamps] LE CHANT DE SELMA;   2119
        "Hélas! sans m'entendre, tu quittes ce bord"; "Ah! why thus forsake me, Rosmala, my own?"
        e, f 149

LEVENSON, ROBERT
    MY BELGIAN ROSE. See 280

LEVERIDGE, RICHARD, 1670?-1758
    BLACK EYED SUSAN; "All in the downs the fleet was moor'd" e 235; "All in the Downs the fleet was   2120
        moored" e 397 words by J. Gay
    THE ROAST BEEF OF OLD ENGLAND; "When mighty roast beef was the Englishman's food" e 14,235,   2121
        349

LEVY, SARA, 1908-
    ALI V'ER; "Ali v'er B'er ali"; "Rise, oh well, Oh well rise up" e, h(tr) 318 words by N. Bailik   2122
    BIKURIM; "P'ri gani hiney heveyti"; "Here I bring my garden's crop" e, h(tr) 318 words by S. Bass   2123

LEWIS, AL, 1901-
    NO! NO! A THOUSAND TIMES NO! See 3451

LEWIS, DAN
    FIFTY CENTS; "I took my girl to a fancy ball"; "A dozen raw, a plate of slaw, a chicken and a   2124
        roast" (ref) e 204

LEWIS, DAVE
    MOTHER PIN A ROSE ON ME; "I love the country air"; "Mother, Mother, Mother, pin a rose on me"   2125
        (ref) e 114,131 joint composers B. Adams and P. Schindler

LEYBOURNE,
    UP IN A BALOON. See 1037

LIANG, CHIEN FONG
    MIDNIGHT, SLEEPING BETHLEHEM; "Midnight, sleeping Bethlehem, stars above are shining bright"   2126
        e 337 words by Yang Ching Chin

LIDDLE, SAMUEL
    "SINCE THOU, O FONDEST" e 344 words by R. Bridges   2127

LIDGEY, C. A.
    "SEE WHERE MY LOVE A-MAYING GOES" e 344   2128
    SUNNY MARCH; "The hedge is full of houses" e 344 words by N. Gale   2129

LIDHOLM, INGVAR, 1821-
    VID MEDELHAVET; "Agaven staar i blom och solen skiner" sw 356 words by H. Gullberg   2130

LIE, SIGURD, 1871-1904
    [SNE] SCHNEE; "Es ist nichts auf dieser Erde"; SNOW; "There is nought on earth so still as the   2131
        snow" e, g 241 words by H. Rode

LIEBE, EDUARD LUDWIG, 1819-1900
    "ICH WANDRE IN DIE WEITE WELT"; "Grüsst mir das blonde Kind am Rhein und sagt" (ref) g 31   2132
        words by H. W. Mertens

Liebe, Ludwig. See LIEBE, EDUARD LUDWIG, 1819-1900

LILIUOKALANI, QUEEN
    ALOHA OE; "Haaheo ka ua ina pali"; FAREWELL TO THEE; "Proudly swept the raincloud by the   2133
        cliff" e, ha 122; "Love like ours was meant to live forever" e 132; "Soaring high, the clouds
        are proudly borne" e 70; AUF WIEDERSEHN; MARIE-MADLEN; HAWAISCHES LIED; "Anker
        auf und aus dem Herz gerissen" g 222; "Now our golden days are at an end" e 28,279,343,366;
        "Farewell to Thee, Farewell to Thee" (ref only) e 236; HAWAIIAN FAREWELL SONG; "Now has
        come the hour of sad parting" e 233

LILJA, BERNHARD
    DET AANGAR SMUTS; "Det aangar smuts och svett mull igenom parken" sw 356   2134

LILJEFORS, INGEMAR, 1906-
    ETT FLICKEBARN; "Spela nu, saa skall jag dansa" sw 356 words by B. Bergman   2135

LINARES, ABBIE BRINK DE
    NOCHE DE CARNIVAL; "Noche divina, Sábado de Carnaval"; CARNIVAL NIGHT; "Oh night   2136
        divine! come you all to carnival" e, s 142 words by A. Linares

LINCKE, PAUL, 1866-1946

    [FRAU LUNA, operetta; words by B. Bäckers] SCHLÖSSER, DIE IM MONDE LIEGEN;   2137
    "Blick doch um dich mit klaren frohen Augen" g 255

    [LYSISTRATA, operetta] GLÜHWÜRCHEN; GLOW WORM; "When the night falls silently";   2138
    "Shine, little glow-worm, glimmer" (ref) e 32,34 words by L. C. Robinson

LINCOLN, ABRAHAM, att to
    ADAM AND EVE'S WEDDING SONG. See 7396A

LINDBERG, OSKAR FREDRIK, 1887-1955
    "HUR SKALL MAN BRUDEN KLÄDA?" sw 356   2139
    "VAD SÖKER DU PAA STRANDEN?" sw 356   2140

LINDBLAD, OTTO JONAS, 1809-1864
    JAG VET ETT LAND; "Jag vet ett land laangt upp i högan nord"; I KNOW A LAND; "I know a land,   2141
    far north, by mountains framed" e, sw 188 words by G. Nyblaeus

    KUNGSSAANGEN; "Ur svenska hjärtans djup en gaang en samfälld och en enkel saang"; THE KING;   2142
    "Let Swedish voices raise this song" e, sw 188 words by C. V. A. Strandberg

    VINTERN RASAT UT; "Vintern rasat ut bland vaara fjällar"; WINTER'S RAGE IS OVER; "Winter's   2143
    rage beyond the hills has vanished" e, sw 188 words by H. Sätherberg

LINDEMAN, LUDWIG M., 1812-1887
    "A BABE IS BORN IN BETHLEHEM"; PUER NATUS e 206   2144

LINDSAY, JENNIE
    "ALWAYS TAKE MOTHER'S ADVICE" e 114,131,132,204   2145

LINLEY, THOMAS, 1732-1795
    "O, BID YOUR FAITHFUL ARIEL FLY" e 276 words by W. Shakespeare   2146

LIPSKY, ALEXANDER
    LILAC-TIME; "So still the lilacs hang" e 85 words by T. S. Jones, Jr.   2147

LISTOWSKI, A.
    RŻY KONICZEK MOJ; "Rży koniczek mój bułany"; THE LANCER'S FAREWELL; "My good steed   2148
    neighs with impatience" e, p 295 words by A. E. Odyniec

LISZT, FRANZ, 1811-1886
    COMMENT, DISAIENT-ILS; "Comment, disaient-ils, avec nos nacelles"; THE ANSWER; "They   2149
    asked, 'How can we, in boat light and fragile'" e, f 211 words by V. Hugo

    "ES MUSS EIN WUNDERBARES SEIN"; "It must be wonderful indeed" e 348; e, g 209 words by   2150
    Redwitz

    DIE LORELEI; "Ich weiss nicht was soll's bedeuten"; THE LORELEY; "I know not what spell is o'er   2151
    me" e, g 276 words by H. Heine

    MIGNONS LIED; "Kennst du das Land wo die Zitronen blüh'n"; MIGNON'S SONG; "Thou know'st   2152
    the land where sweet the citron blows" e, g 274 words by J. W. von Goethe

    [O LIEB', SO LAND DU LIEBEN KANNST] LIEBESTRAUM, no.3; DREAM OF LOVE;   2153
    "My dream of love that rises with the daybreak" e 329; words by M. Whitehill; "My dream of love
    will linger on for ever" e 132

    OH! QUAND JE DORS; "Oh, quand je dors, viens auprés de ma couche"; OH, WHEN I SLUMBER;   2154
    "Oh, when I slumber, come close to my couch" e, f 190,193,195; WHEN IN MY DREAMS;
    "When slumber light in its arms doth enfold me" e, f 211 words by V. Hugo

Literes, Antonio, 1670-1747. See LITERES CARRIÓN, ANTONIO, 1670-1747

LITERES CARRIÓN, ANTONIO, 1670-1747
    [ACCIS Y GALATEA, zarzuela; words by J. de Cañizares] ARIA DE ACIS Y   2155
    GALATEA; "Confiado jilguerillo, mira como importuna"; AIR D'ACIS ET GALATÉE; "Char-
    donneret trop sincère, vois combien importunes" f, s 269

LLOYD, ROBERT
    "GOOD MORNING, MR. ZIP-ZIP-ZIP" e 129,130,236   2156

LOB, OTTO, 1837-1908
    ALTE STUDENTEN; "Nun frisch auf den Tisch einen neuen Pokal"; "Beim goldenen Weine, beim   2157
    schaumenden Bier" (ref) g 31 words by E. Heyck

    AN MEIN VATERLAND; "Kein Baum hörte mir von deinen Wäldern" g 31 words by K. Kretz   2158

    AURA ACADEMICA; "Freunde, trinkt in vollen Zügen musenstädtschen Gerstensaft" g 31 words   2159
    by O. Kamp

    BIERLEIN, RINN!; "Beim Rosenwirt am Grabentor" g 31 words by J. R. Gspandl   2160

    BURSCHENTUM; "Zieht der Bursch die Strass' entlang" g 31 words by E. Heyck   2161

    FILIA HOSPITALIS; "O wonnevolle Jugendzeit mit Freuden ohne Ende"; g 31 words by O. Kamp   2162

    FREUDE; "Auf leichten Füssen kommt gegangen" g 31 words by G. H. Schneider   2163

    HALLO, HERR WIRT; "Hallo, Herr Wirt, noch einen Krug" g 31 words by R. Hermanns   2164

    "IN JEDEM VOLLEN GLASE WEIN" g 31 words by R. Hermanns   2165

    LOBGESANG AUF HEIDELBERG; "Heidelberg, du Jugendbronnen" g 31 words by A. Wickenburg   2166

    "NUN LASS DEIN BRAUNES RÖCKELEIN" g 31 words by H. Freise   2167

    O GOLDNE AKADEMIA; "Als noch Arkadiens goldne Tage mich jungen Burschen angelacht" g 31   2168
    words by G. H. Schneider

LOB, OTTO, 1837-1908 (Continued)
    "VIEL VOLLE BECHER KLANGEN" g 31 words by J. N. Vogl   2169
    ZU HEIDELBERG STUDENT; "Wo zwischen grünen Bergen munter des Nekkars klare Woge rauscht"   2170
      g 31 words by J. Löwenberg

LOCKWOOD, C. T.
    DON'T YOU GO, TOMMY; "You'll rue it my boy, now mind what I say" e 189   2171

LODER, EDWARD JAMES, 1813-1865
    THE BROOKLET; "I heard a brooklet gushing" e 277   2172

LOEFFLER, CHARLES MARTIN TORNOV, 1861-1935
    ADIEU POUR JAMAIS, op. 10, no. 2; "Chère apparence viens"; ADIEU THEN FOR AYE; "Remem-   2173
      bered vision come" e, f 121 words by G. Kahn
    LES PAONS, op. 10, no. 4; "Se penchant vers les dahlias"; THE PEACOCKS; "As they turn to the   2174
      dahlias white" e, f 121 words by G. Kahn

Löw, Johann Jakob, 1628-1703. See LÖWE, JOHANN JAKOB, 1628-1703

LÖWE, JOHANN JAKOB, 1628-1703
    DAS EWIG GRÜNE LAUB DIE PRACHT DER DICHTEREI VERLACHT DER ZEITEN RAUB UND IST VOM   2175
      TODE FREI; "Sollt ich die edle Kunst" g 250 words by M. Kempe

LOEWE, KARL, 1796-1869
    DIE DREI LIEDER, op. 3, no. 3; "In der hohen Hall' sass König Siegfried" g 250 words by L. Uhland   2176
    EDWARD, op. 1, no. 1; "Dein Schwert wie ist's von Blut so rot"; "Why does your brand sae drop wi'   2177
      blude" e, g 272 words by J. G. Herder
    FRIDERICUS REX; "Fridericus Rex, unser König und Herr" g 31 words by G. W. Häring   2178
    HEINRICH DER VOGLER, op. 56, no. 1; "Herr Heinrich sitzt am Vogelherd" g 96, 99, 328 words by   2179
      J. N. Vogl
    PRINZ EUGEN, op. 92; "Zelt, Posten, Werdarufer!" e 99 words by F. Freiligrath   2180
    TOM DER REIMER, op. 135; "Der Reimer Thomas lag am Bach" g 391   2181
    DIE UHR, op. 123, no. 3; "Ich trage, wo ich gehe, stets eine Uhr bei mir" g 326, 327 words by   2182
      G. Seidel

LOHR, FREDERICK N.
    "OUT ON THE DEEP" e 205 words by S. K. Cowan   2183

LONATI, CARLO AMBROGIO, ca1650-ca1710
    KANZONETTE; "Tu partisti, tu partisti, partisti, idolo amato"; "Du gingst fort, geliebtes Idol" g, i 217   2184

LONGÁS, FEDERICO, 1895-
    CIELO AZUL; "Tiene tu risauna canción de cristal"; SKIES ARE BLUE; "Your daughter is a song to   2185
      me, crystal clear" e, s 245 words by S. Vela
    RONDA; "Mazanita mojana, beso de fruta"; ROUND THE NORIA; "Near your fields I am riding,   2186
      watching your labors" e, s 245 words by L. Gongora

LORTZING, ALBERT, 1801-1851
    [CZAAR UND ZIMMERMANN, opera] "LEBE WOHL, MEIN FLANDRISCH MÄDCHEN",   2187
      Act II g 391
    [Ibid] "SONST SPIELT' ICH MIT SZEPTER," Act III g 326, 390   2188
    [DER WAFFENSCHMIED, opera] ARIE DER MARIE, Act II; "Wir armen, armen Mädchen   2189
      sind gar so übel dran" g 311
    [Ibid] AUCH ICH WAR EIN JÜNGLING; "Auch ich war ein Jüngling mit lokkigem Harr" g 326,   2190
      328, 353, 390
    ZAR UND ZIMMERMANN, opera. See 2187-2188

LOTTI, ANTONIO, d1740
    PUR DICESTI, O BOCCA BELLA; "Pur dicesti, o bocca, bocca bella"; MOUTH SO CHARMFUL;   2191
      "Mouth so charmful, O tell me now" e, i 363; ARIETTA; "Sagt es noch einmal, ihr holden,
      schönen Lippen" g, i 167; SPEAK AGAIN LOVE; "Speak again, love, I fain would hear thee
      render" e, i 138

LOUGHBOROUGH, RAYMOND
    HOW LOVELY IS THE HAND OF GOD; "I sometimes think, when silv'ry night" e 241 words by   2192
      D. Dickinson

LOUIS, XIII, KING OF FRANCE, 1610-1643
    AMARYLLIS; "Tu crois, ô beau soleil" f 383; "TU CROIS Ô BEAU SOLEIL" f 108   2193

LOVER, SAMUEL, 1797-1868
    WIDOW MACHREE; "Widow Machree, 'tis no wonder you frown" e 166, 213   2194
    YOUNG RORY O'MORE; RORY O'MORE; "Young Rory O'More courted Kathaleen bawn" e 166,   2195
      213

LOWRY, ROBERT
    AT THE RIVER; "Shall we gather by the river" e 84; "SHALL WE GATHER AT THE RIVER" e 35   2196
    WHERE IS MY BOY TONIGHT?; "Where is my wand'ring boy tonight"; "O where is my boy tonight?"   2197
      (ref) e 34; "WHERE IS MY WANDERING BOY TO-NIGHT" e 114; "WHERE IS MY WAND'RING
      BOY TONIGHT" e 131

LUBOMIRSKI, K., PRINCE, d 1871

    "O GWIAZDECZKO COŚ BŁYSZCZAŁA"; MY DEAR STAR; "My dear star that hung in heaven"   2198
    e, p 159; O GWIAZDECZKO, MY STAR; "Oh, dear star, that glittered brightly" e, p 295
    words by G. Zielinski

LUCA, S. DE., fl 1600

    "NON POSSO DISPERAR"; "I DO NOT DARE RESPOND" e, i 368; ARIETTA; "Ich mag nicht mehr   2199
    verzagen" e, i 168

LUCAS, SAM

    CARVE DAT 'POSSUM; "De 'possum meat am good to eat" e 28,184,366   2200

LUDERS, GUSTAV CARL, 1865-1913

    [THE PRINCE OF PILSEN, opera; words by F. Pixley] THE MESSAGE OF THE   2201
    VIOLET; "The rose's lips are warm and red" e 237

LULLY, J. B.

    AU CLAIR DE LA LUNE. See 4885

LULLY, JEAN BAPTISTE, 1632-1687

    [AMADIS, opera; words by P. Quinault] AIR D'ARCABONNE; "Amour, que veux-tu   2202
    de moi?"; "Oh! Love, what would'st thou with me?" e, f 148

    [Ibid] AIR D'ARCALAUS; "Dans un piège fatal son mauvais sort l'amene"; "He is drawn to the   2203
    snare by cruel fate devised" e, f 146

    [Ibid] BOIS ÉPAIS, Act II; "Bois épais redouble ton ombre" f 88; ALL YOUR SHADES; "All   2204
    your shades ye woods, fold around me" e, f 273; GLOOMY WOODS; "Gloomy woods, redouble
    thy shadow" e, f 404

    [ARMIDE, opera; words by P. Quinault] AIR D'ARMIDE; "Ah! si la liberté me doit   2205
    être ravie"; "Ah! if I have to lose the freedom I prize" e, f 150

    [Ibid] AIR DE RENAUD, Act II; "Plus j'observe ces lieux"; "As I gaze on this spot" e, f 152   2206

    [ATYS, opera; words by P. Quinault] AIR DU SOMMEIL; "Dormons, dormons tous";   2207
    "Come, sleep, to charm us!" e, f 152

    [PROSPERINE, opera; words by P. Quinault] "MA CHÈRE LIBERTÉ"; "TU M'ERI   2208
    UN GRAN TESOR" f, i 411

    [LE SICILIEN OU L'AMOUR PEINTRE, opera; words by J. B. Molière] AIR   2209
    DU BERGER; "Pauvres amants, quelle erreur"; "Foolish indeed is the swain" e, f 152

    [THÉSÉÉ, opera; words by P. Quinault] AIR DE MARS; "Que rien ne trouble ici   2210
    Vénus et les amours"; "Let no alarms disturb this tranquil Paphian grove" e, f 146

    [Ibid] AIR DE VENUS; "Revenez, revenez, amours, revenez"; "Oh! return, oh! return, sweet   2211
    loves, oh! return!" e, f 150

LUTHER, MARTIN, 1483-1546

    EIN' FESTE BURG; "Ein' feste Burg ist unser Gott"; "A MIGHTY FORTRESS IS OUR GOD" e, g   2212
    34,62; e 35,236,343; A MIGHTY FORTRESS e, g 7; "EIN FESTE BURG IST UNSER GOTT"
    g 326 words by M. Luther, harmonized by J. S. Bach

LUZZI, LUIGI, 1828-1876

    AVE MARIA, op.80; "Ave Maria, gratia plena"; "Hail, Mary, full of grace" e, lat 304   2213

LYOFF, ALEXIS THEODORE

    "GLORIOUS YULETIDE, GLAD BELLS PROCLAIM IT" e 244   2214

LYRA, JUSTUS WILHELM, 1822-1882

    MEINE MUSE; "Meine Mus' ist gegangen in des Schenken sein Haus" g 31,99 words by W. Müller   2215
    NUR IN DEUTSCHLAND; "Zwischen Frankreich und dem Böhmerland" g 31,99 words by H. von   2216
    Fallersleben
    REITERLIED; "Die bange Nacht ist nun herum" g 31,99 words by G. Herwegh   2217
    SEHNSUCHT; "Es schienen so golden die Sterne" g 31 words by J. von Eichendorff   2218
    DER WANDERNDE STUDENT; "Bei dem angenehmsten Wetter" g 31 words by J. von Eichendorff   2219
    WANDERSCHAFT; "Der Mai ist gekommen, die Bäume schlagen aus" g 31,99; DER MAI IST   2220
    GEKOMMEN g 42,326,353 words by E. Geibel
    "WO SOLCH EIN FEUER" g 31 words by G. Herwegh   2221

[MACARTHY, HARRY]

    THE BONNIE BLUE FLAG; "We are a band of brothers" e 34,129,130,161; HOMESPUN DRESS;   2222
    "Oh, yes I am a Southern girl" e 161 words by C. B. Sinclair, att to V. Vousden
    THE VOLUNTEER, or IT IS MY COUNTRY'S CALL; "I leave my home and thee, dear" e 161   2223

McCALL, P. J.

    KELLY, THE BOY FROM KILLANN; "What's the news? What's the news? Oh! my bold Shelmalier"   2224
    e 172

McCURRY, JOHN G.

    ZION'S WALLS; "Come fathers and mothers come" e 84   2225

MACDOWELL, EDWARD ALEXANDER, 1861-1908
    [FROM AN OLD GARDEN, song cycle, op. 26] THE BLUE-BELL, no.5; "In love she   2226
        fell, my shy Blue-bell" e 408 words by M. Deland
    [Ibid] THE MYRTLE, no.2; "Its clinging, mournful leaves, I said, seem made to thatch a grave"   2227
        e 408 words by M. Deland
    THE SEA, op.47, no.7; "One sails away to sea, to sea" e 348 words by W. D. Howells   2228
    THY BEAMING EYES, op.40, no.3; "Thy beaming eyes are Paradise to me, my love, to me" e 36   2229
        words by W. H. Gardner
MACGIMSEY, ROBERT, 1898-
    TROUBLE; "Trouble, trouble, trouble, trouble all ah see" e 76   2230
MCGLENNON, FELIX
    AND HER GOLDEN HAIR WAS HANGING DOWN HER BACK; "There was once a simple maiden came   2231
        to New York"; "But, oh, Jane! doesn't look the same" (ref) e 129,130,131 words by M. H.
        Rosenfeld
    ARRAH, GO ON!; "I'm a dacent young colleen just over from Ireland" e 204   2232
    COMRADES; "We from childhood play'd together"; "Comrades, comrades, ever since we were boys"   2233
        (ref) e 114,131,132 (ref only) e 128,129,130
    I'VE WORKED EIGHT HOURS THIS DAY; "Have ye heard the rule me boys?"; "For I've worked eight   2234
        hours this day" (ref) e 114
Machaut, Guillaume de. See GUILLAUME DE MACHAUT, d 1377
Machault, Guillaume de. See GUILLAUME DE MACHAUT, d 1377
MCHUGH, JIMMY, 1894-
    I LOVE TO WHISTLE; "I love to whistle 'cause it makes me merry" e 236 words by H. Adamson   2235
MCKAY, GEORGE FREDERICK
    THE MOON IS UP; "The moon is up, the moon is up! the larks begin to fly" 2 pt round e 343   2236
MACLEOD, ANNIE
    SKYE BOAT SONG. See 4758
MCLEOD, PETER, 1797-1859
    "OH! WHY LEFT I MY HAME?" e 100,349 words by R. Gilfillan   2237
MACKEBEN, THEO
    DIE DUBARRY. See 2451-2452
MADETOJA, LEEVI ANTTI, 1887-1947
    KOSIOVARSA, op.20b, no.3; "Nuori varsa mulla on"; MY WOOING FOAL; "Handsome is my   2238
        yearling foal!" e, fi 124 words by L. Kyösti
MAHLER, GUSTAV, 1860-1911
    [LIEDER AUS DES KNABEN WUNDERHORN] WER HAT DIES LIEDLEIN ERDACHT?;   2239
        "Dort oben am Berg in dem hohen Haus!"; UP THERE ON THE HILL; "Up there on the hill in
        the house so high" e, g 330
    [Ibid] WO DIE SCHÖNEN TROMPETEN BLASEN; "Wer ist denn draussen und wer klopfet an";   2240
        WHERE THE SHINING TRUMPETS BLOW; "Who stands without, where the pale starlight gleams"
        e, g 220
MAI-HSIN
    FAITHFUL UNTO DEATH; "Forward march, no retreat" e 7 joint composer Meng-Po   2241
    SWORD BLADE MARCH; "Forward! Charge! On with sword blades" e 7   2242
MAINVILLE, DENISE
    DEAR LITTLE LADY IN BLUE; "Life is but a fleeting moment" e 71   2243
    THE LORD'S PRAYER; "Our Father Who art in Heaven" e 71   2244
MAJO, GIOVANNI FRANCESCO DE, ca1740-1771
    [IFIGENIA IN TAURIDE, opera; words by M. Verazi] REZITATIV UND ARIE DER   2245
        IPHIGENIE; "Accresca pietoso al viver tuo" (recit); "Si il labbro si lagna" (aria); "Möge der
        barmherzige Himmel deinen Leben hinzusetzen" (recit); "Wenn deine Lippen klagen" (aria) g, i
        218
MARKOVA, NINA VLADIMIROVNA, 1908-
    THE WEREWOLF; "Poor Ivan he was a coward" e, r 342 words by A. Pushkin   2246
MALAN, CÄSAR
    HARRE, MEINE SEELE; "Harre, meine Seele, harre des Herrn!" g 326 words by F. Räder   2247
MALINSKI, J.
    "Z CAŁEGO ŚWIATA TU ZEBRANI"; THE EAGLE OWLS; "We came here, for our country yearning"   2248
        e, p 159
MALOTTE, ALBERT HAY, 1895-
    THE HOMING HEART; "Each day, dear love, my road leads far" e 259 words by D. Henderson   2249
    THE LORD'S PRAYER; "Our Father, which art in heaven" e 364 words from Bible   2250
    THE TWENTY-THIRD PSALM; "The Lord is my shepherd" e 200 words from Bible   2251
Mana-Zucca. See ZUCKERMANN, AUGUSTA, 1890-

MARTINI, JEAN PAUL ÉGIDE, 1741-1816
>PLAISIR D'AMOUR; "Plaisir d'amour ne dure qu'un moment" f 88; THE JOYS OF LOVE; ROMANCE;   2282
"The joys of love endure but for a day" e, f 405; "The joys of love are always quickly passing"
e, f 36; PIACER D'AMOR; "Piacer d'amor piu che un di sol non dura"; "The joys of love so quickly do depart" e, i 329; THE JOY OF LOVE, "The joy of love may not have long to stay" e 348

Martini, Padre. See MARTINI, JEAN PAUL ÉGIDE, 1741-1816

MARX, JOSEPH, 1882-
>MARIENLIED; "Ich sehe dich in tausend Bildern"; SONG OF ST. MARY; "From thousand paintings   2283
though I know thee" e, g 330   words by Novalis

MARX, JULIUS
>MIT MEINER MAPPE; "Mit meiner Mappe unterm Arm wollt' ins Kolleg ich ziehn" g 31   words by   2284
L. Beer

MARX, KARL JULIUS, 1897-
>"DASS ZWEI SICH HERZLICH LIEBEN" g 49   words by H. Claudius   2285
>GLÜCKAUF! GLÜCKAUF! DER SILBERZWEIG; "Glückauf! Glückauf! Der Silberzweig in Bergesnacht   2286
erblüht in unserm tiefen Schacht" g 49   words by F. E. Krauss
>"IHR IN DER LIEBE GEBORGEN" g 49   words by B. von Heiseler   2287
>"JEDEN MORGEN GEHT DIE SONNE AUF" g 49, 326   words by H. Claudius   2288
>KANON ZU VIER STIMMEN; "Sine musica nulla vita" 4 pt round lat 49   2289
>"LAND DER EWIGEN GEDANKEN" g 49   words by H. Claudius   2290
>MEISTERSPRUCH; "Wer allzeit hinterm Ofen sitzt" g 49   words by H. Sachs   2291
>"SCHEIN UNS, DU LIEBE SONNE" g 49   2292

MARZIALS, THEODOR, 1850-?
>THE THREE SAILOR BOYS; "Oh, we're three jolly, jolly, sailor boys" e 28, 205   2293
>TWICKENHAM FERRY; "Ohoiye ho, hoyeho who's for the ferry" e 132   2294

MASCAGNI, PIETRO, 1863-1945
>[CAVALLERIA RUSTICANA, opera; words by G. Menasci and G. Targioni-   2295
Tozzetti] [Fior di Giaggiolo gli angeli] LOLA'S SONG; MY KING OF ROSES;
"My king of roses! Radiant angels stand in heav'n in thousands" e 132
>[Ibid] [Intermezzo sinfonica] AVE MARIA; INTERMEZZO; "Mother, mother, see my   2296
tears are falling" e 132; "Ave Maria, gratia plena"; "Hail, Mary, full of grace" e, lat 304
>[Ibid] O LOLA BIANCA; "O Lola, bianca come fior di spino"; SICILIANA; "O Lola, with thy   2297
lips like crimson berries" e, i 3; O LOLA; "O Lola, with thy cheeks rosier than cherries" e 132
>[Ibid] [Viva il vino] DRINKING SONG; "Hail! The red wine richly flowing" e 132   2298
>[Ibid] VOI LO SAPETE; "Voi lo sapete, o mamma"; "Well do you know, good Mamma" e, i   2299
1, 6
>[IRIS, opera; words by L. Illica] UN DI ERO PICCINA, Act II; "Un di (ero piccina)   2300
al tempio vidi un bonzo"; ONCE IN MY CHILDHOOD; "Once in my childhood within a mighty
temple" e, i 143

MASON, LOWELL, 1792-1872
>MY FAITH LOOKS UP TO THEE; OLIVET; "My faith looks up to Thee Thou Lamb of Calvary" e   2301
28, 35, 236, 279, 366
>"NEARER, MY GOD TO THEE" e 28, 34, 173, 233, 279, 366   words by S. F. Adams   2302
>SAFELY THROUGH ANOTHER WEEK; "Safely thro' another week God has bro't us on our way" e 28,   2303
279, 366   words by J. Newton
>WILDWOOD FLOWERS; "Flowers, wildwood flowers, in a sheltered dell they grow" e 279, 366   2304
>"WORK, FOR THE NIGHT IS COMING" e 28, 233, 236, 279, 366   words by A. L. Walker-Coghill   2305

MASSENET, JULES ÉMILE FRÉDÉRIC, 1842-1912
>[LE CID, opera; words by A. P. Dennery] PLEUREZ! PLEUREZ, MES YEUX! Act   2306
III; "De cet affreux combat" (recit); "Pleurez! Pleurez, mes yeux!" (aria); "Ended at last the
strife" (recit); "Then weep! O grief-worn eyes" (aria) e, f 1
>CRÉPUSCULE; "Comme un rideau sous la blancheur"; TWILIGHT; "As with a veil under the   2307
whiteness" e, f 191, 193, 195   words by A. Silvestre
>ELEGIE; "O doux printemps d'autrefois"; "O spring of days long ago" e, f 122, 329; ELEGY; "Oh,   2308
lovely spring long ago" e 348; "Springtime brings a mem'ry to me" e 357
>[HÉRODIADE, opera; words by P. Milliet and G. Hartmann] IL EST DOUX,   2309
IL EST BON, Act I; "Celui dont la parole efface toutes peines" (recit); "Il est doux, il est bon"
(aria); "He by whose mighty word is banished ev'ry sadness" (recit); "He is kind, he is good (aria)
e, f 1
>[Ibid] NE ME REFUSE PAS, Act I; "Hérode! Hérode! Ne me refuse pas!" (recit); "Ne me   2310
refuse pas" (aria); DO NOT REFUSE MY PLEA; "Ah! Herod! Ah! Herod! Do not deny my plea!"
(recit); "Do not refuse my plea" (aria) e, f 357
>[Ibid] SALOMÉ!, Act III; "C'en est fait! la Judée appartient à Tiberre!" (recit); "Salomé!   2311
Demande au prisonier qui revoit la lumière" (aria); "Is it done! And Judea belongs to Tiberius!"
(recit); "Salome! Then ask the captive freed, who to sunshine returneth" (aria) e, f 364

MASSENET, JULES EMILE FREDERIC, 1842-1912 (Continued)

[Ibid] SALOMÉ! SALOMÉ!, Act I; "Elle a fui le palais elle a quitté ces lieux" (recit); "Salomé!   2312
Salomé! Ah! reviens! je t'attends"(aria); "From the palace she fled, she is no longer here!" (recit);
"Salomé! Salomé! Ah! return! I await" (aria) e, f 4

[Ibid] VISION FUGITIVE, Act II; "Ce breuvage pourrait me donner un tel rêve" (recit); "Vision   2313
fugitive et toujours poursuivie" (aria); "And this potion could bring such a vision before me" (recit);
"Dream so fair, dream I follow while ever 'tis fleeing" (aria) e, f 4

[MANON, opera; words by W. H. Meilhac and P. E. F. Gille] AH! FUYEZ,   2314
DOUCE IMAGE, Act III; "Je suis seul! seul enfin! (recit); "Ah! fuyez, douce image, à mon âme
trop chère" (aria); "I am alone! now, at last!" (recit); "Ah! begone, tender dream, though my
heart still may languish" (aria) e, f 3

[Ibid] EN FERMENT LES YEUX; "Instant charmant, où la crainte fait trève" (recit); "En ferment   2315
les yeux, je vois" (aria); THE DREAM OF DES GRIEUX; "How sweet this hour, when no danger is
low'ring" (recit); "Where the wood sways in the breeze" (aria) e, f 3

[Ibid] ÉPOUSE QUELQUE BRAVE FILLE, Act III, scene 2; "Les grands mots que voilà" (recit);   2316
"Épouse quelque brave fille" (aria); "Mighty curses are those" (recit); "Go marry someone fair
and tender" (aria) e, f 5

[Ibid] "JE SUIS ENCOR TOUT ÉTOURDIE," Act I; "This strange new world fills the soul of me"   2317
e, f 6

[Ibid] OBÉISSONS QUAND LEUR VOIX APPELLE, Act III; "Est-ce vrai? Grand merci!" (recit);   2318
"Obéissons quand leur voix appelle" (aria); "Is that so? Thank you all" (recit); "Come and obey
the voice that is calling" (aria) e, f 1

"OUVRE TES YEUX BLEUS"; "OPEN THY BLUE EYES" e, f 140, 176, 237, 387   words by P. Robiquet   2319
"QUE L'HEURE EST DONC BRÈVE"; HOW BRIEF IS THE HOUR; "The hour swift is flying" e, f 140   2320
words by A. Silvestre

[WERTHER, opera; words by E. Blau, P. Milliet, and G. Hartmann] "VA!   2321
LAISSE COULER MES LARMES," Act III; "No, let all my tears continue" e, f 2

MATOS RODRÍGUEZ, GERARDO H.

LA CUMPARSITA; "La cumparsita de miseria sin fin desfila" s 284   2322
MARGARITA PUNZO; "Caminito del campo por el sendero" s 284   words by F. Silva Valdés   2323

MATTEIS, NICOLA, fl 1672

KANZONETTE; "Caro volto pallidetto"; "Schönes milchweisses Antlitz" g, i 217   2324

MATTHEWS, TIMOTHY R.

"THOU DIDST LEAVE THY THRONE." See 8995

MAUDE CAROLINE, VISCOUNTESS HAWARDEN

MAGDALEN; "Magdelen, at Michael's gate" e 344   words by H. Kingsley   2325

MAURELIA, SISTER, S. P.

THE ENTHRONEMENT OF LOVE; JESUS, KING OF THE HOME; "Heart of Jesus, Thou art pleading"   2326
e 71   words by Sister Rose Angela, S. P.

MAURMEIER, ROBERT, 1862-1931

BURSCHENJAHRZEIT; "Als der Lenz den Blütensegen gross ins maiengrüne Land" g 31   2327
MEIN WÜRZBURG; "Nennt man mir drei Wunderdinge Frauen" g 31   2328

MAYBRICK, MICHAEL, 1844-1913

"BY THE BLUE ALSATIAN MOUNTAINS" e 132; THE BLUE ALSATIAN MOUNTAINS e 279, 366   2329
words by C. (Alington) Barnard

THE HEART OF A SAILOR; "Now who's the lad for a lass to wed" e 205   2330
THE HOLY CITY; "Last night I lay a-sleeping" e 237, 346, 400   words by F. E. Weatherly   2331
THE MIDSHIPMITE; "'Twas in eighty-eight on a winter's night" e 205; "'Twas in 'fifty-five, on a   2332
winter's night" e 28, 366   words by F. E. Weatherly

NANCY LEE; "Of all the wives as e'er you know" e 28, 205, 279, 366   words by F. E. Weatherly   2333
THE STAR OF BETHLEHEM; "It was the eve of Christmas, the snow lay deep and white" e 394   2334
words by F. E. Weatherly

THE TAR'S FAREWELL; "When forc'd to bid farewell to Loo" e 205   2335
THEY ALL LOVE JACK; "When the ship is trim and ready" e 28, 205, 366   words by F. E. Weatherly   2336
A WARRIOR BOLD; "In days of old, when knights were bold" e 28, 366   2337

MAYER, FATHER C.

BOYS, KEEP YOUR POWDER DRY; "Can'st tell who lost the battle" e 161   2338

MAYER, JOSEPH

SHEPHERDS' SONG; "While shepherds watched their flocks by night" e 410   words by N.   2339
Tate

MAZZAFERRATA, GIOVANNI BATTISTA, 17th c

"PRESTO, PRESTO, IO M'INNAMORO"; "SWIFT MY HEART SURRENDERS" e, i 139   2340

MAZZOCCHI, DOMENICO, 1590-1665

KANZONETTE; "Piu non sia, che m'innamori"; "Fernerhin soll es nicht mehr geschehen, dass   2341
mich zur Liebe locken" g, i 217

MEDIŅŠ, JĀNIS
    ABSCHIED; "Deine lieben Hände streichelnd wie ein spater Sonnerstrahl"; LA CARESSE; "Je   2342
        caresse tes mains si douces" f, g 224
    DAS FRAGENDE MÄDCHEN; "Sag', Liebster, mein Liebster, wo nahmst du her so bunte Worte?";   2343
        LA JEUNE FILLE DEMANDE; "Dis, cher ami, d'où viennent donc tes paroles tendres?" f, g 224
    LEBEN DU; "Leben, o Leben du schaukelndes Schweben"; LA VIE; "Où sont, ma vie, tes promesses   2344
        si tendres" f, g 224
MEEN, GEORGE
    O FRED TELL THEM TO STOP; "No doubt you have heard of the Great Fancy Fair" e 115   2345
MÉHUL, ÉTIENNE NICOLAS, 1763-1817
    LE CHANT DU DÉPART; "La victoire, en chantant, nous ouvre la barrière" f 82,91   words by   2346
        J. Chenier
    [UNE FOLIE, opera; words by J. N. Bouilly] "JE SUIS ENCOR DANS MON PRIN-   2347
        TEMPS"; "SUL LIMITAR DEL MITE APRIL" f, i 411
    [JOSEPH, opera; words by A. Duval] AIR DE JOSEPH; "Vainement Pharaon dans sa   2348
        reconnaissance"; "Vainly Pharoah attempts ever with gifts to load me" e, f 153
    ODE ANACRÉONTIQUE; "'e ge melaina pinei de dendrea auten" gr (tr) 278   2349
    STRATONICE, opera; words by F. Benoît Hoffman] AIR D'ERASISTRATE; "Sur   2350
        le sort de son fils" (recit); "Ô des amants deité tutélaire" (aria); "For the fate of his son" (recit);
        "Goddess of Love, oh! protectress of lovers" (aria) e, f 147
MEISEL, WILL
    "TAUSEND ROTE ROSEN BLÜHN, op.112 g 222 words by H. Hannes   2351
MEISSLER, JOSEF
    STOLZENFELS AM RHEIN; "Ein Grenadier auf dem Dorfplatz stand, ein Mädchen ihm zur Seit'"   2352
        g 328
MEJIA-ARREDONDO, ENRIQUE
    FLOR DE MONTAÑA; "Flor de montaña fina y lozana del Indio bravo" s 303   2353
MELANI, ALESSANDRO, ca1630-1703
    VEZZOSA AURORA; "Vezzosa Aurora, vezzosa Aurora deh, sorgi" i 180   2354
MELANI, JACOPO, 1623-1676
    [IL GIRELLO, opera; words by F. Acciaiuoli] ARIE DER DORALBA; "Sconsigliata   2355
        Doralba, ove t'aggiri?"; "Törichte Doralba, wohin verlierst du dich?" g, i 217
    [Ibid] KANZONETTE DER DORALBA; "Inconstante Mustafa?" (recit); "Bionde chiome e bel sem-   2356
        biante la fortuna e il ciel ci da" (aria); "Mustafa unbeständig?" (recit); "Blondes Haar und ein
        schönes Gesicht" (aria) g, i 217
MELARTIN, ERKKI, 1875-1937
    LEIVO, op.138, no.2; "Miks, leivo, lenät Suomehen"; SKYLARK; "Why haste you here, oh joyous   2357
        sprite" e, f 124 words by A. Rahkonen
MELCHERS, HENRIK MELCHER, 1882-
    ZIGENARSAANG, NR.2; "Hochgetürmte Rimaflut" sw 356   2358
MELICHAR, ALOIS, 1896-
    "AN DER DONAU, WENN DER WEIN BLÜHT." See 1403
MELNGAILIS, EMILIS
    DIE GOLDENEN BLÄTTER; "Wie lange zog sich die bleiern träge verdammte Nacht!"; LES FEUILLES   2359
        DORÉES; "La sombre nuit sous sa chappe de plomb pesante se traine" f, g 224
MELVILL, DAVID
    "HEY HO, TO THE GREENWOOD." See 493
    JOLLY SHEPHERD; "Jolly shepherd and up on a hill as he sat" 3 pt round e 144   2360
    MUSING; "Musing, musing, musing, my own self all alone" 4 pt round e 144   2361
    "NOW GOD BE WITH OLD SIMEON" 3 pt round e 144   2362
    O LUSTY MAY; "O lusty May with Flora Queen" e 144   2363
    "SING WE NOW MERRILY" 10 or 11 pt round e 144   2364
    TO PORTSMOUTH; "To Portsmouth! To Portmouth! it is a gallant town" 4 pt round e 144,349   2365
MENA, LUIS E.
    ELILA, piano 303   2366
MENDELSSOHN-BARTHOLDY, FELIX, 1809-1847
    ABSCHIED VOM WALDE, op.59, no.3; "O Täler weit, o Höhen, o schöner grüner Wald" g 31,   2367
        99; O TÄLER WEIT, O HÖHEN g 326 words by J. von Eichendorff; IN HEAVENLY LOVE
        ABIDING; "In heav'nly love abiding, no change my heart shall fear" e 28,366 words by
        A. L. Waring
    AUF FLÜGELN DES GESANGES, op.34, no.2; "Auf Flügeln des Gesanges, Herzliebchen; trag' ich dich   2368
        fort"; ON WINGS OF SONG; "The magic of my singing will carry you far away" e, g 141; "On
        wings of song I'll bear thee, to those fair Asian lands" e, g 277; "On wings of song, my treasure,
        we'll start our voyage from here" e, g 329; "On wings of song I'll take you and bear you far away"
        e 395; "On wings of song the skylark his dewy nest forsakes" e 199; "On wings of song thro' dream-
        land my love afar I bear" e 348 words by H. Heine

MENDELSSOHN-BARTHOLDY, FELIX, 1809-1847 (Continued)

BEI DER WIEGE, op.47, no.6; "Schlummre! Schlummre und träume von kommender Zeit"; BY   2369
  THE CRADLE; "Sleep my dear! Sleep my baby, and dream of the days" e, g 45; CRADLE
  SONG; "Slumber! Slumber and dreams of the fast coming hours" e, g 274 words by C.
  Klingemann

[ELIAS, oratorio] "CAST THY BURDEN UPON THE LORD" e 28,366   2370

[Ibid] "FOR THE MOUNTAINS SHALL DEPART" e 90   2371

[Ibid] IF WITH ALL YOUR HEARTS; "Ye people rend your hearts" (recit); "If with all your   2372
  hearts ye truly seek me" (aria) e 123,200; (aria only) e 394

[Ibid] IT IS ENOUGH; "It is enough, O Lord, now take away my life" e 123,394   2373

[Ibid] LIFT THINE EYES; "Lift thine eyes, O lift thine eyes to the mountains" e 28   2374

[Ibid] "O REST IN THE LORD" e 28,122,123,200,346,394 words from Psalm XXXVII   2375

[Ibid] "THEN SHALL THE RIGHTEOUS SHINE FORTH" e 160   2376

"ES IST BESTIMMT IN GOTTESRAT," op.47, no.4 g 326,328; "IN GOD'S GREAT WISDOM" e, g   2377
  141 words by E. von Feuchtersleben

[FESTGESANG, OP.68, NO.2] "HARK! THE HERALD ANGELS SING" e 28,33,35,38,39,   2378
  125,165,206,233,236,251,296,305,307,315,333,337,366,388; "HARK HOW ALL THE
  WELKIN RINGS" e 410 words by C. Wesley

GRUSS, op.19,no.5; "Leise zieht durch mein Gemuth" g 250; GREETING; "Gently in my thoughts   2379
  I hear" e, g 36; "Leise zieht durch mein Gemüt"; "Soft and clear a silv'ry toll" e, g 141;
  "LEISE ZIEHT DURCH MEIN GEMÜT" g 326 words by H. Heine

[DIE HEIMKEHR AUS DER FREMDE, opera; words by K. Klingemann] I AM   2380
  A ROAMER; "I am a roamer bold and gay" e 273

[ICH WOLLT', MEINE LIEBE ERGÖSSE SICH, OP.63, NO.1] I WOULD THAT MY   2381
  LOVE; "I would that my love could silently flow in a single word" e 28

DER JÄGER ABSCHIED, op.50, no.2; "Wer hat dich, du schöner Wald" g 99,326,328; THE   2382
  HUNTER'S FAREWELL; "Who aloft thy head did raise" e 28 words by J. von Eichendorff

JAGDLIED, op.84, no.3; "Mit Lust tät ich ausreiten durch einen grünen Wald"; HUNTSMAN'S SONG;   2383
  "As gaily I was riding thro' cool and shady wood" e, g 45

LIEBLINGSPLÄTZCHEN, op.99, no.3; "Wisst ihr, wo ich gerne weil'"; THE FAVOURITE SPOT; "In   2384
  the valley, by the mill" e, g 330; THE FAVORITE SPOT; "I a fav'rite spot have found" e 395
  words by F. Robert

[LIEDER OHNE WORTE, OP.3, NO.3] TAKE HEART, YE WEARY; "Take heart, ye weary   2385
  and heavy laden" e 8 words by C. K. Davis

MAIENLIED, op.8, no.7; "Man soll hören süsses Singen in den Auen überall"; MAY SONG; "Listen   2386
  to the silv'ry ringing from the dewy meadow vale" e, g 141 words by V. C. Warte

A MIDSUMMER NIGHT'S DREAM. See 2393-2394

DER MOND; "Mein Herz ist wie die dunkle Nacht"; THE MOON; "My heart is like the gloomy   2387
  night" e, g 45

"OH, WERT THOU IN THE CAULD BLAST," op.63, no.5 e 28,366 words by R. Burns   2388

[PAULUS, oratorio, OP.36] BE THOU FAITHFUL, no.40; "Be thou faithful unto Truth"   2389
  (aria); "And they all persecuted Paul on his way" (recit) e 160

[Ibid] "BUT THE LORD IS MINDFUL OF HIS OWN," no.13, (aria); "And he journey'd with   2390
  companions towards Damascus" (recit) e 394 (aria only) e 28; "BUT THE LORD IS MINDFUL"
  (aria only) e 160

[Ibid] JERUSALEM! THOU THAT KILLEST THE PROPHETS, no.7; "Jerusalem, Jerusalem, thou   2391
  that killest the prophets" e 123

[Ibid] RECITATIVE AND ARIA, no.12; "O Lord, they prophesy against Thee" (recit); "Consume   2392
  them all, Lord God of hosts" (aria) e 160

[EIN SOMMERNACHTSTRAUM] NOCTURNE; "When all the world is sleeping beneath starry   2393
  skies" e 343

[Ibid] YOU SPOTTED SNAKES; "You spotted snakes with double tongue" e 75 words by W.   2394
  Shakespeare, A Midsummer-night's Dream

ST. PAUL ORATORIO. See 2389-2392

[UNGLÜCKSELIGE, OP.94] INFELICE; "In felice! già dal mio sguardo si dileguò!" (recit);   2395
  "Ah, ritorna età felice" (aria); LONE AND JOYLESS; "Lone and joyless! and I may never behold
  him more!"; "Ah, return, ye days of gladness" (aria) e, i 276

WARTEND, op.9, no.3; ROMANZA; "Sie trug einen Falken auf ihrer Hand und hat ihn über den See   2396
  gesandt" g 229

MÉNDEZ-ZEBADÚA, ISMAEL

"NACI EN LA CUMBRE" s 284   2397

MENG-PO

FAITHFUL UNTO DEATH. See 2241

MENOTTI, GIAN CAROL, 1911-

[THE CONSUL, opera] MAGDA'S ARIA; TO THIS WE'VE COME; "To this we've come; that   2398
  men withhold the world from men" e 6

MERCER, JOHN H., 1909-
    "I'M AN OLD COWHAND FROM THE RIO GRANDE" e 236   2399
MERIKANTO, OSKAR, 1868-1924
    REPPURIN LAULU; "Luadogan meren randamil"; SONG OF THE PEDLAR; "Fair the shores of Lodoga"   2400
       e, fi 124
MESSAGER, ANDRÉ CHARLES PROSPER, 1853-1929
    [LA BEARNAISE, opera; words by Leterrier and Vaulvo] BERCEUSE BÉARNAISE;   2401
       "Fais nono, mon bel enfantoux" f 82
METHFESSEL, ALBERT GOTTLIEB, 1785-1869
    BEMOOSTER BURSCHE; "Bemooster Bursche zieh ich aus" g 31 words by G. Schwab   2402
    HINAUS IN DIE FERNE; "Hinaus in die Ferne mit lautem Hörnerklang" g 353; GESANG AUS-   2403
       ZIEHENDER KRIEGER g 99; JÄGER-MARSCHLIED g 31
    MAHNUNG ZUR FREUDE; "Du bist nicht auf der Welt" g 31 words by P. Warncke   2404
    "STIMMT AN MIT HELLEM, HOHEM KLANG" g 31, 326 words by M. Claudius   2405
METZ, THEODORE A.
    A HOT TIME IN THE OLD TOWN; "Come along get you ready wear your bran, bran new gown";   2406
       "When you hear dem a bells go ding, ling, ling" (ref) e 246; THERE'LL BE A HOT TIME; "There'll
       be a hot time in the old town tonight" (ref) e 32, 34 words by J. Hayden
MEYER, GEORGE W., 1884-
    "EVERYTHING IS PEACHES DOWN IN GEORGIA." See 30
MEYER-HELMUND, ERIK, 1861-1932
    BALLGEFLÜSTER; "Sie machen Die Complimente und senden Dir Blumen in's Haus" g 327   2407
MEYERBEER, GIACOMO, 1791-1864
    [L'AFRICAINE, opera; words by A. E. Scribe] O PARADIS SORTI DE L'ONDE, Act   2408
       IV; "Pays merveilleux, jardins fortunés" (recit); "O paradis sorti de l'onde" (aria); "Thou en-
       chanted land, gardens of delight" (recit); "O paradise aris'n from ocean" (aria) e, f 3; LAND
       SO WUNDERBAR!; "Land so wunderbar! Gärten, reich und schön!" (recit); "O Paradise das mir
       zum Ruhme werde" (aria); "O ridente suol! Vago e bel giardin!" (recit); "O Paradiso in terra
       scenso" (aria) g, i 391
    DINORAH. See 2412
    [LES HUGUENOTS, opera; words by A. E. Scribe] "NOBLES SEIGNEURS, SALUT!"   2409
       (recit); "Une dame noble et sage" (aria); LIETI SIGNOR; "Lieti signor, salute!" (recit); "Nobil'
       donna e tanto onesta" (aria); MY NOBLE KNIGHTS; "My noble Knights, I hail you" (recit); "Pure
       and noble is the lady fair" (aria) e, f, i 1, 176
    [Ibid] PARMI LES PLEURS, Act IV; "Parmi les pleurs mon rêve se ranime"; ROMANCE; "Covered   2410
       with tears, my visions reawaken" e, f 1
    [Ibid] PIFF, PAFF, Act I; "Voluntiers, un vieil air huguenot" (recit); "Piff, paff, piff, paff, pour   2411
       les couvents c'est fini" (aria); FOR CONVENTS, IT'S OVER; HUGUENOT SONG; "Listen now,
       here's a Huguenot song" (recit); "Piff, paff, piff, paff, for convents, it's over now" (aria) e, f 5
    [LE PARDON DE PLOËRMEL, opera; words by J. Barbier and M. Carré]   2412
       OMBRE LÉGÈRE, Act II: "La nuit est froide et sombre!" (recit); "Ombre légère qui suis mes pas"
       (aria); "Ahime! che notte oscura!" (recit); "Ombra leggera, non te n'andar" (aria); "Alas!
       how dark the night is!" (recit); "O fleeting shadow upon the meadow" (aria) e, f, i 292;
       OMBRA LEGGERA i 302; OMBRA LEGGIERA; "Ombra leggiera, non te n'andar"; "O tender
       shadow, that hover'st near" (aria only) e, i 6
    [LE PROPHÈTE, opera; words by A. E. Scribe] AH! MON FILS, Act I; "Ah! mon   2413
       fils! sois béni!" "Ah! my son! Blessed be thou!" e, f 2
    [Ibid] DONNEZ, DONNEZ, Act IV; "Donnez, donnez, pour une pauvre âme"; ROMANCE; "Give   2414
       alms, give alms, and one poor soul cherish" e, f 2
MIASKOVSKIĬ, NICOLAĬ IAKOVLEVICH, 1881-1950
    "AT TIMES IT SEEMS TO ME" e, r 342 words by S. Stchipatchev   2415
    ELBRUS AND THE AIRPLANE; "Oh, Mount Elbras you are tall!" e, r 342 words by S. Stchipatchev   2416
    HER PICTURE; "She is as alert as a boy" e, r 342 words by M. Lermontov   2417
    THE RED STAR IS RIDING; SONG OF THE AIR FORCE; "Above verdant steppes and above snow-clad   2418
       mountains" e, r 162 words by I. Frenkel
Miaskovsky, N. See MIASKOVSKIĬ, NIKOLAĬ IAKOVLEVICH, 1881-1950
MICHAELIS, HUGO
    DER GRAF VON RÜDESHEIM; "Das war der Graf von Rüdesheim" g 31 words by E. Bloch and A. G.   2419
       Benda
MICHLEM, T. CARYL, 1925-
    JESUS, BABY WONDERFUL; "Jesus, Baby Wonderful, born among the cattle" e 305 words by H.   2420
       Macnichol
MIESSNER, WILLIAM OTTO, 1880-
    GOD SAVE AMERICA; "Land of our fathers, from ocean to ocean" e 236   2421
    MICHIGAN, MY MICHIGAN; "A song to thee, fair state of mine" e 28   2422

MILAN, LUIS, 16th c
"AL AMOR QUIERRO VENCER"; VILLENCICO EN CASTELLANO; "AH! COULD I BUT CONQUER   2423
LOVE" e, s 403
DURANDARTE; "Durandarte, Durandarte, buen caballero probado" s 12   2424
FALAI, MIÑ' AMOR; VILLANCICO; "Falai, miñ' amor falaime; si non me falais" s 12   2425
SOSPIRASTES, VALDOVINOS; ROMANCE; "Sospirastes, Valdovinos, las cosas que yo mas queria"   2426
s 12
TRISTE ESTABA; ROMANCE; "Trista estaba muy quejosa la trista troyana" s 12   2427
MILFORD, H.
WE NEVER SPEAK AS WE PASS BY; "The spell has passed, the dream is o'er"; "We never speak as   2428
we pass by" (ref) e 114, 131 (ref only) e 128
MILFORD, ROBIN HUMPHREY, 1903-
MEG MERRILIES; "Old Meg she was a gipsy and lived upon the moors" e 199   words by J. Keats   2429
MILIŪTIN, ĪURIĬ SERGEEVICH, 1903-
MY TRUSTY GUN; "My dear sweetheart came to see me when I left by railroad train" e, r 162   2430
words by Uralsky
OUR GENERALS!; "Oh what praises, oh what praises, oh what praises filled the air" e 339   words   2431
by E. Fink
MILLARD, HARRISON, 1830-1895
AVE MARIA; "Ave, Maria, gratia plena"; "Hail, Mary, full of grace" e, lat 304   2432
MY SHIP COMES IN; "My ship comes sailing up the sea" e 205   words by J. Miller   2433
THE PILOT BRAVE; "Our good ship speeds before the gale" e 205   words by G. Cooper   2434
SHIP AHOY!; "Our pennant floats upon the breeze" e 205   words by G. Cooper   2435
THE SHIPS GO SAILING BY; "Two children play'd on the sandy shore" e 205   words by M. C. Doud   2436
VIVA L'AMERICA, HOME OF THE FREE; "Noble Republic! happiest of lands" e 189   2437
MILLER, ALBERT, 1914-
ANIMAL ALPHABET; "A's for the ant, and B's for the bee" e 249   2438
I KNOW AN OLD LADY; "I know an old lady who swallowed a fly" e 249   words by R. Bonne   2439
MILLER, BOB, 1895-
ELEVEN CENT COTTON; "'Leven cent cotton, forty cent meat" e 34   joint composer E. Dermer   2440
MILLER, HARRY S., 1895-
THE CAT CAME BACK; "Dar was ole Mister Johnson he had trouble of his own"; "But the cat came   2441
back" (ref) e 131
MARCHING THRU BERLIN; "The devil put on a different face"; "We'll be singing Hallelujah, march-   2442
ing thru Berlin" (ref) e 7   words by B. Reed
MILLÖCKER, KARL, 1842-1899
[DER BETTELSTUDENT, operetta; words by C. Wäzel and R. Genée] ACH,   2443
ICH HAB' SIE JA NUR; "Und da soll man noch galant sein gegen schöneres Geschlecht" g 254
[Ibid] HÖCHSTE LUST UND TIEFSTES LEID" g 257   2444
[Ibid] ICH HAB KEIN GELD; "Ich hab kein Geld, bin vogelfrei"; "Trotz allem Pech ein lustig   2445
Lied" (ref) g 256
[Ibid] "ICH KNÜPFTE MANCHE ZARTE BANDE" g 254   2446
[GASPARONE, operetta; words by C. Wäzel and R. Genée] ANZOLETTO UND   2447
ESTRELLA, Act I, no. 6; "Anzoletto sang 'Kom mia bella'"; "Wem zuckt es nicht in den Füssen"
(ref) g 254
[Ibid] "DUNKELROTE ROSEN BRING' ICH, SCHÖNE FRAU!" g 255   2448
[Ibid] "ER SOLL DEIN HERR SEIN," Act III g 255   2449
[Ibid] "O DASS ICH DOCH DER RÄUBER WÄRE," Act I, no. 3 g 256   2450
[GRÄFEN DUBARRY, operetta] ICH SCHENK MEIN HERZ; "Ich habe Liebe schon genossen"   2451
g 254
[Ibid] WENN VERLIEBTE BUMMELN GEHN; "Ja, es ist ein alter Vorgang" g 258   2452
[DAS VERWUNSCHENE SCHLOSS, operetta] O, DU HIMMELBLAUER SEE; "Zwischen   2453
Felsen die voll Schnee dulie" g 255
Mills, Alan.   See MILLER, ALBERT, 1914-
MILLS, KERRY
AT A GEORGIA CAMP MEETING; "A camp meeting took place by the colored race"; "When that   2454
band of darkies began to play" (ref) e 114, 115, 131 (ref only) e 128; "When the big brass band
began to play" (ref) e 32, 34
LET'S ALL GO UP TO MAUD'S; "Some say a ride on the trolley is grand" e 204   words by J. C.   2455
Farrell
MINKOVSKY, F.
SHABBAT HAMALKA; "Hachama meyrosh ha-ilanot nistalka"; "The sun has slipped behind the trees"   2456
e, h (tr) 318   words by C. N. Bialik
MIODUSZEWSKI, X.
"KTO SIĘ W OPIEKĘ"; PSALM 90; "Blessed is he whose trust is in the Highest" e, p 295   words by   2457
J. Kochanowski

MIODUSZEWSKI, X
    PIEŚŃ PORANNA; "Kiedy ranne wstają zorze, tobie ziemia, tobie morze"; MORNING SONG; "When   2458
        the dawn from sleep is winging, all the earth of Thee is singing" e, p 295; KIEDY RANNE WSTAJĄ
        ZORZE; IN THE DAWN WITH SKYLARK WINGING; "In the dawn with skylark winging, nature
        bells for Thee are ringing" e 159; PIEŚŃ WIECZORNA; "Wszystkie nasze dzienne sprawy, przyjm
        litośnie Boże prawy"; EVENING SONG; "All our daily plans and deeds, we bring before Thee, God
        Almighty" e, p 295   words by F. Karpinski
MÖNCH VON SALZBURG, 1370-1400
    DIE ZWEI ROSEN. See 4187
MOHR, THEODOR, 1826-1903
    JUGEND; "Nur einmal bringt des Jahres Lauf uns Lenz und Lerchenlieder" g 31   words by R. Von   2459
        Wilpert
MOLLOY, JAMES LYMAN, 1837-1909
    ALICE, WHERE ART THOU? See 93
    THE KERRY DANCE; "O, the days of the Kerry dancing" e 166,237; "O THE DAY OF THE KERRY   2460
        DANCING" e 213
    LOVE'S OLD SWEET SONG; "Once in the dear dead days beyond recall"; "Just a song at twilight"   2461
        (ref) e 28,36,122,131,132,233,236,237,279,329,366   words by G. C. Bingham
    POLLY; "Do you want to know the smartest craft, as ever put from port?" e 205   words by F. E.   2462
        Weatherly
    THE SANDMAN; "When the toys are growing weary and the twilight gathers in" e 129,130   2463
MONACO, JAMES V., 1885-
    "IF WE CAN'T BE THE SAME OLD SWEETHEARTS WE'LL JUST BE THE SAME OLD FRIENDS", (ref)   2464
        e 128; "Once we were sweethearts, not so long ago" (verse) e 131   words by J. McCarthy
    TORPEDO JIM; "Torpedo Jim with an eye like an eagle" e 129,130   2465
MONCRIEF, T. W.
    TONGO ISLAND; "I sailed from port one summer's day" e 225   2466
MONDONVILLE, JEAN JOSEPH CASSANEA DE, 1711-1772
    [TITON ET L'AURORE, opera; words by Abbé de La Marre and Claude   2467
        de Voisenon] ARIETTE DE L'AURORE; "Venez, venez, sous ce riant feuillage"; "Sing
        on, sing on, amid leafy branches" e, f 151
    [Ibid] AIR D'EOLE; "Sur les pâles humains, que le tonnerre gronde!"; "At these mortals   2468
        discharge thy lurid bolts, Oh! Thunder!" e, f 147
MONDRAGÓN, SAMUEL
    SARAPE OAXAQUEÑO; "Sarape que tienes colores del iris"; SONG OF A MEXICAN SARAPE;   2469
        "I'm sending to you, dear, a pretty 'sarape'" e, s 9   words by J. G. Vasconcelos
Moniushko, Stanislav. See MONIUSZKO, STANISLAW, 1819-1872
MONIUSZKO, STANISLAW, 1819-1872
    BŁYSNĄŁ PORANEK; "Błysnął poranek, zniknęły cienie"; AT MORNING; "Morning is rising,   2470
        night shades are fading" e, p 295
    [FLIS, opera; words by S. K. Boguslawski] DUMKA ZOSI; "Ach tyś może wśród   2471
        tej burzy"; ZOSIA'S REVERIE; "O could you have in deep Wisła" e, p 295
    GRAJEK; "Na zagrodzie gospody"; THE FIDDLER; "In the garden of the manor" e, p 295   words   2472
        by Kolankowski
    [HALKA, opera; words by W. Wolski] AYRA JONTKA, Act IV; "Szumią jodły na   2473
        gór szczycie"; JONTEK'S ARIA; "Sadly mountain firs are rustling" e, p 295
    [Ibid] "GDYBY RANNEM SŁONKIEM", Act II, scene 1; "COULD I BUT BE WINGING" e, p 295   2474
    [Ibid] OJCZE Z NIEBIOS; "Ojcze z niebios, Boże Panie!"; LORD, OUR GOD; "Lord, our God,   2475
        Oh Heav'nly Father" e, p 295
    [Ibid] PIEŚŃ Z OPERY "HALKA", Act I, scene 4; "Jako od wichru krzew połamany"; HALKA'S   2476
        ARIA; "Just as by storm-winds plants are uprooted" e, p 295
    KOZAK; "Tam na górze jawor stoi"; THE COSSACK; "On a hillside stands a maple" e, p 295;   2477
        "TAM NA GÓRZE JAWOR STOI"; "ON A HILL A MAPLE'S GROWING" e, p 159
    KRAKOWIACZEK; WESÓŁ I SZCZĘŚLIWY; "Wesół i szczęśliwy Krakowiaczek ci ja"; A KRAKOW   2478
        LAD; "I'm a lad from Krakow, very highly thought of" e, p 295; WESÓŁ I SZCZĘŚLIWY;
        CRACOW CHILD I'M TRULY; "Cracow's child I'm truly, my wit quick and snappy", e, p 159
        words by E. Wasilewski
    KUM I KUMA; "Kuma obiad warzyła"; KUMA; "Kuma supper was making" e, p 295   2479
    "NIECH SIĘ PANIE STROJĄ W PASY"; POLISH MAIDENS; "Let our maidens don their dresses"   2480
        e, p 295
    [PIĘKNA KOBIETA, operetta; words by J. Korzeniowski] PIOSNKA ŻOŁNIERZA;   2481
        "Już matka zasnęła, Już gwiazdka błysnęła"; SOLDIER'S SONG; "Your mother is sleeping, All
        stars vigil keeping" e, p 295
    PIEŚŃ WIECZORNA; "Po nocnej rosie"; EVENING SONG; "Across lush meadows" e, p 295; "PO   2482
        NOCNEJ ROSIE"; "NIGHT'S DEW DROPS GLISTEN" e, p 159

MONIUSZKO, STANISLAW, 1819-1872 (Continued)

POLEĆ PIEŚNI Z MIASTA; "Poleć pieśni z miasta, choć miasto nie nudzi"; FLY SWEET SONG;   2483
"Fly sweet song, sweet love song, Oh fly from city's busy throng" e, p 295; FLY MY SONG TO
HEAVEN; "Fly my song to heaven, leave city walls behind you" e, p 159

PRZYCHODZ MIŁY; "Przychodz miły, dzien już biały"; COME TO ME, MY LOVE; "Come to me,   2484
my love, come back to me"; "Come my loved one, day is pretty" e, p 295 words by J. Czeczott

SOKOŁY; "Przylecieli sokołowie"; FALCONS; "Flying came the swiftest falcons" e, p 295   2485

[STRASZNY DWÓR, opera; words by J. Chęciński] CHÓR KOBIET PRZY   2486
KROSNACH; "Z pod igiełek kwiaty rosną"; WOMEN AT THE LOOM; "Needles deftly stitch
wild flowers" e, p 295

[Ibid] O MATKO MOJA; "O matko moja, matko rodzona"; O MOTHER; "Mother beloved,   2487
mother my dearest" e, p 295

[VERBUM NOBILE, opera; words by W. J. Chęciński] WIEJSKA SERENADA;   2488
"Jak lilija co rozwija"; VILLAGE SERENADE; "Like a lily just unfolding" e, p 295

WĘDROWNA PTASZYNA; "Ptaszku! ptaszku! skąd przylatasz?"; WANDERING BIRD; "Song bird,   2489
song bird, whence came you here?" e, p 295

ZŁOTA RYBKA; "Dołem sinej wody"; GOLDFISH; "In the clear blue current" e, p 295 words by   2490
J. Zacharjasiewicz

MONK, WILLIAM HENRY, 1821-1889

ABIDE WITH ME; "Abide with me! fast falls the eventide" e 28, 233, 236, 279, 366 words by H. F.   2491
Lyte

MONRO, GEORGE, 1680-1731

MY LOVELY CELIA; "My lovely Celia, heav'nly fair, as lilies sweet, as soft as air" e 348   2492

MONROE, ROSE

NOT SO LONG AGO; "Tell me why you turn away so sadly" e 131   2493

MONSIGNY, PIERRE ALEXANDRE, 1727-1817

[LES AVEUX INDISCRETS, opera; words by de La Ribadière] ARIETTE, "Un   2494
jeune coeur nous offre l'image", "A youthful heart seems to our discerning" e, f 151

"Ô MA TENDRE MUSETTE" f 88, 383; "GENTLE AND SWEET MUSETTE" e 45; "PIPES, OH SO   2495
SWEETLY RINGING" e, f 36 words by J. F. de Laharpe

[ON NE S'AVISE JAMAIS DE TOUT, opera; words by J. M. Sedaine] "O MA   2496
TANT DOUCE COLOMBELLE"; I TO MY DOVE; "I to my dove, my tardy sweeting" e, f 175

[LE ROI ET LE FERMIER, opera; words by J. M. Sedaine] IL REGARDAIT MON   2497
BOUQUET; ARIETTA; "Il regardait mon bouquet, sans doute il le désirait"; "His eye was on my
bouquet, no doubt his wish it would say" e, f, p 362; e, f 1

[SANCHO PANÇA, GOUVERNEUR DE L'ÎLE DE BARATARIA, opera; words by   2498
A. A. H. Poinsinet] LE BOUQUET RAVI; "Je ne suis qu'une bergere"; "I AM BUT A
SHEPHERD MAIDEN" e, f 175

MONTÉCLAIR, MICHEL PIGNOLET DE, 1667-1737

[JEPHTÉ, opera; words by S. J. de Pellegrin] AIR D'IPHISE; "Qu'ai-je entendu!   2499
j'en ai frémi"; "Ah! how those words fill me with fear!" e, f 149

[Ibid] AIR DE PHINÉE; "Quel funeste appareil! quel autel!"; "How appalling a sight! She must   2500
die!" e, f 146

MONTEVERDI, CLAUDIO, 1567-1643

AHI, SCIOCCO MONDO; "Ahi, sciocco sciocco, mondo e cieco!" (duet) i 181   2501

[L'ARIANNA, opera; words by O. Rinuccini] LAMENTO D'ARIANNA; "Lasciatemi   2502
morire, lasciatemi morire" i 180, 367; LASCIATEMI MORIRE; LET DEATH NOW COME; "Let
death now come to claim me!" e, i 138; "NO LONGER LET ME LANGUISH" e, i 368; "O
DEATH PRAY COME AND SAVE ME" e, i 404; RECITATIVO E LAMENTO; "O Teseo! O Teseo
mio" (recit); "O mein Theseus! O geliebter Theseus!" (recit); "O lasst, o lasst mich sterben!"
(aria) g, i 167

[IL BALLETTE DELLE INGRATE, cantata] AHI, TROPPO È DURO; "Ahi, troppo, ahi,   2503
troppo è duro"; "ALAS, ALL TO HARSH AND RUTHLESS" e, i 138; ALAS! WHAT SADNESS;
"Alas! What sadness, the sentence is too harsh"; ACH, ZU HART; "Ach, zu hart ist das grausame
Urteil" e, g, i 253

INTERROTTE SPERANZE; "Interrotte speranze eterna fede" (duet) i 181   2504

KANZONE; "Con che soavita, labbra, odorate, e vi bacio e v'ascolto"; "Mit welchem Genuss, ihr   2505
blühenden Lippen, küsse ich euch und höre euch zu" g, i 217

OCCHI, FONTI DEL CORE; "Occhi, fonti del core, occhi piangete" i 180 att to C. Monteverdi   2506

[L'ORFEO, opera; words by A. Striggio] PROLOGO; LA MUSICA; "Dal mio Permesso   2507
amato a voi ne vegno" (recit); "Io la Musica son, ch'ai dolci accenti" (aria) i 179

SI DOLCE È'L TORMENTO; "Si dolce è'l tormento Che in seno mi sta"; SO SWEET IS THE TORMENT;   2508
"So sweet is the torment, that in my heart lies" e, i 404

MONTROSE, PERCY

CLEMENTINE; "In a cavern, in a canyon excavating for a mine" e 35, 225, 402; OH, MY DARLING   2509
CLEMINTINE e 10, 128, 131, 233, 236, 246, 366

MOORAT, JOSEPH
    NOEL, NOEL, NOEL; "'Noel, Noel, Noel', sang the church bell" e 334   words by L. Housman   2510
    THE WORLD IS OLD; "The world is old tonight, the world is old" e 334   words by L. Housman   2511
MOORE, DONALD LEE
    "SILENTLY NOW WE BOW" e 347   2512
MOORE, DOUGLAS STUART, 1893-
    OLD SONG; "I came to the willow alone, I came to the willow alone" e 358   words by T. Roethke   2513
    UNDER THE GREENWOOD TREE; "Under the greenwood tree who loves to lie with me" e 358   words   2514
      by W. Shakespeare
MOORE, FLOYD C.
    "LORD, LET ME LIVE TO-DAY" e 347   words by A. Wyttenbach   2515
MOORE, RAYMOND
    SWEET MARIE; "I've a secret in my heart"; "Come to me, Sweet Marie" (ref) e 131; (ref only)   2516
      e 114,132   words by C. Warman
MORALES, CRISTÓBAL, ca1500-1553
    "DE ANTEQUERA SALE EL MORO" s 12   2517
MORAN, P. K.
    CHIT CHAT; "Pretty little damsels, how they chat" e 225   2518
    PRAY PAPA; "Pray Papa, pray Papa, stay a little longer" e 225   2519
MOREL CAMPOS, JUAN
    FELICES DIAS; "No volverán jamás"; "ONCE THERE WERE HAPPY DAYS" e, s 291   words by S.   2520
      Arce
MORELAND, CHARLES
    THE LITTLE OLD RED SHAWL MY MOTHER WORE; "It now lies on the shelf"; "It is useful no more"   2521
      (ref) e 131,132
MORGAN, CAREY and DAVID LEE
    SUCKIN' CIDER THROUGH A STRAW. See 7795
MORGAN, JAMES
    DON'T BITE THE HAND THAT'S FEEDING YOU; "Last night, as I lay a-sleeping"; "If you don't   2522
      like your Uncle Sammy" (ref) e 129   words by T. Hoier
MORLEY, THOMAS, 1557-1603?
    DOE YOU NOT KNOW; "Doe you not know, doe you not know how love lost first his seeing?" 3 pt   2523
      canzonet e 144
    "FAIRE IN A MORNE" e 144   words by N. Breton   2524
    "FLORA, WILT THOU TORMENT ME?' e 197   2525
    "IT WAS A LOVER AND HIS LASS" e 14,75,235,306,349,397,402; "IT WAS A LOVER AND HIS   2526
      LASSE" e 144,403   words by W. Shakespeare, As You Like It
    "LOVE WING'D MY HOPES" e 107   2527
    MISTERESSE MINE; "Misteresse mine well may you fare" e 144   2528
    "NOW IS THE MONTH OF MAYING" e 14,235,348,349   2529
    "SWEET NYMPH, COME TO THY LOVER" e 196   2530
    "WHAT IF MY MISTRESSE" e 107   2531
    "WHEN LO! BY BREAKE OF MORNING" e 196   2532
    "WITH MY LOVE MY LIFE WAS NESTLED" e 107   2533
MORSE, THEODORE, 1873-1924
    DEAR OLD GIRL; "'Twas a sunny day in June"; "Dear old girl, the robin sings above" (ref) e 131   2534
      (ref only) e 128,236   words by R. H. Buck
    HAIL! HAIL! THE GANGS ALL HERE. See 3669
    M-O-T-H-E-R (A WORD THAT MEANS THE WORLD TO ME); "I've been around the world"; "M"   2535
      is for the million things she gave me" (ref) e 128,131,236   words by H. Johnson
    "MY RED CROSS GIRLIE" e 129,130   words by H. Bewley   2536
    SOLDIER BOY; "Soldier boy, one kiss before you go" e 129,130   words by D. A. Esrom   2537
MORTON, FERDINAND JOSEPH, 1885-1941
    BUDDY BOLDEN'S BLUES; "Thought I heard Buddy Bolden say, 'You're nasty, you're dirty, take   2538
      it away'" e 336
    "DON'T YOU LEAVE ME HERE" e 336   2539
    WININ' BOY BLUES; "I'm a Winin' Boy, don't deny my name" e 336   2540
Morton, Jelly Roll. See MORTON, FERDINAND JOSEPH, 1885-1941
MOSER, HANS JOACHIM, 1889-
    DEUTSCHE UNSTERBLICHKEIT; "Ist es ein Traum nur von versunknem Glück?" g 31   words by   2541
      E. Herzog
    DIE EICHEN; "Abend wird's des Tages Stimmen schweigen" g 31   words by T. Körner   2542
    DIE FREIWILLIGEN VON IJPERN; "Wir haben ein Grab gegraben für lauter junge Knaben" g 31   2543
      words by W. Vesper
    MORGENWEISE; "Wann haben wir im Feld zuletzt gesungen?" g 31   words by H. Heyck   2544

MOSS, E.
    STILL, STILL WITH THEE; "Still, still with Thee, when purple morning breaketh" e 28,366   words   2545
    by H. B. Stowe

MOSSOLOV, ALEXANDER, 1900-
    MOUNTAIN SUMMITS; "Mountain peaks are silent in the night" e, r 342   words by M. Lermontov   2546

MOULINIÉ, ESTIENNE, 1624-
    TIRSIS; "Tirsis au bord des eaux" f 108   2547

MOURET, JEAN JOSEPH, 1682-1738
    [PIRITHOÜS, opera; words by Sequinault] AIR DE L'EUROPÉENNE; "Doux plaisirs,   2548
    tout enchante où vous êtes"; "Let us dwell in these bowers enchanting" e, f 149

Moussorgsky, Modest. See MUSORGSKIĬ, MODEST PETROVICH, 1839-1881

MOZART, JOHANN CHRYSOSTOM WOLFGANG AMADEUS, 1756-1791
    ABENDEMPFINDUNG, K. 523; "Abend ist's, die Sonne ist verschwunden"; THOUGHTS AT   2549
    EVENTIDE; "Evening comes, the sun has lost his glory" e, g 273   words by J. H. Campe
    ALLES SCHWEIGET; "Alles schweiget, Nachtigallen lokken mit süssen Melodien" g 42   2550
    THE ALPHABET, K. Anh. 294d. See 2737
    AN CHLOE, K. 524; "Wenn die Lieb' aus deinen blauen, hellen, off'nen Augen sieht" g 250   words   2551
    by J. G. Jacobi; QUANDO MIRO QUEL BEL CIGLIO; "Quando miro quel bel ciglio nero"; "WITH
    SWANLIKE BEAUTY GLIDING" e, i 274
    "AVE MARIA", K. 554   4 pt canon lat 337   2552
    [AVE VERUM CORPUS, K. 618, motet] AVE VERUM; "Ave, ave verum Corpus natum   2553
    de Maria Virgine" lat 304,382; AVE VERUM CORPUS; "Saviour, source of ev'ry blessing, tune
    my heart to grateful, grateful lays" e, lat 394
    [LA CLEMENZA DI TITO, opera, K.621; words by P. Metastasio] NON PIÙ   2554
    DI FIORI, Act II, no.23; "Ecco il punto, o Vitellia" (recit); "Non più di fiori vaghe catene"
    (aria); "'Tis the moment, O Vitellia" (recit); "No more entrancing garlands of flowers" (aria)
    e, i 2
    [Ibid] PARTO, PARTO, Act I, no.9; "Parto, parto, ma tu, ben mio"; "Dearest, loved one,   2555
    though I am leaving" e, i 2
    CONSERVATI FEDELE, K.23; "Conservati fedele; pensa ch'io resto, e peno" i 308   words by   2556
    P. A. Metastasio
    [COSÌ FAN TUTTE, opera, K.588; words by L. da Ponte] UN' AURA AMOROSA,   2557
    Act I, no.17; "Un' aura amorosa del nostro tesoro"; "My love is a flower, all fragrant before me"
    e, i 3
    [Ibid] COME SCOGLIO, Act II, no.14; "Temerari, sortite fuori di questo loco!" (recit); "Come   2558
    scoglio immoto resta" (aria); "Bold intruders, leave this house this very instant" (recit); "Strongly
    founded, a marble tower" (aria) e, i 1
    [Ibid] "UNA DONNA QUINDICI ANNI," Act II, no.19; "Any girl fifteen or over" e, i 6   2559
    [Ibid] NON SIATE RITROSI, Act II, no.15; "Le nostre pene e sentirne pieta!" (recit); "Non   2560
    siate ritrosi, occhietti vezzosi" (aria); "Because we're suff'ring, we deserve to be heard" (recit);
    "How can you refuse us the light of your gazes" (aria) e, i 4
    [Ibid] PER PIETÀ, BEN MIO, Act II, no.25; "Ei parte senti" (recit); "Per pietà ben mio, perdona   2561
    all' error" (aria); "I hurt him! Should I? ah, no!" (recit); "Dearest love, I beg your pardon" (aria)
    e, i 6
    [EIN DEUTSCHES KRIEGSLIED ICH MÖCHTE WOHL DER KAISER SEIN, K.539]   2562
    ICH MÖCHTE WOHL DER KAISER SEIN; "I'D LIKE TO BE THE EMPEROR" e 395   words by J. Gleim
    [DON GIOVANNI, opera, K.527; words by L. Da Ponte] BATTI, BATTI, Act I,   2563
    no.13; "Batti, batti o bel Masetto"; "Chide me, if thou wilt, Masetto" e, i 6; ARIE DER ZERLINE;
    "Schlage schlag' mich, mein Masetto" g 311
    [Ibid] DALLA SUA PACE, Act I, no.11; "Dalla sua pace la mia dipende"; "On her, my treasure,   2564
    all joy dependeth" e, i 3
    [Ibid] "DEH, VIENI ALLA FINESTRA", Act II, no.17; SERENATA i 298; SERENADE; "From out   2565
    thy casement glancing, oh, smile upon me!" e, i 4
    [Ibid] FINCH' HAN DAL VINO; "Finch' han dal vino calda la testa"; "For a carousal where all is   2566
    madness" e, i 4; AUF DENN ZUM FESTE; "Auf denn zum Feste, froh soll es werden" g, i 390
    [Ibid] "IL MIO TESORO INTANTO," Act II, no.22; "Meanwhile, go seek my darling" e, i 3   2567
    [Ibid] "MADAMINA! IL CATALOGO È QUESTO," Act I, no.4; "Pretty lady! Here's a list I   2568
    would show you" e, i 5; SCHÖNE DONNA; "Schöne Donna! Dies genaue Register" g, i 390
    [Ibid] NON MI DIR, Act II, no.25; "Crudele! ah! no, mio bene!" (recit); "Non mi dir bell'   2569
    idol mio" (aria); "Unkind love? Ah! no, Ottavio!" (recit); "Tell me not my heart's devotion"
    (aria); e, i 6 "Not love thee? Ah, ne'er believe it!" (recit); "Tell me not, oh thou beloved
    one" (aria)
    [Ibid] VEDRAI, CARINO, Act II, no.19; "Vedrai, carino, se sei buonino"; DARLING I'LL SHOW   2570
    YOU; "Darling, I'll show you, something you know too" e, i 36; "Smile! and I'll teach thee"
    e, i 6

MOZART, JOHANN CHRYSOSTOM WOLFGANG AMADEUS, 1756-1791 (Continued)

[DIE ENTFÜHRUNG AUS DEM SERAIL, opera, K.384; words by C. F.   2571
     Bretzner] ACH, ICH LIEBTE, Act I, no.6; "Ach ich liebte was so glücklich"; "Ah, in
     loving I was happy" e, g 6

[Ibid] ARIE DES BLONDCHEN, Act II, no.12; "Welche Wonne, welche Lust regt sich nun in   2572
     meiner Brust" g 311

[Ibid] "DURCH ZÄRTLICHKEIT UND SCHMEICHELN," Act II, no.8; "With tenderness and   2573
     kindness" e, g 6

[Ibid] WIE ÄNGSTLICH, Act I, no.4; "Constanze! Constanze!" (recit); "O wie ängstlich, o wie   2574
     feurig" (aria); "Constanza! Constanza!" (recit); "Oh, so anxious is my heartbeat!" (aria) e, g 3

[Ibid] "SOLCHE HERGELAUFNE LAFFEN," Act I, no.3; "All your tricks are so transparent" e, g 5   2575
[Ibid] "WER EIN LIEBCHEN HAT GEFUNDEN," Act I, no.2; "If you feel you need a woman" e, g 5   2576
[EXULTATE JUBILATE, motet, K.165 (158a) Excerpt] "ALLELUJA!" lat 93, 330, 394;   2577
     "ALLELUIA" 3 pt round lat 337

IM FRÜHLINGSANFANG, K.597; "Erwacht zum neuen Leben steht vor mir die Natur" g 226 words   2578
     by C. Sturm

[IO TI LASCIO, O CARA, ADDIO, K.621a (Anh.245)] ADDIO; "Io ti lascio";   2579
     ADIEU; "Fare thee well" e, i 274

[DAS KINDERSPIEL, K.598] CHILDREN'S PLAY; "We children, we gambol, we dance in a   2580
     ring" e 199

[EINE KLEINE FREIMAURER-KANTATE. LAUT VERKÜNDE UNSRE FREUDE, K.   2581
     623] [Lasst uns mit geschlungnen Händen] "BRÜDER REICHT DIE HAND ZUM
     BUNDE" g 43,326,353; BUNDESLIED g 99; WEIHELIED g 31

"LIEBES MÄDCHEN, HÖR MIR ZU," K.441c; STÄNDCHEN g 99,226,229 att to F. J. Haydn   2582
UN MOTO DI GIOJA, K.579; "Un moto di gioja mi sento in petto"; A TENDER EMOTION; "A   2583
     tender emotion I feel in my bosom" e, i 211

LE NOZZE DI FIGARO, opera, K.492; words by L. da Ponte] DEH VIENI,   2584
     NON TARDAR, Act IV, no.27; "Giunse al fin il momento" (recit); "Deh vieni non tardar, o
     gioja bella" (aria); "This at last is the moment" (recit); "Beloved, don't deny, the night is
     falling" (aria); e, i 1 REZITATIV UND ARIE DER SUSANNE; "Endlich naht sich die Stunde, da ich
     dich, o Geliebter" (recit); "O säume länger nicht, geliebte Seele" (aria) g 311

[Ibid] DOVE SONO I BEI MOMENTI, Act III, no.19; "E Susanna non vien!" (recit); "Dove sono i   2585
     bei momenti" (aria); "And Susanna is late" (recit); "Are they over, those cherished moments"
     (aria) e, i 6

[Ibid] "NON PIU ANDRAI, FARFALLONE AMOROSO," Act I, no.9 i 299; NON PIU ANDRAI;   2586
     "From now on, my adventurous lover" e, i 5; SO, SIR PAGE; "So, Sir Page, now you soon must
     be going" e, i 310; THE BLACKSMITH; "Oh! the blacksmith's a fine sturdy fellow" e 28

[Ibid] "NON SÒ PIÙ COSA SON, COSA FACCIO," Act I, no.6 i 301; NON SÒ PIÙ COSA SON;   2587
     "I can't give you a good explanation for this new and confusing sensation" e, i 2

[Ibid] "PORGI AMOR QUALCHE RISTORO," Act II, no.10; CAVATINA; "Pour, O love, sweet   2588
     consolation" e, i 1; CAVATINE DER GRÄFIN; "Heil'ge Quelle reiner Triebe gib' mir wieder des
     Gatten Herz!" g 311

[Ibid] "SE VUOL BALLARE, SIGNORE CONTINO," Act I, no.3; "Should my dear master want   2589
     some diversion" e, i 5; WILL DER HERR GRAF; "Will der Herr Graf ein Tänzchen nun wagen"
     g, i 390

[Ibid] "VOI, CHE SAPETE," Act II, no.11; "YOU WHO ARE KNOWING" e, i 36; "You know   2590
     the answer, you hold the key" e, i 2; CANZONE DES CHERUBIN; "Ihr, die ihr Triebe des
     Herzens kennt" g 311

[OISEAUX, SI TOUS LES ANS, K.307 (284d)] "OH BIRDS THAT LEAVE EACH YEAR"   2591
     e 395

[IL RÈ PASTORE, K.208, opera; words by P. Metastastio] L'AMERO; "L'Amero   2592
     sarò constante: fedo sposo e fidi amante" i 330

RIDENTE LA CALMA, K.210a (152); "Ridente la calma nell' alma si desti"; HOW CALM IS MY   2593
     SPIRIT; "How calm is my spirit now sweet peace enfolds me" e, i 276; GAY LAUGHTER
     AWAKENS; "Gay laughter awakens my soul from deep sorrow" e, i 405

SEHNSUCHT NACH DEM FRÜHLINGE, K.596; "Komm, lieber Mai, und mache die Bäume wieder   2594
     grün" g 99,229; KOMM, LIEBER MAI g 326,353; LONGING FOR SPRING; "Come lovely May
     with blossoms" e 395; "Come lovely May and make the forests green again" e 209; "Come
     soon, come soon, sweet Mayday!"; VOTI ALLA PRIMAVERA e 199 words by C. A. Overbeck

DAS VEILCHEN, K.476; "Ein Veilchen auf der Wiese stand" g 96,99,226; "A violet grew in   2595
     meadow green" e, g 330; THE VIOLET; "A violet in the meadow green" e, g 275; "A violet
     blooming on the green" e, g 237, 275; "A violet on the meadow grew" e, g 122; "Midst mossy
     banks a violet stood" e 395; "A violet blossomed on the green" e, g 386 words by J. W. von
     Goethe

[WIEGENLIED, K. Anh. 284f (350)] LULLABY. See 1085

MOZART, JOHANN CHRYSOSTOM WOLFGANG AMADEUS, 1756-1791 (Continued)

    [DIE ZAUBERFLÖTE, opera, K.620; words by E. Schikaneder] ACH, ICH   2596
FÜHL'S, Act II, no.17; "Ach ich fühl's es ist verschwunden"; "Ah, I feel, to grief and sadness"
e, g 1,6; ARIE DER PAMINA g 311

    [Ibid] "DIES BILDNIS IST BEZAUBERND SCHÖN," Act I, no.3 g 391; "O image angel like and   2597
fair!" e, g 3

    [Ibid] DER HÖLLE RACHE, Act II, no.14; "Der Hölle Rache kocht in meinem Herzen"; "The   2598
flames of hell are burning now within me" e, g 292; THE QUEEN OF NIGHT'S VENGEANCE
ARIA; "For dire revenge my burning heart is crying"; "Gli angui d'inferno sentomi nel petto"
e, g, i 221; GLI ANGUI D'INFERNO i 302

    [Ibid] "IN DIESEN HEIL'GEN HALLEN," Act II, no.15; g 390; "WITHIN THESE HOLY PORTALS"   2599
e, g 5; "QUI SDEGNO NON S'ACCENDE" i 299; "WITHIN THIS SACRED DWELLING"; WHO
TREADS THE PATH OF DUTY e, g, i 240

    [Ibid] EIN MÄDCHEN ODER WEIBCHEN, Act II, no.20; "Ein Mädchen oder Weibchen wünscht   2600
Papageno sich"; "I'd give my finest feather to find a pretty wife" e, g 4; "ÜB IMMER TREU
UND REDLICHKEIT" g 326,353 words by L. H. C. Hölty

    [Ibid] O ISIS UND OSIRIS, Act II, no.18; "O Isis und Osiris, schenket der Weisheit Geist dem   2601
neuen Paar!" g 390; "O Isis and Osiris, favor this noble pair with wisdom's light!" e, g 5;
POSSENTI NUMI; "O Isis and Osiris, guide them, send down thy spirit on the pair"; "Possenti
Numi I Iside, Osiri, da te a que' petti seno e valor" e, g, i 240; O LORD ON HIGH; "O Lord
on high, we pray Thee guide us" e 123; O LORD, OUR GOD; "O Lord, our God, we seek Thy
guidance" e 160

    [Ibid] "DER VOGELFÄNGER BIN ICH JA," Act I, no.2 g 390; "I am a man of widespread fame"   2602
e, g 4

MÜLLER, KARL LUDWIG, 1749-1818

    DER WÄCHTERRUF; "Loset, was i euch will sage" g 31 words by J. P. Hebel   2603

MÜLLER, WENZEL, 1767-1835

    ABSCHIED; "So leb denn wohl, du stilles Haus!" g 99; "SO LEB DENN WOHL, DU STILLES HAUS"   2604
g 326,353 words by F. Raimund

    [ALINE, opera; words by W. A. Bäuerle] KOMMT A VOGERL GEFLOGEN; "Kommt   2605
a Vogerl gelfogen, setzt sich nieder auf mein Fuss" g 167; FROHE BOTSCHAFT g 99; KOMMT A
VOGEL GEFLOGEN; "Kommt a Vogel feflogen, setzt sich nieder auf mein Fuss" g 326; KOMMT
EIN VOGERL GEFLOGEN; "Kommt ein Vogerl geflogen, setzt sich nieder auf mein' Fuss" g 42

MÜNTZING, PAULA

    LUCIA-VISA; "God morgon, mitt herrskap"; LUCIA'S SONG; "Good morrow my gentles" e, sw 188   2606

MUHLENBERG, WILLIAM AUGUSTUS, 1796-1877

    [GIVE THANKS, ALL YE PEOPLE] THE PRESIDENT'S HYMN; "Give thanks all ye people,   2607
give thanks to the Lord" e 212

MUIR, ALEXANDER

    THE MAPLE LEAF FOR EVER; "In days of yore the hero Wolfe" e 294; "In days of yore, from Britain's   2608
shore" e 28,233,279,366

MULLEN, J. W.

    AFTERWARDS; "After the day has sung its song of sorrow" e 132 words by M. M. Lemon   2609

MULLEN, JAMES B.

    THAT'S HOW I LOVE YOU, MAME; "I'd like to tell you Mame how much I love you"; "I love   2610
you like a 'copper' loves to sleep" (ref) e 204 words by V. Bryan

MURADELI, VANO, 1908-

    THE TWO FRIENDS; "Two good friends went into battle bravely" e 339   2611

MURILLO, EMILIO, 1880-1942

    PAJARILLO; "Pajarillo jilguero abre tus alas"; PRETTY PAHAREELYO, LITTLE BIRD; "Pretty   2612
'Pahareelyo', go flying to my love" e, s 9

MURRAY, FRED and EVERARD, GEORGE

    IT AIN'T ALL HONEY AND IT AIN'T ALL JAM; "With my lovely husband today I landed here" e 131   2613

MUSORGSKIĬ, MODEST PETROVICH, 1839-1881

    [BORIS GODOUNOV, opera] "DOSTIG YA VYSSHEĬ VLASTI," Act II; "I HAVE ATTAINED   2614
TO POWER"; MONOLOGUE e, r (tr) 5

    [Ibid] MARINA'S ARIA, Act III, scene 1; "Skuchno Marinye" (recit); "Kak tomitel'no i vyalo"   2615
(aria); "Ah, poor Marina!" (recit); "Life is empty, life is dreary" (aria) e, r, r (tr) 2

    [Ibid] PIMEN'S TALE, Act IV, scene I; "Smirennyĭ inok vdelakh mirskikh nye mudryĭ sudiya";   2616
"A peaceful monk, who knoweth nought of worldly lore and wisdom" e, r (tr) 5

    [Ibid] VARLAAM'S SONG, Act I, scene I; "Kak vogorodye bylo to Kazani"; "Long ago at   2617
Kazan where I was fighting" e, r (tr) 5

    CHILDREN'S SONG; "In my garden, my green garden raspberries are growing" e, r 340 words by   2618
Mey

    CRADLE-SONG OF THE POOR; "Lullaby, by, lullaby, by, like a modest flower in the field" e 348   2619
words by Nekrassoff

MUSORGSKIĬ, MODEST PETROVICH, 1839-1881 (Continued)

    [THE FAIR AT SOROCHINSK, opera] KHIVRIA'S SONG AND HOPAK, Act II; "Net,   2620
dobryye lyudi" (recit); "Ot kolizh ya Brudeusa vstretila" (aria); "No, good honest people" (recit);
"Since I read his first entrancing billets-doux" (aria) e, r, r (tr) 2

    [THE NURSERY, song cycle] THE EVENING PRAYER, no.5; "Bless O Lord, I pray Thee"   2621
e 121

    [SONGS AND DANCES OF DEATH, song cycle] THE COMMANDER; "The battle   2622
rages, steel shines brightly" e, r 340 words by Golenistchev-Kutuzov

    [SUNLESS, song cycle] IN MY ATTIC, No.1; "Lone is my little room, silent and dear to   2623
me" e 45; WITHIN FOUR WALLS; "I am so peaceful here" e, r 340 words by Golenistchev-
Kutuzov

    "TINY STAR, WHERE ART THOU?" e 407   2624

NÁDOR, GYULA

    JAJ DE BAJOS A SZERELMET TITKOLNI; IT IS HARD TO HIDE LOVE; "It is hard to hide love that   2625
your heart besets" e 164

NÄGELI, HANS GEORG, 1773-1836

    "BLEST BE THE TIE THAT BINDS" e 28,236,279,366 words by J. Fawcett   2626
    "ES KLINGT EIN HELLER KLANG" g 31 words by M. von Schenkendorf, 1783-1817   2627
    "FREUT EUCH DES LEBENS" g 31,99,167,326; "LA FRANCE EST BELLE" f 88 words by M. Usteri   2628
    GOLDNE ABENDSONNE; "Goldne Abendsonne, wie bist du so schön!" g 326 words by B. Urner-Welti   2629

NARDI, N.

    ALEI GIVAH; "Alay givah sham bagalil"; HIGH ON A HILL' "In Galilee high on a hill" e, h (tr) 30   2630
    SHIR AVODAH; "Mi yatsilenu meraav?"; A SONG TO LABOR; "Who will keep hunger from our door"   2631
e, h (tr) 30 words by C. N. Bialik

NARES, JAMES, 1715-1783

    WILT THOU LEND ME; "Wilt thou lend me thy mare to go a mile" 3 pt round e 349   2632

NARVAEZ, LUIS DE, fl 16th c

    ARDÉ, CORAZÓN, ARDÉ; VILLANCICO; "Ardé, corazón, ardé, que no os puedo yo valer" s 12   2633

NATHAN, JOS. S.

    THE MAN WHO FIGHTS THE FIRE; "The summer sun is beaming"; "He's the man who fights the   2634
smoke, the flames and fire" (ref) e 131 words by F. F. Feist

NAUWACH, HANS

    "ACH LIEBSTE, LASS UNS EILEN" g 250 words by M. Opitz   2635

NEANDER, JOACHIM

    "GOTT IST GEGENWÄRTIG" g 326 words by G. Tersteegen   2636

NEEFE, CHRISTIAN GOTTLOB, 1748-1798

    BEIM BURSCHENMAHL; "Wo eine Glut die Herzen bindet" g 31 words by W. Hauff   2637
    HERMANN UND THUSNELDA; "Ha! dort kömmt er mit Schweiss" g 250 words by F. G. Klopstock   2638
    "WAS FRAG ICH VIEL NACH GELD UND GUT" g 353 words by J. M. Miller   2639

NEIDHART VON REUENTHAL, 13th c

    MAY FLIGHT. See 5467

NEIDLINGER, WILLIAM HAROLD, 1863-1924

    THE BIRTHDAY OF A KING; "In the little village of Bethlehem" e 337,346   2640
    SPIRIT OF GOD; "Spirit of God, descend upon my heart" e 398 words by G. Croly   2641

NELLIAM, EDMUND

    SLAVES TO THE WORLD; "Slaves to the world should be toss'd in a blanket" e 235; "Slaves to   2642
the world should be tossed in a blanket" 3 pt round e 349

NELSON, ED G., 1886-

    PEGGY O'NEIL. See 2757
    TEN LITTLE FINGERS AND TEN LITTLE TOES. See 3400

NELSON, SIDNEY

    THE ROSE OF ALLANDALE; "The morn was fair, the skies were clear" e 28 words by C. Jeffery   2643

NESSLER, VIKTOR ERNST, 1841-1890

    [DER TROMPETER VON SÄCKINGEN, opera; words by R. Bunge] "DAS IST   2644
IM LEBEN HÄSSLICH EINGERICHTET"; "BEHÜT' DICH GOTT, ES WÄR AU SCHÖN GEWESEN"
g 31,353; BEHÜT' DICH GOTT, ES WÄR SO SCHÖN GEWESEN g 326; IT WAS NOT TO BE;
"How badly is the course of life adjusted"; "God bless thee love, it was but idle dreaming" (ref)
e 132

NESTLER, FRIEDRICH FERDINAND, 1798-1876

    ENTSCHULDIGUNG; "Wenn wir durch die Strassen ziehen" g 31 words by W. Müller   2645

NEUENDORFF, ADOLF, 1843-1897
    [DER RATTENFÄNGER VON HAMELN, operetta; words by A. Kunz]   2646
        WANDERN, ACH WANDERN; "Wandern, ach wandern weit in die Fern" g 353
NEUMARK, GEORG, 1621-1681
    [GOTTESTROST] "WER NUR DEN LIEBEN GOTT LÄSST WALTEN" g 326   2647
NEVADA, HATTIE
    THE LETTER EDGED IN BLACK; "I was standing by my window; "As I heard the postman" (ref)   2648
        e 114,131
NEVIN, ETHELBERT WOODBRIDGE, 1862-1901
    THE ROSARY; "The hours I spent with thee, dear heart"; DER ROSENKRANZ; "Die Stunden, einst   2649
        mit dir verbracht" e, g 223 words by R. C. Rogers
NEVIN, GEORGE BALCH, 1859-1933
    SONG OF THE ARMOURER; "I forge the sword, I shape the steel" e 240 words by F. V. Hubbard   2650
NEWCOMB, BOBBIE
    THE BIG SUNFLOWER; "There is a charm I can't explain about a girl I've seen" e 34,115   2651
NEWTON, EDDIE WALTER, 1869-1915
    CASEY JONES; "Come, all you rounders, if you want to hear"; "Casey Jones, mounted to the   2652
        cabin" (ref) e 109,225,227; "Come, all you rounders, for I want you to hear" e 184; "Come
        all you rounders that want to hear" e 35 words by W. Saunders, att to T. L. Siebert
NICHOLSON, SYDNEY H., 1875-1947
    "CAROL, SIRS, THE BLESSED BIRTH" e 317 words by M. Howse   2653
    WELCOME YULE; "Welcome Yule, thou merry man" e 334   2654
NICOLAI, OTTO, 1810-1849
    [DIE LUSTIGEN WEIBER VON WINDSOR, opera; words by S. H. Mosenthal]   2655
        ALS BÜBLEIN KLEIN, Act II; DRINKING SONG; "Als Büblein klein an der Mutter Brust"; "When
        that I was and a tiny boy" e, g 5; "ALS BÜBLEIN KLEIN AN DER MUTTER BRUST" g 390
    [Ibid] "NUN EILT HERBEI," Act I, no.3 (recit); "Verführer! Warum stellt ihr so der tugendsamen   2656
        Gatin nach?" (aria); MRS. FORD'S RECITATIVE AND ARIA; "Come to my aid" (recit); "Seducer!
        Why are you intent to lead a virtuous wife astray?" (aria) e, g 6
    THE MERRY WIVES OF WINDSOR. See 2655-2656
NICOLAI, PHILIPP, 1556-1608
    "WACHET AUF, RUFT UNS DIE STIMME" g 326; SLEEPERS WAKE; "Sleepers, wake, for night is   2657
        flying!" e 410 set by J. Praetorius. See also BACH, JOHANN SEBASTIAN Wachet auf, ruft uns
        die Stimme. Gloria sei dir gesungen; arr.
    "WIE SCHÖN LEUCHTET DER MORGENSTERN" g 326 set by J. H. Schein. See also BACH, JOHANN   2658
        SEBASTIAN-WIE SCHÖN LEUCHTET DER MORGENSTERN; WIE BIN ICH DOCH SO HERZLICH
        FROH; arr "WIE SCHÖN LEUCHTET DER MORGENSTERN"
NIEDERMEYER, LOUIS, 1802-1861
    PATER NOSTER; "Pater noster, qui es in coelis" lat 304   2659
NIEH ERH
    CHEE LAI!; "Chee-lai! boo yuan tzo noo lee dee run men"; ARISE; SONG OF THE VOLUNTEERS;   2660
        "Arise! you who refuse to be bond-slaves" c (tr), e 293
NIELSEN, CARL, 1865-1931
    DU DANSKE MAND; "Du danske Mand! af al din Magt syng ud om vor gamle Mor!"; O DANISH   2661
        MAN; "O Danish man! with all your might proclaim now your mother's praise" da, e 87 words
        by H. Drachmann
    MASQUERADE piano 87   2662
NIEWIADOMSKI, STANISLAW, 1859-1936
    EJ DZIEWCZYNO, EJ NIEBOGO; "Ej dziewczyno, ej niebogo jakieś wojsko pędzi drogą skry j się za   2663
        ściany"; LOOK, MY LASSIE; "Look my lassie, have you seen it? troops are coming here this
        minute, our mounted lancers" e, p 159 words by K. Makuszynski
    OJ MAGDALINO, op.44, no.18; "Oj, Magdalino, oj, ty dziwcyno"; MY MAGDALINA; "Oh,   2664
        Magdalina, my Magdalina" e, p 295
NIKOROWICZ, JOSEF, 1827-1890
    Z DYMEM POŻARÓW; "Z dymem pożarów, z kurzem krwi bratniej"; CHORAL; "Feeble our voice,   2665
        Lord, through din of battle" e, p 295; FANNED BY THE FLAMES; "Fanned by the flames, and
        reeking of bloodshed" e, p 159 words by K. Ujejski
NOBLE, RAY
    GOOD NIGHT SWEETHEART; "Good night sweetheart, till we meet tomorrow" e 132,236 joint   2666
        composers J. Campbell and R. Connelly
NOBLE, THOMAS TERTIUS, 1867-1953
    "O LITTLE TOWN OF BETHLEHEM" e 271 words by P. Brooks   2667
NOLAN, MICHAEL
    I WHISTLE AND WAIT FOR KATIE; "After bus'ness you will find me, ev'ry night as sure as fate";   2668
        "I'm waiting here to greet, blue eyed Kate with kisses sweet" (ref) e 246

NOLAN, MICHAEL (Continued)
  LITTLE ANNIE ROONEY; "A winning way, a pleasant smile"; "She's my sweetheart, I'm her beau"   2669
    (ref) e 131,166 (ref only) e 114,128,129,130,132,233
NORKRAAK, RIKARD, 1842-1866
  TONEN; "I skogen smagutten gikk dagen lang, gikk dagen lang" sw 278   words by B. Bjørnson   2670
NORRMAN, JOHN
  BLAAÖGA, SOLÖGA; "Blaaöga, Solöga gullebarn mitt" sw 356   2671
Northey, Carrie. See ROMA, CARO
NORTON, GEORGE A., 1880-1923
  "'ROUND HER NECK SHE WEARS A YELLER RIBBON" e 129   2672
NOSKOWSKI, ZYGMUNT, 1836-1909
  "O WSPOMNIJ BRACIE"; THE OLD MANOR; "Do you recall my dearest brother" e, p 159   2673
  "SKOWRENECZEK ŚPIEWA"; SONG OF THE LARK; "To the lark's sweet singing" e, p 295   2674
NOVÁK, VITĚZSLAV, 1870-1949
  MELANCHOLICKÁ PÍSEŇ O LÁSCE, op.38, no.4; "O, lásky moře bezdné, lze k tvému dospět dnu?";   2675
    MELANCHOLISCHES LIED VON DER LIEBE; "O, Liebe, Meer ohn' Ende, wer fasste deinen Raum?"
    c, g 74 words by J. Vrchlický
NOVELLO, IVOR
  KEEP THE HOME FIRES BURNING; "They were summon'd from the hillside" e 28   2676
NOVOTNÝ, JAROSLAV, 1886-1918
  OD TĚLA TVÉHO, op.2, no.1; "Od těla Tvého mají sněženky vůni"; VON DEINEM LEIBE; "Von   2677
    deinem Leibe leih'n sich Schneeglöcklein Düfte" c, g 73a
NOWAKOWSKI, J. N.
  STARA WISŁA; "Jest kraina w tej krainie"; OLD RIVER WISŁA; "Land of great plains, fertile   2678
    country" e, p 295 words by S. W. Kucz
  TURNIE NASZE, TURNIE; "Turnie nasze, turnie, Hale nasze, hale"; HIGHLANDS, OH OUR   2679
    HIGHLANDS; "Highlands, oh, our highlands, With your dales and mountains" e, p 295
NOWOWIEJSKI, FELIX, 1877-1946
  ROTA; "Nie rzucim ziemi skąd nasz ród"; HYMN OF 1910; "We'll hold our land, our father's land" 2680
    e, p 295; "NIE RZUCIM ZIEMI SKĄD NASZ RÓD"; THE VOW; "We shall not yield our sacred
    soil" e, p 159
NUGENT, MAUD
  SWEET ROSIE O'GRADY; "Sweet Rosie O'Grady, my dear little rose" e 166   2681
NYBERG, MIKAEL, 1871-1940
  PAIMENPOIKA; "Jäi toiset aamulla nukkumaan"; THE YOUNG COWHERD; "Still slept the house   2682
    when I rose this morning" e, fi 124 words by I. Hellén
NYSTROEM, GÖSTA, 1890-
  HÖGA VISAN; "Kom min älskade kom" sw 356   2683
  JUNOS OCH CERES SAANG; "Ära guld till deras fromma" sw 356   2684
  UTE I SKÄREN; "En dag skall komma" sw 356 words by E. Lindqvist   2685

OBERLAND, BERNER
  "A BAUREBÜBLE MAG I NET" g 326   2686
OCHS, SIEGFRIED
  DANK SEI DIR HERR. See 1458
ODYNIEC, A. E., 1804-1885
  "PRECZ, PRECZ OD NAS SMUTEK WSZELKI"; "BE GONE, BE GONE CARES AND TROUBLES"; "Niech   2687
    wesoły z przyjacioły" (ref); "Light your pipes sweet friends make merry" (ref) e, p 159; "PRECZ,
    PRECZ, SMUTEK WSZELKI"; BE GONE, WORRIES; "Begone, worries, troubles!" e, p 295
OFFENBACH, JACQUES, 1819-1880
  [LES CONTES D'HOFFMANN, opera; words by J. Barbier and M. Carré]   2688
    BELLE NUIT, Act III, no.13; BARCAROLLE; "Belle nuit ô nuit d'amour"; "Blissful night, O
    joyous night" e, f 329; "BELLE NUIT, Ô NUIT D'AMOUR"; "BEAUTEOUS NIGHT, O NIGHT
    OF LOVE" e, f 241; O LOVELY NIGHT; "Fairest night of starry ray" e, f 122; "Barcarolle,
    you thrill my poor soul" e 132
    [Ibid] "ELLE A FUI, LA TOURTERELLE!", Act IV; "HE HAS FLOWN, MY PRETTY TURTLE-DOVE"   2689
      e, f 1; ROMANZE DER ANTONIA; "Sie entfloh, die Taube so minnig!" g 311
    [Ibid] "LES OISEAUX DANS LA CHARMILLE," Act II; "Birds upon the branches singing" e, f   2690
      292; "When the birds begin their singing" e, f 6
    [Ibid] SCINTILLE, DIAMANT, Act II; "Allez! Pour te livrer combat" (recit); "Scintille, diamant, 2691
      Miroir où se prend l'alouette" (aria); "Ay, go! The eyes of Giulietta" (recit); "With my diamond
      bright, my magical mirror of light" (aria) e, f 4; LEUCHTE, HELLER SPIEGEL, MIR; "Leuchte,
      heller Spiegel, mir und blende ihn mit deinem Schein" (aria only) g, i 390
  HOFFMANNS ERZÄHLUNGEN. See 2688-2691

OFFENBACH, JACQUES, 1819-1880 (Continued)

    [LA PÉRICHOLE, opera; words by H. Meilhac and L. Halévy] TU N'EST   2692
        PAS BEAU; "Tu n'est pas beau, tu n'est pas riche"; YOU HAVE NO LOOKS; "You have no
        looks, nor have you wealth" e, f 362

O'HARA, GEOFFREY, 1882-

    ART THOU THE CHRIST?; "'Art thou the Christ?' they asked Him" e 123 words by D. S. Twohig   2693

    K-K-K-KATY; "K-K-K-Katy, beautiful Katy, you're the only g-g-g-girl that I adore" e 129,130,   2694
        236

    LEETLE BATEESE; "You bad leetle boy, not moche you care" e 240 words by W. H. Drummond   2695

    THANKS; "For spreading plain and peak that tow'rs, we give thanks" e 123 words by R. G. Dandridge   2696

OHLHANNS, FRANZ, 1861-1910

    STUDENTENLIED; "Wir lugen hinaus in die sonnige Welt" g 31 words by G. H. Bienert   2697

O'KEEFE, WALTER MICHAEL, 1900-

    ALWAYS A BRIDESMAID BUT NEVER A BRIDE; "I once knew a spinster who worked on a plan" e 131   2698

    THE BEARDED LADY; "Let me tell to you the story"; "Love the Bearded Lady" (ref) e 131   2699

    FATHER PUT THE COW AWAY; "Poor Ezra sat on the milking stool"; "Oh, Father put the cow away"   2700
        (ref) e 131

    THE GAMBLER'S WIFE; "Your heart may go out to the woman who's wed"; "Pity the life of a   2701
        gambler's wife" (ref) e 131

    THE MAN ON THE FLYING TRAPEZE; "Oh, once I was happy, but now I'm forlorn"; "He flies thro'   2702
        the air with the greatest of ease" (ref) e 34; "Once I was happy, but now I'm forlorn"; "He flies
        through the air with the greatest of ease" (ref) e 225; "He flies thru the air with the greatest of
        ease" e 128,236; "Oh, he flies through the air with the greatest of ease" (ref) e 115; "Oh! he
        floats thro' the air with the greatest of ease" (ref) e 130,131 also att to A. Lee

    THE TATTOOED LADY; "I just heard a story that rings in my ears"; "Shame on the man who pursued   2703
        her" (ref) e 131

OLCOTT, CHANCELLOR JOHN, 1858-1932

    MOTHER MACHREE; "There's a spot in my heart which no colleen may own" e 233 joint composer   2704
        E. R. Ball, words by R. J. Young

    MY WILD IRISH ROSE; "If you listen, I'll sing you a sweet little song"; "My wild Irish Rose, the   2705
        sweetest flow'r that grows" (ref) e 166

Olcott, Chauncey. See OLCOTT, CHANCELLOR JOHN

OLIVIERI, A.   2706

    [INNO DI GARIBALDI] GARIBALDI'S WAR HYMN; "Si scopron le tombe, si levano i morti";
        "To battle! To battle! The dark earth is gaping, in anguish is riven" e, i 7 words by Mercantini

OLMAN, ABE, 1887-

    DOWN AMONG THE SHELTERING PALMS; "I'm 'way down East"; "Down among the sheltering palms"   2707
        (ref) e 131 (ref only) e 128 words by J. Brockman

OPENSHAW, JOHN

    JUNE BROUGHT THE ROSES; "Red leaves, faded and dead leaves" e 237 words by R. Stanley   2708

OPIE, MARY PICKENS

    COMMUNION HYMN; "Hungry and thirsty, Lord, I come to Thee" e 123   2709

OPIEŃSKI, HENRYK, 1870-1942

    ZASZUMIAŁ CIEMNY GŁĘBOKI LAS; "Zaszumiał ciemny, głęboki las, Załość się po nim niesie";   2710
        DARK IS THE FOREST, SULLEN, DEEP; "Dark is the forest so sullen, deep, its fir-trees sombre,
        scornful" e, p 159 words by K. Tetmajer

ORLANSKY,

    TELL ME WHY; "You've told me all" e, r 287,288 words by K. N. Podrevsky   2711

ORLOWSKI, ANTONI, 1811-1861

    W MOGILE CIEMNEJ; "W mogile ciemnej śpisz na wieki"; IN THY DEEP GRAVE; "In Thy deep   2712
        grave now dost Thou languish" e, p 159

ORTIZ, C. A.

    FLORES NEGRAS; "Oye, bajo las ruinas de mis pasiones"; BLACK FLOWERS; "Black flowers are the   2713
        roses that were so lovely" e, s 9; MIS FLORES NEGRAS; MY SABLE FLOWERS; "Under the wreck
        of passion and love's illusion" e, s 322

OSCIK, J.

    W SŁOŃCU SIĘ DKRZY; "W słońcu się skrzy bagnetów stal"; WHITHER YOU GO?; "Whither you   2714
        go O fighting men" e, p 159 words by A. Semp

OSGOOD, M. R.

    COME, LITTLE LEAVES; "Come, little leaves, said the wind one day" e 129 words by G. Cooper   2715

OSTERLE, MAY

    DUTCH DOLLS; "As the story is related, once some Dutch dolls" e 237 words by H. L. D'Arcy Jaxone   2716

OSTRČIL, OTAKAR, 1879-1935

    SVŮJ CELÝ SMUTEK, op. 14, no. 3; "Svůj celý smutek nelze nikdy říc'"; WAS UNS BEDRÜCKT;   2717
        "Was uns bedrückt, fasst sich in Worte schwer" c, g 73a words by V. Dyk

OTTO, FRANZ, 1809-1842
     UBI BENE, IBI PATRIA; "Überall bin ich zu Hause" g, lat 31   words after F. Hückstädt   2718
OWEN, ANITA
     DAISIES WON'T TELL; "There's a sweet old story"; "Daisies won't tell, dear, come kiss me do"   2719
          (ref) e 114,131 (ref only) e 128
OWENS, HARRY
     LINGER AWHILE. See 3079

PACIUS, FREDRIK, 1809-1891
     MAAMME; "Oi maamme, Suomi, synnyinmaa"; OUR LAND; "Our land, our land, our native land"   2720
          e, fi 124   words by J. L. Runeberg
     SUOMEN LAULU; "Kuule, kuinka soitto kaikuu"; SUOMI'S SONG; "Hear, oh hear the splendid   2721
          singing" e, fi 124   words by E. von Qvanten
PADILLA, JOSÉ, 1889-
     PRINCESITA; "Princesita, Princesita, la de ojos azules y labios de grana"; LITTLE PRINCESS;   2722
          "Little Princess! Little Princess, with eyes like the blue of the skies" e, s 245; "Little Princess,
          Little Princess, with eyes like the sky, mouth a bright crimson flower" e, s 142   words by M. E.
          Palomero
     EL RELICARIO; RENDEZ-VOUS OF LOVE; "I saw you seated there, roses in your hair"; "I'm broken   2723
          hearted for tho' we're parted" (ref) e 236
     LA VIOLETERA; "Como aves precursoras de Primavera"; BUY MY VIOLETS; "Each morn with basket   2724
          laden a Spanish maiden" e, s 132
PAISIELLO, GIOVANNI, 1740-1816
     [LA GROTTA DE TROFONIO, opera; words by Casti] "SI VUOL SAPER CHI SONO";   2725
          THEY WOULD FAIN KNOW WHO I AM i 367
     KAMMERDUETT; LA LIBERTÀ A NICE; "Quando lo stral spezzai"; PALINODIA A NICE; "Lo stral   2726
          gia non spezzai"; "Als ich den Pfeil (Amors) zerbrach"; "Den Pfeil zerbrach ich damals nicht"
          (duet) g, i 218
     [LA MOLINARA, opera; words by G. Palomba] "NEL COR PIÙ NON MI SENTO";   2727
          "WHY FEELS MY HEART SO DORMANT" e, i 368; ARIETTA; "Mich fliehen alle Freuden" g, i
          167
PALACIO, CARLOS
     THE STEEL BATTALIONS; "The steel battalions are marching all singing a fighting song"; "!Las   2728
          Compãnias de Acero Cantando, a la lueha van!" e, s 7   words by L. de Tapia
PALACIOS, CRISTOBAL
     A GRANADA; CANCIÓN ANDALUZA; "Granada la bella nido deamores"; "Granada, my happy,   2729
          beautiful lovenest" e, s 245
PALADILHE, ÉMILE, 1844-1926
     "J'AI DIT AUX ÉTOILES"; SÉRÉNADE; "J'ai dit aux étoiles: Elle est votre soeur"; I SAID TO THE   2730
          STARLETS; "I said to the starlets, she's your sister fair" e, f 407   words by E. Grenier
     PSYCHÉ; "Je suis jaloux, Psyché, de toute la nature!"; PSYCHÉ; "I am jealous, Psyché, of all   2731
          nature!" e, f 190,192,194; "I suffer jealousy at nature's love for Psyche!" e 348   words by P.
          Corneille
PALESTRINA, GIOVANNI PIERLUIGI DA, 1525?-1594
     ADORAMUS TE; "Adoramus te Christe, et benedicimus tibi" lat 206,244; WE DO WORSHIP THEE;   2732
          "We do worship Thee, Jesus, we praise and bless Thy most holy name" e, lat 296
     GLORIA PATRI; "Gloria patri et filio"; "Father of Light, we sing in Thy praise" e, lat 28,366   2733
     THE STRIFE IS O'ER; "Alleluia! Alleluia! Alleliua! The strife is o'er, the battle done" e 346,400   2734
PALMGREN, SELIM, 1878-1951
     JOULULAULU, op.34, no.1; "Ja neitsyt pikku poijuttansa"; CHRISTMAS SONG; "The Virgin hugs   2735
          her little child" e, fi 124   words by S. Nuormaa
     MOTHER; "Mother, thro' the night" e 121   words by C. Engel   2736
PAR, C. F.
     THE ALPHABET; "A b c d e f g" e 28   att to W. A. Mozart   2737
PARADIES, PIETRO DOMENICO, 1707-1791
     QUEL RUSCELLETTO; "Quel ruscelletto che l'onde chiare"; THE BROOKLET; "Where is the course   2738
          of the brooklet" e, i 208; ARIETTA; "Quel ruocelletto che l'onde chiare" i 308
PARKER, HENRY, 1842-1917
     JERUSALEM; "From out their peaceful village" (aria); "Behold, thy King draws near the City gates" 2739
          (recit) e 346,394,398,400
PARKER, HORATIO WILLIAM, 1863-1919
     "ALL MY HEART THIS NIGHT REJOICES" e 251   2740

PARKHURST, (MRS.) E. A.

    THE DRUNKARD'S CHILD; "You ask me why so oft, father"; "But O, my soul is very sad" (ref) e 189   2741

    FATHER'S A DRUNKARD, AND MOTHER IS DEAD; "Out in the gloomy night, sadly I roam"; "Mother,   2742
    oh! why did you leave me alone" (ref) e 189 words by "Stella" of Washington

PARRY, SIR CHARLES HUBERT HASTINGS, 1848-1918

    A HYMN FOR AVIATORS; "Lord, guard and guide our men who fly" e 344 words by M. C. D.   2743
    Hamilton

    JERUSALEM; op.208; "And did those feet in ancient time" e 306 words by W. Blake   2744

    A SPRING SONG, op.21, no.2; "It was a lover and his lass" e 344 words by W. Shakespeare, As   2745
    You Like It

PARRY, JOHN, 1776-1851

    AS BEAUTEOUS AS FLORA; NORAH, THE PRIDE OF KILDARE; "As beauteous as Flora is charming   2746
    young Norah"; "Her eyes with smiles beaming" (ref) e 166,213

PARTLOW, VERN

    NEWSPAPERMEN; "Oh, a newspaper man meets such interesting people" e 293   2747

    TALKING ATOMIC BLUES; "I'm gonna preach to you a sermon 'bout Old Man Atom" e 293   2748

PARTOS, JENÖ

    AZ A SZÉP; "Az a szép, az a szép akinek a szeme szép"; FINE AND TRUE; "Fine and true, fine and   2749
    true, is the girl whose eyes are blue" e, hu 285

PASQUINI, BERNARDO, 1637-1710

    BELLA BOCCA; "Bella bocca, bella bocca, bella bocca mi scocca più strali con cinabro" i 179   2750

    [ERMINIA IN RIVA DEL GIORDANO] ARIE DER ERMINIA; "Verdi tronchi, annose piante";   2751
    "Grüne Stämme, alte Bäume" g, i 217

    KANZONETTE; "Quanto è folle quell' amante"; "Wie töricht ist doch der Verliebte" g, i 217   2752

    "SO BEN S'IO PENO" i 180   2753

PAULSON, GUSTAF, 1898-

    ANNA IMROTH, op.16, no.3; "Korsa händerna här över bröstet saa" sw 356 words by C. Sandburg   2754

PAYNE, JAMES

    MY LAST CIGAR. See 1724

PEARSON, GEORGE C.

    "OH! WHY SHOULD THE SPIRIT OF MORTAL BE PROUD" e 212   2755

PEARSON, W. W.

    THE PLOUGHBOY; "This is the way the ploughboy goes" 3 pt round e 293   2756

PEASE, HARRY, 1886-1945

    PEGGY O'NEIL; "If her eyes are blue as skies" e 236 joint composers E. G. Nelson and G. Dodge   2757

PEERY, ROB ROY, 1900-

    GOD SHALL WIPE AWAY ALL TEARS; "And I heard a great voice" e 123 words from Revelation   2758
    XXI:3,4

PENN, ARTHUR A., 1875-1941

    CARISSIMA; "Oh, hark to the sound of the music and laughter that fills the air" e 237   2759

    THE LAMPLIT HOUR; "Dusk, and the lights of home smile through the rain" e 237 words by T.   2760
    Burke

PÉREZ FREIRE, OSMÁN

    AY, AY, AY; "Asómate a la ventana ay, ay, ay"; "Look out of thy window, please, ay, ay, ay"   2761
    e, s 36; "O come to the window, come, ay, ay, ay" e, s 322; "Si alguna vez en tu pecho, ay-
    ay-ay!" s 284; MY HEART HAS A WINDOW; "My heart has a window, where you can see" e
    237; "Si alguna vez en tu pecho, ay, ay, ay"; "Schlaf ein, liebes Herz, schlaf ein, ei, ei, ei"
    g, s 222; "The moonrays on bayous gleam, ay, ay, ay" e 343; "O come to your window, ay,
    ay, ay" e 279; ALAS; "If ever within your heart" e 350

PERGAMENT, MOSES, 1893-

    VISA I SKYMNING; "Stickorna gaar slamrar och slaar maskorna fogas täta" sw 356 words by A. G.   2762
    Bergman

PERGOLESI, GIOVANNI BATTISTA, 1710-1736

    [MESSA IN FA A 10 VOCI] "QUONIAM TU SOLUS SANCTUS"; FOR THOU ALONE ART   2763
    HOLY lat 367

    [OLIMPIADE, opera; words by P. Metastasio] ARIE DES LICIDAS; "Mentre dormi,   2764
    Amor fomenti"; "Während du schläfst, vermehre Amor" g, i 218

    [Ibid] DUETT DES MEGACLES UND DER ARISTEA; "Ne' giorni tuoi felici"; "In deinen glück-   2765
    lichen" g, i 218

    "PER QUESTE AMARE LACRIME"; "FÜR DIESE BITTERN TRÄNEN"; FOR THESE BITTER TEARS; "In   2766
    exchange for these bitter tears" e, g, i 253

    "QUE NE SUIE-JE LA FOUGÈRE"; "MIGHT I BE THE WOODED FERNBRAKE" e, f 36 words by C. H.   2767
    Riboutte

    SE TU M'AMI; "Se tu m'ami se tu sospiri Sol per me"; SI TU M'AIMES; "Si tu m'aimes si tu soupires   2768
    pour moi"; IF 'TIS FOR ME; "If 'tis for me, for me and me alone thou sighest" e, f, i 208; GENTLE
    SHEPHERD; "Gentle shepherd, will you love me" e, i 276; IF THOU LOVE ME; "If thou love me,

PERGOLESI, GIOVANNI BATTISTA, 1710-1736
    SE TU M'AMI (Continued) if thou be sighing, dying for me" e 348; SE TU M'AMI; SE SOSPIRI;   2768
        IF THOU LOV'ST ME; "If thou lov'st me and sighest ever" e, i 368; ARIETTA; "Wenn du mich
        liebst und heiss nach mir schmachtest" g, i 168
    "TRE GIORNI SON CHE NINA"; NINA; "Three long, long days my Nina" e, i 386; TRE GIORNI;   2769
        "'Tis three long days, that Nina"; "DREI TAGE SIND VERFLOSSEN" e, g, i 138; NINA; "For
        three long days my Nina" e, i 368; NINA; "Drei Tage schon ruht Nina" g 311; ARIA; "Drei
        Tage schon, dass Nina" g, i 167 att to L. V. Ciampi and N. Resta
PERI, JACOPO, 1561-1633
    AL FONTE, AL PRATO; "Al fonte, al prato, al bosco, all' ombra" i 180   2770
    UN DÌ SOLETTO; "Un dì soletto vidd'il diletto" i 180   2771
    [EURIDICE, opera; words by O. Rinuccini] INVOCAZIONE DI ORFEO; "Gioite al   2772
        canto mio"; INVOCATION OF ORPHEUS; "Rejoice ye at my singing" e, i 138; IANO AL SOLE;
        "Erfreut euch meines Sangs" g, i 167
    [Ibid] NEL PURO ARDOR; "Nel puro ardor della più bella stella"; IN PURE PASSION i 367   2773
    O MIEI GIORNI FUGACI; "O miei giorni fugaci, o breve vita" i 180 words by O. Rinuccini   2774
PERTI, GIACOMO ANTONIO, 1661-1756
    BEGLI OCCHI; "A voi che l'accendeste" (recit); "Begli occhi, begli occhi io non me pento" (aria);   2775
        "To you who set me aflame" (recit); "O beautiful eyes, I do not regret" (aria) e, i 134
    DOLCE, SCHERZA; "Dolce, scherza e dolce ride"; "Sweetly play and sweetly laugh" e, i 134   2776
    KANZONETTE; "Io son zitella, Ma sono scaltra"; "Ich bin zwar noch ein Mädchen" g, i 218   2777
    MAI NON INTESI; "Mai non intesi per altro sguardo quel dolce stralle" i 180   2778
    MI FA VEZZI; "Mi fa vezzi e vuol ch'io rida la costanza con amor" i 180   2779
    SCIOGLIE OMAI LE NEVI; "Scioglie omai le nevi e il gelo" i 180   2780
    SPERAR IO NON DOVREI; "Sperar io non dovrei, e pur io vo sperando" i 180   2781
Perti, Jacopo Antonio, 1661-1756. See PERTI, GIACOMO ANTONIO, 1661-1756
PERUCCHINI, GIOVANNI BATTISTA
    [O PESCATOR DELL' ONDE] "DAS SCHIFF STREICHT DURCH DIE WELLEN" g 326,353;   2782
        SCHIFFERLIED g 31 words by J. von Brassier
PESENTI, MARTINO, ca 1600-1648
    COSÌ NILIO CANTÒ; "Così Nilio cantò, fuor d'ogni affanno" i 180   2783
    O BIONDETTA LASCIVETTA; "O biondetta lascivetta pastorella" i 180   2784
PESTALOZZA, ALBERTO, 1851-1934
    CIRIBIRIBIN; CANZONETTA; "Su, finiscila coi baci"; WALZERLIED; "Heute tanzt in der Taverne"   2785
        g, i 223; "Ciribiribin, O come, my love" e 233; "In our gondola reclining" e 343; CIRIBIRIBEE;
        "Ciribiribee, with hearts so free" e 128; VENETIAN SONG; "Ciribiribin, so gaily singing" e 37;
        CHIRIBIRIBEE; "There's a song in dear old Napoli" e, i 132 words by C. Tiochet
PETERS, ANTON
    BURSCHENABSCHIED; "Nun trinkt der Bursch zum letztenmal" g 31   2786
    MAILIED; "Was soll ich tun im wonnigen Mai?" g 31   2787
PETERS, PETER JOHANN, 1820-1870
    RHEINLIED; "Strömt herbei ihr Völkerscharen" g 31 words by O. Inkermann   2788
    WESTFALENLIED; "Ihr mögt den Rhein, den stolzen, preisen, der in dem Schoss der Reben liegt"   2789
        g 31,326 words by E. Ritterhaus
PETRIE, HENRY W., 1857-1925
    I DON'T WANT TO PLAY IN YOUR YARD; "Once there lived side by side, two little maids"; "I don't   2790
        want to play in your yard" (ref) e 114,131,132,204 (ref only) e 128,129,130 words by P. Wingate
PETROCOKINO, PAUL, 1910-
    CANTERBURY CATHEDRAL, piano 306   2791
    CAUX CAROL; "Sheep nor shepherds, none are here" e 307 words by M. Martin   2792
    FARMER'S CAROL; "Come, wife and children, let us see the light" e 307 words by E. Devlin   2793
    WORKERS' CAROL; "Coldly the night winds winging" e 305,307 words by M. Martin   2794
PETRŽELKA, VILÉM, 1889-
    MĚSÍČNÁ NOC, op.10, no.2; "Měsíčná noc, tak jasná noc"; MONDNACHT; "Im Mondenschein so   2795
        klar die Nacht" e, g 73a words by O. Theer
PETTMAN, EDGAR, 1865-1943
    A CAROL OF ADORATION; "O Babe Divine, now will I sing to Thee" e 369 words by W. A.   2796
        Pickard-Cambridge
    THE CAROL OF THE STAR; "A star is brightly burning" e 373 words by S. Baring-Gould   2797
    COME! YE LOFTY; "Come! ye lofty, come! ye lowly" e 374   2798
    "CROWN THE LORD OF GLORY" e 371   2799
    IN JUDAH'S FIELDS; "Long years ago, as men their flocks were tending" e 369 words by J. S.   2800
        Arkwright
    "LOVE CAME DOWN AT CHRISTMAS" e 373 words by C. Rossetti   2801
    "SING, WITH ALL THE SONS OF GLORY" e 371 words by W. J. Irons   2802

PIUFSICH, LAJOS
    NINCS CSEREPES TANYÁM; I HAVE NO TILED HUT; "I have no snug tiled hut, warm clothes I   2831
    possess not" e 164   words by P. Vidor
PLANQUETTE, JEAN-ROBERT, 1848-1903
    [LES CLOCHES DE CORNEVILLE, opera;   words by Clairville and C. Gabet]   2832
    "ON BILLOW ROCKING" e 205
PLATO, GERALD
    MELODIA; "Denkst noch an jene schönen Stunden"; "Hörst du mein heimliches Rufen" (ref) g 222   2833
    words by E. Stöcklein
POCHMURNY, (pseud)
    "NAPRZÓD DO BOJU ZOŁNIERZE"; THE ANTHEM OF UNDERGROUND POLAND (1943); "Soldiers   2834
    of underground Poland" e, p 159   words by Aniela (pseud)
PÖTHKO, GUSTAV EWALD
    WARNUNG VOR DEM RHEIN; "An die Rhein, an die Rhein" g 31,99   words by K. Simrock   2835
POHLENZ, AUGUST
    LUSTIG IST'S MATROSENLEBN. See 5458
POKRASS, DIMITRI YAKOVLEVITCH, 1899-
    MOSCOW; "In the dawn's light faintly gleaming" e, r 287,288; e 35   2836
    PREPARE FOR TOMORROW; IF TOMORROW BRINGS WAR; "If the storm clouds should break" e, r   2837
    7; SHOULD OUR LAND BE ATTACKED; "Should our land be attacked by an enemy's force"; IF
    WAR COMES TOMORROW e, r 287,288   words by V. Lebedev-Kumach
POLA, EDWARD, 1907-
    MARCHING ALONG TOGETHER; "Marching along together sharing ev'ry smile and tear" e 129,130,   2838
    236   joint composer F. Steininger, words by M. Dixon
POLDOWSKI, LADY DEAN PAUL, 1880-1932
    DANSONS LA GIGUE; "Dansons la gigue! J'aimais surtout ses jolis yeux"; LET'S DANCE THE JIG;   2839
    "Let's dance the jig! I loved above all her pretty eyes" e, f 191,193,195   words by P. Verlaine
    L'HEURE EXQUISE; "La lune blanche luit dans les bois"; EXQUISITE HOUR; "The white moon shines   2840
    in the forest" e, f 191,193,195   words by P. Verlaine
POLLACK, LEW
    CHARMAINE. See 2970
    DIANE. See 2971
    LITTLE MOTHER. See 2972
POLOVINKIN, LEONID ALEKSEEVICH, 1894-1949
    WE THANK OUR GREAT LEADER; "All the land is happy land and rejoices" e, r 162   words by I.   2841
    Dobrovolsky
PONCE, MANUEL MARIA, 1882-1948
    ESTRELLITA; "Little star in evening's silver brightness" e 343   2842
    VOY A PARTIR; "Voy a partir al puerto donde se halla"; I'M OFF TO PORT; "I'm off to port, for   2843
    there is a ship lying" e, s 142
PONCHIELLI, AMILCARE, 1834-1886
    [IL FIGLIUOL PRODIGO, opera;   words by A. Zanardini] RACCOGLI E CALMA;   2844
    "La vision spariva! Ove sei" (recit); "Raccogli e calma, sotto alla pia a la dolcissi ma de tuo
    sospir" (aria) i 298
    [LA GIOCONDA, opera;   words by A. Boito] CIELO E MAR, Act II; ROMANZA;   2845
    "Cielo! e mar! l'entereo velo"; "Ocean and sky, radiant in splendor" e, i 3
    [Ibid] OMBRE DI MIA PROSAPIA; "Si morir ella de'!" (recit); "Ombre di mia prosapia" (aria);   2846
    "Yes, her doom is to die!" (recit); "Shades of my fathers around me" (aria) e, i 5
    [Ibid] PESCATOR, AFFONDA L'ESCA, Act II; "Ah! pescator, affonda l'esca" i 298; "Ah!   2847
    Fisher-boy, thy bait be throwing" e, i 4
    [Ibid] STELLA DEL MARINAR; "Ho il cor gonfio di lagrime" (recit); "Stella del marinar!   2848
    Vergine Santa" (aria); "My heart is full of happy tears" (recit); "Star of the mariner! Virgin
    most holy" (aria) e, i 2
    [Ibid] SUICIDIO! Act IV; "Suicidio! In questi fieri momenti" i 301; AH SUICIDE; "Ah!   2849
    Suicide! 'Tis that alone may release me" e, i 143
    [Ibid] "VOCE DI DONNA O D'ANGELO," Act I i 300; THE BLIND GIRL'S SONG; "Ah! 'tis the   2850
    voice of angel bright" e, i 2
PONTET, HENRY
    THE FOG BELL; "Around the lighthouse saps the tide" e 205   words by H. De Burgh   2851
PORPORA, NICOLÀ ANTONIO, 1686-1767?
    "COME LA LUCE È TREMOLA"; "As the light flickers" e, i 134   2852
    [DESTATEVI] "NE' CAMPI E NELLE SELVE" i 180   words by P. Metastasio   2853
    [GIA LA NOTTE S'AVOIEINA] "NON PIU FRA SASSI" i 179   words by P. Metastasio   2854
    [OR CHE UNA NUBE, cantata;   words by P. Metastasio] CONTEMPLAR ALMEN;   2855
    "Contemplar almen chi s'ama è diletto dell' affetto" i 180

PORPORA, NICOLÀ ANTONIO, 1686-1767? (Continued)

[Ibid] SENZA IL MISERO PIACER; "Senza il misero piacer di veder" i 180   words by P.   2856
Metastasio

[QUESTA CHE MIRI, O NICE] SEI MIO BEN;   SEI MIO BEN; "Sei mio ben, sei mio conforto" i 179   words   2857
by P. Metastasio

[TIRSI CHIAMARE A NOME]   "SO BEN CHE LA SPERANZA" i 179; "Ich weiss wohl, dass die   2858
Hoffnung" g, i 218   words by P. Metastasio

[VEGGO LE SELVA]   "POSCIA QUANDO IL PASTOR" (recit); "Ma la selva, il monte intanto van   2859
col bel dell' idol" (aria) i 179   words by P. Metastasio

PORTER, COLE, 1891-

LET'S DO IT (LET'S FALL IN LOVE); "When the little bluebird, who has never said a word"; "Birds   2860
do it, bees do it, even educated fleas do it" (ref) e 345

YOU DO SOMETHING TO ME; "I was mighty blue, thought my life was through"; "You do something   2861
to me. Something that simply mystifies me" (ref) e 345

POULTON, GEORGE R.

AURA LEE; "As the blackbird in the spring"; "Aura Lee! Aura Lee! Maid of golden hair" (ref) e 36,   2862
128, 131, 132   words by W. W. Fosdick

POWELL, JOHN, 1882-

HEARTSEASE, op. 8, no. 2; "Down in the valley there below" e 259   words by L. C. Stiles   2863

PRAETORIUS, MICHAEL, 1571-1621

CANON OF THE MIMES; "Hear the mimes! In olden times" 6 pt round e 337   words by H. W. Simon   2864

I SING THE BIRTH; "I sing the birth was born tonight" e 317   words by B. Jonson   2865

[MUSAE SIONAE]   CHRISTO INCARNATO; "En Trinitatis, speculum illustravit seculum";   2866
CHRIST INCARNATE; "Behold the God-head's Triune blaze shineth on our waning days" e, lat
361

[Ibid]   EIA MEA ANIMA; "Eia mea anima, Bethlehem eamus"; NOW MY SOUL TO BETHLEHEM;   2867
"Now my soul to Bethlehem let our willing way be" e, lat 361

[Ibid]   "EN NATUS EST EMANUEL"; "THIS DAY IS BORN EMMANUEL" e, lat 361   2868

[Ibid]   "ES IST EIN ROS ENTSPRUNGEN" g 49, 326, 354; "BEHOLD A BRANCH IS GROWING" e, g 388;   2869
"ES IST EIN' ROS' ENTSPRUNGEN"; "LO, HOW A ROSE E'ER BLOOMING" e, g 337; e 33, 37, 165, 206;
FLOS DE RADICE JESSE; "I know a flow'r it springeth" e 375; "COME, SEE A ROSE THAT SPRINGETH"
e 333; "A GREAT AND MIGHTY WONDER"; Rosa mystica (tune) e 38, 39; I KNOW A FLOWER; "I know
a flow'r it springeth" e 361; "I KNOW A ROSE TREE SPRINGING" e 307; LO, HOW A ROSE; "Lo, how
a Rose fair blooming" e 125; "Lo, how a Rose upspringing" e 296; THE ROSE; "Hail, Rose of wondrous
virtue" e 410; DAS REIS AUS DER WURZEL JESSE g 99

[Ibid]   MAGNUM NOMEN DOMINI; "Magnum nomen domini Emmannuel!"; GREAT IS OUR LORD   2870
JESU'S NAME; "Great is our Lord Jesu's name Emmanuel!" e, lat 361

[Ibid]   NOBIS EST NATUS; "Nobis est natus hodie"; THIS HAPPY MORN; "This happy morn, to   2871
day is born" e, lat 361

[Ibid]   PARVULUS NOBIS NASCITUR; "Parvulus nobis nascitur, de virgine progreditur"; TO US A   2872
LITTLE CHILD IS BORN; "To us a little Child is born of mother maid before the morn" e, lat 361

[Ibid]   "PUER NOBIS NASCITUR"; "TO ALL MEN A CHILD IS COME" e, lat 361; "UNTO US IS   2873
BORN A SON" e 33

[Ibid]   UNIVERSI POPULI; "Universi populi omnes jam gaudete"; VOICE YOUR JOY TOGETHER   2874
NOW; "Voice your joy, together now, ev'ry ransomed nation" e, lat 361

"VIVA, VIVA LA MUSICA!" lat 326; VIVA LA MUSICA 3 pt round   lat 343   2875

PRATT, CHARLES E., 1841-1902

MY BONNIE LIES OVER THE OCEAN. See 7829

WALKING DOWN BROADWAY; "Walking down Broadway the festive gay Broadway" e 131   words   2876
by W. Lingard

PRESSEL, GUSTAV, 1827-1890

AN DER WESER; "Hier hab ich so manches liebe Mal" g 99, 327; "HIER HAB ICH SO MANCHES LIEBE   2877
MAL" g 326, 353   words by F. Dingelstedt

PRICE, FLORENCE B., 1888-

NIGHT; "Night comes, a madonna clad in scented blue" e 78   words by L. C. Wallace   2878

OUT OF THE SOUTH BLEW A WIND; "Out of the South blew a soft sweet wind" e 78   words by F. C.   2879
Woods

PRICHARD, ROWLAND HUGH, 1811-1887

"COME, THOU LONG-EXPECTED JESUS"; Hyfrydol (tune) e 251; HYFRYDOL; "Love divine, all   2880
love excelling" e 50   words by C. Wesley

PROKOF'EV, SERGEĬ SERGEEVICH, 1891-1954

"INTO YOUR CHAMBER" e, r 342   words by A. Pushkin   2881

"ON THE ARCTIC OCEAN" e, r 342   words by M. Svetloff   2882

SNOWDROPS; "Snowdrops grow on yonder hill" e 121   2883

SNOWFLAKES; "Over field and plain come stealing" e 121   2884

SONG OF FATHERLAND; "Nothing in the whole world can compare with Russia" e, r 342   2885

Prokofieff, S. See PROKOF'EV, SERGEĬ SERGEEVICH, 1891-1953

PROVENZALE, FRANCESCO, ca1627-1704

[LE STELLIDAURA VENDICATA, opera; words by A. Perrucci] DEH, 2886
RENDETEMI; "Deh, rendetemi, ombre care"; O RESTORE TO ME; "O restore to me, shades
forbearing" e, i 139; ARIE DES ARMIDORO; "Ach gebt mir wieder, teure Schatten" g, i 217

PUCCINI, GIACOMO, 1858-1924

[LA BOHÈME, opera; words by G. Giacosa and L. Illica] CHE GELIDA MANINA, 2887
Act I; "Che gelida manina, se la lasci riscaldar"; "How cold your little hand is! Let me warm
it in my own" e, i 3

[Ibid] DONDE LIETA, Act III; "Donde lieta uscì al tuo grido d'amore"; "Once again I'll return 2888
to my own scentless flowers" e, i 6; TO THE HOME THAT SHE LEFT; "To the home that she
left at the voice of her lover" e, i 143

[Ibid] MI CHIAMANO MIMI; "Mi chiamano Mimì, ma il mio nome è Lucia" i 301; "Sì, mi 2889
chiamano Mimi, ma il mio nome è Lucia; I'M ALWAYS CALLED MIMI; "Yes, I'm always
called Mimi, but my name is Lucia" e, i 1; SI, MI CHIAMANO MIMI; THEY CALL ME MIMI;
"They call me Mimi but my name is Lucia" e, i 143

[Ibid] QUANDO M'EN VO SOLETTA, Act II; "Quando m'en vo quando m'en vo soletta"; "Day 2890
after day, when I pass by alone on promenade" e, i 6; AS THRO' THE STREET; "As thro' the
street I wander onward merrily" e, i 143

[Ibid] VECCHIA ZIMARRA, Act IV; "Vecchia zimarra, senti, io resto al pian" i 299; "Faithful 2891
companion, listen, I must remain" e, i 5

[LA FANCIULLA DEL WEST, opera; words by G. Civinini and C. Zangarini] 2892
"MINNIE, DALLA MIA CASA SON PARTITO" i 298

[Ibid] OH, SE SAPESTE, Act II; "Oh, se sapeste come il vivere è allegro!"; OH YOU'VE NO 2893
NOTION; "Oh, you've no notion how exciting my life is!" e, i 143

[GIANNI SCHICCI, opera; words by G. Forzano] O MIO BABBINO CARO; "O mio 2894
babbino caro, mi piace, è bello bello"; OH! MY BELOVED DADDY; "Oh! my beloved daddy, I
love him, I love him" e, i 143

[MADAMA BUTTERFLY, opera; words by L. Illica and G. Giacosa] UN BEL 2895
DÌ, Act II, Scene 1; "Un bel dì, vedremo"; ONE FINE DAY; "One fine day we'll notice" e, i
143

[Ibid] CHE TUA MADRE DOVRA PRENDERTI IN BRACCIO; "Sai cos' ebbe cuore di pensa" (recit); 2896
"Che tua madre dovra prenderti in braccio" (aria); THAT YOUR MOTHER SHOULD TAKE YOU;
"Do you know my sweet" (recit); "That your mother should take you" (aria) e, i 143

[Ibid] ENTRATA DI BUTTERFLY, Act I; "Ancora un passo, or via" (recit); "Spira sul mare e sul 2897
la terra" (aria); "There is one more step to climb" (recit); "Across the earth, and o'er the ocean"
(aria) e, i 143

[MANON LESCAUT, opera; words by M. Praga, D. Oliva, and L. Illica] 2898
DONNA NON VIDI MAI; "Donna non vidi mai simile a questa!"; "Never was woman fairer; thus I
am captured" e, i 3

[Ibid] "IN QUELLE TRINE MORBIDE," Act II; "IN THOSE SOFT SILKEN CURTAINS" e, i 6, 143 2899

[Ibid] L'ORA, O TIRSI, Act II; "L'ora, o Tirsi, è vega e bella"; "THESE ARE HOURS OF JOY'S 2900
CREATING" e, i 143

[TOSCA, opera; words by L. Illica and G. Giacoso] "NON LA SOSPIRI LA 2901
NOSTRA CASETTA"; IN SECRET HIDDEN FROM CARE; "In secret hidden from care and
sadness" e, i 143

[Ibid] SE LA GIURATA FEDE; "Se la giurata fede debbo tradir"; "No, if my plighted fealty I must 2902
betray" e, i 310

[Ibid] "VISSI D'ARTE, VISSI D'AMORE," Act II i 301; "LOVE AND MUSIC, THESE HAVE I 2903
LIVED FOR" e, i 143; "Love for beauty, love and compassion" e, i 6

[TURANDOT, opera, words by G. Adami and R. Simoni] IN QUESTA REGGIA; 2904
"In questa Reggia, or son mill' anni e mille"; WITHIN THIS PALACE; "Within this Palace, a
thousand thousand years ago" e, i 143

[Ibid] SIGNORE, ASCOLTA; "Signore, ascolta! Ah, signore, ascolta!"; OH, I ENTREAT THEE, 2905
SIRE!; "Oh, I entreat thee, Sire, O Sire, to hear me!" e, i 143

[Ibid] "TU CHE DI GEL SEI CINTA"; MORTE DI LIÙ i 301; "THOU WHO WITH ICE ART 2906
GIRDL'D" e, i 143

Purcell, Edward. See COCKRAM, E. PURCELL, d 1932

PURCELL, HENRY, 1658 or 9-1695

[BONDUCA] "HEAR! YE GODS OF BRITAIN" e 273 words by F. Beaumont and J. Fletcher 2907

[DIDO AND AENEAS, opera; words by N. Tate] WHEN I AM LAID IN EARTH, 2908
Act III; "When I am laid, am laid in earth" (aria); "Thy hand, Belinda; darkness shades me"
(recit) e 2

[DON QUIXOTE] "LET THE DREADFUL ENGINES" (recit); "Can nothing, can nothing warm 2909
me?" (aria) e 272 words by T. D'Urfey

"FIE, NAY, PRITHEE, JOHN" 3 pt round e 349 2910

PURCELL, HENRY, 1658 or 9-1695 (Continued)

[A FOOL'S PREFERMENT] "I'LL SAIL UPON THE DOG-STAR" e 277 words by T. D'urfey   2911
"HARK! THE MERRY JINGLING BELLS" 3 pt round e 235   2912
[THE INDIAN QUEEN, opera; words by R. H. Howard] "I ATTEMPT FROM LOVE'S   2913
    SICKNESS TO FLY" e 275,397
[Ibid] "YE TWICE TEN HUNDRED DEITIES," Act III; THE CONJURER'S SONG; "By the croaking   2914
    of the toad, in her cave that makes abode" (aria) e 272
[KING ARTHUR, opera; words by J. Dryden] FAIREST ISLE; "Fairest Isle, all Isles   2915
    excelling" e 235,349,402
[Ibid] LET NOT A MOONBORN ELF; "Let not a moonborn elf mislead ye from your prey and from   2916
    your glory" e 199
[Ibid] YOUR HAY IT IS MOWED; "Your hay it is mowed and your corn is reap'd" e 402   2917
THE KNOTTING SONG; "Hears not my Phillis how the birds" e 277,397,404 words by C. Sedley   2918
LILLIBURLERO. See 4673
MAN IS FOR THE WOMAN MADE; "Man, man, man is for woman made" e 402   2919
[THE MOON, cantata; words by C. Williams] THE MOON REAPPEARS; "Turn, turn,   2920
    turn your eyes" e 199
[Ibid] THE PASSING OF THE MOON; "Bid the sun good morning and bid the moon goodbye" e 199   2921
NYMPHS AND SHEPHERDS; "Nymphs and shepherds, come away, come away" e 237,275,306;   2922
    NYMPHS AND SHEPHERDS, COME AWAY e 397 words by T. Shadwell
THE OWL IS ABROAD; "The owl is abroad, the bat and the toad" e 273   2923
[THE TEMPEST, incidental music; words by W. Shakespeare] ARISE, YE   2924
    SUBTERRANEAN WINDS, Act I; "Arise, arise, ye subterranean winds" e 273
[Ibid] "COME UNTO THESE YELLOW SANDS," Act III e 75,348   2925
[Ibid] FULL FATHOM FIVE; "Full fathom five thy father lies" e 75   2926
TIS WOMEN; "'Tis women makes us love" 4 pt round e 173   2927
UNDER THIS STONE; "Under this stone lies Gabriel John" 3 pt round e 349   2928
WELL RUNG, TOM; "Well rung, Tom, boy, well rung, Tom" 4 pt round e 235   2929

PURDY, ELEANOR, 1925-

SING RHONDDA; "Listen! the ring of men who sing again in the valley" e 306   2930

QUAGLIATI, PAOLO, ca1555-ca1628

KANZONETTE; "Apra il suo verde seno"; "Er erschliesse ihren grünen Schoss" g, i 217   2931

QUEEN, JOHN

JUST BECAUSE SHE MADE DEM GOO-GOO EYES; "A singer in a minstrel show was sitting on the   2932
    end"; "Just because she made dem goo-goo eyes" (ref) e 114; "An actor in a minstrel show"
    e 131 (ref only) e 128

QUILTER, ROGER, 1877-1953

DREAM VALLEY; "Memory, hither come, and tune your merry notes" e 275 words by W. Blake   2933
LOVE'S PHILOSOPHY, op.3, no.1; "The fountains mingle with the river" e 344 words by P. B.   2934
    Shelley
"NOW SLEEPS THE CRIMSON PETAL" e 277 words by A. Tennyson   2935
O MISTRESS MINE, op.6, no.2; "O mistress mine, where are you roaming?" e 272 words by W.   2936
    Shakespeare
[TO JULIA, song cycle, OP.8; words by R. Herrick] THE MAIDEN BLUSH, no.1;   2937
    "So look the mornings when the sun" e 344
[Ibid] THE NIGHT PIECE, no.4; "Her eyes the glow-worm lend thee" e 344   2938

QUIROGA, MANUAL, 1892-

MARIA DE LA O; "Para mis manos tumbagas"; "On wrists and fingers these jewels" e, s 245 words   2939
    by S. Valverde and V. Leon

RACHMANINOFF, SERGEI, 1873-1943

AUX ENFANTS, op.26, no.7; "Chers êtres, jadis quand minuit approchait"; TO THE CHILDREN;   2940
    "How often at midnight" e, f 275; "How oft then I linger'd alone at your bed" e 237 words by
    M. D. Calvocoressi
FRÜHLINGSFLUTHEN, op.14, no.11; "Noch ruh'n die Felder schneebedeckt"; FLOODS OF SPRING;   2941
    "While yet the fields are wrapp'd in snow" e, g 241; "In wintry fields white lies the snow" e 176
HOW FEW THE JOYS, op.14, no.3; "How few the joys that love hath brought me!" e 274   2942
IN THE SILENCE OF THE NIGHT, op.4, no.3; "Night, on her muted lyre" e 121; IN THE SILENT   2943
    NIGHT; "Oh, when in silent night once more I see before me" e 237
THE ISLAND; "A virgin island slumb'ring lies" e 121   2944
"JE LA VIS S'ARRÊTER," op.26, no.15; "WHEN YESTERDAY WE MET" e, f 272   2945

RACHMANINOFF, SERGEI (Continued)

LILACS, op. 21, no. 5; "At the dawn, with the sun on the dew sprinkled lawn" e, r 341; "Morning 2946
skies are aglow"; "Morgenrot schon erglüht" e, g 122   words by E. Beketova

O, DO NOT GRIEVE, op. 14, no. 8; "O, do not grieve for me! For there where ends all sadness" e, r 2947
357   words by A. Apukhtin

L'OMBRE IST TRISTE; "L'ombre ist triste et mon coeur lassé"; NIGHT IS MOURNFUL; "Night is 2948
mournful, mournful as my dreams" e, f 277   words by M. D. Calvocoressi

SUR LA TOMBE ENCORE FRAÎCHE; BY THE GRAVE; "In gloom of night I stand alone in deep despond" 2949
e 273

TOUT EST SI BEAU!, op. 21, no. 7; "Tout est si beau! Tout resplendit aux flammes du couchant"; 2950
HOW FAIR THIS SPOT; "How fair this spot! I gaze to where the golden brook runs by" e, f 276
words by M. D. Calvocoressi

"WE SHALL HAVE PEACE!" e, r 341   words by A. Chekhov 2951

RÁCZ, PÁL

LEHULLOTT A REZGŐ NYÁRFA EZÜST SZINÜ LEVELE; AUTUMN'S COME; "Autumn's come, the 2952
trembling popple trees are all becoming bare" e 164   words by S. Lukaczy

RACZKA, ST., 1893-

"RACH, CIACH, CIACH, OD KOMINA"; RAM, TAM, TAM; "Shrove Tuesday's time for leisure" 2953
e, p 159   words by E. Bieder

RADECKE, ROBERT, 1829-1893

AUS DER JUGENDZEIT; "Aus der Jugendzeit, aus der Jugendzeit klingt ein Lied mir immerdar" g 2954
326, 327   words by F. Rückert

RADOSZEWSKA, A.

CHRYZANTEMY; "O żegnajmi, odchodzę"; CHRYSANTHEMUMS; "Farewell, farewell, I leave 2955
you" e, p 295   words by S. Przesmycki

RAHLFS, LUDWIG

"AUF DER LÜNEBURGER HEIDE" g 326, 353   words by H. Löns 2956

RAKOV, NIKOLAÏ PETROVICH, 1908-

ELEGY; "Why, tell me why my fond affection" e 342   words by N. Yazykov 2957

RAMEAU, JEAN PHILIPPE, 1683-1764

"AH! VOUS DIRAI-JE, MAMAN" See 4874

[CASTOR ET POLLUX, opera; words by P. J. Bernard] AIR DE POLLUX; "Nature, 2958
amour, qui partagez mon coeur"; "Not love alone, Nature, too, shares my heart" e, f 146

[Ibid] AIR DE TÉLAÏRE, Act I; "Tristes apprêts, pâles flambeaux"; "Torches that burn pale in the 2959
gloom" e, f 151

[DARDANUS, opera; words by C. A. L. de la Bruère] O JOUR AFFREUX!; "O 2960
jour affreux! Le ciel met le comble à nos maux"; O TRISTE DI!; "O triste di! Nel mal or c'immerge il destin" f, i 411

[LES FÊTES D'HÉBÉ, opera; words by A. G. de Mondorge] AIR DE MERCURE; 2961
"Tu veux avoir la préférénce"; "You think! oh! Strephon that your piping" e, f 152

[HIPPOLYTE ET ARICIE, opera; words by S. J. de Pellegrin] AIR DE THÉSÉE; 2962
"Puissant maître des flots favorable Neptune"; "Mighty Lord of the deep, oh! benevolent Neptune"
e, f 146

[Ibid] ARIETTE; "Rossignols amoureux répondez à nos voix"; "Nightingales in the wood to our 2963
voice make reply" e, f 150; ROSSIGNOLS AMOUREUX; "Sing of love, nightingales, O reply
to our song" e, f 292

[LA MUSETTE, cantata] THE MUSETTE; "Sous un delicieux ombrage"; (recit); "L'aimbale 2964
Lisette forme des concerts" (aria); "Along a shady forest pathway" (recit); "Lovely, charming
Betty, free from worldly cares" (aria) e, f 404

MUSETTE; "L'echo des bois des sons de la musette" f 88 2965

RAMIREZ, RICARDO

ROMANZA DEL CARIBE; ESTILO QUISQUEYANO   piano 303 2966

RAMOS, SILVANO R.

"ALLÁ EN EL RANCHO GRANDE"; DOWN ON THE BIG RANCH; "Down on the cattle ranches" e, s 2967
219

RANDEGGER, ALBERTO

A MARINER'S HOME'S THE SEA; "Let the hermit dwell in his cloister'd cell" e 205   words by J. P. 2968
Wooler

RANDEL, A.

[VÄRMLÄNNINGARNA] I VILLANDE SKOGEN; "I villande skogen jag vallar min hjord"; 2969
WHERE WILD GROWS THE FOREST; "Where wild grows the forest I pasture my herds" e, sw 188
words by F. A. Dahlgren

RAPEE, ERNO, 1891-1945

CHARMAINE; "I wonder why you keep me waiting" e 128, 129   joint composer L. Pollack 2970
DIANE; "I'M IN HEAVEN WHEN I SEE YOU SMILE" e 128, 129   joint composer L. Pollack 2971
LITTLE MOTHER; "Little Mother Mother mine, there's no other Mother mine" e 129   joint composer 2972
L. Pollack

RASMUSSEN, HOLGER
    DEJLIGE DANMARK; "Dejlige Danmark, hør, hvor det klinger"; BEAUTIFUL DENMARK; "Beautiful   2973
       Denmark, hear its name ringing" da, e 87
RASMUSSEN, P. E.
    "DANMARK, DEJLIGST VANG OG VAENGE"; "DENMARK, LOVELY FIELD AND MEADOW" da, e 87   2974
       words by L. Kok
RATHGEBER, JOHANN VALENTIN, 1682-1750
    BRUDER LIEDERLICH; "Alleweil ein wenig lustig" g 99; "ALLEWEIL EIN WENIG LUSTIG" g 40,309   2975
    VON DER EDLEN MUSIK; "Der hat hingeben das ewig Leben" g 99; "Der hat vergeben das ewig   2976
       Leben" g 226; DER HAT VERGEBEN g 326; "DER HAT VERGEBEN DAS EWIG LEBEN" g 49
    VON EHR-ABSCHNEIDISCHEN ZUNGEN; "So lassen mir die falschen Zungen" g 250   2977
RAVEL, MAURICE, 1875-1937
    CHANSON ESPAGNOLE; "Adieu, va, mon homme"; SPANISH SONG; "Adios, men homíno"; "My   2978
       husband, good-bye" e, f, s 121
    [DEUX ÉPIGRAMMES DES CLEMENT MAROT] D'ANNE JOUANT DE L'ESPINETTE, no.1;   2979
       "Lorsque je voyen ordre la brunette"; MY ANNE AT THE SPINET; "When that my dark-haired
       Anne I see" e, f 121,362
    [Ibid] D'ANNE QUI ME JECTA DE LA NEIGE, no.2; "Anne par jeu me jecta de la neige"; TO   2980
       ANNE, WHO THREW SNOW; "Anne in sport threw me snow" e, f 362
RAVENSCROFT, E. G. S.
    JESUS IN HIS CRADLE; "Jesus in his cradle sleeping must not be awoken" e 377   2981
RAVENSCROFT, THOMAS, ca1590-ca1633
    JOLLY SHEPHERD; "Jolly shepherd and upon a hill he sate" 3 pt round e 235   2982
    LOATH TO DEPART; "Sing with thy mouth, sing with thy heart" 4 pt round e 235   2983
    WHILE SHEPHERDS WATCHED THEIR FLOCKS BY NIGHT. See 9009B
Raye, Don. See WILHOITE, DONALD MAC RAE, 1909-
RAYMOND, EUGENE
    "DEAR LAND OF THE SOUTH" e 189   2984
RAYMOND, FRED
    [BALL DER NATIONEN, operetta; words by G. Schwenn] ABENDS, WENN DIE   2985
       LICHTER GLÜHN; "Bin ich guter Laune, geb ich keine Ruh!" g 258
    [Ibid] "HEUT SCHEINT DIE SONNE INS HERZ MIR HINEIN!" g 255   2986
    [Ibid] "WER SICH DIE WELT MIT EINEM DONNERSCHLAG EROBERN WILL"; "Manchmal, da   2987
       rennt man vor" (verse) g 258
    [MASKE IN BLAU, operetta; words by G. Schwenn] "FRÜHLING IN SAN REMO";   2988
       "Hier leigt ein Leuchten über dem Land!" (verse) g 258
    [Ibid] DIE JULISKA AUS BUDAPEST; "Puszta ist weit! Das ist Juliskas Leid!" g 255   2989
    [Ibid] "SCHAU EINEN SCHÖNEN FRAU NIE ZU TIEF IN DIE AUGEN!" g 257   2990
    [DIE PERLE VON TOKAY, operetta; words by M. Wallner and K. Feltz]   2991
       DULLI-ÖH!; "Beim ersten Glas, das ist man fröhlich"; "Jeder teilt sein Leben ein" (verse) g 258
    [SAISON IN SALZBURG, operetta; words by M.Wallner and K. Feltz] UND   2992
       DIE MUSIK SPIELT DAZU!; "Ma chérie nennt man sein Dirndel"; "Yes, my boy, will you tanz'
       mit mir?" (ref) e, f, g (in pt) 257
    [Ibid] WENN DER TONI MIT DER VRONI; "Wenn sich ein Salzburger Bua und sein Dirndl" g 258   2993
RAYMOND, GENE
    LET ME ALWAYS SING; "Meadows are swaying, wild flowers playing" e 176   2994
READ, JOHN
    DOWN BY THE OLD MILL STREAM; "You must know that my uncle is a farmer" e 205   2995
READING, JOHN, d 1692, supposed composer
    ADESTE FIDELES; "Adeste fideles, laeti triumphantes"; O COME, ALL YE FAITHFUL; "O come,   2996
       all ye faithful, joyful and triumphant" e, lat 35, 79,154,165,206,237,388; e 28,33,37,38,39,
       125,132,233,236,251,296,305,307,315,333,343,366,394,410
REBEL, JEAN FERRY, 1661-1747
    [ULYSSE, opera; words by H. Guichard] AIR DE PÉNÉLOPE; "Souffrirai-je toujours les   2997
       rigueurs de l'absence Ulysse revenez?; "Must I wait here alone, ever mourning thine absence,
       Ulysses, Oh! return" e, f 149
REDNER, LEWIS HENRY, 1831-1908
    "EVERYWHERE, EVERYWHERE, CHRISTMAS TONIGHT" e 296 words by P. Brooks   2998
    "O LITTLE TOWN OF BETHLEHEM," St. Louis (tune) e 28,33,35,38,39,79,125,165,206,233,236,   2999
       251,296,307,315,337,366,388 words by P. Brooks
REED, WILLIAM LEONARD, 1910-
    BUILDING BRITAIN; "Here where the shoulders of the downs" e 306 words by M. Martin   3000
    THE GLOW WITHIN; "Oh, you've gotta get a glory in the work you do" e 76   3001
    "WHEN CHRIST WAS BORN OF MARY FREE" e 307   3002

REGER, MAX, 1873-1916
    GLÜCK, op.15, no.1; "Es ruht mit ernstem Sinnen auf mir dein Blick" g 226   words by K. von   3003
        Rohrscheidt
    HERZENSTAUSCH, op.76, no.5; "Du sagst, mein liebes Mütterlein" g 96   words by K. Enslin   3004
    MARIÄ WIEGENLIED, op.76, no.52; "Maria sitzt am Rosenhag und wiegt ihr Jesuskind" g 96   words   3005
        by M. Doelitz
    UM DICH, op.12, no.5; "Was hat des Schlummers Band zerrissen" g 250   words by I. Kurz   3006
    WIEGENLIED; "Schlaf, Kindlein, balde, schlaf Kindlein, balde" g 229   3007
REGNART, JACOB, 1548-1599
    MEIN MUND, DER SINGT; "Mein Mund, der singt, mein Herz vor Trauern weint" g 41   3008
REICHARDT, JOHANN FRIEDRICH, 1752-1814
    DER BAUM IM ODENWALD, folksong after J. F. Reichardt. See 5237
    BUNDESLIED; "In allen guten Stunden, erhöht von Lieb und Wein" g 99   words by J. W. von Goethe   3009
    "BUNT SIND SCHON DIE WÄLDER" g 49,309,326   words by J. G. von Salis   3010
    CLÄRCHENS LIED; "Freudvoll und leidvoll, gedankenvoll sein" g 99   words by J. W. von Goethe   3011
    HEIDENRÖSLEIN; "Sah ein Knab ein Röslein stehn" g 96   words by J. W. von Goethe   3012
    JÄGERS ABENDLIED; "Im Felde schleich ich still und wild" g 229   words by J. W. von Goethe   3013
    JOHANNA SEBUS; "Der Damm zerreisst, das Feld erbraust" g 250   words by J. W. von Goethe   3014
    "JUNGFRÄULEIN, SOLL ICH MIT EUCH GEH'N?"; "DEAR MAIDEN, SHALL I WITH YOU GO?" g 36   3015
        arr by J. Brahms
    NICHT LOBENSWÜRDIG IST DER MANN (tune). See 5237
    "STERBEN IST EIN HARTE BUSS" g 49   3016
    DAS VEILCHEN; "Ein Veilchen auf der Wiese stand" g 96,99,229   words by J. W. von Goethe   3017
    "WACH AUF, MEINS HERZENS SCHÖNE" g 49,309,326; MORGENSTÄNDCHEN g 99   3018
    "WÄR ICH EIN WILDER FALKE" g 41   3019
REICHARDT, LUISE, 1779-1826
    HOFFNUNG; "Wenn die Rosen blühen"; WHEN THE ROSES BLOOM; "In the time of roses" e, g 122;   3020
        "IN THE TIME OF ROSES" e, g 329; e 28,237,279,366
    SLEEP, MY SAVIOUR, SLEEP; "Sleep, my Saviour, sleep, on Thy bed of hay" e 337   words by S.   3021
        Baring-Gould
    DER SPINNERIN NACHTLIED; "Es sang vor langen Jahren" g 229   words by C. Brentano   3022
REIFF, STANLEY T.
    "LET NOT YOUR HEART BE TROUBLED" e 398   words from St. John XIV:1,2,3   3023
REISSIGER, FRIEDRICH AUGUST, 1809-1883
    "A SCHLOSSER HÔT EN G'SELLE G'HOT" g 326   words by J. C. Grübel   3024
REISSIGER, KARL GOTTLIEB, 1798-1859
    HISTORIA VON NOAH; "Als Noah aus dem Kasten war" g 99   words by A. Kopisch   3025
    STUDENTENLEBEN; "'s gibt kein schöner Leben" g 31   3026
RESPIGHI, OTTORINO, 1879-1936
    NEBBIE; "Soffro Lontan lontano"; MISTS; "Dreamlike, the mists are drifting" e, i 121; "Yonder,   3027
        from swamplands lowly" e, i 408   words by A. Negri
RESTA, NATALE, att to
    TRE GIORNI SON CHE NINA. See 2769
REYLOFF, EDWARD
    "OVER THE ROLLING SEA" e 205   3028
RHAW, GEORG, 1488-1548
    HERZLICH TUT MICH ERFREUEN; "Herzlich tut mich erfreuen die fröhlich Sommerzeit" g 226   3029
Rice, Daddy. See RICE, THOMAS DARTMOUTH, 1806-1860
RICE, GITZ
    MADEMOISELLE FROM ARMENTIERES. See 7665
RICE, THOMAS DARTMOUTH, 1806-1860
    JIM CROW; "Come listen all you gals and boys"; "Weel about and turn about and do jis' so" (ref)   3030
        e 185; "Well about and turn about and do jis' so" (ref) e 225; JUMP JIM CROW e 115; "Wheel
        about, an' turn about, an' do jis so" (ref) e 34; "Come, lis'en all you gals an' boys"; "Wheel
        about an' turn about an' do jes' so" (ref) e 184; JIM CROW; "Come listen all you gals and boys";
        "Weel about and turn about and do jis' so" (ref) e 212
RICHARDSON, T.
    MARY; "Kind, kind and gentle is she" e 385   3031
RICHARTZ, WILLY
    LEISE KLINGT EINE MELODIE; "Du und ich, ich und du sind vom Glück gemeint" g 222   words by   3032
        P. Kirsten
RIDDELL, H. S.
    SCOTLAND YET; "Gae, bring my guid auld harp ance mair" e 17   3033
RIMSKIĬ-KORSAKOV, NIKOLAĬ ANDREEVICH, 1844-1908
    [LE COQ D'OR, opera; words by V. I. Bel'skiĭ] HYMN TO THE SUN; "Salut à   3034
        toi, soleil de flamme!"; "O radiant sun I give you greeting!" e, f 292; "All hail to thee, O sun in
        glory" e, f 176

RIMSKIĬ-KORSAKOV, NIKOLAĬ ANDREEVICH, 1844-1908 (Continued)

 "A FLIGHT OF PASSING CLOUDS," op.42, no.3 e, r 340 words by A. S. Pushkin 3035

 "I HAVE COME TO YOU THIS MORNING", op.42, no.2 e, r 340 words by Fet 3036

 THE NIGHTINGALE AND THE ROSE, op.2, no.2; "The rose has heard the nightingale" e 348; "THE 3037
  NIGHTINGALE CHARM'D BY THE ROSE"; EASTERN ROMANCE e 407

 ON GEORGIAN HILLS, op.3, no.4; "On Georgian hills nocturnal mist has cast its veil" e, r 340 3038
  words by A. S. Pushkin

 [SADKO, opera; words by N. A. Rimskiĭ-Korsakov and V. I. Bel'skiĭ] 3039
  A SONG OF INDIA; "Unnumber'd diamonds lie within the caverns"; CHANSON DU MARCHAND
  HINDOU; "Sans nombre sont les diamants qui brillent" e, f 241; CHANSON INDOUE; "Thy
  hidden gems are rich beyond all measure" e 122; "Once more I hear the song of India" e 132;
  "A wealth of diamonds lie within the caverns" e 329

RINK, JOHANN CHRISTIAN, 1770-1846

 AS EACH HAPPY CHRISTMAS; "As each happy Christmas dawns on earth again" e 206,296 3040

RIVINAC, P.

 OUR FIRST PRESIDENT'S QUICKSTEP, piano 161 3041

ROAT, CHARLES E.

 PAL OF MY DREAMS; "As I turn back the years"; "Dear old pal, how I miss you" e 114 3042

ROBERTS, LEE S., 1884-1949

 SMILES; "There are smiles that make us happy" e 233 words by J. W. Callahan 3043

ROBINSON, EARL, 1910-

 ABE LINCOLN; "Now old Abe Lincoln, a great giant of a man was he" e 293 3044

 JOE HILL; "I dreamed I saw Joe Hill last night" e 35,293 words by A. Hayes 3045

ROCHLITZ, GUSTAV, 1823-1880

 "WEG MIT BÜCHERN UND PAPIEREN" g 31 words by J. Schanz 3046

RODGERS, JIMMIE, 1897-1933

 BLUES LIKE MIDNIGHT; "She left me this morning, midnight was turning day"; "I got the blues 3047
  like midnight" (ref) e 336

 BRAKEMAN'S BLUES; "Portland, Maine, is just the same as sunny Tennessee" e 336 3048

 MY LOVIN' GAL LUCILLE; "If you ever had the blues you know just how I feel" e 336 3049

 TRAVELIN' BLUES; "I had a dream last night"; "I'm goin' away, leavin' today" (ref) e 336 joint 3050
  composer S. L. Alley

RODGERS, RICHARD, 1902-

 MY HEART STOOD STILL; "I laughed at sweethearts I met at schools"; "I took one look at you" (ref) 3051
  e 345 words by L. Hart

 "WITH A SONG IN MY HEART"; "Though I know that we meet ev'ry night" (verse) e 345 words by 3052
  L. Hart

RODNEY, PAUL

 CALVARY; "The pilgrims throng thro' the city gates" (recit); "Rest, rest to the weary" (aria) e 123, 3053
  394,398,400 (aria only) e 132

 THE CLANG OF THE FORGE; "The furnace fires are shining" e 237 words by H. Vaughan 3054

ROE, HORTON

 "SOUL OF MY SAVIOUR" e 71 3055

ROGERS, JAMES HOTCHISS, 1867-1940

 CLOUD-SHADOWS; "I wish I could ride on the shadows of clouds" e 45 words by K. Pyle; 3056

 ROCK OF AGES; "Rock of ages, cleft for me" e 8 words by A. M. Toplady 3057

 THE TIME FOR MAKING SONGS HAS COME; "Surely the time for making songs has come" e 241 3058
  words by H. Hagedorn

ROGERT, D. L.

 KONG KRISTIAN; "Kong Kristian stod ved højen Mast i Røg og Damp"; KING CHRISTIAN; "King 3059
  Christian stood by the lofty mast in mist and smoke" da, e 87 da words by J. Ewald, e words by
  H. W. Longfellow

ROIG, GONZALO, 1890-

 QUIEREME MUCHO; "Quiereme mucho dulce amor mio" s 284 words by A. Rodriguez 3060

ROLAND, MARC, 1894-

 UNTER DEM STERNENZELT; "Unter dem Sternenzelt reich' mir die Hand" g 222 words by P. Frande 3061

ROMA, CARO, 1866-1937

 "CAN'T YO' HEAR ME CALLIN' CAROLINE" e 233 words by W. H. Gardner 3062

ROMBERG, SIGMUND, 1887-1951

 "WHEN I GROW TOO OLD TO DREAM" e 236 words by O. Hammerstein, II 3063

ROME, HAROLD

 THE INVESTIGATOR'S SONG; "I've got a problem that is bothering me" e 293 3064

RONTANI, RAFFAELO, c 1622

 CALDI SOSPIRI; "Caldi sospiri, ch'uscite dal core" i 180 3065

 KANZONETTE; "Or ch'io non segno più"; "Nun, da ich nicht mehr auf den Pfaden wandle" g, i 217 3066

 O PRIMAVERA; "O Primavera, gioventù dell' anno" i 180 words by G. B. Guarini 3067

ROOT, GEORGE FREDERICK, 1820-1895

THE BATTLE-CRY OF FREEDOM; "Yes, we'll rally round the flag, boys"; "The Union forever,   3068
Hurrah! boys, Hurrah!" (ref) e 28,115,129,130,279,366

THE HAZEL DELL; "In the Hazel Dell my Nelly's sleeping"; "All alone my watch I'm keeping in   3069
the Hazel Dell" (ref) e 129,130

JOHNNY SCHMOKER; "Johnny Schmoker, Johnny Schmoker, ich kan spielen" e 225; "Johnny   3070
Schmoker, Johnny Schmoker, ich kann spielen" e 189

"JUST BEFORE THE BATTLE, MOTHER"; "Farewell, Mother, you may never press me to your heart   3071
again" e 28,34,129,130,279,366

THE REAPER ON THE PLAIN; "Bending o'er his sickle, 'mid the yellow grain" e 189 words by C.   3072
G. Eastman

"THERE'S MUSIC IN THE AIR" e 28,129,130,279,366   3073

TRAMP, TRAMP, TRAMP; "In the prison cell I sit" e 10,28,33,34,129,130,233,236,279,366;   3074
TRAMP, TRAMP, TRAMP, THE BOYS ARE MARCHING; "In the prison cell I sat" e 7

THE VACANT CHAIR; "We shall meet, but we shall miss him" e 28,114,366   3075

ROSA, SALVATOR, 1615-1673, att to

"SELVE, VOI CHE LE SPERANZE"; FOREST, THY GREEN ARBORS; "Forest, thy green arbors shaded"   3076
e, i 138

STAR VICINO; "Star vicino al bel' idol che s'ama"; LET ME LINGER NEAR THEE; "Let me linger   3077
near thee forever" e, i 275; "TO BE NEAR THE FAIR IDOL" e, i 139

ROSE, VINCENT, 1880-1944

AVALON; "Ev'ry morning mem'ries stray across the sea where flying fishes play"; "I found my love   3078
in Avalon" (ref) e 345; (ref only) e 233 words by A. Jolson and G. G. De Sylva

LINGER AWHILE; "The stars shine above you, yet linger awhile" e 236 joint composer H. Owens   3079

WHISPERING; "Whispering while you cuddle near me" e 128,236 joint composer J. Schonberger,   3080
words by R. Coburn

ROSENBERG, HILDING CONSTANTIN, 1892-

[KVINNAN I HYLLOS HUS, words by E. Byström-Baekström] GLAUKES   3081
SAANGER, 1. PASTORAL; "Det är middag" sw 356

[Ibid] GLAUKES SAANGER, 2. GLAUKES SAANG OM KÄRLEKEN; "Ack, att jag vore den vaxade   3082
flöjt" sw 356

[Ibid] GLAUKES SAANGER, 3. GLAUKES KLAGOSAANG; "Svalan paa taket" sw 356   3083

ROSENFELD, MONROE H.

LET ME SHAKE THE HAND THAT SHOOK THE HAND OF SULLIVAN; "The Bradys and O'Gradys,   3084
ye may talk about them all" e 204

SHE WAS HAPPY TILL SHE MET YOU; "'Twas a bright and sunny day"; "She was happy till she met   3085
you" (ref) e 114,131,204; (ref only) e 129,130,132

TAKE BACK YOUR GOLD; "I saw a youth and maiden on a lonely city street" e 32,34,246 words   3086
by L. W. Pritzkow

ROSIER, F. W.

THE ALABAMA; "The wind blows off yon rocky shore" e 189 words by E. King   3087

ROSSETER, PHILIP

"IF I URGE MY KIND DESIRES" e 196   3088

"IF SHE FORSAKE ME" e 117,196 words att to T. Campian   3089

ROSSETER'S AYRE; "Christ is born, the Angels tell" e 376 words by J. Philips   3090

"WHAT THEN IS LOVE BUT MOURNING" e 118 words att to T. Campian   3091

WHEN LAURA SMILES; "When Laura smiles her sight revives both night and day" e 36,144,116,196,   3092
199 words by T. Campian

ROSSI, LUIGI, 1598-1653

KANZONE; "Che sventura! Son tant' anni"; "Welch Missgeschick! Seit so vielen Jahren" g, i 217   3093

KANZONE; "Non la volete intendere"; "Du willst es nicht begreifen" g, i 217   3094

[PALAZZO D'ATLANTE INCANTATO, opera; words by G. Rospigliosi]   3095
ARIE DER FIORDILIGI; "Se mi toglie ria sventura"; "Wenn ein unseliges Geschick mir den raubt"
g, i 217

ROSSINI, GIOACCHINO ANTONIO, 1792-1868

[IL BARBIERE DI SIVIGLIA, opera; words by C. Sterbini] "A UN DOTTOR   3096
DELLA MIA SORTE," Act I; "TO A MAN OF MY IMPORTANCE" e, i 5

[Ibid] "LA CALUNNIA È UN VENTICELLO," Act I i 299; DIE VERLEUMDUNG; "Die Verleumdung,   3097
sie ist ein Lüftchen" g, i 390; LA CALUNNIA; "Slander's whisper, when first beginning" e, i 5

[Ibid] LARGO AL FACTOTUM, Act I; "Largo al factotum della città"; I'M THE FACTOTUM;   3098
"I'm the factotum of all the town!" e, i 4,364; "LARGO AL FACTOTUM DELLA CITTÀ" i 298

[Ibid] "UNA VOCE POCO FÀ," Act I i 302; "Though his voice was breath'd afar" e, i 6;   3099
THERE'S A VOICE THAT I ENSHRINE; "There's a voice that I enshrine in my heart" e, i 2,
221; CAVATINA; "See how much a song can do" e, i 292; CAVATINE DER ROSINA; "Frag'
ich mein beklomm'nes Herz" g 311

ROSSINI, GIOACCHINO ANTONIO, 1792-1868 (Continued)

[LA CENERENTOLA, opera; words by J. Ferretti] "NACQUI ALL'AFFANNO E AL   3100
PIANTO," Act II (recit); "Non più mesta accanto al fuoco" (aria) i 300; NON PIÙ MESTA;
"Pain was childhood's sad dower" (recit); "Now farewell, dark days of weeping" e, i 2

[LA GAZZA LADRA, opera; words by G. Gherardini] "DI PIACER MI BALZA IL   3101
COR," Act I; "To my native home I'm near" e, i 6

[GUILLAUME TELL, opera; words by É. de Jouy and H.L.F. Bis] SELVA   3102
OPACA, DESERTA BRUGHIERA, Act II; "S'allontanano alfine! Io sperai rive derlo" (recit); "Selva
opaca, deserta brughiera" (aria) i 301

[L'ITALIANA IN ALGERI, opera; words by A. Anelli] PER LUI CHE ADORO, Act   3103
II; "Per lui che adoro, ch'è il mio tesoro" i 300

[PICCOLA MESSA SOLENNE] CRUCIFIXUS; "Crucifixus crucifixus etiam pro nobis" lat 367   3104

[SEMIRAMIDE, opera; words by G. Rossi] IN SÌ BARBARA; "In sì barbara sciagura";   3105
"In thine ears my sorrow pouring" e, i 2

[SOIRÉES MUSICALES] LA PASTORELLA DELLE ALPI; "Son bella pastorella, che scende ogni   3106
mattino"; THE ALPINE SHEPHERDESS; "I'm the gay and joyful shepherdess who comes with lovely
fruits and flowers" e, i 211   words by C. Pepoli

[Ibid] LA PROMESSA; CANZONETTA; "Ch'io mai vi possa lasciar d'amare"; THE PROMISE;   3107
"How could I ever to love unfaithful be" e, i 211   words by P. A. Metastasio

[STABAT MATER] CUJUS ANIMAM, no.2; "Cujus animam gementem"; "Through his bleeding   3108
side retreating" e, lat 394; e 346,400

[Ibid] INFLAMMATUS, no.8; "Inflammatus, inflammatus et accensus"; "When thou comest, when   3109
thou comest to the judgment" e, lat 394

ROUGET DE LISLE, CLAUDE JOSEPH, 1760-1863

LA MARSEILLAISE; "Allons, enfants de la Patrie!"; "Arise, ye sons of France" e, f 293; f 82,88,91,   3110
127,294,383; "Ye sons of France, awake to glory!" e, f 7; e 35,233; MARSEILLAISE HYMN e 28,
279,366; "Ye sons of Freedom, wake to glory!"; VIRGINIAN MARSEILLAISE; "Virginia hears the
dreadful summons" e 161; CHANT DE GUERRE POUR L'ARMÉE DU RHIN, original version f 294

ROUSSEAU, JEAN JACQUES, 1712-1778

[LE DEVIN DU VILLAGE, opera] AIR DE COLIN; "Je vais revoir ma charmante maitresse";   3111
"To her I go, to my dearest Colette!" e, f 153

ECHO; "Une nymphe était si tant belle qu'elle éfaçoit le plus beau jour" f 278   words by M. de   3112
Corancez

LE ROSIER; "Je l'ai planté, je l'ai vu naître" f 82   words by de Loire   3113

RUBIN, BASYA

YUGNT-HYMN; "Undzer lid iz ful mit troyer"; "Though our song be full of sorrow" e, y 318   words   3114
by S. Kacerginski

RUBINSTEIN, ANTON, 1829-1894

DER ASRA, op.32, no.6; THE ASRA; "Daily walked the lovely daughter of the Sultan in the garden"   3115
e 348

DESIRE; "Open wide my lonely dungeon" e, r 341   words by M. Lermontov   3116

DU BIST WIE EINE BLUME, op.32, no.5; "Du bist wie eine Blume so hold und schön und rein";   3117
THOU'RT LIKE UNTO A FLOWER; "A tender flow'r thou seemest, so pure so fair thou art" e, g
385; "Thou'rt like unto a flower, as fair, as pure, as bright"; "Thou art so like a flower, so pure,
and fair, and kind" e, g 241   words by H. Heine

[MELODY, piano, OP.3, NO.1, F MAJOR] VOICES OF THE WOODS; "Welcome sweet   3118
spring time! We greet thee in song" e 329; WELCOME SWEET SPRINGTIME e 28,366

RUBY, HARRY, 1895-

THINKING OF YOU; "If you were near me I wouldn't dare to say what I'm about to say to you";   3119
"Why is it I spend the day" (ref) e 345   words by B. Kalmar

Rügen, Wizlav, fl 1290. See WIZLAV VON RÜGEN, fl 1290

RUNG, HENRIK, 1807-1871

"I DANMARK ER JEG FØDT"; DENMARK, MY FATHERLAND; "In Denmark I am born" da, e 87   3120
words by H. C. Andersen

MODERS NAVN; "Moders navn er en himmelsk Lyd"; THE MOTHER-TONGUE; "Mother's name has   3121
a blessed sound" da, e 87   words by N. F. S. Grundtvig

RUSSELL, HENRY, 1812-1900

BARBER, SPARE THOSE HAIRS; "O barber, spare those hairs" e 225   words by J. Love   3122

"A LIFE ON THE OCEAN WAVE" e 205   3123

MY MOTHER'S BIBLE; "This book is all that's left me now!" e 129,130,189   words by G. P. Morris   3124

THE OLD ARM CHAIR; "I love it, I love it, and who shall dare" e 130   words by E. Cook; THE   3125
SOLDIER'S GRAVE; "Oh, stranger, tread lightly, tis holy ground here" e 161   words by D. Otto-
lengui

THE SHIP ON FIRE; "The storm o'er the ocean flew furious and fast" e 189; "Hark! what was that"   3126
(last section only) e 212   words by C. Mackay

RUSSELL, HENRY, 1812-1900 (Continued)

WOODMAN, SPARE THAT TREE; "Woodman spare that tree! Touch not a single bough" e 28,115, 129,130,132 words by G. P. Morris — 3127

RUTKOWSKI, NAPOLEON

MÓW DO MNIE JESZCZE; "Mów do mnie jeszcze, za taką rozmową"; SPEAK TO ME ONCE MORE; "Speak to me once more, your voice is like music" e, p 295 words by K. Tetmajer — 3128

RYGAARD, GEORG

DER ER INGENTING, DER MANER; FLAGET; "Der er ingenting, der maner som et Flag"; "THERE IS NOTHING THAT CAN CONJURE"; THE FLAG da, e 87 words by A. Juel — 3129

S. C.

"MOTHER AT YOUR FEET IS KNEELING" e 71 — 3130

SABOLY, NICOLAS, 1614-1675

"SOUN TRES OME FORT SAGE"; "THREE MEN TOWARDS BETHL'EM TURNING" e, f (pr) 52 — 3131

SAINT-SAËNS, CAMILLE, 1835-1921

AIMONS-NOUS; "Aimons-nous et dormons"; LET US LOVE EACH OTHER; "Let us love each other and sleep" e, f 190,192,194 words by T. de Banville — 3132

L'ATTENTE; "Monte, écureuil, monte au grand chêne"; WAITING; "Climb, squirrel climb the big oak tree" e, f 190,192,194 words by V. Hugo — 3133

"LE BONHEUR EST CHOSE LÉGÈRE"; "HAPPINESS IS A FLEETING THING" e, f 190 words by J. Barbier and M. Carré — 3134

LA CIGALE ET LA FOURMI; "La cigale ayant chanté tout l'été, ayant chanté tout l'été" f 278 — 3135

CLAIR DE LUNE; "Dans la forêt que crée un rêve"; MOONLIGHT; "Within the grove so dreamy wending" e, f 140 words by C. Mendes — 3136

DANSE MACABRE; "Zig et zig et zig, la mort en cadence"; DANCE OF DEATH; "Zig and zig and zig, death rhythmically" e, f 192,194 words by H. Cazalis — 3137

THE NIGHTINGALE AND THE ROSE; "Ah!"...(no words) e 208 — 3138

[SAMSON ET DALILA, opera; words by F. Lemaire] AMOUR, VIENS AIDER, Act II; "Samson, recherchant ma présence" (recit); "Amour! viens aider ma faiblesse!" (aria); "Tonight Samson makes his obeisance" (recit); "O love, of thy might let me borrow" (aria) e, f 2 — 3139

[Ibid] "MON COEUR S'OUVRE À TA VOIX," Act II; "MY HEART AT THY SWEET VOICE" e, f 2,122,329; "Like flowers blooming fair" e, f 132 — 3140

[Ibid] PRINTEMPS QUI COMMENCE, Act I; "Printemps qui commence, portant l'espérance"; "The spring, with her dower of bird and of flower" e, f 2 — 3141

SAINTON, CHARLOTTE HELEN (DOLBY), 1821-1885

OCH, GIRLS DEAR; KATEY'S LETTER; "Och, girls dear, did you ever hear, I wrote my love a letter" e 166,213 words by H. S. Dufferin — 3142

SALOMON, SIEGFRIED, 1885-

[LEONORA CHRISTINE, opera; words by A. Barfoed] DER ER TRE HJØRNESTENE; "Der er tre Hjørnestene at bygge paa"; THREE CORNER-STONES ARE TAKEN; "Three corner-stones are taken if house on land shall safely stand" da, e 87 — 3143

SALTER, MARY ELIZABETH (SUMNER), 1856-1938

THE PINE TREE; "O pine tree lonely standing" e 45 — 3144

REMEMBRANCE; "An un-used string in mem'ry's harp" e 45 words by M. E. Sandford — 3145

SAMBURSKY, DANIEL

BA-AH M'NUCHA; "Ba-a m'nucha layagea"; "QUIET AND PEACE COME" e, h (tr) 30; SHIR HA-EMEK; "Ba-a m'nucha layage-a"; "Now rest has come unto the weary" e, h (tr) 318 words by N. Alterman — 3146

SHIR HAKVISH; "Hach patish! Aley!"; "Dud bo-er ba-esh" (verse); "Strike, strike, with hammer in your hand!"; "Pitch boils on the fire" (verse) e, h (tr) 318 words by N. Alterman — 3147

SAMUEL, HAROLD, 1879-1937

DIAPHENIA; "Diaphenia, like the daffadowndilly" e 344 words by H. Constable — 3148

THE FAIRY BOAT; "Sometime a-down a magic stream a little boat comes sailing" e 344 words by A. Horey — 3149

NANNY; "Oh! Nanny, wilt thou go with me" e 344 words by T. Percy — 3150

OH! MY SWETYNGE!; "Oh! My swetynge! My lyttell prety swetynge" e 344 — 3151

SANCES, GIOVANNI FELICE, ca1600-1679

"CHI NEL REGNO ALMO D'AMORE" (duet) i 181 — 3152

PIETOSI, ALLONTANATEVI; "Pietosi, allontanatevi! Dispietati, seguitemi!" i 180 — 3153

Sánchez de Fuentes, Eduardo. See SÁNCHEZ DE FUENTES Y PELÁEZ, EDUARDO, 1874-

SÁNCHEZ DE FUENTES Y PELÁEZ, EDUARDO, 1874-

EN CUBA; "En Cuba, isla hermosa del ardiente sol bajo su cielo azul"; CUBA; "O Cuba, precious island beneath sunny skies that are blue and serene" e, s 322; TU; "En Cuba la isla hermosa del ardiente sol" s 284 words by H. Sánchez — 3154

SANDERS, J.
    ADIÓS MUCHACHOS; "Adiós muchachos, compañeros de mi vida"; FAREWELL COMPANIONS;   3155
       "Farewell companions, all you pals I love so dearly" e, s 9 words by C. F. Vedani
SANDERSON, JAMES, 1769-1841?
    [THE LADY OF THE LAKE, opera; words by W. Scott] HAIL TO THE CHIEF;   3156
       "Hail to the chief, who in triumph advances" e 28,279,366
SÁNDOR, JENÖ
    HALVÁNY SÁRGA RÓZSÁT; "Halvány sárga rózsá bokrétába szedtem"; "DELICATELY TINTED   3157
       ARE THE YELLOW ROSES" e, hu 285
    KÉKSZEMÜ, SZÉPSZEMÜ ANGYALKÁM; "ANGEL WITH EYES THAT ARE BLUE AND BRIGHT"   3158
       e 164 words by A. Szenes
    NEM TUDOD TE, MI A HÜSÉG; THOU BELIEVEST THAT IT IS LOVE; "Thou believest that it is   3159
       love if your cheeks are glowing" e 164 words by A. Szenes
SANDOVAL, MIGUEL, 1903-1953
    SIN TU AMOR; "Mujer de mi vida"; "Amor de mi vida"; WITHOUT YOUR LOVE; "Beloved, O love   3160
       of my life!" e, s 121
SANGER, MARIE JOY
    CHRISTMAS CRADLE SONG; "Still and dark the night about the sheiling" e 307 words by J. Morrison   3161
SANTLY, JOSEPH H., 1886-
    THERE'S YES! YES! IN YOUR EYES; "You fooled me, dear, now for a year"; "Your lips tell me no!   3162
       no! But there's yes! yes! in your eyes" (ref) e 345 words by C. Friend
SANTOS, GONZALO VERA
    ROMANCE DE MI DESTINO; "Todo lo que quise yo" s 284 words by A. R. Castillo   3163
SARONA, F.
    DIP, BOYS, DIP THE OAR; "'Tis moonlight on the sea, boys" e 28,366   3164
SARRI, DOMENICO
    [DIDONE ABBANDONATA, opera; words by P. A. Metastasio] ARIE; "Non   3165
       ha ragione, ingrato"; "Ist denn rechtlos, Undankbarer" g, i 218
SARTI, GIUSEPPE, 1729-1802
    [GIULIO SABINO, opera; words by P. A. Metastasio] ARIA; "Lungi dal caro   3166
       bene vivere non poss' io"; "Fern meiner teuren Schönen kam ich nicht weiter leben" g, i 353
SAS, NÁCI
    "ERDÖSZÉLÉN NAGY A ZSIVAJ"; "AT THE FOREST'S EDGE THERE'S CELEBRATION" e, hu 285;   3167
    HOGYHA SZERETNÉLEK; "Sose mondtam hogy szeretlek"; "NEVER HAVE I SAID I LOVED YOU"   3168
       e, hu 285
SAUVLET, JEAN BAPTISTE, b 1841
    PFÄLZERLIED, op.15; "Am deutschen Strom am grünen Rheine ziehst du dich hin" g 31 words by   3169
       E. Jost
SAVILE, JEREMY, 17th c
    FA LA LA; THE WAITS; "Fa la la la la la la la" e 402   3170
    "HERE'S A HEALTH UNTO HIS MAJESTY" e 14,234,349,402   3171
SAYERS, HENRY J.
    TA-RA-RA-BOOM-DER-È; "A sweet Tuxedo girl you see" e 32,34; TA-RA-RA-BOOM-DE-AY e 233   3172
SCAMMELL, ARTHUR R.
    THE SQUID-JIGGIN' GROUND; "Oh, this is the place where the fishermen gather" e 186   3173
SCANLAN, WILLIAM J.
    "MY NELLY'S BLUE EYES" e 128,131,132   3174
    MOLLY O!; "She's plain Molly O" e 114,131   3175
    PEEK-A-BOO!; "On a cold, winter's ev'ning" e 114,131   3176
    SCANLAN'S ROSE SONG; "This pretty little flow'r which I take from my breast"; "Promise me that   3177
       you'll keep it" (ref) e 129,130,131
SCARLATTI, ALESSANDRO, 1660-1725
    ARMATI; "Armati, mia costanza, segui la mia speranza"; BEWAFFNE DICH; "Bewaffne dich meine   3178
       Standhaftigkeit"; DEVOTION ARISE!; "Devotion arise! and join my hope" e, g, i 253
    BELLEZZA, CHE S'AMA; "Bellezza, che s'ama è gioia cel dore" i 179   3179
    CANZONETTA; "Non dar più peneo caro" i 308   3180
    CARA E DOLCE; "Cara e dolce dolce dolcissima libertà" i 179   3181
    DIFESA NON HA; "Difesa non ha, difesa non ha da un guardo vezzoso" i 179   3182
    "GIA IL SOLE DAL GANGE"; "O'ER GANGES NOW LAUNCHES" e, i 368; SUNRISE ON THE   3183
       GANGES; "The sun on the Ganges" e 348
    IO DISSI; "Io dissi, io dissi che la face che m'arde in sen" i 180   3184
    KANZONETTE; "Chi vuole innamorarsi, chi vuole innamorarsi, ci deve ben pensar"; "Wer sich   3185
       verlieben will, der mag es sich gut überlegen" g, i 217
    NEVI, INTATTE; "Nevi intatte, vie di latte"; "Untouched whiteness, bearers of milk" e, i 134   3186
    "NON VOGL'IO SE NON VEDERTI"; "I WISH NAUGHT BUT TO SURVEY THEE" e, i 139   3187

SCARLATTI, ALESSANDRO, 1660-1725 (Continued)

"O CESSATE DI PIAGARMI" i 181; CEASE, OH CEASE; "Cease, oh, cease to wound and tease me" 3188
e, i 138; "O, I PRAY YOU, DO NOT WOUND ME" e, i 36; "O NO LONGER SEEK TO PAIN ME"
e, i 368; O CESSATE; "O cessate di piegarmi"; CEASE, OH MAIDEN; "Cease, oh maiden, thus
to grieve me!" e, i 272

O, DOLCISSIMA SPERANZA; "O, dolcissima speranza, sei il ristoro" i 179 3189

PENSIERI; "Pensieri, pensieri, Ah, Dio qual pena" i 179 3190

PER FORMARE LA BETTA; "Per formare la Betta che adoro"; "To create Betta whom I adore" e, i 3191
134

[PIRRO E DEMETRIO, opera; words by A. Morselli] "LA FORTUNA E UN PRONTO 3192
ARDIR"; FORTUNE; "Fortune boldly aims at all" e, i 404

RUGIADOSE, ODOROSE; "Rugiadose, odorose, Violette graziose"; EARLY BLOWING, VIOLETS 3193
GROWING; "Early blowing, violets growing, on my heart perfume bestowing" e, i 138; LE
VIOLETTE; DEWY VIOLETS; "Rich in odours, overflowing violets freshly blowing" e, i 274;
THE VIOLETS; "Lowly violet, silent blowing, dewy fragrance sweet bestowing" e, i 368

"SE FLORINDO È FEDELE"; "SHOULD FLORINDO BE FAITHFUL" e, i 368 3194

[IL SEDECIA, RE DI GERUSALEMME] ARIE DES ISMAEL; "Caldo sangue, che bagnando 3195
il sen mi vai"; "Heisses Blut, das du mir die Brust netzend herabfliesst" g, i 217

SENTO NEL CORE; "Sento nel core certo dolore"; LOVING, I BORROW; "Loving, I borrow many a 3196
sorrow" e, i 139; COME UNTO ME; "Come unto me, all ye weary" e 160

LA SPERANZA; "La speranza mi tradisce, mi si mostra e poi svanisce" i 179 3197

TOGLIETEMI LA VITA ANCOR; "Toglietemi la vita ancor, toglietemi la vita ancor crudeli cieli" 3198
i 179; ARIETTA; "Nehmt wiederum mein Leben dar, nehmt wiederum mein Leben dar! Ihr argen
Götter" g, i 168

LA TUA GRADITA FÉ; "La tua gradita fé, che il core m'invaghì" i 180 3199

VA PER LO MARE; "Va per lo Mare, che la circonda"; "The little boat, over wave after wave" e, i 3200
134

SCARLATTI, DOMENICO, 1685-1757

"QUAL FARFALLETTA AMANTE"; "LIKE ANY FOOLISH MOTH I FLY" e, i 274 3201

SCHÄFFER, RICHARD, 1813-1886

LEICHTER WANDERER; "Ein Heller und ein Batzen, die waren beide mein" g 31 words by A. von 3202
Schlippenbach

STUDIO AUF EINER REIS; "Studio auf einer Reis', juchheidi, juchheida, ganz famos zu leben weiss" 3203
g 43,353; URBUMMELLEID g 31 words by G. Weber,

SCHEIDT, SAMUEL, 1587-1654

EI, DU FEINER REITER; "Ei du feiner Reiter, edler Herre mein" g 49 3204

SCHEIN, JOHANN HERMANN, 1586-1630

DER KÜHLE MAIEN; "Der kühle Maien tut Hirt und Schäfelein" g 42 3205
"SIEH DA, MEIN LIEBER CORIDON" g 250 3206

SCHENK, CASPAR

FAREWELL TO GROG; "Come, messmates, pass the bottle 'round" e 225 3207

SCHERTZINGER, VICTOR L.

OUR OWN BELOVED LAND; "America, America, the land of our Fathers' pride"; "Land of our 3208
Fathers, sweet home that we adore" (ref) e 129,130 words by T. H. Ince

SCHILLING, F.

THERE'S A WONDERFUL TREE; "There's a wonderful tree, a wonderful tree" e 244 words by Mrs. 3209
M. N. Meigs

SCHINDLER, PAUL

MOTHER PIN A ROSE ON ME. See 2125

SCHLENKER, ALFRED, 1876-1950

"BRÜDER LASST UNS LUSTIG SEIN" g 31 words by J. C. Günther 3210

FREIBURGER BUMMELLIED; "Brüder, ist das nicht ein Leben"; "Ja, wo Liebe, Lied und Wein" (ref) 3211
g 31 words by R. F. Gagg

GESANG DER JÜNGLINGE; "Heilig ist der Jugendzeit" g 31 words by L. Uhland 3212

HYMNUS AN DEN ZORN; "Kann mir nichts die Harfe stimmen" g 31 words by M. von Strachwitz 3213

DER JUGEND HOCH!; "Noch schäumen die Becher, noch hallen die Lieder" g 31 words by H. von 3214
Treitschke

O JUGENDZEIT; "O Jugendzeit, wie ist mir bang" g 31 words by K. Stieler 3215

SCHWEIZERGEBET; "Ich hab in Nacht und Sturmeswehn" g 31 words by A. Huggenberger 3216

"DIE SONNE SCHIEN VOM HIMMEL" g 31 3217

TRINKLIED; "Lasst mich trinken, lasst mich trinken" g 31 words by F. T. Vischer 3218

WANDERLIED; "Von dem Berge zu den Hügeln niederab das Tal entlang" g 31 words by J. W. von 3219
Goethe

WANDERLIED ZUR LAUTE; "Durch den Wald mit rauschen Schritten trage ich die Laute hin" g 31 3220
words by C. Brentano

WEGELIED ZUM SCHWEIZERFEST; "Drei Ellen gute Bannerseide" g 31 words by G. Keller 3221

SCHLENKER, AUGUST
    JUNGER MUT; "Ein tag ist neu erstanden" g 31 words by A. Huggenberger   3222
SCHLIEBEN, ADOLF, 1828-1896
    HUNDERT SEMESTER; "Als ich schlummernd lag heut Nacht"; "Gaudeamus igitur" (ref) g 31 words   3223
    by A. Katsch
SCHLÖSSER, ADOLPHE, 1830-
    HE THAT KEEPETH ISRAEL; "He that keepeth Israel, slumbers not, nor sleeps" e 123   3224
SCHMELZER, JOHANN HEINRICH, c 1623-1680
    RING GSANGLEIN; "Kombt her in unser Rheyen die treue lieb tut freyen"; "Kommt her in unsern   3225
    Reihen, die treue Lieb tut freien" g 308
SCHMEZER, CHRISTOPH, 1800-1862
    DER ENDERLE VON KETSCH; "Jetzt weicht, jetzt flieht" g 31 words by J. V. Scheffel   3226
    DAS WILDE HEER; "Das war der Herr von Rodenstein" g 31 words by J. V. Scheffel   3227
SCHMID, HEINRICH KASPAR, 1874-
    WIEGENLIED FÜR MEINEN JUNGEN, op.31, no.3; "Schlaf, mein, Küken, Rakker schlafe!" g 226   3228
    words by R. Dehmel
SCHMIDLIN, JOHANNES
    "GEH AUS, MEIN HERZ, UND SUCHE FREUD" g 326 words by P. Gerhardt   3229
SCHMIDSEDER, LUDWIG, 1904-
    [FRAUEN IM METROPOL, operetta; words by G. Schwenn] "KOMM DOCH IN   3230
    MEINE ARME!" g 257
    I HAB DIE SCHÖNEN MADERL'N NET ERFUNDEN; "Es gibt auf der Welt doch erstens kein Geld" g   3231
    222 words by T. Prosel
SCHMITT, GEORG ALOYS, 1827-1902
    SEHNSUCHT NACH DEM RHEIN; "Dort, wo der alte Rhein mit seinen Wellen" g 31; "Dort, wo der   3232
    Rhein mit seinen grünen Wellen" g 99; "DORT WO DER RHEIN MIT SEINEN GRÜNEN WELLEN"
    g 353; DORT WO DER RHEIN g 326 words by J. G. Schmitt
SCHNEIDER, FRIEDRICH, 1786-1853
    "JETZT SCHWINGEN WIR DEN HUT" g 31 words by J. P. Hebel   3233
SCHNOOR, HEINRICH CHRISTIAN
    VOM HOH'N OLYMP; "Vom hohn Olymp herab ward und die Freude" g 99; GESELLSCHAFTSLIED   3234
    g 31
SCHOECK, OTHMAR, 1886-1957
    NACHKLANG; "Es klingt so prächtig" g 250 words by J. W. von Goethe   3235
    DIE VERKLÄRENDE, op.9, no.1; "In mir nur Tod, in dir mein Leben ruht" g 98 words by   3236
    Michelangelo
SCHÖNBERG, ARNOLD, 1874-1951
    ERHEBUNG, op.2, no.3; "Gieb mir deine Hand"; EXULTATION; "Let me have your hand" e, g   3237
    121 words by R. Dehmel
SCHOFIELD, RENA C.
    WAITING ON THE OTHER SHORE; "Side by side we walk together" e 205   3238
SCHOLZE, SPERONTES JOHANN SIG., 1705-1750
    DAS BÖSE MANNSVOLK; "Das Mannsvolk wird doch täglich schlimmer" g 250 words by J. C. Günther   3239
SCHONBERGER, JOHN, 1892-
    WHISPERING. See 3080
SCHOOLCRAFT, LUKE
    SHINE ON; "My ole massa promised me" e 109,110   3240
SCHREINER, HERMANN L.
    "WHEN UPON THE FIELD OF GLORY" g 161 words by J. H. Hewitt   3241
SCHREYER, HERMANN, 1851-1927
    FÜR EHRE, FREIHEIT, VATERLAND!; "Ihr Burschen, schenkt die Becher voll" g 31 words by K.   3242
    Schacko
SCHRÖDER, FRIEDRICH, 1910-
    [HOCHZEITSNACHT IM PARADIES, operetta; words by G. Schwenn] EIN   3243
    GLÜCK, DASS MAN SICH SO VERLIEBEN KANN!; "Oft schon setzte ich des Glückes Becher an
    den Mund" g 258
    [Ibid] ICH SPIEL MIT DIR; "Mir ersetzt ein kleiner Flirt die grosse Leidenschaft" g 256   3244
    [Ibid] "SO STELL ICH MIR DIE LIEBE VOR"; "Ein Zimmer, das verschwiegen ist" (verse) g 256   3245
SCHUBART, CHRISTIAN FRIEDRICH DANIEL, 1739-1791
    DIE HENNE; "Es war einmal 'ne Henne fein" g 250 words by M. Claudius   3246
SCHUBERT, FRANZ PETER, 1797-1828
    ABENDLIED, D. 499; "Der Mond ist aufgegangen"; EVENING SONG; "The little moon is sinking"   3247
    e, g 141 words by M. Claudius
    ADIEU! See 4002
    "ALL HAIL, THOU LOVELY LAUGHING MAY" e 199   3248

DIE ALLMACHT, D.852, op.79,no.2; "Gross ist Jehova, der Herr"; OMNIPOTENCE; "Great is Jehovah, the Lord!" e, g 112,276,348 words by J. L. Pyrker   3249

AN DEN FRÜHLING, D.587; "Willkommen, schöner Jüngling!"; TO THE SPRING; "Good morning, god of springtime" e, g 141 words by J. C. F. Schiller   3250

AN DEN MOND, D.259; The moon; "Soft the moon o'er field and wood" e 199 words by J. W. von Goethe   3251

AN DIE LAUTE, D.905, op.81, no.2; "Leiser, leiser, kleine Laute" g 226,229 words by F. Rochlitz   3252

AN DIE LEIER, D.734, op.56, no.2; "Ich will von Atreus Söhnen"; TO THE LYRE; "I'll sing the bold Atrides" e, g 364 words by Bruchman   3253

AN DIE MUSIK, D.547b, op.88, no.4; "Du holde Kunst, in wie viel grauen Stunden"; TO MUSIC; "Oh lovely muse, how oft in hours of sadness" g 97,99,226,385; "O music come and light my heart's dark places" e 199; "Thou holy art, how oft in hours of sadness" e, g 274; "Thou wondrous art, how oft I look to thee" e, g 220 words by F. Schober   3254

AN MEIN KLAVIER, D.342; "Sanftes Klavier, sanftes Klavier!"; TO MY CLAVIER; "From my clavier, sounds sweet and clear" e, g 141 words by C. F. D. Schubart   3255

AN SYLVIA, D.391, op.106, no.4; "WHO IS SYLVIA?"; "Was ist Sylvia" e, g 277; GESANG AN SYLVIA; "Was ist Sylvia" g 250 "WAS IST SYLVIA" e, g 36,136; "WHO IS SYLVIA?" e 75, 132,237,329 words by W. Shakespeare, Two Gentlemen of Verona   3256

AVE MARIA, D.839, op.52, no.6; "Ave Maria! gratia plena" lat 304; "Ave Maria! Jungfrau mild"; "Ave Maria, maiden mild" e, g, lat 122,123,329; e, lat 394; g 99; e 132,137,346; "Ave Maria! Mother dear" e 395; FATHER IN HEAVEN; "Father in heaven, almighty God" e 89 words by K. K. Davis   3257

DASS SIE HIER GEWESEN!, D.775, op.59, no.2; "Dass der Ostwind Düfte" g 250 words by F. Rückert   3258

[DEM UNENDLICHEN, D.291b] TO THE INFINITE GOD; "How uplifted the heart trusting Thee" e 160 words by M. Harrell   3259

DEUTSCHE MESSE. See 3271

"DU BIST DIE RUH'"; PEACE; "Thou art sweet Peace" e, g 275; "THOU ART REPOSE" e, g 36 words by F. Rückert   3260

DAS ECHO, D.868, op.posth.130; "Herzliebe, gute Mutter"; THE ECHO; "Please listen, dearest mother" e, g 141 words by I. F. Castelli   3261

DER EINSAME, D.800, op.41; "Wenn meine Grillen schwirren"; LONESOME; "When thoughts, like bees, come buzzing" e, g 330 words by C. Lappe   3262

DER ENTFERNTEN, D.350; "Wohl denk ich all enthalben"; TO THE DISTANT BELOVED; "How often sweet remembrance" e, g 141 words by J. G. von Salis   3263

ERLKÖNIG, D.328, op.1; "Wer reitet so spät durch Nacht und wind?" g 96; THE ERL KING; "Who rides there so late through night so wild?" e, g 272 words by J. W. von Goethe   3264

ERNTELIED, D.434; "Sicheln schallen, Ähren fallen unter Sichelschall" g 226 words by H. C. Hölty   3265

DES FISCHERS LIEBESGLÜCK, D.933; "Dort blinket durch Weiden"; FISHERMAN'S BLISS; "A light shining bright thro' the night" e, g 330 words by C. G. von Leitner   3266

DIE FORELLE, D.550, op.32; THE TROUT; "With clear and sparkling waters a brook was flowing by" e 395 words by C. F. D. Schubart   3267

FRÜHLINGSGLAUBE, D.686, op.20, no.2; "Die linden Lüfte sind erwacht" g 99; FAITH IN SPRING; "Awaken'd are the breezes light" e 137 words by L. Uhland   3268

FRÜHLINGSLIED, D.398; "Die Luft ist blau, das Tal ist grün" g 229; SPRING SONG; "The sky is blue and green the dale" e, g 199; "The sky is blue, the valley green" e, g 141   3269

GEHEIMES, D.719, op.14, no.2; "Über meines Liebchens Äuglen"; THE SECRET; "Eyes that shine from my beloved" e, g 220; "All who mark my lady's glances" e, g 277 words by J. W. von Goethe   3270

[GESÄNGE ZUR FEIER DES HEILIGEN OPFERS DER MESSE, D.872] SANCTUS; "Heilig, heilig, heilig, heilig ist der Herr!", no.5 g 326   3271

GOTT IM FRÜHLING, D.448; "In seinem schimmernden Gewand hast du den Frühling uns gesandt"; GOD IN SPRINGTIME; "Now thou hast sent the spring anew, arrayed in robes of lustrous hue" e, g 357 words by J. P. Uz   3272

GRETCHEN AM SPINNRADE, D.118, op.2; "Meine Ruh' ist hin, mein Herz ist schwer"; GRETCHEN AT THE SPINNING WHEEL; "My peace is gone, my heart is sore" e, g 276 words by J. W. von Goethe   3273

HEIDENRÖSLEIN, D.257, op.3, no.3; "Sah ein Knab' ein Röslein stehn" g 42,96,99; HEDGE ROSE; "Once a boy a wild-rose spied" e 132; HEDGE-ROSES; "Once a boy espied a rose" e, g 112; THE WILD ROSE; "Once a boy a wild rose spied" e, g 275; HEDGE-ROSES; "Once a boy a rose espied" e, g 136; THE LITTLE ROSEBUD; "Saw a boy a rose-bud new" e 395 words by J. W. von Goethe   3274

DIE HOFFNUNG, D.637, op.87, no.2; "Es reden und träumen die Menschen viel von bessern künftigen Tagen" g 229 words by J. C. F. von Schiller   3275

HYMN OF PRAISE; "O praise ye the Lord, praise ye Him!" e 160 words by M. Harrell   3276

IM ABENDROTH, D.799; "O wie schön ist deine Welt" g 226,229; IN THE RED OF EVENING;   3277
"O how fair this world of Thine" e, g 112; "O HOW LOVELY IS THY WORLD" e 160; IN
EVENING'S GLOW; "O, how fair thy beauteous world" e, g 209 words by C. Lappe

DIE JUNGE NONNE, D.828, op.43, no.1; "Wie braust durch die Wipfel der heulende Sturm!";   3278
THE NOVICE; "The storm through the forest is roaring amain" e, g 276 words by J. N. Craigher

LEBENSLIED, D.508; "Kommen und Scheiden, Suchen und Meiden"; SONG OF LIFE; "Coming and   3279
leaving, seeking and cleaving" e, g 141 words by F. von Matthisson

LIEBHABER IN ALLEN GESTALTEN, D.558; "Ich wollt', ich wär' ein Fisch"; LOVER IN ALL SHAPES;   3280
"I wish I were a trout" e, g 141; g 226; THE LOVER'S METAMORPHOSES; "I would I were a fish"
e, g 112 words by J. W. von Goethe

LIED DES GEFANGENEN JAGERS, D.843, op.52, no.7; "Mein Ross so müd' in dem Stalle sich steht";   3281
LAY OF THE IMPRISIONED HUNTSMAN; "My hawk is tired of perch and of hood" e, g 273 g words
by P. A. Storck, e words by W. Scott

DAS LIED IM GRÜNEN, D.917, op.posth.115, no.1; "Ins Grüne, ins Grüne, da lockt uns der Frühling";   3282
AWAY TO THE MEADOWS; "Away to the meadows, to dance with our shadows" e, g 330 words by
F. Reil

LITANEI, D.343; "Ruh'n in Frieden alle Seelen"; LITANY; "Rest in peace, all souls departed!" e, g   3283
274; LITANEI AUF DAS FEST ALLER SEELEN; "Ruhn in Frieden alle Seelen" g 99 words by J. G.
Jacobi

DAS MÄDCHEN AUS DER FREMDE, D.252; "In einem Tal bei armen Hirten erschien mit jedem jungen   3284
Jahr"; THE MAIDEN FROM AFAR; "Each spring, one early fragrant morning as larks rise singing in
the air" e, g 141 words by J. C. F. von Schiller

MEERES STILLE, D.216, op.3, no.2; "Tiefe Stille herrscht im Wasser"; CALM AT SEA; "Deepest   3285
stillness on the water" e, g 210 words by J. W. von Goethe

MINNELIED, D.429; "Holder klingt der Vogelsang" g 229; LOVE SONG; "Sweet sings the soaring   3286
lark" e, g 141 words by H. C. Hölty

NACHT UND TRÄUME, D.827, op.43, no.2; "Heil'ge Nacht, du sinkest nieder"; NIGHT AND   3287
DREAMS; "Holy night, thy spell is ended" e, g 112 words by M. von Collin

NACHTVIOLEN, D.752; "Nacht-violen, Nacht-violen"; EVENING VIOLETS; "Evening violets,   3288
evening violets" e, g 112; GILLYFLOWERS; "Gillyflowers, gillyflowers, bring to mind those
vanish'd hours" e 199 words by J. N. Mayrhofer

NATURGENUSS, D.188; "Im Abendschimmer wallt der Quell"; DELIGHT IN THE BEAUTIES OF   3289
NATURE; "The shimm'ring rays of sunset" e, g 141 words by F. von Matthisson

LA PASTORELLA, D.528; "La pastorella al prato contenta se neva" i 308 words by C. Goldoni   3290

PAX VOBISCUM, D.551; "Der Friede sei mit euch, das war dein Abschiedssegen" g 229 words   3291
by F. Schober

RASTLOSE LIEBE, D.138, op.5, no.1; "Dem Schnee, dem Regen, dem Wind entgegen"; RESTLESS   3292
LOVE; "Thro' snow and shower, 'gainst tempest power" e, g 359; "Through snow, through rain
drops" e, g 112 words by J. W. von Goethe

DER SCHIFFER, D.694; "Friedlich lieg' ich hingegossen"; ON THE LAKE; "See my bark, the calm   3293
lake riding" e, g 330 words by F. Schlegel

SCHLUMMERLIED, D.527, op.24, no.2; SCHLAFLIED; ABENDLIED; "Es mahnt der Wald, es ruft   3294
der Strom" g 229 words by J. N. Mayrhofer

DER SCHMETTERLING, D.633, op.57, no.1; "Wie soll ich nicht tanzen?"; THE BUTTERFLY; "And   3295
why should I not dance" e, g 112 words by F. Schlegel

[DIE SCHÖNE MÜLLERIN, song cycle, D.795, OP. 25; words by W. Müller]   3296
MORGENGRUSS, no.8; "Guten Morgen, schöne Müllerin!"; MORNING GREETING; "Good morning,
pretty millermaid" e, g 385

[Ibid] DES MÜLLERS BLUMEN, no.9; "Am Bach viel kleine Blumen stehn" g 229   3297

[Ibid] DER NEUGIERIGE, no.6; "Ich frage keine Blume"; THE QUESTION; "I'll never ask the   3298
flowers" e, g 330

[Ibid] UNGEDULD, no.7; "Ich schnitt' es gern"; IMPATIENCE; "I'd carve it deep" e, g 112,   3299
327

[Ibid] DAS WANDERN; "Das Wandern ist des Müllers Lust" g 42,96   3300

[Ibid] WOHIN, no.2; "Ich hört' ein Bächlein rauschen"; WHITHER; "Among the rocks and   3301
heather" e, g 277; "I heard a brooklet plashing" e, g 359; "I heard a streamlet" e, g 112;
"The streamlet swiftly rushing" e, g 330; WHITHER, LITTLE BROOK?; "I heard a brooklet
rushing along its rocky way" e 395

[SCHWANENGESANG, song cycle, D.957, NO.12] AM MEER; "Das Meer erglänzte   3302
weit hinaus im letzten Abendscheine" g 99; BY THE SEA; "Before us glanc'd the widespread
sea" e, g 240 words by H. Heine

[Ibid] AUFENTHALT, no.5; "Rauschender Strom, brausender Wald"; MY LAST ABODE; "Loud   3303
roaring pines, storm swollen flood" e, g 273 words by Rellstab

[Ibid] DER DOPPELGÄNGER, no.13; "Still ist die Nacht" e 98,250; THE WRAITH; "Still is the   3304
night" e, g 272 words by H. Heine

SCHUBERT, FRANZ PETER, 1797-1828 (Continued)

[Ibid] DIE STADT, no.11; "Am fernen Horizonte"; THE TOWN; "On yonder dim horizon" e, g   3305
407 words by H. Heine

[Ibid] STÄNDCHEN, no.4; "Leise flehen meine Lieder durch die Nacht zu dir"; SERENADE;   3306
"Softly goes my song's entreaty" g 328; e, g 122; "Softly through the night is calling, love,
my song to thee" e, g 387; "Thro' the leaves the night-winds, moving" e, g 237,329; SCHU-
BERT'S SERENADE e 28; "When the shades of night are falling, my love" e 128,132 words by
Rellstab

SELIGKEIT, D.433; "Freuden sonder Zahl blühn im Himmelssaal" g 226; BLISS; "Joy and peace and   3307
love reign in Heav'n above" e, g 330 words by L. H. C. Hölty

SEUFZER, D.198; "Die Nachtigall singt überall" g 229 words by L. H. C. Hölty   3308

STÄNDCHEN, D.889; "HARK, HARK! THE LARK" e 75,132,137,395 words by W. Shapespeare,   3309
Cymbeline

TÄGLICH ZU SINGEN, D.533; "Ich danke Gott und freue mich wie's Kind zur Weihnachtsgabe" g   3310
229 words by M. Claudius

TISCHLERLIED, D.274; "Mein Handwerk geht durch alle Welt"; SONG OF THE CABINET MAKER;   3311
"I am a cabinet maker bold" e, g 141

DER TOD UND DAS MÄDCHEN, D.531, op.7, no.3; "Vorüber, ach, vorüber, geh wilder Knochen-   3312
mann!" g 97,99; DEATH AND THE MAIDEN; "Go by me, Ah! go by me" e, g 274; "Pass
onward, Oh! pass onward" e, g 359 words by M. Claudius

TRAUER DER LIEBE, D.465; "Wo die Taub' in stillen Buchen ihren Tauber sich erwählt"; GRIEF OF   3313
OF LOVE; "Where the beech-tree gently sighing, hides the softly cooing dove" e, g 141 words
by J.G. Jacobi

DIE VÖGEL, D.691, op.posth.172, no.6; "Wie lieblich und fröhlich"; THE BIRDS; "While winging   3314
our flight" e, g 330 words by F. von Schlegel

DER WANDERER, D.493, op.4, no.1; DER UNGLÜCKLICHE; "Ich komme vom Gebirge her" g 97;   3315
THE WANDERER; "I come alone from yonder mountain" e, g 220; "I come here from my mountain lone" e, g 240,272,359 words by G. P. von Lübeck

WANDERERS NACHTLIED I, D.224, op.4, no.3; "Der du von dem Himmel bist" g 97 words by   3316
J. W. von Goethe

WANDERERS NACHTLIED II, D.768, op.96, no.3; "Über allen Gipfeln ist Ruh', in allen Wipfeln   3317
spürest du kaum einen Hauch" g 97 words by J. W. von Goethe

WIEGENLIED, D.498, op.98, no.2; "Schlafe, schlafe, holder süsser Knabe" g 96,226,229; CRADLE   3318
SONG; "Slumber, slumber, dearest sweetest treasure" e, g 275; "Slumber, slumber, sweet my
joy and treasure" e 199; SLUMBER SONG; "Slumber, slumber, tender little flower" e 28,366

[DIE WINTERREISE, song cycle, D.911, OP.89; words by W. Müller] GUTE   3319
NACHT, no.1; "Fremd bin ich eingezogen" g 98

[Ibid] DER LEIERMANN, no.24; "Drüben hinterm Dorfe steht ein Leiermann" g 98 words by W.   3320
Müller

[Ibid] DER LINDENBAUM, no.5; "Am Brunnen vor dem Tore" g 31,97,99,353; "Am Brunnen vor   3321
dem Thore"; THE LIME TREE; "A lime tree by the gateway" e, g 273; "AM BRUNNEN VOR DEM
TORE" g 326; THE LINDEN TREE; "Beside the old stone fountain" e 28,366

[Ibid] DER STÜRMISCHE MORGEN, no.18; "Wie hat der Sturm zerrisen des Himmels graues   3322
Kleid"; THE STORMY MORNING; "How hath the tempest riven the gray robe of the sky" e 45

[DER 23. PSALM, D.706, OP. POSTH.132] "THE LORD IS MY SHEPHERD" e 90   3323
words from Psalm XXIII

SCHÜTKY, FRANZ JOSEPH, 1817-1893
"EMITTE SPIRITUM TUUM" lat 382   3324

SCHÜTZ, A.
CZERWONE MAKI NA MONTE CASSINO; "Czy widzisz te gruzy na szczycie?"; RED POPPIES OF   3325
MONTE CASSINO; "Attention! Your goal's on that mountain" e, p 159 words by Konarski

SCHÜTZ, HEINRICH, 1585-1672
"BRINGT HER DEM HERREN" g 308 words from Psalm XIX:1-2   3326

DANKLIED AN HERZOG WILHELM VON WEIMAR; "Fürstliche Gnade zu Wasser und Lande" g 250   3327
words by C. T. Dufft

"FROM EARTHLY TASKS LIFT UP THINE EYES" e 296   3328
"HOW VAIN THE CRUEL HEROD'S FEAR" e 296   3329
IMMORTAL BABE; "Immortal Babe Who this dear day" e 296 words by J. Hall   3330

SCHULER, GEORGE S.
IN HIS STEPS; "This be our task on life's long rugged way" e 347 words by W. M. Runyan   3331

SCHULTES, W., 1815-1879
COR JESU; "Cor Jesu salus in te sperantium" lat 382   3332

SCHULTZE, NORBERT
LILI MARLEEN; "Vor der Kaserne vor dem grossen Tor" g 43; LILI MARLENE; "Underneath the   3333
lantern by the barrack gate" e 35 words by H. Leip

117

SCHULZ, JOHANN ABRAHAM PETER, 1747-1800

ABENDLIED; "Der Mond ist aufgegangen" g 31,49,99,229,353; DER MOND IST AUFGEGANGEN   3334
g 309,326   words by M. Claudius

AM SYLVESTERABEND; NEUJAHRSLIED; "Des Jahres letzte Stunde ertönt mit ernstem Schlag"   3335
g 99,229; DES JAHRES LETZTE STUNDE g 326   words by J. H. Voss

AN DIE NATUR; "Süsse heilige Natur, lass mich gehn auf deiner Spur" g 96   words by F. L. zu   3336
Stolberg

FREUDE, SCHÖNER GÖTTERFUNKEN; "Freude, schöner Götterfunken, Tochter aus Elysium" g 326,   3337
353; AN DIE FREUDE g 99   words by J. C. F. von Schiller

"HER KOMMER DINE ARME SMAA"; "THY LITTLE ONES, DEAR LORD, ARE WE" da, e 206   words   3338
by H. Brorson

IHR KINDERLEIN KOMMET; "Ihr Kinderlein, kommet, o kommet doch all!" g 326,412; O   3339
COME, LITTLE CHILDREN; "O come, little children, O come, one and all!" e, g 79,251,
388; e 33,165,296; "O come, little children, from cot and from hall" e, g 337   words by C.
von Schmid

IM GRÜNEN; "Willkommen im Grünen!" g 308   words by J. H. Voss   3340

LIEBESZAUBER; "Mädel, schau mir ins Gesicht!" g 99   words by G. A. Bürger   3341

EIN LIED IN DIE HAUSHALTUNG ZU SINGEN, WENN EIN WECHSELZAHN SOLL AUSGEZOGEN   3342
WERDEN; "Wir ziehn nun unsern Zahn heraus" g 250   words by M. Claudius

MAILIED; "Sehn den Himmel, wie heiter!" g 229   words by J. H. Voss   3343

DER SCHMETTERLING; "In einem Tal, bei einem Bach, da flog ein bunter Schmetterling" g 226   3344
words by Andre

SELIGKEIT DER LIEBE; "O Selig, wer liebt!" g 308   words by F. Brun   3345

"WE HAIL THEE WITH REJOICING" e 296   words by C. F. Baum   3346

"WENN KÜHL DER MORGEN ATMET" g 49   words by J. H. Voss   3347

WIEGENLIED; "Schlaf, Kindlein, schlafe sanft und süss in diesem Maien paradies!" g 229;   3348
WIEGENLIED IM MAI g 226   words by F. Brun

"WIR BRINGEN MIT GESANG" g 49; ERNTELIED; "Wir bringen mit Gesang und Tanz dir diesen   3349
blanken Ährenkranz" g 99   words by J. H. Voss

SCHULZ, PAUL

"ES STEHT EINE MÜHLE IM SCHWARZWÄLDER TAL" g 326,353   3350

SCHUMANN, CLARA JOSEPHINE (WIECK), 1819-1896

"WENN ICH EIN VÖGLEIN WÄR" 3 pt round g 40   3351

SCHUMANN, ROBERT ALEXANDER, 1810-1856

DER ABENDSTERN, op. 79, no. 1; "Du lieblicher Stern du leuchtest so fern" g 229; THE EVENING   3352
STAR; "You sweet little star, how tiny you are" e, g 141

AN DEN MOND, op. 95, no. 2; "Schlafloser Sonne melanchol'scher Stern!" g 250   words by F.   3353
Mendelssohn-Bartholdy after G. G. Byron

AN DEN SONNENSCHEIN, op. 36, no. 4; "O Sonnenschein! O Sonnenschein! Wie scheinst du mir in   3354
Herz hinein" g 99; TO THE SUNSHINE; "O sunshine, o sunshine thou shinest in this heart of mine"
e, g 209   words by R. Reinick

AUF DAS TRINKGLAS EINES VERSTORBENEN FREUNDES, op. 35, no. 6; "Du herrlich Glas, nun steht   3355
du leer"; THE LAST TOAST; "Now drear and empty dost thou stand" e, g 273 words by J. Kerner

AUFTRÄGE, op. 77, no. 5; "Nicht so schnelle, nicht so schnelle!"; MESSAGES; "Not so quickly, not   3356
so quickly" e, g 112   words by C. l'Égru

DIE BEIDEN GRENADIERE, op. 49, no. 1; "Nach Frankreich zogen zwei Grenadier'"; THE TWO   3357
GRENADIERS; "For France were making two grenadiers" e, g 122; "To France there journey'd
two grenadiers" e, g 273; "To France were returning two grenadiers"; "Je les aivus ces deux
grenadiers" e, f, g 240; e 137; "Toward France there travelled two grenadiers" e, g 237; g
328   words by H. Heine

BELSATZAR, op. 59; "Die Mitternach zog näher schon"; BELSHAZZAR; "The midnight now is drawing   3358
on" e, g 272   words by H. Heine

DEIN ANGESICHT, op. 127, no. 2; "Dein Angesicht, so lieb und schön"; THE LOVELY FACE; "In   3359
dreams I saw thy face so fair" e, g 272   words by H. Heine

[DICHTERLIEBE, song cycle, op. 48; words by H. Heine] ICH GROLLE NICHT,   3360
no. 7; "Ich grolle nicht und wenn das Herz"; I'LL NOT COMPLAIN; "I'll not complain, tho'
break my heart" e, g 359; WHY BLAME THEE NOW?; "Why blame thee now? Now that my
heart must break?" e, g 272   words by H. Heine

[Ibid] "IM WUNDERSCHÖNEN MONAT MAI." no. 1; IN WONDROUS LOVELY MAY; "In May, in   3361
wondrous lovely May" e, g 36; "'TWAS IN THE LOVELY MONTH OF MAY" e, g 137

[Ibid] "WENN ICH IN DEINE AUGEN SEH'," no. 4; "WHEN GAZING IN THINE EYES SO DEAR"   3362
e, g 387

ER IST'S, op. 79, no. 23; "Frühling lässt sein blaues Band"; 'TIS SPRING; "Springtime flaunts his   3363
banner blue" e, g 359   words by E. Mörike

ERSTES GRÜN, op. 35, no. 4; "Du junges Grün, du frisches Gras!" g 226   words by J. Kerner   3364

SCHUMANN, ROBERT ALEXANDER, 1810-1856 (Continued)

[FRAUENLIEBE UND LEBEN, song cycle, OP.42; words by A. von Chamisso] 3365
ER, DER HERRLICHSTE VON ALLEN; "Er, der Herrlichste von Allen wie so milde wie so gut!"; HE
IS NOBLE, HE IS PATIENT; "He is noble, he is patient, he is tender, true, and kind" e, g 276

FRÜHLINGSGRUSS, op.79, no.4; "So sei gegrüsst viel tausendmal" g 96; GREETING OF SPRING; 3366
"Be greeted in a thousand ways" e, g 141 words by H. von Fallersleben

GEISTERNÄHE, op.77, no.3; "Was weht um meine Schläfe wie laue Frühlingsluft"; THE CALL OF 3367
THE SPIRIT; "What flows around my brow like the soothing spring-like air" e, g 220 words by
Halm

HINAUS IN'S FREIE!, op.79, no.11; "Wie blüht es im Tale, wie grün's auf den Höhn!; OUT INTO 3368
THE OPEN!; "Wild flow'rs in the dell, soft green on the hill!" e, g 141 words by H. von
Fallersleben

JASMINENSTRAUCH, op.27, no.4; "Grün ist der Jasminenstrauch abends eingeschlafen" g 226 words 3369
by F. Rückert

DIE KARTENLEGERIN, op.31, no.2; "Schlief die Mutter endlich ein über ihrer Hauspostille?"; THE 3370
FORTUNE TELLER; "Mother, fin'ly fell asleep as she read her family Bible" e, g 220 words by
A. von Chamisso

KINDERWACHT, op.79, no.21; "Wenn fromme Kindlein schlafen geh'n"; THE CHILDREN'S WATCH; 3371
"When little children close their eyes" e, g 141; g 229

LIED EINES SCHMIEDES, op.90, no.1; "Fein Rösslein, ich beschlage dich" g 229 words by N. Lenau 3372

[LIEDERKREIS, song cycle, OP.39] FRÜHLINGSNACHT, no.12; "Über'm Garten durch die 3373
Lüfte"; SPRING NIGHT; "O'er the garden through the breezes" e, g 112 words by J. von Eichendorff

[Ibid] MIT MYRTHEN UND ROSEN, no.9; "Mit Myrthen und Rosen, lieblich und hold"; WITH 3374
MYRTLE AND ROSES; "With myrtle and roses, lovely and pure" e, g 112 words by H. Heine

[Ibid] MONDNACHT, no.5; "Es war als hätt' der Himmel die Erde still geküsst" g 97,226; BY 3375
MOONLIGHT; "It seemed as though the heaven so softly kissed the earth" e, g 112; MOONLIGHT;
"It seem'd as tho' the heavens had kissed the earth to rest" e, g 359; "It seemed that heaven had
mingled with earth upon a kiss" e, g 277 words by J. von Eichendorff

DIE LÖWENBRAUT, op.31, no.1; "Mit der Myrthe geschmückt" g 250 words by A. von Chamisso 3376

MARIENWÜRMCHEN, op.79, no.13; "Marienwürmchen, setze dich auf meine hand" g 96,229 3377

MEIN SCHÖNER STERN, op.101, no.4; "Mein Schöner Stern! ich bitte dich"; MY LOVELY STAR!; 3378
"My lovely star! I beg of thee" e, g 112 words by F. Rückert

[MYRTHEN, song cycle, OP.25] DU BIST WIE EINE BLUME, no.24; "Du bist wie eine 3379
Blume so hold und schön und rein"; I LIKEN THEE TO A FLOWER; "I liken thee to a flower endow'd
with grace divine" e, g 329; A FLOWER TO ME THOU SEEMEST; "A blossom you are to me dear,
so fragrant and so sweet" e, g 132; THOU ART SO LIKE A FLOWER; "Thou art so like a flower, so
gentle, pure and fair" e, g 122,176; THOU'RT LIKE A LOVELY FLOWER; "Thou'rt like a lovely
flower, so fair, so pure, so dear" e, g 277; THOU'RT LOVELY AS A FLOWER; "Thou'rt lovely
as a flower, so fair and pure thou art" e, g 136,241; YOU ARE JUST LIKE A FLOWER; "You are
just like a flower, so sweet, so pure, so fair" e, g 112; YOU ARE SO LIKE A FLOWER; "You are
so like a flower so fair and pure and kind" e, g 36 words by H. Heine

[Ibid] FREISINN, no.2; "Lasst mich nur auf meinem Sattel gelten!" g 226 words by J. W. von 3380
Goethe

[Ibid] JEMAND, no.4; "Mein Herz ist betrübt"; SOMEBODY; "My heart is sair" e, g 275 g 3381
words by W. Gerhard, e words by R. Burns

[Ibid] LIED DER BRAUT, no.11; "Mutter, Mutter, glaube nicht"; THE BRIDES SONG; "Mother, 3382
Mother, ne'er believe" e, g 275 words by F. Rückert

[Ibid] LIED DER SULEIKA, no.9; "Wie mit innigstem Behagen"; SULEIKA'S SONG; "What a 3383
happiness comes o'er me" e, g 276 words by J. W. von Goethe

[Ibid] DIE LOTOSBLUME, no.7; "Die Lotosblume ängstigt sich vor der Sonne Pracht"; THE LOTUS 3384
FLOWER; "The lotus flow'r doth languish under the sun's fierce light" e, g 136; "The lotus flower
bending, turns from the sun's bright light" e, g 209; "The lotus flower is anxious, fearing the sun
so bright" e, g 112; "The lotus flow'r is anxious, when the hot sun shines bright" e 348; "The
lotus flower trembles, fearing the sun so bright" e, g 36 words by H. Heine

[Ibid] MEIN HERZ IST SCHWER, no.15; "Mein Herz ist schwer, auf von der Wand die Laute"; 3385
MY SOUL IS DARK; "My soul is dark Oh quickly, quickly string the harp" e, g 274 g words by
J. Korner, e words by G. G. Byron

[Ibid] DER NUSSBAUM, no.3; "Es grünet ein Nussbaum vor dem Haus" g 97; THE CHESTNUT; 3386
"A flowering chestnut green and fair" e, g 276; THE WALNUT TREE; "A walnut tree stands
before a cot" e, g 220; "Outside a small house there stands a tree" e, g 112 words by J. Mosen

[Ibid] WIDMUNG, no.1; "Du meine Seele, du mein Herz"; DEDICATION; "Thou art my life, 3387
my soul and heart" e, g 359; "You gentle spirit, heart so true" e, g 112 words by F. Rückert

O IHR HERREN, op.37, no.3; "O ihr Herren, o ihr werten, grossen reichen Herren all'"; TELL ME; 3388
"Tell me, while I crave your pardons, noble gents, that own this dale!" e, g 330; WORTHY FOLK;
"Worthy folk within your towers, great and rich and strong and hale!" e, g 141 words by F. Rückert

SCHUMANN, ROBERT ALEXANDER, 1810-1856 (Continued)

"O WIE LIEBLICH IST DAS MÄDCHEN," op. 138, no. 3; "O HOW LOVELY IS THE MAIDEN" e, g 36   3389
    words by E. Geibel

RÖSELEIN, RÖSELEIN!, op. 89, no. 6; "Röselein, Röselein! müssen denn Dornen sein?"; ROSEBUD RED,   3390
    ROSEBUD RED!; "Rosebud red, rosebud red must thou to thorns be wed?" e, g 330; WILDWOOD
    ROSE; "Wildwood rose, growing free" e, g 407

SCHMETTERLING, op. 79, no. 2; "O Schmetterling, sprich, was fliehest du mich?"; THE BUTTERFLY;   3391
    "Dear butterfly, stay, don't flutter away" e, g 141   words by H. von Fallersleben

SCHNEEGLÖCKCHEN, op. 79, no. 26; "Der Schnee, der gestern noch in Flöcken"; SNOWBELLS; "The   3392
    snow that yesterday so softly" e, g 112; "The snow that yesterday was falling" e, g 209   words by
    F. Rückert

DIE SOLDATENBRAUT, op. 64, no. 1; "Ach, wenn's nur der König auch wüsst" g 99   words by E.   3393
    Mörike

"VIEL GLÜCK ZUR REISE SCHWALBEN!" op. 104, no. 2   g 308   words by E. Kulmann   3394

VOLKSLIEDCHEN, op. 51, no. 2; "Wenn ich früh in den Garten geh' in meinem grünen Hut" g 226,   3395
    229; AS I WALK IN THE GARDEN DEW; "As I walk in the garden dew I wear my green hat gay"
    e, g 36; FOLK SONG; "When I go at the break of day to see my garden grow" e, g 385   words by
    F. Rückert

VOM SCHLARAFFENLAND, op. 79, no. 5; "Kommt, wir wollen uns begeben jetzo ins Schlaraffenland!"   3396
    g 226   words by H. von Fallersleben

DIE WAISE, op. 79, no. 15; "Der Frühling kehret wieder"; THE ORPHAN; "Again the spring brings   3397
    gladness" e, g 141   words by H. von Fallersleben

WANDERLIED, op. 35, no. 3; "Wohlauf! noch getrunken den funkelnden Wein!" g 96   words by J.   3398
    Kerner

WEIHNACHTSLIED, op. 79, no. 16; "Als das Christkind ward zur Welt gebracht"; CHRISTMAS   3399
    SONG; "When the Christ Child came to us on earth" e, g 141   words by H. C. Andersen

SCHUSTER, IRA, 1889-1946

TEN LITTLE FINGERS AND TEN LITTLE TOES; DOWN IN TENNESSEE; "I've got ten little fingers"   3400
    e 128   words by H. Pease and J. White, joint composer E. G. Nelson

SCHWARTZ, JEAN, 1878-

BEDELIA; "Bedelia, I want to steal ye" e 233   words by W. Jerome   3401

THE HAT MY FATHER WORE UPON ST. PATRICK'S DAY; "Where did you get that hat, folks ask   3402
    me ev'ry day"; "It's the hat my dear old father wore upon Saint Patrick's day" (ref) e 166   words
    by W. Jerome

RIP VAN WINKLE WAS A LUCKY MAN; "In the Catskill mountains" e 204   words by W. Jerome   3403

SCHWARTZ, L.

BIRDS FLY DELIGHTFULLY; "Birds fly delightfully, waves roll up frightfully" e, r 287, 288   words   3404
    by S. Bolotin

SCOTT, ALICIA ANN (SPOTTISWOODE), LADY JOHN MONTAGUE-DOUGLAS, 1810-1900   3405

ANNIE LAURIE; "Maxwellton braes are bonnie, where early fa's the dew" e 17, 28, 35, 36, 102, 105,
    132, 163, 233, 235, 236, 240, 279, 349, 366, 402 words by W. Douglas

DURISDEER; "We'll meet nae mair at sunset" e 103, 104   3406

THINK ON ME; "When I no more behold thee, think on me" e 100, 102, 103, 105   3407

SCOTT, CHARLES P.

"GOD IS A SPIRIT" e 398   words from John IV:23, 24   3408

SCOTT, CYRIL MEIR, b 1879

VILLANELLE, op. 33, no. 3; "Come hither, child, and rest" e 344   words by E. Dawson   3409

SCOTT, JOHN PRINDLE, 1877-1932

COME, YE BLESSED; "Then, then shall the King say unto them upon His right hand" e 200   words   3410
    from Matthew XXV:34-36

SCOTT, THOMAS JEFFERSON, 1912-

JOHNNY APPLESEED; "Johnny Appleseed? Sure I knew 'im" e 331   words by J. Scott   3411

PECOS BILL; "Pecos Bill, he had no garments" e 331   words by J. Scott   3412

SCULL, HAROLD

JESUS BORN TO BE A KING; "For Mary's little baby Son" e 378   words by F. Scull   3413

SEAVER, FRED

SOLOMON LEVI; "My name is Solomon Levi, at my store on Chatham Street" e 402; "My name is   3414
    Solomon Levi, at my store on Salem street" e 225; "My name is Solomon Levi and my store's on
    Salem Street" e 366

SECCHI, ANTONIO, 1761-1833

LUNGI DAL CARO BENE; "Lungi dal caro bene vivere non poss' io!"; WHEN FAR FROM MY DEAR   3415
    TREASURE; "When far from my dear treasure life seems a heavy burden" e, i 138

SEDGWICK, A.

BUCKLEYS SLEIGHING SONG; "Oh jump into the sleigh boys"; "While jingle, jingle, jingle, jing,   3416
    The bells so merry ring" (ref) e 189

LITTLE KATY, OR HOT CORN; "Oh hot corn nice hot corn!" e 189   words by J. Simmonds   3417

SEEGER, PETER, 1919-
 "I'M GONNA SING ME A LOVE SONG" e 336 3418
 SIXTY-SIX HIGHWAY BLUES. See 1430
SEEON, KLOSTER
 "ES LIEGT EIN SCHLOSS IN ÖSTERREICH" g 49 3419
SEIFFERT, BERNHARD
 HEIM; "Bin durch die Alpen gezogen" g 31 words by R. Baumbach 3420
SEISMIT-DODA, A.
 QUERIDA; "Yo te vi que bailabas un dia"; MY DARLING; "In the maze of a dance I found you" 3421
  e, s 245
SELBY, B. LUARD
 "A WIDOW BIRD SAT MOURNING" e 344 words by P. B. Shelley 3422
SELLE, THOMAS, 1599-1663
 "ADE, DU EDLES MÜNDLEIN ROT" g 250 3423
SELNER, JOHN C.
 WEDDING HYMN TO OUR LADY; "Dear Mary here before thine altar" e 382 words by D. Dobbyn 3424
SERGEEV, A.
 THE RED ARMY SOLDIER'S SON; "Mother dear, quickly look out of the window" e, r 162 words by 3425
  D. Samarsky
SERMISY, CLAUDIN DE, ca1490-1562
 CHANSON AU LUTH; "Tant que vivray en aage florissant" f 278 words by C. Marot 3426
SERRADELL, NARCISO
 LA GOLONDRINA; "Adónde irá veloz y fatigada" s 284; THE SWALLOW; "O whither now, so 3427
  tired yet swiftly flying" e, s 322; "Whence dost thou fly thou tireless little swallow?" e, s 132;
  "Where will you go, O swift and weary swallow" e 279; "Where wilt thou go, my agile little
  swallow?" e, s 142; O SWALLOW SWIFT; "Oh, swallow swift, on eager pinion flying" e 350
  words by B. N. de Zamacois; "Vuela fugaz la bella golondrina sin parar"; THE SWALLOW;
  "High in the sky at break of dawn I see the swallow fly" e, s 236 words by P. Berrios
Serrano, José, 1873-1941. See SERRANO SIMEÓN, JOSÉ, 1873-1941
SERRANO SIMEÓN, JOSÉ, 1873-1941
 [LA CANCIÓN DEL OLVIDO, zarzuela; words by A. Romero and G. F. Shaw] 3428
  MARINELA; "Marinela, Marinela con su triste"; THE SONG OF FORGETTING; "Marinela sings her
  song of love and sorrow" e, s 245; "Marinela, what a pity" e,s 142
 [EL CARRO DEL SOL, zarzuela] EL CARRO DEL SOL; "Pensan do en el que la quiere"; 3429
  VENETIAN LOVE SONG; "She waits for her lover, sighing" e, s 245 joint composer A. Vives
 [LA DOLOROSA, zarzuela; words by J. J. Lorente] "LA ROCA FRÍA DEL 3430
  CALVARIO"; RAFAEL'S ARIA; "A dark and misty cloud is hiding" e, s 245
 [EL TRUST DE LOS TENORIOS, zarzuela] "TE QUIERO MORENA"; "I LOVE YOU, 3431
  ADORE YOU" e, s 245
SERVAAS DE KONINK, fl 1700
 DRINKLIED; "In het glaasjen of myn Tryntjen, Ik vind weinig onderscheit" d 278 3432
SESSIONS, ROGER, 1896-
 ON THE BEACH AT FONTANA; "Wind whines and whines the shingle" e 85 words by J. Joyce 3433
SEYDLER, L. C.
 HOCH VOM DACHSTEIN; "Hoch vom Dachstein an, wo der Aar noch haust" g 326 words by J. 3434
  Dirnböck
SHACKLEY, F. N.
 THE RESURRECTION AND THE LIFE; "I knelt, I knelt, beside a grassy mound" e 8 words by J. 3435
  Yeames
SHAPORIN, ĪŪRIĬ ALEKSANDROVICH, 1889-
 INVOCATION; "If it be true that in the night" e, r 342 words by A. Pushkin 3436
SHARP, EARL CRANSTON
 JAPANESE DEATH SONG; "Seaweed and sinking sands" e 241 words by H. K. S. 3437
SHATTUCK, C. F.
 CHIMING BELLS OF LONG AGO; "Like a dream ye come to cheer me" e 129,130 3438
SHAW, GEOFFREY TURTON, 1879-1943
 CHRIST IS BORN!; "Christ is born! Christ is born!" e 334 3439
 THE SNOW LIES THICK; "The snow lies thick upon the earth tonight" e 334 words by S. Image 3440
SHAW, MARTIN
 "AS UP THE WOOD I TOOK MY WAY" e 334 words by S. Image 3441
 THE CORPUS CHRISTI CAROL; "Over yonder's a park which is newly begun" e 334 3442
 DOMINUM LAUDES; "Christ, hath Christ's Mother borne" e, lat in pt 334 words by L. Johnson 3443
 THE FALCON CAROL; "Lully, lulley, lully, lulley"; "He bare him up, he bare him down" (verse) 3444
  e 334
 IN EXCELSIS GLORIA; "Christo paremus canticam"; "When Christ was born of Mary free" (verse) e, 3445
  lat in pt 334

SHAW, MARTIN (Continued)
    "THREE KINGS IN GREAT GLORY" e 334   words by S. Image   3446
SHEBALIN, VISSARION IÂKOVLEVICH, 1902-
    'TIS TIME; "'Tis time, my friend, 'tis time" e, r 342   words by A. Pushkin   3447
SHELEM, MATATYAHU
    ROEH VEROAH; "Eysham harheyk beyn heharim"; SHEPHERD AND SHEPHERDESS; "Up in the   3448
        mountains with their sheep" e, h (tr) 36
SHELLEY, HARRY ROWE
    PSALM XCI; "He that dwelleth in the secret place" e 200   words from Bible   3449
SHERFEDINOV, Y.
    THE KOLHOZ; "Wheat is ripe in the fields" e, r 162   words by T. Hussein   3450
SHERMAN, AL, 1897-
    NO! NO! A THOUSAND TIMES NO!; "She was a child of the valley"; "No! No! a thousand times   3451
        no!"(ref) e 131 (ref only) e 128   joint composers A. Lewis and A. Silver
SHERWIN, WILLIAM FISKE, 1826-1888
    "DAY IS DYING IN THE WEST" e 28,35,366   words by M. A. Lathbury   3452
SHIELD, WILLIAM, 1748-1829
    BEFORE YOU MAKE; "Before you make a promise" 4 pt round e 235   3453
    THE FRIAR OF ORDERS GRAY; "I am a Friar of Orders gray" e 240   3454
    THE PLOUGH BOY; "A flaxenheaded cowboy, as simple as may be" e 48   3455
SHIELDS, REN, 1868-1913
    WALTZ ME AROUND AGAIN WILLIE; "Willie Fitzgibbons who used to sell ribbons" e 246   words by   3456
        W. D. Cobb
SHILKRET, NATHANIEL, 1895-
    JEANNINE. See 1251
SHISHOV, I.
    THE SONGSTER; "Oh did you hear a songster's voice at night" e, r 342   words by A. Pushkin   3457
SHOSTAKOVICH, DMITRIĬ DMITRIEVICH, 1906-
    BITTERLY SOBBING; "Bitterly sobbing and grieving a maiden berated her lover" e, r 342   words by   3458
        A. Pushkin
    "COMING THROUGH THE RYE" e 242   words by R. Burns   3459
    MACPHERSON'S FAREWELL; "Sae rantingly, sae wantonly, sae dauntingly gaed he" e, r 342   words   3460
        by R. Burns
    "OH, WERT THOU IN THE CAULD BLAST" e, r 342   words by R. Burns   3461
    RENAISSANCE; "A brush in hand, in dissipation, a vandal smears a work of art" e, r 342   words by   3462
        A. Pushkin
SHTREICHER, LYUBOV
    ALWAYS WORKING; "In a fact'ry I was brought up, always working" e, r 162   words by D. Hofshtein   3463
SIBELIUS, JEAN, 1865-1958
    [FINLANDIA, OP.26] FINLANDIA-HYMNI; "Oi, Herra, annoit uuden päivän koittaa"; FIN-   3464
        LANDIA HYMN; "O, gracious Lord, by whom the morning dawneth" e, fi 124   words by W. Sola;
        FINLANDIA; "The stalwart forests clothe thy rugged mountains" e 343
    NORDEN, op.90, no.1; "Löfven de falla"; FROM THE NORTH; "Bare are the branches" e, fi 121   3465
        words by J. L. Runeberg
SIDENBENDER, FLORENCE
    "I NEEDED GOD" e 347   words by L. R. Beck   3466
SIEBERT, TALLIFERO LAWRENCE, 1877-1917
    CASEY JONES. See 2652
SIECZYNSKI, RUDOLF
    WIEN, DU STADT MEINER TRÄUME, op.1; WIEN, WIEN, NUR DU ALLEIN; "Mein Herz und mein   3467
        Sinn schwärmt stets nur für Wien, " "Dann hört' ich aus weiter Ferne ein Lied" (ref) g 396
SIEGERT, GOTTLOB
    GEBET AN DEN HEILIGEN CHRIST; "Du lieber, heilger, frommer Christ" g 99; PRAYER TO THE   3468
        CHILD JESUS; "O holy Infant, small and dear" e, g 337   words by E. M. Arndt
SIEGMEISTER, ELIE, 1909-
    JOHNNY APPLESEED; "Johnny Appleseed! Johnny Appleseed! Of Jonathan Chapman two things are   3469
        known" e 109,110   words by R. Benét
    A NEW WIND A-BLOWIN'; "There's a brand new wind a-blowin'" e 110   words by L. Hughes   3470
SIEVERT, ALBERT
    GOLDENE BURSCHENZEIT; "Gedenke, o wie weit, wie weit" g 31   words by H. W. Riehl   3471
SILCHER, FRIEDRICH, 1789-1860
    ABSCHIED; "Brüder, sammelt euch in Reihen umden schäumenden Pokal" g 31   3472
    "ACH DU KLARBLAUER HIMMEL" g 326   words by R. Reinick   3473
    ADE, TÜBINGEN; "O Tübingen, du teure Stadt" g 31   words by J. Kerner   3474
    ÄNNCHEN VON THARAU, op.8, no.1; "Ännchen von Tharau ist, die mir gefällt" g 99,309,326;   3475
        "Ännchen von Tharau ist's, die mir gefällt" g 49,353   words by H. Albert

SILCHER, FRIEDRICH, 1789-1860 (Continued)

ALLE JAHRE WIEDER; "Alle Jahre wieder kommt das Christuskind" g 99,326,412; AS EACH 3476
HAPPY CHRISTMAS; "As each happy Christmas dawns on earth again" e, g 388 words by
W. Hey

AM NECKAR, AM NECKAR; "Am Nekker, am Nekker, do isch e Jedes gern" g 326 words by F. 3477
Ritter

DRAUSS IST ALLES SO PRÄCHTIG; "Drauss ist alles so prächtig und es ist mer so wohl" g 326 words 3478
by F. Richter

"E BISSELE LIEB UND E BISSELE TREU" g 326 3479

"HAB OFT IM KREISE DER LIEBEN" g 326,353 words by A. von Chamisso 3480

"ICH HABE DEN FRÜHLING GESEHEN" g 326 3481

IN DER FERNE; "Nun leb wohl, du kleine Gasse" g 31,99; "NUN LEB WOHL, DU KLEINE GASSE" 3482
g 326,327,353 words by J. von Eichendorff

JETZT GANG I ANS BRÜNNELE. See 5421

JUCHHEI, DICH MUSS ICH HABEN; "Ich ging einmal spazieren, spazieren mit einem schönen 3483
Mädchen" g 326

DIE LORELEI; "Ich weiss nicht, was soll es bedeuten" g 42,99,328,353; "ICH WEISS NICHT, WAS 3484
SOLL ES BEDEUTEN" g 326; THE LORELEI; "I know not what spell is enchanting" e 132; THE
LORELEY; "I know not what it presages" e 28,279,366 words by H. Heine

"MAIDLE LASS D'R WAS BERZÄHLE" g 326 3485

MEI MAIDLE; "Mei Maidle hot e G'sichtle als wie ne Roseblatt" g 326 words by F. von Kobell 3486

"MORGEN MUSS ICH FORT VON HIER"; Nun so reis' ich (tune) g 42,326,353; LEBEWOHL g 31,99 3487

"O WIE HERBE IST DAS SCHEIDEN" g 326 3488

"DIE SCHWÄLBLE ZIEHET FORT" g 326 3489

DER SCHWEIZER; "Zu Strassburg auf der Schanz" g 31,99 words by C. Brentano 3490

SO NIMM DENN MEINE HÄNDE; "So nimm denn meine Hände und führe mich" g 326 words by J. 3491
von Hausmann

DER SOLDAT; "Es geht bei gedämpfter Trommel Klang" g 31,99 words by A. von Chamisso 3492

"VÖGLEIN IM HOHEN BAUM" g 353 words by W. Hey 3493

WIE LIEBLICH SCHALLT; "Wie lieblich schallt durch Busch und Wald des Waldhorns süsser Klang" 3494
g 326

SILVER, ABNER, 1899-

NO! NO! A THOUSAND TIMES NO! See 3451

SILVERMAN, AL

LA MANCORNADORA; "Ando ausente del bien que adoré"; BLANCHE OF THE RANCHO; "Blanche 3495
of the Rancho, though yu're so sublime" e, s 248

SILVERMAN, JERRY

DEEP SEA BLUES; "Oh, all day long I'm lookin' for trees" (ref); "Soldiers below layin' cold and 3496
dead" (verse) e 336

ROTATION BLUES; "I'm a lonely soldier sitting here in Korea" e 336 3497

SILICOSIS BLUES; "I said, Silicosis, you made a mighty bad break of me" e 336 3498

SIMA, W. R.

NAVY VICTORY MARCH; "Rah! Fight! Navy blue and gold" e 129,130 words by W. R. Sima, 3499
Collins, and Martin

SIMON, CATEL CHARLES, 1773-1830

[LES BAYADÈRES, opera; words by J. E. de Jouy] "LE SORT PEUT CHANGER SES 3500
DÉCRETS"; "CANGIAR PUÒ DEL FATO IL MISTER" f, i 411

SIMONFFY, KÁLMÁN

HEJ AZ ÉN SZERETŐM; "THIS IS MY BROWN-EYED GIRL" e 164 words by Szelestey 3501

SIMONS, MOÏSÉS

CHIBO QUE ROMPE TAMBÓ; "Yo jabla con ño Fransico"; THE GOAT WHO ATE THE DRUM; "I'll 3502
tell the tale of a nanny" e, s 9

EL MANISERO; "Maní!, Maní!, Caserita no te acuestes a dormir" s 284 3503

SINDING, CHRISTIAN, 1856-1941

SONG OF FREEDOM, op.38, no.1; "Vi vil os et land som er frelst og fritt"; "We want a land that 3504
by right is free" e, n 7

SYLVELIN, op.55, no.1; "Sylvelin, segne Gott Dich auf Erden zu jeder Stund'!"; "Sylvelin, God's 3505
own blessing be on you the whole day through" e, g 122; "Sylvelin, may God's blessing rest ever
upon your head" e, g 137

SJÖBERG, BIRGER

"DEN FÖRSTA GAANG JAG SAAG DIG"; "WHEN FIRST I EVER SAW YOU" e, sw 188 3506

SJÖBERG, C. L.

TONERNA; "Tanke, vars strider blott natten ser"; MUSIC; "Thoughts in their travail the long night 3507
through" e, sw 188 words by E. G. Geijer

SKELLY, J. P.

    A BOY'S BEST FRIEND IS HIS MOTHER; "While plodding on our way"; "Then cherish her with care"   3508
    (ref) e 114,131   words by H. Miller

SKÖLD, YNGVE

    DET HAARDA VILLKORET; "Mitt hjärta längtar till stillhet och ro" sw 356   words by A. Kumlien   3509

ŠKROUP, FRANZ, 1801-1862

    WHERE IS MY HOME? (OVER TATRA); "Kde domov můj?"; "Where is my home?" c, e 7;   3510
    CZECHOSLOVAK NATIONAL ANTHEM c, e 324; combination of Czech and Slovak national
    anthems words by J. K. Tyl; OVER TATRA; "O'er Tatra storms rage and skies are rent asunder"
    e 279,366; WHERE IS MY HOME?; "Where is my home? Where is my home?" e 279,366

SMART, HENRY THOMAS, 1813-1879

    "ANGELS FROM THE REALMS OF GLORY"; Regent Square (tune) e 33,38,39,125,206,251,296,315,   3511
    337,366

SMART, LAUREANO MARTINEZ

    CHOLITA; "Cholita, no te enamores" s 284   words by J. S. Prieto   3512

SMETANA, BEDŘICH, 1824-1884

    [THE BARTERED BRIDE, opera; words by K. Sabina] JENIK'S ARIA, Act II, no.20;   3513
    "Armer Narr, glaubtest Du mich zu fangen?" (recit); "Es muss gelingen! Alles soll nach Wunsch
    und Willen gehen!" (aria); "You are caught! Now I see the way clearly" (recit); "Soon now,
    my dearest, we will leave behind all doubt and sadness!" (aria) e, g 3

    [Ibid] KEZEL'S ARIA, Act II; "Wer in Lieb' entbrannt, hält aus Unverstand Weiber für Engel";   3514
    "Lovers ev'rywhere fatuously swear they've found perfection" e, g 5

    [Ibid] MARENKA'S ARIA, Act I; AH, MY DARLING, WE COULD GROW TOGETHER; "Ah, my   3515
    darling, we could grow together like a single vine" e 6

    [Ibid] MARENKA'S ARIA, Act III; "Endlich allein! Allein mit mir" (recit); "Wie fremd und todt   3516
    ist Alles umher" (aria); "How can I live, bereft of love" (recit); "How strange and dead is every-
    thing here" (aria) e, g 2

    JARO LÁSKY; "Lýry hlas, jenž nitrem mým"; LIEBESFRÜHLING; "Dieses Saitenspiel der Brust" c, g   3517
    73a words by F. Rückert

    WAR SONG; "Válka! Válka! Prapor věje!"; "Up Czechs! War is here!" c, e 7   words by J. J. Kolár   3518

SMITH, CHRIS, 1879-

    GOOD MORNING, CARRIE!; "In sunny South Car'lina lives a kindly old Aunt Dinah"; "Good morning,   3519
    Carrie! how'd you do this morning" (ref) e 114; "In sunny, South Car'lina lives an old Aunt Dinah";
    "Good morning, Carrie! how you do this morning" (ref) e 131   joint composer Bowman, words by
    R. C. McPherson

SMITH, CLAY, 1877-1930

    "ONE NIGHT WHEN SORROW BURDENED" e 394   3520

SMITH, J. E.

    LITTLE BOY BLUE; "The little toy dog is covered with dust" e 129   words by E. Field   3521

SMITH, R. A., 1780-1829

    JESSIE THE FLOWER O' DUNBLANE; "The sun has gane doun o'er the lofty Ben Lomond" e 100   3522
    words by R. Tannahill

    "O WHA'S AT THE WINDOW" e 101   words by A. Carlile   3523

SMITH, THELMA JACKSON

    "BE STILL AND KNOW THAT I AM GOD" e 347   words by L. Downey   3524

SNYDER, TED, 1881-

    TAKE A CAR; "Said Claudie to Maudie, 'Now where shall we go'" e 204   words by E. Rose   3525

SOECHTIG, ELIZABETH DAVIS

    MY PRAYER; "I would not ask for my burden to be lightened" e 347   3526

SÖDERMAN, AUGUST JOHANN, 1832-1876

    [ETT BONDBRÖLLOP] BRÖLLOPSMARSCH; WEDDING MARCH FROM A COUNTRY WEDDING   3527
    piano 188

    [BRÖLLOPET PAA ULFAASA] BRÖLLOPSMARSCH; WEDDING MARCH FROM THE WEDDING   3528
    AT ULFAASA piano 188

    SER JAG STJÄRNORNA; "Ser jag stjärnorna sprida sitt flammande sken"; WHEN THE STARS SHED   3529
    THEIR LIGHT; "When the stars over forest and glimmering lake" e, sw 188   words by H. Sätther-
    berg

SOMERVELL, ARTHUR, 1863-1937

    [LOVE IN SPRING-TIME, song cycle] "DAINTY LITTLE MAIDEN" e 344   words by A.   3530
    Tennyson

    [Ibid] "YOUNG LOVE LIES SLEEPING" e 344   words by C. Rossetti   3531

    [MAUD, song cycle; words by A. Tennyson] "BIRDS IN THE HIGH HALL-GARDEN,"   3532
    no.5 e 272,344

    [Ibid] "COME INTO THE GARDEN, MAUD" e 344   3533

    [A SHROPSHIRE LAD, song cycle; words by A. E. Housman] "IN SUMMER-   3534
    TIME ON BREDON," no.4 e 344

SOMERVELL, ARTHUR, 1863-1937 (Continued)
    [Ibid] "THE LADS IN THEIR HUNDREDS" e 344   3535
SOMMER, W.
    VAGANS SCHOLASTICUS; "Der Sang ist verschollen" g 99; FAHRENDER SCHÜLER g 31   3536
SPALDING, ALBERT, 1888-1953
    THE ROCK OF RUBIES AND THE QUARRIE OF PEARLS; "Some ask'd me where Rubies grew" e 259   3537
        words by R. Herrick
SPEE, FRIEDRICH VON, 1591-1635
    "IN GRÜNEM WALD ICH NEULICH SASS" g 250   3538
SPEIDEL, WILEHLM, 1826-1899
    "FRÜH, WENN DIE HÄHNE KRÄHN" g 326 words by E. Mörike   3539
SPICKER, MAX, 1858-1912
    EVENING AND MORNING, op.56; "Comes at times a stillness as of even" e 123   3540
SPIER, LARRY, 1901-
    MEMORY LANE; "Stars are gleaming, day is o'er"; "I am with you wandering through Memory Lane"   3541
      (ref) e 345 joint composer C. K. Dober, words by B. G. De Silva
SPILMAN, JAMES E.
    FLOW GENTLY SWEET AFTON. See 1733
SPOHR, LOUIS, 1784-1859
    PROUDLY AS THE EAGLE; "Proudly as the eagle wings his flight on high" e 28,366 words by A. Stone   3542
    VANITAS! VANITATUM VANITAS!; "Ich hab mein Scah auf nichts gestellt" g 31 words by J. W.   3543
      von Goethe
SPORLE,
    THE HARRISON SONG; "In days of old, as we've been told"; "With heart and voice we'll gaily sing"   3544
      (ref) e 189 words by T. Power
STADE, WILHELM, 1817-1902
    VOR JENA; "Auf den Bergen die Burgen" g 31 words by L. Dreves   3545
STAINER, SIR JOHN, 1840-1901
    A CRADLE SONG OF THE BLESSED VIRGIN; "The Virgin stills the crying of Jesus sleepless lying"   3546
      e 244
    [THE CRUCIFIXION, oratorio] "FLING WIDE THE GATES" e 400   3547
    [Ibid] "GOD SO LOVED THE WORLD" e 28,346,400   3548
    [THE DAUGHTER OF JAIRUS, oratorio] "MY HOPE IS IN THE EVERLASTING" e 123   3549
STAIRS, LOUISE E.
    "LORD, SPEAK TO ME" e 347 words by F. R. Havergal   3550
STANFORD, SIR CHARLES VILLIERS, 1852-1924
    BOAT SONG, op.19, no.5; "Boat, little boat, a breeze on thy sails shall soon light" e 344 words   3551
      by W. H. Pollock
    [AN IRISH IDYLL, song cycle; words by M. O'Neill] CUTTIN' RUSHES; "Oh   3552
      maybe it was yesterday, or fifty years ago!" e 344
    [Ibid] THE FAIRY LOUGH; "Loughareema! Loughareema lies so high among the heather" e 344   3553
    [Ibid] JOHNEEN; "Sure he's five months old, an' he's two feet long" e 344   3554
    A LULLABY, op.19, no.2; "Golden slumbers kiss your eyes" e 344 words by T. Dekker   3555
    THE RAIN IT RAINETH EVERY DAY, op.65, no.3; "When that I was and a little tiny boy" e 344   3556
      words by W. Shakespeare, Twelfth Night
    [SHAMUS O'BRIEN, opera; words by G. H. Jessop] "OCHONE, WHEN I USED TO   3557
      BE YOUNG" e 344
    [SONGS OF FAITH, song cycle, OP. 97] TO THE SOUL, no.4; "Darest thou now, O   3558
      soul" e 344
    THERE'S A BOWER OF ROSES; "There's a bower of roses by Bendemeer's stream" e 344 words by T.   3559
      Moore
STANGE, MAX, 1856-1932
    DIE BEKEHRTE, op.13, no.1; "Bei dem Glanz der Abendröte ging ich still den Wald entlang";   3560
    DAMON; "As I roam'd the woods at leisure, in the evening hour so still" e 45 words by J. W.
      von Goethe
STANTON, ARNOLD
    THE ROVING KIND. See 623
STAROKADOMSKIĬ, MIKHAIL LEONTÉVICH, 1901-1954
    AN INSCRIPTION IN A BOWER; "Approach with reverent respect" e, r 342 words by A. Pushkin   3561
Starokadomsky, M. See STAROKADOMSKIĬ, MIKHAIL LEONTÉVICH, 1901-1954
STAUCH, RICHARD
    [DIE TATARIN, operetta; words by M. Halvorsen] NIMM MICH IN DEINE ARME;   3562
      "An deinem Herzen will ich vergessen" g 257
STEELE, S. S.
    GUM TREE CANOE; TOM-BIG-BEE RIVER; "On the Tom-Big-Bee River one day I was born" e 185;   3563
    ON TOM-BIG-BEE RIVER; "On Tom-Big-Bee River so bright, I was born" e 343

STEELE, S. S. (Continued)
    WALK, JAWBONE; "In Caroline where I was born" e 185; "In Caroline whar I was born" e 109,110   3564
STEFFE, WILLIAM
    [THE JOHN BROWN SONG] JOHN BROWN'S BODY; "John Brown's body lies a-mouldering in   3565
    the grave" e 293; "John Brown's body lies a-mould'rin' in the grave" e 227; "John Brown's body
    lies a-mould'ring in the grave" e 7,28,35,110,199,294,366; THE BATTLE HYMN OF THE
    REPUBLIC; "Mine eyes have seen the glory of the coming of the Lord" e 7,10,28,32,34,35,109,
    110,115,129,130,233,279,366; MINE EYES HAVE SEEN THE GLORY e 236 words by J. W. Howe;
    "He's gone to be a soldier in the army of the Lord" e 109; SOLIDARITY; "Solidarity forever, solid-
    arity forever" e 293
STEGGALL, CHARLES, 1826-1905
    LIKE SILVER LAMPS; "Like silver lamps in a distant shrine" e 251; THE MANGER THRONE e 410   3566
    words by W. Dix
STEINBRECHER, ALEXANDER, 1910-
    [BRILLANTEN AUS WIEN, comic opera] ICH KENN EIN KLEINES WEGERL IM HELENEN-   3567
    TAL; "Wenn zwei Menschen sich lieben und einig sind" g 223
STEININGER, FRANZ K. W., 1906-
    MARCHING ALONG TOGETHER. See 2838
STENHAMMAR, WILHELM, 1871-1927
    "MIN STAMFAR HADE IN STOR POKAL"; "MY GRANDSIRE, HE HAD A PEWTER CUP" e, sw 188   3568
    words by W. von Heidenstam
    STJÄRNÖGA, op.20, no.1; "Stjärnöga, du som jag mött"; STAR MAIDEN; "Star maiden, you   3569
    that I met" e, sw 188 words by B. Bergman
ŠTĚPÁN, VÁCLAV, 1889-1944
    JÍZDA ŽIVOTEM, op.7, no.5; "Já mladý rytíř jedu v dál, neb cesty rád mám přede dnem"; RITT   3570
    DURCHS LEBEN; "Ein Reiter, der vor Tau und Tag die Strasse liebte, zog ich aus" c, g 74 words
    by H. Bethge
STEPHAN, RUDI, 1887-1915
    ABENDLIED; "Reglos steht der alte Baum, altes Leid verwehet" g 226 words by G. Falke   3571
    DIR; "Meine Seele ist nun still geworden" g 98 words by H. Hinrichs   3572
STEPT, SAM H.
    DON'T SIT UNDER THE APPLE TREE. See 3748
STERN, JOSEPH W.
    THE LITTLE LOST CHILD; "A passing policeman found a little child"; "Do not fear my little   3573
    darling, and I will take you right home" (ref) e 34 words by E. B. Marks
    MOTHER WAS A LADY; "Two drummers sat at dinner in a grand hotel one day"; "My mother was a   3574
    lady like yours you will allow" (ref) e 32,34; IF JACK WERE ONLY HERE e 246 words by E. B.
    Marks
STEVENS, JAMES
    THE FROZEN LOGGER; "As I sat down one evening within a small cafe" e 389   3575
STEVENS, RICHARD JOHN SAMUEL, 1757-1837
    "SIGH NO MORE, LADIES" e 75, 277,349 words by W. Shakespeare, Much Ado About Nothing   3576
STEVENSON, FREDERICK
    I SOUGHT THE LORD; "I sought the Lord, and He heard me" e 398   3577
    LIGHT, op.58; THE WAYFARER'S SONG OF HOPE; "From out the Dawn there came a Voice" e 398   3578
STEVENSON, J.
    VESPERGESANG; "Horch die Wellen tragen bebend sanft und rein den Vesperchor" g 326   3579
STEVENSON, SIR JOHN ANDREW, 1760?-1833
    OFT IN THE STILLY NIGHT; SCOTS AIR; "Oft in the stilly night, ere slumber's chain has bound   3580
    me" e 132,166,213 words by T. Moore
STEWART, HUMPHREY JOHN, 1856-1932
    THE HEAVENLY STAR; "A myriad stars o'erhung the plains" e 8 words by J. H. Rogers   3581
STILL, WILLIAM GRANT, 1895-
    THE BREATH OF A ROSE; "Love is like dew on lilies at dawn" e 259 words by L. Hughes   3582
Stillman-Kelley, Edgar. See KELLEY, EDGAR STILLMAN, 1857-1944
STOLZ, ROBERT, 1882-
    AUF DER HEIDE BLÜH'N DIE LETZTEN ROSEN, op.65; "Versunken ist die Frühlingszeit" g 223   3583
    words by B. Balz
    DANN GEH' ICH HINAUS IN DEN WIENERWALD, op.360a; "Ich geh' durch die Strassen, o mein"   3584
    g 396
    [DER FAVORIT, operetta; words by F. Grünbaum and W. Sterk] DU SOLLST   3585
    DER KAISER MEINER SEELE SEIN; "Ich weiss ein Land das ohne Schranken" g 254
    FRÜHLING IN WIEN, op.300; "Gestern abends ging Frau Grete heim" g 396   3586
    IM PRATER BLÜH'N WIEDER DIE BÄUME, op.247; WIENERLIED; "Kinder schaut's zum Fenster 'raus!"   3587
    g 396

STOLZ, ROBERT, 1882- (Continued)

[IN WEISSEN RÖSSL, singspiel, OP.562] MEIN LIEBESLIED MUSS EIN WALZER SEIN!;   3588
"Was mein Herz zu sagen hat" g 258 words by R. Gilbert

IN WIEN GIBT'S MANCH' WINZIGES GASSERL, op.249; "Alte, zähl' die Kinder z'samm: Glaub es   3589
sind sechs Stück!" g 396

[DAS SPERRSECHSERL, operetta, OP.360c] A KLANE DRAHREREI; "Wenn am Himmel   3590
schön alle Sternderln steh'n" g 396

[WENN DIE KLEINEN VEILCHEN BLÜHEN, OP.590a, singspiel; words by   3591
B. Hardt-Warden] WENN DIE KLEINEN VEILCHEN BLÜHEN; "Wenn der Herbst jeden Baum
taucht in Gelb und Rosa" g 255

WIEN WIRD BEI NACHT ERST SCHÖN!, op.216; WIENER-LIED; "Wenn bekrittelt wird an unsrer   3592
Wienerstadt" g 396 words by W. Sterk

STONEHILL, MAURICE

JUST PLAIN FOLKS; "To a mansion in the city"; "We are just plain folks" (ref) e 131 (ref only)   3593
e 129,130

PEGGY MINE; "It's a long road we have travelled and the end is mighty nigh"; "Balmy Springtide's   3594
left us" (ref) e 131

STORACE, STEPHEN, 1763-1796

[THE PIRATES, opera; words by J. Cobb] PEACEFUL SLUMBERING; "Peaceful   3595
slumbering on the ocean, seamen fear no danger nigh" e 235

[Ibid] THE PRETTY CREATURE; "Oh! the pretty, pretty creature!" e 405   3596

STRADELLA, ALESSANDRO, 1645-1681?

A PORFIRIA VECCHIARELLA; "A Porfiria vecchiarella, a Porfiria vecchiarella, che fu bella" i 179   3597
"COSÌ, AMOR, MI FAI LANGUIR" i 179   3598
[IL FLORIDORO, opera] SZENE DER EURINDA; "Col mio sangue comprarei"; "Rendetemi il   3599
mio bene" (recit); "Per pieta, per pieta, deh torna, deh torna a me" (aria); "Mit meinem Blut
würde ich erkaufen"; "Gebt mir meinen Geliebten wieder" (recit); "Aus Barmherzigkeit, ach
kehre zurück zu mir" (aria) g, i 217; "COL MIO SANGUE COMPREREI"; "I WOULD SPEND MY
BLOOD UNHEEDING" (1st pt only) e, i 139

KANZONETTE; "So ben, che mir saettano"; "Wohl weiss ich, das mich verwunden" g, i 217   3600
OMBRE, VOI CHE CELATE; "Ombre, voi che celate dell' etra i rai" i 179   3601
PIETÀ, SIGNORE!; "Pietà, Signore, di me dolente!"; O LORD, HAVE MERCY; "O Lord, have   3602
mercy, I call upon thee" e, i 368

SE NEL BEN; "Se nel ben, se nel ben sempre inconstante fortuna vagante di far si stabile" i 179   3603

STRAIGHT, NED

LAY MY HEAD BENEATH A ROSE; "Darling fold me to you closer, as you did in days of yore";   3604
"Lay me where sweet flowers blossom" (ref) e 246

STRAUS, OSCAR, 1870-

[EIN WALZERTRAUM, operetta; words by F. Dörmann and L. Jacobson]   3605
LEISE, GANZ LEISE KLINGTS DURCH DEN RAUM; "Da draussen im durtenden Garten" g 257

STRAUSS, JOHANN, 1825-1899

[AN DER SCHÖNEN, BLAUEN DONAU, OP.314] BLUE DANUBE; "Danube so blue,   3606
I'm longing for you" e 132; "Ah! bright birds of June, Oh, light birds of June" e 93; BEAUTI-
FUL BLUE DANUBE; "Beautiful stream with moonlit beam" e 329; MY BLUE DANUBE; "Danube
so blue, I'm longing for you" e 128

[DIE FLEDERMAUS, opera; words by K. Haffner and R. Genée] CHACUN À   3607
SON GOÛT; PRINCE ORLOFSKY'S SONG; "Ich lade gern mir Gäste ein"; "From time to time
I entertain" e, g 2

[Ibid] KLÄNGE DER HEIMAT; "Klänge der Heimat, ihr weckt mir das Sehnen"; "Voice of my   3608
homeland, you waken my longing" e, g 1

[Ibid] MEIN HERR MARQUIS; "Mein Herr Marquis, ein Mann wie Sie sollt besser das verstehn";   3609
LAUGHING SONG; "My dear Marquis, it seems to me you should employ more tact!" e, g 1

[FRÜHLINGSSTIMMEN, OP.410] VOICES OF SPRING; WALTZ-SONG; "The sound of   3610
spring is in the air"; VOCI DI PRIMAVERA; "Comparvero le rondini" e, i 221

[G'SCHICHTEN AUS DEM WIENER WALD, OP.325] TALES FROM THE VIENNA   3611
WOODS; "The bud in bloom will lift its head" e 329 words by M. Whitehill

[INDIGO UND DIE VIERZIG RÄUBER, operetta; words by C. Walzel and   3612
R. Genée] JA, SO SINGT MAN NUR IN WIEN; "Horch, das sind bekannte Klänge!" g 254

[DAS LIED DER LIEBE, operetta] "DU BIST MEIN TRAUM" g 256 joint composer E. W.   3613
Korngold

[DER LUSTIGE KRIEG, opera; words by C. Walzel and R. Genée] NUR FÜR   3614
NATUR; "Nur für Natur hegte sie Sympathie" g 254

[Ibid] "WAS IST AN EINEM KUSS GELEGEN" g 254   3615
[EINE NACHT IN VENEDIG, operetta; words by C. Walzel and R. Genée]   3616
KOMM IN DIE GONDEL, Act I; "Komm in die Gondel, mein Liebchen, o steige nur ein" g 254

[Ibid] LAGUNEN-WALZER, Act III; "Ach, wie so herrlich zu schaun sind all die lieblichen Fraun"   3617
g 255

STRAUSS, RICHARD, 1864-1949

ALL MEIN GEDANKEN, op. 21, no. 1; "All mein Gedanken mein Herz und mein Sinn"; ALL THE   3618
FOND THOUGHTS; "All the fond thoughts that arise in my soul" e, g 330   words by F. Dahn

ALLERSEELEN, op. 10, no. 8; "Stell' auf den Tisch die duftenden Resenden"; ALL SOULS' DAY;   3619
"Beside me set the ruddy glowing heather" e, g 122; "Place here by me the mignonette so
fragrant" e, g 112   words by H. von Gilm

CÄCILIE, op. 27, no. 2; "Wenn du es wüsstest"; CECILIA; "Could you but know, love" e, g 112;   3620
"If you but knew" e, g 121   words by H. Hart

"DU MEINES HERZENS KRÖNELEIN," op. 21, no. 2; PRIDE OF MY HEART; "Pride of my heart its   3621
crown, its joy" e, g 330   words by F. Dahn

DER EINSAME, op. 51, no. 2; "Wo ich bin, mich rings umdunkelt Finsternis so dumpf und dicht";   3622
THE SOLITARY ONE; "Joy is fled, sweet hopes are blighted, darkness shrouds me deep as night"
e, g 274   words by H. Heine

FREUNDLICHE VISION, op. 48, no. 1; "Nicht im Schlafe hab ich das geträumt"; A WELCOME   3623
VISION; "Not in slumber did the dream rise" e, g 272   words by O. J. Bierbaum

GLÜCKES GENUG, op. 37, no. 1; "Wenn sanft du mir im Arme schliefst"; TRUE LOVE'S BLISS;   3624
"When soft asleep I held thee, sweet" e, g 330   words by D. von Liliencron

HEIMKEHR, op. 15, no. 5; "Leiser schwanken die Äste"; HOMECOMING; "Softly branches are   3625
swaying" e, g 112   words by A. F. von Schack

HEIMLICHE AUFFORDERUNG, op. 27, no. 3; "Auf hebe die funkelnde Schale empor zum Mund";   3626
SECRET INVITATION; "Come, once again lift to your red lips the sparkling glass" e, g 112
words by J. H. Mackay

ICH SCHWEBE, op. 48, no. 2; "Ich schwebe wie auf Engelsschwingen"; A FAREWELL; "Like angels   3627
through the ether winging" e, g 276   words by K. Henckell

ICH TRAGE MEINE MINNE, op. 32, no. 1; "Ich trage meine Minne vor Wonne"; I WEAR MY LOVE;   3628
"I wear my love in silence, that none may know" e, g 112   words by K. Henckell

MORGEN, op. 27, no. 4; "Und morgen wird die Sonne wieder scheinen" g 98; TOMORROW; "To-   3629
morrow morn again we'll see the sunshine" e, g 112; "Tomorrow will the sun again be shining"
e 348; "Tomorrow's sun will rise in glory beaming" e, g 121, 330   words by J. H. Mackay

DAS ROSENBAND, op. 36, no. 1; "Im Frühlingsschatten fand ich sie" g 250   words by F. G. Klopstock   3630

RUHE, MEINE SEELE!, op. 27, no. 1; "Nicht ein Lüftchen regt sich leise"; REST NOW, WEARY   3631
SPIRIT; "Not a leaf stirs, all is tranquil" e, g 112   words by K. Henckell

SCHLAGENDE HERZEN, op. 29, no. 2; "Über Wiesen und Felder ein Knabe ging"; LONGING HEARTS;   3632
"Over mountain and dale went a youth, in spring" e, g 330   words by O. J. Bierbaum

STÄNDCHEN, op. 17, no. 2; "Mach' auf, mach' auf, doch leise, mein Kind"; SERENADE; "Come   3633
out! come out! but softly, my child" e, g 112   words by A. F. von Schack

TRAUM DURCH DIE DÄMMERUNG, op. 29, no. 1; "Weite Wiesen im Dämmergrau"; DREAM IN   3634
THE TWILIGHT; "Distant meadows in twilight gray" e, g 112; "Spreading meads in the dusk of
eve" e, g 330   words by O. J. Bierbaum

WALDSELIGKEIT, op. 49, no. 1; "Der wald beginnt zu rauchen"; ALONE IN THE FOREST; "A sound   3635
is in the forest" e, g 275   words by R. Dehmel

WINTERWEIHE, op. 48, no. 4; "In diesen Wintertagen, nun sich das Licht verhüllt"; A WINTER   3636
DEDICATION; "In days of winter dreary, when all is gloom and night" e, g 277   words by K.
Henckell

ZUEIGNUNG, op. 10, no. 1; "Ja, du weisst es, theure Seele"; DEDICATION; "Ah, thou knowest   3637
all my anguish" e, g 112; TO YOU; "Oh my darling, well you know me" e, g 122; "Ja, du
weisst es teure Seele"; DEDICATION; "Sorrow fills my heart, beloved" e, g 45; "Yes, beloved,
well thou knowest" e, g 408   words by H. von Gilm

STRAVINSKIĬ, IGOŘ FEDOROVICH, 1882-

PASTORALE; "Ah Ah Ahoo Ahoo" (without words) 121   3638

SONG OF THE DEW; "Our mother earth is fertile" e, r 341   words by S. Gorodetsky   3639

Stravinsky, Igor. See STRAVINSKIĬ, IGOŘ FEDOROVICH, 1882-

STRECKER, HEINRICH JOSEF, 1893-

[ÄNNCHEN VON THARAU, singspiel; words by B. Hardt-Warden and H.   3640
Strecker] "DRAUSSEN IST FRÜHLING, DRAUSSEN IST MAI"; DU BESITZT MEIN HERZ g 257

[Ibid] FOLG' NUR DEINEM HERZEN!; "Bin verliebt, dass es so 'was gibt" g 257   3641

DRUNT' IN DER LOBAU, op. 290; "Wo die Donau mit silbernen Armen umschlingt's letzte Stükkerl   3642
vom träumenden Wien" g 396

JA, JA DER WEIN IST GUT, op. 99; "Wenn i einmal schlecht aufg'legt bin" g 396   words by J. Gribitz   3643

SING MIR DAS LIED NOCH EINMAL; "In einer Maiennacht" g 222   words by S. Kurzer and H. Robinger   3644

STRICKLAND, LILY TERESA, 1887-1958

"AT EVE I HEARD A FLUTE" e 241   3645

MY LOVER IS A FISHERMAN; "Oh, my lover is a fisherman" e 137   3646

MY SHEPHERD, THOU; "O gentle Shepherd, guide me home" e 347   3647

THE ROAD TO HOME; "Oh, the road to home" e 136   3648

SURZYŃSKI, MIECZYSŁAW, 1866-1924 (Continued)
    JEDNA NUTA; "Czy to zieleń, ruta"; SADNESS; "Is it bitter herb, then?" 4 pt e, p 295   3681
    KOŁYSANKA; "Śpij, dziecinko, Spij, Śliczne oczki zmruź"; LULLABY; "Sleep, my baby, sleep,   3682
        close your eyes in sleep" e, p 295
    LETNI WIECZÓR; "Już zaszedł nad doliną Złocisty słońca krąg"; A SUMMER NIGHT; "When day   3683
        puts out its tapers and silence basks the vale" e, p 295   words by A. Asnyk
    NA STAWIE; "Cicho senno na krysztale"; THE POND; "Dreamy lies the limpid water" e, p 295   3684
        words by K. Glinski
SURZYŃSKI, STEFAN
    MAZURY; "Hej, Mazury hejże ha!"; "Hey, Mazury people strong!" e, p 295   3685
    TANECZNICA; "Czem najładniej grają, Do domu wołają"; THE DANCER; "When music is most   3686
        gay, They call, 'Come home! Don't stay!'" e, p 295
SURZYŃSKI, X. DR.
    CO MI DANO; "Stroiły mi duszę Brzózki, polne grusze"; WHAT IS GIVEN ME; "Music came to my   3687
        soul, From wild pear and peach knoll" e, p 295   words by K. Laskowski
    ORACZ DO SKOWRONKA; "Już śpiewasz skowroneczku"; PLOWER TO THE SKYLARK; "At dawn   3688
        when day is breaking" e, p 295
SUTTON, HARRY O.
    I DON'T CARE; "They say I'm crazy got no sense"; "I don't care, I don't care" (ref) e 204   words   3689
        by J. Lenox
SWAN, EINAR
    TRAIL OF DREAMS; "Down the trail of dreams I'm with you once again" e 132   words by R. Klages   3690
SWIFT, L. E.
    POOR MISTER MORGAN; "Poor Mister Morgan cannot pay his income tax" 3 pt round e 293   3691
    SCHWAB, SCHWAB; "Schwab, Schwab, Charlie Schwab" 4 pt round e 293   3692
    THERE ARE THREE BROTHERS; "There are three brothers named Dupont" 3 pt round e 293   3693
Sygetynski, Tadeusz. See SYGIETYŃSKI, TADEUSZ
SYGIETYŃSKI, TADEUSZ
    IN THE WOOD; "In the woods a-hiding waits my fair Marysia" e 228   3694
    THE VALLEY; "There's a valley, there's a vale" e 228   3695
    WHERE THE ALDERS GROW; "As the night is falling" e 228   3696
    "WHY DID YOU NEVER COME" e 228   3697
SZÁNTO, MIHÁLY
    TIZENHAT ESZTENDÖS BARNA KIS LÁNY; "Nem néz rám a régi babám"; MY SIXTEEN YEAR   3698
        OLD BROWN-EYED YOUNG MAID; "Since my love now loves another" e, hu 285
SZENTIRMAY, ELEMÉR JANOS NÉMETH, 1836-1910
    CSAK EGY KIS LÁNY VAN A VILÁGON; "THERE'S BUT ONE GIRL UNDERNEATH THE SUN" e 164   3699
    ÉLETEMBEN EGYSZER VOLTAM CSAK BOLGOD; "IN MY WHOLE LIFE HAPPY" e 164   3700
    TÚL A TISZÁN DEVECSERBE; B'YOND THE TISZA; "B'yond the Tisza, says the tidings" e 164   3701
SZOPSKI, F., 1865-1939
    LEĆ PIEŚNI W DAL; "Leć pieśni w dal, o leć jak grzmot"; ON WINGS OF SONG; "On wings of   3702
        song fly soul of mine" e, p 159   words by E. Leszczyński
SZULC, JÓSEF ZYGMUNT, 1875-1956
    CLAIR DE LUNE, op.83, no.1; "Votre âme est un paysage choisi"; MOONLIGHT; "Your soul is a   3703
        chosen landscape" e, f 191,193,195   words by P. Verlaine
SZYMANOWSKI, KAROL, 1883-1937
    LIED DES MÄDCHENS AM FENSTER, op.22, no.2; "Ein Wand'rer in der Gassen"; SONG OF THE GIRL   3704
        AT THE WINDOW; "A roamer in the alley" e, g 121   words by A. Paquet

TALAVERA, MARIO
    ARRULLO; "Cierra tus lindos ojos que tienen sueño"; "Cierra pues tus divinos ojos con sueño" (ref);   3705
        MEXICAN LULLABY; "Once, in the long ago, mother rocked my cradle"; "Lullaby with a
        Mexican night above me" (ref) e, s 248   words by R. C. Navarro
TALLEY, THOMAS WASHINGTON
    BEHOLD THAT STAR!; "Behold, behold that star! behold, behold that star up yonder" e 251   3706
TALLIS, THOMAS, ca1505-1585
    TALLIS' CANON; "Praise God, from whom all blessings flow" 2 pt round e 199   3707
TARNOWSKI, (COUNT), 1837-1917
    "JAK TO NA WOJENCE ŁADNIE"; "FOR A LANCER WAR GOES GAILY" e, p 159   3708
TAUBERT, WILHELM KARL GOTTFRIED, 1811-1891
    IN DER FREMDE, op.67; "Es steht ein Baum in jenem Tal"; IN A STRANGE LAND; "In yonder vale   3709
        there stands a tree" e, g 275   words by H. von Fallersleben
    VOM BAUERN UND DEN TAUBEN, op.68, no.3; "Der Bauer hat ein Taubenhaus" g 99   words by   3710
        F. W. Güll

TAYLOR, COLIN, 1881-
        GRASSHOPPER GREEN; "Grasshopper green is a comical chap" e 199   3711
        THE THREE SHIPS; "As I went up the mountain side" e 337 words by A. Noyes   3712
TAYLOR, VIRGIL C.
        LORD OF ALL BEING, THRONED AFAR; "Lord of all being, thron'd afar" e 28,279,366 words by   3713
        O. W. Holmes
Tcherepnin, Alexander. See CHEREPNIN, ALEKSANDR NIKOLAEVICH
TEGNÉR, ALICE CHARLOTTE (SANDSTRÖM), 1864-1943
        BETLEHEMS STJÄRNA; "Gläns över sjö och strand"; "SHINE OVER LAKE AND STRAND" e, sw 188   3714
        words by V. Rydberg
        MORS LILLA OLLE; "Mors lilla Olle i skogen gick"; MOM'S LITTLE OLLE; "Mom's little Olle was in   3715
        the wood" e, sw 188
        "NÄR LILLAN KOM TILL JORDEN"; "WHEN CUCKOOS SANG IN MAYTIME" e, sw 188   3716
        "SOV DU LILLA VIDE UNG"; "SLEEP THOU TENDER WILLOW WAND" e, sw 188 words by Z. Topel-   3717
        ius
TELEMANN, GEORG PHILIPP, 1681-1767
        GLÜCK; "Das Glücke kommt selten per Posta, zu Pferde" g 99; DAS GLÜCK g 98,226 words by   3718
        D. Stoppe
        DIE JUGEND; "Geliebter Frühling meiner Tage, wie voller Anmut blühest du!" g 226   3719
        DIE VERGNÜGUNG; "Gönnt mir doch das bisschen Freude!" g 308 words by D. Stoppe   3720
TERRILL, JESSIE B.
        AN AFRICAN CHRISTMAS CAROL; "Jesus Christ was born on Christmas" e 251   3721
TERRY, SIR RICHARD RUNCIMAN, 1865-1938
        MYN LYKING; "I saw a fair Mayden syttin and sing" e 307; I SAW A FAIR MAYDEN" e 317   3722
TESCHNER, MELCHIOR
        "ALL GLORY, LAUD, AND HONOR" e 35 words by St. Theodulph, Bishop of Orleans   3723
TESSIER, CHARLES, 1550-1610?
        AU JOLI BOIS; "Au joli bois je m'en vais" f 383   3724
THIBAUD I, KING OF NAVARRE, 1201-1253
        J'ALOIE L'AUTRE JOR ERRANT; "J'aloie l'autre jor errant sans compaignon" f 108   3725
THIMAN, ERIC HARDING, 1900-
        A CHILDING SLEPT; "A Childing slept within a bed" e 374   3726
THOMAS, AMBROISE, 1811-1896
        [HAMLET, opera; words by J. Barbier and M. Carré] "O VIN, DISSIPE LA   3727
        TRISTESSE"; DRINKING SONG; "O wine, dispel the heavy sadness" e, f 4
        [MIGNON, opera; words by M. Carré and J. Barbier] ADIEU, MIGNON!, Act II;   3728
        "Adieu, Mignon! courage! Ne pleure pas!"; "Farewell, Mignon! be joyous! Weep not, I pray"
        e, f 3
        [Ibid] CONNAIS-TU LE PAYS; "Connais-tu le pays où fleurit l'oranger?"; "Dost thou know that   3729
        fair land where the lemons bloom?" e, f 2
        [Ibid] "DE SON COEUR J'AI CALMÉ LA FIÈVRE"; "FROM HER HEART THE FEVER DEPARTED";   3730
        BERCEUSE e, f 5
        [Ibid] "ELLE NE CROYAIT PAS", Act III; "Never the maiden dreamed" e, f 3   3731
        [Ibid] JE SUIS TITANIA; "Oui, pour ce soir je suis reine" (recit); "Je suis Titania la blonde"   3732
        (aria); "Yes for this eve I am queen" (recit); "I am Titania, the fairy" (aria) e, f 221; "Yes,
        for this evening I am queen" (recit) e, f 6; "Ah! pour ce soir, je suis reine" (recit); "Ah! for
        tonight, I am queen" (recit); "I'm Titania, the maid with golden hair" (aria) e, f 292
        [Ibid] ME VOICI DANS SON BOUDOIR; "C'est moi! j'ai tout brisé n'importe! m'y voici" (recit);   3733
        "Me voici dans son boudoir" (aria); "Ci son, ho tutto in franto, che monta dentro io sto!" (recit);
        "IN VEDER L'AMATA STANZA" (aria); "'Tis I! all is now broken - no matter! here I am!" (recit);
        "I AM IN HER BOUDOIR FAIR" (aria) e, f, i 357; "'Tis I! all gone to smash!" (recit); "Here am
        I in her boudoir" (aria) e, f 2
THOMAS, JOHN ROGERS, 1829-1896
        "BEAUTIFUL ISLE OF THE SEA" e 129,130,132 words by G. Cooper   3734
        BONNIE ELOISE; "O sweet is the vale where the Mohawk gently glides"; "But sweeter, dearer, yes,   3735
        dearer far than these" (ref) e 10,28,129,130,131,132; BONNY ELOISE e 321 words by C. W.
        Elliott
        CROQUET; "Out on the lawn in the evening gray" e 115,225 words by C. H. Webb   3736
        "'TIS BUT A LITTLE FADED FLOWER" e 129,130 words by E. C. Howarth   3737
THOMPSON, H. S.
        COUSIN JEDEDIAH; "Now, Jacob, get the cows home" e 225; "Oh! Jacob, get the cows home"   3738
        e 28,279,366
        "FAR ABOVE CAYUGA'A WATERS" e 129,130,236   3739
THOMPSON, WILL L.
        COME WHERE THE LILIES BLOOM; "Come away, away, away, come where the lilies bloom so fair"   3740
        e 132

THOMPSON, WILL L. (Continued)

SOFTLY AND TENDERLY; "Softly and tenderly, Love is healing" e 398 3741

THOMSON, (MRS.) D. V.

THE SPINNING WHEEL; "As I sat at my spinning wheel" e 103,104 3742

THOMSON, VIRGIL, 1896-

SUSIE ASADO; "Sweet, sweet, sweet, sweet, sweet tea" e 85 words by G. Stein 3743

THORNTON, JAMES, 1861-1938

MY SWEETHEART'S THE MAN IN THE MOON; "Ev'rybody has a sweetheart underneath the rose"; 3744
"My sweetheart's the man in the moon" (ref) e 114,131; (ref only) e 128,129,130,132

SHE MAY HAVE SEEN BETTER DAYS; "While strolling along with the city's vast throng"; "She may 3745
have seen better days" (ref) e 114,131 (ref only) e 132

THRUPP, J. F., 1827-1867

"BRIGHTEST AND BEST OF THE SONS OF THE MORNING" e 307 words by R. Heber 3746

TIERNEY, HARRY, 1895-

M-I-S-S-I-S-S-I-P-P-I; "M-i-s-s-i-s-s-i-p-p-i that used to be so hard to spell" e 128 words by 3747
B. Hanlon and B. Ryan

TITOV, NIKOLAY ALEXEYEVITCH, 1800-1875

DER ROTE SARAFAN. See 3798

TOBIAS, CHARLES, 1898-

"DON'T SIT UNDER THE APPLE TREE WITH ANYONE ELSE BUT ME" e 236 joint composer S. H. 3748
Stept, words by L. Brown

TOBIN, J. RAYMOND

"OUT IN A STABLE NEAR BETHLEHEM TOWN" e 319 3749

TOMÁŠEK, JAROSLAV, 1896-

POHÁDKA, op.1, no.2; "Jako dítě. Pohádkou ty jsi a já jsem dítě"; EIN MÄRCHEN; "Bin ein Kind 3750
nur. Ein Märchen bist du, und ich ein Kind nur" c, g 74 words by F. Šrámek

TOMER, WILLIAM G.

"GOD BE WITH YOU TILL WE MEET AGAIN" e 28,279,366 words by J. E. Rankin 3751

TONNER, PAUL

"CONCEDE NOBIS GRATIAM"; BLESS US DEAREST LORD; "Bless us, we pray Thee dearest Lord" 3752
e, lat 71 words by S. Hartman

"I FOUND A HEART ALL GOLDEN" e 71 words by C. Bittle 3753

"QUID RETRIBUAM"; WHAT THANKS CAN I RENDER; "O what thanks can I render" e, lat 71 3754
words from Psalm CXV

TOPLIFF, ROBERT

CONSIDER THE LILIES; "Is not the life more than meat, and the body than raiment?" e 200 words 3755
from St. Matthew VI:26,26,28,29

TORELLI, GIUSEPPE, 1658-1709

TU LO SAI; "Tu lo sai Quanto t'amai"; WELL THOU KNOWEST; "Well thou knowest what love 3756
thou owest" e, i 138; "You know how much I have loved you" e, i 134; ASK THY HEART;
"Ask thy heart how I adore thee" e, i 368

TOSTI, SIR FRANCESCO PAOLO, 1846-1916

GOOD-BYE!; "Falling leaf, and fading tree" e 122,237,329,348 words by G. J. White-Melville 3757

MARECHIARE; "Quanno sponta la luna a Marechiare"; NEAPOLITAN SERENADE; "When the moon 3758
rises over Marechiare" e, i 310 words by S. di Giacomo

MATTINATA; "Mary, tremando l'ultima stella"; MATIN SONG; "Mary, the last star quiv'ring and 3759
failing" e, i 241 words by E. Panzacchi

LA SERENATA; "Vola, o serenata"; SERENADE; "Lightly my song, go flying" e, i 386 words by 3760
G. A. Cesareo

VORREI; "Vorrei, allor che tu pallido"; COULD I; "Could I, but come to thee once, but once only" 3761
e, i 386; "Could I come to thee once dear" e, i 329

TOWNE, T. MARTIN

MY DARLING'S LITTLE SHOES; "God bless the little feet that never go astray" e 189 3762

TOZER, A. EDMOND

"AVE MARIA THOU VIRGIN AND MOTHER" e 382 words from St. Patrick Hymnal 3763

TREHARNE, BRYCESON, 1879-1948

CORALS; "My coral beads came from a cave" e 121 words by Z. Akins 3764

"A WIDOW BIRD SAT MOURNING" e 408 words by P. B. Shelley 3765

TREIDLER, HANNS, 1853-1926

EHRE, FREIHEIT, VATERLAND!; "Schwört bei dieser blanken Wehre" g 31 words by R. Baumbach 3766

TREVATHAN, CHARLES E.

MAY IRWIN'S "BULLY" SONG; "Have yo' heard 'bout dat bully"; "When I walk dat levee 'round" 3767
(ref) e 114; BULLY SONG e 131 (ref only) e 128; "Have you heard about dat bully" e 115

MAY IRWIN'S "FROG" SONG; "Away down yonder in the Yankety Yank"; "An jus lots uv folks is like 3768
dis foolish frog" (ref) e 114

132

TROMBONCINO, BARTOLOMEO, fl ca1500
  FROTTOLA; "Ben ch'amor mi faccia torto" i 278   3769
TROTÉRE, H.
  IN OLD MADRID. See 305
TRUHART, ROGER
  THE WABASH CANNON BALL; "From the calm Pacific waters" e 34   3770
TRUHN, FRIEDRICH HIERONYMUS, 1811-1886
  KRANZWIRTSCHAFT; "Der schönste Ort, davon ich weiss" g 31 words by W. Wackernagel 3771
  THE THREE CHAFERS; "There were three young and gallant chafers" e 28,366 3772
TRUNK, RICHARD, 1879-
  IN MEINER HEIMAT, op. 14, no. 2; "In meiner Heimat wird es jetzt Frühling" g 98 words by K. 3773
    Busse
TUCKER, HENRY
  SWEET GENEVIEVE; "O Genevieve, I'd give the world"; "O Genevieve, sweet Genevieve, the days 3774
    may come, the days may go" (ref) e 10,28,36,129,130,233,236,366 words by G. Cooper
  WEEPING, SAD AND LONELY; WHEN THIS CRUEL WAR IS OVER; "Dearest love, do you remember" 3775
    e 109,110,189 words by C. C. Sawyer
TUCKERMAN, SAMUEL PARKMAN, 1819-1860
  "GOD BLESS OUR NATIVE LAND" e 129,130   3776
TUFTS, JOHN WHEELER, 1825-1908
  THE AMERICAN FLAG; "When freedom from her mountain height" e 129,130 words by J. R. Drake 3777
  SONG TO THE FLAG; "Wave, wave, wave, while over land and sea" e 129,130 3778
TULLAR, GRANT COLFAX
  FACE TO FACE; "Face to face with Christ my Saviour" e 346 words by Mrs. F. A. Breck 3779
TURNER, A. J.
  PRAY, MAIDEN, PRAY!; "Maiden, pray for thy lover now" e 161 words by A. W. Kercheval 3780
TURNER, J. W.
  ROLL ON, SILVER MOON; "As I stray'd from my cot at the close of the day" e 131,343 3781
TWIGGS, CHARLES
  MONEY AM A HARD THING TO BORROW; "The times are so tight, for the cash is hard to get"; 3782
    "So take down your shingle and shut up your shop" (ref) e 189

UDDÉN, AAKE
  CHANSON; "Le premier me donna un collier"; "Den förste mig ett kostbart halsband skänkte" f, sw 3783
    356 words by P. Louÿs
  DOCKAN; "Jag gav min väninna en docka"; LA POUPÉE; "Je luis ai donné une poupée" f, sw 356 3784
    words by P. Louÿs
  TENDRESSES; "Ferme doucement tes bras"; "Dina armar slut" f, sw 356 words by P. Louÿs 3785
URBANEK, ED
  WIENIEC MELODJI NARODOWYCH; "A czy znasz ty, bracie młody"; ON WINGS OF POLISH SONG; 3786
    "Do you know, my youthful brother" e, p 295
URUSKI, STANISŁAW
  "OJ, TY WISŁO"; OH, YOU WISŁA; "Wisła, Wisła, azure river" e, p 295   3787

VAGNETTI, ANGIOLO
  GLEANERS SONG; "Ah, young man out there reaping in the field of wheat"; "Reaper of wheat the 3788
    gleaners listen to your song" (ref) e 37
Valderrabano, Enriquez de. See ENRIQUEZ DE VALDERRABANO, ENRIQUE, 16th c
VALDERRAMA, CARLOS, 1887-1950
  LA PAMPA Y LA PUNA; "Des de mi pampa querida salté a la cordillera" s 284 3789
VALERIUS, ADRIANUS, d 1625
  [NEDERLANDTSCHE GEDENCK-CLANCK] WILT HEDEN NU TREDEN; "Wilt heden nu 3790
    treden voor God den Heere" d 201; A PRAYER OF THANKSGIVING; "We gather together to ask
    the Lord's blessing" d, e 236,279,316,343,366; HYMN OF THANKSGIVING e 44; WE'RE
    SINGING OUR PRAISES; "Now singing we're bringing our praises before Him" d, e 34; WIR
    TRETEN ZUM BETEN; "Wir treten zum Beten vor Gott den Herren" g 99; DANKGEBET g 49;
    ALTNIEDERLÄNDISCHES DANKGEBET; "Wir treten zum Beten vor Gott, den Gerechten"
    e, g 31; WIR TRETEN ZUM BETEN e, g 326
VALVERDE, JOAQUIN, 1846-1910
  CLAVELITOS; "Clavelitos, a quien le doy clavelos"; CARNATIONS; "Buy carnations! Who would like 3791
    a carnation" e, s 245; "Fresh carnations! Now for whom can I spare them" e, s 142 words by Estic

VAN ALSTYNE, EGBERT ANSON, 1882-1951
        MEMORIES; "Memories, memories, dreams of love so true" e 233 words by G. Kahn   3792
VAN DE WATER, BEARDSLEY
        THE PENITENT; "A certain man had two sons" e 398 words from St. Luke XV:11-25   3793
        THE PUBLICAN; "Two men went up into the temple to pray" e 398   3794
VANEUF, ANDRÉ
        "KEEP CLOSE TO GOD!" e 398 words by K. Bainbridge   3795
VÁRADY, ALADÁR
        "HAJLIK A JEGENYE"; Zöldül a levele"; "GREEN ARE THE POPLAR LEAVES" e, hu 285   3796
VARELA, CARLOS MARÍA
        "AL RUMOR DE LAS SELVAS HONDUREÑAS" s 284   3797
VARLAMOV, ALEKSANDR IGOROVICH, 1801-1848
        DER ROTE SARAFAN; "Näh nicht, liebes Mütterlein am roten Sarafan" g 99; NÄH NICHT, LIEBES   3798
            MÜTTERLEIN g 353; THE SCARLET SARAFAN; "Mother, darling, mother mine, please let those
            labors be" e 70 words by N. G. Ziganoff, music att also to N. A. Titov
        THE WHIRL-WIND; "Driven by the whirl-wind" e, r 288   3799
VASILENKO, SERGEĬ NIKIFOROVICH, 1872-
        "IN THE CATHEDRAL A GIRL SANG PRAYERS" e, r 341 words by A. Block   3800
Vassilenko, S. See VASILENKO, SERGEĬ NIKIFOROVICH, 1872-
VAUGHAN WILLIAMS, RALPH, 1872-1958
        [THE HOUSE OF LIFE, song cycle] SILENT NOON, no.2; "Your hands lie open in the   3801
            long fresh grass" e 121,358 words by D. G. Rossetti
        [ON WENLOCK EDGE, song cycle] "FROM FAR, FROM EVE AND MORNING", no.2 e 277   3802
            words by A. E. Housman
        THE SNOW IN THE STREET; "From far away we come to you" e 334 words by W. Morris   3803
        [SONGS OF TRAVEL, song cycle, SET II, NO.2] YOUTH AND LOVE; "To the heart   3804
            of youth the world is a highway side" e 272,344 words by R. L. Stevenson
        WHITHER MUST I WANDER?; "Home no more home to me, whither must I wander?" e 344 words   3805
            by R. L. Stevenson
VAZQUEZ, JUAN, fl 16th c
        "COMO QUERÉIS, MADRE?" s 12   3806
        "CON QUÉ LA LAVARÉ?" s 12   3807
        "DE LOS ÁLAMOS VENGO" s 12   3808
        "EN LA FUENTE DEL ROSEL" s 12   3809
        "QUIERO DORMIR Y NO PUEDO" s 12   3810
        "VOS ME MATASTES" s 12   3811
VEGA, AUGUSTO
        JUREMOS LA UNION; "America tu eres de estirpe gloriosa" s 303   3812
VENÉ, RUGGERO
        "O SACRED HEART OF JESUS" e 382 words by X. M. Hayes   3813
        "DEAR SAVIOUR BLESS US ERE WE GO" e 382 words by F. Faber   3814
        PRELUDE piano 382   3815
        PROCESSIONAL piano 382   3816
        RECESSIONAL piano 382   3817
VERACINI, FRANCESCO MARIA, 1690-1750
        NO, TIRSI, TU NON HAI; "No, Tirsi, tu non hai quella che sè decaute"; FAIR TIRSI; "Fair Tirsi,   3818
            you do not possess"; "NEIN, THYRSIS, DU BESITZEST NICHT" e, g, i 253
VERDI, GIUSEPPE, 1813-1901
        [AIDA, opera; words by A. Ghislanzoni] CELESTE AIDA; "Se quel guerrier io fossi!"   3819
            (recit); "Celeste Aida forma divina" (aria); "What if 'tis I am chosen" (recit); "Heav'nly Aida,
            beauty resplendent" (aria) e, i 3; HEAVENLY AIDA (aria only) e, i 132; FAIREST AIDA; "Fair-
            est Aida, Heavenly glory" (aria only) e, i 36; HOLDE AIDA; "O wäre ich erkoren" (recit);
            "Holde Aida, himmelentstammend" (aria) g, i 391
        [Ibid] OH PATRIA MIA, Act III; "Qui Radames vera" (recit); "O patria mia mai piu" (aria); "He 3820
            will ere long be here" (recit); "My native land no more" (aria) e, i 1; O CIELI AZZURI; O
            SKIES CERULEAN; "My native land ne'er more" e, i 143
        [Ibid] RITORNA VINCITOR!; "Ritorna vincitor! E dal mio labbro usci l'empia parola!" i 301;   3821
            MAY LAURELS CROWN THY BROW!; "May laurels crown thy brow! What! can my lips pro-
            nounce language so impious!" e, i 1, 143
        [ATTILA, opera; words by T. Solera] O NEL FUGGENTE NUVOLO; "Liberamente or   3822
            piangi" (recit); "Oh! nel fuggente nuvolo. Non sei tu padre impresso?" (aria); "My tears now flow
            unheeded" (recit); "See, in the cloud a vision. Is it the face of my father?" (aria) e, i 292
        [UN BALLO IN MASCHERA, opera; words by A. Somma] "ERI TU CHE MAC-   3823
            CHIAVI QUELL'ANIMA," Act III (aria); "Alzati! la tuo figlio a te concedo riveder" (recit)
            i 298; IT WAS THOU THE DESTROYER; "Rouse thee now! This I grant thee, to look upon thy
            son once more" (recit); "It was thou the destroyer of her I loved" (aria) e, i 310

VERDI, GIUSEPPE, 1813-1901 (Continued)

[UN BALLO IN MASCHERA] (Continued) ERI TU CHE MACCHIAVI; "Rise! I say! Ere   3823
departing, once more thy son thou mayst behold" (recit); "Is it thou that hast sullied a soul so
pure?" (aria) e, i 4

[Ibid] "MORRÒ, MA PRIMA IN GRAZIA," Act III; "I'll die, yet in this agony" e, i 6   3824

[Ibid] "RE DELL'ABISSO, AFFRÉTTATI," Act I, Scene 2 i 300; INVOCATION ARIA; "King of   3825
the shades, I summon thee" e, i 2

[Ibid] "SAPER VORRESTE DE CHE SI VESTE," Act III i 302; SAPER VORRESTE; IF YOU ARE   3826
ASKING; "If you are asking how he is masking" e, i 143; "No use in guessing how he is dressing"
e, i 292; "You'd fain be hearing what dress he's wearing" e, i 6

[Ibid] "VOLTA LA TERREA FRONTE ALLE STELLE," Act I i 302; "Reading the stars on high eyes   3827
fiercely burning" e, i 6

[DON CARLOS, opera; words by J. Mery and C. du Commun du Locle]   3828
DORMIRÒ SOL NEL MANTO MIO REGAL, Act IV; "Ella giammai m'amò!" (recit); "Dormirò
sol nel manto mio regal" (aria); "Her love was never mine" (recit); "There I shall sleep in
royal state alone" (aria) e, i 5; ELLA GIAMMAI M'AMÒ i 299

[Ibid] LO LA VIDI, Act I; "Io l'ho perduta!" (recit); "Io la vidi e il suo sorriso" (aria); "Oh, I   3829
have lost her" (recit); "When I saw her smile in greeting" (aria) e, i 3

[Ibid] O DON FATALE, Act IV; "O don fatale, o don crudel" i 300; "Oh, fatal dower, oh cruel   3830
gift" e, i 2

[Ibid] PER ME GIUNTO, Act IV; "Son io, mio Carlo" (recit); "Per me giunto è il dì supremo"   3831
(aria); "'Tis I, dear Carlos" (recit); "My last sun today has risen" (aria) e, i 4

[Ibid] "TU CHE LE VANITÀ," Act V; "You who knew worldly pride" e, i 1   3832

[ERNANI, opera; words by F. M. Piave] ERNANI, INVOLAMI; "Sorta è la note, e   3833
non ritorna!" (recit); "Ernani! Ernani, involami" (aria); "Night is approaching, and Silva yet
returns not!" (recit); "Ernani, Ernani, fly with me" (aria) e, i 1

[Ibid] INFELICE! E TUO CREDEVI, Act I; "Che mai vegg'io!" (recit); "Infelice! e tuo credevi"   3834
(aria) i 299; "Do I see rightly?" (recit); "Cruel fortune, to dream that ever" (aria) e, i 5

[Ibid] INFIN CHE UN BRANDO VINDICE, Act I; "L'offeso onor, signore" (recit); "Infin che un   3835
brando vindice" (aria) i 299; AVENGING SWORD; "O Sirs, this must be punished" (recit);
"Avenging sword, still bright and strong" (aria) e, i 5

[Ibid] "LO VEDREMO, VEGLIO AUDACE," Act II; "We shall see, audacious old man" e, i 4   3836

[Ibid] OH! DE' VERD' ANNI MIEI; "Gran Dio! costor sui sepolcrali" (recit); "Oh! de' verd'   3837
anni miei" (aria) i 298

[FALSTAFF, opera; words by A. Boito] È SOGNO? O REALTÀ, Act II, Scene 1; "È   3838
sogno? o realtà...Due rami enormi"; FORD'S DREAM; "Am I awake? Or do I dream?" e, i 4

[Ibid] L'ONORE! LADRI!, Act I, Scene 1; "Ehi! paggio! Andante a impendervi" (recit); "L'onore!   3839
Ladri! Voi state ligi all' onor vostro, voi!" (aria); "Ho! page-boy! Be off and hang yourselves"
(recit); "Your honor! Ruffians! Ye dare to prate about your honor. Ye!" (aria) e, i 4

[Ibid] "SUL FIL D'UN SOFFIO ETESIO," Act IV; "FROM SECRET CAVES AND BOWERS" e, i 143   3840

[LA FORZA DEL DESTINO, opera; words by F. M. Piave] MADRE, PIETOSA   3841
VERGINE, Act II; "Son giunta! gazie, o Dio" (recit); "Madre, Madre, pietosa Vergine" (aria);
"In safety! Heav'n, I thank thee" (recit); "Mother, Mother of mercy, Maiden blest (aria) e, i 1

[Ibid] OH, TU CHE IN SENO AGLI ANGELI, Act III; "La vita è inferno all' infelice" (recit);   3842
"Oh, tu che in seno agli angeli" (aria); "Unhappy men find life infernal" (recit); "You dwell
with angel hosts on high" (aria) e, i 3

[Ibid] PACE, PACE, MIO DIO, Act IV; "Pace, pace, pace, pace, mio Dio" i 301; "Calm me,   3843
calm me, calm me, calm me, O Father" e, i 1

[Ibid] URNA FATALE, Act III; "Morir! Tremenda cosa!" (recit); "Urna fatale del mio destino"   3844
(aria); "To die, appalling fortune" (recit); "Destiny's secret held in your keeping" (aria) e, i 4

[MACBETH, opera; words by F. M. Piave] COME DAL CIEL PRECIPITA, Act II;   3845
"Studia il passo o mio figlio!" (recit); "Come dal ciel precipita" (aria); "O my son, still be
wary!" (recit); "How from the skied e'er darkening" (aria) e, i 5

[Ibid] PIETÀ, RISPETTO, ONORE, Act IV; "Perfidi! All' Anglo contro me v'unite" (recit); "Pietà,   3846
rispetto, onore" (aria); "Traitors all! With England you combine against me!" (recit); "Not love,
nor obedience, nor honor"(aria) e, i 4

THE MASKED BALL. See 3823-3827

[OTELLO, opera; words by A. Boito] AVE MARIA; "Ave Maria, piena di grazie"; "Ave   3847
Maria blest among women" e, i 143; PRAYER; "Hail, Mary, hail! in grace o'erflowing" e, i 1,6

[Ibid] CREDO, Act II; "Vanne; la tua meta gia vedo" (recit); "Credo in un Dio crudel" (aria);   3848
"Go, then; to thy doom thou art going" (recit); "Mine is a cruel God" (aria) e, i 310; CREDO
IN UN DIO e, i 4

[Ibid] SALCE! SALCE!, Act IV; "Mi parea, M'ingiunse di coricarmi" (recit); "Piangea cantando   3849
nell' erma landa" (aria); DESDEMONA'S ARIA; "So it seemed. He bade me soon to await him"
(recit); "The poor soul sat pining, alone and lonely" (aria) e, i 6; THE WILLOW SONG e, i 1;
CANZONE DEL SALICE; THE WILLOW SONG; "Poor soul, she sat sighing" (aria only) e, i 143

135

VERDI, GIUSEPPE, 1813-1901 (Continued)

[RIGOLETTO, opera; words by F. M. Piave] CARO NOME CHE IL MIO COR; "Gual- 3850
tier Maldè! nome di lui si amato" (recit); "Caro nome che il mio cor" (aria) i 302; "I know his
name: Walter Maldè! I love thee!" (recit); "HELD WITHIN MY INMOST HEART" (aria) e, i 221;
"Beloved name, Walter Maldè, I love you" (recit) i 93; "MOST BELOVED NAME OF ALL" (aria);
CARO NOME, DEAREST NAME; "Gualtier Maldè! Name that I love for ever" (recit); "Dearest
name, thy wondrous pow'r" (aria) e, i 143; "Gualtier Maldè! can I forget it?" (recit); "Dearest
name, forever nurs'd" (aria) e, i 6; "O dearest name Walter Maldè I love you" (recit); "Lovely
name that I adore" (aria) e, i 292

[Ibid] CORTIGIANI VIL RAZZA, Act II; "Si la mia figlia" (recit); "Cortigiani, vil razza 3851
dannata" (aria); "Yes, she's my daughter" (recit); "Race of courtiers, vile rabble detested" (aria)
e, i 4; FEILE SKLAVEN!; "Feile Sklaven! Ihr habt sie verhandelt sagt" (aria only) g, i 390

[Ibid] "LA DONNA È MOBILE," Act III; PLUME IN THE SUMMER WIND; "Plume in the summer 3852
wind waywardly playing" e, i 237; WOMAN IS FICKLE; "Woman is fickle, false altogether"
e, i 132,329; WOMAN SO CHANGEABLE; "Woman so changeable, swayed like a feather" e, i
3,122; O, WIE SO TRÜGERISCH; "O wie so trügerisch sind Weiberherzen" g, i 391

[Ibid] PARI SIAMO, Act I; "Pari siamo! io la lingua, egli ha il pugnale"; "Yon assassin is my 3853
equal; he stabs in darkness" e, i 4

[Ibid] PARMI VEDER LE LAGRIME, Act II; "Ella mi fu rapita!" (recit); "Parmi veder la lagrime 3854
scorrenti da quel ciglio" (aria); "Ah, cruel fate, I've lost her" (recit); "Art thou weeping in
loneliness, despairing and unfriended" (aria) e, i 3

[Ibid] QUESTA O QUELLA, Act I; "Questa o quella per me pari sono a quant' altre d'in torno"; 3855
FREUNDLICH BLICK ICH; "Freundlich blick ich auf diese und jene" g, i 391

[SIMON BOCCANEGRA, opera; words by F. M. Piave] "COME IN QUEST' ORA 3856
BRUNA," Act I; "Stars and the sea are smiling" e, i 1

[Ibid] IL LACERATO SPIRITO; "A te l'estremo addio, palagio altero" (recit); "Il lacerato 3857
spirito del mesto genitore" (aria) i 299; ROMANCE; "Farewell to thee for ever, thou haughty
palace" (recit); "Pity a father's wounded heart, torn by pangs of madness" (aria) e, i 5

[LA TRAVIATA, opera; words by F. M. Piave] ADDIO, DEL PASSATO BEI SOGNI 3858
RIDENTI, Act III; "Teneste la promessa...La disfida ebbe luogo" (recit); "Addio, del passato
bei sogni ridenti" (aria) i 301; SZENE UND ARIE DER VIOLETTA; "Ich harre vergebens, seh'
ihn niemals wieder!" (recit); "Leb't wohl jetzt, ihr Gebilde die ihr einst mich umfangen" (aria)
g 311

[Ibid] AH, FORS' È LUI CHE L'ANIMA; "È strano! è strano!" (recit); "Ah, fors' è lui che l'anima" 3859
(aria); IS HE THE ONE; "How strangely, how strangely" (recit); "Is he the one that my sad heart"
(aria) e, i 221; "Surprising! Surprising!" (recit); "Was this the man my fancy saw" (aria) e, i 6;
"How wondrous, how wondrous!" (recit); "Ah, was it he my heart foretold" (aria) e, i 176; AH,
FORSE È LUI; "How curious! How curious!" (recit); "CAN IT BE HE WHOSE IMAGE FAIR" (aria)
e, i 143

[Ibid] "DI PROVENZA IL MAR, IL SUOL," Act II i 298; DI PROVENCE; FAIR PROVENCE; 3860
"To our fair Provence come home" e, i 310; DI PROVENZA IL MAR; "Is the memory erased"
e, i 4

[IL TROVATORE, opera; words by S. Cammarano] "AH SÌ, BEN MIO: COLL' 3861
ESSERE," Act III; CAVATINA; "Oh, come, let links eternal bind" e, i 3

[Ibid] IL BALEN DEL SUO SORRISO, Act II; "Tutto e deserto, ne per l'aure" (recit); "Il balen 3862
del suo sorriso" (aria) i 298; "We are alone here; even in the air I hear not the usual singing"
(recit); "When she smiles, the starlight gleaming" (aria) e, i 4; IHRES AUGES HIMMLISCH
STRAHLEN; "Ihres Auges himmlisch Strahlen leuchtet schöner" (aria only) g, i 390

[Ibid] "CONDOTTA ELL' ERA IN CEPPI," Act II i 300; "In chains to her doom they dragged 3863
her" e, i 2

[Ibid] D'AMOR SULL' ALI ROSEE, Act IV; "Timor de me Sicura, presta è la mia difesa" (recit); 3864
"D'amor sull' ali rosee" (aria); BREEZE OF THE NIGHT; "I tremble not from all I fear'd, shall
this ring now secure me" (recit); "Breeze of the night with your gentlest breath" (aria) e, i 143;
"Why fear for me? My safeguard ever I have thee near me" (recit); "Love, fly on rosy pinions,
float in a dream around him" (aria) e, i 1

[Ibid] DI DUE FIGLI VIVEA PADRE BEATO; "La dirò, venite in torno a me" (recit); "Abbieta 3865
zingara, fosca vegliarda!" (aria); "Yes, I will, draw nearer unto me" (recit); "Swarthy and
threatening a gipsy woman" (aria) e, i 5

[Ibid] DI QUELLA PRIA, Act III; "Di quella pira l'orrendo foco"; LODERN ZUM HIMMEL; 3866
"Lodern zum Himmel seh' ich die Flammen" g, i 391

[Ibid] STRIDE LA VAMPA, Act II; "Stride la vampa la folla indomita" i 300; "Fierce flames 3867
are soaring" e, i 2

[Ibid] "TACEA LA NOTTE PLACIDA," Act I; "The night was calm and peacefully in deep blue 3868
sky reposing" e, i 6; "No star shone in the heav'nly vault" e, i 1; "'TWAS NIGHT AND ALL
AROUND WAS STILL" e, i 143; "TACEA LA NOTTE PLACIDA E BELLA IN CIEL SERENO" i 301

VERDI, GIUSEPPI, 1813-1901 (Continued)

    [Ibid] [Vedi! le fosche, Act II] ANVIL CHORUS; "God of the nations, in glory   3869
enthroned" e 28

    [LES VÊPRES SICILIENNES, opera; words by A. E. Scribe and C. Duvey-   3870
rier] O TU, PALERMO, TERRA ADORATA, Act II; "O patria, o cara patria" (recit); "O tu,
Palermo, terra adorata" (aria) i 299

VILLOLDO, A. G.

    ARRÍMATE, VIDA MIA; "Hace días que ando triste"; DRAW CLOSER, MY LOVE; "Until now each   3871
hour was dreary" e, s 9

    EL CHOCLO; "Allá en Río había un joven muy celoso"; "Ay! Ay! El Choclo" (ref); "Way down in   3872
Rio once there lived a jealous lover" e, s 132

VINCZE, ZSIGMOND

    SZÉP VAGY, GYÖNYÖRÜ VAGY; "Hol szöke sellö, lenge szello"; MAGYAR LAND; "Where nymphs   3873
and breezes on the Tisza" e, hu 285

Violinsky, pseud. See GINSBERG, SOL, 1885-

VIOTTA, JOHANN JOSEPHUS, 1814-1859

    EEN SCHEEPJE; "Een scheepje in de haven landt"; A LITTLE SHIP; "A little ship sails into port"   3874
d, e 316; EEN GANGSPILDEUNTJE d 384

    DE ZILVERVLOOT; "Heb je van de Zilveren Vloot wel gehoord" d 384; PIET HEIN; THE SILVER   3875
FLEET; "Did you ever hear of the great Silver Fleet" d, e 316; HET TRIOMPHANTELIJK LIED
VAN DE ZILVERVLOOT d 201

VITALI, FILIPPO, ca1600-1653

    O BEI LUMI; "O bei lumi, o chiome d'oro" i 180   3876

    PASTORELLA; "Pastorella ove t'ascondi, dove fuggi oimè" i 181   3877

    "S'EL SOL SI SCOSTA" (duet) i 181   3878

Vitols, Joesph. See WIHTOLS, JOSEF, 1863-1948

VIVALDI, ANTONIO, ca1680-1741

    ARIA; "Un certo non so che mi giunge e passa il cor"; "Es schleicht mir was ins Herz und doch ich   3879
weiss nicht was" g, i 168

    [INGRATA] O DI TUA MAN; "O di tua man mi svena" i 181   3880

    [JUDITHA TRIUMPHANS, oratorio] "VULTUS TUI VAGO SPLENDORI"; TO THE RADI-   3881
ANT BEAUTY OF YOUR FACE lat 367

    PIANGO GEMO; PASSACAGLIA; "Piango, gemo, sospiro e peno" i 181   3882

VIVES, AMADEO, 1871-1932

    EL CARRO DEL SOL. See 3429

VOIGT, HERMANN

    [MUTTERLIEBE, OP.148] MOTHER-LOVE; "As in a dream I yet remember" e 122   3883

VOIGTLÄNDER, GABRIEL, ca1591-1643

    WEIBERNEHMEN IST KEIN PFERDEKAUF; "Jungesell, will tu freien" g 250   3884

VOMÁČKA, BOLESLAV, 1887-

    VOJAK V POLI, op.11, no.2; "Vrátimli se domů, půjdu naší ulicí"; DER SOLDAT IM FELDE;   3885
"Wenn ich wieder heimkomm, bieg ich ein in unsre Gasse" c, g 74 words by F. Šrámek

VON TILZER, HARRY, 1872-1946

    THE MANSION OF ACHING HEARTS; "The last dance was over"; "She lives in a mansion of   3886
aching hearts" (ref) e 131 (ref only) e 128 words by A. J. Lamb

    SOMEBODY'S WAITING FOR ME; "It was in a Concert Garden where the fun was at its height";   3887
"Somebody's waiting for me" (ref) e 131 (ref only) e 128 words by A. Sterling

    THE SPIDER AND THE FLY; "Kiss me goodnight mother darling"; "Think of the spider, a man so   3888
false" (ref) e 131 words by A. J. Lamb

    WHERE THE MORNING GLORIES TWINE AROUND THE DOOR; "Down in New England, far, far away";   3889
"Now, the same old moon is shining" (ref) e 131 (ref only) e 128 words by A. Sterling

VOUSDEN, VALENTINE

    THE BONNIE BLUE FLAG. See 2222

    HOMESPUN DRESS. See 2222

VRANKEN, JOSEPH, 1870-1948

    DE HEI; "O de bruine, de geurige, zonige hei" d 384 words by G. H. Priem   3890

VULPIUS, MELCHIOR, ca1560-1615

    "DIE HELLE SONNE LEUCHT' JETZT HERFÜR" g 49 words by N. Herman   3891

    "HINUNTER IST DER SONNEN SCHEIN" g 49 words by N. Herman   3892

VYCPÁLEK, LADISLAV, 1882-

    ZIMNÍ VEČER, op.5, no.2; "Jde k západu slunce a krev lká na ztuhlý sníh"; WINTERABEND; "Die   3893
sinkende Sonne weint blutig auf starren Schnee" c, g 74 words by L. Vycpálek

WAGNER, RICHARD, 1813-1883 (Continued)

    TRÄUME; "Sag' welch' wunderbare Träume"; DREAMS; "Dreams of mystical enchantment"   3921
    e, g 122; "Say, oh say what wondrous dreamings" e, g 220; "Tell me what these dreams of
    wonder" e, g 241; DREAMING; "Ah, what wonder lies in dreaming" e 348   words by M.
    Wesendonck

    [TRISTAN UND ISOLDE, opera] MILD UND LEISE, Act III; "Mild und leise wie er   3922
    lächelt"; ISOLDE'S LIEBESTOD; "Mild and softly he is smiling" e, g 1

    [Ibid] TATEST DU'S WIRKLICH? Act II, Scene 3; "Tatest du's wirklich? Wähnst du das?";   3923
    "Hast thou tho', truly? Think'st thou so?" e, g 5

    [DIE WALKÜRE, opera] LEB' WOHL!, Act III; "Leb' wohl! du kühnes herrliches Kind!";   3924
    WOTAN'S FAREWELL AND FIRE MUSIC; "Fare-well, thou valiant glorious child!" e, g 4

    [Ibid] DER MÄNNER SIPPE, Act I; "Schläfst du Gast?" (recit); "Der Männer Sippe sass hier im   3925
    Saal" (aria); SIEGLINDE'S NARRATIVE; "Sleep'st thou, guest?" (recit); "The kinsmen gathered
    here in the hall" (aria) e, g 1

    [Ibid] "WINTERSTÜRME WICHEN DEM WONNEMOND," Act I, Scene 3; SIEGMUND'S LOVE-   3926
    SONG; "Winter storms have waned to the winsome moon" e, g 3

    [Ibid] "WO IN BERGEN DU DICH BIRGST"; FRICKA'S SCENE; "Where in mountain wilds thou   3927
    hid'st" e, g 2

WAINWRIGHT, JOHN, ca1723-1768

    CHRISTIANS, AWAKE; Yorkshire (tune); "Christians awake, salute the happy morn" e 333,   3928
    337,410; "CHRISTIANS, AWAKE, SALUTE THE HAPPY MORN" e 38,39,251,307   words
    by J. Byrom

WALBE, Y.

    MA-ASEH SEH UG'DI; "Seh ugedi g'di vasch"; THE GOAT AND THE LAMB; "See how the giddy   3929
    goat behaved" e, h (tr) 30

WALDEN, ALFRED J.

    MADEMOISELLE FROM ARMENTIERES. See 7665

WALDMANN, LUDOLF, 1840-1919

    DIE ALTEN DEUTSCHEN TRANKEN JA AUCH!, op.51; "Sitz ich in froher Zecher Kreise" g 31   3930

WALKER, ERNEST, 1870-1949

    CORINNA'S GOING A-MAYING; "Get up, get up for shame, the blooming morn" e 344   words by   3931
    R. Herrick

WALLACE, WILLIAM VINCENT, 1812-1865

    THE FLAG OF OUR UNION; "A song for our banner?" e 189   words by G. P. Morris   3932

WALLEK-WALEWSKI, BOLESLAV, 1885-1940

    "A KIEDY PRZYJDĘ JUŻ DZIEWCZYNO"; "I SHALL MEET YOU TONIGHT" e, p 159   words by   3933
    T. Piotrowski

    FLORYJAŃSKA BRAMA; "Floryjańską bramą, Wjadę otworzoną, biczyskiem se smigam"; FLORIAN'S   3934
    GATE; "Florian's gate wide open, Gee-up, horse my pretty, my whip cracks you gallop" e, p 159

WALTHER, JOHANN, 1496-1570

    ALL' MORGEN; "All' morgen ist ganz frisch und neu" g 49   words by J. Zwick   3935
    "WACH AUF, WACH AUF, DU DEUTSCHES LAND" g 49,326   3936

WALTHER, EMIL, 1867-

    MORGENLIED IM MAI; "Durch die morgenroten Scheiben" g 31   words by W. Flex   3937

WALTHEW, RICHARD HENRY, 1872-1951

    ELDORADO; "Gaily bedight, a gallant knight" e 344   words by E. A. Poe   3938
    MISTRESS MINE; "Oh, Mistress, mine, where are you roaming?" e 344   words by W. Shakespeare,   3939
    Twelfth Night
    "THE SPLENDOUR FALLS" e 344   words by A. Tennyson   3940

WARD, ARTHUR E.

    THE PURPLE ORCHID; "Oh press this purple flow'r close to thy tender heart" e 387   words by M.   3941
    Brainard

WARD, CHARLES B., 1865-1917

    THE BAND PLAYED ON; "Matt Casey formed a social club"; "For Casey would waltz with a   3942
    strawberry blonde" (ref) e 114,115,131,204 (ref only) e 128,132,233,236,   words by J. F.
    Palmer

WARD, CHARLIE L.

    THINK OF YOUR HEAD IN THE MORNING; "Tom Jennings who never could drinking avoid" e 161   3943

WARD, SAMUEL A.

    AMERICA THE BEAUTIFUL; Materna (tune); "O beautiful for spacious skies" e 10,28,129,130,233,   3944
    236,279,284,343,366

Warlamoff, Alexander Jegorowitsch. See VARLAMOV, ALEKSANDR IGOROVITCH,
    1801-1848

Warlock, Peter, pseud. See HESELTINE, PHILIP, 1894-1930

WARNER, THEODOR

    MORGEN; "Herrlich bricht aus Wolkenschleiern schon der Sonne frühster Strahl" g 49   3945

WARREN, GEORGE WILLIAM, 1828-1902
    "GOD OF OUR FATHERS, WHOSE ALMIGHTY HAND" e 129,130,326; GOD OF OUR FATHERS   3946
      e 28,279,343,366   words by D. C. Roberts
WARREN, HARRY, 1893-
    BY THE RIVER SAINTE MARIE; "I left her by the river Sainte Marie" e 236   words by E. Leslie   3947
    DON'T GIVE UP THE SHIP; "Shipmates, stand together, don't give up the ship" e 233   3948
WARSHAVSKY, MORRIS MARK, 1848-1907
    "KINDER, MIR HOBN SIMCHES TOYRE!"; "Children, we'll have a celebration" e, y 318   3949
    DI MEZINKE OYSGEGEBN; "Shtarker, beser! Di rod, di rod macht greser!"; "Larger, longer,   3950
      make the dance-ring stronger" e, y 318
WATERS, SAFFORD
    THE BELLE OF AVENOO A; "I am de belle dey say ov Avenoo 'A'" e 204   3951
WATKINS, MARGERY
    I WILL LIFT UP MINE EYES; "I will lift up mine eyes unto the hills" e 398   3952
WATTS, WINTTER, 1884-
    "BLUE ARE HER EYES" e 137,241   words by M. MacMillan   3953
    ISLE OF BEAUTY; CAPRI; "When beauty grows too great to bear" e 241   words by S. Teasdale   3954
    WINGS OF NIGHT; "Dreamily over the roofs" e 259   words by S. Teasdale   3955
WEATHERLY, F. E.
    TIME WAS; "Time was we were young and life was song and play" e 129,130   3956
WEBB, GEORGE JAMES, 1803-1887
    "HAIL TO THE LORD'S ANOINTED" e 315   words by J. Montgomery   3957
    "STAND UP, STAND UP, FOR JESUS" e 35   words by G. Duffield   3958
WEBB, WILLIAM
    "OF THEE, KIND BOY, I ASKE NO RED AND WHITE" e 106   words by J. Suckling   3959
WEBBE, SAMUEL, 1740-1816
    NOW WE ARE MET; "Now we are met let mirth abound" 3 pt round e 235   3960
    "WOULD YOU KNOW MY CELIA'S CHARMS?" 4 pt round e 349   3961
WEBER, BERNHARD ANSELM, 1766-1821
    MIT DEM PFEIL, DEM BOGEN; "Mit dem Pfeil dem Bogen durch Gebirg und Tal" g 326,353   words   3962
      by F. von Schiller
WEBER, KARL MARIA FRIEDRICH ERNST, FREIHERR VON, 1786-1826
    AN JUNGE SPRÖDE SCHÖNEN, op.15, no.5; "Ich sah ein Röschen am Wege stehn" g 99   words by   3963
      C. Müchler
    [DER FREISCHÜTZ, opera; words by F. Kind] BRAUTJUNGFERNLIED, Act III; "Wir   3964
      winden dir den Jungfernkranz mit veilchenblauer Seide" g 99; "WIR WINDEN DIR DEN JUNGFERN-
      KRANZ" g 326,353
    [Ibid] DURCH DIE WALDER, DURCH DIE AUEN, Act I; "Nein! länger trag' ich nicht die Qualen"   3965
      (recit); "Durch die Walder, durch die Auen" (aria) g 391; DURCH DIE WALDER; "No! I can
      bear my fate no longer" (recit); "Through the forests, through the meadows" (aria) e, g 3
    [Ibid] "LEISE, LEISE, FROMME WEISE", Act II (aria) g 336; EVENING PRAYER; "Softly sighs   3966
      the breath of evening" (aria) e 28,366; SZENE UND ARIE DER AGATHE; "Wie nahte mir der
      Schlummer, bevor ich ihn geseh'n?" (recit); "Leise, leise, fromme Weise" (aria) g 311; WIE
      NAHTE MIR DER SCHLUMMER; "How could I fain have slumbered before his face I saw" (recit);
      "Holy, holy, meek and lowly" (aria) e, g 1
    [Ibid] UND OB DIE WOLKE, Act III; "Und ob die Wolke sie verhülle;" "And though a cloud o'er-   3967
      spread yon heaven" e, g 1; CAVATINE DER AGATHE g 311
    HEIMLICHTER LIEBE PEIN, op.64, no.3; "Mein Schatz der ist auf die Wanderschaft hin" g 99,229   3968
    "ICH LOBE MIR DAS BURSCHENLEBEN" g 31   3969
    [LEYER UND SCHWERT, OP.42, song cycle] LÜTZOWS WILDE JAGD, no.2; "Was   3970
      glänzt dort vom Walde" g 99; LUTZOW'S WILD HUNT; "From yonder dark forest" e 28   words
      by T. Körner
    [Ibid] SCHWERTLIED, no.6; "Du Schwert an meiner Linken" g 99   words by T. Körner   3971
    [OBERON, opera; words by J. R. Planche] "OZEAN! DU UNGEHEUER!," Act II;   3972
      "Ocean! thou mighty monster" e, g 1
    [PRECIOSA, incidental music, OP.78; words by W. A. P. Wolff] "EINSAM   3973
      BIN ICH NICHT ALLEINE," no.6 g 99
    [Ibid] DIE SONN' ERWACHT; "Die Sonn' erwacht, mit ihrer Pracht er füllt sie die Berge" g 326   3974
    "SOFTLY NOW THE LIGHT OF DAY" e 28,132,233,236,366   3975
    UNBEFANGENHEIT, op.30, no.3; "Frage mich immer fragest umsonst!" g 250   3976
    WIEGENLIED, op.13, no.3; "Schlaf, Herzenssöhnchen, mein Liebling bist du" g 99; CRADLE   3977
      SONG; "Sleep, my heart's darling, in slumber repose" e 132   words by F. C. Hiemer
WEBSTER, JOSEPH PHILBRICK, 1819-1875
    GET OUT OF MEXICO; "While old Uncle Sam was busy"; "Oh! poor Max, there's no use talking"   3978
      (ref) e 189   words by E. B. Dewing

WEBSTER, JOSEPH PHILBRICK, 1819-1875 (Continued)

    IN THE SWEET BY AND BY; "There's a land that is fairer than day" e 32,34; SWEET BY-AND-BY   3979
e 129,130 words by S. F. Bennett; THE PREACHER AND THE SLAVE; "Long-haired preachers
come out ev'ry night" e 109,110; PIE IN THE SKY; "Long haired preachers come here every
night" e 225 words by J. Hill

    LORENA; "The years creep slowly by, Lorena" e 36,161,212 words by H. D. L. Webster   3980

WEINER, M.

    HAY'TAH ARTSI; "Lo od yitshal edri vagay"; THE STRANGER TOOK THE LAND I HAD; "My flock   3981
is no longer happy and gay" e, h (tr) 30

    NA-ALZAH V'NISM'CHA; "Na-alzah v'nismechah"; "LET US DANCE WHILE WE REJOICE" e, h (tr)   3982
30

    SE UG' DI; "Se ug' di g'di vase"; "A lamb and a kid, a kid and a lamb" e, h (tr) 318   3983

WEITZNER, GÉZA

    GYERE CIGÁNY; "Gyere cigány, huzzad nékem"; PLAY YOUR MUSIC, GYPSY; "Play your music,   3984
Gypsy, play it" e, hu 285

WELDON, WILLIAM

    OUTSKIRTS OF TOWN; "I'm gonna move 'way out on the outskirts of town" e 336   3985

WELSH, MARY ANNE (WILSON), 1802-1867

    MUSICAL ALPHABET; "A for an apple, an archer, and arrow" e 189   3986

WEMAN, HENRY

    "SE, MEN INTE RÖRA" sw 356 words by H. Gullberg   3987

WENRICH, PERCY, d 1952

    BY THE CAMP FIRE; "Come where the camp-fire is gleaming" e 129,130 words by M. E. Girling   3988

    MOONLIGHT BAY; "We were sailing along on Moonlight Bay" e 233 words by E. Madden   3989

    "PUT ON YOUR OLD GREY BONNET" e 233 words by S. Murphy   3990

    WHEN YOU WORE A TULIP AND I WORE A BIG RED ROSE; "I met you in a garden in an old Kentucky   3991
town"; "When you wore a tulip, a sweet yellow tulip" (ref) e 131; WHEN YOU WORE A TULIP
(ref only) e 128,129,130,236 words by J. Mahoney

    "WHERE DO WE GO FROM HERE?" e 129,130,236 words by H. Johnson   3992

WERNER, HEINRICH, 1800-1833

    HEIDENRÖSLEIN; "Sah ein Knab ein Röslein steht" g 31,42,99; "SAH EIN KNAB EIN RÖSLEIN   3993
STEHN" g 326,353; THE TWO ROSES; "On a bank two roses fair" e 28,132,366 words by
J. W. von Goethe

WESLEY, ALICE P.

    AT REST; "Out of the old life into the new" e 398 words by M. V. Freese   3994

WESLEY, S. S., 1663-1735

    BRIGHTEST AND BEST; "Brightest and best of the sons of the morning" e 379 words by   3995
R. Heber

WESLEY, SAMUEL SEBASTIAN, 1810-1876

    THE CHURCH'S ONE FOUNDATION; Aurelia (tune); "The Church's one foundation Is Jesus Christ   3996
her Lord" e 236 words by S. J. Stone

    "PRAISE THE LORD, O MY SOUL" e 160 words from Psalms   3997

WEST, W. H. C.

    THE JENNY LIND MANIA; "Oh! Manias we've had many" e 189   3998

WESTENDORF, THOMAS P.

    I'LL TAKE YOU HOME AGAIN, KATHLEEN"; "Oh! I will take you back again" (ref) e 128,129,130,   3999
131,132,343; "Oh! I will take you back, Kathleen" (ref) e 10,36,166,329; "I will take you back,
Kathleen" (ref) e 115,233

    WHAT WOULD YOU TAKE FOR ME, PAPA?; "Say what would you take for me, papa?" e 114   4000

WESTON, H. BURGESS

    ROW, BURNIE, ROW; "Row, Burnie, row, through the bracken glen" e 344 words by W. C. Smith   4001

WEYRAUCH, AUGUST HEINRICH VON

    ADIEU!; "Voici l'instant suprême"; FAREWELL; "At last the hour approacheth"; e, f 209 words   4002
by K. F. G.Wetzel, att to F. Schubert

WEYSE, CHRISTOPHER ERNST FRIEDRICH, 1774-1842

    "DAGEN GAAR MED RASKE FJED"; "DAY'S SWIFT STEP WILL NOW SOON CEASE" da, e 87 words   4003
by B. S. Ingemann

    "DANEVANG MED GRØNNE BRED"; "DANEVANG; OH LOVELY SHORE"; da, e 87 words by B. S.   4004
Ingemann

    DER ER ET LAND; "Der er et Land, dets Sted er højt mod Norden"; THERE IS A LAND; "There is   4005
a land, far north in gleaming ocean" da, e 87 words by B. S. Ingemann

    "I ØSTEN STIGER SOLEN OP"; THE SUN IS RISING; "The sun is rising in the sky" da, e 87 words   4006
by B. S. Ingemann

    "MORGENSTUND HAR GULD I MUND"; "MORNING HOUR LIKE GOLD HAS POWER" da, e 87 words   4007
by B. S. Ingemann

WEYSE, CHRISTOPHER ERNST FRIEDRICH, 1774-1842 (Continued)

"NU RINGER ALLE KLOKKER MOD SKY"; "THE BELLS ARE RINGING IN THE SKY" da, e 87   words   4008
by B. S. Ingemann

"NU TITTE TIL HINANDEN"; "NOW PEEP THEY AT EACH OTHER" da, e 87   words by B. S. Inge-   4009
mann

WHITE,

GREAT TOM IS CAST; "Great Tom is cast, and Christ Church Bells ring"   3 pt round   e 235,349   4010

WHITE, CHARLES ALBERT, 1832-1892

"I'SE GWINE BACK TO DIXIE"   e 10,114,129,130,132   4011

WHITE, COOL

LUBLY FAN.   See 7478A

WHITE, MATTHEW

"MY DAME HATH A LAME TAME CRANE"   4 pt round   e 235,349   4012

WHITE, MAUDE VALÉRIE, 1855-1937

"CRABBED AGE AND YOUTH"   e 344   words by W. Shakespeare   4013
KING CHARLES; "Who gave me the goods that went since?"   e 272   words by R. Browning   4014
OPHELIA'S SONG; "How should I your true love know"   e 344   words by W. Shakespeare, Hamlet   4015
TO MARY; "O Mary dear, that you were here"   e 277   words by P. B. Shelley   4016

WHITE EAGLE, CHIEF

HI-YO WITZI; MORNING SONG; "Hi-yo hi-yo witzi nai-yo"   North American Indian dialect and   4017
e mixed 37

WHITING, RICHARD A., 1891-1938

AIN'T WE GOT FUN; "Bill collectors gather 'round and rather haunt the cottage next door"; "Ev'ry   4018
morning, ev'ry evening, ain't we got fun" (ref)   e 345   words by G. Kahn and R. B. Egan
"I WONDER WHERE MY BUDDIES ARE TONIGHT?"   e 129,130   words by B. Rose and R. B. Egan   4019
TILL WE MEET AGAIN; "Smile the while you kiss me sad adieu"   e 233   words by R. B. Egan   4020

WHITNEY, A.

OVER THE RIVER; "Over the river they beckon to me"   e 205   4021

WIANT, BLISS

MOON AND STARS OF CHRISTMAS EVE; "Stars of ice and a wheeling moon"   e 244   words by L. A.   4022
Ely

WIDOR, CHARLES MARIE, 1845-1937

SOUPIR; "J'ai laissé de mon sein de neige"; THE SIGH; "From my breast dropt a lovely flowret"   4023
e, f 140   words by T. Gautier

WIGGINS, KATE DOUGLAS

MORNING PRAYER; "Father, we thank Thee for the night"   e 28   4024

WIHTOLS, JOSEF, 1863-1948

AMARYLLIS ERZÄHLT...; "Herzenkönig und Pikdame sind in meinem Kartenschlosse"; AMARILIS   4025
RACONTE; "Roi de coeur et dame de pique Mon château de rêves habitent"   f, g 224
DER TRAUM DER ORCHIDÉE; "Hinter den Scheiben fiel Dämmerschein nieder"; LE RÊVE   4026
D'ORCHIDÉE; "Sur l'oreiller dans les draps de toile"   f, g 224
DIE WELLE; "Hell strahlt die Sonne am tiefblauen Himmel"; L'ONDE; "Bleu est le ciel si belle la   4027
journée"   f 224

WIKANDER, DAVID

TYST SERENAD; "Bland körsbärsblom i maanens ljus staar vitt"   sw 356   words by S. Agrell   4028

WIKLUND, ADOLF, 1879-1950

"TRE ROSOR HAR JAG PLOCKAT"   sw 356   4029

WILBYE, JOHN, 1574-1638

"ADEW SWEET AMARILLIS"   e 144   4030

WILDER, FRANK

FATHER, DEAR FATHER, COME DOWN WITH THE STAMPS; "O father, dear father, come down   4031
with the stamps"   e 225

WILDNER, OTTO, 1855-1927

DER PRAGER MUSIKANT; "Mit der Fiedel auf dem Rukken"   g 31   words by W. Müller   4032

WILHELM, CARL FRIEDRICH, 1815-1873

DIE WACHT AM RHEIN; "Es braust ein Ruf wie Donnerhall"   g 43   4033

WILHOITE, DONALD MAC RAE, 1909-

OFF TO SEE THE WORLD; "The ships are all shined up"   e 205   joint composer G. de Paul   4034
A SAILOR'S LIFE FOR ME; "We chip the scuppers and paint the hull, and scrub the decks and then";   4035
"A sailor's life is merry" (ref)   e 205   joint composer G. de Paul
"WE'RE IN THE NAVY"   e 205   joint composer G. de Paul   4036

WILLIAMS, THOMAS E., d 1854

LARBOARD WATCH; "At lonely midnight's cheerless hour"   e 205   4037

WILLING, WILLIAM

TWENTY YEARS AGO; "I've wander'd to the village Tom"   e 212,321   4038

WILLIS, RICHARD STORRS, 1819-1900
"IT CAME UPON THE MIDNIGHT CLEAR" e 28,38,39,125,165,206,233,236,251,296,307,315,366,   4039
388,394; "IT CAME UPON A MIDNIGHT CLEAR" e 33,79,337 words by E. H. Sears
WILSON, H. LANE
CARMENA; "Dance and song make glad the night" e 329 words by E. Walton   4040
WILSON, HARRY ROBERT
GRACE; "We thank Thee for our daily bread" 3 pt round e 343   4041
A ROUND OF LAUGHTER; "Laughter makes the world go round" e 343   4042
WILSON, JOHN, 1595-1674
"GAE BRING TO ME A PINT O' WINE" e 100,102 words by R. Burns   4043
LANGUISH AND DISPAIR, MY HEART; "Languish and dispair, my heart, and let thy groans to hills   4044
ascend" e 278
WILSON, WALTER
AIN'T DAT A SHAME; "One dark and stormy night"; "Ain't dat a shame, a measly shame" (ref)   4045
e 114,131 (ref only) e 128 words by J. Queen
WINKLER, GERHARD
CHIANTI-LIED; JA, JA, DER CHIANTIWEIN; "Hoch die Gläser, hoch das Leben" g 223 words by   4046
R. M. Siegel
"MÖWE, DU FLIEGST IN DIE HEIMAT" g 223 words by G. Schwenn   4047
WINNER, JOSEPH E.
LITTLE BROWN JUG; "My wife and I lived all alone" e 32,34,109,110,225,233; "My wife and I   4048
live all alone" e 129,130,131,132; THE UNION WAY; "My wife and I, we lived alone" e 293
words by R. Glaser; MISTER CONGRESSMAN; "Congressman, mister congressman" e 293 words
by A. Cunningham
OIL ON THE BRAIN; "The Yankees boast that they can make clocks" e 225   4049
WINNER, SEPTIMUS, 1827-1902
ABRAHAM'S DAUGHTER; "Oh, kind folks, listen to my song" e 44,110   4050
"GOD SAVE OUR PRESIDENT" e 129,130   4051
LISTEN TO THE MOCKING BIRD; "I'm dreaming now of Hallie" e 32,34,109,110,132; "I'm   4052
dreaming now of Hally, sweet Hally" e 128,129,130,184,279,366
OUT OF WORK; "Out of work without a penny" e 189   4053
"WHAT IS A HOME WITHOUT A MOTHER?" e 129,130   4054
WHISPERING HOPE; "Soft as the voice of an angel" e 122,128,129,130,132,329,346   4055
WINTER, BANKS
WHITE WINGS; "Sail! home as straight as an arrow" e 34,114   4056
WINTER-TYMIAN, EMIL
AM ELTERNGRAB, op.202; "Ich kenn' ein einsam Plätzchen auf der Welt" g 327   4057
WIRÉN, DAG IVAR, 1905-
EN HÖSTENS KVÄLL, op.13b; "En höstens kväll en stormens kväll"; IN HERBSTESNACHT; "In   4058
Herbstesnacht in Sturmesnacht"; AN AUTUMN EVE; "An autumn eve, a stormy eve" e, g, sw
356 words by E. A. Karlfeldt
OM TILL DIN BÄDD, op.13a; "Om till din bädd om till din bädd"; WENN AN DEIN BETT; "Wenn   4059
an dein Bett wenn an dein Bett"; IF O'ER THE FLOOR; "If o'er the floor the softly creaking floor"
e, g, sw 356 words by E. A. Karlfeldt
WITHERS, WILLIAM
HAIL TO THE CHIEF; "Hail to the chief who in triumph advances" e 212   4060
WITT, FRIEDRICH, 1770-1837
AVE MARIA; "Ave Maria gratia plena" lat 382   4061
WIZLAV VON RÜGEN, fl 1290
WEH, ICH HAB GEDACHT; "Weh, ich hab gedacht all diese Nacht an mein so gross Beschwere"   4062
g 226
WOHLGEMUTH, GUSTAV, 1863-1937
WIE'S DAHEIM WAR; "Wie's daheim war, wo die Wiege stand" g 326 words by P. Cornelius   4063
WOLF, HUGO, 1860-1903
ANAKREON'S GRAB; "Wo die Rose hier blüht, wo Reben im Lorbeer sich schlingen" g 226,250;   4064
ANACREON'S GRAVE; "Here where roses still bloom, where tendrils of laurels are twining" e, g
220
AUF DEM GRÜNEN BALCON; "Auf dem grünen Balcon mein Mädchen schaut nach mir"; FROM HER   4065
BALCONY GREEN; "From her balcony green my maiden peeps at me" e, g 112 words by P. Heyse
AUF EIN ALTES BILD; "In grüner Landschaft Sommerflor, bei kühlem Wasser, Schlif und Rohr" g 226   4066
words by E. Mörike
[AUS DER KINDERZEIT. SCHLUMMERLIED] WIEGENLIED; "Su, su, su, du Windchen,   4067
sing' zur Ruh mein Kindchen" g 308 words by A. Wette
BESCHEIDENE LIEBE; "Ich bin wie and're Mädchen nicht"; MODEST HEART; "I'm not as other   4068
lassies" e, g 330; THE UNPRETENTIOUS LOVER; "I am not like other maids" e, g 112

WOLF, HUGO, 1860-1903 (Continued)

DENK ES, O SEELE; "Ein Tännlein grünet wo, wer weiss, im Walde" g 98   words by E. Mörike — 4069

ER IST'S; "Fruhling lässt sein blaues Band"; SONG TO SPRING; "Spring her azure banner flings" — 4070
e, g 359   words by E. Mörike

DER FEUERREITER; "Sehet ihr am Fensterlein dort" g 250   words by E. Mörike — 4071

FUSSREISE; "Am frisch geschnitt'nen Wanderstab"; A-WALKING; "When with my trusty walking- — 4072
stick" e, g 121; TRAMPING; "With fresh-cut staff, at break of day" e, g 359   words by E.
Mörike

DER GÄRTNER; "Auf ihrem Leibrösslein, so weiss wie der Schnee" g 97   words by E. Mörike — 4073

GEBET; "Herr! schicke was du willt, ein Liebes oder Leides" g 98; PRAYER; "Lord, grant me — 4074
what Thou wilt of pleasure or of sorrow" e, g 408   words by E. Mörike

GESANG WEYLA'S; "Du bist Orplid, mein land!"; WEYLA'S SONG; "Hail, sacred Isle! dear — 4075
land!" e, g 121; MY NATIVE LAND; "This is my native land" e 348; REVELATION; "And
there came unto me one of the seven angels" (recit); "I saw the Holy City with tow'rs brightly
glowing" (aria), recit by K. K. Davis   e 89   words from Revelation XXI:9,10

IN DEM SCHATTEN MEINER LOCKEN; "In dem Schatten meiner Locken schlief mir mein Geliebter — 4076
ein"; IN THE FOLDS OF MY EMBRACE; "In the folds of my embrace my dear one has fallen
asleep" e, g 220; IN THE SHADOW OF MY TRESSES; "In the shadow of my tresses, fast asleep
my loved one lies" e, g 112   words by P. Heyse

IN DER FRÜHE; "Kein Schlaf noch kühlt das Auge mir"; AT DAYBREAK; "And still no sleep has — 4077
cooled my eyes" e, g 112   words by E. Mörike

LEBE WOHL!; "Lebe wohl! Du fühlest nicht"; FAREWELL; "Fare you well! You do not know" e, g — 4078
112   words by E. Mörike

MAUSFALLEN-SPRÜCHLEIN; "Kleine Gäste, kleines Haus, liebe Mausin, oder Maus" g 250   words — 4079
by E. Mörike

MIGNON; "Kennst du das Land, wo die Zitronen blühn"; "Know you that land where fruit so richly — 4080
grows" e, g 112   words by J. W. von Goethe

NIMMERSATTE LIEBE; "So ist die Lieb'! So ist die Lieb'! Mit Küssen nicht zu stillen"; INSATIABLE — 4081
LOVE; "'Tis true, alas, that love is not with just a kiss abated" e, g 112   words by E. Mörike

NUN WANDRE, MARIA; DER HEILIGE JOSEF SINGT; "Nun Wandre, Maria, nun Wandre nur fort"; — 4082
GO FORTH NOW SWEET MARY; ST. JOSEPH SINGS; "Go forth now, sweet Mary, go forth without fear" e, g 112   words by P. Heyse

DER SCHÄFER; "Es war ein fauler Schäfer, ein rechter Siebenschläfer" g 226   words by J. W. von — 4083
Goethe

"UND WILLST DU DEINEN LIEBSTEN STERBEN SEHEN"; "IF YOU DESIRE TO SEE A DYING LOVER" — 4084
e, g 112   words by P. Heyse

VERBORGENHEIT; "Lass o Welt, o lass mich sein!"; SECRECY; "Peace O world, O grant me peace!" — 4085
e, g 112; "Tempt me not, O world, again" e, g 359; SOLITUDE e, g 220   words by E. Mörike

DAS VERLASSENE MÄGDELEIN; "Früh, wann die Hähne krähn" g 97,226   words by E. Mörike — 4086

VERSCHWIEGENE LIEBE; "Uber Wipfel und Saaten"; SILENT LOVE; "Thro' the glamor of evening" — 4087
e, g 121   words by J. von Eichendorff

ZUR RUH, ZUR RUH; "Zur, Ruh, zur Ruh ihr müden Glieder!"; TO REST, TO REST; "To rest, to — 4088
rest, the toil is over" e, g 359   words by J. Kerner

WOLFE, JACQUES

DE OLE ARK'S A-MOVERIN'; "Jes wait a little while" e 399 — 4089

WOLFF, BILL

PUT IT ON THE GROUND; "Oh, if you want a raise in pay" e 293   words by R. Glaser — 4090

WOLKENSTEIN, OSWALD VON, 1377?-1445

IM MAI; "O wunniklicher wohl gezierter mai"; O BEAUTIFUL MONTH OF MAY; "Oh blissful, — 4091
wondrous, beautiful month of May" e, g 403

WOLSKI, W., 1824-1882

"NIE MASZ TO WIARY JAK W NASZYM ZNAKU"; "THOUGH BUT A UNIT, WE ARE THE ARMY'S — 4092
GLORY" e, p 159

WOLTERS, GOTTFRIED

DU LIEBE, LIEBE SONNE; "Du liebe, liebe Sonne bescheine mich" g 49   words by H. Claudius — 4093

"WENN EINE MUTTER IHR KINDLEIN TUT WIEGEN" g 49 — 4094

WOOD, CHARLES, 1866-1926

ETHIOPIA SALUTING THE COLOURS; "'Who are you, dusky woman'" e 273   words by W. Whitman — 4095

WOODBURY, ISAAC BAKER, 1819-1858

HE DOETH ALL THINGS WELL; "I remember how I lov'd her" e 212 — 4096

"STARS OF THE SUMMER NIGHT" e 28,129,130,132,233,236,279,366   words by H. W. Longfellow — 4097

WOODMAN, R. HUNTINGTON, 1861-1943

"I AM THY HARP" e 259   words by E. Murray — 4098

WOODS, HARRY M., 1896-

I'M LOOKING OVER A FOUR LEAF CLOVER; "Farewell ev'ry old familiar face"; "I'm looking over a — 4099
four leaf clover" (ref) e 345; (ref only) e 233   words by M. Dixon

WOODS, HARRY M., 1896- (Continued)

    "WHEN THE MOON COMES OVER THE MOUNTAIN" e 132,236 words by H. E. Johnson   4100

WOODWARD, SAMUEL

    THE PATRIOTIC DIGGERS; "Enemies, beware, keep a proper distance" e 173   4101

WOOLER, ALFRED, 1867-1937

    CONSIDER AND HEAR ME; "How long, O Lord, wilt Thou forget me?" e 398 words from Psalm XIII   4102

    "HEAR MY CRY, O LORD!" e 398   4103

WORK, HENRY CLAY, 1832-1884

    DAD'S A MILLIONAIRE; "I wish you joy, my little ragged throng"; "Hurrah! Hurrah! now give us a rousing song" (ref) e 114   4104

    "FATHER, DEAR FATHER COME HOME WITH ME NOW" e 131; COME HOME FATHER! e 114, FATHER DEAR FATHER e 246   4105

    GRAFTED INTO THE ARMY; "Our Jimmy has gone for to live in a tent"; "Oh, Jimmy, farewell! Your brother fell way down in Alabarmy" (ref) e 189   4106

    GRANDFATHER'S CLOCK; "My grandfather's clock was too large for the shelf" e 114,129,130,132, 173,236,279,343,366   4107

    KINGDOM COMING; "Say, darkeys, hab you seen de massa"; "De massa run? ha, ha!" (ref) e 161; KINGDOM COMIN' e 129,130,132,225; "Say, darkies, hab you seen the massa" e 279; YEAR OF JUBILO; KINGDOM COME; "Say, darkies, hab you seen de massa"; "De massa run ha! ha!" (ref) e 109,110; JUBILO; "Say, Uncle, have you ever seen the master"; "The master run, hah, hah" (ref) e 44   4108

    MARCHING THROUGH GEORGIA; "Bring the good old bugle, boys, we'll sing another song" e 7,199   4109

    SONG OF A THOUSAND YEARS; "Lift up your eyes, desponding free men"; "A thousand years! my own Columbia" (ref) e 129,130,279   4110

    WAKE NICODEMUS; NICODEMUS; "Nicodemus, the slave, was of African birth"; "The 'Good time comin' is almost here" (ref) e 34,93,173   4111

WORK, JOHN WESLEY, 1901-

    DUSK AT SEA; "Tonight eternity alone is near" e 78 words by T. S. Jones   4112

    A MONA LISA; "I should like to creep through the long brown grasses that are your lashes" e 78 words by A. Grimke   4113

WOYNA, FRANZ VON

    HANS UND LIESEL; "Und der Hans schleicht umher" g 31,99; "UND DER HANS SCHLEICHT UMHER" g 353   4114

WREDE, ARNO, 1902-

    "DER NEBEL STEIGT, ES FÄLLT DAS LAUB" g 31 words by T. Storm   4115

WRIGHT, A. B.

    THE SOLDIER'S LIFE; "How little you good people know" e 44   4116

WRIGHTON, W. T.

    THE DEAREST SPOT; "The dearest spot on earth to me is home, sweet home" e 28,279,366   4117

    HER BRIGHT SMILE HAUNTS ME STILL; "'Tis years since last we met" e 129,130 words by J. E. Carpenter   4118

YOUNG, PERCY MARSHALL, 1912-

    WELCOME YULE; "Welcome Yule, thou merry man" e 410   4119

YRADIER, SEBASTIAN, 1809-1865

    LA PALOMA; "Cuando salí de la Habana Válgame Dios" s 284; THE DOVE; "One day, when I left Havana" e, s 322; "The day that I left my home for the rolling sea" e 132; "The day when I left the land to sail o'er the sea" e, s 329; "When I from Havana sever'd so long ago" e, s 142; "The day that I left Habana" e 122; "The day that I sailed away on the rolling sea" e 350   4120

ZAHN, CHRISTIAN JACOB, 1765-1830

    REITERLIED; "Wohlauf, Kameraden aufs Pferd" g 99; WOHLAUF KAMERADEN g 31 words by F. Schiller   4121

ZAIRA, M.

    "ADARIM DODI NATAN"; "UNCLE GAVE ME FLOCKS" e, h (tr) 30   4122

    CHANITAH; "Laylah mistarea esh min heha rim"; "See, the light is blazing from the hillside" e, h (tr) 30   4123

    "V'CHI TAVOU"; "WE'LL PLANT A TREE" e, h (tr) 30   4124

ZALESKI, BOHDAN

    ZA NIEMEN HEN PRECZ; "Za Niemen hen precz! Koń gotów i zbroja dziewczyno ty moja"; OVER NIEMEN LET'S GO; "O'er Niemen let's go! My horse stands already, don't cry love, make ready" e, p 159; ZA NIEMEN; "Za Niemen het precz, het precz! Koń gotów i zbroja, dziewczyno ty moja";   4125

ZALESKI, BOHDAN
    ZA NIEMEN HEN PRECZ (Continued) BEYOND NIEMEN; "Far beyond Niemen I go! My steed   4125
    stands awaiting, oh come love, embrace me" e, p 295

ZĀLĪTS, JĀNIS
    DES KRIEGERS BRAUT; "Heuer im Sommer an Sonnentagen hat mir der Garten Blumen getragen";   4126
    FIANCÉE DE GUERRIER; "Dans mon jardin en soleil sont écloses de lis charmants et de belles
    roses" f, g 224
    "SAG', WIE SOLL ICH DIR SCHMEICHELN?"; DIS MOI COMMENT TE CARESSER?; "Mon ange,   4127
    souvent j'ignore quels mots d'amour te dire" f, g 224

ZANETI, FRANCESCO MARIA, ca1680
    AVVEZZATI, MIO CORE; "Avvezzati, mio core, a sospirar a sospirar" i 180   4128

ZDIRA, M.
    KACHA, KACH; "Kacha, kacha, Kacha, Kacha"; "THIS WAY, THIS WAY, LET IT BE" e, h (tr)   4129
    30 words by Ashman

ZELENSKI, WLADISLAW, 1837-1921
    BOGURODZICA; "Bogurodzica Dziewica, Bogiern stawiona Maryja"; MOTHER OF GOD; "Oh, Holy   4130
    Mother Virgin pure, Glorified by Thy son, sweet Mary" e, p 159; BOGU RODZICA; "Bogu Rodzica,
    dzieweca! Bogiem wsławiona Marya"; "Virgin all sinless and fairest, God's lauded Mother, sweet
    Mary" e, p 295 words att to St. Adalbert

ZELLER, KARL, 1842-1898
    [DER OBERSTEIGER, operetta; words by L. Held and M. West] SEI NICHT   4131
    BÖS; "Wo sie war, die Müllerin" g 258
    [DER VOGELHÄNDLER, operetta; words by L. Held and M. West] "ICH BIN   4132
    DIE CHRISTEL VON DER POST" g 258
    [Ibid] "SCHENKT MAN SICH ROSEN IN TIROL," Act I g 258,326   4133
    [Ibid] "WIE MEIN AHNERL ZWANZIG JAHR" Act I g 326; "WIE MEIN AHNL ZWANZIG JAHR"   4134
    g 258

ZELTER, KARL FRIEDRICH, 1758-1832
    BERGLIED; "Am Abgrund leitet der schwindliche Steg" g 250 words by J. C. F. von Schiller   4135
    HERBSTLIED; "Feldeinwärts flog ein Vögelein und sang im muntern Sonnenschein" g 229 words by   4136
    L. Tieck
    "IN ALLEN GUTEN STUNDEN" g 31 words by J. W. von Goethe   4137
    DER KÖNIG VON THULE; "Es was ein König in Thule" g 229,250; DER KÖNIG IN THULE g 96,   4138
    99,226; "ES WAR EIN KÖNIG IN THULE" g 42,326,353 words by J. F. von Goethe
    DAS ROSENBAND; "Im Frühlingsschatten fand ich sie" g 229 words by F. G. Klopstock   4139
    STÄNDCHEN; "Zu meiner Laute Liebesklang"; "Horch auf, zu meiner Laute Klang tönt" (ref) g 229   4140

ZIMMERMANN, CHARLES A.
    ANCHORS AWEIGH; THE SONG OF THE NAVY; "Anchors aweigh, my boys, anchors aweigh" e 129;   4141
    THE SONG OF THE NAVY; "Stand Navy out to sea, fight our battle cry" e 236

ZIMMERMANN, S. ANTON, 1807-1876
    LIED DES TROMPETERS VON SÄCKINGEN; "Altheidelberg, du feine, du Stadt an Ehrenreich" g 31,   4142
    353; ALT HEIDELBERG, DU FEINE; "Alt Heidelberg, du feine, du Stadt an Ehrenreich" g 326;
    ALT HEIDELBERG g 43 words by J. V. Scheffel

ZINCK, HARDENACK OTTO CONRAD, 1746-1832
    LANGT HØJERE BJERGE; "Langt højere Bjaerge saa vide paa Jord man har"; FAR LOFTIER MOUN-   4143
    TAINS; "Far loftier mountains are found on the earth than here" da, e 87 words by N. F. S.
    Grundtvig

ZÍTEK, OTAKAR, 1892-
    V PŘEDTUŠE SMRTI; "Mám často osudné ono tušení"; SCHICKSALSAHNUNG; "Oft belastet bange   4144
    Schicksalsahnung mir das Herz" c, g 73a words by J. Pelikana

ZOECKLER, DOROTHY ACKERMANN
    "WHEN I KNEEL DOWN TO PRAY" e 347   4145

ZÖLLNER, KARL FRIEDRICH, 1800-1860
    "DAS WANDERN IST DES MÜLLERS LUST" g 326,353 words by W. Müller   4146

ZSCHIESCHE, ALFRED
    "WENN DIE BUNTEN FAHNEN WEHEN" g 309,353   4147

ZUCCALMAGLIO, ANTON WILHELM FLORENTIN VON, 1803-1869
    "DORT IN DEN WEIDEN STEHT EIN HAUS" g 353 words after J. Brahms   4148
    "FEINSLIEBCHEN, DU SOLLST MIR NICHT BARFUSS GEHN" g 49,96,226,309,326,353   4149
    KEIN SCHÖNER LAND; "Kein schöner Land in dieser Zeit als hier das unsre Weit und breit" g 49,353;   4150
    KEIN SCHÖNER LAND IN DIESER ZEIT g 31,309,326
    "MEIN MÄDEL HAT EINEN ROSENMUND" g 229,326,353; "YON MAIDEN'S LIPS ARE ROSY RED"   4151
    e, g 406; "MY DARLING'S LIPS ARE A PETALED ROSE" e, g 357; "MY DEAR ONE'S MOUTH IS
    LIKE THE ROSE" e, g 210; "MY MAIDEN'S LIPS ARE LIKE A ROSE" e, g 36 arr by J. Brahms
    NACHTGRUSS; "Verstohlen geht der Mond auf, blau, blau" g 99; VERSTOHLEN GEHT DER MOND   4152
    AUF g 326

ZUCCALMAGLIO, ANTON WILHELM FLORENTIN VON, 1803-1869 (Continued)
>SANDMÄNNCHEN; Zu Bethlehem geboren (tune); "Die Blümelein, sie schlafen schon längst im   4153
>Mondenschein" g 99   arr by J. Brahms g 226; DIE BLÜMELEIN, SIE SCHLAFEN g 309,353; THE
>LITTLE SANDMAN; "The flow'rs have long been sleeping, beneath, the moon so bright" e, g 70;
>DIE BLÜMELEIN ALL SCHLAFEN; "Die Blümelein all schlafen schon längst im Mondenschein" g 326;
>THE SANDMAN; "The flow'rlets have been sleeping long since in moonlight" e 209; THE LITTLE
>DUSTMAN; "The flow'rets all sleep soundly beneath the moon's bright ray" e 28,279,366
>SCHWESTERLEIN; "Schwesterlein, Schwesterlein, wann gehn wir nach Haus?" g 226,229; SISTER   4154
>MINE; "Sister mine, sister mine, when will we go home?" e, g 364; SCHWESTERLEIN, WANN
>GEHN WIR NACH HAUS? g 309,326; DER LETZTE TANZ g 99   att to J. Brahms
>"VERSTOHLEN GEHT DER MOND AUF" g 353   4155
ZUCKERMANN, AUGUSTA, 1890-
>THE BIG BROWN BEAR, op.52, no.1; "I chanced upon a big brown bear" e 364   words by H. A.   4156
>Heydt
ZUKOWSKI, O. M., 1881-
>"WIECZÓR MGLISTY, WIECZÓR BLADY"; IN THE FOREST; "On a foggy evening dreary dusk falls"   4157
>e, p 159   words by M. Konopnicka
ZUMSTEEG, JOHANN RUDOLF, 1760-1802
>RITTER TOGGENBURG; "Ritter, treue Schwesterliebe" g 250   words by J. C. F. von Schiller   4158
ZUÑIGA, J. DANIEL
>CAÑA DULCE; "Caña dulce pa' moler cuando tenga mi casita" s 284   words by J. J. Salas Perez   4159
ZWEIGLE, A.
>TIROL, TIROL, DU BIST MEIN HEIMATLAND. See 1013

ANONYMOUS SONGS AND FOLK SONGS

ABÝSSINIA

SONG OF TRUE MEN; "There's a song that we keep hearing" e 86   4160

(not used)   4161

ARGENTINA

ASÍ ERES TÚ; "Tu garganta es alabastro"; YOU; "The glamorous red of coral" e, s 219   4162

AT THE SIGN OF THE BARBER; "Go ask the barber, he surely will know"; "Come dance my dear one" (ref) e 37   4163

AY, ZAMBA; "Las estrellas del cielo"; "Counting the shining planets" e, s 219   4164

BAILANDO EL GATO; "Cuando los San Juaninos"; COME DANCE THE GATO; "San Juan folk from the mountains"   4165
e, s 207

CHACARERA; "Chacarera, Chacarera, me ha contado un picaflor" s 284   4166

CHACAYALERA; "Carretero, carretero, carretero de juncal"; THE CARTMAN; "'Tis the cartman, 'tis the cart-   4167
man, 'tis the cartman from the marsh" e, s 207

EL CUANDO; "Unay dos me andan queriendo"; WHEN?; "Two there are who seem for me to care" e, s 207; O   4168
WHEN, O WHEN; "When will come the happy morning, sweetest flow'rs the day adorning" e 35

EL PALITO; "No hay corazón como el mio para sufrir" s 284   4169

ROSITA; "Rosita, la chacarera, moza lindaz y ladina"; "Rosita, a rustic maiden, comely, angelic and pleasing"   4170
e, s 207

EL SUEÑO; "Anoche mientras dormia"; MY DREAM; "Last night while slumbering deeply" e, s 207   4171

EL TODO EL TIEMPO PASADO. See 4264

UNA VEZ CLAVELINA; "Una vez clavelina, mi vida, y otra vez clavel"; SOMETIMES A MARIGOLD; "You're   4172
sometimes like a marigold, then you change to mignonette" e, s 322

VIDALITA; "Desde que te fuiste, mi amante bien"; LITTLE SONG OF LIFE; "With you far away, dreary is the day"   4173
e, s 9; "Una noche calma, Vidalita, te robé un beso"; "Lovely was that calm night, Vidalita, when
I stole a fond kiss" e, s 322; "Why in forest deep grieves Vidalita" e 35; LA PLATA SONG;
"Vidalita, dear, Maiden whom I love" e 279

VIDALITA; "No hay rama en el monte, Vidalitá" s 284   4174

LA ZAMBA DE VARGAS; "Batallón cazadores dijo Paunero" s 284   4175

ARMENIA

KHER PAN; "Vay le le vay le le vay kher pan!"; "Thou art standing by the wall" (verse) e 37   4176

AUSTRALIA

BOTANY BAY; "Farewell to old England, the beautiful!" e 34; "Oh, there's Glasgow and Berwick and Penterville"   4177
e 86

DINKY DIE. See 8037A

KOOKABURRA; "Kookaburra sits in the old gum tree" 4 pt round e 214   4178

WALTZING MATILDA; "Once a jolly swagman sat beside the billabong"; "Waltzing Matilda, waltzing Matilda,   4179
you'll come a-waltzing Matilda with me" (ref) e 35

AUSTRIA

DA DROBN AF DEM BERGAL; "Da drobn af dem Bergal gugu, do steht a kloans Wuzerl wie du" g 41   4180

"GROSSER GOTT, WIR LOBEN DICH" g 326   4181

HEUTE BIN ICH ROT; "Heute bin ich rot und morgen bin ich tot"; TODAY MY BLOOD RUNS RED; "Today my   4182
blood runs red, tomorrow's my death-bed" e, g 231

IM MÄRZEN DER BAUER; "Im Märzen der Bauer die Rösslein einspannt" g 40,49,309,326   4183

IN BERLIN, SAGT ER; "In Berlin, sagt er, musst du fein, sagt er" g 99   words by C. von Holtei   4184

"O DU SCHÖNI SÜSSI NACHTIGALL" g 41   4185

'S IST MIR ALLES EINS; Af d'r Ornbank, (tune); "'s ist mir alles eins, 's ist mir alles eins, ob i a Geld hab oder   4186
keins" g 353

DIE ZWEI ROSEN; "Ich hab in einem Garten gesehen"; THE TWO ROSES; "I saw two roses grow on a briar" e, g   4187
231   att to Mönch von Salzburg

BELGIUM

AH, LAMBERT; "Ah! Lambert, que sais-tu donc faire?"; "Lambert, say, can you sing and can you play?" e, f 231   4188

DAAR HAD EEN MEISKEN; THERE WAS A MAIDEN; "There was a maiden who loved a knight" e 86   4189

EL DOUDOU; THE DRAGON; "The festival goes by the crowded market square" e 86   4190

ZEEMANSLEVEN; THE LIFE OF A SAILOR; "All you who sail over the ocean" e 86   4191

THE CHESAPEAKE AND THE SHANNON; The pretty girl of Derby O (tune); "The Chesapeake so bold out of Boston as we're told" e 186 — 4227

CITADEL HILL; BACK BAY HILL; ON CITADEL HILL; "One day in December I'll never forget" e 186 — 4228

THE DAY COLUMBUS LANDED HERE; I NEVER SHALL FORGET; THE OLD TIMER'S SONG; "I never shall forget the day Columbus landed here" e186 — 4229

DONKEY RIDING; "Were you ever in Quebec stowing timber on the deck" e 186, 214 — 4230

AN ESKIMO LULLABY; "Still, now, and hear my singing" e 186 — 4231

THE FALSE YOUNG MAN; A ROSE IN THE GARDEN; "Oh, come, sit down close to me, my dear" e 186 — 4232

THE FARMER'S CURST WIFE. See 4597, A, E

A FROG HE WOULD A-WOOING GO. See 4604B

"A GREAT BIG SEA HOVE IN LONG BEACH" e 186 — 4233

I'LL GIVE MY LOVE AN APPLE; "I'll give my love an apple without any core" e 186 — 4234A

I WILL GIVE MY LOVE AN APPLE; "I will give my love an apple without any core" e 44 — 4234B

I'S THE B'Y; "I's the b'y that builds the boat" e 44; "I'SE THE B'Y THAT BUILDS THE BOAT" e 186 — 4235

THE JAM ON GERRY'S ROCK. See 7724D

JIM WHALEN; "Come gentlemen and ladies, I pray you to draw near" e 186 — 4236

THE KELLIGREWS SOIREE; "You may talk of Clara Nolan's Ball"; "There was birch rine, tar twine, cherry wine, and turpentine" (ref) e 186 words by J. Burke — 4237

LAND OF THE SILVER BIRCH; "Land of the silver birch, home of the beaver" e 186 — 4238

THE LITTLE OLD SOD SHANTY. See 7788C

LOTS OF FISH IN BONAVIST' HARBOUR; "Oh, there's lots of fish in Bonavist' Harbour"; "Catch a-hold this one, catch a-hold that one" (ref) e 186 — 4239

LUKEY'S BOAT; "Oh, Lukey's boat is painted green" e 186 — 4240

THE LUMBER CAMP SONG; "Come all you jolly fellows, and listen to my song" e 186 — 4241

THE MAID ON THE SHORE. See 7810B

THE MORNING DEW; "The pink, the lily, and the blooming rose" e 186 — 4242

NOVA SCOTIA SONG; "The sun was setting in the west" e 186 — 4243

OLD GRANDMA; "Old grandma when the West was new" e 186 — 4244

THE OLD MAN. See 7873B

THE QUAKER'S COURTSHIP; "Madam, I have come a-courting, O dear" e 186 — 4245

THE SHANTYMAN'S LIFE. See 7983B

"SHE'S LIKE THE SWALLOW" e 186 — 4246

SMOKY MOUNTAIN BILL; "Listen for a spell to a story I will tell" e 186 — 4247

TIME TO BE MADE A WIFE; "As I roved out one morning in the lovely month of May" e 186 — 4248

A TRUE LOVER OF MINE. See 4747B

UNFORTUNATE MISS BAILEY. See 4787

WHEN THE ICE WORMS NEST AGAIN; "There's a dusky husky maiden in the Arctic"; "In the land of the pale blue snow" (ref) e 186 — 4249

WHITE MAN, LET ME GO; "Let me go to my home" e 186 — 4250

YE MAIDENS OF ONTARIO; "Ye maidens of Ontario, give ear to what I write" e 186 — 4251

CHILI

ÁMAME MUCHO; "Allá en la noche callada para que se oiga mejor"; LOVE ME AS I LOVE YOU; "The night is so endless, lonely and friendless, who but you will do?" e, s 9; ASÍ AMO YO; AS I LOVE YOU; "Out where the night is still, come and you will hear better my plea" e, s 322 — 4252

A CADA INSTANTE TE MIRO; EACH MINUTE I LOOK AT YOU; "The ways of my girl are charming" e 219 — 4253

ARRULO; LULLABY; "Tell me Santa Anna, why is baby fretful" e 279 — 4254

ASÍ ERES TÚ. See 4162

"AY, AGUITA DE MI TIERRA"; "FLOWS A BROOKLET IN MY HOMELAND" e, s 207 — 4255

CHICHA EN BOTELLA; "Nunca se ha visto en Lima"; A BOTTLE OF CHICHA; "Never before in Lima" e, s 207 — 4256

CORAZONES PARTIDOS; "Corazones partidos, Yo no los quiero"; DIVIDED HEARTS; "Two hearts shouldn't be divided, That's not how it's done" e, s 207 — 4257

CUECA; ZAMACUECA; CHILEAN DANCE SONG; "Your eyes are like fire a-glowing" e 279; DOWN WHERE THE SAMA FLOWS; "Skies that are blue and sunny" e 350 — 4258

EVENING SONG; "The scented twilight across the harbor steals" e 350 — 4259

LA PASTORA; "Al amanecer la aurora anunciando el claro día" e 284 — 4260

LA POLLITA; "Yo tengo, yo tengo, para hacer cria"; MY LITTLE HEN; "On my farm, on my farm I have a pullet" e, s 207 — 4261

RÍO, RÍO; "Qué, grande que viene el río"; s 284; FLOWING RIVER; "How dark the deep flowing river e 350; RIVER, RIVER; "How wide is the flowing river" e, s 322; THE RIVER; "How deep the swift flowing river" e 279 — 4262

LA ROSA Y EL CLAVEL; "La rosa, la rosa con el clavel" s 284 — 4263

EL TODO EL TIEMPO PASADO; IN OLDEN TIMES; "Alone in the twilight visions enchant me" e 219 — 4264

VICTOR; "Victor is afraid of trouble" e 279   4265
YARAVI; LITTLE DOVE; "O my dove, dear, I am yearning" e 279   4266
YO QUISIERA QUERERTE; "Yo quisiera quererte pero tu me has de olvidar"; WOULD YOU WERE MINE; "Would I   4267
    could love and win thee, heedless you are I fear" e, s 207

CHINA

BEAUTIFUL CHINA; "China, China, beautiful land" e 86   4268
CHEE LAI; MARCH OF THE VOLUNTEERS; "Arise ye who refuse to be bond slaves!" e 7   4269
CHEN MEI KE; "Tzu jan fu yu hua t'u seh, Ling hsing hua k'ai shih jen pi"; LORD FOR THY REVEALING GIFTS;   4270
    "Nature is full of color flow'ring from the artistic heart" e, ch (tr), e 244 words by Yang Lin-Liu
COME, FELLOW WORKERS; "Come fellow workers, hung ho hai ho" e 35,293   4271
LONGING FOR HOME; "Sad my heart with yearning" e 37   4272
SPRING FARMING; "March wakes the fields" e 86   4273

COLOMBIA

EL DIA QUE YO NACI; "El dia que yo naci nacieron todas las flores" s 284   4274
GUABINA CHIQUINQUIREÑA; "Vén, vén, niña de mi amor" s 284   4275
"POR UN BESO DE TU BOCA" s 284; OH! TO KISS YOU LIPS; "Oh! to kiss your lips alluring" e, s 322   4276

COSTA RICA

AY TITUY; "Ay tituy, ay tituy, ay tituy, quininuy, quininuy" s 284   4277
CARIÑITOS; "Pasan dias pasan noches"; CARESSES; "Ah, the days and nights go by" e, s 86   4278
DESPRECIO; "Todo sucede en la vida"; SCORN; "All kinds of things have to happen" e, s 86   4279
LOLITA; "Lolita, si tu quisieras, yo te comprara"; "I'll buy you a ship, a marvelous ship" e, s 86   4280
EL PIOJO; "En mi casa mate un Piojo"; THE LOUSE; "I killed a louse in my house" e, s 86   4281
PUNTO GUANACASTECO; "Dicen que viene Guardiola con su tropa" s 284   4282
RUEDE LA BOLA; ROLL THE RED BALL; "Roll the red ball, yes, roll the red ball" e 279   4283
EL TORITO; "Echame ese toro pinto" s 284   4284

CUBA

BAÑADO EL ROSTRO; "Bañado el rostro, en luz divina"; THY RADIANT VISAGE; "Radiant visage, divinely   4285
    shining" e, s 207
BOLERO; "Nadie siembre su fara"; "The grain you plant each year" e, s 86   4286
CUBA; "In a sea that is blue like the heavens" e 350   4287
EN HABANA; LA MORENA TRINIDAD; EPISODE IN HAVANA; "Promenading one fine morning" e 219   4288
KOLIKO; "Hasta lue go me ho gar" s 77   4289
LA MULATA CALLEJERA; "Chiqui, chiqui, chiqui...Ay! quien es esa que viene?"; THE FLIRTATIOUS MULATA;   4290
    "Chiqui, chiqui, chiqui...Who is that, just passing by there?" e, s 207
POTPOURRI SONES; "Alla en el muelle hay una china que me espera"; A MEDLEY OF OLD TIME "SONES";   4291
    "Down on the jetty there is a maiden who is waiting" e, s 207
EL SUNGAMBELO; "De los Sungambelos Que he visto en la Habana"; "Of the Sungambelos I've seen in Havana"   4292
    e, s 86
LA TARDE; "La luz que en tus ojos arde"; AT EVENING; "The light in your dark eyes glowing" e, s 207   4293
UNDER THE SILVER STAR; "Rosita, pretty maid with a laugh like a song"; "Beneath your casement I will tune my   4294
    guitar" (ref) e 350

CZECHOSLOVAKIA

"A NA TOM ZVOLENSKIM MOSTE"; DOWN BY THE BRIDGE; "Down by the bridge in old Zvolen" e, sl 94;   4295
    MOTHER, STOP GRUMBLING!; "Where Zvolen's river goes straying" e 95
ACH, BOŽE MÔJ; "Ach, Bože môj, prebože moj"; GOD IN HEAVEN; "God in heaven, God in heaven" e, sl 94   4296
"ACH, KEBY SOM BOLA"; "WOULD I WERE THAT PIGEON" e, sl 94; "WOULD I WERE A PIGEON" e 95   4297
ACH SYNKU!; "Ach synku, synku, doma li jsi?"; OH MY SON!; "Oh my son, my son, home so soon?" c, e   4298
    324; "Are you at home now, Oh my son?" e 86
A KEĎ SA JANOŠKO; "A keď sa janoško na vojnu bral"; WHEN THE TIME ARRIVED; "When the time arrived and   4299
    the army called John" c, e 324
ANDULÍCKO MOJE; "Andulíčko moje, nedálas pokoje"; MARY ANN, MY PRETTY; "Mary Ann, my pretty, listen   4300
    and have pity" c, e 231; ANDULKO; "Andulko, my darling, Andulko, my darling, though I've
    tried, sleep would not come" e 95

ANDULKO MÉ DÍTĚ; "Andulko mé dítě, Vy se mně líbíte"; LITTLE ANNE; "Little Anne, sweet and true,   4301
Oh if you only knew" c, e 324

"ANIČKA, DUŠIČKA, KDE SI BOLA"; ANICHKA, TELL ME; "Anichka, Anichka, tell me, sweet pet" e, sl 94;   4302
ANITCHKA; "Anitchka, tell me, my pretty sweet pet" e 95; ANIČKA DUŠIČKA; ANNIE, MY
DEAREST ONE; "Annie, my dearest one, where have you been?" e, sl 324

"ANIČKA, DUŠIČKA NEKAŠLI"; ANICHKA, PLEASE; "Anichka, please don't start coughing, dear" e, sl 94;   4303A
"ANNETTE, FILLETTE, NE TOUSSE PAS" f, sl 178

"ANIČKA, DUŠIČKA NEKAŠLI"; ANICHKA, PLEASE; "Anichka, please don't start coughing, dear" e, sl 94;   4303B
COUGHING; "What is that Anitchka?" e 95

ANIČKA MALIČKA; "Anička malička, pod' si ku mne hopkat'"; LITTLE ANN; "Little Ann, pretty Ann" e, sl 94   4304

ANIČKA MLYNÁROVA; "Anička mlynárova, mášli ty húsky doma, mášli, mášli"; "HI, LITTLE MILLER'S ANNA"   4305
e, sl 94; PRETTY MILLER'S DAUGHTER; "Say, pretty miller's daughter" e 95

ANTI-HITLER SONG; "At the edge of our land Czechs are standing guard" e 7   4306

"AŽ JÁ BUDU NADE DVOREM"; "LORSQUE JE VAIS AU DESSUS DE LA FERME" c, f 177   4307

BALZAMINA; "Where will you go, my Johnnie dear?" e 37   4308

BODAJ BY VÁS; "Bodaj by vás, vy mládenci"; OH, YOU WRETCHES; "Oh, you wretches, how I hate you" e, sl   4309
94; "GO AWAY, YOU WICKED FELLOWS!" e 95

BOLERÁZ; "Boleráz, boleráz, zelený boleráz"; LILAC TREE; "Lilac tree, fair to see, Green tree, what a fine   4310
sight!" e, sl 94

THE BIRDS' RETURN; "All the birds are here again with their happy voices" e 28,366 words by J. B. Walters   4311

"BLAHOSLAVENÝ SLÁDEK"; "MAY THE BREWER BE BLESSED" c, e 324   4312

BOLESLAV, BOLESLAV; "Boleslav, Boleslav, to pěkné město"; DO NOT WEEP; "Boleslav, Boleslav, do not weep,   4313
my bride" c, e 86

CEZ TISOVEC; "Cez Tisovec mutná voda pretekáva"; THROUGH TISOVETZ; "Through Tisovetz muddy water   4314
flows in swift streams" e, sl 94

CHODÍ ŠUHAJ; "Chodí šuhaj kolo domu"; AT OUR DOOR; "At our door a lad is waiting" e, sl 94   4315

CHUDOBNÁ DIEVČINA; "Chudobná dievčina tá iného nemá len svoju poctivost' len svoju poctivost'"; "IF A   4316
POOR GIRL IS BORN" e, sl 94

"ČIAŽE JE TO ROLIČKA"; "WHOSE MAY BE THAT FIELD" e, sl 94   4317

CIBULIČKA; "Hop hej! cibuláři"; LE PETIT OIGNON; "Hop hei! V'là les maraîchers" c, f 177   4318

ČIE SÚ TO HÚSKY; "Čie sú to húsky na tej vode?"; WHOSE GEESE ARE THOSE; "Whose geese are those with that   4319
old gander" e, sl 94

"ČIE SÚ TO KONE"; "WHOSE ARE THOSE HORSES" e, sl 94   4320

ČO BUDEME ROBIT'; "Čo budeme robit', chudobní paholci"; WHO WILL HELP?; "Who will help? Where turn   4321
now?" e, sl 94

"ČO SI K NÁM NEPRIŠIEL"; "STILL YOU'VE NOT COME" e, sl 94; COULD YOU NOT COME; "Could you not   4322
come, my dear? Long I was waiting" e 95

"COŽ SE MNĚ, MÁ MILÁ, HEZKÁ ZDÁŠ"; QUE TU ES BELLE; "Que tu es belle, ô mon amour!" c, f 177   4323

ČTYRY HODINY BILY; "Čtyry hodiny bily, dyž sa mládenci bili"; QUATRE HEURES DU MATIN; "Quatre heures   4324
du matin tapaient, lorsque les gars se frappaient" c, f 178

ČTYRY KONĚ JDOU; "Čtyry koně jdou tamhle za vodou pro mou nejmilejší"; AU DELÀ DE L'EAU; "Au delà de   4325
l'eau quatre beaux chevaux vont pour amener ma bienaimée" c, f 178

THE CZARDAS; "When I first was drafted, only last fall, then I did not care for music at all" e 95   4326

DIEVČA, ČOŽE TO MÁŠ; "Dievča, dievča, čože to máš"; LASSIE, WHAT HAVE YOU THERE; "Lassie, lassie,   4327
what have you there?" e, sl 94

DIEVČA, DIEVČA, LASTOVIČKA; "Dievča, dievča, lastovička, vídal som ťa od malička!"; BELLE FILLETTE,   4328
HIRONDELLE; "Belle fillette, hirondelle, enfant je te fus fidèle!" f, sl 94

DIEVČA, LASTOVIČKA; "Dievča, dievča, lastovička, rád t'a vidím od malička"; LASSIE, LITTLE BIRD MINE;   4329
"Lassie, lassie, little bird mine, since our childhood for you I pine" e, sl 94

DOBRI MI; "Dobri mi, dobre mi, mužíček šepce mi"; HAPPY I; "Happy I, happy I, my dear lad passing by" e,   4330
sl 94

DOBRÚ NOC, MÁ MILÁ; "Dobrú noc, má milá, dobrú noc!"; DARLING, GOODNIGHT; "Darling, my darling,   4331
goodnight, goodnight!" e, sl 94; GOODNIGHT e 95

DOLINA; "Dolina, dolina, ej, čože mi je po nej"; VALLEY; "Valley, oh valley low! Ah, why should you   4332
delight me" e, sl 94

DON'T GET MARRIED; "Daughter, don't get married, else you will be sorry" e 95   4333

"DYBYCH VĚDĚL, MÁ ANIČKO"; "SI TU ETAIS, MON ANNETTE"; c, f 177   4334

DYNOM, DÁNOM; "Dynom, dánom, na kopečku stála"; DYNOM, DAŇOM, ON THE HILL A MAIDEN" e, sl 94   4335

EJ, PADÁ ROSIČKA; "Ej, padá, padá rosička"; FALLS NOW THE DEW; "Falls now the dew, dear falls the dew"   4336
e, sl 94

EJ POVEDZ, KATARÍNKA; "Ej povedz, povedz, Katarínka"; OH, KATKA, TELL ME; "Oh, Katka, tell me,   4337
uphill or down" e, sl 94

EŠTE RAZ HOJA; "Ešte raz hoja sloboda moja"; "GIRL I LOVE TO SEE" e, sl 94   4338

THE FALLING DEW; "Falling, falling, falling, now the dew is falling" e 209   4339

HANDKERCHIEF DANCE; "Take now the handkerchief, partner of mine" e 37   4340

HEJ, HAJ, ZELENKÝ HÁJ; "Hej, haj, hej, haj"; HI, HO, THE GREEN GROVE; "Hi, ho, hi, ho" e, sl 94   4341

"HEJ, HORE HÁJ, DOLU HÁJ"; "HEI, LA FORÊT QUI GRONDE" c, f 177   4342

"HEJ, KEĎ SA JANÍČKO NA VOJNU BRAL"; "AFTER HE'D BEEN DRAFTED" e, sl 94   4343

"HEJ, NA PREŠOVSKEJ TURNI"; "OH, HIGH ON PRESHOV'S TOWER" e, sl 94   4344

HEJ, POD KRIVÁŇOM; "Hej, pod Kriváňom toje krásny svet"; THERE BY KRIVAN; "There by Krivan, the world is very bright" e, sl 94   4345

HEJ SLOVANÉ; "Hej Slované, ještě naše slovanská řeč žije"; OH YE SLAVS, REJOICE NOW; "Oh ye Slavs, rejoice now for our mother tongue lives on" e, sl 324; HYMN OF THE SLAVS; "Hail, ye Slavs! Our Slavic language still our souls is greeting" e 279,366   4346

HIKING SONG; "Above a plain of gold and green"; "Huya, huya, huya, ya!" (chorus) e 37   4347

HOLKA MODROOKÁ; "Holka modrooká, nesedávej u potoka"; FILLE AUX YEUX DE PERVENCHE; "Fille aux yeux de pervenche sur le ruisseau ne te penche" c, f 178   4348

HORIČKA ZELENÁ; "Horička zelená, zelenaj sa!"; "HIGH STANDS THE GREEN HILL" e, sl 94   4349

HRÁLY DUDY; "Hrály dudy u Pobudy, já jsem je slyšela"; LA CORNEMUSE; "Aux trois Muses cornemuse jouait, je l'ai entendue" c, f 178; "WHEN I HEAR THE BAGPIPES PLAYING" c, e 324   4350

HUSIČKA DIVOKÁ; "Husička divoká letěla zvysoka"; PLOW DEEPLY; "Plow deeply was the cry coming from geese on high" c, e 324   4351

IŠLA MARÍNA; "Išla Marína do cintorína"; TO THE GRAVEYARD; "To the graveyard goes Mary tripping" e, sl 94; "IŠLA MARÍNA DO CINTORÍNA"; MARINA; "As Marina was swiftly walking" e, sl 86   4352

"IŠLO DIEVČA PRE VODU"; "TO THE WELL A MAIDEN WENT" e, sl 94   4353

JÁ NECHCI ŽÁDNÉHO; "Já nechci žádného jen Honzu samého"; I CARE FOR NO ONE HERE; "I care for no one here, John is my only dear" e, sl 94   4354

"JA SOM BAČA VEL'MI STARY"; "HERE AM I, A SHEPHERD" e, sl 94; "Hej dziny dziny dziny dajdom" (ref); "JE SUIS UN BERGER BIEN VIEUX"; "Eï dziny dziny dziny daïdom" (ref) f, sl 178   4355

"JA SOM DOBRÝ REMESELNÍK"; I'M A TINKER; "I'm a tinker, I'm a good one" e, sl 94   4356

"JEDNA DRUHEJ RIEKLA"; "ONE SAID TO THE OTHER" e, sl 94   4357

JEDÚ CHLAPCI, JEDÚ; "Jedú chlapci, jedú Trenčanskú silnicú"; PAR LA ROUTE DE TRENCIN; "Par la route de Trenčín galopent de beaux gars" c, f 178   4358

KÁČER NA DOLINE; "Káčer na doline, kačka v šachorine"; STANDS A DUCK; "Stands a duck on high hill" e, sl 94   4359

KALINA, MALINA; "Kalina, malina nad Váhom dozrela"; CRANB'RIES AND RASPB'RIES; "Cranb'ries and raspb'ries too down by the river grow" e, sl 94   4360

KDE SI BOLA; "Kde si bola, kde si bola, anulienka moja"; OH, WHERE WERE YOU; "Oh, where were you, Oh, where were you all last night" e, sl 94   4361

"KDYBY MNĚ TO PÁN BŮH DAL"; "SI M'ÉPOUSAIT, GRÂCE À DIEU" c, f 177   4362

KDYŽ JSEM PLELA LEN; "Když jsem plela len, nevěděla jsem, co mě mé srdéčko boli"; EN SOIGNANT LE LIN; "En soignant le lin, je ne savais point, pourquoi mon coeur était triste" c, e 177   4363

KDYŽ TĚ VIDÍM, MÁ PANENKO; "Když tě vidím, má panenko, v tom kostele klečeti"; QUAND JE TE VOIS, MA CHÉRIE; "Quand je te vois, ma chérie à genoux prier ton Dieu" c, f 178   4364

KEĎ JA SMUTNÝ PÔJDEM; "Keď ja smutný pôjdem na tú vojnu"; QUAND M'EN IRAI TRISTE; "Quand m'en irai triste à la guerre" f, sl 177   4365

"KEĎ PÔJDEŠ CEZ HORU"; "AS YOU GO THROUGH THE HILLS" e, sl 94   4366

KEĎ SA DROTÁR; "Keď sa drotár preč do sveta poberá"; TINKERMAN TRUE; "Tinkerman true, starting to roam far and wide" e, sl 94; THE SLOVAK; "When the Slovak started away" e 95   4367

KEĎ SOM IŠIEL; "Keď som išiel od mej milej"; ON THE NIGHT; "On the night I left my sweetheart" e, sl 94   4368

KEĎ SOM JA BOL; "Keď som ja bol prekrásny vojáček"; IF I WERE GOOD-LOOKING; "If I were good-looking, I'd be happy" e, sl 324   4369

"KEĎ SOM TRÁVU KOSIL"; "ONE DAY I HAD TO MOW" e, sl 94   4370

KTO ZA PRAVDU HORÍ; "Kto za pravdu horí v svatej oběti"; HE WHO'S TRUE AND RIGHTEOUS; "He who's true and righteous and who gladly fights" e, sl 324   4371

KUKUČKA; "Kukučka v zelenom hájku kukala"; CUCKOOS SING; "Cuckoos sing in the grove, sing 'cuckoo, cuckoo'" e, sl 94   4372

KUKULIENKA; "Kukulienka, kde si bola"; WHERE, O CUCKOO; "Where, o cuckoo, tell me, were you?" e, sl 94   4373

"MAĆA DIEVČA KONOPE"; SOAKING HEMP; "Soaking hemp a pretty maid" e, sl 94   4374

MAIDEN TELL ME; "Maiden tell me, maiden tell me! What art thou weaving" e 209   4375

MAJERÁN; "Majerán, majerán, zelený majerán"; MARJORAM; "Marjoram, marjoram, fine fresh green marjoram!" e, sl 94   4376

"MAL SOM T'A DIEVČA RAD"; "GIRL, ONCE I LOVED YOU WELL" e, sl 94   4377

MARIŠKA; "Mariška, nepolievaj chodníčky"; MARISHKA; "Marishka, don't you wet the bath today" e, sl 94   4378

MEDZI HORAMI; "Medzy horami lipka zelená"; LONELY A LINDEN STANDS; "Lonely a linden stands on the hillock here" e, sl 94   4379

MĚLA JSEM MILÉHO HULÁNA; "Měla jsem milého hulána, hulána"; AUX UHLANS J'AVAIS UN AMOUREUX; "Aux uhlans j'avais un amoureux, un amoureux" c, f 178   4380

MILY, KADE CHODÍŠ; "Mily, mily, kade chodíš"; LAD BELOVED; "Lad, beloved, would I knew it" e, sl 94   4381

MORAVO!; "Moravo, Moravo, Moravenko milá!"; MORAVIAN FOLK SONG; "Oh, my true nativeland, Oh my dear Moravia!" c, e 324   4382

MY FRIENDS, DO NOT WORRY; "Do not worry, do not worry, my friends, do not worry!" 3 pt round e 37   4383

NA DUNAJI; "Na Dunaji šaty perú"; GIRLS BY DANUBE; "Girls by Danube clothes are washing" e, sl 94   4384

NA KRÁLOVEJ HOLI; "Na Královej Holi, jasná vatra svieti"; THE BARE MOUNTAIN TOP; "High on the mountain-top fires are burning" e, sl 86   4385

NA ZELENEJ LÚČKE; "Na zelenej lúčke šuhaj pasie"; NORTH WIND WHISTLES; "North wind whistles over woods and green wold" e, sl 94   4386

NEOŠIDIL SOM SA; "Neošidil som sa iba na žene: ej!"; MA FEMME EST PEU TENDRE; "Ma femme est peu tendre, qu'en ferai je, hélas: hei!" f, sl 177   4387

NEVYDÁVAJ; "Nevydávaj sa ty dievča ešte"; GIRL, I ADVISE YOU; "Girl, I advise you, don't marry yet" e, sl 94; WIVES AREN'T LIKE MAIDENS; "Daughter, my daughter, don't marry, not yet!" e 95   4388

NITRA, MILÁ NITRA; "Nitra, milá Nitra, ty vysoká, Nitra"; NITRA, DEAREST NITRA; "Nitra, dearest Nitra, there is glory in your name" e, sl 324; NITRA, PROUDEST NITRA!; "Nitra, proudest Nitra, high above the rivers!" e, sl 86; NITRA MINE; "Nitra mine, dear Nitra, noble city Nitra!" e, sl 94   4389

OD ORAVY; "Od Oravy dažď ide, uz môj milý nepride"; DE L'ORAVA; "De l'Orava la pluie vient, mon cher ami tarde bien" f, sl 178   4390

OD OSTROVA; "Od Ostrova usekaná cesta"; OSTROV'S LIMETREES; "Ostrov's limetrees all with bloom are laden" e, sl 94; THERE'S NO ROOM FOR YOU e 95   4391

OSIRELO DÍŤE; "Osirelo díťe, osirelo díťe o pŭldruhém léťe"; L'ORPHELIN; "À peine sur terre, à peine sur terre, l'enfant perd sa mère" c, f 177   4392

OUT ON THE MEADOW; "Out on the meadow green and broad, tall grass is growing"; "Water, sweet water flow" (ref) e 37   4393

PÁSOL JANKO DVA VOLY; "Pásol Janko dva voly u hája"; YANKO GRAZED HIS OXEN; "Yanko grazed his oxen through green meadows" e, sl 94   4394

PO DOLINE; "Po doline tichý vetrík povieva"; WHILE THE BREEZE; "While the breeze the valley grasses bent and swayed" e, sl 94; "PO DOLINE TICHÝ VETRÍK POVIEVA"; "DANS LE VALLON LE VENT SOUFFLE DOUCEMENT" f, sl 178   4395

"POCHVÁLEN BUD' PÁN JEŽIŠ"; GLAD AM I; "Glad I am to find you here" e, sl 94   4396

POD BELEHRADOM; "Pod Belehradom stojí vrany kôň"; NEAR BELGRADE CITY; "Near Belgrade City stands an army steed" e, sl 94   4397

POD NAŠIMA OKNY; "Pod našima okny teče vodička"; SOUS NOS MURS RUISELLE; "Sous nos murs ruisselle l'eau qui court du val" c, f 177   4398

"POD TÝM NAŠIM OKIENEČKOM"; "UNDERNEATH OUR COTTAGE WINDOW" e, sl 94; WE ARE POOR; "By our window blooms a rosebush" e 95   4399

POVEDAL SI; "Povedal si u farára"; "LONG AGO, MY LADDY" e, sl 94   4400

POVEDZ MI; "Povedz mi, dievčatko"; "ONLY YOU CAN TELL ME" e, sl 94   4401

PRELET' SOKOL; "Prelet' sokol cez ten háj, cez háj mariankovy"; FALCON, SPREAD YOUR WINGS; "Falcon, falcon, spread your wings, to the grove go flying" e, sl 94; PRELET' SOKOL; "Prelet', sokol, cez náš dvor, cez háj majránovy"; VOLE, FAUCON; "Vole, faucon, par dessus le bois de marjolaine" f, sl 178   4402

PRELETEL SOKOL; "Preletel sokol s bučka na topol'"; FALCON FLYING WELL; "Falcon flying well in a firtree fell" e, sl 94   4403

PREVEZ, PRIEVOZNÍČKU; "Prevez, prevez, prievozníčku"; FERRY, TAKE ME OVER; "Ferry, ferry, take me over" e, sl 94   4404

PRI DUNAJU; "Pri Dunaju šaty perú"; BY THE STREAM; "By the stream she clothes is washing" e, sl 94   4405

PRI PREŠPORKU; "Pri Prešporku na Dunaji húsky sa perú"; NEAR PRESHPOROK; "Near Preshporok on the Danube" e, sl 94   4406

PRI SKALICI; "Pri Skalici husári verbujú"; IN SKALITZA; "In Skalitza hussars are calling men" e, sl 94   4407

PRÍDI TY, ŠUHAJKO; "Prídi ty, šuhajko, ráno k nám"; LADDIE, COME EARLY; "Laddie, come early to visit me" e, sl 94; "IF YOU WOULD SEE HOW I WORK AND PLAY" e, sl 324; DARLING, COME EARLY; "Darling come early, when I arise" e 95   4408

THE PROMISE; "Adamku dear, what do you fear?" e 95   4409

ROŽNOVSKÉ HODINY; "Rožnovské hodiny smutně bijú"; L'HORLOGE DE ROŽNOV; "L'horloge de Rožnov sonne tristement" c, f 178   4410

SADLA DOLE; "Sadla dole, plakala, aj, jaj"; DOWN SHE SAT; "Down she sat and loud she cried, ay, ay" e, sl 94   4411

SECRET LOVE; "What though my horse proudly doth stride" e 209   4412

SHUSTI FIDDLI; "Shusti, shusti, fiddli, shusti, shusti, fiddli, here's how it plays"; "Children, guess what I have here" (verse) e 37   4413

SIHOTE, ZELENÉ SIHOTE; "Sihote, sihote, zelené sihote"; ISLANDS FAIR; "Islands fair, islands green, oh you fair, green islands!" e, sl 94   4414

SKALICKÁ VEŽA; "Skalická veža, tá je vysoká"; HIGH SKALITZA'S TOWER; "High Skalitza's tow'r, very, very high" e, sl 94   4415

ŠKODA T'A; "Škoda t'a, šuhajko"; SORRY AM I; "Sorry am I you live" e, sl 94 4416
"ŠLA PANENKA K ZPOVÍDÁNÍ"; CONFESSION; "Once a maid went to confession" c, e 324 4417
THE SOLDIER; "Called to the army, my girl I must leave" e 95 4418
"SPIEVAJ SI, SLÁVIČKU"; NIGHTINGALE; "Nightingale who, singing, sets the green grove ringing" e, sl 94 4419
SPIEVAJŽE SI; "Spievajže si, spievaj, spievavé"; SING YOUR SONG; "Sing your song, sing, singer!" e, sl 94 4420
SPIEVANKY; "Spievanky, spievanky, kdeže ste sa vza ly?"; SONGS I SING; "Songs I sing, yet know not" e, sl 94 4421
SPRING MORNING; "Dawning steals softly across the sky" e 343 4422
STODOLA PUMPA; "Far in the hills I hear the nightingale" e 28 4423
"STOJÍ JANO PRI POTOCE"; "YANO DANS L'EAU RUISSELANTE" c, f 177 4424
ŠTYRI HODINY; "Štyri hodiny do dňa"; ONLY FOUR HOURS; "Only four hours till dawn" e, sl 94 4425
"ŠUHAJKO BIJÚ MŇA"; "LADDIE, THEY'RE BEATING ME" e, sl 94 4426
ŠUHAJKO LUTERÁN; "Šuhajko luterán, za teba vôl'u mám"; LUTHERAN LAD; "Lutheran lad, I would marry you 4427
  if I could" e, sl 94
SWALLOWS ARE FLYING; "Swallows are flying, flying now, saying that dawn is near" e 95 4428
TAKÉ ČASY; "Také časy nastávajú"; OH, WHAT TIMES; "Oh, what times are these we live in" e, sl 94 4429
"TAKÚ SOM SI FRAJEROČKU"; "SUCH A REALLY LOVELY SWEETHEART" e, sl 94; EARLY, MY DEAR; "Such a 4430
  really pretty sweetheart" e 95
TANCUJ, VYKRÚCAJ; "Tancuj, tancuj, vykrúcaj, vykrúcaj"; DANCE AND TURN; "Dance and turn, and step 4431
  lightly, step lightly" e, sl 324; DANCE SONG; "Dancing, dancing, whirling 'round, when the
  snow is on the ground" e, 209; TANCUJ; DANCE IT; "Dance it, spin aroundo, aroundo" e, sl 94
"TEČE VODA PROTI VODĚ"; "WHILE THE STREAM FLOWS EVER ONWARD" c, e 324 4432
TEČIE VODA; "Tečie voda, tečie, ej"; "BROOKLET EVER FLOWING" e, sl 94; WATER RUNNING; "Water 4433
  running slowly, finding at last the brookside" e 95
TELL ME DEAR; "Tell me dear, dear, tell me why your brow, white marble" e 95 4434
TENKRATE BUDE VICTORIA; "Tuším, tuším, tuším, Že já umřít musím"; THEN RISE TO VICTORY; "I know, 4435
  I know, I know, that I must die and go" c, e 231
TIE NITRIANSKÉ HODINY; "Tie Nitrianské hodiny vel'mi zle bijú"; BELLS OF NITRA; "Bells of Nitra, ringing, 4436
  chiming, Oh, how sad to me!" e, sl 94; NITRA'S BELLS; "Nitra's bells that ring so sweet" e 95
U STAREJ BŘECLAVY; "U starej Břeclavy na hrází"; NEAR BŘECLAV; "Near Břeclav, close by the river side" 4437
  c, e 324
"U STUDIENKY STÁLA"; "BY THE WELL WE SAW HER" e, sl 94; LET ME KEEP FAITH; "People say, 'Don't 4438
  take him'" e 95
"UMOČIL MA DÁŽDIK NA DVORE"; LASSIE, WON'T YOU; "Lassie, won't you please your door unlock?" e, sl 94 4439
UMREM; "Umrem, umrem, ale neviem, kedy"; SOME DAY; "Some day, some day, though I don't know what 4440
  day" e, sl 94
"UŽ JE SLÚNKO Z TÉJ HORY VEN"; "DÉJÀ LÀ-HAUT PARAIT LE JOUR" c, f 177 4441
V TOM KOUŘIMSKÝM ZÁMKU; "V tom Kouřimským zámku mám já hezkou holku a já rád ji mám"; A KOUŘIM, 4442
  EN VILLE; "A Kouřim en ville j'ai une belle fille et je l'aime bien" c, f 178
VEJE VETOR; "Veje vetor po doline"; THROUGH THE VALE; "Through the vale the wind is hasting" e, sl 94; 4443
  FADING YOUTH; "Through the woods a wind is blowing" e 95
VELICKÝ PÁN FARÁR; "Velický pán farár kázeň káže, dává obrázky"; LE CURÉ DE VELKÁ; "Le curé de Velká 4444
  aime les coeurs pieux" c, f 178
VÍNKO ČERVENÉ; "Vínko, vínko, vínko červené"; WINE SO RUBY-RED; "Wine, O wine, O wine so ruby-red" e, 4445
  sl 94
VODĚNKA STUDENÁ; "Voděnka studená, jako led, jako led"; GAI RUISSEAU; "Gia ruisseau, qui, pressé, court à 4446
  travers les bois" c, f 178
VRÁT' MI, MILÁ; "Vrat' mi, milá, vrát' mi ten dar"; "GIVE IT BACK, GIRL" e, sl 94 4447
VRT' SA DIEVČA; "Vrt' sa dievča vrt' sa dievča okolo mňa"; WHIRL AROUND ME; "Whirl around me, whirl around 4448
  me, lassie whirl, twine" e, sl 94
VYDÁVAJ SA; "Vydávaj sa, moja milá, vydávaj sa"; HURRY NOW, MAKE UP YOUR MIND; "Hurry now, make up 4449
  your mind that you will be wed" e, sl 324
VYSOKO ZORNIČKA; "Vysoko zornička, dobrú noc Anička"; HIGH YOU SHINE; "High you shine, evening star" 4450A
  e, sl 94; EVENING STAR; "High you shine, evening star" e 95
VYSOKO ZORNIČKA; "Vysoko zornička, dobrú noc Anička"; HIGH YOU SHINE; "High the star of evening, now 4450B
  good night my darling" e, sl 94
WATERS RIPPLE AND FLOW; "Waters ripple and flow, past Velecky, sweet home!" e 37 4451
WHERE THE GRASS IS GROWING; "Where the grass is growing, I'll go mowing" e 95 4452
YOU SHALL NEVER HAVE THE RING; "Give it back, dear, give it back, dear!" e 95 4453
YENITCHKU; "Yenitchku, poor fellow, had you then heard Mother, now you'd wear no saber" e 95 4454
Z BREZOVÉHO DREVA; "Z brezového dreva voda kvapká"; SAP IS RUNNING; "Sap is running, running, in the 4455
  birch wood" e, sl 94
ZAHUČALY HORY; "Zahučaly hory, zahučaly lesy"; LES MONTS RETENTISSENT; "Les monts retentissent, les 4456
  forêts mugissent" c, f 177

DENMARK

DOMINICAN REPUBLIC

INCERTIDUMBRE; "Instante supremo de dicha insegurra" s 73   4500
INVITACIÓN; "Venid dorados sueños a mia brazada frente" s 73   4501
MERENGUE; "Merengue, papá Camilio"; "Dance the Merengue, Papa Camilio!" e, s 86   4502
MI BEN QUERIDO; "Lejos de ti mi bien querido" s 73   4503
MIS DELEITES; "Yo me deleito al con templar tu talle" s 73   4504
NADIE SABE; "No alientes celos por que te digan lo que no existe en mi corazón" s 73   4505
NECESITO OLVIDAR; "Los ecos de tus quejas y sollozos porpiedad!" s 73   4506
NO SÉ; "No sé por qué te quiere mi corazón herido" s 73   4507
NUNCA; "En tu ausencia no en cuentro reposo" s 73   4508
LA PALOMA BLANCA; "Yo vi volar una blanca paloma" s 73   4509
PARA TÍ; "Ondina de la fuente de mi vida" s 73   4510
PERFIDIA; "Dios mío! que solo se que da el amor" s 73   4511
PERSUASIÓN; "Allá en el bosque, tórtola mía" s 73   4512
PIEDAD; "Piedad, piedad de mí cuando me lleve" s 73   4513
RENUNCIACION; "Si fuera un astro de la noche umbría" s 73   4514
RESIGNACIÓN; "Olas que el norte arrastra so bre el inmenso mar" s 73   4515
SERENATA; "La noche silenciosa, fuera del templo Diana" s 73   4516
EL SILFO; "Oh dulce castellana! cu yo per fil me muestra en luz arrebolado" s 73   4517
SIN IGUAL; "Todos han dicho que tu hermosura no tiene igual" s 73   4518
TRIGUEÑA; "De amor me hablaron tus ojos trigueña y de amor mi corazón" s 73   4519
TUS CABELLOS; "Negros, brillantes, crespos, tus cabellos" s 73   4520
VEN A MÍ; "Ven, ven Oh lira a calmar mis que brantos" s 73   4521
VISION; "El aliento de tu boca y la risa que a ella asoma" s 73   4522
LA VOZ DE MI DOLOR; "Es cucha amada mía la voz de mi dolor" s 73   4523
YA SOY FELÍZ; "Vuelvo a la vida siempre pensan do en tí" s 73   4524

ECUADOR

ADIOS AMOR; GOODBYE LOVE; "My wish is but to die" e 279   4525
CORAZÓN HERIDO; "Ya no çonfio en tí mi corazón"; MY DAMAGED HEART; "No more shall I entrust to you my heart" e, s 207   4526
IMBABURA; "Imbabura de mi vida, tú serás la preferida" s 284   4527
MELODIA QUE TENÍA; THE SONG I WON'T FORGET piano 207   4528
POBRE CORAZON; "Pobre corazoń entriste cido, ya no puede más surfrir de olvido" s 284   4529
SEPARACIÓN; "Mi madre me dicho no debes llorar"; SEPARATION; "My mother has warned me I never should cry" e, s 207   4530

ENGLAND

ADAM HAD SEVEN SONS; "Adam had seven sons and seven sons had Adam" e 214   4531
ADIEU, SWEET AMARYLLIS; "Adieu, sweet Amaryllis for since to part your will is" 3 pt round e 235,349   4532
ADMIRAL BENBOW; "Oh, we sailed to Virginia, and thence to Fayal" e 234   4533
THE AGINCOURT SONG; "Our King went forth to Normandy" e 235,306; SONG ON THE VICTORY OF AGIN-COURT e 199   4534
A-HUNTING WE WILL GO; "A-hunting we will go, a-hunting we will go, heigho the merry-o" 3 pt round e 343   4535
A-HUNTING WE WILL GO; "The dusky night rides down the sky, and ushers in the morn" e 349; THE DUSKY NIGHT e 234 words by H. Fielding   4536
THE AIRS SUNG BY OPHELIA; "How should I your true love know"; "Lady, he is dead and gone"; "Good morrow, 'tis Saint Valentine's day"; "And will he not come again" e 208 words by W. Shakespeare, ed by F. La Forge   4537
AMO, AMAS; "Amo, amas, I love a lass as a cedar tall and slender" e 225 att to S. Arnold; words by O'Keefe   4538
AS I WAS TRAVELLING THE NORTH COUNTRIE; "As I was a-trav'lling the North Countrie" e 198   4539
"AURORA BOREALIS, THUS SING WE DAWN'S SWEET NAME" 4 pt round e 402   4540
BAA! BAA! BLACK SHEEP; "Baa! Baa! Black sheep, have you any wool" e 28,132,366   4541
THE BAILIFF'S DAUGHTER OF ISLINGTON; "There was a youth, and a well-beloved youth" e 13,215,234,349,397   4542A
THE BAILIFF'S DAUGHTER; "There was a youth, and a well-bred youth" e 126   4542B
THE BANKS OF SWEET PRIMROSES; "As I walked out one summer morning to view the fields and to take the air" e 198   4543
THE BANKS OF THE DEE; "'Twas summer and softly the breezes were blowing"; "Flow on, lovely Dee! Flow on, thou sweet river!" (ref) e 37; 'TWAS WINTER AND BLUE TORY NOSES; "'Twas winter and blue Tory noses were freezing" e 225   4544
BARBARA ALLEN; "All in the merry Month of May" unacc e 212; "In Scarlet town where I was born" e 114; "So early in the month of May" e 115   4545A
BARBARA ALLEN; "In Reading town there I was born" e 198   4545B

DEVILISH MARY; "I went up to London town, to court a fair young lady" e 171   4580A

DEVILISH MARY; "When I first came to town, the boys strove to be near me" e 72   4580B

DICKORY, DICKORY, DOCK; "Dickory, dickory, dock, the mouse ran up the clock" e 28,366   4581

DOWN AMONG THE DEAD MEN; "Here's a health to the King and a lasting peace" e 13,235,273; "Here's a   4582
      health to the king, and lasting peace" e 402

DOWN IN DEMERARA; "There was a man who had a horselum" e 402   4583

DRINK OLD ENGLAND DRY; "Come, drink, my brave boys, and never give o'er" e 198   4584

DUCKS ON A POND; "One duck on a pond, Wibble, wobble" 3 pt round e 28   4585

DULCE DOMUM; "Come, companions, join your voices" e 349   4586

THE DUMB WIFE; "There was a bonny blade, had married a country maid" e 37; THE DUMB WIFE CURED   4587A
      e 234   words and music from T. D'Urfey's Wit and Mirth (1719)

THE WIFE WHO WAS DUMB; "All you that pass along, give ear unto my song" e 72   4587B

"DRINK TO ME ONLY WITH THINE EYES" e 28,35,36,70,122,132,233,236,237,279,297,329,343,366,385,397,   4588
      402; DRINK TO ME ONLY e 13,199,235,349   words by B. Jonson

EARLY ONE MORNING; "Early one morning, just as the sun was rising" e 13,72,199,234,349,397,402; "Early one   4589
      morning just as the sun began to glow" e 343

EARLY TO BED; "Early to bed and early to rise" 3 pt round e 28,279,366   4590

ELSIE MARLEY; "Di ye ken Elsie Marley, honey" e 235   4591

FAIR MARGARET AND SWEET WILLIAM; "There sat two lovers side by side" e 198   4592

FAIR PHOEBE AND HER DARK-EYED SAILOR; "It's of a comely young lady fair; was walking out to take the air"   4593
      e 198

THE FARMER; "Shall I show you how the farmer" e 28,366   4594

"THE FARMER IN THE DELL" e 28,366   4595

THE FARMER'S BOY; "The sun had set behind yon hill" e 402   4596A

THE FARMER'S BOY; "The sun had set behind yon hills" e 198   4596B

THE FARMER'S CURST WIFE; "There was a farmer lived on a hill" e 249; THE WOMEN ARE WORSE THAN THE   4597A
      MEN; "Is it true that the women are worse than the men?" e 172; THE DIVIL AND THE FARMER;
      "A farmer was plowing his field one day" e 173; THE DIVIL AND THE FARMER'S WIFE; "A farmer
      was plowin' his field one day" e 170

THE DEVIL AND THE FARMER'S WIFE; "There was a man lived under the hill" e 110   4597B

THE DEVIL AND THE FARMER'S WIFE; "There was an old man, he owned a small farm" e 72   4597C

THE DEVIL AND THE FARMER'S WIFE; "The devil he came to the farmer one day" e 109   4597D

THE FARMER'S CURST WIFE; "There was an old farmer who lived on a hill" e 186   4597E

THE LITTLE DEVILS; "There was an old man and he lived near Hell" e 312   4597F

THE DEVIL AND THE FARMER'S WIFE; "There was an old man who lived on the hill" e 389   4597G

FARMER'S CURST WIFE; "There was a man and he was born" e 242   4597H

THE FARMER'S CURST WIFE; "There was an old farmer went out for to plow" e 260,263   4597I

THE FARMYARD; "Up was I on father's farm"; "Six pretty maids come gang along o' me" (ref) e 28,366   4598

THE FEMALE HIGHWAYMAN; "Sylva, Sylva, one day, one day" e 198   4599

FIDDLE-DE-DEE; "Fiddle-de-dee, fiddle-de-dee, the fly has married the bumble bee" e 173; THE FLY AND THE   4600
      BUMBLEBEE e 214; FIDDLE-DEE-DEE; "Fiddle-dee-dee, fiddle-dee-dee, the fly has married the
      bumble bee" e 249

THE FOGGY, FOGGY DEW; "When I was a bachelor I lived all alone" e 48; "When I was a bach'lor I lived all   4601A
      alone" e 35,173; "When I was a bach'lor, I lived by myself" e 331; "Oh, I am a bach'lor, I live
      by myself" e 215; THE FOGGY DEW; "When I was a young man I lived all alone" e 399

FOGGY DEW; "I courted her all of the winter" e 109   4601B

THE FOOLISH BOY; "My daddy is dead, and I cannot tell you how" e 249   4602

THE FROG AND THE CROW; "A jolly fat frog liv'd in the river" e 234   4603

FROG WENT A-COURTIN'; "Frog went a-courtin' an' he did ride" e 399; "Oh frog went a-courtin' and he did   4604A
      ride" e 110; FROGGIE WENT A-COURTIN'; "Frog went a-courtin' he did ride" e 331; "A FROG
      HE WOULD A-WOOING GO" e 129,130; MISTER FROGGIE WENT A-COURTIN'; "Mister Froggie
      went a-courtin' and he did ride" e 185; MR. FROGGIE WENT A-COURTING"; "Mister Froggie went
      a-courting and he did ride" e 173

THE FROG AND THE MOUSE; "Frog went a-courtin', he did ride" e 80   4604B

A FROG HE WOULD A-WOOING GO; "A frog he would a-wooing go, 'Heigh-ho!' said Rowley" e 234; "A frog   4604C
      he would a-wooing go, 'Heigh-ho!' says Rowley" e 186; "A frog he would a-wooing go, Hey-ho,
      says Roley" e 249

THE FROG AND THE MOUSE; "There was a frog liv'd in a well" e 199; "There was a frog lived in a well" e 216   4604D

MISSIE MOUSE; "Oh, Missie Mouse, I come to see" e 72   4604E

FROG WENT A-COURTING; "Frog went a-courting and he did ride" e 225   4604F

THE GALLANT HUSSAR; "A damsel possessed of great beauty" e 198   4605

GALLOPING HORSES; "Ride away on your horses, your horses, your horses" e 216   4606

GAN TO THE KYE; "Gan to the kye wi' me, my love"; "Cushie thy pet, is lowing around her poor firstling's   4607
      shed" (verse) e 235

GATHERING NUTS IN MAY; "Here we come gath'ring nuts in May" e 214   4608

GENTLY, JOHNNY, MY JINGALO; "I put my hand all in her own" e 215   4609

GEORGE RIDLER'S OVEN; "The stones that built George Ridler's oven" e 198   4610

GO FROM MY WINDOW; "Go from my window, my love, my love" e 34   4611

GO NO MORE ARUSHING; "Go no more arushing, maids in May" e 95   4612

GO TO JOAN GLOVER; "Go to Joan Glover and tell her I love her" 4 pt round e 36,235,349   4613

GOD SAVE THE KING; "God save our gracious King" e 35,234 setting by T. Arne, no words e 294; authorized   4614
       arr, no words e 294; GOD SAVE THE QUEEN; "God save our gracious Queen" e 13,199,279,366,
       306,349 See also 7408

THE GOLDEN GLOVE; "A wealthy young squire of Tamworth, we hear" e 198   4615

GOLDEN SLUMBERS; Mayfair (tune); "Golden slumbers kiss you eyes" e 234,349,402; I WILL SING A LULLABY   4616
       e 28,37,366

THE GOLDEN VANITY; "There was a ship came from the north country" e 35,199,349; SIR WALTER RALEIGH   4617A
       SAILING IN THE LOWLANDS; "There was a ship that sailed all on the Lowland sea" e 173; THE
       SWEET TRINITY; "There was a ship that sailed upon the Lowland Sea" e 111

THE GOLDEN VANITY; "There was a ship in the North Country" e 235   4617B

THE GOLDEN VANITY; "Oh, I have got a ship in the North Country" e 198   4617C

THE WEEP-WILLOW TREE; THE GOLDEN VANITY; "Oh, my father has a fine ship a-sailin' on the sea" e 260,263   4617D

THE GOLDEN WILLOW TREE; "There was a little ship in South Amerikee" e 84   4617E

THE GOLDEN WILLOW TREE; "There was a ship in the south countree" e 126   4617F

THE GOLDEN WILLOW TREE; "'Twas just as dawn rose o'er the North Sea" e 80   4617G

THE BOLD TRELLITEE; "There was a ship in the North Counteree" e 72   4617H

GOOD MORROW, MISTRESS BRIGHT!; "Good morrow, mistress bright, Thro' lone woods fleeting" e 349 words by   4618
       A. P. Graves

GOOD NIGHT; "Good night to you all, and sweet be thy sleep" 3 pt round e 28,206,279,343,366   4619

GOSSIP JOAN; "Good morrow, Gossip Joan, where have you been a-walking?" e 199,234   4620

GREEN BUSHES. See 5920A

GREENSLEEVES; "Alas, my love, you do me wrong" e 14,111,173,235,402; MY LADY GREENSLEEVES; "Oh who   4621
       is fair as she is fair" e 297 words by J. Irvine; WHAT CHILD IS THIS?; "What child is this, who,
       laid to rest" e 33,35,125,165,206,244,251,296,319,333,334,337,363,366,388,410; "WHAT
       CHILD IS THIS, WHO, LAID TO REST" e 38,39; GREENSLEEVES; "The old year now away is
       fled" e 199,214; "THE OLD YEAR NOW AWAY IS FLED" e 307; "THE OLD YEAR NOW AWAY
       HAS FLED" e 33; A HAPPY NEW YEAR; "The old year now does pass away" e 44

THE GREY MARE; "Young Roger the miller he courted of late" e 198   4622

GROUND FOR THE FLOOR; "I lived in a wood for a number of years" e 198   4623

THE HAPPY CLOWN; The happy farmer (tune); "As Mayday morn laughed care to scorn" e 349 words by A. P.   4624
       Graves

"THE HART, HE LOVES THE HIGH WOOD" 4 pt round e 173   4625

HARVEST HOME; "Come, drink a health to Master"; "Then drink, boys, drink!" (ref) e 37   4626

HARVEST HOME; "Our oats they are hoed, and our barley's reap'd"; "Harvest Home! Harvest Home!" (ref) e 234   4627
       words and music from T. D'Urfey's Wit and Mirth (1719)

"HAVE YOU SEEN BUT A WHITE LILY GROW" e 36; "HAVE YOU SEEN BUT A WHYTE LILLIE GROW" e 106,403;   4628
       "HAVE YOU SEEN BUT THE WHYTE LILLIE GROW" e 386 words by B. Jonson

THE HAWTHORN TREE; "I was a maid of my country" e 13   4629

HELSTON FURRY DANCE; THE WELL OF ST. KEYNE; "A well there is in the West country, and a clearer n'er was   4630
       seena" e 402; THE WELL OF ST. KEYNE e 235 words by R. Southey; ROBIN HOOD; "Robin Hood
       and little John, they are both gone to fare" e 235; ROBIN HOOD AND LITTLE JOHN; "Robin Hood
       and Little John, they both are gone to Fair-o" e 343

HENRY MARTIN; "There were three brothers in Merry Scotland" e 173   4631A

ANDREW BARDEEN; "Three loving brothers in Scotland did dwell" e 126   4631B

HERE'S TO THE MAIDEN; "Here's to the maiden of bashful fifteen"; "Let the toast pass, drink to the lass" (ref)   4632
       e 14,106 words by W. Sheridan

HEY DIDDLE DIDDLE; "Hey, diddle, diddle, the cat and the fiddle, the cow jumped over the moon" e 28,173,366   4633

HEY HO, NOBODY HOME; "Hey ho, nobody home; meat nor drink nor money have I none" 6 pt round e 293   4634

HIGH GERMANY; "O cursed be the wars, love, that ever they began" e 198   4635

THE HIGHWAYMAN; "In Newry town I was bred and born" e 198   4636

THE HIGHWAYMAN OUTWITTED; "It's of a rich farmer in Cheshire, to market his daughter did go" e 198   4637

HOPE, THE HERMIT; Lady Frances Nevill's delight (tune); "Once in a blithe greenwood liv'd a hermit wise and   4638
       good"; "Tho' to care we are born" (ref) e 235,349 words by J. Oxenford

THE HORTICULTURAL WIFE; "She's my myrtle, my geranium, my sunflower, my sweet marjoram"; "Ho! ho!   4639
       she's a fickle wild rose" (ref) e 189

HOW HAPPY THE SOLDIER; "How happy the soldier who lives on his pay" e 110,225   4640

"HOW SHOULD I YOUR TRUE LOVE KNOW?" e 36,215,397 words by W. Shakespeare   4641

HUMPTY DUMPTY; "Humpty Dumpty sat on a wall" e 132   4642

THE HUNT IS UP; "The hunt is up, the hunt is up and it is well nigh day" e 234; THE KING'S HUNT e 13   4643A
     words and music from Musick's Delight on the Cithern (1667)

THE HUNT IS UP; "The hunt is up, the hunt is up and it is well nigh day" e 349   4643B

I DESIGNED TO SAY NO, BUT MISTOOK AND SAID YES; "As I was a-walking in yon shady grove, Young Colin   4644
     came after and spoke of his love" e 198

I DREW MY SHIP; "I drew my ship into the harbour" e 234   4645

"I HAVE HOUSE AND LAND IN KENT"; A WOOING SONG OF A YEOMAN OF KENT'S SON e 234   words and music   4646
     from Melismata (1611)

I MARRIED A WIFE; "I married a wife, O then! O then! I married a wife O then" e 402   4647

I SOWED THE SEEDS OF LOVE; "I sowed the seeds of love, all in the merry spring" e 234   4648

"I THINK, WHEN I READ THAT SWEET STORY" e 28,366   words by J. T. Luke   4649

IF ALL THE WORLD WERE PAPER; "If all the world were paper, and all the sea were ink" e 234   4650

IF THE HEART OF A MAN; Poor Robin's Maggot (tune); Would you have a young virgin (tune); "If the heart of a   4651
     man is depress'd with care" (no. 21 Beggar's Opera) e 397

IN THE MERRY MONTH OF MAY; "In the merry month of May, on a morn at break of day" e 397   4652

"IF YOU WANT TO KNOW WHERE THE PRIVATES ARE" e 225; INFORMATION; "If you want to know where the   4653
     Super is" e 28,366

JACK AND JILL; "Jack and Jill went up the hill" e 132   4654

JACK HALL; "Oh, my name it is Jack Hall, chimney sweep, chimney sweep" e 198   4655

JACK THE SAILOR; "As I walked out one morning fair, one morning as I was a-walking" e 198   4656

"JOAN, COME KISS ME NOW" 3 pt round e 36   4657

JOAN, TO THE MAYPOLE; "Joan, to the Maypole away let us on" e 235,349   4658

JOHN DORY; "As it fell on a holyday, and upon a holy tide-a" e 234   words and music from Playford's Musical   4659
     Companion (1687)

JOHN PEEL; Where will bonnie Annie lie (tune); Bonnie Annie (tune); "D'ye ken John Peel with his coat so gay"   4660
     e 13,28,35,199,233,234,343; "D'ye ken John Peel with his coat so gray" e 402; "D'ye ken John
     Peel with his coat so grey" e 349   words by J. W. Graves

THE JOLLY WAGGONER; "When first I went a-waggoning, a-waggoning did go" e 234   4661A

THE JOLLY WAGGONER; "When first I went a-waggoning, a-waggoning did go" e 145   4661B

THE WARBLING WAGGONER; "When first I went a-waggoning, a-waggoning did go"; e 198; THE JOLLY   4661C
     WAGGONER; "When I first went a-wagoning did go" e 110

JONE O' GREENFIELD'S RAMBLE; "Said Jone to his wife one hot summer day" e 198   4662

JUST AS THE TIDE WAS FLOWING; "One morning in the month of May, down by the rolling river" e 239   4663

THE KEEPER OF THE EDDYSTONE LIGHT; "Oh, my father was the keeper of the Eddystone Light" e 111   4664

THE KEYS OF CANTERBURY; "Madame, I will give to you the keys of Canterbury" e 44   4665

THE KEYS OF HEAVEN; "I will give you the keys of heav'n" e 343   4666

KING ARTHUR; "King Arthur had three sons that he had" e 402   4667

THE KNIGHT'S DREAM; "A gallant young knight once beheld in a dream" e 198   4668

LAVENDER'S BLUE; "Lavender's blue, diddle, diddle, Rosemary's green" e 234   4669A

LAVENDER'S BLUE; "Lavender's blue, diddle, diddle, lavender's green" e 72; "Lavender's blue, dilly, dilly,   4669B
     lavender's green" e 37

THE LEATHER BOTTEL; "When I survey the world around"; "So I wish him joy where'er he dwell" (ref) e 397   4670

"LET SIMON'S BEARD ALONE" 3 pt round e 173   4671

LET'S HAVE A PEAL; "Let's have a peal for John Cook's soul" 9 pt round e 349   4672

LILLIBURLERO; "Ho! broder Teague, dost hear de decree" e 199,294; "Ho! brother Teague dost hear de decree"   4673
     e 402; "Ho! brother Teague dost hear the decree" e 14,235 att to H. Purcell

THE LINCOLNSHIRE POACHER; "When I was bound apprentice in famous Lincolnshire" e 13,111,234,249,402   4674

LITTLE BINGO; "A farmer's dog jumped over the stile" e 249   4675

LITTLE BO-PEEP; "Little Bo-Peep has lost her sheep" e 28,132,366   4676

LITTLE BOY BLUE; "Little boy blue, come blow your horn" e 132   4677

LITTLE JACK HORNER; "Little Jack Horner sat in a corner" e 28,132,366   4678

LITTLE SIR WILLIAM; "Easter day was a holiday of all days in the year" e 46   4679

LITTLE TOM TINKER; "Little Tom Tinker got burned with a clinker" e 28,343   4680

LONDON'S BURNING; "London's burning! London's burning! Look yonder! Look yonder!" 4 pt round e 235   4681

LORD BATEMAN; "Lord Bateman was a noble lord, A noble lord of high degree" e 198 See also 7799A   4682

LORD LOVEL; "Lord Lovel he stood at his castle gate" e 35,215; LORD LOVELL; "Lord Lovell he stood at his   4683
     castle gate" e 185,279,366

LORD RANDALL; "Where have you been all the day, Randall, my son?" e 170,173; LORD RENDAL; "Where have   4684A
     you been all the day, Rendal, my son?" e 14,215; JOHN BRAMBLE; "Where ha' ye been, John
     Bramble, my son?" e 331

LORD RANDAL; "Oh, where have you been, Lord Randal, my son" e 185   4684B

JIMMY RANDAL; "Oh, where have you been, Jimmy Randal, my son" e 260,263   4684C

JIMMY RANDALL; "Where have you bin, Jimmy Randall, my son?" e 343   4684D

LORD WILLOUGHBY; "The fifteenth day of July with glist'ning spear and shield" e 86   4685

LOVE ME LITTLE; "Love me little, love me long" e 235   4686

LOVE WILL FIND OUT THE WAY; "Over the mountains, and over the waves" e 397,402; OVER THE MOUNTAINS   4687
e 297   words from Percy's Reliques

LYE STILL MY DEARE; "Lye still my Deare, why dost thou rise?" e 107   4688

THE MALLOW FLING; "Now the sun is shining brightly" e 235   words by A. H. Body   4689

MAN'S LIFE'S A VAPOUR; "Man's life's a vapour full of woes" e 199; MAN'S LIFE'S A VAPOR; "Man's life's a   4690
vapor full of woes" 3 pt round e 28,343

MARY HAD A LITTLE LAMB; "Mary had a little lamb, little lamb, little lamb" e 132   4691

MERRILY, MERRILY; "Merrily, merrily, greet the morn" e 28,233,366   4692

MICHAEL FINNIGIN; "There once was a man named Michael Finnigin" e 72; "There was an old man called   4693
Michael Finnigin" e 402

THE MILLER OF DEE; The budgeon it is a delicate trade (tune); "There was a jolly miller once liv'd on the river   4694
Dee" e 234; "There was a jolly miller once lived on the river Dee" e 48,404; THE MILLER OF
THE DEE e 402; THE JOLLY MILLER e 37,297; THERE WAS A JOLLY MILLER e 13,349

MISTRESS BOND; "Oh, what shall we have for dinner, Mistress Bond?" e 249   4695

MOWING THE BARLEY; "A lawyer, he went out one day" e 215   4696

MUST I GO BOUND?; "Must I go bound while you go free?" e 215; THE BLUE-EYED BOY; "Must I go bound   4697
while he goes free?" e 243

MY BONNY, BONNY BOY; "Oh, I once loved a boy and a bonny, bonny boy" e 198   4698

MY GOOSE; "Why shouldn't my goose sing as well as thy goose" 4 pt round e 214   4699

"MY JOHNNY WAS A SHOEMAKER" e 86,198   4700

MY LITTLE PRETTY ONE; "My little pretty one, my pretty honey one" e 234; no title; "My lytell prety one,   4701
my pretie boni one" e 106

MY PRETTY LITTLE MISS; "How old are you my pretty little miss" e 171   4702A

HOW OLD ARE YOU?; "How old are you, my pretty little miss"; "Make my living in sandy land" (ref) e 214   4702B

NEAR WOODSTOCK TOWN; "Near Woodstock Town in Oxfordshire, as I walked forth to take the air" e 397   4703

THE NOBLE DUKE OF YORK; "Oh, the noble Duke of York, he had ten thousand men" e 214; O THE NOBLE   4704
DUKE OF YORK; "O the noble Duke of York, he had five thousand men" e 402

NONE CAN LOVE LIKE AN IRISHMAN; THE TURBENTURK; "The turban'd Turk, who scorns the world, may strut   4705
about with his whiskers curled" e 212

"NOW, ROBIN, LEND TO ME THY BOW" e 349   4706

NOW YE SPRINGE IS COME; "Now ye springe is come, turne to thy love, to thy love" e 107   4707

"OH, DEAR WHAT CAN THE MATTER BE" e 36,114,128,234,279,366,402; WHAT CAN THE MATTER BE? e 72   4708

O MY LOVE; "O, my love, lov'st thou me?" 4 pt round e 235,349   4709A

OH, MY LOVE; "Oh, my love, lov'st thou me?" 4 pt round e 36   4709B

O NO, JOHN; "On yonder hill there stands a creature" e 28,136,279,366   4710

O THE BONNY FISHER LAD; "O the bonny fisher lad, that brings the fishes frae the sea" e 235   4711

O THE OAK AND THE ASH; "A North Country lass up to London did pass" e 235; THE OAK AND THE ASH e 14;   4712
OH! THE OAK AND THE ASH; "A north-country maid up to London had stray'd" e 349

O, WON'T YOU BUY MY LAVENDER?; "O won't you buy my blooming lavender?" e 402   4713

O WALY, WALY; "The water is wide I cannot get o'er" e 48   4714

OLD JOHN BRADDLEUM; "Number one, number one, now my song has just begun" e 249   4715

OLD KING COLE; "Old King Cole was a merry old soul and a merry old soul was he" e 44   4716A

OLD KING COLE; "Old King Cole was a merry old soul and a merry old soul was he" e 199,234   4716B

OLD KING COLE; "Old King Cole was a jolly old soul, and this you may know by his larnin'" e 312   4716C

OLD KING COLE; "Old King Cole was a merry old soul, and a merry old soul was he" e 402   4716D

THE OLD MAID'S SONG; "I had a sister, Sally, that was younger than I am" e 215   4717

THE OLD MAN IN THE NORTH COUNTRY; "There was an old man in the North Country, Low down, derry down   4718A
dee" e 198

THE CRUEL SISTER; "There were two sisters sat in a bow'r, Hey ho, my Nannie, oh" e 198   4718B

THE TWO SISTERS; "There lived an old lord by the northern sea, bow down" e 215; THE OLD LORD BY THE   4718C
NORTHERN SEA e 260,264

BINNORIE; "There were two sisters sat in a bow'r, Binnorie, oh Binnorie" e 111   4718D

THE TWA SISTERS O' BINNORIE; "There were twa sisters sat in a bou'r" e 101   4718E

THE OLD WOMAN AND THE PEDLAR; "There was a little woman as I've heard tell" e 249; THERE WAS AN OLD   4719A
WOMAN; "There was an old woman as I've heard tell" e 234

THERE WAS AN OLD LADY; "There was an old lady, as I've heard tell" e 44   4719B

OLIVER CROMWELL; "Oliver Cromwell lay buried and dead" e 46   4720

ON BOARD A NINETY-EIGHT; "When I was young and scarce eighteen" e 198   4721

ON ILKLEY MOOR BAHT 'AT; "Wheear 'as tha been sin' ah saw thee?" e 402   4722

"ONCE I LOVED A MAIDEN FAIR" e 13,36   4723

ONE MAN WENT TO MOW; "One man went to mow, went to mow a meadow" e 402   4724

PSALM OF SION; "O mother dear, Jerusalem, Jehovah's throne on high" e 271   words by W. Prid   4725

THE PASSIONATE SHEPHERD TO HIS LOVE; "Come live with me and be my love" e 215   words by C. Marlowe   4726
PASTIME WITH GOOD COMPANY; "Pastime with good company I love, and shall until I die" e 397   4727
PEAS, BEANS, OATS, AND BARLEY; "There sits the man that plows up the land" e 37   4728
THE PEELERS AND THE PIG; The peelers and the goat (tune); "A bunch of peelers went out one day" e 198   4729
PHILLIS ON THE NEW-MADE HAY; "Phillis on the new-made hay, fair, but lonely still she lay" e 397   4730
PHILLIS WAS A FAIRE MAIDE; "Phillis was a faire maide and she had suitors store" e 196   4731
A POOR BEGGAR'S DAUGHTER; "A poor beggar's daughter did dwell on a green" e 397   4732
THE POOR MAN'S WISH; "Give me a little humble cot" e 198   4733
POOR OLD HORSE; "Oh, when I was a young horse, all in my youthful prime" e198   4734
POP! GOES THE WEASEL; "A penny for a spool of thread" e 32, 34; CORNWALLIS COUNTRY DANCE; "Cornwallis   4735
    led a country dance" e 173; A RIPPING TRIP; "You go aboard of a leaky boat" e 173
THE PRETTY PLOUGHBOY; "As I was a-walking one morning fair in Spring" e 198   4736
PRETTY POLLY OLIVER; "As sweet Polly Oliver lay musing in bed" e 349   words by A. P. Graves; "As pretty   4737
        Polly Oliver sat musing, 'tis said" e 14, 136, 397; POLLY OLIVER e 234; SWEET POLLY OLIVER;
        "As sweet Polly Oliver lay musing in bed" e 48
THE QUEEN OF MAY; "When the winter is gone and the summer is come" e 198   4738
RICHARD OF TAUNTON DENE; "Last New Year's Day, as I've heard say" e 234, 402   4739
ROBIN HOOD AND GUY OF GISBORNE; "When shaws are sheen and shrubs full fair" e 86   4740
THE ROBIN'S LAST WILL; "As I came past by Garrick, and by the bridge o' Dee" e 249; ROBIN'S LAST WILL;   4741
        "As I came past by Garrick, and by the bridge of Dee" e 199
ROCK-A-BYE, BABY; "Rock-a-bye, baby, on the tree top" e 129, 130, 131   4742
THE ROMAN SOLDIERS; "Have you any bread and wine? For we are the Romans" e 216   4743
SALLY IN OUR ALLEY; What though I am a country lass (tune); "Of all the girls that are so smart" e 13, 28, 36, 132,   4744
    279, 366, 402   words by H. Carey
THE SAUCY PLOUGHBOY; "Come all you pretty maidens, and listen unto me" e 198   4745
SAUCY SAILOR; "Come, my own one, come my fond one" e 234   4746
SCARBOROUGH FAIR; "Oh, where are you going? 'To Scarb'ro Fair'"; "Savory, sage, rosemary and thyme" (ref)   4747A
    e 35
A TRUE LOVER OF MINE; "Pray, can you buy me an acre or more"; "Savory, sage, rosemary, and thyme" (ref)   4747B
    e 186
SCOTLAND'S BURNING; "Scotland's burning, Scotland's burning" 4 pt round e 28, 279, 366   4748
SEE-SAW, MARGERY DAW; "See-saw, Margery Daw, Jack shall have a new master" e 28, 132, 366   4749
SEVENTEEN COME SUNDAY; "As I walked out one May morning, one May morning so early" e 198   4750A
SEVENTEEN COME SUNDAY; "As I walked out one May morning so early in the dawning" e 72   4750B
THE SHAMROCK SHORE; "Farewell, dear Erin's native isle, for here I cannot stay" e 198   4751
SHEEP SHEARING; "How delightful to see in those evenings in spring" e 216   4752
A SHEPHERD KEPT SHEEP; "A shepherd kept sheep on a hill so high" e 199   4753
SING A LITTLE; "Sing a little, and play a little" e 249   4754
SING OVY, SING IVY; "My father gave me an acre of land" e 95   4755
SING WE MERRILY; "Sing we now merrily, our purses are empty" 10 pt round e 349   4756
SIR EGLAMORE; "Sir Eglamore, that valiant knight" e 199, 234, 402   4757
SKYE BOAT SONG; "Speed bonnie boat, like a bird on the wing" e 35   words by H. Boulton, att to A. MacLeod   4758
SLEEPE, SLEEPE; "Sleepe, sleepe, though griefe torment thy body, sleep"; e 196   words from G. Earle's Song-   4759
    book (ms 1615)
SONG OF THE WESTERN MEN; "A good sword and a trusty hand!" e 235, 349   words by R. S. Hawkes   4760
THE SPRIG OF THYME; "Come all you pretty fair maids, that are just in your prime" e 198   4761
THE SPRING IS COMING; "The spring is coming resolved to banish the king of the ice with his turbulent train"   4762
    e 349   words by G. MacFarren; THE SPRING'S ACOMING; "The spring is acoming, all nature is
    blooming, and amorous lover does courage recover" e 95
THE SPRINGTIME OF THE YEAR; "As I walked out one morning in the springtime of the year" e 306   4763
STRAWBERRY FAIR; "As I was a-walking to Strawberry Fair" e 145   4764
SUMER IS ICUMEN IN; "Summer is a-coming in" e 235, 402; "SUMER IS I-CUMEN IN" e 199; "SUMER IS   4765
    ICUMEN IN" e, old e 70; SUMMER IS ICUMEN IN e 306; "SUMMER IS A-COMING IN" 4 pt
    round e 13, 37, 44
SUSAN'S COMPLAINT; "As down in the meadows I chanced to pass" e 185   4766
SWEET KITTY CLOVER; "Sweet Kitty Clover, she bothers me so, O, O!" e 402   words by E. Kean   4767
SWEET NIGHTINGALE; "My sweetheart come along, don't you hear the fond song" e 234   4768
THE TAILOR AND THE MOUSE; "There was a tailor had a mouse" e 173, 249   4769
TEN GREEN BOTTLES; "There were ten green bottles hanging on the wall" e 402   4770
"THERE'S A HOLE IN MY BUCKET" e 402   4771
THIS OLD MAN; "This old man, he played one, he played nick nack on my drum" e 402; NICK-NACK-   4772
        PADDY-WHACK e 249; NICK-NACK PADDY WACK e 216
THO' DARK ARE OUR SORROWS; SAINT PATRICK'S DAY; "Tho' dark are our sorrows, today we'll forget them"   4773
    e 166, 213; SAINT PATRICK'S DAY e 15   words by T. Moore

THREE BLIND MICE; "Three blind mice, three blind mice" 3 pt round e 28,233,366,402 4774

THREE PRETTY MAIDS; "Twas three pretty maids walk'd out one afternoon" e 198 4775

THE THREE RAVENS; "There were three ravens sat on a tree" e 14,35,235,397; "There were three ra'ens sat on a tree" e 111 4776A

THE TWA CORBIES; "My lover did come ere evensong" e 262 4776B

TO ALL YOU LADIES; "To all you ladies now at land" e 235; "To all you ladies now on land" e 397 words att to Baron Dorset 4777

TO THE MAYPOLE HASTE AWAY; "Come, ye young men, come along, with your music, dance and song" e 349 4778

TOBACCO; "Tobacco is an Indian weed" e 198 4779A

"TOBACCO'S BUT AN INDIAN WEED" e 173 4779B

THE TREES THEY GROW SO HIGH; "The trees they grow so high and the leaves they do grow green" e 46 4780

TURN AGAIN WHITTINGTON; "Turn again, Whittington, thou worthy citizen" 3 pt round e 235,349,402 4781

TURN THE GLASSES OVER; "I've been to Harlem, I've been to Dover, I've traveled this wide world all over" e 216 4782

TURPIN HERO; "It's bold Turpin hero is my name" e 198 4783

THE TURTLE DOVE; "Fare you well, my dear, I must be gone" e 36 4784

"'TWAS EARLY, EARLY ALL IN THE SPRING" e 198 4785

UNDER THE GREENWOOD TREE; "In summer time, when flow'rs do spring, and birds sit on each tree" e 235,349 4786

UNFORTUNATE MISS BAILEY; "A captain bold of Halifax who lived in country quarters" e 72; "A Captain bold in Halifax who dwelt in country quarters" e 186; MISS BAILEY'S GHOST e 173; THE HUNTERS OF KENTUCKY; "Ye gentlemen and ladies fair, who grace this famous city" e 173 words by S. Woodward 4787

UP THE RAW; "Up the raw, up the raw, up the raw, lass ev'ry day" e 235 4788

UPIDEE; "The shades of night were falling fast" e 402 4789

THE USEFUL PLOUGH; "In praise of the useful plough, from off the ten acre field's brow" e 349 words by A. P. Graves 4790

THE VICAR OF BRAY; The country garden (tune); "In good King Charles' golden days" e 14,235,349 4791

VILLIKINS AND HIS DINAH. See 8037A

THE WAGONER BOY; "Your horses are hungry, pray give them some hay" e 215 4792

THE WATER OF TYNE; "I cannot get to my love if I would dee" e 234 4793

WE ARE JOLLY FELLOWS THAT FOLLOW THE PLOUGH; "At four in the morning we rouse from our slumbers" e 198 4794

THE WEALTHY FARMER'S SON; "Come all you pretty maidens fair, attend unto my song" e 198 4795

WHEN JOAN'S ALE WAS NEW; "There was a jovial tinker, a mighty good ale drinker" e 198 4796

WHEN LOVE IS KIND; "When love is kind, cheerful and free" e 132,136,237,329 words by T. Moore 4797

"WHEN SHALL WE BE MARRIED JOHN?" e 249 4798

WHEN THE BRIGHT GOD OF DAY; "When the bright god of day drove to westward his ray" e 397 4799

WHEN THE KING ENJOYS HIS OWN AGAIN; "What Booker doth prognosticate concerning kings and kindoms' fate" e 294 words by M. Parker 4800

"WHERE ARE YOU GOING TO MY PRETTY MAID?" e 249 4801

WHITE BIRDS; "White birds, white birds, silver in the sun" e 199 words by J. M. Caie 4802

WHITE SAND AND GREY SAND; "White sand and grey sand who'll buy my white sand" e 235; "White sand and grey sand who'll buy my grey sand" e 402; WHITE AND GREY SAND 3 pt round e 349 4803

WHY DOST THOU TURNE AWAY?; "Why dost thou turne away, faire mayde?" e 196 words from G. Earle's Songbook (ms 1615) 4804

WIDDECOMBE FAIR; "Tom Pearce, Tom Pearce, lend me your grey mare" e 35,402; WIDDICOMBE FAIR e 234, 249; "Tom Pearce, Tom Pearce, lend me your gray mare" e 13; TAM PEARCE; "Tam Pearce, Tam Pearce, lend me thy gray mare" e 170 4805

WILLOW SONG; "The poor soul sat sighing by a Sycamore tree" e 75,117; OH! WILLOW!; "A poor soul sat sighing by a sycamore tree" e 235; O, WILLOW, WILLOW e 397; O WILLO, WILLO, WILLO!; "The poore soule sate sighinge by a sickamoore tree" e 208 4806

WITH JOCKEY TO THE FAIR; "'Twas on the morn of sweet May-day, when nature painted all things gay" e 234; AMID THE NEW-MOWN HAY; With Jockey to the fair (tune); "When swallows dart from cottage eaves and farmers dream of barley sheaves" e 349 words by C. MacKay 4807

WON'T IT BE WONDERFUL AFTER THE WAR! See 5878

THE WOODS SO WILD; "Shall I go walk the woods so wild" e 13 4808

THE WORLD TURNED UPSIDE DOWN; "If buttercups buzz'd after the bee" e 173 4809

THE YORKSHIRE FARMER; "A song I will sing unto you" e 198 4810A

THE OLD SPOTTED COW; THE YORKSHIRE BITE; "It is of a wealthy farmer, as you shall hear" e 72 4810B

THE YORKSHIRE BITE; "In London there lived a mason by trade" e 126 4810C

YOU GENTLEMEN OF ENGLAND; "You gentlemen of England that live at home at ease" e 349 4811

YOUNG RILEY THE FISHERMAN; "As I went out one morning down by the river side" e 198 4812

YOUNG ROGER THE PLOUGHBOY; "Young Roger the ploughboy a crafty young swain" e 198 4813

ALLEA ! ALLEO!; "When I was a tiny baby" e 37 — 4814

TULJAK; "All the country was invited"; "Tonni, handsome young Tonni" (ref) e 37 — 4815

FINLAND

ÄLÄ ITKE ÄITINI"; "Älä itke äitini älä äiti kulta"; WEEP NO MORE; "E'en though father from us torn lies beneath the soil now" e, fi 124 — 4816

ALL ALONE; "All alone now I sit here singing" e 95 — 4817

"ARVON MEKIN ANSAITSEMME"; SONG OF PRAISE; "Finland, too, deserves all honour" e, fi 124   words by J. Juteini — 4818

AT THE CHERRY TREE; "Grows by the stream a cherry tree" e 95 — 4819

THE BIRCH TREE; "Lonely in the forest stands a birch tree" e 95 — 4820

FAITH UNDYING; "Sere are the meadows, gray is the sky" e 37 — 4821

FAR FROM ME; "Far from me my loved one went" e 70 — 4822

HÄRMÄN HÄÄT; "Härmässä häät oli kauhiat"; THE WEDDING IN HÄRMÄ; "Frightening and horrible was it all" e, fi 124 — 4823

"ICH BIN DER JUNGE HIRTENKNAB" g 49 — 4824

ILTALAULA; "Tääll' yksinäni laulelen"; EVENING SONG; "My daily work is over" e, fi 124 — 4825

IN DEINES VATERS GÄRTELEIN; "In deines Vaters Gärtelein ein Röslein wuchs all-da" g 49 — 4826

JUOKSE POROSEIN; "Juokse porosein, poikki vuoret, maat!"; SONG OF THE LAPPS; "Run, my reindeer sure, over dale and hill!" e, fi 124   words by F. M. Franzen — 4827

KALEVALA-SÄVELMÄ; "Mieleni minun tekevi, aivoni ajattelevi"; KALEVALA MELODY; "Quickly through my mind go winging thoughts that I should start a singing" e, fi 124 — 4828

KESÄILLALLA; "Kun kävelin kesäillalla"; ON A SUMMER'S EVE; "While walking once on a summer's eve" e, fi 124 — 4829

KESÄILTA; "Ol' kaunis kesäilta, kun laaksossa kävelin"; SUMMER EVENING; "One lovely summer evening while wandering thro' a glade" e, fi 124 — 4830

KOIVISTO POLSKA; Koiviston polska   piano 124 — 4831

KREIVIN SYLISSÄ ISTUNUT; "Minä seisoin korkealla vuorella"; STANDING ON A HILLOCK; "Standing on a hillock well above the lake" e, fi 124 — 4832

KUKAPA SEN SAUNAN LÄMMITTÄÄPI?"; WHO WILL HEAT THE BATH-HOUSE?; "Who will ever heat the sauna bath-house" e, fi 124 — 4833

KUKU KÄKÖSENI; "Kuku, kuku minun käköseni, kuku"; CUCKOO, CUCKOO; "Cuckoo, cuckoo, I can hear you calling Cuckoo" e, fi 124 — 4834

KULLAN YLISTYS; "Minun kultani kaunis on"; MY BEST GIRL; "My best girl's a pretty lass" e, fi 124; MINUM KULTANI; LUMBERMAN'S SONG; "My sweetheart is a gorgeous gal" e, fi 36; WHAT SAY YOU?; "Some folk say we should laugh and play" e 199 — 4835

KUN ENSI KERRAN; "Kun ensi kerran silmäs näin"; MEETING; "I felt a warming burst of sunshine" e, fi 124 — 4836

LAAKSON RUUSU; "Yksi ruusu on kasvanut laaksossa"; THE ROSE IN THE VALE; "All alone in the vale grew a single rose" e, fi 124; THE ROSEBUSH; "In the valley a rosebush is flowering" e 95 — 4837

LÄKSIN MINÄ KESÄYÖNÄ; "Läksin minä kesäyönä käymään"; ONE NIGHT IN SUMMER; "Walking quite alone, one night in summer" e, fi 124 — 4838

LAPPALAISJOIKU; "Elli Nilla la laala laa, jo"; A LAPP JOIKU; "Elli Nilla la-laa la-laa, yo!" e, fi 124 — 4839

LUULLAHAN; "Luullahan jotta on lysti olla"; THE SINGER; "People all think that I am happy" e, fi 124; "GLAUBT IHR DENN, DASS ICH LUSTIG BIN" g 49 — 4840

MANSIKKA; "Mansikka on punanen marja"; STRAWBERRIES; "Red are strawberries, redder than roses" e, fi 124 — 4841

MIES MERTEN MERTA RAKASTAA; EN SJÖMAN ÄLSKAR HAVETS VAAG; "Mies merten merta rakastaa ja kuohuja sen"; THE SAILOR LOVES THE SEA; "The sailor loves the foaming brine, and all the deep-blue sea" e, fi 124 — 4842

NIIN SINULLE LAULAN; "Niin minä neitonen sinulle laulan"; LOVE SONG; "Now let me sing of a secret power" e, fi 124 — 4843

RALLIALEI; "What light is that, shining far at sea?" e 95 — 4844

A RING AROUND HER FINGER; "Azure and white is the endless sky" e 95 — 4845

RUNO; "Brothers, let us sing together" e 37 — 4846

"SO WEIT WIE DIE WEISSEN WOLKEN GEHN" g 49 — 4847

SOUTELIN, SOUTELIN; "Soutelin, soutelin, kultani kanssa"; ONCE I WAS ROWING; "Once I was rowing with my lover" e, fi 124; "KUCKUCK RUFT IM TANNENWALD" g 49 — 4848

SUOMEN RATSUVÄEN MARSSI 30-VUOTISESSA SODASSA; "On Pohjolan hangissa meill' isänmaa"; FINNISH CAVALRY MARCH FROM THE THIRTY YEARS' WAR; "The land of our fathers is in Northern snow" e, fi 124   words by Z. Topelius — 4849

SYNTYMISTÄÄN SUREVA; "Voi äiti parka ja raukka, kun minut synnytit"; ALAS, MY WRETCHED MOTHER; "Alas, my wretched mother, what means this life to me?" e, fi 124 — 4850

TAIVAS ON SININEN; "Taivas on sininen ja valkoinen"; THE SKY IS BLUE; "Countless as all the stars that cover the sky" e, fi 124 — 4851

FRANCE

"AU PRÉ DE LA ROSE"; "AOU PRAT DÉ LA ROSO" f 67   4886

"AUF, AUF, ZUM FRÖHLICHEN JAGEN"; Pour aller à la chasse (tune) g 353   4887

AUPRÈS DE MA BLONDE; "Au jardin de mon père" f 402; "Out in my father's garden" e, f 187; "Dans le jardin   4888
    d'mon père" f 67; NEAR TO MY FAIR ONE; "Oh, in my father's garden" e, f 34; "Dans les jardins
    d'mon père" f 88, 91

L'AUTRE JOUR, EN VOULANT DANSER; "L'autre jour, en voulant danser, gai farira, larira dondé!" f 68   4889

L'AUTRE JOUR, M'ALLANT PROMENER; "L'autre jour, m'allant promener, (Ah, mon mal ne vient que d'aimer!)";   4890
    WALKING ALONE THE OTHER DAY; "Walking alone the other day, (Ah, for love I'm pining away!")
    e, f 174

L'AVOINE; "Qui veut savoir et qui veut voir" f 127   4891

BAD WEATHER; "Ah, Mon Dieu, le temps est nuageux"; "Oh the sky is growing dark!" e, f 86   4892

BAÏLÈRO; "Pastré, dè dèlaï l'aïo, a gaïré dé boun tèn"; CHANT DE BERGERS DE HAUTE-AUVERGNE; "Pâtre, par   4893
    delà l'eau, tu n'as guère de bon temps" f, f(a) 62

LA BELL, SI NOUS ÉTIOM'; "La belle', si nous étiom' dedans stu haut bois"; "Belle, vous m'avez t'embarlifi" (ref)   4894
    f 91

BELLE DOETTE; "Belle Doette as fenestres sesiet" f 108   4895

"LA BELLE EST AU JARDIN D'AMOUR"; "BEAUTY IN LOVE'S GARDEN" e, f 47   4896

LA BELLE TABLE EST MISE; "La belle table est mise dès sous les arbres vert"; BENEATH THE VERDANT ARBOR;   4897
    "Beneath the verdant arbor the table glistens bright" e, f 140   words by F. Mistral

LA BELLE ZOÉ; "C'était un' bell' corvette, Lonla!" f 127; COUSIN MALURON; "C'était un p'tit bonhomm',   4898
    luron!" f 127

BERCEUSE D'AUVERGNE; "Sommeil, vite, vite, vite, sommeil, vite reviens donc" f 91   4899

BERCEUSE DU PETIT GARS; "Dors, dors, mon petit gars" f 91   4900

LA BERGÈRE ANNETTE; "Autrefois la jeune Annette s'en allait sur les coteaux"; ONCE YOUNG CHLOE; "Once   4901
    young Chloe would when roving, on her shepherd's duties bent" e, f 175   words by N. G. Léonard

BERGÈRE LÉGÈRE; "Bergère légère, je crains tes appas"; O FICKLE SHEPHERDESS; "O shepherdess fickle, your   4902
    charms I defy" e, f 36

BERGERS, DANS NOS BOIS; "Bergers, dans nos bois venez vous rendre"; SHEPHERDS, IN THIS GROVE; "Shepherds,   4903
    in this grove come, come and wander" e, f 174

BIÈLH CONTAU; "Jou'l cièu de l'oubernho poulido"; VIEUX CANTAL; "Sous ton ciel, Auvergne jolie" f, f (a) 88   4904

BON VOYAGE, MONSIEUR DUMOLLET; "Bon voyage, cher Dumollet" f 91   4905

BONJOUR GUILLAUME; "Bonjour, Guillaume, as-tu bien déjeuné?" f 127   4906

LA BONNE AVENTURE; "Je suis un petit garçon à la bonne allure"; "Si le roi m'avait donné, Paris sa belle ville"   4907
    f 88; "Je suis un petit poupon de belle figure" f 91; JE SUIS UN PETIT GARÇON; "Je suis un petit
    garçon, de bonne figure" f 127; SI LE ROI M'AVAIT DONNÉ; "Si le Roi m'avait donné Paris sa
    grand' ville" f 127; "Si le roi m'avait donné Paris sa grande ville" f 82

LA BOURRÉE D'AUVERGNE; "Lo bouolé lo Morianno! Lo bouolé maï l'ouraï!"; LA MARIANNE; "Je la veux la   4908
    Marianne! Je la veux, je l'aurai!" f (a) 88

LA BOURRÉE D'AUVERGNE; "La bourrée d'Auvergne, la bourée va bien"; LA BOURRÉE D'AUVERGNHO f 88   4909

LOU BOUSSU; "Dzanètou tsou'l poumièirou què sé souloumbravo"; LE BOSSU; "Jeanneton sous un pommier se   4910
    repose à l'ombre" f, f (a) 64

BREZAIROLA; "Soun, soun, bèni, bèni, bèni, soun, soun, bèni, bèni doun"; BERCEUSE; "Viens, viens, sommeil,   4911
    sommeil, descends, viens, sommeil, viens donc!"; f, f (a) 64; SOUN, SOUN, BÉNI, BÉNI;
    "Sommeil, sommeil, viens, viens, viens, sommeil, sommeil, viens, viens, viens" f, f(a) 88

LE BRICOU; "Ah! l'bricou, l'bricou, l'bricou; qui n'veut pas planter les choux" f 91   4912

BRUNETTE; "La bergère que je sers, ne scait rien de mon martire" f 278   4913

"C'EST À CE JOLI MOIS DE MAY" f 108   4914

"C'EST LES GENS DE BOUZE"; "Bringue, stringue, landerira" (ref) f 91   4915

C'EST MON AMI; "Ah! s'il est dans votre village" f 91; HE IS MY LOVE; "If there's a shepherd in your parish"   4916
    e, f 140   words by J. P. C. de Florian, att to M. Antoinette

C'EST UN PETIT OISEAU; "C'est un p'tit oiseau, qui prit sa volée" f 127   4917

"C'EST UN REMPART QUE NOTRE DIEU" f 82   4918

CADET ROUSSELLE; "Cadet Rousselle a trois maisons"; "Ah! ah! ah! mais vraiment Cadet Rousselle est bon enfant"   4919
    (ref) f 82, 88, 127; "Ah! ah! ah! oui vraiment, Cadet Rousselle est bon enfant" (ref) f 383; CADET
    ROUSELLE; "Ah! ah! ah! mais vraiment, Cadet Rousselle est bon enfant" (ref) f 91

LO CALHÉ; "È, dio mè tu, lo calhé, ound as toun nïou?"; LA CAILLE; "Eh! dis-moi donc, la caille, ou est ton   4920
    nid?" f, f (a) 63

LES CANARDS; "Un canard, déployant ses ail's, coin, coin, coin" f 82   4921A

LES CANARDS; "Un canard déployant ses ailes, en se baignant dans son étang" f 61   4921B

CANTIQUE DES PETITS OISEAUX; "Que chantez vous petits oiseaux?" f 108   words by J. Cassagne   4922

CANTO PER MA MIO; "Sur le pont de Nantes il est un oiseau" f 91   4923

LA CARMAGNOLE; "Madame Véto avait promis de faire égorger tout Paris" f 88; "Madame Veto her promise   4924
    gave, Madame Veto her promise gave, that all of France would be her slave" e, f 7

CELLE QU'ADORE MON COEUR; Des Fraises (tune); Mon mari s'en est allé (tune); Jardinier ne vois-tu pas (tune); 4925
       "Celle qu'adore mon coeur n'est ni brune ni blonde"; SHE WHO HAS MY HEART; "She who has my
       heart is not too fair nor yet too swarthy" e, f 174 words by A. Hamilton

CHANSON DE FORTUNIO; "Si vous croyez que je vais dire" f 127 4926

LA CHANSON DE L'AVEINE; "Voulez-vous savoir comment, comment on sème l'aveine?" f 91 4927

CHANSON DE LA MARIÉE; "Nous somm' venus vous voir" f 91; MADAME LA MARIÉE f 127 4928

CHANSON DE MAI; "Mai revient, tout brille aux cieux" f 82 4929

CHANSON DU COMTE HAMILTON; Mais il est dans la rivière (tune); Quand il est dans la rivière (tune); "C'est 4930
       cet objet pour qui Phébus m'inspire"; COUNT HAMILTON'S SONG; "She, she it is whom Phoebus
       bids me praise" e, f 175 words by A. Hamilton

LA CHANSON DU TAMBOURINEUR; "Qu'on m'apporte ma flûte"; THE SONG OF THE DRUMMER; "Oh bring to me 4931
       my flute" e, f 210

CHANSON TOURANGELLE; "Bonne terre de Touraine, beau jardin et doux verger" f 88 4932

CHANTONS LES AMOURS DE JEAN; "Chantons, chantons les amours de Jeanne"; OH SING OF THE LOVE OF JOHN; 4933
       "Oh sing, oh sing of the love of Jeanne!" e, f 36

CHARMANTE MARIANNE; "Où vas-tu donc, Marianne charmante?" f 88 4934

CHAUDRON TROUÉ; "Chaudron troué, Madame a reparer"; "Somm' venus dans votre vile" (verse) f 91 4935

LE CHEVALIER DU GUET; "Qu'est-c'qui passe ici si tard" f 91,127; LA MARJOLAINE f 383 4936

"CHEVALIERS DE LA TABLE RONDE" f 383 4937

CHEZ NOUS IL Y A CINQ PETITS CHATS; "Chez nous y a cinq p'tits chats" f 127 4938

CHUT, CHUT; "Moun païré mé n'o lougado"; "Mon père m'a trouvé un' place" f, f (a) 65 4939

COLINETTE; "Colinette au bois s'en alla" f 60 4940

COME, GOOD WIND; V'la l'bon vent (tune); "Come, good wind, come fair wind" e 279,366 4941

COMPÈRE ET COMMÈRE; "Mon compère, quand je danse, mon cotillon va-t-il bien?" f 82; MA COMMÈRE 4942
       QUAND JE DANSE; "Ma commère quand je danse, mon cotillon va-t-il bien?" f 127

COMPÈRE GUILLERI; "Il etait un p'tit homme, qui s'app'lait Guilleri" f 91,127,383 4943

LE COUCOU; "Dans la forêt lointaine, on entend le coucou" f 383 4944

LE COUCOU; "Le coucou a fait son nid sur l'arbre" f 91 4945

LOU COUCUT; "Lou coucut oqu'os un áuzel"; LE COUCOU; "Le coucou c'est un bel oiseau" f, f (a) 65 4946

LA COUMAIRE; "Tu vas voir la commère"; TO MONTELIMAR; "You'll visit that old dame?" e, f 86 4947

LE CURÉ DE POMPONNE; "Un jour, m'en allant confesser" f 60 4948

D'OÙ VENEZ-VOUS, FILLETTE?; "D'où venez-vous, fillette, le rossignol qui vole?"; D'OUND V'ENANATZ, 4949
       FILHETO?; "D'ound v'enantz, filheto, lou roussignóu que volo?" f (a) 67

DAME TARTINE; "Il était un' Dame Tartine" f 91 4950

DANCING DOLLIES; "So we tap, tap, tap, tap the feet of dancing dollies" e 214 4951

DANS CE BEAU VALLON; "Dans ce beau vallon, sur le gazon" f 59 4952

DANS MON BERGER; "Dans mon berger tout m'enchante" f 59 4953

LA DANSE DES GORETS; "L'autre jour étant seulette près des vertes forêts"; "Youp la la, larirette, ô gué!" (ref) 4954
       f 82; YOUP, LA! LA!; "Quand j'étais avec mon père, Youp lala, lalira!"; "Youp lala lalirette,
       Oh! gai!" (ref) f 127

DANSONS LA CAPUCINE; "Dansons la capucine, n'y a pas de pain chez nous" f 127 4955

DEBOUT, SAINTE COHORTE; "Debout, sainte cohorte, Soldats du Roi des rois!" f 82 4956

LA DELAÏSSÁDO; "Uno pastourèlo, èspèr' olaï al capt del bouès"; LA DÉLAISSÉE; "Une bergère, attend, là-bas 4957
       en haut du bois" f, f (a) 63

DÉLICIEUSES CÎMES; "Délicieuses cîmes, celles du Canigou"; MONTANYAS REGALADAS; "Montanyas regaladas 4958
       son las del Canigó" f 68

LES DEUX MANIÈRES D'AIMER; "Être soumis, fidèle et sincère"; THE TWO WAYS OF LOVING; "Gentle and 4959
       faithful, truthful and tender" e, f 174

DIALOGUE DES MÉTAMORPHOSES; "O belle Marguerite, Reine de mes amours" f 91 4960

DIS-MOI, M'AMOUR LA CAILLE; "Dis-moi, m'amour la caille, ou t'as ton nid?" f 91 4961

LOU DIZIOU BÉ; "Lou diziou bé, Pierrou, qu'aymay ley drolloy"; ON DISAIT BIEN; "On disait bien, que tu 4962
       aimais les filles" f, f (a) 66

DODO, NANETTE; "Dodo, dodo, Nanette, landerirette!" f 68 4963

DONNER LE BONJOUR; "Le chat à la promenade, doit donner le bonjour" f 127 4964

DU ROSSIGNAL QUI CHANTE; "Du rossignol qui, chante j'ai entendu la voix"; O NIGHTINGALE; "O nightingale, 4965
       pray sing that I may hear thy voice" e, f 406

EHO! EHO!; "Eho! Eho! Eho! Les agneaux vont aux plaines"; "Eho! Eho! Eho! Keep your lambs in the valley" e, f 47 4966

"EN PASSANT PAR LA LORRAINE" f 82,88,91,127; "PASSING ONCE THRU FAIR LORRAINE" e, f 7; LES TROIS 4967
       CAPITAINES f 383

"EN REVENANT D'AUVERGNE" f 88,91 4968

ES LEBEN DIE STUDENTEN; "Es leben die Studenten stets in den Tag hinein" g 31 words by C. Dehn 4969

EST-CE QUE ÇA SE DEMANDE; "Sois donc sensible à mes soupirs"; WHY, WHAT A THING TO MENTION; "Why 4970
       not my sighs sweetly requite?" e, f 174

FAIS DODO, COLAS; "Fais dodo, Colas, mon p'tit frère" f 91 4971

LA FANFAN LA TULIPE; FANFAN LA TULIPE; "Call me Fanfan la Tulipe"; "When my stepfather sent me away 4972
    from home" (verse) e 86

FARANDOLE; "Straight from the dairy, fresh as a fairy" e 95   4973

FILEUSE; "Lorsque j'étais jeunette, je gardais les moutons"; "When I was young and pretty, I watched over my 4974A
    flock" e, f 47

LO FIOLAIRE; "Ton qu'èrè pitchounèlo Gordavè loui mou-tous"; LA FILEUSE; "Tant que j'étais petite je gardais 4974B
    les moutons" f, f (a) 64

LA FILLE AU CRESSON; "Margotton vat-à l'iau avec que son cruchon!" f 61   4975

LA FILLE DE PARTHENAY; "A Parthenay, il y avait une tant belle fille" f 383   4976

LA FILLE DU ROI LOYS; "Le roi Loys est sur son pont" f 91   4977

FIND WORK, MY DAUGHTER; "Find work, my daughter, you can milk a cow" e 95   4978

LE FORGERON; "Sous ton lourd marteau, mon voisin" f 82,88   4979

FRÈRE JACQUES; "Frère Jacques, frère Jacques, dormez vous, dormez vous?" f 82,91,127,383,402; BROTHER 4980
        JOSEPH; "Brother Joseph, Brother Joseph, do you sleep?" e 235; BROTHER JOHN; "Are you sleeping,
        are you sleeping, brother John" e, f 187; ARE YOU SLEEPING? 4 pt round e 28,233,366

GAI LON LA, GAI LE ROSIER; "Par derrièr' chez ma tante"; GAY AS THE ROSE; "Out by my aunt's own cottage" 4981
    e, f 187

LES GARS DE LOCMINÉ; "Mon père et ma mère, De Lyon ils sont"; "Sont, sont, sont les gars de Locminé" f 127 4982

GENTIL COQUELICOT; "Je descendis dans mon jardin" f 127; GENTIL COQU'LICOT f 91   4983

GENTILLE BATELIÈRE; "Gentille batelière laisse là ton bateau"; "Non! non! non! j'aime mieux mon bateau" (ref) 4984
    f 383

"GRAND DIEU, NOUS TE BÉNISSONS" f 82   4985

GUIGNOLOT DE ST. LAZOT; "C'est Guignolot d'Saint Lazot"; THE FEAST OF ST. LAZARUS; "We're the 4986
    Lazarus mummers" e, f 231

HANS DE SCHNÖCKELOCH; "Hans, Hans de Schnöckeloch a tout c'qu'il veut en mains" f 88   4987

HÉ! BEYLA-Z-Y DAU FÉ!; "Hé! Beyla-z-y dau fé an aquel azé!; HÉ! DONNE-LUI DU FOIN!; "Hé! Donne-lui 4988
    du foin à ce pauvre âne!" f, f(a) 66

"IL COURT, IL COURT LE FURET" f 82,127; LE FURET DU BOIS JOLI f 91   4989

"IL EST QUELQU'UN SUR TERRE"; "THERE'S SOMEONE IN MY FANCY" e, f 47   4990

IL ÉTAIT TROIS MATELOTS; "Il était trois mat'lots de Groix" f 127   4991A

LES TROIS MATELOTS DE GROIX; "Il était trois mat'lots de Groix" f 88   4991B

"IL ÉTAIT UN' BERGÈRE" f 82,91; IL ÉTAIT UNE BERGERE f 127,383; "There was a little maiden" e, f 70; 4992
        "Il était une bergère" f 88; THE SHEPHERDESS; "A shepherdess was watching ding-dong, ding-
        dong" e 199

IL ÉTAIT UN' FRÉGATE; "Il était un' frégate lon la" f 68   4993

"IL ÉTAIT UN PETIT NAVIRE" f 88,91,127; THERE WAS ONCE A LITTLE SHIP; "Oh, there was once a little 4994
        ship" e, f 187; LE PETIT NAVIRE f 82,383

IL ÉTAIT UNE FILLE; "Il était une fille, une fille d'honneur"; "Oh! Mais on ne voit plus guèrre" (ref) f 91 4995

IL PLEUT, BERGÈRE; "Il pleut, il pleut, bergère" f 383; "IL PLEUT, IL PLEUT, BERGÈRE" f 82,88,91,127 4996

"J'AI CUELLI LA BELLE ROSE"; "I HAVE PICKED A LOVELY ROSEBUD" e, f 187   4997

J'AI DU BON TABAC; "J'ai du bon tabac dans ma tabatière" f 88,91   4998

J'AI PERDU LE DO; "J'ai perdu le do de ma clarinette" f 88; "J'AI PERDU LE DO DE MA CLARINETTE" f 127 4999

J'AIME UN BRUN; "J'aime un brun depuis un jour"; "I HAVE LOVED FOR HALF A DAY" e, f 175   5000

J'ENTENDS LE MOULIN; Frit à l'huile (tune); "J'entends la moulin, tique, tique, taque"; I HEAR THE MILL- 5001
        WHEEL; "I hear the mill-wheel, tick-a, tick-a, tack-a" e, f 187

JACQUES, JACQUES; "Jacques, Jacq' hélas, mon ami Jacques" f 60   5002

LE JARDIN D'AMOUR; "Quand je vais au jardin, jardin d'amour"; THE GARDEN OF LOVE; "When through love's 5003
        garden at nightfall I glide" e, f 45; JARDIN D'AMOUR f 383; GEH ICH ZUM GRÜNEN HAIN; "Geh
        ich zum grünen Hain Liebeshain" g 226

JE T'AURAI, MA BRUNETTE; "Je t'aurai, ma brunette, je t'aurai, oui, ma foi!" f 91   5004

JEANNETTE, OÙ IRONS-NOUS?; "Jeannette, où irons-nous garder?" f 383   5005

UNO JIONTO POSTOURO; "Uno jionto postouro, un d'oquèce motis"; UNE JOLIE BERGÈRE; "Une jolie bergère, 5006
        par un de ces matins" f, f (a) 66

JOLI TAMBOUR; "Trois jeun' tambours s'en revenant de guerre" f 127; THE DRUMMER-BOY; "A drummer-boy 5007A
        from war came marching gaily" e 199

LE JOLI TAMBOUR; "Trois jeun' tambours s'en rev'nant de la guerre" f 88; "Trois jeun' tambours s'en revenaient 5007B
        de guerre" f 91; "Trois jeun's tambours s'en revenant de guerre" f 82

JOU L'POUNT D'O MIRABEL; "Jou l'pount d'o Mirabel Cotorino lobabo"; AU PONT DE MIRABEL; "Au pont de 5008
        Mirabel Catherine, un jour lavait" f, f (a) 65

LÀ-HAUT SUR LA MONTAGNE; "Là-haut sur la montagne, était un vieux chalet" f 88   5009

LÀ-HAUT, SUR LE ROCHER; "Là-haut, sur le rocher là-haut, sur la montagne" f 66   5010

LÀ-HAUT, SUR LES MONTAGNES; "Là-haut, sur les montagnes, un pâtre malheureux" f 91   5011

LANGUIRAY-JE TOUJOURS?; "Mon père m'a mariée avec un vieillard jaloux" f 61   5012

LE LEVER DU SOLEIL; "La douce lumière de l'astre du jour" f 88   5013

LISETTE; "En menant paître mon troupeau"; "As off to pasture I did go" e, f 36   5014

"LORSQUE J'AVIONS DES NOISETTES" f 91   5015

LORSQUE J'ÉTAIS TANT AMOUREUSE; "Lorsque j'étais tant amoureuse de mon galant"; QUOAND JOU N'ÈRI   5016
AMOUROUSETE; "Quoand jou n'èri amourousete d'acet galant" f, f (p) 68

LULLABY; "Never, never in our mountain was there born so sweet a baby" e 95   5017

"MA CULOTTE A DEUX BOUTONS" f 127   5018

MA GRAND' MÈRE; "Ma grand'mère qui n'avait qu'un' dent" f 91   5019

"MALBROUGH S'EN VA-T-EN GUERRE" f 82,88; MALBROUGH f 383; MARLBOROUGH; "Marlborough has gone   5020
to battle" e, f 7; "MALBROUGH S'EN VA-T-EN f 91; "MALBROUCK S'EN VA-T-EN GUERRE" f 127;
"For he's a jolly good fellow" (2nd verse); "The bear went over the mountain" (3rd verse) e, f 70;
MALBROUCK; "Malbrouck has gone to battle" e, f 34; "TO WAR HAS GONE DUKE MARLBOROUGH"
e 279,366; "FOR HE'S A JOLLY GOOD FELLOW" e 128,132,233,236,366

"MALUROUS QU'O UNO FENNO"; "MALHEUREUX QUI A UNE FEMME" f, f (a) 64   5021

MAMAN, DITES-MOI; "Maman, dites-moi ce qu'on sent quand on aime"; MOTHER, PLEASE EXPLAIN; "Mother   5022
please explain, what is love? Won't you tell me?" e, f 176

MAMAN, LES P'TITS BATEAUX; "Maman, les p'tits bateaux qui vont sur l'eau, ont-ils des jambes?" f 91   5023

MARCHONS AVEC JOIE; "Marchons avec joie dans le bon chemin" f 82   5024

LA MARGUERITE; "Où est la Marguerite? Ho gué! ho gué! Ho gué!" f 82   5025

"MARIANNE S'EN VA-T-AU MOULIN"; MARIE WENT TO THE MILL; "One day, Marie went to the mill" e, f 187   5026

LA MARION ET LE BOSSU; "La Marion sous un pommier qui se guinganave" f 91   5027

MARQUIS ET MARQUISE; "Madame la Marquise, votre bras est bien fait" f 88   5028

MATIN; "Il fait jour, le ciel est rose" f 82   5029

LA MAUMARIÉE; LA MAL MARIÉE; "Mon per' m'a mariée a la Saint Nicolas" f 383   5030

MAYDAY; "Mayday is come, now welcome May!" e 95   5031

LA MÈR' MICHEL; "C'est la mèr' Michel qui a perdu son chat" f 82,91; LA MÈRE MICHEL f 383; C'EST LA   5032
MÈRE MICHEL f 127

MEUNIER, TU DORS; "Meunier, tu dors! Ton moulin va trop vite" f 127   5033

"MIGNONNE, ALLONS VOIR SI LA ROSE" f 88   5034

LA MIST'-EN L'AIRE; "Bonhomme, bonhomme, que savez-vous faire?" f 88,127   5035

LE MOIS DE MAI; "C'est le mai, mois de mai" f 91; IT IS MAY; "It is May, lovely May" e 95   5036

LE MOIS DE MAI; "Il est de retour, le joyeux mois de mai!" f 88   5037

MON BEAU SAPIN; "Mon beau sapin, roi des forêts" f 88   5038

"MON PÈR' M'A DONNÉ UN MARI" f 82   5039

MON PETIT OISEAU; "Mon petit oiseau a pris sa volée" f 91   5040

MONA; "Sous les saules de la rivière" f 91   5041

LA MONACO; "A la Monaco, l'on chasse, l'on déchasse" f 91   5042

MONSIEUR DE LA PALISSE; "Messieurs, vous plait-il douir l'air du fameux la Palisse" f 127; "Cherries grow   5043
inside the park of Monsieur de la Palisse" e 86; LA PALISSE f 88

LA MOUCHE ET LA FOURMI; "Je suis, disait la mouche, a la table des Rois" f 82   5044

"MOUÉ, QUAND J'ÉTAIS CHEZ MON PÈRE" f 68   5045

LOU MOULET; "O joucat sus lo ribieriro escoundut dins les vernhats"; LE MOULIN; "Sur le bord de la rivière   5046
caché dans les aulnes verts" f, f(p) 88

LE MOULIN; "Je sais au bord du Rhin (Fa-le-ri de-ri di-ra, la la la la!)" f 82   5047

N'AÏ PAS IÈU DE MÏO; "N'aï pas ïeu dè mio, soui qu'un' pastourel"; JE N'AI PAS D'AMIE; "Je n'ai pas d'amie,   5048
je ne suis qu'un berger" f, f (a) 63

"NE PLEURE PAS, JEANNETTE" f 383   5049

LA NÉCESSITÉ D'AIMER; "Un peu d'amour est nécessaire"; THE NEED TO LOVE; "Life without love is dull and   5050
dreary" e, f 174

LE NEZ DE MARTIN; "Martin prend sa serpe, au bois il s'en va" f 82   5051

NID D'HIRONDELLE; "Pauvre petit, pourquoi pleurs-tu?"; THE SWALLOW'S NEST; "Poor little one, tell me why   5052
you cry" e, f 86

LES NOCES DU PAPILLON; "Il faut te marier, Papillon couleur de neige" f 82,383 words by M.   5053
Boucher

NOTRE ALSACE ADORÉE; "Notre Alsace adorée, risant et clair séjour" f 88   5054

NOTRE ÂNE; "Notre âne, notre âne avait grand mal aux pieds" f 127   5055A

NOTRE ÂNE; "Notre âne, notre âne a grand mal à sa tête" f 91   5055B

NOTRE BON DUC DE SAVOIE; "Notre bon duc de Savoie n'est-il pas un bon enfant?" f 91   5056

"NOUS N'IRONS PLUS AU BOIS" f 82,88,91,127,383   5057

"O DIEU, S'IL FAUT QU'ON TE CRAIGNE" f 82   5058

"OBAL, DIN LO COUMBELO"; "AU LOIN, LÀ-BAS DANS LA VALLÉE" f, f (a) 66   5059

OBAL, DIN LOU LIMOUZI; "Obal, din lou Limouzi, pitchoun' obal din lou Limouzi"; LÀ-BAS DANS LE LIMOU-   5060
SIN; "Là-bas dans le Limousin, petit', là-bas dans le Limousin" f, f (a) 62

L'OCCASION MANQUÉE; "Margueridette au bord du bois" f 383   5061

OÏ AYAÏ; "Oï, ayaï, couci ïeu foraï?"; "Oh! yayaï! Qu'est c'que je ferai?" f, f (a) 65   5062

L'OISEAU CAPTIF; "Depuis bien des années, la nuit comme le jour" f 91   5063

OÙ IRAI-JE ME PLAINDRE?; "Où irai-je me plaindre? Moi, pauvre infortuné?" f 67   5064

OUND' ONORÈN GORDA?; "Ound' onorèn gorda, pitchouno drooulèto?"; OÙ IRONS-NOUS GARDER?; "Où irons-   5065
nous garder, petite fillette?" f, f (a) 62

PASSO PEL PRAT; "Lo lo lo...Passo pel prat, bèloto"; VIENS PAR LE PRÉ; "Lo lo lo...Viens par le pré, ma belle"   5066
f, f (a) 64

PASTORALE; "Baïlèro, lèro, lèro! Pastré, de delaï l'aïo!"; "Baïlèro, lèro, lèro, Pâtre, par delà l'eau!" f, f (a) 65   5067

PASTORALE; "Viens, charmante, Annette, sauter sur l'herbette" f 108   5068

LA PASTOURA ALS CAMPS; "Quon lo pastouro s'en bo os cams"; LA BERGÈRE AUX CHAMPS; "Quand la bergère   5069
s'en va-t-aux champs" f, f (a) 62

PASTOURELLE; "È passo dè dessaï! È passo dellaï l'aïo!"; "Ah! viens auprès de moi! Et passe la rivière!" f, f(a)63   5070

LA PASTROULETTA È LOU CHIBALIÉ; "Lougarias bous un'gardaïré, pastrouletto?"; LA BERGÈRE ET LE CAVALIER;   5071
"Voulez-vous un petit pâtre, bergère?" f, f (a) 63

LE PAUVRE LABOUREUR; "Le pauvre laboureur, il a bien du malheur"; THE MAN BEHIND THE PLOUGH; "The man   5072
behind the plough, he has trouble and to spare" e, f 297

LE PETIT PIERRE; "Je suis le petit Pierre du Faubourg Saint-Marceau" f 127   5073

PETITE ABEILLE; "Petite abeille ménagère, si vous ne cherchez que des fleurs" f 59   5074

LA PETITE ROBE; "J'avais pris une maîtresse et bonne maison, Gai!" f 91   5075

LE PEUREUX; "En passant dans un p'tit bois où le coucou chantait" f 91; ET MOI DE M'ENCOURIR; "En passant   5076
près d'un bois où le coucou chantait" f 383

PIERROT ET MARGOT; "Pierrot et Margot sont recrus" f 61   5077

PLANTONS LA VIGNE; "Plantons la vigne, la voilà la joli' vigne" f 82,91; CHANSON À BOIRE; "Le vigneron va   5078
planter sa vigne" f 88

LA POLICHINELLE; "Pan! qu'est-c'qu'est là?" f 82,91   5079

LE POMMIER D'AOÛT; "Derrièr' chez mon père y a t'un pommier d'août" f 91   5080

"POSTOURO, SÉ TU M'AYMO"; "BERGÈRE, SI TU M'AIMES" f, f (a) 66   5081

LES POULETTES; "C'est un' poulett' blanche, qui va pondre dans la grange" f 127   5082

POUR L'ENFANT; "Soun, soun, minou mináuno, soun, soun, bèi o l'efon!"; "Sommeil, sommeil, viens à   5083
l'enfant!" f, f (a) 65

POUR SE TROUVER SUR LA FOUGÈRE; "Pour se trouver sur la fougère seule avec Colin, la jeune Catin"; ALL ON A   5084
SHINY SUMMER MORNING; "All on a shiny summer morning Chloe's pretty crook pretty Chloe took"
e, f 174

PSAUME 68; "QUE DIEU SE MONTRE SEULEMENT" f 82   5085

"PUISQUE ROBIN J'AY A NOM" f 108   5086

"QUAND J'ÉTAIS CHEZ MON PÈRE" f 91   5087A

"QUAND J'ÉTAIS CHEZ MON PÈRE"; HEIGH HO, HEIGH HI!; "Oh I lived with my daddy" e, f 47   5087B

"QUAND J'ÉTAIS CHEZ MON PÈRE"; "WHEN I WAS HOME WITH FATHER" e, f 187   5087C

"QUAND LA MARIE S'EN VA-T-À L'IAU" f 68   5088

QUAND TU VENAIS; "Quand tu venais, le soir chez nous" f 88   5089

QUAND VIENT LE PRINTEMPS; "Quand vient le printemps la verte fougère" f 88   5090

QUAND Z'EYRO PETITOUNE; "Quand z'eyro petitoune, ma miouna bourda do viouleta"; LORSQUE J'ÉTAIS   5091
PETITE; "Lorsque j'étais petite, ma mignonne entourée de violettes" f, f (a) 66

"QUE VOULEZ-VOUS, LA BELLE?" f 82   5092

QUE VOUS ME COÛTEZ CHER; "Que vous me coûtez cher, mon coeur, pour vos plaisirs" f 108   5093

RAGOTIN; "Ragotin, ce matin, a tant bu de pots de vin" f 91   5094

RAMÈNE TES MOUTONS; "La plus aimable, à mon gré, je vais vous la présenter" f 91   5095

LE RETOUR; "La nuit s'approche et mon village s'en dort là-bas silencieux" f 88   5096

LE RETOUR DU MARIN; "Quand le marin revient de guerre, tout doux" f 91,383   5097

RÉVEILLEZ-VOUS; "Réveillez-vous, belle endormie" f 67   5098

LE ROI D'YVETOT; "Il était un roi d'Yvetot" f 127,383 words by Beranger; LES INSTRUMENTS DE MUSIQUE;   5099
"Accourez tous, tambours, clairons" f 82 words by F. Henry

LE ROI DAGOBERT; "C'est le roi Dagobert qui met sa culotte à l'envers" f 91,127; "Le bon roi Dagobert avait sa   5100
culotte à l'envers!" f 82

"LE ROI S'EN VA-T'EN CHASSE"; "THE KING IS GONE A-HUNTING" e, f 47   5101

LA RONDE DE LA VIEILLE; "A Paris, dans une ronde composé' de jeunes gens"; "Oh! la vieille, la vieille, la   5102
vieille" (ref) f 91

ROSSIGNOLET DU BOIS; "Rossignolet du bois qui chantes d'une voix douce et plaisante" f 88, 91   5103

LES ROSSIGNOLS; "Les rossignols, dans leur tendre ramage"; THE NIGHTINGALES; "Sweet nightingales, with   5104
their accents entrancing" e, f 174

LE SABOTIER; "Écoutez, amis, écoutez, Tran lar di rèno" f 91   5105

LES SABOTS; "Combien coûtèrent, combien coûtèrent" f 91   5106

SARABANDE; "Amours, amours, tant tu m'y faictz de mal" f 88   5107

"SAVEZ-VOUS PLANTER LES CHOUX" f 82,88,91,127   5108A

"SAVEZ-VOUS PLANTER LES CHOUX"; "CAN YOU PLANT YOUR CABBAGE SO?" e, f 187   5108B

SEMONS LA SALADE; "Semons, semons la salade; le jardinier est malade!" f 82   5109

SI L'AMOUR PRENAIT RACINE; "Tout garçon qui sert bien son maître"; IF LOVE WOULD GROW; "Ev'ry young   5110
man who serves a master" e, f 187

SI TU LES VOYAIS; "Si tu les voyais, Térolé, Téroléro, léro" f 91   5111

LE SOLDAT FRANÇAIS; "Où t'en vas-tu soldat de France" f 82   5112

SONG OF JOAN OF ARC; "Children of God, be brave" e 37   5113

SONT TROIS JEUN' CAPITAINES; "Sont trois jeun' capitaines a la chasse s'en vont" f 91   5114

SUNRISE SERENADE; "Lo! how the sun climbs to the sky!" e 37   5115

"SUR LE PONT D'AVIGNON" f 82, 88, 91, 127, 383   5116

SWEET NIGHTINGALE; "Sweet nightingale, forever faithful" e 95   5117

TAISEZ-VOUS, MA MUSETTE; "Taisez-vous, ma musette, vos chantes ne sont plus doux" f 108   5118

TÈ, L'CO, TÈ!; "Tè, l'co, tè! Tè, l'co, tè! Tè, l'co, tè! Arresto lo baco!"; VA, L'CHIEN, VA!; "Va, l'chien,   5119
va! Va, l'chien, va! Va, l'chien, va! Arrête la vache!" f, f (a) 66

THREE DRUMMERS; "Rat-a-plan, rat-a-plan, rat-a-plan, plan plan"; "Three drummer boys were from the war   5120
returning" (verse) e 37

LES TISSERANDS; "Les tisserands sont plus que les évêques" f 91   5121

TONTAINE, TONTON; "Mes amis, partons pour la chasse" f 127   5122

LA TOUR, PRENDS GARDE; "La tour, prends garde, la Tour prends garde de te laisser abattre" f 82, 127   5123

TREMP' TON PAIN; "Tremp' ton pain, Marie, tremp' ton pain" f 91, 127   5124

"LA TRENT-ET-UN DU MOIS D'AUÔT" f 88   5125

TUROLURETO, VOI LAN LA!; "La bas, la bas, il y a une petite prairie"; "Over the hill and down by the meadow"   5126
e, f 86

UN, DEUX, TROIS; "Un, deux, trois, nous irons au bois" f 127   5127

VIE DU CHASSEUR; "Avec ma gibecière, je cours bois et bruyère" f 88   5128

VIENS DANS CE BOCAGE; "Viens dans ce bocage, belle Aminte" f 61; TAMBOURIN f 91   5129

LE VIGNERON; "Dieu! quel métier de galère" f 91   5130

VIVE HENRI IV; "Vive Henri Quatre, vive ce roi vaillant!" f 91   5131

VIVE L'AMOUR; "Let ev'ry good fellow now fill up his glass"; "Vive la, vive la, vive l'amour" (ref) e 402   5132

VIVE LA ROSE!; "Adieu l'hiver morose: Vive la rose!" f 82   5133

VIVONS HEUREUX; "Vivons heureux, aimons nous, bergère!" f 59   5134

VOICI LE PRINTEMPS; "Voici le printemps qui passe"; HEAR THE VOICE OF SPRING; "Hear the voice of spring   5135
who passeth" e, f 47

VOUS QUI DONNEZ DE L'AMOUR; "Vous qui donnez de l'amour au coeur le moins tendre" f 59; MUSETTE f 108   5136

WITH SOUND OF FIFE; "With sound of fife and bagpipes too, they pass along in gay procession" e 37; SPRING-   5137
TIME IS HERE; "The fifers play, the pipers too, follow we all, it is the hour!" e 95

FRENCH CANADA

"A LA CLAIRE FONTAINE" f 82, 383; "By the clear running fountain" e, f 186, 187   5138A

"A LA CLAIRE FONTAINE"; THE CRYSTAL FOUNTAIN; "In the crystal fountain" e, f 86   5138B

"À SAINT-MALO, BEAU PORT DE MER"; "AT SAINT MALO BESIDE THE SEA" e, f 186, 187   5139

"AH! SI MON MOINE VOULAIT DANSER"; COME AND DANCE WITH ME; "If you will come and dance with me"   5140
e, f 186, 187

ALOUETTE; "Alouette, gentille alouette, alouette, je te plumerai" f 44, 82, 233, 236, 383, 402; "Skylark, pretty   5141
skylark, I will pluck you" e, f 35; "O, Alouette, gentille Alouette, Alouette, je t'y plumerai"
f 186, 187; "Alouette, gentile Alouette, Alouette, je te plumerai" f 28, 279, 343, 366

AUPRÈS DE MA BLONDE. See 4888

AVOINE, AVOINE!; "Quand le bonhomme a semé son avoine"; SOWING HIS GOOD GRAIN; "When the old farmer   5142
was sowing his good grain" e, f 21

LE BAL CHEZ BOULÉ; "Dimanche, après les vêpr's, y aura bal chez Boulé"; "Vogue, marinier, vogue, vogue"   5143
(ref); BOULE'S BALL; "When Sunday vespers end we all then have our chance" e, f 186, 187

BIEN TRAVAILLER; "Bien travailler, c'est s'amuser"; DO YOUR WORK WELL; "Do your work well, and you will   5144
find" e, f 21

BLANCHE COMME LA NEIGE; "La belle s'est endormi sur un beau lit de roses"; WHITE AS A SNOWFLAKE; "A   5145
maiden lay asleep upon a bed of roses" e, f 187

BOITEUX D'HERMITE; "Où vas-tu, boiteux d'hermite?"; LIMPY LEE, LIMPY LOW; "Tell us true, where are you   5146
going, Limpy low, limpy lee?" e, f 21

BON CORDONNIER; "Mesdemoiselles, où allez-vous donc comm' ci?"; GOOD COBLER, SIR!; "Good gracious me!   5147
Tell me, where you're going like this?" e, f 21

BONHOMME! BONHOMME!; "Bonhomm', bonhomm', sais-tu jouer?"; MY FRIEND! MY FRIEND!; "My friend, my   5148A
friend, can you play this?" e, f 186, 187

BONHOMME, BONHOMME!; "Bonhomme, bonhomme, que sais-tu donc faire?"; WHAT CAN YOU DO?; "Hey,   5148B
mister! Hey, mister! Tell us, what can you do?" e, f 21

BOUM BADIBOUM; "J'ai un' méchante mère"; "I have a wicked mother" e, f 187   5149

C'EST L'AVIRON; "M'en revenant de la jolie Rochelle"; "C'est l'aviron qui nous mène" (ref); PULL ON THE OARS;   5150
    "Riding along the road from Rochelle city"; "Pull on the oars as we glide along together" (ref) e, f
    186, 187; STRONG IS THE OAR; "Home from Rochelle one morning I came riding"; "Strong is the
    oar that can hold us in the current" (ref) e, f 219

C'EST LA BELLE FRANÇOISE; "C'est la belle Françoise, lon, gai!"; THE FAIR FRANÇOISE; "The fair Françoise   5151
    has one wish, ah me!" e, f 187

A CANADIAN BOAT SONG; Dans mon chemin j'ai rencontré (tune); "Faintly as tolls the evening chime" e 186;   5152
    "Faintly as toll the evening chime" e 279, 366   words by T. Moore

UN CANADIEN ERRANT; Si tu te mets anguille (tune); "Un canadien errant, banni de ses foyers"; ONCE A   5153
    CANADIAN LAD; "Once a Canadian lad, exiled from hearth and home" e, f 186, 187   words
    by M. A. Gérin-Lajoie

CASSONS LES OEUFS; "J'ai des poul's à vendre, des roug's et des blanches"; BUY MY FRESH EGGS; "Will you   5154
    buy my fresh eggs? White or brown, they're fresh eggs!" e, f 21

CÉCILIA; "Mon pèr' n'avait fille que moi"; "My father has no child but me" e, f 187   5155

COUVRE-FEU; "Veillez, veillez, veillez, Marie Picard!"; FORWARD MARCH!; "Come on, can't you come on,   5156
    Marie Picard!" e, f 21

DANS LES CHANTIERS; "Voici l'hiver arrivé"; THE WINTER CAMP; "When the winter comes at last" e, f 186,   5157
    187

DANS PARIS Y A-T-UNE BRUNE; "Dans Paris, y a-t-une brune plus bell' que le jour"; NOW IN PARIS LIVES A   5158
    MAIDEN; "Now in Paris lives a maiden fairer far than day" e, f 187

DANS TOUS LES CANTONS; "Dans tous les cantons ya des fill's et des garçons"; THROUGH ALL THE COUNTRY   5159
    'ROUND; "Through all the country 'round where young boys and girls are found" e, f 186, 187

EN ROULANT MA BOULE; "En roulant ma boule roulant"; "Derrièr' chez nous, ya-t-un étang" (verse); "Behind   5160
    our house we have a pond" (verse) e, f 186, 187; ON, ROLL ON; "On, roll on, my ball, roll on";
    "Behind our house there is a pond" (verse) e 214

ENTENDEZ-VOUS SUR L'ORMEAU; "Etendez-vous sur l'ormeau chanter le petit oiseau?"; HEAR THE LITTLE   5161
    BIRD; "Hear the little bird singing in the old elm tree" 4 pt round e, f 187

ENVOYONS D' L'AVANT, NOS GENS!; "Quant nous partons du chantier"; PADDLE YOUR CANOE, MY BOYS;   5162
    "When the work's all done at last" e, f 187

LE FORGERON; "Le forgeron revat le fer"; THE BLACKSMITH; "See how the blacksmith shapes the steel" e, f 187   5163

ISABEAU S'Y PROMÈNE; L'ENLÈVEMENT EN MER; "Isabeau s'y promène le long de son jardin"; ONE DAY ISABEL   5164
    WANDERED; "One day Isabel wandered down in her garden fair" e, f 187

"J'AI TANT DANSÉ, J'AI TANT SAUTÉ"; "I'VE DANCED AND DANCED THE LIVELONG DAY" e, f 187   5165

JE SAIS BIEN QUELQUE CHOSE; "C'est en m'y promenant le long de ces prairies"; I KNOW SOMETHING; "When   5166
    I was walking by down where the grass is growing" e, f 187

LE LONG DE LA MER JOLIE; "Belle, embarquez, belle, embarquez"; BESIDE THE BRIGHT SEA; "Please come   5167
    on board my little ship" e, f 187

LUNDI, JOUR DE LAVAGE; "Lundi, c'est jour de lavage, frottons, bri bron bron!"; HOW THE DAYS GO; "Mon-   5168
    day is the day for washing in the old oak tub" e, f 21

LE MARCHAND DE VELOURS; L'ALOUETTE CHANTA LE JOUR; "Mon père m'y mari' avec un marchand de   5169
    velours"; "Ah! gai lon la, vive la roulette" (ref); THE MERCHANT I MARRIED; "My father made
    me wed a merchant whom he chose for me"; "Oh, gay are we! Tra la la la, la la!" (ref) e, f 187

"MARIEZ-MOI, MA PETITE MAMAN"; MAMAN, FIND ME A HUSBAND; "Maman, please find me a husband"   5170
    e, f 219

MICHAUD A TOMBÉ; "Michaud a monté dans un pommier"; GET UP NOW; "Wee Willie has climbed our apple   5171
    tree" e, f 21

MON ONCLE, MON ONCLE; "Mon oncl', mon oncle a bien mal à sa têt'"; NO SCHOOL TODAY; "Hooray!   5172
    Hooray! We'll have no school today" e, f 21

MONSIEUR LE CURE; SIMONE; "D'où venez vous si crotté, Monsieur le curé?"; "Where have you been, sir, I   5173
    pray, Monsieur le curé?" e, f 187

NANETTE; "Au beau clair de la lun', m'en allant promener"; "As I went walking out, beneath the soft moonlight"   5174
    e, f 187

"NOUS ÉTIONS TROIS CAPITAINES"; "WE ARE THREE YOUNG CAPTAINS JOLLY" e, f 187   5175

OMELETTE AU LARD; "Si j'avais des oeufs, du lard"; SCRAMBLED EGGS; "If I had some nice fresh eggs" e, f 21   5176

"PAPILLON, TU ES VOLAGE!"; "Butterfly, oh, you are fickle!" e, f 187; PAPILLON; BUTTERFLY; "Butterfly,   5177
    you fickle creature" e, f 219

LE PÂTÉ DE ROUEN; "C'est dans la ville de Rouen"; THEY MADE A PIE; "Once in the village of Labelle" e, f 21   5178

UNE PERDRIOLE; "Le premier jour de mai, que donn'rai-je à ma mie?" f 383   5179

PETITE BOITEUSE; "Où vas-tu, ma petit' boiteuse?"; THE LAME DUCK; "Whither bound, limping like a lame   5180
    duck?" e, f 21

PETITE HIRONDELLE; "Petite hirondelle qui n'as qu'une aile"; FLYING, SINGING; "A thrush or a starling? isn't   5181
    he darling!" e, f 21

PETITE SOURIS GRISE; "Enfin, nous te tenons, petite souris grise"; LITTLE GREY MOUSE; "At last, we've caught   5182
    you stealing from our kitchen cupboard" e, f 21

PETITS DORIONNES; "Qu'est-c' qui passe, ici, si tard?"; LET US PASS; "Who's that passing by, so late?" e, f   5183
    21

LA POULETTE GRISE; "C'est la poulette grise"; THE LITTLE GREY HEN; "The little hen that's grey e, f 187   5184
    "QUAND J'ETAIS CHEZ MON PERE." See 5087C

LES RAFTSMEN; "Là ousqu'y sont, tous les raftsmen?"; THE RAFTSMEN; "The gay raftsmen, oh where are they?"   5185
    e, f 186, 187

RONDE DU LOUP; "Promenons-nous dans le bois"; WHERE IS THE WOLF?; "Let's take a walk through the woods"   5186
    e, f 21

LA ROSE BLANCHE; "Par un matin, je me suis levée"; THE WHITE ROSE; "I rose early one summer morn" e, f 86   5187
    "SAVEZ-VOUS PLANTER LES CHOUX." See 5108B

"SUR LE PONT D'AVIGNON"; "ACROSS THE REDWOOD BRIDGE" e, f 21   5188

VIVE LA CANADIENNE!; Par derrièr' chez mon père (tune); "Vive la Canadienne! Vole, mon coeur, vole!"; OF   5189
    MY CANADIAN GIRL I SING; "Of my Canadian girl I sing, gaily our voices ring!" e, f 186, 187, 383

VOYAGEUR'S SONG; "Joy to thee, my brave canoe" e 279, 366; PADDLING SONG e 86   5190

THE WRECK OF THE JULIE PLANTE; "On wan dark night on Lac San Pierre" e 186 words by W. H. Drummond   5191

YOUPE! YOUPE! SUR LA RIVIÈRE!; "Par un dimanche au soir m'en allant promener"; "'Twas on a Sunday night   5192
    when I went for a walk" e, f 186, 187

GERMANY

"A.B.C. DIE KATZE LIEF IN DEN SCHNEE" g 40   5193

ABA HAIDSCHI BUMBAIDSCHI; "Aba haidschi bumbaidschi schlaf lange" g 326   5194

ABENDLIED; "Nun wollen wir singen das Abendlied" g 33; NUN WOLLEN WIR SINGEN DAS ABENDLIED g 309,   5195
    326

ABENDSTÄNDCHEN; "Und jetzo kommt die Nacht herbei" g 49   5196

ABREDE; Ich ging wohl nächten späte (tune); "Ein Knäblein ging spazieren ins Rosengärtelein"; DORT NIED'N IN   5197
    JENEM HOLZE; "Dort nied'n in jenem Holze leit sich ein Mühlen stolz" g 99; DORT NIEDN IN
    JENEM HOLZE; "Dort niedn in jenem Holze da liegt ein Mühlen stolz" g 41; "Dort niedn in jenem
    Holze leit sich ein Mühlen stolz" g 49, 309, 326

ABSCHIED; "Liebchen, ade! Scheiden tut weh!" g 99; LIEBCHEN, ADE! g 326, 353; WINTER, ADE!; "Winter   5198
    ade! Scheiden tut weh!" g 326, 353; WINTERS ABSCHIED g 99 words by H. H. von Fallersleben

ABSCHIED; "Was klinget und singet die Strass' herauf?" g 31 words by L. Uhland   5199

ACH BITTRER WINTER; "Ach bitter Winter, wie bist du kalt!" g 49, 309, 326   5200

ACH BLÜMLEIN BLAU; "Ach Blümlein blau verdore nicht!" g 41   5201

ACH ELSLEIN, LIEBES ELSELEIN; "Ach Elslein, liebes Elselein, wie gern wär ich bei dir!" g 229; ACH ELSLEIN   5202
    g 41; ACH ELSLEIN, LIEBES ELSLEIN; "Ach Elslein, liebes Elslein, wie gern wär ich bei dir!" g
    326; ACH ELSLEIN, LIEBES ELSELEIN; "Ach Elslein, liebes Elselein mein, wie gern wär ich bei
    dir!" g 49; ACH ELSLEIN, LIEBES ELSLEIN MEIN; "Ach Elslein, liebes Elslein mein, wie gern wär
    ich bei dir!" g 309

[Ach lieber Herre Jesu Christ] "O JESU, JOY OF LOVING HEARTS" e 50 arr by J. Brahms   5203

ACH SCHATZ; "Ach Schatz wenn du über die Gasse gehst" g 49   5204

"ACH, WIE IST'S MÖGLICH DANN" g 309; TREUE LIEBE g 99   5205

ADE ZUR GUTEN NACHT; "Ade zur guten Nacht, jetzt wird der Schluss gemacht" g 42, 49, 309, 326, 353; ADE   5206
    g 99; ADE ZUR GUTEN NACHT; "Ade zur guten Nacht, jetzt ist der Schluss gemacht" g 31

ALL MEIN GEDANKEN; "All mein Gedanken, die ich hab, die sind bei dir" g 49, 226, 229, 309, 353; NUR DU;   5207
    "All' mein Gedanken, die ich hab, die sind bei dir" g 99; THOU ONLY; "My thoughts and all my
    memories belong to thee" e, g 35

ALLE LEUT GEHN JETZT NACH HAUS; "Alle Leut, alle Leut gehn jetzt nach Haus" g 326   5208

"ALLE VÖGEL SIND SCHON DA"; Nun so reis' ich (tune) g 49, 309, 326, 353; words by H. H. von Fallersleben   5209
    ABSCHIED VON DER GELIEBTEN; "Nun so reis ich weg von hier" g 99; tune similar to Ah! vous
    dirai-je, maman

ALLES NEU MACHT DER MAI; Fahret hin (tune); "Alles neu macht der Mai, macht die Seele frisch und frei"   5210
    g 326, 353; HÄNSCHEN KLEIN GING ALLEIN; "Hänschen klein ging allein in die weite Welt
    hinein" g 353; JÄGERLIED; "Fahret hin, fahret hin, Grillen geht mir aus dem Sinn!" g 326;
    LIGHTLY ROW; "Lightly row! lightly row! O'er the glassy waves we go" e 28, 366

"ALLEWEIL KA MER NET LUSTIG SEI" g 49, 309, 326, 353   5211

"ALS DER GROSSVATER DIE GROSSMUTTER NAHM" g 326   5212

"ALS ICH EIN JUNG GESELLE WAR" g 40, 309, 326, 353; DER TOD VON BASEL g 31, 99   5213

"ALS ICH EINMAL REISTE" g 309   5214

"ALS WIR JÜNGST IN REGENSBURG WAREN" g 49, 309, 326, 353; DONAUSTRUNDEL g 31; FRÄULEIN KUNIGUND   5215
    g 99

ALTES WIENER FIAKERLIED; "I hab halt zwa kohlschwarze Rappen" g 396   5216

AM SONNTAG, DA KOCHT DIE MEISTRIN BOHNEN; "Am Sonntag, am Sonntag, da kocht die Meistrin Bohnen";   5217
    "Falteri, so muss das sein" (ref) g 309

DER CORTESAN; "Die Lieb will ein Comedi spillen" g 250   5260

COUNT AND NUN; "I stood upon a mountain high" e 95   5261

"D'BÄURE HÔT D'KATZ VERLORE" g 326   5262

DA DROBEN AUF JENEM BERGE; "Da droben auf jenem Berge, da stehet ein goldenes Haus" g 49   5263A

DAS MÜHLRAD; "Da droben auf jenem Berge, da steht ein hohes Haus"; THE MILL-WHEEL; "Afar and aloft on   5263B
    yon mountain top a house tow'rs high in the air" e, g 210; g 99 words att to W. Ehlers

DA UNTEN IM TALE; "Da unten im Tale läuft's Wasser so trüb"; BELOW IN THE VALLEY; "Below in the valley   5264
    dark waters run cold" e, g 210 arr by J. Brahms

"DAT DU MIN LEEVSTEN BÜST"; Dat du myn Schätsken bist (tune); Lasst und, ihr Brüder (tune) g 49,309,326,353   5265

DEINE SCHÖNHEIT WIRD VERGEHN; "Deine Schönheit wird vergehn, wie die Rosen im Garten stehn" g 309   5266

DEN ACKERMANN SOLL MAN LOBEN; "Den Akkermann soll man loben und preisen auf dieser Erde" g 49   5267

DEN LIEBEN LANGEN TAG; Um hoalber Neune (tune); "Den lieben langen Tag hab i nur Not und Plag" g 353   5268
    words by P. J. Düringer

DEUTSCHES FREIHEITSLIED AUS BÖHMEN; "Du hast ein Zeil vor den Augen" g 43   5269

DORNRÖSCHEN; "Dornröschen war ein schönes Kind" g 49   5270

"DORT, WO DIE KLAREN BÄCHLEIN RINNEN" g 42   5271

DREH DICH, RÄDCHEN; "Dreh dich, dreh dich, Rädchen" g 49   5272

DREI KLÄNGE SIND'S; "Drei Klänge sind's, sie tönen hold und rein" g 31 words by H. Seidel   5273

DREI LAUB AUF EINER LINDEN; "Drei Laub auf einer Linden blühen also wohl" g 49,309,326   5274

DREI LILIEN; "Drei Lilien, drei Lilien, die pflanzt ich auf mein Grab" g 31,42,49,99,309,326,353; IM   5275
    SCHÖNSTEN WIESENGRUNDE; "Im schönsten Wiesengrunde ist meiner Heimat Haus" g 31,49
    326,353 words by W. Ganzhorn

DIE DREI REITER; "Es ritten drei Reiter zum Tore hinaus g 31; ES RITTEN DREI REITER g 42,326,353; DER REITER   5276
    AM TOR g 99; "ES KLAPPERT DIE MÜHLE AM RAUSCHENDEN BACH" g 353

DREIMOL OMS STÄDELE; "Dreimol oms Städele dreimol oms Haus" g 309,326   5277

DROBA AUF DR RAUHE ALB; "Droba auf dr rauhe Alb jubeidi, jubeida"; SCHÖN IST EIN ZYLINDERHUT; "Schön   5278
    ist ein Zylinderhut, juchheidi, juchheida" g 326

DROBA IM OBERLAND; "Droba im Oberland, ei, da ist's so wunderschön!" g 309; DROBEN IM OBERLAND;   5279
    "Droben im Oberland, ei, da ist es wunderschön!" g 326; "Droben im Oberland, hei, da ist
    es wunderschön!" g 353

DRUNT IN DER GRÜNEN AU; "Drunt in der grünen Au steht a Birnbaum, schau, schau, juhe" g 309   5280A

DRUNTEN IN DER GRÜNEN AU; "Drunten in der grünen Au, steht ein Birnbaum,tragt Laub, juchhe!" g 49,326   5280B

DRUNTEN IM UNTERLAND; Draussen im Schwabeland wächst a schöns Holz (tune); "Drunten im Unterland, da ist's   5281
    halt fein" g 42,309,326,353; UNTERLÄNDERS HEIMWEH g 31,99 words by G. Weigle

DU, DU DALKETER JAGERSBUA; "Du, du dalketer Jagersbua, i, i werd dir's auszahln!" g 353   5282

"DU, DU LIEGST MIR IM HERZEN' g 42,99,326,353; "YOU, YOU, IN MY HEART LIVING" e, g 36   5283

"DU GABST UNS UNSER TÄGLICH BROT"; Vater unser im Himmelreich (tune) g 49   5284

DUDELDEI; "Das Schwarzbraune Bier das trink ich so gern" g 31   5285

"DURCHS WIESETAL GANG I JETZ NA" g 309,326,353   5286

"EI BAUR, WAS KOST DEI HEU" g 49   5287

EI MÄDCHEN VOM LANDE; "Ei Mädchen vom Lande, wie bist du so schön!" g 326   5288

EI WIE SO TÖRICHT; "Ei wie so töricht ist, wenn man's betrachtet" g 49; EI WIE SO TÖRICHT IST g 309   5289

EIA, PEIA, WIEGENSTROH; "Eia, peia, Wiegenstroh, schläft mein Kind, so bin ich froh" g 49   5290

EIA, POPEIA; "Eia, popeia, das Breile ist gut" g 49   5291

DER EIFERSÜCHTIGE KNABE; "Es stehen drei Sterne am Himmel" g 99   5292

EINMAL NOCH STUDENT ZU SEIN; "Sei's im Westen, sei's im Osten, nimmer schläft der Wunsch mir ein" g 31   5293
    words by H. Dreckschmidt

DIE ERDE BRAUCHT REGEN; "Die Erde braucht Regen, der Tag braucht ein Licht" g 49   5294

ERLAUBE MIR, FEINS MÄDCHEN; "Erlaube mir, feins Mädchen, in den Garten zu gehn" g 229 arr by J. Brahms   5295

"ES BLIES EIN JÄGER WOHL IN SEIN HORN" g 309; ES BLIES EIN JÄGER g 49   5296A

"ES BLIES EIN JÄGER WOHL IN SEIN HORN" g 309,326; ES BLIES EIN JAGER g 49   5296B

"ES DUNKELT SCHON IN DER HEIDE" g 49,309,326,353   5297

ES, ES, ES, UND ES; "Es, es, es, und es, es ist ein harter Schluss" g 49,309,326,353; HANDWERKSBURSCHEN-   5298
    ABSCHIED g 99

ES FREIT'EIN WILDER WASSERMANN; "Es freit'ein wilder Wassermann in der Burg wohl über dem See" g 49,309,   5299A
    353; DIE SCHÖNE LILOFEE g 99

ES FREIT EIN WILDER WASSERMANN; "Es freit ein wilder Wassermann von der Burg bis über den See" g 49   5299B

"ES GEHT EIN' DUNKLE WOLK HEREIN" g 309; "Es geht eine dunkle Wolk herein" g 49; "ES GEHT EINE DUNKLE   5300
    WOLK HEREIN" g 326; "THE HEAVY CLOUDS BLOW UP AGAIN" e, g 231

ES GEHT EIN RUNDGESANG; "Es geht ein Rundgesang an unserm Tisch herum" g 353   5301

"ES GIBT KEIN SCHÖNRES LEBEN" g 40   5302

"ES GING EIN' JUNGFRAU ZARTE" g 309   5303

"ES HATT EIN BAUER EIN SCHÖNES WEIB" g 42,353; INS HEU; "Es hatte ein Bauer ein schönes Weib" g 31   5304

"ES IST AUF ERD KEIN SCHWERER LEIDEN" g 226   5305

GELÜBDE; "Ich hab mich ergeben, mit Herz und mit Hand" g 99; ICH HAB MICH ERGEBEN g 326   words by   5347
      H. F. Massmann; WIR HATTEN GEBAUET; "Wir hatten gebauet ein stattliches Haus" g 99; AM 26.
      NOVEMBER 1819 g 31   words by D. A. von Binzer

GESTERN BEI MONDENSCHEIN; "Gestern bei Mondenschein ging ich spazieren" g 41,326; GESTERN BEIM MON-   5348
      DENSCHEIN; "Gestern beim Mondenschein ging ich spazieren" g 49,309; DIE KRANZBINDERIN g 99

"GESTERN, BRÜDER, KÖNNT IHR'S GLAUBEN" g 31; DER TOD g 99   words by G. E. Lessing   5349

GLOCKEN KLINGEN; "Glocken klingen hoch vom Turm" 2 pt round g 40   5350

GLÜCK AUF; "Glück auf! Glück auf! Der Steiger kommt" g 99; GLÜCK AUF, GLÜCK AUF! g 49,326,353;   5351
      GLÜCK AUF! DER STEIGER KOMMT g 309

GOLD UND SILBER LIEB ICH SEHR; "Gold und Silber lieb ich sehr, kann's auch wohl gebrauchen" g 326,353   5352

GOOD NIGHT; "Sweetheart mine, good night, dearest love, good night!" e 95   5353

DER GRIMMIG TOD; "Der grimmig Tod mit seinem Pfeil" g 49   5354

"GRÜN, GRÜN, GRÜN SIND ALLE MEINE KLEIDER" g 326   5355A

GREEN, GREEN, GREEN; "Green, green, green are all of my gay dresses" e 37   5355B

"GRÜSS GOTT DU SCHONER MAIEN" g 40,309,326,353   5356

HAB MIR MEIN WEIZEN AUFS BERGL GSÄT" g 309; "HAB MIR MEIN WEIZEN AM BERG GESÄT" g 326   5357

HÄNSEL UND GRETEL; "Hänsel und Gretel verliefen sich im Wald" g 49   5358

HÄTT ER GESCHWIEGEN STILL; "Es waren mal drei Gesellen" g 31   5359

HANKA; "Hanka, with heavy dark-brown hair" e 95   5360

HANS NABER; "Hans Naber, ick hebb et ju togebracht" g 41   5361

HANS UND VERENE; "Es g'fallt mer nummen eini" g 31   words by J. P. Hebel   5362

HEIM WOLLEN WIR GEHN; "Heim Heim Heim wollen wir gehn" g 40   5363

HEIMLICHE LIEBE; "Kein Feuer, keine Kohle kann brennen so heiss als heimliche Liebe" g 99; KEIN FEUER,   5364
      KEINE KOHLE g 42,49,309,326,353

HEISSA KATHREINERLE; "Heissa Kathreinerle schnür dir die Schuh" g 49,309,326,353   5365

HEITERER LEBENSLAUF; "Mein Lebenslauf ist Lieb und Lust" g 31; "MEIN LEBENSLAUF IST LIEB UND LUST"   5366
      g 353   words by S. A. Mahlmann

EIN HELLER UND EIN BATZEN; "Ein Heller und ein Batzen, die waren beide mein, ja mein" g 326,353   words by   5367
      A. von Schlippenbach

HERZIG SCHÖNS RÖSELEIN; "Herzig schöns Röselein schmeckt uns der Wein so gut" g 49   5368

HERZLIEB, ICH HAB VERNOMMEN; "Herzlieb, ich hab vernommen, dass du sollst scheiden von mir" g 49   5369

HEUT GEHT ES AN BORD; "Heut geht an Bord, heut segeln wir fort" g 326   words by P. Vollrath   5370

"HEUT IST EIN FEST BEI DEN FRÖSCHEN AM SEE" 3 pt round g 326   5371

"HEUT IST EIN FREUNDENREICHER TAG"; I kumme dahea von Estarei (tune) g 49,309,326   5372

"HEUT NOCH SIND WIR HIER ZU HAUS" g 309,326   5373

HOCH SOLL ER LEBEN; "Hoch soll er leben, hoch soll er leben, dreimal hoch!" g 353; TRINKSPRÜCHE g 326   5374

HÖRT, IHR HERRN; "Hort, ihr Herrn und lasst euch sagen" g 49; "HÖRT, IHR HERRN, UND LASST EUCH SAGEN"   5375A
      g 309,326

NACHTWACHTERLIED; "Hört, ihr Herrn und lasst euch sagen"; SONG OF THE NIGHT WATCHMAN; "Hear all   5375B
      men and mark ye well!" e, g 230

HOPP, MARIANNELE; "Hopp, Mariannele, hopp, Mariannele, kumm, mr wolle danze" g 49   5376

HOPSA, SCHWABENLIESEL; "Hopsa, Schwabenliesel dreh dich rum und tanz a bissel" g 353   5377

"HORCH, ES RUFT DER GLOCKE TON" 3 pt round g 40   5378

HORCH, WAS KOMMT; "Horch, was kommt von draussen rein" g 43; "HORCH, WAS KOMMT VON DRAUSSEN   5379A
      REIN" g 309,326,353; VERSTÄNDIGE LIEBE g 31

DER VERLASSENE LIEBHABER; "Horch, was kommt von draussen rein?" g 99   5379B

"ICH BIN DER BUB VOM ELSTERTAL" g 326   5380

"ICH BIN DER DOCTOR EISENBART" g 309,326,353   5381

"ICH BIN EIN DEUTSCHER KNABE" g 326   5382

"ICH BIN EIN FREIER WILDBRETSCHÜTZ" g 326,353   words by H. Löns   5383

ICH BIN EIN MUSIKANTE; "Ich bin ein Musikante und komm aus Schwabenland" g 353   5384

ICH FAHR DAHIN; "Ich fahr dahin, denn es muss sein" g 99; "Ich fahr dahin, wann es muss sein" g 49; "Ich   5385
      fahr dahin, wenn es muss sein" g 326

"ICH GING DURCH EINEN GRASGRÜNEN WALD" g 49,309,326,353   5386

ICH GING EMOL SPAZIERE; "Ich ging emol spaziere, nanu, nanu, nanu" g 309,353   5387

"ICH GING IM WALDE SO FÜR MICH HIN"; Frisch auf, frisch auf, der Bergmann kommt (tune) g 309   5388

ICH HAB DIE NACHT GETRÄUMET; Es wollt ein Jäger jagen (tune); "Ich hab die Nacht geträumet wohl einen   5389
      schweren Traum" g 41,49,309,326; THE DREAM; "Last night while I was sleeping, there came a
      dream to me" e 95; DER SCHWERE TRAUM g 99; THE HEAVY DREAM; "I dreamed as I lay
      sleeping a heavy dream of woe" e, g 230; WASSERSNOT; "Zu Koblenz auf der Brücken, da lag
      ein tiefer Schnee" g 99

ICH HAB MIR MEIN WEIZEN; "Ich hab mir mein Weizen am Berg gesät" g 49   5390

"ICH HABE DEN FRÜHLING GESEHEN" g 326,328   5391

"ICH HABE MEIN FEINSLIEBCHEN" g 40   5392

ICH HATT EINEN KAMERADEN; "Ich hatt einen Kameraden, einen bessern findst du nit" g 43,49,309,326,353;   5393
      DER GUTE KAMERAD; "Ich hatt einen Kameraden, einen bessern find'st du nit" g 99   words by L.
      Uhland

ICH HÖRT EIN SICHELEIN; "Ich hört ein Sichelein rauschen, wohl rauschen durch das Korn" g 41; ICH HÖRT EIN   5394A
      SICHELEIN RAUSCHEN g 49,309,353; I HEARD A SCYTHE; "I heard a scythe go sighing, go sighing
      through the corn" e 95

ICH HÖRT EIN SICHLEIN RAUSCHEN; "Ich hört ein Sichlein rauschen, wohl rauschen durch das Korn" g 326   5394B

"ICH REIT AUF EINEM RÖSSLEIN" g 49   5395

ICH SCHELL MEIN HORN; "Ich schell mein Horn in Jammerton" g 41   5396

ICH SCHIESS DEN HIRSCH; "Ich schiess den Hirsch im wilden Forst" g 353; "ICH SCHIESS DEN HIRSCH IM   5397
      WILDEN FORST" g 326; JÄGERS LEIBESLIED g 99; SIEBENBÜRGISCHES JÄGERLIED g 31   words
      by F. Schober

"ICH TRAG EIN GOLDNES RINGELEIN"; Des Abends, wenn ich schlafen geh (tune) g 309   5398

"ICH WOLLT, DASS ICH EIN JÄGER WÄR" g 49   5399

"ICH WOLLT, DASS'S KOHLEN SCHNEIT" g 309; "ICH WOLLT, WENN'S KOHLEN SCHNEIT" g 49   5400

"ICH WOLLT EIN BÄUMLEIN STEIGEN" g 49   5401

IHR KLEINEN VÖGELEIN; "Ihr kleinen Vögelein, ihr Waldergötzerlein" g 42   5402

IHR LUSTIGEN HANNOVERANER; "Ihr lustigen Hannoveraner seid ihr alle beisammen?" g 99   5403

"IHREN SCHÄFER ZU ERWARTEN" g 326; PHYLLIS UND DIE MUTTER g 31,99,353 words by J. W. von Goethe   5404

"IM GRÜNEN WALD, DA WO DIE DROSSEL SINGT"; Ungetreuer du (tune) g 353; "IM GRÜNEN WALD, DORT   5405
      WO DIE DROSSEL SINGT" g 326

IM MAIEN DIE VÖGELEIN SINGEN; "Im Maien, im Maien die Vögelein singen" g 309; IM MAIEN, IM MAIEN   5406
      g 49

IM SCHWARZEN WALFISCH; War einst ein jung, jung Zimmergesell (tune); "Im schwarzen Walfisch zu   5407
      Ascalon da trank ein Mann drei Tag" g 31; "IM SCHWARZEN WALFISCH ZU ASKALON";
      "Im schwarzen Walfisch zu Askalon da trank ein Mann drei Tag" g 353; JONAS g 99
      words by J. V. Scheffel

"IM WALD UND AUF DER HEIDE" g 49,309,326,353; JÄGERLEBEN g 99; JÄGERLIED g 31 att to F. L.   5408
      Gehricke, words by W. Bornemann

INNSBRUCK; "In grüner Berge Kranze die Silberschnee umsäumt" g 31 words by G. Doehler   5409

INS MUETERS STÜBELI; "In Mueters Stübeli, do goht der hm, hm, hm" g 49; INS MUETERS STÜEBELI; "Ins   5410
      Muetters Stüebeli, do goht der hm, hm, hm" g 309

IST ES DENN NUN; "Ist es denn nun wirklich wahr" g 43   5411

EIN JÄGER AUS KURPFALZ; "Ein Jäger aus Kurpfalz, der reitet durch den grünen Wald" g 42,49,309,326,353;   5412
      DER JÄGER AUS KURPFALZ g 31,99

"DER JÄGER IN DEM GRÜNEN WALD" g 49,309,353   5413

"DER JÄGER LÄNGS DEM WEIHER GING" g 49,309,353; DER JÄGER UND DIE NIXE g 99; "EIN JÄGER LÄNGS   5414
      DEM WEIHER GING" g 326 words by A. W. von Zuccalmaglio

JÄNSKEN VON BREMEN; "Jänsken von Bremen de hadde ne koh met eene breden Snute" g 41   5415

JANUARY AND FEBRUARY; "When January days are here" e 28,366 words by J. B. Walters   5416

JE HÖHER DER KIRCHTURM; "Je höher der Kirchturm desto schöner das Geläute" g 42,309,326   5417

JEDER BRAVE FUHRMANN; Eenen Berg'schen Fohrmann (tune); "Jeder brave Fuhrmann der muss sein' Wagen han"   5418
      g 309

"JETZT FÄNGT DAS SCHÖNE FRÜHJAHR AN" g 40,49,309,326   5419

"JETZT FAHRN WIR ÜBERN SEE" g 49,309   5420

"JETZT GANG I ANS BRÜNNELE" g 31,41,99,309,326,327,353; DIE DREI RÖSELEIN g 31,99 att to F. Silcher   5421

"JETZT KOMMEN DIE LUSTIGEN TAGE" g 49,309,326,353   5422

"JETZT KOMMT DIE FRÖHLICHE SOMMERZEIT" g 49   5423

JETZT KOMMT DIE ZEIT; "Jetzt kommt die Zeit dass ich wandern muss" g 49   5424A

"JETZT KOMMT DIE ZEIT, DASS ICH WANDERN MUSS" g 309   5424B

JETZT STEIGT HAMPELMANN; "Jetzt steigt Hampelmann, jetzt steigt Hampelmann aus seinem Bett heraus" g 49   5425

"JETZUND NEHM ICH MEINE BÜCHSE" g 42   5426

KAMERADEN, WIR MARSCHIEREN; "Kameraden, wir marschieren wollen fremdes Land durchspüren" g 49 words   5427
      by J. Riel

"KEHR' ICH EINST ZUR HEIMAT WIEDER" g 31,326   5428

DER KEHRAUS; "Dr Kehrüs, dr Kehrüs, die Maide gehn jetz heim" g 49   5429

KEIN BESSER LEBEN IST; "Kein besser Leben ist auf dieser Welt zu denken" g 43   5430

KEIN' SCHÖNERN BAUM GIBT'S; "Kein' schönern Baum gibt's wie ein' Vogelbeerbaum" g 40   5431

"KEIN SCHÖNRER TOD IST IN DER WELT" g 43 words by M. von Silcher   5432

"KENNT IHR DAS LAND IN DEUTSCHEN GAUEN?" g 326   5433

"KENNT JI AL DAT NIJE LEÏD"; "IST EUCH SCHON DAS LIED BEKANNT" g 309   5434

"KINDLEIN MEIN, SCHLAF DOCH EIN" g 309; "KINDLEIN MEIN, SCHLAF NUR EIN" g 49   5435

KLEINES WALDVÖGELEIN; "Es flog ein kleines Waldvögelein" g 49   5436

KLINGE LIEBLICH UND SACHT; "Klinge lieblich und sacht, klinge leis durch die Nacht!" g 309   5437

KOMMT, IHR GSPIELEN; "Kommt, ihr Gspielen wir wolln uns kuhlen bei diesem frischen Taue" g 49   5438

KRÄHT DER GOKKEL; "Kräht der Gokkel, auf dem Mist" 2 pt round g 40   5439

"DER KUCKUCK AUF DEM ZAUNE SASS"; Der Gutzgauch auf dem Zaune sass (tune) g 41,309   5440A

HOCHZEITSLIED; "Der Kuckuck auf dem Zaune sass" g 99   5440B

"KUCKUCK, KUCKUCK RUFT'S AUS DEM WALD"; Stieglitz, Stieglitz, 's Zeiserl is Krank (tune) g 353; words   5441
by H. H. von Fallersleben; THE CUCKOO; "Cuckoo, cuckoo, from the woods sing!" e 37;
"Cuckoo, cuckoo, welcome thy song" e 28,366

LANDESVATER; "Alles schweige! Jeder neige ernsten Tönen nun sein Ohr!" g 31   5442

LASS NUR DER JUGEND IHREN LAUF!; "Lass nur der Jugend, der Jugend, der Jugend ihren Lauf" g 49,326;   5443
LASST DOCH DER JUGEND IHREN LAUF; "Lasst doch der Jugend, der Jugend, der Jugend ihren
Lauf" g 309,353

LATERNE; "Laterne, Laterne, Sonne, Mond und Sterne" g 49   5444

DIE LEINEWEBER; "Die Leineweber haben eine saubere Zunft" g 353; "DIE LEINEWEBER HABEN EINE SAUBERE   5445
ZUNFT" g 309,326; VON DEN LEINEWEBERN g 99

"DAS LIEBEN BRINGT GROSS FREUD" g 49,309,326,353; LIEBESFREUD; "Das Lieben bringt gross Freud" g 31;   5446
MEIN EIGEN SOLL SIE SEIN g 99

LIEBESGRUSS AUS DER FERNE; "Sind wir geschieden und leb ich ohne dich" g 229   5447

LIEBLICH ERGRÜNEN; "Lieblich ergrünen so Auen als Felder" g 42   5448

LIED DER LANDSKNECHTE; "Wir zogen in das Feld" 2 versions g 99; "WIR ZOGEN IN DAS FELD" g 43   5449

LIEDERWERK; "Es geht wohl zu der Sommerzeit" g 43   5450

LIPPE-DETMOLD; "Lippe-Detmold, eine wunderschöne Stadt, darinnen ein Soldat" g 31,43,99   5451

LOB DER EDLEN MUSICA; Die Binsgauer wollten wallfahrten gahn (tune); "Ein lust'ger Musikante marschierte am   5452
Nil" g 99; LOB DER EDLEN MUSIKA g 31; EIN LUST'GER MUSIKANTE g 42; EIN LUSTGER
MUSIKANTE; "Ein lustger Musikante marschierte einst am Nil" g 353

"LOBE DEN HERREN, DEN MÄCHTIGEN KÖNIG" g 49,326 words by J. Neander   5453

"LOBE DEN HERREN, O MEINE SEELE" g 326 words by J. D. Herrnschmidt   5454

LORE, DES FÖRSTERS TÖCHTERLEIN; "Im Wald, im grünen Walde, da steht ein Försterhaus" g 328   5455

LUSTIG, IHR BRÜDER; "Lustig, ihr Brüder, lasst Grillen und Sorgen sein!" g 309   5456

LUSTIG IST DAS ZIGEUNERLEBEN; "Lustig ist das Zigeunerleben, faria, faria" g 326,353   5457

LUSTIG IST'S MATROSENLEBN; "Lustig ist's Matrosenlebn, haltojo, ist mit lauter Lust umgebn, haltojo" g 309,   5458
326,353; MATROSENLEBEN; "Lustig ist's Matrosenleben, haltojo, ist mit lauter Lust umgebn,
haltojo" g 49 words by W. Gerhard, att to A. Pohlenz

"DER MÄCHTIGSTE KÖNIG IM LUFTREVIER" g 326   5459

MÄDCHENPREIS; "Ich spring an diesem Ringe aufs beste so ich kann" g 99   5460

EIN MÄNNLEIN STEHT IM WALDE; "Ein Männlein steht im Walde ganz still und stumm" g 326 words by H. von   5461
Fallersleben; A LITTLE MAN; "A tiny little man stands in forest dim" e 28,366

DER MAI, DER LUSTIGE MAI; "Der Mai, der Mai, der lustige Mai" g 49; "DER MAI, DER MAI, DER LUSTIGE   5462
MAI" g 309

DER MAIEN IST KOMMEN; "Der Maien ist kommen, und das ist ja wahr!" g 49,326   5463

MARIA THERESIA; "Maria Theresia, zeuch nicht in den Kreig!" g 43   5464

MARIA UND DIE ARME SEELE VOR DER HIMMELSTÜR; "Dort oben, dort oben vor der himmlischen Tür" g 99   5465

MARIA ZU LIEBEN; "Maria zu lieben ist allzeit mein Sinn" g 326   5466

MAY FLIGHT; "Now Spring will come and greet us" e 37 tune att to N. von Reuental   5467

MEERSTERN, ICH DICH GRÜSSE; "Meerstern, ich dich grüsse! O Maria, hilf!" g 49,326   5468

MEI SCHÄTZLE IST FEI; "Mei Schätzle ist fei, 's könnt feiner net sei" g 326   5469

MEIN BÜCHSLEIN AM ARM; "Mein Büchslein am Arm, drei Federn auf dem Hut" g 49   5470

MEIN CHRISTIAN; Wilhelm, komm an meine Seite (tune); "Wo mag denn nur mein Christian sein" g 49; WO   5471
MAG DENN NUR MEIN CHRISTIAN SEIN g 309,353

"MEIN HANDWERK FÄLLT MIR SCHWER" g 309   5472

MEIN HUT, DER HAT DREI ECKEN; Oh cara mamma mia (tune); "Mein Hut, der hat drei Ecken, drei Ecken hat   5473
mein Hut" g 353

"MEIN SCHÄTZLEIN KOMMT VON FERNE" g 309   5474

"MIR IST EIN FEINS BRAUNS MAIDELEIN"; g 49,326; "MIR IST EIN SCHÖNS BRAUNS MAIDELEIN" g 309   5475

"MIR SAN JA DIE LUSTIGEN HAMMASCHMIEDSGSÖLLN" g 309; MIR SAN JA DIE LUSTIGEN HAMMER-   5476
SCHMIEDSGSELLN" g 326

MIT LAUTEM JUBEL BRINGEN WIR; "Mit lautem Jubel bringen wir die schöne Erntekron'" g 49   5477

MOORSOLDATEN; "Wohin auch das Auge blicket"; THE PEAT BOG SOLDIERS; "Far and wide as the eye can   5478
wander" e, g 7,293; e 35,293

MORGEN MARSCHIEREN WIR; "Morgen marschieren wir zu dem Bauer ins Nachtquartier" g 43   5479

"MORGEN WILL MEIN SCHATZ ABREISEN" g 326; "HAMBURG IST EIN SCHÖNES STÄDTCHEN" g 326   5480

MORGENLIED DER SCHWARZEN FREISCHAR; "Heraus, heraus der Klingen, lasst Ross und Klepper springen" g 31,   5481
99 words by G. A. Salchow

MUDDER WITTSCH; "Mudder Wittsch, Mudder Wittsch, kik mi mal an" g 49   5482

MUSS I DENN; "Muss i denn, muss i denn zum Städtele naus" g 43; "Must I then, must I then, leave this dear 5483
    little town" e, g 70; MUSS I DENN ZUM STÄDTELE NAUS g 309,326,353; MUSS I DENN, MUSS
    I DENN g 49; MUSS I DENN; "Muss i denn, muss i denn zum Städtle hinaus"; MUST I THEN;
    "Must I then, must I then to the city away" e, g 35; ABSCHIED; "Muss i denn, muss i denn zum
    Städtele naus" g 99; ABSCHIEDSLIED g 31 words by H. Wagner

MUSS I DENN STERBEN; "Muss i denn sterben, bin noch so jung" g 42 5484
"NACH GRÜNER FARB MEIN HERZ VERLANGT" g 49,309 5485
NACH SÜDEN NUN SICH LENKEN; "Nach Süden nun sich lenken die Vöglein allzumal" g 43; DER PRAGER 5486
    STUDENTEN WANDERSCHAFT g 31 words by J. von Eichendorff; WENN ALLE UNTREU WERDEN;
    "Wenn alle untreu werden, so bleiben wir doch treu" g 31 words by M. von Schenkendorf

DIE NACHTIGALL IM TANNENWALD; Sitz ein schöner Vogel im Tannenwald (tune); "Sitzt e klois Vogerl im 5487
    Tannewald" g 99; "'S SITZT A KLEI'S VOGELE IM TANNAWALD" g 309

"NÄHER, MEIN GOTT, ZU DIR" g 326 words att to L. Mason 5488
DER NIBELUNGENHORT; "Es war einmal ein König" g 31 words by K. Simrock 5489
NOW WE MUST PART; "If but the moon will fail this evening" e 95 5490
"NUN ADE, DU MEIN LIEB HEIMATLAND" g 42,49,309,326,353; LIEB HEIMATLAND, ADE g 99 words by 5491
    A. Disselhoff

"NUN LASST UNS SING'N DAS ABENDLIED"; "NUN LAET UNS SENG'N DAT ABENDLEED" g 309 5492
"NUN LEB WOHL, DU SCHÖNE STADT" g 49 5493
NUN RUHEN ALLE WÄLDER; "Nun ruhen alle wälder, Vieh, Menschen, Städt und Felder" g 49 5494
NUN SINGT MIR EIN LIED; "Nun singt mir ein Lied, dass ich scheiden muss" g 31 5495
"NUN WILL DER LENZ UNS GRÜSSEN" g 49,309,326 5496
O ALTE BURSCHENHERRLICHKEIT; "O alte Burschenherrlichkeit! Wohin bist du entschwunden" g 43,326,353; 5497
    "O alte Burschenherrlichkeit! wohin bist du verschwunden?" g 31; RUCKBLICK g 99 words by
    E. Höfling

O DU LIEBER AUTUSTIN; "O du lieber Augustin, 's Geld is hin, 's Madl is hin" g 353; "O du lieber Augustin, 5498
    Augustin, Augustin" g 42,326; LIEBER AUGUSTIN g 132; ACH, DU LIEBER AUGUSTIN; "Ach,
    du lieber Augustin, Augustin, Augustin"; "Oh, my dear old Augustin, Augustin, Augustin" e, g
    70; O TOI, CHER AUGUSTIN; "O toi, mon cher Augustin, tout mon bien, il est tien" f 88;
    WHEN I WAS A LADY; "When I was a lady, a lady, a lady" e 28,366

O DU SCHÖNER ROSENGARTEN; Stets in Trauern muss ich leben (tune); "O du schöner Rosengarten, o du schöner 5499
    Lorienstrauss" g 309; SCHONER ROSENGARTEN; "O du schöner Rosengarten, o du schöner Strauss"
    g 353

O DU SCHÖNER WESTERWALD; "Heute wollen wir marschiern, einen neuen Marsch probiern" g 326 5500
O SCHIPMANN; "O Schipmann, o Schipmann, o Schipmann du" g 41 5501
O STRASSBURG; "O Strassburg, o Strassburg, du wunder schöne Stadt!" g 31,43; DER UNERBITTLICHE 5502A
    HAUPTMANN g 99

O STRASSBURG, O STRASSBURG; "O Strassburg, o Strassburg, du wunderschöne Stadt" g 158 5502B
O WIE SCHÖN; "O wie schön die hellen Lieder klingen!" 4 pt round g 40 5503
"O WIE WOHL IST MIR AM ABEND" g 40,353; DIE ABENDGLOCKE; THE EVENING BELLS; "Oh, how lovely is 5504
    the evening" e, g 34; "O WIE WOHL IST'S MIR AM ABEND"; "O, HOW LOVELY IS THE EVENING"
    e, g 337; LOVELY EVENING e 28,37,114,233,366; CHRISTMAS BELLS; "Oh, how lovely is the
    evening, when the Christmas bells are ringing" 3 pt round e 206

THE OPEN ROAD; "Come sling your pack and stride along" e 37 5505
PRINZ EUGEN; "Prinz Eugen, der edle Ritter" g 43,49,99; PRINCE EUGENE; "Prince Eugene, the noble 5506
    Marshal" e, g 7; "Prinz Eugenius, der edle Ritter" g 31

EIN PROSIT DER GEMÜTLICHKEIT; "Ein Prosit, ein Prosit der Gemütlichkeit" g 43,353 5507
RÄTSELLIED; "Ach Jungfer, ich will ihr was aufzuraten geben" g 99 5508
REGIMENT SEIN STRASSEN ZIEHT; "Regiment sein Strassen zieht, auch mein Bursch in Reih und Glied" g 309 5509
DER REICHSTE FÜRST; "Preisend mit viel schönen Reden ihrer Länder Wert und Zahl" g 31,326 words by J. 5510
    Kerner

DIE REISE NACH JUTLAND; "Die Reise nach Jutland, ei die fällt uns so schwer" g 43 5511
REITERS MORGENLIED; "Morgenrot, Morgenrot! leuchtest mir zum frühen Tod?" g 99 words by W. Hauff 5512
RINGLEIN, RINGLEIN, DU MUSST WANDERN; "Ringlein, Ringlein, du musst wandern von dem einen zu dem 5513
    andern" g 49

RÖSLEIN AUF DER HEIDEN; Freut euch, freut euch in dieser Zeit (tune); "Sie gleicht wohl einem Rosenstock" 5514
    g 99; "SIE GLEICHT WOHL EINEM ROSENSTOCK" g 309,326

ROSE GARDEN; "Your garden grows so lovely, girl!" e 95 5515
"ROSEL, WENN DU MEINE WÄRST" g 309; "RUSLA, WENN DU MEINE WARST" g 49,326 5516
ROSESTOCK, HOLDERBLÜH; "Rosestock, Holderblüh, wenn i mein Dirndel sieh" g 353; "Rosestock, Holderblüh! 5517
    Wann i mein Dirnderl sieh" g 42; ROSESTOCK, HOLDERBLÜT; "Rosestock, Holderblüt, wenn i
    mein Dienderl sieh" g 31; "Rosestock, Holderblüt, wenn i mei Dirnderl sieh" g 326; "Rosestock,
    Holderblüt, wann i mein Dirnderl sieht" g 327; ROSASTOCK, HOLDERBLÜT; "Rosastock, Holder-
    blüt, wenn i mei Dirnderl sieh" g 49; ROSASTOCK, HOLDERBLÜH; "Rosastock, Holderblüh, wenn

ROSESTOCK, HOLDERBLÜH (Continued)   i mei Dirndel sieh" g 309; OBERSCHWÄBISCHER LÄNDLER;   5517
    "Rosestock, Holderblüh, wenn i mein Dirnderl sieh" g 99; LOVELY ROSEBUSH; "Lovely little
    rosebush sweet, when I my darling meet" e 37

ROTE LIPPEN UND GOLDNER WEIN; "Im Arm ein frisches ros'ges Kind" g 31   words by E. Rittershaus   5518

RUNDGESANG; RUNDADINELLA; "Ihr lieben Brüder mein, Rundadinella" g 49   5519

RUNDGESANG UND GERSTENSAFT; "Rundgesang und Gerstensaft lieben wir ja alle" g 353   5520

'S IST ALLES DUNKEL; "'s ist alles dunkel, 's ist alles trübe" g 353; WORAN ICH MEINE FREUDE HAB g 99   5521

SABINCHEN; "Sabinchen was ein Frauenzimmer" g 353; "SABINCHEN WAR EIN FRAUENZIMMER" g 326   5522

ST. MICHAEL; "Unüberwindlich starker Held St. Michael" g 49   5523

"SCHÄFER SAG, WO TUST DU WEIDEN?" g 49, 309, 326   5524

SCHÄFERMÄDCHEN, KOMM MIT MIR; "Schäfermädchen, komm mit mir, komm mit mir, komm mit mir" g 309   5525

DAS SCHÄFERMÄDCHEN UND DER KUCKUCK; "Ein Schäfermädchen weidete zwei Lämmer an der Hand" g 99;   5526
    EIN SCHÄFERMÄDCHEN WEIDETE"; "Ein Schäfermädchen weidete zwei Lämmlein an der Hand" g
    353; THE SHEPHERDESS AND THE CUCKOO; "It was a fair young shepherdess that fed her lamb-
    kins two" e 199

SCHÄFERS KLAGELIED; "Da droben auf jenem Berge, da steh ich tausendmal" g 42   words by J. W. von Goethe   5527

"EINES SCHICKT SICH NICHT FÜR ALLE" 4 pt round g 326   words by J. W. von Goethe   5528

EIN SCHIFFLEIN SAH ICH FAHREN; "Ein Schifflein sah ich fahren, Kapitän und Leutenant"; "Kapitän, Leutenant,   5529A
    Fähnrich, Sergeant, nimm das Mädel, nimm das Mädel bei der Hand" (ref) g 309, 326

KAPITÄN UND LEUTENANT; "Ein Schifflein sah ich fahren, Kapitän und Leutenant"; "Kapitän, Leutenant,   5529B
    Fähnderich, Sergeant, nimm das Mädel, nimm das Mädel, nimm das Mädel bei der Hand"
    g 99

SOLDATEN; "Ein Schifflein sah ich fahren, Kapitän und Leutenant"; "Kapitän, Leutenant, Fähnderich, Sergeant,   5529C
    nimm das Mädel bei der Hand" (ref) g 31

SCHLAF', KINDLEIN, SCHLAF'; CRADLE SONG; "Sleep, baby sleep, thy father minds the sheep" e 199   arr by   5530A
    J. Brahms

SLEEP, BABY, SLEEP; "Sleep, baby sleep! Thy father guards the sheep" e 114, 132, 279, 366   5530B

SCHLENDRIAN; "Ich gehe meinen Schlendrian und trinke meinen Wein" g 31   5531

DER SCHNEIDER JAHRSTAG; "Und als die Schnieder Jahrstag hattn" g 99   5532

SCHNEIDRI, SCHNEIDRA, SCHNEIDRUM; "Schneidri, schneidra, schneidrum, schneidri, schneidra, schneidrum"   5533
    g 309, 353; LOB DES SCHNEIDERS g 49

SCHÖN IST DIE JUGEND; "Schön ist die Jugend bei frohen Zeiten" g 326, 353   words by E. Schoch   5534

DAS SCHÖNSTE LAND DER WELT; "Das schönste Land der Welt ist mein Tirolerland" g 326   5535

SCHÖNSTER ABESTÄRN; "Schönster Abestärn, o, wie gesehn i di so gärn!" g 157; WEEP NO MORE; "Lovely   5536
    evening star, queen of all my thoughts you are" e 95

SCHWARZBRAUN IST DIE HASELNUSS; "Schwarzbraun ist die Haselnuss, schwarzbraun bin auch ich" g 326, 353   5537

"EINE SEEFAHRT, DIE IST LUSTIG" g 326, 353   5538

SEHT, WIE DIE SONNE DORT SINKET; "Seht, wie die Sonne dort sinket hinter dem nächtlichen Wald!" g 326,   5539
    353; SÜSSER DIE GLOCKEN NIE KLINGEN; "Süsser die Glocken nie klingen als zu der Weihnachts-
    zeit" g 353; NEVER DO BELLS RING MORE SWEETLY; "Never do bells ring more sweetly than at
    the Christmas time" e 165

SIEBENSCHRITT; SEVEN STEPS; "One, two, three, four, five, six, sev'n" e 37   5540

SILVESTERLIED; "So singen wir, so trinken wir" g 31   words by H. H. von Fallersleben   5541

"SIND WIR NICHT ZUR HERRLICHKEIT GEBOREN" g 31   words by H. Wollheim   5542

SING SANG UND KLING KLANG; "Ein treues Herz voll Liebeslust, an Liedern reich und Sangeslust" g 31   words   5543
    by J. John

"SINGET DEM HERRN EIN NEUES LIED" 3 pt round g 326   5544

"SITZT A SCHÖNS VOGERL IM TANNABAUM" g 309   5545

"SO GEHT ES IM SCHNÜTZELPUTZ-HÄUSEL" g 309   5546

"SO GRÜN ALS IST DIE HEIDEN" g 99   5547

SO PÜNKTLICH ZUR SEKUNDE; "So pünktlich zur Sekunde trifft keine Uhr wohl ein" g 31   words by O. von   5548
    Reichert

"SO SCHEIDEN WIR MIT SANG UND KLANG" g 353   words by H. H. von Fallersleben   5549

"SO TREIBEN WIR DEN WINTER AUS"; Bewaht mich Gott vorm Interim (tune) g 49, 309, 326   5550

"SOLL ICH DIR MEIN LIEBSCHEN NENNEN?" g 326   5551

SOMMERSEGEN; "Himmels-au, licht und blau, wieviel zählst du Sternlein?" g 49   5552

DIE SPINNERIN; "Spinn, spinn, meine liebe Tochter" g 99; "SPINN, SPINN, MEINE LIEBE TOCHTER" g 309;   5553
    SPINN, SPINN g 41; WENN DER TOPP; "Wenn der Topp aber nu en Loch hat" g 40; WENN DER
    TOPP ABER NU EN LOCH HAT g 353

STANDING ON THE MOUNTAIN; "Standing on the mountain, gaze far down the valley"; "Rum-de-re-dum, the   5554
    drums are beating" (ref) e 37

STEH NUR AUF, DU HANDWERKSGESELL; "Steh nur auf, steh nur auf, du Handwerksgesell" g 309; WACH AUF,   5555
    DU HANDWERKSGESELL; "Wach auf, wach auf, du Handwerksgesell" g 49, 326

"STEHN ZWEI STERN AM HOHEN HIMMEL" g 49, 309, 326   5556

"STEIG ICH DEN BERG HINAUF" g 326 5557

STUDENT SEIN; "Student sein, wenn die Veilchen blühen, das erste Lied die Lerche singt" g 31   words by J. 5558
    Buchhorn

STUDENTENSINN; "Gesungen und gesprungen, gelacht, geküsst, geherzt" g 31 5559

DER SUMMA IST UMMA; "Der Summa ist umma, fallen d'Laba vom Baum" g 41 5560

SUSY, LITTLE SUSY; "Susy, little Susy, now what is the news" e 28,366 5560*

DER TAG IS HIN; "Der Tag is hin, die Nacht bricht an" 3 pt round g 40 5561

TANZ RÜBER, TANZ NÜBER; "Tanz rüber, tanz nüber, tanz nauf und tanz no" g 41,309; "Tanz rüber, tanz 5561*
    nüber, tanz rauf und tanz no" g 326

TANZLIED; "O, wie so schön und gut ist doch ein freier" g 99 5562

TEUTOBURGER SCHLACHT; "Als die Römer frech geworden, sim serim sim sim sim sim" g 31   words by J. V. 5562*
    Scheffel

TEUTS SÖHNE; "Auf, singet und trinket den köstlichen Trank!" g 31 5563

TIEF IN DEM BÖHMERWALD; "Tief in dem Böhmerwald, da liegt mein Heimatort" g 326   words by M. Schmid 5563*

EIN TIROLER WOLLTE JAGEN; "Ein Tiroler wollte jagen einen Gemsbock, Gemsbock silbergrau" g 326 5564

"TRARA, DAS TÖNT WIE JAGDGESANG" 4 pt round g 40,326 5564*

"TRARIRO, DER SOMMER, DER IST DO" g 49,309,326 5565

TREUE LIEBE; "Es kommt die Zeit zum Offenbaren" g 49 5565*

TREUE LIEBE; O du Deutschland (tune); "Soviel Stern am Himmel stehen, an dem blauen Himmelszelt" g 99; 5566
      WEISST DU, WIEVIEL STERNLEIN STEHEN; "Weisst du wieviel Sternlein stehen an dem baluen
      Himmelszelt?" g 326,353   words by W. Hey

TREUE LIEBE; "Steh ich in finstrer Mitternacht" g 31,99   words by W. Hauff 5566*

"TRINK ICH WEIN, SO VERDERB ICH" g 43   words att to H. Dedekind 5567

TRINK, KAMERAD!; "Trink, Kamerad! trink, trink, trink, Kamerad" g 31   words by H. H. von Fallersleben 5567*

TRINKERS TESTAMENT; "Ihr Brüder, wenn ich nicht mehr trinke" g 31 5568

TRINKLIED IM FREIEN; "Brüder, lagert euch im Kreise" g 31 5568*

TRITTZU; "Wenn alle Brünnlein fliessen, so muss man trinken" g 99; WENN ALLE BRÜNNLEIN g 41; WENN 5569
      ALLE BRÜNNLEIN FLIESSEN g 49,309,326,353

DAS TUMBE BRÜDERLEIN; "Wo sol ich mich hinkeren, ich tumbes Brüderlein?" g 31 5569*

ULANEN; "Ulanen, stolz von Lützow her" g 43 5570

UN JETZ ISCH US; "Un jetz isch us un nüt meh"; UND JETZT ISTS AUS; "Und jetzt ists aus und nichts mehr" 5570*
    g 309

"UND AUF-A-MA BÜSCHELE HABERSTROH" g 326 5571

UND IN DEM SCHNEEGEBIRGE; "Und in dem Schneegebirge da fliesst ein Brünnlein kalt" g 41,49,309,326,353 5571*

"UND JETZT GANG I ANS PETERS BRÜNNELE" g 41,49; "UND JETZT GANG I ANS PETERSBRÜNNELE" g 309,326 5572

"UND WENN DAS GLÖCKLEIN FÜNFMAL SCHLÄGT" g 49,309 5572*

UNSER HANS; "Unser Hans hat Hosen an, und die sind zu klein" g 41 5573

UNSER LIEBE FRAUE; "Unser liebe Fraue vom klaten Brunnen" g 49 5573*

UNTREUE; "Was hab ich denn meinem Feinsliebchen getan?" g 99; "WAS HAB ICH DENN MEINEM FEINSLIEB- 5574
      CHEN GETAN?" g 326,353

VAIN SERENADE; "Came a lad to see his sweetheart" e 95 5574*

VERSTEHST; "Ei Bübla, wennst mich so gern häst, verstehst?" g 99 5575

VETTER MICHEL; "Gestern abend war Vetter Michel hier" g 99 5575*

VIEL FREUDEN MIT SICH BRINGET; "Viel Freuden mit sich bringet die fröhlich Sommerzeit" g 309; "Viel 5576
      Freuden mit sich bringet die schöne Sommerzeit" g 49

VIVE LA COMPAGNEIA; "Ich nehm mein Gläschen in die Hand"; "Vive la Compagneia! Vive la, vive la, vive 5576*
      la va" (ref) g 99; VIVE LA SENIOR CLASS; "Let ev'ry Freshman now vow to the last!"; "Vive la
      compagnie! Vive le, vive le, vive l'amour" (ref) e 343

VO LUZERN; "Vo Luzern uf Wägis zue Jodler" g 41 5577

VÖGELE IM TANNEWALD; "Vögele im Tannewald pfeifet so hell, tireli" g 326; "Vögele im Tannwald pfeifet so 5577*
      hell, tirili" g 309; VÖGELEIN IM TANNENWALD; "Vögelein im Tannenwald pfeifet so hell!" g 99

EIN VOGEL WOLLTE HOCHZEIT MACHEN; Es wollt' ein Vogel Hochzeit machen (tune); "Ein Vogel wollte 5578
      Hochzeit machen in dem grünen Walde" g 40,49,309,353; VOGELHOCHZEIT g 99; DIE VOGEL-
      HOCHZEIT g 326; THE WEDDING OF THE BIRDS; "The birds they held a wedding fine, deep in
      the leafy woodland green" e, g 230

"VON DEN BERGEN RAUSCHT EIN WASSER" g 326 5578*

VON DER ALPE RAGT EIN HAUS; "Von der Alpe ragt ein Haus niedlich übers Tal hinaus" g 353; AUF DER ALM, 5579
      DA GIBT'S KOA SÜND g 326   words by J. N. Vogl

WACH AUF, MEIN HERZ, UND SINGE; "Wach auf, mein Herz, und singe dem Schöpfer aller Dinge" g 49   words 5579*
      by P. Gerhardt

WACHET AUF; "Wachet auf, wachet auf, es krähte der Hahn" 2 pt round g 40 5580

WAHRE FREUNDSCHAFT; "Wahre Freundschaft soll nicht wanken" g 49; "WAHRE FREUNDSCHAFT SOLL NICHT 5581
      WANKEN" g 309,326

WALDESLUST; "Waldeslust, Waldeslust, o wie einsam schlägt die Brust" g 326,353 5582

GREECE

CANELLA; "By the seashore there dwells a fair maid" e 86   5633
THE CURSE; "Damnation fall upon the man" e 95   5634
DIAMANTO; "Rouse thee, Diamanto! Haste, to the mill you must go!" e 37   5635
THE FERRYMAN OF LAKE OKHRIDA; "Happy he, girl, he who calls you daughter" e 95   5636
MOUNT AGRAFA; "Upon Mount Agrafa let me go" e 95   5637
TO TSOBANOPOULO; "Tsobanakos imoona provatakya fylaga"; THE YOUNG SHEPHERD; "I was once a shepherd   5638
      lad keeping sheep, was always glad" e, gr (tr) 36
YOUNG CONSTANTINE; "When Constantine was five years old" e 86   5639

GUATEMALA

CENZONTLE DE HAUTAL; SONG OF THE REED-BIRDS; "Reed-birds are singing in the marshes" e 86   5640
EL MISHITO; "Yo quisiera ser mishito"; THE KITTEN; "I would like to be your kitten" e, s 322   5641
VAMOS A LA MAR; "Vamos a la mar, tum, tum, a comer pescado, tum, tum" s 284   5642

HAITI

ANGELIQUE, Ô!; "Angelique, ô, Angelique, ô, Alé caille mamman ou" f 284   5643
BAINYIN; "Bainyin, bainyin, na pe bainyin Poule a Maitresse" f 284   5644
CHOUCONNE; "Of anything I have done" e 86; "In woodland so green and sweet" e 279   5645

HAWAII

FEASTING BY THE OCEAN; "Comes the day of feasting and dancing" e 279   words by W. Hughes   5646
ISLAND SONG; "Isles of Hawaii, verdant in the ocean" e 279   words by W. Hughes   5647
SONG OF LIHUE; "O fairest village of Lihue" e 279   words by W. Hughes   5648

HONDURAS

CANCION DEL MARINERO HONDUREÑO; "Marinero Hondureño que ya te vas" s 284   5649

HUNGARY

ABLAKOMBA, ABLAKOMBA; "Ablakomba, ablakomba besütött a holdvilág" hu 23   5650
ABLAKOMBA HÁROM BOKOR; IN MY WINDOW THREE POTS; "In my window three pots of geranium" e 164   5651
ALÁZATOS SZOLGÁJA; I WISH YOU GOOD EVENING; "One, two, three, four, five and six and seven eight!"   5652
      e 164
AZ ALFÖLDÖN HALÁSZLEGÉNY VAGYOK ÉN; I'M A FISHER; "I'm a fisher, in the lowlands I reside" e 164   5653
"ÁLTAL MENNÉK ÉN A TISZÁN LADIKON" hu 23   5654
ANYNYI BÁNAT AS SZŰVEMEN; "Anynyi bánat az szűvemen Kétrét hajlott az egeken"; "Skies above are heavy   5655
      with rain, Sad my heart and weary with pain"; "All das Leid in meinem Herzen Drängt zum
      Himmel meine Schwerzen" e, g, hu 22
ÁROK, ÁROK; "Árok, árok, de mély árokba estem" hu 289   5656
ÁROK IS VAN; THERE ARE PITS; "There are pits and there are ditches" e 164   5657
ÁRVA LEÁNY MENYASSZONYI BÚCSÚZTATÓJA; "A paszulya szára felfuttott a fára" hu 289   5658
ASZSZONYOK; "Aszszonyok, aszszonyok, had' legyek tarsatok"; "Women, women, listen, let me share your   5659
      labour"; "Frauen, Frauen lasst mich euch Genossin heissen" e, g, hu 22
AZÉRT CSILLAG; "Azért csillag, hogy ra gyogjon"; "STERNE SIND, DAMIT SIE STRAHLEN"; STARS SHINE   5660
      BRIGHT; "Stars shine bright their light to give us" e, g, hu 92; STARS ARE SHINING; "Stars are
      shining to relieve us" e 164
"AZÉRT, HOGY ÉN HUSZÁR VAGYOK" hu 23; THE DRAFTEE; "Hello, sweetheart! Yes, I'm drafted!" e 95   5661
BABOT VITTEM; BEANS I TO THE MILL; "Beans I to the mill was taking" e 164   5662
BEFORDULTAM A KONYHÁRA; "I INTO THE HOUSE WAS TURNING" e 164; TO THE DOOR I STROLLED; "To   5663
      the door of my girl I strolled" e 37
BESZEGŐDTEM TARNÓCÁRA; "Beszegődtem Tarnócára bojtárnak"; GING INS DORF; "Ging ins Dorf, jetzt will   5664
      ich einmal Schäfer sein"; ALWAYS FOR A SHEPHERD'S; "Always for a shepherd's life I've been in-
      clined" e, g, hu 92; TO TARNÓCA I WENT; "To Tarnóca I went as a farmer's hand" e 164
BIRÓ URAM, PANASZOM VAN; LEARNED JUDGE; "Learned judge I am complaining, my love for my husband's   5665
      waning" e 164
BORDAL; "Ó én édes pintes üvegem"; TRINKLIED; "Komm mein liebes Fläschchen, komm doch her" g, hu 26   5666
BORSÓT VITTEM A MALOMBA; "Borsót vittem a malomba, azt gondoltam, tiszta búza" hu 289   5667
BUJDOSIK A KEDVES RÓZSÁM; SOMEWHERE FAR; "Somewhere far my dearest rose is wandering" e 164   5668
BUJDOSO-ÉNEK; "Erdők, völgyek, szűk ligetek, Sokat bujdostam bennetek"; DER FLÜCHTLING; "Hab durch-   5669
      zogen Berg und Täler, Bin gewandert durch die Welt weit" g, hu 24

BUZA; "Buza, buza, buza, de szép tábla buza"; "Weizen, Weizen, Weizen, prächtig anzusehen" g, hu 27   5670

CHERRY GATHERING; "Not that way, my pretty!" e 95   5671

A CSAP UCCÁN VÉGIG; "A Csap uccán végig, végig, végig"; WHEN ALONG THE VILLAGE; "When along the   5672
village street I'm going"; LÄNGS DER SCHENKENGASS' ENTLANG; "Längs der Schenken-gass'
entlang, der losen" e, g, hu 92; DOWN THE VILLAGE STREET; "Down the village street I wandering go" e 164

"CSÁRDÁS KIS KALAPOT VESZEK"; "SETZ' HEUT' FROH DEN NEUEN HUT AUF"; ON MY HEAD; "On my head   5673
my new hat so neat" e, g, hu 92

CSEREBOGÁR; "Cserebogár, sárga cserebogár"; MAIENKÄFER; "Maienkäfer, Maienkäfer, goldner"; CHAFER,   5674
CHAFER; "Chafer, Chafer, all the day you're humming" e, g, hu 92; COCKCHAFER; "Brown
cockchafer, buzzing friend, have no fear" e 164

"CSICSÓNÉNAK HÁROM LÁNYA"; "TÖCHTER HAT FRAU CSICSÓ DREI"; MADAM CSICSO'S DAUGHTERS;   5675
"Madam Csicso's daughters three, oh!" e, g, hu 92

DE SZERETNÉK; "De szeretnék rámás csizmát viselni"; EIN PAAR SCHMUCKE STIEFEL; "Ein Paar schmucke   5676
Stiefel nähm' ich gern in Kauf"; I HAVE COME; "I have come a handsome pair of boots to buy"
e, g, hu 92

DEBRECENBE KÉNE MENNI; "Debrecenbe kéne menni, pulykakakast kéne venni"; WE'VE TO DEBRECHEN BEEN;   5677
"We've to Debrecen been hieing, there a monster turkey buying"; LASST NACH DEBREZIN UNS
LAUFEN; "Lasst nach Debrezin uns laufen, einen Truthahn dort zu kaufen" e, g, hu 92; WE
MUST GO TO DEBRECEN; "We must go to Debrecen fair, we must buy a turkey hen there" e 164

DEBRECENNEK VAN EGY VIZE; "Debrecennek van egy vize, Kinek Hortobágy a neve" hu 289   5678

DERES A FÜ...; DEWY IS THE GRASS; "Dewy is the grass, my dear horse do not feed" e 164   5679

DO NOT CARE; "Do not worry, it is not worthwhile" e 37; THE FISHERMAN; "By the river stands a little shed"   5680
e 95

[EDDIG VALÓ DOLGOM]; "Eddig való dolgom a tavaszi szántás"; "Spring begins with labour, then's the time for   5681
sowing"; "Meines Lebens Arbeit warden Pflug zu halten" e, g, hu 22

ÉDES ANYÁM A KENDŐM; MOTHER DEAR; "Mother dear, the love of mine asks me for my kerchief fine!" e 164   5682

ÉDES KEDVES FELESÉGEM; "Édes kedves feleségem, jaj de sovány vagy"; LIEBE FRAU, DU BIST SO MAGER;   5683
"Liebe Frau, du bist so mager wie ein Besenstiel"; DARLING WIFE; "Darling wife, it vexes me that
you so thin should be" e, g, hu 92

ÉDESANYÁM; "Édesanyám hol van az az ides téj" hu 289   5684

ÉG A KUNYHÓ; "Eg a kunyhó, ropog a nád"; LIEB' NICHT BLONDE; "Lieb' nicht Blonde, lieb' nicht Braune";   5685
NEITHER DARK NOR FAIR; "Neither dark nor fair one shall you woo" e, g, hu 92; HUT IS
BURNING; "Hut is burning, thatch is blazing, in two brown eyes you are gazing" e 164

"AZ EGRI MÉNES MIND VERES"; ERLAU HAT PFERDE; "Erlau hat Pferde, die gut geh'n"; ERLAU HAS HORSES;   5686
"Erlau has horses good and fleet" e, g, hu 92

ELINDULTAM SZÉP HAZÁMBUL; "Elindultam szép hazámbul, Hires kis Magyarországbul" hu 23   5687

AZ ÉN RÁCSÓS KAPUM; "Az én rácsos kapum sárgára van festve" hu 289   5688

ERDŐ, ERDŐ, SŰRŰ ERDŐ ÁRNYÁBAN; SHADOWS O'ER THE FOREST; "Shadows o'er the forest spread their thick,   5689
dark veil" e 164

"ERESZ ALATT FÉSZKEL A FECSKE"; UNDERNEATH THE EAVES; "Underneath the eaves the swallows dwell";   5690
SCHWÄLBCHEN UNTER'M DACH; "Schwälbchen unter'm Dach ihr Nestlein baut" e, g, hu 92;
UNDER EAVES; "Under eaves their nest the swallows made" e 164

ERESZKEDIK LE A FELHŐ; CLOUDS ARE SINKING; "Clouds are sinking low and lower" e 164   5691

"ÉRIK A ROPOGÓS CSERESZNYE"; "Kirschen, wie Knorpel hart pflück ich heut'" g, hu 27   5692

ERRE GYERE RÓZSÁM; "Erre gyere rózsám, nincsen az" hu 289   5693

ESTE VAN A FALUBAN; VILLAGE EVENING, IT IS LATE; "Village evening it is late, it is late" e 164   5694

ESZTENDÖBE EGYSZER ESIK VIZKERESZT; TWELFTH NIGHT COMES; "Twelfth night comes again, when once   5695
the year is round" e 164

EZ A KIS LÁNY AZT HISZI; THIS GIRL; "This girl took it in her head, that she'll by her love be wed" e 164   5696

EZ A KIS LÁNY MEGY A KÚTRA; FROM THE WELL; "From the well this girl brings water" e 164   5697

EZÉRT A LEGÉNYÉRT; "Ezért a legényért nem adnék egy krajcárt"; THAT LAD IS NOTHING WORTH; "That   5698
lad is nothing worth who shyness can't o'ercome"; NICHT EINEN GROSCHEN WERT; "Nicht einen
Groschen wert ist solch ein trüber Held" e, g, hu 92; NOT A RUSH THIS LAD; "Not a rush, not
a rush, this lad, this lad is worth" e 164

EZT A KEREK ERDŐT; "Ezt a kerek erdöt járom én"; WHERE THE BROOKLET FLOWS; "Where the brooklet   5699
flows there stands a tree"; DURCH DEN WALD AN'S BÄCHLEIN; "Durch den Wald an's Bächlein
führt mein Weg" e, g, hu 92

FAGGYU GYERTYÁT ÉGETEK ÉN; TALLOW CANDLE; "Tallow candle I am burning, for a brown girl I am yearn-   5700
ing" e 164

FALU VÉGÉN EGY KIS HÁZ; THERE'S A HOUSE; "There's a house far out of town, 'what do'th thou my maiden   5701
brown?'" e 164

FALU VÉGÉN VAN EGY HÁZ; ON THE VILLAGE END; "On the village end quite far, there an old Jew runs a bar"   5702
e 164

A FALUBA NINCS TÖBB KIS LÁNY; "A faluba nincs több kis lány csak kettő"; ONLY TWO GIRLS; "Only two   5703
girls in the village, only two"; NUR ZWEI MÄDCHEN GAB'S IM DORFE; "Nur zwei Mädchen gab's
im Dorfe, sonderbar" e, g, hu 92; IN THE WHOLE TOWN; "In the whole town there are neat maids
only two" e 164

"FEHÉR LÁSZLÓ LOVAT LOPOTT" hu 23   5704

[FEKETE FOD]; "Fekete föd, fehér az én zsebkendőm"; "Snow-white kerchief, dark both field and furrow show";   5705
"Schwarz die Erde, schneeweiss ist mein Taschentuch" e, g, hu 22

FEKETE SZEM ÉJSZAKÁJA; "Fekete szem éjszakája, hány csillag ragyog ki rája"; BRIGHT YOUR EYES; "Bright   5706
your eyes as stars above you, dearest maiden, how I love you!"; SCHWARZ LEUCHTET IHR, AUGEN-
STERNE; "Schwarz leuchtet ihr, Augensterne, Mädel, hab' dich gar so gerne" e, g, hu 92; IN THE
NIGHT OF DARK EYES' WONDER; "In the night of dark eyes' wonder are those all stars shining yonder?" e 164

FEKETESZÁRU CSERESZNYE; "Feketeszáru cseresznye, rabod vagyok te menyecske"; BEAUTIFUL DARK-EYED   5707
MAID; "Beautiful dark-eyed maid, I pray you will your heart give me someday"; DUNKELFAR-
BIGE SCHÖNE DU; "Dunkelfarbige Schöne du, warum raubtest du mir die Ruh'?" e, g, hu 92

FÉRE TÖLEM BUBÁNAT; "Fére tölem bubánat, bubánat! kajcsót hajtok utánnad, utánnad" hu 23; FORGET THE   5708
WORLD; "Grief, I want to drown it, to drown it, I drown it in my goblet, my goblet" e 95

FÜRDIK A HOLDVILÁG; "Fürdik a holdvilág az ég tengerében"; O'ER THE GLOOMY FOREST; "O'er the gloomy   5709
forest moonbeams bright are falling"; 'S STRAHLT DES VOLLEN MONDES; "'S strahlt des vollen
Mondes silbernes Gefunkel" e, g, hu 92

GERENCSÉRI UTCA; "Gerencséri ucca végig piros rózsa" hu 23   5710

GIMBELEM, GOMBOLOM; I'M BUTT'NING; "Butt'ning up, butt'ning down on my breast" e 164; ONE BUTTON,   5711
TWO BUTTONS; "One button, two buttons, and the rest, thirteen on my vest" e 37

GIPSY TINKER; "Damn that village I've been through there, couldn't get a job to do there!" e 95   5712

GYERE BE RÓZSÁM; COME IN; "Come in my sweetest, come in here" e 164   5713

A GYULAI KERT ALATT; "A gyulai kert alatt, kert alatt" hu 23; A KERTMEGI KERT ALATT; "A kertmegi   5714
kert alatt setaltam" hu 23

HA FELÜLÖK, CSUHAJ; "Ha felülök, csuhaj, ha felülök kis pej lovam hátára" hu 23   5715

HA BEMEGYEK, HA BEMEGYEK A TEMPLOMBA; WHEN E'ER TO THE CLERGYMAN'S HOUSE; "When e'er to the   5716
clergyman's house I myself betake" e 164

[HA KIMEGYEK]; "Ha kimegyek arr' a magos tetőre"; "If I climb the rocky mountains all day through"; "Wollt   5717
ich in die blauen Berge suchen gehn" e, g, hu 22

HÁRMAT RIKKANTOTT MÁR; "Hármat rikkantott már, hármat rikkantott már"; THRICE I HEARD THE THRUSH;   5718
"Thrice I heard the thrush call"; DREIMAL PFIFF DIE AMSEL; "Dreimal pfiff die Amsel, dreimal
pfiff die Amsel" e, g, hu 92; THRICE THE BLACKBIRD; "Thrice the blackbird whistled" e 164

HÁROM BOKOR SALÁTA; THREE GREEN LETTUCE-HEADS; "Three green, three green lettuce-heads, Angel of   5719
mine" e 164; LATZIKA AND MARISHKA; "Currants hanging on the stem, Latzikam dear" e 95

HATFORINTOS NÓTA; "A cseroldalt öszszejártam, Sehol párom nem találtam"; SECHSGULDENTANZ; "Such'   5720
im Wald seit vielen Stunden, Hab' Mädel nicht gefunden" e, g, hu 25

HÁZUNK ELÖTT MENNEK EL; "Házunk elött mennek el a huszárok"; RIDING THROUGH OUR VILLAGE; "Riding   5721
through our village gay hussars I see"; DURCH DAS DORF, HEI!; "Durch das Dorf, hei! traben die
Husaren hin" e, g, hu 92; HÁZUNK ELÖTT MENNEK EL A HUSZÁROK; LOOK, THE HUSSARS
ARE MARCHING; "Look, the hussars are marching down the street right here" e 164

[HEJ, ÉDES ANYÁM]; "Hej, édes anyám, kedves édes anyám"; "Mutter, du liebe, lass dir, lass dir sagen" g, hu   5722
27

"HÉT CSILLAGBÓL VAN A GÖNCÖL SZEKERE"; BRIGHTLY SHINE; "Brightly shine the Great Bear's seven stars on   5723
high"; SIEBENSTERNIG ZIEHT DER BÄR; "Siebensternig zieht der Bär am Himmel weit" e, g, hu
92; HÉT CSILLAGBÓL VAN A GÖNCZÖL SZEKERE; SEVEN WHITE STARS; "Seven white stars in
the greater bear do shine" e 164

HULLÁMZÓ BALATON TETEJÉN; "Hullámzó Balaton tetején csónakázik egy halászlegény"; IN HIS SHALLOP;   5724
"In his shallop on Lake Balaton floats the young fisher lad, pale and wan"; SCHAUKELND AM
BALATON; "Schaukelnd am Balaton zieht ein Boot, drin ein Fischer, so bleich wie der Tod" e,
g, hu 92; HIGH THE WAVES OF LAKE BALATON; "High the waves of Lake Balaton ran, his boat
there drove a young fisherman" e 164

THE HUSSAR; "Now I know October first will be my marching day, dear" e 95   5725

DIE HUSSITEN VOR NAUMBURG; "Die Hussiten zogen vor Naumburg über Jena her und Kamburg" g 31   5726

HUZZAD CSAK; "Huzzad csak, huzzad csak keservesen"; PLAY, GYPSY, PLAY; "Play, Gypsy, play strains of   5727
sorrow and woe"; SPIELE, ZIGEUNER; "Spiele, Zigeuner, voll Weh und voll Schmerz" e, g, hu
92; DID YOU PLAY GIPSY; "Did you play, gipsy, as hard as you durst?" e 164

I HAVE TORN MY SUNDAY JACKET; "I have torn my Sunday jacket, picking berries, one, two and three!" e 95   5728

IN MY YARD VIOLETS; "In my yard violets blossom now so thickly" e 95   5729

ISTEN HOZZÁD SZÜLÖTTEM FOLD; "Isten hozzád szülöttem föld, én miattam lehetsz már zöld" hu 23   5730

[ISTENEM, ISTENEM]; "Istenem, istenem, áraszd meg a vizet"; "Coldly runs the river, reedy banks o'erflowing";   5731
"Gott, ach Gott im Himmel, lass die Wasser schwellen" e, g, hu 22

I'VE A PURSE; "I've a purse, but not a penny, can I order wine, then?" e 95   5732

JAJ BE MAGAS, JAJ BE MAGAS; OH HOW LOFTY; "Oh how lofty, oh how lofty, lofty is this wayside inn" e 164   5733

JAJ, DE BÚSAN HARANGOZNAK; "Jaj, de busan harangoznak Tarjánba"; HARK, THE BELLS ARE RINGING;   5734
    "Hark, the bells are ringing in the dawning red"; TRAURIG KLINGT DER GLOCKEN TON; "Traurig
    klingt der Glokken Ton beim Morgenrot" e, g, hu 92; MOANFULLY IN TARJÁN; "Moanfully in
    Tarján they the bells do ring" e 164

JER AZ ABLAKOMRA, KEDVES; COME TO ME; "Come to me, dear, I am lonely" e 164   5735

JER ÖLEMBE TUBICAM; COME INTO MY ARMS; "Come into my arms, my sweet" e 164   5736

JÓ BOR, JÓ EGÉSZSÉG; GOOD WINE, GOOD HEALTH; "Good wine, good health in life" e 164   5737

JÖN A ROZSÁM; "FROM THE FARM BACK THERE COMES MY ROSE" e 164   5738

JUHÁSZ LEGÉNY; "Juhász legény, szegény juhász legény"; O POOR SHEPHERD LAD; "O poor shepherd lad with-   5739
    out a penny"; SCHÄFERKNABE, ARMER SCHÄFERKNABE; "Schäferknabe, armer Schäferknabe,
    sieh' das viele Geld" e, g, hu 92

KÁKA TÖVÉN; "Káka tövén költ a ruca"; DUCKS ARE HATCHED; "Ducks are hatched where reeds grow   5740
    thickly"; "ENTE LEGT INS SCHIF DIE EIER" e, g, hu 92; KÁKA TÖVEN KÖLT A RUCA; DUCKS
    AMONGST THE RUSH; "Ducks amongst the rush are pairing" e 164; AUTUMN; "From the gray
    branches leaves are falling" e 406

KÁLLAI KETTÖS I; "Felülről fuj az öszi szél" hu 289   5741

KÁLLAI KETTÖS II; "Kincsem komám aszszoszóroszórossz asszony" hu 289   5742

KANÁSZTÁNC; "Megösmerni a kanászt az ö járásáról"; SCHWEINEHIRTENTANZ; "Welche Tracht Schweine-   5743
    hirt, Welche mag ihm ziemen?" g, hu 25

KÉK NEFELEJCS; "Kék nefelejcs, el ne felejts, virágzik a tó mentén"; FAIR BLUE FLOWERS; "Fair blue flowers,   5744
    gentle streamlet, from my love I soon must part"; LIEBLICH BLÜH'N VERGISSMEINNICHT; "Lieb-
    lich blüh'n Vergissmeinnicht blau weithin dort den Bach entlang" e, g, hu 92

"KERTEM ALATT DOLGOZNAK AZ ÁCSOK"; ALL DAY LONG; "All day long till evening without stopping";   5745
    HÖR' VON FRÜH BIS SPÄT; "Hör' von früh bis spät zum Abenddämmern" e, g, hu 92

KÉTSZER NYILIK AZ AKÁCFA VIRÁGA; TWICE BLOOM THE ACACIA TREES; "Twice bloom the acacia trees   5746
    along the lane" e 164

KI VOLT ITT; WHO WAS HERE?; "Who was here? Who was here? Who was it whose pipe has been left here?"   5747
    e 164

KIAPADT A RÉTBÖL; "Kiapadt a rétböl, Mind a sár, mind a viz" hu 289   5748

KIS SZEKERES, NAGY SZEKERES; "Kis szekeres, nagy szekeres mind megiszsza"; ALL GOOD COACHMEN; "All   5749
    good coachmen, short ones or tall never fail for good wine to call"; IST DER KUTSCHER; "Ist der
    Kutscher gross oder klein trinkt er für sein Leben gern Wein" e, g, hu 92; COACHMAN SMALL
    AND BIG; "Coachman small and big on his van wets his whistle whene'er he can" e 164

A KIS TARDI LEÁNYOK; "A kis tardi leányoknak nincs párja" hu 289   5750

KITETTÉK A HOLTTESTET; "Kitették a holttestet az udvarba"; SLOWLY, SLOWLY DOWN; "Slowly, slowly   5751
    down the path they bear his bier"; LANGSAM IN DEN HOF; "Langsam in den Hof trägt man den
    Sarg hinaus" e, g, hu 92; KITETTÉK A HOLTTESTET AZ UDVARRA; WHEN THEY LAID THE
    BODY; "When they laid the body on the courtyard floor" e 164

KOSSUTH LAJOS AZT ÜZENTE; FATHER KOSSUTH WORD IS SENDING; "Father Kossuth word is sending, that   5752
    his regiments are ending" e 164; LOUIS KOSSUTH; "Kossuth Lajos azt izente"; "Kossuth a mes-
    sage is speeding, half his regiment lies bleeding" e, hu 7

KUTYA, KUTYA TARKA; "Kutya, kutya tarka, se füle, se farka"; CROP-EARED MONGREL; "Crop-eared   5753
    mongrel prowling, what is this you're growling"; HÜNDCHEN, KURZ GESCHOREN; "Hündchen, kurz
    geschoren, ohne Schwanz und Ohren" e, g, hu 92

LÁTTAD E TE BABÁM; "Láttad e te babám, azt a száraz nyárfát" hu 23   5754

LÁTTÁL-E VALAHA; "Láttál-e valaha Csipkebokor rózsát" hu 289   5755

LEKASZÁLTÁK MÁR A RÉTET; "Lekaszálták már a rétet, nem hagytak rajt virágot"; ALL MOWN DOWN; "All   5756
    mown down is now the meadow, not one blossom can I see"; ABGEMÄHT IST SCHON DIE WIESE;
    "Abgemäht ist schon die Wiese, alle Blümlein sind gefällt" e, g, hu 92; ALL THE FLOWERS ON
    THE MEADOW; "All the flowers on the meadow were cut by the mowers knife" e 164

LOVE'S MY PERMIT; "Through the streets how bravely they come" e 95   5757

A MADÁRKA A PÁRJÁVAL SZÁLLDOGÁL; WITH HIS PAIR THE BIRD FLIES; "With his pair the bird flies to and   5758
    fro and sings" e 164

MAGASAN REPÜL A DARU; "HIGH THE CRANES ARE FLYING"; "High the cranes are flying, I can hear them   5759
    shriek" e 164; FLYING CRANES; "Farewell calls of flying cranes sound in the air" e 37; THE
    HERON; "Far up above flies the heron" e 279

MAGOS A RUTAFA; "Magos a rutafa, ága elágazik, Selyem sárhaja" hu 23   5760

MAGYAR LEADERS; "Hej Rákóczi! Hej Bercsényi! Régi vitéz magyaroknak"; "Hey, Rakoczi! Hey, Berczenyi!   5761
    Magyar leaders unforgotten!" e, hu 7

[MÁR DOBOZON]; "Már Dobozon, már Dobozon régen leesett a hó"; "Dort in Dobos, ja in Dobos fiel schon längst   5762
    der erste Schnee" g, hu 27

MAROS VIZE FOLYIK; "Maros vize folyik csendesen, borulj a vállamra, kedvesem"; TRANQUILLY THE MAROS; 5763
    "Tranquilly the Maros waters flow, to you jasmine bower let us go"; LANGSAM FLIESST DER MAROS
    FLUSS; "Langsam fliesst der Maros Fluss dahin, Schatz, komm in die Laube von Jasmin" e, g, hu 92;
    MAROS VIZE FOLYIK CSENDESEN; MAROS RIVERS WATER; "Maros rivers water slowly flows, on my
    bosom come and rest, my rose" e 164

MÉG AZT MONDJÁK PICI KIS BABÁM; YES, THEY TELL ME; "Yes, they tell me, oh my sweetheart dear" e 164 5764

MÉLY A RIMA, ZAVAROS, HA MEGÁRAD; DEEP'S THE RIMA; "Deep's the Rima, turbid if its waters swell" e 5765
    164

"MENYECSKÉNEK NEM JÓ LENNI" hu 289 5766

MONDJA MEG ANNAK A KIS LEÁNYNAK; GO AND TELL THAT LITTLE MAIDEN; "Go and tell that little blue- 5767
    eyed maiden she should cure my poor heart sorrow-laden" e 164

MOST JÖTTEM MEG PÁRISBÓL; "I JUST NOW FROM PARIS CAME" e 164 5768

A NÁD JANCSI CSÁRDÁBAN; "A Nád Jancsi csárdábavan, pandúroknak izenve van" hu 23 5769

NAGY A FEJE; "Nagy a feje, busuljon a ló"; HORSES HANG THEIR HEADS; "Horses hang their heads down, it is 5770
    true"; 'S PFERD KANN TRAUERN; "'S Pferd kann trauern, denn sein Kopf ist gross" e, g, hu 92;
    NAGY A FEJE, BÚSULJON A LÓ; HIS HEAD IS BIG; "His head is big, let the horse be sad" e 164

NAGYPÉNTEKEN MOSSA HOLLÓ A FIÁT; "ON GOOD FRIDAY RAVEN GIVES HIS YOUNG ONE A BATH" e 164 5771

"NE MENJ RÓZSÁM A TARLÓRA"; GO NOT THROUGH THE STUBBLE; "Go not through the stubble, my dear"; 5772
    GEH' NICHT AUF DAS STOPPELFELD; "Geh' nicht auf das Stoppelfeld, Kind" e, g, hu 92; "IS
    IT TO THE FIELDS YOU'RE GOING?" e 164

NÉHA-NÉHA; "Néha csendes alkony órán"; NOW AND THEN; "As the silent twilight deepens" e, hu 285 5773

NÉKEM OLYAN ASSZONY KELL; I WANT SUCH A WIFE; "I want such a wife, you bet, sick or not who up will 5774
    get" e 164

NEM MESSZE VAN IDE; "Nem meszsze van ide kis Margitta" hu 23 5775

NEM ÜTIK A JOGÁSZT AGYON; "NO ONE KILLS THE COLLEGE SCHOLAR" e 164 5776

NINCSEN ANNYI TENGERCSILLAG; MILLION STARS ARE SHINING; "Million stars are shining on the skies above" 5777
    e 164

NYISD KI BABÁM AZ AJTÓT; OPEN THE DOOR; "Open the door, baby sweet!" e 164 5778

"AZ ÖCSÉNYI KERTEK ALSÓ VÉGÉN" hu 289 5779

ŐSSZEL SZALL A GÓLYA MADÁR; STORKS IN AUTUMN; "Storks in autumn on their voyage sally forth" e 164 5780

[OLVAD A HÓ]; "Olvad a hó, csárdás kis angyalom"; "Snow is melting, oh, my dear, my darling"; "Winter 5781
    scheidet, holdes Liebchen" e, g, hu 22

PANASZ; "Beteg az én rózsám nagyon, Talán meg is hal"; KLAGE; "Krank zum Sterben ist mein Liebster, und 5782
    er leidet schwer" g, hu 26

PÁR-ÉNEK; "Ne hagyj el, angyalom, megöregszem"; WECHSELGESANG; "Täubchen, verlass mich nicht, werd' 5783
    ich jetzt alt" g, hu 26

PÁROSÍTÓ (1); "Sárga csikó, csengő rajta, Vajjon hová megyünkrajta?"; LIED, EIN PAAR ZU BESINGEN (1); 5784
    "Scheck, lass deine Schellen läuten, Sag, wohin wir heute reiten" g, hu 26

PÁROSÍTÓ (2); "Virágéknál ég a világ, Sütik már a rántott békát"; LIED, EIN PAAR ZU BESINGEN (2); "Bei 5785
    den Wirag's brennt das Feuer, Frösche bäckt man ungeheuer" g, hu 26

PÁSZTORNÓTA; "Mikor guláslegény voltam, Zöld mezőre kihajtottam"; HIRTENLIED; "Rinder hüten macht mir 5786
    viel Spass, Treib' das Vieh auf grüne Weide" g, hu 24

PÉNTEKEN ESTE; ON FRIDAY EVENING; "On Friday evening, or Sabbat maybe, when it gets dark I go to my 5787
    baby" e 164

PIROS ALMA CSÜNG; "Piros alma csüng az ágon"; ROSY ARE MY APPLES; "Rosy, are my apples growing"; 5788
    ROSIG, WIE DIE ÄPFEL HANGEN" e, g, hu 92

PIROS, PIROS, PIROS; "Piros, piros, piros, háromszor is piros"; ROSY, ROSY, RED WINE; "Rosy, rosy, red wine, 5789
    fill me thrice the red wine"; ROTEN, ROTEN, ROTEN WEIN; "Roten, roten, roten, dreimal just
    schenkt roten" e, g, hu 92; "Rosy, rosy, rosy, rosy, rosy, rosy, glows the red wine in my glass"
    e 164

PLEASED TO MEET YOU!; "So much pride in one small maiden" e 95 5790

A RÁTÓTI LEGÉNYEK; "A rátóti legények libát fogtak szégenyek"; NEULICH SAGTE KUNZ ZUM HANS; "Neu- 5791
    lich sagte Kunz zum Hans: 'Heut stehl'n wir des Nachbars Gans'"; HANS SAID 'KUNTZ'; "Hans said
    'Kuntz, I think we might steal our neighbor's geese tonight'" e, g, hu 92

RECECE; "Recece, I'm no captain of the force" e 164 5792

RÉGI KESERVES; "Olyam árva vagyok, mint út mellett az ág"; TRAURIGE WEISE; "Einsam leid' ich, einsam, 5793
    gleich dem Ast am Bergweg" g, hu 24

REPÜLJ FECSKÉM; "Repülj fecském ablakára, kérjed, ny issa meg szavadra"; FROM MY WINDOW FLY; "From 5794
    my window fly, dear swallow, how I wish that I could follow"; FLIEG' ZUR LIEBSTEN; "Flieg' zur
    Liebsten, Schwälbchen, flieg' zu, fleh' dass sie ihr Fenster auftu'" e, g, hu 92

RÉSZEG VAGYOK; "Részeg vagyok rózsám mint a csap"; FULL OF WINE; "Full of wine, my rosebud, like yon 5795
    vat"; SCHATZ, ICH BIN BETRUNKEN; "Schatz, ich bin betrunken wie ein Fass" e, g, hu 92;
    RÉSZEG VAGYOK ROZSAM; I AM TIPSY; "I am tipsy sweetheart, like a top" e 164

RITKA BUZA, RITKA ÁRPA; "Ritka buza, ritka árpa, ritka rozs"; RARE AND RIPE; "Rare and ripe the barley, 5796
    rare and ripe the wheat"; GOLDNER WEIZEN, GOLDNE GERSTE; "Goldner Weizen, goldne Gerste,
    goldnes Korn" e, g, hu 92; SCARCE IS BARLEY; "Scarce is barley, scarce is corn and scarce is
    wheat" e 164

ROZSABIMBÓ, TULIPÁN; "ROSES, TULIPS, GOLD AND PEARL" e 164   5797

RÓZSABOKORBAN JÖTTEM A VILÁGRA; IN A ROSEBUSH; "In a rosebush I the daylight first did see" e 164 5798

[SÁRGA KUKORICASZÁL]; "Sárga kukoricaszál, Kapálatlan kapálatlan maradtál"; "Gelber Mais, verdorrter 5799
    Strauch, Blieb dein Boden, blieb dein Boden unbehaun" g, hu 27

SARKON VAN A HÁZAM; I LIVE ON THE CORNER; "I live on the corner, there my house you see" e 164 5800

SÜRÜ CSILLAG RITKÁN RAGYOG AZ ÉGEN; SELDOM SHINE THE STARS; "Seldom shine the stars all on the 5801
    milky way" e 164

SZALMASZÁL A VIZBE; ONE STRAW SWIMS; "One straw swims forsaken in the water forsaken" e 164 5802

"SZÁNT A BABÁM CSIREG, CSÖRÖG" hu 23   5803

A SZÁNTÓI UTCA; "A szántói híres utca, Cimbalommal van kirakva" hu 289   5804

SZÁRAZ ÁGON BÚS GERLICE; ON A DRY BRANCH; "On a dry branch sadly coos a turtle-dove" e 164 5805

"SZÁRAZ ÁGTÓL MESSZE VIRÍT" hu 23   5806

SZARKA CSÖRÖG; ON THE ROOF A MAGPIE; "On the roof a magpie shrieks and not a stork" e 164 5807

SZÉKELY "FRISS"; "Ne busuljon, komámasz-szony"; SEKLER SCHNELLTANZ; "Nachbarin, was soll denn dein 5808
    Zorn" g, hu 25

SZÉKELY "LASSÚ"; "Azt akartam énmegtudni, Szabade másét szeretni, jaj, jaj, ja-ja-jaj"; SEKLER LANGSAM- 5809
    TANZ; "Dieses wollt' ich gerne wissen, Darf des andern Weib ich küssen, ach ja, ach ja, ach" g,
    hu 25

SZÉP SZAKMÁRI LÁNYOK; "Szép szakmári lányok, Isten veletek!" hu 289   5810

SZERELEM, SZERELEM; "Szerelem, szerelem, Átkozott gyötrelem" hu 289   5811

"SZERELMES A NAP A HOLDBA; SUN TO MOON; "Sun to moon his light has given"; "SONNE HAT DEN MOND 5812
    SO GERNE" e, g, hu 92

SZERETNÉK SZÁNTANI; "Szeretnék szántani, hat ökröt hajtani"; WITH MY SIX BROWN OXEN; "With my six 5813
    brown oxen I my fields plough daily"; WOLLT' MIT SECHS OCHSEN; "Wollt' mit sechs Ochsen,
    bunt, pflügen das Feld, den Grund" e, g, hu 92; HOW I WOULD PLOUGH; "How I would plough
    the land! Oxen drive through the sand" e 164

SZILVÁS VILLAGE; "Szilvás village mourns today. Dead the shepherd, once so gay!" e 95   5814

SZÓL A KAKAS MÁR; HARK THE COCK DO'TH CROW; "Hark the cock do'th crow, day is breaking now" e 164 5815

TE VAGY A LEGÉNY; "Te vagy a legény, Tyukodi pajtás!"; FREUND TYIKODI, HEI!; "Freund Tyukodi, hei! ist 5816
    der rechte Mann!"; TYUKODI, MY LAD; "Tyukodi, my lad, you're our comrade true" e, g, hu 92

TEMETÖBE LÁTTALAK MEG; "Temetöbe láttalak meg legelébb, mikor az édesanyádat temették"; FIRST I SAW 5817
    YOU; "First I saw you in the churchyard, and you wept, standing by the grave wherein your mother
    slept"; DORT, IM FRIEDHOF, SAH ICH DICH; "Dort, im Friedhof, sah ich dich zum erstenmal,
    weintest an der Mutter Grab in tiefster Qual" e, g, hu 92; TEMETÖBEN LÁTTALAK MEG
    LEGELEBB; IN THE CHURCHYARD; "In the churchyard I caught first sight of thee maid, When
    thy mother in her grave to rest they laid" e 164

THAT'S MY GIRL; "That's my girl, what a girl!" e 95   5818

[TÖLTIK A NAGY]; "Töltik a nagy erdö út ját"; "All the lads to war they've taken"; "Wege schüttet man im 5819
    Walde" e, g, hu 22

A TÖMLÖCBEN; "Minden ember szerencsésen; Csak én élek keservesen"; IM KERKER; "Alle Welt beglückt und 5820
    freudvoll, Ich allein betrübt und leidvoll" g, hu 24

TÖRIK MÁR A RÉTEKET; "Törik már a réteket, ripeg ropog a járom" hu 23   5821

TRÉFÁS NÓTA; "Két krajcárom volt nékem"; SCHERZLIED; "Sieben Kreuzer waren mein" g, hu 26   5822

VALAMIT SUGOK MAGÁNAK; "Valamit sugok magának vállaljon el babájának"; HEAR ME WHISPER; "Hear me 5823
    whisper low in your ear, let me be your sweetheart, my dear"; HÖR', WAS LEIS' INS OHR; "Hör',
    was leis' ins Ohr ich dir raun', will dein Schatz sein, kannst mir vertrau'n" e, g, hu 92; SOMETHING
    IN YOUR EAR; "Something in your ear I would say, 'Choose me for your sweetheart, I pray'!" e 164

VAN NEKI; "Van neki, van neki van neki, van, karikagyűrűje"; OH YES, SHE HAS; "Oh yes, she has, yes, 5824
    she has, yes, she has, yes, she has a lover"; SEHT NUR, SIE HAT; "Seht, nur, sie hat, ja, sie hat,
    ja, sie hat einen Ring, der Gold ist" e, g, hu 92; SURE HE HAS; "Sure he has, sure he has, sure he
    has, sure, a ring with stones laid in" e 164

VÉGIG MENTEM A TÁRKÁNYI; "Végig mentem a tárkányi sej, haj, nagy uccán" hu 23   5825

"VÉGIG MENTEM AZ ORMÓDI TEMETÖN"; THROUGH THE CHURCHYARD; "Through the churchyard, sad and 5826
    lone, I went one day"; DEM ORMODER FRIEDHOF; "Dem Ormoder Friedhof galt jüngst mein Besuch"
    e, g, hu 92; THROUGH ORMÓD'S GRAVEYARD; "Through the graveyard, Ormod's graveyard, my
    path lead" e 164

VÉKONY DESZKA KERITÉS; OF THIN LATH'S; "Of thin laths this fence is made" e 164   5827

VIRÁGÉNEK A XVI. SZÁZADBÓL; "Ej, haj! gyöngyvirág, teljes szegfű, szarkaláb"; FLOWER SONG FROM THE 5828
    XVITH CENTURY; "Oh, oh, lily white, pink carnation, poppy bright"; BLUMENLIED AUS DEM
    XVI. JAHRHUNDERT; "Ei, hei! Veilchen schlicht, Nelken und Vergissmeinnicht" e, g, hu 92

VIRÁGOM, VÉLED ELMEGYEK; "Vetekedik vala háromféle virág" hu 23   5829
WINE I DRINK; "Wine I drink, despite your warning, lovely star, darling dove, beauty mine!" e 95   5830
WISH YOU A GOOD EVENING; "Wish you a good evening, brave Hussars of Hungary arriving" e 37   5831
WOE, WOE, MOTHER MINE; "Woe, woe, mother mine, he's left me! Oh these soldiers!" e 95   5832
ZAVAROS A BODROG; TURBID IS THE BODROG; "Turbid is the Bodrog if its swelling" e 164   5833
ZÖLDRE VAN A RÁCSOS KAPUM FESTVE; AT THE GREEN GATE; "At the green gate, at the green gate, under   5834
    branches cover" e 164
ZSÁLYA, ZSÁLYA; "Zsálya, zsálya, fehér zsálya" hu 289   5835
ZSINDELYEZIK A KASZÁRNYA TETEJÉT; "Zsindelyezik a kaszárnya tetejét, mind elvitték a legények elejét";   5836
    BUSILY THE BARRACK ROOF; "Busily the barrack roof they mend today, nearly all the soldiers have
    been sent away"; FRISCHE SCHINDELN SCHLÄGT MAN; "Frische Schindeln schlägt man ans Kaser-
    nendach, all die Burschen man uns fortnahm nach und nach" e, g, hu 92; IN THE BARRACKS; "In
    the barracks, look the roofs they now do tile, they the pick of youth' took off to rank and file" e 164
ZUHÁSZCSÚFOLÓ; "Volte olyan juhász, Volte olyan juhász"; DER SCHÄFER; "War einmal ein Schäfer, War   5837
    einmal ein Schäfer" g, hu 26

ICELAND

"BI BI OG BLAKA"; "BYE BYE AND HUSHABYE" e, ic 231   5838
LITLU BÖRNIN LEIKA SJER; "Litlu börnin leika sjer liggja mónum i"; LITTLE CHILDREN RUN TO PLAY; "Little   5839
    children run to play out across the hill" e, ic 231
SPEED, MY REINDEERS; "Autumn winds blow from the lea" e 37   5840
"STÓDUM TVAU Í TÚNI"; "There in the field we parted" e, ic 230   5841
"WOLLT IHR HÖREN NUN MEIN LIED" g 49   5842

INDIA

KASHMIR LULLABY NO. 1; "Drink thy milk, leaving none in the cup" e 86   5843
KASHMIR LULLABY NO. 2; "In my lap I'll lay thee" e 86   5844
TUMRI; HOW CAN I FETCH THEE WATER?; "How can I go, mother dear" e 86   5845

INDIANS OF NORTH AMERICA

BEFORE DAWN; "Owl, wise gray owl, will you tell?" e 37   5846
CHIC-A-BOOM; "Chic-a-boom, boom, boom, Chic-a-boom boom" e 242   5847
GHOST DANCE SONG; "Pity me, pity me! Father pity me!" e 37   5848
HIAWATHA'S WOOING; "And then added Hiawatha" e 279   5849
MY BARK CANOE; "In the still night, the long hours through I guide my bark canoe"; "Chekahbay tebick   5850
    ondandeyan Chekahbay tebick ondandeyan" e, Ojibway Indian 186
PRAYER TO THE GREAT SPIRIT; "To Gitchi Manitou praises be" e 279   5851
YAH-NAH-NEE; "Yah-nah, ha-way-ee, yah-nah-nee-nah!" Omaha Indian 321   5852

IRAN

KABÚ TAR; THE DOVE; "Gentle dove, thou hast flown away" e 86   5853
RUN TO ME; "Run to meet me, greet me, dear, with a kiss" e 86   5854
SHALL I BRING THEE BEETS?; "Shall I bring beets to thee" e 86   5855

IRAQ

BETAIHH; THE GAZELLE; "The swift gazelle has enchanted me" e 86   5856
LAHN; LAMENT; "There are no more men who force the fates" e 86   5857

IRELAND

A EIBHLÍN; "A Eibhlín siúd mise thar sáile!"; EILEEN; "Dear Eileen, I'm going to leave you" e, ir 280   5858
AN BÓITHRÍN BUIDHE; "Do fuaireas féin, do fuaireas féin"; THE YELLOW BOREEN; "And what do you think one   5859
    day I found" e, ir 280 words by H. Boulton
AN CAILIN DEAS 'CRÚDHADH A BÓ; "Chuadhas thart le Druim-Chiaráin le déidheanaighe"; THE PRETTY GIRL   5860
    MILKING HER COW; "I wander'd by lonely Dunkerron whose ruin adorns the lake shore" e, ir 280;
    CAILÍN DEAS CRÚITE NA MBO; "It being on a fine summer's morning, as the birds sweetly tuned
    on each bough" e 172; IT WAS ON A FINE SUMMER MORNING; Cailin Deas (tune); "It was on a
    fine summer's morning, the birds sweetly tun'd on each bough" e 166,213 words by T. Moore

THE CRUISKEEN LAWN (Continued)   let the hunter praise his hounds"; "Little jug, my heart's love" (ref)   5892
    e 172; LET THE FARMER PRAISE HIS GROUNDS; "Gramachree macruiskeen" (ref) e 166, 213
    See also 7081

THE CUCKOO MADRIGAL; "Cuckoo! cuckoo! our joyful rover, at last you're over the ocean blue" e 349   words   5893
    by A. P. Graves

DARBY KELLY; "My grandsire beat the drum complete" e 349   words by C. Dibdin   5894

THE DAWNING OF THE DAY; "One morning early I walked forth, by the margin of Lough Lene" e 16; "One   5895
    morning early as I walked forth, by the margin of Lough Lene" e 133

DEAR HARP OF ERIN; Daniel the Worthy (tune); "Dear harp of Erin, let thy strain re-echo through the land again"   5896
    e 234   words by D. Weir

DERMOT AND SHELAH; "O who sits so sadly, and heaves the fond sigh?" e 406   words by T. Toms   5897

DERMOT, HIDE NOT THY ANGUISH; "Hide not thy anguish, Thou must not deceive me" e 86   5898

DOWN BY THE SALLY GARDENS; "It was down by the Sally gardens my love and I did meet" e 215; DOWN BY   5899
    THE SALLEY GARDENS; "It was down by the salley gardens my love and I did meet" e 36; THE
    SALLY GARDENS; "Down by the Sally gardens my love and I did meet" e 46   words by W. B. Yeats

DUBLIN CITY; "As I was a-walkin' thru Dublin City" e 349   5900

EILEEN AROON; "When, like the early rose, Eileen Aroon!" e 210   words by G. Griffin; "ERIN! THE TEAR AND   5901
    THE SMILE IN THINE EYES" e 166, 213   words by T. Moore   See also 7158

THE FAMINE SONG; "Oh, the praties they are small, over here, over here" e 172; THE PRATIES THEY GROW   5902
    SMALL; "Oh, the praties they grow small, over here, over here" e 111, 173; OVER THERE; "Oh!
    potatoes they grow small over there!" e 34

"FAREWELL! BUT WHENEVER YOU WELCOME THE HOUR"; Moll Roone (tune) e 166, 213, 349 words by T. Moore   5903

FEAGH MACHUGH; "Feagh MacHugh of the mountain; Feagh MacHaugh of the glen" e 133 words by T. D. McGee   5904

THE FIDDLER; Among the heather (tune); "My name is Mick Molloy, in clear and cloudy weather" e 133   words   5905
    by F. A. Fahy

FILL THE BUMPER FAIR; Bob and Joan (tune); "Fill the bumper fair, ev'ry drop we sprinkle o'er the brow of care,   5906
    smooths away a wrinkle" e 166, 213   words by T. Moore

THE FLIGHT OF THE EARLS; "To other shores across the sea we speed with swelling sail" e 349   words by A. P.   5907
    Graves

THE FLOWER OF FINAE; "Bright red is the sun on the waves of Lough Sheelin" e 133   words by T. Davies   5908

THE FLOWER OF KILLARNEY; The Gentle maiden (tune); "Mavourneen's the flow'r of Kilarney" e 235   5909

THE FLOWER OF MAGHERALLY, O; "One pleasant summer morning, when the flowers all were springing, O!"   5910
    e 133

FLY NOT YET; Planxty Kelly (tune); "Fly not yet; 'tis just the hour when pleasure, like the midnight flow'r"   5911
    e 166, 213   words by T. Moore

THE FOGGY DEW; "The wisest soul by anguish torn will soon unlearn the lore it knew" e 16; OH! A WAN   5912
    CLOUD WAS DRAWN; THE FOGGY DEW; "Oh! a wan cloud was drawn o'er the dim weeping
    dawn" e 166, 213   words by A. P. Graves

FOLLOW ME UP TO CARLOW; "Lift, Mac Cahir Oge, your face" e 172   words by P. J. McCall   5913

FORGET NOT THE FIELD; The lamentation of Aughrim (tune); "Forget not the field where they perish'd" e 166,   5914
    213, 349   words by T. Moore

THE GARDEN WHERE THE PRATIES GROW; "Have you ever been in love, my boys"; "She was just the sort of   5915
    creature" (ref) e 172

GARRY OWEN; "Let Ireland's sons be not dismayed"; "Instead of Spa, we'll drink brown ale and pay the reck'ning   5916
    on the nail" (ref) e 37; GARRYOWEN; "Let Bacchus's sons be not dismayed" e 172; WE MAY
    ROAM THRO' THIS WORLD; "We may roam thro' this world like a child at a feast"; "Then remember
    wherever your goblet is crown'd" (ref) e 15; THE DAUGHTERS OF ERIN e 166, 213

THE GIRL I LEFT BEHIND ME; Brighton Camp (tune); "I'm lonesome since I cross'd the hill" e 15, 28, 128, 132,   5917
    235, 279, 349, 366; "The dames of France are fair and free" e 172; "The dames of France are fond
    and free" e 95; "THE DAMES OF FRANCE ARE FOND AND FREE" e 166, 213; AS SLOW OUR SHIP;
    "As slow our ship her foamy track" e 349   words by T. Moore

THE GIRLS OF COLERAINE; "There's a sweet little spot in the County of Derry" e 172   5918

GO WHERE GLORY WAITS THEE; Maid of the valley (tune); "Go where glory waits thee, but while fame elates   5919
    thee Oh! still remember me" e 166, 213, 349   words by T. Moore

THE GREEN BUSHES; "As I was a-walking one morning in May, to hear the birds whistle and see lambkins play"   5920A
    e 172; BRIAN O LINN; "Brian O Linn had no breeches to wear" e 172

GREEN BUSHES; "As I was a-walking one morning in May, To hear the birds whistle and see the lambs play"   5920B
    e 198

The groves of Blarney (tune); The grooves of Blarney (tune); THE LAST ROSE OF SUMMER; "'Tis the last rose of   5921
    summer, left blooming alone" e 15, 28, 36, 93, 128, 132, 279, 292, 366, 402; QUI SOLA VERGIN ROSA;
    "Qui sola vergin rosa, come puoi tu fiorir?" e 122; 'TIS THE LAST ROSE OF SUMMER e 166, 213,
    329; DES SOMMERS LETZTE ROSE; "Letzte Rose, wie magst du so einsam hier blühn?" g 326;
    LETZTE ROSE g 353   words by T. Moore; OH BAY OF DUBLIN!; "Oh Bay of Dublin! my heart
    you're troublin'" e 349   words by H. S. Dufferin; WITH DEEP AFFECTION; THE BELLS OF

The groves of Blarney (Continued) SHANDON; "With deep affection and recollection I often think of   5921
    those Shandon Bells" e 166,213   words by F. S. Mahony
THE HARP THAT ONCE THRO' TARA'S HALLS; Gramachree (tune); Will you go to Flanders (tune); "The harp   5922
    that once thro' Tara's halls the soul of music shed" e 128,132,166,213; MOLLY MY TREASURE;
    e 15,349; "The harp that once thro' Tara's halls its soul of music shed" e 402; THE HARP THAT
    ONCE e 235; THE HARP THAT ONCE THROUGH TARA'S HALLS; "The harp that once through
    Tara's halls the soul of music shed" e 199; THE HARP THAT ONCE THROUGH TARA'S HALLS;
    "The harp that once thro' Tara's halls the soul of music shed" e 28,279,366   words by T. Moore
"HAS SORROW THY YOUNG DAYS SHADED"; Sly Patrick (tune) e 172,166,172,213   words by T. Moore   5923
THE HEATHER GLEN; "There blooms a bonnie flower up the heather glen" e 133   words by Dr. Sigerson;   5924
    O'DONNELL'S MARCH; THE BROWN LITTLE MALLET; "Oh have you heard the tidings? Limerick's
    aflame" e 349   words by A. P. Graves
THE HEROES OF THE SEA; "I'll tell you of a wonder that will stiffen up your hair" e 349   words by A. P. Graves   5925
HEY, HO, THE MORNING DEW; "My father bought at great expense a grand high stepping grey" e 349   5926
THE 'HOLLY AND IVY' GIRL; The Maid of Wicklow (tune); "Come, buy my nice fresh ivy" e 133   words by   5927
    J. Keegan
"HOW DEAR TO ME THE HOUR WHEN DAYLIGHT DIES"; The twisting of the rope (tune) e 213   words by T.   5928
    Moore
HOW PLEASANT, SWEET BIRDIES; "How pleasant, sweet birdies, to wake in the dawn" e 133   5929
I KNOW MY LOVE; "I know my love by his way o'walkin'" e 36,215; "I know my love by his way of walking"   5930
    e 72,172
I KNOW WHERE I'M GOIN'; "I know where I'm goin' and I know who's goin' with me" e 36,172,215; I KNOW   5931
    WHERE I'M GOING; "I know where I'm going and I know who's goin' with me" e 169; "I know where
    I'm going and I know who's going with me" e 389
"I LOVE MY LOVE IN THE MORNING"; The mountains high (tune) e 166,213   words by G. Griffin   5932
"I SAW THY FORM IN YOUTHFUL PRIME"; Domhnall (tune) e 213   words by T. Moore   5933
I THANK YOU, MA'AM, SAYS DAN; "What brought you into my house" e 172   5934
"I WISH I HAD THE SHEPHERD'S PET"; "O, Guirrim, guirrim hoo" (ref); "And O I beseech and beseech you"   5935
    (ref) e, ir 172
"I WISH I WERE ON YONDER HILL"; Shule Aroon (tune) e 166,213; ON AND ON e 95   5936
"I'D MOURN THE HOPES THAT LEAVE ME"; The rose tree (tune) e 166,213,349   words by T. Moore   5937
IF I WERE A BLACKBIRD; "If I were a blackbird and could whistle and sing" e 312   5938
IN GLENDALOUGH LIVED A YOUNG SAINT; "In Glendalough lived a young saint, in an odor of sanctity dwelling"   5939
    e 172
INIS A BHFAD I GCÉIN; "Inis a bhfad i gcéin san iarthar aoibhinn tá"; I KNOW AN ISLE; "I know an isle, a pearl   5940
    in ocean's diadem" e, ir 280   words by H. Boulton; IRISH TUNE FROM COUNTY DERRY, LONDON-
    DERRY AIR; "From far away I hear sweet voices calling me" e 402; MY GENTLE HARP; "My gentle
    harp, once more I waken" e 35   words by T. Moore; LONDONDERRY AIR; "WOULD GOD I WERE
    THE TENDER APPLE BLOSSOM" e 128,132,329; "WOULD GOD I WERE THE TENDER APPLE BLOS-
    SOM" e 122,166,213,237   words by K. T. Hinkson; AN OLD DERRY AIR; "Across the bay some
    lonely bird is calling" e 397   words by W. Ransom; EMER'S LAMENT FOR CUCHYLAIN; "'Tis
    fair and good the beauty of this head was" e 16
INISHOWEN; "God bless the grey mountains of dark Donegal" e 133   words by C. G. Duffy   5941
IRISH GIRL; "When first I came to the county Limrick" e 95   5942
IS AITHNE DÚINN GO LÉIR; "'San mBealtaine breágh buidhe"; WHAT ANYBODY KNOWS; "In Maytide, with   5943
    the bloom on the bramble and the broom" e, ir 280   words by H. Boulton
IT IS NOT THE TEAR; THE SIXPENCE; "It is not the tear, at this moment shed, when the cold turf has just been   5944
    laid o'er him" e 349   words by T. Moore
"I'VE FOUND MY BONNY BABE A NEST" e 349   words by A. P. Graves   5945
THE JOLLY PLOUGHBOY; "'Twas Jack, the jolly ploughboy, was ploughing in his land" e 199; WHEN FIRST I   5946
    SAW SWEET PEGGY; THE LOW-BACKED CAR; "When first I saw sweet Peggy, 'twas on a market
    day" e 28,166,213,279,366; THE LOW-BACK'D CAR e 172   words by S. Lover
KEVIN BARRY; Rolling home (tune); "Early on a Monday morning, high up on the gallows tree" e 34; "Early on   5947
    a Sunday morning, high upon a gallows tree" e 293; "In Mountjoy jail one Monday morning high
    upon the gallows tree" e 7; ROLLING HOME; "Call all hands to man the capstan, see that your
    cable, it go clear" e 401   words by L. Hansen; "Call all hands to man the capstan, see the cable
    run down clear" e 320; "Up aloft, amid the rigging swiftly blows the fav'ring gale" e 173
KILGARY MOUNTAIN; "As I was goin' over the famed Kilgary Mountain" e 172   5948
KILKENNY AND THE GIANT BODEGH; "The giant Bodegh roam'd o'er Erin's green lea" e 37   5949
KITTY OF COLERAINE; Paddy's resource (tune); "As beautiful Kitty one morning was tripping" e 235; AS   5950
    BEAUTIFUL KITTY e 166,213   words by E. Lysaght
LAY HIS SWORD BY HIS SIDE; IF THE SEA WERE INK; "Lay his sword by his side, it hath served him too well"   5951
    e 349   words by T. Moore

THE LEAFY COOL-KELLURE; THE WHITE-BREASTED BOY; "Just between the day and dark, o'er the green of   5952
    the glimm'ring park" e 349 words by A. P. Graves; THE LARK IN THE CLEAR AIR; "Dear
    thoughts are in my mind and my soul soars enchanted" e 172 words by S. Ferguson

THE LEPREHAUN; "In a shady nook one moonlight night, a Leprehaun I spied" e 15 words by P. W. Joyce   5953

LESBIA HATH A BEAMING EYE; Nora Creina (tune); "Lesbia hath a beaming eye, but no one knows for whom it   5954
    beameth" e 166,213 words by T. Moore

LET ERIN REMEMBER; Red Rose (tune); "Let Erin remember the days of old" e 172,235; THE LITTLE RED FOX   5955
    e 16; "LET ERIN REMEMBER THE DAYS OF OLD" e 349; The red fox (tune) e 166,213 words by
    T. Moore

LIKE THE BRIGHT LAMP; Thamama Hulla (tune); ERIN! OH ERIN!; "Like the bright lamp that lay on Kildare's   5956
    holy fane" e 166,213 words by T. Moore

LIMERICK IS BEAUTIFUL; "Oh, then, Limerick is beautiful as ev'rybody knows" e 172   5957

THE LITTLE RED FOX; "The little red fox is a raider sly, in the misty moonlight creeping" e 133 words by F. A.   5958
    Fahy

THE LITTLE RED LARK; "Oh swan of slenderness, dove of tenderness" e 349,397; OH SWAN OF SLENDERNESS   5959
    e 166,213 words by A. P. Graves

THE MAID OF SLIEVENAMON; THE LASS FROM THE COUNTY DOWN; "Alone, all alone by the wave-washed   5960A
    strand" e 133

THE MAID OF SLIEVENAMON; "Alone, all alone, by the wave-wash'd strand" e 172   5960B

THE MAID OF THE SWEET BROWN KNOWE; "Come all ye lads and lasses and listen to me awhile" e 172   5961

MARCHING TO CANDAHAR; "Marching, forc'd marching, at stretch of speed, so strong the need" e 349 words   5962
    by A. P. Graves

THE MEETING OF THE WATERS; The Old Head of Denis (tune); The Old Head of Dennis (tune); "There is not   5963
    in the wide world a valley so sweet" e 15,28,235,349,402; THERE IS NOT IN THE WIDE WORLD
    e 166,213 words by T. Moore

THE MELODY OF THE HARP; "Oh Harp of Erin! what glamour gay" e 349 words by A. P. Graves   5964

THE MEN OF THE WEST. See 7882

THE MINSTREL BOY; The Moreen (tune); "The minstrel boy to the war is gone" e 15,28,35,128,166,199,213,   5965
    233,234,279,366

MRS. McGRATH; "Oh, Missis McGrath!, the sergeant said, 'Would you like to make a soldier of your son, Ted"   5966
    e 172

MOLLY BRANNIGAN; "Ma'am dear, and did you ever hear of Molly Brannigan" e 172   5967

MOLLY MALONE; "In old Dublin city where colleens are pretty" e 215; COCKLES AND MUSSELS; "In Dublin   5968
    City where the girls, they are so pretty" e 166; COCKLES AND MUSSELS; "In Dublin's fair city,
    where girls are so pretty" e 35; MOLLY MALONE e 249; "In Dublin's fair city, where the girls
    are so pretty" e 172,402

MORE OF CLOYNE; "Little sister, whom the Fay hides away within his dun" e 349 words by A. P. Graves   5969

MUSIC IN THE STREET; "It rose upon the sordid street, a cadence sweet and lone" e 133   5970

MY BONNY CUCKOO; The little and great mountain (tune); "My bonny cuckoo I tell thee true that through the   5971
    groves I'll rove with you" e 234

MY GENTLE HARP; THE CAOINE OR LAMENT; "My gentle harp! once more I waken e 133,349 words by T.   5972
    Moore

MY LOVE'S AN ARBUTUS; Coola shore (tune); "My love's an arbutus by the borders of Lene" e 136,166,213,349   5973
    words by A.P. Graves

MY NAME IS PADDY LEARY; OFF TO PHILADELPHIA; "My name is Paddy Leary, from a shpot call'd Tipperary"   5974
    e 166,213; OFF TO PHILADELPHIA; "My name is Paddy Leary from a place called Tipperary" e 172

NAY, TELL ME NOT DEAR; Dennis, don't be threatening (tune); "Nay, tell me not dear, that the goblet drowns";   5975
    "Then fancy not, dearest, that wine can steal" (ref) e 166,213 words by T. Moore

NELLY, MY LOVE, AND ME; "There's a beech tree grove by the riverside" e 16   5976

NI MAGADH SIN A BHRIGHDIN; "Bíonn imnidhe orm, a chroidhe, nuair fheicim thu id' shuidhe"; BIDDY, I'M   5977
    NOT JESTING; "I'm grieving, gramachree, when your lovely form I see" e, ir 280 words by H.
    Boulton

NIGHT CLOSED AROUND; Thy fair bosom (tune); AFTER THE BATTLE; "Night clos'd around the conqu'ror's way"   5978
    e 166,213 words by T. Moore

NO! NOT MORE WELCOME; Luggelaw (tune); "No! not more welcome the fairy numbers of music fall on the   5979
    sleeper's ear" e 166,213 words by T. Moore

NOW, THERE ONCE WAS A YOUNG GIRL; "Now, there once was a young girl diggin' potatoes in her father's   5980
    garden" e 321

OH, BREATHE NOT HIS NAME; The brown maid (tune); "Oh! breathe not his name, let it sleep in the shade"   5981
    e 166,213,349 words by T. Moore

"OH, DID YOU NE'ER HEAR OF THE BLARNEY" e 166,213 words by S. Lover   5982

"OH! DID YOU NOT HEAR OF KATE KEARNEY?"; The beardless boy (tune); KATE KEARNEY e 166,213 words   5983
    by O. Morgan

OH FOR THE SWORDS; "Oh for the swords of former time!" e 349; OH, FOR THE SWORDS OF FORMER TIME   5984
  e 166, 213   words by T. Moore

OH! HAD WE SOME BRIGHT LITTLE ISLE; Sheela Na Guira (tune); "Oh! had we some bright little isle of our   5985
  own" e 166, 213   words by T. Moore

OH! IRISHMEN! NEVER FORGET; The Carabhat Jig (tune); OUR OWN LITTLE ISLE; "Oh! Irishmen! never forget!   5986
  'tis a foreigner's farm your own little isle" e 213   words by J. E. Pigot

O SLEEP, MY BABY; "O sleep, my baby, you are sharing with the sun in rest repairing" e 349   words by A. P.   5987
  Graves

OH THE MOMENT WAS SAD; SAVOURNEEN DEELISH; "Oh! the moment was sad when my love and I parted"   5988
  e 166, 213   words by G. Colman; 'TIS GONE, AND FOR EVER; SAVOURNEEN DEELISH; "'Tis
  gone, and for.ever, the light we saw breaking like Heaven's first dawn" e 349   words by
  T. Moore

OH!'TIS SWEET TO THINK; Donall na Greine (tune); Thady, you gander (tune); "Oh! 'tis sweet to think that   5989
  where e'er we rove" e 166, 213, 297   words by T. Moore

OH! WEEP FOR THE HOUR; The pretty girl of Derby O (tune); EVELEEN'S BOWER; "Oh! weep for the hour when   5990
  to Eveleen's bow'r the Lord of the valley with false vows came" e 166, 213   words by T. Moore See
  also 4227

OF PRIESTS WE CAN OFFER; The Yorkshire lasses (tune); FATHER O'FLYNN; "Of priests we can offer a charmin'   5991
  variety" e 166, 213   words by A. P. Graves

ON BOARD THE KANGAROO; "O, once I was a waterman and lived at home at ease" e 172   5992

ONE BUMPER AT PARTING; Moll Roe in the morning (tune); "One bumper at parting! tho' many have circled   5993
  the board since we met" e 166, 213   words by T. Moore

ORIGIN OF IRISH SURNAMES; "There was Gormac O'Con, of the great Con grandson" e 86   5994

THE OULD ORANGE FLUTE. See 8037B

OVER THE MORNING DEW; "It is the sweetest hour for love" e 133   words by R. D. Joyce   5995

THE PALATINE'S DAUGHTER; "To Castle Hyde to market I was going out one morning" e 172   5996

PÍOBAIREACHT SIDHE; "A mháthair is ait an ceól pibe"; THE PIPING ON THE HILL; "Dear mother, Oh! what   5997
  is that piping I hear when I wander alone?" e, ir 280   words by H. Boulton

THE QUERN TUNE; "Maids, at morn, grind the good corn" e 349   words by A. P. Graves   5998

QUICK! WE HAVE BUT A SECOND; Paddy Snap (tune); "Quick! we have but a second, fill round the cup, while   5999
  you may" e 166, 213   words by T. Moore

RAISE US A RIDDLE; THE FLOATING TRIBUTE; "Raise us a riddle as spinning we sit" e 349   words by A. P.   6000
  Graves

THE RAKES OF MALLOW; "Bold and reckless, wild and daring, lawless, rough and overbearing" e 15; BEAUING,   6001
  BELLEING, DANCING, DRINKING; "Beauing, belleing, dancing, drinking, breaking windows, cursing, sinking" e 166, 213

"REMEMBER THE GLORIES OF BRIEN THE BRAVE"; Molly Macalpin (tune); e 166, 213; MOLLY MCALPIN e 349   6002

REMEMBER THE POOR; "Oh! remember the poor when your fortune is sure" e 349   words by A. P. Graves   6003

REMEMBER THEE; CASTLE TIROWEN; "Remember thee? yes, while there's life in this heart" e 349   words by   6004
  T. Moore

"RICH AND RARE WERE THE GEMS SHE WORE"; The summer is coming (tune); e 70, 166, 213 words by T. Moore   6005

ROISIN DUBH; "O my sweet little rose, cease to pine for the past" e 95   6006A

OH! MY SWEET LITTLE ROSE; ROISIN DUBH; "Oh! my sweet little rose, cease to pine for the past" e 166, 213   6006B

THE ROVER; "No more, no more in Cashel town I'll sell my health a-raking" e 133   6007

SAILING IN THE LOWLANDS LOW; "Dunmore, we quitted, Michaelmas gone by" e 133   words by P. J. McCall   6008

"ST. PATRICK WAS A GENTLEMAN" e 234   6009A

"ST. PATRICK WAS A GENTLEMAN"; e 16, 166, 213   words by H. Bennet and Toleken   6009B

SEOITHÍN; "Éist! insan gcoill tá sídheógai ag obair"; LULLABY, LILY-BUD; "Hush! Hush! In the hazel wood,   6010
  good people stirring" e, ir 280   words by H. Boulton

THE SHAN VAN VOCHT; "O the French are on the sea says the Shan Van Vocht" e 199; THE SHAN VAN   6011A
  VOGHT; "'Oh! the French are on the sea', says the Shan Van Voght" e 294

THE SHAN VAN VOCHT; "Oh, the French are on the sea, says the Shan Van Vocht" e 235; SHAN VAN   6011B
  VOGHT; "Oh! the French are on the sea, says the Shan Van Voght" e 172; "OH! THE DAYS ARE
  GONE WHEN BEAUTY BRIGHT"; The old woman (tune); LOVE'S YOUNG DREAM e 166, 213   words
  by T. Moore

THE SHAN VAN VOGHT; THE POOR OLD WOMAN; "'O the French are on the sea', says the Shan Van Voght"   6011C
  e 16

SHE IS FAR FROM THE LAND; Open the door (tune); "She is far from the land where her young hero sleeps" e   6012A
  166, 213   words by T. Moore

SHE IS FAR FROM THE LAND; OPEN THE DOOR SOFTLY; "She is far from the land where her young hero sleeps"   6012B
  e 349   words by T. Moore

SHULE AGRA; "His hair was black, his eye was blue" e 34; HIS HAIR WAS BLACK; SHULE AGRA e 166, 213   6013
  words by A. P. Graves

SILENT, OH MOYLE; Arah my dear Ev'len (tune); "Silent, oh Moyle, be the roar of thy water" e 235; ARRAH,   6014
     MY DEAR EVELEEN e 349; ARRAH, MY DEAR EILEEN; "Silent, O Moyle be the roar of thy waters"
     e 16; "SILENT, O MOYLE! BE THE ROAR OF THY WATER"; SONG OF FIONNUALA e 166, 213
     words by T. Moore

SING, SWEET HARP; "Sing, sweet harp, oh sing to me some song of ancient days" e 349 words by T. Moore   6015

THE SNOWY-BREASTED PEARL; Pearl of the white breast (tune); "There's a Colleen fair as May, for a year   6016
     and for a day" e 16, 172; OH! SHE IS NOT LIKE THE ROSE; "Oh! she is not like the rose, that
     proud in beauty grows" e 166, 213 words by S. E. De Vere

SUMMER IN ERIN; "The hills are glowing with bloom and blossom" e 133 words by W. Rooney   6017

THE SONGS ERIN SINGS; "I've heard the lark's cry thrill the sky" e 349 words by A. P. Graves   6018

"SWEET BABE, A GOLDEN CRADLE HOLDS THEE"; THE FAIRIES' LULLABY e 199   6019

SWEET INNISFALLEN; THE CAPTIVATING YOUTH; "Sweet Innisfallen, fare thee well" e 349 words by T.   6020
     Moore

THO' THE LAST GLIMPSE OF ERIN; THE COULIN; "Tho' the last glimpse of Erin with sorrow I see" e 166, 213   6021
     words by T. Moore

THOSE EVENING BELLS; "Those evening bells! those evening bells! How many a tale their music tells" e 28, 279,   6022
     366 words by T. Moore

"THE TIME I'VE LOST IN WOOING"; Pease upon a trencher (tune) e 166, 213 words by T. Moore   6023

'TIS BELIEVED THAT THIS HARP; Gage fane (tune); THE ORIGIN OF THE HARP; "'Tis believed that this harp,   6024
     which I wake now for thee" e 166, 213 words by T. Moore

"'TIS PRETTY TO BE IN BALLINDERRY" e 133, 166, 213; "'TWAS PRETTY TO BE IN BALLINDERRY" e 349   6025
     words by A. P. Graves

TO LADIES EYES; Fague A Ballagh (tune); "To ladies' eyes around, boy, we can't refuse, we can't refuse";   6026
     "But fill up the cup! where e'er, boy" (ref) e 166, 213

TRA BHUAIL MAC RÓIGH AN SGIATH; "Bhí gártha cogaidh ar an ngaoith"; WHEN FERGUS SMOTE THE SHIELD;   6027
     "Loud rang the challenge through the land" e, ir 280 words by H. Boulton

'TWAS ONE OF THOSE DREAMS; THE SONG OF THE WOODS; "'Twas one of those dreams that by music are   6028
     brought" e 349 words by T. Moore

VAN DIEMEN'S LAND; "Come all you gallant poaching boys that ramble free from care" e 172   6029

WEARING OF THE GREEN; The tulip (tune); "O Paddy dear, and did you hear the news that's going round"   6030
     e 7, 15, 28, 37, 172, 233, 279, 366; THE WEARIN' O' THE GREEN; "Oh, Paddy dear! an' did ye
     hear the news that's goin' round?" e 294; WEARIN' OF THE GREEN e 34; OH! PADDY DEAR;
     "O Paddy dear, and did you hear the news that's going round" e 166, 213 words by D.
     Boucicault

WEEP ON, WEEP ON; Ullachan Dubh (tune); THE SONG OF SORROW; "Weep on, weep on, your hour is past"   6031
     e 166, 213 words by T. Moore

THE WEST'S AWAKE; "When all beside a vigil keep, the West's asleep" e 235 words by T. Davies   6032

WHEN COLD IN THE EARTH; Limerick's lamentation (tune); The Irish tune (tune); Lochaber no more (tune);   6033
     "When cold in the earth lies the friend thou hast lov'd" e 213 words by T. Moore

WHEN HE WHO ADORES THEE; The fox's sleep (tune); "When he who adores thee, has left but the name" e 172,   6034
     166, 213 words by T. Moore

WHEN IN DEATH I SHALL CALM RECLINE; "The bard's legacy (tune); "When in death I shall calm recline, Oh,   6035
     bear my heart to my mistress dear" e 213; THE LEGACY e 16, 212 words by T. Moore

"WHEN SHE ANSWERED ME HER VOICE WAS LOW" e 166, 213, 349 words by A. P. Graves   6036

WHEN THRO' LIFE UNBLEST WE ROVE; Banks of Banna (tune); ON MUSIC; "When thro' life unblest we rove,   6037
     losing all that made life dear" e 166, 213, 349 words by T. Moore

WHENE'ER I SEE THOSE SMILING EYES; Father Quinn (tune); "When'er I see those smiling eyes, so full of hope   6038
     and joy, and light" e 166, 213, 349 words by T. Moore

WHILE GAZING ON THE MOON'S LIGHT; Oonagh (tune); "While gazing on the moon's light, a moment from   6039
     her smile I turned" e 166, 213 words by T. Moore

WHILE HISTORY'S MUSE; Paddy Whack (tune); "While history's muse the memorial was keeping" e 166, 213   6040
     PADDY WHACK e 15 words by T. Moore

THE WOMEN ARE WORSE THAN THE MEN. See 4597A

WREATHE THE BOWL; Nora Kista (tune); "Wreathe the bowl with flow'rs of soul" e 166, 213 words by T.   6041
     Moore

THE YOUNG MAY MOON; The dandy O! (tune); "The young May moon is beaming, love" e 166, 213 words   6042
     by T. Moore

A CARIGNANO; "S'a ven ël Lünes da matin"; À CARIGNAN; "Lundi matin la branle sonne" f, i 338   6043

A LA MODA D'J MUNTAGNUN; "'Nbel giù de la muntagna vuria piế milié" i 238   6044

A LA VITALÒRA; "E s'io fossi pesce, il mare passerei"; LIED AUS S. VITO; "Könnt' ich doch mit starkem Arm die Wogen teilen!" g, i 51   6045

ABBALLA; "Abballa 'oje nennam io canto vedennote abballà"; TANZLIED; "Die Rebenhügel hüllen sich ins purpurfarb'ne Kleid!" g, i 51   6046

L'ADDIO; "Addio per sempre albergo avventurato"; ABSCHIED; "Leb' wohl auf immer dar Du Haus voll Licht und Sonne!" g, i 51   6047

ADDIO A NAPOLI; "È pronta la partenza"; ABSCHEID VON NEAPEL; "Wie glänzt das Meer so blau" g, i 51   6048

ADESSO I COSTUMA I ABITI BIANCHI; ORA SI PORTANO GLI ABITI BIANCHI; "Adesso i costuma i abiti bianchi, streti sui fianchi, li vogio, li vogio, li vogio anca mi!" i 325   6049

"AI PREÀT LA BIELE STELE" i 238   6050

AL CHANTE IL GIAL; "Al chante il gial al criche il di"; WHEN THE COCK CROWS; "When the cock crows at break of day" e, i 36   6051

"ALLA MATTINA MI ALZO ALLE NOVE" i 325   6052

AMAR IL CARO BENE; "Amar il caro bene ancor in lontananza è gran fede d'un cor è gran costanza" i 235   6053

AMORE A QUINDICI ANNI; "L'è na fieta di quindes ani"; "C'est une fillette de quinz'ans à peine" f, i 338   6054

AMORE AL CONVENTO; "Voglio lasciar l'amure per farmi monigheta"; AMOUR AU COUVENT; "Je ne veux plus soucis d'amour, je veux me faire nonnette" f, i 338   6055

L'AMOROSO GIARDINO; "Sun 'ndait ant ël giardin"; JARDIN D'AMOUR; "J'allais dans le jardin" f, i 338   6056

LA BARCHËTTA; GUARDA CHE BIANCA LUNA; "Guarda che bianca lüña, guarda che ciel seron" i 325 •words by A. Brofferio   6057

"BEFORE I HAD FOUND A SWEETHEART" e 95   6058

LA BELLA DEL RE DI FRANCIA; "A Türin, a la Rösa Bianca"; "A Turin, à la Rose blanche" f, i 338   6059

LA BELLA LEANDRA; "Nel bosco di Leandra na tan bela fia j'è"; LA BELLE LÉANDRE; "Dans le bois de Léandre jolie fill' est bien cachée" f, i 338   6060

LA BELLA NINA; "Come ti vidi appeno, o Nina bella"; DIE SCHÖNE NINA; "Als ich dich, schöne Nina, sah von ferne" g, i 51   6061

LA BELLA VENEZIANA; "Se vuol talun saper chi sia?"; DIE SCHÖNE VENEZIANERIN; "Wo ich daheim bin, soll ich euch künden?" g, i 51   6062

LA BIONDINA IN GONDOLETA; GONDOLIERA; "La Biondina in gondoleta l'altra sera gomena" i 325; LA GONDOLETTA; "La Biondina in gondoletta l'altra sera gomenà"; THE GONDOLA; "In my boat at eventide with my love I slowly glide" e, i 406   6063

LA BRANDULIÑA; "L'an mariã la Branduliña, për anel l'an daie na tiña" i 325   6064

LA CANZONE DEL VINO; "Da'n tera an pianta, oh che bela piantra"; CHANSON DU VIN; "De terr'en plante, oh la jolie plante" f, i 338   6065

LA CANZONE DELLA VEGLIA; "'Buna séira, vioire, larà"; CHANSON DE LA VEILLE; "Bonsoir, bonsoir, com- mères, larà" f, i 338   6066

CANZONETTA; "Quando la man mi premi"; "Als du Hand mir drücktest" g, i 51   6067

IL CARDELLINO; "Sto crescendo un gentil cardellino"; DER ZEISIG; "Hab' gezähmt einen muteren Zeisig" g, i 51   6068

CARE MIE SELVE; "Care mie selve, addio, ricevete quest' ultimi sospiri" i 181   words by G. B. Guarini   6069

LA CAROLINA; "Ho veduta una fanciulla"; CAROLINA; "Kenn' ein Mädchen hübsch und zierlich" g, i 51   6070

CHE BEL GOGNIN LA 'PEPPINETTA; CHE BEL VISIN LA 'PEPPINETTA'; "Che bel gognin la Peppinetta, corpo del diavol voeui fagh l'amor" e 325   6071

CHESTE VIOLE; "Cheste viole palidute ciolte sù dal vâs cumò" i 238   6072

"CHI BELLE TRECCE CHI TTE' LA CAMPAGNÒLE"; CHE BELLE TRECCE HA LA CAMPAGNOLA i 325   6073

CHIAGNARRÒ LA MIA SVENTURA; PIANGERÒ LA MIA SVENTURA; "Chiagnarrò la mia sventura si non tuorne cchiù" i 325   6074

COME, BUY MY FLOWERS; "Come buy my lovely flowr's" e 37   6075

CRUDEL!; "Crudel! Di che peccato a doler t'hai" i 325   6076

DE SA TURR' 'E SU FORTI; DALLA TORRE DEL FORTE; "De sa turr' 'e su forti si bibi Barberia dongu sa bona notti a sa picciocca mia" i 325   6077

"DONNA LOMBARDA PERCHÉ NUN M'AMI?" i 325   6078

"DOVE SEI STATO MIO BELL'ALPINO?" i 238   6079

DRUNGHE, DRUNGHETE!; "La forosetta mia mi viene a far la spia"; LIEBESLIEDCHEN; "Heut' kam mein junges Liebchen zu mir ins kleine Stübchen" g, i 51   6080

E C'ERAN TRE ALPIN; "E c'eran tre alpin tornavan dalla guerra" i 238   6081

"È COL SIFFOLO DEL VAPORE" i 238   6082

L'È BEN VER; "L'è ben ver, l'è ben ver ch'jo mi slontani"; IT'S VERY TRUE; "I am far from my home but not my sweetheart" e, i 36; "L'e ben ver l'e ben ver che me slontani" i 238   6083

E LA VIOLETTA; "E la violetta la va, la va, la va, la va" i 238; LA LIONETTA; "E la Lioneta l'era nël camp"; LA LIONNETTE; "Et la Lionnette coupait le blé" f, i 338   6084

FANCIULLA DAGLI OCCHI CELESTI; "O fanciulla dagli occhi celesti perchè a tuti tu neghi amor?"; TOS-   6085
    KANISCHES LIED; "Deine Augen, die himmlischen blauen, sag' warum seh'n sie so ernst in die
    Welt?" g, i 51

FENESTA CHE LUCIVE; "Fenesta che lucive e mò non luci"; "Finestra che lucevi ed or non luci"; THE   6086
    LIGHTED WINDOW; "I stand beneath your window vigil keeping" e, i 310; FENESTA
    CA LUCIVE; FINESTRA CHE SPLENDEVI; "Fenesta ca lucive e mò non luce" i 325;
    FINESTRA CHE LUCEVI; DAS TOTE LIEBCHEN; "Wie freundlich glühte ihres Fensters Schimmer!"
    g, i 51

LA FESTA DI PIEDIGROTTA; "Quest' anno anch'io vò andar alla Madonna a Piedigrotta"; DAS FEST VON   6087
    PIEDIGROTTA; "Zur lieben Frau von Piedigrotta will ein jedes Mädchen geh'n" g, i 51

FINESTRA BASSA; "Finestra bassa e patrona crudela"; STÄNDCHEN; "Dein Herz ist kalt, dein Fenster bleibt   6088
    verschlossen" g, i 51

FINGO PER MIO DILETTO; "Fingo per mio diletto vezzi lusinghe amor"; DITES, QUE FAUT-IL FAIRE?; "Dites,   6089
    que faut-il faire pour rendre un coeur constant?"; HOW SHALL AN ARTLESS MAIDEN?; "How shall
    an artless maiden hold her lover true?" e, f, i 211

FIOR DI TOMBA; "Là darè di cui bocage na tan bela fia j'è"; FLEURE DE TOMBE; "Là derrière ces bocages, jolie   6090
    fille est à marier" f, i 338

THE FISHERMAN; "Lightly floats my little boat" e 37   6091

FRÀ PATALUC; "'Cosa fastü li, fratin"; FRÈRE PATALOUC; "'Petit frère que fais tu là'" f, i 338   6092

IL GENOVESE; "Bel Genovéis a völ maridesse"; LE BEAU GÉNOIS; "Le beau Génois d'épouser s'avise" f, i 338   6093

GIOVANOTTINA CHE VIENI ALL FONTE; "Giovanottina che vieni alla fonte, due stelle in fronte ti vedo brillar"   6094
    i 325

GIROMETTA; "Girometta de la montagna, turna al to pais"; GIROMETTE; "Giromette de la montagne, rentre   6095
    à ton pays" f, i 338

IL GONDOLIERO; "Brilla, brilla in ciel sereno"; DER GONDOLIER; "Goldner Stern, deinen Schimmer breite"   6096
    g, i 51

IN CIMA AI MONTICELLI; "In cima ai monticelli ci sta un bel palazzo" i 238   6097

"IN DUV'ÈLA 'STA RUMAGNÒLA?"; DOV'È QUESTA ROMAGNOLA? i 325   6098

IN PIZZ' E CUDDU MONTI; SULLA CIMA DI QUEL MONTE; "In pizz'e cuddu monti mi sezzu a fai arrunda"   6099
    i 325

INVITO ALL DANZA; "'O ciao, ciao, Maria Catlina, dumje'"; INVITATION À LA DANSE; "'Viens ici, Marie   6100
    Cath'rine, viens danser le Rigodon" f, i 338

IU PARTU; IO PARTO; "Iu partu e su' custrittu di partiri" i 325   6101

JI VAJJ' ALL'ORT' A COJJE LE RŌSE; VADO IN GIARDINO A COGLIER LE ROSE; "Ji vajj' all'ort' a cojje le rōse   6102
    e scontre lu spose"; "Cinghe, la bella seji" (ref) i 325

JOLICOEUR; "Di'me'n po', bel galant, bel giuvo"; "Dites moi, beau galant, beau chevalier" f, i 338   6103

"LÄSST SICH AMOR BEI EUCH SCHAUEN" g 226   6104

LEE L'ANDAVA E MI VEGNEVA; LEI ANDAVA ED IO TORNAVO; "Lee l'andava e mi vegneva su la strada de   6105
    Moltrâs" i 325

LITANIA; "El prim ch'a l'è stáit an s'mund l'è stáit nost car Signur"; LITANIES; "Le premier qui fut au monde,   6106
    c'est notre cher Seigneur" f, i 338

LU GUARRACINO; "Lu guarracino che jeva pe' mare le venne voglia'" i 325   6107

LULLABY; "Lullaby, now lullaby, dear; Angels watch you from the sky, dear" e 95   6108

LA MARCIA DEL PRINCIPE TOMMASO; "Prinssi Tomà ven da Milan"; MARCHE DU PRINCE THOMAS; "Prince   6109
    Thomas vient de Milan" f, i 338

I ME DISE CHE IL TEMPO XE BELO; MI DICONO CHE IL TEMPO È BELLO; "I me dise che il tempo xe belo,   6110
    xela una cana, o xelo un capelo?" i 325

MI VOTU E MI RIVOTU SUSPIRANNU; MI VOLTO E MI RIVOLTO SOSPIRANDO; "Mi vōtu e mi rivōtu suspirannu,   6111
    passu la notti 'ntera senza sonnu" i 325

LES MONTAGNARDS; "Montagnes de ma vallée, vous êtes mes amours" f 238   6112

MONTE CANINO; "Non ti ricordi quel mese d'Aprile" i 238   6113

MONTE NERO; "Spunta l'alba del sedici giugno" i 238   6114

MOONLIGHT; "See what a night of moonlight" e 37   6115

MORNING; Marianina (tune); "When from out the darkness of the night" e 343   6116

MOTHER, THE BELLS ARE RINGING; "Mother, mother, the bells are ringing" e 95   6117

NEOPOLITAN FISHER'S SONG; "You know I love you madly" e 95   6118

OH, DIO DEL CIELO; "Oh, Dio del cielo, se fossi una rondinella vorrei volare, vorrei volare" i 238   6119

O MARIOLIN; O MARIOLINA; "O Mariolin, la mama te dimanda, la mama me dimanda" i 325   6120

OI BELA, VORÉISSI VNI; O BELLA, VORRESTI VENIRE; "Oi bela, voréissi vni al pucio, ai pucio" i 325   6121

LA PASTORA; "E lassù su la montagna gh'era su 'na pastorèla" i 238   6122

PERCHÈ MIA BELL' ANNINA; "Perchè mia bell' Annina abbassi gli occhi lorquando tu m'incontri per la via?"   6123
    i 325

PIDOCCHIO E PULCE; "Èl pui e ansem la püles a Ruma vōlo'ndè"; LE POU ET LA POUCE; "Le pou et la puce   6124
    pour Rome sont partis" f, i 338

PIGRA; "Mia mama völ ch'i fila d' festa"; LA PARESSEUSE; "Le jourd' fête, ma mère veut quej' file" f, i   6125
     338

PUNCHINELLO; "Ho, there you are, Punchinello" e 214   6126

QUANDO NASCESTE VOI; "Quando nasceste voi nacque un giardino"; "Vien, vien, vien ricciolino d'amor" (ref)   6127
     i 325

QUANTO SO' BELLI L'ÔMINI MORETTI; "Quanto sô' belli l'ômini moretti, e speciarmente quelli ggiovinotti" i   6128
     325

QUEL MAZZOLIN DI FIORI; "Quel mazzolin di fiori che? vien da la montagna" i 238   6129

"QUEL OSELIN DEL BOSCH" i 238   6130

RATTO AL BALLO; "An sü la riva de lo mar j'è na dona che canta"; L'ENLEVEMENT AU BAL; "Sur le rivage,   6131
     au bord d'la mer il y'a une femme qui chante" f, i 338

IL REGGIMENTO PIEMONTE; "Al Lünes da matin bato la generala"; LES RÉGIMENT PIÉMONT; "Lundi, au grand   6132
     matin on bat la générale" f, i 338

LE REPLICHE DI MARION; LES RÉPLIQUES DE MARION; "'O la corbleu, la morbleu, Marion" f, i 338   6133

LA ROSA È IL PIÙ BEL FIORE; "La rosa è il più bel fiore, fiore di gioventù" i 325   6134

RUSINEIN, A SEAN QUE DA VÔ; ROSETTA, SIAMO QUI DA VOI; "Rusinein, a sean que da vô, Rusinein, a   6135
     sean que da vô" i 325

SALTARELLA; "All together, dance together" e 95   6136

LA SCILLITANA; THE GIRL FROM SCILLA; "Deep in the darksome forest, I saw a tiger" e 95   6137

SEI BELLA NEGLI OCCHI; "Sei bella negli occhi, sei bella nel core" i 325; ALL BEAUTY WITHIN YOU; "All   6138
     beauty within you, all graces around you" e 95

SÌ, SÌ MIO COR; "Sì, sì, mio cor, sì, sì, penar" (duet) i 181   6139

SOCCORRETEMI PER PIETA; "Soccorretemi per pietà, soccorretemi per pietà, occhi belli" (duet) i 181   6140

"IL SOLE DIETRO AI MONTI" i 238   6141

DIE SORGLOSE; "In Wiesen und in Auen ich froh und glücklich bin" g 226   6142

LA SPOSA MORTO; "Don don don don Gentil galant s'l'aute muntagne" i 238   6143

"'STA NOTTE È BELLO LO MARE"; BARKAROLE; "Das Meer glänzt heute so helle" g, i 51   6144

SU E GIÒ DEL CORRIDOR; SU E GIÙ PER IL CORRIDOIO; "Su e giò del corridor, per vedé gh'é el pittor su e giò,   6145
     in ponta de pé" i 325

SU LA PIÙ ALTA CIMA; "Su la più alta cima cantava un lugherin" i 238   6146

SUL CAPPELLO; "Sul cappello sul cappello che noi portiamo" i 238   6147

SUL PONTE DI BASSANO; "Sul ponte di Bassano là ci darem la mano" i 238   6148

SUN CUMPRÀME ÜN UMNETIN; HO ACQUISTATO UN MARITINO; "Sun cumpràme ün umnetin grand e gross   6149
     me'l dil mamlin, tüti j'áutri van a fné" i 325

TARANTELLA; THE SHARK; "Bright and early ev'ry morning I would stroll along the shore" e 95   6150

TENGO 'NU CHIUOVO 'MPIETTO; HO UN DOLORE IN SENO; "Tengo 'nu chiuovo 'mpietto e nun ce pare" i   6151
     325

TERESINA, VA, TI VESTI; "Teresina, va, ti vesti, ché al bal te vol menar" i 325   6152

IL TESTAMENTO DEL CAPITANO; "Il Capitano l'è ferito si l'è ferito e sta per morir" i 238   6153

TIRITOMBA; "Sera jette, sera jette a la marina"; "I went out one pleasant evening by the seashore" e, i 34;   6154
     "I went out one pleasant evening to the seashore" e 37

LE TRE COLOMBE; "S'a sun tre culumbe bianche"; LES TROIS COLOMBES; "Ce sont trois colombes blanches"   6155
     f, i 338

TU VUOI MARITO, O NINA; "Tu vuoi marito, o Nina, ma questa è grossa assai" i 325   6156

VA L'ALPIN; "Va l'alpin su l'alte cime" i 238   6157

LA VECCHIA GALANTE; VIEILLE GALANTE; "An Türin a j'e na veja, pum, pum"; "A Turin il y a-t une   6158
     vieille, pum, pum" f, i 338

LA VENDEMMIA; "Svegghiache vi da'issonno, o briaconi"; WEINLESE; "Ihr trunk'nen Schläfer, auf zum Fest   6159
     der Trauben!" g, i 51

LA VERA SORRENTINA; "Io la vidia Piedigrotta"; DIE SCHÖNE VON SORRENT; "Jüngst beim Piedigrottafeste"   6160
     g, i 51

VIENI, MIA BELLA BIONDINA; "Vieni, vieni mia bella biondina"; SERENADE; "Komm' o komm' meine   6161
     reizende Blonde" g, i 51

VIENI SUL MAR; "Deh! ti desta, fanciulla, la luna spande un raggio si'chiaro sul mar"; COME TO THE SEA;   6162
     "Wake my lov'd one the silvery moonlight lights a pathway out, over the sea" e, i 132

VOCA, VOCA; "Voca, voca, tira 'nterra, che m'aspetta" i 325; VOGA, VOGA!; "Voga, voga, tira a terra,   6163
     chè m'aspetta"; IN DER BARKE; "Schnell, ihr Wogen, rasch, ihr Wellen!" g, i 51

WHEN I RAISE MY EYES; "When I raise my eyes and see you" e 95   6164

JAPAN

HAIL OUR GRACIOUS EMPEROR!; "Hail our gracious Emperor! May he reign ten thousand, thousand years and   6165
     more! e 37

FISHELECH KOYFN; "Bin ich mir gegangen fishelech koyfn"; "I went to market to buy fish" e, y 318 — 6197

FORN FORSTU FUN MIR AVEK; "Forn forstu fun mir avek, tayer lebn mayns"; "You are leaving me behind, my own true love" e, y 318 — 6198

FUNEM SHEYNEM VORTSL AROYS; "Funem sheynem vortsl aroys iz a sheyner boym aroys"; "Out of the lovely root grew a lovely tree" e, y 318 — 6199

GENZELECH; "Dort baym taychi, nit vayt fun dem shtetl"; "On the banks of the river, near by the village" e, y 318 — 6200

GIBN DIR MAYN TOCHTER; "Gibn dir mayn tochter, A shuster far a man?"; "My dear, my darling daughter, will you be a cobbler's wife?" e, y 318 — 6201

DI GILDERNE PAVE; "Es iz gefloygn, di gilderne pave"; "The golden peacock came a-flying" e, y 318 — 6202

GILU HAGALILIM; "Gilu haGililim, giborey hachayil"; "Sing Galileans, ye heroes of battle" e, h (tr) 318; GLEE REIGNS IN GALILEE; "Glee reigns in Galilee, the Galil rejoices" e 35 — 6203

GIRLS OF TODAY; "Girls these days don't even mind their elders" e 95 — 6204

HATIKVAH; "Kol od baleyvav p'nima, Nefesh Y'hudi homiya"; "Od lo avda tikvateynu" (ref); "As long as in a Jewish breast, the soul's stirring has not ceased"; "Our ancient hope will not perish" (ref) e, h (tr) 318; "Kolod balevav p'nimah Nefesh yehudi homiyah"; "Od lo avdah tikvantenu" (ref); SONG OF HOPE; "While in the beating Jewish hearts there is a soul that hope imparts"; "Our one hope, our aspiration" (ref) e, h (tr), y 30; THE HOPE; "As long as deep within the heart the soul of Judea is turbulent and strong" e 35   words by N. H. Imber, att to S. Cohen — 6205

HAYO, HAYA; "Hayo, haya, melech rasha, melech rasha"; "Once there was a wicked, wicked king" e, h (tr) 318 — 6206

HOB ICH A POR OKSN; "Hob ich a por oksn, oksn"; "I've a pair of poodles, poodles" e, y 318 — 6207

"HOB ICH MIR A KLEYNEM MICHALKE"; "Macht er mir a fayfele" (verse); "I've a friend called Michalke, Michalke"; He makes for me a whistle" (verse) e, y 318 — 6208

HOP! MAYNE HOMNTASHN!; "Yachne-Dvoshe fort in mark, Zi halt zich in eyn pakn, bakn"; "Yachne-Dvoshe's in a dither, packing for the market-place" e, y 318 — 6209

HORAH   no words 30 — 6210

"ICH HOB GE-AKERT UN GEZEYT"; "I have plowed and I have sowed" e, y 318 — 6211

IN DER KUZNYE; "In der kuznye, bay dem fayer, Shteyt der shmider un er shmit"; "In the smithy at the fire stands the blacksmith stout and strong" e, y 318   words by M. Rosenfeld — 6212

"INDROYSN GEYT A DROBINKER REGN"; "Outdoors the rain is dropping slow" e, y 318 — 6213

"INDROYSN IZ A TRIBER TOG"; "'Tis miserable out of doors" e, y 318 — 6214

KEGN GOLD FUN ZUN; "Kegn gold fun zun, geyt oyf mayn gold fun veytsn"; "Towards the golden sun springs my golden wheat" e, y 318 — 6215

KI TAVO-U EL HA-ARETS; "Ki tavo-u el ha-arets Un-tatem kol ets t'chila"; "Eyt linto-a ilanot" (ref); "And when you come unto the land, May you forthwith plant trees"; "This is the time for planting" (ref) e, h (tr) 318 — 6216

KIRYA Y'FEYFIYA; "Kirya y'feyfiya, ma sos learayich"; "Lovely walled city, delight of cities" e, h (tr) 318 — 6217

KRU-IM ANU; "Kru-im anu, bluyim anu, Lichvod yomtov na-ade tlay al gabey tlay!"; "Our clothes are worn, tattered and torn, for the holiday we've patched our rags to wear" e, h 318 — 6218

KUM AHER, DU FILOZOF; "Kum aher, du filozof, Mit dayn ketsishn moychl"; "Come my fine philosopher, you're a trifle dense" e, y 318 — 6219

LAMA SUKKA ZU?; "Lamma sukka zu? Aba tov sheli?"; "What is this hut for, daddy, dear?" e, h (tr) 318 — 6220

LAYTISHE MAZOLES; "Laytishe mazoles tuen oyfn vasershvimen"; "I keep seeking my fortune, but it passes me by" e, y 318 — 6221

LET US LIGHT THE CANDLES; "Let us light the candles and tell the wondrous story" e 216 — 6222

LOMIR ALE ZINGEN - A ZEMERL; "Lomir ale zingen, Lomir ale zingen"; "Zog-zhe mir tatenyu, vos iz lechem?" (verse); "Let's all sing together, let's all sing together"; "Tell me, daddy, what does lechem mean?" (verse) e, y 318 — 6223

LULLABY; "Sleep my baby, sleep my jewel, mother rocks the cradle" e 95 — 6224

DI MAME IZ GEGANGEN; "Di mame iz gegangen in mark arayn noch koyln"; "My mother went to market for to buy some coal" e, y 318 — 6225

MAMENYU, LYUBENYU; "Mamenyu, lyubenyu, kroynele hartsele"; "Mother, dear Mother, stand by me now" e, y 318 — 6226

MAYN YINGELE; "Ich hob a kleynem yingele, A zunele gor fayn"; "I have a little boy, and whenever I see him" e, y 318   words by M. Rosenfeld — 6227

MECHUTENESTE MAYNE; "Mechuteneste mayne, mechuteneste getraye, Lomir zayn oyf eybig mechutonim"; "Dear relation, sweet relation, Oh let us always be good relations" e, y 318 — 6228

MI YIVNE HAGAGIL?; "Mi yivne haGalil? El yivne haGalil"; "Banim yivnu haGalil!" (verse); "Who will build Galilee"; "The sons will build Galilee" (verse) e, h (tr) 318 — 6229

MI Y'MALEL?; "Mi y'malel g'vurot Yisrael? Otan mi yimne?"; "Stories are told by prophets of old" e, h (tr) 318; "Who can retell your feats, Israel?" e, h (tr) 318; WHO CAN RETELL?; "Who can retell the things that befell us?" e 35 — 6230

"MIT A NODL, ON A NODL"; "Here I sit and cross my feet" e, y 318 — 6231

MOLAD'TI; "Molad'ti hi erets K'na-an"; "My place of birth is the land of Canaan" e, h (tr) 318   6232

MO-OZ TSUR; ROCK OF STRENGTH; "Rock of strength, Thou art our aid" e 37   6233

MY DREYDL; "I have a little dreydl, I made it out of clay" e 214   6234

"NEM AROYS A BER FUN VALD"; "Lead a bear out of the woods" e, y 318   6235

"OT AZOY NEYT A SHNAYDER"; "He sews and sews the whole week long" e, y 318   6236

"OY, DORTN, DORTN, IBERN VASERL"; "Far off, far off, across the bridge" e, y 318   6237

"OYF DEM YAM VEYET A VINTELE"; "A breeze is blowing across the sea" e, y 318   6238

OYFN BARG, IBERG BARG; "Oyfn barg, ibern barg, Flien toybn porn"; "Over the hill, beyond the hill, doves in pairs do fly" e, y 318   6239

"OYFN OYVN ZITST A MEYDL"; "On the oven, there sits a maiden" e, y 318   6240

PAPIR IZ DOCH VAYS; "Papir iz doch vays, un tint iz doch shvarts"; "Oh, paper is white, and ink is black or blue" e, y 318   6241

PINCHOSL UN CHANTSCHELE; "Se pinchosl, o pinchosl, Se kum doch zu dein meidele"; PINCHOSSEL AND HANNAH; "O Pinchossel, dear Pinchossel, O come to me, your loving girl" e, y 230   6242

RAISINS AND ALMONDS; "A daughter of Zion, from the holy temple"; "Ah! beside Yidele's cradle there stands" (ref) e 37; "To my little one's cradle in the night" (ref only) e 214   6243

R'KOD HAT'LAIM; "Bimtsiltayim v'tupim meh meh meh meh kolnarim"; OUR FLOCK WILL DANCE; "Hear the drums and cymbals playing! 'Baa, baa, baa, baa! go the sheep" e, h (tr) 30   6244

RUCHOT HAYAM; "Ruchot hayam m'zamz'mim"; "The winds chant across the sea" e, h (tr) 318   6245

"S'DREMLEN FEYGL OYF DI TSVAYGN"; "Birds are sleeping on the branches" e, y 318   words by L. Rudnitsky   6246

"S'HOT GELEBT MIT UNDZ A CHAVER"; "Once, living in our midst we had a comrade" e, y 318   6247

"SHA, SHTIL, MACHT NISHT KAYN GERUDER!"; "Quiet, be still! make no commotion" e, y 318   6248

SHABES LICHT UN SHABES LOMPN; "Shabes licht un shabes lompn, O, vi zis iz ayer shayn!"; "Sabbath candles, Sabbath lamps, oh, how pleasant is your glow!" e, y 318   6249

SHALOM CHAVERIM; "Shalom Chaverim, Shalom Chaverim, Shalom, Shalom"; GLAD TIDINGS; "Glad Tidings we bring of peace on earth good will toward men" e, y 389   6250

SHIR HA-PALMACH; "Beyn g'vulot bidrachim l'lo derech"; "La-olel, v'larach She-arim po niftach" (ref); "Between the borders, on pathless byways"; "For the helpless and the young, wide the gates we fling" (ref) e, h (tr) 318   6251

"SHLOF MAYN KIND, SHLOF KESEYDER"; "Sleep my child, sleep" e, y 318   6252

SHLOF MAYN ZUN; "Shlof mayn zun, mayn tayer feygele"; "Sleep, my child, my baby chick" e, y 318   6253

"SHIPILT-ZHE MIR DEM NAYEM SHER"; "Play, play the latest tune" e, y 318   6254

SHU-ALIM M'YAL'LIM; "Shu-alim m'yal'lim, K'var chatsot"; "The jackals howl. It is midnight" e, h (tr) 318   6255

SIMCHU NA; "Simchu na, simchu na, B'simchat haTora"; Let us rejoice, let us rejoice, in the joy of Torah" e, h (tr) 318   6256

SPRING CALLS; "Come and greet the sweet spring fair" e 37   6257

TIF IN VELDELE; "Tif in veldele shteyt a beymele Un di tsvaygelech blien"; "Deep in the heart of the forest a young tree is leaving" e, y 318; THE TAILOR BOY; "Stands a maple tree, deep in the forest" e 95   6258

TOG AZOY VI NACHT; "Tod azoy vi nacht, un nacht azoy vi tog"; "Day the same as night, night the same as day" e, y 318   6259

TRETI, TRETI, TRETI; "Treti, treti, treti, vos in Treti zang?"; "Treti, treti, treti, What's the Treti song?" e, y 318   6260

TSVEY TAYBELECH; "Tsvey taybelech zenen ibern vaser gefloygn"; "There were two doves flew over the water" e, y 318   6261

TUM-BALALAYKA; "Shteyt a bocher uner tracht"; "A lad stood thinking all the night through" e, y 36, 318   6262

"UN DU AKERST UN DU ZEYST"; "You are the plowmen and you sow" e, y 318   words by C. Zhitlowsky   6263

UNTER DEM KIND'S VIGELE; "Unter dem kind's vigele Shteyt a klorvays tsigele"; "Under baby's cradle here there's an all-white nanny, dear" e, y 318   6264

VI AZOY KON ICH LUSTIG ZAYN?; "Vi azoy kon ich lustig zayn? As farshtert zenen mir mayne vegn"; "Then how can I merry be, now my love is gone" e, y 318   6265

VIGNDIG A FREMD KIND; "Zolst azoy lebn un zayn gezint"; "May you live long and well my lady" e, y 318   6266

WHAT MAIDENS WANT; "Mother, mother, come sing a song" e 95   6267

Y'MEY HANOAR; "Y'mey hanoar Chalfu avaru"; "The days of my bloom have gone and passed" e, h (tr) 318   6268

"YAFIM HALEYLOT BI-CHNA-AN"; "Lovely are the nights in Canaan" e, h (tr) 318   6269

YESH LI GAN; "Yesh li gan uv'er yesh li"; I'VE A GARDEN; "I've a garden and a well" e, h (tr) 30   words by N. Bialik   6270

YIS'M'CHU ADIRIM; "Yis'm'chu adirim, adirim, B'simchat matan Tora"; "Rejoice, O ye mighty men, in the great gift of the Torah" e, h (tr) 318   6271

YOM L'YABASHA (SHIR HAG'ULA); "Yom l'yabasha nehefchu m'tsulim"; "Hitba-ata b'tarmit ragley bat Anamit" (verse); "The day that the sea by God's might became dry"; "With guile the Egyptian into the deep Thou did cast" (verse) e, h (tr) 318   6272

ZAMRI-LI; "Zamri-li, zamri, Zamri-li, zamri Yona t'mima"; "Sing unto me, O sing, innocent dove, sing to me of the joy of Yemen" e, h (tr) 318   6273

ZAYT GEZUNTERHEYT; "Zayt gezunterheyt, mayne libe eltern"; "Goodbye, my dear parents, goodbye" e, y 318   6274

ZEMER LACH; "Zemer, zemer lach! Zemer, zemer lach!"; "Har-rayich hema yismachu" (ref); "We sing a   6275
    song to you, a song to you"; "The hills and mountains too, rejoice" (ref) e, h (tr) 318

ZHAMELE; "Du vest zayn a g'vir, mayn Zhamele"; "You'll be rich one day, my Zhamele" e, y 318   6276

ZIRMU GALIM; "Zirmu galim, peleg z'rom, Derech harva gay"; "Flow, O waves, O stream flow on" e, h (tr)   6277
    318

ZITS ICH MIR OYFN BENKELE; "Zits ich mir oyfn benkele Un farkem mir mayne herelech"; "Sitting on the   6278
    bench, combing out my hair" e, y 318

ZOG NIT KEYNMOL; "Zog nit keynmol az du geyst dem letstn veg"; "Oh, never say that you have reached the   6279
    very end" e, y 318   words by H. Glik

ZUM, GALI, GALI; "Zum, gali, gali, gali"; "Hechalutz le' man avodah" (verse) h (tr) 293   6280

ZUNTIG BULBE; "Zuntig bulbe, Montig bulbe, Dinstig un mitovch bulbe"; "Sunday 'taters, ever 'taters, always,   6281
    always, always 'taters" e, y 318

LATIN AMERICA

A CANTAR A UNA NIÑA; "A cantar a una niña yo le ensenaba"; WHEN I TEACH SINGING; "When to an eager   6282
    maiden music I'm teaching" e, s 219

AL PASAR LA BARCA; "Al pasar la barca me dijo el barquero"; THE BOATMAN; "Do you know the boatman of   6283
    the river ferry?" e, s 219

ALALIMÓN; "Alalimón, alalimón, la fuente se rompió"; "Alalimón, alalimón! The fountain will not play"   6284
    e, s 219

ARROZ CON LECHE; "Arroz con leche; me quiero casar con una viudita de la capital"; RICE PUDDING; "I like   6285
    rice pudding with milk or with cream" e, s 219; "I want rice pudding and not a thing more" e 86

CAMINO DE VALENCIA; "Camino de Valencia, Soledad"; ON THE ROAD TO VALENCIA; "Trooping into   6286
    Valencia, Soledad" e, s 219

EL CAPOTÍN; "No me mates, no me mates, déjame viviren paz"; "Do not hate me, nor beráte me, I will do   6287
    my best to please" e, s 219

"CARTA DEL REY HA VENIDO"; A LETTER FROM THE KING; "Now from the king comes a letter" e, s 219   6288

COMO UNA ESTRELLA FUGAZ; "Como una estrella fugaz que luce en noche sombria"; LIKE A SHOOTING STAR;   6289
    "As bright as a shooting star released from the bow of evening" e, s 219

CORRIDO DE LA CANELERA; "Sírvame una o dos canelas endulzadas con sus manos"; "Serve canelas, drink so   6290
    famous in this hamlet on the mountain" e, s 219

DOÑA ANA; "Doña Ana no está aquí que está en su vergel"; "Doña Anna is not here, she works in her garden"   6291
    e, s 219

IF I HAD ONE ROSE; "If I had one rose, of all, the sweetest" e 350   6292

"MAMBRÚ SE FUÉ A LA GUERRA"; MAMBRÚ IS WITH THE ARMY" e, s 219   6293

MATARILE; "Ambos a dos, Matarile"; "Oh, I choose John, Matarile" e, s 219   6294

NO HAY ÁRBOL; "No hay árbol que no tenga sombra en verano"; NO TREE BUT HAS A SHADOW; "No tree but   6295
    has a shadow when June o'ertakes it" e, s 219

"EL PATIO DE MI CASA"; MY COURTYARD; "My cottage has a courtyard" e, s 219   6296

"RAMÓN DEL ALMA MÍA"; DON RAMÓN; "Ramón, my one and only Ramón" e, s 219   6297

SAN SERENÍ; "San Serení de la buena, buena vida"; "San Serení, this is not the time for napping" e, s 219   6298

LA TARDE ERA TRISTE; "La tarde era triste, la nieve caía"; HOW SAD WAS THE EVENING; "How sad was the   6299
    evening, with snowflakes descending" e, s 322

LA VIUDITA DEL CONDE LAUREL; "Yo soy la Viudita del Conde Laurel"; THE COUNTESS OF LAUREL; "Oh, I   6300
    am a widow, the Countess of Laurel" e, s 219

VUELA, SUSPIRO; "Vuela, suspiro do está mi amada"; FLY MY AFFECTION; "Fly, my affection, fly to my dear   6301
    one" e, s 219

WHITE LLAMAS; "White as clouds at noonday, Llama flocks are grazing" e 219   6302

YO SOY FAROLERO; "Yo soy farolero de la Puerta' el Sol"; THE LAMPLIGHTER; "Up and down the city streets at   6303
    fall of night" e, s 219

LATVIA

THE SONG OF THE ROOSTER; "Why your crowing, why your crowing"; "Cock-a-doodle, cock-a-doodle-doo!"   6304
    (ref) e 37

LITHUANIA

THE BEE TREE; "Down the river floats a bee tree" e 95   6305
BY MY WINDOW; "By my window sitting, through my window staring" e 95   6306
HUSBAND AND WIFE; "Wife", I said, "you'll never find me into tempers flying" e 95   6307
I WILL TELL YOU; "I will tell you, I will tell you what the flowing brooklet whispers" e 95   6308
LITTLE HORSE OF MINE; "Little horse of mine, what means this neighing?" e 95   6309

LONG HAVE I WOVEN; "Long have I woven, woven and woven" e 95   6310
OH HOW HE SCOLDED; "Oh how he scolded, oh how he hit me!" e 95   6311
PIGEONS AND FAIRIES; "Pigeons flying to and fro" e 37   6312
THE PLEDGED HORSE; "Heaven guard my horse and keep him!" e 95   6313
ROSMARIN UND SALBEIBLÄTTER; "Rosmarin und Salbeiblätter send ich dir zum Abschiedsgruss" g 31   6314
SISTER, THE SUN IS RISING; "Sister, the sun is rising, Sister the dawn is breaking" e 95   6315
WHO IS CRYING!; "Who is crying? What lamenting sounds so sadly through the night?" e 95   6316

LUXEMBURG

U LETZEBURG; LUXEMBURG; "Luxemburg, O sacred homeland, come break the chains that bind" e 86   6317

MEXICO

A LA ORILLA DE UN PALMAR; "A la orilla de un palmar yo vide una joven bella"; IN THE GROVE AMONG THE   6318
    PALMS; "In the grove among the palms I once saw a maiden roaming" e, s 248; A LA ORILLA DEL
    PALMAR; IN A PALM GROVE; "In a palm grove by the sea I met such a lovely maiden" e, s 322
ADELITA; "Adelita se llama la joven"; s 284; "Sí, Adelita se llama la joven"; "Yes, she's the girl that they   6319
    call Adelita" e, s 322; "Adelita's the name of my loved one" e 279; LA ADELITA s 247;
    ADELITA; "Si Adelita se fuera con otro"; "Oh Adelita, I pray, do not leave me" e, s 248;
    "Adelita se llama la ingrata"; DEPARTURE SONG; "When the dawn comes again, Adelita" e, s 350
ALBORADA; "Que amanece, que amanece, mira que ya amaneció" s 247   6320
AMAPOLA DEL CAMINO; "Novia del campo amapola, que estas abierta en el trigo"; YOU'RE MY PRETTY WAY-   6321
    SIDE FLOWER; "Like a poppy that is growing in a field of wheat before me" e, s 248
EL ANTE COLIMOTE; "Cuatro palomas azules paradas en un romero" s 247   6322
AURELIA; "El día quince de Abril, voy a contártelo Aurelia" s 247   6323
BELLA Y FELICE; "Bella y felice, gallar day seductora comoel otoño" s 247   6324
EL BORRACHITO; "Si el amarte fué delito; Ay!; Si!" s 247   6325
EL BUTAQUITO; "Arrima tu butaquito cielito lindo sienta te en frente"; THE FOOTSTOOL; "O, pull up your   6326
    footstool, my fair and sweet one" e, s 86
EL CABALLITO; "Santiago, como buen charro, le dijo a San Miguelito" s 247   6327
CANCIÓN DE MORELOS; "Rema, Nenita, rema y remay vamos remando" s 247   6328
EL CARAMBA; "Mañana me voy; Caramba! para Veracruz" s 247   6329
CARMELA; "Asi cual mueren en occidente"; "As die at ev'ning on far horizons" e, s 36; "As in the skies of the   6330
    west are dying" e, s 142; "As now the evening draws nigh" e 279; CAREM CARMELA; "The
    golden splendor is fading" e, s 350
EL CARRERITO; "Dicen que me han de quitar las veredas por dondeando Hum" s 247   6331
EL CARRETERO; "El carretero se vá, Ya se va para Sayula" s 247   6332
EL CEFIRO; "Céfiro, que por la tarde"; THE BREEZE; "Breeze, when at eve you are passing" e, s 142;   6333
    ANDULUSIA; "Where honey'd blossoms are growing" e, s 350
LOS CHAMULITAS; "Chumeltic tabalumil chumeltic la binajel" s 247   6334
LAS CHAPARRERAS; "Las muchachas de mi tierra, ésas si saben querer" s 247   6335
EL CHARRO; "Estaba un charro sentado en las trancas de un corral"; "There was a charro a-sitting on the fence of 6336
    a wide corral" e, s 219
LA CHINITA MADERISTA; "Era china, china, china, como una estopa de coco" s 247   6337
CHULA LA MAÑANA; "Chula la mañana, chula la mañana"; MERRY IS THE MORNING; "Merry is the morning,   6338
    merry is the morning" e, s 219
CIELITO LINDO; "De la Sierra Morena, cielito lindo"; "Ay, ay, ay, ay! Canta y no llores" (ref) s 284; "From   6339A
    la Sierra Morena, Cielito Lindo"; "Ay, ay, ay, ay! Sing sorrow never!" (ref) e, s 36; "From the
    dark Sierra Mountain"; "Ay, ay, ay, ay! Sing, no more sighing" (ref) e 37; "Ay! Ay! Ay! Ay!
    Vienen bajando" (ref); "I'm waiting near by the fountain here"; "Ay, ay, ay, ay, come, come
    to your window" (ref) e, s 350; "Some birds can find in wide skies their mates"; "Ay! Ay! Ay!
    Ay! Sing, do not weep dear" (ref) e 343; BEAUTIFUL HEAVEN; "From the dark mountain comes
    a fair maiden" e 279; "There is a garden, a wonderful garden"; "Garden of love, beautiful heav-
    en" (ref) e 132 (ref only) e 128; CIELITO LINDO; "Debajo de mi ventana"; "Ay, ay, ay, ay!
    Canta y no llores" (ref); DEAR LITTLE HEAVEN; "Under my window a cowboy"; "Ay, ay, ay, ay!
    Sing lest you're tearful" (ref) e, s 322
CIELITO LINDO; "Todas las ilusiones, todas las ilusiones"; "Ay ay ay ay ay, forman y crecen" e, s 247   6339B
CLARÍN DE CAMPAÑA; "Mientras tengan licor las botellas" s 247   6340
LA CUCARACHA; "Con las barbas de Carranza" e, s 247; "Una cosa me da risa"; "Soldiers marching down the   6341
    highway" e, s 128, 132, 236; "Cuando uno quiere a una"; "When a fellow loves a maiden" e, s
    110; THE COCKROACH e, s 34
DE MEXICO HA VENIDO; "De Mexico ha venido un nuevo despacho"; "From Mexico there's just come a strange   6342
    new decree" e, s 109, 110

DÉJAME, OH! DÉJAME; "Déjame, Oh! Déjame deleitar en tus miradas" s 247   6343

DEL JARABE TAPATÍO; "¡Ay! Querido Guadalajara, ciudad de las ansias mías" s 247   6344

DIOS BENDIGA ESTE DÍA; "Dios bendiga este día venturoso y bendiga la prenda que adoro" s 247   6345

EN LAS BARRANCAS; "En las barrancas te aguardo a orillas" s 247   6346

FIESTA; "There's a silver moon shining brightly" e 350   6347

FLOR, BLANCA FLOR; "Flor, blanca flor, flor de las flores" s 247   6348

FLOR DE LIMON; "Hermosa flor de limón, dame de tu medicina"; LEMON BLOSSOM; "Oh lemon blossom so   6349
fair, you have the secret of healing" e, s 9

EL GALLO; "Aquí está un gallo de alzada" s 247   6350

GORGONIO ESPARZA; GREGORIO ESPARZA; "Ay nahual, cara de perro!" s 247   6351

EL GUACO CHANO; "Estaba mi guaco Chano arriba de las anonas" s 247   6352

LA GUASANGA; "Cupido Cupido, como traidor" s 247   6353

HACE UN AÑO; "Hace un año que yo tauve una ilusión" s 247   6354

HERACLIO BERNAL; "Año de noventa y cuatro y Puerto de Mazatlán" s 247   6355

MOY MIRO SÓLO ABROJOS; "Hoy miro sólo abrojos, espinas por doquiera" s 247   6356

IF I COULD FLY; "If I could fly across the sky" e 350   6357

JARABE TAPATIO; "O what a parrot! such frivolity!" e 279   6358

LA JESUSITA; "Y quiéreme, Jesusita, y quiéreme por favor"; "Vamos al baile y verás qué bonito" (verse) s 247;   6359
LA JESUCITA; "Come let us go to the dance (verse); "So favor me, Jesucita" (ref) e 35

LINO ZAMORA; "Pobrede Lino Zamora! Ah! qué suerte le ha tocado" s 247   6360

EL LIRIO; "Hay in lirio que el tiemp no consume" s 247   6361

LLORAR, LLORAR; "llorar, llorar es mi único consuelo" s 247   6362

LA LLORONA; "Salías del Templo un día llorona cuando al pasar yo te vi"; CRY BABY; "Oh why the tears? Pretty   6363
cry baby, cry baby, dry your tears lose your sorrow" e, s 9

MACARIO ROMERO; "Voy a cantar estos versos con cariño verdadero" s 247   6364A

CORRIDO DE MACARIO ROMERO; "Voy a cantar estos versos con cariño verdadero"; "Hark to the verses I sing   6364B
you! Hark to the tale of a hero" e, s 219

LA MALAGUEÑA; "Qué bonitos ojos tienes"; THE MALAGANIAN; "How your two eyes can enchant me" e, s 322   6365

MAMBRÚ; "Un niño nació en Francia en Dominusté Quéelegancia!" s 247   6366

LAS MAÑANITAS; "Estas son las mañanitas"; BIRTHDAY MORNING SONG; "This, the song of David's making"   6367
e, s 322

MI MAMÁ ME ACONSEJABA; "Mi mamá me aconsejaba que no fuera enamorado"; MY MOTHER'S ADVICE;   6368
"My good mother often tells me not to be too bold or daring" e, s 219

MIGUEL RUBALCABA; "Serían las tres de la tarde" s 247   6369

MODESTA AYALA; "Esta tar dea Modesta encontré por las calles hermosas de Iguala"; s 247; CORRIDO DE   6370
MODESTA AYALA; "Una tarde a Modesta encontré por las calles hermosas de Iguala"; "Oh, a
lovely young girl I encountered in the beautiful town of Iguala" e, s 219

EL MOSCO; "No te prodigues en dar, porque a quí, como en Cuquío" s 247   6371

LA MUERTE DE MORELOS; "Oíd, hijos de Mexico, la historia triste y mísera" s 247   6372

LA NEGRA; "Si estás dor mida, mi negra, levánte, ya no duermas" s 247   6373

¡OH, BLANCA VIRGEN!; "¡Oh blanca virgen, a tu ventana asoma el rostro, ven a escuchar!" s 247   6374

PAJARILLO BARRANQUEÑO; "Pajarillo, pajarillo pajarillo barranqueño" s 284; LITTLE BIRDLING OF THE   6375
FOREST; "Little birdling of the forest, Oh my love, my little darling" e, s 248; LITTLE BIRD OF
THE CLIFF; "Little bird, upon the headland, far away from busy cities" e, s 219

EL PAJARILLO ERRANTE; "Yo soy pajarillo errante lejos del nido, lejos del nido" s 247   6376

LA PALOMA AZUL; THE BLUE DOVE; "O lovely dove, you are so beautiful" e 279   6377

EL PASTELERO; "Mi vecina de ahi enfrente se llamaba doña" s 247   6378

LA PERLA DE MAZATLAN; PEARL OF MAZATLAN; "Sweet and disarming, graceful and charming" e 86   6379

PREGUNTALE Á LAS ESTRELLAS; "Pregúntale á las estrellas, si no de noche me ven llorar"; O ASK OF THE   6380A
STARS ABOVE YOU; "O ask of the stars above you if these my tears did not flow all night" e, s 142

PREGÚNTALE A LAS ESTRELLAS; "Pregúntale á las estrellas si por la noche me ven llorar"; O ASK ALL THE   6380B
STARS; "O ask all the stars if they have not seen me weeping throughout the night" e, s 322

¿QUÉ TIENES, CORAZÓN?; "¿Qué tienes corazón? ¿por qué suspiras?" s 247   6381

EL QUELITE; "¡Qué bonito es el quelite!" s 247   6382

SAN JUAN DEL RÍO; "Paloma¿ de dónde vienes?" s 247   6383

SANDUNGA DE YERANESA; "Antenoche fui a tu casa, tres golpes le dí al candado" s 247   6384

SHY INCOGNITA; "'Tis the day for the fiesta!"; "Hear the castanets loudly ringing" (ref) e 37   6385

SI ALGUNA VEZ; "Si alguna vez amas a un hombre" s 247   6386

EL SOMBRERO ANCHO; "De Celaya traje el hule" s 247   6387

SON LOS OJITOS; "Son los ojitos de la vida mía los que ando buscando" s 247   6388

STREET CRY; "Dark the night is, all is silent"; "Loudly I'm calling! Good hot tamales" (ref) e 37   6389

"TE QUIERO PORQUE TE QUIRO"; "YOU ARE MY LOVE, FOR I LOVE YOU" e, s 322   6390

TECOLOTE; "Tecolote de guadaña, pájaro madrugador"; "Little owlet of Mexico, singing to me from above"   6391A
e, s 44; EL TECOLOTE; LAMENT OF THE OWL; "Oh the harvest moon is shining on the field of
new-mown hay" e, s 9

EL TECOLOTE; "Tecolote, tecolote, pájaro madrugador"; THE OWL; "Tecolote, moping owlet, rising so early   6391B
        each day" e, s 322

TENGO UNA NOVIA; "Tengo una novia muy alta muy delgadita" s 247   6392

LAS TORRES DE PUEBLA; "¿Dónde están esas torres de Puebla?" s 247   6393

TÚ ERES LA LUZ; "Tú eres la luz de la existencia mía" s 247   6394

EL TURRONERO; "Chinita, pelito ne gro, te mando sólo avisar" s 247   6395

VALENTÍN MANCERA; "Yo soy Valentín Mancera, borrega nixtamalera" s 247   6396

LA VALENTINA; "Una pasión me domina, es la que me ha hecho venir" s 247   6397

VASITO DE AGUA DE COCO; "Vasito de agua de coco, la boca me has endulzado" s 247   6398

EL VENADITO; "Soy un pobre venadito que habita en la serranía"; THE DEER; "Like a deer that lives in hiding   6399
        on the distant craggy mountain" e, s 219

LA VERDAD Y LA MENTIRA; "En los campos de Amaltea donde las flores regaba" s 247   6400

"YO NO SE SI ME QUIERES"; "SECRET LONGING ENTHRALLS ME" e, s 142   6401

NETHERLANDS

"ADIEU NATUURLIJK LEVEN MIJN" d 384   6402

"ADIEU, REIN BLOEMKEN ROSIERE" d 202   6403

AENHOORT ALLE MIJN GHECLAGH; "Aenhoort doch mijn geclagh, ghij ruyters fraey van sinnen" d 384   6404

AENWAKKERING TOT VREUGD; "Is dit niet wel een vremde gril?" d 384; LET US QUAFF; "The strangest thing   6405
        I ever heard!" e 95

EEN AERDIG VROUKEN; "Een aerdig vrouken hevet mij bedroghen" d 384   6406

AFZIJN; "Een scheepje zag ik varen" d 384   6407

"AL DIE WILLEN TE KAP'REN VAREN" d 203   6408

"AL IS ONS LANDJE NOG ZOO KLEIN" d 384   6409

AL VAN DEN DROGEN HARING; "Al van den drogen haring willen wij zingen" d 202   6410

"AL WAT DEN MENSCH BEJEGENT" d 201   6411

ALIE BRAND; "Alie Brand, die liefste van my land" d 384   6412

"ALL THE FISH ARE SWIMMING IN THE WATER" e 214   6413

"ALLE DIE WILLEN NAAR ISLAND GAAN" d 203; "WER WILL MIT UNS NACH ISLAND GEHN" g 49   6414

DIE ALLERZOETSTE JEZUS; "Die allerzoetste Jezus, die allerliefste Heer" d 384   6415

"ALS DE GROOTE KLOKKE LUIDT" d 203   6416

ALS DE ROMBOM HEEFT GESLAGEN; "Als de rombom heeft geslagen dat wij marcheeren moeten gaan" d 201   6417

ALS IK KRIJG; "Als ik krijg mijn beminde glaasje" d 384   6418

ALS JEZUS IN ZIJN MAJESTEIT; "Als Jezus in zijn majesteit zal komen" d 384   6419

"ALS 'T VOOR EEN MAN IS TE ZWAAR"; "IS A TASK TOO GREAT FOR ONE?" 4 pt round d, e 316   6420

"ANNE MARIE WAAR GA JE NAAR TOE?" d 202   6421

AUSWANDERERLIED; "Nach Ostland wollen wir fahren" g 99   6422

HET AVONDKLOKJE; "'T Sonnetje gaat van ons scheiden" d 384   6423

BEDROEFDE HARTEN; "Bedroefde harten, wilt vreudge rapen" d 384   6424

DE BESTE STUURLUI STAAN AAN WAL" d 384   6425

DE BEZEM; "De bezem, de bezem, wat doe je er mee?"; THE BROOM; "The broom, the broom! What is it for?"   6426
        d, e 316; "The broom, the broom, what do you with it" 4 pt round d, e 28,366

"CASTIJDEN STERKT DEN CRANCKEN MOET" d 384   6427

"DAAR BOVEN UIT HET VENSTERKE" d 202   6428

"DAAR GING EEN MEID OM WATER UIT" d 203   6429

"DAAR GING EEN PATERTJE LANGS DE KANT"; "Hei, 'twas in de mei!" (ref) d 202   6430

"DAAR KWAM EENEN BOER VAN ZWITSERLAND" d 203   6431

"DAAR VAART EEN MAN OP ZEE" d 203   6432

"DAAR WAS E WUF DIE SPON" d 203   6433

DAAR WAS EEN MEISKEN; "Daar was een meisken zoo jonk en gezond" d 203   6434

"DAAR WAS EEN SNEEUWWIT VOGELTJE" d 202; DE MINNEBODE; "Daer zat een sneeuwwit vogeltje" d 384   6435

DAAR WAS EENEN MAN; "Daar was eenen man, Eenen fraaien man" d 202   6436

"DAAR WAS LAATST EEN MEISJE LOOS" d 384   6437

"DAAR ZOU EEN MEISJE GAAN HALEN WIJN" d 202   6438

DAER SPRUYT EEN BOOM; "Daer spruyt een boom in ghenen dal" d 384   6439

DAER WAS EEN KWEZELTJE; "Daer was een kwezeltje, die 'tal wil verstaen" d 384   6440

DAG VROUW, DAG MAN; "Dag vrouw, dag man, dag al tegaar" d 203   6441

HET DAGET IN DEN OOSTEN; "Het daget in den Oosten, het lichet overal" d 202; HET DAGHET IN DEN   6442
        OOSTEN; "Het daghet in den Oosten, het licht nu overal" d 384

"DAT CRANSELIJN DAT HI DRAGHET" d 384   6443

DAUWT GIJ HEMELEN!; "Dauwt, gij hemelen van boven" d 384   6444

"DEN DAGH EN WIL NIET VERBORGHEN ZIJN" d 384   6445

"DEN UIL DIE OP DEN PEERBOOM ZAT" d 203   6446

"DO, DO, KINDJE VAN DE MINNE" d 203; DO, DO KINDJE, CRADLE SONG; "Du, du, little baby child" d, e   6447
   316

"DRIE MAAL DRIE IS NEGEN"; "Three times eight is twenty-four" d, e 316   6448

DE DRIE RUITERTJES; "Ik stond op hoogen bergen" d 384   6449

DRIE SCHUINTAMBOERS; "Drie schuintamboers die kwamen uit het Oosten" d 201   6450

EEN EDEL FONTEIN; "Een edel fontein is ons ontsloten" d 384   6451

EEN, TWEE, DRIE, VIER; "Een, twee, vier, hoedje van, hoedhe van"; PAPER HAT; "One, two, three, four,   6452
   paper hat, paper hat" d, e 316

"EI, WILDER DAN WILD, WIE ZAL MIJ TEMMEN?" d 202   6453

EK SAL JOU KRY; "Hiers ek weer, hiers ek weer met my rooi rok voor jou deur" f (a) 384   6454

EN DAAR ZAT EENEN UIL; "En daar zat eenen uil en spon, willewon" d 203   6455

EN 'S AVONDS, EN 'S AVONDS; "En 's avonds, en 's avonds, en 's avonds is het goed" d 203   6456

"ER WAS EEN OORLOGSSCHIP" d 203, 384   6457

FERME JONGENS; "Ferme jongens, stoere knapen" d 384   6458

FRED'RIK HENDRIK VAN NASSAU; Baise may ma Janneton (tune); "Fred'rik Hendrik van Nassau, Prince van   6459
   Oranje" d 201

FRIJSK FOLKSLIET; "Frijsk bloed, tsoch op! wol nou ris bruwzein in siede"; FRIESCH VOLKSLIED; "Friesch   6460
   bloed, stuif op! wil nu eens bruisen, koken" d, f 384

"GEEFT WAT OM DEN ROMMELPOT" d 203   6461

"GELDELOOS GIJ DOET MIJ PIJN" d 203   6462

GEPEYS VOL FANTASIËN; "Gepeys, gepeys vol van enuien welk oorspronc is dat menich treurt" d 384   6463

DE GEUZEN IN BOMLER WEERDT; "De Geuzen zijn in Bomler Weerdt ghevallen" d 384   6464

DE GEZELLEN UIT ROSENDAEL; "Wie wil hooren een nieu liet?" d 384   6465

"GHEQUETST BEN IK VAN BINNEN" d 384; "GHEQUETST BEN IC VAN BINNEN"; MY HEART IS SORE; "My   6466
   heart is wounded sore" d, e 86; "GEKWETST BEN IK VAN BINNEN" d 202

"GIJ DIE DE STERREN HEBT GESTICHT"; Creator alme siderum d 384   6467

GILDEBROEDERS MAAKT PLEZIEREN; "Gildebroeders maakt plezieren met muziek vroeg ende laat" d 203   6468

G'LIJK DEN GROOTSTEN RAPSACK; Almande, Guerre guerre gay (tune); "G'lijk den grootsten Rapsack, vloot   6469
   den Speck verbaast" d 201

"GROOTE GOD, WIJ LOVEN U" d 384   6470

'T HAESKEN; "Willen wij, willen wij 't Haesken jagen door de hei?" d 384; WILLEN WIJ 'T HAASKEN JAGEN?;   6471
   "Willen wij, willen wij 't Haasken jagen door de hei?" d 202

HAND EN HOOFD; "Een kloeke hand, een rappe hand" d 384   6472

"HEER HALEWIJN ZONG EEN LIEDEKIJN" d 202   6473

HEF OP MIJN KRUIS; "Hef op mijn kruis wel zoete bruid" d 384   6474

HELPT NU U SELF; FIRST HELP YOURSELF; "First help yourself, unsheath your blade" e 86   6475

HEMELS VADER; "Hemels Vader ontferm U mij" d 384   6476

"HIER IS ONZE FIERE PINKSTERBLOM" d 203   6477

HOE LUIDE ZONG DE LEERAAR; "Hoe luide zoo zong de leeraar al op de tinnen" d 384   6478

HOE RIJ DIE BOERE?; "Hoe rij die Boere? Sit, sit, so!" d 384   6479

"HOE ZACHTJES GLIJDT ONS BOOTJE" d 384   6480

HONGER; "Honger is de beste saus" d 384   6481

"ICK HAD EEN GESTADICH MINNEKEN" d 384   6482

ICK SEG ADIEU; "Ick seg adieu, wij twee wi moeten sceyden" d 384; IK ZEG ADIEU; "Ik zeg adieu, wij twee   6483
   wij moeten scheiden" d 202

ICK SIE DE MORGENSTERRE; "Ick sie de morgensterre mijns lievekens claer aenschijn" d 384; IK ZIE DIE   6484
   MORGENSTERRE; "Ik zie die morgensterre, mijn liefkens klaar aanschijn" d 202

ICK VRIJDD' EEN VRAUWKIN ALSO FIJN; "Ick vrijdd' een vrauken also fijn" d 384; IK VRIJDE EEN VROUWKEN   6485
   ALZOO FIJN; "Ik vrijd' een vrouwken alzoo fijn" d 202

IK HEB DE GROENE STRAATJES; "Ik heb de groene straatjes Zoo dikwijls ten eind gegaan!" d 202   6486

IK HOORDE DEES DAGEN; "Ik hoorde dees dagen een magetje klagen" d 202   6487

IK VINDE MIJ GEDRONGEN; "Ik vinde mij gedrongen, dat ik zingen moet" d 202   6488

IK VOER LAATST OVER SEE; "Ik voer laatst over zee, wil je mee?" d 203   6489

IK WEET EEN REIN KASTEEL; "Ik weet een rein kasteel in een zeer schoon landouwe" d 202   6490

"IK WIL MIJ GAAN VERTROOSTEN" d 201, 384   6491

IK ZAG CECILIA KOMEN; "Ik zag Cecilia komen langs eenen waterkant" d 202   6492

IMMACULATE HEART OF MARY; OUR LADY OF FATIMA; "All clothed with light, in rainbow sky" e 71   6493

IN DE HEILIGE SCHRIFTURE; "In de heilige Schrifture vind ik een exempel schoon" d 384   6494

"IN DEN HEMEL IS EENEN DANS" d 203   6495

"IN HOLLAND STAAT EEN HUIS" d 203   6496

IN 'T SOETSTE VAN DEN MEIJE; "In 't soetste van den meije al daer ick quam gegaen" d 384; IN 'T ZOETSTE   6497
   VAN DEN MEIE; "In 't zoetste van den meie, aldaar ik kwam gegaan" d 202

'T IS DE BAZINNE; "'t Is de bazinne van al de bazinnen" d 203   6498

"'T IS SINT ANNA DIE KOMT AAN" d 203   6499

"JAN BROEDER VRIJT EEN MEISJE ZOET" d 384 6500

JAN DE MULDER; "Jan de Mulder, met zijnen leeren kulder" d 203 6501

JAN HINNERK; "Jan Hinnerk wahnt up de Lammer, lammerstraat" d 49, 203; JAN HINNERK UP DE LAMMER- 6502
 STRAAT; DE MAN, DE SICK WAT MAKEN KUNN d 99

JAN MIJNE MAN; "Jan mijne man zou ruiter worden" d 384 6503

"JEUGDIG VOLKJE, RAS, RAS, RAS"; Qu'il est bon bon bon (tune) d 203 6504

JEUGDIGE NIMPHEN; "Jeugdige nimphen die 't boerten bemint" d 384 6505

"JONGE DOCHTER WILT NIET TREUREN" d 203 6506

"'K HEB EEN STUIVER IN MIJN HAND"; "LOOK, A NICKEL IN MY HAND" d, e 316 6507

"'K HEB MIJN WAGEN VOLGELADEN"' d 203, 384; THE WAGON; "Once, I loaded in my wagon" d, e 316; 6508
 "HAB MEIN WAGE VOLLGELADE" e 309, 326, 353; HAB MEIN WAGE g 49; SEE MY WAGON,
 IT'S FULL-LADEN; "See my wagon, it's well laden" d, e 34

"'K KWAM LAESTMAEL DOOR EEN GROENE WEIJ" d 384 6509

"'K PASSEERDE VOOR DE VISSCHEMERKT" d 202 6510

'K ZAG TWEE APEN; "'k Zag twee apen wortels schrapen"; I SAW TWO KITTENS; "I saw two kittens wearing 6511
 mittens" d, e 316

DE KABELS LOS; "De kabels los, de zeilen op" d 384 6512

EEN KALEMANDEN ROK; "Een kalemanden rok een wit mantlijntje d'rop" d 203 6513

KARELTJE, TJIP, TJIP, TJIP!; "Kareltje, Kareltje, tjip, tjip, tjip" d 203 6514

KLEIN, KLEIN KLEUTERTJE; "Klein, klein kleutertje, wat doe je in mijn hof?" d 384 6515

KLEIN VOGELIJN; "Klein vogelijn op groenen tak" d 384 6516

HET KLOOSTER VAN SINT ARJAAN; "Lize kloeg: 'Zoo gansch alleen'" d 384 6517

KOM MEE NAAR BUITEN; "Kom mee naar buiten allemaal"; THE WIELEWAAL; "Come to the country, join us 6518
 all" 4 pt round d, e 316 att to A. Hartsuiker

"KOMT HIER AL BIJ, AANHOORT DEES KLUCHT" d 203; PIERLALA; "Come listen all and hear my tale" e 95 6519

"KOMMT NU MET ZANG VAN ZOETE TONEN"; Bransle Guinee (tune) d 201 6520

"KOMT, VRIENDEN, IN HET RONDE" d 203 6521

DE KONING VAN FRANKRIJK EN DE STAD MAESTRICHT; "Maestricht, gij schoone stede" d 384 6522

LAET ONS VROOLICK ZIJN; "Laat ons te samen vroolijk zijn" d 384 6523

"LANG ZAL DIE LEVEN"; A BIRTHDAY SONG; "Long may he (she) live" d, e 316 6524

LUCHTIGE MAAGDEN; "Luchtige Maagden! Dat men u vraagden" d 202 6525

"MAMA, 'K WIL EEN MAN HÈ!"; "MOTHER, I WANT A HUSBAND" d, e 316 6526

MANE, STERREN, NACHTPLANETEN; "Mane, sterren, nachtplaneten, nooit en was uw glans zoo klaar" d 384 6527

MATROZENLIED; "Daar dreunt het geschut en de vlag gaat in top" d 384 6528

DIE MEI PLEIZANT; "Die mei pleizant willen wij planten" d 202 6529

"EEN MEISJE DAT VAN SCHEVENINGEN KWAM" d 202 6530

MERK TOCH HOE STERK; "Merk toch hoe sterk nu in 't werk zich al stelt" d 201; BERG OP ZOOM; "Merk, 6531
 toch hoe sterck, nu in 't werck sich al steldt!"; "See, how with might they would fright us in
 fight" d, e 7

"MIJN LIEFKEN SIET MIJ OVEL AAN" d 384 6532

MIJN TIJD GAAT WEG; "Mijn tijd gaat weg en ik daarmet" d 384 6533

"DE MINNE DIE IN KIJN HARTJE LEIT"; Ik bender een arme Pelgrim ziet (tune) d 202 6534

MITTE CONFITTE; "Mitte confitte kom t'avond thuis" d 203 6535

"MOE GEWERKT EN MOE GESPEELD" d 384 6536

"MOEDER, IK WIL HEBBEN EEN MAN"; "Warme garnars, garnars, garnars" (ref) d 202 6537

MUSICA, ALDERZOETSTE CONST; "Musica, aldezoetste, const, terecht wordt gij verheven" d 384 6538

"NAAR BRABANT WILLEN WE RIJDEN" d 384 6539

"DE NACHTEGAAL DIE ZANK EEN LIED" d 202 6540

EENS NADERDE ONS VAN FRANKRIJK'S GRENS; Het koekoeklied (tune); "Eens naderd' ons van Frankrijksgrens, 6541
 een troep" d 201

"NU LAAT ONS ALLEN VROLIJK ZIJN"; "JOIN WITH US AND HAPPY BE" d, e 316 6542

"NI WIL IK EEN LIEDEKEN ZINGEN" d 202 6543

"NU TREKT DEN BOER EEN PAAR KLOMPJES AAN" d 384 6544

O ANGENIETJE; "O Angenietje, Mijn honighbietje" d 384; "O ANGENIETJE, MIJN HONINGBIETJE" d 202 6545

"O FRIESLAND, ZOO VOL DEUGDEN; "O Friesche aard, recht edel land" (ref) d 201 6546

"O HEER, DIE DAAR DES HEMELS TENTE SPREIDT"; Gallarde Sint Margriet (tune); d 201; O HEER DIE DAER; 6547
 O LORD ABOVE; "O Lord above, who has spread Heaven's blue" e 86

O NACHT, JALOERSE NACHT!; "O nacht, jalourse nacht, die tot mijn leet gesworen" d 384 6548

O NEDERLAND, LET OP UW ZAAK; 's Nachts toen een blauw gestarde kleed (tune); "O Nederland, let op uw 6549
 zaak, de tijd en stond is daar" d 201

"O NOACH, GOEDE OUDE HEER" d 384 6550

O ZONNE, HEERLIJK OVERTOGEN; "O zonne, heerlijk overtogen met purper van het morgenrood" d 384 6551

OCH, LIEVE HEER; "Och, lieve Heer, il heb geleden mijn zondig schip met vollen last" d 384 6552

"ONS LIESJE ZAT TE TREUREN" d 202 6553

ORANJE-LIEDJE; "Oranjehoutje kan geen kwaad!" d 384   6554

OU TANTE KOBA; "Ou tante Koba ba die is so dom" d 384   6555

"OUD EN JONG, ELK IS VERHEUGD"; Schoonste Nimphje van het woud (tune) d 201   6556

POLLIE, ONS GAAN PÊREL-TOE; "Pollie gaan mos Pêrel-toe" d 384; "Pollie ons gaan Pêrel-toe"; "POLLY, COME WITH ME TO PAARL" e, f (a) 239   6557

RECHT OP; "Recht op van lijf, recht op van ziel" d 384   6558

REIN MAEGDEKEN; "Rein maegdeken met eeren" d 384   6559

"RIJCK GOD, HOE MACH DAT WESEN" d 384   6560

'T ROS BEIJAARD; "'T Ros Beijaard doet zijn ronde In de stad van Dendermonde" d 201   6561

"ROSA, WILLEN WIJ DANSEN?"; d 202; ROSA; "Come, dance with me, my Rosa" e 37   6562A

ROSA; "Rosa, willen wy dansen?"; "Rosa let us be dancing" d, e 109,110; "Rosa, we will go dancing" e 279   6562B

DE RUYTER; "Ik zing er al van een Ruyter koen" d 384   6563

"'S AVONDS ALS IK SLAPEN GA" d 384   6564

"'S NACHTS RUSTEN MEEST DE DIEREN" d 202   words by G. A. Bredero   6565

"SA, BOER, GAAT NAAR DEN DANS" d 202   6566

SCHALT BAZUINEN; "Schalt bazuinen over d'aard!" d 384   6567

SCHIPPERSDEUN; "De wind waait uit den Oosten" d 384   6568

SCHOON BOVEN ALLE SCHOONE; "Schoon boven alle schoone, hoe mag't geschien" d 201   6569

SCHOON JONCKVROUW; "Schoon jonckvrouw, ick moet u clagen" d 384; "SCHOON JONKVROUW, IK MOET U KLAGEN" d 202   6570

"SCHOON LIEF, HOE LIGT GIJ HIER EN SLAAPT" d 202   6571

SCHOON LIEVEKEN, WAAR WAARDE GIJ?; "Schoon lieveken, waar waarde gij den eersten meiennacht" d 202, 384   6572

SINTE MERTEN; "Sinte Merten van deze genuchten" d 203   6573

SLAET OP DEN TROMMELE; "Slaet op den trommele van dirredomdeijne" d 384   6574A

SLAAT OP DEN TROMMELE; "Slaat op den trommele van dirredomdeine" d 201   6574B

"SPRINGT OP EN TOONT UW SCHOEN" d 203   6575

STAP AN!; "Stap an, stap an, stap an, recht naar de kroeg" d 384   6576

DIE STEWELJIES VAN SANNIE; "Pas altyd vir 'n vroumens op" d 384; DIE STEWELTJES VAN SANNIE, BE ON YOUR GUARD; "Be on your guard with ev'ry girl" e 86   6577

"SUZE NANJE, IK WAIGE DI" d 203   6578

TE DUINKERK; "Te Duinkerk gaat het al verkeerd" d 203   6579

TE KIELDRECHT; "Te Kieldrecht, te Kieldrecht, daar zijn de meiskens koene" d 203; "Te Kieldrecht, te Kieldrecht, daer zijn de meiskens koene" d 384   6580

THIJSKEN VAN DEN SCHILDE; "Het is goed pays, goed vrede in alle Vlaamsche landen" d 384   6581

DE TOEBACK; "Is er iemand uit Oost Indien gekomen" d 384; EEN LIEDJE VAN DE ZEE; "Wie gaat mee, gaat mee over zee!"; A SONG OF THE SEA; "Come to sea with us" d, e 316; "When the wind blows free 'cross the key from the sea" e 86; HINAUS AUF DIE SEE; "Wer geht mit, juchhe! über See?" g 99   6582

"TOEN HANSELIJN OVER DE HEIDE REED" d 202   6583

TRIP A TROP A TRONJES; "Trip a trop a Tronjes, up and down and over" e 214   6584

TUSSCHEN KEULEN EN PARIJS; "Tusschen Keulen en Parijs leit de weg naar Rome" d 384   6585

TWEE VOERLUI; "Een karretje op een zandweg reed" d 384   6586

VAN DEN BRIEL; "Wij Geuskens willen nu singhen" d 384   6587

VAN EEN SMIDJE; "Wir wilt hooren een historie" d 384   6588

VAN JESUKE EN SINT JANNEKEN; "Lesmael op eenen zomerschen dag" d 384; JESUKEN EN JANNEKEN; "Letsmael op eenen zomerschen dag"; LITTLE JESUS AND ST. JOHN; "And once upon a time on a bright summer's day" d 231; "LESTMAAL OP EENEN ZOMERSCHEN DAG" d 201   6589

VAN LIEFDE KOMT GROOT LIJDEN; "Van liefde komt groot lijden en onderwijlen groot leed" d 384; "Van liefde komt groot lijden en onderwijl groot leid" d 201   6590

"DE VASTENAVOND DIE KOMT AN" d 203   6591

VER BOVEN'T PRACHTIG STERGEWELF; "Ver boven 't prachtig stergewelf daar is een heerlijk oord" d 384   6592

VERLANGEN; "Verlangen, gij doet mijn der harten pijn" d 384   6593

HET VIEL EEN COELEN DOUWE; "Het viel een coelen douwe tot eender veynster in" d 384   6594

HET VIEL EEN HEMELSDAUWE; "Het viel een hemelsdauwe voor mijn liefs vensterkijn" d 384; HET VIEL EENS HEMELS DOUWE; "Het viel eens hemels douwe voor mijn liefs vensterkijn" d 202; A DEW FROM HEAVEN; "Before my true love's window, a dew from heaven falls" e 95   6595A

HET VIEL EENS HEMELS DOUWE; ALL HEAVEN ON A MAIDEN; "All heaven on a maiden distill'd as 'twere the dew" e 361   6595B

VIER WEVERKENS; "Vier weverkens zag men ter botermarkt gaan" d 203   6596

VLAGGELIED; "O schitt'rende kleuren van Nederlands vlag" d 384   6597

DIE VOGELKENS IN DER MUITEN; "Die vogelkens in der muiten zij zingen haren tijd" d 202   6598

"VREUGD EN DEUGD MIJN HERT VERHEUGT" d 202   6599

213

WAAR DAT MEN ZICH AL KEERT; Pots hondert duisent slapperment (tune); "Waar dat men zich al keert of wendt" 6600
    d 201

"WAAR IS ER KERKE ZONDER ZANK" d 203; "WAER IS ER KERKE ZONDER ZANK?" d 384 6601

"WAAR STAAT JOUW VADERS HUIS EN HOF" d 202 words by W. D. Hooft 6602

"WAAROM KOKEN DE BOEREN DIE PAP ZOO DUN" d 203 6603

WAARVAN GAAN DE BOEREN ZOO MOOI?; "Waarvan gaan de boeren, de boeren" d 203 6604 ·

"HET WAREN TWEE CONINCSKINDEREN" d 384; "HET WAREN TWEE KONINGSKINDEREN" d 202 6605

"WAT DOET GIJ AL IN 'T GROENE VELD?" d 203 6606

WAT VOOR VIJAND DURFT ONS NAKEN?; "Wat voor vijand durft ons naken, vier gebroeders op een peerd!" 6607
    d 201

"WAT ZULLEN ONZE PATRIOTJES ETEN"; "Kapitein, luitenant, vaanderig, sergeant" (ref) d 201 6608

WEEST NU VERBLIJD; "Weest nu verblijd, te dezer tijd" d 201 6609

WEK OP! WEK OP!; "Wek op! Wek op! dat herte mijn" d 202 6610

WEL ANNE MARIEKEN; "Wel Anne Marieken, waar gaat gij naar toe?" d 202 6611

"WEL, WAT ZEG JE VAN MIJN KIPPEN?"; "COME AND SEE MY LITTLE CHICKENS" d, e 316 6612

DER WERELD RAAD; "Der wereld raad is dikwijls kwaad" d 384 6613

WIEN NEERLANDSCH BLOED; "Wien Neerlandsch bloed in d'andren vloeit" d 384 6614

WIJ BOEREN EN BOERINNEN; "Wij boeren en boerinnen, wij werken dag en nacht" d 203,384 6615

"WIJ KLOMMEN OP HOOGE BERGEN" d 202 6616

WIJ LEVEN VRIJ; "Wij leven vrij, wij leven blij Op Neerlands dierb'ren grond" d 384 6617

WIJ ZIJN AL BIJEEN; "Wij zijn al bijeen, al goe kadulletjes" d 203 6618

"EEN WIJF HAD EEN KABAAS" d 203 6619

WILHELMUS VAN NASSOUWE; "Wilhelmus van Nassouwe ben ik van Duitschen bloed" d 201; HET WILHELMUS; 6620
    "Wilhelmus van Nassouwe ben ick van duytschen bloet"; WILLIAM OF NASSAU; "I, William of
    Nassau, scion of a Dutch and ancient line" d, e 316; "Wilhelmus van Nassouwe ben ick van
    duytschen bloet"; WILHELMUS OF NASSAU; "Wilhelmus, Prince of Nassau, of old Dutch blood
    am I" d, e 7 words by P. van Marnix

"WINDEKEN, DAAR HET BOSCH AF DRILT" d 202 words by P. C. Hooft 6621

"DE WINTER IS VERGANGHEN". d 384; "DE WINTER IS VERGANGEN" d 202; "ONCE MORE THE WINTER'S 6622
    LEFT US" d, e 316; "DER WINTER IST VERGANGEN" g 41,49,309,326; SCHEIDELIED g 31

"DES WINTERS ALS HET REGHENT" d 384; "DES WINTERS ALS HET REGENT" d 202 6623

HET ZANDMANNETJE; "De bloempjes gingen slapen, zij waren geurensmoe" d 384 6624

ZEEMANSLIED: KOM HIER GIJ PRONKERT KIJKEN; Ick ginck op eenen morgen (tune); "Kom hier gij pronkert 6625
    kijken, die kost' lijk zijt bekleed" d 201

"ZEG KWEZELKEN, WILDE GIJ DANSEN?" d 202; ZEG KWEZELKEN d 384; HET KWEZELKEN; "Zeg, kwezel- 6626
    ken, wilde gy dansen?"; LITTLE HYPOCRITE; "Say, Kwezelken, will you go dancing" d, e 34

ZIE ONS WACHTEN; "Zie ons wachten aan de stroomen" d 384 6627

"ZIJN VRIENDELIC OOGEN SCHINEN" d 384 6628

"ZIJT VROOLIJK, GROOT EN KLEINE" d 202 6629

"HET ZOU EEN JAGER UIT JAGEN GAAN" d 202 6630

NEW ZEALAND

HOKIHOKI TONU MAI; ONCE WHEN I AWOKE; "Once when I awoke, there still were stars brilliantly gleaming" 6631
    e 86

NICARAGUA

I SAW YOUR FACE; "I saw your face in a rippling stream" e 86 6632

EL TORITO; "Quién fuera como el zompopo para no tener pereza" s 284 6633

VEN DULCE AMADO MÍO; "Ven dulce amado mío, no tardes en venir" s 284 6634

NORWAY

COWHERD'S SONG; "My calling sounds over the moorland" e 95 6635

EG HEITER ANNE KNUTSDATTER; "Eg heiter Anne Knutsdatter, Kari er mi Mor"; MY NAME IS ANNIE 6636
    CAMPBELL; "My name is Annie Campbell, my mothers' is the same" e, n 231

FISHING SONG; "One morning bright I rowed out for fishing"; "He had no right near my nets to anchor" (ref) 6637
    e 37

HJURINGSVISA; "Kella bukk, Kella blakk, Kella liten Neva tapp"; HERDMAID'S SONG; "Nanny-goat, billy-goat, 6638
    Little kid with fluffy coat" e, n 230

HOMECOMING FROM SUMMER PASTURES; "Ended now our summer toil, the butter churned, the cheeses made" 6639
    e 95

[Jeg lagde mig saa silde] ICH LEGTE MICH ZUR RUH; "Ich legte mich zur Ruh, es war spät in der   6640
    Nacht" g 226

KJAERRINGA MAE STAVEN; OLD WOMAN WITH A CANE; "See her come a-walking while to herself she's   6641
    talking" e 86

EIN LITEN GUT IFRA TISTEDAL'N; A LITTLE BOY FROM TISTEDAL'N; "A little boy from the Tistedal'n asked   6642
    his mother" e 86; A GIRL FIFTEEN; "A girl fifteen does not know her heart" e 95

LOVE'S ORACLE; "BY OUR DOOR A ROSE-TREE BLOWS" e 199   6643

"NAA SKA' EN LITEN FAA SOVA SAA SÖDT"; THE CRADLE IS READY; "The cradle is ready and there you shall   6644
    sleep" e, n 231

OLD NORWAY; Gamele norge (tune); "How can you forget old Norway, land of rock and narrow fjord" e 279, 366   6645

PAAL PAA HAUGEN; "Paal sine höno paa haugan utslepte"; PAUL AND THE HEN; "Paul let the hens out to run in   6646
    the orchard" e, n 230

SONG OF THE HOMEFRONT; "Vaer nordmann, la tyskerne føle ditt hatt"; "We're Norsemen! The Nazis shall   6647
    feel how we hate" e, n 7

STEV FRA TELEMARKEN; "Naer eg vi' sitja einstas aa kvea"; LOVE LAMENT FROM TELEMARKEN; "Whene'er   6648
    I long to sit and sing" e, n 230

THANK YOU, NO!; "When I once make up my mind to wed, boy" e 95   6649

TO FOLD, YE LAMBKINS; "To fold, ye lambkins come, the day is done" e 406   6650

PANAMA

ADIOS, FLORECITA BLANCA; "Para qué quieres cariño, si lo despreciaste así" s 284   6651

COCO DE LOS SANTOS; "Una vieja me dio un coco para que se lo pelara"; THE COCOA-NUT; "An old woman   6652
    gave a cocoanut to me, and said to peel it" e, s 322

HOJITA DE GUARUMAL; "Hojita de guarumal donde vive la langosta" s 284   6653

MI POLLERA; "Mi pollera, mi pollera, mi pollera es colorado" s 284   6654

SEÑO' GALLOTE; "Seño' Gallote, Seño' gallote, Dice tu mama que venga aca"; MR. ROOSTER; "Oh, Mister   6655
    Rooster, your mother's calling" e, s 86

TIENE PLATA; "Tiene plata, tiene plata, tiena plata y no me da"; HE HAS SILVER; "He has silver, he has   6656
    silver, but he never gives me any!" e, s 86

PERU

BLOW ON THE SEA SHELL; "Blow on the sea shell, full and strong" e 219   6657

THE INDIAN FLUTE; "Lonely calls the Indian flute, like the wood dove's coo" e 219   6658

LLANTO DEL INDIO; "Somos los indios rojos puro Atahualpa"; THE CRY OF THE INDIAN; "Indians are we   6659
    descended from Atahualpa" e, s 207

MUCHACHA BONITA; "Muchacha bonita lunar en la cara"; THE MAID WITH THE MOLE ON HER CHEEK; "A   6660
    man loved a maid with a mole on her cheek" e, s 9

LA OLLANTA; THE INDIAN PRINCESS piano 207   6661

LA PALOMA CUENCANA; THE DOVE; "My own love, Paloma, little dove" e 279   6662

PALOMITA; "Palomita donde estás que te busca mi querer?"; LITTLE DOVE; "Lovely dove, where have you   6663
    fled? Searching you, my heart does yearn" e, s 207

SERENADE; "Glow-worm, light your lamp" e 350   6664

SONG OF THE GOLDEN CORN; "Bend thy rays upon the cornfields" e 219   6665

SUNG AT HARVEST TIME; "Come, my sisters, come, my brothers, at the sounding of the horn" e 219   6666

SUSPIROS DEL CHANCHAMAYO; "Amorcito nuevo quisiera tener, pero no lo tengo por no padecer"; BY THE   6667
    RIO CHANCHAMAYO; "By the Rio Chanchamayo in Peru, where the Andes rise into the distant
    blue" e, s 9

LA YUNSITA; "Yunsita, yunsita, yunsita, yunsita, ¿quién te tumbará?" s 284   6668

PHILIPPINE ISLANDS

EL CUNDIMAN; "May dusa payata na lalo ng hapdi"; IS THERE ANY SADNESS?; "Is there any torment, is   6669
    there any sadness" e, t 86

THE PHILIPPINES; "Slender palms are beckoning and calling"; "Garden isles ever bright where the charms of   6670
    the night" (ref) e 350

POLAND

"A JAK BĘDZIE SŁOŃCE I POGODA"; ONE FINE DAY; "One fine day when flowers are a-blowing" e, p 159   6671

"A JAK PRZYJDĄ DO MNIE CHŁOPCY"; "WHEN THE BOYS SHALL COME A-WOOING" e, p 159   6672

"A JAK ŻOŁDU NIE DOSTANĘ"; IF I DON'T GET MY PAY; "Soldier's payment, I must get it" e, p 295   6673

A NASZA KOMPANJA; "A nasza kompanja, tam w okopach stoi"; OUR COMPANY; "Our company is now   6674
    standing in the ramparts" e, p 295

"A SAPERY GRÓB MURUJA"; MY TOMB; "Men are building a tomb for me" e, p 295   6675

AKACJI KWIAT; "Białej akacji kwiat, budzi w spomnienia"; THE WHITE ACACIA FLOWER; "The white acacia's   6676
flow'r brings back memories" e, p 295   words by Z. Bajkowska

ALBOŚMY TO JACY TACY; "Albośmy to jacy tacy, jacy tacy, jacy tacy"; WE ARE SMART, OUR DRESS IS   6677
PRETTY; "We are smart, our dress is pretty, yes it's pretty, yes it's pretty" e, p 159

BARTOSZU, BARTOSZU; "Bartoszu, Bartoszu, oj, nie traćwa nadziei"; LET US NOT LOSE ALL HOPE; "Let us   6678
not lose all hope, hey, Bartosz our dear master" e, p 159

BYŁA BABULINKA; "Była babulinka z rodu bogatego"; BABULINKA; "Once a babulinka from a wealthy family"   6679
e, p 295

BYWAJ DZIEWCZE ZDROWA; "Bywaj dziewczę zdrowa, Ojczyzna mnie woła"; FAREWELL MAIDEN; "Farewell   6680
lass, I'm leaving, for my country calls me" e, p 295

BYWAJ ZDROWY KRAJU KOCHANY; "Bywaj mi zdrowy, kraju kochany"; FAREWELL, MY COUNTRY; "Farewell,   6681
my country, beloved homeland" e, p 295

CEMU ŻEŚ TAK; "Cemu żeś tak womsy odon?"; WHY SO SAD; "Why are your mustaches drooping?" e, p 295   6682

CHAŁUPECZKA NISKA; "Chałupeczka niska, Ojciec matkę ściska"; A LOWLY HUT; "O, our hut is tiny, Father   6683
hugs my mother" e, p 295

CHCIAŁO SIĘ ZOSI JAGODEK; "Chiało się Zosi jagódek, Kupić ich za co nie miała"; ZOSKA WANTED SOME   6684
CHERRIES; "Zoska once wanted some cherries, growing on neighbor Jasko's trees" e, p 295

CHŁOPEK CI JA CHŁOPEK; "Chłopek ci ja chłopek; Wpołu dobrze orze!"; THE THRIFTY FARMER; "I'm a   6685
thrifty farmer, and my field I plow well" e, p 295; JAK TO W NASZEM POLU; "Jak to w
naszem polu, Świecą ranne rosy"; ON THE BATTLE FIELD; "See in our green meadow gleaming
early dews"; CANDLE SONG; "I'm the fire to guide you burning through the dark" e, p 295

CHOĆ BURZA HUCZY WKOŁO NAS; "Choć burza huczy wkoło nas, do góry wznieśmy skroń!"; THOUGH   6686
STORMS ARE RAGING; "Though storms are raging round our ship, a course still true we steer"
e, p 159

CHODZIŁ SENNEK; "Chodził sennek i drzemo tał luli, luli cyt"; COMES THE SANDMAN; "Round the fence and   6687
round the cabin, luli, luli cyt" e, p 295

CHUSTECZKA; "Ta chusteczka brata mego"; THE KERCHIEF; "Oh, this kerchief of my brother" e, p 295   6688

CIEBIE, BÓŻE, CHWALIMY; "Ciebie, Boże, chwalimy, Ciebie, Panie wyznawamy"; THEE, O LORD; "Thee,   6689
O Lord, we humbly praise, Lord, our God, Creator eternal" e, p 295

CIĘŻKIE LOSY LEGIONERA; "Ciężkie losy legionera, Raz, dwa, trzy!"; THE HARD LOT OF A LEGIONNAIRE;   6690
"Legionnaires are always busy, Hup, two, three" e, p 295; W DZIEŃ DESZCZOWY I PONURY;
"W dzień deszczowy i ponury raz, dwa, trzy"; WHEN IT'S RAINY; "When it's rainy, when it's
mournful, left, right, left" e, p 159

CÓRUŚ, CZEGO CI JESZCZE TRZA; "Córuś, córuś, czego ci jeszvze trza?"; DAUGHTER, WHAT DO YOU   6691
WANT TODAY?; "Daughter, daughter, what do you want today?" e, p 159; SMUTNA DOLA;
"Smutna, smutna, Smutna jest dola ma"; SAD IS MY FATE; "Oh sad, so sad! Sad is my fate,
indeed" e, p 295

COŚ TAM W LESIE STUKNĘŁO; "Coś tam w lesie stuknęło, cos tam w lesie huknęło"; FOREST TREES STAND   6692
TALL AND BARE; "Forest trees stand tall and bare, a queer noise went thro' the air" e, p 159

CZEMU TY DZIEWCZYNO; "Czemu ty dziewczyno Pod zaworem stoisz?"; WHY DEAR MAIDEN; "Why do you,   6693
dear maiden by the oak stand lonely?" e, p 295; WHY STAND YOU, DEAR MAIDEN?; "Why
stand you, dear maiden, by the maple lonely" e, p 159

CZERWONE JABŁUSZKO; "Czerwone jabłuszko po stole się toczy"; "Oberek, obereczek, mazurek mazureczek"   6694
(ref); RIPE AND RED THE APPLE; "Ripe and red the apple rolling off the table"; "'Oberek' hold
on steady, 'Mazurek' all is ready" e, p 159; RED APPLE; "Pretty ripe red apple on the table
rolling" e, p 295

CZERWONY PAS; "Czerwony pas za pasem broń"; "Dia Hucuła niema życia jak na połoninie" (ref); RED IS   6695
THE BELT; "Red is the belt holding his gun"; "Houtzouls' life in highlands only" (ref) e, p
159   words by J. Koreniowski

CZTERY LATA WIERNIEM SŁUŻYŁ; "Cztery lata wierniem służył gospodarzowi"; I WAS FARMHAND FOR A   6696
FARMER; "I was farmhand for a farmer, toiled four years at least" e, p 159

CZY TO PANNA, CZY MĘŻATKA; "Czy to panna, czy mężatka, Hu! ha ha ha!"; WHETHER MAIDEN OR A   6697
YOUNG WIFE; "Whether maiden or a young wife, Hu! ha ha ha!" e, p 295

CZY TO W DZIEŃ, CZY TO W NOC; "Czy to w dzień, czy to w noc, zawszem wesół"; BE IT DAY OR BE IT   6698
NIGHT; "Be it day or be it night, at my side my faithful sword" e, p 159

"DAJ SWĄ RĄCZKĘ DO MEJ DŁONI"; FAREWELL; "In my hand your hand so slender" e, p 159   6699

DALEJ BRACIA, DALEJ ŻYWO; "Dalej bracia, dalej żywo, otwiera się dla nas zniwo"; COME ON, LADS, THE   6700
COUNTRY'S CALLING; "Come on, lads, the country's calling, fight's on, no use idly strolling"
e, p 159

DALEJ CHŁOPCY; "Dalej chłopcy, bierzmy kosy"; "AT THEM, BOYS, WITH SCYTHES MADE READY" e, p   6701
295; PATRZ MARJACKA WIEŻA STOI; "Patrz Mariacka wieża stoi dla miasta strażnica"; LOOK,
ST. MARY'S CHURCH; "Look, St. Mary's Church is standing with a spire so slender" e, p 159

DOROTKA; "Ta Dorotka, ta maluśka, ta maluśka"; "My Dorotka, my maluśka, my maluśka" e, p 295   6702

DYL, DYL; "Dyl, dyl, dy lu, dy lu, dy lu, Na skrzypeczkach Jasio gra"; "Dyl, dyl, dy lu, dy lu, dy lu, On   6703
his fiddle Jasio plays" 4 pt round e, p 295

DZIEWCYNO, DZIEWCYNO; "Dziewcyno, dziewcyno zal sercu memu"; O MY LASS, O MY LASS; "O my lass,   6704
O my lass, I am in deep despair" e, p 159

DZISIAJ BAL U WETERANÓW; "Dzisiaj bal u weteranów kużdy zna tych panów"; WE ALL LOVE THOSE VETERANS   6705
PARTIES; "We all love those Vet'rans parties, best place for your leisure" e, p 159; MARYŚKA,
MOJA MARYŚKA; "Towarzystwo weteranów, Każdy zna tych panów"; PRETTY MARYŚKA; "Jolly
men are we the vet'rans, gay with all our patrons" e, p 295

GAICZEK; "Gaiczek, zielony, pięknie przystrojony"; HARVESTING SONG; "Gaik's here, gaik's here, berry   6706
bright and bonny" e, p 159

GAUDE MATER POLONIA; "Gaude Mater Polonia, prole foecunda nobili"; REJOICE MOTHER POLAND; "Rejoice   6707
Mother Poland, abundant in noble progeny" e, lat 159

GDY MUZYKA GRA WESOŁO; "Gdy Muzyka gra wesoło, Husia usia, husia usia"; HUSIA USIA; "While the music   6708
plays so gayly, Husia usia, husia usia" e, p 295

GDY WIECZOREM IDĘ SAM; "Gdy wieczorem idę sam to w mej wyobraźni"; "Gaudeamus igitur iuvenes dum   6709
sumus" (ref); IN THE EVENING TWILIGHT'S DUSK; "In the evening twilight's dusk, as I walk at
leisure" e, lat, p 159

GDYBY ORŁEM BYĆ; "Gdyby orłem być, lot sokoli mieć"; GIVE ME EAGLE WINGS; "Give me eagle's wings,   6710
or a falcon's flight" e, p 159; HAD I AN EAGLE'S WING; "Had I an eagle's wing! Or a falcon's
flight!" e, p 295 words by M. Goslawski

GDZIE TO JEDZIESZ JASIU?; "Gdzie to jedziesz Jasiu? Na wojenkę, Kasiu, na wojenkę daleczką"; MUST YOU   6711
GO, MY JOHNNIE?; "'Must you go, my Johnnie?' 'Yes, I must, my bonnie, I must go to war alone'"
e, p 159

GÓRALU, CZY CI NIE ŻAL; "Góralu, czy ci nie żal odchodzić od stron ojczystych"; LAD FROM THE HIGHLANDS;   6712
"Lad from the highlands, art grieving that thou art leaving thy mountains?" e, p 159; HIGHLAND
SONG; "My laddie, are you not grieving to leave your fair native mountains" e, p 295 words by
M. Balucki

HANIŚ MOJA, HANIŚ; "Haniś moja, haniś, cóżeś za Hanisia"; I AM NOT PLEASED WITH YOU; "I am not   6713
pleased with you, Hanis my girl so dear" e, p 159

HEJ, FLISACZA DZIATWO; "Hej, flisacza dziatwo, hej dalejże, dalej"; SONG OF THE RAFTSMEN; "Rafts-   6714
men's life a pleasure, their crafts they well master" e, p 159

HEJ! GÓRALU; "Hej! Góralu, czemuś smutny"; MOUNTAIN LADDIE; "Mountain lad, Hej! Why the sadness"   6715
e, p 295

"HEJ, GÓROL CI JA, GÓROL"; "HEY, I AM A HIGHLAND LADDIE" e, p 159   6716

HEJ! IDEM W LAS; "Hej! idem w las, Piórko mi się migoce!"; HEY! TO THE WOODS; "Hey! to the woods,   6717
gleams my feather like the sleet!" e, p 295; I GO TO WOODS; "I go to woods, feathers flutter
in my cap" e, p 159 words by K. Tetmajer

HEJ LUDZIZKA, POSŁUCHAJCIE; "Hej ludziska, posłuchajcie, Hej!"; HEY FOLKS, HEARKEN; "Hej folks,   6718
hearken, listen to me, Hej!" e, p 295

HEJ, MAZURZE; "Hej, Mazurze, bij nóżkami"; MAZURKA; "Hey, Mazurze, who's that prancing" e, p 295   6719

HEJ STRZELCY WRAZ; "Hej strzelcy wraz, nad nami orzeł biały"; MARCH, SOLDIERS, MARCH; "March,   6720
soldiers, march, our luck again we're trying" e, p 159 words by W. Anczyc

HEJ TAM NA GÓRZE; "Hej nam na górze, stoja rycerze"; BRAVE KNIGHTS CAME ONE DAY; "Brave knights   6721
came one day, up a hill in May" e, p 159

HEJ, TAM POD LASEM; "Hej, tam pod lasem, Coś błyska zdala"; IN THE WOODLAND; "Hej, in the wood-   6722
land, what gleams with wonder?" e, p 295

HEJ TAM W KARCZMIE; "Hej tam w karczmie za stołem, siadł przy dzbanie Jan stary"; OLD YAN ONCE IN HIS   6723
GLORY; "Old Yan once in his glory, in the inn yard made merry" e, p 159 words by W. Pol

HEJ TAM W POLU JEZIORO; "Hej tam w polu jezioro, za jeziorem ciemny las"; THERE BEHIND THAT LAKE   6724
AWAY; "There behind that lake away, dark the woods at end of day" e, p 159

HEJ TY BACA, BACA NASZ; "Hej ty baca, baca nasz, Dobrych na zbój chłopców masz"; HEY, OUR CHIEF-   6725
TAIN; "Hey, our chieftain, chieftain old, your lads are we, brigands bold" e, p 159

HEJ, ŻEGLARZU!; "Hej, żeglarzu! żeglujze całą nockę po morze"; SAILORS' SONG; "Hej, good sailor! Sail   6726
along, sail the whole night on the sea" e, p 295

"HEJŻE INO, FIJOŁECKU LEŚNY"; HEIGH-HO, BLUE BELL; "Heigh-ho, blue-bell, blue-bell in the bower" e,   6727
p 159; PRETTY VIOLET; "Pretty violet, pretty woodland violet" e, p 295

I DLA MNIE WIOSNY WRÓCI CZAR; "Wiosenny wkoło słychać gwar"; RUSTLINGS OF SPRING; "Rustlings of   6728
spring sound here and there" e, p 295 words by Z. Lubicz

I SOWED MILLET; "I sowed millet in my meadow, millet never got" e 95   6729

I ZABUJAŁY SIWE ŁABĘDZIE; "I zabujały białe łabędzie na wodzie"; WHITE ARE THE SWANS; "White are the   6730
swans on dark waters sleepily" e, p 159

IDZIE MACIEK; "Idzie Maciek bez wieś"; MACIEK; "There goes Maciek through town" e, p 295   6731

"IDZIE ŻOŁNIERZ BOREM, LASEM"; "IN DEEP FOREST MARCHING IS DREARY" e, p 159   6732

I'M THE MAN FROM KRAKOW; "I'm the man from Krakow, all the world may know it" e 37   6733

IS THAT SO?; "Past my gate, all in state, ride the gallant suitors" e 228   6734

JA KRAKOWIAK, TY KRAKOWIAK; "Ja Krakowiak, ty Krakowiak i co z tego będzie"; CRACOW KINSMAN;   6735
    "Cracow kinsman cease your labour, swift to leave your farmstead" e, p 159

JAK DOBRZE NAM; "Jak dobrze nam zdobywać góry"; HOW GOOD IT IS; "How good it is to conquer mountains"   6736
    e, p 295

"JAK SIĘ, MACIE, BARTŁOMIEJU?"; "HOW ARE YOU, MY GOOD FRIEND BARTEK?" e, p 295   6737

"JAK WSPANIAŁA NASZA POSTAĆ"; "TO DEPART WE ARE NOW READY" e, p 159   6738

JAKEM MASZEROWAŁ; "Jakem maszerował, muzyczka grała"; I WAS MARCHING SMARTLY; "I was marching   6739
    smartly as the music played" e, p 159; JAKIEM MASZEROWAŁ; "Jakiem maszerował Muzyka
    grała; WHEN I WAS A-MARCHING; "When I was a-marching, To the music clear" e, p 295

JANKO MUZYKANT; "W naszej wiosce uciechy Oj niemało to będzie"; JAN, THE MUSICIAN; "In our little   6740
    village dear, folks will gather bright and gay" e, p 295

JASIEK; "Jasiek konie napawał"; JASIEK AND THE MAIDEN; "Jasiek brought his horse to drink" e, p 295   6741

JECHAŁ KOSAK ZAPOROSKI; "Jechał Kozak zaporowski przez krakowskie błonie"; THROUGH A CRACOW   6742
    FLOWERING MEADOW; "Through a Cracow flowering meadow rode a Cossack straying" e, p 159

JEDZIE JASIO OD TORUNIA; "Jedzie Jasio od Torunia, Czarny wąsik ma"; JASIO RIDES FROM TORUN; "Jasio   6743
    rode all way from Toruń, Sporting a mustache" e, p 295

JESTEM SOBIE CHŁOPAK MŁODY; "Jestem sobie chłopak młody, dy, dy"; I AM YOUNG AND NOT TOO OLD;   6744
    "I am young and not too old, old, old, old" e, p 159

JESZCZE JEDEN MAZUR DZISIAJ; "Jeszcze jeden mazur dzisiaj, choć poranek świta"; THE LAST MAZUR;   6745
    "Come, let's dance the ball's last mazur" e, p 159; OSTATNI MAZUR; "Come, let's dance
    another mazur" e, p 295

"JESZCZE POLSKA NIE ZGINEŁA"; POLISH NATIONAL ANTHEM; "Our dear Poland shall not perish" e, p 159;   6746
    "Mighty Poland will not perish" e, p 7; NATIONAL ANTHEM; "Oh, our Poland shall not perish"
    e, p 295 att to K. Ogiński, words by J. Wybicki

JUŻ DZIŚ OSTATNIĄ NOCKĘ; "Już dziś ostatnią nockę u dziadunia spała"; "Dziś jeszcze swoje szmatki" (ref);   6747
    WEDDING SONG; "This is the last night she'll spend in grandfather's old place"; "Today she'll
    pack her linens" (ref) e, p 295

JUŻ TY O MNIE ZAPOMNIAŁEŚ; "Już ty o mnie zapomniałeś, Jasiuleńku mój"; YOU HAVE FORGOTTEN ME;   6748
    "How soon you forgot about me, Jasiuleńku mine" e, p 295

JUŻ TY ŚPIEWASZ, SKOWRONECZKU; "Już ty śpiewasz, skowroneczku, już i ja też orzę"; WELCOME,   6749
    SKYLARK; "Early at dawn I'm at work, and high up you are winging" e, p 159

KIEDYM JECHAŁ DO DZIEWECZKI; "Kiedym jechał do dzieweczki, brzękały mi podkóweczki"; WHEN I SAID   6750
    GOOD-BYE AND PARTED; "When I said good-bye and parted, and my horses shoes had started" e,
    p 159; KIEDYM JECHOŁ OD DZIEWECZKI; "Kiedym jechoł od dziewecki, Brzękały mi podkó-
    wecki"; WHEN I SAID GOOD-BYE; "When I said good-bye and parted, and my horses hoofs had
    started" e, p 295

"KOŁO MEGO OGRÓDECKA"; "IN MY GARDEN, IN THE BOWER" e, p 295; IN MY GARDEN e, p 159   6751

KOŁYSANKA; "Śpij, siostrzyczko moja mała"; CRADLE SONG; "Sleep, my little baby sister" e, p 295   6752

KORALIKI; "Chodziłam se kole rzecki, pogubiłam koralicki"; CORALS; "I lost, walking by the river, coral   6753
    beads prettiest ever" e, p 295

KRAKOWIACZEK CI JA; "Krakowiaczek ci ja! Krakowskiej natury"; A LAD FROM KRAKOW; "Here's a lad   6754
    from Krakow, he is quite a dandy" e, p 295; "Krakowiaczek ci ja, wKrakowiem się rodził";
    I AM A LAD FROM CRACOW; "I'm a lad from Cracow, born in Cracow city" e, p 159

KRAKOWSKIE WESELE; "Jedzie, jedzie, wesele"; A KRAKOW WEDDING; "See the wedding party ride"   6755
    e, p 295

KSIĄDZ MI ZAKAZOWAŁ; "Ksiądz mi zakazował, abym nie całował"; MY CONFESSOR TOLD ME; "My con-   6756
    fessor told me, that hell will enfold me, if I kiss" e, p 159; "Ksiądz mi zakazował, Zebym nie
    całował"; MY CONFESSOR WARNED ME; "My confessor warned me not to kiss on Sunday" e, p 295

KTÓREDY JASIU POJEDZIESZ; "Którędy Jasiu, którędy Jasiu pojedziesz, pojedziesz"; WHICH WAY, MY   6757
    JOHNNIE; "Which way, my Johnny, which way my Johnny will you take, will you take?" e, p 159

KUMA SOBIE SIEDZIAŁA; "Kuma sobie siedziała, motek nici zwijała"; KUM AND KUMA; "Kuma sat and was   6758
    spinning, old Kum's heart was she winning" e, p 159

KURDESZ; "Każ nam dać wina"; "Come let us drink wine" e, p 295   words by Father Bohomolec   6759

ŁĄCZKO, ŁĄCZKO ZIELONA; "Łączko, łączko, łączko zielona"; MEADOW FRESH AND GREEN; "Meadow,   6760
    meadow, meadow fresh and green" e, p 159; ROLIŚ, ROLIŚ; "Roliś, roliś, roliś kochana";
    FURROW, FURROW; "Furrow, forrow, furrow straight and true" e, p 295

LEĆ GLOSIE PO ROSIE; "Leć głosie po rosie, prostu ku traktowi"; FLY MY VOICE SO LOVING; "Fly my voice so   6761
    loving, towards that road yonder" e, p 159; WIND OF NIGHT; "Wind of night, rover, come bend
    the grass over" e 95

LITTLE CUCKOO; "In the springtime, cuckoo! Ev'ry lad goes wooing" e 228   6762

ŁÓDKO, MOJA ŁÓDKO; "Łódko moja łódko, Suwaj po głębinie"; SAIL ON; "Sail on, sail on, my boat, sail over   6763
    the deep sea" e, p 295; BOAT, MY GOOD COMPANION; "Boat, my good companion, now obey
    your master" e 95

LOVE ORACLE; "Linden, green linden, tall in the meadow, bend, let your branches hang down" e 95   6764

LŚNI BLASKIEM; "Lśni blaskiem kwietna błon"; LOST LOVE; "Bright flowers bloom round me" e, p 295   6765

MAŁGORZATKA; "Za górami, za lasami, za lasami, Tańcowała Małgorzatka z husarzami"; MARGARETA;   6766
    "Beyond high hills, beyond forest, danced our lovely Margareta with the hussars" e, p 295

MAM CHUSTECZKĘ HAFTOWANĄ; "Mam chusteczkę haftowaną Co ma cztery rogi"; I HAVE AN EMBROIDERED   6767
    KERCHIEF; "I have an embroidered kerchief Stitched all o'er and so neat" e, p 295

MARSZ, MARSZ ME SERCE; "Marsz, marsz me serce, pobudkę biją"; MARCH, MARCH, MY HEART; "March,   6768
    march, my heart, the bugles sound loudly" e, p 159; "March, march my stout heart when trumpet
    calls day" e, p 295

MARSZ PIERWSZEJ BRYGADY; "Legiony to, żołnierska nuta"; MARCH OF THE FIRST BRIGADE; "We legionnaires,   6769
    the army's music" e, p 295; "LEGJONY TO ZOŁNIERSKA NUTA"; "We legionnaires - fight's our
    aim only" e, p 159

MARY, TIME YOU WERE WEDDED!; "Apples be ripe and ready, falling all, falling already" e 228   6770

MARYSIU, MARYSIU; "Marysiu,"Marysiu, gotuj pirogi"; "Marysiu, Marysia, cook some pirogi" e, p 295   6771

MATUŚ MOJA, MATUŚ; "Matuś moja matuś, Wydaj mnie za Jasia"; MOTHER MINE, OH MOTHER; "Mother   6772
    mine, oh mother, let me marry Johnny!" e, p 295; MOTHER DEAR; "Mother dear, please let
    me go with Hans" e 221

MAZUREK; "See the sun yonder shining in beauty" e 279,366   6773

MIAŁA BABA KOGUTA; "Miała baba koguta, koguta, koguta"; AN OLD WOMAN HAD A COCK; "An old woman   6774
    had a cock, had a cock, had a cock" e, p 159; ONCE THERE WAS A BABA; "Once there was a
    baba who, baba who, baba who" e, p 295

MÓJ WIONECKU Z BARWINECKU; "Mój wionecku z barwinecku Wiesiałak cie na kołecku"; PERIWINKLE   6775
    WREATH, I HAD THEE HUNG; "Periwinkle wreath, I had thee hung On a wooden peg, I had
    thee hung" e, p 295

NA DOLINIE; "Na dolinie zawierucha"; IN THE VALLEY; "In the valley blows a wild storm" e, p 295   6776

NA GANKU STAŁA MANIA; "Na ganku stała mania, w ogrodku kwitły bzy"; FAIR MARY; "Fair Mary through   6777
    the garden went in a languid stride" e, p 159

NA GRZYBKI; "Nie teraz, nie teraz, na grzybki chodzą"; MUSHROOM PICKING; "Not now, oh, not now for   6778
    mushrooms do we go" e, p 295

NA POŻEGNANIE; "Jak szybko mija chwile"; FAREWELL TO THE OLD YEAR; "How quickly flies ev'ry moment"   6779
    e, p 295

NA WAWEL; "Na Wawel, na Wawel, Krakowiaku żwawy"; TO WAWEL; "To Wawel, to Wawel, little lad of   6780A
    Krakow" e, p 295

NA WAWEL, NA WAWEL; "Na Wawel, na Wawel Krakowiaku żwawy"; LITTLE LAD OF CRACOW; "Little lad of   6780B
    Cracow, leave the city's bustle" e, p 159

"NAD PIĘKNYM RUCZAJEM U WZGÓRZA"; YOUNG SOPHIE; "Young Sophie, of all girls the fairest" e, p 159   6781

NAD WODĄ W WIECZORNEJ PORZE; "Nad wodą w wieczornej porze za gaskami chadzała"; BY THE WATER,   6782
    IN THE EVENING; "By the water, in the evening to a flock of geese did tend" e, p 159

NAPRZÓD DRUŻYNO STRZELECKA; "Naprzód drużyno strzelecka, sztandar do góry swój wznieś"; QUICK   6783
    MARCH, OH SOLDIERS OF FREEDOM; "Quick march, o soldiers of freedom, Our banner waves in
    the blast" e, p 159

NASZ CHŁOPICKI; "Nasz Chłopicki wojak dzielny, śmiały"; OUR CHŁOPICKI; "Our Chłopicki fights hard, leads   6784
    men boldly" e, p 295   words by J. Słowaczynski

NASZA SPUŚCIZNA; "Cztery rzeczy w Polsce słyna"; OUR LEGACY; "Four things that our Poles are famed for"   6785
    e, p 295   words by W. Pol

NIC MNIE TAK NIE GNIWA!; "Nic mnie tak nie gniwa, Jak psiapara Kaśka!"; THE LITTLE VIXEN; "No one   6786
    vexes me more than my pretty Kasiu" e, p 295

NIE CHCĘ CIĘ, KASIUNIU; "Nie chcę cię Kasiuniu, nie chcę cię"; NOT TO YOU MY KATE; "Not to you my   6787
    Kate, will I be wed" e, p 159; KASIENKA; "I won't have you, Kasiu, No! No! No!" e, p 295

NIE CHODŹ, MARYSIU; "Nie chodź, Marysiu, do lasa"; MARYŚ, DO NOT GO TO THE WOODS" e, p 295   6788

NIE DALEKO JEZIORA; "Niedalkeo jeziora, stała lipka zielona!"; BY THE LAKE ON YONDER LEA; "By the   6789
    lake on yonder lea, stood the greening linden tree" e, p 295; NIEDALEKO JEZIORA; BY THE
    LAKE; "By the lake, on yonder lea, stood a greening linden tree" e, p 159

"NIE DBAM JAKA SPADNIE KARA"; "I DON'T CARE IF MY FATE IS ABJECT" e, p 159   words by A. Mickiewicz   6790

NIE MASZ NAD MAZURA; "Nie masz nad mazura, Nie masz tańca nad mazura"; LET US ALL OUR WORRIES   6791
    BANISH; "Let's all worries banish, Let us all worries banish" e, p 159

NIE OGLĄDAJ SIĘ MARYSIU; "Nie oglądaj się Marysiu Za tym wojskiem, za pancernym"; FROM YOUR DREAMS   6792
    DELIGHTFUL MARY; "From your dreams, delightful Mary, boys from armoured cars do vanish"
    e, p 159   words by K. Makuszyński

NIE OPUSZCZAJ NAS; "Nie opuszczaj nas, Nie opuszczaj nas"; DO NOT FORSAKE US; "Do not forsake us, Do   6793
    not forsake us" e, p 295

"NIE TAK TO ILLO TEMPORE BYWAŁO"; TIMES HAVE NOW CHANGED; "Times have now changed, and worries   6794
    now are many" e, p 159

NIECHAJ WESOŁO;   "Niechaj wesoło zabrzmi nam echo";   JOYOUSLY ECHOES RING;   "Joyously echoes ring to   6795
each measure" e, p 295

NIEMASZ NAD ŻOŁNIERZA;   "Niemasz nad żołnierza dzielniejszego człeka";   NO ONE LIKE A SOLDIER;   "No   6796
one's like a soldier quite so brave and glorious" e, p 159

"O MÓJ ROZMARYNIE ROZWIJAJ SIĘ";   BLOOM MY SWEET ROSEMARY;   "Bloom my sweet Rosemary, my heart   6797
to cheer" e, p 159; O MOJ ROZMARYNIE; ROSEMARY; "Bloom my lovely plant of sweet rosemary"
e, p 295

"O SIADAJ, SIADAJ, KOCHANIE MOJE";   IT'S PARTING TIME;   "It's parting time for you, our lady fair" e, p   6798
159

OD KRAKOWA CZARNA ROLA;   "Od Krakowa czarna rola, Ja jej orał nie będę";   FROM OUT KRAKOW;   "From   6799
out Krakow, rich dark furrows, I shall not be plowing more" e, p 295; POD KRAKOWEM CZARNA
ROLA; "Pod Krakowem czarna rola, ja jej orał nie będę"; DARK THE SOIL NEAR CRACOW CITY;
"Dark the soil near Cracow city, it will not be ploughed by me" e, p 159

"OD KRAKOWA CZARNY LAS";   NEAR KRAKOW;   "Near Krakow are forests dark" e, p 295; NEAR CRACOW;   6800
"Near Cracow the forest's dark" e, p 159

OD WARSZAWY DO KRAKOWA;   "Od Warszawy do Krakowa, Wszędy droga nam gotowa";   FROM WARSAW TO   6801
KRAKOW; "From Warsaw to fairest Krakow open roads all beckon to us" e, p 295; FROM WARSAW
TO CRACOW GOING; "From Warsaw to Cracow going, soldier's life is easy flowing" e, p 159

OWCZARECZEK;   "Nie wyganiaj, owczareczku";   THE LITTLE SHEPHERD;   "Do not tarry, little shepherd" e, p   6802
295

PANIENECZKA;   "Panieneczka, panieneczka, Czesze złoty w łos";   LOVELY MAIDEN;   "Lovely maiden, lovely   6803
maiden, combing golden tresses" 4 pt round e, p 295

PANNA MŁODA;   "Panna młoda, jak jagoda, Stoi w drzwiach i płacze";   YOUNG MAIDEN;   "Maiden young and   6804
sweet as springtime, at her door stands sighing" e, p 295; PANNA MŁODA JAK JAGODA; AT HER
DOOR THERE STANDS A MAIDEN; "At her door there stands a maiden, dim her eyes with weeping"
e, p 159   words by W. Pol

PIĘKNY JEST WISŁY BRZEG;   "Piękny jest wisły brzeg, suną się tam andry";   VISTULA'S BANKS ARE FINE;   6805
"Vistula's banks are fine, our boys often walk there" e, p 159

PIJE KUBA DO JAKUBA;   "Pije Kuba do Jakuba, Jabuk do Michała";   DRINKING SONG;   "Kuba drinks to his   6806
friend Jacob, Jacob drinks to Marty" e, p 159; KUBA; "Kuba drinks to his friend Jacob, Jacob
drinks to Michael" e, p 295; JACOB, DRINK!; "Jacob, drink! Your glass now clink" e 279,366

PINE CONES;   "Barn holds only fir cones" e 228   6807

PŁONIE OGNISKO;   "Płonie ognisko i szumią knieje, Druzynowy siadł wśród nas";   THE FLAMING CAMP FIRE;   6808
"As we sit round the camp fire flaming, forest murmurs fill the night" e, p 295

PŁYNIE WISŁA, PŁYNIE;   "Płynie Wisła płynie, po polskiej krainie";   THROUGH THE POLISH LAND;   "Through   6809
the Polish land rolls Vistula her waters" e, p 159; PLYNIE WISLA; VISTULA, FLOW ON; "Over
Polish soil the Vistula is flowing" e 86

"POCZEKAJ HANKA TAM U CHRUSTU";   WAIT FOR ME, HANIU;   "Wait for me, Haniu, there by the square"   6810
e, p 295

POD KOPIECZKIEM GRUSZKA ROŚNIE;   "La, la, la, la, la";   "Na Kopieczku gruszka rośnie" (verse);   ON A   6811
HILL; "On a hill a pear tree's growing"(verse) e, p 159

POD ZIELONYM DĘBEM;   "Pod zielonym dębem stoi koń siodłany";   UNDERNEATH THE GREEN OAK;   "Under-   6812
neath the green oak a saddled horse is standing" e, p 159; "Underneath the green oak stands a
saddled brown steed" e, p 295

PODKÓWECZKI DAJCIE OGNIA;   "Podkóweczki, dajcie ognia, Bo dziewczyna tego godna";   LITTLE HEEL PLATES;   6813
"Little heel plates, strike with fire, for the lady I admire" e, p 295; "Dziś, dziś, dziś, dziś, dziś,
dziś, dziś, dziś, Podkóweczki, dajcie ognia, bo dziewczyna tego godna"; CLICK YOUR HEELS;
"Hey, hey, hey, hey, hey, hey, hey, hey, Click your heels till sparks are flying, let your dance
be bright and snappy" e, p 159

"POGNAŁA WÓŁKI NA BUKOWINE";   SHE TENDED HER OXEN;   "She took her oxen to Bukowine" e, p 295   6814

POJADĘ, MARYSIU, NA BOJE;   "Pojadę Marysiu, na boje nic tu nie pomogą łzy twoje";   I MUST GO TO WAR;   6815
"I must go to war, my Mary dear, I will come back to you, have no fear" e, p 159

POJEDZIEMY NA ŁÓW;   "Pojedziemy na łów, na łów, towarzyszu mój";   HUNTING SONG;   "We shall go a   6816
hunting, hunting, friend of mine we'll go!" e, p 295

PÓKI LWIE SERCA;   "Póki lwie serca sokole poloty";   STOUT HEARTS;   "The while our stout hearts dream of   6817
falcon winging"; HEART OF MINE; "Break, break if you must, it is better so" e, p 295   words
by V. Janda

PONURO JĘCZY WICHER;   "Ponuro jęczy wicher na dworze";   RISING WINDS;   "Sullenly raging, wild winds are   6818
moaning" e, p 295   words by Z. Bajkowska

POSZŁA BABA DO FAROŻA;   "Poszła baba do faroza i pytała się o radę";   AN OLD WOMAN;   "An old woman fond   6819
of liquor came for help unto her vicar" e, p 159

PRAGNĄ OCKI PRAGNĄ;   "Pragną ocki pragną, za dziewczyną ładną";   OH, I LOVE A MAIDEN;   "Oh, I love a   6820
maiden, my heart's with grief laden" e, p 159

ŻYŁ TU PRZED LATY; "Żył tu przed laty, Mazur bogaty"; THE MAZOVIAN; "Once a mazur gay, young and prosperous" e, p 295   6886

PORTUGAL

A MARCELA; "Eu fui apanhar marcela a marcela marcelinha. Ai!" e 57   6887
ACORDEI DE MADRUGADA; "Acordei de madrugada Fui varrer a Conceição"; I WOKE AT DAWN; "At the silent break of dawn I woke and crossed the village square" e, po 219   6888
O ADRO TEM QUATRO QUINAS; "Ai o adro tem quatro quinas" po 58   6889
AI! MENINA; "Ai! s'eu te déra dava dava" po 57   6890
O´ALENDROEIRO; "O´ alendroeiro, Ond'es tá teu lendroal?" po 58   6891
AO SALTAR DA RIBEIRINHA; "Ao saltar da 'Ribeirinha' Puz o pé molhei a meia" po 58   6892
BOINA BOINA!; "Boina, boina! O´ ra paz da boina boina" po 57   6893
CANÁRIO LINDO; "Canário, lindo Canário, Canário meu lindo bem" po 57   6894
CANÇÃO DA VINDIMA; "Oh! Videira dám'um cacho" po 58   6895
CANÇÃO DE TECEDEIRAS; "A´gua do rio que lá vai" po 57   6896
CANTIGA DA AZEITONA; "Os amores da azeitona" po 58   6897
CANTIGA DA CEIFA; "Ai, andando eu a cavari" po 58   6898
CANTIGA DE ALVISSARAS PELA PÁSCOA; "Cachopas levantaivos cêdo vinde colher" po 58   6899
CHORA VIDEIRA; "O meu amor me diexou por outra mais bonitinha" po 58   6900
'CHULA'; "Salto e brinco de contente" po 58   6901
O CUCO; "Se houver de tomar amores" po 57   6902
O DERRIÇO; "Meu amor quèstás tão triste" po 58   6903
ÉS O MEU AMOR E NÃO DIGAS QUE NÃO; "Adeus ó vila d'Idanha" po 57   6904
"EU HEI-DE CANTAR BEM ALTO" po 58   6905
THE HABAÑERA; "A strain of music is sounding" e 350   6906
JÁ CÁ VAI ROUBADA; "Já um ladrão novo P'ra roda entrou" po 58   6907
JOSÉZITO; "Josézito já te tenho dito que não é" po 58   6908
O´ LIMÃO; "O´ limão verde limão" po 57   6909
LOUREIRO, VERDE LOUREIRO; "Loureiro verde loureiro Não te ponhas triste assim" po 58   6910
MACELADA; "Eu venho da macelada venho de colher (u)ma flor(i)" po 57   6911
MANGERICO; "Mangerico revira a fôlha Mangerico" po 58   6912
MARIA DA CONCEIÇÃO; "Maria da Conceição o´ que palavra tão doce" po 57   6913
O´ MEU AMORZINHO; "O´ meu amorzinho Eu venho d'arada c'o chapeu" po 57   6914
"O MEU MENINO É D'OIRO" po 57   6915
MILHO GROSSO; "Milho grosso, milho grosso, milho grosso" po 57   6916
NOSSA SENHORA DAS DÔRES; "Virgem Senhora das Dôres" po 57   6917
OH! QUE CALMA; "Oh! que calma vai caindo" po 57   6918
OLH'O´ MÊ AMÔRI; "Do poial da tua porta, Olh'ó mê amôri" po 57   6919
ROMANCE DE DOM FERNANDO; "Tu que tens oh Dom Fernando" po 57   6920
THE ROVER; "I hear a gay voice calling wherever I go" e 350   6921
SANTA CRUZ; "Oh! divina Santa Cruz A´ vossa porta cheguei" po 58   6922
SANTA LUZIA; "Senhora Santa Luzia Senhora Santa Luzia Vizinha do Castelejo" po 57   6923
SÃO JOÃO; "São João não come peras por não estarem bem maduras" po 58   6924
SENHOR DA SERRA; "Fostes ao Senhor da Serra" po 58   6925
O SENHOR DO MEIO; "O senhor do meio cuida que é alguem" po 57   6926
SENHORA DA PÓVOA; "Senhora da Póvoa Virgem Senhora da Póvoa" po 58   6927
SENHORA DO ALMURTÃO; "Senhora do Almurtão Minha linda rosa branca" po 57   6928
"SETE ANOS QUE ANDEI NA GUERRA"· po 57   6929
'SINHORA' DO ALMURTÃO; "'Sinho-ora do Almurtão Quem vos varreu a capela?" p 57   6930
SISARÃO; "Sisarão, Sisarão, Sisarão meu lindo bem"; O SIZIRÃO; "Sizirão, Sizarão, Sizirão meu lindo bem" po 58   6931
"TENHO BARCOS, TENHO REMOS" po 58   6932
"UM AI, MEU AMOR" po 58   6933

PUERTO RICO

BORINQUEN; "Land of Borinquen, the fair land where I was born" e 279   6934
LA PERLA; THE PEARL; "A pearl is born in the sea" e 279   6935

ARDELEANA; "Hear the fledgling cuckoo singing" e 95 — 6936
CUCKOO; "Cuckoo, cuckoo, gray as shadow" e 95 — 6937
STANCUTZA; "In the hut beside the corssroads" e 95 — 6938
WE MUST PART; "Though our hearts are but one heart" e 95 — 6939
WHAT A WORLD!; "Priest says, 'Drinking makes men quarrel'" e 95 — 6940

RUSSIA

AH, THAT DAY; "Ah, that day I went out walking!" e 95 — 6941
ALLAHWERDY; "Out of the old and timeless ages" e, r 352 — 6942
ALONE; "Through the night the wind is howling" e 70 — 6943
BANDURA; "Lonely with my bandura" e 37 — 6944
CHARM; "Where the woods the valley bounded" e 95 — 6945
THE CLIFF; "There's a cliff climbing high to a place in the sky" e 86 — 6946
"COME, BOYS, UNSADDLE THE HORSES" e 86 — 6947
COSSACK CRADLE SONG; "Slumber now, my pretty wee one, Bahyushskeebahyou" e 406 — 6948
THE COSSACK RIDES BEYOND THE DANUBE; "Now beyond the Danube where the Cossack must be riding" e, r — 6949
    352; PERTTY MINKA; "Minka, darling, now I leave you, duty's calling, I must grieve you" e 343
COSSACK'S FAREWELL; "Farewell now, my sweetheart" e 95 — 6950
DREAMING BY THE HANDMILL; "Hackadook, hackadook, hackadook" e, r 287,288 words by A. Globa — 6951
DAS DREIGESPANN; "Seht ihr drei Rose vor dem Wagen und diesen jungen Postillon?" g 31; THE TROIKA; — 6952
    "As lightly as the snowflakes settle" e 343
ELDER BLOOMING; "Elder blooming, all in flower, spring has brought fair weather" e 95 — 6953
FAREWELL MY GYPSY CAMP; "Farewell, my camp and gypsy sweetheart"; "Farewell! farewell! my little gypsy — 6954
    sweetheart" (ref) e, r 352
"HARK! THE VESPER HYMN IS STEALING" e 28,366 words by T. Moore — 6955
HARVEST HYMN; "Harvest time has come once more" e 37 — 6956
HOW IT RAINS; "Like the rain from gray Autumn skies" e 37 — 6957
I CROSSED THE WORLD; "Once I crossed the world to find a sweetheart" e, r 352 — 6958
I SHALL WAKEN EARLY; "I shall waken early in the morning" e 86 — 6959
THE KAZBEK; "Where the Kazbek sleeps white robed deep in snow"; "Sweet our legends and our stories" (ref) — 6960
    e, r 352
THE LAST DAY; "The day has come when for the last time I meet you, my jolly jolly friends" e, r 352 — 6961
THE LETTER WRITER; "If my mother had not seen me" e 95 — 6962
LITTLE GATE; "As soon as darkness drifts down the blue evening" e, r 352 — 6963
THE MOUSTACHED HUSSARS; "With spears in the bright sunlight flaring" e, r 352 — 6964
NIGHT IS STILL; "Night is still, slow go the minutes" e, r 352 — 6965
NOVGOROD'S BELLS; "Novgorod's bells were ringing" e 95 — 6966
OCHY CHORNIA; "Ochy chornia, Ochy iasnia, Ochy sjguchia"; DARK EYES; "Eyes of fire and dew, eyes of — 6967
    darkest hue, how I thrill with love" e, r (tr) 36; "I've one memory of across the sea from a bal-
    cony" e 132; "Where the northern lights gleam in Russian skies" e 343; "Dear dark eyes that
    shine, I once thought were mine" e 128,236
ON, ALWAYS ONWARD; "On, always onward we surge to the light for land" e 86 — 6968
"ONE IS HIGH AND ONE IS LOW" e 95 — 6969
ROARS AND MOANS THE DNIEPPER; "The Dneipper roars and loudly moaning" e, r 352 — 6970
ROUND-DANCE; "Here upon a stone I'm sitting" e 95 — 6971
"SEE ALAILA DIP HER FEET" e, r 287,288 words by A. Globa — 6972
SING A MERRY NEW SONG; "Sing a merry new song, brother, of a new and happy order" e 86 — 6973
SONG OF THE VOLGA BOATMEN; "Ay-yukh-nyem! ay-yukh-nyem! Eshtchyo rahzeek, eshtchyo rahz!"; "Yo, — 6974
    heave ho! yo heave ho! Pull once more, lads, pull once more!" e, r (tr) 122; VOLGA BOAT
    SONG; "Heave-a-way, heave-away, let us pull lads" e 132; VOLGA BOATMEN; "Pull our
    boat, men! Pull our boat, men! Give your strength to the task" e 279,366
THE SUN HID BEHIND THE MOUNTAIN; "The sun was hiding its light" e 86 — 6975
TACHANKA; "See, a cloud of dust is rising" e 35, 288 att to K. Listov — 6976
TAKE ME EARTH; "From no forest comes this rustling" e 95 — 6977
THE TROIKA; "Coachman, get my troika ready" e 95; THE FROST; "See the white frost, how it glitters" e 37 — 6978
TROIKA; "I drive my troika, hear the silver bells ring" e 37 — 6979
TWO GUITARS; "While the fields we strayed dear"; "When night's falling, those two guitars are calling" (ref) — 6980
    e 132,236
THE VILLAGE PEDDLAR; "Oh, you pack upon my back" e, r 352 — 6981
WHY WAS I BORN A BOY?; "Ah, me! Why was I born a boy!" e, r 352 — 6982
WOMAN'S SAD LOT; "Through the fields as I was going" e 95 — 6983
YOU ARE A BRIDE; "You are a bride, girl, yet you look woeful" e 95 — 6984

LA PUPUSERA; "La pupusera junto al comal hace pupusas de chicharrón" s 284   words by M. T. de Cobos   6985

SCOTLAND

AE FOND KISS; "Ae fond kiss, and then we sever" e 102,397   words by R. Burns   6986A

AE FOND KISS; "Ae fond kiss, and then we sever" e 101,105   words by R. Burns   6986B

AE FOND KISS; Rory Dall's port (tune); "Ae fond kiss, and then we sever" e 232   words by R. Burns   6986C

AFTON WATER; "Flow gently, sweet Afton, amang thy green braes" e 101,102,105,163,234,349; "Flow gently, sweet Afton, among thy green braes" e 365; SWEET AFTON e 232   words by R. Burns   6987A

AFTON WATER; "Flow gently, sweet Afton among thy green braes" e 100   words by R. Burns   att to A. Hume   6987B

AIR FAL-AL-AL O; "Air fal-al-al o horo air fal-al-al é"; "Oh merry young maiden, come and merrily dance" (verse) e 199   6988

"AN' O FOR ANE AND TWENTY TAM"; The moudiewart (tune); "They snool me sair, an' hand me doun" (verse) e 101   words by R. Burns   6989

"AND YE SHALL WALK IN SILK ATTIRE" e 101,341   words by S. Blamire   6990

"THE AUBURN HAIRED BONNY DEY"; "And lo'es my bonny dey" (ref) e 86   6991

THE AULD HOOSE; "Oh! the auld hoose, the auld hoose" e 163,349; THE AULD HOUSE; "Oh! the auld house, the auld house" e 101,103   words by B. Nairne   6992

AULD JOE NICOLSON'S BONNIE NANNIE; "The daisy is fair, the daylily rare"; "O my Nannie! my dear little Nannie!" (ref) e 101,105   words by J. Hogg   6993

AULD LANG SYNE; "Sould auld acquaintance be forgot" e 17,28,35,70,100,128,132,163,234,236,279,343,349, 366; SHOULD AULD ACQUAINTANCE BE FORGOT e 233; "Should old acquaintance be forgot" e 44   6994A

AULD LANG SYNE; "Should auld acquaintance be forgot" e 232,365   6994B

AYE WAUKIN, O!; "Aye waukin' O! Waukin' aye, an' wearie"; "Spring's a pleasant time" (verse); e 100,103, 104; AY WAUKIN, O; "Ay waukin, O, waukin still and weary"; "Simmer's a pleasant time" (verse) e 232   words by R. Burns   6995

BALOO, BALOO; "Baloo, baloo, my wee, wee thing" e 101,103   words by R. Gall   6996

BE GUDE TO ME; "Be gude to me as langs I'm here"; "For a' that, and a' that and thrice a mickle's a' that" (ref) e 103,104   6997

BIDE YE YET; "Gin I had a wee hoose and a canty wee fire"; "Sae bide ye yet, and bide ye yet" (ref) e 101,105   6998

THE BIRKS OF ABERFELDY; "Bonnie lassie, will ye go, will ye go, will ye go"; "Now simmer blinks on flow'ry braes" (verse) e 100,105   words by R. Burns   6999

THE BLUE BELLS OF SCOTLAND; "Oh where, and oh where is your Highland laddie gone?" e 17,28,35,366; THE BLUE BELL OF SCOTLAND e 233; "Oh! where, tell me where, is your Highland laddie gone?" e 234; THE BLUE BELLS OF SCOTLAND e 100,104   words by A. McVicar and Mrs. Grant   7000

THE BLUE BONNETS; "March, march, Etrick and Tiviotdale" e 7; THE BLUE BONNETS OVER THE BORDER e 101   words by W. Scott   7001

"BLYTHE, BLYTHE AN' MERRY WAS SHE"; Andro and his cutty gun (tune) e 101,105   words by R. Burns   7002

THE BOATIE ROWS; "O weel may the boatie row" e 100,103,104,349   words by J. Ewen   7003

THE BOATMAN; "How often haunting the highest hilltop I scan the ocean thy sail to see" e 103   7004

BONIE LADDIE, HIGHLAND LADDIE; The Old Highland laddie (tune); "I hae been at Crookieden" e 365   words by R. Burns   7005

BONNIE BANKS O' LOCH LOMON'; "By yon bonnie banks and by yon bonnie braes"; e 102,103; "O, you'll tak' the high road" (ref) e 104,105,163; THE BONNIE BANKS O' LOCH LOMOND; "By yon bonnie banks an' yon bonnie braes"; "O ye'll tak' the high road" (ref) e 18; LOCH LOMOND e 357; "By yon bonnie banks and by yon bonnie braes"; "O ye'll tak' the high road" (ref) e 70,233,234,385,397, 402; "Oh! ye'll take the high road" e 28,236,277,343,366; "Oh, you'll take the high road" (ref only) e 35,128,132   7006

THE BONNIE BRIER BUSH; For lack of gold (tune); "There grows a bonnie brier bush in oor kailyaird" e 101,103; "There grows a bonnie brier-bush in our kailyard" e 163,349; THE BONNIE BRIAR BUSH; "There grows a bonnie briar bush in our kailyard" e 234   7007

BONNIE DUNDEE; The band at a distance (tune); "To the Lords of Convention 'twas Claverhouse spoke"; "Come fill up my cup, come fill up my can" (ref) e 17,163,235,349   words by W. Scott; THE BONNETS OF BONNIE DUNDEE e 28; RIDING A RAID; "Tis old Stonewall the Rebel that leans on his sword"; "Come tighten your girth and slacken your rein" (ref) e 161   7008

THE BONNIE EARL O' MURRAY; "Ye Hielands and ye Lowlands, O whaur ha'e ye been?" e 101; THE BONNY EARL O' MORAY; "Ye Hielands and ye Lowlands, O where hae ye been?" e 46   7009

BONNIE GEORGE CAMPBELL; "High upon Hielands and laigh upon Tay" e 102; "Hie upon Hielands, and laigh upon Tay" e 35   7010

BONNIE LADDIE; "Where ha'e ye been a' the day" e 235; HIGHLAND LADDIE e 17; HIELAND LADDIE; "Whaur ha'e ye been a' the day?" e 101   See also 9448A   7011

A BONNIE WEE LASSIE; "A bonnie wee lassie, whose name it was Nell"; "That nice little window, the cute little window" (ref) e 173; CUTE LITTLE WINDOW e 170   7012

BONNIE WEE THING; "Bonnie wee thing, cannie wee thing"; "Wistfully I look and languish in that bonnie face   7013
    o' thine" (verse) e 100,105; "Wishfully I look and languish in that bonnie face o' thine" (verse)
    e 17   words by R. Burns

"THE BONNIEST LASS IN A' THE WARLD" e 102,105   7014

THE BORDER WIDOW'S LAMENT; "My love built me a bonnie bow'r" e 101,103   7015

THE BRAES O' BALQUHIDDER; "Will ye go, lassie go to the braes o' Balquhidder?"; "Where the deer and the   7016
    rae" (verse) e 235   words by R. Tannahill

BRAW BRAW LADS; "Braw, braw lads on Yarrow braes" e 100,103,104   words by R. Burns   7017

THE BROOM O' THE COWDENKNOWES; "How blythe was I ilk morn to see"; "O, the broom, the bonnie, bonnie   7018
    broom" (ref) e 100,104

THE BUSH ABOON TRAQUAIR; "Hear me, ye nymphs, and ev'ry swain" e 101   words by R. Crawford   7019

"CA' THE YOWES TO THE KNOWES"; "Hark the mavis' evening sang" (verse) e 100,102,104,105,297; "Hark,   7020
    the mavis' e'ening sang" (verse) e 232; "As I gaed down to the waterside" (verse) e 235; CA' THE
    YOWES; "Hark the mavis' ev'nin' sang" (verse) e 199; "Will ye gang down the waterside" (verse)
    e 17; "CA' THE EWES TO THE KNOWES"; "Hark, the mavis ev'nin' sang" (verse) e 349; "Hark
    the mavis ev'ing sang" (verse) e 163; CA' THE EWES; "Hark, the mavis ev'nin' song" (verse) e
    36   words by R. Burns

THE CAMPBELLS ARE COMIN'; "The Campbells are comin', oho, oho"; "Upon the Lomonds I lay, I lay" (verse)   7021
    e 17,100,199,163,349; "The great Argyle he goes before" (verse) e 7,279,366; THE CAMPBELLS
    ARE COMING; "Upon the Lomonds I lay, I lay" (verse) e 235

"THE CARLE HE CAM' O'ER THE CRAFT" e 104   7022

CASTLES IN THE AIR; "The bonnie, bonnie bairn, wha sits poking in the ase" e 100   words by J. Ballantine   7023

CHARLIE IS MY DARLING; "O! Charlie is my darling, my darling, my darling!"; "'Twas on a Monday morning"   7024
    (verse) e 17,100,102,104,163,199,297,349,402; "'Twas on a Sunday morning" e 234; O
    CHARLIE IS MY DARLING; "When first his standard caught the eye" (verse) e 132,366

COLIN'S CATTLE; "Cro Chalain will gi'e, me sae cannie and free" e 101,103   words by M. MacFarlane   7025

"COME OWRE THE STREAM, CHARLIE"; The Maclean's welcome (tune); "We'll bring down the red deer" (verse)   7026
    e 100,104   words by J. Hogg

COME UNDER MY PLAIDIE; "Come under my plaidie, the nicht's gaun to fa'" e 100   words by H. Macneil   7027

COMIN' THRO' THE RYE; The miller's daughter (tune); "Gin a body meet a body" e 17,36,100,104,128,163,   7028A
    176,233,402; "If a body meet a body" e 28,279,366; COMIN' THRU THE RYE; "Gin a body,
    meet a body" e 132   words by R. Burns

COMIN THRO' THE RYE; Miller's wedding (tune); "Comin thro' the rye, poor body" e 365   words by R. Burns   7028B

CORN RIGS; "It was upon a Lammas nicht"; "Corn rigs and barley rigs" (ref) e 100,102; A LAMMAS NIGHT;   7029
    "It was upon a Lammas night"; "Corn rigs an' barley rigs" (ref) e 285   words by R. Burns

CRAIGIE-BURN WOOD; "Sweet fa's the eve on Craigie-burn" e 101   words by R. Burns   7030

CUCKOO OF THE GROVE; "Small bird in that tree, have you pity for me" e 95   7031

DAINTY DAVIE; "Meet me on the warlock knowe"; "Now rosy May comes in wi' flow'rs" (verse) e 101   words   7032
    by R. Burns

DANCE TO YOUR DADDY; "Dance to your daddy, my bonnie laddie" e 104,105,234   7033A

DANCE TO YOUR DADDY; "Dance to your daddy, my little laddie" e 44   7033B

THE DE'IL'S AWA'; The Hemp-dresser (tune); "The De'il cam' fiddlin thro' the toun" e 18,101; "The deil cam   7034
    fiddlin thro' the town" e 365   words by R. Burns

DUNCAN GRAY; "Duncan Gray cam' here to woo" e 102,232; "Weary fa' you, Duncan Gray" e 365   words by   7035
    R. Burns

DUNDEE; "O God of Bethel, by Whose hand Thy people still are fed" e 279,366   words by P. Doddridge and J.   7036
    Logan

ELIBANKS AND ELIBRAES; Killiecrankie (tune); "O, Elibanks and Elibraes, it was but aince I saw ye" e 365   7037
    words by R. Burns

FAREWELL TO FIUNARY; "The wind is fair, the day is fine and swiftly, swiftly runs the time"; "We must up and   7038
    haste away" (ref); "Eirigh agus tiugainn O" (ref); Scotch (in part) e 103,105   words by N. MacLeod

FLORA MACDONALD'S LAMENT; "Far over yon hills of the heather so green" e 100,235; THE LAMENT OF   7039
    FLORA MACDONALD; "Far over yon hills of the heather sae green" e 349   words by J. Hogg

THE FLOWERS O' THE FOREST; "I've heard a liltin' at oor yowe milkin'" e 100,103,104; "I've heard them   7040A
    lilting at our yowe-milking" e 199; "I've heard them liltin' at the ewe milkin'" e 17; THE
    FLOWERS OF THE FOREST; "I've heard them liltin' at owr ewe milkin'" e 235; "I've heard
    them lilting at our yowe-milking" e 349; words by J. Elliot; "I've seen the smiling of Fortune
    beguiling" e 163   words by Mrs. Cockburn

THE FLOWERS O' THE FOREST; "I've seen the smiling o' Fortune beguiling" e 100   words by Mrs. Cockburn   7040B

THE FORNICATOR; Clout the cladron (tune); "Ye jovial boys who love the joys" e 365   words by R. Burns   7041

THE GALLANT WEAVER; "Where Cart rins rowin' to the sea" e 100,104   words by R. Burns   7042

GLENLOGIE; "Three score o' nobles rade up the King's ha'" e 101   7043

GLOOMY WINTER; "Gloomy winter's noo awa' saft the westlan' breezes blaw" e 100   words by R. Tannahill   7044

GREEN GROW THE RASHES O!; "There's naught but care on ev'ry han'" e 17,235,402; "There's nocht but care   7045
    on ev'ry han'" e 163; "There's nocht but care on ev'ry hand" e 101; GREEN GROW THE RASHES;
    "There's nought but care on ev'ry han'" e 365   words by R. Burns

GUID NICHT AND JOY BE WI' YE A'; "The best o' joys maun ha'e an end" e 101   words by A. Boswell   7046

HAME, HAME, HAME; Auld Robin Gray (tune); "It's hame, an' it's hame" e 101   words by A. Cunningham   7047

HAPPY WE ARE A' THE GITHER; O Willie was a wanton (tune); "Here aroond the ingle breezing" e 101   words   7048
    att to R. Burns

HELEN OF KIRKCONNELL; "I wish I were where Helen lies" e 102; "I WISH I WERE WHERE HELEN LIES" e 235   7049

HERE AWA', THERE AWA'; "Here awa', there awa', wandering Willie" e 349,365; WANDERING WILLIE e 100   7050
    words by R. Burns

"HERE'S A HEALTH TO ANE I LO'E DEAR"; "Although thou maun never be mine" (verse) e 101   words by R.   7051
    Burns

HEY, CA' THRO'; "Up wi' the carls of Dysart and the lads o' Buckhaven"; "Hey, ca' thro', ca' thro', for we   7052
    hae mickle ado!" (ref) e 232; "UP WI' THE CARLS O'DYSART" e 101,104   words by R. Burns

HEY THE BONNIE BREIST-KNOTS; "Hey the bonnie, how the bonnie, hey the bonnie breist-knots!"; "There   7053
    was a bridal in the toun" (verse) e 103,104

HEY THE DUSTY MILLER; "Hey the dusty miller and his dusty coat" e 104   words by R. Burns   7054

HIGHLAND MARY; Katherine Ogie (tune); "Ye banks, and braes, and streams around" e 101   7055

"HO, RO! MY NUT-BROWN MAIDEN" e 100,102   7056

HOLLIN GREEN HOLLIN; "Alone in greenwood must I roam" e 86   7057

"HOW LANG AND DREARY IS THE NICHT"; Cauld kail in Aberdeen (tune); "For, Oh! her lanely nichts are   7058
    lang" (ref) e 101   words by R. Burns

A HUNDRED PIPERS; "Wi' a hundred pipers an' a', an' a'" e 17; THE HUNDRED PIPERS e 100,102,163,235,   7059
    349; WI' A HUNDRED PIPERS; JACOBITE SONG e 37; "WI' A HUNDRED PIPERS AN' A'" e 279,
    366   words by B. Nairne

HUSH-A-BY, BAIRNIE; "Hush-a-by, bairnie, my bonnie wee laddie"; e 101,103   words from Fionn's Celtic Lyre   7060

"I GAED A WAEFU' GATE YESTREEN"; My only jo, and dearie O (tune); e 100,102   words by R. Burns   7061

"I HA'E LAID A HERRIN' IN SAUT" e 105   7062

"I LEFT MY DEARIE LYING HERE"; "Hòvan, hòvan, Gorry òg O" (ref) sc in part e 101,103,104   7063

"I LO'E NA A LADDIE BUT ANE"; My lodging is on the cold ground (tune) e 100,104; "I LO'E NE'ER A LADDIE   7064
    BUT ANE" e 406   words by H. Macneil

"I WISH I WERE WHERE GADIE RINS"; "Ance mair to hear the wild birds sang" (verse) e 100   words by J. Park   7065

"I WOULD I WERE THE LIGHT FERN GROWING" e 105   words by Mrs. Norton   7066

ILKA BLADE O' GRASS; "Confide ye aye in Providence" e 100   words by J. Ballantine   7067

"I'LL AY CA' IN BY YON TOON"; I'll gae nae mair to your toon (tune); "There's nane shall ken, there's nane   7068
    can guess" (verse) e 101,105   words by R. Burns

"I'LL BID MY HEART BE STILL" e 349   words by T. Pringle   7069

I'M A' DOUN FOR LACK O' JOHNNIE; "I'm a' doun, doun, doun, I'm doun for lack o' Johnnie"; "Gin Johnnie   7070
    kent I was na weel" (verse) e 101,103,104

I'M OWRE YOUNG TO MARRY YET; "I'm owre young, I'm owre young"; "I am my mammie's ae bairn" (verse)   7071
    e 100,104,235   words by R. Burns

IN PRAISE OF ISLAY; "See afar yon hill Ardmore"; "O, my island! O, my Isle!" (verse) e 102,103,104,105   7072
    words by T. Pattison

IN YON GARDEN; "In yon garden fine and gay" e 104   7073

THE ISLE OF MULL; "Thou Isle o' Moola, austere and awesome"; "Thou kingly island of towering mountains"   7074
    (verse) e 105   words by K. MacLeod

JENNIE'S BAWBEE; "I met four chaps yon birks amang" e 101   words by A. Boswell   7075

JENNY NETTLES; "I met ayont the cairnie, Jenny Nettles trig and braw" e 102   words by A. C. Bunten   7076

JESS MACFARLANE; Ay waukin O (tune); "When first she cam' to toun" e 101   7077

JOCK O' HAZELDEAN; "Why weep ye by the tide, ladye?" e 100,104,163,349   words by W. Scott   7078

"JOCKIE'S TAEN THE PARTING KISS"; Bonnie lass tak' a man (tune) e 101   words by R. Burns   7079

"JOCKY FOU AND JENNY FAIN" e 232   words by R. Burns   7080

JOHN ANDERSON, MY JO; "John Anderson, my jo, John, when we were first acquent" e 100,103,235; JOHN   7081A
    ANDERSON e 365   See also 5892

JOHN ANDERSON MY JO; "John Anderson my jo, John, when we were first acquent" e 232   words by R. Burns   7081B

JOHN GRUMLIE. See 7878C

JOHNNIE COPE; "Cope sent a challenge frae Dunbar" e 101; "Sir John Cope trode the north right far" e 294   7082

KATE DALRYMPLE; "In a wee cot house far across the main" e 235; "In a wee cot hoose far across the muir"   7083
    e 100   words by W. Watt

KELVIN GROVE; O the shearin's no for you (tune); "Let us haste to Kelvin Grove, bonnie lassie, O" e 100,105,   7084
    234,349

KIND ROBIN LO'ES ME; Robin Cushie (tune); "O Robin is my only jo" e 101   7085

THE LAIRD O' COCKPEN; When she came ben, she bobbed (tune); "The Laird o' Cockpen he's prood and he's   7086
    great" e 100, 104; "The laird o' Cockpen he's prood an' he's great" e 18, 163; "The Laird o'
    Cockpen, he's proud an' he's great" e 234 words by B. Nairne

THE LAND O' THE LEAL; Hey tuttu tatti (tune); "I'm wearin' a wa', John, like snaw-wreaths in thaw" e 100,   7087
    103 words by B. Nairne

THE LASS O' GOWRIE; Loch-Eroch side (tune); "'Twas on a simmer's afternoon" e 18, 100 words by W. Reid   7088

THE LASS O' PATIE'S MILL; "The lass o' Patie's mill sae bonnie, blythe and gay" e 100, 102 words by A.   7089
    Ramsay

"LASSIE WI' THE LINT-WHITE LOCKS"; Rothiemurche's rant (tune); "Now nature cleads the flow'ry lea" (verse)   7090
    e 101 words by R. Burns

LAST MAY A BRAW WOOER; The Lothian lassie (tune); "Last May a braw wooer cam' doun the lang glen" e 101,   7091
    103, 104; "Last May a braw wooer cam down the lang glen" e 365 words by R. Burns

THE LEA RIG; My ain kind dearie O (tune); "When owre the hill the eastern star" e 100, 105; "When o'er the   7092
    hill the evening star" e 95 words by R. Burns; MY AIN KIND DEARIE, O; "Will ye gang o'er
    the learig" e 18

LEEZIE LINDSAY; "Will ye gang to the Hielans, Leezie Lindsay?" e 36, 163, 349; "Will ye gang to the Hielands,   7093
    Leezie Lindsay?" e 18, 28, 37, 45, 101, 104, 199, 235, 366 words by R. Burns

LENACHAN'S FAREWELL; "Fare thee weel, my native cot" e 294   7094

LEWIE GORDON; "O send Lewie Gordon hame" e 101 words by A. Geddes   7095

LOCK THE DOOR LARISTON; "Lock the door, Lariston, lion of Liddesdale" e 18, 101, 102 words by J. Hogg   7096

LOGAN WATER; "By Logan's streams, that rin sae deep" e 100 words by J. Mayne   7097

LOGIE O' BUCHAN; "O, Logie o' Buchan, O Logie the laird" e 100, 103 words by G. Halket   7098

LOUDON'S BONNIE WOODS AND BRAES; "Loudan's bonnie woods and braes, I maun lea' them a', lassie" e 100   7099
    words by R. Tannahill

MAC CRIMMON'S LAMENT; "O'er Coolin's face the night is creeping" e 102, 105   7100

MCPHERSON'S FAREWELL; McPherson's rant (tune); "Farewell, ye dungeons dark and strong, the wretch's   7101
    destinie!" e 365 words by R. Burns

MAGGIE LAUDER; "Wha wadna be in love wi' bonnie Maggie Lauder?" e 100, 102 words by F. Semple   7102

A MAN'S A MAN FOR A' THAT; "Is there for honest poverty that hangs his heid, an' a' that?" e 100, 102; "Is   7103
    there for honest poverty that hangs his head an' a' that?" e 18; "Is there for honest poverty that
    hangs his head and a' that?" e 163, 349; IS THERE FOR HONEST POVERTY; "Is there for honest
    poverty that hings his head, an' a' that?" e 232 words by R. Burns

THE MARCH OF THE CAMERON MEN; "There's many a man of the Cameron clan" e 17, 163   7104

MARY MORISON; "O Mary, at thy window be, it is the wish'd, the trysted hour" e 100, 102 words by R. Burns   7105

MARY OF ARGYLE; "I have heard the mavis singing" e 18   7106

MAY FORTUNE AYE BE KINDLY; "May fortune aye be kindly my bonnie lass, to thee" e 105 words by J. M.   7107
    Diack

THE MIST COVERED MOUNTAINS OF HOME; "Horo! Soon shall I see them, O, Heero!"; "There I shall visit   7108
    the place of my birth" (verse) e 105

MO MARY; "Out on the hillside by the sheiling" e 111   7109

MOLLY!; "First when I came to this place of troubles I was free"; "Oh, fy! fain wad I stay at home wi' thee,   7110
    Molly!" (ref) e 102, 105 words by W. Christie

MUIRLAND WILLIE; "O hearken and I will tell you hoo" e 100   7111

MY AIN HOOSE; "Sing cheerilie, couthilie, cantie and free"; "Ayont by the ferry whaur woodlands are free"   7112
    (verse) e 105

MY BONNIE MARY; "Go fetch to me a pint o' wine" e 397 words by R. Burns   7113

MY BOY TAMMIE; "Whaur hae ye been a' day, my boy Tammie?" e 100, 103, 104, 235 words by H. Macneill   7114

MY DEAR HIELAND LADDIE; "Blythe was the time when he fee'd wi' my faither, O!" e 101, 104 words by R.   7115
    Tannahill

MY FAITHFU' JOHNNIE; "When will you come again" (duet) e 101   7116

MY FAITHFUL FAIR ONE; MO RÙN GEAL DILEAS; "My faithful fair one, my own, my rare one" e 100, 105   7117

MY HEART IS SAIR FOR SOMEBODY; "My heart is sair, I daurna tell" e 100, 103 words by R. Burns   7118

MY HEART'S IN THE HIGHLANDS; "My heart's in the Highlands, my heart is not here"; "Farewell to the High-   7119
    lands, farewell to the North!" (verse) e 102, 105 words by R. Burns

MY JO JANET; "Sweet sir, for your courtesie, when ye come by the Bass" e 100, 105   7120

MY LOVE IS LIKE A RED, RED ROSE; Low down in the broom (tune); "O, my love is like a red, red rose" e 163,   7121A
    402; "MY LUVE IS LIKE A RED, RED ROSE" e 17; "O, my luve is like a red, red rose" e 36; "O,
    MY LOVE IS LIKE A RED, RED ROSE" e 101, 102, 105 words by R. Burns

A RED, RED ROSE; Major Graham's Strathspey (tune); "My luve is like a red, red rose" e 232; "O my luve's like   7121B
    the red, red rose" e 365 words by R. Burns

"MY LOVE, SHE'S BUT A LASSIE YET"; Put up your dagger, Jamie (tune) e 100, 102, 232, 235   7122

MY LUVE'S IN GERMANIE; "My luve's in Germanie, send him hame, send him hame" e 100 words by H.   7123
    MacNiel

MY NANNIE, O; "Behind yon hills where Lugar flows" e 100 words by R. Burns   7124

MY NANNIE'S AWA'; "Noo in her green mantle blythe Nature arrays" e 100, 102; "Now in her green mantle   7125
    blythe Nature arrays" e 18   words by R. Burns

MY OWN DEAR ONE'S GONE; "Since my dear one's gone, all the joy of morning" e 103, 104   words by J. Diack   7126

"MY WIFE'S A WINSOME WEE THING" e 101   words by R. Burns   7127

"NOW NATURE HANGS HER MANTLE GREEN"; Mary Queen of Scots lament (tune) e 232   words by R. Burns   7128

O' A' THE AIRTS; Miss Admiral Gordon's Strathspey (tune); "O' a' the airts the wind can blaw" e 105, 163, 365   7129
    words by R. Burns (1st verse) and J. Hamilton (2nd verse)

O! ARE YE SLEEPIN', MAGGIE; "Mirk an' rainy is the nicht" e 100   words by R. Tannahill   7130

O CAN YE SEW CUSHIONS; "O can ye sew cushions, and can ye sew sheets?" e 17, 46, 100, 103, 199, 235, 274;   7131
    CAN YE SEW CUSHIONS e 44, 402

"O DINNA THINK, BONNIE LASSIE"; Clunie's reel (tune) (duet) e 101   words by H. Macneil   7132

"O KENMURE'S ON AND AWA', WILLIE" e 102, 105   words by R. Burns   7133

"O GIN MY LOVE WERE YON RED ROSE" e 101, 102, 105   words by R. Burns   7134

"O, LAY THY LOOF IN MINE, LASS"; Cordwainer's March (tune); "A slave to Love's unbounded sway" (verse)   7135
    e 101, 232   words by R. Burns

O LOVE WILL VENTURE IN; "O love will venture in, where it daurna weel be seen" e 100, 105   words by R. Burns   7136

O MOUNT AND GO; "O mount and go, mount and make ye ready"; "When the drums do beat" (verse) e 100   7137
    words by R. Burns

OH, MY BONNY HIGHLAND LADDIE; "Our gallant prince is now come hame" e 294   7138

"O NANCY'S HAIR IS YELLOW LIKE GOWD" e 102   7139

OH! OPEN THE DOOR; The braes of Boyndlie (tune); "Oh, open the door, some pity to shew" e 100, 105   words   7140
    by R. Burns

O PUIRITH CAULD; I had a horse (tune); "O puirith cauld, an' restless love" e 101   words by R. Burns   7141

O, RATTLIN', ROARIN' WILLIE; "O, rattlin', roarin' Willie, O he held to the fair" e 101   words by R. Burns   7142

O SAW YE BONNIE LESLEY?; "O saw ye bonnie Lesley as she gaed owre the border?" e 101; "O saw ye bonnie   7143
    Lesley as she ga'ed o'er the border?" e 18

O THIS IS NO MY AIN LASSIE; This is no my ain house (tune); "O this is no my ain lassie, fair tho' the lassie be"   7144
    e 18, 100, 105

"O TRUE LOVE IS A BONNIE FLOWER"; Twine the Plaiden (tune) e 105   words by C. Gray   7145

O WALY, WALY; "O waly, waly, up the bank, and waly, waly doun the brae" e 100, 103   7146

"O, WERT THOU IN THE CAULD BLAST"; Lennox love to Blantyre (tune) e 101, 105, 232, 365   words by R. Burns   7147

"O, WILLIE BREWED A PECK O' MAUT" e 101   words by R. Burns   7148

OCH, HEY! JOHNNIE LAD; "Och, hey! Johnnie lad, ye're no sae kind's ye should hae been" e 101, 103   words   7149
    by R. Tannahill

O'ER THE WATER TO CHARLIE; "Come boat me o'er, come row me o'er" e 365   words by R. Burns   7150

ON A BANK OF FLOWERS; "On a bank of flowers in a summer day" e 95   words by R. Burns   7151

ON CESSNOCK BANKS; The cardin' o't (tune); "On Cessnock banks there lives a lass" e 105   words by R. Burns   7152

"ON THE BANKS OF ALLAN WATER" e 18; ALLAN WATER e 402   7153

PIBROCH O' DONUIL DHU; Lochiel's march (tune); "Pibroch o' Donuil Dhu, pibroch o' Donuil, wake thy wild   7154
    voice anew" e 101; "Pibroch of Donald Dhu, pibroch of Donuil, wake thy wild voice anew" e 235;
    PIBROCH OF DONUIL DHU; "Pibroch of Donuil Bhu, Pibroch of Donuil, wake thy wild voice anew"
    e 18   words by W. Scott

THE PIPER O' DUNDEE; The drummer (tune); "The piper cam' to oor toon" e 163; "The piper cam' to oor toon"   7155
    e 18, 101, 102; "The piper came to our town" e 234; THE PIPER OF DUNDEE e 349

THE POOR AULD MAIDENS; "There's three score and ten of us, poor auld maidens" e 103, 104   7156

THE QUEEN'S MARIES; "Yestreen the Queen had four Maries"; "Oh! often hae I dress'd my Queen" (verse) e 100,   7157
    103, 104

ROBIN ADAIR; Eileen Aroon (tune); "What's this dull town to me?" e 28, 34, 235, 279, 349, 366, 402   words by R.   7158
    Burns See also 5901

ROBIN TAMSON'S SMIDDY; "My mither ment my auld breeks" e 102; words by A. Rodgers   7159

"A ROSEBUD BY MY EARLY WALK"; The shepherd's wife (tune) e 100, 104   words by R. Burns   7160

THE ROWAN TREE; "Oh! Rowan tree, oh! Rowan tree!" e 100, 104, 163, 349   words by B. Nairne   7161

"ROY'S WIFE O' ALDIVALLOCH"; The ruffian's rant (tune); "She vow'd, she swore she would be mine" (verse)   7162
    e 101   words by Mrs. Grant

SAW YE JOHNNIE COMIN'; "Saw ye Johnnie comin'? quo' she" e 101   7163

SCOTS WHA HAE; Hey Tuttie Tattie (tune); "Scots, wha hae wi' Wallace bled" e 17, 100, 102, 105, 232, 235, 365;   7164
    "SCOTS, WHA HAE WI' WALLACE BLED!" e 7, 163, 279, 349   words by R. Burns

SEE THE SMOKING BOWL; Jolly mortals, fill your glasses (tune); "See the smoking bowl before us" e 365   words   7165
    by R. Burns

SHE'S FAIR AND FAUSE; "She's fair and fause that causes my smart" e 100   words by R. Burns   7166

SIR PATRICK SPENS; "The King sits in Dumfernline Town" e 86   7167

THE SODGER'S RETURN; The mill, mill, O (tune); "When wild war's deadly blast was blawn" e 100   words by   7168
    R. Burns

WILL YE NO COME BACK AGAIN?; "Bonnie Charlie noo awa', safely owre the friendly main" e 163; "Bonnie   7206
    Charlie's noo awa', safely owre the friendly main" e 100,104; "Bonnie Charlie's now awa', safely
    owre the friendly main" e 349 words by B. Nairne
WILLIE'S GANE TO MELVILLE CASTLE; "O Willie's gane to Melville Castle" e 100,102   7207
"WILLIE'S RARE AND WILLIE'S FAIR" e 100,103,104   7208
"WILT THOU BE MY DEARIE?"; The Sutor's dochter (tune) e 18,101,105 words by R. Burns   7209
"THE WINTER IT IS PAST" e 101   7210
WITH LAUGHING LOOKS; JENNY; "With laughing looks I once arose, how dark soe'er the day" e 166,213   7211
    words by A. P. Graves
THE WRAGGLE-TAGGLE GYPSIES, O!; "There were three gypsies a-come to my door" e 35,70; THE GYPSIE   7212
    LADDIE; "He was a highborn gentleman" e 215
YE BANKS AND BRAES; Caledonian Hunt's delight (tune); "Ye banks and braes o' bonnie Doon, how can ye bloom   7213
    sae fresh and fair" e 34,100,103,104,235,297; YE BANKS AND BRAES O' BONNIE DOON e 163,
    399,402; THE BANKS O' DOON e 232,365; YE BANKS AN' BRAES; "Ye banks an' braes o' bonnie
    Doon, how can ye bloom sae fresh an' fair" e 17 words by R. Burns
THE YELLOW-HAIRED LADDIE; "The yellow-haired laddie sat on yon burn brae" e 100,104   7214

SOUTH AFRICA

AUNTIE MINA'S COOKING THE SIRUP; "Auntie Mina's cooking, cooking, the sirup"; "Tante Mins kook, o si   7215
    kook, o sy kook nou" af, e 239
THE CAPETOWN GIRLS; "The Capetown girls are pretty as can be"; "Die kaapse nooiens is wonderlik jaloers"   7216
    af, e 239
GERTJIE; "Set our wedding day, my Gertjie" e 86   7217
JAN PIERIEWIET; "Jan Pieriewiet, Jan Pieriewiet, Poor Jannie full of shame"; "Jan Pieriewiet, Jan Pieriewiet, Jan   7218
    Pieriewiet staan stil" af, e 239
MARCHING TO PRETORIA; "I'm with you and you're with me"; "Klap julle handjies"; "We are marching to   7219
    Pretoria" (ref) af, e 239
MEISIESFONTEIN; "By Meisiesfontein, die ware fontein"; "At Meisiesfontein I met her again" af, e 239   7220
"ON THE TOP OF THE HILL"; "Daar vêr oor die berg daar staan 'n blom" af, e 239   7221
ONIONS AND POTATOES; "Onions and potatoes, oh, ev'rybody here knows"; "Asrtappels en uiwe, waatlemoen   7222
    en druiwe" af, e 239
SARIE MARAIS; "My Sarie Marais is so vêr van my hart"; "Sarie Marais is so dear to my heart"; "O bring my   7223
    terug na die ou Transvaal" (ref); "Oh, take me back to the old Transvaal" (ref) af, e 239,384
SIEMBAMBA; "Siembamba mam se kindjie"; "Siembamba mammy's baby" af, e 239   7224
SUGARBUSH; "Sugarbush come dance with me"; VASTRAP; "Suikerbos ek wil jou hê" af, e 239   7225
THERE'S A CAPE-CART; "There's a Cape-cart! The cart has a load"; "Daar kom die wa" af, e 239   7226
TRAIN TO KIMBERLY; "Here comes the train, it's here again"; "So ry die trein" af, e 239   7227
TRANSVAALSCH VOLKSLIED; "Kent gij dat volk vol heldenmoed" d 384   7228
WIMOWEH; "Hey-yup! Boy. Wimoweh" e 389   7229
"THE WORLD IS VERY, VERY BIG"; "Die wereld die is baie groot" af, e 239   7230

SPAIN

"A MÍ ME GUSTA LO BLANCO" s 282   7231
AL PASAR POR SEVILLA; "Al pasar por Sevilla via a una chiquilla y me enamoré"; PASSING THROUGH SEVILLE;   7232
    "As I strolled through the busy park, waiting for my ship soon to go" e, s 219
"EL AMOR ES COMO UN NIÑO"; "L'AMOUR EST ENFANT VOLAGE" f, s 270   7233
ANDA, RESALADA; "Eres alta y delgadita como junco de ribera" s 282   7234
¡ARRE, BUEY!; "Desde la mi ventana te he visto arando"; GET UP, MY OX; "Under my window, hark to the   7235
    voice of plowman" e, s 219
ARRIBA CON ÉL; "Arriba con él, vamos a Viana arriba con él" s 282   7236
ARRIBA LAS BERZAS; "Arriba las berzas, abajo las coles" s 283   7237
ARROYO CLARO Y RONDÍN RONDANDO; "Arroyo claro, fuente serena" s 283; ARROYO CLARO; CLEAR BROOK;   7238
    "Oh, clear-running brook whose stream hurries by" e, s 219
"AY CON SAL, CON SAL" s 283   7239
¡AY! LINDA AMIGA; "¡Ay! linda amiga, que no vuelvo a verte"; AH! LOVELY LADY; "Ah! Lovely lady, to see   7240
    thee I sigh now" e, s 36
"AYER ME DIXO TU MADRE" s 283   7241
BAILACHE; "Bailache, bailache, bailache" s 283   7242
BAILE A LO ALTO; "Eres hija del sueño paloma mia" s 281   7243
BAILES DEL PANDERO; "Sal a bailar, buena moza" s 283   7244
BENDENKLICHKEITEN; "Grad aus dem Wirtshaus nun komm ich heraus" g 31,99; GRAD AUS DEM WIRTSHAUS   7245
    g 353; "GRAD AUS DEM WIRTSHAUS NUN KOMM ICH HERAUS" g 326

AA JÄNTA AA JA' "Aa jänta aa ja, aa janta aa ja, allt uppaa ländavagen, aa ja"; THE MAIDEN AND I; "The   7294
   maiden and I, the maiden and I, strolled where the flow'rs were growing, oh my!" e, sw 135

ACK, HÖR DU LILLA FLICKA; "Tra la la la la la"; "Ack, hör du lilla flicka, kom och laat oss dansa" (verse);   7295
   COME WITH ME; "Come with me my pretty little maiden, come with me a-dancing" (verse) e,
   sw 188; DAL-POLSKA; DALECARLIAN POLKA; "Come my fair maiden to me, let us join the
   dancing" (verse) e, sw 135

ACK VÄRMELAND, DU SKÖNA; "Ack Värmeland, du sköna, du härliga land!"; O VÄRMELAND; "O Värmeland,   7296
   of Sweden's fair counties the crown" e, sw 188; OH VAERMELAND, THE FAIREST; "Oh, Vaermeland, the fairest, the grandest of all" e, sw 135; VÄRMELAND; "O Värmeland, O homeland, O
   fair, happy land" e 95; VERMELAND; "Oh Vermeland, all praise to the wonderful land" e 279,366

ALL DAY WHILE I'M AT WORK; "All day while I'm at work, my love, I think and think of you" e 95   7297

"ALLS INGEN FLICKA LASTER JAG"; "I'LL NEVER PLAGUE A MAIDEN FAIR" e, sw 135   7298

ALLT UNDER HIMMELENS FÄSTE; "Allt under himmelens fäste där sitta stjärnor smaa"; THE STARS THEY   7299
   SHINE SO BRIGHTLY; "The stars they shine so brightly all in the sky above" e, sw 188; IN
   HEAVEN'S VAULT ABOVE ME; "In heaven's vault above me the little stars do shine" e, sw 45

BRÖLLOPSMARSCH FRAAN DELSBO; OLD DELSBO WEDDING MARCH piano 188   7300

BRUDSTASSEN; "Ja'minns ett bröllop i näste gaur"; THE WEDDING ARRAY; "I mind a wedding in yonder farm"   7301
   e, sw 230

DOMAREDANSEN; "Nu vilja vi begynna en domaredans"; THE JUDGE'S DANCE; "Let's start the judge's dance   7302
   he's come home to stay" e, sw 135

DU GAMLA, DU FRIA; "Du gamla, du fria, du fjällhöga Nord"; THOU ANCIENT, THOU FREE-BORN; "Thou   7303
   ancient, thou free-born, thou mountainous North" e, sw 188; "DU GAMLA, DU FRIA, DU FJÄLL-
   HÖGA NORD"; "OH BEAUTIFUL NORTHLAND, MY MOUNTAINOUS HOME" e, sw 135 words
   by R. Dybeck

FÄDERNESLANDET; "Härliga land, Frihetens stamort paa jorden!"; OH, FATHERLAND; "Beautiful land of   7304
   freedom and power and glory" e, sw 135

"EN GAANG I BREDD MED MIG"; "WHEN WE COME HAND IN HAND" e, sw 135   7305

GLÄDJENS BLOMSTER; "Glädjens blomster i jordens mill, ack visst aldrig gro"; FLOWERS OF JOY; "Flowers   7306
   of joy in the earth's dark mould, they can never thrive" e, sw 188; LITTLE FLOWERS SO BRIGHT
   AND GAY; "Little flowers so bright and gay, you no longer grow" e, sw 135

GODNATT; "Godnatt, godnatt, godnatt, O Sol!"; GOOD-NIGHT; "Good-night, good-night, good-night! Oh   7307
   sun" e, sw 135

GÖKVISA; "Du lilla spaaman, svara: O säg hur maanga aar"; OH LITTLE WIZARD, TELL ME; COO-COO SONG;   7308
   "Oh little wizard tell me: How long yet must I wait?" e, sw 135

GOTLANDSKADRILJ; GOTLAND QUADRILLE piano 188   7309

"HEUT SOLL DAS GROSSE FLACHSERNTEN SEIN"; Ny ska vi skörda linet i dag (tune) g 49,309   7310

I SIT ALONE; "I sit alone, all my friends are gone" e 95   7311

I SOMMARENS SOLIGA DAGAR; "I sommarens soliga dagar vi gaa genom skogar och hagar"; IN SUMMER THE SUN   7312
   SHINES SO CLEARLY; "In summer the sun shines so clearly through the meadow and wood we go
   cheering" e, sw 188 words by G. E. Johansson

IM FRÜHTAU ZU BERGE; "Im Frühtau zu Berge wir gehn, fallera" g 49,309,353; "Im Frühtau zu Berge wir ziehn,   7313
   falera" g 326

IT CANNOT BE; "My dear, I truly love you, and will for all my life" e 95   7314

"JAG TROR JAG FAAR BÖRJA ÖFVERGE ATT SÖRJA"; CARES I'LL TRY TO BANISH; "Cares I'll try to banish,   7315
   sorrows all must vanish" e, sw 135; COME PRETTY; "What's the use of grieving, though the
   world's deceiving?" e 95

"JAG VET EN DEJLIG ROSA"; "I KNOW A ROSE SO COMELY" e, sw 188   7316

JÖSSEHÄRADSPOLSKA; JÖSSEHÄRAD REEL piano 188   7317

JOY IN HEAVEN; "Joy's a flower can never grow till earth's troubles cease" e 95   7318

KRISTALLEN DEN FINA; "Kristallen den fina som solen maand' skina"; THOUGH CRYSTAL SHINES FAIRLY;   7319
   "Though crystal shines rarely like sunlight so clearly" e. sw 188; "Kristallen den fina sum solä
   maand' stijina"; LIKE A CRYSTAL SO FINE; "Like a crystal so fine, reflecting the sunshine" e,
   sw 230

LAMMEN HAR JAG; "Lammen har jag, baa' stora och smaa"; LAMBS HAVE I; "Lambs have I, both large and   7320
   small" e, sw 230

LILLA STINA; "Stina här här du mig"; STINA DEAR; "Stina dear, take my arm" e, sw 135   7321

MANDOM, MOD OCH MORSKE MÄN; "Mandom, mod och morske män Fins i gamla Sverige än"; MEN OF   7322
   COURAGE, STRENGTH, AND BRAWN; "Men of courage, strength, and brawn, Live in Sweden
   since the dawn" e, sw 135

MIDSUMMER NIGHT; "Come boys, now we'll light the fires" e 37   7323

NÄFVERVISEN; "Eja mit hjerta hur innerlig er fröjden"; THE BIRCHBARK SONG; "My heart, with inward peace,   7324
   adores creation" e, sw 231 words by E. Annersdatter

NÄR JAG BLEF SJUTTON AAR; "Fjorton aar tror jag visst att jag va'"; WHEN I WAS SEVENTEEN; "At the time I   7325
was fourteen years old" e, sw 135; "Fourteen years I had seem'd just to be" e, sw 137; "FJORTON
AAR TROR JAG VISST AAT JAG VAR"; FOURTEEN YEARS, I SHOULD SAY, WAS MY AGE" e, sw
188   words by H. Lilljebjörn

NECKEN; "Necken, han sjunger paa bölja blaa"; NEPTUNE; "I hear old Neptune with great delight" e, sw 135   7326

NECKENS POLSKA; "Djupt i hafvet paa demantehällen"; NEPTUNE'S POLKA; "On a diamond throne beneath   7327
the ocean" e, sw 135

OCH FLICKEN HON GAAR I DANSEN; "Och flickan hon gaar i dansen med rödan gullband"; A MAID, GOING   7328
TO A DANCE; "A maid, going to a dance, took red ribbons along" e, sw 135; ZUM TANZE, DA
GEHT EIN MÄDEL; "Zum Tanze da gehte ein Mädel mit güldenem Band" g 49,309,326

OCH HÖR DU UNGA DORA; "Och hör du unga Dora, vill du gifta dig i aar?"; OH ANSWER ME, MY DORA; "Oh   7329
answer me, my Dora, will this year find you wed?" e, sw 135; O LISTEN, PRETTY DORA; "O
listen, pretty Dora! Wilt thou marry me this year?" e, sw 188

"OCH JUNGFRUN GICK AAT KILLAN"; "THE MAIDEN TO THE WELL HAS GONE" e, sw 188   7330

ÖSTGÖTAPOLSKA; ÖSTGÖTA REEL piano 188   7331

OM SOMMAREN SKÖNA; "Om sommaren sköna, när marken hon gläds"; WHEN BRIGHT DAYS OF SUMMER;   7332
"When bright days of summer the earth do rejoice" e, sw 188   words by A. Wallenius

OXDANSEN; OX DANCE piano 188   7333

PER SVINAHERDE; "Per Svinaherde satte sig paa tufvan och sang"; PETER, THE SWINEHERD; "The swineherd   7334
Peter, sitting on the grass, sang this song" e, sw 135

PERHAPS WHEN LILIES BLOOM; "I have no mind for grieving, but grief holds me fast" e 95   7335

SJUNG; "Hvarför skall man tvinga mig att sjunga"; THE SINGER; "Why must I be singing, always singing?" e,   7336
sw 135

STOR OLA, LILL' OLA; "Stor Ola, lill' Ola! Nu körer jag vall"; BIG OLA, DEAR OLA; "Big Ola, dear Ola, I'm   7337
tending my flock" e, sw 230

SWEDISH CRADLE SONG; "Light and rosy by thy slumbers" e 343   7338

"TÄNKER DU, ATT JAG FÖRLORADER ÄR"; DO YOU THINK THAT I; "Do you think that I of heart-ache will   7339
die" e, sw 188

"TILL ÖSTERLAND VILL JAG FARA"; "I WOULD GO TO THAT EASTERN COUNTRY" e, sw 188   7340

TRÄSKODANSEN; CLOG DANCE piano 188   7341

UTI VAAR HAGE; "Uti vaar hage där växa blaa bär"; HERE IN OUR GROVE; "Here in our grove are blue bill-   7342
berries fair" e, sw 188; OUT IN THE GARDEN; "Out in our garden the blueberries grow" e, sw
231

VAART LAND; "Vaart land, vaart land, vaart fosterland"; "MY LAND, MY LAND, MY FATHERLAND" e, sw 135   7343
(not used)   7344

VAARVINDAR FRISKA, LEKA OCH HVISKA; "Vaarvindar friska, leka och hviska lunderna om likt älskander par";   7345
SPRING'S BREEZES PLAYING; "Spring's breezes playing over the spraying of tiny brooklets all
through the land" e, sw 135

"VI GAA ÖVER DAGGSTÄNKTA BERG"; "WE ROAM OVER HILLS DRENCHED WITH DEW" e, sw 188 words by   7346
O. Thunman

"VI SKA' STÄLLA TE'EN ROLIGER DANS"; LET US FROLIC IN DANCE LIGHT AND GAY; "Let us frolic in a dance   7347
light and gay" e, sw 135

VINDARNA SUCKA UTI SKOGARNA; "Vindarna sucka uti skogarna, forsarna brusa uti älvarna"; SOFT WINDS   7348
SIGH; "Soft winds sigh through the woods in Dalarna, swift-flowing rapids join the rivers" e, sw
188 words by O. Fredrik

VINGAAKERSDANSEN; VINGAAKER DANCE piano 188   7349

SWITZERLAND

ADDIO LA CASERMA; "Addio la caserma, con tutti gli ufficiali, sergentie caporali" i 155   7350

DAS ALTE GRENCHNER LIED; "Es het e Buur es Töchterli, mit Name heisst es Bäbeli" g 156   7351

DAS ALTE GUGGISBERGER LIED; "'s isch äben e Mönsch uf Ärde, Similibärg" g 156   7352

ALTES EMMENTALER KÜHERLIED; "Un uf der Wält si kener Lüt wie üser Chüejerknabe" g 158   7353

DAS BICOCCALIED DES NIKLAUS MANUEL; "Potz marter, Kueri Velti, du hast vil lieder gmacht" g 157   7354

CHANSON DES GUERRES DE FLANDRE; "Malgré la bataille qu'on donne demain" f 155   7355

CHELLELÄNDLER SPINNERLIEDLI; "Schnurre, schnurrenum und um, Rädle, trüll di umme" g 157   7356

COUCOU, CANARI JALOUX!; "Un soldat revenant de guerre et coucou!" f 155   7357

CUCÙ; "L'inverno l'è passato l'aprile non c'è più" i 155   7358

"DURD'S WIESETAL GANG I DURAB" g 156   7359

EMMENTALER HOCHZEITSTANZ; "Bin alben e wärti Tächter gsi" g 156   7360

ENTLEBUCHER KUHREIGEN; "Üsen Ätti dass er täti mit dem Chueli" g 156   7361

ES BUREBÜEBLI MAH-N-I NID; "Es Burebüebli man-n-i nid, das gseht me mir wohl a juhe!" g 49,156; HAG-   7362
ESTOLZIN g 31; ES BUREBÜEBLI MAN-N-I NIT; "Es Burebüebli man-n-i nit, das gseht me mir
wohl a, juhe!" g 41

ES ISCH KEI SÖLIGER STAMME; "Es isch kei söliger stamme, Oweder der Chüherstamm"; NO RACE THERE IS TO   7363
      VIE; "No race there is to vie, with our mountain herdsman stock" e, g 230
"ES KAM EIN HERR ZUM SCHLÖSSLI"; g 49,156; "TO A LITTLE CASTLE THERE CAME A KNIGHT" e, g 230   7364
DIE GEDANKEN SIND FREI; "Die Gedanken sind frei! Wer kann sie erraten?" g 49,309,353   7365
GSÄTZLI; "Durd's Oberland uf und durd's Oberland ab" g 156   7366
"HA AN EM ORT ES BLÜEMELI GSEH" g 158   7367
LA JARDINIÈRE DU ROI; "L'on dit, que la plus belle c'est toi, c'est toi" f 155   7368
KÜHERLIED DER EMMENTALER; "Was kann schöner sein, was kann edler sein" g 157   7369
KUHREIGEN; "Har Chüeli zum Brunne Gar wenig schint d'Sunne"; ALPINE COWHERD SONG; "Come, cows, to   7370
      the stream, in the sun's gentle gleam" e, g 230
LIEBESKLAGE; "Schätzeli, was trurist du weinist du, chlagist du?" g 157   7371
LIED AUF DIE SCHLACHT BEI NANCY; "Nun wend wir aber heben an das best" g 157   7372
MARION ET LE DRAGON; "Marion, joli Marion, veux tu faire campagne" f 155   7373
O, DU LIEBS ÄNGELI; "O, du liebs Ängeli, Rosmarinstängeli, o du liebs Härzeli, tue du nit eso!" g 156   7374
O, TAKE ME BACK TO SWITZERLAND; "By the dark waves of the rolling sea" e 279,366   7375
QUATTRO CAVAI CHE TROTTANO; "Quattro cavai che frottano sotto la timonella" i 155   7376
ROSSIGNOLET GENTIL, RAMÈNE-MOI MON AMI; "Auprès d'une fantaine était un peuplier" f 155   7377
'S HEIDELIDOMM; "Dei oben uff em Bergli stoht e bruni Heidelidomm" g 158; DEI OBEN UFF EM BERGLI g 41   7378
DER SCHEERSCHLEIFER; "Es chunt e frömde Schlyfer daher, er schlyft die Messer und die Scher" g 157   7379
SCHÖ IST DAS HENNELI; "Schö ist das Henneli am Morge off em Stengeli" g 158   7380
SCHÖNSTER ABESTÄRN. See 5536
SCHWYTZER HEIWEH; "Härz, mys Herz, warum so trurig?" g 158   7381
SKATE WITH ME; "Will you come and skate today with me?" e 343   7382
SON TRE MESI, CHE FO IL SOLDATO; "Son tre mesi, son tre mesi che fo il soldato" i 155   7383
SORGEN UND TRAUREN; "Sorgen und Trauren schikket sich allezeit numme für Bauren und gar nicht für mich"   7384
      g 158
"STETS IN TRURE MUESS I LEBE" g 158   7385
ULLI U ELSI; "Ulli, myn Ulli, chum du zu mir z'Chilt" g 158   7386
LA VA IN FILANDA; "La va in filanda perchè l'è bella l'èmorettinella la mi piace al cuor" i 155   7387
"VON LUZERN UF WEGGIS ZU" g 326   7388
VON MEINEN BERGEN MUSS ICH SCHEIDEN; "Von meinen Bergli muss i scheiden, wos so liebli is, so schön" g   7389
      326; ABSCHIED; "Von meinen Bergen muss ich scheiden, wo's gar so lieblich ist und schön " g 31
"WIE CHRISTUS, DER HERR, AM OELIBERG GING" g 157   7390
ZU STRASSBURG AUF DER SCHANZ; "Zu Strassburg auf der Schanz, da fängt mein Unglück an" g 158   7391

SYRIA

THE SUN OF SUNS; "O see, how dazzling is the glory of the risen sun!" e 37   7392

TURKEY

BUY MY SWEETS; "Bright shining star they call me"; "Who will buy my sweets" (chorus) e 37   7393

UNITED STATES

ABALONE; "In Carmel Bay the people say" e 321   words by G. Sterling   7394
ABDUL ABULBUL AMIR; "The sons of the Prophet are brave men and bold" e 225; ABDULLAH BULBUL AMEER;   7395
      IVAN PETRUSKI SKIVAR; "The sons of the Prophet were hardy and bold" e 343
ADAM AND EVE'S WEDDING SONG; "When Adam was created, he dwelt in Eden's shade" e 212   tune and words   7396A
      att to A. Lincoln
WHEN ADAM WAS CREATED; "When Adam was created, he dwelt in Eden's shade" e 109,110   7396B
ADIÓS MI SUEÑO; "Adiós mi sueño de venturanza"; FAREWELL MY DREAM; "Farewell my dream of joy and for-   7397
      tune" e, s 113
AH, POOR BIRD; "Ah, poor bird, take your flight far above the sorrows of this sad night" 4 pt round e 293   7398
AIN'T GONNA RAIN; "It ain't gonna rain, it ain't gonna snow" e 321; IT AIN'T GONNA RAIN e 132   7399A
AIN'T GONNA RAIN NO MO'; "Oh, it ain't gonna rain, it ain't gonna snow" e 185   7399B
'T AINT GWINE RAIN NO MO'; "'Taint gwine hail, 'taint gwine snow" e 80   7399C
ALABADO; "Praised and exalted be the Divine Sacrament"; "Alabado y ensalzado sea el Divino Sacramento"   7400
      e, s 109,110
ALL ROUND THE KITCHEN; "All around the kitchen, Cocky doodle doodle do"; "Now stop right still Cocky   7401
      doodle doodle do" (verse) e 214
"ALL DAY SINGIN' SUPPER ON THE GROUND" e 381   7402
ALL THE PRETTY LITTLE HORSES; "Hush-a-by, don't you cry, go to sleepy little baby" e 216; "Hush-you-bye   7403
      don't you cry, go to sleepy little baby" e 227; THE LITTLE HORSES e 84

"ALL WE DO IS SIGN THE PAY-ROLL" e 129,130   7404

THE ALPHABET SONG; "Mother may I go out to swim?" e 249   7405

AMAR, AMAR; "Amar, amar como nunca jamás habrán amado"; LOVE SONG; "To love and love as no one has   7406
  ever loved before" e, s 113

AMAZING GRACE; "Amazing grace, how sweet the sounds" e 227   7407

AMERICA; "My country 'tis of thee" e 7,10,32,233,236,279,343; "MY COUNTRY 'TIS OF THEE" e 28,129,130, 7408
  321,366 words by S. F. Smith; "God bless our native land" e 28,321; "God save America" e 321;
  "There are no lice on us" e 321 See also 4614

AN AMERICAN FRIGATE; "An American frigate called Richard by name" e 44   7409A

PAUL JONES; "An American frigate from Baltimore came" e 72   7409B

PAUL JONES' VICTORY; "An American frigate, a frigate of fame" e 110   7409C

ANALIZATION; "What are mortals made of?" e 225   7410

ANDREW BARDEEN. See 4631B

THE ANGEL BAND; "There was one, there was two, there was three little angels" e 332; BAND OF ANGELS;   7411
  "There was one, there were two, there were three little angels" e 216

THE ANIMAL FAIR; "I went to the animal fair" e 225   7412

"ARE YOU ANGRY WITH ME DARLING"; "Time will change in knowledge" (ref) e 132   7413

ARKANSAS TRAVELER; "Down on a farm in Arkansas" e 185; "O once upon a time in Arkansas" e 35; ARKAN-   7414
  SAS TRAVELLER; "How do you do stranger?" (words spoken) e 225

AS I WALKED OUT ONE MAY MORNING; "As I walked out one May morning just as the sun was rising"; "I'm   7415
  going to the meeting, do you want to come along" (ref) e 44

AUNT RHODY; "Go tell Aunt Rhody" e 170,173,389; "GO TELL AUNT RHODIE" e 185,216; "GO TELL AUNT   7416
  NANCY"; GO TELL AUNT RHODY; THE OLD GREY GOOSE e 249; "GO TELL AUNT NANCY"
  e 227

AUNT SAL'S SONG; "A gentleman came to our house" e 312   7417

AWAKE, AWAKE; "Awake, awake, ye drowsy sleepers" e 72   7418A

THE DROWSY SLEEPER; "Awake, awake, you drowsy sleeper" e 312   7418B

A-WALKIN' AND A-TALKIN'; "A-walkin' and a-talkin', a-walkin' goes I" e 72   7419

AWAY DOWN EAST; "There's a famous fabled country never seen by mortal eyes" e 189   7420

BACON ON THE RIND; "A soldier in the cavalry lay on a canvas bunk" e 225   7421

THE BALLAD OF THE TEA PARTY; Come and listen to my ditty (tune); The sailor's complaint (tune); "Tea ships 7422
  near to Boston lying" e 173

THE BALLAD OF THE THUNDERHEAD; "There were two wild stallions on the mountain" e 170 words by B. Ives   7423

BANJO SAM; "Catfish, catfish, goin' up stream" e 392   7424

THE BANKS OF SWEET DUNDEE; UNDAUNTED MARY; "There was an orphan female whose fortune was not told"   7425A
  e 81

THE BANKS OF SWEET DUNDEE; "It's of a wealthy farmer, lived on the banks of sweet Dundee" e 72   7425B

THE BANKS OF THE SACRAMENTO; "Ho! Boys Ho! For California Ho!" e 115   7426

BARBARA ALLEN. See 4545A,F,G,H,I,J,K

BARBER'S CRY; "Lather and shave, lather and shave" e 110   7427

THE BATCHELOR'S LAMENT; "Returning home at close of day" e 189   7428

THE BATTLE OF SARATOGA; "Come unto me, ye heroes, and I the truth will tell" e 173   7429

BE QUIET DO! I'LL CALL MY MOTHER; "As I was sitting in a wood" e 189   7430

BEANS, BACON AND GRAVY; "I was born long ago in 1894" e 293   7431

THE BEE; "As Cupid in a garden strayed; Transported with the damask shade" e 109,110   7432

THE BEE AND THE PUP; "There was a bee-i-ee-i-ee" e 28,366   7433

THE BELL COW; "Partridge in the pea patch picking up the peas" e 214   7434

"THE BELL DOTH TOLL" 3 pt round e 28,114,366   7435

THE BELL IS RINGING; "Hark! the bell is ringing, calling us to singing" 3 pt round e 28,366   7436

BENEATH THE WILLOWS; "Oh, my heart is sad and lonely, where is now the one I love? e 242   7437

BETSY B.; "O Betsy B. was a lady fair that late came from Lancashire" e 72   7438

BIBLE STORIES; "Young folks, old folks, ev'rybody come"; "God made the world in six days and rested on the 7439
  seventh" (verse) e 72

THE BIG CORRAL; "That big husky brute from the cattle chute"; "Press along, cowboy, Press along with a cowboy 7440
  yell" (ref) e 214; "That chuck wagon brute from the cattle chute"; "Press along, cowboy, press
  along, press along with a cowboy yell" (ref) e 335

BIG-EYE RABBIT; "The rabbit is the kind of thing that travels in the dark"; "Big-eye Rabbit, Boo! Boo!" (ref) 7441
  e 214

BIG ROCK CANDY MOUNTAIN; "Oh, the buzzin' of the bees and the cigarette trees" (ref); "On a summer's day 7442A
  in the month of May" (verse) e 171; "On a summer day in the month of May" (verse); "Oh! the
  buzzin' of the bees in the cigarette trees" (ref) e 129,130

BIG ROCK CANDY MOUNTAINS; "One evening, as the sun went down"; "In the Big Rock Candy mountains,   7442B
  there's a land that's fair and bright" (ref) e 34,227

THE BILLBOARD; "As I was walking down the street a billboard met my eye" e 225   7443

BILLY BOY. See 4549B

BILLY THE KID; "I'll sing you a true song of Billy the Kid" e 80 — 7444

BINGO; "Here's to good old Yale, drink it down, drink it down" e 225 — 7445

BINGO; "There was a farmer had a dog and Bingo was his name-o" e 216 — 7446

BIRD COURTSHIPS; THE BIRD SONG; THE BIRD'S COURTING SONG; DIL-DO-DAY; "'Hi!' said the blackbird — 7447
    sittin' on a chair" e 406; BIRD SONG; "'Hi', says the blackbird, sittin' on a chair" e 225; THE
    BIRDS' COURTING SONG; "'Hi!' said the blackbird sitting on a chair" e 110; "Hi, says the black
    bird sitting on a chair" e 216

BIRDIE; "There's others that are much more handsome" e 381 — 7448

THE BIRD'S BALL; "The brook once said to the nightingale" e 249 — 7449

BLACK IS THE COLOR; "Black, black, black, is the color of my true love's hair" e 227; BLACK IS THE COLOR — 7450A
    OF MY TRUE LOVE'S HAIR e 264

BLACK, BLACK, BLACK IS THE COLOR; "Black, black, black is the color of my true love's hair" e 215; BLACK — 7450B
    IS THE COLOR OF MY TRUE LOVE'S HAIR e 36

BLACK IS THE COLOR; "Black is the color of my true love's hair" e 72 — 7450C

BLACK IS THE COLOR OF MY TRUE LOVE'S HAIR; "But black is the color of my true love's hair" e 312 — 7450D

BLACK JACK DAVY; "Black Jack Davy came a-riding thro' the woods" e 243 — 7451

BLACK TAIL RANGE; "I am a roving cowboy from off the western Plains" e 120 — 7452

THE BLACKBIRD AND THE CROW; "Blackbird says unto the crow" e 392 — 7453

BLACKEYED SUSIE; "All I want in the creation, pretty little wife and a big plantation" e 227 — 7454

BLEEDING SAVIOUR; "Alas! and did my Saviour bleed" e 212 — 7455

BLENDON; "Jesus, my all, to heav'n is gone" e 212 — 7456

BLOOD ON THE SADDLE; "There was blood on the saddle" e 186; "There was bul-led on the saddle" e 80 — 7457
    words by E. Cheetham

BLUE MOUNTAIN LAKE; "Come all you good fellers, wherever you be" e 227 — 7458

THE BLUE TAIL FLY; "When I was young I used to wait on my master and give him his plate"; "Jimmie crack — 7459A
    corn and I don't care" (ref) e 173; "When I was young I used to wait on master and hand him the
    plate"; "Jimmy crack corn, but I don't care" (ref) e 44; "When I was young, I used to wait on
    master and give him his plate"; "Jimmy crack corn, and I don't care" (ref) e 293; YOU WHO
    DON'T BELIEVE IT; "There is no land upon the earth, contains the same amount of worth"; "You
    who don't believe it" (ref) e 173

DE BLUE-TAIL FLY; "When Ah was young Ah use' to wait on Massa and hand him de plate"; "Jimmy crack corn — 7459B
    an' Ah don' care" (ref) e 80; THE BLUE-TAIL FLY; "When I was young I use' to wait on Massa an'
    hand him his plate" e 35; "When I was young I used to wait, on my ole Massa, hand him de plate";
    "Jimmy crack corn an' I doan care" (ref) e 399; "When I was young I used to wait on master and
    hand him his plate"; "Jim crack corn, I don't care" (ref) e 216

THE BLUE-TAIL FLY; JIM CRACK CORN; "When I was young, I used to wait on my old Massa and hand his plate"; — 7459C
    "Jim crack corn, I don't care" (ref) e 185

THE BLUE TAIL FLY; "When I was young I used to wait on old massa and hand him his plate"; "Jim crack corn, — 7459D
    I don't care" (ref) e 331; JIM CRACK CORN; THE BLUE TAIL FLY; "When I was young I us'd to
    wait on Massa and hand him de plate" e 212

THE BOATMEN'S DANCE; "High row the boatmen row" (ref); "The boatmen dance, the boatmen sing" e 83; — 7460A
    THE BOATMEN'S SONG; "High ho, the boatmen row"; "Then dance, the boatmen, dance!" (ref)
    e 335 words att to D. D. Emmett

DE BOATMAN DANCE; "De boatman dance, de boatman sing"; "Dance de boatman dance" (ref) e 185 — 7460B

DE BOATMAN; "Hio, Hio, Hio de boatman row" (ref); "O de boatman dance, de boatman sing" e 343 words — 7460C
    att to D. D. Emmett

THE BOLD FISHERMAN; "There was a bold fisherman who sailed out from Pimlico"; "Singing twinkeedoodleum, — 7461
    twinkeedoodleum" (ref) e 44; "There was a bold fisherman who sailed out from Pimbeco"; "Sing-
    ing 'Twinkidoodledum, twinkidoodledum'" (ref) e 335; "'Twinkidoodledum, twinkidoodledum'"
    (ref) e 214

THE BOLD SOLDIER; "Soldier, O soldier, a-comin' from the plain" e 173 — 7462A

THE BOLD SOLDIER; "There was a bold soldier that lately came from war" e 72 — 7462B

THE BOLD TRELLITEE. See 4617H

THE BONNY LABORING BOY; "As I strolled out one morning all in the bloom of spring" e 72 — 7463

EL BORRACHITO; "Por la calle van vendiendo"; THE LITTLE DRUNKARD; "Down the street I hear them selling" — 7464
    e, s 113

BOSTON BURGLAR; "I belong to Boston City, boys, a place you all know well" e 172 — 7465

THE BOSTON TEA TAX; "I snum I am a Yankee lad, and I guess I'll sing a ditty" e 173; TEA TAX SONG; "The — 7466A
    other day the folks round here were mad about the taxes" e 145

TEA TAX; "I snum I am a Yankee lad, and I guess I'll sing a ditty" e 225 — 7466B

BOTANY BAY; "I was brought up in London town" e 126 — 7467

BOUND FOR CANAAN; "O when shall I see Jesus" e 212 — 7468

THE BRATS OF JEREMIAH; UNHAPPY JEREMIAH; "I've oft-times heard of married life and pleasures without 7469
    equal" e 72

BRAVE WOLFE; "Cheer up your hearts, young men" e 110; "Come, all you old men all" e 186 7470A

BRAVE WOLFE; "Bad news has come to town" e 227 7470B

BRENNAN ON THE MOOR. See 5882C

"BRIGHT MORNING STARS ARE RISING" e 332 7471

BRIGHT PHOEBE; "Bright Phoebe was my true love's name" e 72 7472

THE BRIGHT SUNNY SOUTH; "The bright sunny South was in peace and content" e 72 7473

"BRING ME ON MY SUPPER, BOYS" e 321 7474

LA BRISA; "Brilla la noche serena"; THE BREEZE; "Quietly gleams the starlit night" e, s 113 7475

BROKEN ENGAGEMENT; "They were standing by the window" e 243 7476

BUCKEYE JIM; "Way up yonder above the moon, a jaybird lived in a silver spoon"; "Go limber, Jim; you can't 7477A
    go" (ref) e 34

BUCKEYE JIM; "'Way up yonder above the sky, a bluebird lived in a jaybird's eye"; "Buckeye, Jim, you can't 7477B
    go" (ref) e 227

BUFFALO GALS; "As I was lumb'ring down de street, down de street"; "Buffalo gals, can't you come out tonight?" 7478A
    (ref) e 10,129,130,132; "As I was lumb'ring down the street, down the street" e 399; "Oh, Buffalo
    Gals, won't you come out tonight" (ref) e 185; LUBLY FAN; "As I was lumb'ring down de street,
    down de street"; "Den lubly Fan will you cum out tonight" e 109,110; RIG-A JIG-JIG; "As I was
    lumb'ring down the street, down the street"; "Oh, Rig-a jig-jig and away we go" (ref) e 214; "As
    I was walking down the street, heigh-o, heigh-o"; "Rig-a-jig-jig, and away we go" (ref) e 343

BUFFALO GALS; "Buffalo gals, woncha come out tonight"; "I danced with a gal with a hole in her stockin'" 7478B
    (ref) e 227

BUFFALO GALS; "Buffalo gals, won't you come out tonight"; "Oh, won't you, won't you, won't you, won't you" 7478C
    (ref) e 173

LOUISIANA GIRLS; "As I was walkin' down the street, down the street"; "O Lou'siana girls, won't you come out 7478D
    tonight" (ref) e 37

THE BUFFALO SKINNERS; "'Twas in the town of Jacksboro in the year of seventy three" e 227; "'Twas in the 7479
    town of Jacksboro in the spring of seventy three" e 129; THE JOLLY LUMBERMEN; "Come all you
    jolly lumbermen and listen to my song" e 110

THE BULL-DOG; "Oh, the bulldog on the bank and the bullfrog in the pond" e 28,225,233,279,366 7480

BURRY ME BENEATH THE WILLOW; "My heart is sad and I am weeping"; "Oh, burry me beneath the willow" 7481
    (ref) e 129,130,132

BURY ME NOT ON THE LONE PRAIRIE; Hind Horn (tune); "Oh, bury me not on the lone prairie" e 186; THE 7482A
    DYING COWBOY e 10; THE LONE PRAIRIE e 120; "O BURY ME NOT ON THE LONE PRAIRIE"
    e 399

BURY ME NOT ON THE LONE PRAIRIE; "Oh, bury me not on the lone prairie" e 227; "OH BURY ME NOT ON 7482B
    THE LONE PRAIRIE" e 155

BURY ME NOT ON THE LONE PRAIRIE; THE DYING COWBOY; "Oh, bury me not on the lone prairie" e 129,130 7482C

BURY ME NOT ON THE LONE PRAIRIE; "Oh bury me not on the lone prairie" e 109,110 7482D

"OH, BURY ME NOT ON THE LONE PRAIRIE"; e 132; THE DYING COWBOY e 279,366 7482E

OH BURY ME NOT; "Oh bury me not on the lone prairie" e 236 7482F

THE BUTCHER BOY; "In yonder city where I did dwell" e 243; THE BUTCHER'S BOY; "In London City a lady 7483
    did dwell" e 81

BUY A BROOM; "Pretty lady, pretty gentleman, from mine Vaterland I do bring" e 189 7484

BYE, BABY BUNTING; "Bye baby bunting, Daddy's gone a-hunting" e 109,110 7485

THE CALIFORNIA PIONEERS; "I love this land, its sunny clime" e 189 7486

CANTO DE CUNA; "Arriba en el cielo esta una ventana"; CRADLE SONG; "There's an open window high up in 7487
    God's heaven" e, s 113

CAPTAIN JINKS; "I'm Captain Jinks of the Horse Marines" e 28,366; CAPTAIN JINKS OF THE HORSE MARINES 7488
    e 225

CAPTAIN KIDD; "Oh! My name was Robert Kidd, as I sailed, as I sailed" e 34,109,110; THROUGH ALL THE 7489A
    WORLD; "See springs of water rise, fountains flow, rivers run" e 109

THROUGH ALL THE WORLD; Captain Kidd (tune); "Through all the world below, God is seen all around" e 110 7489B

CAPTAIN KIDD; "Oh, my name was William Kidd, as I sailed, as I sailed" e 173; WONDROUS LOVE; "What 7489C
    wondrous love is this, oh! my soul, oh, my soul!" e 173

CARELESS LOVE; "Love, oh, love, oh, careless love" e 109,110,173,215,293,331; KELLY'S LOVE e 35; 7490A
    "Oh love, oh love, oh careless love" e 185; "Oh, it's love, oh, love, oh, careless love" e 399

CARELESS LOVE; "Love, O love, O careless love" e 227 7490B

CARELESS LOVE; "Mother, mother, tell me, do"; "Careless love, oh, careless love" (ref) e 242 7490C

CARELESS LOVE; "Captain, Captain, tell me true"; "Love, O love, O careless love" (ref) e 243 7490D

CAROLINE; "Aine, de, trois, Caroline"; "One, two, three, Caroline" e, f 219,279,366 7491

THE CARRION CROW; "A carrion crow sat on an oak" e 179 7492A

THE CARRION CROW; THE TAILOR AND THE CROW; "A carrion crow sat on an oak" e 267 7492B

CENTRAL WILL SHINE; "Central will shine tonight, Central will shine" e 28,366   7493

CHANSON DES FLEURS; "Cantons, chantons en choeur, Marguerites et Violettes"; FLOWER SONG; "Come now, let us join hands, Marguerites and Morning Glories" e, f 21   7494

THE CHEAT; "Up in Horse-pasture we used to go fishin'" e 381   7495

THE CHICKENS ARE A-CROWING; "The chickens they are crowing, a-crowing" e 109,110   7496

EL CHIFLIDO; "A la noche voy a verte"; THE WHISTLE; "Tonight in the cold and darkness" e, s 113   7497

CHING-A-RING CHAW; "Ching-a-ring-a ring ching ching"; "Brothers gather round, listen to this story" (verse) e 84   7498

CHRISTOPHER COLUMBO; "In fourteen hundred ninety-two, three ships set out to sea" e 44   7499

"CIGARETTES WILL SPOIL YOUR LIFE" e 321   7500

CINDY; "I wish I was a' apple, a-hangin' on a tree" e 80; "I wish I was an apple, a hangin' in a tree" e 110; "You ought-a see my Cindy, she lives away down South" e 227; "You ought to see my Cindy, she lives way down south" e 293   7501

LA CIRIACA; "Ay! Ciriaca tú no com prendes"; "AH! CIRIACA YOU DO NOT UNDERSTAND" e, s 113   7502

CO-CA-CHE-LUNK; "When we first came on this campus" e 225   7503

"COFFEE GROWS IN WHITE OAK TREES"; "Two in the center and turn about" (ref) e 185   7504A

"COFFEE GROWS ON WHITE OAK TREES"; "Two in the middle and I can't jump Josie" (verse); "Railroad, steamboat, river an' canoe" (finale) e 227   7504B

THE COLORADO TRAIL; "Eyes like the morning star, cheek like a rose"; "Weep all ye little rains" (ref) e 321   7505A

THE COLORADO TRAIL; "Eyes like the morning star, cheeks like a rose"; "Weep all ye little rains" (ref) e 321; ALONG THE COLORADO TRAIL; "Weep, all ye little rains"; "Eyes like the morning star, cheeks like the rose" (verse) e 389   7505B

"COME ALL YOU FAIR AND TENDER LADIES"; e 227; THE LITTLE SPARROW e 72   7506A

"COME ALL YE FAIR AND TENDER LADIES" e 265   7506B

COME HASTE TO THE WEDDING   unacc fiddle tune   212   7507

COME, O MY LOVE; "The winter has gone and the leaves turn green"; "Come, O my love, so fare you well" (ref) e 243   7508

COME OUT, YE CONTINENTALERS; "Come out, ye continentalers, we're going for to go" e 44   7509

COME, SAINTS AND SINNERS; "Come, saints and sinners, hear me tell the wonders of Immanuel" e 32,34   7510

CONFESS JEHOVAH; "Confess Jehovah thankfully, for He is good" e 109,110,173   7511

THE CONSTITUTION AND THE GUERRIERE; "It oft-times has been told that the British seamen bold" e 173   7512

THE CORDWOOD CUTTER; "Last Monday morning, 'bout half past five" e 72   7513

CORRIDO DE ELENA; "Elena, querida mía, y una cosa has de escuchar"; "Elena, dearest Elena, there's one thing that you must hear" e, s 314   7514

CORRIDO DE LA MUERTE DE ANTONIO MESTAS; "Año de milochocientos ochenta y nuéve pasó"; "In the year of eighteen hundred and eighty-nine in July" e, s 314   7515

COTTON-EYE JOE; "Where did you come from, Where did you go?" e 214   7516

COUNTING SONG; "Come let us sing. What shall we sing?" e 230   7517

THE COWBOY; "Now all the day long on the prairies I ride" e 120   7518

THE COWBOY; "Oh a man there lives on the western plain" e 129,130   7519

THE COWBOY'S CHRISTMAS BALL; "Way out in Western Texas where the Clear Fork waters flow" e 80   7520

COWBOY'S GETTIN'-UP A HOLLER; "Wake up, Jacob, day's a-breakin'" e 109,110   7521

COWBOY'S HEAVEN; "Last night as I lay on the prairie" e 120   7522

COWBOY'S LAMENT; "My home's in Montana, I wear a bandana" e 120   7523

THE COWBOY'S MEDITATION; "At midnight when the cattle are sleeping" e 10   7524

THE COWMAN'S PRAYER; "O Lord, please lend me now Thine ear" e 80   7525

CRAWDAD; "You get a line and I'll get a pole, baby" e 145; "You get a line and I'll get a pole, honey" e 44; THE CRAWDAD HOLE; "Now, you get a line and I'll get a pole, honey" e 216   7526A

THE CRAWDAD; "Ah got a hook and you got a line" e 32,34; THE CRAWDAD SONG; "Ah got a hook an' you got a line" e 80   7526B

SWEET THING; "What you gonna do when the liquor gives out, sweet thing?' e 227; CRAWDAD SONG; "Wake up, old man, you slept too late, this mornin'" e 227   7526C

THE CRAWFISH MAN; "Wake up darlin', don't sleep so late" e 216   7526D

CROOKED WHISKEY; "In the highest toned society"; "Come join us in the chorus while we sing" (ref) e 189   7527

CROW SONG; "There were three crows sat on a tree, O Billy Magee Magar" e 28,366   7528

THE CRUEL MOTHER; "Three little babies dancin' at the ball" e 262   7529A

DOWN BY THE GREENWOOD SHADY; "There was a maiden lived in New York" e 72   7529B

THE CUCKOO; "A boy went out to shoot one day" e 392   7530

THE CUCKOO; "The cuckoo is a funny bird" e 44; "The cuckoo she's a pretty bird" e 264   7531A

THE CUCKOO; "The cuckoo is a pretty bird, she sings as she flies" e 242   7531B

CUMBERLAND GAP; "Me an' my wife an' my wife's gran'pap all raise hell in Cumberland Gap" e 115; "Me and my wife and my wife's gran'pap all raise hell in Cumberland Gap" e 225   7532

THE CURTAINS OF NIGHT; "When the curtains of night are pinned back by the stars" e 132,343; "WHEN THE CURTAINS OF NIGHT ARE PINNED BACK" e 321   7533

CUTTING DOWN THE PINES; The Bigler's crew (tune); "Friends, if you will listen, I'll sing to you a song" e 72;   7534
    CRUISE OF THE BIGLER; "Come all my boys and listen a song I'll sing to you"; "Watch her! Catch
    her! Jump up her juberju!" e 145; THE BIGLER e 227

DANDOO; "There was a man lived in the west" e 110   7535

THE DARBY RAM. See 4578B, C, D

DARKY SUNDAY SCHOOL; "The earth was made in six days" e 225   7536

DARLIN' COREY; "Wake up, wake up, darlin' Corey" e 227; DARLIN' CORY; "Wake up, wake up, darlin' Cory"   7537A
    e 34

DARLING CORA; "Go dig a hole in the meadow" e 109, 110   7537B

DARLING COREY; "Wake up, wake up, Darling Corey" e 389   7537C

LITTLE CORY; "Wake up, wake up, little Cory!" e 312   7537D

THE DAYS OF '49; "I'm old Tom Moore from the bummer's shore" e 227; IN THE DAYS OF 'FORTY-NINE;   7538
    "There was old Bob Cloy, that could out-roar a buffalo bull, you bet" e 126

DEAF WOMAN'S COURTSHIP; "Old woman, old woman, are you fond of smoking?" e 216; "Old woman, old   7539
    woman, are you fond of spinning?" e 185; "Old woman, old woman, will you go a-shearing?"
    e 313

THE DEAR COMPANION; "I used to love in fond affection"; "O, go and leave me if you want to" e 81   7540

DEAR EVELINA, SWEET EVELINA; "Way down in the meadow where the lily first blows" e 129, 130; DEAR   7541
    EVELINA e 343

DEAREST BILLIE; "Yonder comes my dearest Billie" e 392   7542

DEATH; "Vain man, thy fond pursuits forbear" e 212   7543

THE DEATH OF QUEEN JANE; "Queen Jane lay in labor for six days or more" e 263; "Queen Jane was in labour   7544
    full six weeks and more" words by P. Papers; "Queen Jeanie, Queen Jeanie traveld six weeks and
    more" e 260 words by Kinloch, Ancient Scottish Ballads

THE DENS OF YARROW; "There were seven sons, and two of them twins" e 72   7545

DESVENTURADO; "Huyó veloz un tiempo de ventura"; THE TRAGIC LOVER; "Swiftly flies life's moment brief   7546
    of happiness" e, s 113

THE DEVIL'S NINE QUESTIONS; "Oh, you must answer my questions nine" e 44   7547A

THE DEVIL'S NINE QUESTIONS; "You must answer me questions nine" e 171, 173   7547B

RIDDLES WISELY EXPOUNDED; THE DEVIL'S TEN QUESTIONS; "If you don't answer my questions well" e 262   7547C

THE DODGER; "Yes the candidate's a dodger" e 83; THE DODGER SONG e 293   7548

DOG AND CAT; "Bought me a dog, bought me a cat" e 242   7549

THE DOG-CATCHER'S CHILD; "Oh, the moon shines tonight on the river" e 225   7550

A DOLLAR AIN'T A DOLLAR ANYMORE; "I was feeling kind of hungry" e 293 words by T. Glazer   7551

THE DONKEY; "Sweetly sings the donkey at the break of day" 3 pt round e 28, 343   7552

DOWN IN A COAL MINE; "Down in a coal mine, underneath the ground" e 115, 129, 130, 132, 214   7553

DOWN IN THE VALLEY; "Down in the valley, the valley so low" e 173   7554A

DOWN IN THE VALLEY; "Down in the valley, valley so low" e 227   7554B

DOWN IN THE VALLEY; "Down in the valley, the valley so low" e 35, 37   7554C

DOWN IN THE VALLEY; "Down in the valley, valley so low" e 393   7554D

THE VALLEY SO LOW; "Down in the valley, valley so low" e 242   7554E

DOWN IN THE VALLEY; "Down in that valley, that valley so low" e 267   7554F

"DOWN IN THE WILLOW GARDEN" e 227   7555

DOWN THE RIVER; "The water is bright and shining" e 44   7556

DREARY LIFE; "Come, all you jolly cowboys" e 120   7557

DRILL YE TARRIERS, DRILL. See 612

THE DRUNKARD; "At an early dawn I spied a man" e 243   7558

THE DURANT JAIL; "The Durant jail beats no jail at all" e 227   7559

DUTCH WARBLER; DER DEITCHER'S DOG; In Lauterbach hab' ich mein' Strumpf verloren (tune); "Oh where, oh   7560
    where ish mine little dog gone" e 225; WHERE IS MY LITTLE DOG GONE; "Oh where, oh where
    is my little dog gone" e 128, 132 words by S. Winner

THE DYING CALIFORNIAN; "Lay up nearer, brother, nearer" e 110   7561

THE DYING SERGEANT; "Come all you heroes, where'er you be" e 126   7562

EATING GOOBER PEAS; "Sitting by the roadside on a summer day" e 225; GOOBER PEAS e 44, 161; "Sitting by   7563
    the roadside on a summer's day" e 169 att to P. Nutt, words by A. Pindar

EDWARD; "How come that blood on your own coat sleve"; "What bluid's that on thy coat lap" e 260 words from   7564A
    Motherwell's MS.

EDWARD; "What makes that blood on the point of your knife?" e 173   7564B

EF I HAD A RIBBON BOW; "Ef I had a ribbon bow to bind my hair" e 265   7565

EGGS AND MARROWBONE; "There was an old woman in our town" e 111   7566

EL-A-NOY; "'Way down upon the Wabash, Sich land was never known" e 34, 110, 145, 279   7567A

THE PLAINS OF ILLINOIS; "Come all you good old farmers that on your plow depend" e 72   7567B

EL CHARRO. See 6336

ELENA; "Estaba una niña"; "A MAIDEN EMBROIDERED" e, s 113   7568

GEORDIE (A TRAGIC LEGEND); "As I walked over London Bridge, one morning that was foggy" e 267   7607A

GEORGIE, O; "Come bridle me up my milkwhite steed" e 392   7607B

GEORGE COLON; "George Colon rode home one cold winter night" e 243   7608

GEORGIA; "I'm going back to Georgia, I'm going back to Rome" e 242   7609

GET OFF THE TRACK!; "Ho! the car emancipation rides majestic thro' our nation" e 189   7610

GET THE MONEY; "It makes no diff'rence where you are" e 321   7611

GILES COLLINS; GEORGE COLLINS; JOHNNY COLLINS; "Giles Collins said to his mother one day" e 81   7612

GIPSY LADDIE; "A gipsy lad was a-ridin' one day" e 399   7613

GIT ALONG LITTLE DOGIES; "As I was a-walking one morning for pleasure" e 120, 227; "When I was a walking   7614A
one morning for pleasure" e 145; WHOOPI-TI-YI-YO; "As I was a-walking one morning for pleasure" e 216

WHOO-PEE TI YI YO; GIT ALONG, LITTLE DOGIES; "As I was a-walking one morning for pleasure" e 129, 130,   7614B
236; WHOOPEE TI-YI-YO! GIT ALONG LITTLE DOGIES! e 10, 279, 366

WHOOPEE TI-YI-YO; "As I was a-walkin' one mornin' for pleasure" e 35   7614C

YIPPY TI-YI-YO, GIT ALONG, LITTLE DOGIES; "As I was a-walkin' one mornin' for pleasure" e 185   7614D

THE GLORIOUS FOURTH; "We'll march and shout hurrah!" e 129, 130   7615

THE GLORY TRAIL; HIGH CHIN BOB; "'Way up high in the Mogollons, among the mountain tops" e 80   words   7616
by B. Clark

GO GET THE AXE; "Peepin' through the knot-hole of grandpa's wooden leg" e 110   7617

GO TER SLEEP; "Go ter sleep, go ter sleep, go ter sleepy, mammy's baby" e 95; GO TO SLEEPY e 109, 110   7618A

GO TO SLEEP; "Go to sleep, go to sleep, go to sleep little baby" e 242   7618B

THE GOAT SONG; "There was a man, now please take note" e 249   7619

GOD, OUR FATHER; "God, our Father, gives to each one" e 242   7620

GOD SAVE AMERICA; "God save us from ev'ry foe" e 189   7621

GOD SAVE THE PEOPLE; "When wilt Thou save the people?" e 321   words by E. Elliot   7622

GOIN' DOWN TO TOWN; "I used to have a ol' gray hoss, he weigh' ten thousand pound " e 80   7623

GOIN' TO BOSTON; "Goodbye girls, I'm goin' to Boston"; "Won't we look pretty in the ballroom?" (ref) e 312;   7624
"Come on, girls, I'm goin' to Boston"; "Don't we look pretty when we're dancing" (ref) e 185;
GOING TO BOSTON; "Come along girls, we're going to Boston"; "Don't we look pretty when we're
dancing" (ref) e 216

GOIN' UP THE RIVER; "Goin' up the river from Catlettsburg to Pike" e 110   7625

THE GOLDEN WILLOW TREE. See 4617E, F, G

LAS GOLONDRINAS; "Volverán las oscuras golondrinas"; THE SWALLOWS; "Dusky wingéd swallows will return   7626
again" e, s 113

GOODBYE, MY LOVER, GOODBYE!; "The ship goes sailing down the bay" e 205, 236, 366   7627

GOOD-BYE, OLD PAINT; "Good-bye, old Paint, I'm a-leaving Cheyenne" e 109, 110, 236; "Good-bye, Old   7628A
Paint, I'm leaving Cheyenne" e 214; GOOD-BY, OLD PAINT; "Good-by, old Paint, I'm a-leaving
Cheyenne" e 335; OLD PAINT; "Good-by, old Paint, I'm a-leavin' Cheyenne" e 227

GOODBYE OLD PAINT; "Good-by, you old Paint, I'm a-leaving Cheyenne" e 120   7628B

GOOD-NIGHT, LADIES; "Good-night, ladies! good-night, ladies!"; "Merrily we roll along, roll along, roll along"   7629
(ref) e 28, 132, 233, 236, 279, 343, 366, 402

GRADUATION SONG; "Our school-days now are past and gone" e 28, 366   words by G. Cooper   7630

GRANDMA GRUNTS; "Grandma Grunts said a curious thing" e 392   7631

THE GRAVE IN THE CLEARIN'; "Oh, follow the stream to the clearin'" e 381   7632

THE GRAVE OF BONAPARTE; "On a lone barren isle, where the wild roaring billow assail the stern rock" e 212   7633

GREAT BIG STARS; SHINE, SHINE; "Great big stars, 'way up yonder" e 332   7634

GREAT GRAND-DAD; "Great grand-dad when the land was young" e 120   7635A

GREAT GRANDAD; "Great Grandad when the West was young" e 225   7635B

GREAT-GRANDDAD; "Great-granddad, when the land was young" e 44, 80   words by J. Lambert   7635C

THE GREAT PACIFIC RAILROAD; "The great Pacific railroad for California hail!" e 145   7636

THE GREAT ROUND UP; "When I think of the last great round up" e 10   7637

GREEN CORN; "Wake, snake, dawn's a-breakin'" e 389   7638

GREEN GROW THE LILACS; "Green grow the lilacs, all covered with dew" e 44; "Green grow the lilacs, all   7639
sparkling with dew" e 35

GREEN GROW THE RUSHES, HO; "I'll sing you one-ho! Green grow the rushes-ho" e 35; GREEN GROW THE   7640
RUSHES-O; "I'll sing you one-o. Green grow the rushes-o" e 44

THE GREEN MOUNTAIN YANKEE; "I'm right from the mountain just from Vermont" e 189   7641

GREENFIELDS; "How tedious and tasteless the hours" e 34, 212   words by J. Newton   7642

GROUND-HOG; "Get out your gun and call your dog" e 185; "Old Joe Digger, Sam and Dave" e 227; "Shoulder   7643A
up your gun and call your dog" e 109, 110; "Shoulder up yuh gun an' call up yuh dog" e 80; JIM
CROW; "Lincoln set the Negro free" e 293   words by Almanac Singers

GROUND-HOG; "Whet up your knife and whistle up your dog" e 393; "Whet up your knives and whistle up your   7643B
dogs" e 313

A GROUNDHOG; "Get up your gun an' call up your dawg" e 242   7643C

GROUNDHOG; "Get up your guns and call up your dogs" e 243   7643D

GUAJITO; "Guajito a dónde te vas Guajito"; "Guajito, where do you go tomorrow my handsome Guajito" e, s   7644
113

"GUIDE ME, O THOU GREAT JEHOVAH" e 312   7645

HA, HA, MY DARLIN' CHILE; "Somebody stole my li'l black dog" e 37   words by G. A. Miller   7646

HA, HA THIS-A-WAY; "When I was a little boy" e 214; HA, HA, THISAWAY e 44   7647

HAD A LITTLE ROOSTER; "Had a little rooster by the barnyard gate" e 214   7648

HALLELUJAH, I'M A BUM; "Oh, why don't I work like other men do?" e 35; "Oh, why don't you work like other   7649
     men do?" e 109,110,335; HALLELUJAH, I'M A-TRAVELIN'; "Stand up and rejoice!" e 293

THE HAND-CART SONG; "Ye saints who dwell on Europe's shore" e 173   7650

HANGSAMAN; "Slack your rope, hangsaman, O, slack it for awhile" e 109,110; THE MAID FREED FROM THE   7651A
     GALLOWS e 321

O JUDGES; THE HANGMAN'S TREE; "O judges, O judges, just hold your ropes a little little while" e 243   7651B

HARK! I HEAR A VOICE; "Hark I hear a voice Way up on the mountain top"; "Let us all unite in love" (ref)   7652
     e 28,366

HAVE YOU STRUCK ILE?; "From California ocean laved to old Virginia's shore"; "Hurrah! Hurrah! Rich treasures   7653
     in our 'Sile'" e 189   words by J. B. Quinby

HE CAME FROM HIS PALACE GRAND; "He came from his palace grand and he came to my cottage door"; "But I   7654
     am nothing to him" (ref) e 321

HEARSE SONG; The worms crawl in (tune); "Have you ever thought as the hearse goes by" e 225; "THE SCABS   7655
     CRAWL IN" e 293

HEIRLOOMS; "My mother she has an old spinning wheel" e 242   7656

HELLO! HELLO!; "Hello! Hello! Well, well, here we come singing" 2 pt round e 343   7657

"HERE COME THREE DUKES A-RIDING" e 185   7658

"HERE COME THREE MERCHANTS A-RIDING" e 109,110   7659

HE'S A FOOL; "One day while walking down Thirty Fifth Street" e 293;   words by United Wholesale and Ware-   7660
     house Workers Local 65, N.Y.

HE'S GONE AWAY; "I'm goin' away for to stay a little while" e 109,110,321; TEN THOUSAND MILES e 215   7661

HEY, BETTY MARTIN!; "Hey, Betty Martin, tippy toe, tippy toe"; "Skip with me, I'll skip with you" (verse)   7662
     e 216; "Hey, Betty Martin, tip-toe, tip-toe"; "Dance and play, let's be gay" (ref) e 185

HI HO THE PREACHER MAN; "Hi ho the Preacher Man! He can preach and he can pray" e 265   7663

THE HILLS OF GLENSHEE; "On a bright summer's morning the day was a-dawning" e 72   7664

HINKY DINKY PARLEY VOO; "Mademoiselle from Armentieres, parley voo" e 225; MADEMOISELLE FROM AR-   7665
     MENTIERES e 10; MADEMOISELLE FROM ARMENTIERES e 233; "Mademoiselle from Armentieres,
     parlay-vous?" e 227; "The Waves and Wacs will win the war" e 227; HINKY DINKY PARLAY-
     VOO; "Oh farmer have you a daughter fair, parlay voo" e 7; HINKY DINKY e 109,110; HINKY
     DINKY PARLEE VOO; "Two German officers crossed the Rhine, parlee-voo" e 132

HIRAM HUBBARD; "Hiram Hubbard was not guilty, I've heard great many say" e 312   7666

DE HISTORY OB DE WORLD; "O, I come from ole Virginny wid my head full ob knowledge" e 189   7667

HOG DROVERS; "Hog drovers, hog drovers, hog drovers are we" e 44   7668

HOLD ON; "Some of these days about four o'clock" e 231   7669

HOLD THE FORT; "We meet today in freedom's cause and raise our voices"; "Hold the fort for we are coming"   7670
     (ref) e 293

HOME ON THE RANGE; "Oh, give me a home where the buffalo roam" e 10,28,35,37,70,115,120,129,130,132,   7671
     227,233,236,279,329,343,364,366

HOOSEN JOHNNY; "De little black bull kem down de medder, Hoosen Johnny" e 216   7672

HOP UP, MY LADIES; "Hop up, my ladies, three in a row" e 214   7673

HORNET AND PEACOCK; "Ye Demo's attend and ye Federals, too" e 109,173   7674

THE HORSE NAMED BILL; "Oh, I had a horse and his name was Bill" e 321; THE CRAZY DIXIE; "I had a hoss,   7675
     his name was Bill" e 80

HOUND DOG; "Ev'ry time I come to town, the boys keep kickin' my dog around" e 171   7676

HOW ARE YOU GREEN-BACKS; "We're coming, Father Abram, one hundred thousand more" e 189   words by   7677A
     E. Bowers

WE ARE COMING, FATHER ABRA'AM; "We are coming, Father Abra'am, three hundred thousand more" e 279,   7677B
     366

HOW D'YE DO; "How d'ye do, Mister Johnson?" e 28,236,366   7678

HOW FIRM A FOUNDATION; "How firm a foundation, ye saints of the Lord" e 32,34   7679

HOW OLD ARE YOU. See 4702B

THE HUNTERS OF KENTUCKY. See 4787

THE HUNTSMEN; "A southerly wind and a cloudy sky proclaim it a hunting morning" 3 pt round e 28,366   7680

HUSH, LITTLE BABY; "Hush, little baby, don't say a word" e 389; THE MOCKING BIRD e 216; HUSH, LI'L'   7681A
     BABY; "Hush, li'l' baby, don' say a word" e 77

HUSH LITTLE BABY; "Hush, little baby, don't say a word" e 313   7681B

HYMN TO THE DAWN; "The dawn is breaking"; ALABADO; "Ya viene el alba" e, s 113   7682

I AM A CUCKOO; "I am a cuckoo, my name is cuckoo" e 189	7683
"I BUILT MY LOVE A BIG FINE HOUSE" e 313	7684
I CAN'T MAKE UP MY MIND; "I can't make up my mind, Mama in such unseemly haste" e 225	7685
I CATCHA DA PLENTY OF FEESH; "I sail over the ocean blue" e 109, 110	7686
"I DON'T LIKE NO RAILROAD MAN" e 321	7687
I DON'T WANT NO MORE ARMY; "The officers live on top of the hill" e 225	7688
I DON'T WANT TO GET ADJUSTED; "In this world we have our troubles" e 389	7689
I HAD A SISTER SUSAN; "I had a sister Susan, she was ugly and misshapen" e 267	7690
I HAD AN OLD HOUND; "I had an old hound with a cold, wet nose" e 145	7691
I LIVED IN A TOWN; "I lived in a town way down South by the name of Owensb'ro" e 110	7692
I LOVE LITTLE WILLIE; "I love little Willie, I do mamma" e 185	7693A
LITTLE WILLIE; "I love little Willie, I do, mama" e 267	7693B
I MUST AND I WILL GET MARRIED; "One morning, one morning, the weather being fine" e 225	7694
I RIDE AN OLD PAINT; "I ride an old paint, I lead an old Dan" e 109, 110, 145, 214, 279, 366; "I ride and old paint, I lead an old dam" e 120; OLD PAINT; "I ride an old paint, I lead an old Dan" e 169, 227	7695
I SPURRED MY HORSE; "I spurred my horse to make him trot"; "Coymalindo, Killkokillko, Coymalindo, Killkome" (ref) e 185	7696
I WANT TO BE A FARMER; "I want to be a farmer, a farmer, a farmer" e 214	7697
"I WAS BORN ABOUT TEN THOUSAND YEARS AGO" e 227	7698A
I WAS THERE; "I was born almost ten thousand years ago" e 72	7698B
"I WASH MY FACE IN A GOLDEN VASE" e 262	7699
"I WISH I WERE A LITTLE BIRD" e 216	7700
I WON'T BE A NUN; "Now is it not a pity such a pretty girl as I" e 212	7701
"IF YOU WANT TO GO A-COURTING" e 109, 110	7702
"IF YOUR FOOT IS PRETTY, SHOW IT" e 189	7703
"I'LL PLAY SOMETHING FOR YOU; "I'll play something for you. What will you play for me?" e 44	7704
"I'M BOUND TO FOLLOW THE LONGHORN COW" e 120	7705
I'M GOING TO GET MARRIED NEXT SUNDAY; "Good morning, good morning, good morning in spring" e 392	7706
I'M SAD AND I'M LONELY; "I'm sad and I'm lonely, my heart it will break" e 109, 110, 173	7707
IN DE VINTER TIME; "In de vinter, in de vintertime, ven de vin' blows on de vindowpane" e 321	7708A
IN THE VINTER; "In the vinter, in the vintertime, ven the vind blows on the vindowpanes" e 44	7708B
IN MY LITTLE CABIN; "In my little cabin haint ne'er a glass" e 265	7709
"IN THE DAYS WHEN WE WENT GOLD-HUNTING!" e 189	7710
IN THE SHADOW OF THE PINES; "We were wand'ring 'neath the shadow of the pines" e 393	7711
INDITA DE AMARANTE MARTÍNEZ; "Año de mil nuévecientos veintiséis tan afamado"; "Ah, the year of nineteen hundred twenty-six" e, s 314	7712
THE ISLAND OF JAMAICA; "One evening, as I roamed a-shore from my galliant brigantine" e 72	7713
IT IS SPRING; "It is spring, the daisies are busting out" e 44	7714
ITISKIT, ITASKIT; "Itiskit, itaskit, a green and yellow basket" e 109, 110	7715
IT'S RAINING, IT'S POURING; "It's raining it's pouring, the old man is snoring" e 109, 110	7716
"IT'S THE SYME THE WHOLE WORLD OVER" e 34, 109, 110; IT'S THE SYME THE 'OLE WORLD OVER; "She was just a parson's daughter" e 225	7717
I'VE GOT NO USE FOR WOMEN; "I've got no use for women, a true one may never be found" e 173	7718
JACK O' DIAMONDS; "Jack o' Diamonds, Jack o' Diamonds, I know you of old" e 263, 392; MY HORSES AIN'T HUNGRY; "Oh, my horses ain't hungry, they won't eat your hay" e 267; RABBLE SOLDIER; "I've rambled and gambled all my money away" e 321	7719
JACK WILSON; JAMES IRVING; "I am a boatman by my trade, Jack Wilson is my name" e 81	7720
JACKARO; "There was a silk merchant" e 313	7721
THE JACKET SO BLUE; "A reg'ment of soldiers came down from Yorkshire" e 72	7722
JACKIE ROVER; "On business to market, butter and cheese to buy" e 72	7723
THE JAM ON GERRY'S ROCKS; "Come all you jolly fellows, wherever you may be" e 227	7724A
THE JAM ON GERRY'S ROCKS; "Come all ye jovial shanty boys, wherever you may be" e 34	7724B
THE JAM AT GERRY'S ROCKS; "Come, all you jolly river lads, I'll have you to draw near" e 72	7724C
THE JAM ON GERRY'S ROCK; "Come all of you bold shanty boys, and list while I relate" e 186	7724D
JAMES MACDONALD; "'Twas late one Sunday evening as you can plainly see" e 126	7725
JAMIE'S ON THE STORMY SEA; "Ere the twilight bat was flitting" e 189	7726
JEFFERSON AND LIBERTY; "The gloomy night before us flies" e 44, 109, 110, 115, 293	7727
JENNIE JENKINS; "Will you wear white, O my dear, O my dear?" e 216, 227	7728
JENNY GET AROUND; "The days are long and lonesome"; "O get around, Jenny" (ref) e 312	7729
JENNY PUT YOUR KETTLE ON; "Jenny, put your kettle on, a little one and big one" e 312	7730
JESSE JAMES; "Jesse James was a lad who killed many a man" e 120; "Jesse James was a lad that killed a many a man" e 227	7731A
JESSE JAMES; "Jesse James was a lad who killed many a man" e 34, 109, 110	7731B
JESSE JAMES; "Jesse James was a lad he killed many a man" e 399	7731C

JIM FISK; "I'll sing of a man who's now dead in his grave" e 115 7732
JIMMY RANDAL. See 4684C
JOE BOWERS; "My name it is Joe Bowers, I've got a brother Ike" e 109,110 7733A
JOE BOWERS; "My name it is Joe Bowers, and I've got a brother Ike" e 173 7733B
JOE BOWERS; "My name it is Joe Bowers, I have a brother Ike" e 312 7733C
JOHN ADKIN'S FAREWELL; "Poor drunkards, poor drunkards, take warning by me" e 321; JOHN ANDERSON'S 7734
 LAMENTATION; "O sinners! Poor sinners! Take warning by me" e 212
THE JOHN B. SAILS; "Oh, we come on the sloop John B." e 321; THE WRECK OF THE JOHN B.; "We come on 7735
 the sloop 'John B.'" e 389
JOHN BARLEYCORN; "John Barleycorn was a hero born" e 126 7736
JOHN BRAMBLE. See 4684A
JOHN HARDY; "John Hardy was a brave and a desperated boy" e 109,110 7737A
JOHN HARDY; "John Hardy was a desp'rate little man" e 170 7737B
JOHN HARDY; "John Hardy was a desp'rate little man" e 227 7737C
JOHN WHIPPLE'S MILL; "I went to John Whipple and asked for a job"; "With a down, down, down derry-down" 7738
 (ref) e 72
JOHNNY HAS GONE FOR A SOLDIER; Shule Aroon (tune); "Here I sit on Buttermilk Hill" e 173; "Sad I sit on 7739
 Butternut Hill" e 227; "There I sat on Buttermilk Hill" e 35
THE JOHNSON BOYS; "Johnson Boys was raised in the ashes"; "Sight of a pretty girl makes them afraid" (ref) e 7740
 389 words by P. Campbell
THE JOLLY BOATSWAIN; "There was a jolly boatswain in our town did dwell" e 72 7741
JOLLY MILLER; "There once was a miller who lived by his mill" e 242 7742
THE JOLLY STAGE DRIVER; "A story, a story to you I will tell" e 72 7743
THE JOLLY THRASHER; "As I walked out one morning along the highway" e 72 7744
THE JOLLY WAGONER. See 4661C
JOSEPHUS ORANGE BLOSSUM; "My name is Josephus Orange Blossom" e 225 7745
JOYFUL; "Am I a soldier of the cross" e 212 7746
JUBILEE!; "All out on the old railroad"; "Swing'n turn, Jubilee" (ref) e 313 7747
THE JUNIPER TREE; "Oh, sister Phoebe, how merry were we" e 44 7748A
OLD SISTER PHOEBE; "Old Sister Phoebe, how happy were we" e 212 7748B
"JUST KICK THE DUST OVER MY COFFIN"; "Oh ain't it a wonderful story" (ref) e 392 7749
KAFOOZELUM; "In ancient days there dwelt a Turk" e 80 7750
KANSAS BOYS; "Come along girls, listen to my voice" e 80 7751
KATE AND HER HORNS; "You that in merriment delight, pray listen unto what I recite" e 72 7752
KATEY MOREY; "Come, all you sly and crafty rogues, come listen to my story" e 72 7753
THE KEEPER; "A keeper did a-shooting go" e 393 7754
KENTUCKY MOONSHINER; "I've been a moonshiner for sev'nteen long years" e 109,110 7755
THE KILLER; "O, liquor will cause you to murder" e 381 7756
KING ALCOHOL; King Andrew (tune); "King Alcohol has many forms by which he catches men" e 115,189 7757
KING AND QUEEN; "A-walking on the green grass, a-talking side by side" e 37 7758
KING HENRY FIFTH'S CONQUEST OF FRANCE; "A king was sitting on his throne" e 126 7759
KING WILLIAM; "King William was King James' son" e 242 7760
KISSING SONG; "When a man falls in love with a little turtle dove" e 225 7761
THE KNICKERBOCKER LINE; "Oh, I wrote my love a letter, and I sealed it with a weafer"; "And the rig, jig, 7762
 the rig, jig, jig" (ref) e 72
A LADIE GAY; "A ladie gay and a gay ladie, and children she had three" e 393 7763
LADY ISHBEL AND THE ELFIN-KNIGHT; "He followed her up and he followed her down" e 263 7764
LADY MARGARET; "Come all ye wild rovers and sit ye down" e 393 7765
LAKES OF COL FIN; "Airly one morning young William arose" e 126 7766
LARDY DAH; "Let me introduce a fellah, Lardy dah!" e 225 7767
THE LASS FROM THE LOW COUNTREE; "Oh, he was a lord of high degree" e 263 7768
"LAST WINTER WAS A HARD ONE"; WHEN MCGUINNESS GETS A JOB; "Rise up, Missus Reilly, don't give away 7769
 to blues" (ref) e 72
LATHER AND SHAVE; "It's into the city, not far from this spot"; "With his lather and shave" (ref) e 72 7770
LAVENDER COWBOY; "He was only a lavender cowboy" e 169 7771
LAZY JOHN; "Lazy John, Lazy John, will you marry me?" e 313 7772
LAZY MAN; "Oh, who will shuck my corn" e 381 7773
LEATHER BRITCHES BEANS; "Leather britches beans and sow belly grits and black-eyed peas" e 381 7774
LEATHERWING BAT; "Hi! said the little leatherwing bat" e 227; THE LEATHER-WINGED BAT; "Hi! said the 7775
 little leather-winged bat" e 72; "Hi, says the little leather-winged bat" e 169
LET US ALL SPEAK OUR MINDS IF WE DIE FOR IT; "Men tell us 'tis fit that wives should submit" e 189 words 7776
 by W. Brough
LET'S GO TO THE ZOO; "Let's go to the zoo and see the shiny black seals" e 214 7777
LET'S HAVE ANOTHER ROUND; "I'm a celebrated lumberman, my duty I never shirk" e 72 7778

LI'L LIZA JANE; "I knows a gal that you don't know, Li'l Liza Jane"; "O Eliza, Li'l Liza Jane!" (ref) e 26,402;   7779A
    "You got a gal and I got none, Li'l Liza Jane"; "Oh, li'l Liza, li'l Liza Jane" (ref) e 185; "I'se
    got a gal an' you got none Li'l Liza Jane"; "Ohe Liza, Li'l Liza Jane" (ref) e 128,129,130,131,
    236; "You got a gal an' I got none"; "O Eliza, Li'l 'Liza Jane!" e 279,366

LIZA JANE; "When I go a-courtin', I go on the train"; "Oh, Liza, po' gal" (ref) e 171; "When I go a-courtin',   7779B
    I'll go on the train"; "Oh, Lord, Liza poo' gal" (ref) e 225

MOUNTAIN TOP; "I'll go up on the mountain top"; "Oh pore Liza, pore gal" (ref) e 80   7779C

LIZA JANE; "Our horse fell down the well"; "Oh, it's good-bye, Liza Jane" (ref) e 214; GOOD-BYE LIZA JANE   7779D
    e 145

HURRY UP, LIZA JANE; "I'll go up on the mountain top and plant me a patch of cane"; "Hurry up, pretty little   7779E
    gal, hurry up Liza Jane" (ref) e 214

THE LILY OF THE WEST; "When first I came to Louisville" e 321   7780

LISTEN, MISTER BILBO; "Listen, Mister Bilbo, where ever you may be" e 293   words by R. and A. Claiborne   7781

LISTEN TO THE BELLS; "Listen to the bells, come, bow thy head" 2 pt round e 44   7782

LITTLE BOY; "Little boy, little boy, who made your britches?" e 242   7783

LITTLE BRASS WAGON; "Ride her up and down in your little brass wagon" e 185; THE LITTLE RED WAGON;   7784
    "Jolting up and down in the little red wagon" e 216; SKIP TO MY LOU; "Three wheels off, the
    bed's a-draggin'" e 242

THE LITTLE CABIN BOY; "'Tis of a lady so gay and possessed of beauty bright" e 72   7785

THE LITTLE DEVILS. See 4597F

LITTLE LADY FROM BALTIMORE; "I know a little lady from Baltimore" e 214   7786

THE LITTLE MOHEE; "As I was a-walking along the seashore" e 44; "One day I sat musing alone on the grass"   7787A
    e 331; "As I went out walking upon a fine day" e 170,173; MY LITTLE MOHEE; "As I went out
    walking alone one fine day" e 257; LITTLE MAWHEE; "As I was a-walking for pleasure one day"
    e 392; THE LITTLE MOHEE e 279,366

THE LITTLE MOHEE; "As I was out walking for pleasure one day" e 399   7787B

LITTLE MOHEE; "As I went a-walking all by the seashore" e 185   7787C

LITTLE MOHEE; "One day when out walking, I happened to see" e 242   7787D

PRETTY MAUMEE; "As I was a-roving for pleasure one day" e 81   7787E

LITTLE MOHEE; "As I was walking for pleasure one day" e 243   7787F

THE LITTLE OLD SOD SHANTY; "I'm looking rather seedy now while holding down my claim"; "Oh, the hinges   7788A
    are of leather and the windows have no glass" (ref) e 173; BALLAD OF HARRY BRIDGES; "Let me
    tell you of a sailor, Harry Bridges is his name" e 293   words by Almanac Singers

THE LITTLE OLD SOD SHANTY ON MY CLAIM; "I am looking rather seedy now while holding down my claim";   7788B
    "Oh, the hinges are of leather and the windows have no glass" e 129

THE LITTLE OLD SOD SHANTY; He's the lily of the valley, the bright and morning star (tune); "I am looking   7788C
    rather seedy now while holding down my claim"; "Oh, the hinges are of leather and the windows
    have no glass" (ref) e 186

LITTLE PIGS; "Little pigs lie in the best of straw" e 111   7789

LITTLE PINK; "Come, little Pink, and tell me what you think" e 81   7790

LITTLE SALLY SAND; "Little Sally Sand, sittin' in the sand" e 109,110   7791

THE LITTLE SCOTCH GIRL; "There was a little Scotch girl, she went down town" e 72   7792

LOCKS AND BOLTS; "Young men and maids, pray tell your age" e 109,110   7793

LOLLY TOO DUM; "As I went out one mornin' to take the pleasant air" e 173; "As I went out one morning to   7794A
    breathe the morning air" e 72,227

LOLLY TOO DUM; "As I went out one mornin' to take the pleasant air" e 169   7794B

ROLLY TRUDUM; "As I went out walking to breathe the pleasant air" e 321   7794C

THE LONE FISH-BALL; "There was a man went up and down to seek a dinner through the town" e 225; "There   7795
    was a man went up and down, to seek a dinner thro' the town" e 402; SUCKING CIDER THRO' A
    STRAW; "The sweetest girl I ever saw, sat sucking cider thro' a straw" e 402; SUCKIN' CIDER
    THROUGH A STRAW; "The prettiest gal that ever I saw" e 109

THE LONESOME GROVE; "One day in a lonesome grove" e 109,110   7796

LONESOME VALLEY; "You got to walk that lonesome valley" e 227   7797

LONG TIME AGO; "Once there was a little kitty, white as the snow" e 216   7798

LORD BATESMAN OR THE TURKISH LADY; "There was a man who lived in England He was of some high degree"   7799A
    e 393   See also 4682

THE TURKISH LADY; "Thar was a man, and he lived in England" e 331   7799B

LORD THOMAS AND FAIR ELINORE; THE BROWN GIRL; "Lord Thomas rose early one morning in May and dress'd   7800A
    himself in blue" e 173

LORD THOMAS AND FAIR ELLENDER; "The brown girl she hath house and lands" e 262   7800B

THE LEGEND OF FAIR ELEANOR AND THE BROWN GAL; "The Brown Gal she hath cabins and farms" e 265   7800C

LORD THOMAS; "Lord Thomas rose up one merry morning and dressed himself in blue" e 243   7800D

"THE LORDS OF CREATION MEN WE CALL" e 225   7801

LOVE IS TEASIN'; "O love is teasin' and love is pleasin'" e 312   7802

246

"LOVE SOMEBODY, YES I DO" e 36,321   7803

A LOVELORN YOUTH; "A lovelorn youth one day did go" e 331   7804

LOVERS, MOTHER, I'LL HAVE NONE; "To her daughter t'other day" e 189   7805

"LULU IS OUR DARLING PRIDE" e 132   7806

THE LUMBERMAN IN TOWN; "When the lumberman comes down, ev'ry pocket bears a crown" e 227   7807

LYDIA PINKHAM; "Let us sing of Lydia Pinkham" e 225   7808

THE MAID ON THE MOUNTAIN'S BROW; "Come, all young men and maidens, come listen to my song" e 72   7809

THE MAID ON THE SHORE; "There was a fair maiden I dearly adored" e 72   7810A

THE MAID ON THE SHORE; THE SEA CAPTAIN; "There was a young maiden who lived all alone" e 186   7810B

THE MAIL BOAT; "Bye-o-baby bye. Bye-o-baby bye" e 216   7811

MARCHING ALONG; "The flag of our country is floating on high" e 44   7812

MARINER'S HYMN; "Hail you! and where did you come from" e 332   7813

THE MARINES' HYMN; "From the Halls of Montezuma to the shores of Tripoli" e 7,114,233,236,279 words by   7814
        H. C. Davis

MARY WORE A RED DRESS; "Mary wore a red dress, red dress" e 216   7815

ME JOHNNY MITCHELL MAN; "Oh, you know Joe Silovatsky" e 110   7816

THE MENAGERIE; "Joe Johnson was a fellow, the bravest ever found"; "The elephant walks around, around" (ref)   7817
        e 185; "Vanburgh is the man who goes to all the shows"; "The elephant now goes 'round" (ref) e
        225; "Van Amburgh is the man who goes to all the shows" e 279,366

MI CARRO FORD; "Tengo mi carro paseado"; "It's a banged-up car I'm driving" e, s 314   7818

THE MILK MAID; "Where be ye goin', sweet little maid" e 263   7819

THE MILL WHEEL; "The mill wheel's frozen in the stream" e 145   7820

A MINCE PIE OR A PUDDING; "Welcome here, welcome here" e 332   7821

THE MIST IT CAME; "The mist it came, the mist it came, it settled over the town" e 242   7822

MONEY; "O money is the meat in the cocoanut" e 321   7823

THE MOULDERING VINE; "Hail! Ye sighing sons of sorrow" e 86   7824

EL MUCHACHO ALEGRE; "Yo soy el muchacho alegre que me divierto cantando"; "I am a happy young fellow   7825
        who finds contentment in singing" e, s 314

THE MUFFIN MAN; "Oh, do you know the muffin man, the muffin man, the muffin man" e 216   7826

THE MULE SONG; "A story has come down from old Mathusem" e 72   7827

MUSIEU BAINJO; "Voyez ce mulet là, Musieu Bainjo"; MONSIEUR BANJO; "Look at the stylish man, Monsieur   7828
        Banjo" e, f 219; MUSIEU BAINJO; "Look at that darkey, Mister Banjo" e, f 225; "See that
        mulatto playing the banjo" e 279,366; MISTER BANJO; "Voyez ce mulet là, M'sieu Bainjo";
        "Is'nt that dandy neat, Mister Banjo" e, f 331; MUSIEU BANJO; "Look who's a-comin' here,
        Musieu Banjo" e 77

"MY BONNIE LIES OVER THE OCEAN" e 36,205; BRING BACK MY BONNIE e 236; MY BONNIE e 233; "My   7829
        Bonnie is over the ocean" e 28,366; THE COWBOY'S DREAM; "Last night as I lay on the prairie"
        e 10,227; SOUP SONG; "I'm spending my nights at the flophouse" e 293 words by M. Sugar

MY DUCKSIE HAS FLED; "As I went a-walking on a fair summer's day in London's fair city" e 72   7830

MY GOOD OLD MAN; "Where are you going, my good old man?" e 216   7831

MY LADY; "I hear, I hear, I hear, my lady ha!" e 132   7832

MY LOVE IS LIKE A DEWDROP; "My love is like a dewdrop setting out upon a thorn" e 72   7833

MY OLD MAN; "My old man, number one, He plays, knick-a-knick on the drum" e 242   7834

MY PRETTY LITTLE MAID; "Oh, where are you going, my pretty little maid?"; "Sing ree, sing low, sing fair   7835
        you well" (ref) e 72

"MY SWEETHEART'S A MULE IN THE MINES" e 145   7836

NANCY; "Come rise ye up ye, Nancy, and go along with me" e 242   7837

NEEDLE'S EYE; "Needle's eye that doth supply, the thread that runs so smoothly" e 242   7838A

NEEDLE'S EYE; "Needle's eye doth supply thread that runs so true" e 185   7838B

"NEVER WAS A CHILD SO LOVELY" e 262   7839

NEW MONMOUTH; "Come thou fount of ev'ry blessing" e 212   7840

NEW RIVER TRAIN; "I'm riding on that new river train" e 214   7841

THE NEWBURGH JAIL; "Come listen, kind friends and I'll sing you a song"; "Says right! fal the diddle daddle"   7842
        (ref) e 72

THE NICE YOUNG MAN; "There was a young man by the name of Brown" e 189   7843

NIGHT-HERDING SONG; "Oh, slow up dogies, quit roving around" e 110,216,335   7844A

NIGHT HERDING SONG; "Oh, say, little dogies, why don't you slow down?" e 120   7844B

THE NIGHT-HERDING SONG; "Oh, say, little dogies, quit your rovin' around" e 80   7844C

THE NIGHTINGALE; "One morning, one morning, one morning in May" e 81   7845A

ONE MORNING IN MAY; THE NIGHTINGALE; "One morning, one morning, one morning in May" e 267   7845B

THE BOLD GRENADIER; THE NIGHTINGALE'S SONG; "As I went a-walking one morning in May, I spied a fair   7845C
        couple as they were at play" e 72

900 MILES; "I'm a-walkin' down the track, I got tears in my eyes" e 227   7846

NINETY-FIFTH; "When I can read my title clear to mansions in the sky" e 212   7847A

THE SAINT'S DELIGHT; "When I can read my title clear to mansions in the skies" e 110   7847B

NO MORE BOOZE; "There was a little man and he had a little can" e 109,110   7848

THE NOBLE SKEWBALL; "Ye galliants and nobles, I pray listen all" e 126   7849

NOBODY; "If to force me to sing it be your intention" e 225   7850

NOTHING LIKE GROG; "A plague of those musty old lubbers" e 225   7851

NOTTAMUN TOWN; "In Nottamun Town not a soul would look up" e 312   7852

THE NURSE PINCHED THE BABY; "Oh, the nurse pinched the baby" e 321   7853

NUT BROWN MAIDEN; "Nut brown maiden, thou hast a bright blue eye for love" e 28,279,366   7854

O.P.A. DITTY; "Oh, we'll roll back the prices" e 321   7855

O DEATH; "What is this that I can see" e 95,110; OH DEATH e 109   7856

O' DINAH; "There was a rich merchant in London did dwell" e 243   7857

O I'M A GOOD OLD REBEL; Joe Bowers (tune); "O I'm a good old Rebel, now that's just what I am" e 161   words   7858
         by I. Randolph

"O, MADAM, I HAVE COME A-COURTIN'" e 393   7859

O ME! O MY!; "O me! O my! we'll get there by and by" e 28,366   7860

OH, MISTRESS SHADY; "Oh, Mistress Shady, she is a lady" e 28,366   7861

OH, SHE'S GONE, GONE, GONE; "Sent my brown jug down-town"; "Railroad, steamboat, river and canoe" (ref)   7862
         e 214

OH, WATCH THE STARS; "Oh, watch the stars, see how they run" e 332   7863

"OH, WHO'S GOIN' TO SHOE YOUR PRETTY LITTLE FOOT" e 262   7864A

WHO WILL SHOE YOUR PRETTY LITTLE FOOT?; "O, who will shoe your pretty little foot" e 36   7864B

SHOES AND GOWNS; "Oh! who will shoe your pretty little feet?" e 242   7864C

OL' TEXAS; "I'm goin' to leave Ol' Texas now" e 34   7865

OLD ADAM; "I'm so sorry for old Adam, just as sorry as can be" e 216   7866

OLD BETTY LARKIN; "Hop around, skip around old Betty Larkin" e 312   7867

OLD BLUE; "I had an old dog and his name was Blue" e 173   7868A

OLD BLUE; "I had an ol' dog an' his name was Blue" e 169   7868B

OLD BLUE; "I raised a dog and his name was Blue" e 227   7868C

THE OLD CHISHOLM TRAIL; "Come along boys, and listen to my tale" e 34,185,227; CHISHOLM TRAIL e 145   7869A

THE OLD CHISHOLM TRAIL; "Come along, boys and listen to my tale" e 331   7869B

THE OLD CHISHOLM TRAIL; "Come gather 'round me, boys and I'll tell you a tale" e 115   7869C

THE OLD CHISHOLM TRAIL; "Come along, boys, and listen to my tale" e 227   7869D

THE CHISHOLM TRAIL; "Well, come along boys and listen to my tale" e 109,110; THE OLD CHISHOLM TRAIL   7869E
         e 279,366

THE CHISHOLM TRAIL; "Oh come along, boys, and listen to my tale" e 120   7869F

THE OLD CHISHOLM TRAIL; "Oh, come along boys and listen to my tale" e 236   7869G

OLD COLONY TIMES; "In good old colony times, when we were under the King" e 34,185; THREE JOLLY   7870
         ROGUES OF LYNN; "In good old colony days, when we lived under the King" e 111

THE 'OLD GRANITE STATE'; "We have come from the mountains" e 189   7871

THE OLD GRAY MARE; "Oh, the old gray mare she ain't what she used to be" e 129,130,131,132,185,233; OLD   7872
         ABE LINCOLN; "Old Abe Lincoln came out of the wilderness" e 34,109,110; "Old Abe Lincoln,
         he came out of the wilderness" e 44; "OLD ABE LINCOLN CAME OUT OF THE WILDERNESS" e
         321

OLD GREYBEARD; "There was an old man who came over the lea" e 242; THERE WAS AN OLD MAN; "There   7873A
         was an old man came over the lea" e 243

THE OLD MAN; "There was an old man came over the lea" e 186   7873B

OLD JOE CLARK; "Old Joe Clark, the preacher's son, preached all over the plain"; "Fare thee well, old Joe   7874A
         Clark" (ref) e 227; "I went down to old Joe Clark's, I'd never been there before"; "Oh, fare
         you well, Old Joe Clark" (ref) e 185; OLD JOE CLARKE; "I used to live on mountain top,
         but now I live in town"; "Fare you well, old Joe Clarke" (ref) e 109,110; ROUND AND ROUND
         HITLER'S GRAVE; "Wish I had a bushel,wish I had a peck" e 227; 'ROUND AND 'ROUND THE
         PICKET LINE; "I wish I had a needle" e 293

OLD JOE CLARK; "I would not go to Old Joe's house, tell you the reason why"; "Fare you well, Old Joe Clark"   7874B
         (ref) e 225

OLD MAC DONALD; "Old MacDonald had a farm" e 249; "OLD MACDONALD HAD A FARM" e 236; MAC-   7875
         DONALD'S FARM e 28,233,366

THE OLD MAID SONG; "I wonder I never got married" e 126; THE OLD MAID; "Oh, I wonder I never got   7876A
         married" e 111

I WONDER WHEN I SHALL BE MARRIED; "I wonder I never got married, um, ah!" e 72   7876B

"I WONDER WHEN I SHALL BE MARRIED" e 393   7876C

THE OLD MAID'S LAMENT; "Come all you pretty maidens, some old and some younger" e 72   7877

THE OLD MAN IN THE WOOD; "There was an old man that lived in the wood" e 214; THE OLD MAN IN THE   7878A
         WOODS; "There was an old man who lived in the woods" e 313; FATHER GRUMBLE; "There was an
         an old man who lived in a wood" e 249

OLD GRUMBLER; "Old Grumbler swore by the shirt he wore" e 44   7878B

JOHN GRUMLIE; "John Grumlie swore by the licht o' the mune" e 101   words by A. Cunningham   7878C

FATHER GRUMBLE; "There was an old man and he lived in the wood" e 262   7878D

THE OLD MINER'S REFRAIN; "I'm getting old and feeble and I can work no more" e 115   7879

OLD RILEY; "Old Riley crossed the water"; "Old Rattler, Rattler, there's a prisoner gone" (verse) e 389   7880

OLD ROGER IS DEAD; "Old Roger is dead and gone to his grave" e 216   7881A

OLD ROGER IS DEAD; "Old Roger is dead and he lies in his grave" e 313   7881B

OLD ROSIN THE BEAU; "I live for the good of my nation" e 173; ACRES OF CLAMS; "No longer the slave of
     ambition" e 173; "I've wander'd all over this country" e 293; LINCOLN AND LIBERTY; "Hurrah
     for the choice of the nation" e 44,109,110; THE MEN OF THE WEST; "While ye honor in song
     and in story" e 172; THE OLD SETTLER'S SONG; "I've travelled all over this country" e 227   7882

OLD SHIP OF ZION; "What ship is this that will take us all home?"; "'Tis the old ship of Zion" (ref) e 32,34   7883A
     att to S. Hauser

THE SHIP OF ZION; "What ship is this that you're going on board?"; "'Tis the Old Ship Zion, Hallelujah!" (ref)   7883B
     e 72

THE OLD SHOEMAKER; "I'm an old shoemaker by my trade" e 242   7884

OLD SMOKY; "On top of old Smoky, all covered in snow" e 227; ON TOP OF OLD SMOKY; "On top of old   7885A
     Smoky all covered with snow" e 169,389; "On top of old Smoky all cover'd with snow" e 35,
     293; WAY UP ON OLD SMOKY; "Way up on old Smoky, all covered with snow" e 110; PLAN-
     TONIO; "I'll tell you a story, there is one I know" e 120; PLANTONIO, THE PRIDE OF THE
     PLAIN; "I'll tell you a story, there's one that I know" e 214

ON TOP OF OL' SMOKY; "On top of ol' Smoky, all covered with snow" e 171   7885B

ON TOP OF OLD SMOKY; "On top of Old Smoky, all covered with snow" e 242   7885C

OLD SMOKY; "On top of Old Smoky, all covered with snow" e 243   7885D

OLD SMOKY; "Out on Old Smoky, Old Smoky so low" e 393   7885E

OLE SMOKY; "Goin' up on ole Smoky, all kiver'd with snow" e 331   7885F

THE OLD SOAP-GOURD; "Here we go 'round the old soap-gourd" e 313   7886

THE OLD SOLDIERS OF THE KING; "Since you all must have singing and won't be said 'Nay'" e 44   7887

THE OLD SPOTTED COW. See 4810B

OLD TYLER; "Old Tyler was a good old dog, we thought he'd treed a coon" e 312   7888

OLD VIRGINNY; "I was born in old Virginny to North Carolina I did go" e 312   7889A

EAST VIRGINIA; Greenback dollar (tune); "I was born in East Virginia; North Carolina, I did go" e 293; "I   7889B
     DON'T WANT YOUR MILLIONS, MISTER" e 293

THE OLD WHITE MARE; "Once I had an old white mare" e 185   7890

OLD WOMAN ALL SKIN AND BONE; "There was an old woman all skin and bone" e 109,110   7891A

SKIN AND BONES; "There was an old woman all skin and bones" e 312,313   7891B

OLD WOMAN AND THE PIG; "There was an old woman and she had a little pig" e 216,313   7892A

THERE WAS AN OLD WOMAN; "There was an old woman and she had a little pig" e 264   7892B

OLD ZIP COON; TURKEY IN THE STRAW; "O ole Zip Coon he is a larned skoler" e 109,110; OLE ZIP COON;   7893
     "Ole Zip Coon he is a larned skolar" e 115 words att to B. Farrell; ZIP COON e 212; "Oh, ole
     Zip Coon he is a learned scholar" e 225; "I was goin' down the road" e 185; "I went down to
     sandy hook toder arter noon" e 10; ANOTHER LITTLE DRINK; "Oh, we had an old hen and she
     had a wooden leg" e 109,110; THERE WAS AN OLD SOLDIER; "Oh! There was an old soldier
     and he had a wooden leg" e 110; TURKEY IN THE STRAW; "As I was a gwine on down de
     road" e 129,130,132,225; "As I was gwine down the road" e 184; "As I was a gwine on down
     the road" e 35; "As I was goin' down the road" e 173

THE OLE GREY GOOSE; "Monday was my wedding day" e 34   7894

ON MEESH-E-GAN; "Frainchman he don't lak to die in de fall" e 109,110   7895

ON SPRINGFIELD MOUNTAIN; "On Springfield Mountain there did dwell" e 173,243; SPRINGFIELD MOUNTAIN   7896A
     e 80,109,110; THE PESKY SARPENT e 34

ON SPRINGFIELD MOUNTAIN; "On Springfield Mountain there did dwell" e 242   7896B

SPRINGFIELD MOUNTAIN; "On Springfield mountain there did dwell" e 227   7896C

ON THE BANKS OF SWEET LOCH RAE; "I am as poor a distressed maid as ever yet was known" e 126   7897

"ON THE BANKS OF THAT LONELY RIVER"; "Then blame me not for weeping" (ref) e 81   7898

ON THE BANKS OF THE OHIO; "I asked my love to take a walk" e 243   7899

ON THE FIRST THANKSGIVING DAY; "On the first Thanksgiving day Pilgrims went to church to pray" e 129,130   7900

ONCE MORE A-LUMB'RING GO; "Come all you sons of freedom that run the Saginaw stream" e 227   7901

ONE MORE DRINK FOR THE FOUR OF US; "I was drunk last night, drunk the night before" e 225   7902

ONE SUMMER EVENING; "I went out one summer evening" e 37   7903

"OUR BOYS WILL SHINE TONIGHT" e 233   7904

OUR FLAG IS THERE; "Our flag is there! Our flag is there!" e 129,130   7905

"OUR HOME IS ON THE MOUNTAIN'S BROW" e 189 att to The Alleghanians   7906

"OUT THE WINDOW HE MUST GO" e 128   7907

OVER THE RIVER AND THROUGH THE WOODS; "Over the river and through the woods to grandfather's house we   7908
     go" e 129,130

OVER THE RIVER TO FEED MY SHEEP; "Charlie's neat and Charlie's sweet" e 313   7909

OX-DRIVER'S SONG; "Pop my whip and I bring the blood" e 171; THE OX-DRIVING SONG e 173   7910

THE OXEN SONG; "Come all you bold ox teamsters" e 34; TEAMSTER'S SONG e 110 words att to L. Gorman   7911

OYSTERS, SIR; "Many a knight and lady gay will stay me as I cry" e 189   7912

PADDY WORKS ON THE ERIE; "In eighteen hundred and forty one" e 35,227; PADDY WORKS ON THE RAILWAY   7913
e 293; PADDY; "In eighteen hundred and sixty-one" e 145; PADDY WORKS ON THE RAILROAD;
"In eighteen hundred and forty-wan" e 115,225; PAT WORKS ON THE RAILWAY; "In eighteen
hundred forty-one" e 44; "In eighteen hundred and forty-one" e 110,335; PATRICK ON THE
RAILROAD e 173

"PALOMITA QUE VIENES HERIDA"; "Little dove that has come to me wounded" e, s 314   7914

PAPER OF PINS; "I'll give to you a paper of pins" e 36   7915A

PAPER OF PINS; "I'll give to you a paper of pins" e 173   7915B

PAPER OF PINS; "I'll give to you a paper of pins" e 185   7915C

A PAPER OF PINS; "I will give to you a paper of pins" e 264   7915D

THE PATRIOTIC DIGGERS; "Johnny Bull, beware, keep your proper distance" e 44   7916

PAUL BUNYAN; "Come gather 'round, my shanty boys" e 331 words by J. Scott   7917

"PAUVRE PETITE MAMZELLE ZIZI" f 383   7918

THE PEANUT STAND; "Come, listen to me closely, while I rehearse a ditty" e 44   7919

THE PENITENTIARY BLUES; "As I sat down to a game o' cooncan" e 80   7920

PETER GRAY; "Once on a time there lived a man, his name was Peter Gray" e 35,170,173; "Once on a time,   7921
there was a man, his name was Peter Gray" e 28,366

PETTICOAT LANE; THE CAMBRIC SHIRT; "As I walked out in Petticoat Lane, oh me rose, be married in time"   7922
e 72

PILGRIM STRANGER; "I'm a pilgrim, and I'm a stranger" e 212   7923

THE PILGRIMS' LEGACY; "The Mayflower, on New England's coast, has furl'd her tattered sail"; "And to a   7924
dreary wilderness this glorious boon they bring" (ref) e 189

THE PIRATE SONG; "My boat's by the tower, and my bark's on the bay" e 173   7925

PIRI-MIRI-DICTUM DOMINI; "I had three cousins over the sea" e 264   7926A

"I HAD FOUR BROTHERS OVER THE SEA" e 279,366   7926B

PLANTATION SONG; "Had a little banjo, E string made of twine" e 242   7927

POLLY-WOLLY-DOODLE; "O I went down South for to see my Sal" e 402; "Oh, I went down South for to see my   7928
Sal" e 115,129,130,132,225,236,279,366

THE POOR COUNTRYMAN; "I'm a poor countryman from the town of Athlone" e 72   7929

POOR HOWARD; "Poor Howard's dead and gone, left me here to sing this song" e 389   7930

POOR LONESOME COWBOY; "I'm a poor lonesome cowboy" e 321   7931A

POOR LONESOME COWBOY; "I'm a poor lonesome cowboy" e 120   7931B

POOR LONESOME COWBOY; "I ain't got no father" e 145   7931C

LONESOME COWBOY; "I ain't got no father" e 129,130   7931D

POOR WAYFARING STRANGER; "I am a poor wayfaring stranger" e 321; WAYFARING STRANGER; "I'm just a   7932A
poor wayfaring stranger" e 44,173,227

POOR AND FOREIGN STRANGER; "I am a poor and a foreign stranger" e 72; POOR WAYFARING STRANGER; "I   7932B
am a poor wayfaring stranger" e 110

"I AM A POOR WAYFARING STRANGER" e 35   7932C

POOR WAYFARIN' STRANGER; "I am a poor wayfarin' stranger" e 399   7932D

"I'M JUST A POOR WAYFARIN' STRANGER" e 331   7932E

THE POOR WORKING GIRL; "The poor working girl, may heaven protect her" e 115   7933

'POSSUM TREE; "My dog did bark and I went to see"; "Although you know it is nothing to me" (ref) e 392   7934

PRAIRIE FLOWER; "I'm a little prairie flow'r" e 366   7935

PRETTY FAIR MISS; "A pretty fair miss a-working in the garden" e 313   7936

PRETTY POLLY; "Good morning, Pretty Polly, we met in due time" e 393   7937

PRETTY POLLY; "I courted Pretty Polly the live-long night" e 227   7938A

PRETTY POLLY; "I courted Pretty Polly the live-long night" e 173   7938B

THE GOSPORT TRAGEDY; "Oh, Polly, pretty Polly, Oh, yonder she stands" e 81   7938C

PRETTY POLLY; "Oh, where is Pretty Polly? Oh, yonder way she stands" e 264   7938D

THE GOSPORT TRAGEDY; "Oh, Polly, pretty Polly, Oh yonder she stands" e 81   7938E

PRETTY SARO; "Down in some lone valley in a lonesome place" e 34,313; "I came to this country in seventeen   7939
forty-nine" e 392

THE PROMISED LAND; "On Jordan's stormy banks I stand" e 109,110,115; BOUND FOR THE PROMISED LAND   7940
e 32,34,227 att to Miss Durham

PSALM III; "I laid me down and slept" e 173   7941

PUTTIN' ON THE STYLE; "Young man in a carriage driving like he's mad"; "Puttin' on the agony, it's puttin'   7942
on the style" (ref) e 72

RAGGLE-TAGGLE; "Three gypsies came to the castle gate" e 321   7943

THE RAILROAD CORRAL; "We're up in the morning ere breaking of day" e 109,110   7944

THE RAINBOW; "The last I was in London, I heard the happy news" e 72   7945

RED RIVER VALLEY; "In the bright Mohawk Valley (tune); "From this valley they say you are going" e 10, 35,   7946
109, 110, 133, 227, 233, 331; "'Tis a long time that I have been waiting" e 186

THE REGULAR ARMY, OH!; "Three years ago, this very day" e 225   7947

REMEMBER THE ALAMO; "When sounds the thrilling bugle blast" e 145   7948

RÉMON; "Mo parlé Rémon, Rémon"; "I heard from Rémon, Rémon" e, f 110   7949

THE RESURRECTION; "Man had his first creation in heevin's guarded place" e 72   7950

REUBEN JAMES; Wildwood flower (tune); "Have you heard of the ship called the good Reuben James" e 293;   7951
THE GOOD REUBEN JAMES e 7

REVOLUTIONARY TEA; "There was an old lady lived over the sea" e 28   7952

RIDDLE SONG. See also 4234, 4612, 7926

THE RIDDLE SONG; "I gave my love a cherry that has no stone" e 171, 173, 331; "I gave my love a cherry without   7953
a stone" e 215; THE RIDDLE; "I gave me love a cherry that had no stone" e 242; "I gave my love
a cherry that has no stone" e 35

RIDING DOWN FROM BANGOR; "Riding down from Bangor on an Eastern train" e 402   7954

RIDING SONG; "Draw near, young men and learn from me my sad and mournful tale" e 129, 130   7955

THE RIFLEMEN'S SONG AT BENNINGTON; "Why come ye hither, Redcoats, your mind what madness fills?" e 173;   7956
RIFLEMEN AT BENNINGTON; "Why come ye hither, stranger? Ye know 'tis madness still" e 145

THE RIO GRANDE; "Oh, the Rio Grande is flowing" e 129, 130   7957

RISE AND SHINE; "Rise and shine, brothers, rise and shine, rise and shine" e 109   7958

RISSELDY, ROSSELDY; "I married my wife in the month of June" e 145, 214   7959

ROBIN; "Robin, he married a wife from the West" e 173   7960

THE ROCK ISLAND LINE; "As I 'rived in St. Louis on April the tenth" e 72   7961

THE RODEO RIDER'S LAMENT; "I long to ride the range once more" e 37   words by F. Bell   7962

ROLL THE UNION ON; "We're gonna roll, we're gonna roll"; "If the boss is in the way" (verse) e 293   words by   7963
L. Hays and C. Williams

ROLLING IN THE DEW; "Oh, where are you bound, my pretty fair maid" e 72   7964

THE ROLLING STONE; "Since the times have grown harder, I've a mind to leave home" e 72   7965

THE ROMISH LADY; "There was a Romish lady, brought up in popery" e 212   7966

THE ROSEWOOD CASKET; "In a little rosewood casket" e 392; "There's a little rosewood casket" e 243   7967

THE ROVING GAMBLER; "I'm a roving gambler" e 170; "I am a roving gambler" e 109, 110   7968

THE ROVING PEDLER; "I am a roving pedlar man, I've roved the country round" e 72   7969

ROW, ROW, ROW YOUR BOAT; "Row, row, row your boat gently down the stream" 4 pt round e 28, 114, 233,   7970
236, 366

RUSTY JIGGS AND SANDY SAM; "Away up high in the Sirey Peaks" e 225   7971

RYE WHISKEY; "I'll eat when I'm hungry, I'll drink when I'm dry" e 110, 225   7972

SAILING ON THE SEA; "Christopher Columbus didn't have a compass" e 44   7973

SALANGADOU; "Salangadou, Salangadou, Salangadou. Salangadou, Coté piti fille la yé"; "Salangadou,   7974
Salangadou, Salangadou, Slangadou, Oh where is my darling gone" e, f 109, 110

SAM BASS; "Sam Bass was born in Indiana, it was his native home" e 227   7975

SAM HALL; "Oh, my name it is Sam Hall" e 399   7976

SANDOVALITO; "Sandovalito toda tu gente ya acabó, ya acabó"; "Sandovalito, of all your people you're bereft,   7977
you're bereft" e, s 314

SCHLOF, BOBBELI; "Schlof, bobbeli, schlof, der Dawdi hiet die schof"; "Sleep, little one, sleep, your Daddy's   7978
watching the sheep" e, g 109, 110

SCHOOL; "I wish I was in Boston City" e 225   7979

SERENE IS THE NIGHT; "The night is fair and still dear" e 279   7980

SEVENTEEN COME SUNDAY. See 4750B

SHADY GROVE; "Cheeks as red as a bloomin' rose"; "Shady Grove my little love" (ref) e 313   7981

THE SHANTY-BOY AND THE PINE; "Come all ye jolly good shanty-boys" e 335   7982

THE SHANTY MAN'S LIFE; "Oh a Shanty man's life is a wearisome life" e 115; A SHANTYMAN'S LIFE; "Oh a   7983A
shantyman's life is a wearisome life" e 109, 110

THE SHANTYMAN'S LIFE; "The shantyman's life is a wearisome one" e 186   7983B

THE PINERY BOY; A SHANTYMAN'S LIFE; A SHANTY LAD; "A pinery boy's life is a wearisome one" e 335   7983C

A SHANTYMAN'S LIFE; "A shanty lad, he leads a dreadful dreary life" e 72   7983D

SHE PERISHED IN THE SNOW; "It's on a dark and stormy night, the snow was falling fast" e 72   7984

"SHE'LL BE COMIN' ROUND THE MOUNTAIN"; e 10, 35, 128, 145, 185, 233, 236, 402; "SHE'LL BE COMIN'   7985
ROUND THE MOUNTAIN WHEN SHE COMES" e 129, 130, 132

SHINE LIKE A STAR IN THE MORNING; "Shine, shine, shine, like a star..." e 332   7986

'SHINNING' ON THE STREET; "Rushing 'round the corners, chasing every friend" e 189   7987

THE SHIP'S CARPENTER; THE HOUSE CARPENTER; "It's pretty well met to my own true love" e 72   7988

SHO 'NOUGH STEAMBOATS; "Ting-a-ling, ting-a-ling, ting-a-ling, ting-a-ling, blow!"; "Dese steamboats   7989
on de Hudson, I guess dey's mighty fine"; "De steamboats on de Hudson Lawd know what make 'em
go" (ref) e 191   words by G. L. Eskew

THE SHOEMAKER; "I am a shoemaker by my trade" e 109, 110, 335   7990

SHOOT THE BUFFALO; "And it's ladies to the center, and it's gents around the row" e 227   7991A

SHOOT THE BUFFALO; "Come all ye young fine fellows" e 145   7991B

SHOOT THE BUFFALO; "Rise you up, my dearest dear, and present to me your hand" e 109, 110   7991C

SHOOT THE BUFFALO; "Rise you up my partner dear, and present to me your hand" e 185   7991D

ON THE BANKS OF THE OHIO; "Come all you brisk young fellows" e 331; WE'LL HUNT THE BUFFALO! e 189   7991E

SHORT RATIONS; "Fair ladies and maids of all ages" e 161   words by J. A. Augustin   7992

THE SHUCKING OF THE CORN; "The sun shines down on the cornfield"; "I'm a-going to the shucking of the   7993
corn" (ref) e 44; SHUCKIN' OF THE CORN; "I have a ship on the ocean"; "I'm a-goin' to the
shuckin' of the corn" (ref) e 32, 34

SIERRA NEVADA; "A orillas de una laguna se quejaba un triste león"; "By the margin of a lake a lonely lion sat   7994
and said" e, s 314

SIMPLE GIFTS; "'Tis the gift to be simple" e 83   7995

SIMPLE LITTLE NANCY BROWN; "Simple little Nancy Brown, from 'way down East come into town" e 72   7996

SINDY; "Sindy is a pretty little girl" e 242   7997

SING-A-LING-A-LING; "O Mister we sing-a-ling-a-ling with all our hearts to you" e 343   7998

'SING', SAID THE MOTHER; "Over in the meadow in the nest in the tree" e 216   7999

THE SIOUX INDIANS; "I'll sing you a song, though it may be a sad one" e 173   8000

SIR HUGH OR THE JEW'S DAUGHTER; "It rained, it rained, it rained, it rained all over town" e 243   8001

SIR PETER PARKER; "My Lords, with your leave an account I will give" e 173   8002

"SISTER, THOU WAST MILD AND LOVELY" e 321   8003

SKATING SONG; "Some may sigᴜ, for summer's sky" e 189   8004

SKIP TO MY LOU; "Choose your partner, skip to my Lou" e 249, 343; "Flies in the buttermilk, skip to my Lou" e   8005
36, 109, 110, 115, 227; "Flies in the buttermilk, two by two" e 173; "Lost my partner, what'll I do";
"Lou, Lou, skip to my Lou" e 216; "Oh, mouse in the buttermilk, skip to my Lou" e 212; "She's
gone again, skip to my Lou" e 169; "Skip to my Lou, my chosen one" e 185; "Swing your partner,
hold her tight" e 399; SKIP-TURN-A-LOO!; "Choose you partners, skip-turn-a-loo!" e 37

SLAGO TOWN; "Oh, once I knew a pretty little girl when pretty girls were but few"; "Oh, once I courted a   8006
pretty little girl way down in Waterloo" (variant 1st line) e 81

SOLDIER BOY; "Soldier boy, soldier boy, where are you going" e 28   8007

SOLDIER, SOLDIER, WILL YOU MARRY ME?; "Soldier, soldier, won't you marry me with your musket, fife and   8008A
drum?" e 215; SOLDIER WON'T YOU MARRY ME e 249

SOLDIER, SOLDIER, WILL YOU MARRY ME?; "Soldier, soldier, will you marry me with you musket, fife and   8008B
drum?" e 331

SOLDIER, SOLDIER, WON'T YOU MARRY ME?; "Now, now, soldier, won't you marry me? For o the fife and   8008C
drum" e 34

O SOLDIER, SOLDIER; "O soldier, soldier, won't you marry me?" e 236   8008D

SOMEBODY; "Somebody's tall and handsome" e 321   8009

SONG OF PRAISE; "To our Father dear, Sing a song of praise" e 242   8010

SOON ONE MORNIN'; "Soon one mornin' death comes creepin' in my room" e 227   8011

SORGUMS; SORGHUM; "Some like 'em light, some like 'em brown" e 381   8012

SOURKRAUT; "If you want to know how for to make the sourkraut" e 225   8013

SOURWOOD MOUNTAIN; "Chicken a-crowin' on Sourwood Mountain" e 109, 110; "Chicken a-crowing on Sour-   8014A
wood Mountain" e 173; "Chickens a-crowin' on Sourwood Mountain" e 242

SOURWOOD MOUNTAIN; "Chickens a-crowin' in Sourwood Mountain" e 399; "My true love lives over the   8014B
mountain" e 225

SOURWOOD MOUNTAIN; "Chickens a-crowin' on Sourwood Mountain" e 227   8014C

SOURWOOD MOUNTAIN; "Chickens a-crowin' on Sourwood Mountain" e 185   8014D

SOURWOOD MOUNTAIN; "I got a gal at the head of the holler" e 331; "Chickens are crowing on Sour Wood   8014E
Mountain" e 279, 366

SOURWOOD MOUNTAIN; "Chickens a-crowin' on Sourwood Mountain" e 343   8014F

THE SOUTHERN SOLDIER BOY; The boy with the auburn hair (tune); "Bob Roebuck is my sweetheart's name"   8015
e 189   words by G. W. Alexander

THE SOW TOOK THE MEASLES; "How do you think I began in the world?" e 173   8016

THE SPIDER AND THE SPOUT; "The blasted, bloomin' spider ran up the bloomin' spout" e 28, 366   8017

THE SPORTING BACHELORS; "Come all you sporting bach'lors" e 227   8018

THE SQUIRE OF EDINBORO TOWN; "There was a squire in Edinboro town" e 126   8019

THE SQUIRREL; "The squirrel is a pretty thing" e 214   8020

THE STAR-SPANGLED BANNER; Anacreon in Heaven (tune); "Oh, say can you see, by the dawn's early light"   8021
e 1, 10, 28, 32, 34, 35, 44, 129, 130, 233, 236, 279, 293, 294, 343, 366; words by F. S. Key; EULOGY
TO GENERAL GEORGE WASHINGTON; "Should the tempest of war overshadow our land" e 44

STARS IN THE HEAVEN; BYE AND BYE; "Bye and bye, stars in the heav'n, number one, number two, number   8022
three, number four" e 332

STARVING TO DEATH ON A GOVERNMENT CLAIM; The Irish washerwoman (tune); "My name is Tom Hight,   8023A
an old bach'lor I am"; "Hurrah for Greer County! the land of the free" (ref) e 227; THE LANE
COUNTY BACHELOR; "My name is Frank Bolar, 'n ol' bach'lor I am"; "But hurrah for Lane
County, the land of the free" (ref) e 80

THE GOVERNMENT CLAIM; "Ernest Smith is my name, an old bach'lor I am"; "Hurrah for B. County, the land   8023B
of the free" (ref) e 81

THE STATE OF ARKANSAS; "My name is Stamford Barnes, I come from Nobleville town" e 227; "My name is   8024
Stanford Barnes, I come from Nobleville town" e 110

STEAMBOAT DOWN TO TOWN; "Steamboat down to town, steamboat down to town" e 145   8025

STEEL-LININ' CHANT; "Ho bend yo' backs and line it straight" e 331   8026

STRAWBERRY GIRL; "Who'll buy my strawberries ripe and red?"; FRAISES DU BOIS JOLI; "Qui veut des fraises du   8027
bois joli" e, f 21

THE STRAWBERRY ROAN; "I was hanging 'round town" e 186   words by C. W. Fletcher   8028

STREAK O' LEAN; "Streak o' lean, streak o' fat, a-kill ma dog and kill ye cat"; "Done cawn, raw cawn, bring   8029
along ma jummy john" (ref) e 242

STREET CRIES; DOUGHNUTS; "Here comes the doughnut man"; CLAMS; "Clams, clams, ten cents for your   8030
clams"; JUNK MAN; "Buy all the old furniture" e 335

STREET URCHINS' MEDLEY; "Sing a song of cities, cities great and small" e 28,366   8031

THE STREETS OF LAREDO; "As I walked out in the streets of Laredo" e 34,171,227; THE COWBOY'S LAMENT   8032A
e 173

COWBOY'S LAMENT; "As I walk'd out in the streets of Laredo" e 170; "As I walked out in the streets of Laredo"   8032B
e 129

STYLE ALL THE WHILE; "They say that _____ he ain't got no style" e 28,366   8033

SUEÑO DE UN MARINO; "Quisiera verte un día"; A SAILOR'S DREAM; "I wish that I might see thee" e, s 113   8034

SUGAR AND TEA; "You are my sugar and tea" e 242   8035

SWAPPING SONG; "When I was a little boy, I lived by myself" e 145,313   8036A

THE SWAPPING SONG; "Oh when I was a little boy I lived by myself" e 216   8036B

SWEET BETSY FROM PIKE; "Did you ever hear tell of Sweet Betsy from Pike" e 35,109,227; "O did you hear   8037A
tell of sweet Betsy from Pike?" e 279; "Do you remember sweet Betsy from Pike?" e 170; "Oh,
do you remember sweet Betsy from Pike" e 170; "Oh, don't you remember sweet Betsy from Pike"
e 80,110,215,331,335; BETSY FROM PIKE e 185; THE GRAND HOTEL; "There's a place in
Vancouver the loggers know well" e 186; LINCOLN CAMPAIGN SONG; "There once was old
Abram, lived out in the West" e 321; SQUARIN' UP TIME; "Oh, the fish are all caught and
the squids are all jigged" e 186 words by A. Scammell; DINAH AND VILLIKINS; "There was
a rich merchant in London did dwell" e 111; VILIKINS AND HIS DINAH; "It is of a rich merchant I am going to tell" e 402; VILLIKINS AND HIS DINAH; "'Tis of a rich merchant I am
going to tell" e 185; DINKY DIE; "He went up to London and straight-a-way strode" e
293

THE OULD ORANGE FLUTE; "In the County Tyrone, in the town of Dungannon" e 172   8037B

SWEET BETSY FROM PIKE; "Do you know sweet Betsy, our Betsy from Pike" e 242   8037C

WILLIAM AND DINAH; "There was a rich margent, from London did dwell" e 81   8037D

SWEET FERNS; "The birds are returning, their sweet notes of spring"; "Sweet ferns, sweet ferns, they tell me my   8038
lover is true" (ref) e 243

SWEET JANE; "Farewell, sweet Jane, I now must go across the roaming sea" e 262   8039

SWEET VIOLETS; "Sweet violets, covered all over with shnow" e 321   8040

SWEET WILLIE; EARL BRAND; "He rode up to the old man's gate" e 243   8041

SWING ON THE CORNER; "First young lady all around in town" e 110   8042

THE T.V.A.; "My name is William Edwards" e 110   8043

TADDLE DIDDLE DINK-DINK; "Wunst I had an old grey mare" e 145   8044

TAKE A WHIFF ON ME; "Walked up Ellum and I come down Main" e 227   8045

TALKING UNION; "If you want higher wages let me tell you what to do" (no tune) e 293,336   words by   8046
Almanac Singers

TAPS; "Fades the light, falls the night" e 37; "Soldier rest, gently pressed" e 343; "Day is done, gone the   8047
sun" e 28,366

TELL ME WHY; "Tell me why the stars do shine" e 233   8048

THE TENDERFOOT; THE HORSE WRANGLER; "One day I thought I'd have some fun" e 186 words by D. J.   8049
O'Malley

THE TEUTON'S TRIBULATION; "Mine Cot! Mine Cot! Vot language dot" e 225; "Mine Cot! Mine Cot! Vot   8050
language dat" e 189 words att to A. Dodge

TEXAS COWBOY; "Oh, I'm a Texas cowboy" e 120   8051

"THERE ARE MANY FLAGS IN MANY LANDS" e 28,366 words by M. H. Howliston   8052

"THERE IS A TAVERN IN THE TOWN" e 10,114,233,402; FARE-THEE-WELL, FOR I MUST LEAVE THEE e 128,   8053
129,131

"THERE'S A LITTLE WHEEL A-TURNIN' IN MY HEART" e 216   8054

THE THREE FISHERMEN; "Once there were three fishermen" e 28,366	8055
THREE GRAINS OF CORN; "Give me three grains of corn, mother" e 242	8056
THREE JOLLY BOOCHERS; "There is three jolly boochers, three jolly boochers, three" e 126	8057
THREE LITTLE PIGS; "Oh, the farmer had one, and the farmer had two" e 267	8058
THREE LITTLE PIGS; "There was an old sow who had three little pigs" e 249	8059
TIL-A-MI-CRAC-IN; "Til-a-mi-crac-in, 'tis a fine song" e 242	8060
TIM FLAHERTY; "I'm a light hearted Paddy, a rale Irish laddy" e 189	8061
THE TINKER'S SONG; "'Twas jolly old Roger, the tin-maker man" e 335	8062
TODAY IS MONDAY; SOUP SONG; "Today is Monday, today is Monday, Monday bread and butter" e 10; SOUP SONG; ALL YOU LITTLE ROOKIES, WE WISH THE SAME TO YOU e 129,130; SOUP SONG; "Ev'ry-body happy! Well I should say" e 366	8063
TOM BOLYNN; "Tom Bolynn was a Scotchman born, his shoes worn out, his stockings torn" e 109,110	8064
TOM DOOLEY; "Hang down your head, Tom Dooley"; "I met her on the mountain, and there I tuck her life" e 227	8065
TOM JOAD; "Tom Joad got out of the old McAlester Pen" e 109,110 words by W. Guthrie	8066
TOM TACKLE; "Tom Tackle was noble, was true to his word" e 225	8067
TOY DANCE; "Waltz with your partners, boys" e 37	8068
THE TRAIL TO MEXICO; "I made up my mind to change my way" e 335; "It was in the merry month of May, when I started for Texas far away" e 331	8069
THE TREE IN THE WOOD; "All in the wood there was a tree" e 44	8070A
THE TREE IN THE WOOD; "Now on the ground there was a tree" e 249	8070B
THE TREE IN THE VALLEY-O; "There was a tree and a very fine tree" e 313	8070C
THE TREE IN THE WOOD; "All in a wood there grew a tree" e 28,279,366	8070D
THE TROOPER AND THE TAILOR; "There was a good blacksmith in London did dwell" e 72	8071
THE TURTLE DOVE; "Poor little turtle dove setting on a pine" e 173	8072
THE TWA CORBIES. See 4776B	
'TWAS MAY DAY IN THE MORNING; "There was a crow sat on a stone" e 44	8073
TWO DUKES; "Two dukes were a-walking down by the seaside" e 126	8074
TWO DUKES A'RIDING; "Here come two dukes a-riding" e 313	8075
TWO IN THE MIDDLE; "Two in the middle and you can't jump, Josie" e 214	8076
THE TWO SISTERS. See 4718C	
UNCLE SAM'S FARM; "Of all the mighty nations in the east and in the west" e 44; "Of all the mighty nations in the east or in the west" e 189	8077
UNCLE TOM'S RELIGION; "Far away from wife and children" e 189	8078
THE UNCONSTANT LOVER; "O come, all my young lovers, whomsoever wants to gao" e 109,110	8079
UNFORTUNATE MISS BAILEY. See 4787	
UNION MAID; Redwing (tune); "There once was a union maid"; "Oh, you can't scare me, I'm sticking to the union" (ref) e 293 words by W. Guthrie	8080
UNION TRAIN; The old ship of Zion (tune); "Oh, what is that I see yonder coming" e 293 words by Almanac Singers	8081
UP ON THE MOUNTAIN; "Up on the mountain, two by two" e 216	8082
THE UTAH IRON HORSE; "The Iron Horse draws nigh with its smoke-nostrils high" e 173	8083
EL VISTIDO AZUL; "Deja niña que te mire porque te quiero mirar"; THE BLUE DRESS; "Dearest let me gaze forever for I love to look at you" e 113	8084
VOREEMA; "When first I saw Voreema combing out her locks"; "With a whoop, whoop, and a holler" (ref) e 37	8085
THE WAGONER'S LAD; "Oh, I am a poor girl, my fortune's been bad" e 72	8086
THE WASHING DAY, A BALLAD FOR WET WEATHER; "The sky with clouds was overcast" e 189	8087
THE WATER-CRESSES; "Oh, up yonder way Cinch Mountain" e 263	8088
WAY DOWN THE OHIO; "Way down the Ohio my little boat I steered" e 110	8089
WAY UP ON CLINCH MOUNTAIN; "Way up on Clinch Mountain, I wander alone"; "Rye whiskey, rye whiskey, I know you of old" (verse 3) e 321	8090A
WAY UP ON CLINCH MOUNTAIN; "Way up on Clinch Mountain where the wild geese fly high" e 321	8090B
RYE WHISKEY; CLINCH MOUNTAIN; "Way up on Clinch Mountain I wander alone" e 109,110	8090C
WE ARE ALL NODDIN'; "We are all noddin' nid, nid, noddin'" e 343	8091
"WE ARE CLIMBING THE HILLS OF ZION"; "Oh, breth'ren, go get ready" (verse) e 129	8092
WE GOT TO ALL GET TOGETHER; "There's a farmer in the country and a worker in the town" e 293	8093
WE WHOPPED AND WE HOLLERED; "We whooped and we hollered and the first thing we did find" e 214	8094
THE WEALTHY OLD MAID; THE WARRANTY DEED; "A lawyer there was I will call Mister Clay" e 171	8095
THE WEDDING OF MISS DUCK; "In come the duck and drake" e 392	8096
A WEDDING SONG; "There's going to be a wedding" e 243	8097
WEEP ALL YE LITTLE RAINS; "Weep all ye little rains, wail, wind, wail" e 215	8098
WEEPING WILLOW; "My heart is sad and I am lonely" e 243	8099
WEEVILY WHEAT; "I don't want none of your weevily wheat" e 109,110	8100A
WEEVILY WHEAT; "I won't have none of your weevily wheat"; "Charlie is a handsome man" (ref) e 185	8100B

WE'LL ALL WORK TOGETHER; "Working on the railroad, working in the mine" e 44   8101

WE'LL FIGHT FOR UNCLE ABE; "Way down in old Varginni, I suppose you all do know" e 189   words by C. E.   8102
Pratt

WENT UP TO THE MOUNTAIN; "Went up to the mountain to give my horn a blow" e 37   8103

THE WEST VIRGINIA BOYS; "Come, all you Virginia girls and listen to my noise" e 72   8104

WESTERN RANGERS; "Come all you western rangers bound to that distant land" e 126   8105

WHAT A COURT HATH OLD ENGLAND; Down, Derry, Down (tune); "What a court hath Old England of folly   8106
and sin" e 109, 110, 173, 225; DERRY DOWN e 44; GOODY BULL; "Goody Bull and her daughter
together fell out" e 225; YOU SIMPLE BOSTONIANS; "You simple Bostonians, I'd have you
beware" e 110; "Our fleet and our army, they soon will arrive" e 109

WHAT ARE YOU MADE OF?; "What's old women made of, made of" e 145   8107

"WHAT WAS YOUR NAME IN THE STATES?" e 173; "Oh what was your name in the States?" e 34   8108

WHAT'S THE MATTER WITH _____?; "What's the matter with _____ he's all right" e 366   8109

WHEN BOYS GO A-COURTING; "When boys go a-courting they dress up so fine" e 109, 110   8110

WHEN I FIRST CAME TO THIS LAND; "When I first came to this land, I was not a wealthy man" e 44   8111

"WHEN I LAYS DOWN AND I DO DIE" e 265   8112

WHEN I WAS SINGLE; "When I was single, oh then, oh then" e 170; "When I was single, o then, o then" e 173;   8113A
WHEN I WAS SINGLE (II) (MAN'S COMPLAINT) e 227; OH, WHEN I WAS SINGLE; "Oh, when I
was single, oh then, oh, then" e 111

I WISH I WAS SINGLE AGAIN; "I wish I was single again, again"; "Oh, Nancy O, my Nancy O" (ref) e 72   8113B

I WISH I WAS SINGLE AGAIN; "When I was single, oh then, oh then" e 185   8113C

WHEN I WAS SINGLE (I) (WOMAN'S STORY); "When I was single, went dressed all so fine" e 227; I WISH I   8113D
WAS A SINGLE GIRL; "When I was single, marrying was my crave" e 72

THE SINGLE GIRL; "When I was single, went dressed all so fine" e 109, 110   8113E

WHEN THE SAINTS GO MARCHING IN; "We are trav'ling in the footsteps of those who've gone before" e 389   8114

WHEN THE WORK'S ALL DONE; "A group of jolly cowboys, discussing plans at ease" e 44; WHEN THE WORK'S   8115
ALL DONE THIS FALL e 10, 129, 130

WHEN YOU GO A-COURTIN'; "When you go a-courtin', I'll tell you where to go" e 227; THE TEXIAN BOYS;   8116
"Lou'siana gals, come and listen to my noise" e 227

"WHERE ARE YOU GOING TO, MY PRETTY MAID?" e 214   8117

WHERE AWAY, STRANGER; "'Where away?' said a stranger to a lad of eighteen" e 145   8118

WHERE, O WHERE; "Where, O where are the verdant Freshman?" e 28, 279, 366   8119

"WHERE, OH WHERE IS DEAR LITTLE SUSIE?"; Ten little Indians (tune) e 170; THE PAW PAW PATCH; "Where,   8120
oh where, is dear little Nellie?" e 216

WHERE SHALL I BE?; "When Judgment Day is drawing nigh, where shall I be?" e 321   8121

WHICH SIDE ARE YOU ON?; Lay the lily low (tune); "Come all you good workers. Good news to you I'll tell"   8122
e 293, 335 words by F. Reece

WHISTLE, DAUGHTER, WHISTLE; "Oh, whistle, daughter, whistle, and you shall have a sheep" e 267   8123

THE WHITE CAPTIVE; AMANDA AND ALBIN; "The moon had gone down o'er the hills in of the west" e 126   8124
words by T. C. Upham

WHO IS THE MAN?; "Who is the man, that life doth will" e 35, 109, 110 tune Ainsworth Psalter   8125

WHOEVER SHALL HAVE PEANUTS; "Whoever shall have some good peanuts" e 214   8126

WHO'S THAT A CALLING; "The moon is shining on the window-sill" e 132; "WHO'S THAT A-CALLING?";   8127
"The moon is beaming o'er the sparkling rill" (verse) e 343

WHY, SOLDIERS, WHY; WOLFE'S SONG; "How stands the glass around?" e 173   8128

THE WICKED REBELS; "On the ninth day of November, at the dawning in the sky" e 44   8129

THE WIFE OF USHER'S WELL; "There was a woman, she lived alone" e 260, 262   8130

THE WIFE'S LAMENT; "I ain't got a fine dress of satin" e 381   8131

WILD AMERICAY; "You gentle birds of Erin's Isle who crossed the Atlantic sea" e 72   8132

WILD BILL JONES; "One night while I was a-ramblin' around, met up with that Wild Bill Jones" e 81   8133

WILL, THE WEAVER; "Mamaw, mamaw, now I'm married, a single life I wish I'd tarried" e 312   8134A

WILLIE THE WEAVER; "Mother, mother, now I'm married, don't you wish I'd longer tarried?" e 72   8134B

WILL YOU GO OUT WEST?; "Where is the girl who will go out west with me?" e 72   8135

WILL YOU LOVE ME THEN AS NOW?; "You have told me that you love me" e 132   8136

WILLIAM RILEY; "Come all young men and maidens and hark to what I tell" e 212   8137A

CAPTAIN WALKER'S COURTSHIP; "It's of a rich man's daughter who lived in Maiden Lane" e 72; FAIR JULIAN   8137B
BOND; WILLIAM REILLY AND HIS COLLEEN BAWN; "'Twas on a pleasant morning all in the bloom
of Spring" e 72

JOHN REILLY; "As walking out one summer morning to take the cool and pleasant air" e 263; JOHN RILEY;   8137C
"On walking out one summer's morning to take the cool and pleasant air" e 215

JOHNNY RILEY; "As I walked forth in my father's garden, a worthy young gentleman I spied" e 72   8137D

WILLIE THE WEEPER; "Oh, hark to the story of Willie the Weeper" e 80; "Hark to the story of Willie the Weeper"   8138A
e 109; COCAINE LIL e 110

WILLY, THE WEEPER; "Did you ever hear the story 'bout Willy, the Weeper?" e 35   8138B

WILLOWBEE; "This way, you willowbee, you willowbee, you willowbee" e 216   8139

"THE WIND BLEW UP, THE WIND BLEW DOWN" e 264   8140

WINDSOR; "God, my heart prepared is" e 34   8141

WINDY BILL; "Oh, Windy Bill was a Texas boy" e 120   8142

WINTER HAS COME; "Winter has come upon our loved ones" e 44   8143

THE WISCONSIN EMIGRANT; "Since times are so hard, I've thought" e 126   8144

WONDROUS LOVE; "What wondrous love is this, Oh! my soul, oh, my soul!" e 32,34,110,227   8145

WON'T YOU SIT WITH ME AWHILE?; "As I walked out one May morning I met with a nice young girl" e 72   8146

THE WOODMEN'S ALPHABET; "A is for axes, we very well know" e 72   8147

WOOLIE BOOGIE BEE; "I wish I was the sun up above" e 171   8148

WORKIN' ON THE ROAD; "The days are too long while I'm workin' the road" e 381   8149

YANKEE DOODLE; "Father and I went down to camp" e 10,7,32,34,129,130,173,294; "Fath'r and I went down   8150
 to camp" e 28,109,110,233,279; e 236 (text only); e 366; "FATHER AND I WENT DOWN TO
 CAMP"; YANKEE DOODLE e 115; YANKEE DOODLE; "If, Yankees, you would have a song" e
 173; "Walk in my tall-haired Indian gal" e 173; "The wars are o'er and peace is come" e 173;
 THE BATTLE OF THE KEGS; "Gallants, attend, and hear a friend" e 173,225 words by F. Hop-
 kinson; CORNWALLIS'S COUNTRY DANCE; "Cornwallis led a country dance" e 110; FAIR AND
 FREE ELECTIONS; "While some on rights and some on wrongs" e 44; THE PRESIDENTS; "George
 Washington, first president, by Adams was succeeded" e 44

YANKEE MAID; "Oh! I am a Yankee maid my lot O! tis happy and free" e 189   8151

THE YANKEE MAN-OF-WAR; "'Tis of a gallant Yankee ship that flew the stripes and stars" e 173   8152

YANKEE MANUFACTURES; "I wish I was in Yankeeland" e 189   8153

YANKEE TARS; "When Nature, kind Goddess, first form'd this big ball" e 145   8154

YE PARLIAMENT OF ENGLAND; "Ye Parliament of England, Ye Lords and Commons too" e 34; YE PARLIA-   8155
 MENTS OF ENGLAND; "Ye parliaments of England, ye Lords and Commons too" e 173

THE YELLOW ROSE OF TEXAS; "There's a yellow rose in Texas" e 161,236   8156

YONDERS TREE; "I love my rooster, my rooster loves me" e 44; THE BARNYARD FAMILY; "I have a rooster,   8157A
 my rooster loves me" e 28,366

BARNYARD SONG; "I had a cat and the cat pleased me" e 110,216,225,249   8157B

I BOUGHT ME A CAT; "I bought me a cat, my cat pleased me" e 83   8157C

YORK; "Ye men of earth in God rejoice" e 32,34   8158

THE YORKSHIRE BITE. See 4810B

YOUNG CHARLOTTE; "Young Charlotte lived in her father's home" e 242   8159A

THE FROZEN GIRL; "Young Charlotte lived on a mountain top, in a bleak and lonely spot" e 44   8159B

THE YOUNG COUNSELOR; "'Tis of a counselor I write" e 126   8160

THE YOUNG MAN WHO WOULDN'T HOE CORN; "I'll sing you a song and it's not very long" e 173,227   8161

THE YOUNG VOYAGEUR; "From the wilds of the North comes the young voyageur" e 35   8162

YOU'RE IN THE ARMY NOW; "You're in the Army now, you're not behind the plow" e 129,130,225; "You're   8163
 in the Army now, no longer behind the plow" e 10

ZAMBOANGA; "Oh, the monkeys have no tails in Zamboanga" e 225   8164

ZEBRA DUN; "We was camped on the plains at the head of the Cimarron" e 120,225   8165

UNITED STATES NEGRO

AFTER HOURS; "I was sittin' down here thinkin' all in my lonesome cell" e 336   8166

AFTER 'WHILE; "After 'while, after 'while, Some sweet day after 'while" e 409   8167

AH'M BROKE AN' HUNGRY; "Ah'm broke an' hungry, ragged an' dirty too" e 110   8168A

BROKE AND HUNGRY; "I am broke and hungry, ragg'd and dirty too" e 336   8168B

AIN' NO MO' CANE ON DIS BRAZIS; "It ain't no mo' cane on dis Brazis" e 227   8169

AIN'T GOIN' TO STUDY WAR NO MORE; "Goin' to lay down my burden down by the river side" e 76; STUDY   8170
 WAR NO MORE; "I'm a-going to lay down my sword and shield down by the riverside" e 409; I
 AIN'T GWINE STUDY WAR NO MORE; "Gwine to lay down my burden, down by the riverside" e
 28,366

AIN'T I GLAD I'VE GOT OUT THE WILDERNESS; "O, ain't I glad I've got out the wilderness"; "Come a-leaning   8171
 on the Lord" (ref) e 409

AIN'T THAT GOOD NEWS?; "I've a crown up in the Kingdom" e 409; AIN'T DAT GOOD NEWS?; "I got a   8172
 crown up ina dat Kingdom" e 290

AIN'T YOU GLAD YOU GOT GOOD RELIGION?; "Ain't you glad, ain't you glad"; "O sinner, sinner you will   8173
 feel" (verse) e 409

ALABAMA BOUND; "Oh, de boats on de ribber turn roun' an' roun'" e 80   8174

ALASKA HAHVES' MOON; "Hahves' moon, Hahves' moon, shine on" e 321   8175

"ALBERTA, LET YOUR HAIR HANG LOW" e 336   8176

ALL GOD'S CHILLUN GOT SHOES; "I gotta shoes, you gotta shoes, all God's chillun got shoes" e 351; ALL   8177
     GOD'S CHILLUN GOT WINGS; "I got a robe, you got a robe, all o' God's chillun got a robe"
     e 115; "I got shoes, you got shoes, all God's chillun got shoes" e 216; GOIN' TO SHOUT ALL
     OVER GOD'S HEAB'N; "I got a robe, you got a robe, all o' God's chillun got a robe" e 183;
     GOIN' TO SHOUT ALL OVER GOD'S HEAV'N; "I got a robe, you got a robe, all of God's child-
     ren got a robe" e 70; GOING TO SHOUT ALL OVER GOD'S HEAV'N; "I've got a robe, you've
     got a robe, all of God's children got a robe" e 409; HEAV'N, HEAV'N e 28,366; ALL GOD'S
     CHILDREN; "I've got a robe, you've got a robe, all God's children got a robe" e 233,236;
     HEAV'N, HEAV'N GOIN' TO SHOUT ALL OVER GOD'S HEAV'N e 129,130,132; I GOT A
     ROBE; "I gotta robe, you gotta robe, all of God's children gotta robe" e 402; "I got a robe,
     you got a robe, all God's chillun got a robe" e 76

ALL MAH SINS BEEN TAKEN AWAY; "Mary wove three links of chain" e 80   8178A
"MARY WORE THREE LINKS OF CHAIN" e 321   8178B
"ALL OVER THIS WORLD"; "All my troubles will soon be over with" (verse) e 409   8179
ALMOST DONE; "Take these stripes from, stripes from around my shoulders" e 227   8180
THE ANGELS DONE BOWED DOWN; "O the angels done bowed down"; "While Jesus was a-hanging upon the   8181
     cross" (verse) e 409
DE ANGELS LOOKIN' AT ME; "Hol' de light, hol'de light" e 184   8182
ANOTHER MAN DONE GONE; "Another man done gone, another man done gone, from the county farm" e 227,   8183
     321
AT THE BAR OF GOD; "O mourner! O mourner, O mourner look at the people at the bar of God" e 409   8184
BABY, DID YOU HEAR?; "Baby, did you hear? Your sweetie's gonna leave you" e 169   8185
BABY IN A GUINEA-BLUE GOWN; "O, I ain't gwine stay no longuh" e 321   8186
BAD LUCK BLUES; "I wanna go home and I ain't got sufficient clothes" e 336   8187
BALLAD OF THE BOLL WEEVIL; "Oh have you heard de latest de lates' of the songs?" e 225; BALLET OF THE   8188A
     BOLL WEEVIL; "O have you heard de lates', de lates' of de songs?" e 34; THE BOLL WEEVIL
     e 227; "Dat weevil is a little bug from Mexico" e 343; I'M A-LOOKING FOR A HOME; "Five
     long years in the army" e 293
BALLAD OF THE BOLL WEEVIL; "Oh, de boll weevil am a little black bug" e 109,110; THE BOLL WEEVIL   8188B
     e 335
THE BOLL WEEVIL; "The first time I seen the boll weevil he was a-sitting on the square" e 389   8188C
BOLL WEEVIL;·"The first time I saw the boll weevil, he was standin' on the square" e 171   8188D
THE BOLL WEEVIL; "Oh, de boll weevil am a li'l black bug" e 80,115   8188E
BOLL WEEVIL BLUES; "Farmer asked the boll weevil 'Where you been so long?'" e 336   8188F
BALM IN GILEAD; "Dere's a balm in Gilead to make de wounded whole" e 76; "There is a balm in Gilead, to   8189
     make the wounded whole" e 409; THERE IS A BALM IN GILEAD e 182
DE BAND O' GIDEON; "Oh, de band o' Gideon, band o' Gideon, band o' Gideon over in Jordan" e 183   8190
BE WITH ME; "Be with me Lord! Be with me!" e 409   8191
BEEN IN DE PEN SO LONG; "Been in de pen so long, O Honey, I'll be long gone" e 184   8192A
BEEN IN THE PEN SO LONG; "Been in the pen so long, Honey, I'll be long gone" e 336   8192B
BEFORE THIS TIME ANOTHER YEAR; "Before this time another year I may be gone"; "My mother's broke the   8193
     ice and gone" (verse) e 409
BELSHAZZA' HAD A FEAS'; "Belshazza' had a feas' 'n' dazza han' writ'n' on de wall" e 182   8194
BET ON STUBALL; "Ol' Stuball fastes' race horse, he goes 'roun like show'rin' rain" e 409   8195
BETTY AND DUPREE; "Betty told Dupree, 'I want a diamond ring'" e 336   8196
BILE DEM CABBAGE DOWN; "Massa had a old gray rooster" e 80   8197
BIRD IN A CAGE; "Bird in a cage, love, bird in a cage" e 184   8198
BLIND MAN STOOD ON THE WAY AND CRIED; "O the blind man stood on the way and cried" e 366; DE BLIN'   8199A
     MAN STOOD ON DE ROAD AN' CRIED; "O de blin' man stood on de road an' cried" e 52
BLIND MAN; "Blin' man stood on de road an' cried" e 109,110   8199B
BLUEBERRIES; "Blueberries, fresh an' fine, I got juicy blueberries, lady" e 184   8200
THE BLUES AIN' NOTHIN'; "Ah'm gonna build mahself a raft an' float dat ribbah down" e 109,110; THE   8201
     BLUES AIN'T NOTHIN'; "I'm gonna build myself a raft and float that river down" e 336
BRICKS IN MY PILLOW; "I've got bricks in my pillow and my head can't rest no more" e 336   8202
THE BROOM MAN; "Here goes the broom man" e 184   8203
BY AN' BY; "Oh by an' by, by an' by, I'm goin' to lay down dis heavy load" e 52,76; BYE AND BYE; "O bye   8204
     and bye, bye and bye, I'm goin' to lay down my heavy load" e 409
BYE AND BYE; "Bye an' bye we all shall meet again" e 409   8205
BY'M BY; "By'm by, by'm by, stars shinin' number, number one" e 216; "By'm by, by'm by, stahs shinin',   8206
     numbah numbah one" e 321
CALL DAT RELIGION? NO, NO, NO - NO, NO, NO!; "Do you call dat religion?"; "Come on, my dear steward"   8207
     (verse) e 184
CALVARY; "Calvary, Calvary, Calvary"; "Ev'ry time I think about Jesus" (verse) e 409   8208

CAMP MEETIN'; "Oh, walk together chillun, don' you get weary" e 351; THERE'S A GREAT CAMP MEETING;   8209
    "O walk together children don't you get weary" e 409

CAN'CHA LINE 'EM; "Ho, boys, is you right? Done got right" e 227   8210

CAN'T YOU LIVE HUMBLE; "Can't you live humble? Praise King Jesus!"; "Lightning flashes, thunders roll"   8211
    (verse) e 409

CAPTAIN, O CAPTAIN; "Captain, O captain, you must be cross" e 409   8212

CAPTAIN SAYS HURRY; "Captain says hurry! Straw boss says run!" e 409   8213

CASEY JONES; BEEN ON THE CHOLLY SO LONG; "On a Sunday mornin' it begins to rain" e 227   8214

CHAIN GANG BLUES; "Paper boy holl'rin' 'Extra! Have you read the news'"; "That's why I'm singin'" (ref) e 336   8215

CHARCOAL MAN; "Mah mule is white, mah charcoal is black" e 110   8216

CHICKEN REEL; FIDDLER'S TUNE   piano 184   8217

CHILLY WATER; "Chilly water, chilly water, hallelujah to that Lamb"; "I know that water is chilly and cold"   8218
    (ref) e 28,366

CHILLY WINDS; "I'm goin' where them chilly winds don' blow, darlin' baby" e 110   8219A

CHILLY WINDS; "I'm goin' where those chilly winds don't blow, darlin' baby" e 336   8219B

CHIMNEY SWEEPER; "Chimney Sweeper, sweep out yo' chimney" e 184   8220

DE CHURCH BELL TOLLIN', DING DONG; "Oh, don't you hear that mournful soun'" e 184   8221

THE CITY BLUES; "Cloudy in the west looks like rain" e 336   8222

CL'AR DE KITCHEN; "There is a gal in our town, she wears a yaller striped gown"; "Ol' folks, young folks,   8223
    cl'ar de kitchen!" (ref) e 80

CLIMB TO GLORY; "Oh, de Lo'd says to Noah, 'It's gwine-a be a little floody'" e 80   8224

COLD RAINY DAY; "Cold rainy day, some old cold rainy day, I'll be back some old cold rainy day" e 321   8225

COLLECTOR MAN BLUES; "Hey, hey, hey, somebody knockin' at my door" e 336   8226

COME DOWN; "Come down, Come down, my Lord!"; "Jesus Christ, He died for me" (verse) e 409   8227

COME HERE JESUS IF YOU PLEASE; "No harm have I done you on my knees" e 409   8228

COME HERE LORD; "Come here, Lord! Come here, Lord!"; "O, little did I think He was so nigh" (verse) e 409   8229

CONVICT SONG; "Ev'ry mail day I get a letter, says 'Son come home'" e 409   8230

CONVICT SONG; "Lawd I wonder if I'll ever get back home, get back home" e 409   8231

COTTON-EYED JOE; "Don't you remember, don't you know" e 185   8232

CRUCIFIXION; "They crucified my Lord, an' He never said a mumballin' word" e 290; HE NEVER SAID A   8233A
    MUMBALIN' WORD; "They crucified my Lord, and He never said a mumbalin' word" e 76

CRUCIFIXION; "Oh dey whupped him up de hill" e 95; NEVER SAID A MUMBALIN' WORD e 109,110; NEVER   8233B
    SAID A MUMBLIN' WORD e 227

HE NEVER SAID A MUMBALIN' WORD; "They led Him to Pilate's bar, not a word, not a word" e 409   8233C

DANGEROUS WOMAN; "Well, I got a sweet woman" e 336   8234

DANIEL SAW THE STONE; "Daniel saw the stone, rolling, rolling"; "Never saw such a man before, cut out   8235A
    the mountain without hands" (verse) e 409

DANIEL SAW THE STONE; "Daniel saw the stone, hewn out the mountain" e 409   8235B

DARLIN'; "If I'd a-known my captain was blind" e 336   8236

DAT SUITS ME; "Oh, come on, Elder, let's go roun' de wall, dat suits me" e 182   8237

"DEATH AIN'T NOTHIN' BUT A ROBBER"; "Death came to my house" (verse) e 409   8238

"DEATH, AIN'T YOU GOT NO SHAME?" e 321   8239

DEATH'S GOIN' TO LAY HIS HAND ON ME; "O sinner, sinner, you better pray"; "Crying, 'O Lord!' crying 'O   8240
    my Lord!'" (ref) e 409

DEEP RIVER; "Deep river, my home is over Jordan" e 10,76,109,110,129,130,132,183,236,252,279,343,366   8241

DEPRESSION BLUES; "If I could tell my troubles, it may would give my poor heart ease" e 336   8242

DESE BONES AM GWINETER RISE AGAIN; "I know it, 'deed I know it"; "De Lawd He thought He'd make a   8243A
    man" (verse) e 184

DESE BONES GONNA RISE AGAIN; "Lawd he thought he'd make a man"; "I know it, 'deed I know it" (ref)   8243B
    e 185

DESE BONES GWINE TO RISE AGAIN; "De Lawd He thought He'd make a man"; "Ah knows it, brudder, yes Ah   8243C
    knows it" (ref) e 80

"DIDN'T MY LORD DELIVER DANIEL?" e 76,83; "DIDN' MY LORD DELIVER DANIEL?" e 110   8244A

MY LORD DELIVERED DANIEL; "My Lord deliver'd Daniel"; "I met a pilgrim on the way" (ref) e 28,366   8244B

DO LORD REMEMBER ME; "Do Lord, do Lord, do remember me" e 409   8245

"DOES YO' CALL DAT RELIGION"; "Some preachers is out a-preachin'" (verse) e 266   8246

A DOLLAR AND A HALF A DAY; "Five dollars a day is a white man's pay" e 109,110   8247

"DONE MADE MY VOW TO THE LORD"; "Sometimes I'm up, sometimes I'm down" (verse) e 409   8248

DONE WRITTEN DOWN MY NAME; "Oh, members, rise, oh, rise, an' don't you be ashame'" e 182   8249

"DON'T LET YO' WATCH RUN DOWN" e 184   8250

DON'T LIE, BUDDY; "Mammy Logan, she had a daughter" e 336   8251

"DON'T YOU HEAR THE LAMBS A-CRYING?"; "Some for Paul and some for Silas" (verse) e 332   8252

"DON'T YOU LET NOBODY TURN YOU 'ROUN'"; "'Twas at the river of Jordan" (verse) e 409   8253

DOWN BY THE RIVER; "Oh, we'll wait till Jesus comes" e 28,366   8254

DOWN BY THE RIVERSIDE; "I'm gonna lay down my sword and shield" e 44   8255

DOWN ON ME; "Down on me Down on me"; "Talk about me, much as you please"(verse) e 409   8256

THE DOWNWARD ROAD IS CROWDED; "O the downward road is crowded"; "The win' blows East, an' the win'   8257
      blows West" (verse) e 409

DRAFTEE'S BLUES; "When you look into your mailbox" e 336   8258

DRIVIN' STEEL; "Drivin' steel, (huh) drivin' steel (huh)" e 184   8259

DRY BONES; "Dem bones, dem bones, dem dry bones"; "Toe bone connected to de foot bone" (verse) e 76   8260A

ANATOMICAL SONG; "Didn't it rain-a, rain-a, rain-a, rain-a, rain-a, rain-a, rain?"; "Oh, the toe bone   8260B
      connected to the foot bone" (verse) e 216

THE DUMMY LINE; "Some folks say dat de Dummy don' run" e 80   8261

EASY RIDER; "Easy rider, see what you done done" e 227; "Easy Rider, just see what you have done" e 336,389   8262A

C.C. RIDER; "C.C. Rider, just see what you have done" e 336   8262B

CORINNA BLUES; "C.C. Rider just see what you done done" e 336   8262C

"EVERY NIGHT WHEN THE SUN GOES IN" e 35,109,110,336   8263

EVIL-HEARTED MAN; "When the sun rose this morning I was feelin' mighty bad"; "Because I was evil. Evil-   8264
      hearted me" (ref) e 336

EV'RY DAY'LL BE SUNDAY; "Bye an' bye an' bye, good Lord!"; "One o' these mornin's bright an' fair" (verse)   8265
      e 409

"EV'RY TIME I FEEL DE SPIRIT" e 76,52,182; "O, ev'ry time I feel de spirit" e 183; I WILL PRAY; "Ev'ry   8266
      time I feel the Spirit" e 409; EVERY TIME I FEEL THE SPIRIT; "Yes, ev'ry time I feel the spirit"
      e 366

EV'RYBODY GOT TO DIE; "Ev'rybody who am living, ev'rybody got to die" e 76   8267

EZEKIEL SAW DE WHEEL; "Ezekiel saw de wheel, 'way up in de middle of de air" e 183,185; EZEK'EL SAW   8268
      THE WHEEL; "Ezek'el saw the wheel 'way up in the middle o' the air" e 409

FARMLAND BLUES; "I woke up this morning between one and two" e 336   8269

FEEL SO SAD AND SORROWFUL; "Feel so sad and sorrowful running over with the blues"; "Goin' to the mountain   8270
      top, throw myself down to the sea" (ref) e 77

FOUND MY LOST SHEEP; "Done found my lost sheep"; "My Lord had one hundred sheep" (verse) e 332   8271

FREE AT LAST; "Free at last, free at last, I thank God I'm free at last"; "'Way down yonder in the grave-yard   8272
      walk" (verse) e 409

GET RIGHT, STAY RIGHT; "Oh, get right, an' stay right" e 184   8273

THE GIFT OF GOD; "O the gift of God is eternal life"; "When I was seeking Jesus" (verse) e 409   8274

"GIMME DAT OLD TIME RELIGION" e 183; "GIMME DAT OL'-TIME RELIGION" e 115   8275

GIVE ME JESUS; "I heard my mother say" e 409; "O, when I come to die" e 76   8276

GIVE ME YOUR HAND; "O give me your hand"; "You say you're aiming for the skies" (verse) e 409   8277

GO DOWN IN DE LONESOME VALLEY; "My brother, want to get religion?" e 184   8278

GO DOWN, MOSES; "When Israel was in Egypt land"; "Go down Moses, way down in Egypt land" (ref) e 227;   8279
      "When Israel was in Egypt's land"; "Go down, Moses, way down in Egypt's land" (ref) e 28,76,
      233,366,409; "When Israel was in Egyp' Lan'"; "Go down, Moses, way down in Egyp' Lan'" (ref)
      e 35; "Go down, Moses, way down in Egypt land"; "When Israel was in Egypt land" (verse) e 293;
      "When Israel was in Egypt's land" (verse) e 183; "Go down Moses, way down in Egypt's land";
      "When Israel was way down in Egypt's land"; "When Israel was in Egypt's land" (verse) e
      109,110

GO DOWN 'N THE VALLEY AND PRAY; "Brother didn't conscience come and tell you"; "No I ain't a-shame"   8280
      (ref) e 409

GOD IS A GOD; "God is a God! God don't never change!"; "He made the sun to shine by day" (verse) e 409   8281

"GOD'S GOIN' TO SET THIS WORLD ON FIRE" e 321   8282A

"GOD, HE'S GWINE TO SET DIS WORLD ON FIRE" e 80   8282B

GOD'S GOIN' TO STRAIGHTEN THEM; "We got deacons in de church" e 409   8283

GOIN' DOWN THE ROAD FEELIN' BAD; "I'm goin' down this road feelin' bad" e 227   8284A

GOIN' DOWN THE ROAD; "I'm goin' down the road feelin' bad" e 293   8284B

"I'M GOIN' DOWN THIS ROAD FEELIN' BAD" e 109,110   8284C

GOING HOME IN THE CHARIOT; "Going home in the chariot in the morning"; "O never you mind what Satan   8285
      say" (verse) e 409

GONNA LEAVE BIG ROCK BEHIND; "Nine mo' months an' two mo' days"; "Heave ho! heave ho! I'm gonna leave   8286
      Big Rock behind" (ref) e 409

GOOD MORNING EVERYBODY; "Good morning everybody, O children! Good morning everybody, Lord" e 409   8287

"GOOD LORD I DONE DONE"; "You told me to pray and I done that too" (verse) e 409   8288

THE GOSPEL TRAIN; "Get on board, little children, get on board"; "That Gospel Train is comin'" (verse) e 110;   8289
      DE GOSPEL TRAIN; "De gospel train's a-comin'" (verse) e 76; "GIT ON BO'D LITTLE CHILD'EN"
      "De Gospel train am comin'" e 183; DE GOSPEL TRAIN; GIT ON BO'D LIT'L' CHILDREN; "De
      gospel train am a-comin'"; "Den git on bo'd lit'l' children" (ref) e 52; GOSPEL TRAIN; "De
      gospel train is a-comin'"; "Oh, git on boa'd, little child'n" (ref) e 182

"GOT MY LETTER"; "Fisherman Peter out on the sea" (verse) e 409   8290

GOT NO MONEY; "Got no money but I will have some Susie" e 409	8291
GOT RELIGION ALL AROUND THE WORLD; "Christians, hold up your heads!" e 409	8292
GOT THEM BLUES; "Got them blues, but I'm too mean, Lordy, I'm too damn' mean to cry" e 336	8293
"GOT TO GO TO JUDGMENT" e 409	8294
GREAT DAY; "Great day! great day, the righteous marching"; "Chariot rode on the mountain top" (verse) e 409; "Oh, Great Day! Great Day! de righteous marchin'"; "Chariot moved on de mountaintop" (verse) e 182	8295
GREAT GITTIN' UP MORNIN'; "In that great gittin' up mornin'"; "Stop and lemme tell you 'bout the coming of the Savior" (verse) e 227	8296A
THAT GREAT GETTING-UP MORNING; "Come and let me tell you 'bout the rising of the Saviour"; "On that great getting up morning" (ref) e 44	8296B
THE GREY GOOSE; "Last Sunday morning, Lord, Lord, Lord" e 173	8297A
THE GREY GOOSE; "Well, las' Monday mornin', Lawd, Lawd, Lawd" e 227	8297B
THE GREY GOOSE; "It was one Sunday mornin', Lawd, Lawd, Lawd" e 216	8297C
GWINE TO ALABAMY; "I'm gwine to Alabamy" e 110	8298
GWINTER SING ALL ALONG DE WAY; "Oh, I'm a-gwinter sing all de way" e 351	8299
"HAD TO GET UP THIS MORNIN'"; "'Woke up this mornin' in such big haste" (verse) e 409	8300
HALLELU; "Hallelu hallelu O yes the storm is passin' over" e 409	8301
HALLELUJAH; "Hallelujah! Hallelujah"; "I have a sister, in that day she'll take wings and fly away" (verse) e 409	8302
HALLELUJAH TO DE LAM'; "Come, my sisters, bretheren too" e 184	8303
HAMMER SONG; "Nine poun' hammer, Wham!" e 331	8304
HAMMERING; "Those cruel people! Hammering!"; "They crucified my Lord" (verse) e 409	8305
THE HAMMERS KEEP RINGING; "The hammers keep ringing on somebody's coffin" e 409	8306
HAN' ME DOWN YO' SILVAH TRUMPET, GABRIEL; "Oh, han' me down, han' me down" e 184	8307
"HE IS KING OF KINGS"; "He built his throne up in the air" (verse) e 409	8308
HEAR ME PRAYING; "Lord, oh, hear me praying"; "Like Peter when you said to him" (verse) e 409	8309
HEAVE AWAY; "Heave away, heave away! I'd rather court a yellow gal than work for Henry Clay" e 109,110	8310
"HE'S A MIGHTY GOOD LEADER" e 409	8311
"HE'S A-CHOPPIN' IN DE NEW GROUN'" e 184	8312
"HE'S GOT HIS EYES ON YOU"; "I would not be a sinner" (verse) e 409	8313
HE'S JUS' DE SAME TODAY; "When Moses an' his soldiers from Egypt's land did flee" e 76	8314
HI HO, JERUM; "There was a rich man and he lived in Jerusalem" e 72	8315A
THE RICH MAN AND THE POOR MAN; "There was a rich man and he lived in Jerusalem" e 293	8315B
HIE AWAY HOME; "Possum settin' on a hick'ry limb" e 225	8316
HIGH-PRICED BLUES; "I'll tell you something, ain't no joke"; "Prices goin' higher, 'way up higher" (ref) e 336	8317
HOLD ON; "Norah, Norah, lemme come in" e 266	8318
"HOLD THE WIND!"; "I got my Jesus, going to hold Him fast" (verse) e 409	8319
HOLY BIBLE; "Holy Bible, Holy Bible"; "Before I'd be a slave, I'd be buried in my grave" (ref) e 409	8320
HONEY, TAKE ONE ON ME; "I was comin' down State Street" e 184	8321
HOT BOILIN' SUN COMIN' OVER; "Look-a yonder! Hot boilin' sun comin' over" e 409	8322
HOUSE OF THE RISING SUN; "There is a house in New Orleans they call the Rising Sun" e 336,389	8323
HOW LONG TRAIN BEEN GONE?; "Oh, how many members gone? Gone, gone" e 182	8324
A HUND'ED LIT'L ANGELS IN THE BAN'; "There's one, there's two, there's three lit'l angels" e 184	8325
HUSH, SOMEBODY CALLIN' MY NAME; "Hush, hush, somebody callin' my name" e 184	8326
I AIN'T GOIN' TO DIE NO MO'; "Oh! ain't I glad, Oh! ain't I glad" e 129	8327
I AIN'T GONNA GRIEVE MY LORD NO MORE; "Oh, you can't go to heav'n" e 343	8328
"I AM THE TRUE VINE"; "I am in Him, and He's in me" (verse) e 409	8329
"I BEEN IN DE STORM, SO LONG" e 183,307	8330
"I BELIEVE THIS IS JESUS"; "The light of God shines in His face" (verse) e 409	8331
I COULDN'T HEAR NOBODY PRAY; "An' I couldn't hear nobody pray, O, Lord"; "In de valley I couldn't hear nobody pray" (verse) e 183; "And I couldn't hear nobody pray"; "In the valley, on my knees" (verse) e 76; "Lord, I couldn' hear nobody pray, Oh, Lord"; "In the valley, couldn' hear nobody pray" (verse) e 182; "And I couldn't hear nobody pray"; "In the valley, couldn't hear nobody pray" (verse) e 409; COULDN'T HEAR NOBODY PRAY; "An' I couldn't hear nobody pray" e 52; "I couldn't hear nobody pray" e 28,37,279,366	8332
I DON'T BELIEVE SHE'D KNOW ME; "I don't believe my baby'd know me" e 336	8333
I DON'T WAN' TO BE BURIED IN DE STAWM; "O I don' wan' be buried in de stawm, O Lawdy" e 227	8334
I FEEL LIKE MY TIME AIN'T LONG; "I feel like, I feel like"; "Went to the graveyard the other day" (verse) e 409	8335
"I GOT A HOME IN-A DAT ROCK" e 76; GOT A HOME IN THAT ROCK; "I've got a home in a-that Rock" e 409	8336
"I GOT A HOUSE IN BALTIMO'" e 409	8337
"I GOT A LETTER FROM JESUS" e 321	8338

I HAVE ANOTHER BUILDING; "I know I have another building"; "I want to go to heaven, and I want to go right" (verse) e 409 — 8339

"I HEARD THE PREACHING OF THE ELDER"; "How long did it rain?" (verse) e 409 — 8340

I KNOW THE LORD'S LAID HIS HANDS ON ME; "O I know the Lord, I know the Lord"; "Did ever you see the like before" (verse) e 409 — 8341

I MOURNED IN DE VALLEY; "I mourned in de valley, didn't I mourn" e 184 — 8342

"I MUST WALK MY LONESOME VALLEY" e 409 — 8343

"I NEVER FELT SUCH LOVE IN MY SOUL BEFO'" e 409 — 8344

"I WANT TO BE READY"; "Walk in Jerusalem just like John" (ref) e 28,76,279,366,409 — 8345

I WENT DOWN IN THE VALLEY; "O brothers let's go down, let's go down, let's go down" e 409 — 8346

I WHEEL TO DE BUZZARD"; JUMP JIM CROW; "Snake bake hoe cake" (ref) e 242 — 8347

I WISH I HAD DIED IN EGYPT LAND; "'O, I can't stay away'"; "Children grumbled on the way" (verse) e 409 — 8348

I WON'T STOP PRAYING; "And I won't stop praying"; "Old Satan's mad and I am glad" (verse) e 409 — 8349

"IF I HAD WINGS LIKE NORA'S DOVE" e 321; DINK'S SONG; "Ef I had wings like Norah's dove" e 227 — 8350

I'LL BE READY WHEN DE GREAT DAY COME; "Oh, I'll be ready, I'll be ready" e 184 — 8351

I'LL BE THERE; "I'll be there in the mornin'"; "When the gen'l roll is called" (verse) e 409 — 8352

I'M A STRANGER HERE; "Ain't it hard to stumble when you've got no place to fall?" e 336 — 8353

"I'M A-GOING TO DO ALL I CAN" e 409 — 8354

"I'M A-GOING TO JOIN THE BAND"; "The more come in with a free goodwill" (verse) e 409 — 8355

I'M A-ROLLIN'; "I'm a-rollin', I'm a-rollin', I'm a-rollin' through an unfriendly world" e 183; I'M A-ROLLING; "O brothers, won't you help, yes, help me" e 366 — 8356

I'M GOIN' TO SING; "I'm goin' to sing when the spirit says sing" e 409 — 8357

I'M GOING BACK WITH JESUS; "I'm going back with Jesus when He comes" e 409 — 8358

I'M JUST A-GOIN' OVER THERE; "I'm just a-goin' 'way over Jordan" e 409 — 8359A

OVER JORDAN; "I'm just a-goin' over Jordan" e 95 — 8359B

I'M LOOKIN' FOR MY JESUS; CAN'T STAY AWAY; "Steal away an' pray, I'm lookin' for my Jesus" e 184; STEAL AWAY AND PRAY; "O, steal away and pray, I'm looking for my Jesus" e 409 — 8360

I'M ON MY WAY; "I'm on my way, (I'm on my way) and I won't turn back" e 293 — 8361

I'M SO GLAD; "I'm so glad, I'm so glad"; "I'll tell you how I the Lord" (verse) e 409 — 8362

I'M TRAMPIN'; "I'm trampin', trampin' tryin' to make heab'n my home"; "I never been to heab'n" (verse) e 184 — 8363

"I'M WORKING ON THE BUILDIN'"; "If I was a sinner" (verse) e 409 — 8364

IN THE PINES; "True love, true love, don't lie to me" e 336 — 8365A

IN THE PINES; "True love, true love, don't lie to me" e 336 — 8365B

IN THIS LAN'; "Lord help the po' and the needy" e 409 — 8366

INCHING ALONG; "Keep a-inching along, keep a-inching along"; "It was inch by inch that I sought the Lord" (verse) e 409; KEEP A-INCHIN' ALONG; "Keep a-inchin' along, Keep a-inchin' along"; "It was inch by inch dat I sought de Lord" (verse) e 182 — 8367

IS THERE ANYBODY HERE?; "Is there anybody here who loves my Jesus?"; "This world's a wilderness of woe" (verse) e 409 — 8368

"IT MAKES A LONG-TIME MAN FEEL BAD" e 336 — 8369

I'VE BEEN WORKING ON THE RAILROAD; "I've been working on the railroad, all the livelong day" e 216; "I once did know a girl named Grace"; "I been wukkin' on de railroad all de live long day" (ref) e 114; I BEEN WUKKIN' ON DE RAILROAD; "Oh, I was bo'n in Mobile town" e 35; LEVEE SONG e 28,366; WUKKIN' ON DE RAILROAD (ref only) e 278; I'VE BEEN WUKKIN' ON DE RAILROAD (ref only) e 236; I BEEN WORKIN' ON DE LEVEE; "Oh, I been workin' on de levee all de livelong day"; "Oh, sing a song of de city" (verse) e 184; THE LEVEE SONG; "I had a girl that called me 'Dear'"; "I've been working on the levee, all the livelong day" e 44 — 8370

I'VE DONE WHAT YOU TOLD ME TO DO; "O Lord, I've done what you told me to do"; "In a-that morning, O my Lord" (ref) e 409 — 8371

"I'VE JUST COME FROM THE FOUNTAIN"; "O brothers, I love Jesus" (ref) e 129,409; "I JES' COME FROM DE FOUNTAIN" e 184 — 8372

JACOB'S LADDER; "We are climbing Jacob's ladder" e 32,34,233; "WE ARE CLIMBING JACOB'S LADDER" e 409 — 8373

JEHOVAH, HALLELUJAH; "Jehovah, hallelujah, the Lord will provide" e 332 — 8374

JERRY; "Got to pull this timber 'fore the sun goes down"; "Haulin' timber, timber" (ref) e 336 — 8375

JESUS GOIN' TO MAKE UP MAH DYIN' BED; "Oh, in mah dyin' hour, ah don' want nobody to moan"; "Well, well, well, so ah kin die easy" (ref) e 80 — 8376A

JESUS GOIN' TO MAKE UP MY DYING BED; "You needn't min' my dyin'" e 409 — 8376B

JESUS IS RISEN FROM THE DEAD; "In-a this-a band we have sweet music"; "Go tell Mary and Martha" (verse) e 409 — 8377

JIM ALONG, JOSEY; "Oh, I'm from Lou'siana, as you all know" e 185; "Oh! I'se from Lucianna as you all know" e 212 — 8378

JIM CROW BLUES; "I'm tired of bein' Jim Crowed" e 336 — 8379

JIM STRANGE KILLED LULA; "Let me tell you baby, let me tell you right" e 409 — 8380

JOE TURNER; "They tell me Joe Turner's come and gone" e 336; JOE TURNER BLUES; "Dey tell me Joe Turner's   8381
    come and gone" e 109,110

JOHN HENRY; "John Henry tol' his Cap'n" e 184; "John Henry told his cap'n" e 77; "John Henry told his Captain"   8382A
    e 335; "John Henry said to his captain" e 35; "Captain said to big old John Henry" e 115; "John
    Henry had a little baby" e 409; "John Henry was a little baby" e 227; "John Henry was about three
    days old" e 145; "When John Henry was about three days old" e 264,293 (none of these tunes are
    exactly alike but they have similarities not found in the following)

JOHN HENRY; "When John Henry was a baby" e 331   8382B

JOHN HENRY; "This is the hammer that killed John Henry" e 409   8382C

JOHN HENRY; "This ol' hammer killed John Hnery!" e 409   8382D

JOHN HENRY; "Listen to my story 'tis a story true" e 109,110   8382E

JOHN HENRY; "Well, ev'ry Monday mornin' when the bluebirds begin to sing" e 227   8382F

JOHN HENRY; "People out west heard of John Henry's death" e 77   8382G

"JOSHUA FIT THE BATTLE OF JERICHO" e 145,227,293; "JOSHUA FIT THE BATTLE O' JERICO" e 183;   8383A
        "JOSHUA FIT DE BATTLE OF JERICHO" e 185; "JOSHUA FIT DE BATTLE OB JERICHO" e 35;
        "JOSHUA FIGHT DE BATTLE OB JERICHO" e 76; SLAVERY'S CHAIN; "Slavery Chain done broke
        at last" e 293

SLAV'RY CHAIN; "Slav'ry chain broke at las'"; JOSHUA FIT DE BATTLE; "Joshua fit de battle of Jericho" e 110   8383B

JUBILEE; "Jubilee, jubilee, O Lordy jubilee"; "What is the matter the church won't shout, O Lordy" (verse) e 409   8384

KEEMO KIMO; "In South Carolina on Possum Creek" e 185; KEMO KIMO; "Way down yonder on Beaver Creek"   8385A
    e 343

KEMO-KIMO; "There was a frog lived in a pool" e 173   8385B

KEEP ME FROM SINKING DOWN; "O Lord, O my Lord, O my good Lord, keep me from sinking down" e 129,409;   8386
        KEEP ME F'OM SINKING DOWN; "Oh, Lawd! Oh, mah Lawd! Oh, mah good Lawd! Keep me f'om
        sinkin' down" e 351

KEEP YOUR HAND ON THE PLOW; "Mary wo' three links of chain"; "United Nations make a chain" (version II)   8387
    e 227; UNITED NATIONS e 293

"KING JESUS BUILT ME A HOUSE ABOVE" e 409   8388

KING JESUS IS A-LIS'ENIN'; "King Jesus is a-lis'enin' all night long"; "I know I've been converted" (verse) e   8389
    184; KING JESUS IS A-LISTENING; "King Jesus is a listening, all day long"; "That gospel train
    is coming" (verse) e 366

LAST FAIR DEAL GONE DOWN; "It's the last fair deal gone down" e 336   8390

"LAY TEN DOLLARS DOWN"; "I went down to Macon, an' I did not go to stay" (verse) e 409   8391

LEAD ME TO THE ROCK; "Lead me, Lead me, my Lord"; "The man who loves to serve the Lord" (verse) e 409   8392

LEANIN' ON DAT LAMB; "Oh, longtime mo'ner, won't you come out de wilderness"; "I'm leanin' on dat Lamb"   8393
    (ref) e 182

"LET DE HEB'N-LIGHT SHINE ON ME" e 182   8394

"LET THE CHURCH ROLL ON"; "Hypocrite in the church, now that ain't right" (verse) e 409   8395

"LET US CHEER THE WEARY TRAVELLER"; "I'll take my gospel trumpet" (verse) e 409   8396

LINK O'DAY; "Massa bin an' sol'yeh" e 109,110   8397

LISTEN TO THE ANGELS SHOUTIN'; "Where do you think I foun' my soul" e 409   8398

LISTEN TO THE LAMBS; "Listen to the lambs, all a-crying" e 409; LISTEN TO DE LAM'S; "Listen to de lam's   8399
    all a-cryin'" e 76; LIS'EN TO DE LAM'S; "Lis'en to de lam's all a-cryin'" e 183,351

"LITTLE DAVID, PLAY ON YOUR HARP" e 76,185; LITTLE DAVID e 409; "Little David, play on yo' harp"   8400
    e 109,110,366; "LIT'LE DAVID PLAY ON YO' HARP" e 183

A LITTLE MORE FAITH IN JESUS; "All I want, all I want, all I want is a little more faith in Jesus" e 76   8401

A LITTLE TALK WITH JESUS; "Pray mourner pray may the Lord help you pray" e 409   8402

A LITTLE TALK WITH JESUS; "O a little talk with Jesus makes it right"; "My brother, I remember when I was   8403
    a sinner lost" (verse) e 409

LIVE A HUMBLE; "Live a-humble, humble"; "Watch that sun, how steady he runs" (verse) e 409   8404A

LIVE A-HUMBLE; "Ol' man Adam were de fus' man invented" e 80   8404B

LONESOME BLUES; "I woke up this mornin', feelin' sad and blue"; "You know I'm lonesome and the blues is in   8405
    my way" (ref) e 336

LONESOME HOUSE BLUES; "I had a dream last night all about my gal" e 336   8406

LONG-HANDLED SHOVEL; "It takes a long-handled shovel to dig a nine-foot hole" e 336   8407

THE LONG-LINE SKINNER BLUES; "I've got a belly full of whisky and a head full of gin" e 336   8408

LONG TIME AGO; "On the lake where droop'd the willow" e 83   8409

LOOK DOWN THAT LONESOME ROAD; "Look down, look down that lonesome road" e 215; LONESOME ROAD   8410A
    e 35

THAT LONESOME ROAD; "Look up, look down that lonesome road" e 81   8410B

TO THE PINES; "Look down, look down that lonesome road" e 242   8410C

LORD I WANT TO BE A CHRISTIAN; "Lord, I want to be a Christian in a my heart" e 409; I WANT TO BE A   8411
        CHRISTIAN IN MY HEART; "Lord, I want to be a Christian in my heart" e 76; LAWD, AH WANTS
        TO BE A CHRISTIAN; "Laws, Ah wants to be a Christian in-a ma heart" e 351

THE LORD IS MY SHEPHERD; "The Lord, the Lord, the Lord is my shepherd" e 409	8412
"LORD MAKE ME MORE HOLY" e 409	8413
THE LORD'S BEEN HERE; "The Lord's been here and blessed my soul" e 409	8414
THE LORD'S PRAYER; "Our Father, which art in Heaven" e 76	8415
LULLABY; "O mother Glasco where's yo' lamb?" e 409	8416
MAH MAMMY STOLED A COW; "Steal up, young ladies, mah mammy stoled a cow" e 80	8417
MAMMA DINAH; "Mamma Dinah, O ho do mamma Dinah" e 409	8418
MANY THOUSAN' GONE; "No mo' auction block for me" e 35, 184	8419A
AUCTION BLOCK; "No more auction block for me" e 186	8419B
MARCH ON; "'Way over in Egypt's land, you shall gain the victory!" e 409	8420
"MARCHING UP THE HEAVENLY ROAD"; "My sister, have you got your sword and shield" e 409	8421
MARRYIN' BLUE YODEL; "Well, I don't mind marry'n, but I can't stand settlin' down" e 336	8422
MARY AND MARTHA; "Mary and-a Martha's just gone 'long"; "Crying free grace and dying love" (ref) e 28, 279	8423
ME AND MY CAPTAIN; "Me and my captain don't agree"; "He don't know, he don't know my mind" (ref) e 336	8424
MICHIGAN WATER BLUES; "Michigan water tastes like sherry wine (sweet sherry wine)" e 336	8425
THE MIDNIGHT SPECIAL; "If you ever go to Houston, you better walk right"; "Let the Midnight Special shine its light upon me" (ref) e 80; "Now, you wake up in the mornin', you hear the ding-dong ring"; "Oh, let the Midnight Special shine her light on me" (ref) e 389; "Well, you wake up in the morning, hear the ding-dong ring"; "Let the midnight special shine her light on me" (ref) e 32, 34, 293; "Well, you wake up in the morning, hear the big bell ring" e 336; "Well, you wake up in de • monrin', hear de ding-dong ring"; "Let de Midnight Special shine its light on you" (ref) e 227; "Yonder comes Roberta! Tell me how do you know?"; "Let the Midnight Special shine a light on me" (ref) e 184	8426
MIDNIGHT TRAIN; "De midnight train an' de fo' day train"; "De I.C. carried my baby" (verse) e 77	8427
MISTAH RABBIT; "Mistah Rabbit, Mistah Rabbit, yo' ears mighty long"; "Ev'ry little soul must shine" (ref) e 216; MISTER RABBIT; "Mister Rabbit, Mister Rabbit, your tail's mighty white"; "Ev'ry little soul gwine-a shine" (ref) e 227	8428
"MONKEY MARRIED THE BABOON'S SISTER" e 184; MONKEY'S WEDDING e 145	8429
MULE SKINNER BLUES; "Well, it's good morning, Captain" e 336	8430A
MULE SKINNER BLUES; "Good morning, Captain, Good morning, Shine" e 336	8430B
MY GOOD LORD'S DONE BEEN HERE; "Oh, my Good Lord's done been here!"; "When I get up in Heaven and a my work is done" (verse) e 409	8431
MY LITTLE BLACK STAR; "Oh, my baby is lak' a little black star" e 266	8432
"MY LORD, WHAT A MORNING" e 35, 76; "MY LORD, WHAT A MORNIN'" e 182; "MY LORD WHAT A MOURNING" e 28, 366, 409	8433
"MY LORD'S GOIN' MOVE THIS WICKED RACE"; "Nicodemus he desired to know" (verse) e 409	8434
MY NAME'S WRITTEN ON HIGH; "Hail! Hail! I belong to the blood-washed army"; "O hallelujah to the lamb!" (verse) e 409	8435
MY SINS BEEN TAKEN AWAY; "My Lord's done just what He said" e 409	8436
"MY SOUL IS A WITNESS FOR MY LORD"; "You read in de Bible, an' you understan'" (verse) e 76; WITNESS; "You read in the Bible and you understand" (verse) e 409	8437
MY SOUL'S BEEN ANCHORED IN THE LORD; "O, my soul's been anchored in the Lord"; "Where've you been, poor sinner" (verse) e 409	8438A
MY SOUL'S BEEN ANCHORED IN THE LORD; "In the Lord, in the Lord"; "I'm born of God I know I am" (verse) e 409	8438B
NAW I DON'T; "Naw I don't, naw I don't" e 409	8439
NEVER NO MORE HARD TIMES BLUES; "I got a barrel of flour, Lord; I got a bucket of lard" e 336	8440
NEW BORN AGAIN; "I found free grace an' dying love, I'm new born again"; "Been long time a-talking 'bout my trials here below" (ref) e 409	8441
NEW STRANGER'S BLUES; "I'm a stranger here, just blowed in your town" e 336	8442
NEW YORK CITY; "I'm in New York City, gonna lay my line" e 336	8443
NINE FOOT SHOVEL; "Got a nine foot shovel" e 77	8444
NO HIDING PLACE; "There's no hiding place down here"; "Went to the rocks for to hide my face" (verse) e 409	8445
"NOBODY KNOWS THE TROUBLE I'VE SEEN" e 115, 236; "Oh, nobody knows the trouble I've seen" e 28, 279, 336; "NOBODY KNOWS THE TROUBLE I SEE" e 10; "NOBODY KNOWS DE TROUBLE I'VE SEEN" e 52; "NOBODY KNOWS DE TROUBLE I SEE" e 35, 76, 183; "NOBODY KNOWS THE TROUBLE I'VE HAD" e 129, 130, 132	8446
NOBODY KNOWS WHO I AM; "O, nobody knows a who I am"; "Heav'n bells a-ringing in my soul" (verse) e 409	8447
NOBODY'S BUT MINE; "Gwine down to mah shack, chicken on mah back" e 80	8448
NOONDAY ON DE RIBBER; "Noonday on de ribber, fishin' wid a hook an' line" e 80	8449
NOW LET ME FLY; "Way down yonder in de middle o' de fiel'" e 35, 183, 184	8450
NUMBER 12 TRAIN; "Number twelve train took my baby, I could not keep from cry'n" e 336	8451

O FREEDOM; "O freedom, O freedom, O freedom after awhile" e 227   8452A

OH, FREEDOM; "Oh, freedom! Oh, freedom! Oh, freedom over me" e 34,182   8452B

OH, FREEDOM; "Oh freedom, Oh freedom, Oh freedom over me" e 293   8452C

OH, GRAVEYARD; "Oh, graveyard, oh, graveyard, I'm walkin' through de graveyard" e 182   8453

"OH, I WANT TWO WINGS"; "Oh, meet me, Jesus, meet me, Lord" (ref) e 184   8454

"O IT'S GOIN' TO BE A MIGHTY DAY"; "Yes the book of Revelations to be brought forth on that day" (verse) e 409   8455

O LAMB, BEAUTIFUL LAMB; "O Lamb, beautiful Lamb! I'm going to serve God till I die"; "Down on my knees when the light passed by" (verse) e 409   8456

O LORD; "Oh, boss man, tell me, what have you done?" e 109   8457

O LORD I'M HUNGRY; "O Lord I'm hungry I want to be fed" e 409   8458

O, LULA!; "O Lula, O Lord, gal, I want to see you so bad" e 227   8459

O MAKE ME HOLY; "O make-a-me ho-holy"; "Did you ever see such love before" (verse) e 409   8460

"O MARY, DON'T YOU WEEP, DON'T YOU MOURN"; "Some o' dese mornin's 'bout ten o'clock" (verse) e 184; "Some of these mornings bright and fair" (verse) e 236,409; O MARY, DON'T YOU WEEP; "If I could I surely would" (verse) e 293; "The way of evil doing is a-wide and fair" (ref) e 28,366; "Oh, Mary don't you weep, don't you moan"; "Now don't you believe that the Bible ain't true" (verse) e 185   8461

OH, MONAH; "If you wanna get to Heaven, I'll tell you how to go" e 185   8462

O MOTHER DON'T YOU WEEP; "When I'm gone, when I'm gone"; "For I'm goin' to Heav'n above" (verse) e 409   8463

O MY LITTLE SOUL; "I don't care where you bury my body"; "O my little soul's goin' to shine, shine" (ref) e 409   8464

"O PETER, GO RING-A DEM BELLS" e 176; PETER, GO RING-A DEM BELLS e 183; "OH, PETER GO RING DEM BELLS" e 28   8465

OH, ROCK-A MY SOUL; "Oh, rock-a my soul, in de bosom of Abraham"; "When I went down in de valley to pray" (verse) e 184; OH, A-ROCK-A MY SOUL; "Oh, a-rock-a my soul, in de bosom of Abraham"; "When I went down in the valley to pray" e 35   8466

"O ROCKS DON'T FALL ON ME"; "Look over yonder on Jerricho's wall" (verse) e 409; "I look over yondah on Jerico's walls" (verse) e 183   8467

"OH, WASN'T THAT A WIDE RIVER" e 28,76,366; "OH! WASN'T DAT A WIDE RIBBER" e 129   8468

O WRETCHED MAN; "O wretched man that I am" e 409   8469

OH, YOU BETTAH MIND!; "Oh, you bettah mind, Oh, you bettah mind" e 184   8470

OL' ELDER GREEN; "Ol' Elder Brown's in town" e 409   8471

THE OLD ARK'S A MOVERING; "O, the old ark's a-movering"; "See that sister dressed so fine?" (verse) e 409; THE OL' ARK'S A-MOVERIN'; "Oh, the ol' ark's a-moverin'"; "Noah built the ark upon dry land accordin' to command" e 77   8472A

THE OLD ARK A-MOVERIN' ALONG; "Just wait little while I'm gwine to tell 'bout the ark" e 28,279,366   8472B

THE OLD CABIN HOME; "I am going far away, far away to leave you now" e 184   8473

OLD KING CROW; "Now listen here what I'se goin' to say" e 185   8474

"OLD ZION'S CHILDREN MARCHIN' ALONG"; "I hailed my mother in the morning" (verse) e 409   8475

OLE MASSA; "Ole Massa, he am gone"; "Oh! yes, I'se a-gwine dar too" (ref) e 37   8476

ON A MONDAY; "On a Monday, Monday I was arrested"; "Well it's all. Almost done" (ref) e 336   8477

ONE MORE RIVER; "Old Noah once he built the ark"; "One more river, and that's the river of Jordan" (ref) e 35; "Old Noah once he built an ark" e 402; ONE MORE RIVER TO CROSS; "A man named Noah built an Ark"; "There's just one more river, and that one river is Jordan" (ref) e 185; ONE MORE RIVER; "One more river, and that's the river of Jordan"; "Old Noah once he built the Ark" (verse) e 249; NOAH'S ARK; "Old Noah built himself an ark"; "There's one wide river, and that wide river is Jordan" (ref) e 28,225,279,366   8478

"OPEN THE WINDOW NOAH"; "The little dove flew in the window and mourned" (verse) e 409   8479

ORIGINAL TALKING BLUES; "If you want to go to heaven let me tell you what to do" e 336; TALKING BLUES; "Now you wanna go to heaven, lemme tell you what to do" e 389 (verses spoken with accompaniment)   8480

OVER YONDER; "I got a sister over yonder" e 182   8481

PAY DAY AT COAL CREEK; "Pay day, pay day, oh, pay day; pay day at Coal Creek tomorrow" e 336   8482

PEANUT-PICKIN' SONG; "You kin do jes'-a what you please"; "Den I'se gwine home" (ref) e 37,129,130,279, 366; COTTON-PICKING SONG; "This cotton want a-pickin' so bad" e 335   8483

PETER ON DE SEA, SEA, SEA, SEA; "Peter, Peter, Peter on de sea, sea, sea, sea" e 183,184   8484

PICAYUNE BUTLER; "Away down souf whar I was born" e 212   8485A

PICAYUNE BUTLER; "Now here I am a gwine to sing" e 321   8485B

PICK A BALE OF COTTON; "You got to jump down, turn around" e 34,227   8486

PLENTY GOOD ROOM; "There's plenty good room"; "My Lord's done just what he said" (verse) e 409   8487

PO' LAZ'US; "High Sheriff tol' de deputy, (Hanh)" e 227   8488

PO' OL' LAZ'RUS; "Po' ol' Laz'rus layin' in between two mountains" e 409   8489

POOR BOY; "As I went down to the river, poor boy"; "Bow down your head and cry, poor boy" (ref) e 173; PO'   8490A
 BOY; "As I went down to the river, po' boy"; "Bow down your head and cry, po' boy" (ref) e 171

PO' BOY; "As I sat down t' play a game o' coon can"; "Run away with another man, po' boy" (ref) e 109, 110   8490B

PO' BOY; "My mammy's in the cold, cold ground"; "She ran away with another man, po' boy" (ref) e 184   8490C

POOR MAN BLUES; "I never had a barrel of money" e 336   8491

POOR ME; "I'm sometimes up, I'm sometimes down" e 409   8492

POOR MOURNER; "Charley went out huntin' on a moonshiney night" e 266   8493

POOR MOURNER'S GOT A HOME; "M... m... my Lord! m... Poor mourner's got a home at last"; "O mourner,   8494A
 mourner, ain't you tired a mourning" (verse) e 409

PO' MO'NER GOT A HOME AT LAS'; "Oh, no harm, no harm, no harm"; "Oh, mo'ner mo'ner, ain't you tired   8494B
 o' mo'nen?" (verse) e 182

POOR SINNER; "O poor sinner, O now is your time"; "Fire in the east, fire in the west" e 409   8495

PRAY ON; "In the river of Jordan John baptized" e 409   8496

PRAYER IS DE KEY; "Oh, prayer is de key, bretheren"; "On yo' knees, down on yo' knees" (verse) e 182   8497

PRISON BOUND; "It was early one mornin', Lord" e 336   8498

RABBIT-FOOT BLUES; "Blues, jumped a rabbit and he ran a solid mile" e 336   8499

RAILROAD BILL; "Railroad Bill, he was so bad" e 409   8500

RAISE A RUCKUS; "My ol' mistiss promise me" e 227   8501

READ IN DE BIBLE; "Read in de Bible, understan', Methus'lah was de oldes' man"; "Oh! Methus'lah was a   8502
 witness" (ref) e 37

RELIGION IS A FORTUNE; "O religion is a fortune, I really do believe" e 182, 409   8503

THE RELIGION THAT MY LORD GAVE ME; "O the religion that my Lord gave me, Shines like a mornin' star";   8504
 "O brother you'd better believe" (verse) e 409

RIDE ON, JESUS; "Oh, ride on, Jesus! Ride on, Jesus!"; "If you see my sister, Oh, yes!" (verse) e 182   8505

RIDE ON, KING JESUS; "Ride on, King Jesus! No man can-a hinder me"; "For He is King of kings" (verse) e 76;   8506
 "Ride on King Jesus! No man can hinder him"; "King Jesus rides on a milk-white horse" (verse)
 e 409

RISE, SHINE FOR THY LIGHT IS A-COMIN'; "O, 'rise! shine! for thy light is a-comin'"; "This is the year of   8507
 Jubilee" (verse) e 409

ROAD GANG SONG; "Pick 'em up, pick 'em up, let 'em fall down" e 409   8508

ROCK ABOUT MY SARO JANE; "I've got a wife an'-a five li'l chillun'" e 227   8509

ROCK ISLAND LINE; "I may be right and I may be wrong"; "Oh, well, the Rock Island, it is a mighty good   8510
 road" (ref) e 389; "I got sheep, I got goats"; "Oh, the Rock Island line is a mighty good road"
 e 216

ROCK OF AGES; "My lovin' brother when the world's on fire" e 409   8511

ROCKIN' JERUSALEM; "O Mary, O Martha, O Mary ring dem bells"; "Church gettin' higher, rockin' Jerusalem!"   8512
 (verse) e 409

THE ROCKS AND THE MOUNTAINS; "O the rocks and the mountains shall all flee away"; "Sinner, sinner give   8513
 up your heart to God" (verse) e 409

ROLL, JORDAN, ROLL; "Roll, Jordan, roll, roll, Jordan, roll"; "O brother, you ought t' have been there" (verse)   8514
 e 129, 130, 132; "O brother you ought to been there" (verse) e 233, 409; "Oh, brothers, you ought
 t' have been there" (verse) e 10, 29, 366; "O brothers you ought to ha' been there" (verse) e 76;
 "Oh, brothers you oughter been there" (verse) e 183; "O brothers, you ought t' have been there"
 e 32, 34

ROLL ON; "Roll on, roll on, sweet moments roll on"; "When I was blind and could not see" (verse) e 366, 409   8515

ROSA LEE; "Oh, when I lived in Tennessee" e 184   8516

RUN, MOURNER, RUN; "There's singing here, there's singing there" e 409   8517

RUN, NIGGER, RUN; "Run, Nigger, run, de patter roller get yuh" e 80   8518A

RUN, SAMMY, RUN; "Run, Sammy, run, de patter roll'll catch yuh" e 185   8518B

RUN TO DE CITY OF REFUGE; "Read 'bout Samson from his birth"; "He had to run, run, run" (ref) e 184   8519

RUN TO JESUS; "Run to Jesus, shun the danger"; "He will be our dearest friend" (verse) e 366   8520

RUN, TO MY LORD; "Oh, Christians, Christians, what yer gwineter do"; "Goin' to moan, moan" (ref) e 184   8521

SAME TRAIN; "Same train, same train, same train, carry my mother" e 37   8522

SATAN'S A LIAR; "Satan's a liar an' a conju'h too" e 80   8523

SATISFIED; "Rich folks worries 'bout trouble" e 184   8524

SATURDAY NIGHT AND SUNDAY TOO; "Saturday night and Sunday too, true love on my mind" e 169   8525

SCANDALIZE' MY NAME; "Well, I met my sister de other day" e 182   8526

SCREW THIS COTTON; "Screw this cotton, screw this cotton, screw this cotton, screw it tight" e 409   8527

SEBEN TIMES; "All the way 'roun, seben times" e 409   8528

SEE CAN'T YOU JUMP FOR JOY; "My Lord calls me, see can't you jump for joy" e 184   8529

"SEE THE SIGNS OF JUDGMENT" e 409   8530

SET DOWN, SERVANT!; "'Set down, servant!' 'I can't set down'" e 331; "'Set down, servant' 'I cain' set   8531
 down'" e 227

"SEVEN LONG YEARS IN STATE PRISON"; "Sad, sad and lonely, sittin' in my cell" (ref) e 184   8532

SHEPHERD, SHEPHERD; "Shepherd, shepherd, where'd you leave your lambs?" e 332; "Shepherd, Shepherd, where'd you lose your sheep?" e 409 8533

SHORT'NIN' BREAD; "Two little darkies lyin' in bed"; "Mamma's little baby loves short'nin'" (ref) e 225; "Mammy's little baby loves short'nin'" (ref) e 237; "Three li'l babies lyin' in bed" e 343; "Two little chillun a lyin' in bed" e 249; "Two little pickaninnies lyin' in bed" e 37; "Put on de skillet, put on de led" e 128,236,246; "Hog got away in my backyard"; "Mammy's baby loves short'nin'" (ref) e 184 8534

SHORTY GEORGE; "Well-a Shorty George, he ain' no friend of mine" e 227; "Well-a, Shorty George, he ain't no friend of mine" e 336 8535

SHOUT FOR JOY; "O Lord! Shout for joy!"; "Early in the morning" (verse) e 409 8536

SHOW ME THE WAY; "O my good Lord, show me the way"; "Enter the chariot, travel along" (verse) e 409 8537

SHUCKIN' SUGAR BLUES; "I've got your picture, and I'm goin' to put it in a frame" e 336 8538

"SING A HO THAT I HAD THE WINGS OF A DOVE"; "Virgin Mary had one son" (verse) e 409 8539

SINNER MAN; "O sinner man where are you going" e 230 8540

SINNER-MAN SO HARD TO BELIEVE; "Ain't dat a pity, Lord, ain't dat a shame"; "Dives was a rich man" (verse) e 182 8541

"SINNER, PLEASE DON'T LET THIS HARVEST PASS"; "I know that my Redeemer lives" (verse) e 321,409; "SINNER, PLEASE DON'T LET DIS HARVEST PASS"; "Sinner, O see dat cruel tree" (verse) e 76 8542

SISTERN AND BRETHREN; "Sistern and brethren, stop foolin' wid pray" e 109,110 8543

"SIT DOWN SERVANT, SIT DOWN"; "Know you mighty tired so sit down" (verse) e 409 8544A

SIT DOWN, SERVANT, SIT DOWN; "Oh, sit down, servant, sit down"; "I know you're tired, sit down" e 77 8544B

SIT DOWN, SISTER; "Oh, won't you sit down?"; "Who's that yonder dressed in red?" (verse) e 35.214; WON'T YOU SIT DOWN; "Who's dat yonder dressed in red?"; "Oh, won't you sit down?" (ref) e 343 8545A

SIT DOWN, SISTER, SIT DOWN; "Sit down, sister, sit down, walk right in an' sit down" e 184 8545B

SITTIN' DOWN BESIDE O' THE LAMB; "New Jerusalem! Sittin' down beside o' the Lamb"; "Before I'd lay in hell, one day, good Lord!" (verse) e 409 8546

SKILLET GOOD AND GREASY; "I'm goin' downtown, gonna get me a sack of flour" e 336 8547A

GOIN' KEEP MY SKILLET GREASY; "O de times is very hard"; "If I can, can, can" (ref) e 409 8547B

SOME OF THESE DAYS; "I'm goin' down to the river of Jordan" e 409 8548

"SOMEBODY GOT LOST IN DE STORM" e 184 8549

"SOMEBODY'S BURIED IN THE GRAVEYARD"; "Although you see me coming along so" (verse) e 409 8550

"SOMEBODY'S KNOCKING AT YOUR DOOR"; "Knocks like Jesus" (verse) e 76,409 8551

"SOMETIMES I FEEL LIKE A MOTHERLESS CHILD" e 183,227,284; "Sometimes I feel like a motherless chile" e 52 8552

SOON A WILL BE DONE; "Soon-a will be done-a with the troubles of the world"; "No more weeping and a-wailing" (verse) e 409 8553A

SOON A WILL BE DONE; "Soon-a will be done with the trouble of this world" e 409 8553B

SPORTIN' LIFE BLUES; "I got a letter from my home" e 336 8554

STAGOLEE DONE KILL DE BULLY; "Got up one mornin' 'bout four o'clock" e 184 8555

STAN' STILL JORDAN; "Stan' still Jordan, stan' still Jordan"; "I got a mother in heaven" (verse) e 182; "You may bury my body" (verse) e 52 8556

STAND THE STORM; "O stand the storm, it won't be long"; "My ship is on the ocean" (verse) e 409 8557

STANDIN' IN THE NEED OF PRAYER; "It's me, it's me, it's me, O Lord"; "Tain't my mother or my father" (verse) e 183; STANDIN' IN DE NEED OF PRAYER; "It's me, it's me, O Lord"; "Not my brother, nor my sister" (verse) e 76; STAN'IN' IN DE NEED OF PRAYER; "'Tain' ma brother nor ma sister" (verse) e 182; IT'S ME; "It's me it's me, O Lord"; "Not my brother, but it's me" e 409 8558A

IT'S A ME, O LORD; "It's a me it's a me O Lord"; "Not my brother it's a me O Lord" (verse) e 129,130,132; "Not my brother, (no) it's a-me, O Lord" (verse) e 28,279,366 8558B

"STEADY, JESUS LISTENIN'"; "Stop po' sinner, don't you run" (verse) e 409 8559

STEAL AWAY; "Steal away, steal away, steal away to Jesus!"; "My Lord calls me, He calls me by the thunder" (verse) e 10,28,35,76,129,279,366; "My Lord, He calls me, He calls me by the thunder" (ref) e 233; STEAL AWAY TO JESUS e 183,402,409 8560

STEEL GOT TO BE DROVE; "You can't look it down" e 77 8561

STEP IT UP AND GO; "With a girl, havin' a little fun" e 336; BORROW LOVE AND GO; BOTTLE UP AND GO; "She got to borrow love and go" e 336 8562

THE STORY OF NORAH; "Now didn't ole Norah build himself an Ark?" e 266 8563

STREET SONG; "Rag man, bone man come's your way" e 409 8564

SUGAR BABE BLUES; "Take your arm from 'round my neck" e 336 8565

THE SUN MOWS DOWN; "Hurry mourner! The sun mows down"; "Now what do you think about dyin' children?" (verse) e 409 8566

SUNDAY MORNIN' BAN; "What ban' that Sunday mornin'"; "Jordan's deep an' Jordan's wide" (verse) e 409 8567

SWEET ORANGES; "Sweet oranges, sweeter than de honey" e 184 8568

SWING ALONG, SUE; "Oh, the wind blew up an' the wind blew down" e 77 8569

SWING LOW; "Swing low, sweet chariot, coming for to carry me home"; "I looked over Jordan and what did I   8570
    see" (verse) e 409; SWING LOW SWEET CHARIOT; "I look over Jordan and what do I see?" (verse)
    e 78; "I looked over Jordan, what did I see?" (verse) e 402; "I look over Jordan an what did I see"
    (verse) e 183; "Swing low, sweet chariot, comin' for to carry me home" e 10; "I looked over Jor-
    dan and what did I see" (verse) e 76, 129, 130, 132, 233, 236; "I look'd over Jordan an' what did I
    see" (verse) e 35; "Oh, swing low, sweet chariot, comin' fer ter carr' me home"; "I looked over
    Jerd'n an' what did I see" e 182; "Swing low, sweet chariot, comin' fo' to carry me home"; "I looked
    over Jordan and what did I see" (ref) e 28, 279, 343, 366
T.B. BLUES; "Too late, too late, too late"; "When I was on my feet, I couldn't walk down the street" (ref)   8571
    e 336
TAKE THIS HAMMER; "Take this hammer (huh!) carry it to the captain" e 34, 227, 293, 335   8572
TAKE YO' TIME; "Honey baby, take yo' time" e 77   8573
TAKE YO' TIME, MISS LUCY; "Oh, I jes' come out before you, to sing a little song" e 184; TAKE YOUR   8574
    TIME, MISS LUCY; "Miss Lucy, she is handsome, Miss Lucy, she is tall" e 214; MISS LUCEY
    LONG; "Oh, I just come out afore you" e 212
TALKING COLUMBIA BLUES; "Down along the river just a-settin' on a rock" (no tune) e 336   words by W.   8575
    Guthrie
TALKING DUST BOWL BLUES; "Back in nineteen twenty-seven" (no tune) e 336   words by W. Guthrie   8576
TALKING MINER; "I'm just a miner in a mining town" (no tune) e 336   words by W. Guthrie   8577
TALKING SAILOR; "In bed with my woman just singin' the blues" (no tune) e 336   words by W. Guthrie   8578
TALKING SUBWAY BLUES; "I struck out for old New York" (no tune) e 336   words by W. Guthrie   8579
TEACHER'S BLUES; "Teacher, teacher, why are you so poor" e 336   8580
"TELL ALL THE WORLD, JOHN"; "What kind o' shoes are those you wear" (verse) e 409   8581
THANK GOD I'M ON MY WAY TO HEAVEN; "You may talk about me jes as much as you please" e 409   8582
THEN MY LITTLE SOUL'S GONNA SHINE; "I'm gonna rise up high and higher" e 185   8583
THERE WAS AN OLD FISH; "Was an old fish and his name was Whale" e 214   8584
THERE'S A MEETING HERE TONIGHT; "Get you ready, there's a meeting here tonight"; "Camp meeting in the   8585
    wilderness" (verse) e 409
THERE'S ROOM ENOUGH; "O brothers, don't stay away!" e 409   8586
THERE'S SOMETHING ON MY MIND; "There's something on my mind that's worryin' me" e 409   8587
"THEY LED MY LORD AWAY"; "The Jews and Romans, in-a one band" (verse) e 409   8588
THINGS ABOUT COMIN' MY WAY; "Ain't got no money, can't buy no grub"; "Now after all my hard trav'lin'"   8589
    (ref) e 336
THIS IS A SIN-TRYING WORLD; "O, this is a sin-trying world"; "O Heav'n is so high and I am so low" (verse)   8590
    e 409; THIS IS A SIN-TRYIN' WORLD; "O, this is a sin-tryin' world" e 109, 110
THIS IS DE HEALIN' WATER; "Oh, this is de healin' water"; "Come along, mo'ner" (verse) e 182   8591
THIS OL' TIME RELIGION; "O this ol' time religion"; "It was good for the prophet Daniel" (verse) e 409   8592
TILL I FIND MY DEN; "Till ah fin' mah den Ahm goin' up de river" e 109   8593
TOLD MY CAPTAIN; "Told my captain my hands were cold" e 336   8594A
TOLD MY CAP'N; "Told my cap'n my hands wuz cold" e 77   8594B
TRACK-LINING CHANT; "Hey! boys, I want the linin' bars!" e 335   8595
TRIP TO RALEIGH; "Now I went down to Raleigh" e 226   8596
TRYIN' TO CROSS THE RED SEA; "Didn't ol' Pharoah get lost"; "I went down in the valley" (verse) e 409   8597
TRYIN' TO GET HOME; "Lord I'm bearin' heavy burdens" e 409   8598
TURN BACK PHARAOH'S ARMY; "Going to write to Massa Jesus"; "To turn back Pharaoh's army" (ref) e 28   8599
"'TWAS ON ONE SUNDAY MORNING" e 409   8600
TWO WINGS; "O Lawd, I want two wings to hide my face" e 331   8601
UPON DE MOUNTAIN; "Upon de mountain, chillun call" e 110; "'Pon de mountain, childlun call" e 77   8602
VENDOR'S CALL; "Heah's yo' coal, heah's yo' coal" e 409   8603
VICKSBURG BLUES; "I've got those Vicksburg blues and I'm singin' it ev'rywhere I go" e 336   8604
WADE IN DE WATER; "Wade in de water, wade in de water, children" e 52   8605
WAKE ME; "Wake me, shake me, don't let me sleep too late"; "Get to de lot befo' I do, catch my mule I'll   8606
    be there too" (verse) e 409
WANDERIN'; "My daddy is an engineer, my brother drives a hack"; "And it looks like I'm never gonna cease my   8607
    wanderin'" (ref) e 293, 321, 336; "There's snakes on the mountain and eels in the sea" e 321
"WANT TO GO TO HEAVEN WHEN I DIE" e 409   8608
WARTIME BLUES; "What you gonna do when they send your man to war?" e 336   8609
WATERMELONS; "Watermelons watermelons fresh from de vine" e 184   8610A
WATERMELONS; STREET CRIES; "Watermelons off de vine" e 335   8610B
WAY DOWN YONDER IN THE CORNFIELD; "Some folks say dat a darkey won't steal" e 114   8611
'WAY OVER IN THE PROMISED LAND; "Where O where is old Elijah?" e 80   8612
WE SHALL NOT BE MOVED; "We shall not, we shall not be moved" e 293   8613
"WE SHALL WALK THROUGH THE VALLEY"; "If Jesus Himself shall be our leader" (ref) e 409   8614
WEEPIN' MARY; "If there's anybody here like weepin' Mary" e 52   8615

"WERE YOU THERE WHEN THEY CRUCIFIED MY LORD?"; WERE YOU THERE e 34,52,76,115,182,183,409   8616

WHAT KIND OF SHOES; "What kind of shoes you going to wear?"; "Yes, yes, my Lord, I'm going to join the   8617
    heav'nly choir" (ref) e 28

WHAT SHALL I DO?; "I'm so glad trouble don't last alway" e 409   8618

WHEN I LAY DOWN; "When I lay down and die on my old tired hunkers" e 336   8619

WHEN I LAY MY BURDEN DOWN; "Oh, glory, glory! Hallelujah! When I lay my burden down" e 182   8620

"WHEN I'M DEAD, DON'T YOU GRIEVE AFTER ME"; "Pale horse an' Rider have taken my mother away" (verse)   8621
    e 184; WHEN I'M DEAD; "Pale Horse and Rider have taken my mother away" (verse) e 409

WHEN MY BLOOD RUNS CHILLY AND COLD; "When-a my blood runs chilly an' col'" e 227   8622

"WHEN THE TRAIN COMES ALONG"; "I may be blind an' cannot see" (verse) e 409   8623

"WHERE SHALL I GO?"; "I went to the rock for to hide my face" (verse) e 409   8624

"WHO BUILT DE ARK?"; "Now didn't ol' Noah build de ark?" (verse) e 184   8625

WHO DID?; "Who did, who did, who did, who did, who did swallow Jo-Jo-Jo-Jo?" e 216   8626

WHO LAID DE RAIL; "Hit's a mighty dry year when de crab grass fail" e 212   8627

WHO MOU'N FO' ME?; "Ridin' in de buggy, Miss Mary Jane" e 80   8628

WHOA BUCK; "Sometimes I plow my old grey horse" e 227   8629

WIDE, DEEP, TROUBLED WATER; "I know a wide river, 'taint no Mississippi" e 266   8630

WINNSBORO COTTON MILL BLUES; "Old man Sargent, sittin' at the desk"; "I got the blues, I got the blues, I   8631
    got the Winnsb'ro Cotton Mill blues" (ref) e 336

"WISH I'S IN HEAVEN SETTIN' DOWN" e 409   8632

WORK ALL DE SUMMER; "Work all de summer, summer, work all de fall, fall" e 335   8633

WORKIN' ON THE RAILROAD LINE; "Listen Big Boy if you wanna be a man" e 409   8634

WORRIED BLUES; "I've got the worried blues, Lord" e 336   8635

WORRIED MAN BLUES; "It takes a worried man to sing a worried song" e 293   8636

"YO' LOW DOWN WAYS"; "You talk about yo' elder when he's tryin' to preach the word" (verse) e 409   8637

"YONDER COMES THE HIGH SHERIFF" e 184   8638

YOU DON'T KNOW MY MIND; "You don't know, you don't know, you don't know my mind" e 336   8639

"YOU HEAR THE LAMBS A-CRYING"; "My Saviour spoke these words so sweet" (verse) e 409   8640

"YOU MAY BURY ME IN THE EAST"; "In-a that morning my Lord" (ref) e 409; I'LL HEAR THE TRUMPET   8641
    SOUND e 366

YOU SHALL REAP; "You shall reap jes what you sow" e 409   8642

YOU'D BETTER MIN'; "You'd better min' how you talk" e 409   8643

YOU'D BETTER RUN; "You'd better run, run, run-a-run"; "God sent ol' Jonah to the Nineveh lan'" (verse) e 409   8644

YOU'RE MY BROTHER SO GIVE ME YOUR HAN'; "It makes no diff'rence what church you may belong to" e 409   8645

ZION'S CHILDREN; "Oh! Zion's children comin' along" e 129   8646

URUGUAY

ESTILO; "La aurora empieza a brillar" s 284   8647

SERENATA; "En medio de esta noche callada y placentera" s 284   8648

LA VIDALITA. See 4173

VENEZUELA

CANTEMOS, CANTEMOS; "Cantemos, cantemos gloria al Salvador" s 284   8649

ESTA NOCHE SERENA; "Esta noche serena, Sin luz de luna" s 284   8650

LIGHT AS A SWALLOW; "Light as a swallow gracefully flying, dance to the gay guitars" e 219   8651

LA MONICA PEREZ; "Senora Monicz Pérez, a mi me parece bien"; MONICA PEREZ; "Tell me, oh Monica   8652
    Pérez, where is all our love today" e, s 9

RIQUI, RIQUI, RIQUIRRÁN; "Aserrín, aserrán, los maderos de San Juan"; SUGAR-CANE; "Sugarcane, sugarbeet,   8653
    all good dhildren like a treat" e, s 322; "Lirolín, lirolán! All good children of San Juan" e, s 219

EL SAN PEDRO; "Si San Pedro se muriera todo el mundo" s 284   8654

TOWARD THE SUNRISE; "Lightly the breezes at morning are blowing" e 350   8655

WALES

YR ALLTUD O GYMRU; "Mae yr Alltud o Gymru yn gwylied y lloer"; THE EXILE OF CAMBRIA; "O Wales as I   8656
    leave you the light fades away" e, w 349

AR HYD Y NOS; "Holl amrantau'r sêr ddywedant"; ALL THROUGH THE NIGHT; "Fiery day is ever mocking"   8657
    e, w 349; "With the stars my watch I'm keeping" e, w 19; "While the stars are shining brightly"
    e, w 402; "Sleep, my child, and peace attend thee" e 28,34,70,233,236,279,366; "While
    the moon her watch is keeping" e 199,234

BEDD FY RHIAINT; Yr helig gân (tune); "Ryw dro yn y gwanwyn ar derfyn y dydd"; MY PARENTS' GRAVE; The   8658
    willow song (tune); "The radiance of sunset was dim in the West" e, w 20   words by D. Rowlands

THE BLOSSOM OF THE THORN; "How fondly I gaze on the fast falling leaves" e 406   8659

BREUDDWYD Y FRENHINES; "Breuddwyd y frenhines oedd gwel'd ei hun yn dlawd"; THE QUEEN'S DREAM;   8660
"In her gilded chamber, the jewel'd Queen lay dreaming" e, w 20; "From the starving city she
turn's her couch to seek" e, w 20

CADAIR IDRIS; "Bûm inau'n rhodianna, yn nyffryn Llangollen"; ONE MORNING IN SPRING TIME; "One morning   8661
in spring-time, when sunlight lay gleaming" e, w 20

CLYCHAU ABERDYFI; "Os wyt ti yn bur i mi"; THE BELLS OF ABERDOVEY; "If to me as true thou art" e, w 349;   8662
"When the night sinks over all" e, w 19; "E'en as thou art true to me" e 37; "Stay thou true my
dear to me" e 235   words by Ceiriog

CNOT Y COED; "Yn y dyddiau gynt, pan chwareuai'r gwynt"; THE MISTLETOE; "In the days of old, when the   8663
streams ran gold" e, w 349   words by Tegid, Llew

CODIAD YR HEDYDD; "Clyw! clyw! foreol glod"; THE RISING OF THE LARK; "Hark, hark, at morning-tide"   8664
e, w 19; "Clyw! clyw! foreuol glod"; "Hark! hark! his matin praise" e, w 349; "RISE, RISE
THOU MERRY LARK" e 199, 234   words by Ceiriog

COUNTING THE GOATS; "Ho! Goatherd, Ho! Ho! Goatherd, Ho!" e 249   8665

DAFYDD Y GARREG WEN; "Cariwch medd Dafydd fy nhelyn i mi"; DAVID OF THE WHITE ROCK; "David, the   8666
Bard, on his bed of death lies" e, w 19, 234; DAFYDD Y GAREG WEN e, w 349   words by Ceiriog

Y DERYN PUR; "Y deryn pur â'r adain las"; THE DOVE; "Arise, sweet dove on airy wing" e, w 19; "Fair dove,   8667
on blue, far glancing wing" e, w 349; "My dove with wings so fair, so blue" e 235

DIFYRRWCH GWYR DYFI; Woe to the day (tune); "Difyrrwch gwyr Dyfi yr hen amser gynt"; THE MEN OF   8668
DOVEY'S DELIGHT; "By Dovey's banks in the dim, olden days" e, w 349

DIFYRRWCH Y BRENIN; "Beth mae'r brenin yn fwynhau"; ON THIS DAY; "On this day our King was born" e, w   8669
349

DYCHWELIAD Y TELYNOR; Y Brython (tune); "Yn ymyl y dre' o ddiffyg gwell lle"; THE MINSTREL'S RETURN;   8670
The Briton (tune); "One calm moon-lit night, away from the light" e, w 20   words by D. Rowlands

DYNESIAD Y GAUAF; Craig y Tyle (tune); "Mae Natur i gyd yn newid ei phryd"; WINTER IS NEAR; The rock   8671
of the steep (tune); "Dame Nature's array no longer is gay" e, w 20   words by D. Rowlands

ELEGY OF IVOR OF KERI; "Dare I ask you, dear, to love me" e 95   8672

ERYRI WEN; "Eryri Wen, Eryri Wen, Hen gaer fy nhadau gynt"; WHITE SNOWDON; "Their's was no dream, oh!   8673
monarch hill, with Heav'n's own azure crown'd" e, w 20; "Eryri Wen, Frenhines bur, Daearol Ferch
y ne" e, w 349   words by T. G. Jones

Y FWYALCHEN; "O gwrando! y beraidd fwyalchen"; THE BLACKBIRD; "Dear blackbird, I'll list while thou   8674
singest" e, w 19; "O gwrandaw! y beraidd fwyalchen"; "O sweetest of blackbirds, come listen!"
e, w 349

GWCW FACH; "Gwcw fach, ond wyt tin ffolog"; CUCKOO, DEAR; "Cuckoo dear, what means this folly?"   8675
e, w 19

HELA'R 'SGYFARNOG; "Awn i hela'r ysgyfarnog"; HUNTING THE HARE; "Over hill and plain they're bounding"   8676
e, w 19, 234   words by Ceiriog; "Dewch i'r helfa, mae'r udgyrn yn canu"; "O the yelping of
hounds, the skelping" e, w 349   words by Ceiriog

YR HEN DDRAENEN DDA; "Mwynen Cynnwyd (tune); "Yr hen ddraenen ddu wrth dalcen y tŷ"; THE OLD CHES-   8677
NUT TREE; "The pleasing melody of Cynnwyd; "The old chesnut tree, which stand on the lea"
e, w 20   words by D. Rowlands

HUN GWENLLIAN; A gentle maid in secret sighed (tune); "Gwellian fach, fy nghalon dlos"; GWENDOLEEN'S   8678
REPOSE; "My Gwendoleen, my heart's delight" e, w 349

I BLAS GOGERDDAN; "I Blas Gogerddan heb dy dad!"; THIS GARDEN NOW; "Without the Sire has thou return'd?"   8679
e, w 349

I COULD NOT FIND MY BABY-O!; "I left my baby darling lying there" e 321   8680

I WISGO AUR-GORON; "I wisgo aur-goron y byd ar ei phen"; NOW STRIKE THE HARP GENTLY; BE MERRY BUT   8681
WISE; "Now strike the harp gladly, let music respond" e, w 349

LLANDYFRI; "Yn iach i ti Gymru"; ADIEU TO DEAR CAMBRIA; "Farewell to thee, Cymru" e, w 349   8682

LLWYN ONN; "Ym Mhalas Llwyn Onn gynt"; THE ASH GROVE; "The ash-grove how graceful" e, w 19, 343;   8683
LLWYN ON; "Yn Mhalas Llwyn on gynt" e, w 349; e 234, 279, 349, 366; "Away in the shadows
a lone bird is singing" e 297; "Down yonder green valley" e, w 402; e 46, 199

"MAE CROESAWIAD GWRAIG Y TY"; Welcome of the hostess (tune); Under yonder oaken tree (tune); LADY   8684
GWENNY; "County by county for beauty and bounty" e, w 349

Y MARCH A'R GWDDW BRITH; "Caradog eilw'i ddeiliaid"; THE SNOW-WHITE STEED; "Caradoc's horn is   8685
sounding" e, w 19; "I HEAR THE TRUMPET SOUNDING"; The camp (tune) e 235

MENTRA, GWEN; "Am danat ti mae son, Wennaf Wen, Wennaf Wen"; VENTURE GWEN; THE STARS IN   8686
HEAVEN ARE BRIGHT; "O'er Cymru, like a star, brightest Gwen, whitest Gwen" e, w 349;
GOLEUDDYDD; "The smiling spring, profusely gay" e 86

MERCH MEGAN; "Mi welais fy merch"; MEGAN'S FAIR DAUGHTER; "I see her in dreams" e, w 20   8687

MERCH Y MELINYDD; "Os yw fy anwyl gariad, Yn caru dwy neu dair"; THE MILLER'S DAUGHTER; "Because   8688
my sweetheart flatters Gwenllian, Kate, and Clare" e, w 349

MORFA RHUDDLAN; "Cilia'r haul draw dros ael bryniau hael Arfon"; THE MARSH OF RHUDDLAN; "Over   8689
    Eryri the setting sun flashes" e, w 349; "Du ac arswydus yw'r hanes am heddiw"; "Dark was the
    hour when our heroes were dying" e, w 20; WHERE ARE THE MEN; "Where are the men who
    went forth in the morning" e 235

MORFUDD; Consêt Dafydd ab Gwilym (tune); "Tyrd gyda mi, Forfudd, i rodio'n yrardd"; MORVUDD; Davydd   8690
    ab Gwilym's conceit (tune); "O come to the garden, sweet Morvudd awhile" e, w 20 words by
    D. Rowlands

Y MYNACH DU; "Hen Fynach Du Caerlleon Gawr"; THE BLACK MONK; "The old black monk stood still to   8691
    hear" e, w 349; CLYCHAU'R LLAN; Y Mynach Du (tune); "Dros gaerau'r nen diflanna'r dydd";
    VILLAGE BELLS; The black monk (tune); "While day recedes beyond the main" e, w 20

PANT CORLAN YR WYN; "Mehefin ddaeth fugeiliaid mwyn"; LET NOW THE HARP; "Let now the harp and   8692
    voice unite" e, w 349 words by J. Thomas

PE CAWN I HON; "Pe cawn i hon yn eiddoi mi"; SHE MUST BE MINE; "If she would turn her eyes that spurn"   8693
    e, w 349

RHYFELGYRCH CADBEN MORGAN; "Rhwym wrth dy wregys, gleddyf gwyn dy dad"; CAPTAIN MORGAN'S   8694
    MARCH; "Forth to the battle, onward to the fight" e, w 19; RHYFELGYRCH CAPTEN MORGAN;
    FORTH TO THE BATTLE; "Fast to thy girdle fix thy father's brand!" e, w 349 words by Ceiriog

RHYFELGYRCH GWYR HARLECH; "Harlech cyfod dy faneri"; MARCH OF THE MEN OF HARLECH; "Hark, I   8695
    hear the foe advancing" e, w 7, 19, 199; "Wele goelcerth wen yn fflamio"; MEN OF HARLECH;
    "Fierce the beacon light is flaming" e, w 349; e 234; "Men of Harlech, in the hollow" e, w
    402; e 233, 397; MARCH OF THE MEN OF HARLECH e 34; "Men of Harlech! honor calls us"
    e 28, 279, 366

SERCH HUDOL; "Serch hudol swyn, Sy'n llanw'r llwyn"; WEEP NOT, I PRAY; "Weep not, I pray, though on   8696
    this day" e, w 349

SYR HARRI DDU; "Du oedd ei bryd a'i darian gref"; BLACK SIR HARRY; "Black was his plume, black was his   8697
    shield" e, w 349

THREE JOLLY HUNTERS; "There were three jolly hunters a-hunting one fine day"; "One said it was a lighthouse,   8698
    the second said Nay" (ref) e 44

TROS Y GARREG; "Tros y garreg gamfa gu"; OVER THE ROCK; "Over the rock afar I roam" e, w 20; TROS Y   8699
    GAREG; "Tros y gareg gamfa gu"; OVER THE STONE; "O that happy summer week" e, w 349;
    THE GREY OLD STONE; "O'er the stone, the grey old stone" e 95; SAINT DISTAFF'S DAY;
    "Partly work and partly play ye must on St. Distaff's day" e 235

Y TŶ AR Y BRYN; Tôn Alarch (tune); "Mae'r tŷ ar y bryn, fu'n drystfawr cyn hyn"; THE HOUSE ON THE HILL;   8700
    The swan's tune (tune); "The house on the hill is order'd and still" e, w 20

Y TYLWYTH TEG; Y Gofid Glâs (tune); "Tra byddo'r byd mewn hyfryd hwyl"; THE FAIRIES; Blue devils (tune);   8701
    "When all the world is fast asleep" e, w 20 words by T. T. Jones

WRTH EDRYCH YN OL; Lady Owen's delight (tune); "Wrth edrych yn ôl y mae'r galon yn dwend"; WHY LINGERS   8702
    MY GAZE?; "Why lingers my gaze where the last hues of day" e, w 235, 349 words by F. Hemans

YMADAWIAD Y BRENIN; "Cariwyd y dydd! rhown gân a chainc"; THE DEPARTURE OF THE KING; "Loudly we   8703
    call, 'Justice for all!'" e, w 19; LOUDLY PROCLAIM; "Loudly proclaim o'er land and sea" e, w
    349 words by Ceiriog; FREE MEN, ARISE; "Heroes of Wales! Free men arise!" e 235

YN NYFFRYN CLWYD; The missing boat (tune); "Yn Nyffryn Clwyd nid oes"; VALE OF CLWYD; "By Clwyd,   8704
    all hoar with moss" e, w 349

YN NYFFRYN LLANGOLLEN; "Yn Nyffryn Llangollen ac ochor y Glyn"; IN THE VALE OF LLANGOLLEN; "In   8705
    the vale of Llangollen the story runs still" e, w 349

YSTAFELL CYNDDYLAN; "Boed curiad y stwffwl yn araf a gwan"; THE HALL OF CYNDDYLAN; "The Hall of   8706
    my Chieftain is gloomy tonight" e, w 20

WEST INDIES

ADA; "All de call me call Ada" e 252   8707

ALWAYS ONE RAIN; "I saw you in the bright sunlight"; "Always One Rain a day, to wash my tears away" (ref)   8708
    e 11

L'ANNÉE PASSÉE; "L'année passée moen té yon fille"; LAST YEAR; "Last year I was a little girl" e, f 286   8709

BALL GAWN ROUN'; "De play begin an' de ball gawn roun'" e 252   8710

A BAND OF BIRDS; COME DE BIRD; "A band of birds, come a-singing" e 11   8711

BID BAMBOO; "I ask my woman what I could do"; "Cause a Big Bamboo hangin' on the wall" (ref) e 11   8712

BORDE, C'EST VRAI; "Borde, c'est vrai, Trinidadien pas ni compassion"; TRINIDAD RACE TRACK SONG;   8713
    "Trinindad is the hardest of the towns I know" e, f 286

BROWN SKIN GIRL; "Brown skin girl stay home and mind baby"; "Ev'rything to keep me from sleepin'" (verse)   8714
    e 11

CALL DINAH; "All de call wa me dah call Dinah" e 252   8715

CHI-CHI BUD OH!; "A Chi-Chi Bud oh! Some a dem a halla, some a bawl" e 252   8716

COME, LITTLE DONKEY; "Ah! Come, little donkey, come"; "My donkey walk, my donkey talk, my donkey   8717
    eat with a knife and fork" e 77

CORDELIA BROWN; "Oh, Cordelia Brown What makes your head so red" e 11; CUDELIA BROWN; "Oh Cudelia   8718
    Brown, Wa meck yuh head so red?" e 252

DALLAS GAWN; "Dallas gawn a Cuba, Dallas gawn a Cuba" e 252   8719

DAY DAH LIGHT; BANANA LOADER'S SONG; "Day oh! Day oh! Day dah light an' me wan' go home" e 252;   8720
    BANANA BOAT LOADER'S SONG e 11

DEATH, OH ME LAWD; "Death, oh death, oh me Lawd" e 323   8721

DÉVIRÉ KATIE; "Déviré Katie déviré l'en caille mama ou"; KATIE COME HOME; "Katie come home now,   8722
    Katie come home right away!" e, f 286

DOCTA BUD; "Docta Bud, a cunning bud, Hard bud fe dead" e 252   8723

FAN ME SOLJA MAN; "Fan me solja man, fan me" e 252   8724

FISHERMAN'S SONG; "Fishermen sleep when the fish don't bite"; "Weigh up Susianna, 'Round the Bay of   8725
    Montserray" (ref) e 11

FYAH BUN; "Oh, yuh buil' yuh house pon san' an'de breeze come blow i' dung, Nancy" e 252   8726

GIMME BACK MY SHILLING; "I tell the Tommy to go home" e 11   8727

HAVE YOU HEARD?; LAS KANT FIND; LOST AND CANNOT BE FOUND; "Have you heard, Oh have you heard?"   8728
    e 11; LAS KEAN FINE; DIGGING SONG; "Yuh no yeary weh me yeary sey?" e 252

HER REPUTATION; "She found a soldier man, a soldier man she found"; "'Cause a soldier man he won't marry"   8729
    (ref) e 11

HILL AND GULLY; "Hill an' Gully rider Hill an' Gully" e 11; HILL AN' GULLY; "Hill an' Gully ride-a, Hill   8730
    an' Gully" e 252

HOL' YUH HAN'; "Dis long time gal me never see you" e 252   8731

HOSANNA; "Hosanna, me build a house, oh Hosanna, me build a house, oh" e 11; HOSSANNA; "Hossanna!   8732
    Me buil' me home oh, Ha-ha, Me buil' i' pon a sandy groun'" e 252

HOUSE AN' LAN'; "Edohedoh, oh oh oh oh, Edohedoh, house an' lan' a buy fambly oh!" e 252   8733

IN THE BOND; "Sally in the bond, bond-a-larry" e 37   8734

INVOCATION; "O ken Karanga, Karanga, Karanga day" f 286   8735

JUDY DROWNDED; "Judy drownded, Judy drownded, Whai of!" e 252; JUDY DROWNED; "Judy drowned, Judy   8736
    drowned Whai Oh!" e 11

LIZETTE; "Lizette, when you leave me here alone"; "All day long, while chopping cane" (verse) e 406   8737

LEMME GO, MELDA MARCY; "Well I cried all night, and not a policeman was in sight"; "Stop it! boy I angry"   8738
    (ref) e 11

LINSTEAD MARKET; "Carry me ackee go a Linstead Market"; "Oh Lawd! Not a mite not a bite" (ref) e 252   8739

THE LORD'S PRAYER; "Our Father, which art in heaven, hallowed a-be thy Name" e 323   8740

LOUIS CAMILLE; "Louis Camille, Où esti Elligon passé?"; "Louis Camille, have you seen Elligon today?" e, f   8741
    286

LOVELY CRICKET; "Where will you rest when the bright stars shine"; "When you are dressed in green" (ref) e 11   8742

MADA CANTINNY; ANANCY; "Dem sey dah me dah Cantinny" e 252   8743

MAN SMART, WOMAN SMARTER; "Let us put man and woman together" e 11   8744

MARTINIQUE BRULÉE; "Mart'nique brûlee chez moen"; MARTINIQUE HAS BURNED; "Mart'nique has burned"   8745
    e, f 286

MARY ANN; "When Mary Ann walks in the woods"; "Why do we boys love Mary Ann?" (ref) e 11   8746

MATILDA; "Matilda, Matilda, Matilda she take me money and run Venezuela" e 11   8747

MATTY WALLA-LEF'; "Me no wan', me nowan' wa Matty walla-lef" e 252   8748

MERCY POURIN' DOWN; "What a mercy pourin' down" e 323   8749

MISSA RAMGOAT; "Missa Ramgoat oh! Barba deh yah, Missa Ramgoat, oh!" e 252   8750

MONGOOSE DEAD OH; "Mongoose stealin' blackbird told me so"; "Mongoose gone, mongoose, gone; Not my   8751
    fault he dead" (ref) e 11

MONKEY DRAW BOW; MONKEY JAW BONE; "One day me go dung a Lnag-Pan Fe wata" e 252   8752

MOURNING SONG; "Wo yo yoi, wa ya yai Mama moen mort dans Kalenda Roche"; "Wo yo yoi, wa ya yai,   8753
    Mother has died in Kalenda Rock" e, f 286

MURDER IN DE MARKET; "Murder in de market, murder, murder in de market, murder" e 323   8754

NOBODY'S BUSINESS; "Solomon granpa gawn a Equador" e 252   8755

OH, NOT A CENT; "Oh, not a cent, not a cent" e 286   8756

OGOUN BELELE; "Ogoun Belele O yea, Ogoun Belele" e 323   8757

ONE SOLJA MAN; "One solja man come fe court me" e 252   8758

"PACK SHE BACK TO SHE MA" e 286   8759

PAPA DIDN'T KNOW; "One night they rowed without a man, papa didn't know, mama didn't know" e 323   8760

PETITE BRUN DOUX-DOUX; "Moen c'est un petite brun doux-doux"; I'M DARK-EYED AND PETITE; "I'm   8761
    dark-eyed and petite to hold" e, f 286

RATTA MADAN-LAW; "Ratta Madan-law cut one night shut" e 252   8762

RIBBER BEN COME DUNG; DIGGING SONG; "De ribber ben come dung" e 252   8763A

"DE RIBBER BEN COME DUNG"; DIGGING SONG e 252   8763B

ROOKOOMBINE; "Train top a bridge jus-a run like a breeze" e 252   8764
SAMMY DEAD OH!; "A no tief Sammy tief meck dem kill him" e 252   8765
"SEE ME LITTLE BROWN BOY?" e 286   8766
SOUND THE FIRE ALARM; "Out in the country where I come from"; "Fire! Fire! Put out the fire" (ref) e 11   8767
STORM WARNING; "When the storm warning posted in St. Croix"; "Hurricane is an angry thing" (ref) e 11   8768
SWEET CHACOUN; "I still am pining sweet Chacoun"; "I have searched for our star Chacoun" (ref) e 11   8769
TEACHER LICK DE GAL; "One shif me got Ratta cut i'" e 252   8770
"TIME FOR MAN GO HOME"; THE MONKEY SONG e 323   8771
TINGA LAYO; "Tinga layo Marré bourriq ba moen"; DONKEY SONG; "Tinga layo come, little donkey, come"   8772
        e, f 286
TO CARMENCITA; "Go, little message to Camencita" e 350   8773
WATA COME A ME Y'EYE; "Ev'ry time me memba Liza, Wata come a me y'eye"; "Come back Liza, come back   8774
        gal" (ref) e 252; WATER COME A ME EYE; "Ev'ry time I 'member Liza water come a me eye" e 11
WATER IN ME RUM; "CAPITAL OFFENCE; "One day I woke up feelin' weak" e 11   8775

YUGOSLAVIA

COIN I NEED; "Coin I need today, wife, not tomorrow" e 95   8776
DOMOVINA; "Kad u borbu mi i demo"; "When our battle flag is flying" e, cr 293   8777
"THE DOVE HAS TWIN WHITE FEET" e 36   8778
DUBROVNIKU GOD; DUBROVNIK; "Oh, Dubrovnik! Oh Dubrovnik! wake" e 86   8779
GUERRILLA SONG; "Mrka četa, mrka četa Srpskijeh junaka"; "Softly rustling, softly rustling thru the Serbian   8780
        valley" e, cr 7
HAJDUK VELJKO I CARAPIĆ VASO; GUERILLA FIGHTER VELJKO; "We sing how Guerilla Veljko sent word" e 86   8781
JUNAČKA PJESMA; SIRDAR JANKO; "Sirdar Janko, get a move on" e 86   8782
JUNAK JANKO; KNIGHT JANKO; "Deep in the forest, Mother stopped three bearers" e 86   8783
JUNAK JANKO; KNIGHT JANKO; "Who here has seen my son" e 86   8784
KOLO; "Come along and dance this dance now, a ha ha" e 95   8785
KRALJEVIĆ MARKO I TRI NIEMČIĆA; MARKO AND THE THREE GERMANS; "On the very night that Marko   8786
        married" e 86
LULLABY; "Lullaby, lullaby, so I rock, rock my boy" e 95   8787
MERCY, BEAUTY; "Mercy, beauty, mercy, hear me" e 95   8788
PEOPLE AWAKE!; "Zdrami se rod, Kvišku povsod"; "People Awake! Hear the earth shake" e, cr 7   8789
RISE, GUERILLAS, RISE; "Četnička truba zatrubi"; "Hear how the chetnik's bugle calls" e, cr 7 8790
RISES THE SUN; "Rises the sun but gray clouds make the light unsteady" e 95   8791
YANKO; "Yesterday Yanko fell upon our village" e 95   8792

CAROLS

ALSACE

AT THE NATIVITY; "Gloomy night embraced the place wherein the noble Infant lay" e 361   8793
"THE SHEPHERDS WENT THEIR HASTY WAY" e 333,361   words by S. T. Coleridge   8794
SLUMBER, DEAR JESUS; "O slumber, slumber softly, dear Jesus" e 271   8795

ARGENTINA

LITTLE SHEPHERDS; "Little shepherds, come forth from the vale" e 244   8796

AUSTRIA

AUF, AUF NUN, IHR HIRTEN; "Auf, auf nun ihr Hirten, nicht schlaft mir so lang!" g 354; AS LATELY WE   8797
     WATCHED; "As lately we watch'd o'er our fields thro' the night" e 79,296
ES WIRD SCHO GLEI DUMPA; "Es wird scho glei dumpa, es wird jå schon Nåcht"; THE DARKNESS IF FALLING;   8798
     "The darkness is falling, the day is nigh gone" e, g 388; TIROLER CHRISTKINDL WIEGENLIED;
     "Es wird schon gleich dunkel, es wird ja schon Nacht" g 40
GÖTTLICHS KINDLEIN; "Göttlich's Kindlein, dich zu grüssen" g 40   8799
GRÜNET FELDER; "Grünet Felder, grünet Wiesen, weil der Heiland ist geborn" g 40; GRÜNET, FELDER,   8800
     GRÜNET WIESEN g 354
HIRTEN, AUF UM MITTERNACHT!; "Hirten, auf um Mitternacht, erhebt euch aus dem Schlafe!"; SHEPHERDS,   8801
     UP!; "Shepherds, up, your watch to take! your time of sleep is ending" e, g 388
LIED DER KINDER ZU BETHLEHEM; "Bist einmal kommen, du Heiland der Welt"; CAROL OF THE CHILDREN OF   8802
     BETHLEHEM; "We bid Thee welcome, Thou Saviour of all" e, g 388
LIPPAI; "Lippai, steh auf vom Schlaf!"; "Lippai, don't play you're dead!" e, g 337   8803
O HEILIG KIND; WE GREET THEE, HEAVENLY DOVE; "We greet Thee, blessed heavenly Dove" e 79   8804
WEIHNACHTS-WIEGENLIED; "Schlafe mit Ruh'! Göttliches Kindelein"; CHRISTMAS LULLABY; "Soundly now   8805
     sleep, Heavenly Child of love" e, g 154
WER KLOPFET AN?; "'Wer klopfet an?' 'O, zwei gar arme Leut!'"; WHO'S KNOCKING THERE?; "'Who's   8806
     knocking there?'; 'Two folk in sorry plight'" e, g 388

BASQUE

ABETS ZAGUN GUZIEK; BETHLEHEM'S STALL; "Bethlehem's darkened city Mary and Joseph sought" e 361   8807
     words by K. W. Simpson
AT CHRISTMAS-TIDE; "At Christmas-tide all Christians sing to hail the news" e 373   8808
AUR TXIKI; "LOVELY BABY, MARY BORE HIM" e 244,361   8809
"BEARING MYRRH AND SPICES SWEET" e 371   8810
BELENEN SORTU ZAIGU; IN MIDDLE WINTER THEY SET OUT; "In middle winter they set out from home to be   8811
     enroll'd at Bethlehem" e 361
BEUDE BAZTER EGUN; WHY SHOULD WE GO GRIEVING?; "Why should we go grieving? This is Christmas Day!";   8812
     "O Christ Jesus! Lovest us so dearly" (verse) e 361
BIBA JESUS GOURE JAONE; "PRAISE JESUS CHRIST WHO CAME THIS NIGHT" e 361; BORN THIS DAY; "Dear   8813
     little Infant, born this day" e 373
BIRJINA GAZTETTOBAT ZEGOEN; "A MAIDEN WAS ADORING GOD THE LORD" e 244,361; "THE ANGEL   8814
     GABRIEL FROM HEAVEN CAME"; GABRIEL'S MESSAGE e 317; GABRIEL'S MESSAGE e 363,369
CHANTEZ BIEN NÖEL; Pour l'amour de Marie (tune); "All ye who are to mirth inclined"; "Chantez! Chantez   8815
     bien Nöel! 'Jesus is born' the angels tell" (ref) e 372
EASTER FLOWERS; "Easter flow'rs are blooming bright" e 371   8816
EGUBERRIREN JITIAZ; GODS OF THE HEATHEN; "Gods of the heathen, bronze and stone"; "Eve was our mother,   8817
     low she fell" (verse) e 361; WHENCE COMES THIS RUSH OF WINGS?; "Whence comes this rush of
     wings afar" e 296,337; CAROL OF THE BIRDS e 165,206
THE EMPTY TOMB; "Awake, arise and greet the dawning day" e 371   8818
ETZEN BADA MARIA?; "WHO WERE THE SHEPHERDS MARY?" e 361   8819
EZ DUKEZU; "LEAD ME TO THY PEACEFUL MANGER" e 361   8820
HASTEN TO BETHLEHEM; "Come list to the story I tell you" e 370   words by S. Baring-Gould   8821
HIROUR ERREGEREKI; WHEN DAVID'S DAUGHTER; "When David's daughter to David's city bore Christ the   8822
     strong to save" e 361
HOTS AINGURIEKIN, ARKANJELIEKIN; HOW THE BANNER'D ANGELS; "How the banner'd angels down the night   8823
     go singing!" e 361
I SAW A MAIDEN; "I saw a maiden sitting and sing" e 317,370   8824
JAON HANDIAK IKHOUSAZIE; "Great gentlefolk hold and bethink you" e 361   8825
JOSEPH AND GENTLE MARY CAME; "Joseph and gentle Mary came, unto the town of Bethlehem" e 377   8826A
TO BETHLEHEM; "Joseph and gentle Mary came unto the town of Bethlehem" e 370   8826B
THE JOYS OF CHRISTMAS; "May joy come from God above"; "Sing we merrily, sing Nowell" (ref) e 372   8827

KHANTA BEZA BITORIA; SING THE UNIVERSAL GLORY; "Sing the universal glory Lo! the serpent's triple head" 8828
    e 361
KHANTA ZAGUNGUZIEK; "WE SING OF DAVID'S DAUGHTER" e 361; "COMPANIONS, ALL SING LOUDLY" 8829
    e 165,296
KHIRISTIAK ORDUDA; "CHRISTIAN MEN, LOOK UP ON HIGH"; "Jesus, and is Thine hour come?" (verse) e 361 8830
O EGUBERRI GAUA; "THERE CAME A SHY INTRUDER" e 361 8831
OI! BETLEEM!; O BETHLEHEM; "O Bethlehem! 'Tis not the rosebud's time to open" e 39,361; THE INFANT 8832
    KING; "Sing lullaby! Lullaby baby, now reclining" e 363,370; SING LULLABY! LULLABY BABY
    e 317
OI! GAU DOATSU; "STARS AND HILLS ARE HOARY" e 361 8833

BELGIUM

DE AENBIDDING DER HERDERS; "Wat zang, wat klang van d'engelsche schaeren"; SHEPHERD'S CHRISTMAS 8834
    SONG; "Hear how the angels sing all in chorus" e, fl 154
GENTLE SAVIOUR, DAY AND NIGHT; "Gentle Saviour day and night, ride three Princes great in might" e 378 8835
JESUS IN THE STALL; "Come ye shepherds, hear the call of your Jesus in the stall" e 361 8836
"A LITTLE CHILD ON THE EARTH HAS BEEN BORN" e 307 8837
THREE KINGS; "Three Kings are here, both wealthy and wise" e 199 8838
WIR DREI HIRTENMÄDCHEN; "Wir drei Hirtenmächen sahen aus der grünen Wiese klein" g 354 8839

BRAZIL

REPOUSA TRANQUILO O MEIGO JESUS; LULLABY FOR BABY JESUS; "Sleep quietly, my Jesus, now close Thy 8840
    dear eyes" e 165
SENHORA DONA SANCHA; "Senhora Dona Sancha coberta d'ouro e prata"; OH HEAR THE HEAV'NLY ANGELS; 8841
    "Oh hear the heav'nly angels in soft and wondrous chorus" e, po 154

CANADA

THE CHERRY TREE CAROL. See 8911J

CATALONIA

ALLÁ SOTA UNA PENYA; "Allá sota una penya n'es nat un Jesuset pobret, pobret"; ALLÍ BAJO UNA PEÑA; 8842
    "Allí, bajo una peña, nació ya Jesusín pobrin, pobrin!" ca, s 54
L'ANGEL I ELS PASTORS; "Pastorets, de la muntanya que viviu amb gran rezel"; EL ANGEL Y LOS PASTORES; 8843
    "Pastores de la Montaña, que vivis con gran recelo" ca 54
LES BESTIES EN EL NAIXEMENT; "Les gallinas van pujant, juntas van; el gall cantant"; LAS ANIMALES ANTE 8844
    EL NACIMIENTA; "Las gallinas van subiendo, juntas van el gallo canta" ca, s 55
EL BON JESUSET; "El bon Jesuset volina sabates"; EL BUEN NIÑO JESÚS; "El buen Jesusín quería zapatos" ca, 8845
    s 56
EL CANT DELS OCELLS; "Al veure despuntar el major lluminar"; EL CANTO DE LOS PÁJAROS; "Cuando ven 8846
    despuntar el mayor luminar" ca, s 56
CAP A BETLHEM CAMINÉN; "Pastors tots aném, amb gran reverencia a adorar a Jesús"; HACIA BELÉN ANDAMAS; 8847
    "Pastores, venid con gran reverencia adorad a Dios" ca, s 55
LO DESEMBRE CONGELAT; "El desembre congelat confús se retira"; EL HELADO DICIEMBRE; "El diciembre ya 8848
    se va consus crudos días" ca, s 53; CANSÓ DE NADAL; "Lo desembre congelat, confús se retira";
    CHRISTMAS SONG; "Winter now has passed away, storms have all abated" ca, s 154; THE
    ANNUNCIATION; "To a virgin meek and mild came an angel holy" e 244 words by V. E. Boe;
    NATIVITY SONG; "When December's winds were stilled, past the month of snowing" e 244
LES DOLCES FESTES; "Digues, xic ¿com es que riuen tan contents tots els minyons?"; LAS DULCES FIESTAS; 8849
    "Hijo, dime ¿por qué rien los niños con tal humor?" ca, s 54
LES DOTZE VAN TOCANT; "Les dotze van tocant; ja es nat el Rei Infant"; VAN DANDO LAS DOCE; "Las 8850
    doce dando van; nació el Rey celestial" ca, s 56
ESTANT EN LA CAMBRA; "Estant en la cambra amb son Fill aimat"; RECOGIDA CON EL NIÑO; "Sola en su 8851
    aposento con el Hijo amado" ca, s 53
FUM FUM FUM; "A vint i cinc de desembre fum, fum, fum"; "Veinticinco de diciembre fum, fum, fum" ca, 8852
    s 53; FOOM, FOOM, FOOM!; "On December twenty-five, sing foom, foom, foom!" e, s 337;
    "On December twenty-fifth, sing fum, fum, fum" e, s 388; "On December twenty-fifth, fum, fum,
    fum" e 165; "On December five and twenty, fum, fum, fum" e 33
LA GITANA; "Cuan el bon Jesús founat els angels l'anunciaven"; "Cuando el buen Jesús nació angelitos lo 8853
    anunciaban" ca, s 56

JESÚS ES NAT; "Quan Sant Josep se'n anava am María gran pena tenía veientla plorant"; JESÚS HA NACIDO; 8854
    "Al ir José con la Vírgen María gran pena sufría viéndola llorar" ca, s 56

JOSEP I MARIA VAN A PASSEJAR; "Josep i María van a passejar en una font fresca varen reposar"; JOSÉ Y 8855
    MARÍA SALEN DE PASEO; "José con María van a pasear, en la fresca fuente van a descansar"
    ca, s 53

NIT DE VETLLA; "Esta nit es nit de vetlla"; NOCHE EN VELA; "Esta noche es noche en vela" ca, s 55 8856

EL NOI DE LA MARE; "Que li darém a n'el Noi de la Mare?"; EL HIJO DE LA VIRGEN; "¿Qué le daremos al 8857
    Niño divino" ca, s 55; WHAT SHALL WE GIVE TO THE BABE?; "What shall we give to the Babe
    in the manger" e 33

LA PASTORA; "Den vos guard Josep i la vostra esposa"; "Dios guardea José y a su santa esposa" ca, s 53 8858

PASTORELLA DE NADAL; "Ohinme pastors ohinme una estona, que us vinc a portar una bona nova"; PASTORAL 8859
    DE NAVIDAD; "Pastores oid; oid una nueva que os alegrará una buena nueva" ca, s 55

ELS PASTORETS; "Allá dalt de la muntanya un angel als pastors diu"; LOS PASTORCILLOS; "Arriba de la mon- 8860
    taña a un angel se oye decir" ca, s 54

EL PETIT BAILET; "Yo soc el petit bailet cansadet de molt cami"; EL PEQUEÑO ZAGAL; "El pequeño zagal soy 8861
    cansado de tanto andar" ca, s 53

EL POBRET ALEGRE; "Jo tinc una jupa tota de vellut"; EL POBRECILLO ALEGRE; "De tela de pana yo tengo un 8862
    jubón" ca, s 55

EL RABADÁ JOANET; "Llevat, llevat Joanet! llevat au fora del llit"; EL PASTOR JUAN; "Levántate presto, Juan, 8863
    que tenemos el deber de correr hacia Belén" ca, s 53

SANT JOSEP I LA MARE DE DEU; "Sant Josep i la Mare de Deu feren companyia bona partiren de Nazarteh"; 8864
    SAN JOSÉ Y LA VIRGEN; "San José y la Vírgin María van en buena compañia, partieron de Nazaret"
    ca, s 54

ELS TRES PASTORETS; "Si n'hi han tres pastorets tots a dintre d'una cova"; LOS TRES PASTORCILLOS; "Tres 8865
    pastorcillos había metidos en una cueva" ca, s 54

EL TUNCH QUE TAN TUNCH; "Anem pastors a Betlhem; caminem anem anem"; EL TUÑC QUE TAN TUNC; 8866
    "Pastores hacia Belén caminemos presto ya" ca, s 56

CZECHOSLOVAKIA

"CAROL HIGH, AND CAROL LOW" e 379 words by E. M. Dawson 8867

CAROL OF THE BIRDS; "From out of a wood did a cuckoo fly" e 214,410; THE BIRDS e 199,271 8868

CO TO ZNAMENÁ?; "Co to znamená medle nového?"; WHAT IS THE MEANING?; "What is the meaning of 8869
    this new glory?" c, e 154

"HAJEJ, NYNEJ, JEŽÍŠKU"; ROCKING SONG; "Little Jesus, sweetly sleep, do not stir" c, e 388; e 33,337, 8870
    410; ROCKING e 199,271,319,337,410

IN EINEM KRIPPLEIN; "In einem Kripplein lieget das Kindlein" g 354 8871

KAMPAK BEZIS; "Kampak běžíš Jeníčku, a nejdeš pomaličku chodníčkem k nám"; "WHERE ARE YOU BOUND, 8872
    JOHNNY DEAR" c, e 324

"LET OUR GLADNESS KNOW NO END" e 79,165,296; "FREU DICH, ERD UND STERNENZELT" g 354 8873

MARY WAS WATCHING; "Mary was watching tenderly her little son" e 319 8874

MORNING STAR; "Morning star, O cheering sight" e 214 8875

NARODIL SE KRISTUS PÁN; "Narodil se Kristus, Pán, veselme se!"; CHRIST WAS BORN; "Christ was born and 8876
    lives anew! Oh, rejoice, all!" c, e 324

NESEM VÁM NOVINY; "Nesem vám noviny, poslouchejte"; COME ALL YE SHEPHERDS; "Come, all ye shep- 8877
    herds, come hark unto me!" c, e 388; HEAR WHAT GREAT NEWS WE BRING; "Hear what great
    news we bring to all the earth" c, e 154; ANGELS AND SHEPHERDS; "Come all ye shepherds and
    hark to our song!" e 165; CAROL OF THE SHEPHERDS; "Come, all ye shepherds and be not dis-
    mayed" e 251; COME, ALL YE SHEPHERDS; MESEM VAM NOVING; "Come, all ye shepherds,
    come hark unto me!" e 33; COLD IS THE MORNING; "Cold is the morning and bleak is the day"
    e 337 words by W. P. Kent; KOMMET, IHR HIRTEN; "Kommet, ihr Hirten, Männer und Fraun"
    g 40,354; COME, ALL YE SHEPHERDS; "Come, all ye shepherds, your flocks will not stray" e 296
    words by M. L. Hohman

"PÁSLI OVCE VALAŠI"; "SHEPHERDS WATCHED THEIR FLOCKS BY NIGHT" c, e 337; "UNDER BETHLEM'S 8878
    STAR SO BRIGHT" e 319

"PŮJDEM SPOLEM DO BETLÉMA"; "ALLONS ENSEMBLE À BETHLÉEM" c, f 177 8879

"SEL BYCH RÁD K BEGLÉMU"; "TO BETHL'EM I WOULD GO" c, e 337 8880

SLEEP, MY SAVIOR; "Sleep, my Savior, sleep on Thy bed of hay" e 165; SLEEP, MY SAVIOUR, SLEEP; "Sleep, 8881
    my Saviour, sleep, on Thy bed of hay" e 378

DENMARK

A BABE IS BORN IN BETHLEHEM; "A Babe is born in Bethlehem, Bethlehem" e 244 8882

EIN KIND GEBORN ZU BETHLEHEM; "Ein Kind geborn zu Bethlehem, Bethlehem, des freuet sich Jerusalem" g 354 8883

DER NEUE TAG; Dag visen (tune); "Der neue Tag, der nun anbricht" g 354   8884
THE PERFECT ROSE; "The roses bloom then fade away" e 279,366   8885
DEN YNDIGSTE ROSE; THE FAIREST OF ROSES; "The fairest of roses is growing" e 206   8886

DOMINICAN REPUBLIC

ABREME LA PUERTA; "Abreme la puerta, abreme la puerta"; LET ME CROSS YOUR THRESHOLD; "Let me cross   8887
     your threshold, do this one thing for me" e, s 154; EL AGUINALDO s 284

ECUADOR

DULCE JESUS MIO; "Dulce Jesus mio, minino adorado"; SWEET AND PRECIOUS JESUS; "Sweet and precious   8888
     Jesus, infant loved and cherished" e, s 154

ENGLAND

AH MAN, AH SAY; "Ah man, ah say, ah say, ah say"; "Man have in mind how here before" (verse) e 360   8889
"ALL HAIL TO THE DAYS THAT MERIT MORE PRAISE" e 38,39; THE PRAISE OF CHRISTMAS e 271,334   8890
     words by T. Durfey
ALL YOU THAT IN THIS HOUSE; Essex's last good-night (tune); "All you that in this house be here" e 410   8891
"ALLELUYA PRO VIRGINE MARIA"; "ALLELUYA, THE JOY OF VIRGIN MARY"; "Diva natalicia, nostra purgat   8892
     vincia" (verse); "Joy divine of Christmas Day, does our very sins away" e, lat 360,361
"ALMA REDEMPTORIS MATER" (ref); AS I LAY UPON A NIGHT; "As I lay upon a night, My thought was on a   8893
     berd so bright" (verse) e, lat in pt 360,361
THE ANGEL GABRIEL; "The Angel Gabriel from God was sent to Galilee" e 319,337,363,410; "WHEN RIGHT-   8894A
     EOUS JOSEPH WEDDED WAS" e 361; WHEN RIGHTEOUS JOSEPH e 334
"WHEN RIGHTEOUS JOSEPH WEDDED WAS" e 361   8894B
AS I LAY UPON A NIGHT; "As I lay upon a night, Forsooth I saw a seemly sight" e 360,361   8895
AS IT FELL OUT UPON ONE DAY; DIVES AND LAZARUS; "As it fell out upon one day, rich Dives he made a   8896A
     feast" e 333
DIVES AND LAZARUS; "As it fell out upon a day, rich Dives made a feast" e 361   8896B
"AS JACOB WITH TRAVEL WAS WEARY ONE DAY" e 333; JACOB'S LADDER e 334   8897
"AVE DOMINA CELI REGINA"; "Worshipt be the birth of thee" (verse) e, lat 360,361   8898
"AWAKE, AND JOIN THE CHEERFUL CHOIR" e 377   8899
THE BABE IN BETHLEM'S MANGER; "The Babe in Bethlem's manger laid"; "Nowell, Nowell, O sing a Saviour's   8900
     birth" e 361; "THE BABE IN BETHLEM'S MANGER LAID" e 319; "Nowell, Nowell, now sing a
     Saviour's birth" (ref) e 333; "Nowell, Nowell, Lord, sing a Saviour's birth" (ref) e 334; THE
     BABE OF BETHLEHEM; "Noël, Noël, Now sing the Savior giv'n" (ref) e 296; THE SAVIOUR'S
     WORK; "Nowell, Nowell, now sing a Saviour's birth" (ref) e 337
A BABE IS BORN; "A Babe is born all of a may, in the savasyoun of us" e 33,337; "A Babe is born all of a   8901
     maid, to bring salvation unto us" e 410; "Nowell el el el, now is well" (solo); "A Babe is born
     all of a may, who brings salvation unto us" e 334; "GLORY TO GOD IN HEIGHTS OF HEAVEN"
     e 361
THE BABE IS LORD OF ALL; "Infant Holy, Son of God most Holy" e 372   8902
BE MERRY, BE MERRY; "Be merry, be merry, be merry I pray you ev'ry one"; "A principal point of charity it   8903
     is, it is merry to be" (verse) e 360,361
THE BLACK DECREE; "Let Christians all with one accord rejoice" e 361   8904
THE BOAR'S HEAD CAROL; "The boar's head in hand bear I"; "Caput apri defero" (ref) e, lat 206,334,337;   8905
     "The boar's head in hand bring I" e, lat 79,165; "THE BOAR'S HEAD IN HAND BEAR I"; BOAR'S
     HEAD CAROL e, lat 307,333; THE BORE'S HEED; "The bore's heed in hand bring I"; "Caput apri
     differo" (ref) e, lat 410
CANDLEMAS EVE; "Down with the rosemary and bays" e 334 words by R. Herrick   8906A
CANDLEMAS EVE CAROL; "Down with the rosemary and bays" e 378 words by R. Herrick   8906B
CAROL, CHILDREN CAROL; "Carol, children, carol, carol joyfully" e 79   8907
CAROL OF THE BEASTS; "Jesus, our brother, kind and good" e 214; THE FRIENDLY BEASTS e 79,165,249;   8908
     "Jesus, our brother, strong and good" e 33 words by R. Davis
THE CEDAR OF LEBANON; "The cedar of Lebanon plant of renown"; "All glory to God in the highest we wing"   8909
     (ref) e 333
CEREMONIES FOR CHRISTMAS; "Come bring with a noise, my merry, merry boys" e 374 words by R. Herrick   8910
THE CHERRY TREE CAROL; "Joseph was an old man, and an old man was he" e 334; "When Joseph was an old   8911A
     man, an old man was he" e 154; JOSEPH WAS AN OLD MAN; THE CHERRY TREE CAROL, PART I;
     "Joseph was an old man, and an old man was he" e 361; ST. JOSEPH AND THE ANGEL; "Saint
     Joseph was an old man an old, old man was he" e 363; AS JOSEPH WAS A-WALKING; THE
     CHERRY TREE CAROL; "As Joseph was a-walking, he heard an angel sing" e 333

THE CHERRY TREE CAROL; "Joseph was an old man, an old man was he" e 363; AS JOSEPH WAS A-WALKING; 8911B
    THE CHERRY TREE CAROL; "As Joseph was a-walking, he heard angels sing" e 296

THE CHERRY TREE CAROL; "O, Joseph was an old man" e 393   8911C

JOSEPH AND THE ANGEL; THE CHERRY TREE CAROL, PART II; "As Joseph was a-walking, he heard an angel 8911D
    sing" e 361

THE CHERRY-TREE CAROL; "St. Joseph was an old man an old man was he" e 126   8911E

AS JOSEPH WAS A-WALKING; "As Joseph was a-walking, he heard an angel sing" e 33,337,388   8911F

AS JOSEPH WAS A-WALKING; "As Joseph was a-walking, he heard an angel sing" e 319, 79; MARY'S QUES- 8911G
    TION; THE CHERRY TREE CAROL, PART III; "Then Mary took her young Son and set Him
    on her Knee" e 361

JOSEPH AND MARY; THE CHERRY TREE CAROL; "Joseph was an old man, an old man was he" e 332   8911H

THE CHERRY TREE; "When Joseph was an olden man" e 268,261   8911I

THE CHERRY TREE CAROL; "Oh, Joseph took Mary up on his right knee" e 186   8911J

THE CHERRY TREE; "When Joseph war an olden man" e 265   8911K

A CHILD THIS DAY IS BORN; "A Child this day is born, a Child of high renown" e 296,307,333,334,337,363, 8912
    410; NOVELS e 361; NOWELL, SING ALL WE MAY; "Nowell, Nowell, Nowell, Nowell, sing all
    we may" e 319

"CHRIST THE LORD IS RISEN TODAY"; Easter Hymn (tune); e 28,346,343,366,400 words by C. Wesley   8913

CHRISTMAS IS COMING; "Christmas is coming, the geese are getting fat" e 33,343; "Christmas is coming, 8914
    the goose is getting fat" e 44,214,337 3 pt round words by E. Nesbitt

COME ALL YOU WORTHY GENTLEMEN; "Come all you worthy gentlemen that may be standing by" e 307; 8915
    SOMERSET CAROL e 334

CORNISH MAY SONG; "Ye country maidens, gather dew, while yet the morning breezes blow"; "Arise, arise, 8916
    the night is past" (ref) e 70 words by A. Boswell

COVENTRY CAROL; "Lully, lulla, thou little tiny child" e 38,39,334; "Lully, lulla you little tiny child" 8917A
    e 61; "Lullay, thou little tiny child" e 35,165,206,333,410; "Lully, lullay, thou little tiny
    child" e 33; LULLY, LULLAY; COVENTRY CAROL e 307,337; "LULLAY, THOU LITTLE TINY
    CHILD" e 35,206,296,307,319 words by R. Croo

LULLE LULLAY; "Lullay, Thou tiny little Child" e 261,268   8917B

CRADLE SONG; "Hush! my dear, lie still and slumber" e 271 words by I. Watts   8918

"DAME GET UP AND BAKE YOUR PIES"; e 35,79; DAME GET UP; "O Dame get up and bake your pies" e 216 8919

DAVID EX PROGENIE; "David ex progenie, nata fuit hodie"; FROM THE ROYAL SHEPHERD'S LINE; "From the 8920
    royal shepherd's line, came one day a maiden fine" e 360,361; "Verbum caro factum est; habi-
    tavit in nobis"; "See the Word our flesh become, and among us make His home" part II set to
    same tune as above e 360,361

DOWN IN YON FOREST; "Down in yon forest there stands a hall"; "The bells of Paradise I heard them ring" (ref) 8921
    e 307; THE BELLS OF PARADISE; "What are those bells that chime so clear" e 165

EYA MARTYR STEPHANE; "Eya martyr Stephane, pray for us we pray to thee"; "Of this martyr make we mend" 8922
    (verse) e, lat in pt 360,361

THE FIRST NOEL; "The first Noel, the angel did say" e 28,79,251,315,366,388; "The first Noel the angels 8923
    did say" e 165,206,296; THE FIRST NOWEL; "The first Nowel the Angel did say" e 361; "THE
    FIRST NOWELL THE ANGEL DID SAY" e 38,39; THE FIRST NOWELL e 33,35,125,199,233,236,
    244,271,307,319,337,349,363,410; "The first Nowell that the Angel did say" e 334; "The first
    Nowell the angels did say" e 333; "The first Noel, the Angel did say" e 154; WHENE'ER THOU
    ART IN NEED OF ME; "When Thou wouldst pour the living stream" e 244 words by P. Hsi

FOR JOY OF HEART; "For joy of heart, come, bear apart" e 371   8924

FURRY DAY CAROL; "Remember us poor Mayers all" e 39; "God bless the master of this house" e 319; "GOD 8925
    BLESS THE MASTER OF THIS HOUSE"; THE FURRY DAY CAROL e 307,333

FYFE'S NOEL; THE FIRST NOEL; "The first Noel an angel sung" e 361   8926

A GALLERY CAROL; "Rejoice and be merry in songs and in mirth" e 334; REJOICE AND BE MERRY e 317 8927

GLAD CHRISTMAS BELLS; "Glad Christmas bells, your music tells" e 28,206,244,296,366   8928

GLORY TO GOD; "Glory to God in the Highest" 3 pt round e 319   8929

"GOD GIVE YE MERRY CHRISTMAS TIDE"; "Our blessed Master Jesus Christ, was born on Christmas Day" (ref) 8930
    e 244

"GOD REST YOU MERRY, GENTLEMEN" e 33,35,79,125,165,199,206,251,271,296,305,307,315,319,333,334, 8931A
    337,363,366,388,402,410; GOD REST YOU MERRY e 38,39,361; "GOD REST YE, MERRY
    GENTLEMEN" e 349

"GOD REST YOU, MERRY GENTLEMEN" e 333,334; GOD REST YOU MERRY e 361   8931B

GOD'S DEAR SON; "God's dear Son without beginning" e 334; "GOD'S DEAR SON WITHOUT BEGINNING" e 333, 8932
    361

GOLDEN MORNINGS; "They saw the light shine out afar" e 271 words by P. Dearmer   8933

GOOD DAY SIR CHRISTMAS; "Good day, good day, good day my Lord Sir Cristemas"; "Good day Sir Cristemas 8934
    our King" (verse) e 360

GOOD KING WENCESLAS; Tempus adest florideum (tune); "Good King Wenceslas look'd out" e 28,33,35,35,38, 8935
    39,79,125,154,199,206,296,305,315,319,334,349,361,363,366,388; "Good King Wenceslas looked
    out" e 165,271,307,337,410; "GOOD KING WENCESLAS LOOKED OUT" e 333 words by J. M.
    Neale; FLOWER CAROL; "Spring has now unwrapped the flowers" e 199,271 words by P. Dearmer;
    SPRING CAROL; "Spring is here with all her joys" e 44; "GENTLE MARY LAID HER CHILD" e 251
    words by J. S. Cook

THE GREAT GOD OF HEAVEN; "The great God of Heaven is come down to earth" e 363 words by H. R. Bramley 8936
GREEN GROW'TH THE HOLLY; "Green grow'th the holly, so doth the ivy" e 333 words att to King Henry VIII 8937
"HAIL MARY FULL OF GRACE"; "The Holy Ghost is to thee sent" (verse) e 360,361 8938A
"HAIL MARY FULL OF GRACE"; "The Holy Ghost is to thee sent" (verse) e 360 8938B
AN HEAVENLY SONG; "An heavenly song I dare well say"; "This is the song that ye shall hear" (verse) e 360,361 8939
HOLD, MEN HOLD!; "Hold, men, hold! We are very cold" e 337 8940
"THE HOLLY AND THE IVY" e 33,38,39,271,293,305,307,319,333,337,363,388,410; "DER STECHDORN UND 8941A
    DER EFEU" e, g 354
"THE HOLLY AND THE IVY" e 206,296,333,334 8941B
THE HOLY WELL; "As it fell out one May morning, and upon a bright holiday" e 334; "As it fell out one May 8942
    morning, on one bright holiday" e 410; AS IT FELL OUT ONE MAY MORNING; "As it fell out
    one May morning, and upon a bright holiday" e 333; AS IT FELL OUT UPON A DAY; "As it
    fell out upon a day, on a high and a holy day" e 319; "THE LORD AT FIRST DID ADAM MAKE"
    e 363; A CHILD MY CHOICE; "Let folly praise what fancy loves, I praise and love that Child"
    e 361

HOW FAR IS IT TO BETHLEHEM; "How far is it to Bethlehem? Not very far" e 38,39; CHILDREN'S SONG OF 8943
    THE NATIVITY e 271 words by F. Chesterton
"I HEARD THE BELLS ON CHRISTMAS DAY" Illsley (tune) e 337 att to H. Bishop, words by H. W. 8944
    Longfellow
I SAW THREE SHIPS; "I saw three ships come sailing in" e 33,125,206,244,271,296,305,307,333,334,363,375, 8945A
    410; "I saw three ships come sailing by" e 199; "I saw three ships came sailing in" e 317
I SAW THREE SHIPS; "I saw three ships come sailing in" e 216,333,337,361 8945B
"AS I SAT ON A SUNNY BANK" e 79; "ALS EINST ICH STAND AN FLUSSES RAND" e, g 354; CHRISTMAS DAY 8945C
    IN THE MORNING e 332
I SAW THREE SHIPS; "I saw three ships come sailing by" e 334 8945D
"DREI SCHIFFE SAH ICH FAHREN VORBEI" g 354 8945E
IN BETHLEHEM CITY; "In Bethlehem city, on Christmas day morn" e 361 words by G. R. Woodward 8946
IN THEE IS GLADNESS; "In Thee is gladness amid all sadness" e 410 words by C. Winkworth 8947
IN THOSE TWELVE DAYS; "In those twelve days let us be glad" e 361,410 8948
"IT CAME UPON THE MIDNIGHT CLEAR" e 305,307,319,363,410 words by E. H. Sears; "AS SHEPHERDS LAY 8949
    WITHIN THE FOLD" e 333
JOY TO THE WORLD; Antioch (tune); "Joy to the world! the Lord is come" e 28,33,35,79,125,165,206,233, 8950
    236,251,315,337,343,366; "Joy to the world! the Lord has come" e 296; "JOY TO THE WORLD!
    THE LORD IS COME" e 38,39 att to J. F. Händel, words by I. Watts
"LET ALL THAT ARE TO MIRTH INCLINED"; "For to redeem our souls from thrall; Christ is the Saviour of us 8951
    all" (ref) e 361
LISTEN LORDLINGS; "Listen, lordlings, unto me, a tale I will you tell" e 154; LISTEN, LORDLINGS, UNTO 8952
    ME e 165
"THE LORD AT FIRST DID ADAM MAKE" e 333,334,361 8953A
"THE LORD AT FIRST DID ADAM MAKE" e 334; "THE LORD AT FIRST HAD ADAM MADE" e 361; A CAROL 8953B
    FOR CHIRSTMAS EVE e 154
LULLAY MY LIKING; "I saw a fair maid as she sat and did sing" e 363 8954
"LITTLE CHILDREN CAN YOU TELL" e 296 8955
"MAKE WE JOY NOW IN THIS FEST"; "A patre unigenitus" (verse) e, lat 360,361,374 8956
MASTERS IN THIS HALL; "Masters in this hall, hear ye news today" e 35,165,337 words by W. Morris; "RISE 8957
    UP NOW, YE SHEPHERDS" e 363; "SHEPHERDS FROM THE MOUNTAINS" e 361
THE MAY CAROL; "This morning is the month of May" e 44 8958
THE MAY DAY CAROL; "Awake, awake, oh pretty maid" e 214; "Awake, awake, O, pretty, pretty maid" 8959
    e 215
THE MAY-DAY GARLAND; "I've brought you here a bunch of may!" e 334 8960
NO ROOM IN THE INN; "When Caesar Augustus had raised a taxation" e 337 8961
NOEL, NOEL; "'Tis the day, the blessed day, on which our Lord was born" e 296,410 8962
NOW MAKE WE MERTHE; "Now make we merthè all and some"; "Now God Almighty down hath sent" (verse) 8963
    e 360,361
"NOW MAY WE SINGEN AS IT IS"; "The Babe to us that now is bore" e 360,361 8964
NOW WELL MAY WE MERTHIS MAKE; "Alleluya, Now well may we (our) merthis make" e 360,361 8965
NOWEL. OUT OF YOUR SLEEP ARISE; "Nowel, Nowel, Nowel"; "Out of your sleep arise" (verse) e 360,361 8966

"NOWEL, SING WE BOTH ALL AND SOME"; "Exortum est in love and lysse" e, lat 360, 361; "NOWEL SING WE   8967
      NOW ALL AND SOME"; "In Bedleem, in that fair city" (verse) e, lat 360

NOWEL, THIS IS THE SALUTATION; "Nowel, Nowel, Nowel, this is the salutation of the angel Gabriel" e 360,   8968
      361; NOWELL, NOWELL; "Nowell, Nowell, Nowell, Nowell! This is the salutation of the angel
      Gabriel" e 333; THE SALUTATION CAROL e 334; NOWELL, NOWELL: TIDINGS TRUE; BRING
      US IN GOOD ALE; "Nowell, Nowell, Nowell, Nowell"; "Tidings true there be come new" (verse)
      e 379

NOWEL, TO US IS BORN; "Nowel, Nowel, To us is born"; "In Bedlem that Child of life is born of Mary" (verse)   8969
      e 360, 361; NOWEL, TO US IS BORN OUR GOD EMANUEL; "Nowel, Nowel, Nowel, To us is born
      our God Emmanuel; "In Bedlem this Berd of life is born of Mary" (verse) e 360

NUNS IN FRIGID CELLS; "Nuns in frigid cells at this holy tide" e 337   words by H. W. Longfellow   8970

"O LITTLE TOWN OF BETHLEHEM"; Forest Green (tune) e 305, 307, 317, 319, 410; "O BETHLEHEM, DU KLEINE   8971A
      STADT" e, g 354   words by P. Brooks

"O LITTLE TOWN OF BETHLEHEM" e 369   words by P. Brooks   8971B

"O MORTAL MAN, REMEMBER WELL"; SUSSEX MUMMERS' CAROL e 307   8972

"OH, WHO WOULD BE A SHEPHERD BOY" e 361   words by J. Gray   8973

OF A ROSE SING WE; "Of a rose singe we, Misterium mirabile" e 360, 361   8974

"THE OLD YEAR NOW AWAY IS FLED"   See 4621

OLD YORKSHIRE GOODING CAROL; "Well-a-day! Well-a-day! Christmas too soon goes away" e 79   8975

"ON CHRISTMAS NIGHT ALL CHRISTIANS SING" e 307, 410; ON CHRISTMAS NIGHT e 296, 319, 361   8976A

ON CHRISTMAS NIGHT; "On Christmas night all Christians sing"; "O CHRISTENHEIT, TU AUF DAS OHR" e, g   8976B
      354

OUR BLESSED LADY'S LULLABY; Sellenger's round (tune); "Upon my lap my sovreigh sits" e 361   words by R.   8977
      Rowland

PAST THREE O'CLOCK; London waits (tune); "Past three o'clock, and a cold frosty morning" e 410; PAST   8978
      THREE A CLOCK; "Past three a clock, and a cold frosty morning" e 307

"PRAY FOR US THE PRINCE OF PEACE"; "To thee now Christès dere derling" (verse) e, lat 361   8979

PSALLIMUS CANTATES; "Psallimus cantantes, nova cantica dantes"; CAST AWAY THE OLDEN; "Cast away the   8980
      olden, sing a new and golden song" e, lat 360, 361

"REMEMBER, O THOU MAN" e 333, 334   8981

"RING OUT, O BELLS, YOUR PEALS TODAY" e 244   8982

"SAINT STEPHEN WAS AN HOLY MAN" e 361; SAINT STEPHEN e 410; "O LOVELY VOICES OF THE SKY"   8983
      e 244; O LOVELY VOICES e 334

"SEE, AMID THE WINTER'S SNOW"; "Hail, thou ever blessed morn!" (ref) e 361   8984

THE SEVEN JOYS OF MARY; "The first good joy our Mary had" e 334; "The first good joy that Mary had" e   8985A
      35, 296, 337, 361, 363, 410; "THE FIRST GOOD JOY THAT MARY HAD" e 307, 333; THE SEVEN
      JOYS OF CHRISTMAS; "The first good joy that Christmas brings" e 337

THE SEVEN REJOICES OF MARY; "The first rejoice Our Ladye got" e 361   8985B

THE SEVEN JOYS OF MARY; "The very first joy that Mary had" e 173   8985C

THE SEVEN JOYS OF MARY; "The very first blessing that Mary had" e 261, 268   8985D

THE SEVEN JOYS OF MARY; "The first joy of Mary was the joy of one" e 388   8985E

THE BLESSINGS OF MARY; "The very first blessing Mary had" e 332   8985F

"SING WE TO THIS MERRY COMPANY"; "Holy maiden blessed thou be" (verse) e 360, 361   8986

SIR CHRISTMAS; "Nowel, Nowel, Nowel, Nowel, Who is this that singeth so" e 360, 361   8987

"THE SNOW LAY ON THE GROUND"; VENITE ADÓREMUS e 38, 39   8988

SWEET BABY, SLEEP; "Sweet baby sleep! What ails my dear" e 271   words by G. Wither   8989

"THERE IS NO ROSE OF SUCH VIRTUE" e, lat 360, 361   8990

"THERE WAS A STAR IN DAVID'S LAND" e 333   8991

THIS ENDERS NIGHT; "This enders night I saw a sight" e 360, 361; THIS ENDRIS NIGHT; "This endris night I   8992
      saw a sight" e 333, 334; THE OTHER NIGHT; THIS ENDERS NYZGT; "The other night I saw a
      sight" e 296; THIS ENDRIS NYZGT e 206

THIS NEW CHRISTMAS CAROL; Me anvez eur goulmik (tune); "This new Christmas carol let us bravely sing"   8993
      e 361; "This new Christmas carol let us cheerfully sing" e 334, 410

"THIS THE TRUTH SENT FROM ABOVE" e 307   8994

"THOU DIDST LEAVE THY THRONE; Margaret (tune) e 39   att to T. Matthews, words by E. E. S. Elliott   8995

"TODAY OUR GOD OF HIS GREAT MERCIE" e 370   8996

"TOMORROW SHALL BE MY DANCING DAY" e 361, 410   8997

THE TWELVE DAYS OF CHRISTMAS; "On the first day of Christmas" e 33, 35, 215, 249, 337; "ON THE FIRST   8998A
      DAY OF CHRISTMAS" e 268

THE TWELVE DAYS OF CHRISTMAS; "On the first day of Christmas" e 378   8998B

THE TWELVE DAYS OF CHRISTMAS; "The first day of Christmas" e 332   8998C

"THE FIRST DAY OF CHRISTMAS" e 307; THE TWELVE DAYS OF CHRISTMAS e 333; "On the first day of   8998D
      Christmas" e 410

DAYS OF CHRISTMAS; "First day of Christmas my true love sent to me" e 242   8998E

A VIRGIN MOST PURE; "A Virgin most pure, as the prophets do tell" e 319,333,334,361,375   8999A

A VIRGIN MOST PURE; "A Virgin most pure, as the prophet do tell" e 334; "A Virgin most pure, as the prophet   8999B
foretold" e 332; THE JOYFUL SOUNDS OF SALVATION; "In the reign of great Caesar" e 361

A VIRGIN MOST PURE; "A Virgin most pure, as the prophets do tell" e 307,361,410; A VIRGIN MOST BLESSED;   8999C
"A Virgin most blessed, the prophet foretold" e 244; A VIRGIN UNSPOTTED; "A Virgin unspotted,
the prophet foretold" e 165,363

THE WAITS' SONG; "The moon shines bright and the stars give a light" e 334; THE MOON SHINES BRIGHT   9000
e 333; THE WAITS' e 361; "The moon shines bright and the stars give light" e 307

THE WASSAIL SONG; "Here we come a-wassailing among the leaves so green" e 33,35,44,125,337,349; HERE   9001A
WE COME A-WASSAILING e 38,39,79,165,214,333,334,410; HERE WE COME A-CAROLING;
"Here we come a-caroling among the leaves so green" e 206,296

WASSAIL SONG; "Here we come a-wassailing among the leaves so green" e 271; HERE WE COME A-WASSAILING   9001B
e 333,334; WE'VE BEEN AWHILE A-WANDERING; "We've been a-while a-wandering, amongst the
leaves so green" e 319

HERE WE COME A-WASSAILING; "Here we come a-wassailing, among the leaves so green" e 319   9001C

"WASSAIL, WASSAIL, ALL OVER THE TOWN"; GLOUCESTERSHIRE WASSAIL e 38,39,271,307; WASSAIL,   9002A
WASSAIL e 79; WASSAIL ALL OVER THE TOWN e 319; GLOUCESTERSHIRE WASSAIL e 337;
WASSAIL SONG e 199

WASSAIL, WASSAIL; "Wassail, Wassail all over the town!" e 296; GLOUCESTERSHIRE WASSAILERS'SONG e   9002B
154

THE KENTUCKY WASSAIL SONG; "Wassail, wassail all over the town" e 267   9002C

"WE SAW A LIGHT SHINE OUT AFAR" e 361   9003

"WE WISH YOU A MERRY CHRISTMAS" e 33,44,165,214,249,296; A MERRY CHRISTMAS e 319   9004

WELCOME YULE; "Welcome be thou, Heaven King" e 132   9005

WHAT CHILD IS THIS? See 4621

"WHAT TIDINGS BRINGEST THOU MESSENGER?" e 360,361; WHAT TIDINGS BRINGEST THOU? e 333 att to   9006
J. Dunstable

"WHEN CHRIST WAS BORN OF MARY FREE" e 79,296   9007

"WHEN JESUS CHRIST WAS TWELVE YEARS OLD"; "Then praise the Lord, both high and low" (ref) e 334,361   9008

"WHILE SHEPHERDS WATCHED THEIR FLOCKS" e 271,333; WHILE SHEPHERDS WATCHED e 361 words by   9009A
N. Tate

"WHILE SHEPHERDS WATCHED THEIR FLOCKS"; Winchester old (tune) e 206,305,333; "WHILE SHEPHERDS   9009B
WATCHED THEIR FLOCKS BY NIGHT" e 307 words by N. Tate, att to Ravenscroft

"WHILE SHEPHERDS WATCHED THEIR FLOCKS" e 333 words by N. Tate   9009C

"WHILE SHEPHERDS WERE FEEDING THEIR FLOCKS IN THE FIELD" e 379   9010

WITH PRAISES ABOUNDING; "With praises abounding, sing we the great birth" e 380   9011

THE WORLD'S DESIRE; "The Christ-child lay on Mary's lap" e 271 words by G. K. Chesterton   9012

A YOEMAN'S CAROL; "Let Christians all with joyful mirth" e 334   9013

EUROPE

ANGELUS AD VIRGINEM; "Angelus ad Virginem Subintrans in conclave"; GABRIEL TO MARY WENT; "Gabriel   9014
to Mary went, a mighty message bare he" e, lat 360,361; "Came th' Archangel to the Maid of
lowly mien and station" e, lat 334

ANGELUS EMITTITUR; "Angelus emittitur, ave dulce promitur"; "Igitur porta coeli panditur" (ref); GABRIEL   9015
FROM HEAVEN HAS FLOWN; "Gabriel from Heav'n has flown, solemn ave to intone"; "Evermore
henceforth opens Heaven's door" (ref) e, lat 361

AVE MARIS STELLA LUCENS; "Ave maris stella alleluia, alleluia"; HAIL! THOU STAR THAT GUIDEST; "Hail!   9016
thou star that guidest alleluia, alleluia" e, lat 361; EARTH TO-DAY REJOICES; "Earth today rejoices, alleluya, alleluya" e 333 words by J. M. Neale

"CONGAUDEAT TURBA FIDELIUM"; COME, YE FAITHFUL; "Come, ye faithful, sing we right merrily" e, lat   9017
361; FROM CHURCH TO CHURCH; "From church to church the bells' glad tidings run" e 319

DIES EST LETICIAE; "Dies est leticiae in ortu regali"; CHRISTIAN FOLK A DAY OF JOY; "Christian folk, a day   9018
of joy bid ye one another" e, lat 361; HET IS EEN DAG DER VROOLIJKHEID; "Het is een dag der
vroolijkheid in des Konings hove" d 201; HET IS EEN DACH DER VROOLIKHEIT; "Het is een dach
der vroolikheit in des coninx hove" d 384

DONA NOBIS PACEM; "Dona nobis pacem, pacem" 3 pt round lat 337; GRANT US THY PEACE; "Grant to us   9019
Thy peace, O Lord" e 233

ECCE NOVUM GAUDIUM; "Ecce novum gaudium, ecce novum mirum"; HERE IS JOY FOR EV'RYONE; "Here is   9020
joy for ev'ry one, here is wondrous shewing" e, lat 361; HERE IS JOY FOR EVERY AGE; "Here is
joy for ev'ry age, ev'ry generation" e 377

ECCE QUOD NATURA; "Ecce quod natura mutat sua jura"; "Ecce novum gaudium, ecce novum mirum" (verse)   9021
THOUGH THEY CANNOT PALTER; "Though they cannot palter, nature's canon's alter"; "Lo, a
blithe and novel joy, an unheard of wonder" e, lat 360,361

JERUSALEM GAUDE; "Jerusalem gaude gaudio magno"; JERUSALEM REJOICE; "Jerusalem rejoice, be glad and   9022
     joyful" e, lat 388

JESU REDEMPTOR OMNIUM; "Jesu, Redemptor omnium, quem lucis ante originem"; JESUS, REDEEMER OF THE   9023
     WORLD; "Jesus, Redeemer of the world, who, ere the earliest dawn of light" e, lat 388

LAETABUNDUS; "Laetabundus Exsultet fidelis chorus"; FAITHFUL PEOPLE; "Faithful people Season all your song   9024
     with gladness" e, lat 360

O SANCTISSIMA; "O sanctissima, O piissima"; O THOU JOYFUL DAY; "O thou joyful day, O thou blessed day"   9025
     e, lat 35,79,337; e 33; OH, HOW JOYFULLY; "Oh, how joyfully, Oh how merrily" e 296; O YE
     JOYFUL PEOPLE; "O ye joyful people, O ye happy people" e 165; O DU HEILIGE; "O du Heilige,
     Hochgebenedeiete!"; "O DU FRÖHLICHE, O DU SELIGE" g, lat 354; O DU FRÖHLICHE g 326,
     353,412; DIE DREI GROSSEN CHRISTLICHEN FESTE g 99; YEARS OF PEACE; "Years of peace
     are coming, speed them onward!" e 28,366

"OF THE FATHER'S LOVE BEGOTTEN" e 333   9026

"OMNES UNA GAUDEAMUS"; "LET US ALL BE GLAD TOGETHER" e, lat 360   9027

"OMNIS MUNDUS JUCUNDETUR"; "LET THE EARTH REJOICE IN CHORUS" e, lat 361   9028

"PANGAMUS MELOS GLORIAE"; "SING OUT A SONG OF VICTORY" e, lat 361   9029

PERSONENT HODIE; "Personent hodie voces puerelae"; LIFT YOUR VOICES AND SING; "Lift your voices and   9030
     sing, let the glad tidings ring" e, lat 361

PSALLITE UNIGENITO; "Psallite unigenito, Christo Dei Filio"; SING, O SING!; "Sing, o sing! Hail the Holy   9031
     One! Jesus Christ, of God the Son" e, lat 388

"PUER NATUS IN BETHLEHEM"; "A CHILD IS BORN IN BETHLEHEM" e, lat 363,388   9032A

"PUER NATUS IN BETHLEHEM"; "A BOY IS BORN IN BETHLEHEM" e, lat 361   9032B

"QUEM PASTORES LAUDAVERE"; "HE, WHOM JOYOUS SHEPHERDS PRAISED" e, lat 388; "SHEPHERDS LOUD   9033
     THEIR PRAISES SINGING" e 333; "SHEPHERDS TELL YOUR BEAUTEOUS STORY" e, lat 361

"QUI CREAVIT COELUM"; "HE BY WHOM THE HEAVENS WERE MADE" e, lat 361; LULLY, LULLY, LU; "He   9034
     Who heav'n hath made for all" e, lat 206; CAROL OF THE NUNS OF SAINT MARY'S, CHESTER;
     "Qui creavit caelum"; "He who heav'n created" e, lat 388

RESONET IN LAUDIBUS; "Resonet in laudibus cum jucundis plausibus"; NOW WITH GLADNESS CAROL WE; "Now   9035
     with gladness carol we, with the voice of jubilee" e, lat 361

VENI, EMMANUEL; "Veni, veni, Emmanuel, captivum solve Israel"; O COME, O COME, EMMANUEL; "O come,   9036
     O come, Emmanuel, and ransom captive Israel" e, lat 33,38,39; e 125,337; O COME, O COME,
     IMMANUEL; "O come, O come, Immanuel, and ransom captive Israel" e 296

VERBUM CARO FACTUM EST; "Verbum caro factum est de virgine"; GOD'S OWN WORD OUR FLESH DID TAKE;   9037
     "God's own Word our flesh did take, O Maidenhood" e, lat 361

FINLAND

IN DULCI JUBILO; "In dulci jubilo, nun singet und seid froh" g 354   9038

EIN KINDELEIN SO LÖBELICH; "Ein Kindelein so löbelich ist uns geboren heute" g 354   9039

FRANCE

AH! QUE JE GOÛTE DE DOUCEUR; FAIR IS MY LOT; "Fair is my lot, sweet is my part" e 361   9040

AIMABLE ENFANT, QUI NAIS POUR MOI; "O LOVELY INFANT, BORN FOR ME" e 361   9041

ALLONS ÉCOUTER L'AUBADE; "Allons écouter l'aubade qui commence à résoner"; ANAN AUZI LAS AUBADOS;   9042
     "Anan auzi las aubados que s'en benoun de souna" f 69

LES ANGES DANS NOS CAMPAGNES; "Les anges dans nos campagnes, ont entonné l'hymne des cieux" f 79;   9043A
     ANGELS WE HAVE HEARD ON HIGH; "Angels we have heard on high, sweetly singing o'er the
     plains" e, f 388; LES ANGES; HÖRT DER ENGEL HELLE LIEDER; "Hört der Engel helle Lieder
     klingen das weite Feld entlang" f, g 354; NOËL CHAMPENOIS; "Les anges dans nos campagnes
     ont entonné des choeurs joyeux" f 88; "Angels we have heard on high, sweetly singing o'er the
     plain" e 38,39; ANGELS, WE HAVE HEARD YOUR VOICES; "Angels, we have heard your voices,
     sweetly singing o'er the plains" e 361; ANGELS, FROM THE REALMS OF GLORY; "Angels from
     the realms of glory, wing you flight o'er all the earth" e 307,410; GLORIA IN EXCELSIS DEO
     e 305 words by J. Montgomery; HEARKEN, ALL! WHAT HOLY SINGING; "Hearken all! what
     holy singing now is sounding from the sky!" e 251; WHEREFORE THIS GREAT JOY; "Wherefore
     this great joy and singing? Why these songs of Holy mirth?" e 370; TO THE CHILD JESUS;
     "Children, vie with one another singing clear the hymn of praise" e 244

LES ANGES DANS NOS CAMPAGNES; "Les anges dans nos campagnes ont entonné l'hymne des cieux"; ANGELS   9043B
     WE HAVE HEARD ON HIGH; "Angels we have heard on high, sweetly singing o'er the plains" e, f
     35,125,165,206,244,296,337,366; BERGERS, POUR QUI CETTE FETE? e 79; GLORIA IN EX-
     CELSIS DEO e 33

LA BALLADE DE JÉSUS CHRIST; "Jésus Christ s'habille en pauvre" f 88; "JESUS DRESSED IN GARB SO LOWLY"   9044
     e 319; PICARDY NOËL; "Jesus Christ lay sweetly sleeping" e 376

BARGIES OLLANS; "IF YOU SHEPHERDS WATCH THE LAMBING" e 361   9045

BERGERS PAR LES PLUS DOUX ACCORD; "O HINDS, TUNE UP YOUR PIPES"; "In manger bare and lowly lying"   9046
    (verse) e 361

CAROL OF SERVICE; "Up, my neighbor, come away"; "Up and get us gone, to help the world along" (ref) e 271   9047
    words by S. Wilson

CAROL OF THE FLOWERS; "Come with us, sweet flow'rs, and worship Christ the Lord" e 79; COME WITH US   9048
    SWEET FLOWERS e 244; CAROL OF THE FLOWERS; THE SONG OF THE THREE WISE MEN; "In the
    early morning as I went my way" e 337   words by W. P. Kent

CÉLÉBRONS LA NAISSANCE; Chantons je vous en prie (tune); "Célébrons la naissance nostri salvatoris"; O PUB-   9049
    LISH THE GLAD STORY; "O publish the glad story nostri salvatoris" e, f, lat in pt 388; ADAM E
    SA COUMPAGNO; ADAM AND HIS HELPMATE; "Within a lovely garden dwelt Adam long ago"
    e 361; IN THE TOWN; "Take heart, the journey's ended; I see the twinkling lights" e 337; OR
    DITES-NOUS, MARIE; NOW TELL US, GENTLE MARY; "Now tell us, gentle Mary, what did
    Gabriel say to Thee?" e 165; A DAY, A DAY OF GLORY; "A day, a day of glory! A day that
    ends our woe" e 319, 333, 363, 379   words by M. Neale

CHANTANS! BARGIES, NOUÉ, NOUÉ; HAIL! SHEPHERDS HAIL; "Hail! Shepherds hail! A King is born!" e   9050
    361   words by K. W. Simpson; "SHEPHERDS! SHAKE OFF YOUR DROWSY SLEEP" e 79, 125, 296,
    315, 333; CHANTONS, BERGERS NOEL, NOEL; e 165; SHEPHERDS, SHAKE OFF e 319; PEOPLE,
    LOOK EAST; "People, look East. The time is near" e 38, 39

CHANTONS, JE VOUS EN PRIE; "NOW LET US SING, I PRAY THEE" e 361; THE GOLDEN CAROL OF MELCHIOR,   9051
    CASPER AND BALTHAZAR; "We saw a light shine out afar" e 296; THE GOLDEN CAROL OF THE
    THREE KINGS e 379; THE GOLDEN CAROL OF THE THREE WISE MEN e 244

CHRIST WAS BORN; "Christ was born on Christmas day" e 374   words by J. M. Neale   9052

THE CITIZENS OF CHÂTRES; "The citizens of Châtres a curious story tell" e 363   9053

COURONS VOIR L'ENFANT JÉSUS; "COME AND SEE THE HOLY ONE" e 361   9054

DANS CETTE ÉTABLE; "Dans cette étable que Jésus est charmant"; IN THAT POOR STABLE; "In that poor   9055
    stable how charming Jesus lies" e, f 307; BETHLEHEM; "In that poor stable, how charming Jesus
    is" e, f 334; "Jesus in stable! What music may profess" e 361   words by Flechier

DEJOUST UNO TÉOULADO; "Dejoust uno téoulado qué tant ès maou traoucado"; DANS UNE HUMBLE MASURE;   9056
    "Dans une humble masure sans porte ni toiture" f 69

DESSU IN POU DE PEILLE; UPON A WISP OF LITTER; "Upon a wisp of litter, not far from Bethlehem" e 361   9057

DIÉU VOUS GARD', NOSTE MÈSTRE; THE GOSSOON AND THE GAFFER CAROL; "God save you kindly gaffer"   9058
    e 361

"D'OÙ VIENS-TU, BERGÈRE?" f 383; WHENCE COME YOU, SHEPHERD MAIDEN?; "Whence O shepherd maiden,   9059A
    whence come you?" e, f 186, 187; "WHENCE, O SHEPHERD MAIDEN?" e, f 388; "WHERE WERE
    YOU, OH MAIDEN?" e, f 154; THE SHEPHERDESS; "From whence shepherdess, do you now come?"
    e 165; TELL ME, SHEPHERD MAIDEN; "Tell me, shepherd maiden, whence come you?" e 33;
    "SHEPHERDESS, WHENCE COME YOU?" e 244

"D'OU VIENS-TU BERGÈRE?" f 127   9059B

"D'OÙ VIENS-TU, BERGÈRE?" f 82   9059C

"D'OÙ VIENS-TU, BELLE BERGÈRE"; "SAG, O HIRTEN, SAG UNS NUR" f, g 354   9059D

DOUX SAUVEUR, ENFANT D'AMOUR; SAVIOUR SWEET, O BABE OF LOVE; "Saviour sweet, O Babe of love, in   9060
    whom the world hath gladness" e 361; OÙ S'EN VONT CES GAIS BERGERS?; "Whither now the
    shepherds fare so gaily o'er the heather" e 244

EASTER CAROL; "Cheer up, friends and neighbours, now it's Easter tide" e 271   words by P. Dearmer   9061

THE ECHO CAROL; "While the shepherds watched, nor slept" e 363   9062

"L'ENFANT JÉSUS S'ENDORT"; WHILE JESUS SLEEPS; "While Jesus sleeps at night" e, f 337   9063

"ENTRE LE BOEUF ET L'ÂNE GRIS" f 91; "DORT ZWISCHEN OCHS UND ESELEIN" f, g 354; "HERE BETWIXT   9064
    ASS AND OXEN MILD"; GEVAERT e 38, 39; OXEN AND SHEEP; "Oxen and sheep Thy guardians
    mild" e, f 337; "TWIXT GENTLE OX AND ASS SO GRAY" e, f 79; "HERE WITH THE ASS AND
    OXEN MILD" e 33; LE SOMMEIL DE L'ENFANT JESUS; THE SLEEP OF THE CHILD JESUS; "Cradl'd
    amid a herd of kine" e 296

FANNE, CORAIGE; LA DIALE À MORT; CHEER UP OLD WOMAN; "Cheer up old woman, Satan is dead" e 361   9065

"UN FLAMBEAU, JEANNETTE, ISABELLE" f 82, 383; "BRING A TORCH, JEANNETTE, ISABELLA" e, f 337; e   9066
    38, 39, 125, 165, 296; "BRING YOUR TORCHES, JEANNETTE, ISABELLA" e, f 388; BRING YOUR
    TORCHES e 79; HERE A TORCH; "Here a torch, Jeannette, Isabella" e 271; JEANNETTE,
    ISABELLA; "Torches here, Jeannette, Isabella" e 33, 35

GRAN DEI, RIBON, RIBÉNE; THE TRUMPET CAROL; "Tan-ta-ra! Mighty God! Let me shatter the silence" e 361   9067

GRAND DIEU! QUE DE MERVEILLES; "Grand Dieu! que de merveilles s'accomplissent pour moi!"; ACH GOTT,   9068
    SIEH, DEINE WUNDER; "Ach, Gott, sieh, deine Wunder erfüllen sich an mir!" f, g 354

HAUT, HAUT PEYROT; UP, UP PIERRE; "Up, up Pierre, awaken! Dost hear that magic sound?" e 361   9069

"IL EST NÉ LE DIVIN ENFANT"; "Depuis plus de quatre mille ans" (verse) f 82, 91, 127, 383; "BORN IS JESUS,   9070
    THE INFANT KING"; "More than four thousand years' delay" (verse) e, f 388; "HE IS BORN, LITTLE
    INFANT KING"; "More than four thousand years, they say" (verse) e 33; "HE IS BORN, THE HOLY

"IL EST NE LE DIVIN ENFANT" (Continued)   ONE!"; "Full four thousand years ago" (verse) e 39,361; "YEA,   9070
    THE HEAVENLY CHILD IS BORN"; "Over four thousand years have passed" (verse) e, f 154

"IN THE ENDING OF THE YEAR" e 363   9071

INFANT SO GENTLE; "Infant so gentle, so pure and so sweet" e 165,244,296   9072

J'ANTAN PO NOTE RUĒ; I HEAR UPON THE HIGHWAY; "I hear upon the highway resounding minstrelsy" e 361   9073

JE SAIS, VIERGE MARIE; "Je sais, Vierge Marie ce que je dois"; MARIA, DER JUNGFRAUE; "Maria, der Jung-   9074
    fraue, wir benedein und danken" f, g 354; I KNOW, O BLESSED MARY; "I know, O Blessed Mary,
    all I would bring" e 361

JE SUIS L'ARCHANGE DE DIEU; "I THE ANGEL AM OF GOD"; "He is come, come, come!" (ref) e 361   9075

JESU VE'N TREZELON SAI FÉTE; ELOQUENT BELLS IN EVERY STEEPLE; "Eloquent bells in ev'ry steeple scatter   9076
    good news to all the people" e 361

KINGS AND SHEPHERDS; "We Eastern Kings from afar" e 373   9077

LAISSE QUY TAS AIFFARES; "PUT BY YOUR BUSINESS WORRY"; "The Lord most High vouchsafed to lie" (verse)   9078
    e 361

"LAVOU QU'TU CÔRR' DON SI VITE?"; "LÀ OÙ QU'TU COURS DONC SI VITE?" f 69   9079

LA LÉGENDE DE SAINT NICOLAS; "Il était petits enfants" f 88,383; SAINT NICOLAS f 127   9080

LEI PLUS SAGE; STEADY NEIGHBORS; "Steady neighbors give up their labours" e 361   9081

LI A PROUN DE GENT; THE GOUTY CAROL; "There's many folk agait o' pilgrim errand"; "My leg is aching   9082
    worse! Out and saddle, out and saddle" (ref) e 361

MARCHE DES ROIS; "Ce matin, j'ai rencontre le train" f 79,82; "De bon matin j'ai rencontré le train" f 91;   9083
    LA MARCHE DES ROIS; "De grand matin j'ai rencontré le train"; THE MARCH OF THE KINGS;
    "At dawn of day, I met them on the way" e, f 337; "At break of day I met upon the way" e 33;
    "Three great Kings I met at early morn" e 79,244; "De matin ai rescountra lou trin"; "Once
    at dawn I met the brave array" e, f 210; MARCH OF THE THREE KINGS; "Three great kings
    came from the Orient" e 296

MARIE ET JOSEPH; "Marie et Joseph attendant l'heureux moment de voir le Messie"; MARIA UND JOSEF;   9084
    "Maria und Josef warten auf die Gnadenzeit, da kāme der Messias" f, g 354

MICOULAU NOSTE PASTRE; NICHOLAS THE SHEPHERD; "Old Nicholas our shepherd (A crazed and simple   9085
    wight)" e 361

MORTEL, ENTENDS MARIA; MARY'S MAGNIFICAT; "Mortals give ear to Mary hymning her ecstasy" e 361   9086

NODAU; "Lou saubodou sus tèrro ques tonuèt es bengut"; "Cette nuit sur la terre nous arrive un sauvier" ca, f 88   9087

NOEL; THE BIRTHDAY; "When it was midnight on Noel" e 86   9088

NOËL ALSACIEN; "Près de ta mère, clos ta paupière"; I'LL BE BESIDE YOU; "I'll be beside You, ready to guide   9089
    You" e, f 154; SLAAP, MIJN KINDJELIEF; LULLABY OF MARY AND THE ANGELS; "Sleep, my
    little one, sleep, my dearest one" e 79; SLEEP, MY LITTLE ONE e 244; SLEEP, LITTLE DOVE;
    "Sleep, little dove of mine, sleep while the stars shine" e 271

NOËL DES BERGERS; "Michaut, qui cause ce grand bruit" f 127   9090

NOËL NOUVELET; "Noël nouvelet, noël chantons ici"; f 88,383; SING NOËL, NOËL; "Sing Noël, Noël, Noël   9091
    sing joyfully" e 33; NOEL! A NEW NOEL!; "Noel! A new Noel! here together sing!" e 361; SING
    WE NOW OF CHRISTMAS; "Sing we now of Christmas, Noël sing we here!" e 79

LA NOËL PASSÉE; "La Noël passée, povret orphelin"; THE ORPHAN AND KING HENRY; "One Christmas I'm   9092
    starving, the orphan child said" e, f 47

NOËL PROVENÇAL; "Guillaume, Antoine et Pierre"; "Les anges dans le gloire Du ciel pur qui resplendit" (ref)   9093
    CAROL; "Come Will and Jack and John"; "For angels from the high Citadel of the heav'ns above"
    (ref) e, f 231

NOIE, NOIE, EST VENU; "NOW HAS CHRISTMAS COME AGAIN" e 165   9094

NOUS ALLONS, MA MIE; COME WITH HEARTS AFIRE; "Come, with hearts afire, seek Him where He lies" e   9095
    361; LASST UNS ALLE GEHEN; "Lasst uns alle gehen zu dem Kindelein" g 354

O BIENHEUREUSE NUIT; "O NIGHT, RESTFUL AND DEEP" e 361   9096

"O COME, THE LORD'S ANNOINTED" e 333   9097

O VOUS DONT LES TENDRES ANS; "COME ALL YE OF TENDER YEARS" e 361   9098

O, WHO ARE THEY?; "Oh, who are they, so pure and bright" e 377   9099

"OFT AS THEE, MY INFANT SAVIOUR" e 376   9100

ON ENTEND PARTOUT; "On entend partout carillon sur le mont de Judée" f 82; "FROM O'ER THE HILLS OF   9101
    FAIR JUDEA"; NOËL e 79

ON THIS DAY WAS BORN; "On this day was born Christ Jesus" e 363   9102

ON VINT DE NOUS AIPOUTHA; "WE'VE BEEN TOLD A JOYFUL THING" e 361   9103

PAS TRE DEI MOUNTAGNO; THE WEATHER CAROL; "Shepherd of the mountain, Lo! the Godhead true" e 361   9104

"LE PASTRASSOU DIEN SA TSABANO"; "IL SOMMEILLAIT, LE PAUVRE PÂTRE" f(a) 69   9105

PATAPAN; Ma mere mariez-moi (tune); "Guillô, pran ton tambourine"; "Willie take your little drum" e, f   9106
    33,337; "Take thy tabor and thy flute" e 376; "Now we'll play upon the drum" e 216; GUILLÔ
    PRAN TON TAMBOURINE; "Davie get you tambourine" e 361; "GUILLAUME, TAKE THY TABOR"
    e 319; TAKE THY TABOR; "Take thy tabor and thy flute" e 333; WILLIE, TAKE YOUR DRUM;
    "Willie, take your little drum" e 165; "WILLIE, TAKE YOUR LITTLE DRUM" e 307

PATHANS VITE DE BESANÇON; "SHEPHERDS, LEAD ON TO BETHLEHEM" e 361 — 9107

PER NOUN LANGUI; THE BAGPIPE CAROL; "This is a tedious road we're in"; "Sing we Nowell, Nowell, Nowell" (ref) e 361 — 9108

PROMPTEMENT LEVEZ-VOUS MA VOISIN; NEIGHBOUR MINE; "O rise and come away (Neighbour run!); "Rouse ye! run a pace! to behold His sleeping face!" (ref) e 361 — 9109

QUAND LA MIÈJO-NUE SOUNAVO; I WOKE, FROM MY COUCH UPRISING; "I woke, from my couch upspringing" e 361 — 9110

"QUELLE EST CETTE ODEUR AGRÉABLE?" f 88; "WHENCE IS THAT GOODLY FRAGRANCE" e, f 307; WHAT IS THIS FRAGRANCE?; "What is this fragrance softly stealing" e 361; WHAT IS THIS ODOUR?; "What is this odour round us flowing?" e 333; "WHAT IS THIS RARE AND PLEASANT ODOUR?" e 363; CAROL OF BEAUTY; "Praise we the Lord, who made all beauty" e 271 words by S. Wilson — 9111

QUITTEZ, PASTEURS; "Quittez, pasteurs, vos brébis, vos houlettes"; LAY DOWN YOUR STAFFS, O SHEPHERDS; "Lay down your staffs, Oh shepherds, leave your sheep!" e, f 79; "O leave your sheep, your lambs that follow after" e 319; O LEAVE YOUR SHEEP e 307, 363; THE ANGEL SANG; "The angel sang the shepherds for to waken" e 333; "LEAVE, SHEPHERDS, LEAVE YOUR PEACEFUL FLOCKS" e 361; YE SHEPHERDS, LEAVE YOUR FLOCKS; "Ye shepherds, leave your flocks upon the mountains" e 317 — 9112

QUOI, MA VOISINE, ES-TU FACHEE?; WHERE GO YE NOW?; "Where go ye now, my friend, my neighbor" e 165 — 9113

QUIQUE SOYEZ PETIT ENCORE; ALTHOUGH YOU ARE SO TINY; "Although you still are but an infant" e 79 — 9114

REJOICE, REJOICE; "Rejoice, rejoice divine Maria" e 380 — 9115

SHEPHERDS, BE JOYFUL; "Shepherds be joyful, your Saviour is come" e 361 — 9116

SILENCE CIEL! SILENCE TERRE!; BE SILENT HEAVEN! BE SILENT EARTH!; "Be silent Heav'n! Be silent earth!" e 361 — 9117

SING OF MAIDEN MARY; "Sing of Maiden Mary, and of Christ our Lord" e 244 — 9118

SING WE NOËL; "Sing we Noël this holy Christmas morn" e 125 — 9119

SUS, LEVETE PORRENOT; "UP AND SHAKE THEE PETERKIN" e 361 — 9120

THERE CAME THREE KINGS; "There came three kings, at break of day" e 369 — 9121

"THOU, WHOSE BIRTH ON EARTH" e 373 — 9122

THREE KINGS SONG; "The Magi came out of the Orient Land" e 244 — 9123

TÔ LES AN QUAN NOEI S'EPRÔCHE; "EVERY YEAR AS ROUND COMES CHRISTMAS" e 361 — 9124

TOURO-LOURO-LOURO! LOU GAU CANTO; THE PEASANT'S PILGRIMAGE; "Turelurelu! The cock doth crow" e 361 — 9125

TU QUE CERQUES TEI DELICE; "YOU THAT MAKE A TOIL OF PLEASURE" e 361 — 9126

UNE VAINE CRAINTE; GLAD TIDINGS; "Fearfulness and sadness shadoweth thy heart" e 361 — 9127

VECI LE SAINTAM' ME FRAIRE; "BROTHERS, 'TIS THE HOLY SEASON" e 361 — 9128

VENEZ, VENEZ, VITE!; "Venez, venez, vite mon garçon!"; BÉNI, BÉNI, BÉNI; "Béni, béni, béni, joubencel" f 69 — 9129

LE VERMEIL, DU SOLEIL; MORNING HUSH; "Morning hush, first a blush faintly telling day is welling" e 361 — 9130

VIVEN UROUS E COUNTÈNT; THE LAUNDRY CAROL; "Why not be forever gay, Bregado?" e 361 — 9131

VOICI LA NOËL; "Voici la Noël, faites la veillée" f 82; CHRISTMAS EVE IS HERE; "Christmas Eve is here, see the moon is waking" e 79 — 9132

VOICI QUE LES PÂTRES; "Voici que les pâtres et les bergères"; SALTEN I BALLEN; "Salten i ballen els pastorells, dones" f 69 — 9133

THE WINTER SEASON; "The winter season of the year" e 44 — 9134

WITH HAPPY HEARTS UNITED; Faisans rejouissance (tune); "With happy hearts united in gladness let us sing" e 361 — 9135

WITHIN THIS HUMBLE SHELTER; "Within this humble shelter, 'neath a poor thatching" e 380 — 9136

Y M'EN VAI QUITTE; "I'M LEAVING HOME SEEKING MY FORTUNE" e 361 — 9137

FRENCH CANADA

"D'OÙ VIENS-TU, BERGÈRE?" See 9059A

LA GUIGNOLEE; CAROL OF THE MISTLETOE SINGERS; "Greetings, good master, mistress, children" e 165 — 9138

ON THE CORNER; "On the corner, get together" 3 pt round e 337 — 9139

GERMANY

"ALS ICH BEI MEINEN SCHAFEN WACHT"; "WHILE BY MY SHEEP I WATCHED AT NIGHT" e, g 337; WHILE BY MY SHEEP e 79; ECHO CAROL; "While I my sheep did watch one night" e 165; MY SHEEP WERE GRAZING; THE CHRISTMAS HYMN; "My sheep were grazing on a plain" e 296 — 9140

AM WEIHNACHTSBAUM DIE LICHTER BRENNEN; 'TIS THE EVE OF CHRISTMAS; "O festive night, 'tis the eve of Christmas" e 165 — 9141

AN WEIHNACHTEN; REJOICE THEE, O HEAVEN; "Rejoice thee, O heaven, with all the world singing" e 79 — 9142

"ANGELS SINGING, CHURCH BELLS RINGING" e 244 — 9143

AUF IHR HIRTEN; "Auf ihr Hirten, von dem Schlaf" g 40   9144

AUF, IHR HIRTENSLEUT!; "Auf, ihr Hirtensleut! Hört ein' grosse Freud" g 49   9145

A BABE IS BORN; Herr Jesu Christ, mein Leben's Licht (tune); "A Babe is born, all of a Maid to bring salvation   9146
    unto us" e 361

"DER CHRISTBAUM IST DER SCHÖNSTE BAUM"; g 412; THE BEAUTIFUL CHRISTMAS TREE; "The Christmas   9147
    tree's more beautiful" e, g 251

CHRISTMAS BELLS. See 5504

CRADLE SONG OF THE INFANT JESUS; "Soft to the manger stealing, beside the Christ-Child kneeling" e 244,   9148
    361 words by K. W. Simpson

"DEN GEBOREN HAT EIN MAGD"; "Su, su su su su, schlaf, mein liebes Kindelein" (ref) g 354   9149

EIA, EIA; "To us in Bethlem city was born a little son" e 337   9150

ES BLÜHN DREI ROSEN; "Es blühn drei Rosen auf einem Zweig" g 412   9151

ES HAT SICH HALT ERÖFFNET; "Es hat sich halt eröffnet das himmlische Tor" g 40, 412   9152

ES KOMMT EIN SCHIFF; "Es kommt ein Schiff, geladen bis an sein' höchsten Bord" g 40, 49; THERE COMES A   9153
    GALLEY SAILING; SONG OF THE SHIP; "There comes a galley sailing with angels flying fast" e
    206; THERE COMES A VESSEL LADEN; "There comes a vessel laden with full sail flying fast" e
    296

"FOR US THIS DAY IS GIV'N A SON" e 333   9154

HEIDEL, BUBEIDEL; "DEAR BABY JESUS, NOW REST IN SLEEP" e 79   9155

DER HEILAND IST GEBOREN; THE CHRIST-CHILD IS BORN; "The Christ-Child is born, Oh Hallelujah!" e 79   9156

HERBEI, O IHR GLÄUBIGEN; "Herbei, o ihr Gläubigen, fröhlich triumphierend" g 326 words by F. H. Ranke   9157

EIN HIRTENSANG; THE SHEPHERD'S STORY; "Come ev'ryone rejoicing, O neighbors come and hear" e 79   9158

IN DULCI JUBILO; "In dulci jubilo let us our homage shew" e 307, 319, 375; "In dulci jubilo, let us our homage   9159
    show" e 337, 361; "In dulci jubilo, now sing we all Io" e 199; "In dulci jubilo, now sing with
    hearts aglow" e 34; "In dulci jubilo, we lift our voice to Thee" e 37; "IN DULCI JUBILO, NUN
    SINGET UND SEID FROH" g 354; NUN SINGET UND SEID FROH; "Nun singet und seid froh,
    jauchzt alle und sagt so" g 49; IN DULCI IUBILO; "In dulci iubilo, now sing we all Io!"
    e 334; NOW SING WE, NOW REJOICE; "Now sing, we, now rejoice, now raise to heaven
    our voice" e 206; GOOD CHRISTIAN MEN, REJOICE; "Good Christian men, rejoice with
    heart and soul and voice" e 33, 35, 38, 39, 79, 125, 206, 251, 271, 296, 307, 315, 333, 349, 361,
    363, 410 words by J. M. Neale

INMITTEN DER NACHT; "Inmitten der Nacht, als Hirten erwacht" g 40   9160

JAHRESLIED; "Wir hassen die Sorgen und jagen sie gar!" g 49   9161

JODEL, SING, MAXEL, SPRING!; "Jodel, sing, Maxel, spring! Ich hör drauss Wunderding" g 49   9162

JOSEPH, LIEBER JOSEPH MEIN; "Joseph, lieber Joseph mein, hilf mir wiegen mein Kindelein" g 412; MARIA   9163
    UND JOSEPH g 79; WEIHNACHTSWIEGENLIED g 99; JOSEPH, LIEBER JOSEPH; JOSEPH, DEAREST
    JOSEPH; "Joseph dearest Joseph sweet, help me rock my babe to sleep" e, g 34; "Joseph, dearest
    Joseph sweet, help me rock my child to sleep" e 33; JOSEPH DEAREST; "Joseph dearest, Joseph
    mild, help me rock my little child" e 79; JOSEPH DEAREST, JOSEPH MINE; SONG OF THE
    CRIB; "Joseph dearest, Joseph mine, help me cradle the Child divine" e 307; SONG OF THE
    CRIB e 271; JOSEPH, JOSEPH, HUSBAND MINE; "Joseph, Joseph, husband mild, help me rock my
    little child" e 333; JOSEPH, O DEAR JOSEPH MINE; SONG OF THE CRIB; "Joseph, O dear
    Joseph mine, help me rock the Child divine" e 296; CHRIST WAS BORN ON CHRISTMAS DAY;
    "Christ was born on Christmas day, wreathe the holly twine the bay" e 79, 296, 315, 337

EIN KINDELEIN IN DER WIEGEN; THE WORLD'S DESIRE; "THE CHRIST-CHILD LAY ON MARY'S LAP" e 361;   9164
    words by G. K. Chesterton; "HE SMILES WITHIN HIS CRADLE" e 271, 307, 410; THE CRADLE e
    251 words by R. Graves; "A BABE LIES IN THE CRADLE" e 333

"LASST UNS DAS KINDELEIN WIEGEN" g 412; DER HIRTEN WIEGENLIED; SHEPHERDS AT THE CRADLE; "Come,   9165A
    shepherd brothers, come silently near" e 79

"LASST UNS DAS KINDLEIN WIEGEN" g 40   9165B

LAUFET, IHR HIRTEN; COME, HASTEN, YE SHEPHERDS; "Come hasten, ye shepherds, come one and come all"   9166
    e 79

MACHT HOCH DIE TÜR; "Macht hoch die Tür, die Tor macht weit" g 49 words by G. Weissel   9167

MARIA AUF DEM BERGE; "Uf 'm Berge, da geht der Wind" g 99; "Auf dem Berge da geht der Wind"; MARY ON   9168
    THE MOUNTAIN; "On the mountain where breezes sigh" e, g 154, 337; "Auf dem Berge da gehet
    der Wind"; MARIA ON THE MOUNTAIN; "On the mountain the wind bloweth wild" e, g 388; "AUF
    DEM BERGE DA GEHT DER WIND" g 410; AUF DEM BERGE DA GEHT'S DER WIND; "Ufm Berge, da
    geht der Wind" g 40; "AUF DEM BERGE, DA WEHET DER WIND" g 326

"MARIA DURCH EIN DORNWALD GING" g 49; "MARIA WALKS AMID THE THORN" e, g 388; "MARIA WAN-   9169
    DERED THROUGH A WOOD" e, g 337; "Maria durch 'nen Dorenwald ging"; "SWEET MARY
    THROUGH A THORN-GROVE DID GO" e, g 230; JESUS SWEET AND MARY; "As through the
    thorn-brake Mary wander'd" e 376

MENSCHEN, DIE IHR WAR'T VERLOREN; "MAN, REJOICE! YOUR SEARCH IS OVER!" e 165   9170

"MORGEN, KINDER, WIRDS WAS GEBEN!" g 326,412 words by K. F. Splittegarb, att to C. G. Herig   9171A

DIE WEIHNACHTSFREUDE; "Morgen, Kinder, wirds was geben" g 99 words by C. F. Splittegarb   9171B

"MORGEN KOMMT DER WEIHNACHTSMANN"; Ah! vous dirai-je, Maman (tune) g 412; DER WEIH-   9172
NACHTSMANN g 99 words by H. von Fallersleben

MY SPIRIT BEHOLDETH; "My spirit beholdeth a wonderful sight" e 333   9173

O FREUDE ÜBER FREUDE; "O Freude über Freude ihr Nachbarn kommt und hört" g 49   9174

O TANNENBAUM; Lauriger Horatius (tune); "O Tannenbaum, o Tannenbaum, wie treu sing deine Blätter" g 40,   9175A
326,353,412; "O Evergreen, O Evergreen! How faithful are your branches!" e, g 34; "O Tannenbaum, o Tannenbaum, your leaves are ever faithful!" e, g 388; THE CHRISTMAS TREE; "We
stand before the Christmas tree, a symbol for the faithful" e, g 337; O CHRISTMAS TREE; "O
Christmas Tree, O Christmas Tree, forever true your color" e 206; "Oh, Christmas tree, Oh
Christmas tree, how ever green your branches" e 216; "O Christmas tree, O Christmas tree, how
steadfast is thy foliage" e 251; "O Christmas tree, O Christmas tree, O tree of green, unchanging"
e 165; "O Christmas tree, O Christmas tree! Thou tree most fair and lovely!" e 296; "O Christmas tree! O Christmas tree! Thy leaves are so unchanging" e 315; "O Christmas Tree, O Christmas Tree, Your branches green delight us!" e 33; "O Tannenbaum, O Tannenbaum! Your leaves
are faithful ever!" e 79; O CHRISTMAS PINE; "O Christmas pine, O Christmas pine, forever
true your color!" e 279,366; O TANNEBAUM; "O Tannebaum, o Tannebaum! wie treu sind
deine Blätter!" g 99; MARYLAND, MY MARYLAND; "The despot's heel is on thy shore, Maryland! my Maryland!" e 161; "Thou wilt not cower in the dust, Maryland! my Maryland!" e
129,130 words by J. R. Randall; THE RED FLAG; "The people's flag is deepest red" e 294
words by J. M. Connell

O TANNENBAUM; "O Tannenbaum, o Tannenbaum, du trägst ein grünen Zweig" g 49; O TANNENBAUM,DU   9175B
TRÄGST EIN GRÜNEN ZWEIG g 326; O TANNENBAUM, DU BIST EIN EDLER ZWEIG; "O Tannenbaum, o Tannenbaum, du bist ein edler Zweig" g 309

PREIS DER HIMMELSKÖNIGIN; "Wunderschön prächtige, grosse und mächtige" g 99   9176

STILL, STILL, STILL!; "Still, still, still, weils Kindlein schlafen will!" g 40,412; "STILL, STILL, STILL,   9177A
WEIL'S KINDLEIN SCHLAFEN WILL" g 353

STILL, STILL, STILL; "Still, still, still, wer Gott erkennen will" g 49   9177B

SÜSSER DIE GLOCKEN NIE KLINGEN. See 5539

THREE HOLY WOMEN; "One morning before the sun mounted" e 37   9178

"TO US IS BORN A LITTLE CHILD"; "O Jesus darling of my heart" (ref) e 244,296   9179

TUET EILENDS ERWACHEN; "Tuet eilends erwachen, ihr Hirten vom Schlaf" g 40   9180

"UNTO US A BOY IS BORN" e 307; PUER NOBIS e 38,39; "UNTO US A BOY WAS BORN" e 337; "UNTO US   9181
A CHILD IS BORN" e 363,377; "UNTO US IS BORN A SON" e 319,334

"VOM HIMMEL HOCH, DA KOMM ICH HER"; g 326; "FROM HEAVEN HIGH I COME TO YOU" e, g 251; e 33,   9182
38,39,125; FROM HEAVEN HIGH e, g 337; VOM HIMMEL HOCH g 49,79,412; FROM HEAVEN
ABOVE; "From heav'n above to earth I come" e, g 206,296,319,410; FROM HEAVEN HIGH;
"From heaven high I come to earth" e, g 388; "DIES IST DER TAG DEN GOTT GEMACHT"
g 412

"VOM HIMMEL HOCH, O ENGLEIN, KOMMT" g 40,49; CHRISTKINDLEINS WIEGENLIED; "Vom Himmel hoch,   9183
ihr Engel kommt" g 99; SUSANI; "From heaven high the angels come" e 33; SUSANI, SUSANI;
"Come, Angels, come from Heav'n descend" e 372; "From highest heaven come, angels come!"
e 361; CHRIST CHILD'S SLUMBER SONG; "From heaven above, O angels draw nigh" e 165; "A
LITTLE CHILD THERE IS Y-BORN" e 333

WACH, NACHTIGALL, WACH AUF!; "Wach, Nachtigall, wach auf! Wach auf, du schönes Vögelein" g 49;   9184
WACH NACHTIGALL g 40; DIE WEIHNACHTSNACHTIGALL; "Lieb Nachtigall, wach auf, Wach
auf, du schönes Vögelein"; THE CHRISTMAS NIGHTINGALE; "Sweet nightingale awake, come
forth fair warbler now" e, g 388; "O nightingale awake! And ev'ry songster sing with thee"
e 79

WAS SOLL DAS BEDEUTEN?; "Was soll das bedeuten? Es taget ja schon" g 86   9185

"WE GOT A LOT FOR CHRISTMAS!" e 337   9186

WHEN THE CRIMSON SUN; "When the crimson sun descended" e 333   9187A

"WHEN THE CRIMSON SUN HAD SET" e 373   9187B

WINTER NAHT; "Winter naht, Sommer zieht, darum übt ein neues Weihnachtslied" 2 pt round g 40   9188

"YE WATCHERS AND YE HOLY ONES"; Lasst uns erfreuen (tune); VIGILES ET SANCTI e 38,39; ALLELUIA;   9189
"Come all ye people, come and sing" e 37

ZU BETHLEHEM GEBOREN; "Zu Bethlehem geboren ist uns ein Kindelein" g 412   9190

HUNGARY

MENYBÖL AR ANGYAL; "Menyböl ar angyal leyött hozzátok"; ANGELS FROM HEAVEN; "Angels from Heaven   9191
come to you, shepherds" e, hu 154; "ES KAM EIN ENGEL VOM HOHEN HIMMEL" g 354; HARK
TO THE ANGELS; "Hark to the angels from heaven calling" e 165

INDIA

LINA AWATARA; "Lína awatárá soí jagaraijá"; HE BECAME INCARNATE; "He became incarnate, Christ the King of glory" e 244 9192

INDIANS OF NORTH AMERICA

JESOUS AHATONHIA; "Chrétiens, prenez courage"; THE HURON CAROL; "'Twas in the moon of winter-time" e, f 186,244; JESUS AHATONHIA e 154; "'TWAS IN THE MOON OF WINTER TIME" e 251; THE INDIAN CHRISTMAS CAROL e 173; JESUS IS BORN; JESOUS AHATONNIA; "Let Christian hearts rejoice today" e 33; "TO JESUS, FROM THE ENDS OF EARTH"; JESOS AHATONHIA e 165; A HURON CHRISTMAS CHANT; "To Thee, dear Jesus, now we raise our song of praise" e 279 9193

IRELAND

DUAN NOLLAIG; "Heire Bannag Hoire Bannag"; CHRISTMAS INVOCATION; "Hey the Bannock, Ho the Bannock" e, ir 154 9194

IRISH CAROL; "Christmas day is come; let's all prepare for mirth" e 337 words att to L. Wadding 9195

ITALY

ALMA CHE SCORGI; THREE KINGS CAME RIDING; "Three Kings came riding from the east, led by a star" e 361 9196

CANTIAM TUTTI; O SHEPHERDS SING TOGETHER; "O shepherds sing together, Sing! O beloved brothers" e 361 9197

CANZONE D'I ZAMPOGNARI; "Quanno nascette Ninno a Bettelem me"; CAROL OF THE BAGPIPERS; "When Christ our Lord was born at Bethlehem a far" e 388; "And when the child was born at Bethlehem" e 337; "A star shone up in heaven the night the child was born" e 165; "The night the child was born, was born in Bethlehem" e, i 33; ZU BETHLEHEM GEBOREN; "Zu Bethlehem geboren was das Kindelein" g 354 9198

"DORMI, DORMI, O BEL BAMBIN"; "SLEEP, O HOLY CHILD OF MINE" e, i 154,337; "SLEEP, SLEEP, LOVELY BABE" e 165 9199

GESÙ BAMBIN L'E NATO; "Gesù Bambin l'e nato, nato in Betelem"; JESUS WAS BORN TO MARY; "Jesus was born to Mary, Mary in Bethlehem" e, i 154 9200

HARK YE SHEPHERDS; "Hark ye shepherds, hasten to the manger" e 296 words by H. W. Davis 9201

IN BETHLEHEM; "In Bethlehem is born, is born the Holy Child" e 165 9202

LIETI PASTORI; O JOYFUL SHEPHERDS; "O joyful shepherds, make haste, with footsteps flying" e 361 9203

MARIA VERGIN BEATA; "HOW MANY A KING A-DREAMING" e 361 9204

"MARY, DEAR MOTHER OF JESUS" e 296 9205

MORTO ERODE; "Morto Erode Gesù torna"; HEROD DEAD; "Herod dead, Our Lord returneth" e, i 388 9206

NINNA NANNA; "Ninna Nanna Ninna Nanna dormi figlio dormi amore"; SLEEP MY DARLING; "Sleep my Darling, sleep my Baby" e, i 361 9207

OH! DEAR JESUS; "Thou camest from heav'n we are told" e 296 9208

OH! INFANT JESUS; "Oh! Infant Jesus, Thee I love" e 296 9209

"OH! NIGHT AMONG THE THOUSANDS" e 296 9210

POICHÉ L'UMIL CAPANNA; TO WEARY SHEPHERDS SLEEPING; "To weary shepherds sleeping, a blinding light appeared" e 244,386 9211

LA ROSELLINA; DARK IS THE EVEN; "Dark is the even! Yet is the heaven" e 361 9212

"SHEPHERDS, THE DAY IS BREAKING"; Ecco bella regina (tune) e 361 9213

"SHEPHERDS, WHY DO YE TARRY?"; Chio può mirar (tune); "To the manger, this day O hasten away" (ref) e 361 9214

"THE SNOW LAY DEEP UPON THE GROUND" e 244 9215

TU SCENDI DALLE STELLE; "Tu scendi dalle stelle, o Re del Cielo"; FROM STARRY SKIES DESCENDING; "From starry skies descending, Thou comest, glorious King" e, i 388 words by Pope Pius IX 9216

JAPAN

JAPANESE CHRISTMAS SONG; "Missionaries us have told, 'tis a story to you old" e 244 9217

"LOWLY SHEPHERDS OF JUDEA"; "Yoodahyah noh hetsoo jee woe" e, j (tr) 244 words by S. Ojima 9218

"SWEET AND HOLY JESUS' NAME"; Jasmine (tune) e 244 9219

LITHUANIA

EIN KIND GEBORN ZU BETHLEHEM; "Ein Kind geborn zu Bethlehem, Bethlehem; des freuet sich Jerusalem" g 354 9220

NETHERLANDS

HET VIEL EENS HEMELS DOUWE. See 6595B

KOMT, VERWONDERT U HIER MENSEN; "KOMMT, VERWUNDERT EUCH, IHR LEUTE" g 354   9258

"KOMT, WILT U SPOEDEN NAAR BETHLEHEM" d 384   9259

LAET ONS MIT HERTEN REYNE; "WITH HEART AND SPIRIT RECONCILED"; "To us a Son is given" (verse) e 361   9260

"MARIA DIE ZOUDE NAAR BETHLEHEM GAAN" d 201; "OUR LADY ON CHRISTMAS DAY" e 244,361   9261A

"MARIA DIE ZOUDE NAER BETHLEEM GAEN"; LA VIERGE MARIE VA À BETHLÉEM" d, f 69   9261B

MET DEZEN NIEUWEN JARE; "Met dezen nieuwen jare zoo wordt ons openbare" d 201; MIT DESEN NIEWEN   9262
         JARE; A YEAR BEGINS OF JOY AND GRACE; "A year begins of joy and grace, like ev'ry year that
         sees His face" e 361

NU ZIJT WELLEKOME; "Nu zijt wellekome, Jesu lieven Heer" d 201; "Nu zijt wellekomme, Jesu lieve Heer";   9263
         WELCOME, DEAREST JESUS; "Welcome, dearest Jesus, from the heav'n above" d, e 316; NU
         SIJT WILLEKOME JESU LIEVEN HEER; WELCOME, SON OF MARY; "Welcome Son of Mary, 'Tis
         from far you come" e 361

O, BLIJDE NACHT; "O, blijde nacht! De Christus is geboren" d 384   9264

"O GIJ, DIE JEZUS' WIJNGAARD PLANT" d 384   9265

"O HERDERS, LAAT UW BOKSKENS EN SCHAAPKENS" d 384   9266

O JESUS SOETE AENDACHTICHEIT; "O Jesus, true and fervent friend" e 361; "O JESUS, ZOETE AANDACH-   9267
         TIGHEID" d 384

"O KERSTNACHT, SCHOONER DAN DE DAGEN" d 201,384   9268

O ZALIG, HEILIG BETHLEHEM; "O zalig, heilig Bethlehem, o onder duizend uitverkorer" d 384   9269

"ONS IS GEBOREN EEN KINDEKIJN"; Puer nobis nascitur (tune) d 201; "ONS IS GHEBOREN EEN KINDEKIJN";   9270
         "A CHILD OF BEAUTY IS BORN TO US" d, e 154

EEN SERAPHIJNSCHE TONGE; "Een seraphijnsche tonge mij nu wel dienst voorwaar" d 384   9271

"SINT JOSEPH GING AL TREUREN" d 201   9272

"SINT NIKLAAS, GOED HEILIG MAN" d 203; "SINTERKLAAS KAPOENTJE"; "SINTERKLAAS; YOU GOOD OLD   9273
         MAN" d, e 316

THIS JOYFUL EASTERTIDE; "This joyful Eastertide, away with sin and sorrow!" e 319; "Let joy your carols fill;   9274
         away with sin and sadness!" e 319

"VAN VROUDEN ONS DIE KINDERKENS ZINGEN"; Conditor alme siderum (tune) d 201   9275

WIJ KOMEN VAN OOSTEN; "Wij komen van Oosten, wij komen van ver" d 203   9276

THE WORLD HAS WAITED LONG; "The world has waited long to hear the heavenly story" e 361 words by J. Gray   9277

ZIE GINDS KOMT DE STOOMBOOT; "Zie ginds komt de stoomboot uit Spanje weer aan"; LOOK, THERE IS THE   9278
         STEAMER; "Look, there is the steamer arriving from Spain" d, e 316

ZINGT, ENG'LEN ZINGT!; "Zingt, eng'len zingt! Straks zuit g'ons welkom heeten" d 384   9279

ZINGT MET VREUGDE; "Zingt met vreugde, gij hemelen" d 384   9280

NICARAGUA

VENID PASTORCILLOS; "Venid pastorcillos venid a adoraral Rey de los cielos" s 284   9281

NORWAY

BETHLEHEM LAY HUSHED AND STILL; "Dark the night o'er field and hill" e 374 words by J. Phillips   9282

"I DENNE SØDE JULETID"; "AT CHRISTMAS TIME WHEN ALL IS GAY" e, n 154   9283

JER ER SAA GLAD HVER JULEKVELD; "I AM SO HAPPY ON CHRISTMAS EVE" e 165; "HOW GLAD I AM EACH   9284
         CHRISTMAS EVE" e 244; "ICH FREU MICH HEUTE AM WEIHNACHTSFEST" g 354

O JUL MED DIN GLAEDE; CHRISTMAS, O HAPPIEST DAY!; "O Christmas, O Christmas, O happiest day!" e 165   9285

PHILIPPINE ISLANDS

PAGKA-TÁO; "Tálang napakaliwanag"; CHRISTMAS CAROL; "'Twas a brilliant star in the sky" e, t 154   9286

POLAND

"ANIÓŁ PASTERZOM MÓWIŁ"; "SHEPHERDS HEARD THE ANGELS SAY" e, p 295   9287

BÓG SIĘ RODZI; "Bóg sięrodzi, moc truchleje"; GOD IS BORN; "God is born on earth, powers tremble" e, p   9288
         295 words by F. Karpinski

DZISIAJ W BETLEJEM; "Dzisiaj w Betlejem, dzisiaj w Betlejem, Wesoła nowina!"; IN BETHLEHEM; "In Bethle-   9289
         hem, in Bethlehem, tidings ring triumphant!" e, p 295; HEAR THE GLAD TIDINGS!; "Hear the
         glad tidings, hear the glad tidings!" e 165

GDY SIĘ CHRYSTUS RODZI; "Gdy się Chrystus rodzi I na świat przychodzi"; CHRIST IS BORN; "Christ the King   9290
         is born on an early morn" e, p 295; ALS DIE WELT VERLOREN; "Als die Welt verloren, Christus
         ward geboren" g 354; JESUS CHRIST IS BORN; "Jesus Christ is born, now unto the world" e, p 388;
         ON THE NIGHT WHEN JESUS CAME; "On the night when Jesus came to earth from heaven" e 165

LULAJŻE, JEZUNIU; "Lulajże, Jezuniu, moja perełko"; LULLABY, SWEET JESUS; "Lullaby, sweet Jesus, pearl very precious" e, p 295; LULLABY JESU; "Lullaby, Jesu, my pearl and my dear one" e 165   9291A

LULAJŻE JEZUNIU; "Lulajże Jezuniu moja perełko"; ROCKABYE JESUS; "Rockabye Jesus, my soul's fairest treasure" e, p 388   9291B

LULAJŻE JEZUNIU; "Lulajże Jezuniu moja perełko"; POLISH LULLABY; "Sleep, little Jesus, my treasure, my blessing" e, p 337; "Lulajze Jesuniu moja peretko" p 79   9291C

MĘDRCY ŚWIATA; "Mędrcy świata, monarchowie"; THREE GOOD WISE MEN; "Three good wise men, earthly monarchs" e, p 295   9292

PASTERZE MILI; "Pasterze mili, coście widzieli?"; SHEPHERDS DEAR; "Shepherds dear, oh pray, what saw you this day?" e, p 295   9293

PÓJDŹMY WSZYSCY; "Pójdźmy wszyscy do stajenki"; HASTEN YONDER; "To the stable, hasten yonder" e, p 295   9294

PRZYBIEŻELI DO BETLEJEM; "Przybieżeli do Betlejem pasterze"; QUICKLY ON TO BETHLEHEM; "Quickly on to Bethlehem the shepherds came" e, p 295; "PRZYBIEZELI DO BETLEEM PASTERZE"; SHEPHERDS, COME A-RUNNING; "Shepherds, come a-running to Bethlehem" e, p 388   9295

SEHT, DAS KINDLEIN WIENET; "Seht, das Kindlein weinet dort im Krippelein" g 354   9296

"SLEEP NO MORE, THE GLAD HEAVENS ARE BLAZING"; Virginelle, fide ancelle (tune) e 361   9297

ŚLICZNA PANIENKA; "Śliczna Panienka, Jezusa zrodziła"; FAIREST OF MAIDENS; "Fairest of maidens, bore the Infant this day" e, p 295   9298

W ŻŁOBIE LEŻY; "W żłobie leży! któż pobieży"; IN A MANGER; "In a manger sleeps the Infant" e, p 295; INFANT HOLY, INFANT LOWLY; "Infant holy, Infant lowly, for His bed a cattle stall" e 251,319; "IN A MANGER HE IS LYING" e 296; TELL, O SHEPHERDS; "Tell, O shepherds, tell the story" e 361   9299A

W ŻŁOBIE LEŻY; "W żłobie leży! któż pobieży"; IN A MANGER; "In a manger sleeps the Infant" e, p 295   9299B

WŚRÓD NOCNEJ CISZY; "Wśród nocnej ciszy, głos się rozchodzi"; IN THE STILL OF THE NIGHT; "Angels from heaven sang a thrilling psalm" e, p 295; ECHOES ARE SOUNDING; "Echoes are sounding through the silent skies" e, p 154; MIDST THE DEEP SILENCE; "Midst the deep silence of that holy night" e 165; IN THE SILENCE OF THE NIGHT; "In the silence of that night so bright" e 244   9300

PORTUGAL

AO MENINO DEUS; "Entrac, entrac pastorinhos"; OH ENTER DEAR SHEPHERDS; "Oh enter, enter, dear shepherds" e 154   9301

JESUS, MARIA E JOSÉ; "Estando a Virgem á borda do rio" po 57   9302

PUERTO RICO

AGINALDO NO. 2; "Tra la la la la la la la"; "A la media noche al rigor del hielo"; A CHRISTMAS SONG; "In the deep of midnight Christ was born a-crying" e, s 291   9303

ALEGRÍA; "Hacia Belén se encaminan María con su amante esposo"; REJOICING; "With her tender, loving husband, young María went to Bethl'em" e, s 291   9304

EL NIÑO JESUS; "Madre a la puerta hay un niño mas hermosa que el sol bello"; THE CHILD JESUS; "Mother dear, a Child at our door step has a beauty past comparing" e, s 154,337   9305

VILLANCICO; "Vamos, pastorcitos, vamos a Belén"; CHRISTMAS CAROL; "Let us go, oh shepherds, to the town of Bethl'hem" e, s 219; VAMOS, PASTORCITOS; HASTEN NOW; YE SHEPHERDS; "Hasten now, ye shepherds, hasten to the manger" e 165; AGUINALDO NO. 1; "De tierra lejana venimos a verte"; A CHRISTMAS GIFT; "From a far-off land we come to see you yearly" e, s 291   9306

RUSSIA

THE ANGELICAL HYMN; "From the hallow'd belfry tow'r" e 410   9307

IN A MANGER; "In a manger poor sleeps the Christ Child" e 337   words by C. Engel   9308

IN BETHLEHEM'S MANGER; "In Bethlehem's manger Jesus Christ is born us" e 244   9309

KOLYADA; "Kolyada, Kolyada walks about on Christmas Eve" e 214   9310

SLAWA; LET US PRAISE THEE; "Let us praise Thee, of God in heavens" e, r 154; "PRAISE TO GOD IN THE HIGHEST" e 307   9311

UNSER HEILAND IST GEBOREN; "Unser Heiland ist geboren, Halleluja" g 354   9312

WIEGENLIED; "Schlaf, mein Kindlein, schlaf ein Schläfchen" g 354   9313

SCOTLAND

BALOO, LAMMY; "This day to you is born a Child of Mary meek, the Virgin mild" e 337; BALOO LOO, LAMMY; "I come from heaven good news to tell, good news, the best news that e'er befell" e 165   9314

LEANABH AN AIGH; "Leanabh an aigh! Leanabh bh'aig Mairi"; CHILD IN THE MANGER; "Child in the manger! Infant of Mary" e, sc 154   9315

A LA NANITA NANA; "A la nanita nana, nanita ea"; "Mi Jesús tiene sueño" (verse); "My Jesus, He is sleeping" (verse) e, s 388   9316

BUENOS REYES; GOOD KINGS; "Good kings, now sing and be joyful" e 33   9317

CAMINA LA VIRGEN PURA; "Camina la virgen pura, camina para Belén" s 283   9318

COME, ALL YE CHILDREN; "Come, all ye children, your voices raise on this morn" e 296   9319

DIE HEILIGE NACHT; "Heute nacht ist heilige Nacht" g 354   9320

"IST ES NOCH STILL IN DER RUNDE" g 354   9321

PASTORES A BELEN; "Pastores a Belen vamos con alegria" s 79; GO YE TO BETHLEHEM; "Go ye to Bethlehem, O shepherds, leave your sheep" e 165   9322

VILLANCICOS DE NAVIDAD; "Brincan y lailan los peces en el río" s 281   9323

VILLANCICOS DE NAVIDAD; "La Virgen está lavando y tendiendo el romero" s 281   9324

VILLANCICOS DE NAVIDAD; "La virgen lava pañales y los tiencleen el romero" s 281   9325

LA VIRGEN VA CAMINANDO; "La Virgen va a caminando, alepún"; OUR PURE VIRGIN WAS GOING; "Darker the mountain was growing" e, s 154   9326

SWEDEN

THE ANGEL'S ANTHEM; "There was music on the hillside and singing in the glen" e 412   words by H. Kemp   9327

"ETT BARN ÄR FÖTT PAA DENNA DAG"; "A TENDER CHILD WAS BORN THIS DAY" e, sw 154   9328

HEJ, TOMTEGUBBAR; "Hej, tomtegubbar, slaan i glasen"; HO! JOLLY GNOMES; "Ho! jolly gnomes fill up the glasses" e, sw 188   9329

EN JUNGFRU FÖDDE ETT BARN I DAG; "TODAY THE VIRGIN HAS BORNE A CHILD" e 165   9330

JUNGFRU MARIA TILL BETLEHEM GICK; "Jungfru Maria till Betlehem gick lovat vare Guds heliga namn!"; MARY THE VIRGIN TO BETHLEHEM WENT; "Mary the Virgin to Bethlehem went; Prais'd be God's holy name evermore" e, sw 388   9331

NÄR JULDAGSMORGON GLIMMAR; "När juldagsmorgon glimmar, jag vill till stallet gaa"; I TURN UNTO A STABLE; "I turn unto a stable when Christmas day doth dawn" e, sw 188   9332

NU ÄR DET JUL IGEN; "Nu är det Jul igen, och Nu är det Jul igen"; DANCE CAROL; "Yuletide is here again, and Yuletide is here again" e, sw 388; "Christmas is here again oh Christmas is here again" e, sw 79; NOW IT IS CHRISTMASTIME; "Now it is Christmastime, vacation will start again" e, sw 337; CHRISTMAS HAS COME AGAIN; "Christmas has come again, Christmas has come again" e 165; CHRISTMAS IS HERE AGAIN; "Christmas is here again and Christmas is here again" e, sw 188   9333

O BLESSED YULETIDE; "O blessed Yuletide, light from the heavens" e 244   9334

STAFFAN WAR EIN STALLKNECHT; "Staffan war ein Stallknecht mal" g 354   9335

STAFFANSVISA; "Sankt Staffan han rider sina hästar tell vanns"; SAINT STEPHEN WAS RIDING; "Saint Stephen was riding and he travel'd afar" e, sw 388; ZUR WEIHNACHTSZEIT; "Sankt Steffan, der reitet zu der Tränke sein Pferd" g 354   9336

EN STJÄRNA GICK PAA HIMLEN FRAM; THE STAR THAT LED TO BETHLEHEM; "A star in heaven shone one night" e, sw 165   9337

SWITZERLAND

DORMI, DORMI, BEL BAMBIN; "Dormi, dormi, bel bambin, re divin" i 155   9338

"KOMMT ALL HEREIN, IHR ENGELEIN" g 157; KOMMT ALL' HEREIN! g 412   9339

MEIN MUND, DER SINGT; "Mein Mund, der singt, mein Stimm erklingt" g 354   9340

"SCHLAF WOHL, DU HIMMELSKNABE DU" g 354   9341

"THE SHEPHERDS HAD AN ANGEL" e 380   words by C. G. Rossetti   9342

I TRE RE; "Noi siamoi tre re, noi siamoi tre re" i 155   9343

UNITED STATES

A LA RU; "Duérmete, Niño lindo en los brazos del amor"; CRADLE SONG; "Oh sleep, Thou Holy Baby, with Thy head against my breast" e, s 314   9344A

CANTO DE CUNA AL NIÑO JESUS; "Duérmete Niño lindo en los brazos del amor"; "Sleep thou beauteous Child within the arms of love" e, s 113   9344B

AWAKE; "Awake, my soul, to joyful lays" e 332   9345

AWAY IN A MANGER; "Away in a manger, no crib for a bed" e 33, 79, 165, 206, 244, 251, 296, 315, 337, 388 music att to J. R. Murray   9346A

AWAY IN A MANGER; "Away in a manger, no crib for a bed" e 319, 369   9346B

BABE OF BETHLEHEM; "Ye nations all, on you I call" e 332   9347

THE BITTER WITHY; "As it fell out, one holiday small rain from sky did fall" e 261   9348

THE CHERRY TREE CAROL. See 8911C, 8911E, 8911F, 8911H, 8911I, 8911K

CHILD OF GOD; THE LITTLE CRADLE ROCKS TONIGHT IN GLORY; "If anybody ask you who I am" e 33,332   9349

CHILDREN OF THE HEAVENLY KING; "Children of the heav'nly King, as we journey let us sing" e 332   9350

CHRIST WAS BORN; "Christ was born in Bethlehem, in a lowly stable lay" e 242   9351

CRADLE HYMN; "Hush, my babe, lie still and slumber" e 332   words by I. Watts   9352

"CUANDO POR EL ORIENTE SALE LA AURORA"; WHEN IN THE EAST THE SUN ARISES; "When in the east the   9353
     mighty sun no more did tarry" e, s 314   9353

A DAY OF JOY AND FEASTING; "A day of joy and feasting, of happiness and mirth" e 337   9354

DAYS OF CHRISTMAS. See 8998E

DE LA REAL JERUSALÉN; "De la real Jerusalén salió una estrella brillando"; FROM ROYAL JERUSALEM; "From   9355
     Jerusalem proceeding, to the Christ Child's manger going" e, s 314

DOWN IN YON FOREST; "Down in yon forest be a hall, sing May, Queen May, sing Mary" e 261,268   9356A

DOWN IN YON FOREST; "Down in yon forest stands a hall, sing May, sing May, sing Mary" e 44   9356B

EXULTATION; "Come away to the skies my beloved, arise" e 332   9357

"HOW MANY MILES TO BETH-E-LE-HEM?"; "How many miles to London Town?" e 332   9358

I WONDER AS I WANDER; "I wonder as I wander, out under the sky" e 267,357   9359

JANUARY, FEBRUARY; THE LAST MONTH OF THE YEAR; "What month was my Jesus borned in?" e 332   9360

JESUS BORNED IN BETHLEA; "Jesus borned in Bethlea, Jesus borned in Bethlea" e 332   9361A

JESUS BORN IN BETH'NY; "Jesus born in Beth'ny, Jesus born in Beth'ny" e 268   9361B

JESUS BORN IN BETHLEA; "Jesus born in Bethlea, Jesus born in Bethlea" e 331; "CHRIST WAS BORN IN BETHLE-   9361C
     HEM" e 165,312

JESUS, JESUS, REST YOUR HEAD; "Jesus, Jesus, rest your head, you has got a manger bed"; "Have you heard   9362
     about our Jesus?" (verse) e 268

JESUS THE CHRIST IS BORN; "Jesus the Christ is born, Give thanks now, ev'ry one" e 268   9363

JOLLY OLD SAINT NICHOLAS; "Jolly old Saint Nicholas, lean your ear this way!" e 28,206,366   9364

JUDAS; "'Twas in the merry month of May, the Easter time was near" e 261   9365

KENTUCKY WASSAIL SONG. See 9002C

LA LEVANTADA DE BARTOLO; "En Belén está la gloria"; THE AWAKING OF BARTOLO; "In Bethlehem there is   9366
     glory" e, s 314

LITTLE BITTY BABY; "Children, go, where I send thee" e 313,332   9367A

ONE FOR THE LITTLE BITTY BABY; "Children, go, where I send thee!" e 33,389   9367B

HOLY BABE; "Children, go, and I will send thee" e 332   9367C

LOWLY BETHLEHEM; "Not Jerusalem lowly Bethlehem"; "Nicht Jerusalem, sondern Bethlehem" e, g 109,110   9368

LULLE LULLAY. See 8917B

MAY CAROL; "I've been a-wand'ring all the night" e 312; "I've been a-wandrin' all the night" e 313   9369

OFRECIMIENTO DE LOS PASTORES; "Voy para Belén a ver a mi amada"; OFFERING OF THE SHEPHERDS; "Now   9370
     I go to Bethlehem, o'er the cradle hover" e, s 314

OLD CHRISTMAS; FIDDLE TUNE no words 332   9371

PEDIMENTO DE LAS POSADAS; "¿Quién les da posada a estos peregrinos"; THE SEARCH FOR LODGINGS; "Who,   9372
     to these poor pilgrims, shelter will be grudging" e, s 314

REJOICE MY FRIENDS; "Rejoice my friends, the Lord is King!" e 332   9373

SEE JESUS THE SAVIOUR; "No shelter for Mary, who Jesus did carry" e 268   9374

THE SEVEN JOYS OF MARY. See 8985D, 8985E, 8985F

THE SEVEN VIRGINS; "As walking out upon a day, small rain did fall from Heaven" e 261   9375

SHEPHERDS IN JUDEA; "The God sent an angel from heaven so high" e 332   9376

SHEPHERDS REJOICE; "Shepherds, rejoice, lift up your eyes" e 332   9377

SHIP A-SAILING; "A little ship was on the sea" e 242   9378

SING ALL MEN!; "Sing all men! 'tis Christmas morning" e 268   9379

SING WE THE VIRGIN MARY; "Sing we the Virgin Mary, sing we that matchless one" e 261   9380

STAR IN THE EAST; "Hail the blest morn, see the great Mediator"; "Brightest and best of the sons of the   9381
     morning" (ref) e 332

THE STORY OF TWELVE; "Come and I will sing you" e 216,331   9382A

THE TWELVE APOSTLES; "Stay and I'll sing! What'll you sing?" e 332   9382B

THE TWELVE DAYS OF CHRISTMAS. See 8998C

VAMOS TODOS A BELÉN; "Vamos todos a Belén; con amor y gozo"; LET US ALL GO TO BETHLEHEM; "Let us   9383
     go to Bethlehem as our spirits soar" e, s 314

UNITED STATES NEGRO

AIN'T THAT A ROCKING ALL NIGHT; "Mary had the little Baby, born in Bethlehem" e 332   9384

ALMOST DAY; "Chicken crowing for midnight, and it's almost day" e 332; LOOKA DAY; "Oh, true believer,   9385
     oh, looka day" e 332

BABY BORN TODAY; "Mother Mary, what is the matter?" e 332   9386

GLORY HALLELUJAH TO DE NEW-BORN KING; "Tell me who do you call de Wonderful Counsellor?" e 182   9387

GLORY TO THE NEWBORN KING; "O Mary what you goin' to name that pretty little baby?"; "Glory! glory! glory   9388A
    to that newborn King" (ref) e 409; GLORY TO THAT NEWBORN KING e 244

MARY, WHAT YOU GOING TO NAME THAT PRETTY LITTLE BABY?; "The Virgin Mary had-a one Son" (ref)   9388B
    e 332

"GO TELL IT ON THE MOUNTAIN"; "In the time of David some called him a King" (verse) e 332; "When I   9389A
    was a sinner, I prayed both night and day" (verse) e 33; "When I was a seeker, I sought both night
    and day" (verse first) e 337; "While shepherds kept their watching o'er silent flocks by night" (verse)
    e 409; GO, TELL IT ON THE MOUNTAINS; "When I was a learner, I sought both night and day" e
    296; TELL IT ON DE MOUNTAIN; "When I was a seeker, I sought both night an' day" e 154

"GO, TELL IT ON DE MOUNTAIN"; "Sing, Glory, Hallelujah, over de hills an' ev'rywhere" (verse) e 184   9389B

HEARD FROM HEAVEN TODAY; "Hurry on, my weary soul, and I heard-a from heaven today"; "A Baby born   9390
    in Bethlehem" (verse) e 332

HEAVEN BELL RING; "Oh, Christmas come but once a year" e 332   9391

LOOK AWAY TO BETHLEHEM; "Look, look away, look away" e 332   9392

MARY HAD A BABY; "Mary had a Baby, Aye, Lord"; "The people keep a-coming and the train done gone" (ref)   9393
    e 332; "Mary had a baby, yes Lord"; "De people keep a-comin' an' de train done gone" (ref) e 182

THE NEW BORN BABY; "Baby born in Bethlehem" e 332   9394

"OH, MARY AND THE BABY, SWEET LAMB" e 332   9395

O MARY, WHERE IS YOUR BABY?; "Read in the gospel of Math-a-yew" e 332   9396

POOR LITTLE JESUS; "It was poor little Jesus, yes, yes" e 33, 332; PO' LIL JESUS; "It was po' little Jesus, yes,   9397
    yes" e 227

RISE UP, SHEPHERD AN' FOLLER; "Dere's a star in de Eas' on Christmas morn" e 154, 244; "There's a star in the   9398
    east on Christmas morn" e 35, 165; RISE UP, SHEPHERD AND FOLLOW e 216, 332, 337; RISE UP,
    SHEPHERDS, AN' FOLLER; "Dere's a star in de Eas' on Christmas morn" e 296; RISE UP, SHEP-
    HERDS, AND FOLLOW; "There's a star in the East on Christmas morn" e 33

SING-A-LAMB; "Oh, that Lamb, sing-a-lamb"; "Bring Mary and the Baby" (verse) e 332   9399

SING HALLELU; "Down in a valley, sing hallelu" e 332   9400

"SINGING IN THE LAND"; "O sister, don't you want to go to heaven?" e 332   9401

'TWAS A WONDER IN HEAVEN; "O Lord, I wonder, bye and bye" e 332   9402

"WASN'T THAT A MIGHTY DAY"; "Well, Jesus was a baby" (verse) e 332; (ref only) e 244, 409   9403

YONDER COMES SISTER MARY; "Yonder comes Sister Mary, How do you know it is her?" e 332   9404

VENEZUELA

AGUINALDO; "San José y María van para Belén"; "Noche pre cursora de La Navidad" (verse); "Saint Joseph   9405
    and Mary go to Bethlehem"; "Evening, the forerunner of the Saviour's birth" (verse) e, s 244

GLORIA EN LAS ALTURAS; GLORY IN THE HIGHEST; "Go in adoration, go to Bethlehem" e 165   9406

THE JOURNEY; DIN, DIN, DIN; "Din, din, din, came the awaited day" e 165   9407

WALES

NOS GALAN; "Oer yw'r gwr sy'n methu caru"; NEW YEARS EVE; "Soon the hoar old year will leave us" e 19,   9408
    349; "SOON THE HOAR OLD YEAR WILL LEAVE US" e 333; DECK THE HALL; "Deck the hall with
    boughs of holly" e 37, 165, 306, 234, 296, 315, 319, 366; "Deck the halls with boughs of holly" e 125,
    236; "DECK THE HALLS WITH BOUGHS OF HOLLY" e 233; DECK THE HALLS e 28, 33, 35, 79, 337,
    388; DÍAS DE NAVIDAD; "Navidad, Navidad!"; "Christmas! Christmas!" e, s 244

SUO-GAN; "Suo-gan, do not weep" e 165   9409

"SWEETLY SANG THE GLORIOUS ANGELS" e 315   9410

TÔN GAROL; "Mae'r flwyddyn yn marw, ei hamser a ddaeth"; A WELSH CAROL; "The old year is fading, and   9411
    and soon will be past" e, w 20

WEST INDIES

THE VIRGIN MARY HAD A BABY BOY; "De Virgin Mary had a baby boy" e 323   9412

YUGOSLAVIA

ČESTIT SVIETU; "Čestit svietu danas svemu"; "HAPPINESS THE SUN IS BRINGING" e, cr 154   9413

FREUET EUCH ZUR STUND; "Freuet euch, freuet euch, freuet euch zur Stund" g 354   9414

OJ PASTIRI; "Oj pastiti, čudo novo"; HEAR, O SHEPHERDS; "Hear, O shepherds; hear while I tell you" sc 337   9415A

"HIRTEN, HABT IHR ES GESEHEN" g 354   9415B

SIEH GOTTES GESTIRN; "Sieh gottes Gestirn, o wie blinkt's heut so schön!" g 354   9416

ZVIM NA ZEMLJI MIR; TO ALL THE EARTH; "To all the earth comes the song of angels" e 165   9417

SEA CHANTIES

HAND O'ER HAND; "A handy ship and a handy crew, Handy, my boys, so handy!" e 29   9443A

SO HANDY, MY BOYS, SO HANDY; "A handy ship and a handy crew, Handy, my boys, so handy" e 320   9443B

HANGING JOHNNY; "And they calls me hanging Johnny" e 205; "O they call me hanging Johnny" e 235; "Oh they   9444
       call me Hanging Johnny" e 320; HANGIN' JOHNNIE; "Now they calls me Hangin' Johnnie" e 401

HAUL AWAY JOE; "Way, haul away, haul away, my rosies" e 331; "Way, haul away, Oh, haul and sing to-   9445A
       gether" e 214; "Way, haul away, we'll haul away the bowlin'" e 35,199; "When I was a little
       lad and so my mother told me" e 173

HAUL AWAY, JOE; "Away, haul away, come haul away together" e 293   9445B

HAUL AWAY, JOE; "Away, haul away, we'll haul away together" e 320,366   9445C

HAUL ON THE BOWLINE; "Haul on the bowline, the Yankee ship's arollin" e 335; "Haul on the bowline, the   9446A
       ship she is a rollin'" e 29; HAUL ON THE LINE BOYS; "Haul on the line boys, Our bully ship's
       a rollin'" e 205; HAULING ON THE BOWLINE; "Haul upon the bowline the fore and main top
       bowline" e 320; HAUL ON THE BOWLIN'; "Haul on the bowlin', our bully ship's a rollin'!"
       e 28; "Haul on the bowlin' the fore and maintop bowlin'" e 279,366

HAUL ON THE BOWLIN'; "Haul on the bowlin', O Mary you are my darlin'" e 205   9446B

HIGH BARBAREE; "There were two lofty ships from old England came" e 169,173,235,401 att to C. Dibdin   9447A

HIGH BARBAREE; "There was a gallant English ship a-sailing on the sea" e 320   9447B

HIGHLAND LADDIE; "Where have you been all the day"; "Way, hay, and away we go, Highland laddie" (ref)   9448A
       e 320

HIGHLAND LADDIE; "Was you ever in Quebec?"; "Heigh-ho and away she goes, Bonny laddie" (ref) e 171   9448B

HOLTOYO!; "Merry is a life at sea" e37   9449

HOMEWARD BOUND; "We're homeward bound I hear them say" e 320   9450A

HOMEWARD BOUND; "We're homeward bound, I heard them say" e 29   9450B

HULLABALOO BELAY; "My mother kept a boarding house" e 320   9451

HURRAH, SING FARE-YOU-WELL; "Sing fare-you-well my bonny young girl" e 320   9452

JACK THE SAILOR; "'Twas twenty five or thirty years since Jack first saw the light"; "Jack was ev'ry inch a   9453
       sailor" (ref) e 249; JACK WAS EVERY INCH A SAILOR; "Now 'twas twenty-five, or thirty years,
       since Jack first saw the light" e 171,186

JOHNNY BOKER; "Oh do my Johnny Boker, come rock and roll me over" e 320,366   9454

JOHNNY COME DOWN TO HILO; "Was you ever down in Mobile bay"; "O, take, O, shake, O, who's that gal   9455A
       with a blue dress on?" (ref) e 145; WHEN JOHNNY COMES DOWN; "I nebber seen de like since
       I bin born"; "Oh wake her, Oh shake her, Oh wake dat girl wid de blue dress on" (ref) e 234;
       WHEN JOHNNY COMES DOWN TO HILO; "I nebber see de like since I bin born" e 320

JOHNNY COME TO HILO; "Oh, a poor man came a-riding by"; "Oh, wake her, oh, shake her; Oh, shake that   9455B
       girl with the blue dress on" (ref) e 214

JOHN'S GONE TO HILO; "Oh, Johnnie's gone, what shall I do? Away to Hilo" e 320; HILO; "Tommy's gone: 9456
       What shall I do?; "Tommy's gone to Hilo" e 29; TOM'S GONE TO HILO; "Tommy's gone, what
       shall I do? Away down Hilo" e 235; TOM'S GONE TO ILO; "My Tommy's gone, what shall I
       do?" e 366

JULIA; "A sailor has one pleasure dear" e 37   9457

LEAVE HER JOHNNIE LEAVE HER; "I thought I heard the old man say Leave her Johnnie" e 320   9458A

LEAVE HER JOHNNY; "I thought I heard the skipper say, Leave her Johnny" e 234; "I thought I heard the captain   9458B
       say, Leave her Johnny" e 29; LEAVE HER, JOHNNY, LEAVE HER; "Oh, the times are hard and the
       wages low" e 366

LIVERPOOL GIRLS; "When I was a youngster I sail'd with the rest" e 29   9459

THE LIVERPOOL SONG; "'Twas in the cold month of December, when all of my money was spent" e 29   9460

A LONG TIME AGO; "A long, long time and a long time ago" e 29   9461A

A LONG TIME AGO; "A long, long, time and a very long time" e 320   9461B

A LONG TIME AGO; "Oh, a long time, a very long time" e 401   9461C

THE LOSS OF THE ELIZA; THE HERONS; "Fort Amherst's hardy youthful crew" e 186   9462

LOWLANDS; "Lowlands, lowlands, away, my John" e 109,110,227; "Lowlands, my lowlands away my John"   9463A
       e 320; LOWLANDS AWAY; "I dream'd a dream the other night, lowlands, my lowlands away my
       John!" e 235

LOWLANDS; "I dreamed a dream the other night, lowlands, lowlands, away my John" e 35   9463B

LOWLANDS; "Lowlands, lowlands, away, my John" e 401   9463C

LOWLANDS; "I dreamt a dream the other night; lowlands, lowlands, alas, my John!" e 29   9463D

MAINSAIL HAUL; "One morning in the month of cold December" e 320   9464

THE MARINER; "Light blew the breeze and smooth the tide" e 205   9465

MARY ANN; "Oh, fare thee well, my own true love" e 186   9466

THE MERMAID; "One Friday morn, when we set sail" e 234,349   9467A

THE MERMAID; "O, 'twas in the broad Atlantic in an equinoctial gale" e 402   9467B

THE MERMAID; "One Friday morn when we set sail" e 199   9467C

THE MERMAID; "One Friday morn as we set sail" e 249   9467D

THE MERMAID; "'Twas Friday morn when we set sail!" e 205   9467E

MISTER STORMALONG; "Old Stormy he is dead and gone" e 320; STORMALONG e 235; "Old Stormy's dead   9468
       and gone to rest" e 29; OLD STORMY; "Old Stormy he is dead and gone" e 331

NASSAU BOUND; "We sailed the Sloop John B."; "There's no better place than a sailing ship" (verse) e 11   9469

ONE MORE DAY; "Only one more day, my Johnny" e 320   9470A

ONE MORE DAY; "Oh have you heard the news, my Johnny?" e 35   9470B

PADDY DOYLE; "To me, way! and we'll furl, and we'll pay Paddy Doyle for his boots!" e 29; "To me way, hay, hay, hay, yah, We'll pay Paddy Doyle for his boots" e 320   9471A

PADDY DOYLE'S BOOTS; "Yeo, ho, and we'll haul, aye, we'll hang Paddy Doyle for his boots" e 366   9471B

REUBEN RANZO; "Oh, poor old Reuben Ranzo, Ranzo, boys, Ranzo!" e 320; RANZO e 29; REUBEN RANZO; "Hurrah for Reuben Ranzo, Ranzo, boys, Ranzo" e 279,366   9472

RIO GRANDE; "Oh, New York town is no place for me!" e 401; "O say, were you ever in Rio Grande?" e 29,35, 109,110,234,335; "O were you ever in Rio Grande?" e 37,320; "Were you ever in Rio Grande?" e 115; "WERE YOU EVER IN RIO GRANDE?" e 205,366   9473

ROLL THE COTTON DOWN; "Away down South where I was born" e 320; "Oh, were you ever in Mobile Bay" e 29; ROLL DE COTTON DOWN; "Oh, roll de cotton, roll it down" e 37   9474

ROLLING HOME. See 5947

SACRAMENTO; Camptown races (tune); "As I was walking on the Quay, Hoodah, to my hoodah" e 320; "A bully ship and a bully crew, dooda, dooda!" e 34,109,227; "We've formed our band and we are well manned, dooda, dooda!" e 109,110; "Sing and heave, and heave and sing, doo da, doo da" e 173; HO FOR CALIFORNIA; "We've formed our band and we are all well manned" e 335   9475

THE SAILOR LIKES HIS BOTTLE O; "So early in the morning"; "A bottle of rum and a bottle of gin" (verse) e 205; "SO EARLY IN THE MORNING"; "A bottle o' rum, and a bottle o' beer" (verse) e 235   9476

THE SAILOR'S FAREWELL; "Farewell! farewell, my Polly dear!" e 86   9477

SAILOR'S HORNPIPE piano 205   9478

SALLY BROWN; "I shipped on board of a Liverpool liner" e 205; "O Sally Brown I love your daughter" e 320; "O Sally Brown's a Creole lady" e 29; "Sally Brown she's a bright mulatter" e 235   9479

SANTA ANNA; "Oh, Santa Anna won the day" e 235; SANTY ANNA; "O Santy Anna gained the day" e 34; "Oh, Santy Anna won the day" e 29; SANTY ANNO; "We're sailing down the river from Liverpool" e 227   9480A

SANTA ANNA; "Oh Santa Anna won the day" e 320   9480B

SHENANDOAH; "O Shenandoah, I long to hear you" e 227,235; O SHENANDOAH e 37; "Oh, Shenandoah I long to hear you" e 35,199,335; THE WIDE MISSOURI e 109,110; "Oh, Shenandoah! I love your daughter" e 279,366,401; "Oh Shenandoah's my native valley" e 29; "Missouri she's a mighty river" e 320; "The old Mizzoo, she's a mighty river" e 173; THE WIDE MISSOURI; SHENANDOAH; "Oh, Shenandoah, I love your daughter" e 129; THE WIDE MIZZOURA; "O Shannadore, I love your daughter" e 321   9481

A SONG OF THE SEA; "A sailor's life is a roving life" e 205   9482

SPANISH LADIES; "Farewell and adieu to you fine Spanish ladies" e 29; "Farewell and adieu to you, fair Spanish ladies" e 235; "Farewell and adieu unto you, Spanish ladies" e 402; "Farewell and adieu to you, Spanish ladies" e 34   9483A

SPANISH LADIES; "Farewell and adieu to you Spanish ladies" e 320   9483B

WE'LL RANT AND WE'LL ROAR; THE RYANS AND THE PITTMANS; "My name it is Robert, they call me Bob Pittman" e 186   9483C

THE SPANISH LADIES; "Farewell and adieu to you, fair Spanish ladies" e 44   9483D

SPANISH LADIES; "Farewell and adieu to you, fair Spanish ladies" e 401   9483E

THE STATELY SOUTHERNER; "It was a stately Southern ship and she flew the Stripes and Stars" e 320   9484

"THE STORMY SCENES OF WINTER" e 186   9485

THREE PIRATES; "Three pirates came to London Town, Yo-ho! Yo-ho!" e 37; THREE PIRATES CAME TO LONDON TOWN e 214   9486

VENEZUELA; "I met her in Venezuela" e 169   9487

WE BE THREE MARINERS; "We be three poor mariners" e 37; "WE BE THREE POOR MARINERS" e 235,349,397; THREE POOR MARINERS; "O we be three poor mariners" e 297   words by T. Ravenscroft   9488

WE'RE ALL BOUND TO GO; "One day as I was strolling, unthinking by the quay" e 234; "One day as I was walk- ing down by the Clarence Dock" e 320   9489

"A WET SHEET AND A FLOWING SEA" e 205   9490

THE WHALE; "It was in the year of forty-four" e 173   9491

WHISKEY JOHNNIE; "Whiskey is the life of man" e 34; WHISKY! JOHNNY! e 29; WHISKY FOR MY JOHNNY; "Whisky is the life of man" e 205   9492A

WHISKY; "O whisky is the life of man" e 320   9492B

WHISKEY, JOHNNY; "Whiskey is the life of man" e 225   9492C

YEO, HEAVE HO!; "Yeo, heave ho! 'Round the capstan go" e 35   9493

INDEX TO ALL TITLES AND FIRST LINES

ABENDLIED (Schulz) 3334 (31,49,99,229,353)
ABENDLIED (Stephan) 3571 (226)
ABENDS 1148 (45)
ABENDS, WENN DIE LICHTER GLÜHN 2985 (258)
"Abends, will ich schlafen gehn" 1736 (96,237,236,328)
ABENDSEGEN 1736 (96,236,237,328)
ABENDSTÄNDCHEN 5196 (49)
DER ABENDSTERN 3352 (141,229)
ABETS ZAGUN GUZIEK 8807 (361)
ABGEMÄHT IST SCHON DIE WIESE 5756 (92)
"Abgemäht ist schon die Wiese, alle Blümlein sind gefällt"
    5756 (92)
ABIDE WITH ME (Bennett) 279 (160)
ABIDE WITH ME (Monk) 2491 (28,233,236,279,366)
"Abide with me, fast breake the morning light" 279 (160)
"Abide with me! fast falls the eventide" 2491 (28,233,
    236,279,366)
ABLAKOMBA, ABLAKOMBA 5650 (23)
"Ablakomba, ablakomba besütött a holdvilág" 5650 (23)
ABLAKOMBA HÁROM BOKOR 5651 (164)
THE ABOLITIONIST HYMN 379 (109,110,173)
"ABOUT THE SWEET BAG OF A BEE" 2059 (106)
"Above a plain of gold and green" 4347 (37)
"Above the country thickets, the summer moon is bright"
    24 (93)
"Above verdant steppes and above snowclad mountains"
    2418 (162)
ABRAHAM'S DAUGHTER 4050 (44,110)
ABREDE 5197 (99)
ABREME LA PUERTA 8887 (154)
"Abreme la puerta, abreme la puerta" 8887 (154,284)
"ABSCHEULICHER! WO EILST DU HIN?" 229 (1)
ABSCHIED (Folksongs, German "Liebchen ade!...") 5198
    (99)
ABSCHIED (Folksongs, German "Muss i denn") 5483 (99)
ABSCHIED (Folksongs, German "Was klinget und singet...")
    5199 (31)
ABSCHIED (Folksongs, Italian) 6047 (51)
ABSCHIED (Folksongs, Swiss "Von meinen Bergen...")
    7389 (31)
ABSCHIED (Medinš) 2342 (224)
ABSCHIED (Müller) 2604 (99)
ABSCHIED (Silcher) 3472 (31)
ABCHIED VOM WALDE 2367 (31,99)
ABSCHIED VON DER GELIEBTEN 5209 (99)
ABSCHIED VON NEAPEL 6048 (51)
ABSCHIEDSLIED 5483 (31)
ABSENCE (Berlioz) 289 (190,192,194,362)
L'ABSENCE (Berlioz) 289 (190,192,194,362)
ABSENCE MAKES THE HEART GROW FONDER 842 (114,
    128,131)
Accis y Galatea (Literes Carrión) 2155 (269)
ACCORDING TO THE ACT 9418 (320)
ACCORTA LUSINGHIERA 520 (179)
"Accorta lusinghiera gia m'annodasti il cor" 520 (179)
"ACCOUREZ, HÂTEZ-VOUS" 571 (411)
"Accourez tous, tambours, clairons" 5099 (82)
"Accresca pietoso al viver tuo" 2245 (218)
ACH BITTRER WINTER 5200 (49,309,326)
"Ach bittrer Winter wie bist du Kalt!" 5200 (49,309,326)
ACH BLÜMLEIN BLAU 5201 (41)
"Ach Blümlein blau verdore nicht!" 5201 (41)
ACH, BOŽE MÔJ 4296 (94)
"Ach, Bože môj, prebože môj" 4296 (94)
"Ach, das Exmatrikulieren ist ein böses Ding ja" 5334
    (31)

"Ach, die Wiederkehr der schönen Morgenröte" 679 (218)
"ACH DU KLARBLAUER HIMMEL" 3473 (326)
ACH, DU LIEBER AUGUSTIN 5498 (70)
"Ach, du lieber Augustin, Augustin, Augustin" 5498 (70)
ACH ELSLEIN 5202 (41)
ACH ELSLEIN, LIEBES ELSELEIN 5202 (49,229)
"Ach Elslein, liebes Elselein mein, wie gern wär ich bei
    dir!" 5202 (49)
"Ach Elslein, liebes Elselein, wie gern wär ich bei dir!"
    5202 (41,229)
ACH ELSLEIN, LIEBES ELSLEIN 5202 (326)
ACH ELSLEIN, LIEBES ELSLEIN MEIN 5202 (309)
"Ach Elslein, liebes Elslein mein, wie gern wär ich bei
    dir!" 5202 (309)
"Ach Elslein, liebes Elslein, wie gern wär ich bei dir!"
    5202 (326)
"Ach gebt mir wieder, teure Schatten" 2886 (217)
ACH GOTT, SIEH, DEINE WUNDER 9068 (354)
"Ach, Gott, sieh, deine Wunder erfüllen sich an mir!"
    9068 (354)
ACH, ICH FÜHL'S 2596 (1,6)
"Ach ich fühl's es ist verschwunden" 2596 (1,6,311)
ACH, ICH HAB' SIE JA NUR 2443 (254)
ACH, ICH LIEBTE 2571 (6)
"Ach ich liebte war so glücklich" 2571 (6)
"Ach Jungfer, ich will ihr was aufzuraten geben" 5508 (99)
"ACH, KEBY SOM BOLA" 4297 (94)
"Ach, kehre zurück, goldenes Zeitalter" 1280 (218)
Ach lieber Herre Jesu Christ 5203 (50)
"ACH LIEBSTE, LASS UNS EILEN" 2635 (250)
Ach Mutter, liebe Mutter (tune) 5321A
"Ach Mutter, liebe Mutter, mein Kopf tut mir so weh"
    5321A (49)
ACH SCHATZ 5204 (49)
"Ach Schatz wenn du über die Gasse gehst" 5204 (49)
ACH! SO FROMM 1089 (391)
"Ach! so fromm, ach! so traut" 1089 (391)
ACH, SYNKU! 4298 (324)
"Ach synku, synku doma li jsi?" 4298 (324)
"Ach tyś może wśród tej burzy" 2471 (295)
Ach was soll ich Sünder machen? 112 (337)
"Ach, wenn's nur der König auch wüsst" 3393 (99)
"ACH, WIE IST'S MÖGLICH DANN" (Folksongs, Germany)
    5205 (99,309)
"ACH WIE IST'S MÖGLICH DANN" (Kücken) 1987 (42,
    99,326,353,402)
Ach, wie so herrlich zu schaun sind all die lieblichen
    Fraun" 3617 (255)
ACH, ZU HART 2503 (253)
"Ach, zu hart ist das grausame Urteil" 2503 (253)
Acis and Galatea 1440 (277)
"Ack, ännu synes icke morgonljuset" 1936 (355)
"Ack, att jag vore den vaxade flöjt" 3082 (356)
ACK, HÖR DU LILLA FLICKA 7295 (188)
"Ack, hör du lilla flicka, kom och låt oss dansa" 7295
    (135,188)
ACK VÄRMELAND, DU SKÖNA 7296 (135,188)
"Ack Värmeland, du sköna du härliga land!" 7296 (135,
    188)
ACORDEI DE MADRUGADA 6888 (219)
"Acordei de madrugada Fui varrer a Conceição" 6888
    (219)
ACRES OF CLAMS 7882 (173,293)
"Across lush meadows" 2482 (295)
"Across the bay some lonely bird is calling" 5940 (397)
"Across the earth, and o'er the ocean" 2897 (143)

"Agnus Dei! qui tollis peccata mundi" 315 (123,237,304, 346,394)

"Água do rio que la vai" 6896 (57)

EL AGUINALDO ("Abreme la puerta...") 8887 (284)

AGUINALDO ("San José y María...") 9405 (244)

AGUINALDO NO. 1 ("De tierra lejana...") 9306 (291)

AGUINALDO NO. 2 ("Tra la la...") 9303 (291)

Ah. See also I

"Ah, ah, ah, ah, ah, again. Prepare your boat for sailing, O faithful gondolier" 278 (221)

"Ah, ah, ah, ah, ah, ancor. La bruna gondoletta appresta o barcarol" 278 (221)

"Ah! ah! ah! mais vraiment, Cadet Rousselle est bon enfant" 4919 (82,88,91,127)

"Ah! Ah! Ah! minha machadinha" 4201 (219)

"Ah! ah! ah! oui vraiment, Cadet Rousselle est bon enfant" 4919 (383)

"Ah Ah Ahoo Ahoo" 3638 (121)

"Ah! Ah! Where is my hatchet hidden?" 4201 (219)

"Ah! All are aware" 866 (221)

"Ah! Along the forest pathway" 812 (292)

"Ah! begone, tender dream, though my heart still may languish" 2314 (3)

"Ah! beside Yidele's cradle there stands" 6243 (37)

"Ah! bright birds of June, Oh, light birds of June" 3606 (93)

AH! ÇA IRA! 4872 (7,88,91)

"Ah! ça ira, ça ira, ça ira! Les aristocrats à la lanterne" 4872 (7,88,91)

"Ah! Chacun le sait" 866 (221,292)

"Ah! Ciascun lo dice" 866 (6,221)

"AH! CIRIACA YOU DO NOT UNDERSTAND" 7502 (113)

"Ah! Come, little donkey, come" 8717 (77)

"Ah come to town de udder night" 1002 (80)

"AH! COULD I BUT CONQUER LOVE" 2423 (403)

"Ah, cruel fate, I've lost her" 3854 (3)

"Ah! E strano poter il viso suo veder" 1317 (221)

"Ah! Eu entrei na roda" 4199 (219)

"Ah! Fisher-boy, thy bait be throwing" 2847 (4)

"Ah! for tonight, I am queen" 3732 (292)

"AH, FORS' È LUI CHE L'ANIMA" 3859 (6,143,176,221)

AH, FORSE È LUI 3859 (143)

AH! FUYEZ, DOUCE IMAGE 2314 (3)

"Ah! fuyez, douce image, à mon âme trop chère" 2314 (3)

"Ah! gai lon la, vive la roulette" 5169 (187)

"Ah, good evening, fair maiden, good evening my dear" 430 (359)

"Ah got a hook an' you got a line" 7526B (80)

"Ah got a hook and you got a line" 7526B (32,34)

"Ah! Herod! Ah! Herod! Do not deny my plea!" 2310 (357)

"Ah! how those words fill me with fear" 2499 (149)

"Ah, I am worn with my sorrow" 646 (6)

"Ah, I feel, to grief and sadness" 2596 (1,6)

"Ah! I see. Ah! I see my trust was folly" 570 (148)

"Ah! I wish I could live in daydreams" 1336 (93)

AH! I WOULD LINGER 1336 (221)

"Ah! I would linger in this daydream" 1336 (221)

"Ah! if I have to lose the freedom I prize" 2205 (150)

"Ah, in loving I was happy" 2571 (6)

"Ah! In my fairy dream" 1336 (6)

"Ah! Je ris de me voir si belle en ce miroir" 1317 (1,6, 22)

AH! JE VEUX VIVRE 1336 (6,93,221,292)

"Ah! je veux vivre dans ce rêve" 1336 (6,93,221,292)

"Ah knows it, brudder, yes Ah knows it" 8243C (80)

"Ah! l'bricou, l'bricou, l'bricou, qui n'veut pas planter les choux" 4912 (91)

AH, LAMBERT 4188 (231)

"Ah! Lambert, que sais-tu donc faire?" 4188 (231)

AH, LÈVE-TOI, SOLEIL! 1337 (3)

"Ah, how can I leave thee?" 1898 (28,279,366)

AH, LOVE OF MINE 1255 (348)

"Ah, love of mine, canst thou divine" 1255 (348)

"Ah! love thou art a willful wild bird" 318 (132)

AH! LOVELY LADY 7240 (36)

"Ah! Lovely lady, to see thee I sigh now" 7240 (36)

AH MAN, AH SAY 8889 (360)

"Ah man, ah say, ay say, ah say" 8889 (360)

"Ah! Marìa, Marì! Quanta suonno che perdo pe te" 578 (132)

"Ah! me, what bitter tears I shed while yet an exile" 823 (150)

"Ah, me! Why was I born a boy!" 6982 (352)

AH! MON BEAU CHÂTEAU 4873 (91)

"Ah! mon bon chateau, ma tant', tire, lire, lire" 4873 (91)

"Ah, Mon Dieu, le temps est nuageux" 4892 (86)

AH! MON FILS 2413 (2)

"Ah! mon fils! sois béni!" 2413 (2)

AH, MY DARLING, WE COULD GROW TOGETHER 3515 (6)

"Ah, my darling, we could grow together like a single vine" 3515 (6)

"Ah! my son! Blessed be thou!" 2413 (2)

"Ah! ne repousse pas mon âme pécheresse" 1330 (123,394)

AH! NELLA CALMA 1336 (221)

"Ah! nella calma d'un bel sogno" 1336 (221)

"Ah! never 'Till life and mem'ry perish" 1510 (132)

"AH! NON CREDEA MIRARTI..." 258

"AH, NON GIUNGE" 258

"Ah! None can gainsay it" 866 (6)

"Ah! now I know! Dear friends for whom I sing" 645 (2)

"Ah! Où va la jeune indoue" 812 (221,292)

"Ah! pescator, affonda l'esca" 2847 (4,298)

AH, POOR BIRD 7398 (293)

"Ah, poor bird, take your flight far above the sorrows of this sad night" 7398 (293)

"Ah, poor Marina!" 2615 (2)

"Ah! pour ce soir, je suis reine" 3732 (292)

AH! QUANTO È VERO 630 (139)

"Ah! quanto è vero, che il nundo arciero" 630 (139)

AH! QUE JE GOÛTE DE DOUCEUR 9040 (361)

"Ah, return, ye days of gladness" 2395 (276)

"Ah, ritorna, età dell' oro" 1280 (218)

"Ah, ritorna età felice" 2395 (276)

"AH SÌ, BEN MIO: COLL' ESSERE" 3861 (3)

"Ah! si la liberté me doit être ravie" 2205 (150)

"AH! SI MON MOINE VOULAIT DANSER" 5140 (186,187)

"Ah! s'il est dans votre village" (Folksongs, French) 4916 (91,140)

"Ah! s'il est dans votre village" (Godard) 1289 (136,237, 348)

"Ah, so belated" 870 (292)

AH! SO PURE 1089 (329)

"Ah! so pure, Ah! so bright" 1089 (329)

AH SUICIDE 2849 (143)

"Ah! Suicide! 'Tis that alone may release me" 2849 (143)

"Ah, tardai troppo" 870 (6,292)

AH, THAT DAY 6941 (95)

"Ah, that day I went out walking!" 6941 (95)

"Ah! That's what they say" 866 (292)

"Ah, the days and nights go by" 4278 (86)

"Ah! the joy past compare, these jewels bright to wear!"
1317 (1,6,221)
"Ah, the year of nineteen hundred twenty-six" 7712 (314)
"Ah, thou knowest all my anguish" 3637 (112)
AH, 'TIS A DREAM 2048 (28,366)
"Ah, 'tis a tiny bird which never ceases flying" 1769 (208)
"Ah! 'tis the voice of angel bright" 2850 (2)
"Ah, 'tis too late" 870 (292)
"Ah tornar la belle aurora" 679 (218)
"Ah! turn me not away, receive me tho' unworthy" 1330
(123,394)
"AH, UN FOCO INSOLITO" 857 (5)
"Ah! viens auprès de moi! Et passe la rivière!" 5070 (63)
"AH! VOUS DIRAI-JE, MAMAN" 4874 (36,88,91)
Ah! vous dirai-je, Maman (tune) 9172
"Ah! wake me never, dreaming ever" 1336 (292)
"Ah, was it he my heart foretold" 3859 (176)
"Ah! what a price I pay" 655 (148)
"Ah, what wonder lies in dreaming" 3921 (348)
"Ah! Where roams the dusky maiden" 812 (221)
"Ah! who could dream it of you" 258 (292)
"Ah! why thus forsake me, Rosmala, my own?" 2119
(149)
"Ah, wild thoughts come throngingly" 857 (5)
"Ah, young man out there reaping in the field of wheat"
3788 (37)
AHI, SCIOCCO MONDO 2501 (181)
"Ahi, sciocco, sciocco, mondo e cieco!" 2501 (181)
"Ahi, troppo, ahi, troppo è duro" 2503 (138,253)
AHI, TROPPO È DURO 2503 (138,253)
"Ahimè! che notte oscura!" 2412 (292)
"Ahime! dove trascorsi" 1274 (2)
Ah'm. See also I'm
AH'M BROKE AN' HUNGRY 8168A (110)
"Ah'm broke an' hungry, ragged an' dirty too" 8168A (110)
"Ah'm gonna build mahself a raft an' float dat ribbah down"
8201 (109,110)
A-HUNTING WE WILL GO ("A-hunting we will go...")
4535 (343)
A-HUNTING WE WILL GO ("The dusky night rides...")
4536 (349)
"A-hunting we will go, a-hunting we will go, heighho the
merry-o" 4535 (343)
"AI, AI, DER REBE GEIT" 6167 (230)
"Ai, andando eu a cavari" 6898 (58)
AI! MEMINA 6890 (57)
"Ai o adro tem quatro quinas" 6889 (58)
"AI PREÀT LA BIELE STELE" 6050 (238)
"Ai! s'eu te déra dava dava" 6890 (57)
Aida 3819-3821
AIMABLE ENFANT, QUI NAIS POUR MOI 9041 (361)
"L'aimable Lisette forme des concerts" 2964 (404)
AIME-MOI, BERGÈRE 2088 (383)
"Aime-moi, bergere, et je t'aimerai" 2088 (297,383)
AIMONS-NOUS 3132 (190,192,194)
"Aimons-nous et dormons" 3132 (190,192,194)
Ain'. See also Ain't
AIN' NO MO' CANE ON DIS BRAZIS 8169 (227)
"Aine, dé, trois, Caroline" 7491 (219,279,366)
"Ainoa olen talon tyttö" 4852 (124)
"AINSI PARFOIS NOS SEUILS" 385 (85)
Ain't. See also Ain'
"Ain't dat a pity, Lord, ain't dat a shame" 8541 (112)
AIN'T DAT A SHAME 4045 (114,128,131)
"Ain't dat a shame, a measly shame" 4045 (114,128,131)
AIN'T DAT GOOD NEWS? 8172 (290)

AIN'T GOIN' TO STUDY WAR NO MORE 8170 (76)
AIN'T GONNA RAIN 7399A (321)
AIN'T GONNA RAIN NO MO' 7399B (185)
"Ain't got no money, can't buy no grub" 8589 (336)
AIN'T I GLAD I'VE GOT OUT THE WILDERNESS 8171 (409)
"Ain't it hard to stumble when you've got no place to fall?"
8353 (336)
AIN'T THAT A ROCKING ALL NIGHT 9384 (332)
AIN'T THAT GOOD NEWS? 8172 (409)
AIN'T WE GOT FUN 4018 (345)
AIN'T YOU COMING BACK TO OLD NEW HAMPSHIRE,
MOLLY 1613 (246)
"Ain't you glad, ain't you glad" 8173 (409)
AIN'T YOU GLAD YOU GOT GOOD RELIGION? 8173
(409)
L'AÏO DÈ ROTSO 4875 (62)
"L'aïo dè rotso té foro mourir" 4875 (62)
AIR (Lambert) 2029 (278)
AIR A BOIRE 381 (278)
AIR D'ACIS ET GALATÉE 2155 (269)
AIR D'ANAÏS 1365 (151,292)
AIR D'APOLLON 1368 (153)
AIR D'ARCABONNE (Lully) 2202 (148)
AIR D'ARCALAUS 2203 (146)
AIR D'ARMIDE 2205 (150)
AIR D'EMILIE 824 (150)
AIR D'EOLE 2468 (147)
AIR D'ERASISTRATE 2350 (147)
AIR D'IPHIGÉNIE 822 (148)
AIR D'IPHISE 2499 (149)
AIR D'ORESTE 383 (152)
AIR DE COLIN 3111 (153)
AIR DE COUR 351 (378)
AIR DE GLAUCUS 2075 (152)
AIR DE GULISTAN 754 (153)
AIR DE JOSEPH 2348 (153)
AIR DE L'AMOUR 572 (150)
AIR DE L'EUROPÉENNE 2548 (149)
AIR DE MARGOT 770 (151)
AIR DE MARS 2210 (146)
AIR DE MÉDÉE 655 (148)
AIR DE MERCURE 2961 (152)
AIR DE PARIS 378 (152)
AIR DE PÉNÉLOPE 2997 (149)
AIR DE PHINÉE 2500 (146)
AIR DE POLLUX 2958 (146)
AIR DE POLYCRATE 1366 (147)
AIR DE RENAUD 2206 (152)
AIR DE RICIMER 756 (147)
AIR DE ROSINE 1307 (149)
AIR DE SCYLLA 2076 (149)
AIR DE TELAÏRE 2959 (151)
AIR DE THÉSÉE 2962 (146)
AIR DE THÉTIS 698 (148)
AIR DE VALÈRE 825 (146)
AIR DE VÉNUS (Desmarets) 823 (150)
AIR DE VENUS (Lully) 2211 (150)
AIR DE ZÉPHIRE 573 (152)
Air des bijoux 1317 (1,6,221)
AIR DU BERGER 2209 (152)
AIR DU SOMMEIL 2207 (152)
AIR FAL-AL-AL O 6988 (199)
"Air fal-al-al o horo air fal-al-al é" 6988 (199)
THE AIR FORCE 440 (44)
"The Air Force, the Air Force, that's the force for me"
440 (44)

ALL HAIL! OH NORTHERN STRAND! 738 (124)
"All hail! Oh Northern Strand! Our fathers' joyous land!"
738 (124)
"All hail the power of Jesus' name" 1680 (35)
"All hail, thou dwelling pure and lowly" 1321 (3)
"ALL HAIL, THOU LOVELY LAUGHING MAY" 3248 (199)
"ALL HAIL TO THE DAYS THAT MERIT MORE PRAISE"
8890 (38,39,271,334)
"All hail to thee, O sun in glory" 3034 (176)
ALL HEAVEN ON A MAIDEN 6595B (361)
"All heaven on a maiden distill'd as 'twere the dew" 6595B
(361)
"All I want, all I want, all I want is a little more faith in
Jesus" 8401 (76)
"All I want in the creation, pretty little wife and a big
plantation" 7454 (227)
"All in a wood there grew a tree" 8070D (29,279,366)
"All in the downs the fleet was moor'd" 2120 (235)
"All in the Downs the fleet was moored" 2120 (397)
"All in the merry month of May" 4545A (212), 4545I (393)
"All in the wood there was a tree" 8070A (44)
"ALL IS STILL WHILE NATURE SLEEPS" 429 (220)
"All kinds of things have to happen" 4279 (86)
"All kinds of trouble will find you some day" 1558 (336)
"ALL LOOKES BE PALE" 532 (144)
ALL MAH SINS BEEN TAKEN AWAY 8178A (80)
ALL MEIN GEDANKEN (Folksongs, German) 5207 (49,226,
229,307,353)
ALL MEIN GEDANKEN (Strauss) 3618 (330)
"All' mein Gedanken, die ich hab, die sind bei dir" 5207
(35,49,99,226,229,309,353)
"All mein Gedanken mein Herz und mein Sinn" 3618 (330)
"All men should once with love grow tender" 639 (5)
ALL' MORGEN 3935 (49)
"All' morgen ist ganz frisch und neu" 3935 (49)
ALL MOWN DOWN 5756 (92)
"All mown down is now the meadow, not one blossom can I
see" 5756 (92)
ALL MY HEART THIS NIGHT (Ebeling) 973 (317)
"ALL MY HEART THIS NIGHT REJOICES" (Ebeling) 973
(271,317)
"ALL MY HEART THIS NIGHT REJOICES"(Parker) 2740
(251)
ALL MY SINS BEEN TAKEN AWAY 8178A (80)
"All my troubles will soon be over with" 8179 (409)
ALL ON A SHINY SUMMER MORNING 5084 (174)
"All on a shiny summer morning Chloe's pretty crook pretty
Chloe took" 5084 (174)
"All our daily plans and deeds, we bring before Thee, God
Almighty" 2458 (295)
"All out on the old railroad" 7747 (313)
"ALL OVER THIS WORLD" 8179 (409)
"All people that on earth do dwell" 379 (173)
ALL QUIET ALONG THE POTOMAC 1644 (161)
"All quiet along the Potomac tonight" 1644 (109,110,161)
ALL QUIET ON THE POTOMAC 1644 (109,110)
All saints 746 (28,343)
ALL SOULS' DAY 3619 (112,122)
"All the birds are here again with their happy voices"
4311 (28,366)
"All the country was invited" 4815 (37)
"ALL THE FISH ARE SWIMMING IN THE WATER" 6413
(214)
ALL THE FLOWERS ON THE MEADOW 5756 (164)
"All the flowers on the meadow were cut by the mowers
knife" 5756 (164)

ALL THE FOND THOUGHTS 3618 (330)
"All the fond thoughts that arise in my soul" 3618 (330)
"All the lads to war they've taken" 5819 (22)
"All the land is happy land and rejoices" 2841 (162)
ALL THE PRETTY LITTLE HORSES 7403 (216,227)
"ALL THE SKIES TONIGHT SING O'ER US" 137 (361)
"All the way 'roun, seben times" 8528 (409)
"All the winter earth lay bare, snow and ice lay ev'rywhere"
9228 (371)
"All the world is sad and dreary" 1129 (35,115,284)
"All thro' life we're looking for you" 1239 (344)
ALL THROUGH THE NIGHT 8657 (19,28,34,70,199,233,
234,236,279,349,366,402)
"All together, dance together" 6136 (95)
"ALL WE DO IS SIGN THE PAY-ROLL" 7404 (129,130)
"All who mark my lady's glances" 3270 (277)
"All ye that grieve, O come to Him relief he giveth" 1051
(400)
"All ye who are to mirth inclined" 8815 (372)
ALL YOU LITTLE ROOKIES, WE WISH THE SAME TO YOU
8063 (129,130)
ALL YOU THAT IN THIS HOUSE 8891 (410)
"All you that in this house be here" 8891 (410)
"All you that pass along, give ear unto my song" 4587B
(72)
"All you who sail over the ocean" 4191 (86)
ALL YOUR SHADES 2204 (273)
"All your shades ye woods, fold around me" 2204 (273)
"All your tricks are so transparent" 2575 (5)
"Allá dalt de la muntanya un angel als pastors diu" 8860
(54)
"Allá en el bosque, tórtola mía" 4512 (73)
"Allá en el muelle hay una china que me espera" 4291
(207)
ALLÁ EN EL RANCHO GRANDE 2967 (219)
"Allá en la noche callada para que se oiga mejor" 4252
(9,322)
"Allá en Río había un joven muy celoso" 3872 (132)
"ALLA MATTINA MI ALZO ALLE NOVE" 6052 (325)
ALLÁ SOTA UNA PENYA 8842 (54)
"Allá sota una penya n'es nat un Jesuset pobret, pobret"
8842 (54)
ALLAHWERDY 6942 (352)
ALLAN WATER 7153 (402)
"ALLE DIE WILLEN NAAR ISLAND GAAN" 6414 (203)
"Alle gute Gabe kommt oben her von Gott" 682* (49)
ALLE JAHRE WIEDER 3476 (99,326,388,412)
"Alle Jahre wieder kommt das Christuskind" 3476 (99,
326,388,412)
"Alle Leut, alle Leut, gehn jetzt nach Haus" 5208 (326)
ALLE LEUT GEHN JETZT NACH HAUS 5208 (326)
Alle Menchen müssen sterben 113 (337)
"ALLE VÖGEL SIND SCHON DA" 5209 (49,309,326,353)
"Alle Welt beglückt und freudvoll, Ich allein betrübt und
leidvoll" 5820 (24)
ALLEA! ALLEO! 4814 (37)
L'allegro, il penseroso ed il moderato 1450-1451
"Allein! Wieder allein!" 2105 (254)
ALLELUIA 9189 (37)
"ALLELUIA" (Mozart) 2577 (337)
"Alleluia! Alleluia! Alleluia! The strife is o'er, the
battle done" 2734 (346,400)
"ALLELUJA!" (Mozart) 2577 (93,330,394)
ALLELUJA-AMEN 1452 (308)
"Alleluya, Now well may we (our) merthis make" 8695
(360,361)

THE ANIMAL FAIR 7412 (225)

LOS ANIMALES ANTE EL NACIMIENTO 8844 (55)

"ANIOŁ PASTERZOM MÓWIŁ" 9287 (295)

ANITCHKA 4302 (95)

"Anitchka, tell me, my pretty sweet pet" 4302 (95)

"Anker auf und aus dem Herz gerissen" 2133 (222)

"Ann hini gouz eva dous, Ann hini gouz essur" 4880 (91)

ANN HINNI GOUZ 4880 (91)

ANNA IMROTH 2754 (356)

"Anne in sport threw me snow" 2980 (362)

"ANNE MARIE WAAR GA JE NAAR TOE?" 6421 (202)

"Anne par jeu me jecta de la neige" 2980 (362)

L'ANNÉE PASSÉE 8709 (286)

"L'année passée moen té yon fille" 8709 (286)

"ANNELI, WO BIST GESTER GSI?" 353 (156)

"ANNETTE, FILLETTE, NE TOUSSE PAS" 4303A (178)

ANNIE LAURIE 3405

ANNIE, MY DEAREST ONE 4302 (324)

"Annie, my dearest one, where have you been?" 4302 (324)

THE ANNUNCIATION 8848 (244)

"Año de mil nuévecientos vientiséis tan afamado" 7712 (314)

"Año de milochocientos ochenta y nuéve paso" 7515 (314)

"Año de noventa y cuatro y Puerto de Mazatlán" 6355 (247)

"Anoche mientras dormia" 4171 (207)

ANOTHER LITTLE DRINK 7893 (109, 110)

ANOTHER MAN DONE GONE 8183 (227, 321)

"Another man done gone, another man done gone, from the county farm" 8183 (227, 321)

THE ANSWER 2149 (211)

EL ANTE COLIMOTE 6322 (247)

ANTE UNA TUMBA 4479 (73)

"Antenoche fuí a tu casa, tres golpes le dí al candado" 6384 (247)

THE ANTHEM OF UNDERGROUND POLAND (1943) 2834 (159)

ANTI-CALOMEL 1740 (189)

ANTI-CONFEDERATION SONG 4220 (186)

ANTI-HITLER SONG 4306 (7)

Antioch (tune) 8950

L'ANTOINE 4881 (63)

L'ANTOUÈNO 4881 (63)

ANVIL CHORUS 3869 (28)

"Any girl fifteen or over" 2558 (6)

ANY RAGS? 49 (114, 131)

ANYNYI BÁNAT AZ SZÜVEMEN 5655 (22)

"Anynyi bánat az szüvemen Kétrét hajlott az egeken" 5655 (22)

"Anzoletto sang 'Komm mia bella'" 2447 (254)

ANZOLETTO UND ESTRELLA 2447 (254)

AO MENINO DUES 9301 (154)

AO SALTAR DA RIBEIRINHA 6892 (58)

"Ao saltar da 'Ribeirinha' Puz o pé molhei a meia" 6892 (58)

"AOU PRAT DÉ LA ROSO" 4886 (67)

"DER APFEL IST NICHT GLEICH AM BAUM" 1925 (49)

"Apples be ripe and ready, falling all, falling already" 6770 (228)

"Approach with reverent respect", 3561 (342)

"Apra il suo verde seno" 2931 (217)

APRÈS UN RÊVE 1041 (121)

APRIL SONG 322 (362)

"Aquí es ta un gallo de alzada" 6350 (247)

"Aquíestan todos los negros" 1364 (284)

"Ar an talamh, i n-áit 'tá láimh leis an tráigh" 5862 (280)

AR HYD Y NOS 8657 (19, 349, 402)

ARABIAN MELODY 370 (407)

Araby's daughter 1891

Arah my dear Ev'len (tune) 6014

ARBEIT IST AUS 5221 (40)

"Arbeit ist aus, nach Haus, nach Haus!" 5221 (40)

ARCHIPOETA 5222 (31)

ARDÉ, CORAZÓN, ARDÉ 2633 (12)

"Ardé, corazón, ardé, que no os puedo yo valer" 2633 (12)

ARDELEANA 6936 (95)

"The ardent, romantic, the charming god of song" 1196 (189, 329)

ARDON GL'INCENSI 871 (302, 221)

"Ardon gl'incensi splendon le sacre faci...Spargi d'amaro pianto" 871 (302)

"Are they over, those cherished moments" 2585 (6)

"ARE YOU ANGRY WITH ME DARLING" 7413 (132)

"Are you at home, now, Oh, my son?" 4298 (86)

ARE YOU SLEEPING? 4980 (28, 233, 366)

"Are you sleeping, are you sleeping, Brother John" 4980 (28, 187, 233, 366)

ARE YOU THERE MO-RI-AR-I-TY? 391 (172)

AREN'T YOU THE GIRL I MET AT SHERRY'S 707 (131)

ARGONNERWALD 1305 (43)

"Argonnerwald! Um Mitternacht ein Pionier stand auf der Wacht" 1305 (43)

ARGWOHN 5223 (99)

ARIA ("Diese Flamme die mich senget") 2263 (168)

ARIA ("Drei Tage schon, dass Nina") 2769 (167)

ARIA ("Gleich wie der Sonne...") 516 (168)

ARIA ("Lasciar d'amarti...") 1211 (168)

ARIA ("Lungi dal caro...") 3166 (353)

ARIA ("Piangete ohime!...") 585 (168)

ARIA ("Quel neo, quel vago neo...") 1743 (278)

ARIA ("Un certo non so che...") 3879 (168)

ARIA DE ACIS Y GALATEA 2155 (269)

Aria di Giovanni 115

ARIA DI MARGHERITA 1317 (221)

L'Arianna 2502

ARIE ("Ah tornar la belle aurora") 679 (218)

ARIE ("Mirti, faggi, tronchi...") 514 (218)

ARIE ("Non ha ragione, ingrato") 3165 (218)

ARIE ("Seele meines Herzens...") 517 (218)

ARIE ("Vaghe luci, è troppo crudo") 515 (218)

ARIE ("Vuoi, che parta!...") 72 (218)

ARIE DE ISMENE 1548 (218)

ARIE DER BALTASARA 3 (217)

ARIE DER DALINDA 364 (217)

ARIE DER DORALBA 2355 (217)

ARIE DER ERIXENA 2810 (218)

ARIE DER ERMINIA 2751 (217)

ARIE DER FIORDILIGI 3095 (217)

ARIE DER LARISSA 1280 (218)

ARIE DER MARIE 2189 (311)

ARIE DER MARZELLINE 230 (311)

ARIE DER PAMINA 2596 (311)

ARIE DER ZERLINE 2563 (311)

ARIE DES ARMIDORO 2886 (217)

ARIE DES BLONDCHEN 2572 (311)

ARIE DES ISMAEL 3195 (217)

ARIE DES LICIDAS 2764 (218)

ARIETTA ("Caro laccio, dolce nodo") 1212 (167)

ARIETTA ("Caro mio ben...") 1255 (167)

ARIETTA ("Che fiero costume...") 2089 (167)

ARIETTA ("Chi vuol comprar...") 1810 (167)

319

"AUF, AUF ZUM FRÖHLICHEN JAGEN" (Folksongs, German)
5227 (49, 309, 326)

AUF DAS TRINKGLAS EINES VERSTORBENEN FREUNDES
3355 (273)

AUF DE SCHWÄB'SCHE EISEBAHNE 5228 (326)

AUF DE SCHWÄBSCHE EISEBAHNE 5228 (309, 353)

"Auf de schwäb'sche Eisebahne gibt's gar viel Halstatione"
5228 (326)

"Auf de schwäbsche Eisebahne gibts gar viele Halstatione"
5228 (309, 353)

"Auf dem Berg so hoch da droben, da steht ein Schloss"
5252 (326)

"Auf dem Berge da gehet der Wind" 9168 (388)

"AUF DEM BERGE DA GEHT DER WIND" 9168 (154, 337,
410)

AUF DEM BERGE DA GEHT'S DER WIND 9168 (40)

"AUF DEM BERGE, DA WEHET DER WIND" 9168 (326)

AUF DEM GRÜNEN BALCON 4065 (112)

"Auf dem Grünen Balcon mein Mädchen schaut nach mir"
4065 (112)

AUF DEM KIRCHHOFE 396 (97, 112, 250)

"Auf den Bergen die Burgen" 3545 (31)

AUF DEN SCHWÄB'SCHEN EISENBAHNEN 5228 (309, 353)

"Auf den schwäb'schen Eisenbahnen gibts gar viele
Haltstationen" 5228 (309, 353)

AUF DENN ZUM FESTE 2566 (390)

"Auf denn zum Feste, froh soll es werden" 2566 (390)

AUF DER ALM, DA GIBT'S KOA SÜND 5579 (326)

AUF DER HEIDE BLÜH'N DIE LETZTEN ROSEN 3583 (223)

"AUF DER LÜNEBURGER HAIDE" (Jöde) 1792 (31)

"AUF DER LÜNEBURGER HEIDE" (Rahlfs) 2956 (326, 353)

AUF DER OFENBANK 1926 (49)

"Auf der Ofenbank in der Abendzeit" 1926 (49)

"AUF DER TREPPE SITZEN MEINE ÖHRCHEN" 1665 (250)

"Auf die Nacht in der Spinnstub'n, da singen die Mädchen"
406 (226)

AUF, DU JUNGER WANDERSMANN 5229 (49, 309, 326)

"Auf, du junger Wandersmann! jetzo kommt die Zeit heran"
5229 (49, 309, 326)

AUF EIN ALTES BILD 4066 (226)

"AUF EINEM BAUM EIN KUCKUCK SASS" 5230 (49, 309,
326)

AUF FLÜGELN DES GESANGES 2368 (141, 277, 329)

"Auf Flügeln des Gesanges, Herzliebchen, trag' ich dich
fort" 2368 (141, 277, 329)

"AUF GEHEIMEM WALDESPFADE" 1396 (121)

"Auf hebe die funkelnde Schale empor zum Mund" 3626
(112)

"Auf, ihr Brüder, lasst uns wallen in den grossen, heiligen
Dom" 3652 (31)

AUF IHR HIRTEN 9144 (40)

"Auf ihr Hirten, von dem Schlaf" 9144 (40)

AUF, IHR HIRTENSLEUT! 9145 (49)

"Auf, ihr Hirtensleut! Hört ein' grosse Freud" 9145 (49)

AUF, IHR MÄNNER, AUFGEWACHT 5231 (309)

"Auf, ihr Männer, aufgewacht, und seid auf die Jagd
bedacht!" 5231 (309)

"Auf ihrem Leibrösslein, so weiss wie der Schnee" 4073 (97)

"Auf leichten Füssen kommt gegangen" 2163 (31)

"Auf nach drüben, alles ist gut disponiert!" 1989 (254)

"Auf, singet und trinket den köstlichen Trank!" 5563 (31)

"Auf und ab, kreuz und quer" 1918 (222)

AUF WIEDERSEHN, MARIE-MADLEN 2133 (222)

AUFENTHALT 3303 (273)

AUFM WASA 5232 (41)

"Aufm Wasa graset d'Hasa, ond em Wasser gambet d'Fisch"
5232 (41)

AUF'M WASE GRASET D'HASE 5232 (326)

"Auf'm Wase graset d'Hase ond em Wasser gambet
d'Fisch" 5232 (326)

AUFTRÄGE 3356 (112)

THE AULD HOOSE 6992 (163, 349)

THE AULD HOUSE 6992 (101, 103)

AULD JOE NICHOLSON'S BONNIE NANNIE 6393 (101, 105)

AULD LANG SYNE 6994A (17, 28, 35, 70, 100, 128, 132, 163,
234, 236, 279, 343, 349, 366), 6994B (232, 365)

AULD ROBIN GRAY (Leeves) 2087 (100, 103)

Auld Robin Gray (tune) 7047

AUNT HARRIETT BECHA STOWE 1646 (189)

AUNT RHODY 7416 (170, 173, 389)

AUNT SAL'S SONG 7417 (312)

"Auntie Mina's cooking, cooking the sirup" 7215 (239)

AUNTIE MINA'S COOKING THE SIRUP 7215 (239)

AUPRÈS DE MA BLONDE 4888 (34, 67, 88, 91, 187, 402)

"Auprès d'une fantaine était un peuplier" 7377 (155)

AUR' AMOROSA 502 (181)

"Aur' amorosa, che dolcemente spiri al bel matin" 502
(181)

AUR TXIKI 8809 (244, 361)

AURA ACADEMICA 2159 (31)

UN' AURA AMOROSA 2557 (3)

"Un' aura amorosa del nostro tesoro" 2557 (3)

AURA LEE 2862 (36, 128, 131, 132)

"Aura Lee! Aura Lee! Maid of golden hair" 2862 (36, 128,
131, 132)

AURELIA 6323 (247)

Aurelia (tune) 3996

AURORA 1043 (121)

"AURORA BOREALIS, THUS SING WE DAWN'S SWEET
NAME" 4540 (402)

"La aurora empieza a brillar" 8647 (284)

AURORE 1043 (121)

L'AURORE 1042 (278)

"L'Aurore s'allume, l'ombre epaisse fuit" 1042 (278)

"Aus Barmherzigkeit, ach kehre zurück zu mir" 3599
(217)

AUS DEM HAUS 5233 (40)

"Aus dem Haus! Die Glock hat geschlagen" 5233 (40)

AUS DER JUGENDZEIT 2954 (326, 327)

"Aus der Jugendzeit, aus der Jugendzeit klingt ein Lied mir
immerdar" 2954 (326, 327)

Aus der Kinderzeit. Schlummerlied 4067 (308)

"Aus Feuer ist der Geist geschaffen" (Arndt) 75 (31)

"Aus Feuer ist der Geist geschaffen" (Hempel) 1617 (99)

"Aus Liebe, aus Liebe, aus Liebe will mein Heiland sterben" 128 (311)

AUS LIEBE, WILL MEIN HEILAND STERBEN 128 (311)

AUS MEINEN GROSSEN SCHMERZEN 1150 (36, 98, 136,
250)

"Aus meinen grossen Schmerzen mach' ich die kleinen
Lieder" 1150 (36, 98, 136, 250)

AUS MEINES HERZENS GRUNDE 5234 (49)

"Aus meines herzens Grunde sag ich dir Lob und Dank"
5234 (49)

"Aus winkligen Gassen" 1181 (31)

DIE AUSERWÄHLTE 5235 (99)

AUSWANDERERLIED 6422 (99)

AUSZUG AUS PRAG 1409 1181 (31)

AUTHOR OF ALL MY JOYS 1276 (274)

"Author of all my joys, their crown and splendor" 1276
(274)

AWAY IN A MANGER (Hume) 1733 (38,39,125)
AWAY IN A MANGER (Kirkpatrick) 1900 (305,307,410)
"Away in a manger, no crib for a bed" (Carols, United
    States) 9346A (33,79,165,206,244,251,296,315,337,
    388) 9346B (319,369)
"Away in a manger, no crib for a bed" (Kirkpatrick) 1900
    (305,307,410)
"Away in a manger, no crib for His bed" (Herbert) 1631
    (28,366)
"Away in a manger, no crib for His bed" (Hume) 1733
    (38,39,125)
"Away in the shadows a lone bird is singing" 8683 (297)
AWAY, RIO 9420 (173)
AWAY TO RIO 9421 (242)
AWAY TO THE MEADOWS 3282 (330)
"Away to the meadows, to dance with our shadows" 3282 (330)
AWAY TO THE WARS 5871 (349)
"Away up high in the Sirey Peaks" 7971 (225)
"Away, way down on the old Swanee" 1667 (128)
"AWAY WITH THESE SELF-LOVING LADS" 891 (197)
"AWAY WITH THESE SELFE LOVING LADS" 891 (144)
"Away, ye gay landscapes, ye gardens of roses" 1247
    (101,103)
"Awn i hela'r ysgyfarnog" 8676 (19)
"AY, AGUITA DE MI TIERRA" 4255 (207)
AY, AY, AY 2761 (36,284,322)
"Ay ay ay ay ay, forman y crecen" 6339B (247)
" Ay, ay, ay, ay! Canta y no llores" 6339A (36,284,322)
"Ay, ay, ay, ay, come, come to your window" 6339A
    (350)
"Ay! Ay! Ay! Ay! Sing, do not weep dear" 6339A (343)
"Ay, ay, ay, ay! Sing lest you're tearful" 6339A (322)
"Ay, ay, ay, ay! Sing, no more sighing" 6339A (37)
"Ay, ay, ay, ay! Sing sorrow never" 6339A (36)
"Ay! Ay! Ay! Ay! Vienen bajando" 6339A (350)
"Ay! Ay! El Choclo" 3872 (132)
"AY, AY, THE RABBI'S HERE!" 6167 (230)
"Ay! Ciriaca tu no com prendes" 7502 (113)
"AY CON SAL, CON SAL" 7239 (283)
"Ay, go! The eyes of Giulietta" 2691 (4)
¡AY! LINDA AMIGA 7240 (36)
"¡Ay! linda amiga, que no vuelvo a verte" 7240 (36)
AY-LYE, LYU-LYE, LYU-LYE 6175 (318)
"Ay-lye, lyu-lye, lyu-lye Shlofzhe, shlof mayn g'dule"
    6175 (318)
"Ay-lye, lyu-lye, lyu-lye sleep my pride and joy" 6175
    (318)
AY! MAMA INES 1364 (284)
"Ay nahual, cara de perro!" 6351 (247)
"¡Ay! Querido Guadalajara, ciudad de las ansias mias"
    6344 (247)
"Ay, tear her tattered ensign down!" 2040 (129,130)
AY TITUY 4277 (284)
"Ay tituy, ay tituy, ay tituy, quininuy, quininuy" 4277
    (284)
AY WAUKIN, O 6995 (232)
Ay waukin O (tune) 7077 (101)
"Ay waukin, O waukin still and weary" 6995 (332)
"Ay-yukh-nyem! ay-yukh-nyem! Eshtchyo rahzeek,
    eshtchyo rahz!" 6974 (122)
AY, ZAMBA 4164 (219)
AYE WAUKIN', O! 6995 (103,104)
"Aye waukin' O! Waukin' aye, an' wearie" 6995 (103,104)
"AYER ME DIXO TU MADRE" 7241 (283)
"Aymer est ma vie, Aymer est ma vie" 685 (278)
AYN CHAROD 1021 (30)

"Ayont by the ferry whaur woodlands are free" 7112 (105)
AYRA JONTKA 2473 (295)
AYRE (Bull) 468 (294)
AYRE (Campion) 533 (278)
AYRE (Dowland) 903 (278)
"Ayzeh pele ayze pele im yeshnam leloth kaeleh" 6176
    (30)
AYZEH PELEH 6176 (30)
AZ A SZEP 2749 (285)
"Az a szép, az a szép akinek a szeme szép" 2749 (285)
AZ ALFÖLDÖN HALÁSZLEGÉNY VAGYOK ÉN 5653 (164)
"AŽ JÁ BUDU NADE DVOREM" 4307 (177)
AZ MEN FORT KAYN SEVASTOPOL 6177 (318)
"Az men fort kayn Sevastopol, Iz nit vayt fun Simferopol"
    6177 (318)
"Az men fort kine Sevastopol, Iz nit veit fan Simfereopol"
    6177 (293)
"AZ ÖCSÉNYI KERTEK ALSÓ VÉGÉN" 5779 (289)
AZÉRT CSILLAG 5660 (92)
"Azért csillag, hogy ra gyogjon" 5660 (92)
"AZÉRT, HOGY ÉN HUSZÁR VAGYOK" 5661 (23)
"Azt akartam énmegtudni, Szabade máset szeretni, jaj,
    jaj, ja-ja-jaj" 5809 (25)
"Azure and white is the endless sky" 4845 (95)

"Ba-a m'nucha layagea" 3146 (30,318)
BA-AH M'NUCHA 3146 (30)
"Ba-Galil, b'tel Chay, Trumpeldor nafal" 6184 (318)
"Ba jo la ardiente cúspide don de sin par naciste" 4493
    (73)
BAA! BAA! BLACK SHEEP 4541 (28,132,366)
"Baa! Baa! Black sheep, have you any wool" 4541 (28,
    132,366)
THE BABE IN BETHLEM'S MANGER 8900 (361)
"The Babe in Bethlem's manger laid" 8900 (296,319,333,
    334,337,361)
A BABE IS BORN (Carols, English) 8901 (33,334,337,410)
A BABE IS BORN (Carols, Germany) 9146 (361)
"A BABE IS BORN ALL OF A MAID" (Grimes) 1399 (372)
"A Babe is born all of a Maid to bring salvation unto us"
    (Carols, England) 8901 (410)
"A Babe is born, all of a Maid, to bring salvation unto us"
    (Carols, Germany) 9146 (361)
"A Babe is born all of a may, in the savasyoun of us"
    8901 (33,337)
"A Babe is born all of a may, who brings salvation unto us"
    8901 (334)
A BABE IS BORN IN BETHLEHEM (Carols, Denmark) 8882
    (244)
"A BABE IS BORN IN BETHLEHEM" (Lindeman) 2144 (206)
"A Babe is born in Bethlehem, Bethlehem" 8882 (244)
"A BABE IS BORNE I WYS" 147 (369)
THE BABE IS LORD OF ALL 8902 (372)
"A BABE LIES IN THE CRADLE" 9164 (333)
THE BABE OF BETHLEHEM ("The Babe in Bethl'hem's
    manger...") 8900 (296)
BABE OF BETHLEHEM ("Ye nations, all...") 9347 (322)
"The Babe to us that now is bore" 8964 (360,361)
BABOT VITTEM 5662 (164)
BABULINKA 6679 (295)
"A Baby born in Bethlehem" (HEARD FROM HEAVEN TO-
    DAY) 9390 (332)
"Baby born in Bethlehem" (THE NEW BORN BABY) 9394
    (332)

BABY BORN TODAY 9386 (332)

BABY, DID YOU HEAR? 8185 (169)

"Baby, did you hear? Your sweetie's gonna leave you" 8185 (169)

BABY FACE 37 (233)

"Baby face, you've got the cutest baby face" 37 (233)

"Baby, how long, baby, how long has that evening train been gone" 605 (336)

BABY IN A GUINEA-BLUE GOWN 8186 (321)

"BABY, PLEASE DON'T GO" 453 (336)

A BABY WAS SLEEPING 5872 (166,213)

"A baby was sleeping, its mother was weeping" 5872 (166, 213,397)

"BACCHUS, GOD OF MIRTH AND WINE" 80 (273)

IL BACIO 70 (93,329)

BACK BAY HILL 4228 (186)

"Back in nineteen twenty-seven" 8576 (336)

"Backward, still backward, oh time, in your flight" (Hewitt) 1648 (212)

"Backward, turn backward, Oh! time in your flight" (Hewitt) 1648 (161)

"Backward, turn backward, oh time in your flight" (Leslie) 2118 (129,131)

BACON ON THE RIND 7421 (225)

THE BAD GIRL'S LAMENT 4221 (186)

BAD LUCK BLUES 8187 (336)

"Bad news has come to town" 7470B (227)

BAD WEATHER 4892 (86)

THE BADGER DRIVE 4222 (186)

THE BAGPIPE CAROL 9108 (361)

BAILACHE 7242 (283)

"Bailache, bailache, bailache" 7242 (283)

BAILANDO EL GATO 4165 (207)

BAILE A LO ALTO 7243 (281)

BAÏLÈRO 4893 (62)

"Baïlèro, lèro, lèro! Pastre, de delaï l'aïo!" 5067 (65)

"Baïlèro, lèro, lèro, Pâtre, par delà l'eau!" 5067 (65)

BAILES DEL PANDERO 7244 (283)

THE BAILIFF'S DAUGHTER 4542B (126)

THE BAILIFF'S DAUGHTER OF ISLINGTON 4542A (13,215, 234,349,397)

BAINYIN 5644 (284)

"Bainyin, bainyin, na pé bainyin Poule a Maitresse" 5644 (284)

Baise may ma Janneton (tune) 6459 (201)

"BAK MIR NIT KAYN BULKELECH" 6178 (318)

"Bake no sweet rolls for me" 6178 (318)

"BAKONY ERDÖN SIR A GERLE" 2002 (285)

LE BAL CHEZ BOULÉ 5143 (186,187)

BALD GRAS I AM NECKAR 5236A (326)

"Bald gras i am Nekkar, bald gras i am Rhein" 5236A (326)

BALD GRAS ICH AM ACKER 5236A (309)

"Bald gras ich am Acker, bald gras ich am Rain" 5236A (309)

BALD GRAS ICH AM NECKAR 5236A (309,353), 5236B (309)

"Bald gras ich am Neckar, bald gras ich am Rhein" 5236A (99,309,353), 5236B (309)

"Bald gras ich am Nekkar, bald gras ich am Rhein" 5236A (31)

"IL BALEN DEL SUO SORRISO" 3862 (4,298,390)

Balkanliebe 1866-1867

Ball der Nationen 2985-2987

BALL GAWN ROUN' 8710 (252)

BALLAD OF HARRY BRIDGES 7788A (293)

THE BALLAD OF THE BOLL WEEVIL 8188A (225), 8188B (109,110)

BALLAD OF THE FAT TURKEYS 632 (190,192,194)

THE BALLAD OF THE TEA PARTY 7422 (173)

THE BALLAD OF THUNDERHEAD 7423 (170)

LA BALLADE DE JÉSUS CHRIST 9044 (88)

BALLADE DES GROS DINDONS 632 (190,192,194)

BALLATELLA 2115 (1,176)

BALLET OF THE BOLL WEEVIL 8188A (34)

Il ballette delle ingrate 2502

BALLGEFLÜSTER 2407 (327)

Un ballo in maschera 3823-3827

BALM IN GILEAD 8189 (76,409)

A BALMY AFTERNOON IN MAY 7283 (219)

"Balmy Springtide's left us" 3594 (131)

BALOO, BALOO 6996 (101,103)

"Baloo, baloo, my wee, wee thing" 6996 (101,103)

BALOO, LAMMY 9314 (337)

BALOO LOO, LAMMY 9314 (165)

BALULALOW 1641 (307)

BALZAMINA 4308 (37)

BAÑADO EL ROSTRO 4285 (207)

"Bañado el rostro en luz divina" 4285 (207)

BANANA BOAT LOADER'S SONG 8720 (252)

BANANA LOADER'S SONG 8720 (11)

BANATER SCHWAGENLIED 1899 (31)

The band at a distance (tune) 7008

DE BAND O' GIDEON 8190 (183)

BAND OF ANGELS 7411 (216)

A BAND OF BIRDS 8711 (11)

"A band of birds, come a-singing" 8711 (11)

THE BAND PLAYED ON 3942 (114,115,128,131,132,204, 233,236)

BANDURA 6944 (37)

"Die bange Nacht ist nun herum" 2217 (31,99)

"Banim yivnu haGalil!" 6229 (318)

BANJO SAM 7424 (392)

THE BANKS O' DOON 7213 (232,365)

Banks of Banna (tune) 6037

THE BANKS OF NEWFOUNDLAND 4223 (186)

THE BANKS OF SWEET DUNDEE 7425A (81), 7425B (72)

THE BANKS OF SWEET PRIMROSES 4543 (198)

THE BANKS OF THE DAISIES 5867 (213)

THE BANKS OF THE DEE 4544 (37)

THE BANKS OF THE SACRAMENTO 7426 (115)

BARBARA ALLEN 4545A,B,C,D,E,F,G

BARBARA ALLEN'S CRUELTY 4545H (242)

BARBAROSSA 1240 (31)

BARBARY ALLEN 4545I (393)

BARBARY ELLEN 4545J (264)

BARBER, SPARE THOSE HAIRS 3122 (225)

THE BARBERRY 1950 (295)

BARBER'S CRY 7427 (110)

Der barbier von Bagdad 715 (5)

Il barbiere di Siviglia 3096-3099

BARB'RA ALLAN 4545L (101)

BARB'RA ELLEN 4545C (331)

BARB'RY ELLEN 4545C (215), 4545I (312) 4545K (34)

BARCAROLLE 2688 (329)

"Barcarolle, you thrill my poor soul" 2688 (132)

LA BARCHËTTA 6057 (325)

THE BARD OF ARMAGH 5873A (172)

The bard's legacy (tune) 6035

"Bardzo raniuchno wschodziło słoneczko" 670* (295)

"Bare are the branches" 3465 (121)

THE BARE MOUNTAIN TOP 4385 (86)

BARGIES OLLANS 9045 (361)

BARKAROLE 6144 (51)

THE BARKSHIRE TRAGEDY 4546 (14)

THE BARLEY MOW 4547 (13,235,349)

"ETT BARN ÄR FÖTT PAA DENNA DAG" 9328 (154)

"Barn holds only fir cones" 6807 (228)

BARNEY BUNTLINE 9422 (401)

BARNEY THE PIPER 5874 (280)

THE BARNYARD FAMILY 8157A (28,366)

BARNYARD SONG 8157B (110,216,225,249)

The bartered bride 3513-3516

BARTOSZU, BARTOSZU 6678 (159)

"Bartoszu. Bartoszu, oj, nie traćwa nadziei" 6678 (159)

"Batallón cazadores dijo Paunero" 4175 (284)

THE BATCHELOR'S LAMENT 7428 (189)

"A battalion its way was wending" 100 (288)

BATTI, BATTI 2563 (6)

"Batti, batti, o bel Masetto" 2563 (6)

THE BATTLE-CRY OF FREEDOM 3068 (28,115,129,130, 279,366)

BATTLE HYMN OF THE HUSSITES 577 (7)

THE BATTLE HYMN OF THE REPUBLIC 3565 (7,10,28,32, 34,35,109,110,115,129,130,233,236,279,366)

THE BATTLE OF SARATOGA 7429 (173)

BATTLE OF THE KEGS 8150 (173,225)

"The battle rages, steel shines brightly" 2622 (340)

"Der Bauer hat ein Taubenhaus" 3710 (99)

DAS BAUERNLIED 682* (49)

DER BAUM IM ODENWALD 5237 (31,99)

BAVARIAN YODEL 5238 (132)

BAY DEM SHTETL 6179 (318)

"Bay dem shtetl a shtibl mit a grinem dach" 6179 (318)

"Bay mayn Rebn iz gevezn, Iz gevezn, bay mayn Rebn" 6166 (318)

THE BAY OF BISCAY 785 (234,366)

Les Bayadères 3500 (411)

BAYT-ZHE MIR OYS A FINF-UN-TSVANTSIGER 6180 (318)

"Bayt-zhe mir oys a finf-un-tsvantsiger, Oyf samerodno drayer" 6180 (318)

BE CONTENT 368 (253)

"Be content, live happily" 368 (253)

"BE GONE, BE GONE CARES AND TROUBLES" 2687 (159)

BE GONE, WORRIES 2687 (295)

"Be greeted in a thousand ways" 3366 (141)

BE GUDE TO ME 6997 (101,105)

"Be gude to me as langs I'm here" 6997 (101,105)

BE IT DAY OR BE IT NIGHT 6698 (159)

"Be it day or be it night, at my side my faithful sword" 6698 (159)

BE MERRY, BE MERRY 8903 (360,361)

"Be merry, be merry, be merry I pray you ev'ry one" 8903 (360,361)

BE MERRY BUT WISE 8681 (349)

BE NEAR ME STILL 1656 (123)

BE ON YOUR GUARD 6577 (86)

"Be on your guard with ev'ry girl" 6577 (86)

BE QUIET DO! I'LL CALL MY MOTHER 7430 (189)

BE SILENT HEAVEN! BE SILENT EARTH 9117 (361)

"Be silent Heav'n! Be silent earth" 9117 (361)

"Be silent, my turbulent passions" 1262 (340)

"BE STILL AND KNOW THAT I AM GOD" 3524 (347)

BE STILL AND LISTEN 1677 (76)

BE THOU FAITHFUL 2389 (160)

"Be thou faithful unto Truth" 2389 (160)

BE THOU WITH ME 116 (160)

"Be thou with me, dear Lord and Father" 116 (160)

BE WITH ME 8191 (409)

"Be with me Lord! Be with me!" 8191 (409)

BEANS, BACON AND GRAVY 7431 (293)

BEANS I TO THE MILL 5662 (164)

"Beans I to the mill was taking" 5662 (164)

"The bear went over the mountain" 5020 (70)

BEARÁI PÍOBAIRE 5874 (280)

THE BEARDED LADY 2699 (131)

THE BEARDLESS BOY (tune) 5983

"BEARING MYRRH AND SPICES SWEET" 8810 (371)

La Béarnaise 2401 (82)

LE BEAU GÉNOIS 6093 (338)

"Le beau Génois d'épouser s'avise" 6093 (338)

BEAU SOIR 790 (112,237,408)

BEAUING, BELLEING, DANCING, DRINKING 6001 (166, 213)

"Beauing, belleing, dancing, drinking, breaking windows, cursing, sinking" 6001 (166,213)

THE BEAUREGARD 324 (161)

"BEAUTEOUS NIGHT, O NIGHT OF LOVE" 2688 (241)

"Beautiful, beautiful lake, deep is your water and clear" 6826 (95)

BEAUTIFUL BLUE DANUBE 3606 (329)

BEAUTIFUL CHINA 4268 (86)

THE BEAUTIFUL CHRISTMAS TREE 9147 (251)

BEAUTIFUL DARK-EYED MAID 5707 (92)

"Beautiful dark-eyed maid, I pray you will your heart give me someday" 5707 (92)

BEAUTIFUL DENMARK 2973 (87)

"Beautiful Denmark, hear its name ringing" 2973 (87)

BEAUTIFUL DREAMER 1107 (10,28,36,129,130,132,329, 343,385)

"Beautiful dreamer, wake unto me" 1107 (10,28,36,129, 130,132,329,343,385)

BEAUTIFUL EVENING 790 (408)

BEAUTIFUL HEAVEN 6339A (279)

"BEAUTIFUL ISLE OF THE SEA" 3734 (129,130,132)

"Beautiful land of freedom and power and glory" 7304 (135)

BEAUTIFUL SAVIOR 5239 (296)

"Beautiful Savior, King of Creation" 5239 (296)

"Beautiful stream with moonlit beam" 3606 (329)

"BEAUTY IN LOVE'S GARDEN" 4896 (47)

"BEAUTY IS BUT A PAINTED HELL" 534 (197)

BEAUTY LATELY 1444 (199)

"Beauty lately dropped her sandal" 1444 (199)

BEAUTY SATE BATHING 1814 (144)

"Beauty sate bathing by a spring" 1814 (144)

"Because all men are brothers" 1550 (293)

"Because I have been given much" 1671 (123)

"Because I was evil. Evil-hearted me" 8264 (336)

"Because my sweetheart flatters Gwenllian, Kate and Clare" 8688 (349)

BECAUSE OF THY GREAT BOUNTY 1671 (123)

"Because we're suff'ring, we deserve to be heard" 2560 (4)

BEDD FY RHIAINT 8658 (20)

BEDELIA 3401 (233)

"Bedelia, I want to steal ye" 3401 (233)

BEDENKLICHKEITEN 7245 (31,99)

BEDOUIN LOVE SONG 2824 (237)

BEDROEFDE HARTEN 6424 (384)

"Bedroefde harten, wilt vreugde rapen" 6424 (384)

THE BEE 7432 (109,110)

THE BEE AND THE PUP 7433 (28,366)

THE BEE TREE 6305 (95)

BEEN IN DE PEN SO LONG 8192A (184)

BEWAFFNE DICH 3178 (253)
"Bewaffne dich meine Standhaftigkeit" 3178 (253)
Bewahr mich Gott vorm Interim (tune) 5550
"Beyn g'vulot bidrachim l'lo derech" 6251 (318)
BEYN N'HAR PRAT UN'HAR CHIDEKEL 6181 (318)
"Beyn n'har prat un'har chidekel, Al hahar mitamer dekel" 6181 (318)
"Beyond high hills, beyond forest, danced our lovely Margareta with the hussars" 6766 (295)
BEYOND NIEMEN 4125 (295)
DE BEZEM 6426 (28,316,366)
"De bezem, de bezem, Wat doe je er mee?" 6426 (28,316, 366)
"Bhí gartha cogaidh ar an ngaoith" 6027 (280)
"BI BI OG BLAKA" 5838 (231)
"Białej akacji kwiat, budzi w spomnienia" 6676 (295)
BIAŁE RÓŻE 1964 (295)
BIBA JESUS GOURE JAONE 8813 (361)
BIBLE STORIES 7439 (72)
Biblické písně 954-955
DAS BICOCCALIED DES NIKLAUS MANUEL 7354 (157)
A BICYCLE BUILT FOR TWO 749
"Bid me but live and I will live thy votary to be" 2061 (106)
BID ME TO LIVE 2061 (106,348)
"Bid me to live, and I will live thy Protestant to be" (Hatton) 1555 (272)
"Bid me to live and I will live thy protestant to be" (Lawes) 2061 (348)
"Bid the sun good morning and bid the moon goodbye" 2921 (199)
BIDDY, I'M NOT JESTING 5977 (280)
BIDE YE YET 6998 (101,105)
BIÈLH CONTAU 4904 (88)
BIEN TRAVAILLER 5144 (21)
"Bien travailler, c'est s'amuser" 5144 (21)
BIER HER! 477 (43,353)
"Bier her! Bier her! oder ich fall' um, juchhe!" 477 (43, 353)
BIERLEIN, RINN! 2160 (31)
BIG BAMBOO 8712 (11)
THE BIG BROWN BEAR 4156 (364)
THE BIG CORRAL 7440 (214,335)
BIG-EYE RABBIT 7441 (214)
"Big-eye Rabbit, Boo! Boo!" 7441 (214)
BIG OLA, DEAR OLA 7337 (230)
"Big Ola, dear Ola, I'm tending my flock" 7337 (230)
BIG ROCK CANDY MOUNTAIN 7442A (129,130,171)
BIG ROCK CANDY MOUNTAINS 7442B (34,227)
THE BIG SUNFLOWER 2651 (34,115)
THE BIGLER 7534 (227)
The Bigler's crew (tune) 7534
BIKURIM 2123 (318)
BILE DEM CABBAGE DOWN 8197 (80)
BILL BAILEY, WON'T YOU PLEASE COME HOME? 576 (34, 114,131,132)
"Bill collectors gather 'round and rather haunt the cottage next door" 4018 (345)
THE BILLBOARD 7443 (225)
BILLIE BOY 4549B (242)
BILLY BOY 4549A,B,C
"Billy broke locks, and Billy broke bolts" 7576 (173)
BILLY MAGEE MAGAW 1253 (109)
BILLY THE KID 7444 (80)
"BIM, BAM, BIM, BAM! HORCH ES SINGT DER GLOKKE TON" 5244 (326)

"Bimtsiltayim v'tupim meh meh meh meh kolnarim" 6244 (30)
"Bin alben e wärti Tächter gsi" 7360 (156)
"Bin durch die Alpen gezogen" 3420 (31)
BIN EIN FAHRENDER GESELL (Folksongs, German) 5245 (43,326)
BIN EIN FAHRENDER GESELL (Keller) 1880 (31)
"Bin ein fahrender Gesell, kenne keine Sorgen" (Folksong, German) 5245 (43,326)
"Bin ein fahrender Gesell, kenne keine Sorgen" (Keller) 1880 (31)
"Bin ein Kund nur. Ein Märchen bist du, und ich ein Kind nur" 3750 (74)
BIN I NET A BÜRSCHLE 5246 (309,326)
"Bin i net a Bürschle auf der Welt?" 5246 (309,326)
"Bin ich guter Laune, geb ich keine Ruh!" 2985 (258)
"Bin ich mir gegangen fishelech koyfn" 6197 (318)
"Bin verliebt, dass es so 'was gibt" 3641 (257)
"BIND' AUF DEIN HAAR" 1560 (122,329)
BINGO ("Here's to good old Yale...") 7445 (225)
BINGO ("There was a farmer...") 7446 (216)
BINNORIE 4718D (111)
DIE BINSCHGAUER WALLFAHRT 5247 (31)
"Die Binschgauer wollten wallfahrten gehn" 5247 (31,99)
Die Binsgauer wollten wallfahrten gahn (tune) 5452
DIE BINZGAUER WALLFAHRT 5247 (99)
"Bion imnidhe orm, a chroidhe, nuair fheicim thy id' shuidhe" 5977 (280)
"Bionde chiome e bel sembiante la fortuna e il ciel ci da" 2356 (217)
LA BIONDINA IN GONDOLETA 6063 (325)
"La Biondina in gondoleta l'altra sera gomena" 6063 (325)
"La Biondina in gondoletta l'altra sera gomenà" 6063 (406)
THE BIRCH TREE 4820 (95)
THE BIRCHBARK SONG 7324 (231)
THE BIRD AND THE ROSE 1706 (385)
BIRD COURTSHIPS 7447 (406)
BIRD IN A CAGE 8198 (184)
"Bird in a cage, love, bird in a cage" 8198 (184)
BIRD OF BLUE 1239 (344)
BIRD OF THE WILDERNESS 1707 (259)
BIRD SONG (Folksongs, American) 7447 (225,406)
BIRDIE 7448 (381)
THE BIRDS (Carols, Czech) 8868 (199,271)
THE BIRDS (Schubert) 3314 (330)
"The birds are returning, their sweet notes of spring" 8038 (243)
"Birds are sleeping on the branches" 6246 (318)
THE BIRD'S BALL 7449 (249)
BIRDS' COURTING SONG 7447 (110,216,406)
"Birds do it, bees do it, even educated fleas do it" 2860 (345)
BIRDS FLY DELIGHTFULLY 3404 (287,288)
"Birds fly delightfully, waves roll frightfully" 3404 (287, 288)
"BIRDS IN THE HIGH HALL-GARDEN" 3532 (272,344)
THE BIRDS' RETURN 4311 (28,366)
"The birds sleeping gently" 93 (132)
"The birds they held a wedding fine, deep in the leafy woodland green" 5578 (230)
"Birds upon the branches singing" 2690 (292)
BIRJINA GAZETTOBAT ZEGOEN 8814 (361)
BIRKAT AM (TECH'ZAKNA) 6182 (318)
THE BIRKS OF ABERFELDY 6999 (100,105)
BIRÓ URAM, PANASZOM VAN 5665 (164)

BLUE BIRD 730 (385)

THE BLUE BONNETS 7001 (7)

THE BLUE BONNETS OVER THE BORDER 7001 (7)

BLUE DANUBE 3606 (93,132)

Blue devils (tune) 8701

THE BLUE DOVE 6377 (279)

THE BLUE DRESS 8084 (113)

THE BLUE-EYED BOY 4697 (243)

THE BLUE JUNIATA 3673 (185,279,366)

BLUE MOUNTAIN LAKE 7458 (227)

THE BLUE TAIL FLY 7459A (44,173,293), 7459B (35,80, 216,399), 7459C (185), 7459D (212,331)

BLUEBERRIES 8200 (184)

"Blueberries, fresh an' fine, I got juicy blueberries, lady" 8200 (184)

THE BLUEBIRD 1769 (208)

BLÜH, NUR, BLÜH 5251 (49)

"Blüh, nur, blüh, mein Sommerkorn" 5251 (49)

DIE BLÜMELEIN ALL SCHLAFEN 4153 (326)

"Die Blümelein all schlafen schon längst im Mondenschein" 4153 (326)

DIE BLÜMELEIN, SIE SCHLAFEN 4153 (309)

"Die Blümelein, sie schlafen schon längst im Mondenschein" 4153 (70,99,226,309,353)

"Blümlein traut, sprecht für mich recht inniglich" 1319 (311)

THE BLUES AIN' NOTHIN' 8201 (109,110)

THE BLUES AIN'T NOTHIN' 8201 (336)

"Blues, jumped a rabbit and he ran a solid mile" 8499 (336)

BLUES LIKE MIDNIGHT 3047 (336)

BLUME VON HAWAII 4 (258)

Die Blume von Hawaii 4-5

BLUMENLIED AUS DEM XVI. JAHRHUNDERT 5828 (92)

BŁYSNAŁ PORANEK 2470 (295)

"Błysnął poranek, zniknęły cienie" 2470 (295)

"BLYTHE, BLYTHE AN' MERRY WAS SHE" 7002 (101,105)

"Blythe was the time when he fee'd wi' my father, O!" 7115 (101,104)

THE BOAR'S HEAD CAROL 8905 (79,165,206,334,337)

"THE BOAR'S HEAD IN HAND BEAR I" 8905 (206,333,334, 337)

"The boar's head in hand bring I" 8905 (79,165)

A BOAT, A BOAT 1772 (235,349)

"A boat, a boat, haste to the ferry" 1772 (235,349)

"Boat, little boat, a breeze on thy sails shall soon light" 3551 (344)

BOAT, MY GOOD COMPANION 6763 (95)

"Boat, my good companion, now obey your master" 6763 (95)

BOAT SONG (Grieg) 1386 (348)

BOAT SONG (Pierné) 2812 (364)

BOAT SONG (Stanford) 3551 (344)

THE BOATIE ROWS 7003 (100,103,104,349)

THE BOATMAN (Folksongs, Latin America) 6283 (219)

THE BOATMAN (Folksongs, Scotland) 7004 (103)

DE BOATMAN (Folksongs, United States) 7460C (343)

DE BOATMAN DANCE 7460B (185)

"De boatman dance, de boatman sing" 7460B (185)

"The boatmen dance, the boatmen sing" 7460A (83)

THE BOATMEN'S DANCE 7460A (83)

THE BOATMEN'S SONG 7460A (335)

Bob and Joan (tune) 5906

"Bob Roebuck is my sweetheart's name" 8015 (189)

BOBBIN' AROUND 1086 (189)

BOBBY SHAFTO 4550 (402)

BOBBY SHAFTOE 4550 (234)

"Bobby Shaftoe's gone to sea, silver buckles on his knee" 4550 (234)

"Bobby Shafto's gone to sea, silver buckles on his knee" 4550 (402)

Boccaccio 3675-3676

BODAJ BY VÁS 4309 (94)

"Bodaj by vás, vy mládenci" 4309 (94)

DAS BODENSEELIED 5252 (326)

"Boed curiad y stwffwi yn araf a gwan" 8706 (20)

DAS BÖSE MANNSVOLK 3239 (250)

BÓG SIĘ RODZI 9288 (295)

"Bóg się rodzi, moc truchleje" 9288 (295)

BOGU RODZICA 4130 (295)

"Bogu Rodzica, dzieweca! Bogiem wsławiona Marya" 4130 (259)

BOGURODZICA 4130 (159)

"Bogurodzica Dziewica, Bogiem stawiona Maryja" 4130 (159)

La bohème 2887-2891

The Bohemian girl 158-159

BOINA BOINA! 6893 (57)

"Boina, boina! Ora paz da boina boina" 6893 (57)

BOIS ÉPAIS 2204 (88,273,404)

"Bois épais redouble ton ombre" 2204 (88,273,404)

LE BOITEUSE AU MARCHE 167 (21)

BOITEUX D'HERMITE 5146 (21)

"Bokrétát kötöttem mezei virágbol" 2056 (285)

"Bold and reckless, wild and daring, lawless, rough and overbearing" 6001 (15)

BOLD BRENNAN ON THE MOOR 5882B (35)

THE BOLD FISHERMAN 7461 (44,214,335)

THE BOLD GRENADIER 7845C (172)

"Bold intruders, leave this house this very instant" 2558 (1)

BOLD PHELIM BRADY 5873B (133)

THE BOLD "PRINCESS ROYAL" 4551 (198)

THE BOLD SOLDIER 7462A (173), 7462B (72)

THE BOLD TRELLITEE 4617H (263)

THE BOLD VOLUNTEER 387 (44)

BOLDLY, WITH METTLE 341 (235)

"Boldly with mettle if you seize a nettle" 341 (235)

BOLERÁZ 4310 (94)

"Boleráz, boleráz, zelený boleráz" 4310 (94)

BOLERO 4286 (86)

BOLESLAV, BOLESLAV 4313 (86)

"Boleslav, Boleslav, do not weep my bride" 4313 (86)

"Boleslav, Boleslav, to pěkné město" 4313 (86)

THE BOLL WEEVIL 8188A (343), 8188B (335), 8188C (389), 8188D (171), 8188E (80,115)

BOLL WEEVIL BLUES 8188F (336)

BON CORDONNIER 5147 (21)

EL BON JESUSET 8845 (56)

"El bon Jesuset volina sabates" 8845 (56)

"Le bon roi Dagobert avait sa culotte à l'envers!" 5100 (82)

"Bon voyage, cher Dumollet" 4905 (91)

BON VOYAGE, MONSIEUR DUMOLLET 4905 (91)

THE BONDMAID 2027 (121)

Bonduca 2907 (273)

BONEY 9429 (29,320)

"Boney was a warrior" 9429 (29,320)

"LE BONHEUR EST CHOSE LÉGÈRE" 3134 (190)

"Bonhomm', bonhomm', sais-tu jouer?" 5148A (186,187)

BONHOMME, BONHOMME! 5148A (186,187), 5148B (21)

"Bonhomme, bonhomme, que sais-tu donc faire?" 5148B (21)

"The Bradys and O'Gradys, ye may talk about them all"
  3084 (204)
THE BRAES O' BALQUIDDER 7016 (235)
The braes of Boyndlie (tune) 7140
"Brahma, Dieu des croyants" 269 (140)
"Brahma, thou mighty god" 269 (140)
BRAKEMAN'S BLUES 3048 (336)
LA BRANDULIÑA 6064 (325)
Bransle Guinee (tune) 6520
THE BRATS OF JEREMIAH 7469 (72)
DAS BRAUNE MAIDELEIN 5253 (99)
BRAUTJUNGFERNLIED 3964 (99)
BRAUTLIED 3908 (328)
BRAVE KNIGHTS CAME ONE DAY 6721 (159)
"Brave knights came one day, up a hill in May" 6721
  (159)
BRAVE WOLFE 7470A (110,186), 7470B (227)
BRAW BRAW LADS 7017 (100,103,104)
"Braw, braw lads on Yarrow braes" 7017 (100,103,104)
BRAZILIAN SAILOR'S SONG 4205 (86)
"The bread of angels becomes the bread of men" 1141
  (304)
"Break, break if you must, it is better so" 6817 (295)
"BREAK FORTH, O BEAUTEOUS HEAVENLY LIGHT" 135
  (307,319,337)
BREAK THE NEWS TO MOTHER 1532 (32,34)
"BREAKE NOW, MY HEART, AND DIE" 535 (144)
"BREAKE NOW, MY HEART, AND DYE" 535 (197)
BREAKFAST IN MY BED ON SUNDAY MORNIN' 1344 (131)
"The breaking waves dashed high" 459 (129,130)
THE BREATH OF A ROSE 3582 (259)
THE BREEZE (Folksongs, Mexico) 6333 (142)
THE BREEZE (Folksongs, United States) 7475 (113)
"A breeze is blowing across the sea" 6238 (318)
"Breeze of night with your gentlest breath" 3864 (1)
BREEZE OF THE NIGHT 3864 (143)
"Breeze, when at eve you are passing" 6333 (142)
BRENNAN ON THE MOOR 5882A (172,173), 5882C (72)
BREUDDWYD Y FRENHINES 8660 (20)
"Breuddwyd y frenhines oedd gwel'd ei hun yn dlawd"
  8660 (20)
BREZAIROLA 4911 (64)
BRIAN O LINN 5920A (172)
"Brian O Linn had no breeches to wear" 5920A (172)
"BRICH AN, DU SCHÖNES MORGENLICHT" 135 (337)
BRICKS IN MY PILLOW 8202 (336)
LE BRICOU 4912 (91)
BRIDAL CHORUS 3908 (132)
The brides of Venice 277
THE BRIDE'S SONG 3382 (275)
BRIDE'S WALTZ 1187 (87)
THE BRIGANDS 6862 (295)
"Bright a star in heav'n was shining" 6841 (37)
"Bright and early ev'ry morning I would stroll along the
  shore" 6150 (95)
"Bright banner of freedom" 1236 (161)
"Bright flowers bloom round me" 6765 (295)
"Bright is this new day, come let us be gay" 6840 (295)
"Bright moonbeams came streaming through the window"
  6824 (295)
"BRIGHT MORNING STARS ARE RISING" 7471 (332)
BRIGHT PHOEBE 7472 (72)
"Bright Phoebe was my true love's name" 7472 (72)
"Bright red is the sun on the waves of Lough Sheelin"
  5908 (133)
"Bright shining star they call me" 7393 (37)

"The bright stars fade, the morn is breaking" 1553 (132)
THE BRIGHT SUNNY SOUTH 7473 (72)
"The bright sunny South was in peace and content" 7473
  (72)
BRIGHT YOUR EYES 5706 (92)
"Bright your eyes as stars above you, dearest maiden, how I
  love you!" 5706 (92)
BRIGHTEST AND BEST (Wesley) 3995 (379)
"Brightest and best of the sons of the morning" (Carols,
  United States) 9381 (332)
"BRIGHTEST AND BEST OF THE SONS OF THE MORNING"
  (Harding) 1525 (38,39)
"BRIGHTEST AND BEST OF THE SONS OF THE MORNING"
  (Thrupp) 3746 (307)
"Brightest and best of the sons of the morning" (Wesley)
  3995 (379)
BRIGHTLY SHINE 5723 (92)
"Brightly shine the Great Bear's seven stars on high" 5723
  (92)
Brighton Camp (tune) 5917
"Brilla, brilla in ciel sereno" 6096 (51)
"Brilla la noche serena" 7475 (113)
Brillanten aus Wien 3567 (273)
"Brille le soleil et les champs effleure" 1857 (224)
"Brillez dans ces beaux lieux" 824 (150)
"Brincan y lailan los peces en el rio" 9323 (281)
"BRING A TORCH, JEANNETTE, ISABELLA" 9066 (38,39,
  125,165,251,296,337)
BRING BACK MY BONNIE 7829 (236)
"Bring Mary and the Baby" 9399 (332)
"BRING ME ON MY SUPPER, BOYS" 7474 (321)
"Bring the good old bugle, boys, we'll sing another song"
  4109 (7,199)
BRING US IN GOOD ALE 8968 (379)
BRING YOUR TORCHES 9066 (79)
"BRING YOUR TORCHES, JEANNETTE, ISABELLA" 9066
  (79,388)
"BRINGT HER DEM HERREN" 3326 (308)
"BRINGT MIR BLUT DER EDLEN REBEN" 74 (31)
"Bringue, stringue, landerira" 4915 (91)
LA BRISA 7475 (113)
THE BRISK AND SPRIGHTLY LAD 4553 (234)
"A BRISK YOUNG SAILOR COURTED ME" 4554 (198)
Britania, the gem of the ocean (tune) 221
Britania, the pride of the ocean (tune) 221
THE BRITISH GRENADIERS 4555 (7,13,35,199,234,349)
The Briton (tune) 8670
BROADWAY SIGHTS 2050 (189)
Bröllopet paa Ulfaasa 3528 (188)
BRÖLLOPSMARSCH ([Bröllopet paa Ulfaasa]) 3528 (188)
BRÖLLOPSMARSCH ([Ett bondbröllop]) 3527 (188)
BRÖLLOPSMARSCH FRAAN DELSBO 7300 (188)
BROKE AND HUNGRY 8168B (336)
BROKEN ENGAGEMENT 7476 (243)
"Brokenhearted world, brokenhearted children" 1437 (76)
"The brook once said to the nightingale" 7449 (249)
THE BROOKLET (Loder) 2172 (277)
THE BROOKLET (Paradies) 2738 (208)
"BROOKLET EVER FLOWING" 4433 (94)
THE BROOM 6426 (28,316,366)
BROOM, GREEN BROOM 4556A (234)
THE BROOM MAN 8203 (184)
THE BROOM O' THE COWDENKNOWES 7018 (100,104)
"The broom, the brier, the birken bush" 185 (100,349)
"The broom, the broom, what do you with it" 6426 (28,
  366)

"Butterfly, oh, you are fickle" 5177 (187)
"Butterfly, you fickle creature" 5177 (219)
"Butt'ning up, butt'ning down on my breast" 5711 (164)
BUY A BROOM 7484 (189)
"Buy all the old furniture" 8030 (335)
"Buy carnations! Who would like a carnation" 3791 (245)
BUY MY FRESH EGGS 5154 (21)
BUY MY SWEETS 7393 (37)
BUY MY VIOLETS 2724 (132)
BUZA 5670 (27)
"Buza, buza, buza, de szép tábla buza" 5670 (27)
"BY A LONELY FOREST PATHWAY" 1396 (121)
"By a well in yonder bower, stood Mary fair as a flower"
6838 (159)
BY AN' BY 8204 (52,76)
"BY CHANCE, IN THE BALLROOM" 635 (341)
"By Clwyd, all hoar with moss" 8704 (349)
"By Dovey's green banks in the dim, olden days" 8668
(349)
BY KILLARNEY'S LAKES AND FELLS 160 (132,166,213)
"By Killarney's lakes and fells, em'rald isles and winding
bays" 160 (15,28,128,132,166,213,233,237,279,
366,402)
"By Logan's streams, that rin sae deep" 7097 (100)
"By Meisiesfontein, die ware fontein" 7220 (239)
BY MOONLIGHT 3375 (112)
BY MY WINDOW 6306 (95)
"By my window sitting, through my window staring"
6306 (95)
BY OUR COTTAGE 6185 (95)
"By our cottage, mother mine, mother mine, as I stood
one morning" 6185 (95)
"BY OUR DOOR A ROSE-TREE BLOWS" 6643 (199)
"By our window blooms a rosebush" 4399 (95)
"By silent hearth in wintertide" 3909 (3)
BY THAT LAKE WHOSE GLOOMY SHORE 5883 (213)
"By that lake whose gloomy shore skylark never warbles
o'er" 5883 (213)
"BY THE BLUE ALSATIAN MOUNTAINS" 2329 (132,279,
366)
BY THE BROOK 1383 (121)
BY THE CAMP FIRE 3988 (129,130)
"By the clear running fountain" 5138A (186,187)
BY THE CRADLE 2369 (45)
"By the croaking of the toad, in her cave that makes
abode" 2914 (272)
"By the dark waves of the rolling sea" 7375 (279,366)
BY THE FEAL'S WAVE BENIGHTED 5884 (166,213)
"By the Feal's wave benighted, not a star in the skies"
5884 (166,213)
BY THE GRAVE 2949 (273)
BY THE LAKE 6789 (159)
BY THE LAKE ON YONDER LEA 6789 (295)
"By the lake, on yonder lea, stood a greening, linden tree"
6789 (159)
"By the lake on yonder lea, stood the greening linden tree"
6789 (295)
BY THE LIGHT OF THE MOON 4885 (210)
"BY THE LIGHT OF THE SILVERY MOON" 982 (233)
"By the lore of ages far" 1552 (274)
"By the margin of a lake a lonely lion sat and said" 7994
(314)
BY THE PALE MOONLIGHT 4885 (35)
BY THE RIO CHANCHAMAYO 6667 (9)
"By the Rio Chanchamayo in Peru, where the Andes rise
into the distant blue" 6667 (9)

BY THE RIVER SAINTE MARIE 3947 (236)
"By the river stands a little shed" 5680 (95)
"By the rivers of Babylon we wept" 6168 (318)
BY THE SAD SEA WAVES 277 (205)
"By the sad sea waves I listen while they moan" 277 (205)
BY THE SEA 3302 (240)
"By the seashore there dwells a fair maid" 5633 (86)
BY THE STREAM 4405 (94)
"By the stream she clothes is washing" 4405 (94)
BY THE WATER, IN THE EVENING 6782 (159)
"By the water, in the evening to a flock of geese did tend"
6782 (159)
BY THE WATERS OF BABYLON 1717 (398)
"By the waters of Babylon we sat down and wept" 1717
(398)
"BY THE WELL WE SAW HER" 4438 (94)
"By thy rivers gently flowing Illinois, Illinois" 1830 (28)
"By yon bonnie banks an' yon bonnie braes" 7006 (18)
"By yon bonnie banks, and by yon bonnie braes" 7006 (28,
70,102,103,104,105,163,233,234,236,279,343,366,
385,397,402)
"Bye an' bye an' bye, good Lord!" 8265 (409)
"Bye an' bye we all shall meet again" 8205 (409)
BYE AND BYE ("Bye an' bye we all shall meet") 8205 (409)
BYE AND BYE ("Bye and bye, stars in the heav'n...") 8022
(332)
BYE AND BYE ("O, bye and bye") 8204 (409)
"Bye and bye, stars in the heav'n, number one, number two,
number three, number four" 8022 (332)
BYE, BABY BUNTING 7485 (109,110)
"Bye baby bunting, Daddy's gone a-hunting" 7485 (109,
110)
"BYE BYE AND HUSHABYE" 5838 (231)
"Bye-low, baby, go to sleep, my dear!" 1766 (124)
"Bye-o-baby bye. Bye-o-baby bye" 7811 (216)
BYŁA BABULINKA 6679 (295)
"Była babulinka z rodu bogatego" 6679 (295)
BY'M BY 8206 (216,321)
"By'm by, by'm by, stahs shinin', numbah, numbah one"
8206 (321)
"By'm by, by'm by, stars shinin', number, number one"
8206 (216)
B'YOND THE TISZA 3701 (164)
"B'yond the Tisza, says the tidings" 3701 (164)
BYWAJ DZIEWCZE ZDROWA 6680 (295)
"Bywaj dziewcze zdrowa, Ojczyzna mnie woła" 6680
(295)
"Bywaj mi zdrowy, kraju kochany" 6681 (295)
BYWAJ ZDROWY KRAJU KOCHANY 6681 (295)

C-A-F-F-E-E 1634 (42)
"C-a-f-f-e-e trink nicht so viel" 1634 (42)
C. C. RIDER 8262B (336)
"C. C. Rider just see what you done done" 8262C (336)
"C. C. Rider, just see what you have done" 8262B (336)
ÇA, ÇA GESCHMAUSET 5259 (31)
"Ça ça geschmauset, lasst uns nicht rappelköpfisch sein"
5259 (31,99)
CA' HAWKIE 4558 (235)
"Ca', Hawkie, Ca' Hawkie, Ca' Hawkie through the watter"
4558 (235)

334

CARNIVAL NIGHT 2136 (142)
CARNIVAL OF VENICE 278 (221)
"Caro laccio, dolce nodo" 1212 (167)
CARO MIO BEN 1255 (36,122,138,167,237,329,368, 385,405)
"Caro mio ben credimi almen" 1255 (36,122,138,167, 237,329,368,385,405)
CARO NOME 3850 (143)
"CARO NOME CHE IL MIO COR" 3850 (6,93,143,221, 292,302)
CARO VOI SIETE 1480 (180)
"Caro voi siete all' alma" 1480 (180)
"Caro volto pallidetto" 2324 (217)
CAROL 9093 (231)
CAROL, CHILDREN CAROL 8907 (79)
"Carol, children, carol, carol joyfully" 8907 (79)
A CAROL FOR CHRISTMAS EVE 8953B (154)
"CAROL HIGH, AND CAROL LOW" 8867 (379)
A CAROL OF ADORATION 2796 (369)
CAROL OF BEAUTY 9111 (271)
CAROL OF SERVICE 9047 (271)
CAROL OF THE BAGPIPERS 9198 (33,165,337,388)
CAROL OF THE BEASTS 8908 (214)
CAROL OF THE BIRDS (Carols, Basque) 8817 (165,206)
CAROL OF THE BIRDS (Carols, Czechoslovakia) 8868 (214,410)
CAROL OF THE CHILDREN OF BETHLEHEM 8802 (388)
CAROL OF THE FLOWERS 9048 (79,337)
CAROL OF THE MISTLETOE SINGERS 9138 (165)
CAROL OF THE NUNS OF ST. MARY'S, CHESTER 9034 (388)
CAROL OF THE SHEPHERDS 8877 (251)
CAROL OF THE SKIDDAW YOWES 1418 (344)
A CAROL OF THE STAR 2797 (373)
"CAROL, SIRS, THE BLESSED BIRTH" 2653 (317)
CAROLINA 6070 (51)
LA CAROLINA 6070 (51)
"Carolina, Carolina, at last they're got you on the map" 1799 (345)
CAROLINA IN THE MORNING 853 (345)
CAROLINE 7491 (219,279,366)
EL CARRERITO ("Dicen que me han...") 6331 (247)
EL CARRETERO ("El carretero se vá...") 6332 (247)
"Carretero, carretero, carretero de juncal" 4167 (207)
CARRETERO ES MI AMANTE 7250 (282)
"Carretero es mi amante de cuatro mulas" 7250 (282)
"El carretero se vá, Ya se va para Sayula" 6332 (247)
THE CARRION CROW 7429A (179), 7429B (267)
"A carrion crow sat on an oak" 7429A (179), 7429B (267)
EL CARRO DEL SOL 3429 (245)
"Carry me ackee go a Linstead Market" 8739 (252)
"CARRY ME BACK TO OLD VIRGINNY" 330 (10,28,35, 114,122,128,129,130,132,184,233,236,343,366)
"CARTA DEL REY HA VENIDO" 6288 (219)
THE CARTMAN 4167 (207)
"Carve a little bit off the top for me, for me!" 2107 (204)
CARVE DAT 'POSSUM 2200 (28,184,366)
CASEY JONES (Folksongs, United States Negro) 8214 (227)
CASEY JONES (Newton) 2652 (35,109,184,225,227)
"Casey Jones! Mounted to the cabin" 2652 (35,109,184, 225,227)
A CASINHA PEQUENINA 4196 (284,322)
LAS CASITA 801 (248)
LA CASQUETTE DE BUGEAUD 4882 (88)
Cassandre 383 (152)

CASSONS LES OEUFS 5154 (21)
CAST AWAY THE OLDEN 8980 (360,361)
"Cast away the olden, sing a new and golden song" 8980 (360,361)
"CAST THY BURDEN UPON THE LORD" 2370 (28,366)
CASTA CIVA, CHE INARGENTI 254 (6)
"Casta Diva, casta Diva, che inargenti" 254 (6)
"CASTIJDEN STERKT DEN CRANCKEN MOET" 6427 (384)
CASTLE TIROWEN 6004 (349)
CASTLES IN THE AIR 7023 (100)
Castor et Pollux (2958-2959
THE CAT CAME BACK 2441 (131)
"Catarina, while you sham a-sleep" 1323 (5)
"Catfish, catfish, goin' up stream" 7424 (392)
"Cauld blaws the wind frae north to sooth" 7186 (101,102)
Cauld kail in Aberdeen 7058
"Cause a Big Bamboo hangin' on the wall" 8712 (11)
"'Cause a soldier man he won't marry" 8729 (11)
CAUX CAROL 2792 (307)
The cavalcade of the Boyne (tune) 5868A
Cavalleria rusticana 2295-2299
CAVALRY OF THE STEPPES 1922 (7)
CAVATINA (Bellini) 254 (6)
CAVATINA (Donizetti) 873 (4)
CAVATINA (Donizetti, Don Pasquale) 857 (5)
CAVATINA (Donizetti, Don Pasquale) 860 (292)
CAVATINA (Gounod, "Ah, leve-toi, soleil!") 1337 (3)
CAVATINA (Gounod, "Dio possente Dio d'amor") 1318 (237)
CAVATINA (Halévy) 1508 (5)
CAVATINA (Mozart) 2588 (1)
CAVATINA (Rossini) 3099 (292)
CAVATINA (Verdi) 3861 (3)
CAVATINE DER AGATHE 3967 (311)
CAVATINE DER GRÄFIN 2588 (311)
CAVATINE DER ROSINA 3099 (311)
"Ce breuvage pourrait de donner un tel rêve" 2313 (4)
"CE CHER ENFANT SUR MES GENOUX" 753 (411)
"Ce matin, j'ai rencontré le train" 9083 (79,82)
CE QUE JE SUIS SANS TOI 1314 (276)
"Ce qu'est le lierre sans l'ormeau" 1314 (276)
"Ce sont trois colombes blanches" 6155 (338)
CEASE, OH CEASE 3188 (138)
"Cease, oh cease to wound and tease me" 3188 (138)
CEASE, OH MAIDEN 3188 (272)
"Cease, oh maiden, thus to grieve me!" 3188 (272)
"Cease ye, oh cease these sounds of gladness!" 874 (5)
"Cease your neighing, pawing, my steed" 673* (295)
CECILIA (Folksongs, French Canada) 5155 (187)
CECILIA (Strauss) 3620 (112,121)
THE CEDAR OF LEBANON 8909 (333)
"The cedar of Lebanon plant of renown" 8909 (333)
EL CEFIRO 6333 (142,350)
"Céfiro, que por la tarde" 6333 (142,350)
CÉLÉBRONS LA NAISSANCE 9049 (388)
"Célébrons la naissance nostri salvatoris" 9049 (388)
CELESTE AIDA 3819 (3,36,132,391)
"Celeste Aïda, forma divina" 3819 (3,36,132,391)
CELLE QU'ADORE MON COEUR 4925 (174)
"Celle qu'adore mon coeur n'est ni brune ni blonde" 4925 (174)
"Celui dont la parole efface toutes peines" 2309 (1)
CEMU ŻEŚ TAK 6682 (295)
"Cemu żeś tak womsy odon?" 6682 (295)
"C'en est donc fait et mon coeur va changer" 868 (292)
"C'en est fait! la Judée appartient à Tiberre!" 2311 (364)

La cenerentola 3100 (2, 300)

"Cent esclaves ornaient ce superbe festin" 754 (153)

CENTRAL WILL SHINE 7493 (28, 366)

"Central will shine tonight, Central will shine" 7493 (28, 366)

CENZONTLE DE HUATAL 5640 (86)

CEREMONIES FOR CHRISTMAS 8910 (374)

"Certain coucou certain hibou au rossignol dans un bocage" 1368 (153)

"A certain man had two sons" 3793 (398)

"Un certo non so che mi giunge e passa il cor" 3879 (168)

"Cesi, ah cesi quel contento!" 874 (5)

"C'EST À CE JOLI MOIS DE MAY" 4914 (108)

"C'est cet objet pour qui Phébus m'inspire" 4930 (175)

"C'est dans la ville de Rouen" 5178 (21)

"C'est des contrebandiers le refuge ordinaire" 319 (93)

"C'est en m'y promenant le long de ces prairies" 5166 (187)

"C'EST FORCE, FAIRE LE WEIL" 1413 (403)

"C'est Guignolot d'Saint Lazot" 4986 (231)

C'EST L'AVIRON 5150 (186, 187, 219)

"C'est l'aviron qui nous mène" 5150 (186, 187, 219)

"C'EST L'EXTASE LANGOUREUSE" 786 (121)

C'EST LA BELLE FRANÇOISE 5151 (187)

"C'est la belle Françoise, lon, gai! 5151 (187)

"C'est la mer' Michel qui a perdu son chat" 5032 (82, 91, 127, 383)

C'EST LA MÈRE MICHEL 5032 (127)

"C'est la poulette grise" 5184 (187)

"C'est le mai, mois de mai" 5036 (91)

"C'est le roi Dagobert qui met sa culotte à l'envers" 5100 (91, 127)

"C'EST LES GENS DE BOUZE" 4915 (91)

"C'est moi! j'ai tout brisé n'importe! m'y voici!" 3733 (357)

C'EST MON AMI 4916 (91, 140)

C'EST UN PETIT OISEAU 4917 (127)

"C'est un' poulett' blanche, qui va pondre dans la grange" 5082 (127)

"C'est un p'tit oiseau, qui prit sa volée" 4917 (127)

"C'EST UN REMPART QUE NOTRE DIEU" 4918 (82)

"C'est une fillette de quinz'-ans à peine" 6054 (338)

ČESTIT SVIETU 9413 (154)

"Čestit svietu danas svemu" 9413 (154)

"Cet étang qui s'étend dans la plaine" 1020 (383)

"C'était un' bell' corvette, Lonla!" 4898 (127)

"C'était un p'tit bonhomm', luron!" 4898 (127)

"Četnička truba zatrubi" 8790 (7)

"Cette nuit sur la terre nous arrive un sauvier" 9087 (88)

CEZ TISOVEC 4314 (94)

"Cez Tisovec mutná voda pretekáva" 4314 (94)

CHACARERA 4166 (284)

"Chacarera, Chacarera, me ha contado un picaflor" 4166 (284)

CHACAYALERA 4167 (207)

CHACUN À SON GOÛT 3603 (2)

CHACUN LE SAIT 866 (221, 292)

CHAD GADYA 6186 (318)

"Chad gadya, Chad gadya D'zabin aba, bitrey zuzey" 6186 (318)

CHAFER, CHAFER 5674 (92)

"Chafer, Chafer, all the day you're humming" 5674 (92)

DE CHAIN GANG 1801 (184)

CHAIN GANG BLUES 8215 (336)

CHAIRS TO MEND 1585 (235, 343, 349)

"Chairs to mend, old chairs to mend" 1585 (235, 343, 349, 402)

CHAŁUPECZKA NISKA 6683 (295)

"Chałupeczka niska, Ojciec matkę ściska" 6683 (295)

THE CHAMARRITA 4197 (350)

CHAMPAGNE CHARLIE 2085 (225)

LOS CHAMULITAS 6334 (247)

"Change me this twenty-fiver, into equal pieces of three" 6180 (318)

CHANITAH 4123 (30)

CHANSON (Uddén) 3783 (356)

CHANSON À BOIRE 5078 (88)

CHANSON À MANGER 2109 (364)

CHANSON AU LUTH (Clemens non Papa, Jacobus) 685 (278)

CHANSON AU LUTH (Sermisy) 3426 (278)

CHANSON D'AMOUR 1791 (73)

CHANSON D'AVRIL 322 (191, 195, 362)

CHANSON DE FLORIAN 1289 (136, 237)

CHANSON DE FORTUNIO 4926 (127)

CHANT DE GUERRE POUR L'ARMÉE DU RHIN 3110 (294)

LA CHANSON DE L'AVEINE 4927 (91)

CHANSON DE LA MARIÉE 4928 (91)

CHANSON DE LA VEILLE 6066 (338)

CHANSON DE MAI 4929 (82)

CHANSON DE MARIE ANTOINETTE 1761 (208)

CHANSON DES FLEURS 7494 (21)

CHANSON DES GUERRES DE FLANDRE 7355 (155)

CHANSON DU COMTE HAMILTON 4930 (175)

CHANSON DU MARCHAND HINDOU 3039 (241)

LA CHANSON DU TAMBOURINEUR 4931 (210)

CHANSON DU VIN 6065 (338)

CHANSON ESPAGNOLE 2978 (121)

CHANSON INDOUE 3039 (122)

CHANSON PROVENCALE 24 (93)

CHANSON TOURANGELLE 4932 (88)

CHANSON TRISTE 940 (362)

Chansons de Bilitis 791-792

Les chansons de Miarka 1237-1238

Chansons grises 1503

CHANT DE BERGERS DE HAUTE-AUVERGNE 4893 (62)

LE CHANT DE SELMA 2119 (149)

LE CHANT DU DÉPART 2346 (82, 91)

CHANT HINDOU 269 (140)

CHANTANS! BARGIES, NOUÉ, NOUÉ 9050 (361)

CHANTEZ BIEN NOEL 8815 (372)

"Chantez! Chantez bien Noël! 'Jesus is born' the angels tell" 8815 (372)

"Chantez, chantez l'amour" 2075 (152)

"CHANTEZ, OISEAUX, CHANTEZ" 826 (411)

CHANTONS, BERGERS NOEL NOEL 9050 (165)

"Chantons, chantons en choeur, Marguerites et Violettes" 7494 (21)

"Chantons, chantons, les amours de Jeanne" 4933 (36)

CHANTONS, JE VOUS EN PRIE 9051 (361)

Chantons je vous en prie (tune) 9049

Chantons L'Hymen 831 (82)

"Chantons la Belle au bois dormant" 831 (82)

CHANTONS LES AMOURS DE JEAN 4933 (36)

CHANUKE, O CHANUKE! 6187 (318)

"Chanuke, O Chanuke, a yontev a sheyner" 6187 (318)

"Chanukkah, O Chanukkah, O holiday so fair" 6187 (318)

LAS CHAPARRERAS 6335 (247)

CHARCOAL MAN 8216 (110)

LE CHARDONNERET AU BEC D'OR 2042 (269)

"Chickens are crowing on Sour Wood Mountain" 8014E
  (279,366)
"The chickens they are crowing, a-crowing" 7496 (109,
  110)
"Chide me, if thou wilt, Masetto" 2563 (6)
EL CHIFLIDO 7497 (113)
CHILD IN THE MANGER 9315 (154)
"Child in the manger! Infant of Mary" 9315 (154)
"A CHILD IS BORN IN BETHLEHEM" (Carols, Latin) 9032A
  (363,388)
"A CHILD IS BORN IN BETHLEHEM" (Carols, Netherlands)
  9257A (165), 9257B (379)
THE CHILD JESUS 9305 (154,337)
"CHILD JESUS CAME TO EARTH THIS DAY" 1186 (296)
"Child Jesus in his garden" 649 (121)
A CHILD MY CHOICE 8942 (361)
"A CHILD OF BEAUTY IS BORN TO US" 9270 (154)
CHILD OF GOD 9349 (33,332)
A CHILD THIS DAY IS BORN 8912 (296,307,333,334,337,
  363,410)
"A Child this day is born, a Child of high renown" 8912
  (296,307,333,334,337,361,363,410)
"A CHILD WAS BORN UPON THIS EARTH" 9238 (316)
CHILDHOOD DAYS 1863 (295)
A CHILDING SLEPT 3726 (374)
"A Childing slept within a bed" 3726 (374)
"Children, go, and I will send thee" 9367C(332)
"Children, go, where I send thee" 9367A (313,332),
  9367B (33,389)
"Children grumbled on the way" 8348 (409)
"Children, guess what I have here" 4413 (37)
"Children of a fold that bled" 1972 (124)
"Children of God, be brave" 5113 (37)
CHILDREN OF THE HEAVENLY KING (Carols, United States)
  9350 (332)
"Children of the heav'nly King, as we journey let us sing"
  (Carols, United States) 9350 (332)
CHILDREN SING A CAROL SPLENDID 9256 (361)
"Children sing a carol splendid, ecce mundi gaudia" 9256
  (361)
"Children, vie with one another, singing clear the hymn of
  praise" 9043A (244)
"Children, we'll have a celebration" 3949 (318)
CHILDREN'S PLAY 2580 (199)
CHILDREN'S SONG 2618 (340)
CHILDREN'S SONG OF THE NATIVITY 8943 (271)
THE CHILDREN'S WATCH 3371 (141)
CHILEAN DANCE SONG 4258 (279)
CHILLY WINDS 8219A (110), 8219B (336)
CHILLY WATER 8218 (28,336)
"Chilly water, chilly water, hallelujah to that Lamb"
  8218 (28,366)
CHIMING BELLS OF LONG AGO 3438 (129,130)
CHIMNEY SWEEPER 8220 (184)
"Chimney Sweeper, sweep out yo' chimney" 8220 (184)
"China, China, beautiful land" 4268 (86)
"Ching-a-ring-a-ring ching ching" 7498 (84)
CHING-A-RING CHAW 7498 (84)
LA CHINITA MADERISTA 6337 (247)
"Chinita, pelito ne gro, te mando sólo avisar" 6395 (247)
"Ch'io mai vi possa lasciar d'amare" 3107 (211)
Chio può mirar (tune) 9214 (361)
"Chiqui, chiqui, chiqui... Ay! quien es esa que viene?"
  4290 (207)
"Chiqui, chiqui, chiqui... Who is that, just passing by
  there?" 4290 (207)
CHIRIBIRIBEE 2785 (132)

THE CHISHOLM TRAIL 7869A (145), 7869E (109,110)
CHIT CHAT 2518 (225)
CHŁOPEK CI JA CHŁOPEK 6685 (295)
"Chłopek ci ja chłopek, Wpołu dobrze orze!" 6685 (295)
CHOĆ BURZA HUCZY WKOŁO NAS 6686 (159)
"Choć burza huczy wkoło nas, do góry wzniesmy skroń"
  6686 (159)
EL CHOCLO 3872 (132)
CHODÍ ŠUHAJ 4315 (94)
"Chodí šuhaj kolo domu" 4315 (94)
"Chodziłam se kole rzecki, pogubiłam koralicki" 6753
  (295)
CHODZIŁ SENNEK 6687 (295)
"Chodził sennek i drzemo tał luli, luli cyt" 6687 (295)
CHOLITA 3512 (284)
"Cholita, no te enamores" 3512 (284)
"Choose your partner, skip to my Lou" 8005 (249,343)
"Choose your partners, skip-turn-a-loo!" 8005 (37)
CHÓR KOBIET PRZY KROSNACH 2486 (295)
CHORA VIDEIRA 6900 (58)
CHORAL 2665 (295)
DIE CHOSSID BEIM BOJN SI SUKE 6189 (230)
CHOUCOUNE 5645 (86,279)
"Chrétiens, prenez courage" 9193 (186,244)
CHRIST BE WITH ME! 672 (123)
"Christ be with me, Christ within me" 672 (123)
THE CHRIST-CHILD IS BORN 9156 (79)
"The Christ-Child is born, Oh Hallelujah!" 9156 (79)
"The Christ-child lay on Mary's lap" (Carols, England)
  9012 (271)
"THE CHRIST-CHILD LAY ON MARY'S LAP" (Carols,
  Germany) 9164 (361)
CHRIST CHILD'S SLUMBER SONG 9183 (165)
"Christ, hath Christ's Mother borne" 3443 (334)
CHRIST INCARNATE 2866 (361)
CHRIST IS BORN (Carols, Poland) 9290 (295)
CHRIST IS BORN! (Shaw) 3439 (334)
"Christ is born! Christ is born!" 3439 (334)
"Christ is born, the angels tell" 3090 (376)
CHRIST IS RISEN, THEN LET US SING 9228 (371)
"Christ the King is born on an early morn" 9290 (295)
"CHRIST THE LORD IS RISEN TODAY" (Carols, England)
  8913 (28,343,346,366,400)
"CHRIST THE LORD IS RISEN TODAY" (Gordon) 1304
  (371)
CHRIST WAS BORN (Carols, Czechoslavakia) 8876 (324)
CHRIST WAS BORN (Carols, France) 9052 (374)
CHRIST WAS BORN (Carols, United States) 9351 (242)
"Christ was born and lives anew! Oh, rejoice, all!" 8876
  (324)
"CHRIST WAS BORN IN BETHLEHEM" (Carols,United States)
  9361C (165,312)
"Christ was born in Bethlehem, in a lowly stable lay"
  9351 (242)
"Christ was born on Christmas day" (Carols, France) 9052
  (374)
CHRIST WAS BORN ON CHRISTMAS DAY (Carols, Ger-
  many) 9163 (79,296,315,337)
"Christ was born on Christmas day, wreathe the holly,
  twine the bay" 9163 (79,296,315,337)
"DER CHRISTBAUM IST DER SCHÖNSTE BAUM" 9147
  (251,412)
CHRISTIAN FOLK, A DAY OF JOY 9018 (361)
"Christian folk, a day of joy bid ye one another" 9018
  (361)
"CHRISTIAN MEN, LOOK UP ON HIGH" 8830 (361)

CHRISTIANS AWAKE 3928 (333,337,410)
"CHRISTIANS, AWAKE, SALUTE THE HAPPY MORN" 3928 (38,39,251,307)
"Christians, hold up your heads!" 8292 (409)
CHRISTKINDLEINS WIEGENLIED 9183 (99)
CHRISTMAS ANTHEM 9254 (244)
CHRISTMAS BELLS 5504 (206)
CHRISTMAS CAROL (Carols, Mexico) 9225 (279)
CHRISTMAS CAROL (Carols, Philippine Islands) 9286 (154)
CHRISTMAS CAROL (Carols, Puerto Rico) 9306 (219)
"Christmas! Christmas! 9408 (244)
CHRISTMAS CRADLE SONG 3161 (307)
CHRISTMAS DAY IN THE MORNING 8945C (332)
"Christmas Day is come, let's all prepare for mirth" 9195 (337)
CHRISTMAS EVE CANON 1570 (337)
CHRISTMAS EVE IS HERE 9032 (79)
"Christmas Eve is here, see the moon is waking" 9032 (79)
A CHRISTMAS GIFT 9306 (291)
CHRISTMAS HAS COME AGAIN 9333 (165)
"Christmas has come again, Christmas has come again" 9333 (165)
THE CHRISTMAS HYMN (Carols, Germany) 9140 (296)
CHRISTMAS HYMN (Kaiper) 1849 (251)
CHRISTMAS INVOCATION 9194 (154)
CHRISTMAS IS COMING (Carols, England) 8914 (33,44, 214,337,343)
CHRISTMAS IS COMING (Davies) 775 (307)
"Christmas is coming, the geese are getting fat" (Carols, England) 8914 (343)
"Christmas is coming, the geese are getting fat" (Davies) 775 (307)
"Christmas is coming, the goose is getting fat" (Carols, England) 8914 (44,214,337)
CHRISTMAS IS HERE AGAIN 9333 (188)
"Christmas is here again and Christmas is here again" 9333 (188)
"Christmas is here again oh Christmas is here again" 9333 (79)
CHRISTMAS LULLABY 8805 (154)
THE CHRISTMAS NIGHTINGALE 9184 (79,388)
CHRISTMAS, O HAPPIEST DAY 9285 (165)
CHRISTMAS SONG (Adam) 26
CHRISTMAS SONG (Bach) 122 (388)
CHRISTMAS SONG (Carols, Catalan) 8848 (154)
A CHRISTMAS SONG (Carols, Puerto Rico) 9303 (291)
CHRISTMAS SONG (Palmgren) 2735 (124)
CHRISTMAS SONG (Schumann) 3399 (141)
THE CHRISTMAS TREE 9175A (337)
"The Christmas tree's more beautiful" 9147 (251)
CHRISTO INCARNATO 2866 (361)
"Christo paremus canticum" 3445 (334)
CHRISTOPHER COLUMBO 7499 (44)
"Christopher Columbus didn't have a compass" 7973 (44)
CHRISTUS IS OPGESTANDEN 9229A (384), 9229B (201)
"Christus is opgestanden al van de Joden hun handen" 9229A (201)
"Christus is opgestanden al van der Joden heur handen" 9229B (384)
CHRYSANTHEMUMS 2955 (295)
CHRYSIS 1861 (74)
CHRYZANTEMY 2955 (295)
"Chuadhas thart le Druim-Chiaráin le déidheanaighe" 5860 (280)
CHUDOBNÁ DIEVČINA 4316 (94)

"Chudobná dievčina tá iného nemá len svoju poctivost' len svoju poctivost'" 4316 (94)
'CHULA' 6901 (58)
CHULA LA MAÑANA 6338 (219)
"Chulala mañana, chula la mañana" 6338 (219)
"Chumeltic tabalumil chumeltic la binajel" 6334 (247)
DE CHURCH BELL TOLLIN', DING DONG 8221 (184)
"Church gettin' higher, rockin' Jerusalem" 8512 (409)
THE CHURCH'S ONE FOUNDATION 3996 (236)
"The Church's one foundation is Jesus Christ her Lord" 3996 (236)
"The churning, foaming ocean waves are rolling towards the shore" 1952 (162)
CHUSTECZKA 6688 (295)
CHUT, CHUT 4939 (65)
"Ci son, ho tutto in franto, che monta dentro io sto!" 3733 (357)
CIASCUN LO DICE 866 (6,221)
"ČIAŽE JE TO ROLIČKA" 4317 (94)
CIBULIČKA 4318 (177)
"Cicho senno na krysztale" 3684 (295)
CICHY WIECZÓR 3680 (295)
"Cichy wieczór już zapada" 3680 (295)
Le Cid 2306 (1)
ČIE SÚ TO HÚSKY 4319 (94)
"Čie sú to húsky na tej vode?" 4319 (94)
"ČIE SÚ TO KONE" 4320 (94)
CIEBIE, BOŻE, CHWALIMY 6689 (295)
"Ciebie, Boże, chwalimy, Ciebie, Panie wyznawamy" 6689 (295)
"Cieco, cieco, cieco si finse amor" 2817 (134)
CIECO SI FINSE AMOR 2817 (134)
La ciel a visité la terre 1315 (394)
"Le ciel, par d'éclatants miracles" 1272 (5)
CIELITO LINDO 6339A, 6339B
CIELO AZUL 2185 (245)
CIELO E MAR 2845 (3)
"Cielo! e mar! l'entereo velo" 2845 (3)
"Cierra pues tus divinos ojos con sueño" 3705 (248)
"Cierra tus lindos ojos que tienen sueño" 3705 (248)
CIĘŻKIE LOSY LEGIONERA 6690 (295)
"Ciężkie losy legionera, Raz, dwa, trzy!" 6690 (295)
"La cigale ayant chanté tout l'ete, ayant chanté tout l'été" 3135 (278)
LA CIGALE ET LA FORMI 3135 (278)
LES CIGALES 633 (190,192,194)
"CIGARETTES WILL SPOIL YOUR LIFE" 7500 (321)
"Cilia'r haul draw dros ael bryniau hael Arfon" 8689 (349)
CINDY 7501 (80,110,227,293)
"Cinghe la bella seji" 6102 (325)
LA CIRIACA 7502 (113)
CIRIBIRIBEE 2785 (128)
"Ciribiribee, with hearts so free" 2785 (128)
CIRIBIRIBIN 2785 (223,233,343)
"Ciribiribin, O come, my love" 2785 (233)
"Ciribiribin, so gaily singing" 2785 (37)
CITADEL HILL 4228 (186)
THE CITIZENS OF CHÂTRES 9053 (363)
"The citizens of Châtres, a curious story tell" 9053 (363)
THE CITY BLUES 8222 (336)
"The city skies are clouded" 926 (287,288)
"Clad in verdure green thy branches as once more, friend, I greet thee" 1485 (2)
CLÄRCHENS LIED 3011 (99)
CLAIR DE LUNE (Debussy) 794 (211)
CLAIR DE LUNE (Saint-Saëns) 3136 (140)

CLAIR DE LUNE (Szulc) 3703 (191,193,195)
CLAMS 8030 (335)
"Clams, clams, ten cents for your clams" 8030 (335)
THE CLANG OF THE FORGE 3054 (237)
CL'AR DE KITCHEN 8223 (80)
CLARE'S DRAGOONS 5886 (235,349)
Clari 308
CLARIN DE CAMPAÑA 6340 (247)
"Clasped to your heart in a loving embrace" 2118 (129, 131)
"Un clavel corté por la sierra fui" 802 (248)
CLAVELITOS 3791 (142,245)
"Clavelitos, a quien le doy clavelos" 3791 (142,245)
CLEAR BROOK 7238 (219)
CLEAR THE TRACK 9434 (335)
CLEAR THE TRACK LET THE BULLGINE RUN 9434 (320)
"Clear the way for the Calf of Gold!" 1322 (5)
CLEMENTINE 2509 (35,225,402)
La clemenza di Tito 2554-2555
CLICK YOUR HEELS 6813 (159)
THE CLIFF 6946 (86)
"Climb, squirrel, climb the big oak tree" 3133 (190, 192,194)
CLIMB TO GLORY 8224 (80)
CLINCH MOUNTAIN 8090C (109,110)
Clivia 879-881
LES CLOCHES 793 (140)
Les cloches de Corneville 2832 (205)
"LES CLOCHETTES DES MUGUETS" 1727 (191,193,195)
CLOCKMAKER'S SONG 671 (295)
CLOG DANCE 7341 (188)
CLORIS HERMOSA 952 (269)
CLORIS SIGH'D 4565 (107)
"Cloris sigh'd and sung and wept" 4565 (107)
"Close your eyes, Lena, my darling" 999 (28,114,129, 130,131,132,233,366)
CLOUD-SHADOWS 3056 (45)
CLOUDS ARE SINKING 5691 (164)
"Clouds are sinking low and lower" 5691 (164)
"Cloudy in the west looks like rain" 8222 (336)
Clout the cladron (tune) 7041
"Clown in a costume and face masked with makeup" 2116 (132)
Clunie's reel (tune) 7132
CLYCHAU ABERDYFI 8662 (19,349)
CLYCHAU'R LLAN 8691 (20)
"Clyw! clyw! foreol glod" 8664 (19)
"Clyw! clyw! foreuol glod" 8664 (349)
CNOT Y COED 8663 (349)
ČO BUDEME ROBIT' 4321 (94)
"Čo budeme robit', chudobní paholci" 4321 (94)
CO-CA-CHE-LUNK 7503 (225)
CO MI DANO 3689 (295)
"ČO SI K NÁM NEPRIŠIEL" 4322 (94)
"Co tak mocno pukneło?" 6835 (295)
"CO TAM MARZYC O KOCHANUI" 939 (159)
CO TO ZNAMENÁ? 8869 (154)
"Co to znamená medle nového?" 8869 (154)
"Coachman, get my troika ready" 6978 (95)
COACHMAN SMALL AND BIG 5749 (164)
"Coachman small and big on his van wets his whistle whene'er he can" 5749 (164)
THE COASTS OF HIGH BARBARY 4566 (35)
The cobbler's jig (tune) 4568 (234)
COCAINE LIL 8138A (110)
"Cock-a-doodle, cock-a-doodle-doo!" 6304 (37)

COCK ROBIN 4567 (249,402)
COCKCHAFER 5674 (164)
COCKLES AND MUSSELS 5968 (35,166,172,349,402)
THE COCKROACH 6341 (34)
COCO DE LOS SANTOS 6652 (322)
THE COCOA-NUT 6652 (322)
COCONITO 170 (248)
COD LIVER OIL 5887 (171)
CODIAD YR HEDYDD 8664 (19,349)
"COFFEE GROWS IN WHITE OAK TREES" 7504A (185)
"COFFEE GROWS ON WHITE OAK TREES" 7504B (227)
"The coffee that they give us, they say is mighty fine" 7605 (227)
COIN I NEED 8776 (95)
"Coin I need today, wife, not tomorrow" 8776 (95)
"Col mio sangue comprarei" 3599 (217)
"COL MIO SANGUE COMPREREI" 3599 (139)
COLD IS THE MORNING 8877 (337)
"Cold is the morning and bleak is the day" 8877 (337)
COLD RAINY DAY 8225 (321)
"Cold rainy day, some old cold rainy day, I'll be back some old cold rainy day" 8225 (321)
"The cold wind swept the mountain's height" 1601 (189)
"Cold winter may go and gay springtime depart" 1389 (395)
"Coldly runs the river, reedy banks o'erflowing" 5731 (22)
"Coldly the night winds winging" 2794 (305,307)
COLD'S THE WIND 4568 (234)
"Cold's the wind and wet's the rain" 4568 (234)
COLIN AND PHOEBE 4569 (198)
COLINETTE 4940 (60)
"Colinette au bois s'en alla" 4940 (60)
COLIN'S CATTLE 7025 (101,103)
COLLECTOR MAN BLUES 8226 (336)
THE COLORADO TRAIL 7505A (321) 7505B (321)
"Columbia, Columbia, to glory arise" 951 (109,110)
COLUMBIA THE GEM OF THE OCEAN 221
COM' È GENTIL 859 (3)
"Com' è gentil la notte e mezzo april" 859 (3)
"Combien coûtèrent, combien coûtèrent" 5106 (91)
COME AGAIN 893 (36,196)
COME AGAIN, SWEET LOVE 893 (272,348)
"COME AGAIN, SWEET LOVE DOTH NOW INVITE" 893 (117,272,348)
"Come again, sweete love doth now invite" 893 (36,196)
"Come a-leaning on the Lord" 8171 (409)
"Come all my boys and listen a song I'll sing to you" 7534 (145,227)
"Come all of you bold shanty boys, and list while I relate" 7724D (186)
"Come all ye bold fishermen, listen to me" 9430 (173)
COME, ALL YE CHILDREN 9319 (296)
"Come, all ye children, your voices raise on this morn" 9319 (296)
"COME ALL YE FAIR AND TENDER LADIES" 7506B (265)
"Come all ye jolly fellows, how would you like to go" 4226 (186)
"Come all ye jolly good shanty-boys" 7982 (335)
"Come, all ye jolly shepherds, that whistle thro' the glen" 7199 (100,105)
"Come all ye jovial shanty boys, wherever you may be" 7724B (34)
"Come all ye lads and lasses and listen to me awhile" 5961 (172)
"COME ALL YE OF TENDER YEARS" 9098 (361)

"Come all ye people, come and sing" 9198 (37)

COME ALL YE SHEPHERDS 8877 (33,296,388)

"Come, all ye shepherds and be not dismayed" 8877 (251)

"Come all ye shepherds and hark to our song!" 8877 (165)

"Come all ye shepherds, come hark unto me!" 8877 (33, 388)

"Come, all ye shepherds, your flocks will not stray" 8877 (296)

"Come all ye weary, cease from your sighing" 1311 (394)

"Come all ye wild rovers and sit ye down" 7765 (393)

"Come all ye young fellows that follow the sea" 9426 (173, 233)

"Come all ye young fine fellows" 7991B (145)

"Come all ye young sailormen, listen to me" 9430 (35,109, 110,145,214)

"Come all you bold ox teamsters" 7911 (34,110)

"Come all you brisk young fellows" 7991E (189,331)

"COME ALL YOU FAIR AND TENDER LADIES" 7506A (72, 227)

"Come all you gallant poaching boys that ramble free from care" 6029 (172)

"Come all you good fellers, wherever you be" 7458 (227)

"Come all you good old farmers that on your plow depend" 7567B (72)

"Come all you good workers, Good news to you I'll tell" 8122 (293,335)

"Come all you heroes, wher'er you be" 7562 (126)

"Come, all you jolly cowboys" 7557 (120)

"Come all you jolly fellows, and listen to my song" 4241 (186)

"Come all you jolly fellows, wherever you may be" 7724A (227)

"Come all you jolly lumbermen and listen to my song" 7479 (110)

"Come, all you jolly river lads, I'll have you to draw near" 7724C (72)

"Come, all you old men all" 7470A (186)

"Come all you pretty fair maids, that are just in your prime" 4761 (198)

"Come all you pretty maidens, and listen unto me" 4745 (198)

"Come all you pretty maidens fair, attend unto my song" 4795 (198)

"Come all you pretty maidens, some old and some younger" 7877 (72)

"Come, all you rounders, for I want you to hear" 2652 (184)

"Come, all you rounders, if you want to hear" 2652 (109, 225,227)

"Come all you rounders that want to hear" 2652 (35)

COME ALL YOU ROVING BACHELORS 4570 (198)

"Come all you roving bachelors that want to take a wife" 4570 (198)

"Come, all you sly and crafty rogues, come listen to my story" 7753 (72)

"Come all you sons of freedom that run the Saginaw stream" 7901 (227)

"Come all you sporting bach'lors" 8018 (227)

"Come, all you Virginia girls and listen to my noise" 8104 (72)

"Come all you western rangers, bound to that distant land" 8105 (126)

COME ALL YOU WORTHY GENTLEMEN 8915 (307)

"Come all you worthy gentlemen that may be standing by" 8915 (307,334)

"Come all young men and maidens and hark to what I tell" 8137A (212)

"Come, all young men and maidens, come listen to my song" 7809 (72)

"Come along and dance this dance now, a ha ha" 8785 (95)

"Come along boys, and listen to my tale" 7869A (34,145, 185,227), 7869B (331), 7869D (227)

"Come along get you ready wear your bran, bran new gown" 2406 (32,34,246)

"Come along girls, listen to my voice" 7751 (80)

"Come along girls, we're going to Boston" 7624 (216)

"Come along, mo'ner" 8591 (182)

COME AND DANCE WITH ME 5140 (186,187)

"Come and greet the sweet spring fair" 6257 (37)

"Come and I will sing you" 9382A (216)

"Come and let me tell you 'bout the rising of the Saviour" 8296B (44)

Come and listen to my ditty (tune) 7422

"Come and obey the voice that is calling" 2318 (1)

"COME AND SEE MY LITTLE CHICKENS" 6612 (316)

"COME AND SEE THE HOLY ONE" 9054 (361)

COME AND TRIP IT 1450 (404)

"Come and trip it as you go" 1450 (404)

"Come, Angels, come, from Heav'n descend" 9183 (372)

COME AWAY 894 (197)

"Come away, away, away, come where the lilies bloom so fair" 3740 (132)

"COME AWAY, COME SWEET LOVE" 894 (144)

"Come away to dreamin' town, Mandy Lou" 1512 (78)

"Come away to the skies my beloved, arise" 9357 (332)

"Come away with me Lucile in my merry Oldsmobile" 983 (233)

"Come back, come back, my beloved!" 289 (190,192, 194)

"Come back Liza, come back gal" 8774 (11,252)

"Come back, my love! O be persuaded" 289 (362)

COME BACK TO ERIN 175 (132,166,213,343)

"Come back to Erin, Mavoureen, Mavoureen" 175 (132, 166,213,343)

COME BACK TO ME 4855 (95)

COME BACK TO SORRENTO 745 (132,233)

COME BELOVED 1453 (276)

"Come boat me o'er, come row me o'er" 7150 (365)

"Come boys, now we'll light the fires" 7323 (37)

"COME, BOYS, UNSADDLE THE HORSES" 6947 (86)

"Come bridle me up my milkwhite steed" 7607B (392)

"Come bring with a noise, my merry, merry boys" 8910 (374)

COME, BUY MY FLOWERS 6075 (37)

"Come buy my lovely flowr's" 6075 (37)

"Come, buy my nice fresh ivy" 5927 (133)

"Come, cheer up, my lads, 'tis to glory we steer" 386 (14,173,235,349)

COME, COME AWAY WITH ME 6875 (295)

"Come, come away with me, lady so fair and sweet" 6875 (295)

"COME, COME, YE SAINTS" 684* (34)

"Come, companions, join your voices" 4586 (349)

"Come, cows, to the stream, in the sun's gentle gleam" 7370 (230)

"COME DAL CIEL PRECIPITA" 3845 (5)

"Come dance my dear one" 4163 (37)

COME DANCE THE GATO 4165 (207)

"Come, dance with me, my Rosa" 6562A (37)

COME DE BIRD 8711 (11)

COME DOWN 8227 (409)

"Come down, Come down, my Lord!" 8227 (409)

"Come, drink a health to Master" 4626 (37)

"Come, drink, my brave boys, and never give o'er" 4584 (198)

"Come ev'ryone rejoicing, O neighbors come and hear" 9158 (79)

"Come fathers and mothers come" 2225 (84)

COME, FELLOW WORKERS 4271 (35, 293)

"Come fellow workers, hung ho hai ho" 4271 (35, 293)

"Come fill up my cup, come fill up my can" 7008 (17, 28, 163, 235, 349)

"Come, follow, follow, follow, follow" 1658 (235, 349)

"COME FOLLOW ME" 1658 (235, 349)

"COME, FOLLOW ME, THE SAVIOUR SPAKE" 1862 (50)

"COME, FOR THY LOVE IS WAITING" 1278 (357)

Come friends who plow the sea 3669

"Come gather 'round me, boys and I'll tell you a tale" 7869C (115)

"Come gather 'round, my shanty boys" 7917 (331)

"Come gentlemen and ladies, I pray you to draw near" 4236 (186)

"Come gie's a sang Montgomery cried" 7184 (101)

"COME, GOOD PEOPLE, LET US SING" 9230 (372)

COME, GOOD WIND 4941 (279, 366)

"Come, good wind, come fair wind" 4941 (279, 366)

COME HASTE TO THE WEDDING 7507 (212)

COME, HASTEN, YE SHEPHERDS 9166 (79)

"Come hasten, ye shepherds, come one and come all" 9166 (79)

COME HEAVY SLEEPE 895 (144)

"Come heavy sleepe, the image of true death" 895 (144)

COME HERE JESUS IF YOU PLEASE 8228 (409)

COME HERE LORD 8229 (409)

"Come here, Lord! Come here, Lord!" 8229 (409)

COME HERE, VITÚ 4216 (219)

"Come here, Vitú, come here, Vitú" 4216 (219)

"Come hither, child, and rest" 3409 (344)

COME HOME FATHER! 4105 (114)

COME IN 5713 (164)

"Come in my sweetest, come in here" 5713 (164)

"COME IN QUEST' ORA BRUNA" 3855 (2)

COME INTO MY ARMS 5736 (164)

"Come into my arms, my sweet" 5736 (164)

"COME INTO THE GARDEN, MAUD" 3533 (344)

"Come, Jesus, my love" 665 (304)

"Come, join hand in hand, brave Americans all" 386 (44)

"Come, join the circle!" 4199 (219)

"Come join us in the chorus while we sing" 7527 (189)

"COME LA LUCE E TREMOLA" 2852 (134)

"COME, LANDLORD, FILL THE FLOWING BOWL" 4571 (402)

COME LASSES AND LADS 4572 (13, 199, 234, 349, 402)

"Come, lasses and lads, get leave of your dads" 4572 (199, 234, 349, 402)

"Come, lasses and lads, take leave of your dads" 4572 (13)

"COME, LET US ALL A-MAYING GO" 1659 (235)

"Come let us drink wine" 6759 (295)

"Come, let us go to the dance" 6359 (35)

"Come let us sing. What shall we sing?" 7517 (230)

"Come, let's dance another mazur" 6745 (295)

"Come, let's dance the ball's last mazur" 6745 (159)

"Come, lis'en all you gals an' boys" 3030 (184)

"Come list to the story I tell you" 8821 (370)

"Come, list ye, landsmen, all to me, to tell the truth I'm bound" 9435 (173)

"Come listen all and hear my tale" 6519 (95)

"Come listen all you gals and boys" 3030 (115, 185, 212)

"Come listen, kind friends and I'll sing you a song" 7842 (72)

"Come, listen to me closely, while I rehearse a ditty" 7919 (44)

COME, LITTLE DONKEY 8717 (77)

COME, LITTLE LEAVES 2715 (129)

"Come, little leaves, said the wind one day" 2715 (129)

"Come, little Pink, and tell me what you think" 7790 (81)

"Come live with me and be my love" 4726 (215)

"Come lovely May and make the forests green again" 2594 (209)

"Come, lovely May with blossoms" 2594 (395)

"Come, messmates, pass the bottle 'round" 3207 (225)

"Come, my beloved! Through the sylvan gloom" 1453 (276)

COME MY CELIA 1062 (144)

"Come, my Celia, let us prove" 1062 (144)

"Come, my comrade fair" 942 (121)

"Come my fair maiden to me, let us join the dancing" 7295 (135)

"Come my fine philosopher, you're a trifle dense" 6219 (318)

"Come, my love, the stars are shining" 305 (132)

"Come my loved one, day is pretty" 2484 (295)

"Come, my own one, come, my fond one" 4746 (234)

"Come, my sisters, bretheren too" 8303 (184)

"Come, my sisters, come my brothers, at the sounding of the horn" 6666 (219)

"Come now, let us join hands, Marguerites and Morning Glories" 7494 (21)

"COME NOW, SHEPHERDS, COME AWAY" 763 (33)

COME, O MY LOVE 7508 (243)

"Come, O my love, so fare you well" 7508 (243)

COME O'ER THE SEA 5888 (16, 213)

"Come o'er the sea, maiden with me" 5888 (16, 213)

COME ON AND JOIN INTO THE GAME 528 (389)

"Come on, can't you come on, Marie Picard!" 5156 (21)

"Come on, girls, I'm goin' to Boston" 7624 (185)

COME ON, LADS, THE COUNTRY'S CALLING 6700 (159)

"Come on, lads, the country's calling, fight's on, no use idly strolling" 6700 (159)

"Come on, my dear steward" 8207 (184)

"Come on you lads of old Lorraine" 1202 (35)

"Come, once again lift to your red lips the sparkling glass" 3626 (112)

"Come out! come out! but softly, my child" 3633 (112)

COME OUT, YE CONTINENTALERS 7509 (44)

"Come out, ye continentalers, we're going for to go" 7509 (44)

"COME OWRE THE STREAM, CHARLIE" 7026 (100, 104)

"COME PER ME SERENO" 259 (302)

COME PHILLIS 1097 (119, 196)

"Come, Phillis, come into these bowers" 1097 (119, 196)

"COME, PHYLLIS, COME INTO THESE BOWERS" 1097 (119, 196)

"Come, praise, come, praise the Lord" 124 (160)

COME PRAISE THE LORD 124 (160)

COME PRETTY 7315 (95)

COME RAGGIO DI SOL 516 (139, 168, 274, 368)

"Come raggio di sol mite e sereno" 516 (139, 168, 274, 368)

COME, REST IN THIS BOSOM 5889 (95)
"Come, rest in this bosom, my own stricken deer" 5889
(95)
COME, REST ON THIS BOSOM 5889 (166,213)
"Come, rest on this bosom, my own stricken deer!" 5889
(166,213)
"Come, rise ye up ye, Nancy, and go along with me" 7837
(242)
COME, SAINTS AND SINNERS 7510 (32,34)
"Come, saints and sinners, hear me tell the wonders of Im-
manuel" 7510 (32,34)
COME SCOGLIO 2558 (1)
"Come scoglio immoto resta" 2558 (1)
"COME, SEE A ROSE THAT SPRINGETH" 2869 (333)
"COME, SEE WHERE THE GOLDEN-HEARTED SPRING"
1456 (199)
COME SETE IMPORTUNI 586 (179)
"Come sete importuni, come sete improtuni, amorosi
pensieri! 586 (179)
"Come, shepherd brothers, come silently" 9165A (79)
"Come shipmates and brothers, Ho yo!" 9441 (205)
COME, SISTER DEAR 7289 (219)
"Come, sister, dear, come walking along the shore with
me" 7289 (219)
"Come, sleep and with thy sweet deceiving" 1420 (277)
"Come, sleep, to charm us!" 2207 (152)
"Come sling your pack and stride along" 5505 (37)
"Come soon, come soon, sweet Mayday!" 2594 (199)
"Come, swallow your bumpers, ye tories" 386 (115)
COME SWEET REPOSE 123 (386)
COME, SWEETEST DEATH 123 (346,400)
"Come, sweetest Death! Come, blessed rest!" 123 (346,
400)
"Come ti vidi appeno, o Nina bella" 6061 (51)
"Come tighten your girth and slacken your rein" 7008
(161)
"COME, THOU ALMIGHTY KING" 1244 (28,233,236,346,
366)
"Come, thou fount of ev'ry blessing" 7840 (212)
"COME, THOU LONG-EXPECTED JESUS" (Prichard) 2880
(251)
"Come thou, sweet rest, come sweet repose" 123 (386)
COME TO ME (Beethoven) 246 (123)
COME TO ME (Folksongs, Hungary) 5735 (164)
"Come to me, come to me, all ye that need rest" 246
(123)
"Come to me, dear, I am lonely" 5735 (164)
"Come to me in my dreams and then by day I shall be well
again" 1053 (78)
COME TO ME, MY LOVE 2484 (295)
"Come to me, my love, come back to me" 2484 (295)
"Come to me, Sweet Marie" 2516 (114,131,132)
"Come to my aid" 2656 (6)
"Come to sea with us" 6582 (316)
"Come to the church in the wildwood" 2830 (28,233,236,
279,343,366)
"Come to the country, join us all" 6518 (316)
COME TO THE LAND 6171 (30)
"Come to the land with joy and with spirit, Come to the
holy land" 6171 (30)
COME TO THE SEA 6162 (132)
COME TO THE WATERS 663 (89)
"Come to town the other night" 1002 (185)
COME UNDER MY PLAIDIE 7027 (100)
"Come under my plaidie, the nicht's gaun to fa'" 7027
(100)

COME UNTO HIM (Händel) 1466 (200,394)
"Come unto Him, all ye that labor" 1466 (200)
"Come unto Him, all ye who weep; for He too weepeth"
1051 (123)
COME UNTO ME (Coenen) 688* (200)
COME UNTO ME (Scarlatti) 3196 (160)
"Come unto me, all ye that labour and are heavy laden"
688* (200)
"Come unto me, all ye weary" 3196 (160)
"Come unto me, ye heroes, and I the truth will tell"
7429 (173)
"COME UNTO THESE YELLOW SANDS" 2925 (75,348)
"COME, WHERE MY LOVE LIES DREAMING" 1109 (28,129,
130,132)
"Come where the camp-fire is gleaming" 3988 (129,130)
COME WHERE THE LILIES BLOOM 3740 (132)
"Come, wife and children, let us see the light" 2793 (307)
"Come Will and Jack and John" 9093 (231)
COME WITH HEARTS AFIRE 9095 (361)
"Come, with hearts afire, seek Him where He lies" 9095
(361)
COME WITH ME 7295 (188)
"Come with me my pretty little maiden, come with me
a-dancing" 7295 (188)
"Come with me where moonbeams light Tahitian skies"
457 (132,236)
"Come with the night and lonliness" 1138 (385)
COME, WITH THY LUTE 4573 (28,366)
"Come, with thy lute to the fountain" 4573 (28,366)
COME WITH US SWEET FLOWERS 9048 (244)
"Come with us, sweet flow'rs, and worship Christ the
Lord" 9048 (79,244)
COME, YE BLESSED (Gaul) 1217 (394)
COME, YE BLESSED (Scott) 3410 (200)
"Come ye, come to the waters" 663 (89)
COME YE FAITHFUL 9017 (361)
"Come, ye faithful, sing we right merrily" 9017 (361)
COME! YE LOFTY (Pettman) 2798 (374)
"COME! YE LOFTY, COME! YE LOWLY" (Jude) 1836
(315)
"Come! ye lofty, come! ye lowly" (Pettman) 2798 (374)
"Come ye shepherds, hear the call of your Jesus in the
stall" 8836 (361)
COME, YE THANKFUL PEOPLE 998 (28,279,343,366)
"Come, ye thankful people, come, raise the song of
harvest home" 998 (28,279,343,366)
"Come ye that weep, to Him bow down, who sin forgiveth"
1051 (394)
"Come, ye young men, come along, with your music,
dance and song" 4778 (349)
"Come you dear little sonny boy, come close your sleepy
blue eyes" 743 (241)
"COME YOU NOT FROM NEWCASTLE?" 4574 (48,234)
"COME, YOU PRETTY FALSE-EYED WANTON" 536 (197)
"Comes at times a stillness as of even" 3540 (123)
"Comes the day of blood and glory" 2001 (295)
"Comes the day of feasting and dancing" 5646 (279)
COMES THE SANDMAN 6687 (295)
"Comfort ye, comfort ye, my people" 1465 (89)
COMFORT YE MY PEOPLE 1465 (89)
La comica del cielo 3 (217)
COMIN' THRO' THE RYE 7028A (17,28,36,100,104,128,
132,163,176,233,279,366,402) 7028B (365)
"Comin thro' the rye, poor body" 7028B (365)
COMIN' THRU THE RYE 7028A (132)
"Coming and leaving, seeking and cleaving" 3279 (141)

346

"Così Nilio cantò, fuor d'ogni affanno" 2783 (180)

"Così volete, così sarà" 588 (217)

THE COSSACK 2477 (295)

COSSACK CRADLE SONG 6949 (406)

THE COSSACK RIDES BEYOND THE DANUBE 6949 (352)

COSSACK'S FAREWELL 6950 (95)

COSSACK'S LULLABY 140 (343)

La costanza in amor vince l'inganno 517-518

THE COTTAGE WELL THATCHED WITH STRAW 4545 (198)

COTTON-EYE JOE 7516 (214)

COTTON-EYED JOE 8232 (185)

COTTON-PICKING SONG 8483 (335)

LE COUCOU ("Le coucou a fait son nid...") 4945 (91)

LE COUCOU ("Lou coucut oqu'os...") 4946 (65)

LE COUCOU ("Dans la foret...") 4944 (383)

"Le coucou a fait son nid sur l'arbre" 4945 (91)

"Le coucou c'est un bel oiseau" 4946 (65)

COUCOU, CANARI JALOUX! 7357 (155)

LOU COUCUT 4946 (65)

"Lou coucut oqu'os un auzel" 4946 (65)

COUGHING 4303B (95)

COULD I 3761 (329, 386)

"COULD I BUT BE WINGING" 2474 (295)

"Could I, but come to thee once, but once only" 3761 (386)

"Could I come to thee once dear" 3761 (329)

COULD I FORGET? 675 (140)

COULD MY SONGS THEIR WAY BE WINGING 1505 (140)

"Could you but know, love" 3620 (112)

COULD YOU NOT COME 4322 (95)

"Could you not come, my dear? Long I was waiting" 4322 (95)

COULDN'T HEAR NOBODY PRAY 8332 (28, 37, 52, 279, 366)

THE COULIN 6021 (166, 213)

LA COUMAIRE 4947 (86)

COUNT AND NUN 5261 (95)

COUNT HAMILTON'S SONG 4930 (175)

THE COUNT OF CABRA 7291 (219)

THE COUNTESS OF LAUREL 6300 (219)

COUNTING SONG 7517 (230)

COUNTING THE GOATS 8665 (249)

"Counting the shining planets" 4164 (219)

"Countless as all the stars that cover the sky" 4851 (124)

The country garden (tune) 4791

THE COUNTRY LASS 4852 (124)

COUNTRY SONG 24 (93)

"County by county for beauty and bounty" 8684 (349)

THE COUNTY OF MAYO 5890 (349)

COUPLETS DU MYSOLI 772 (292)

COURONS VOIR L'ENFANT JÉSUS 9054 (361)

COUSIN JEDEDIAH 3738 (28, 225, 279, 366)

COUSIN MALURON 4898 (127)

COUVRE-FEU 5156 (21)

COVENTRY CAROL 8917A (33, 35, 38, 39, 165, 206, 333, 334, 337, 361, 410)

"Covered with tears, my visions reawaken" 2410 (1)

"Cow meat am good and sweet" 1780 (114, 131)

THE COWBOY ("Now all the day long...") 7518 (120)

THE COWBOY ("Oh a man there lives...") 7519 (129, 130)

COWBOY CAROL 446 (305, 307)

THE COWBOY'S CHRISTMAS BALL 7520 (80)

THE COWBOY'S DREAM 7829 (227)

COWBOY'S GETTIN'-UP A HOLLER 7521 (109, 110)

COWBOY'S HEAVEN 7522 (120)

COWBOY'S LAMENT ("As I walked out...") 8032A (173), 8032B (129, 170)

COWBOY'S LAMENT (!My home's in Montana...") 7523 (120)

THE COWBOY'S MEDITATION 7524 (10)

COWHERD'S SONG 6635 (95)

THE COWMAN'S PRAYER 7525 (80)

"Coymalindo, Killkokillko, Coymalindo, Killkome" 7696 (185)

"COŽ SE MNĚ, MÁ MILÁ, HEZKÁ ZDÁŠ" 4323 (177)

"CRABBED AGE AND YOUTH" 4013 (344)

CRACOW CHILD I'M TRULY 2478 (159)

CRACOW KINSMAN 6735 (159)

"Cracow kinsman cease your labour, swift to leave your farmstead" 6735 (159)

"Cracow's child I'm truly, my wit quick and snappy" 2478 (159)

"Cradl'd amid a herd of kine" 9064 (296)

THE CRADLE 9164 (251)

CRADLE HYMN (Carols, United States) 9352 (332)

THE CRADLE IS READY 6644 (231)

"The cradle is ready and there you shall sleep" 6644 (231)

CRADLE SONG (Brahms) 436 (28, 132, 136, 210, 241, 329, 366)

CRADLE SONG (Carols, England) 8918 (271)

CRADLE SONG (Carols, United States) 9344A (314)

CRADLE SONG (Flies) 1085 (209)

CRADLE SONG (Folksongs, Germany, "Sleep baby sleep, thy father...") 5530A (199)

CRADLE SONG (Folksongs, Germany, "Sleep, little darling...") 5612 (231)

CRADLE SONG (Folksongs, Netherlands) 6447 (316)

CRADLE SONG (Folksongs, Poland) 6752 (295)

CRADLE SONG (Folksongs, United States) 7487 (113)

CRADLE SONG (Grimes) 1400 (374)

A CRADLE SONG (Heseltine) 1641 (307)

CRADLE SONG (Howells) 1720 (274)

A CRADLE SONG (Hughes) 1730 (344)

CRADLE SONG (Mendelssohn-Bartholdy) 2369 (274)

CRADLE SONG (Schubert) 3318 (199, 275)

CRADLE SONG (Weber) 3977 (132)

A CRADLE SONG OF THE BLESSED VIRGIN 3546 (244)

CRADLE SONG OF THE INFANT JESUS (Carols, Germany) 9148 (244, 361)

CRADLE-SONG OF THE POOR 2619 (348)

"Cradled all lowly, behold the Saviour Child" 1312 (376)

THE CRADLES 1044 (140, 210)

Craig y Tyle (tune) 8671

CRAIGIE-BURN WOOD 7030 (101)

CRANB'RIES AND RASB'RIES 4360 (94)

"Cranb'ries and raspb'ries too down by the river grow" 4360 (94)

CRAWDAD 7526A (44, 145) 7526B (32, 34)

THE CRAWDAD HOLE 7526A (216)

CRAWDAD SONG 7526B (80), 7526C (227)

THE CRAWFISH MAN 7526D (216)

THE CRAZY DIXIE 7675 (80)

CREATION HYMN 228

CREATOR ALME SIDERUM 6467 (384)

CREDO (Verdi) 3848 (310)

CREDO IN UN DIO 3848 (4)

"Credo in un Dio crudel" 3848 (4, 310)

CREEPING JANE 4576 (198)

CRÉPUSCULE 2307 (191, 193, 195)

LE CRI DES EAUX 530 (259)

THE CRICKETS 633 (190, 192, 194)

"DALEKO, DALEKO, ZA GÓRĄ, ZA RZEKĄ" 1873 (159)

DALLA SUA PACE 2564 (3)

"Dalla sua pace la mia dipende" 2564 (3)

DALLA TORRE DEL FORTE 6077 (325)

DALLAS GAWN 8719 (252)

"Dallas gawn a Cuba, Dallas gawn a Cuba" 8719 (252)

DALLE STANZE, OVE LUCIA 874 (5)

"Dalle stanze, ove Lucia tratta a vea col suo consorte" 874 (5)

DAME GET UP 8919 (216)

"DAME, GET UP AND BAKE YOUR PIES" 8919 (33,79)

"Dame Nature's array no longer is gay" 8671 (20)

"Une dame noble et sage" 2409 (176)

DAME TARTINE 4950 (91)

"The dames of France are fair and free" 5917 (172)

"THE DAMES OF FRANCE ARE FOND AND FREE" 5917 (95, 166,213)

"Der Damm zerreisst, das Feld erbraust" 3014 (250)

DAMMI PACE 1492 (181)

"Dammi pace, oh volto amato" 1492 (181)

"Damn that village I've been through there, couldn't get a job to do there!" 5712 (95)

Le damnation de Faust. Marche hongroise 287

"Damnation fall upon the man" 5634 (95)

DAMON 3560 (45)

"D'AMOR SULL' ALI ROSEE" 3864 (1,143)

"D'AMOUROUS CUER VOEL CANTER" 28 (403)

"A damsel possessed of great beauty" 4605 (198)

"Da'n tera an pianta, o che bela pianta" 6065 (338)

"Dance and play, let's be gay" 7662 (185)

"Dance and song make glad the night" 4040 (329)

DANCE AND TURN 4431 (324)

"Dance and turn, and step lightly, step lightly" 4431 (324)

DANCE CAROL 9333 (79,388)

"Dance de boatman dance" 7460B (185)

DANCE IT 4431 (94)

"Dance it, spin aroundo, aroundo" 4431 (94)

DANCE, LASSIES 6850 (295)

"Dance now, all you lassies" 6850 (295)

"DANCE, O DANCE, GENTLE MAIDEN" 947 (139)

"DANCE, O DANCE, MAIDEN GAY" 947 (368)

DANCE OF DEATH 3137 (192,194)

Dance of the blessed spirits 1275 (123)

DANCE SONG 4431 (209)

"Dance the Merengue, Papa Camilio!" 4502 (86)

DANCE TO YOUR DADDY 7033A (104,105,234) 7033B (44)

"Dance to your daddy, my bonnie laddie" 7033A (104,105, 234)

"Dance to your daddy, my little laddie" 7033B (44)

THE DANCER 3686 (295)

"Dancing, dancing, whirling 'round, when the snow is on the ground" 4431 (209)

DANCING DOLLIES 4951 (214)

DANDOO 7535 (110)

The dandy O! (tune) 6042

"DANEVANG MED GRØNNE BRED" 4004 (87)

"DANEVANG, OH LOVELY SHORE" 4004 (87)

DANGEROUS WOMAN 8234 (336)

DANIEL SAW THE STONE 8235A (409), 8235B (409)

"Daniel saw the stone, hewn out the mountain" 8235B (409)

"Daniel saw the stone, rolling, rolling" 8235A (409)

Daniel the Worthy (tune) 5896

Dank sei dir Herr 1458 (160)

DANKGEBET 3790 (49)

DANKLIED AN HERZOG WILHELM VON WIEMAR 3327 (250)

"DANMARK, DEJLIGST VANG OG VAENGE" 2974 (87)

DANN GEH' ICH HINAUS IN DEN WIENERWALD 3584 (396)

"Dann hört' ich aus weiter Ferne ein Lied" 3467 (396)

D'ANNE JOUANT DE L'ESPINETTE 2979 (121,362)

D'ANNE QUI ME JECTA DE LA NEIGE 2980 (362)

DANS CE BEAU VALLON 4962 (59)

"Dans ce beau vallon, sur le gazon" 4952 (59)

DANS CETTE ÉTABLE 9055 (307,334)

"Dans cette étable que Jésus est charmant" 9055 (307,334)

"Dans l'ennui si désolément vert" 797 (362)

"Dans la forêt lointaine, on entend le coucou" 4944 (383)

"Dans la forêt que crée un rêve" 3136 (140)

"Dans la plaine immense" 1049 (408)

"Dans le bois de Léandre jolie fill' est bien chachée" 6060 (338)

"Dans le bois ténébreux, la princesse aux si doux yeaux" 372 (278)

"Dans le jardin d'mon père" 4888 (34,67)

DANS LE PAYS NATAL 1857 (224)

"DANS LE PRINTEMPS DE MES ANNÉES" 1205 (411)

"DANS LE VALLON LE VENT SOUFFLE DOUCEMENT" 4395 (178)

DANS LES CHANTIERS 5157 (186,187)

"Dans les jardins d'mon père" 4888 (88,91)

DANS LES RUINES D'UNE ABBAYE 1045 (362)

DANS MON BERGER 4953 (59)

"Dans mon berger tout m'enchante" 4953 (59)

Dans mon chemin j'ai recontré (tune) 5152

"Dans mon jardin en soleil sont écloses de lis charmants et de belles roses" 4126 (224)

DANS PARIS, Y A-T-UNE BRUNE 5158 (187)

"Dans Paris y a-t-une brune plus bell' que le jour" 5158 (187)

"Dans ton coeur dort un clair de lune" 940 (362)

DANS TOUS LES CANTONS 5159 (186,189)

"Dans tous les cantons ya des fill's et des garçons" 5159 (186,189)

"Dans un piège fatal son mauvais sort l'amène" 2203 (146)

"Dans un sommeil que charmait ton image" 1041 (121)

"Dans un soupir, l'onde au rivage" 773 (278)

DANS UNE HUMBLE MASURE 9056 (69)

"Dans une humble masure sans porte ni toiture" 9056 (69)

"Dans Venise la rouge Pas un bateau qui bouge" 1341 (190, 192,194)

LA DANSE DES GORETS 4954 (82)

DANSE MACABRE 3137 (192,194)

DANSONS LA CAPUCINE 4955 (127)

"Dansons la capucine, n'y a pas de pain chez nous" 4955 (127)

DANSONS LA GIGUE 2839 (191,193,195)

"Dansons la gigue! J'aimais surtout ses jolis yeux" 2839 (191,193,195)

"Danube so blue, I'm longing for you" 3606 (128,132)

"DANZA, DANZA, DANZA, FANCIULLA" 947 (168)

"Danza, danza, fanciulla, al mio cantar" 947 (139,368)

DANZA, DANZA, FANCIULLA GENTILE 947 (139,368)

Dar. See also There

"Dar was ole Mister Johnson he had trouble of his own" 2441 (131)

DARBY KELLY 5894 (349)

THE DARBY RAM 4578B (249), 4579C (216), 4578D (44)

Dardanus 2960 (411)

"Dare I ask you, dear, to love me" 8672 (95)

"Darest thou now, O soul" 3558 (344)

"A dark and misty cloud is hiding" 3430 (245)

DARK EYES 6967 (36,128,132,236,343)
DARK IS THE EVEN 9212 (361)
"Dark is the even! Yet is the heaven" 9212 (361)
"Dark is the forest, so sullen deep, its fir-trees sombre,
        scornful" 2710 (159)
DARK IS THE FOREST, SULLEN, DEEP 2710 (159)
"The dark, starless midnight was quiet and peaceful" 154
        (340)
"Dark the night is, all is silent" 6389 (37)
"Dark the night o'er field and hill" 9282 (374)
DARK THE SOIL NEAR CRACOW CITY 6799 (159)
"Dark the soil near Cracow city, it will not be ploughed by
        me" 6799 (159)
"Dark was the hour when our heroes were dying" 8689 (20)
"Darker the mountain was growing" 9326 (154)
"A darkey heard the praises sung" 1780 (114)
"Darkness hath fallen on forest and stream" 432 (274)
THE DARKNESS IS FALLING 8798 (388)
"The darkness is falling, the day is nigh gone" 8798 (388)
"Darkness, what darkness in forest and dale" 432 (112)
THE DARKTOWN STRUTTERS' BALL 452 (236)
"A darky left his happy home" 689* (114)
DARKY SUNDAY SCHOOL 7536 (225)
DARLIN' 8236 (336)
DARLIN' COREY 7537A (227)
DARLIN' CORY 7537A (34)
DARLING, COME EARLY 4408 (95)
"Darling come early, when I arise" 4408 (95)
DARLING CORA 7537B (109,110)
DARLING COREY 7537C (389)
"Darling fold me to you closer, as you did in days of yore"
        3604 (246)
DARLING, GOODNIGHT 4331 (94)
"Darling, I am growing old" 762 (10,32,34,129,130,131,
        132,233,236,343)
DARLING I'LL SHOW YOU 2570 (36)
"Darling, I'll show you, something you know too" 2570
        (36)
"Darling, my darling, goodnight, goodnight!" 4331 (94,
        95)
DARLING NELLIE GRAY 1515 (10,28,32,34,109,110,129,
        130,132,184,233,236,279,366)
DARLING WIFE 5683 (92)
"Darling wife, it vexes me that you so thin should be" 5683
        (92)
"DAS IST IM LEBEN HÄSSLICH EINGERICHTET" 2644 (31,
        326,353)
"Das war der Graf von Rüdesheim" 2419 (31)
"Das was der Zwerg Perkéo im Heidelberger Schloss" 1411
        (31)
"Dashing thro' the snow in a one horse open sleigh" 2814
        (28,128,132,279,296,315,343,366,402)
"Dashing through the snow, in a one horse open sleigh"
        2814 (337)
"Dass der Ostwind Düfte" 3258 (250)
DASS SIE HIER GEWESEN! 3258 (250)
"DASS ZWEI SICH HERZLICH LIEBEN" 2285 (49)
Dat. See also That
"DAT CRANSELIJN DAT HI DRAGHET" 6443 (384)
"DAT DU MIN LEEVSTEN BÜST" 5265 (49,309,326,353)
Dat du myn Schätsken bist (tune) 5265
DAT SUITS ME 8237 (182)
"Dat weevil is a little bug from Mexico" 8188A (343)
DATTI PUR PACE 368 (253)
"Datti pur pace e vivi lieto" 368 (253)
"Daughter, daughter, what do you want today?" 6691 (159)

"Daughter, don't get married, else you will be sorry" 4333
        (95)
"Daughter, my daughter, don't marry, not yet!" 4388 (95)
The daughter of Jairus 3549 (123)
THE DAUGHTER OF PEGGY O'NEIL 1901 (128)
THE DAUGHTER OF ROSIE O'GRADY 854 (166,233)
"A daughter of Zion, from the holy temple" 6243 (37)
DAUGHTER, WHAT DO YOU WANT TODAY? 6691 (159)
THE DAUGHTERS OF ERIN 5916 (166,213)
DAUWT GIJ HEMELEN! 6444 (384)
"Dauwt, gij hemelen van boven" 6444 (384)
DAVID EX PROGENIE 8920 (360,361)
"David ex progenie, nata fuit hodie" 8920 (360,361)
DAVID OF THE WHITE ROCK 8666 (19,349)
"David, the Bard on his bed of death lies" 8666 (19,349)
"David the king was grieved and moved" 300 (109,110)
DAVID'S LAMENTATION 300 (109,110)
"Davie get your tambourin" 9106 (361)
Davydd ab Gwilym's conceit (tune) 8690
DAWN 1511 (78)
"The dawn is breaking" 7682 (113)
THE DAWNING OF THE DAY 5895 (16,133)
"Dawning steals softly across the sky" 4422 (343)
A DAY, A DAY OF GLORY 9049 (319,333,363,379)
"A day, a day of glory! A day that ends our woe" 9049
        (319,333,363,379)
"Day after day, when I pass by alone on promenade" 2890
        (6)
THE DAY COLUMBUS LANDED HERE 4229 (186)
DAY DAH LIGHT 8720 (11)
"The day has come when for the last time I meet you, my
        jolly jolly friends" 6961 (352)
"The day I left my mother's house" 7572 (242)
"The day is broke, my boys, march on" 7591 (44)
"Day is done, gone the sun" 8047 (28,366)
"DAY IS DYING IN THE WEST" 3452 (28,35,366)
THE DAY IS ENDED 201 (398)
"The day is ended ere I sink to sleep" 201 (398)
DAY NOW IS OVER 1624 (87)
"Day now is over, church bells are ringing and sunset and
        peace bless our earth anew" 1624 (87)
"Day oh! Day oh! Day dah light an' me wan' go home"
        8720 (11,252)
"Day of fame and blood is breaking" 2001 (159)
A DAY OF JOY AND FEASTING 9354 (337)
"A day of joy and feasting, of happiness and mirth" 9354
        (337)
"The day that I left Habana" 4120 (122)
"The day that I left my home for the rolling sea" 4120 (132)
"The day that I sailed away on the rolling sea" 4120 (350)
"The day that the sea by God's might became dry" 6272
        (318)
"Day the same as night, night the same as day" 6259 (318)
"The day was cold with rain" 396 (112)
"The day when I left the land to sail o'er the sea" 4120
        (329)
DAYDREAMS 1336 (93)
DAYENU 6190 (44)
"Daylight is fading, as the Cossacks start parading" 1923
        (237)
"The days are long and lonesome" 7729 (312)
"The days are too long while I'm workin' the road" 8149
        (381)
"Days I knew with you, are just a memory" 1621 (345)
"Days of autumn, days of autum" 202 (121)

352

DEN LIEBEN LANGEN TAG 5268 (353)
"Den lieben langen Tag hab i nur Not und Plag" 5268 (353)
"Den lubly Fan will you cum out tonight" 7478A (109,110)
"Den Pfeil zerbrach ich damals nicht" 2726 (218)
DEN RIDDER 4470 (86)
DEN SLAEP VAN'T KINDEKEN JESU 9234 (384)
"DEN UIL DIE OP DEN PEERBOOM ZAT" 6446 (203)
"Den vos guard Josep i la vostra esposa" 8858 (53)
DENK ES, O SEELE 4069 (98)
"Denk' ich zurück, drei Jahre sind's g'rad" 2102 (255)
"DENKST DU DARAN?" 847 (31)
"Denkst noch an jene schönen Stunden" 2833 (222)
"DENMARK, LOVELY FIELD AND MEADOW" 2974 (87)
DENMARK, MY FATHERLAND 3120 (87)
Dennis, don't be threatening (tune) 5975 (166,213)
THE DENS OF YARROW 7545 (72)
DEPARTURE OF THE KING 8703 (19)
DEPARTURE SONG 6319 (350)
LE DÉPIT 928 (108)
DEPRESSION BLUES 8242 (336)
"Depuis bien des années, la nuit comme le jour" 5063 (91)
"Depuis hier je cherche en vain mon maître" 1338 (2)
"Depuis plus de quatre mille ans" 9070 (82,91,127,154,383,
	388)
"Der du von dem Himmel bist" (Kayser) 1872 (42)
"Der du von dem Himmel bist" (Schubert) 3316 (97)
DER ER ET LAND 4005 (87)
"Der er et Land, dets Sted er højt mod Norden" 4005 (87)
"DER ER ET YNDIGT LAND" 1981 (87)
DER ER INGENTING, DER MANER 3129 (87)
"Der er ingenting, der maner som et Flag" 3129 (87)
DER ER TRE HJØRNESTENE 3143 (87)
"Der er tre Hjørnestene at bygge paa" 3143 (87)
"Der hat hingeben das ewig Leben" 2976 (99)
DER HAT VERGEBEN 2976 (326)
"DER HAT VERGEBEN DAS EWIG LEBEN" 2976 (49,226,326)
DER WERELD RAAD 6613 (384)
"Der wereld raad is dikwijls kwaad" 6613 (384)
THE DERBY RAM 4578A (14,231)
"Dere was an old Nigga, dey call'd him Uncle Ned" 1130 (129)
DERES A FÜ 5679 (164)
"Dere's a star in de Eas' on Christmas morn" 9398 (154,244,
	296)
"Dere's balm in Gilead to make de wounded whole" 8189 (76)
DERMOT AND SHELAH 5897 (406)
DERMOT, HIDE NOT THY ANGUISH 5898 (86)
"Derrièr' chez mon père y a t'un pommier d'août" 5080 (91)
"Derrièr' chez nous, ya-t-un étang" 5160 (186,187)
DERRY DOWN 8106 (44)
"Derweil ich schlafend lag ein Stündlein wohl vor Tag"
	1162 (226)
Y DERYN PUR 8667 (19)
"Y Deryn pur à'r adain las" 8667 (19)
Des Abends, wenn ich schlafen geh (tune) 5398 (309)
Des Fraises (tune) 4925
DES JAHRES LETZTE STUNDE 3335 (326)
"Des Jahres letzte Stunde ertönt mit ernstem Schlag" 3335
	(99,229,326)
"Des jardins de la nuit" 1043 (121)
DES KRIEGERS BRAUT 4126 (224)
"Des le mi pampa querida salté a la cordillera" 3789 (284)
DES MÜLLERS BLUMEN 3297 (229)
DES SOMMERS LETZTE ROSE 5921 (326)
"DES WINTERS ALS HET REGENT" 6623 (202)
"DES WINTERS ALS HET REGHENT" 6623 (202)
"DESCEND CREATOR, HOLY DOVE" 6885 (159)

"Desde la mi ventana te he visto arando" 7235 (219)
"Desde que te fuiste, mi amante bien" 4173 (9)
DESDEMONA'S ARIA 3849 (6)
Dese. See also These
DESE BONES AM GWINETER RISE AGAIN 8243A (184)
DESE BONES GONNA RISE AGAIN 8243B (185)
DESE BONES GWINE TO RISE AGAIN 8243C (80)
"Des steamboats on de Hudson, I guess dey's mighty fine"
	7989 (191)
"El desembre congelat confús se retira" 8848 (53)
DESENGAÑÉMONOS YA 2274 (269)
"Desengañémonos ya, mal pagado pensamiento" 2274 (269)
El deseo de la pulpillo 2043-2044
THE DESERTER 4579 (198)
DESESPERACIÓN 4486 (73)
DESESPERANZA 4487 (73)
DESIRE 3116 (341)
DESMOND'S SONG 5884 (166,213)
"The despot's heel is on thy shore, Maryland! my Maryland!"
	9175A (161)
DESPRECIO 4279 (86)
DESSU IN POU DE PEILLE 9057 (361)
"Déšť drobný šelestí na listech osik" 2006 (73)
DÉŠŤ V SAMOTĚ 2006 (73)
Destatevi 2853 (180)
"Destiny's secret held in your keeping" 3844 (4)
DESVENTURADO 7546 (113)
DEUTSCHE UNSTERBLICHKEIT 2541 (31)
DEUTSCHES FREIHEITSLIED AUS BÖHMEN 5269 (43)
Ein deutsches Kriegslied ich möchte wohl der Kaiser sein
	2562 (395)
"DEUTSCHLAND, DEUTSCHLAND ÜBER ALLES" 1563 (31,
	42,49,294,326,353)
DEUTSCHLAND ÜBER ALLES 1563 (294)
DAS DEUTSCHLANDLIED 1563 (49)
DEUTSCHMEISTER-REGIMENTS-MARSCH 1839 (396)
Les deux avares 1367 (211)
Deux épigrammes des Clement Marot 2979-2980
LES DEUX MANIÈRES D'AIMER 4959 (174)
THE DEVIL AND THE FARMER'S WIFE 4597B (110), 4597C
	(72), 4597D (109), 4597G (389)
"The devil he came to the farmer one day" 4597D (109)
"The devil put on a different face" 2442 (7)
DEVILISH MARY 4580A (171), 4580B (72)
THE DEVIL'S NINE QUESTIONS 7547A (44), 7547B (171,173)
THE DEVIL'S TEN QUESTIONS 7547C (262)
Le devin du village 3111 (153)
DÉVIRÉ KATIE 8722 (286)
"Déviré Katie, déviré l'en caille mama ou" 8722 (286)
DEVOTION ARISE! 3178 (253)
"Devotion arise! and join my hope" 3178 (253)
A DEW FROM HEAVEN 6596A (95)
"Dewch i'r helfa, mae'r udgyrn yn canu" 8676 (349)
DEWY IS THE GRASS 5679 (164)
"Dewy is the grass, my dear horse do not feed" 5679 (164)
DEWY VIOLETS 3193 (274)
Dey. See also They
"Dey tell me Joe Turner's come and gone" 8381 (109,110)
DI DUE FIGLI VIVEA PADRE BEATO 3865 (5)
UN DI ERO PICCINA 2300 (143)
"Un di (ero piccina) al tempio vidi un bonzo" 2300 (143)
"Di 'me'n po, bel galant, bel giuvo" 6103 (338)
DI MEZINKE OYSGEGEBN 3950 (318)
"DI PIACER MI BALZA IL COR" 3101 (6)
DI PROVENCE 3860 (310)
DI PROVENZA IL MAR 3860 (4)
"DI PROVENZA IL MAR, IL SUOL" 3860 (4,298,310)

THE DONKEY 7552 (28,343)
DONKEY RIDING 4230 (186,214)
DONKEY SONG 8772 (286)
DONN' INGRATA 1027 (180)
"Donn' ingrata, senza amore" 1027 (180)
"UNA DONNA A QUINDICI ANNI" 2558 (6)
"LA DONNA È MOBILE" 3852 (3,122,132,237,329,391)
"DONNA LOMBARDA PERCHÉ NUN M'AMI?" 6078 (325)
DONNA NON VIDI MAI 2898 (3)
"Donna non vidi mai simile a questa!" 2898 (3)
DONNER LE BONJOUR 4964 (127)
"Les donneurs de sérénades et les belles écouteuses" (Debussy)
        796 (208)
"Les donneurs de sérénades et les belles écouteuses" (Dupont)
        946 (190,192,194,357)
DONNEZ, DONNEZ 2414 (2)
"Donnez, donnez, pour une pauvre âme" 2414 (2)
DON'T BITE THE HAND THAT'S FEEDING YOU 2522 (129)
DON'T GET MARRIED 4333 (95)
DON'T GIVE UP THE SHIP 3948 (233)
"DON'T LET YO' WATCH RUN DOWN" 8250 (184)
DON'T LIE, BUDDY 8251 (336)
"DON'T SIT UNDER THE APPLE TREE WITH ANYONE ELSE
        BUT ME" 3748 (236)
"Don't we look pretty when we're dancing" 7624 (185,216)
DON'T YOU GO, TOMMY 2171 (189)
"DON'T YOU HEAR THE LAMBS A-CRYING?" 8252 (332)
"DON'T YOU LEAVE ME HERE" 2539 (336)
"DON'T YOU LET NOBODY TURN YOU 'ROUN'" 8253 (409)
"Don't you remember, don't you know" 8232 (185)
"Don't you remember with emotion and devotion" 4196
        (284,322)
DONZELLE, FUGGITE 616 (138)
"Donzelle, fuggite procace beltà" 616 (138)
DER DOPPELGÄNGER 3304 (98,250,272)
DORMI, DORMI, BEL BAMBIN 9338 (155)
"Dormi, dormi, bel bambin re divin" 9338 (155)
"DORMI, DORMI, O BEL BAMBIN" 9199 (154,337)
"Dormi Jesu, mater ridet" 1178 (344)
"DORMIRÒ SOL NEL MANTO MIO REGAL" 3828 (5,299)
"Dormons, dormons tous" 2207 (152)
DORNRÖSCHEN 5270 (49)
"Dornröschen war ein schönes Kind" 5270 (49)
DOROTKA 6702 (295)
"Dors, dors, mon petit gars" 4900 (91)
"Dors entre mes bras, enfant plein de charmes!" 3898 (275)
"Dors, mignon, près de ta mère" 1360 (136,241)
DORS, MON ENFANT 3898 (275)
"Dors mon enfant, clos ta paupière" 1307 (149)
"Dort baym taychi, nit vayt fun dem shtetl" 6200 (318)
"Dort blinket durch Weiden" 3266 (330)
DORT, IM FRIEDHOF, SAH ICH DICH 5817 (92)
"Dort, im Friedhof, sah ich dich zum erstenmal, weintest
        an der Mutter Grab in tiefster Qual" 5817 (92)
"DORT IN DEN WEIDEN STEHT EIN HAUS" 4148 (353)
"Dort in Dobos, ja in Dobos fiel schon längst der erste Schnee"
        5762 (27)
DORT NIED'N IN JENEM HOLZE 5197 (41,49,99,309,326)
"Dort niedn in jenem Holze da liegt ein Mühlen stolz" 5197
        (41)
"Dort nied'n in jenem Holze leit sich ein Mühlen stolz"
        5197 (49,99,309,326)
"Dort oben am Berg in dem hohen Haus!" 2239 (330)
"Dort oben, dort oben vor der himmlischen Tür" 5465 (99)
"Dort Saaleck, hier die Rudelsburg" 54 (31,99)

"Dort unten im Talle läuft's Wasser so trüb" 5223 (99)
DORT UNTEN IN DER MÜHLE 1281 (326)
"Dort unten in der Mühle sass ich in süsser Ruh" 1281 (326)
"Dort, wo der alte Rhein mit seinen Wellen" 3232 (31)
DORT WO DER RHEIN 3232 (326)
"DORT WO DER RHEIN MIT SEINEN GRÜNEN WELLEN" 3232
        (99,353)
"DORT, WO DIE KLAREN BÄCHLEIN RINNEN" 5271 (42)
"DORT ZWISCHEN OCHS UND ESELEIN" 9064 (354)
"Dost thou know that fair land where the lemons bloom"
        3729 (2)
"Dost thou recall thy wistful promise?" 1291 (140)
"Dost thou remember Erin, on the alien shore today" 5861
        (280)
"DOSTIG YA VYSSHEĬ VLASTI" 2614 (5)
LES DOTZE VAN TOCANT 8850 (56)
"Les dotze van tocant; ja es nat el Rei Infant" 8850 (56)
D'OÙ VENEZ-VOUS, FILLETTE 4949 (67)
"D'où venez-vous, fillette, le rossignole qui vole?" 4949
        (67)
"D'où venez vous si crotté, Monsieur le curé?" 5173 (187)
"D'OÙ VIENS-TU, BELLE BERGÈRE" 9059D (354)
"D'OÙ VIENS-TU, BERGÈRE" 9059A (154,186,187,383,388)
        9059B (127), 9059C (82)
DOUBT 1262 (340)
"DOUCE DAME JOLIE" 1414 (36)
"La douce lumière de l'astre du jour" 5013 (88)
"Douce nuit, Sainte nuit dans le ciel tout reluit" 1408 (88)
EL DOUDOU 4190 (86)
DOUGHNUTS 8030 (335)
DOUN THE BURN 1691 (100,103)
D'OUND V'ENANATZ, FILHETO? 4949 (67)
"D'ound v'enanatz, filheto, lou roussignóu que volo?" 4949
        (67)
"Doux plaisirs, tout enchante où vous êtes" 2548 (149)
DOUX SAUVEUR, ENFANT D'AMOUR 9060 (361)
THE DOVE (Folksongs, Iran) 5853 (86)
THE DOVE (Folksong, Peru) 6662 (279)
THE DOVE (Folksongs, Wales) 8667 (19,235,349)
THE DOVE (Yradier) 4120 (122,132,142,322,329,350)
"Dove, dove sei gita" 294 (180)
"THE DOVE HAS TWIN WHITE FEET" 8778 (36)
DOV'È QUESTA ROMAGNOLA? 6098 (325)
DOVE SEI GITA 294 (180)
"DOVE SEI STATO MIO BELL' ALPINO?" 6079 (238)
"DOVE SONO I BEI MOMENTI" 2585 (6)
THE DOVER SAILOR 9438 (198)
"Down a down, down a down, thus Phyllis sung" 2820 (118)
DOWN A DOWN THUS PHYLLIS SUNG 2820 (118)
"Down along the river just a-settin' on a rock" 8575 (336)
DOWN AMONG THE CANE BRAKES 1111 (129)
DOWN AMONG THE DEAD MEN 4582 (13,235,273,402)
DOWN AMONG THE SHELTERING PALMS 2707 (128,131)
DOWN BY THE BRIDGE 4295 (94)
"Down by the bridge in old Zvolen" 4295 (94)
DOWN BY THE GREENWOOD SHADY 7529B (72)
DOWN BY THE OLD MILL STREAM 2995 (205)
DOWN BY THE RIVER 8254 (28,366)
DOWN BY THE RIVERSIDE 8255 (44)
DOWN BY THE SALLEY GARDENS 5899 (36)
DOWN BY THE SALLY GARDENS 5899 (215)
"Down by the Sally gardens my love and I did meet" 5899
        46)
DOWN BYE STREET 1689 (259)
"Down Bye Street, in a little Shropshire town" 1689 (259)

DOWN DE ROAD 958 (132)

"Down de road, down de road, on my way to home" 958 (132)

"DOWN DEEP WITHIN THE CELLAR" 1077 (240)

"Down Derry down (tune) 8106 (109,110,173,225)

DOWN, DOWN, DOWN 1875 (227)

"DOWN, DOWN, PROUD MIND" 709 (116)

"DOWN FROM HEAVEN ON YOUR PEOPLE" 171 (159)

DOWN IN A COAL MINE 7553 (115,129,130,132,214)

"Down in a coal mine, underneath the ground" 7553 (115, 129,130,132,214)

"DOWN IN A VALLEY" 624 (144)

"Down in a valley, sing hallelu" 9400 (332)

"Down in Alabama when the breeze begins to sigh" 830 (129,130)

"Down in de cornfield hear dat mournful sound" 1118 (28, 128,129,130,132,233,279,366)

DOWN IN DEMERARA 4583 (402)

"Down in New England, far far, away" 3889 (131)

"Down in some lone valley in a lonesome place" 7939 (34, 313)

DOWN IN TENNESSEE 3400 (128)

"Down in that valley, that valley so low" 7554F (267)

"Down in the jungles lived a maid" 1808 (32,34)

"Down in the lonely churchyard where the violets fade and bloom" 7589C (243)

DOWN IN THE VALLEY 7554A (173), 7554B (227), 7554C (35,37), 7554D (393), 7554F (267)

"Down in the valley, the valley so low" 7554A (173), 7554C (35,37)

"Down in the valley there below" 2863 (259)

"Down in the valley, valley so low" 7554B (227), 7554D (393), 7554E (242)

"DOWN IN THE WILLOW GARDEN" 7555 (227)

DOWN IN YON FOREST (Carols, England) 8921 (307)

DOWN IN YON FOREST (Carols, United States) 9356A (261,268), 9356B (44)

"Down in yon forest be a hall, sing May, Queen May, sing Mary" (Carols, United States) 9356A (261,268)

"Down in yon forest stands a hall, sing May, sing May, sing Mary" (Carols, United States) 9356B (44)

"Down in yon forest there stands a hall" (Carols, England) 8921 (307)

"Down on a farm in Arkansas" 7414 (185)

"Down on de Mississippi" 1121 (129,130)

DOWN ON ME 8256 (409)

"Down on me Down on me" 8256 (409)

"Down on my knees when the light passed by" 8456 (409)

DOWN ON THE BIG RANCH 2967 (219)

"Down on the cattle ranches" 2967 (219)

"Down on the jetty there is a maiden who is waiting" 4291 (207)

DOWN SHE SAT 4411 (94)

"Down she sat and loud she cried, ay, ay" 4411 (94)

"Down the mountainside doth a streamlet glide" 5238 (132)

DOWN THE RIVER 7556 (44)

"Down the river floats a bee tree" 6305 (95)

"Down the street I hear them selling" 7464 (113)

"Down the trail of dreams I'm with you once again" 3690 (132)

DOWN THE VILLAGE STREET 5672 (164)

"Down the village street I wandering go" 5672 (164)

DOWN WENT McGINTY 1093 (114,128,131,225)

"Down went McGinty to the bottom of the wall" 1093 (114, 128,131,225)

DOWN WHERE THE SAMA FLOWS 4258 (350)

"Down where the verdant meadows lie" 4194 (86)

"Down with the rosemary and bays" 8906A (334), 8906B (378)

"Down yonder green valley" 8683 (46,199,402)

DOWNE-A-DOWNE 2820 (197)

"Downe-a-downe, downe-a-downe, thus Phillis sung" 2820 (197)

THE DOWNWARD ROAD IS CROWDED 8257 (409)

DOXOLOGY 379 (233)

"A dozen raw, a plate of slaw, a chicken and a roast" 2124 (204)

THE DRAFTEE 5661 (95)

DRAFTEE'S BLUES 8258 (336)

THE DRAGON 4190 (86)

DRAUSS IST ALLES SO PRÄCHTIG (Jürgens) 1838 (31)

DRAUSS IST ALLES SO PRÄCHTIG (Silcher) 3478 (326)

"Drauss ist alles so prächtig und es ist mir so wohl" (Jürgens) 1838 (31)

"Drauss ist alles so prächtig und es ist mer so wohl" (Silcher) 3478 (326)

"Draussen im Schwabeland wächst a schöns Holz (tune) 5281 (42,309,326,353)

"DRAUSSEN INS FRÜHLING, DRAUSSEN IST MAI" 3640 (257)

DRAW CLOSER, MY LOVE 3871 (9)

"Draw near, young men and learn from me my sad and mournful tale" 7955 (129,130)

THE DREADNOUGHT 9439A (173), 9439B (320)

THE DREAM 5389 (95)

DREAM CRADLE SONG 448 (199)

DREAM FACES 1741 (129,130,132)

DREAM IN THE TWILIGHT 3634 (112,330)

THE DREAM OF DES GRIEUX 2315 (3)

DREAM OF LOVE 2153 (329)

A DREAM OF PARADISE 1356 (394)

"Dream so fair, dream I follow while ever 'tis fleeing" 2313 (4)

DREAM SONG 434 (343)

DREAM VALLEY 2933 (275)

DREAM-WORLD 942 (121)

DREAMES AND IMAGINATIONS 1815 (144)

"Dreames and imaginations are all the recreations abscence can gaine me" 1815 (144)

"Dreamily over the roofs" 3955 (259)

DREAMING (Dailey) 752 (114,128,131,236)

DREAMING (Wagner) 3921 (348)

DREAMING BY THE HANDMILL 6951 (287,288)

"Dreaming, dreaming, of you sweetheart I am dreaming" 752 (114,128,131,236)

"Dreaming, to thee my heart I surrender" 1041 (121,348)

"Dreamlike, the mists are drifting" 3027 (121)

DREAMS (Wagner) 3921 (122,220,241)

"Dreams of mystical enchantment" 3921 (122)

"Dreamy lies the limpid water" 3684 (295)

DREARY LIFE 7557 (120)

"Dreh dich, dreh dich, Rädchen" 5272 (49)

DREH DICH, RÄDCHEN 5272 (49)

DIE DREI DÖRFER 67 (31)

"Drei Ellen gute Bannerseide" 3221 (31)

DIE DREI GROSSEN CHRISTLICHEN FESTE 9025 (99)

DREI KLÄNGE SIND'S 5273 (31)

"Drei Klänge sind's, sie tönen hold und rein" 5273 (31)

"Drei Könge wandern aus Morgenland" 719 (97,337)

DREI KONINGENLIED 9237 (384)

DREI LAUB AUF EINER LINDEN 5274 (49,309,326)
"Drei Laub auf einer Linden blühen also wohl" 5274 (49, 309,326)
DIE DREI LIEDER 2176 (250)
DREI LILIEN 5275 (31,42,49,99,309,326,353)
"Drei Lilien, drei Lilien, die pflanzt ich auf mein Grab" 5275 (31,42,49,99,309,326,353)
DIE DREI REITER 5276 (31)
DIE DREI RÖSELEIN 5421 (31,99)
"DREI SCHIFFE SAH ICH FAHREN VORBEI" 8945E (354)
"Drei Tage schon, dass Nina" 2769 (167)
"Drei Tage schon ruht Nina" 2769 (311)
"DREI TRAGE SIND VERFLOSSEN" 2769 (138)
Der 23. Psalm 3323 (90)
DAS DREIGESPANN 6952 (31)
DREIMAL PFIFF DIE AMSEL 5718 (92)
"Dreimal pfiff die Amsel, dreimal pfiff die Amsel" 5718 (92)
DREIMOL OMS STÄDELE 5277 (309,326)
"Dreimol oms Städele dreimol oms Huas" 5277 (309,326)
DRIE KONINGEN, DRIE KONINGEN 9236 (203)
"Drie Koningen, drie Koningen, geeft mij een nieuwen hoed" 9236 (203)
"DRIE MAAL DRIE IS NEGEN" 6448 (316)
DE DRIE RUITERTJES 6449 (384)
DRIE SCHUINTAMBOERS 6450 (201)
"Drie schuintamboers die kwamen uit het Oosten" 6450 (201)
DRILL, YE TARRIERS, DRILL 612
DRINK OLD ENGLAND DRY 4584 (198)
"Drink thy milk, leaving none in the cup" 5843 (86)
DRINK TO ME ONLY 4588 (13,199,235,349)
"DRINK TO ME ONLY WITH THINE EYES" 4588 (13,28,35, 36,70,122,132,199,233,235,236,237,279,297, 329,343,349,366,385,397,402)
DRINKING (Fischer) 1077 (273)
DRINKING SONG (Folksongs, Poland) 6806 (159)
DRINKING SONG (Mascagni) 2298 (132)
DRINKING SONG (Nicolai) 2655 (5)
DRINKING SONG (Thomas) 3727 (4)
"Drinking songs, what an old, old, story!" 2109 (364)
DRINKLIED (Servaas de Konink) 3432 (278)
"Driven by the whirl-wind" 3799 (288)
DRIVIN' STEEL 8259 (184)
"Drivin' steel, (huh) drivin' steel, (huh)" 8259 (184)
DROBA AUF DR RAUHE ALB 5278 (326)
"Droba auf dr rauhe Alb jubeidi, jubeida" 5278 (326)
DROBA IM OBERLAND 5279 (309)
"Droben im Oberland, ei, da ist es wunderschön!" 5279 (326)
"Droba im Oberland, ei, da ist's so wunderschön!" 5279 (309)
DROBEN IM OBERLAND 5279 (326,353)
"Droben im Oberland, hei, da ist es wunderschön!" 5279 (353)
"DROBEN STEHET DIE KAPELLE" 1834 (326)
DROOP NOT, YOUNG LOVER 1460 (273)
"Droop not, young lover; pine not in sadness" 1460 (273)
"Dros gaerau'r nen diflanna'r dydd" 8691 (20)
Drot og Marsk 1608 (87)
THE DROWSY SLEEPER 7418B (312)
"Drüben hinterm Dorfe steht ein Leiermann" 3320 (98)
The drummer (tune) 7155
THE DRUMMER-BOY 5007A (199)
"A drummer-boy from war came marching gaily" 5007A (199)

DRUNGHE, DRUNGHETE! 6080 (51)
THE DRUNKARD 7558 (243)
THE DRUNKARD'S CHILD 2741 (189)
THE DRUNKEN SAILOR 9440A (29,35,173,235,320)
DRUNT IN DER GRÜNEN AU 5280A (309)
"Drunt in der grünen Au steht a Birnbaum, schau, schau, juhe" 5280A (309)
DRUNT' IN DER LOBAU 3642 (396)
DRUNTEN IM UNTERLAND 5281 (42,309,326,353)
"Drunten im Unterland, da ist's halt fein" 5281 (31,42, 99,309,326,353)
DRUNTEN IN DER GRÜNEN AU 5280B (49,326)
"Drunten in der grünen Au, steht ein Birnbaum tragt Laub, juchhe!" 5280B (49,326)
DRY BONES 8260A (76)
DRYADS, SYLVANS 1497 (275)
"Dryads, Sylvans with fair Flora" 1497 (275)
"Du ac arswydus yw'r hanes am heddiw" 8689 (20)
DU ÄR MIN AFRODITE 1176 (355)
"Du är min Afrodite, den ur havet födda" 1176 (355)
"Du all mein Hort, glaub' meinem Wort" 1255 (167)
DU BESITZT MEIN HERZ 3640 (257)
"Du bist das Land wo von den Hängen der Freiheit Rosengarten lacht" 1373 (31)
"DU BIST DIE RUH'" 3260 (36,275)
"DU BIST MEIN TRAUM" 3613 (256)
DU BIST MÎN 1945 (49)
"Du bist mîn ich bin dîn" 1945 (49)
"Du bist nicht auf der Welt" 2404 (31)
"Du bist Orplid, mein land!" 4075 (121)
DU BIST WIE EINE BLUME (Rubinstein) 3117 (241,385)
DU BIST WIE EINE BLUME (Schumann) 3379 (36,112,122, 132,136,176,241,277,329)
"Du bist wie eine Blume, so hold und schön und rein" (Rubinstein) 3117 (241,385)
"Du bist wie eine Blume so hold und schön und rein" (Schumann) 3379 (36,112,122,132,136,176,241, 277,329)
DU DANSKE MAND 2661 (87)
"Du danske Mand! af al din Magt syng ud om vor gamle Mor!" 2661 (87)
"DU, DU DALKETER JAGERSBUA" 5282 (353)
"Du, du dalketer Jagersbua, i, i werd dir's auszahln!" 5282 (353)
"DU, DU LIEGST MIR IM HERZEN" 5283 (36,42,99,326, 353)
"Du, du, little baby child" 6447 (316)
"Du fjärilsmö av rosigt Yoshiwara" 1061 (355)
"DU GABST UNS UNSER TÄGLICH BROT" 5284 (49)
DU GAMLA, DU FRIA 7303 (188)
"DU GAMLA, DU FRIA, DU FJÄLLHÖGA NORD" 7303 (135,188)
"Du gingst fort, geliebtes Idol" 2184 (217)
"Du hast ein Zeil vor den Augen" 5269 (43)
"Du hast mir gehört, du warst mein Weib" 1991 (222)
"Du Heissgeliebte, ob ich nah oder ferne" 2263 (168)
"Du herrlich Glas, nun steht du leer" 3355 (273)
"Du holde Kunst, in wie viel grauen Stunden" 3254 (97, 99,220,226,274,385)
"Du junges Grün, du frisches Gras!" 3364 (226)
"DU KUNDE JU EJ VETA" 1007 (355)
DU LIEBE, LIEBE SONNE 4093 (49)
"Du liebe, liebe Sonne bescheine mich" 4093 (49)
"Du lieber, heilger, frommer Christ" 3468 (99,337)
"Du lieblicher Stern du leuchtest so fern" 3352 (141,229)

"Dziewcyno, dziewcyno al sercu memu" 6704
   (159)
"DZIEWCZĘ A BUZIĄ JAK MALINA" 1199 (295)
"Dziś, dziś, dziś, dziś, dziś, dziś, dziś, dziś, Poskoweczki
   dajcie ognia, bo dziewczyna tego godna" 6813
   (159)
"Dziś jeszcze swoje szmatki" 6747 (295)
DZISIAJ BAL U WETERANÓW 6705 (159)
"Dzisiaj bal u weteranów kuzdy zna tych panów" 6705
   (159)
DZISIAJ W BETLEJEM 9289 (295)
"Dzisiaj w Betlejem, dzisiaj w Betlejem, Wesoła nowina!"
   9289 (295)

L'È BEN VER 6083 (36,238)
"L'è ben ver, l'è ben ver ch'jo mi slontani" 6083
   (36)
"L'e ben ver l'e ben ver che me slontani" 6083 (238)
"E BISSELE LIEB UND E BISSELE TREU" 3479 (326)
E C'ERAN TRE ALPIN 6081 (238)
"E c'eran tre alpin tornavan dalla guerra" 6081 (238)
"È COL SIFFOLO DEL VAPORE" 6082 (238)
"È, dio mè tu, lo calhé, ound as toun nïou?" 4920
   (63)
"E DOVE T'AGGIRI" 631 (139)
"'e ge melaina pinei de dendrea auten" 2349
   (278)
"E la Lioneta l'era něl camp" 6084 (338)
"E lassù su la montagna gh'era su 'na pastorèla" 6122
   (238)
E LA VIOLETTA 6084 (238)
"E la violetta la va, la va, la va, la va" 6084
   (238)
"L'è na fieta di quindes ani" 6054 (338)
"È passo de dessa'l! È passo della'l l'a'io!" 5070 (63)
"È pronta la partenza" 6048 (51)
THE E-RI-E 7574A (32,34,227)
"E s'io fossi pesce, il mare passerei" 6045 (51)
"E SARÒ DUNQUE OGNOR" 296 (411)
È SOGNO? O REALTÀ 3838 (4)
"È sogno? o realtà...Due rami enormi" 3838 (4)
"È strano! È strano! 3859 (6,143,176,221)
"E Susanna non vien!" 2585 (6)
"È TORNATO IL MIO BEN" 479 (180)
"E tu di'ci 'lo parto, adio!" 745
"Each day, dear love, my road leads far" 2249
   (259)
EACH MINUTE I LOOK AT YOU 4253 (219)
"Each morn with basket laden a Spanish maiden" 2724
   (132)
"Each spring, one early fragrant morning as larks rise
   singing in the air" 3284 (141)
THE EAGLE OWLS 2248 (159)
EARL BRAND 8041 (243)
THE EARL OF SALISBURY'S PAVAN 492 (306)
"Early at dawn I'm at work, and high up you are winging"
   6749 (159)
EARLY BLOWING, VIOLETS GROWING 3193 (138)
"Early blowing, violets growing, on my heart perfume
   bestowing" 3193 (138)
"Early in the morning, just like bees they're swarming"
   6882 (295)

EARLY, MY DEAR 4430 (95)
"Early in the morning" 8536 (409)
"Early on a Monday morning, high up on the gallows tree"
   5947 (34)
"Early on a Sunday morning, high upon a gallows tree"
   5947 (293)
EARLY ONE MORNING 4589 (13,72,199,234,343,349,
   397,402)
"Early one morning as sunlight rose glist'ning" 670* (295)
"Early one morning just as the sun began to glow" 4589
   (343)
"Early one morning, just as the sun was rising" 4589 (13,
   72,199,234,349,397,402)
EARLY TO BED 4590 (28,279,366)
"Early to bed and early to rise" 4590 (28,279,366)
EARTH AND SKY 399 (98,273)
EARTH TO-DAY REJOICES 9016 (333)
"Earth today rejoices, alleluya, alleluya" 9016 (333)
"The earth was green, the sky was blue" 1597 (344)
"The earth was made in six days" 7536 (225)
EAST VIRGINIA 7889B (293)
EASTER CAROL 9061 (271)
"Easter day was a holiday of all the days in the year"
   4679 (46)
EASTER FLOWERS 8816 (371)
"Easter flow'rs are blooming bright" 8816 (371)
Easter hymn (tune) 8913
EASTER SONG 1349 (123,346,398,400)
EASTERN ROMANCE 3037 (407)
EASY RIDER 8262A (227,336,389)
"Easy Rider, just see what you have done" 8262A (336,
   389)
"Easy rider, see what you done done" 8262A (227)
EATING GOOBER PEAS 7563 (225)
L'EAU DE SOURCE 4875 (62)
"L'eau de la source te fera mourir" 4875 (62)
"EBBEN, N'ANDRO LONTANA" 613 (301)
"EBBEN? NE ANDRÒ LONTANTA" 613 (143)
"Ecce gratum et optatum" 1374 (321)
ECCE NOVUM GAUDIUM 9020 (361)
"Ecce novum gaudium, ecce novum mirum" (ECCE NOVUM
   GAUDIUM) 9020 (361)
"Ecce novum gaudium, ecce novum mirum" (ECCE QUOD
   NATURA) 9021 (360,361)
ECCE QUOD NATURA 9021 (360,361)
"Ecce quod natura mutat sua jura" 9021 (360,361)
Ecco bella regina (tune) 9213
Ecco, Dorinda, il giorno 361 (134)
"Ecco il petto! Ah, non fuggite" 2261 (218)
"Ecco il punto, o Vitellia" 2554 (2)
"Echame ese toro pinto" 4284 (284)
ECHO (Rousseau) 3112 (278)
DAS ECHO (Schubert) 3261 (141)
THE ECHO (Schubert) 3261 (141)
THE ECHO CAROL (Carols, France) 9062 (363)
ECHO CAROL (Carols, Germany) 9140 (165)
"L'echo des bois des sons de la musette" 2965 (88)
ECHOES ARE SOUNDING 9300 (154)
"Echoes are sounding through the silent skies" 9300 (154)
L'éclair 1506
"Los ecos de tus quejas y sollozos porpiedad!" 4506 (73)
"Écoutez, amis, écoutez, Tran lar di rèno" 5105 (91)
ECSTACY 941 (121,140,237)
EDDIG VALÓ DOLGOM 5681 (22)
"Eddig való dolgom a tavaszi szántás" 5681 (22)
EEN EDEL FONTEIN 6451 (384)

ES FREIT' EIN WILDER WASSERMANN 5299A (49,309, 353), 5299B (49)

"Es freit' ein wilder Wassermann in der Burg wohl über dem See" 5299A (49,99,309,353), 5299B (49)

"Es geht bei gedämpfter Trommel Klang" 3492 (31,99)

"ES GEHT EIN' DUNKLE WOLK HEREIN" 5300 (49,309)

ES GEHT EIN RUNDGESANG 5301 (353)

"Es geht ein Rundgesang an unserm Tisch herum" 5301 (353)

"ES GEHT EINE DUNKLE WOLK HEREIN" 5300 (49,231, 326)

Es geht eine helle Flöte 206 (326)

"Es geht wohl zu der Sommerzeit" 5450 (43)

"Es geyt shoyn avek zich der heyliger" 1004 (318)

"Es g'fallt mer nummen eini" 5362 (31)

"Es gibt auf der Welt doch erstens kein Geld" 3231 (222)

"ES GIBT KEIN SCHÖNRES LEBEN" 5302 (40)

"ES GING EIN' JUNGFRAU ZARTE" 5303 (309)

"Es grünet ein Nussbaum vor dem Haus" 3386 (97,112, 220)

"ES HAT DIE ROSE SICH BEKLAGT" 1154 (36,98,99,136)

ES HAT SICH HALT ERÖFFNET 9152 (40,412)

"Es hat sich halt eröffnet das himmlische Tor" 9152 (40, 412)

"ES HATT EIN BAUER EIN SCHÖNES WEIB" 5304 (42,353)

"Es hatte ein Bauer ein schönes Weib" 5304 (31)

"Es hatten drei Gesellen ein Kein Kollegium" 445 (31,99)

"Es het e Buur es Töchterli, mit Name heisst es Bäbeli" 7351 (156)

ES ISCH KEI SÖLIGER STAMME 7363 (230)

"Es isch kei söliger stamme, Oweder der Chüherstamm" 7363 (230)

"ES IST AUF ERD KEIN SCHWERER LEIDEN" 5305 (226)

"ES IST BESTIMMT IN GOTTESRAT" 2377 (141,326,328)

ES IST EIN REIS ENTSPRUNGEN 2869 (412)

ES IST EIN' ROS' ENTSPRUNGEN (Brahms) 398 (307)

"ES IST EIN ROS ENTSPRUNGEN" (Praetorius) 2869

"ES IST EIN SCHNEE GEFALLEN" 5306 (41)

ES IST EIN SCHNITTER 5307 (41,49)

ES IST EIN SCHNITTER, DER HEISST TOD" 5307 (309)

"Es ist ein Schnitter, der heisst Tod, hat Gwalt vom grossen Gott" 5307 (41,99,309)

"Es ist ein Schnitter, heisst der Tod, hat G'walt vom grossen Gott" 5307 (226)

"Es ist ein Schnitter, heisst der Tod, hat Gwalt vom grossen Gott" 5307 (49)

"ES IST NICHT WAHR, DASS AUF DEM THRON" 110 (218)

"Es ist nichts auf dieser Erde" 2131 (241)

"ES IST VOLLBRACHT" 131 (330)

"Es iz gefloygn, di gilderne pave" 6202 (318)

"ES KAM EIN ENGEL VOM HOHEN HIMMEL" 9191 (354)

"ES KAM EIN HERR ZUM SCHLÖSSLI" 7364 (49,156,230)

"Es kann ja nicht immer so bleiben" 1661 (99)

"Es kommt die zeit zum Offenbaren" 5565* (49)

ES KOMMT EIN SCHIFF 9153 (40,49)

"Es kommt ein Schiff, geladen bis an sein' höchsten Bord" 9153 (40,49)

"Es kommt ein wundersamer Knab" 2011 (31)

"ES KLAPPERT DIE MÜHLE AM RAUSCHENDEN BACH" 5276 (353)

"ES KLINGT EIN HELLER KLANG" 2627 (31)

"Es klingt so prächtig" 3235 (250)

"ES LAGEN IM FELDE DIE HIRTEN BEI NACHT" 2017 (49)

ES LEBEN DIE STUDENTEN 4969 (31)

"Es leben die studenten stets in den Tag hinein" 4969 (31)

"ES LEBT DER SCHÜTZE FROH UND FREI" 5308 (326)

"Es lebt' eine Vilja, ein Waldmägdelein" 2098 (254)

"ES LIEGT EIN SCHLOSS IN OESTERREICH" (Folksongs, Germany) 5309 (309)

"ES LIEGT EIN SCHLOSS IN ÖSTERREICH" (Seeon) 3419 (49)

"Es liegt eine Krone im grünen Rhein" 1654 (31,327)

"ES LIESS SICH EIN BAUER EIN' FALTROCK SCHNEIDN" 5333 (309)

"Es lockt und säuselt um den Baum" 400 (275)

"Es mahnt der Wald, es ruft der Strom" 3294 (229)

"ES MUSS EIN WUNDERBARES SEIN" 2150 (209,348)

"Es muss gelingen! Alles soll nach Wunsch und Willen gehen!" 3513 (3)

ES MUSS WAS WUNDERBARES SEIN, VON DIR GELIEBT ZU WERDEN 273 (257)

ÉS O MEU AMOR E NÃO DIGAS QUE NÃO 6904 (57)

"Es reden und träumen die Menschen viel von bessern künftigen Tagen" 3275 (229)

"Es regt sich was im Oderwald" 1633 (31)

ES REITEN ITZT 5310 (49)

"Es reiten itzt die ungrischen Husaren" 5310 (49)

ES RITTEN DREI REITER 5276 (42,326,353)

"Es ritten drei Reiter wohl über den Rhein" 5590 (49)

"Es ritten drei Reiter zum Tore hinaus" 5276 (31,42,99, 326,353)

"Es ruht mit ernstem Sinnen auf mir dein Blick" 3003 (226)

"Es sang vor langen Jahren" 3022 (229)

"Es sass ein Salamander" 421 (250)

"ES SASS EIN KLEIN WILD VÖGELEIN" 5311 (41,49)

"Es schienen so golden die Sterne" 2218 (31)

"ES SCHLÄGT EINE NACHTIGALL AN EINEM WASSERFALL" 5312 (326)

"Es schleicht mir was ins Herz und doch ich weiss nicht was" 3879 (168)

"Es stehen drei Sterne am Himmel" 5292 (99)

"ES STEHN DREI BIRKEN AUF DER HEIDE" 1793 (31)

ES STEHT EIN BAUM IM ODENWALD 5237 (31,99,309, 353)

ES STEHT EIN LIND IN JENEM TAL 5313 (49)

"Es steht ein Lind in jenem Tal, ach Gott, was tut sie da?" 5315 (326)

"Es steht ein Lind in jenem Tal, ist oben breit und unten schmal" 5313 (49)

"Es steht ein Baum in jenem Tal" 3709 (275)

"Es steht ein Soldat am Wolgastrand" 2105 (254)

"ES STEHT EIN WIRTSHAUS AN DER LAHN" 5314 (353)

ES STEHT EINE LIND IN JENEM TAL 5315 (326)

"ES STEHT EINE MÜHLE IM SCHWARZWÄLDER TAL" 3350 (326,353)

ES TAGET VOR DEM WALDE (Bürki) 466 (156)

ES TAGET VOR DEM WALDE (Folksongs, Germany) 5326 (49,326)

"Es taget vor dem Walde, stand auf Kätterlin!" 5316 (326)

"Es taget vor dem Walde, stand uf, Kätterlin" (Bürki) 466 (156)

"Es taget vor dem Walde, stand uf, Kätterlin!" (Folksongs, Germany) 5316 (49)

"ES TAGT, DER SONNE MORGENSTRAHL" 1282 (49)

"ES TANZT EIN BI-BA-BUTZEMANN" 5317 (40,49)

ES TÖNEN DIE LIEDER 5318 (326)

"Es tönen die Lieder, der Frühling kehrt wieder" 5318 (326)

"Far away from wife and children" 8078 (189)
"Far away, in ancient Krakow" 6849 (295)
"Far away in sunny meadows" 761 (129,130,132)
"Far away, into the sea, the sun goes down" 1747 (191, 193,195)
"Far beyond Niemen I go! My steed stands awaiting, oh come love, embrace me" 4125 (295)
FAR CALIFORNIA 7580 (242)
FAR FROM ME 4822 (70)
"Far from me my loved one went" 4822 (70)
"Far in the hills I hear the nightingale" 4423 (28)
FAR IS MY LOVE 4855 (36)
"Far is my love to the castle he's taken" 4855 (36)
FAR LOFTIER MOUNTAINS 4143 (87)
"Far loftier mountains are found on the earth than here" 4143 (87)
"Far off, far off, across the bridge" 6237 (318)
FAR OFF IS OUR LAND 759 (7)
"Far off within the sombre forest" 812 (292)
"Far over yon hills of the heather sae green" 7039 (100, 349)
"Far over yon hills of the heather so green" 7039 (100,349)
"Far up above flies the heron" 5759 (279)
FAR YONDER 1873 (295)
"Far yonder, out yonder, From forest's green bower" 1873 (295)
FARANDOLE 4973 (95)
"Fare thee weel, my native cot" 7094 (294)
"Fare thee well" (Mozart) 2579 (274)
FARE-THEE-WELL, FOR I MUST LEAVE THEE 8053 (128, 129,131)
"Fare thee well, old Joe Clark" 7874A (227)
FARE YOU WELL 7581 (72)
"Fare you well, my dear, I must be gone" 4784 (36)
"Fare you well, my own true love, and it's fare you well for awhile" 7581 (72)
"Fare you well, Old Joe Clark" 7874B (225)
"Fare you well, Old Joe Clarke" 7874A (109,110)
"Fare you well! You do not know" 4078 (112)
FAREWELL (Folksongs, Poland) 6699 (159)
FAREWELL! (Franz) 1156 (210)
A FAREWELL (Strauss) 3627 (276)
FAREWELL (Weyrauch) 4002 (209)
FAREWELL (Wolf) 4078 (112)
"Farewell and adieu to you, fair Spanish ladies" 9483A (29), 9482D (44), 9483E (401)
"Farewell and adieu to you fine Spanish ladies" 9483A (29)
"Farewell and adieu to you, Spanish ladies" 9483A (34), 9483B (320)
"Farewell and adieu unto you, Spanish ladies" 9483A (402)
"FAREWELL! BUT WHENEVER YOU WELCOME THE HOUR" 5903 (166,213,349)
"Farewell calls of flying cranes sound in the air" 5759 (37)
FAREWELL COMPANIONS 3155 (9)
"Farewell companions, all you pals I love so dearly" 3155 (9)
"Farewell, dear Erin's native isle, for here I cannot stay" 4751 (198)
"Farewell ev'ry old familiar face" 4099 (345)
"Farewell, farewell, I leave you" 2955 (295)
"Farewell! farewell! my little gypsy sweetheart" 6954 (352)
"Farewell! farewell, my Polly dear!" 9477 (86)

FAREWELL GRANADA 186 (245)
"Farewell, Granada, from you I'm going" 186 (142)
"Farewell, Granada! Our bonds I sever" 186 (245)
"Farewell lass, I'm leaving, for my country calls me" 6680 (295)
FAREWELL MAIDEN 6680 (295)
FAREWELL, MANCHESTER! 1059 (294,349)
"Farewell, Manchester! Noble town, farewell!" 1059 (294,349)
"Farewell, Mignon! be joyous! Weep not, I pray" 3728 (3)
"Farewell, Mother, you may never press me to your heart again" 3071 (28,34,129,130,279,366)
"Farewell, my camp and gypsy sweetheart" 6954 (352)
FAREWELL, MY COUNTRY 6681 (295)
"Farewell, my country, beloved homeland" 6681 (295)
FAREWELL, MY DEAR BRETHREN 7582 (86)
"Farewell, my dear brethren, the time is at hand" 7582 (86)
FAREWELL MY DREAM 7397 (113)
"Farewell my dream of joy and fortune" 7397 (113)
FAREWELL MY GYPSY CAMP 6954 (352)
"Farewell now, my sweetheart" 6950 (95)
"Farewell, sweet Jane, I now must go across the roaming sea" 8039 (262)
FAREWELL TO FIUNARY 7038 (103,105)
FAREWELL TO GROG 3207 (225)
FAREWELL TO MY HOME 613 (143)
"Farewell to old England, the beautiful!" 4177 (34)
FAREWELL TO SUMMER 5335 (28,366)
"Farewell to the Highlands, farewell to the North!" 7119 (102,105)
FAREWELL TO THE OLD YEAR 6779 (295)
FAREWELL TO THEE 1233 (122)
"Farewell to thee, Cymru" 8682 (349)
"Farewell to Thee, Farewell to Thee" 2133 (236)
"Farewell to thee for ever, thou haughty palace" 3857 (5)
"Fare-well, thou valiant glorious child!" 3924 (4)
"FAREWELL, UNKIND, FAREWELL" 897 (197)
"Farewell, ye dungeons dark and strong, the wretch's destinie!" 7101 (365)
"Farewell, ye mountains, ye beloved meadows" 644 (2)
THE FARMER (Folksongs, England) 4594 (28,366)
THE FARMER (Folksongs, United States) 7583 (145)
"Farmer asked the boll weevil, 'Where you been so long?'" 8188F (336)
"A farmer came to camp one day" 281 (161,225)
THE FARMER COMES TO TOWN 7583 (109,110,335)
"A farmer he lived in the West Countree" 4546 (14)
"THE FARMER IN THE DELL" 4595 (28,366)
"THE FARMER IS THE MAN" 7583 (109,110,293,335)
THE FARMER-LABOR TRAIN 1426 (293)
"A farmer was plowin' his field one day" 4597A (170)
"A farmer was plowing his field one day" 4597A (173)
THE FARMER'S BOY 4596A (402), 4596B (198)
FARMERS' CAROL 2793 (307)
THE FARMER'S CURST WIFE 4597A (249), 4597E (186), 4597H (242), 4597I (260,263)
"A farmer's dog jumped over the stile" 4675 (249)
THE FARMER'S SON 7584 (126)
THE FARMER'S SONG 7585 (37)
FARMLAND BLUES 8269 (336)
THE FARMYARD 4598 (28,366)
"Fast to thy girdle fix thy father's brand!" 8694 (349)
"The fat turkeys across the fields" 632 (190,192,194)

"Fiddle-de-dee, fiddle-de-dee, the fly has married the
    bumblebee" 4600 (173,214)
FIDDLE-DEE-DEE 4600 (249)
"Fiddle-de-dee, fiddle-de-dee, the fly has married the
    bumble bee" 4600 (249)
FIDDLE TUNE 9371 (332)
THE FIDDLER (Folksongs, Ireland) 5905 (133)
THE FIDDLER (Moniuszko) 2472 (295)
FIDDLER'S TUNE 8217 (184)
Der fidele Bauer 1031 (256)
Fidelio 229-233
FIDUCIT 445 (31,99)
"FIE, NAY, PRITHEE, JOHN" 2910 (349)
"Fierce flames are soaring" 3867 (2)
"Fierce the beacon light is flaming" 8695 (234,349)
FIERO, ACERBO DESTIN 948 (181)
"Fiero, acerbo destin dell' alma mia" 948 (181)
"Fiery day is ever mocking" 8657 (349)
FIESTA 6347 (350)
"The fifers play, the pipers too, follow we all, it is the
    hour! 5137 (95)
"The fifteenth day of July with glist'ning spear and shield"
    4685 (86)
FIFTY CENTS 2124 (204)
FIGLIA MIA, NON PIANGER 1494 (181)
"Figlia mia, non pianger, no no" 1494 (181)
Il figliuol prodigo 2844 (298)
FILEUSE 4974A (47), 4974B (64)
FILIA HOSPITALIS 2162 (31)
FILL THE BUMPER FAIR 5906 (166,213)
"Fill the bumper fair, ev'ry drop we sprinkle o'er the brow
    of care, smooths away a wrinkle" 5906 (166,213)
LA FILLE AU CRESSON 4975 (61)
FILLE AUX YEUX DE PERVENCHE 4348 (178)
"Fille aux yeux de pervenche sur le ruisseau ne te penche"
    4348 (178)
LA FILLE DE PARTHENAY 4976 (383)
La fille du régiment 866-868
LA FILLE DU ROI LOYS 4977 (91)
LES FILLES DE CADIX 809 (93,191,193,195,208)
"Filli, Filli, nol niego" 628 (218)
FINCH' HAN DAL VINO 2566 (4)
"Finch' han dal vino calda la testa" 2566 (4)
FIND WORK, MY DAUGHTER 4978 (95)
"Find work, my daughter, you can milk a cow" 4978 (95)
FINE AND TRUE 249 (285)
"Fine and true, fine and true, is the girl whose eyes are
    blue" 2749 (285)
FINE KNACKS FOR LADIES 898 (119,144,196)
"Fine knacks for ladies, cheap, choice, brave and new!"
    898 (119,196)
"Fine knacks for ladies, cheape choise brave and new" 898
    (144)
THE FINE OULD IRISH GINTLEMAN 456 (189)
FINESTRA BASSA 6088 (51)
"Finestra bassa e patrona crudela" 6088 (51)
FINESTRA CHE LUCEVI 6086 (51)
"Finestra che lucevi ed or non luci" 6086 (51,310)
FINESTRA CHE SPLENDEVI 6086 (325)
FINETTA FAIR AND FEAT 626 (119)
"Finetta, Finetta, fair and feat" 626 (119)
FINGO PER MIO DILETTO 6089 (211)
"Fingo per mio diletto vezzi lusinghe amor" 6089 (211)
"Die Finken schlagen, der Lenz ist da" 1652 (328)
"Finland too, deserves all honour" 4818 (124)
Finlandia 3464 (124,343)

FINLANDIA HYMN 3464 (124)
FINLANDIA-HYMNI 3464 (124)
FINNEGAN'S WAKE 7586 (109,110)
FINNISH CAVALRY MARCH FROM THE THIRTY YEARS'
    WAR 4849 (124)
FIOCCA LA NEVE 677* (121)
LO FIOLAIRE 4974B (64)
Fior di Giaggiolo gli angeli 2295 (132)
FIOR DI TOMBA 6090 (338)
FIORE INGRATO 95 (180)
"Fiore ingrato, ingrato fiore, perche t'armi di rigore" 95
    (180)
FIRE DOWN BELOW 9442A (234), 9442B (205), 9442C
    (216)
FIRE, FIRE 540 (144)
"Fire, fire, fire, fire, loe here I burne" 540 (144)
"Fire! Fire! Put out the fire!" 8767 (11)
"Fire in the east, fire in the west" 8495 (409)
"Fire in the galley, fire down below" 9442A (234)
THE FIREMAN'S SONG 7587 (189)
"THE FIRST DAY OF CHRISTMAS" 8998C (332), 8998D
    (307)
"First day of Christmas my true love sent to me" 8998E
    (242)
"The first day of the week, cometh Mary Magdalene" 742
    (200)
"The first good joy our Mary had" 8985A (334)
"The first good joy that Christmas brings" 8985A (337)
"THE FIRST GOOD JOY THAT MARY HAD" 8985A (35,
    296,307,333,337,361,363,410)
FIRST HELP YOURSELF 6475 (86)
"First help yourself, unsheath your blade" 6475 (86)
FIRST I SAW YOU 5817 (92)
"First I saw you in the churchyard, and you wept, standing
    by the grave where in your mother slept" 5817 (92)
"The first joy of Mary was the joy of one" 8985E (888)
"First night when I come home" 7594 (243)
THE FIRST NOEL 8923 (28,79,165,206,251,296,315,366,
    388)
THE FIRST NOEL (FYFE'S NOEL) 8926 (361)
"The first Noel an angel sung" 8926 (361)
"The first Noel, the angel did say" 8923 (28,79,154,251,
    315,366,388)
"The first Noel the angels did say" 8923 (165,206,296)
THE FIRST NOWEL 8923 (361)
"The first Nowell the Angel did say" 8923 (361)
THE FIRST NOWELL 8923 (33,35,125,154,199,233,236,
    244,271,305,307,319,333,334,337,349,363,410)
"The first Nowell that the Angel did say" 8923 (334)
"THE FIRST NOWELL THE ANGEL DID SAY" 8923 (33,35,
    38,39,125,199,233,236,244,271,305,307,319,337,
    349,363,410)
"The first Nowell the angels did say" 8923 (333)
THE FIRST PRIMROSE 1385 (209)
"The first rejoice Our Ladye got" 8985B (361)
THE FIRST SNOWDROPS 4461 (37)
"The first time I saw the boll weevil, he was standin' on the
    square" 8188D (171)
"The first time I seen the boll weevil he was a-sitting on the
    square" 8188C (389)
"First when I came to this place of troubles I was free" 7110
    (102,105)
"First when Maggie was my care" 7202 (101,105)
"First young lady all around in town" 8042 (110)
DES FISCHERS LIEBESGLÜCK 3266 (330)
"FISH, FISH, FISH, TINY LITTLE FISH" 6828 (159,295)

FISHELECH KOYFN 6197 (318).

THE FISHERMAN (Folksongs, Hungary) 5680 (95)

THE FISHERMAN (Folksongs, Italy) 6091 (37)

"Fisherman Peter out on the sea" 8290 (409)

FISHERMAN'S BLISS 3266 (330)

THE FISHERMAN'S SONG (Bellman) 265 (135)

FISHERMAN'S SONG (Folksongs, West Indies) 8725 (11)

"Fishermen sleep when the fish don't bite" 8725 (11)

FISHING SONG 6637 (37)

FISKAFANGET 265 (135)

"Five dollars a day is a white man's pay" 8247 (109,110)

"Five long years in the army" 8188A (293)

"FJÄRILN VINGAD SYNS PAA HAGA" 262 (188)

FJÄRRAN I SKOG 283 (188)

"Fjärran i skog, laangt fraan dig skiljd" 283 (188)

Fjeldlieder 1894 (124)

"Fjorton aar tror jag visst att jag va'" 7325 (135,137)

"FJORTON AAR TROR JAG VISST ATT JAG VAR" 7325 (188)

THE FLAG 3129 (87)

"The flag of our country is floating on high" 7812 (44)

THE FLAG OF OUR UNION 3932 (189)

THE FLAG OF OUR UNION FOREVER 702 (129,130)

FLAG OF THE FREE 3908 (28,366)

"Flag of the free, fairest to see" 3908 (28,366)

FLAGET 3129 (87)

"UN FLAMBEAU, JEANNETTE, ISABELLA" 9066 (82,337, 383,388)

"The flame we adore in this temple" 825 (146)

"The flames of hell are burning now within me" 2598 (292)

THE FLAMING CAMP FIRE 6808 (295)

FLAMME EMPOR! 1258 (31,326)

"Flamme empor! Flamme empor! Steige mit lodern dem Scheine" 1258 (31,326)

"Die Flamme lodert, milder Schein" 243 (99)

THE FLAT RIVER RAFTSMAN 7588 (72)

"A flaxenheaded cowboy, as simple as may be" 3455 (48)

Die Fledermaus 3607-3609

"LA FLEUR QUE TU M'AVAIS JETÉE" 317 (3)

FLEURE DE TOMBE 6090 (338)

FLIEG' ZUR LIEBSTEN 5794 (92)

"Flieg' zur Liebsten, Schwälbchen, flieg' zu, fleh' dass sie ihr Fenster auftu'" 5794 (92)

Der fliegende Holländer 3899-3901

"Flies in the buttermilk, skip to my Lou" 8005 (36,109, 110,115)

"Flies in the buttermilk, two by two" 8005 (173)

"A FLIGHT OF PASSING CLOUDS" 3035 (340)

THE FLIGHT OF THE EARLS 5907 (349)

FLING OUT THE BANNER (Marshall) 2280 (129,130)

"FLING OUT THE BANNER! LET IT FLOAT" (Calkin) 523 (28)

"Fling out the banner on the breeze" 2280 (129,130)

"FLING WIDE THE GATES" 3547 (400)

THE FLIRTATIOUS MULATA 4290 (207)

Flis 2471 (295)

THE FLOATING TRIBUTE 6000 (349)

"Flocks are sporting, doves are courting" 584 (208,348)

FLOODS OF SPRING 2941 (176,241)

FLOR, BLANCA FLOR 6348 (247)

"Flor, blanca flor, flor de las flores" 6348 (247)

FLOR DE LIMÓN 6349 (9)

FLOR DE MONTAÑA 2353 (303)

"Flor de montaña fina y lozana del Indio bravo" 2353 (303)

FLOR ENTRE FLORES 4496 (73)

LA FLOR QUE COGISTE 4497 (73)

La Flora 1192 (217)

FLORA MACDONALD'S LAMENT 7039 (235)

"FLORA, WILT THOU TORMENT ME?" 2525 (197)

FLORELLA 7589A (81), 7589B (81)

FLORES NEGRAS 2713 (9)

FLORIAN'S GATE 3934 (159)

"Florian's gate wide open, Gee-up, horse my pretty, my whip cracks you gallop" 3934 (159)

FLORIAN'S SONG 1289 (136,237,348)

FLORIDA CAKEWALK 1802 (184)

Il Floridante 1461 (211)

Il floridoro 3599

FLORILLA 7589C (243)

FLORYJAŃSKA BRAMĄ 3934 (159)

"Floryjańską bramą, Wjadę otworzoną, biczyskiem se smigam" 3934 (159)

FLOS DE RADICE JESSE 2869 (375)

FLOW GENTLY SWEET AFTON (Hume) 1733 (28,35,132, 233,279,336,366)

"Flow gently, sweet Afton, amang thy green braes" (Hume) 1733 (28,233,279,366)

"Flow gently, sweet Afton, amang thy green braes" (Folksongs, Scotland) 6987A (101,102,163,234,349)

"Flow gently sweet Afton, among thy green braes" (Folksongs, Scotland) 6987A (232,367), 6987B (100)

"Flow gently, sweet Afton among thy green braes" (Hume) 1733 (35,132,336)

FLOW MY TEARES 899 (144)

"Flow my teares fall from your springs" 899 (144)

FLOW MY TEARS 899 (116)

"Flow my tears, fall from your springs" 899 (116)

"FLOW NOT SO FAST YE FOUNTAINES" 900 (196)

"Flow, O waves, O stream flow on" 6277 (318)

"Flow on, lovely Dee! Flow on, thou sweet river!" 4544 (37)

"Flow teares from your springs" 899 (107)

FLOWER CAROL 8935 (199,271)

THE FLOWER OF FINAE 5908 (133)

THE FLOWER OF KILLARNEY 5909 (235)

THE FLOWER OF MAGHERALLY, O 5910 (133)

FLOWER SONG (Folksongs, United States) 7494 (21)

FLOWER SONG FROM THE XVITH CENTURY 5828 (92)

A FLOWER TO ME THOU SEEMEST 3379 (132)

"A flowering chestnut green and fair" 3386 (276)

FLOWERS O' THE FOREST 7040A (17,100,103,104,199), 7040B (100)

FLOWERS OF JOY 7306 (188)

"Flowers of joy in the earth's dark mould, they can never thrive" 7306 (188)

THE FLOWERS OF THE FOREST 7040A (163,235,349)

"THE FLOWERS THAT BLOOM IN THE SPRING" 3664 (132)

"Flowers, wildwood flowers, in a sheltered dell they grow" 2304 (279,366)

FLOWING RIVER 4262 (350)

"The flow'rets all sleep soundly beneath the moon's bright ray" 4153 (28,279,366)

"The flow'rlets have been sleeping long since in moonlight" 4153 (209)

"The flow'rs have long been sleeping, beneath the moon so bright" 4153 (70)

"FLOWS A BROOKLET IN MY HOMELAND" 4255 (207)

Die Flucht ins Glück 882-883
DER FLÜCHTLING 5669 (24)
DER FLUG DER LIEBE 5339 (99)
LA FLÛTE DE PAN 792 (362)
THE FLUTE OF PAN 792 (362)
THE FLY AND THE BUMBLEBEE 4600 (214)
FLY AWAY, CROW 1034 (199)
FLY, BIRDIE, FLY 1539 (87)
"Fly, birdie, fly! o'er Fura's waters flowing" 1539 (87)
FLY MY AFFECTION 6301 (219)
"Fly, my affection, fly to my dear one" 6301 (219)
FLY MY SONG TO HEAVEN 2483 (159)
"Fly my song to heaven, leave city walls behind you" 2483 (159)
FLY MY VOICE SO LOVING 6761 (159)
"Fly my voice so loving, towards that road yonder" 6761 (159)
FLY NOT YET 5911 (166, 213)
"Fly not yet; 'tis just the hour when pleasure, like the midnight flow'r" 5911 (166, 213)
FLY, SWEET SONG 2483 (295)
"Fly sweet song, sweet love song, Oh fly from city's busy throng" 2483 (295)
"Flying came the swiftest falcons" 2485 (295)
FLYING CRANES 5759 (37)
FLYING, SINGING 5181 (21)
FLYV, FUGL, FLYV 1539 (87)
"Flyv, Fugl, flyv over Furesøens Vove" 1539 (87)
Die Försterchristel 1770 (256)
FOG 1535 (358)
THE FOG BELL 2851 (205)
"The fog comes on little cat feet" 1535 (358)
FOGGY DEW ("I courted her all of the winter") 4601B (109)
THE FOGGY DEW ("Oh! a wan cloud...") 5912 (166, 213)
THE FOGGY DEW ("Over the hills...") 7590 (72)
THE FOGGY DEW ("When I was a young man...") 4601A (399)
THE FOGGY DEW ("The wisest soul by anguish torn...") 5912 (16)
THE FOGGY, FOGGY DEW 4601A (35, 48, 173, 215, 331)
"Foi numa léva que a cabocla Maringá" 611 (284)
FOLG' NUR DEINEM HERZEN! 3641 (257)
Une folie 2347 (411)
FOLK SONG 3395 (385)
FOLLOW ME UP TO CARLOW 5913 (172)
FOLLOW THE DRINKIN' GOURD 529 (389)
FOLLOW THE GLEAM 889 (343)
"FOLLOW THY FAIR SUN" 542 (119)
FOLLOW WASHINGTON 7591 (44)
FOLLOW YOUR SAINT 541 (117, 144)
"Follow your saint, follow with accents sweet" 541 (117, 144)
"FOLLOWE THY FAIRE SUNNE" 542 (144)
FONTEINE MOEDER MAGHET REINE 9240 (361)
THE FOOLISH BOY 4602 (249)
"Foolish indeed is the swain" 2209 (152)
A fool's preferment 2911 (277)
FOOM, FOOM, FOOM! 8852 (337)
THE FOOTSTOOL 6326 (86)
"For a carousal where all is madness" 2566 (4)
"FOR A LANCER WAR GOES GAILY" 3708 (159)
"For a lover's caprice, love will be revenged" 770 (151)
"For a' that, and a' that and thrice a mickle's a' that" 6997 (101, 105)

"For a toast, your own will avail me" 321 (4)
"For angels from the high Citadel of the heav'ns above" 9093 (231)
FOR BALES 1253 (161)
"For Casey would waltz with a strawberry blond" 3942 (114, 115, 128, 131, 132, 204, 233, 236)
FOR CONVENTS, IT'S OVER 2411 (5)
"For dire revenge my burning heart is crying" 2598 (221)
"For France were making two Grenadiers" 3357 (122)
"For He is King of kings" 8506 (76)
"FOR HE'S A JOLLY GOOD FELLOW" 5020 (70, 128, 132, 233, 236)
"For I'm goin' to Heav'n above" 8463 (409)
"For I'm old, and I'm helpless and feeble" 393 (114, 129, 130, 131)
"For it's fair weather when good fellows get together" 470 (240)
"For I've worked eight hours this day" 2234 (114)
FOR JOY OF HEART 8924 (371)
"For joy of heart, come, bear apart" 8924 (371)
For lack of gold (tune) 7007
"For love that hovers o'er your pathway" 572 (150)
"For Mary's little baby son" 3413 (378)
"For me her hand, the heart disclosing" 1140 (210)
FOR MUSIC 1155 (136, 209)
"For, Oh! her lanely nichts are lang" 7058 (101)
"For Robin was a rovin' boy" 7175A (100, 102)
"For spreading plain and peak that tow'rs, we give thanks" 2696 (123)
"FOR THE BEAUTY OF THE EARTH" 1938 (28, 233, 343)
"For the fate of his son" 2350 (147)
"For the helpless and the young, Wide the gates we fling" 6251 (318)
"FOR THE LOVE MY HEART DOTH PRIZE" 363 (368)
"FOR THE MOUNTAINS SHALL DEPART" 2371 (90)
"For the sunshine that kisses your beautiful lips is my rival" 2037 (248)
"For there's the white house yonder" 7598 (189)
FOR THESE BITTER TEARS 2766 (253)
FOR THOU ALONE ART HOLY 2763 (367)
"For three long days my Nina" 2769 (368)
"For to redeem our souls from thrall, Christ is the Savior of us all" 8951 (361)
"FOR US THIS DAY IS GIV'N A SON" 9154 (333)
"For you said goodbye we parted" 745 (233)
"For your last sleep you leave us now" 673 (295)
FORD'S DREAM 3838 (4)
"Foreboding fears of ill my wonted courage vanquish" 1272 (5)
DIE FORELLE 3267 (395)
Forest Green (tune) 8971A
FOREST SOLITUDE 402 (112)
FOREST, THY GREEN ARBORS 3076 (138)
"Forest, thy green arbors shaded" 3076 (138)
"FOREST TREES ARE SWAYING" 1893 (124)
FOREST TREES STAND TALL AND BARE 6692 (159)
"Forest trees stand tall and bare, a queer noise went thro' the air" 6692 (159)
LE FORGERON ("Le forgeron rebat le fer") 5163 (187)
LE FORGERON ("Sous ton lourd...") 4979 (82, 88)
"Le forgeron rebat le fer" 5163 (187)
FORGET NOT THE FIELD 5914 (166, 213, 349)
"Forget not the field where they perish'd" 5914 (166, 213, 349)

FORGET THE WORLD 5708 (95)

FORGOTTEN 726 (236)

"Forgotten you? Well, if forgetting" 726 (236)

"Forier di morte già il crepuscol cade" 3920 (237, 240, 298)

FORN FORSTU FUN MIR AVEK 6198 (318)

"Forn forstu fun mir avek, tayer lebn mayns" 6198 (318)

THE FORNICATOR 7041 (365)

"La forosetta mia mi viene a far la spia" 6080 (51)

FORSAKEN (Folksongs, United States) 7592 (243)

FORSAKEN (Koschat) 1955 (132, 279)

"Forsaken, forsaken, forsaken am I" 1955 (132, 279)

"Forse vien fuor l'aurora, e queste dolci note e questi accenti" 1746 (278)

"Fort Amherst's hardy youthful crew" 9462 (186)

"Forth from its scabbard pure and bright" 327 (161)

FORTH TO THE BATTLE 8694 (349)

"Forth to the battle, onward to the fight" 8694 (19)

"LA FORTUNA E UN PRONTO ARDIR" 3192 (404)

FORTUNE 3192 (404)

"Fortune boldly aims at all" 3192 (404)

"FORTUNE FLOURISHED IN OUR CIRCLE" 6845 (295)

THE FORTUNE TELLER 3370 (220)

FORTY YEARS ON 384 (402)

"Forty years on, when afar and a-sunder" 384 (402)

"Forward! Charge! On with sword blades" 2242 (7)

FORWARD MARCH! 5156 (21)

"Forward march, no retreat" 2241 (7)

La forza del destino 3841-3844

"Fostes ao Senhor da Serra" 6925 (58)

FOUND MY LOST SHEEP 8271 (332)

THE FOUNTAIN THE PARK 1509 (114)

"The fountains mingle with the river" 2934 (344)

FOUR CORN FIELDS 1781 (248, 322)

"Four fascist rebel gen'rals" 7251 (7)

THE FOUR GENERALS 7251 (7, 35, 293)

FOUR IN ONE 7593 (86)

"The four insurgent generals" 7251 (293)

"The four insurgent gen'rals" 7251 (35)

FOUR NIGHTS 7594 (243)

"Four things that our Poles are famed for" 6785 (295)

FOUR WINDS 693 (78)

"Four winds blowing through the sky" 693 (78)

"Fourteen years I had seem'd just to be" 7325 (137)

"FOURTEEN YEARS, I SHOULD SAY, WAS MY AGE" 7325 (188)

THE FOX 7595A (173), 7595C (242), 7595D (216)

"The fox started out one moonshiny night" 7595C (242)

"Fox went out on a chilly night" 7595A (173)

THE FOX WENT OUT ON A MOONSHINY NIGHT 7595B (399)

"The fox went out on a starlit night" 7595D (216)

THE FOX WENT THROUGH THE TOWN, OH! 7595D (80)

The fox's sleep (tune) 6034

FRÀ PATALUC 6092 (338)

FRA POCO A ME RICOVERÒ 875 (3)

"Fra poco a me ricoverò" 875 (3)

"Fräulein Goldfisch schwamm in dem Goldfischglas wohl über den weissen Sand" 1829 (255)

FRÄULEIN KUNIGUNG 5215 (99)

"Frag' ich mein beklomm'nes Herz" 3099 (311)

FRAG' OB DIE ROSE 1490 (36)

"Frag' ob die Rose süss von Duft" 1490 (36)

"Frage mich immer fragest umsonst!" 3976 (250)

DAS FRAGENDE MÄDCHEN 2343 (224)

FRAGMENT EINER SOLO-KANTATE 588 (217)

"The fragrance of pine boughs perfumes all the air" 1395 (208)

"FRAGRANT MALVA, PERTTY FLOW'R" 1879 (285)

"Fragt di welt an alte kasche" 6169 (231)

A FRAIL WILDWOOD FLOWER 7596 (243)

"Frainchman he don't lak to die in de fall" 7895 (109, 110)

FRAISES DU BOIS JOLI 8027 (21)

"Fran flydda dar jag än har kvar" 609 (135)

"LA FRANCE EST BELLE" 2628 (88)

FRANKIE AND ALBERT 7597B (227)

FRANKIE AND JOHNNIE 7597A (32)

"Frankie and Johnnie were lovers" 7597A (32, 34)

FRANKIE AND JOHNNY 7597A (109, 110, 128, 129, 131)

"Frankie and Johnny were lovers" 7597 (109, 110, 128, 129, 131)

"Frankie was a good woman, ev'rybody knows" 7597B (227)

FRATRICIDE 4859 (124)

Frau Luna 2137 (255)

FRAU MUSICA SINGT 5243 (42, 49)

"Frauen, Frauen lasst mich euch Genossin heissen" 5659 (22)

Frauen in Metropol 3229 (257)

Frauenliebe und Leben 3365 (276)

FRED'RIK HENDRIK VAN NASSAU 6459 (201)

"Fred'rik Hendrik van Nassau, Prince van Oranje" 6459 (201)

FREE AMERICA 4555 (115, 173)

FREE AMERIKAY 4555 (44)

FREE AT LAST 8272 (409)

"Free at last, free at last, I thank God I'm free at last" 8272 (409)

FREE MEN, ARISE 8703 (235)

"FREEDOM IS THE THING MOST DEAR" 1831 (188)

"Fregt di velt an alte kashe" 6169 (318)

FREIBURGER BUMMELLIED 3211 (31)

FREIHEIT (Daniel) 759 (7, 35, 293)

FREIHEIT (Gansser) 1203 (31)

FREIHEIT (Groos) 1402 (31, 49, 99, 326)

"FREIHEIT, DIE ICH MEINE" 1402 (31, 49, 326)

Der Freischütz 3964-3967

FREISINN 3380 (226)

DIE FREIWILLIGEN VON IJPERN 2543 (31)

"Fremd bin ich eingezogen" 3319 (98)

FREMONT CAMPAIGN SONG 7598 (189)

FRENCH CATHEDRALS 7599 (343)

THE FRENCH GIRL 721 (132)

FRÈRE JACQUES 4980 (82, 91, 127, 187, 383, 402)

"Frère Jacques, Frère Jacques, dormez vous, dormez vous?" 4980 (82, 91, 127, 187, 383, 402)

FRÈRE PATALOUC 6092 (338)

"Fresh carnations! Now for whom can I spare them" 3791 (142)

"FREU DICH, ERD UND STERNENZELT" 8873 (354)

FREUDE 2163 (31)

FREUDE, SCHÖNER GÖTTERFUNKEN 3337 (326, 353)

"Freude, schöner Götterfunken, Tochter aus Elysium" (Beethoven) 248 (99)

"Freude, schöner Götterfunken, Tochter aus Elysium" (Schulz) 3337 (99, 326, 353)

"Freuden sonder Zahl blühn im Himmelssaal" 3307 (226, 330)

"Freudvoll und leidvoll, gedankenvoll sein" 3011 (99)

"Freuet euch, freuet euch, freuet euch zur Stund" 9414 (354)

FREUET EUCH ZUR STUND 9414 (354)

FREUND TYUKODI, HEI! 5816 (92)

"Freund Tyukodi, hei! ist der rechte Mann!" 5816 (92)

"FREUNDE, DAS LEBEN IST LEBENSWERT!" 2093 (222)

"Freunde, trinkt in vollen Zügen musenstädtschen Gerstensaft" 2159 (31)

"FREUNDE, VERNEHMET DIE GESCHICHTE" 27 (391)

FREUNDLICH BLICK ICH 3855 (391)

"Freundlich blick ich auf diese und jene" 3855 (391)

FREUNDLICHE VISION 3623 (272)

FREUNDSCHAFT UND LIEBE 1083 (99)

"FREUT EUCH DES LEBENS" 2628 (31, 99, 167, 326)

Freut euch, freut euch in dieser Zeit (tune) 5514

FREUT EUCH IHR SCHÄFERSLEUT 5340 (49, 309)

"Freut euch, ihr Schäfersleut, freut euch ins Feld" 5340
(49, 309)

"Freut, ihr Brüder, freut euch jtzt" 1009 (250)

THE FRIAR OF ORDERS GRAY 3454 (240)

FRICKA'S SCENE 3927 (2)

FRIDERICUS REX 2178 (31)

"Fridericus Rex, unser König und Herr" 2178 (31)

"Der Friede sei mit euch, das war dein Abschiedssegen"
3291 (229)

Friederike 2091-2092

"Friedlich lieg' ich hingegossen" 3293 (330)

FRIENDLESS BLUES 1518 (109, 110)

THE FRIENDLY BEASTS 8908 (33, 79, 165, 249)

FRIENDS AND NEIGHBORS 7600 (72)

"Friends and neighbors, I'm going for to leave you" 7600
(72)

"Friends, if you will listen, I'll sing to you a song" 7534
(72)

"Friesch bloed, stuif op! wil nu eens bruisen, koken" 6460
(384)

FRIESCH VOLKSLIED 6460 (384)

FRIESENSANG 53 (31)

"Frightening and horrible was it all" 4823 (124)

"Frihet är det bästa ting" 1831 (188)

"Frijsk bloed, tsoch op! wol nou ris bruwzein siede" 6460
(384)

FRIJSK FOLKSLIET 6460 (384)

"Frisch als Fuchs fuhr ich ins Leben" 1292 (31)

Frisch auf, frisch auf, der Bergmann kommt (tune) 5388

"FRISCH AUF! FRISCH AUF ZUM JAGEN" 5341 (42)

Frisch auf, juhhe! wen's Schiessen freut (tune) 5602 (309)

"Frisch frölich wend wir singen" 1669 (156)

FRISCHE SCHINDELN SCHLÄGT MAN 5836 (92)

"Frische Schindeln schlägt man ans Kasernendach, all die
Burschen man uns fortnahm nach und nach" 5836
(92)

DIE FRIST IST UM 3899 (4)

"Die Frist ist um, und abermals verstrichen sind sieben
Jahr" 3899 (4)

Frit à l'huile (tune) 5001

THE FROG AND THE CROW 4603 (234)

THE FROG AND THE MOUSE 4604B (80), 4606D (199, 216)

"A FROG HE WOULD A-WOOING GO" 4604A (129, 130),
4604C (186, 234, 249)

"A frog he would a-wooing go, 'Heigh-ho!' said Rowley"
4604C (234)

"A frog he would a-wooing go, 'Heigh-ho!' says Rowley"
4604C (186)

"A frog he would a-wooing go, Hey-ho, says Roley" 4604C
(249)

FROG WENT A-COURTIN' 4604A (110, 399)

"Frog went a-courtin' an' he did ride" 4604A (399)

"Frog went a-courtin', he did ride" 4604A (331)

"Frog went a-courtin', he did ride" 4604A (331), 4604B
(80)

FROG WENT A-COURTING 4604F (225)

"Frog went a-courting and he did ride" 4604F (225)

FROGGIE WENT A-COURTIN' 4604 (331)

FROH ZU SEIN 5342 (40)

"FROH ZU SEIN BEDARF ES WENIG" 5342 (326)

"Froh zu sein, bedarf man Wenig" 5342 (40)

FROHE BOTSCHAFT 2605 (99)

DER FROHE WANDERSMANN 1174 (99)

"From a far-off land we come to see you yearly" 9306 (291)

FROM A KRAKOW SMITHY'S FORGE 6879 (295)

"From a Krakow smithy's forge, clamor sounds each morning"
6879 (295)

"From all that dwell below the skies" 379 (132)

From an old garden 2226 (408)

FROM BORDER UNTO BORDER 846 (288)

"From California ocean laved to old Virginia's shore" 7653
(189)

FROM CHURCH TO CHURCH 9017 (319)

"From church to church the bells' glad tidings run" 9017
(319)

"FROM EARTHLY TASKS LIFT UP THINE EYES" 3328 (296)

"FROM EVERY SPIRE ON CHRISTMAS EVE" 694 (28, 296,
366)

FROM FAR AWAY COMING 1873 (159)

"From far away coming, o'er streams and hills roaming"
1873 (159)

"From far away I hear sweet voices calling me" 5940 (402)

"From far away we come to you" 3803 (334)

"FROM FAR, FROM EVE AND MORNING" 3802 (277)

"From groves of spice, o'er fields of rice" 448 (199)

FROM HEAVEN ABOVE 9182 (206, 296, 319, 410)

"From heaven above, O angels draw nigh" 9183 (165)

FROM HEAVEN HIGH 9182 (337, 388)

"From heaven high I come to earth" 9182 (388)

"FROM HEAVEN HIGH I COME TO YOU" 9182 (33, 38, 39,
125, 251, 337)

"From heaven high the angels come" 9183 (33)

"From Heav'n above to earth I come" 9182 (206, 296, 319,
410)

FROM HER BALCONY GREEN 4065 (112)

"From her balcony green my maiden peeps at me" 4065
(112)

"FROM HER HEART THE FEVER DEPARTED" 3730 (5)

"From highest heaven come, angels come!" 9183 (361)

"From Jerusalem proceeding, to the Christ Child's manger
going" 9355 (314)

"From la Sierra Morena, Cielito Lindo" 6339A (36, 284, 350)

"From Mexico there's just come a strange new decree" 6342
(109, 110)

"From my breast dropt a lovely flowret" 4023 (140)

"From my clavier, sounds sweet and clear" 3255 (141)

FROM MY WINDOW FLY 5794 (92)

"From my window fly, dear swallow, how I wish that I could
follow" 5794 (92)

"From no forest comes this rustling" 6977 (95)

"From now on, my adventurous lover" 2586 (5)

"FROM O'ER THE HILLS OF FAIR JUDEA" 9101 (79)

FROM OUT KRAKOW 6799 (295)

"From out Krakow, rich dark furrows, I shall not be plowing
more" 6799 (295)

"From out of a wood did a cuckoo fly" 8868 (199, 214, 271,
410)

"From out the Dawn there came a Voice" 3578 (398)

"From out their peaceful village" 2739 (346, 348, 394, 400)

GEBET (Foerster) 1094 (73)

GEBET (Hiller) 1656 (123)

GEBET (Wolf) 4074 (98,408)

GEBET AN DEN HEILIGEN CHRIST 3468 (99,337)

GEBET WÄHREND DER SCHLACHT 1662 (43)

"Gebt mir meinen Geliebten wieder" 3599 (217)

DIE GEDANKEN SIND FREI 7365 (49,309,353)

"De Gedanken sind frei! Wer kann sie erraten?" 7365 (49,
309,353)

"GEDENKE DOCH, MEIN GEIST, ZURÜCKE" 117 (308)

"Gedenke, o wie weit, wie weit" 3471 (31)

GEE, BUT I WANT TO GO HOME 7605 (227)

"Gee, I wish that I had a girl like the other fellows had"
1847 (128,129,130,131,236)

GEE, MOM, I WANT TO GO HOME 7605 (44)

"GEEFT WAT OM DEN ROMMELPOT" 6461 (203)

DIE GEFANGENEN REITER 5346 (99)

"GEH AUS, MEIN HERZ" 1629 (49)

"GEH AUS, MEIN HERZ, UND SUCHE FREUD" 3229 (326)

GEH ICH ZUM GRÜNEN HAIN 5006 (226)

"Geh ich zum grünen Hain Liebeshain" 5003 (226)

GEH' MACH DIE FENSTERL AUF 1840 (346)

GEH' NICHT AUF DAS STOPPELFELD 5772 (92)

"Geh' nicht auf das Stoppelfeld, Kind" 5772 (92)

GEHEIMES 3270 (220,277)

Die Geisha 1829 (255)

GEISTERNÄHE 3367 (220)

"GEKWETST BEN IK VAN BINNEN" 6466 (202)

"Gelber Mais, verdorrter Strauch, Blieb dein Boden, blieb
dein Boden unbehaun" 5799 (27)

"GELDELOOS GIJ DOET MIJ PIJN" 6462 (203)

"Geliebter Frühling meiner Tage, wie voller Anmut blühest
du!" 3719 (226)

GELIJK ALS DE WITTE ZWANEN 9242 (384)

"Gelijk als de witte zwanen zingen op haar levensend"
9242 (284)

La gelosia 628 (218)

GELÜBDE 5347 (99)

IL GENOVESE 6093 (338)

"Gentil cavallero dadme agora un beso" 2829 (278)

GENTIL COQUELICOT 4983 (127)

GENTIL COQU'LICOT 4983 (91)

GENTILLE BATELIÈRE 4984 (383)

"Gentille batelière laisse là ton bateau" 4984 (383)

"Gentle and faithful, truthful and tender" 4959 (174)

"GENTLE AND SWEET MUSETTE" 2495 (45)

GENTLE ANNIE 1114 (28,36,129,130,212,279,366)

"Gentle dove, thou hast flown away" 5853 (86)

GENTLE FAIR JENNY 7606 (312)

"Gentle flow'rs in the dew, bear love from me" 1319 (2)

GENTLE LADY 679* (85)

"Gentle lady, do not sing" 679* (85)

A gentle maid in secret sighed (tune) 8678

The gentle maiden (tune) 5909

"GENTLE MARY LAID HER CHILD" 8935 (251)

GENTLE SAVIOUR, DAY AND NIGHT 8835 (378)

"Gentle Saviour day, and night, ride three Princes great in
might" 8835 (378)

GENTLE SHEPHERD 2768 (276)

"Gentle shepherd, will you love me" 2768 (276)

"Gentle slumbers o'er thee glide" 1112 (129,132)

"A gentleman came to our house" 7417 (312)

GENTLY FLOW 1584 (199)

"Gently flow, O lovely stream" 1584 (199)

"Gently in my thoughts I hear" 2379 (36)

GENTLY, JOHNNY, MY JINGALO 4609 (215)

GENZELECH 6200 (318)

GEORDIE (A TRAGIC LEGEND) 7607A (267)

GEORGE COLLINS 7612 (81)

GEORGE COLON 7608 (243)

"George Colon rode home one cold winter night" 7608
(243)

GEORGE RIDLER'S OVEN 4610 (198)

"George Washington, first president, by Adams was succeeded" 8150 (44)

GEORGIA 7609 (242)

GEORGIE, O 7607 (392)

"Gepeys, gepeys vol van enuien welk oorspronc is dat
menich treurt" 6463 (384)

GEPEYS VOL FANTASIËN 6463 (384)

GERECHTER GOTT 3915 (2)

"Gerechter Gott! So ist's entschieden schon!" 3915 (2)

"Gerencséri ucca végig piros rózsa" 5710 (23)

GERENCSÉRI UTCA 5710 (23)

"GERN HAB' ICH DIE FRAU'N GEKÜSST" 2099 (254)

"Gernbeim Morgenscheine wandl' ich durch die Haine"
1273 (308)

GERTJIE 7217 (86)

Gesänge zur Feier des heiligen Opfers der Messe 3272 (326)

GESANG AN SYLVIA 3256 (250)

GESANG AUZIEHENDER KRIEGER 2403 (99)

GESANG DER JÜNGLINGE 3212 (31)

GESANG WEYLA'S 4075 (121)

GESELLSCHAFTSLIED 3234 (31)

"Gestern abend war Vetter Michel hier" 5575* (99)

"Gestern abends ging Frau Grete heim" 3586 (396)

GESTERN BEI MONDENSCHEIN 5348 (41,326)

"Gestern bei Mondenschein ging ich spazieren" 5348 (41,
326)

GESTERN BEIM MONDENSCHEIN 5348 (49,309)

"Gestern beim Mondenschein ging ich spazieren" 5348
(49,99,309)

"GESTERN, BRÜDER, KÖNNT IHR'S GLAUBEN?" 5349 (31,
99)

GESÙ BAMBIN L'E NATO 9200 (154)

"Gesù Bambin l'e nato, nato in Betelem" 9200 (154)

"Gesungen und gesprungen, gelacht, geküsst, geherzt"
5559 (31)

GET OFF THE TRACK! 7610 (189)

"Get on board, little children, get on board" 8289 (110)

GET OUT OF MEXICO 3978 (189)

"Get out your gun and call your dog" 7643A (185)

GET RIGHT, STAY RIGHT 8273 (184)

GET THE MONEY 7611 (321)

GET THEE BEHIND ME, SATAN 57 (293,336)

"Get to de lot befo' I do, catch my mule I'll be there too"
8606 (409)

"Get up, get up for shame, the blooming morn" 3931 (344)

GET UP, MY OX 7235 (219)

GET UP NOW 5171 (21)

"Get up your gun an' call up your dawg" 7643C (242)

"Get up your guns and call up your dogs" 7643D (243)

"Get you ready, there's a meeting here tonight" 8585
(409)

"EIN GETREUES HERZE WISSEN" 1241 (326)

"Ein getreues Herze wissen hat die höchsten Schatzes
Preis" 1241 (326)

DE GEUZEN IN BOMLER WEERDT 6464 (384)

"De Geuzen zijn in Bomler Weerdt ghevallen" 6464 (384)

GEVAERT 9064 (38,39)

DE GEZELLEN UIT ROSENDAEL 6465 (384)

"GHEQUETST BEN IC VAN BINNEN" 6466 (86)

"GHEQUETST BEN IK VAN BINNEN" 6466 (384)
GHOST DANCE SONG 5848 (37)
"GIA IL SOLE DAL GANGE" 3183 (368)
Gia la notte d'avoieina 2854 (179)
Gianni Schicci 2894
"The giant Bodegh roam'd o'er Erin's green lea" 5949 (37)
Giasone 621 (181)
GIBN DIR MAYN TOCHTER 6201 (318)
"Gibn dir mayn tochter, A shuster far a man?" 6201 (318)
"Gibt's a schönres Platzerl weit und breit" 1765 (222)
"Gieb mir deine Hand" 3237 (121)
THE GIFT OF GOD 8274 (409)
"GIJ ŁIE DE STERREN HEBT GESTICHT" 6467 (384)
GILDEBROEDERS MAAKT PLEZIEREN 6468 (203)
"Gildebroeders maakt plezieren met muziek vroeg ende
        laat" 6468 (203)
DI GILDERNE PAVE 6202 (318)
GILES COLLINS 7612 (81)
"Giles Collins said to his mother one day" 7612 (81)
GILLYFLOWERS 3288 (199)
"Gillyflowers, gillyflowers, bring to mind those vanish'd
        hours" 3288 (199)
GILU HAGALILIM 6203 (318)
"Gilu haGalilim, giborey hachayil" 6203 (318)
GIMBELEM, GOMBOLOM 5711 (164)
GIMME BACK MY SHILLING 8727 (11)
"GIMME DAT OL'-TIME RELIGION" 8275 (115)
"GIMME DAT OLD TIME RELIGION" 8275 (183)
"Gin a body meet a body" 7028A (17,36,100,104,128,132,
        163,176,233,402)
"Gin I had a wee hoose and a canty wee fire" 6998 (101,
        105)
"Gin Johnnie kent I was na weel" 7070 (101,103,104)
GING INS DORF 5664 (92)
"Ging ins Dorf, jetzt will ich einmal Schäfer sein"
        5664 (92)
"Gioco di rea fortuna" 861 (298)
La gioconda 2845-2850
"Gioite al canto mio" 2772 (138,167)
GIOVANOTTINA CHE VIENI ALLA FONTE 6094 (325)
"Giovanottina che vieni alla fonte, due stelle in fronte ti
        vedo brillar" 6094 (325)
"The Gipsy fires are burning" 683 (237)
"A gipsy lad was a-ridin' one day" 7613 (399)
GIPSY LADDIE 7613 (399)
GIPSY MELODY 960 (122,237,329)
GIPSY TINKER 5712 (95)
Il girello 2355-2356
A GIRL FIFTEEN 6642 (95)
"A girl fifteen does not know her heart" 6642 (95)
A GIRL FROM DABROWA 6847 (159)
THE GIRL FROM SCILLA 6137 (95)
GIRL, I ADVISE YOU 4388 (94)
"Girl, I advise you, don't marry not yet" 4388 (94)
THE GIRL I LEFT BEHIND ME 5917 (15,28,95,128,132,
        172,235,279,349,366)
"GIRL I LOVE TO SEE" 4338 (94)
"GIRL, ONCE I LOVED YOU WELL" 4377 (94)
THE GIRL THAT WAITS FOR ME 1842 (339)
GIRLS BY DANUBE 4384 (94)
"Girls by Danube clothes are washing" 4384 (94)
THE GIRLS OF CADIZ 809 (93,191,193,195)
THE GIRLS OF COLERAINE 5918 (172)
"The girls of my native country" 1789 (291)
"The girls of old Cadiz, we know" 809 (93)
GIRLS OF TODAY 6204 (95)

GIRLS' SONG 1718 (275)
"Girls these days don't even mind their elders" 6204 (95)
GIROMETTA 6095 (338)
"Girometta de la montagna, turna al to pais" 6095 (338)
GIROMETTE 6095 (338)
"Giromette de la montagne, rentre à ton pays" 6095 (338)
GIT ALONG LITTLE DOGIES 7614A (120,145,227), 7614B
        (129,130,236)
GIT ON BO'D LIT'L' CHILDREN 8259 (52)
"GIT ON BO'D LITTLE CHILD'EN" 8289 (183)
LA GITANA 8853 (56)
GITANERIAS 1378 (176)
Gitanjali 601 (121)
"Gitano soy, el destino me ha privao de sus favores" 1378
        (176)
Giuditta 2093 (222)
Giulio Sabino 3166 (353)
"Giunse al fin il momento" 2584 (1)
"Give a rouse, then, in the May-time" 470 (240)
"Give alms, give alms, and one poor soul cherish" 2414
        (2)
"Give it back, dear, give it back, dear!" 4553 (95)
"GIVE IT BACK, GIRL" 4447 (94)
"Give me a little humble cot" 4733 (198)
GIVE ME A NIGHT IN JUNE 1172 (345)
GIVE ME EAGLE WINGS 6710 (159)
"Give me eagle's wings, or a falcon's flight" 6710 (159)
GIVE ME JESUS 8276 (76,409)
"Give me three grains of corn, mother" 8056 (242)
GIVE ME YOUR HAND 8277 (409)
Give thanks, all ye people 2607 (212)
"Give thanks all ye people, give thanks to the Lord"
        2607 (212)
GLAD AM I 4396 (94)
"Glad I am to find you here" 4396 (94)
GLAD CHRISTMAS BELLS 8928 (28,206,244,296,366)
"Glad Christmas bells, your music tells" 8928 (28,206,
        244,296,366)
GLAD SASOM FAGELN 1421 (188)
"Glad saasom faageln i morgonstunden" 1421 (188)
GLAD TIDINGS (Carols, France) 9127 (361)
GLAD TIDINGS (Folksongs, Jewish) 6250 (389)
"Glad Tidings we bring of peace on earth good will toward
        men" 6250 (389)
GLÄDJENS BLOMSTER 7306 (135,188)
"Glädjens blomster, i jordens mull, ack visst aldrig gro"
        7306 (135,188)
"Gläns över sjö och strand" 3714 (188)
"The glamorous red of coral" 4162 (219)
"GLAUBT IHR DENN, DASS ICH LUSTIG BIN" 4840
        (49)
GLAUKES SAANGER, 1. PASTORAL 3081 (356)
GLAUKES SAANGER, 2. GLAUKES SAANG OM KÄRLEKEN
        3082 (356)
GLAUKES SAANGER, 3. GLAUKES KLAGOSAANG 3083
        (356)
GLEANERS SONG 3788 (37)
GLEE REIGNS IN GALILEE 6203 (35)
"Glee reigns in Galilee, the Galil rejoices" 6203 (35)
"Gleich wie der Sonne Strahl, heiter und selig" 516
        (168)
DER GLEICHSINN 1561 (226)
GLENLOGIE 7043 (101)
G'LIJK DEN GROOTSTEN RAPSACK 6469 (201)
"G'lijk den grootsten Rapsack, vloot den Speck verbaast"
        6469 (201)

GLOCKEN KLINGEN 5350 (40)

"Glocken klingen hoch vom Turm" 5350 (40)

"Glömma, glömma bara glömma allt som var ditt liv" 1522 (355)

"The gloomy night before us flies" 7727 (44, 109, 110, 115, 293)

"Gloomy night embraced the place wherein the noble Infant lay" 8793 (361)

GLOOMY WINTER 7044 (100)

"Gloomy winter's noo awa' saft the westlan' breezes blaw" 7044 (100)

GLOOMY WOODS 2204 (404)

"Gloomy woods, redouble thy shadow" 2204 (404)

GLORIA EN LAS ALTURAS 9406 (165)

"Gloria, gloria in excelsis" 1562 (343)

GLORIA IN EXCELSIS (Haydn) 1562 (343)

GLORIA IN EXCELSIS DEO (Carols, France) 9043A (305), 9043B (33)

GLORIA PATRI 2733 (28, 366)

"Gloria patri et filio" 2733 (28, 366)

THE GLORIOUS FOURTH 7615 (129, 130)

GLORIOUS SUMMER NIGHT 1996 (87)

"Glorious summer night, cool springs in elfin light" 1996 (87)

"GLORIOUS YULETIDE, GLAD BELLS PROCLAIM IT" 2214 (244)

"Glory! glory! glory to that newborn King" 9388A (244, 409)

GLORY HALLELUJAH TO DE NEW-BORN KING 9387 (182)

GLORY IN THE HIGHEST (Carols, Venezuela) 9406 (165)

THE GLORY OF GOD IN NATURE 228

GLORY TO GOD (Carols, England) 8929 (319)

GLORY TO GOD (Gebhardi) 1228 (337)

"GLORY TO GOD IN HEIGHTS OF HEAVEN" 8901 (361)

"Glory to God in the Highest" (Carols, England) 8929 (319)

"Glory to God in the highest!" (Gebhardi) 1228 (337)

GLORY TO THAT NEWBORN KING 9388A (244)

GLORY TO THE NEWBORN KING 9388A (409)

THE GLORY TRAIL 7616 (80)

GLOUCESTERSHIRE WASSAIL 9002A (38, 39, 271, 307, 337)

GLOUCESTERSHIRE WASSAILERS' SONG 9002B (154)

THE GLOW WITHIN 3001 (76)

GLOW WORM (Lincke) 2138 (32, 34)

"Glow-worm, light your lamp" 6664 (350)

GLÜCK (Reger) 3003 (226)

GLÜCK (Telemann) 3718 (98, 99, 226)

GLÜCK AUF 5351 (99)

GLÜCK AUF! DER STEIGER KOMMT 5351 (49, 326, 353)

GLÜCK AUF, GLÜCK AUF 5351 (49, 326, 353)

"Glück auf! Glück auf! Der Steiger kommt!" 5351 (49, 99, 309, 326, 353)

"Das Glück, das uns im Wachen nicht gegeben" 886 (257)

EIN GLÜCK, DASS MAN SICH SO VERLIEBEN KANN! 3243 (258)

DAS GLÜCK IS A VOGERL 1968 (396)

"GLÜCKAUF! GLÜCKAUF! DER SILBERZWEIG" 2286 (49)

"Glückauf! Glückauf! Der Silberzweig in Bergesnacht erblüht in unserm tiefen Schacht" 2286 (49)

"Das Glücke kommt selten per Posta, zu Pferde" 3718 (98, 99, 226)

GLÜCKES GENUG 3624 (330)

"Des Glückes ungemess'ne Stunden hab' ich im Leben oft gesucht" 883 (257)

"GLÜCKLICH BLÜHE UNSER LAND" 1673 (326)

GLÜCKLICHE REISE 1989 (254)

Glückliche Reise 1988-1989

GLÜHWÜRMCHEN 2138 (32, 34)

"Go and tell that little blue-eyed maiden she should cure my poor heart sorrow-laden" 5767 (164)

GO AND TELL THAT LITTLE MAIDEN 5767 (164)

"Go ask the barber, he surely will know" 4163 (37)

"GO AWAY, YOU WICKED FELLOWS!" 4309 (95)

"Go by me, Ah! go by me" 3312 (274)

GO CALL THE DOCTOR, & BE QUICK, or ANTI-CALOMEL 1740 (189)

"Go, child, do not fail to hit your mark" 9223 (244)

GO CHRISTALL TEARES 901 (144)

"Go christall teares, like to the morning showers" 901 (144)

"Go dig a hole in the meadow" 7537B (109, 110)

GO DOWN IN DE LONESOME VALLEY 8278 (184)

GO DOWN MOSES! 8279 (28, 35, 76, 109, 110, 183, 227, 233, 293, 366, 409)

"Go down, Moses, way down in Egyp' Lan'" 8279 (35)

"Go down Moses, way down in Egypt land" 8279 (227, 293)

"Go down Moses, way down in Egypt's land" 8279 (28, 76, 109, 110, 233, 366, 409)

GO DOWN 'N THE VALLEY AND PRAY 8280 (409)

"Go fetch to me a pint o' wine" 7113 (397)

GO FORTH NOW SWEET MARY 4082 (112)

"Go forth now, sweet Mary, go forth without fear" 4082 (112)

GO FROM MY WINDOW 4611 (34)

"Go from my window, my love, my love" 4611 (34)

GO GET THE AXE 7617 (110)

"Go in adoration, go to Bethlehem" 9406 (165)

Go Javten, go Javten! Tilsammen i en Slump (tune) 4463

"Go limber, Jim; you can't go" 7477A (34)

"Go, little message to Camencita" 8773 (350)

"Go marry someone fair and tender" 2316 (5)

GO NO MORE ARUSHING 4612 (95)

"Go no more arushing, maids, in May" 4612 (95)

GO NOT THROUGH THE STUBBLE 5772 (92)

"Go not through the stubble, my dear" 5772 (92)

"Go now, my own, my sweet, good-bye!" 1890 (339)

"GO TELL AUNT NANCY" 7416 (227, 249)

"GO TELL AUNT RHODIE" 7416 (185, 216)

"GO TELL AUNT RHODY" 7416 (170, 173, 249, 389)

"GO, TELL IT ON DE MOUNTAIN" 9389B (184)

"GO TELL IT ON THE MOUNTAIN" 9389A (33, 332, 337, 409)

GO TELL IT ON THE MOUNTAINS 9389A (296)

"Go tell Mary and Martha" 8377 (409)

GO TER SLEEP 7618A (95)

"Go ter seep, go ter sleep, go ter sleepy, mammy's baby" 7618A (95, 109, 110)

"Go, then; to thy doom thou art going" 3848 (4, 310)

"Go to bed and good night, with roses bedight" 436 (28, 136, 241, 329, 366)

"GO TO BED, SWEET MUSE" 1816 (196)

GO TO JOAN GLOVER 4613 (36, 235, 349)

"Go to Joan Glover and tell her I love her" 4613 (36, 235, 349)

GO TO SLEEP 7618B (242)

"Go to sleep, go to sleep, go to sleep little baby" 7618B (242)

GO TO SLEEP, LENA DARLING 999 (28, 129, 130, 131)

GO TO SLEEPY 7618A (109, 110)

"Go to the western gate, Luke Havergal" 930 (358)

GO 'WAY BACK AND SIT DOWN 1796 (204)

GO WHERE GLORY WAITS THEE 5919 (166, 213, 349)

"Go where glory waits thee, but while fame elates thee Oh! still remember me" 5919 (166,213,349)

GO YE TO BETHLEHEM 9322 (165)

"Go ye to Bethlehem, O shepherds, leave your sheep" 9322 (165)

THE GOAT AND THE LAMB 3929 (30)

THE GOAT SONG 7619 (249)

THE GOAT WHO ATE THE DRUM 3502 (9)

GOD AND MAN 120 (89)

"GOD BE WITH YOU TILL WE MEET AGAIN" 3751 (28, 279,366)

GOD BLESS MY BOY AT SEA 313 (205)

"God bless our native land" (tune: America) 7408 (28,321)

"GOD BLESS OUR NATIVE LAND" (Tuckerman) 3776 (129, 130)

"God bless the grey mountains of dark Donegal" 5941 (133)

"God bless the little feet that never go astray" 3762 (189)

"GOD BLESS THE MASTER OF THIS HOUSE" 8925 (307,319, 333)

"God bless thee love, it was but idle dreaming" 2644 (132)

"GOD GIVE YE MERRY CHRISTMAS TIDE" 8930 (244)

GOD HATH MADE US ALL 1763 (90)

"GOD, HE'S GWINE TO SET DIS WORLD ON FIRE" 8282B (80)

GOD IN HEAVEN 4296 (94)

"God in heaven, God in heaven" 4296 (94)

GOD IN SPRINGTIME 3272 (357)

"GOD IS A SPIRIT" 3408 (398)

GOD IS A GOD 8281 (409)

"God is a God! God don't never change!" 8281 (409)

GOD IS BORN 9288 (295)

"God is born on earth, powers tremble" 9288 (295)

"GOD IS MY SHEPHERD" 954 (89)

GOD IS SPIRIT 1311 (90)

"God made the world in six days and rested on the seventh" 7439 (72)

"God Morgon, mitt herrskap" 2606 (188)

"God, my heart prepared is" 8141 (34)

"God of justice ever with us" 1774 (7)

GOD OF OUR FATHERS 3946 (28,279,343)

"GOD OF OUR FATHERS, WHOSE ALMIGHTY HAND" 3946 (129,130,326)

"GOD OF THE EARTH, THE SKY, THE SEA" 1684 (28,366)

"God of the nations, in glory enthroned" 3869 (28)

GOD, OUR FATHER 7620 (242)

"God, our Father, gives to each one" 7620 (242)

"God, our help in ages past" (Davis) 782 (89)

"God prosper long our noble King" 4564 (14)

"GOD REST YE, MERRY GENTLEMEN" 8931A (349)

GOD REST YOU MERRY 8931A (38,39,361), 8931B (361)

"GOD REST YOU MERRY, GENTLEMEN" 8931A (33,35,38, 39,79,125,165,199,206,251,271,296,305,307,315, 319,333,334,337,361,363,366,402,410), 8931B (333,334,361)

GOD SAVE AMERICA ("God save us from ev'ry foe") 7621 (189)

GOD SAVE AMERICA (Miessner) 2421 (236)

"God save America" (Tune: America) 7408 (321)

"God save our gracious King" 4614 (35,234)

"God save our gracious Queen" 4614 (13,199,279,306, 349,366)

"GOD SAVE OUR PRESIDENT" 4051 (129,130)

GOD SAVE THE KING 4614 (35,234,294)

GOD SAVE THE PEOPLE 7622 (321)

GOD SAVE THE QUEEN 4614 (13,199,279,306,349,366)

"GOD SAVE THE SOUTH" 995 (161)

"God save us from ev'ry foe" 7621 (189)

"God save you kindly gaffer" 9058 (361)

"The God sent an angel from heaven so high" 9376 (332)

"God sent ol' Jonah to the Nineveh lan'" 8644 (409)

GOD SHALL WIPE AWAY ALL TEARS (Peery) 2758 (123)

GOD SHALL WIPE AWAY ALL TEARS FROM THEIR EYES (Sullivan) 3661 (398)

GOD SO LOVED THE WORLD (Händel) 1485 (90)

"GOD SO LOVED THE WORLD" (Stainer) 3548 (28,346, 400)

"God so loved the world, God so loved the world" 1485 (90)

GOD, THOU KEPT'ST POLAND 1998 (159)

"God, Thou kept'st Poland always in Thy power" 1998 (159)

GOD, WHO HELD POLAND 1998 (295)

"God, who held Poland for so many ages" 1995 (295)

"Goddess fairest, goddess fairest, so brightly gleaming" 254 (6)

"Goddess of Love, oh! protectress of lovers" 2350 (147)

GODNATT 7307 (135)

"Godnatt, godnatt, godnatt! O Sol!" 7307 (135)

GOD'S DEAR SON 8932 (334)

"GOD'S DEAR SON WITHOUT BEGINNING" 8932 (333, 334,361)

GOD'S GLORY IN NATURE 228

"GOD'S GOIN' TO SET THIS WORLD ON FIRE" 8282A (321)

GOD'S GOIN' TO STRAIGHTEN THEM 8283 (409)

"The gods have foreshewn me the future" 1272 (5)

GODS OF THE HEATHEN 8817 (361)

"Gods of the heathen, bronze and stone" 8817 (361)

GOD'S OWN WORD OUR FLESH DID TAKE 9037 (361)

"God's own Word our flesh did take, O Maidenhood" 9037 (361)

"GOE TO BED SWEETE MUZE" 1816 (144)

GÖKVISA 7308 (135)

"Gönnt mir doch das bisschen Freude!" 3720 (308)

Die Götterdämmerung 3902 (2)

GÖTTLICHS KINDLEIN 8799 (40)

"Göttlich's Kindlein, dich zu grüssen" 8799 (40)

Y Gofid Glâs (tune) 8701

GOIN' DOWN THE ROAD 8284C (293)

GOIN' DOWN THE ROAD FEELIN' BAD 8284A (227)

GOIN' DOWN TO TOWN 7623 (80)

GOIN' KEEP MY SKILLET GREASY 8547B (409)

GOIN' TO BOSTON 7624 (185,312)

"Goin' to lay down my burden down by the river side" 8170 (76)

"Goin' to moan, moan" 8521 (184)

GOIN' TO SHOUT ALL OVER GOD'S HEAB'N 8177 (183)

GOIN' TO SHOUT ALL OVER GOD'S HEAV'N 8177 (70)

"Goin' to the mountain top, throw myself down to the sea" 8270 (77)

"Goin' up on ole Smoky, all kiver'd with snow" 7885F (331)

GOIN' UP THE RIVER 7625 (110)

"Goin' up the river from Catlettsburg to Pike" 7625 (110)

GOING HOME IN THE CHARIOT 8285 (409)

"Going home in the chariot in the morning" 8285 (409)

"Going in the early evening to the deacon's house" 1954 (162)

GOING TO BOSTON 7624 (216)

GOING TO SHOUT ALL OVER GOD'S HEAV'N 8177 (28, 366,409)

"Going to write to Massa Jesus" 8599 (28)

Going. See also Gwine

GOLD UND SILBER LIEB ICH SEHR 5352 (326, 353)

"Gold und Silber lieb ich sehr, kann's auch wohl gebrauchen" 5352 (326, 353)

THE GOLDEN CAROL OF MELCHIOR, CASPER AND BALTHAZAR 9051 (296)

THE GOLDEN CAROL OF THE THREE KINGS 9051 (379)

THE GOLDEN CAROL OF THE THREE WISE MEN 9051 (244)

THE GOLDEN GLOVE 4615 (198)

"The golden haired princess sat high in her tow'r" 1390 (395)

GOLDEN MORNINGS 8933 (271)

"The golden peacock came a-flying" 6202 (318)

GOLDEN SLUMBERS 4616 (234, 349, 402)

"Golden slumbers kiss your eyes" (Folksongs, England) 4616 (28, 37, 234, 349, 366, 402)

"Golden slumbers kiss your eyes" (Stanford) 3555 (344)

"The golden splendor is fading" 6330 (350)

THE GOLDEN SUNLIGHT 579 (343)

"The golden sunlight, from a blue sky beaming" 579 (343)

THE GOLDEN VANITY 4617A (35, 111, 173, 199, 349), 4617B (235), 4617C (198), 4617D (260, 263)

THE GOLDEN WILLOW TREE 4617E (84), 4617F (126), 4617G (80)

GOLDENE BURSCHENZEIT 3471 (31)

DIE GOLDENEN BLÄTTER 2359 (224)

GOLDFISH 2490 (295)

GOLDNE ABENDSONNE 2629 (326)

"Goldne Abendsonne, wie bist du so schön!" 2629 (326)

"Goldner Stern, deinen Schimmer breite" 6096 (51)

GOLDNER WEIZEN, GOLDNE GERSTE 5796 (92)

"Goldner Weizen, goldne Gerste, goldnes Korn" 5796 (92)

GOLEUDDYDD 8686 (86)

GOLIARDENLIED 1374 (31)

LA GOLONDRINA 3427 (132, 142, 236, 284, 322)

LAS GOLONDRINAS 7626 (113)

THE GONDOLA 6063 (406)

LA GONDOLETTA 6063 (406)

DER GONDOLIER 6096 (51)

GONDOLIERA 6063 (325)

IL GONDOLIERO 6096 (51)

"Gone are the days" 1127 (28, 129, 130, 132, 233, 236, 279, 366)

GONNA LEAVE BIG ROCK BEHIND 8286 (409)

GOOBER PEAS 7563 (44, 161, 169)

GOOD-BY, OLD PAINT 7628A (335)

"Good-by, Old Paint, I'm a-leavin' Cheyenne" 7628A (227)

"Good-by, old Paint, I'm a-leaving Cheyenne" 7628A (335)

"Good-by, you old Paint, I'm a-leaving Cheyene" 7628B (120)

Good-bye. See also Goodbye

GOOD-BYE! 3757 (122, 237, 329, 348)

"GOOD-BYE BROADWAY, HELLO FRANCE" 203 (129, 130)

"Good-bye, good-bye to summer, for summer's nearly done" 1986 (28)

GOOD-BYE LIZA JANE 7779D (145)

GOOD-BYE, OLD PAINT 7628A (109, 110, 214, 236)

"Good-bye, old Paint, I'm a-leaving Cheyenne" 7628A (109, 110, 236)

"Good-bye, Old Paint, I'm leaving Cheyenne" 7628A (214)

GOOD CHRISTIAN MEN REJOICE 9159 (33, 35, 38, 39, 79, 125, 206, 251, 271, 296, 307, 315, 333, 349, 361, 363, 410)

"Good Christian men rejoice with heart, and soul, and voice" 9159 (33, 35, 38, 39, 79, 125, 206, 251, 271, 296, 307, 315, 333, 349, 361, 363, 410)

GOOD COBLER, SIR! 5147 (21)

"Good day, good day, good day my Lord Sir Cristemas" 8934 (360)

GOOD DAY SIR CHRISTMAS 8934 (360)

"Good day Sir Cristemas our King" 8934 (360)

GOOD EVENING, MY PRETTY 4462 (95)

"Good evening, my pretty! So now your love's a soldier" 4462 (95)

"Good evening my treasure" 430 (276)

"Good gracious me! Tell me, where you're going like this?" 5147 (21)

"Good health, good cheer, May you live a hundred years" 6843 (295)

GOOD KING WENCESLAS 8935 (28, 33, 35, 38, 39, 79, 125, 154, 165, 199, 206, 269, 271, 305, 307, 315, 319, 334, 337, 349, 361, 363, 366, 388, 410)

"Good King Wenceslas look'd out" 8935 (28, 33, 35, 38, 39, 79, 125, 154, 199, 206, 269, 305, 315, 319, 334, 349, 361, 363, 366, 388)

"GOOD KING WENCESLAS LOOKED OUT" 8935 (165, 271, 307, 333, 337, 401)

GOOD KINGS 9317 (33)

"Good kings, now sing and be joyful" 9317 (33)

"GOOD LORD I DONE DONE" 8288 (409)

"Good men and true in this house who dwell" 5891 (16)

GOOD MORNING, BLUES 2080 (336)

"Good morning, Blues, Blues, how do you do?" 2080 (336)

"Good morning, Captain, Good morning, Shine" 8430B (336)

GOOD MORNING, CARRIE! 3519 (114, 131)

"Good morning, Carrie! how you do this morning" 3519 (131)

"Good morning, Carrie! how'd you do this morning" 3519 (114)

GOOD MORNING EVERYBODY 8287 (409)

"Good morning everybody, O children! Good morning everybody, Lord" 8287 (409)

"Good morning, god of springtime" 3250 (141)

"Good morning, good morning, good morning in spring" 7706 (392)

"Good morning, good morning, warblers" 1726 (191)

"GOOD MORNING, MR. ZIP-ZIP-ZIP" 2156 (129, 130, 236)

"Good morning, pretty millermaid" 3296 (385)

"Good morning, Pretty Polly, we met in due time" 7937 (393)

"GOOD MORNING TO YOU" 1653 (28)

"Good morrow, Gossip Joan, where have you been a-walking?" 4620 (199, 234)

GOOD MORROW, MISTRESS BRIGHT! 4618 (349)

"Good morrow, mistress bright, Thro' lone woods fleeting" 4618 (349)

"Good morrow, my gentles" 2606 (188)

"Good morrow, 'tis Saint Valentine's day" (from THE AIRS SUNG BY OPHELIA) 4537 (208)

GOOD NIGHT! (Abraham) 7 (258)

GOOD NIGHT (Folksongs, England) 4619 (28, 206, 279, 343, 366)

GOOD NIGHT (Folksongs, Germany) 5353 (95)

GOOD-NIGHT (Folksongs, Sweden) 7307 (135)

"Good-night, good-night, good-night! Oh sun" 7307 (135)

GOOD-NIGHT LADIES 7629 (28, 132, 233, 236, 279, 343, 366, 402)

"Hahves' moon, Hahves' moon, shine on" 8175 (321)

HAI CORE, O CRUDELE 2257 (134)

"Hai core, o crudele, per farmi morir" 2257 (134, 179)

HAIL COLUMBIA! 2808 (10, 34, 44, 115, 129, 130, 212)

"Hail Columbia, happy land!" 2808 (10, 28, 34, 44, 115, 129, 130, 212, 233, 279, 366)

"Hail! Hail! I belong to the bloodwashed army" 8435 (409)

"HAIL! HAIL! THE GANG'S ALL HERE!" 3669 (10, 28, 129, 130, 131)

"HAIL, HOLY QUEEN" 971 (304)

"Hail Mary full of grace" (Abt) 9 (304)

"Hail, Mary, full of grace" (Arcadelt) 69 (304)

"HAIL MARY FULL OF GRACE" (Carols, England) 8938A (360), 8938B (360)

"Hail, Mary, full of grace" (Cherubini) 662 (304)

"Hail, Mary, full of grace" (Gounod-Bach) 1310 (304)

"Hail Mary, full of grace" (Luzzi) 2213 (304)

"Hail, Mary, full of grace" (Mascagni) 2296 (304)

"Hail, Mary, full of grace" (Millard) 2432 (304)

"Hail, Mary, hail! in grace o'erflowing" 3847 (1, 6)

HAIL OUR GRACIOUS EMPEROR! 6165 (37)

"Hail our gracious Emperor! May he reign ten thousand, thousand years and more!" 6165 (37)

"Hail, Queen, Heavenly Mother, hear our voices raised to Thee" 6868 (295)

"Hail, Rose of wondrous virtue" 2869 (410)

"Hail, sacred Isle! dear land!" 4075 (121)

HAIL! SHEPHERDS HAIL 9050 (361)

"Hail! Shepherds hail! A King is born!" 9050 (361)

"Hail the blest morn, see the great Mediator" 9381 (332)

"Hail! The red wine richly flowing" 2298 (132)

"Hail, thou ever blessed morn!" 8984 (361)

HAIL! THOU STAR THAT GUIDEST 9016 (361)

"Hail! thou star that guidest alleluia, alleluia" 9016 (361)

HAIL TO THE CHIEF (Sanderson) 3156 (28, 279, 366)

HAIL TO THE CHIEF (Withers) 4060 (212)

"Hail to the chief, who in triumph advances" (Sanderson) 3156 (38, 279, 366)

"Hail to the chief who in triumph advances" (Withers) 4060 (212)

"HAIL TO THE LORD'S ANNOINTED" 3957 (315)

"Hail! Ye sighing sons of sorrow" 7824 (86)

"Hail, ye Slavs! Our Slavic language still our souls is greeting" 4346 (279, 366)

"Hail you! and where did you come from" 7813 (332)

HAJDUK VELJKO I CARAPIC VASO 8781 (86)

"HAJEJ, NYNEJ, JEŽÍŠKU" 8870 (388)

"HAJLIK A JEGENYE" 3796 (285)

Halka 2473-2476

HALKA'S ARIA 2476 (295)

"Halk'illan ruskon auermaan käy lento joutsenen" 987 (124)

THE HALL OF CYNDDYLAN 8706 (20)

"The Hall of my Chieftain is gloomy tonight" 8706 (20)

HALLELU 8301 (409)

"Hallelu hallelu O yes the storm is passin' over" 8301 (409)

HALLELUJAH 8302 (409)

"Hallelujah! Hallelujah" 8302 (409)

HALLELUJAH, I'M A BUM 7649 (35, 109, 110, 335)

HALLELUJAH, I'M A-TRAVELIN' 7649 (293)

HALLELUJAH TO DE LAM' 8303 (184)

HALLO, HERR WIRT 2164 (31)

"Hallo, Herr Wirt, noch einen Krug" 2164 (31)

HALVÁNY SÁRGA RÓZSÁT 3157 (285)

"Halvány sárga rózsa bokretaba szedtem" 3157 (285)

"HAMBURG IST EIN SCHÖNES STÄDTCHEN" 5480 (326)

HAME, HAME, HAME 7047 (101)

Hamlet 3727

HAMMER SONG 8304 (331)

HAMMERING 8305 (409)

THE HAMMERS KEEP RINGING 8306 (409)

"The hammers keep ringing on somebody's coffin" 8306 (409)

HAN' ME DOWN YO' SILVAH TRUMPET, GABRIEL 8307 (184)

THE HAND-CART SONG 7650 (173)

HAND EN HOOFD 6472 (384)

"HAND ME DOWN MY WALKING CANE" 331 (129)

HAND O'ER HAND 9443A (29)

A HANDFUL OF EARTH 682 (114)

HANDKERCHIEF DANCE 4340 (37)

"Handsome is my yearling foal!" 2238 (124)

HANDSOME LADDIE 672* (295)

HANDWERKSBURSCHEN-ABSCHIED 5298 (99)

"A handy ship and a handy crew, Handy, my boys, so handy!" 9443A (29), 9443B (320)

"Hang down your head, Tom Dooley" 8065 (227)

HANGIN' JOHNNIE 9444 (401)

HANGING JOHNNY 9444 (205, 235, 320)

THE HANGMAN'S TREE 7651 (243)

HANGSAMAN 7651 (109, 110)

HANIS MOJA, HANIS 6713 (159)

"Haniś moja, haniś, čoześ za Hanisia" 6713 (159)

HANKA 5360 (95)

"Hanka, with heavy dark-brown hair" 5360 (95)

HANS DE SCHNÔCKELOCH 4987 (88)

"Hans, Hans de Schnôckeloch a tout c'qu'il veut en mains" 4987 (88)

HANS NABER 5361 (41)

"Hans Naber, ick hebb et ju togebracht" 5361 (41)

HANS SAID 'KUNTZ' 5791 (92)

"Hans said 'Kuntz, I think we might steal our neighbor's geese tonight'" 5791 (92)

HANS UND LIESEL 4114 (31, 99)

HANS UND VERENE 5362 (31)

HANUKKAH SONG 6187 (33, 35)

"HAPPINESS IS A FLEETING THING" 3134 (190)

"HAPPINESS THE SUN IS BRINGING" 9413 (154)

HAPPY BIRTHDAY 1788 (291)

"THE HAPPY CHRISTMAS COMES ONCE MORE" 164 (165, 296)

THE HAPPY CLOWN 4624 (349)

The happy farmer (tune) 4624 (349)

"Happy he, girl, he who calls you daughter" 5636 (95)

A HAPPY HEART 820 (128, 132)

HAPPY I 4330 (94)

"Happy I, happy I, my dear lad passing by" 4330 (94)

A HAPPY NEW YEAR (Folksongs, England) 4621 (44)

"Happy the man who has not sinned" 6174 (318)

THE HAPPY VAGABOND 461 (191, 193, 195)

HAPPY WE ARE A' THE GITHER 7048 (101)

"Har Chîeli zum Brunne Gar wenig schint d'Sunne" 7370 (230)

"Har-rayich hema yismachu" 6275 (318)

THE HARD LOT OF A LEGIONNAIRE 6690 (295)

HARD TIMES COME AGAIN NO MORE 1115 (28, 236, 279, 366)

HARD TRAVELIN' 1427 (293)

"HARK, FROM THE MIDNIGHT HILLS AROUND" 312 (296)

HAULING ON THE BOWLINE 9446A (320)
HAUT, HAUT PEYROT 9069 (361)
"Have pity and release my soul" 2257 (134)
"Have ye heard the rule me boys?" 2234 (114)
"Have yo' heard 'bout dat bully" 3767 (114,131)
"Have you any bread and wine? For we are the Romans" 4743 (216)
"Have you ever been in love, me boys" 5915 (172)
"Have you ever thought as the hearse goes by" 7655 (225)
HAVE YOU HEARD? 8728 (11)
"Have you heard about dat bully" 3767 (115)
"Have you heard about our Jesus?" 9362 (268)
"Have you heard how in the Negev" 375 (318)
"Have you heard of the ship called the good Reuben James" 7951 (7,293)
"Have you heard, Oh have you heard?" 8728 (11)
HAVE YOU SEEN 4882 (37)
"HAVE YOU SEEN BUT A WHITE LILY GROW" 4628 (36)
"HAVE YOU SEEN BUT A WHYTE LILLIE GROW" 4628 (106,403)
"HAVE YOU SEEN BUT THE WHYTE LILLIE GROW" 4628 (386)
"Have you seen my bonny boy" 1387 (208)
"Have you seen the white night-cap" 4882 (37)
HAVE YOU STRUCK ILE? 7653 (189)
"DET HAVER SAA NYLIGEN REGNET" 4464 (231)
HAWAIIAN FAREWELL SONG 2133 (233)
HAWAISCHES LIED 2133 (222)
"Hawkie is a bonny cow" 4558 (235)
THE HAWTHORN TREE 4629 (13)
"Hay un lirio que el tiempo no consume" 6361 (247)
HAYNAS MOZAS 7260 (283)
"Haynas mozas, haynas mozas, haynas mozas na ribeira" 7260 (283)
"HAYNT IZ PURIM, BRIDER" 1296 (318)
HAYO, HAYA 6206 (318)
"Hayo, haya, melech rasha, melech rasha" 6206 (318)
HAY'TAH ARTSI 3981 (30)
THE HAZEL DELL 3069 (129,130)
HÁZUNK ELÖTT MENNEK EL 5721 (92)
"Házunk elött mennek el a huszárok" 5721 (92,164)
"He bare him up, he bare him down" 3444 (334)
HE BECAME INCARNATE 9192 (244)
"He became incarnate, Christ the King of glory" 9192 (244)
HÉ! BEYLA-Z-Y DAU FÉ! 4988 (66)
"Hé! Beyla-z-y dau fé an aquel azé!" 4988 (66)
"He built his throne up in the air" 8308 (409)
"HE BY WHOM THE HEAVENS WERE MADE" 9034 (361)
"He by whose mighty word is banished ev'ry sadness" 2309 (1)
HE CAME FROM HIS PALACE GRAND 7654 (321)
"He came from his palace grand and he came to my cottage door" 7654 (321)
HE CARVED HIS MOTHER'S NAME UPON THE TREE 779 (131)
HE DOETH ALL THINGS WELL 4096 (212)
HÉ! DONNE-LUI DU FOIN! 4988 (66)
"He! Donne-lui du foin à ce pauvre âne!" 4988 (66)
"He don't know, he don't know my mind" 8424 (336)
"He flies thro' the air with the greatest of ease" 2702 (34)
"He flies through the air with the greatest of ease" 2702 (225)
"He flies thru the air with the greatest of ease" 2702 (128,236)

"He followed her up and he followed her down" 7764 (263)
"He had no right near my nets to anchor" 6637 (37)
"He had to run, run, run" 8519 (184)
"HE HAS FLOWN, MY PRETTY TURTLE-DOVE" 2689 (1)
HE HAS SILVER 6656 (86)
"He has silver, he has silver, but he never gives me any" 6656 (86)
"HE IS BORN, LITTLE INFANT KING" 9070 (33)
"HE IS BORN, THE HOLY ONE!" 9070 (39,361)
"He is come, come, come!" 9075 (361)
"He is drawn to the snare by cruel Fate devised" 2203 (146)
"He is kind, he is good" 2309 (1)
HE IS KING OF KINGS 8308 (409)
HE IS MY LOVE 4916 (140)
HE IS NOBLE, HE IS PATIENT 3365 (276)
"He is noble, he is patient, he is tender, true, and kind" 3365 (276)
"He kissed, he kissed, he kissed her!" 1709 (237)
"He made the sun to shine by day" 8281 (409)
"He makes for me a whistle" 6208 (318)
HE NEVER SAID A MUMBALIN' WORD 8233A (76), 8233B (409)
"He once did love with fond affection" 7592 (243)
"He rode up to the old man's gate" 8041 (243)
"He sang a hymn, when He was facing Calv'ry's cruel cross" 817 (398)
"He sews and sews the whole week long" 6236 (318)
HE SHALL FEED HIS FLOCK 1466 (123,200,337)
"He shall feed His flock like a shepherd" 1466 (123,200, 337)
"HE SMILES WITHIN HIS CRADLE" 9164 (251,271,307, 410)
"He that dwelleth in the secret place" 3449 (200)
HE THAT KEEPETH ISRAEL (Schlösser) 3224 (123)
"He that keepeth Israel, slumbers not, nor sleeps" (Schlösser) 3224 (123)
HE VENIDO A DESPEDIRME 1363 (284)
"He was a highborn gentleman" 7212 (215)
"He was handed up his orders at Monroe, Virginia" 1235 (109)
"He was her man, but he done her wrong" 7597B (227)
"He was only a lavender cowboy" 7771 (169)
"He went up to London and straight-a-way strode" 8037A (293)
"He who heav'n created" 9034 (388)
"He Who heav'n hath made for all" 9034 (206)
"He who is noble, kind in thought and action" 1083 (28)
"HE, WHOM JOYOUS SHEPHERDS PRAISED" 9033 (388)
HE WHO'S TRUE AND RIGHTEOUS 4371 (324)
"He who's true and righteous and who gladly fights" 4371 (324)
"He will be our dearest friend" 8520 (366)
"He will ere long be here" 3820 (1)
"Heah's yo' coal, heah's yo' coal" 8603 (409)
"Hear all men and mark ye well!" 5375B (230)
"Hear how the angels sing all in chorus" 8834 (154)
"Hear how the chetnik's bugle calls" 8790 (7)
HEAR ME PRAYING 8309 (409)
HEAR ME WHISPER 5823 (92)
"Hear me whisper low in your ear, let me be your sweetheart, my dear" 5823 (92)
"Hear me, ye nymphs, and ev'ry swain" 7019 (101)
"HEAR MY CRY, O LORD!" 4103 (398)
"Hear, oh hear the splendid singing" 2721 (124)
HEAR, O SHEPHERDS 9415A (337)

"Heraus, heraus der Klingen, lasst Ross und Klepper springen" 5481 (31,99)
"L'herbe est molle au sommeil" 945 (362,364)
HERBEI, O IHR GLÄUBIGEN 9157 (326)
"Herbei, o ihr Gläubigen, fröhlich triumphierend" 9157 (326)
HERBST 11 (31)
HERBSTLIED (Köhler) 1946 (49)
HERBSTLIED (Zelter) 4136 (229)
HERDERS HIJ IS GEBOOREN 9244 (361)
HERDERS HIJ IS GEBOOREN 9244 (201,384)
"Herders, hij is geboren in't midden van den nacht" 9244 (201,384)
DE HERDERTJES 9245 (201)
"De herdertjes lagen bij nachte" 9245 (201)
HERDMAID'S SONG 6638 (230)
"Here, a sheer hulk, lies poor Tom Bowling" 834 (205, 235,349,402)
HERE A TORCH 9066 (271)
"Here a torch, Jeanette, Isabella" 9066 (271)
"HERE AM I, A SHEPHERD" 4355 (94)
"Here am I in her boudoir" 3733 (2)
"HERE AMID THE SHADY WOODS" 1447 (275)
"Here are fruit, flowers, leaves, and branches" 1504 (191,193,195)
"Here aroond the ingle breezing" 7048 (101)
"Here at the portal shall my garland" 404 (272)
HERE AWA', THERE AWA' 7050 (349,365)
"Here awa', there awa', wandering Willie" 7050 (100, 349,365)
HERE BELOW 1047 (362)
"Here below, lilacs die and never is bird song more than a short refrain" 1047 (362)
"Here beside the stream I weep" 4856 (124)
"HERE BETWIXT ASS AND OXEN MILD" 9064 (38,39)
"HERE BY THIS SPRING RECLINING" 267 (188)
"Here come the crows to steal the corn" 1034 (199)
"HERE COME THREE DUKES A-RIDING" 7658 (185)
"HERE COME THREE MERCHANTS A-RIDING" 7659 (109,110)
"Here come two dukes a-riding" 8075 (313)
"Here comes the doughnut man" 8030 (335)
"Here comes the train, it's here again" 7227 (239)
"Here goes the broom man" 8203 (184)
"Here he swore to love me, ever, spoke his love and went away" 255 (292)
"Here I bring my garden's crop" 2123 (318)
"Here I sit and cross my feet" 6231 (318)
"Here I sit on Buttermilk Hill" 7739 (173)
HERE IN OUR GROVE 7342 (188)
"Here in our grove are blue billberries fair" 7342 (188)
HERE IN THE TWILIGHT 1303 (132)
HERE IS JOY FOR EVERY AGE 9020 (377)
"Here is joy for ev'ry age, ev'ry generation" 9020 (377)
"Here is joy for ev'ry one, here is wondrous shewing" 9020 (361)
HERE IS JOY FOR EV'RYONE 9020 (361)
"HERE IS THE LITTLE DOOR" 1719 (307)
"Here is the usual place for the smugglers to gather" 319 (1)
"HERE SHE HER SACRED BOWER ADORNES" 545 (196)
"HERE THE PRETTY BIRDS" 827 (175)
"Here upon a stone I'm sitting" 6971 (95)
HERE WE COME A-CAROLING 9001A (206,296)
"Here we come a-caroling among the leaves so green" 9001A (206,296)

HERE WE COME A-WASSAILING 9001A (38,39,79,165, 333,334,410), 9001B (333,334), 9001C (319)
"Here we come a-wassailing, among the leaves so green" 9001A (33,35,38,39,44,79,125,165,333,334, 337,349,410) 9001B (271,333,334) 9001C (319)
"Here we come gath'ring nuts in May" 4608 (214)
"Here we go 'round the old soapgourd" 7886 (313)
"Here where roses still bloom, where tendrils of laurels are twining" 4064 (220)
"Here where the shoulders of the downs" 3000 (306)
"HERE WITH THE ASS AND OXEN MILD" 9064 (33)
"HERE'S A HEALTH TO ANE I LO'E DEAR" 7051 (101)
"Here's a health to the Barley Mow, my boys" 4547 (13, 235,349)
"Here's a health to the king and a lasting peace" 4582 (13,235,273)
"Here's a health to the king, and lasting peace" 4582 (402)
"HERE'S A HEALTH UNTO HIS MAJESTY" 3171 (14,234, 349,402)
"Here's a lad from Krakow, he is quite a dandy" 6754 (295)
"Here's to good old Yale, drink it down, drink it down" 7445 (225)
HERE'S TO THE MAIDEN 4632 (14,106)
"Here's to the maiden of bashful fifteen" 4632 (14,106)
"Here's to the Squire that goes on parade" 387 (44)
HERE'S YOUR MULE 281 (161)
Herlich thut mich verlangen 1550
HERLIGT EN SOMMERNAT 1996 (87)
"Herligt en Sommernat drage til Elverkrat" 1996 (87)
HERMANN UND THUSNELDA 2638 (250)
"Hermosa flor de limón, dame de tu medicina" 6349 (9)
HEROD DEAD 9206 (388)
"Herod dead, Our Lord returneth" 9206 (388)
"Hérode! Hérode! Ne me refuse pas!" 2310 (357)
Hérodiade 2309-2313
"Heroes are threading through meadowlands" 1923 (288)
THE HEROES OF THE SEA 5925 (349)
"Heroes of Wales! Free men arise!" 8703 (235)
THE HERON 5759 (279)
THE HERONS 9462 (186)
"Herr Abt, ich fühle mich" 245 (42)
"Herr, den ich tief im Herzen trage" 1656 (123)
Der Herr denket an uns 119 (50)
"Herr Heinrich sitzt am Vogelherd" 2179 (96,99,328)
Der Herr ist mein getreuer Hirt 1612 (50)
Herr Jesu Christ, mein Leben's Licht (tune) 9146
"Herr! schicke was du willt, ein Liebes oder Leides" 4074 (98,408)
"DER HERR SEGNE EUCH" 119 (50)
"Herrlich bricht aus Wolkenschleiern schon der Sonne frühster Strahl" 3945 (49)
DAS HERZ AM RHEIN 1654 (31,327)
Herz und Mund und Tat und Leben. Wohl mir, dass ich Jesum habe 120
"Herzenkönig und Pikdame sind in meinem Kartenschlosse" 4025 (224)
HERZENSTAUSCH 3004 (96)
HERZIG SCHÖNS RÖSELEIN 5368 (49)
"Herzig schöns Röselein schmeckt uns der Wein so gut" 5368 (49)
HERZLICH TUT MICH ERFREUEN 3029 (226)

"Herzlich tut mich erfreuen die fröhlich Sommerzeit"
      3029 (226)
HERZLIEB, ICH HAB VERNOMMEN 5369 (49)
"Herzlieb, ich hab vernommen, dass du sollst scheiden von
      mir" 5369 (49)
"HERZLIEBCHEN MEIN UNTERM REBENDACH" 701 (326,
      327)
"Herzliebe, gute Mutter" 3261 (141)
"HE'S A-CHOPPIN IN DE NEW GROUN'" 8312 (184)
HE'S A FOOL 7660 (293)
"HE'S A MIGHTY GOOD LEADER" 8311 (409)
HE'S GONE AWAY 7661 (109, 110, 215, 321)
"He's gone to be a soldier in the army of the Lord" 3565
      (109)
"HE'S GOT HIS EYES ON YOU" 8313 (409)
HE'S JUS' DE SAME TODAY 8314 (76)
"He's such a li'l' fellow" 838 (136)
"He's the man who fights the smoke, the flames and fire"
      2634 (131)
"HÉT CSILLAGBÓL VAN A GÖNCÖL SZEKERE" 5723 (92)
HÉT CSILLAGBÓL VAN A GÖNCZÖL SZEKERE 5723 (164)
HET IS EEN DACH DER VROOLIKHEIT 9018 (384)
"Het is een dach der vroolikheit in des coninx hove" 9018
      (384)
HET IS EEN DAG DER VROOKIJKHEID 9018 (201)
"Het is een dag der vroolijkheid in des Konings hove"
      9018 (201)
"Heuer im Sommer an Sonnentagen hat mir der Garten
      Blumen getragen" 4126 (224)
L'HEURE EXQUISE (Hahn) 1503 (121, 140, 191, 193, 195,
      237, 241)
L'HEURE EXQUISE (Poldowski) 2840 (191, 193, 195)
L'HEUREUX VAGABOND 461 (191, 193, 195)
"Heut geht an Bord, heut segeln wir fort" 5370 (326)
HEUT GEHT ES AN BORD 5370 (326)
HEUT' HAB' ICH DAS GLÜCK GEFUNDEN! 199 (222)
"HEUT IST EIN FEST BEI DEN FRÖSCHEN AM SEE" 5371
      (326)
"HEUT IST EIN FREUDENRIECHER TAG" 5372 (49, 309, 326)
"Heut' kam mein junges Liebchen zu mir ins kleine Stübchen"
      6080 (51)
"HEUT' MACHT DIE WELT SONNTAG FÜR MICH" 884
      (396)
"HEUT NOCH SIND WIR HIER ZU HAUS" 5373 (309, 326)
"HEUT SCHEINT DIE SONNE INS HERZ MIR HINEIN!" 2986
      (255)
"HEUT SOLL DAS GROSSE FLACHSERNTEN SEIN" 7310
      (49, 309)
HEUTE BIN ICH ROT 4182 (231)
"Heute bin ich rot und morgen bin ich tot" 4182 (231)
HEUTE IST HEUT 220 (31)
"Heute nacht ist heilige Nacht" 9320 (354)
Heute scheid ich (tune) 1067
"Heute scheid ich, morgen wandr ich" 1067 (99)
"Heute tanzt in der Taverne" 2785 (223)
"Heute wollen wir marschiern, einen neuen Marsch
      probiern" 5500 (326)
HEY, BETTY MARTIN! 7662 (185, 216)
"Hey, Betty Martin, tip-toe, tip-toe" 7662 (185)
"Hey, Betty Martin, tippy toe, tippy toe" 7662 (216)
"Hey! boys, I want the linin' bars!" 8595 (335)
HEY, CA' THRO' 7052 (232)
"Hey, ca' thro', ca' thro', for we hae meikle ado" 7052
      (101, 104, 232)
HEY, DIDDLE DIDDLE 4633 (28, 173, 366)

"Hey, diddle, diddle, the cat and the fiddle, the cow
      jumped over the moon" 4633 (28, 173, 366)
HEY FOLKS, HEARKEN 6718 (295)
"Hey! Get out the way, Ol' Dan Tucker" 1002 (170)
"Hey, hey, hey, hey, hey, hey, hey, hey, Click your
      heels till sparks are flying, let your dance be bright
      and snappy" 6813 (159)
"Hey, hey, hey, somebody knockin' at my door" 8226
      (336)
HEY, HEY, HO 659 (296)
"Hey, hey, ho, the north winds blow" 659 (296)
HEY HO, NOBODY HOME 4634 (293)
"Hey ho, nobody home, meat nor drink nor money have I
      none" 4634 (293)
HEY, HO, THE MORNING DEW 5926 (349)
"HEY, HO! TO THE GREENWOOD" 493 (37, 144, 235)
"HEY, I AM A HIGHLAND LADDIE" 6716 (159)
"Hey, Mazury people strong!" 3685 (295)
"Hey, Mazurze, who's that prancing?" 6719 (295)
HEY, MR. HACHA 1784 (7)
"Hey, mister! Hey, mister! Tell us, what can you do?"
      5148B (21)
HEY, OUR CHIEFTAIN 6725 (159)
"Hey, our chieftain, chieftain old, your lads are we,
      brigands bold" 6725 (159)
"Hey, Rakoczi! Hey, Berczenyi! Magyar leaders unfor-
      gotten!" 5761 (7)
"Hey, Red Navy! The Baltic Fleet of glory" 336 (339)
"Hey the Bannock, Ho the Bannock" 9194 (154)
HEY THE BONNIE BREIST-KNOTS 7053 (103, 104)
"Hey the bonnie, how the bonnie, hey the bonnie breist-
      knots!" 7053 (103, 104)
HEY THE DUSTY MILLER 7054 (104)
"Hey the dusty miller and his dusty coat" 7054 (104)
HEY! TO THE WOODS 6717 (295)
"Hey! to the woods, gleams my feather like the sleet"
      6717 (295)
Hey tutti tatti (tune) 7087
Hey tutti tatti (tune) 7164
"Hey-yup! Boy. Wimoweh" 7229 (389)
HEY! ZHANKOYE 6177 (293)
"Hi, ho, hi, ho" 4341 (94)
HI HO, JERUM 8315A (72)
HI, HO, THE GREEN GROVE 4341 (94)
HI HO THE PREACHER MAN 7663 (265)
"Hi ho the Preacher Man! He can preach and he can pray"
      7663 (265)
"HI, LITTLE MILLER'S ANNA" 4305 (94)
"'Hi!' said the blackbird sittin' on a chair" 7447 (406)
"Hi! said the blackbird sitting on a chair" 7447 (110)
"Hi! said the little leather-winged bat" 7775 (72)
"Hi! said the little leatherwing bat" 7775 (227)
"'Hi', says the blackbird, sittin' on a chair" 7447 (225)
"Hi, says the blackbird, sitting on a chair" 7447 (216)
"Hi, says the little leather-winged bat" 7775 (169)
HI, THERE, MUSICIAN 263 (135)
"Hi, there, musician! Come blow your trumpet" 263 (135)
HI-YO WITZI 4017 (37)
"Hi-yo, hi-yo witzi nai-yo" 4017 (37)
HIAWATHA'S WOOING 5849 (279)
"Hide not thy anguish, Thou must not deceive me" 5898
      (86)
HIE AWAY HOME 8316 (225)
"Hie upon Hielands and laigh upon Tay" 7010 (35)
HIELAND LADDIE 7011 (101)

"HIER HAB ICH SO MANCHES LIEBE MAL" 2877 (99,326, 327,353)
"Hier habt ihr mein Herz! Ach fliehet nicht" 2261 (218)
"HIER IN DES ABENDS TRAULICH ERNSTER STILLE" 1083 (326)
"HIER IS ONZE FIERE PINKSTERBLOM" 6477 (203)
"Hier leigt ein Leuchten über dem Land!" 2988 (258)
"Hier ob dem Eingang seid befestiget" 404 (272)
"HIER SIND WIR VERSAMMELT" 976 (43,353)
"Hier sind wir versammelt zu löblichem Tun" 976 (31, 43,99,353)
"Hiers ek weer, hiers ek weer met my rooi rok voor jou deur" 6454 (384)
HIGH BARBAREE 9447A (169,173,235,401), 9447B (320)
HIGH CHIN BOB 7616 (80)
HIGH GERMANY 4635 (198)
"High heav'n hath stoop'd to earth so lowly" 1315 (394)
"High, high up she rises!" 9440B (225)
"High in the sky at break of dawn I see the swallow fly" 3427 (236)
"High ho, the boatmen row" 7460A (335)
HIGH ON A HILL 2630 (30)
"High on the mountaintop fires are burning" 4385 (86)
HIGH-PRICED BLUES 8317 (336)
"High row the boatmen row" 7460A (83)
"High Sheriff tol' de deputy, (Hanh)" 8488 (227)
HIGH SKALITZA'S TOWER 4415 (94)
"High Skalitza's tow'r, very, very, high" 4415 (94)
"HIGH STANDS THE GREEN HILL" 4349 (94)
HIGH THE CRANES ARE FLYING 5759 (164)
"High the cranes are flying, I can hear them shriek" 5759 (164)
"High the star of evening, now good night my darling" 4450B (94)
HIGH THE WAVES OF LAKE BALATON 5724 (164)
"High the waves of Lake Balaton ran, his boat there drove a young fisherman" 5724 (164)
"High upon Hielands and laigh upon Tay" 7010 (102)
HIGH YOU SHINE 4450A, 4450B (94)
"High you shine, evening star" 4450A (94,95)
THE HIGHER THE PLUM-TREE 2062 (235)
"The higher the plum-tree, the riper the plum" 2062 (235)
HIGHLAND FOLK WERE SOWING 6883 (295)
"Highland folk were sowing all oats, all oats" 6883 (295)
A HIGHLAND LAD 7203 (100,103,104,235)
"A HIGHLAND LAD MY LOVE WAS BORN" (O gin ye were dead, Gudeman, tune) 7175A (232)
"A Highland lad my love was born" (The White Cockade, tune) 7203 (17,100,103,104,235)
HIGHLAND LADDIE (Folksongs, Scotland) 7011 (17)
HIGHLAND LADDIE (Sea chanty) 9448A (320), 9448B (171)
HIGHLAND MARY 7055 (101)
HIGHLAND SONG 6712 (295)
HIGHLANDS, OH OUR HIGHLANDS 2679 (295)
"Highlands, oh our highlands, With your dales and mountains" 2679 (295)
THE HIGHWAYMAN 4636 (198)
THE HIGHWAYMAN OUTWITTED 4637 (198)
EL HIJO DE LA VIRGEN 8857 (55)
"Hijo, dime ¿por qué rien los niños con tal humor?" 8849 (54)
HIKING SONG 4347 (37)
"Hildebrand und sein Sohn Hadubrand" 12 (31)
DAS HILDEBRANDLIED 12 (31)

HILL AN' GULLY 8730 (252)
"Hill an' Gully ride-a, Hill an' Gully" 8730 (252)
"Hill an' Gully rider Hill an' Gully" 8730 (11)
HILL AND GULLY 8730 (11)
"The hills and mountains too, rejoice" 6275 (318)
"The hills are glowing with bloom and blossom" 6017 (133)
THE HILLS OF GLENSHEE 7664 (72)
HILO 9456 (29)
DIE HIMMEL RÜHMEN 228
DIE HIMMEL RÜHMEN DES EWIGEN EHRE 228
"Himmels-au, licht und blau, wieviel zählst du Sternlein?" 5552 (49)
HINAUS AUF DIE SEE 6582 (99)
HINAUS IN DIE FERNE 2403 (353)
"Hinaus in die Ferne mit lautem Hörnerklang" 2403 (31, 99,353)
HINAUS IN'S FREIE! 3368 (141)
Hind horn (tune) 7482A
HINDOO SONG 269 (140)
"Hingestreckt im hohen Gras" 1931 (49)
HINKY DINKY 7665 (109,110)
HINKY DINKY PARLAY-VOO 7665 (7)
HINKY DINKY PARLEE VOO 7665 (132)
HINKY DINKY PARLEY VOO 7665 (10,225)
"Hinter den Scheiben fiel Dämmerschein nieder" 4026 (224)
"HINUNTER IST DER SONNEN SCHEIN" 3892 (49)
"Hio, Hio, Hio, de boatman row" 7460C(343)
Hippolyte et Aricie 2962-2963
HIRAM HUBBARD 7666 (312)
"Hiram Hubbard was not guilty, I've heard great many say" 7666 (312)
HIROUR ERREGEREKI 8822 (361)
DIE HIRTEN 718 (97,250)
HIRTEN, AUF UM MITTERNACHT! 8801 (388)
"Hirten, auf um Mitternacht, erhebt euch aus dem Schlafe" 8801 (388)
"HIRTEN, HABT IHR ES GESEHEN" 9415B (354)
DIR HIRTEN UND DIE ENGEL 9248 (354)
"Hirten wachen im Feld, Nacht ist rings auf der Welt" 718 (97,250)
DIE HIRTEN WIEGENLIED 9165A (79)
HIRTENLIED 5786 (24)
EIN HIRTENSANG 9158 (79)
HIRTENSYMPHONIE 1469
HIS COMING 1153 (137)
HIS EYE IS ON THE SPARROW 1185 (398)
"His eye was on my bouquet, no doubt his wish it would say" 2497 (1,362)
"His eyes with fire were flaming" 2115 (1,176)
"HIS GOLDEN LOCKS TIME HATH TO SILVER TURNDE" 902 (144)
HIS HAIR WAS BLACK 6013 (166,213)
"His hair was black, his eye was blue" 6013 (34,166,213)
HIS HEAD IS BIG 5770 (164)
"His head is big, let the horse be sad" 5770 (164)
HISTORIA VON NOAH 3025 (99)
DE HISTORY OB DE WORLD 7667 (189)
"Hitba-ata b'tarmit ragley bat Anamit" 6272 (318)
"Hit's a mighty dry year when de crab grass fail" 8627 (212)
L'HIVER 1939 (192,194)
HJARTATS SAANGER 1522 (355)
HJURINGSVISA 6638 (230)
HO ACQUISTATO UN MARITINO 6149 (325)

"Ho bend yo' backs and line it straight" 8026 (331)
"Ho! Boys Ho! for California Ho!" 7426 (115)
"Ho, boys, is you right? Done got right" 8210 (227)
"Ho, broder Teague, dost hear de decree" 4673 (199, 294)
"Ho! brother Teague dost hear de decree" 4673 (402)
"Ho! brother Teague dost hear the decree" 4673 (14, 235)
HO FOR CALIFORNIA 9475 (335)
HO FOR THE KANSAS PLAINS 681*. (189)
"Ho! Goatherd, Ho! Ho! Goatherd, Ho!" 8665 (249)
"Ho! ho! she's a fickle wild rose" 4639 (189)
"Ho il cor gonfio di lagrime" 2848 · (2)
HO! JOLLY GNOMES 9329 (188)
"Ho! jolly gnomes fill up the glasses" 9329 (188)
"Ho! page-boy! Be off and hang yourselves" 3839 (4)
"HO, RO! MY NUT-BROWN MAIDEN" 7056 (100, 102)
"Ho, the car emancipation rides majestic thro' our nation" 7610 (189)
"Ho, there you are Punchinello" 6126 (214)
HO UN DOLORE IN SENO 6151 (325)
"Ho veduta una fanciulla" 6070 (51)
HO! WESTWARD HO! 851 (189)
HOB ICH A POR OKSN 6207 (318)
"Hob ich a por oksn, oksn" 6207 (318)
"HOB ICH MIR A KLEYNEM MICHALKE" 6208 (318)
HOBELLIED 1976 (99, 326, 353)
"Hoch die Gläser, hoch das Leben" 4046 (223)
Hoch droben auf'm Berge (tune) 5584
HOCH SOLL ER LEBEN 5374 (353)
"Hoch soll er leben, hoch soll er leben, dreimal hoch!" 5374 (326, 353)
HOCH VOM DACHSTEIN 3434 (326)
"Hoch vom Dachstein an, wo der Aar noch haust" 3434 (326)
"Hochgetürmte Rimaflut" 2358 (356)
Hochzeit in Samarkand 1991 (222)
HOCHZEITSLIED 5440B (99)
Hochzeitsnacht im Paradies 3244-3246
HOE LEIT DIT KINDEKEN 9248 (201)
"Hoe leit dit kindeken hier in de kou" 9248 (201)
HOE LUIDE ZONG DE LEERAAR 6478 (384)
"Hoe luide zoo zong de leeraar al op de tinnen" 6478 (384)
HOE RIJ DIE BOERE? 6479 (384)
"Hoe rij die Boere? Sit, sit so!" 6479 (384)
"HOE ZACHTJES GLIJDT ONS BOOTJE" 6480 (384)
"HÖCHSTE LUST UND TIEFSTES LEID" 2444 (257)
HÖGA VISAN 2683 (356)
"Die Höh'n und Wälder schon steigen" 1156 (210, 226, 229)
DER HÖLLE RACHE 2598 (221, 292)
"Der Hölle Rache kocht in meinem Herzen" 2598 (221, 292)
HØR, UNGERSVEND, SIIG IKKE NEI 1540 (87)
"Hør Ungersvend, slig ikke nei, leeg Tavlebord med mig!" 1540 (87)
HÖR' VON FRÜH BIS SPÄT 5745 (92)
"Hö'r' von früh bis spät zum Abenddämmern" 5745 (92)
HÖR', WAS LEIS' INS OHR 5823 (92)
"Hör', was leis' ins Ohr ich dir raun', will dein Schatz sein, kannst mir vertrau'n" 5823 (92)
HÖRE MIT SINN 3902 (2)
"Höre mit Sinn, was ich dir sage" 3902 (2)
"Hörst du mein heimliches Rufen" 2833 (222)
HÖRT DER ENGEL HELLE LIEDER 9043A (354)
"Hört der Engel helle Lieder klingen das weite Feld entlang" 9043A (354)
HÖRT, IHR HERRN 5375A (49)

"HÖRT, IHR HERRN UND LASST EUCH SAGEN" 5375A (49, 309, 326), 5375B (230)
"Hösten är kommen, hör stormarnes gny!" 751 (135)
HOFFNUNG (Reichardt) 3020 (122, 329)
DIE HOFFNUNG (Schubert) 3275 (229)
"Der Hoffnung letzter Schimmer sinkt dahin" 225 (272)
HOG DROVERS 7668 (44)
"Hog drovers, hog drovers, hog drovers are we" 7668 (44)
"Hog got away in my back yard" 8534 (184)
"HOGYHA OLYKOR ÉJFÉLTÁJBAN" 1846 (285)
HOGYHA SZERETNÉLEK 3168 (285)
"HOHE NACHT DER KLAREN STERNE" 206 (326)
HOJITA DE GUARUMAL 6653 (284)
"Hojita de guarumal donde vive la langosta" 6653 (284)
HOKIHOKI TONU MAI 6631 (86)
"Hol' de light, hol' de light" 8182 (184)
"Hol szöke sellö, lenge szello" 3873 (285)
HOL' YUH HAN' 8731 (252)
"Hold me tightly, waltz me lightly" 2097 (329)
HOLD, MEN HOLD! 8940 (337)
"Hold, men, hold! We are very cold" 8940 (337)
HOLD ON! ("Norah, Norah, lemme...") 8318 (266)
HOLD ON ("Some of these days...") 7669 (231)
HOLD THE FORT 7670 (293)
"Hold the fort for we are coming" 7670 (293)
"HOLD THE WIND!" 8319 (409)
HOLD THOU MY HAND 740 (123)
HOLDE AÏDA 3819 (391)
"Holde Aïda, himmelentstammend" 3819 (391)
HOLDE FRÜHLINGSZEIT 1277 (229)
"Holde Frühlingszeit scheuch alles Leid!" 1277 (229)
"Holde Schöne, hör' diese Töne" 3676 (255)
"Holder klingt der Vogelsang" (Brahms) 410 (137, 277)
"Holder klingt der Vogelsang" (Schubert) 3286 (141, 229)
"HOLDER MOND, DU SILBERN SCHIFFLEIN" 1285 (49)
HOLKA MODROOKÁ 4348 (178)
"Holka modrooká, nesedávej u potoka" 4348 (178)
"Holl amrantau'r sêr ddywedant" 8657 (19, 349, 402)
HOLLIN GREEN HOLLIN 7057 (86)
THE 'HOLLY AND IVY' GIRL 5927 (133)
"THE HOLLY AND THE IVY" 8941A (33, 38, 39, 271, 293, 305, 307, 319, 333, 337, 354, 363, 388, 410), 8941B (206, 296, 333, 334)
HOLTOYO! 9449 (37)
HOLY BABE 9367C (332)
HOLY BIBLE 8320 (409)
"Holy Bible, Holy Bible" 8320 (409)
THE HOLY BOY 1752 (337)
The holy city (Gaul) 1217-1221
THE HOLY CITY (Maybrick) 2331 (237, 346, 400)
"Holy Father, we Thy children" 120 (89)
"The Holy Ghost is to thee sent" 8938A (360), 8938B (360)
"HOLY GHOST! WITH LIGHT DIVINE" 1308 (28, 366)
"Holy Infant, in Thy cradle" 1178 (344)
HOLY, HOLY, HOLY 968 (28, 233, 236, 346, 366)
"Holy, holy, holy, Lord God Almighty" 968 (28, 233, 236, 346, 366)
"Holy, holy, meek and lowly" 3966 (1)
"Holy maiden blessed thou be" 8986 (360, 361)
HOLY NIGHT, PEACEFUL NIGHT 1408
HOLY NIGHT, SILENT NIGHT 1408
"Holy night, thy spell is ended" 3287 (112)
THE HOLY WELL 8942 (334, 410)
HOME AGAIN 2818 (205)

"How cold your little hand is! Let me warm it in my own" 2887 (3)

"How cold your little hand is! May I keep it warm in mine?" 2887 (3)

"How come that blood on your own coat sleve" 7564A (260)

"How could I ever to love unfaithful be" 3107 (211)

"How could I fain have slumbered before his face I saw" 3966 (1)

"How curious! How curious!" 3859 (143)

"How dark the deep flowing river" 4262 (350)

"HOW DEAR TO ME THE HOUR WHEN DAYLIGHT DIES" 5928 (213)

"How dear to my heart are the scenes of my childhood" 1891 (28,32,34,279,366)

"How dear to the heart are the scenes of my childhood" 1891 (129,130,132)

"How dear to this heart are the scenes of my childhood" 1891 (233)

"How deep the swift flowing river" 4262 (279)

"How delightful to see in those evenings in spring" 4752 (216)

"How do you do stranger?" 7414 (225)

"How do you like to go up in a swing" 1835 (199)

"How do you think I began in the world?" 8016 (173)

HOW D'YE DO 7678 (28,236,366)

"How d'ye do, Mister Johnson?" 7678 (28,236,366)

HOW FAIR THIS SPOT 2950 (276)

"How fair this spot! I gaze to where the golden brook runs by" 2950 (276)

"How far, how far, how far ye seem behind me" 640 (3)

HOW FAR IS IT TO BETHLEHEM 8943 (38,39)

"How far is it to Bethlehem? Not very far" 8943 (38,39, 271)

HOW FEW THE JOYS 2942 (274)

"How few the joys that love hath brought me!" 2942 (274)

HOW FIRM A FOUNDATION 7679 (32,34)

"How firm a foundation ye saints of the Lord" 7679 (32,34)

"How fondly I gaze on the fast falling leaves" 8659 (406)

"How from the skies e'er darkening" 3845 (5)

"HOW GLAD I AM EACH CHRISTMAS EVE" 9284 (244)

HOW GOOD IT IS 6736 (295)

"How good it is to conquer mountains" 6736 (295)

HOW HAPPY THE SOLDIER 4640 (110,225)

"How happy the soldier who lives on his pay" 4640 (110, 225)

"How hath the tempest riven the gray robe of the sky" 3322 (45)

"How I shrink! how I quail! yet must the deed be done" 656 (148)

HOW I WOULD PLOUGH 5813 (164)

"How I would plough the land! Oxen drive through the sand" 5813 (164)

HOW IT RAINS 6957 (37)

"HOW LANG AND DREARY IS THE NICHT" 7058 (101)

"How little you good people know" 4116 (44)

HOW LONG 605 (336)

"How long did it rain?" 8340 (409)

"How long, O Lord, wilt Thou forget me?" 4102 (398)

HOW LONG TRAIN BEEN GONE? 8324 (182)

HOW LOVELY IS THE HAND OF GOD 2192 (241)

"HOW MANY A KING A-DREAMING" 9204 (361)

"HOW MANY MILES TO BETH-E-LE-HEM?" 9358 (332)

"How many miles to London Town?" 9358 (332)

"How oft then I linger'd alone at your bed" 2940 (237)

"How often at midnight" 2940 (275)

"How often haunting the highest hilltop I scan the ocean thy sail to see" 7004 (103)

"How often sweet remembrance" 3263 (141)

HOW OLD ARE YOU? 4702B (214)

"How old are you my pretty little miss" 4702A (171), 4702B (214)

HOW PLEASANT, SWEET BIRDIES 5929 (133)

"How pleasant, sweet birdies, to wake in the dawn" 5929 (133)

"How quickly flies ev'ry moment" 6779 (295)

HOW SAD WAS THE EVENING 6299 (322)

"How sad was the evening, with snowflakes descending" 6299 (322)

"How seldom will you meet a man" 691 (114)

HOW SHALL AN ARTLESS MAIDEN? 6089 (211)

"How shall an artless maiden hold her lover true?" 6089 (211)

"HOW SHALL I FITLY MEET THEE?" 140 (337)

"HOW SHOULD I YOUR TRUE LOVE KNOW?" (Folksongs, England) 4641 (36,215,397)

"How should I your true love know" (from the AIRS SUNG BY OPHELIA) 4537 (208)

"How should I your true love know" (White) 4015 (344)

"How soon you forgot about me, Jasiuleńku mine" 6748 (295)

"How stands the glass around?" 8128 (173)

"How still the twilight draped in evening shadow" 3920 (364)

"How strange and dead is everything here" 3516 (2)

"How strangely, how strangely" 3859 (221)

"How sweet is the shepherd's sweet lot!" 451 (199)

"How sweet this hour, when no danger is low'ring" 2315 (3)

"How tedious and tasteless the hours" 7642 (34,212)

HOW THE BANNER'D ANGELS 8823 (361)

"How the banner'd angels down the night go singing!" 8823 (361)

HOW THE DAYS GO 5168 (21)

"How uplifted the heart trusting Thee" 3259 (160)

"HOW VAIN THE CRUEL HEROD'S FEAR" 3329 (296)

HOW VOID OF COMPASSION 2089 (368)

"How void of compassion is Cupid his fashion" 2089 (368)

"How wide is the flowing river" 4262 (322)

"How wondrous, how wondrous!" 3859 (176)

"How your two eyes can enchant me" 6365 (322)

HOY MIRO SÓLO ABROJOS 6356 (247)

"Hoy miro sólo abrojos, espinas por doquiera" 6356 (247)

HRÁLY DUDY 4350 (178,324)

"Hrály dudy u Pobudy, já jsem je slyšěla" 4350 (178,324)

HÜNDCHEN, KURZ GESCHOREN 5753 (92)

"Hündchen, kurz geschoren, ohne Schwanz und Ohren" 5753 (92)

HUGUENOT SONG 2411 (5)

Les Huguenots 2409-2411

HULANKA (Chopin) 668 (295)

"Hull az eső sűrű cseppje" 1167 (285)

HULLABALOO BELAY 9451 (173)

HULLÁMZÓ BALATON TETEJÉN 5724 (92)

"Hullámzó Balaton tetején csónakázik egy halászlegény" 5724 (92)

HUMORESQUE 956 (132,329)

"Humoresque my heart's at rest" 956 (329)

HUMPTY DUMPTY 4642 (132)

"Humpty Dumpty sat on a wall" 4642 (132)

Hun er saa hvid 1381 (229)

HUN GWENLLIAN 8678 (349)
A HUND'ED LIT'L ANGELS IN THE BAN' 8325 (184)
HUNDERT SEMESTER 3223 (31)
HUNDRED CANDLES, HUNDRED BOTTLES 1167 (285)
"A hundred lovely slaves did the festival grace" 754 (153)
A HUNDRED PIPERS 7059 (17,100,102,163,235,349)
"Hungry and thirsty, Lord, I come to Thee" 2709 (123)
THE HUNT IS UP 4643A (234), 4643B (349)
"The hunt is up, the hunt is up and it is well nigh day"
    4643A (234), 4643B (349)
THE HUNTER'S FAREWELL 2382 (28)
THE HUNTER'S HORN 3679 (295)
THE HUNTERS OF KENTUCKY 4787 (173)
HUNTING SONG 6816 (295)
HUNTING THE HARE 8676 (19,234,349)
HUNTSMAN'S SONG 2383 (45)
THE HUNTSMEN 7680 (28,366)
"HUR SKALL MAN BRUDEN KLÄDA?" 2139 (356)
THE HURON CAROL 9193 (186,244)
A HURON CHRISTMAS CHANT 9193 (279)
"Hurrah for B. County, the land of the free" 8023B (81)
"Hurrah for Greer County, the land of the free" 8023A
    (227)
"Hurrah for our own native isle, Newfoundland!" 4220
    (186)
"Hurrah for Reuben Ranzo, Ranzo, boys, Ranzo" 9472
    (279,366)
"Hurrah for the choice of the nation" 7882 (44,109,110)
"Hurrah! Hurrah! now give us a rousing song" 4104 (114)
"Hurrah! Hurrah! Rich treasures in our 'Sile'" 7653 (189)
HURRAH, SING FARE-YOU-WELL 9452 (320)
"Hurricane is an angry thing" 8768 (11)
"Hurroo! boys, here we are again!" 599 (189)
"Hurry mourner! The sun mows down" 8566 (409)
HURRY NOW, MAKE UP YOUR MIND 4449 (324)
"Hurry now, make up your mind that you will be wed"
    4449 (324)
"Hurry on, my weary soul, and I heard-a from heaven
    today" 9390 (332)
HURRY UP, LIZA JANE 7779E (214)
"Hurry up, pretty little gal, hurry up, Liza Jane" 7779E
    (214)
HUSARENLIEBE 5625B (31)
HUSBAND AND WIFE 6307 (95)
"HUSH A BA, BIRDIE, CROON, CROON" 449 (199)
HUSH-A-BY, BAIRNIE 7060 (101,103)
"Hush-a-by, bairnie, my bonnie wee laddie" 7060 (101,
    103)
"Hush-a-by, don't you cry, go to sleepy little baby" 7403
    (216)
HUSH BABY 6858 (159)
"Hush! Hush! In the hazel wood, good people stirring!"
    6010 (280)
"Hush, hush, somebody callin' my name" 8326 (184)
"Hush! Hush! with lovely eyes" 372 (121)
HUSH, LI'L' BABY 7681A (77)
"Hush, li'l' baby, don' say a word" 7681A (77)
HUSH, LITTLE BABY 7681A (389), 7681B (313)
"Hush, little baby, don't say a word" 7681A (216,389),
    7681B (313)
"Hush, my babe, lie still and slumber" (Carols, United
    States) 9352 (332)
"HUSH, MY DEAR, LIE STILL AND SLUMBER" (Bach) 112
    (337)
"Hush! my dear, lie still and slumber" (Carols, England)
    8918 (271)

"Hush! my dear, lie still and slumber" (Grimes) 1400
    (374)
"Hush, my little birdie, Hush, my little baby" 6170
    (318)
HUSH, SOMEBODY CALLIN' MY NAME 8326 (184)
"Hush-you-bye, don't you cry, go to sleepy little baby"
    7403 (84,227)
HUSIA USIA 6708 (295)
HUSIČKA DIVOKÁ 4351 (324)
"Husička divoká letěla zvysoka" 4351 (324)
HUSKER DU I HOEST 1609 (36)
"Husker dui Hoest, da vi hjemad fra Marken gik" 1609
    (36)
THE HUSSAR 5725 (95)
DIE HUSSITEN VOR NAUMBURG 5726 (31)
"Die Hussiten zogen vor Naumburg über Jena her und
    Kamburg" 5726 (31)
HUT IS BURNING 5685 (164)
"Hut is burning, thatch is blazing, in two brown eyes you
    are gazing" 5685 (164)
"Huya, huya, huya, ya!" 4347 (37)
"Huyó veloz un tiemp de ventura" 7546 (113)
"Huzza for the prairies wide and free" 681* (189)
HUZZAD CSAK 5727 (92)
"Huzzad csak, huzzad csak keservesen" 5727 (92)
"Hvarför skall man tvinga mig att sjunga" 7336 (135)
HVORFOR SVÖMMER DIT OGE? 1392 (407)
"Hvorfor svömmer dit öge tidt i en tareglans?" 1392
    (407)
"Hyacinthia, festival time" 792 (362)
HYFRYDOL 2880 (50)
Hyfrydol (tune) 2880 (251)
A HYMN FOR AVIATORS 2743 (344)
HYMN OF LOVE 958 (343)
HYMN OF 1910 2680 (295)
HYMN OF PRAISE 3276 (160)
A HYMN OF THANKS TO THE BLESSED VIRGIN MARY
    2272 (71)
HYMN OF THANKSGIVING 3790 (44)
HYMN OF THE LAST SUPPER 817 (398)
HYMN OF THE SLAVS 4346 (279,366)
HYMN TO THE DAWN 7682 (113)
HYMN TO THE SACRED HEART 3678 (295)
HYMN TO THE SUN (Georges) 1237 (190,192,194)
HYMN TO THE SUN (Rimskii-Korsakov) 3034 (176,292)
HYMNE AN DIE NACHT 235 (326)
HYMNE AU SOLEIL 1237 (190,192,194)
HYMNUS AN DEN ZORN 3213 (31)
"Hypocrite in the church, now that ain't right" 8395
    (409)

I. See also Ah
"I a fav'rite spot have found" 2384 (395)
"I ain't been long in this here army" 1299 (225)
I AIN'T GOIN' TO DIE NO MORE 8327 (129)
I AIN'T GONNA GRIEVE MY LORD NO MORE 8328 (343)
"I ain't got a fine dress of satin" 8131 (381)
"I ain't got no father" 7931C (145), 7931D (129,130)
I AIN'T GWINE STUDY WAR NO MORE 8170 (28,366)
"I ALLE DE RIGER OG LANDE" 1227 (87)
"I am a boatman by my trade, Jack Wilson is my name"
    7720 (81)

"I am a brisk and sprightly lad" 4553 (234)
"I am a cabinet maker bold" 3311 (141)
I AM A CUCKOO 7683 (189)
"I am a cuckoo, my name is cuckoo" 7683 (189)
"I am a Friar of Orders gray" 3454 (240)
"I am a happy young fellow who finds contentment in
    singing" 7825 (314)
"I am a jolly Irishman" 599 (189)
I AM A LAD FROM CRACOW 6754 (159)
"I am a lonely and a lonesome traveler" 1580 (389)
"I am a man of widespread fame" 2602 (4)
"I am a poor and a foreign stranger" 7932B (72)
"I am a poor unlucky chap, I'm very fond of rum" 984
    (72)
"I am a poor wayfarin' stranger" 7932D (399)
"I AM A POOR WAYFARING STRANGER" 7932A (321),
    7932B (110), 7932C (35)
I AM A ROAMER 2380 (273)
"I am a roamer bold and gay" 2380 (273)
"I am a roving cowboy from off the western plains" 7452
    (120)
"I am a roving gambler" 7968 (109,110)
"I am a roving pedlar man, I've roved the country round"
    7969 (72)
"I am a shoemaker by my trade" 7990 (109,110,335)
"I am alone! now, at last!" 2314 (3)
"I am as poor a distressed maid as ever yet was known"
    7897 (126)
"I am, as you know a Madison belle" 1039 (189)
"I am broke and hungry, ragg'd and dirty too" 8168B (336)
"I AM BUT A SHEPHERD MAIDEN" 2498 (175)
"I am confirm'd a woman can, Love this or that or any
    man" 2062 (106)
"I am de belle dey say ov Avenoo A" 3951 (204)
"I am far from my home but not my sweetheart" 6083
    (36)
"I am from gay Paree, I sing a melody" 721 (132)
"I am going far away, far away to leave you now" 8473
    (184)
"I am happy to see you tonight, dear friends" 59 (189)
"I AM IN HER BOIDOIR FAIR" 3733 (357)
"I am in Him, and He's in me" 8329 (409)
"I am in truth a country youth" 582 (235)
"I am jealous, Psyche, of all Nature" 2731 (190,192,194)
"I am looking rather seedy now while holding down my
    claim" 7788B (129), 7788C (186)
"I am my mammie's ae bairn" 7071 (100,104,235)
"I am not like other maids" 4068 (112)
I AM NOT PLEASED WITH YOU 6713 (159)
"I am not pleased with you, Hanis my girl so dear" 6713
    (159)
"I AM SO HAPPY ON CHRISTMAS EVE" 9284 (165)
"I am so peaceful here" 2623 (340)
"I AM THE CAPTAIN OF THE PINAFORE" 3656 (132,205)
"I am the monarch of the sea" 3658 (205)
"I AM THE TRUE VINE" 8329 (409)
"I AM THY HARP" 4098 (259)
I AM TIPSY 5795 (164)
"I am tipsy sweetheart, like a top" 5795 (164)
"I am Titania the fairy" 3732 (221)
"I am waiting here to greet, Blue eyed Kate with kisses
    sweet" 2668 (246)
"I am weary, for you've left me here" 937 (287,288)

"I am with you wandering through Memory Lane" 3541
    (345)
"I am writing to you, Molly while the fair moon softly
    shines" 1613 (246)
I AM YOUNG AND NOT TOO OLD 6744 (159)
"I am young and not too old, old, old, old" 6744 (159)
"I ask my woman what I could do" 8712 (11)
"I asked my love to take a walk" 7899 (243)
"I ATTEMPT FROM LOVE'S SICKNESS TO FLY" 2913
    (275,397)
"I been a-havin' some hard travelin'" 1427 (293)
"I BEEN IN DE STORM, SO LONG" 8330 (183,307)
I BEEN WORKIN' ON DE LEVEE 8370 (184)
I BEEN WUKKIN' ON DE RAILROAD 8370 (35)
"I been wukkin' on de railroad all de live long day" 8370
    (28,35,114,236,278,366)
"I believe that the gods, being justly incensed" 614 (151)
"I BELIEVE THIS IS JESUS" 8331 (409)
"I belong to Boston City, boys, a place you all know well"
    7465 (172)
"I BID MY LAST FAREWELL" 2271 (134)
I BLAS GOGERDDAN 8679 (349)
"I Blas Gogerddan heb dy dad!" 8679 (349)
I BOUGHT ME A CAT 8157C (83)
"I bought me a cat, my cat pleased me" 8157C (83)
"I BUILT MY LOVE A BIG FINE HOUSE" 7684 (313)
"De I.C. carried my baby" 8427 (77)
"I came from Alabama wid my banjo on my knee" 1126
    (10,28,109,110,128,129,130,225,236,366)
"I came to Alabama, wid my banjo on my knee" 1126
    (184,279)
"I came to the willow alone, I came to the willow alone"
    2513 (358)
"I came to this country in seventeen forty-nine" 7939
    (392)
"I came to town de udder night" 1002 (34)
"I cannot get to my love if I would dee" 4793 (234)
"I CANNOT SING THE OLD SONGS" 176 (28,132)
"I can't give you a good explanation for this new and con-
    fusing sensation" 2587 (2)
I CAN'T MAKE UP MY MIND 7685 (225)
"I can't make up my mind, Mama in such unseemly haste"
    7685 (225)
I CARE FOR NO ONE HERE 4354 (324)
"I care for no one here, John is my only dear" 4354 (324)
"I CARE NOT FOR THESE LADIES" 546 (144)
I CATCHA DA PLENTY OF FEESH 7686 (109,110)
"I chanced upon a big brown bear" 4156 (364)
"I climb the long trail of the mountain" 7280 (37)
"I come alone from yonder mountain" 3315 (220)
"I come from Alabama with my banjo on my knee" 1126
    (35,233)
"I come from heaven good news to tell, good news, the
    best news that e'er befell" 9314 (165)
"I come from reaping, I've reaped my grain" 7259 (95)
"I come here from my mountain lone" 3315 (240,272,
    359)
"I come to town de udder night" 1002 (28,109,110,115,
    212,279,366)
I COULD NOT FIND MY BABY-O 8680 (321)
"I COULDN'T HEAR NOBODY PRAY" 8332 (28,37,76,
    182,183,279,366,409)
"I courted her all of the winter" 4601B (109)
"I courted Pretty Polly the livelong night" 7938A (227),
    7938B (173)

I CROSSED THE WORLD 6958 (352)

"I danced with a gal with a hole in her stockin'" 7478B (227)

"I DANMARK ER JEG FØDT" 3120 (87)

"I DENNE SØDE JULETID" 9283 (154)

I DESIGNED TO SAY NO, BUT MISTOOK AND SAID YES 4644 (198)

"I did not send them to school to be taught" 5344 (230)

I DLA MNIE WIOSNY WRÓCI CZAR 6728 (295)

"I DO NOT DARE DESPOND" 2199 (368)

"I don't believe my baby'd know me" 8333 (336)

I DON'T BELIEVE SHE'D KNOW ME 8333 (336)

I DON'T CARE 3689 (204)

"I don't care, I don't care" 3689 (204)

"I DON'T CARE IF MY FATE IS ABJECT" 6790 (159)

"I don't care where you bury my body" 8464 (409)

"I don't know why I cry" 1807 (184)

"I don't know why you're angry, and why you pout and frown" 6183 (318)

"I DON'T LIKE NO RAILROAD MAN" 7687 (321)

I DON'T WAN' TO BE BURIED IN DE STAWM 8334 (227)

I DON'T WANT NO MORE ARMY 7688 (225)

"I don't want none of your weevily wheat" 8100A (109, 110)

I DON'T WANT TO GET ADJUSTED 7689 (389)

I DON'T WANT TO PLAY IN YOUR YARD 2790 (114, 128, 129, 130, 131, 132, 204)

"I DON'T WANT YOUR MILLIONS, MISTER" 7889B (293)

"I dream of Jeanie with the light brown hair" 1116 (10, 28, 35, 37, 109, 110, 114, 129, 130, 131, 233, 236, 329, 343)

I DREAM OF LILAC TIME 1252 (236)

"I dream'd a dream the other night, lowlands, my Lowlands away my John!" 9463A (235)

"I dreamed a dream the other night, lowlands, lowlands, away my John" 9463B (35)

"I dreamed as I lay sleeping a heavy dream of woe" 5389 (230)

"I dreamed I saw Joe Hill last night" 3045 (35, 293)

"I dreamt a dream the other night; lowlands, lowlands, alas, my John!" 9463D (29)

I DREW MY SHIP 4645 (234)

"I drew my ship into the harbour" 4645 (234)

"I drive my troika, hear the silver bells ring" 6979 (37)

"I DRÖMMER TRÄDEN STAA" 1179 (355)

"I envy not the golden crown" 727 (240)

"I fear the magic of the night" 1369 (211)

"I feel I also know the knack" 860 (6)

"I feel, I feel, I feel, I feel like a mornin' star" 527 (184)

"I feel, I feel, I feel, I feel like a morning star" 527 (32, 34)

"I feel, I feel, I feel like a morning star" 527 (216)

"I feel, I feel the Deity within" 1462 (123)

"I feel like, I feel like" 8335 (409)

I FEEL LIKE MY TIME AIN'T LONG 8335 (409)

"I felt a warming burst of sunshine" 4836 (124)

"I flee from pleasures" 2014 (259)

"I forge the sword, I shape the steel" 2650 (240)

"I FOUND A HEART ALL GOLDEN" 3753 (71)

"I found free grace an' dying love, I'm new born again" 8441 (409)

"I found my love in Avalon" 3078 (233, 345)

"I GAED A WAEFU' GATE YESTREEN" 7061 (100, 102)

"I gave my love a cherry that had no stone" 7953 (242)

"I gave my love a cherry that has no stone" 7953 (35, 171, 173, 331)

"I gave my love a cherry without a stone" 7953 (215)

I GO TO WOODS 6717 (159)

"I go to woods, feathers flutter in my cap" 6717 (159)

"I got a barrel of flour, Lord, I got a bucket of lard" 8440 (336)

"I got a crown up ina dat Kingdom" 8172 (290)

"I got a gal at the head of the holler" 8014E (331)

"I GOT A HOME IN-A DAT ROCK" 8336 (76)

"I GOT A HOUSE IN BALTIMO'" 8337 (409)

"I GOT A LETTER FROM JESUS" 8338 (321)

"I got a letter from my home" 8554 (336)

"I got a mother in heaven" 8556 (182)

"I got a mule, and her name is Sal" 50

I GOT A ROBE 8177 (76, 402)

"I got a robe, you got a robe, all God's chillun got a robe" 8177 (76)

"I got a robe, you got a robe, all o' God's chillun got a robe" 8177 (115, 183)

"I got a robe, you got a robe, all of God's children got a robe" 8177 (70)

"I got a sister over yonder" 8481 (182)

"I got my Jesus, goint to hold Him fast" 8319 (409)

"I got sheep, I got goats" 8510 (216)

"I got shoes, you got shoes, all God's chillun got shoes" 8177 (216)

"I got the blues, I got the blues, I got the Winnsb'ro Cotton Mill blues" 8631 (336)

"I got the blues like midnight" 3047 (336)

"I got the dust pneumonee, pneumonee in my lung" 1425 (336)

"I gotta robe, you gotta a robe, all of God's children gotta robe" 8177 (402)

"I gotta shoes, you gotta shoes, all God's chillun got shoes" 8177 (351)

I GUESS I'LL HAVE TO TELEGRAPH MY BABY 689* (114, 128, 131, 204)

I HAB DIE SCHÖNEN MADERL'N NET ERFUNDEN 3231 (222)

"I hab halt zwa kohlschwarze Rappen" 5216 (396)

"I had a cat and the cat pleased me" 8157B (110, 216, 225, 249)

"I had a dream last night" 3050 (336)

"I had a dream last night all about my gal" 8406 (336)

"I had a girl that called me, 'Dear'" 8370 (44)

I had a horse (tune) 7141

"I had a hoss, his name was Bill" 7675 (80)

"I had a sister, Sally, that was younger than I am" 4717 (215)

I HAD A SISTER SUSAN 7690 (267)

"I had a sister Susan, she was ugly and misshapen" 7690 (267)

"I had an ol' dog an' his name was Blue" 7868B (169)

"I had an old dog and his name was Blue" 7868A (173)

I HAD AN OLD HOUND 7691 (145)

"I had an old hound with a cold, wet nose" 7691 (145)

"I HAD FOUR BROTHERS OVER THE SEA" 7926B (279, 366)

"I had three cousins over the sea" 7926A (264)

"I hae been at Crookieden" 7005 (365)

"I HA'E LAID A HERRIN' IN SAUT" 7062 (105)

"I hailed my mother in the morning" 8475 (409)

"I hate to see de ev'nin' sun go down" 1519 (34)

"I have a little boy, and whenever I see him" 6227 (318)
"I have a little dreydl, I made it out of clay" 6234 (214)
"I have a rooster, my rooster loves me" 8157A (28,366)
"I have a ship on the ocean" 7993 (32,34)
"I have a sister, in that day she'll take wings and fly away" 8302 (409)
"I have a wicked mother" 5149 (187)
I HAVE AN EMBROIDERED KERCHIEF 6767 (295)
"I have an embroidered kerchief Stitched all o'er and so neat" 6767 (295)
I HAVE ANOTHER BUILDING 8339 (409)
"I HAVE ATTAINED TO POWER" 2614 (5)
I HAVE COME 5676 (92)
"I have come a handsome pair of boots to buy" 5676 (92)
"I HAVE COME TO YOU THIS MORNING" 3036 (340)
"I have heard the mavis singing" 7106 (18)
"I HAVE HOUSE AND LAND IN KENT" 4646 (234)
"I HAVE LOVED FOR HALF A DAY" 5000 (175)
I HAVE MADE A FINE BOUQUET 2056 (285)
"I have made a fine bouquet of meadow flowers" 2056 (285)
"I have no mind for grieving, but grief holds me fast" 7335 (95)
"I have no snug tiled hut, warm clothes I possess not" 2831 (164)
I HAVE NO TILED HUT 2831 (164)
"I HAVE PICKED A LOVELY ROSEBUD" 4997 (187)
"I have plowed and I have sowed" 6211 (318)
"I have searched for our star Chacoun" 8769 (11)
"I have seen a blue bird winging his flight to the greenwood tree" 730 (385)
"I HAVE SEEN DAWN" 1965 (259)
"I have studied all the stars" 463 (131)
I HAVE TORN MY SUNDAY JACKET 5728 (95)
"I have torn my Sunday jacket, picking berries, one, two and three" 5728 (95)
"I have travelled many miles" 707 (131)
I HAVE TWELVE OXEN 1753 (276)
"I have twelve oxen that be fair and brown" 1753 (276)
I HAVE WEPT IN MY DREAM 1728 (191,193,195)
"I have wrapped my dreams in a silken cloth" 692 (78)
"I hear a gay voice calling wherever I go" 6921 (350)
"I hear dem angels a callin' loud" 1591 (10)
"I hear dem angels callin' loud" 1591 (185)
"I hear, I hear, I hear, my lady ha!" 7832 (132)
"I hear old Neptune with great delight" 7326 (135)
I HEAR THE MILL WHEEL 5001 (187)
"I hear the mill wheel, tick-a, tick-a, tack-a" 5001 (187)
"I HEAR THE TRUMPET SOUNDING" 8685 (235)
"I hear them angels a-calling loud" 1591 (343)
"I hear tonight the old bells chime" 2111 (129,130)
I HEAR UPON THE HIGHWAY 9073 (361)
"I hear upon the highway resounding minstrelsy" 9073 (361)
"I heard a brooklet gushing" 2172 (277)
"I heard a brooklet plashing" 3301 (359)
"I heard a brooklet rushing along its rocky way" 3301 (395)
"I HEARD A CRY" 1079 (137,241)
I HEARD A SCYTHE 5394A (95)
"I heard a scythe go sighing, so sighing through the corn" 5394A (95)
"I heard a sound in the night" 1911 (241)
"I heard a streamlet" 3301 (112)
"I heard from Rémon, Rémon" 7949 (110)
"I heard my mother say" 8276 (409)
I HEARD OF LATE 190 (197)

"I heard of late that Love had fall'n asleepe" 190 (197)
"I HEARD THE BELLS ON CHRISTMAS DAY" (Calkin) 524 (28,206,236,296,366)
"I HEARD THE BELLS ON CHRISTMAS DAY" (Carols, England) 8944 (337)
"I HEARD THE PREACHING OF THE ELDER" 8340 (409)
"I HEARD THE VOICE OF JESUS SAY" 1537 (123)
"I hurt him! Should I? ah, no!" 2561 (6)
"I INTO THE HOUSE WAS TURNING" 5663 (164)
"I JES' COME FROM DE FOUNTAIN" 8372 (184)
"I just heard a story that rings in my ears" 2703 (131)
"I JUST NOW FROM PARIS CAME" 5768 (164)
"I keep seeking my fortune, but it passes me by" 6221 (318)
"I killed a louse in my house" 4281 (86)
"I knelt, I knelt, beside a grassy mound" 3435 (8)
"I know a charmer, a gay señorita" 4211 (350)
I KNOW A FLOWER 2869 (361)
"I know a flow'r it springeth" 2869 (375)
I KNOW A LAND 2141 (188)
"I know a land, far north, by mountains framed" 2141 (188)
"I know a little lady from Baltimore" 7786 (214)
"I know a lovely land" 1981 (87)
"I know a place where an old castle stands" 4467 (231)
"I KNOW A ROSE SO COMELY" 7316 (188)
"I KNOW A ROSE TREE SPRINGING" 2869 (307)
"I know a wide river, 'taint no Mississippi" 8630 (266)
I KNOW AN ISLE 5940 (280)
"I know an isle, a pearl in ocean's diadem" 5940 (280)
I KNOW AN OLD LADY 2439 (249)
"I know an old lady who swallowed a fly" 2439 (249)
"I know his name: Walter Maldè! I love thee!" 3850 (221)
"I know I have another building" 8339 (409)
"I know, I know, I know, that I must die and go" 4435 (231)
"I know it, 'deed I know it" 8243A (184), 8243B (185)
"I know I've been converted" 8389 (184)
"I know my lads that smiles are sweet" 1248 (205)
I KNOW MY LOVE 5930 (36,72,172,215)
"I know my love by his way o' walkin'" 5930 (36,215)
"I know my love by his way of walking" 5930 (72,172)
"I know not how lovely your face is" 635 (121)
"I know not what it presages" (Silcher) 3484 (28,279, 366)
"I know not what spell is enchanting" 3484 (132)
"I know not what spell is o'er me" 2151 (276)
I KNOW, O BLESSED MARY 9074 (361)
"I know, O Blessed Mary, all I would bring" 9074 (361)
I KNOW SOMETHING 5166 (187)
"I know that my Redeemer lives" 8542 (321,409)
"I KNOW THAT MY REDEEMER LIVETH" 1468 (123,346, 394,400)
"I know that water is chilly and cold" 8218 (28,366)
I KNOW THE LORD'S LAID HIS HANDS ON ME 8341 (409)
I KNOW WHERE I'M GOIN' 5931 (36,172,215)
"I know where I'm goin', and I know who's goin' with me" 5931 (36,172,215)
I KNOW WHERE I'M GOING 5931 (169,389)
"I know where I'm going and I know who's goin' with me" 5931 (169)
"I know where I'm going and I know who's going with me" 5931 (389)
"I know you're tired, sit down" 8544B (77)
"I knows a gal that you don't know, Li'l Liza Jane" 7779A (36,402)

"I knows a little stunner" 666 (204)
I kumme dahea von Estarei (tune) 5372
"I laid me down and slept" 7941 (173)
"I laughed at sweethearts I met at schools" 3051 (345)
"I leave my home and thee, dear" 2223 (161)
"I left her by the river Sainte Marie" 3947 (236)
"I left my baby darling lying there" 8680 (321)
"I LEFT MY DEARIE LYING HERE" 7063 (101, 103, 104)
"I LIE QUITE STILL IN GRASS SO GREEN" 399 (348)
"I like rice pudding with milk or with cream" 6285 (219)
I LIKE THEM ALL 7263 (406)
"I like them all, the pretty girls" 7263 (406)
I LIKEN THEE TO A FLOWER 3379 (329)
"I liken thee to a flower endow'd with grace divine" 3379 (329)
"I live for the good of my nation" 7882 (173)
I LIVE ON THE CORNER 5800 (164)
"I live on the corner, there my house you see" 5800 (164)
I LIVED IN A TOWN 7692 (110)
"I lived in a town way down South by the name of Owensb'ro" 7692 (110)
"I lived in a wood for a number of years" 4623 (198)
"I LO'E NA A LADDIE BUT ANE" 7064 (100, 104)
"I LO'E NE'ER A LADDIE BUT ANE" 7064 (406)
"I long to ride the range once more" 7962 (37)
"I look over Jordan an what did I see" 8570 (183)
"I look over Jordan and what do I see?" 8570 (78)
"I look over yondah on Jerico's walls" 8467 (183)
"I look'd over Jordan an' what did I see" 8570 (35)
"I looked over Jerd'n an' what did I see" 8570 (182)
"I looked over Jordan and what did I see" 8570 (409)
"I looked over Jordan, what did I see?" 8570 (402)
"I lost, walking by the river, coral beads prettiest ever" 6753 (295)
"I love but thee as thou dost me" 250 (210)
"I love ev'ry inch of her prairie land" 985 (233)
"I love it, I love it, and who shall dare" 3125 (130)
I LOVE LITTLE WILLIE 7693A (185)
"I love little Willie, I do, mama" 7693A (185), 7693B (267)
"I LOVE MY LOVE IN THE MORNING" 5932 (166, 213)
"I love my rooster, my rooster loves me" 8157A (44)
I LOVE NOBODY ELSE BUT YOU, DEAR 2026 (285)
"I love the country air" 2125 (114, 131)
"I love the sound of the horn" 1082 (193)
I LOVE THEE (Beethoven) 250 (210, 387)
I LOVE THEE (Grieg) 1382 (122, 132, 176, 237, 241, 329, 387)
"I love thee as thou lovest me" 250 (387)
"I love this land, its sunny clime" 7486 (189)
I LOVE TO WHISTLE 2235 (236)
"I love to whistle 'cause it makes me merry" 2235 (236)
I LOVE YOU (Beethoven) 250 (36, 122, 141)
I LOVE YOU (Grieg) 1382 (36)
"I LOVE YOU, ADORE YOU" 3431 (245)
"I love you, dear, as you love me" 250 (141)
"I love you like a 'copper' loves to sleep" 2610 (204)
"I made up my mind to change my way" 8069 (335)
I MARRIED A WIFE 4647 (402)
"I married a wife in the month of June" (Jennifer gently) 7606 (72)
"I married a wife, O then! O then! I married a wife O then!" 4647 (402)
"I married me a wife and took her home" 7606 (312)
"I married my wife in the month of June" (Risseldy, rosseldy) 7959 (145, 214)

"I may be blind an' cannot see" 8623 (409)
"I may be right and I may be wrong" 8510 (389)
"I may? So please you! My ladies and gentlemen!" 2114 (4)
"I met a pilgrim on the way" 8244B (28, 366)
"I met a singer on the hill" 1599 (276)
"I met ayont the cairnie, Jenny Nettles trig and braw" 7076 (102)
"I met four chaps yon birks amang" 7075 (101)
"I met her in Venezuela" 9487 (169)
"I met her on the mountain, and there I tuck her life" 8065 (227)
"I met you in a garden in an old Kentucky town" 3991 (131)
"I mind a wedding in yonder farm" 7301 (230)
"I mind meself a wee boy wi' no plain talk" 1543 (344)
I MOURNED IN DE VALLEY 8342 (184)
"I mourned in de valley, didn't I mourn" 8342 (184)
I MUST AND I WILL GET MARRIED 7694 (109, 110)
"I must clown to get rid of my unhappiness" 2116 (132)
"I must go down to the seas again, to the lonely sea and the sky" 65 (45)
"I MUST GO GATHER COMFORT" 9250 (361)
I MUST GO TO WAR 6815 (159)
"I must go to war, my Mary dear, I will come back to you, have no fear" 6815 (159)
"I MUST HAVE A SWEETHEART" 849 (285)
"I MUST WALK MY LONESOME VALLEY" 8343 (409)
"I nebber see de like since I bin born" 9445A (320)
"I nebber seen de like since I bin born" 9445A (234)
"I NEEDED GOD" 3466 (347)
"I never been to heab'n" 8363 (184)
"I NEVER FELT SUCH LOVE IN MY SOUL BEFO'" 8344 (409)
"I never had a barrel of money" 8491 (336)
"I never, never worry" 1344 (131)
"I never saw a moor, I never saw the sea" 1168 (358)
I NEVER SHALL FORGET 4229 (186)
"I never shall forget the day Columbus landed here" 4229 (186)
"I ØSTEN STIGER SOLEN OP" 4006 (87)
"I once did know a girl named Grace" 8370 (114)
"I once knew a spinster who worked on a plan" 2698 (131)
"I pled with Chloe, maid supreme" 238 (405)
"I pray you, I pray you, sing me the scale of D flat" 236 (199)
"I PRETHEE, SEND ME BACK MY HEART" 2062 (36)
I PRETHEE SWEET 2065 (107)
"I prethee sweet to me be kind" 2065 (107)
"I PRITHEE KEEP MY SHEEP FOR ME" 2032 (106)
"I put my hand all in her own" 4609 (215)
"I raised a dog and his name was Blue" 7868C (227)
"I RECEIVED A DRESS" 850 (285)
"I remember how I lov'd her" 4096 (212)
"I remember the days of our youth and love" 1132 (129)
I RIDE AN OLD PAINT 7695 (109, 110, 145, 214, 279, 366)
"I ride an old paint, I lead an old dam" 7695 (120)
"I ride an old paint, I lead an old Dan" 7695 (109, 110, 145, 169, 214, 227, 279, 366)
"I rose early one summer morn" 5187 (86)
"I SAID 'I WILL FORGET THEE!'" 411 (273)
"I said, Silicosis, you made a mighty bad break of me" 3498 (336)
I SAID TO THE STARLETS 2730 (407)
"I said to the starlets, she's your sister fair" 2730 (407)

"I sail over the ocean blue" 7686 (109,110)

"I sail'd in the good ship, the Kitty" 837 (235)

"I sailed from port one summer's day" 2466 (225)

"I saw a fair maid as she sat and did sing" 8954 (363)

I SAW A FAIR MAYDEN 3722 (317)

"I saw a fair Mayden syttin and sing" 3722 (307,317)

I SAW A MAIDEN 8824 (317,370)

"I saw a maiden sitting and sing" 8824 (317,370)

"I saw a youth and maiden on a lonely city street" 3086 (32,34,246)

"I saw gay, festive dancing within my dwelling" 1095 (245)

"I SAW MY LADY WEEP" 903 (119,279)

"I SAW MY LADY WEEPE" 903 (144)

"I saw the Holy City with tow'rs brightly glowing" 4075 (89)

"I saw the native land I lov'd and knew" 2048 (348)

"I saw three black pigs riding" 1718 (275)

I SAW THREE SHIPS 8945A (33,125,199,206,244,271,296, 305,307,317,333,334,363,375,410), 8945B (216, 333,337,361), 8945C (334)

"I saw three ships came sailing in" 8945A (317)

"I saw three ships come sailing by" 8945A(199), 8945D (334)

"I saw three ships come sailing in" 8945A (33,125,206, 244,271,296,305,307,333,334,363,375,410), 8945B (216,333,337,361)

"I SAW THY FORM IN YOUTHFUL PRIME" 5933 (213)

I SAW TWO KITTENS 6511 (316)

"I saw two kittens wearing mittens" 6511 (316)

"I saw two roses grow on a briar" 4187 (231)

"I saw you in the bright sunlight" 8708 (11)

"I saw you seated there, roses in your hair" 2723 (236)

I SAW YOUR FACE 6632 (86)

"I saw your face in a rippling stream" 6632 (86)

"I say, old man, your horse is dead; we say so and we hope so" 9437C (29)

"I say that nothing shall deter me" 319 (1)

"I see her face in the flames of the camp-fire" 1842 (339)

"I see her in dreams" 8687 (20)

"I SHALL MEET YOU TONIGHT" 3933 (159)

"I shall not go tomorrow, girl" 5605 (95)

I SHALL WAKEN EARLY 6958 (86)

"I shall waken early in the morning" 6958 (86)

"I shipped on board of a Liverpool liner" 9479 (205)

"I should like to creep through the long brown grasses that are your lashes" 4113 (78)

I SING THE BIRTH (Praetorius) 2865 (317)

"I sing the birth was born tonight" (Boughton) 377 (334)

"I sing the birth was born tonight" (Praetorius) 2865 (317)

I SIT ALONE 7311 (95)

"I sit alone, all my friends are gone" 7311 (95)

"I skogen smagutten gikk dagen lang, gikk dagen lang" 2670 (278)

"I snum I am a Yankee lad, and I guess I'll sing a ditty" 7466A (173), 7466B (225)

"I sometimes think, when silv'ry night" 2192 (241)

I SOMMARENS SOLIGA DAGAR 7312 (188)

"I sommarens soliga dagar vi gaa genom skogar och hagar" 7312 (188)

I SOUGHT THE LORD (Galbraith) 1198 (8)

I SOUGHT THE LORD (Stevenson) 3577 (398)

"I sought the Lord, and He heard me" 3577 (398)

"I sought the Lord, but afterwards I knew" 1198 (8)

I SOWED MILLET 6729 (95)

"I sowed millet in my meadow, millet never got" 6729 (95)

I SOWED THE SEEDS OF LOVE 4648 (234)

"I sowed the seeds of love, all in the merry spring" 4648 (234)

I SPURRED MY HORSE 7696 (185)

"I spurred my horse to make him trot" 7696 (185)

"I stand beneath your window vigil keeping" 6086 (310)

"I stand beside Thy cradle here" (Bach) 122 (388)

"I still am pining sweet Chacoun" 8769 (11)

"I stood on the station platform" 55 (7)

"I stood upon a mountain high" 5261 (95)

"I struck out for old New York" 8579 (336)

"I suffer jealousy at nature's love for Psyché!" 2731 (348)

"I tell the Tommy to go home" 8727 (11)

I THANK YOU, MA'AM, SAYS DAN 5934 (172)

"I THE ANGEL AM OF GOD" 9075 (361)

"I think I hear the angels sing" 527 (129,130,131,185, 225,399)

"I think I've got a song here" 2279 (114)

I THINK, OH MY LOVE 2269 (78)

"I THINK, WHEN I READ THAT SWEET STORY" 4649 (28,366)

"I thought I heard the captain say, Leave her Johnny" 9458B (29)

"I thought I heard the Captain say, 'We'll sail for Rio'" 9421 (242)

"I thought I heard the old man say Leave her Johnnie" 9458A (320)

"I thought I heard the skipper say, Leave her Johnny" 9458B (234)

"I thought my heart would break" 807 (121)

I TO MY DOVE 2496 (175)

"I to my dove, my tardy sweeting" 2496 (175)

"I told her, 'no Baby, you know I don't wanna go'" 2083 (336)

"I took my girl to a fancy ball" 2124 (204)

"I took one look at you" 3051 (345)

"I tremble not from all I fear'd, shall this ring now secure me" 3864 (143)

I TRIUMPH! I TRIUMPH! 598 (273)

"I triumph! I triumph! I triumph! The last word is spoken" 598 (273)

I TURN UNTO A STABLE 9332 (188)

"I turn unto a stable when Christmas day doth dawn" 9332 (188)

"I understand you, indeed I understand you well" 519 (134)

"I used to have a ol' gray hoss, he weigh' ten thousand pound" 7623 (80)

"I used to live on mountain top, but now I live in town" 7874A (109,110)

"I used to love in fond affection" 7540 (81)

I VILLANDE SKOGEN 2969 (188)

"I villande skogen jag vallar min hjord" 2969 (188)

"I VOW I'LL DO ALL IN MY POWER" 319 (93)

I VOW TO THEE, MY COUNTRY 1688 (306)

"I vow to thee, my country, all earthly things above" 1688 (306)

I WALKED THE ROAD AGAIN 984 (72)

"I wander over the roads" 461 (191,193,195)

I WANDER THIS SUMMER MORNING 1149 (137)

"I wander this summer morning here in my garden alone" 1149 (137)

"I wander'd by lonely Dunkerron whose ruin adorns the lake shore" 5860 (280)

"I wander'd today to the hill" 483 (28,32,34,132,233, 236,279,343,366)

"I wanna go home and I ain't got sufficient clothes" 8187 (336)

"I want rice pudding and not a thing more" 6285 (86)

I WANT SUCH A WIFE 5774 (164)

"I want such a wife, you bet, sick or not who up will get" 5774 (164)

I WANT TO BE A CHRISTIAN IN MY HEART 8411 (76)

I WANT TO BE A FARMER 7697 (214)

"I want to be a farmer, a farmer, a farmer" 7697 (214)

"I WANT TO BE READY" 8345 (28,76,279,366,409)

"I want to go to heaven, and I want to go right" 8339 (409)

I WAS A FARMHAND FOR A FARMER 6696 (159)

"I was a maid of my country" 4629 (13)

"I WAS BORN ABOUT TEN THOUSAND YEARS AGO" 7698A (227)

"I was born almost ten thousand years ago" 7698B (72)

"I was born in East Virginia North Carolina, I did go" 7889B (293)

"I was born in old Virginny to North Carolina I did go" 7889A (312)

"I was born in this country in eighteen forty-nine" 7580 (242)

"I was born long ago in 1894" 7431 (293)

"I was brought up in London town" 7467 (126)

"I was comin' down State Street" 8321 (184)

"I was drunk last night, drunk the night before" 7902 (225)

"I was farmhand for a farmer, toiled four years at least" 6696 (159)

"I was feeling kind of hungry" 7551 (293)

"I was goin' down the road" 7893 (185)

"I was hanging 'round town" 8028 (186)

I WAS MARCHING SMARTLY 6739 (159)

"I was marching smartly as the music played" 6739 (159)

"I was mighty blue, thought my life was through" 2861 (345)

"I was once a shepherd lad keeping sheep, was always glad" 5638 (36)

"I was seeing Nellie home" 1084 (28,32,34,129,130,131, 233,236,279,366)

"I was sittin' down here thinkin' all in my lonesome cell" 8166 (336)

"I was standing by my window" 2648 (114,131)

I WAS THERE 7698B (72)

"I WASH MY FACE IN A GOLDEN VASE" 7699 (262)

I WEAR MY LOVE 3628 (112)

"I wear my love in silence, that none may know" 3628 (112)

"I, WENN I GELD GNUAG HÄTT" 1882 (326)

I WENT DOWN IN THE VALLEY 8346 (409)

"I went down in the valley" (TRYIN' TO CROSS THE RED SEA) 8597 (409)

"I went down to Macon, an' I did not go to stay" 8391 (409)

"I went down to old Joe Clark's, I'd never been there before" 7874A (185)

"I went down to Sandy Hook toder arter noon" 7893 (10)

"I went out one pleasant evening by the seashore" 6154 (34)

"I went out one pleasant evening to the seashore" 6154 (37)

"I went out one summer evening" 7903 (37)

"I went to John Whipple and asked for a job" 7738 (72)

"I went to market to buy fish" 6197 (318)

"I went to New York City a month or two ago" 1646 (189)

"I went to see my Susan" 1594 (185)

"I went to the animal fair" 7412 (225)

"I went to the dance and the animals come" 1428 (389)

"I went to the rock for to hide my face" 8624 (409)

"I went up to London town, to court a fair young Lady" 4580A (171)

"I WEPT, BELOVED, AS I DREAMED" 1728 (121)

"I wept in my dream" 1728 (191,193,195)

"I WHEEL TO DE BUZZARD" 8347 (242)

I WHISTLE AND WAIT FOR KATIE 2668 (246)

I WISGO AUR-GORON 8681 (349)

"I wisgo aur-goron y byd ar ei phen" 8681 (349)

I WILL GIVE MY LOVE AN APPLE 4234B (44)

"I will give my love an apple without any core" 4234B (44)

"I will give you a paper of pins" 7915D (264)

"I will give you the keys of heav'n" 4666 (343)

"I WILL GO WITH MY FATHER A-PLOUGHING" 1419 (344)

"I WILL LIFT UP MINE EYES" (Dvořák) 955 (90)

I WILL LIFT UP MINE EYES (Watkins) 3952 (398)

"I will lift up mine eyes unto the hills" (Watkins) 3952 (398)

I WILL PRAY 8266 (409)

"I will return he said to me" 1711 (114,204)

I WILL SING A LULLABY 4616 (28,37,366)

"I will take you back, Kathleen" 3999 (115,233)

"I WILL TELL NO ONE" 765 (340)

I WILL TELL YOU 6308 (95)

"I will tell you, I will tell you, what the flowing brooklet whispers" 6308 (95)

"I, William of Nassau, scion of a Dutch and ancient line" 6620 (316)

"I wish I could but know who was he that addressed me" 1320 (6)

"I wish I could ride on the shadows of clouds" 3056 (45)

I WISH I HAD A GIRL 1847 (128,129,130,131,236)

"I wish I had a needle" 7874A (293)

I WISH I HAD DIED IN EGYPT LAND 8348 (409)

"I WISH I HAD THE SHEPHERD'S PET" 5935 (172)

"I wish I ken'd my Maggie's mind" 7173 (102,105)

"I wish I was a' apple, a-hangin' on a tree" 7501 (80)

I WISH I WAS A SINGLE GIRL 8113D (72)

"I wish I was an apple, a hangin' in a tree" 7501 (110)

"I wish I was in Boston City" 7979 (225)

"I wish I was in de land ob cotton" 1000 (7,10,28,35,184, 212,233,236,294,343,366)

"I wish I was in de land of cotton" 1000 (279)

"I wish I was in the land of cotton" 1000 (109,110,115, 129,130,284)

"I wish I was in Yankeeland" 8153 (189)

I WISH I WAS SINGLE AGAIN 8113B (72), 8113C (185)

"I wish I was single again, again" 8113B (72)

"I wish I was the sun up above" 8148 (171)

"I WISH I WERE A LITTLE BIRD" 7700 (216)

"I wish I were a trout" 3280 (141)

"I WISH I WERE ON YONDER HILL" 5936 (95,166,213)

"I WISH I WERE THE LIGHT FERN GROWING" 7066 (105)

"I WISH I WERE WHERE GADIE RINS" 7065 (100)

"I WISH I WERE WHERE HELEN LIES" 7049 (102,235)

"I WISH NAUGHT BUT TO SURVEY THEE" 3187 (139)

"I wish that I might see thee" 8034 (113)

I WISH YOU GOOD EVENING 5652 (164)

"I wish you joy, my little ragged throng" 4104 (114)

"I wish you joy on your birthday" 1788 (291)

"I wôas nit, wie mir is, i wôas nit, wie mir is" 1848 (99)

I WOKE AT DAWN 6888 (219)

I WOKE, FROM MY COUCH UPRISING 9110 (361)

"I woke, from my couch upspringing" 9110 (361)

"I woke up this mornin', feelin' sad and blue" 8405 (336)

"I woke up this morning between one and two" 8269 (336)

I WONDER AS I WANDER 9359 (267,357)

"I wonder as I wander, out under the sky" 9359 (267,357)

"I wonder I never got married" 7876A (126)

"I wonder I never got married, um, ah!" 7876B (72)

I WONDER WHEN I SHALL BE MARRIED 7876B (72)

"I WONDER WHEN I SHALL BE MARRIED" 7876C (393)

"I WONDER WHERE MY BUDDIES ARE TONIGHT?" 4019 (129,130)

I WONDER WHO'S KISSING HER NOW? 1713 (34)

"I wonder why you keep me waiting" 2970 (128,129)

I WON'T BE A NUN 7701 (212)

"I won't have none of your weevily wheat" 8100B (185)

"I won't have you, Kasiu, No! No! No!" 6787 (295)

I WON'T STOP PRAYING 8349 (409)

I WORKED FOR MY MASTER 6834 (159)

"I worked for my master for one whole season" 6834 (295)

"I worked for my master one year so steady" 6834 (159)

"I WOULD GO TO THAT EASTERN COUNTRY" 7340 (188)

"I would I were a fish" 3280 (112)

"I would I were Actaeon whom Diana did disguise" 1642 (272)

"I WOULD KISS YOU" 660 (341)

"I would like to be your kitten" 5641 (322)

"I would not ask for my burden to be lightened" 3526 (347)

"I would not be a sinner" 8313 (409)

"I would not go to Old Joe's house, tell you the reason why" 7874B (225)

"I would not wed the finest lass that ever sway'd on beauty's throne" 1606 (129)

"I WOULD SPEND MY BLOOD UNHEEDING" 3599 (139)

I WOULD THAT MY LOVE 2381 (28)

"I would that my love could silently flow in a single word" 2381 (28)

I ZABUJAŁY SIWE ŁABĘDZIE 6730 (159)

"I zabujały biale łabędzie na wodzie" 6730 (159)

IANO AL SOLE 2772 (167)

"The ice is floating in the stream" 7570 (189)

"ICH BETE AN DIE MACHT DER LIEBE" 374 (326)

"ICH BIN DER BUB VOM ELSTERTAL" 5380 (326)

"ICH BIN DER DOKTOR EISENBART" 5381 (309,326, 353)

"ICH BIN DER JUNGE HIRTENKNAB" 4824 (49)

"ICH BIN DIE CHRISTEL VON DER POST" 4132 (258)

"ICH BIN EIN DEUTSCHER KNABE" 5382 (326)

"ICH BIN EIN FREIER WILDBRETSCHÜTZ" 5383 (326, 353)

ICH BIN EIN MUSIKANTE 5384 (353)

"Ich bin ein Musikante und komm aus Schwabenland" 5384 (353)

ICH BIN GUT AUFGELEGT! 271 (396)

"ICH BIN NUR EIN ARMER WANDERGESELL" 1993 (254)

ICH BIN VERLIEBT, ICH WEISS NICHT WIE MIR GESCHAH 880 (254)

"Ich bin vermundt" 1978 (250)

"Ich bin wie and're Mädchen nicht" 4068 (112,330)

"Ich bin zwar noch ein Mädchen" 2777 (218)

Ich bitt' dich, schreib' mir die Es-Scala auf 236 (199)

"Ich danke Gott und freue mich wie's Kind zur Weihnachts- gabe" 3310 (229)

ICH FAHR DAHIN 5385 (49,99,326)

"Ich fahr dahin, denn es muss sein" 5385 (99)

"Ich fahr dahin, wann es muss sein" 5385 (49)

"Ich fahr dahin wenn es muss sein" 5385 (326)

"Ich fahre von hinnen auf meine Weis" 349 (31)

"Ich flüchte mich in meine Klause" 2014 (259)

"Ich frage keine Blume" 3298 (330)

"ICH FREU MICH HEUTE AM WEIHNACHTSFEST" 9284 (354)

"Ich geh' durch die Strassen, o mein" 3584 (396)

"Ich gehe meinen Schlendrian und trinke meinen Wein" 5531 (31)

"Ich ging den Weg entland" 2807 (250)

"ICH GING DURCH EINEN GRASGRÜNEN WALD" 5386 (49,309,326,353)

"Ich ging einmal spazieren, spazieren mit einem schönen Mädchen" 3483 (326)

ICH GING EMOL SPAZIERE 5387 (309,353)

"Ich ging emol spaziere, nanu, nanu, nanu" 5387 (309, 353)

"ICH GING IM WALDE SO FÜR MICH HIN" 5338 (309)

Ich ging wohl nächten späte (tune) 5197

ICH GROLLE NICHT 3360 (272,359)

"Ich grolle nicht und wenn das Herz" 3360 (272,359)

ICH HAB DIE NACHT GETRÄUMET 5389 (41,49,309,326)

"Ich hab die Nacht geträumet wohl einen schweren Traum" 5389 (41,49,99,230,309,326)

ICH HAB' HEIMWEH NACH WIEN 1765 (222)

"Ich hab in einem Garten gesehen" 4187 (231)

"Ich hab in Nacht und Sturmeswehn" 3216 (31)

ICH HAB KEIN GELD 2445 (256)

"Ich hab kein Geld, bin vogelfrei" 2445 (256)

"Ich hab mein Sach auf nichts gestellt" 3543 (31)

ICH HAB MICH ERGEBEN 5347 (326)

"Ich hab mich ergeben, mit Herz und mit hand" 5347 (99,326)

ICH HAB MIR MEIN WEIZEN 5390 (49)

"Ich hab mir mein Weizen am Berg gesät" 5390 (49)

"ICH HABE DEN FRÜHLING GESEHEN" (Folksongs, Germany) 5391 (326,328)

"ICH HABE DEN FRÜHLING GESEHEN" (Silcher) 3481 (326)

"Ich habe fünf liebe Söhne gehabt" 5344 (99)

"Ich habe in deutschen Gauen" 1768 (31)

"Ich habe Liebe schon genossen" 2451 (254)

"ICH HABE MEIN FEINSLIEBCHEN" 5392 (40)

Ich halte treulich still 121

"Ich harre vergebens, seh' ihn niemals wieder!" 3858 (311)

ICH HATT EINEN KAMERADEN 5393 (43,49,309,326,353)

"Ich hatt einen Kameraden, einen bessern find'st du nit" 5393 (99)

"Ich hatt einen Kameraden, einen bessern findst du nit" 5393 (43,49,309,326,353)

"ICH HATT NIN MEI TRUTSCHEL" 2018 (49)

Ich hatte einst ein schönes Vaterland 2048

"Ich hob a kleynem yingele, A zunele gor fayn" 6227 (318)

"ICH HOB GE-AKERT UN GEZEYT" 6211 (318)

"Ich hör' meinen Schatz" 423 (275)

"Ich hört' ein Bächlein rauschen" 3301 (112,277,330,359)

ICH HÖRT EIN SICHELEIN 5394A (41)

ICH HÖRT EIN SICHELEIN RAUSCHEN 5394A (49,309, 353)

"Ich hört ein Sichelein rauchen, wohl rauschen durch das Korn" 5394A (41,49,309,353)

ICH HÖRT EIN SICHLEIN RAUSCHEN 5394B (326)

"Ihr Freunde, stimmt an unser Friesenlied" 53 (31)
"IHR IN DER LIEBE GEBORGEN" 2287 (49)
IHR KINDERLEIN KOMMET 3339 (79,251,326,337,388, 412)
"Ihr Kinderlein kommet, o kommet doch all!" 3339 (79, 251,326,337,388,412)
IHR KLEINEN VÖGELEIN (Folksongs, Germany) 5402 (42)
IHR KLEINEN VÖGELEIN (Gneist) 1286 (49)
"Ihr kleinen Vögelein, ihr Waldergötzerlein" (Folksongs, Germany) 5402 (42)
"Ihr kleinen Vögelein, ihr Waldergötzerlein" (Gneist) 1286 (49)
"Ihr lieben Brüder mein, Rundadinella" 5519 (49)
IHR LUSTIGEN HANNOVERANER 5403 (99)
"Ihr lustigen Hannoveraner seid ihr alle beisammen?" 5403 (99)
"Ihr mögt den Rhein, den stolzen, preisen, der in dem Schoss der Reben liegt" 2789 (31,326)
"Ihr schönen Augen, zu grausam ist" 515 (218)
"Ihr trunk'nen Schläfer, auf zum Fest der Trauben!" 6159 (51)
"IHREN SCHÄFER ZU ERWARTEN" 5404 (31,99,326,353)
IHRES AUGES HIMMLISCH STRAHLEN 3862 (390)
"Ihres Auges himmlisch Strahlen leuchtet schöner" 3862 (390)
Ik bender een arne Pelgrim ziet (tune) 6534
IK HEB DE GROENE STRAATJES 6486 (202)
"Ik heb de groene straatjes Zoo dikwijls ten eind gegaan!" 6486 (202)
IK HEB GEJAAGD 9251 (384)
"Ik heb gejaagd mijn leven lank" 9251 (384)
IK HEBB SE NICH 5344 (41)
"Ik hebb se nich op de Scholen gebracht" 5344 (41)
"Ik hef se nicht up de Scholen gebracht" 5344 (230)
IK HOORDE DEES DAGEN 6487 (202)
"Ik hoorde dees dagen, een magetje klagen" 6487 (202)
"Ik stond op hoogen bergen" 6449 (384)
IK VINDE MIJ GEDRONGEN 6488 (202)
"Ik vinde mij gedrongen, dat ik zingen moet" 6488 (202)
IK VOER LAATST OVER ZEE 6489 (203)
"Ik voer laatst over zee, Wil je mee?" 6489 (203)
IK VRIJDE EEN VROUWKEN ALZOO FIJN 6485 (202)
"Ik vrijd' een vrouwken alzoo fijn" 6485 (202)
IK WEET EEN REIN KASTEEL 6490 (202)
"Ik weet een rein kasteel in een zeer schoon landouwe" 6490 (202)
"IK WIL MIJ GAAN VERTROOSTEN" 6491 (201,384)
IK ZAG CECILIA KOMEN 6492 (202)
"Ik zag Cecilia komen Langs eenen waterkant" 6492 (202)
IK ZEG ADIEU 6483 (202)
"Ik zeg adieu, Wij twee, wij moeten scheiden" 6483 (202)
IK ZIE DIE MORGENSTERRE 6484 (202)
"Ik zie die morgensterre mijn liefkens klaar aanschijn" 6484 (202)
"Ik zing er al van een Ruyter koen" 6563 (384)
"IL COURT, IL COURT LE FURET" 4989 (82,91,127)
"Il est au loin une colline" 1313 (123)
"Il est de retour, le joyeux mois de mai!" 5037 (88)
"IL EST DOUX, IL EST BON" 2309 (1)
"IL EST NÉ, LE DIVIN ENFANT" 9070 (82,91,127,154, 383,388)
"IL EST QUELQU'UN SUR TERRE" 4990 (47)
"Il est un tout petit oiseau qui toujours vole" 1769 (208)
IL ÉTAIT TROIS MATELOTS 4991A (127)
"Il était trois mat'lots de Groix" 4991A (127), 4991B (88)

"Il était trois petits enfants" 9080 (88,127,383)
"IL ÉTAIT UN' BERGÈRE" 4992 (82,91)
"Il était un' Dame Tartine" 4950 (91)
IL ÉTAIT UN' FRÉGATE 4993 (68)
"Il était un' frégate lon la" 4993 (68)
"IL ÉTAIT UN PETIT NAVIRE" 4994 (82,88,91,127,187, 383)
"Il etait un p'tit homme, qui s'app'lait Guilleri" 4943 (91,127,383)
"Il était un roi de Thulé" 1320 (1,6)
"Il était un roi d'Yvetot" 5099 (127,383)
"IL ÉTAIT UNE BERGÈRE" 4992 (70,88,127,383)
EL ÉTAIT UNE FILLE 4995 (91)
"Il était une fille, une fille d'honneur" 4995 (91)
"Il fait jour, le ciel est rose" 5029 (82)
IL FAUT PARTIR 867 (292)
"Il faut partir mes bons compagnons d'armes" 867 (292)
"Il faut te marier, Papillon couleur de neige" 5053 (82,383)
"Il m'a dit: 'Cette nuit, j'ai rêvé'" 791 (362)
IL N'AIME QUE MOI 977 (221)
IL NEIGE 270 (191,193,195)
"Il neige, il neige de gros flocons" 270 (191,193,195)
"IL PLEURE DANS MON COEUR" 788 (121)
IL PLEUT, BERGÈRE 4996 (383)
"IL PLEUT DES PÉTALES DE FLEURS" 1439 (259)
"IL PLEUT, IL PLEUT, BERGÈRE" 4996 (82,88,91,127, 383)
IL REGARDAIT MON BOUQUET 2497 (1,362)
"Il regardait mon bouquet, sans doute il le désirait" 2497 (1,362)
"IL SOMMEILLAIT, LE PAUVRE PÂTRE" 9105 (69)
L'ILE INCONNUE 290 (275)
ILKA BLADE O' GRASS 7067 (100)
"I'LL AY CA' IN BY YON TOON" 7068 (101,105)
I'LL BE BESIDE YOU 9089 (154)
"I'll be beside you, ready to guide you" 9089 (154)
"I'll be down to get you in a taxie, honey" 452 (236)
I'LL BE READY WHEN DE GREAT DAY COME 8351 (184)
I'LL BE THERE 8352 (409)
"I'll be there in the mornin'" 8352 (409)
"I'll be true to my baby" 1017 (246)
I'LL BE TRUE TO MY HONEY BOY 1017 (246)
"I'LL BID MY HEART BE STILL" 7069 (349)
"I'll buy you a ship, a marvelous ship" 4280 (86)
"I'll die, yet in this agony" 3824 (6)
"I'll eat when I'm hungry, I'll drink when I'm dry" 7972 (110,225)
I'll gae nae mair to your toon (tune) 7068
I'LL GIVE MY LOVE AN APPLE 4234A (186)
"I'll give my love an apple without any core" 4234A (186)
"I'll give to you a paper of pins" 7915A (36), 7915B (173), 7915C (185)
"I'll go up on the mountain top" 7779C (80)
"I'll go up on the mountain top and plant me a patch of cane" 7779E (214)
I'LL HEAR THE TRUMPET SOUND 8641 (366)
"I'll never ask the flowers" 3298 (330)
I'LL NEVER ASK YOU TO TELL 1138 (385)
"I'LL NEVER PLAGUE A MAIDEN FAIR" 7298 (135)
I'LL NOT COMPLAIN 3360 (359)
"I'll not complain, tho' break my heart" 3360 (359)
I'LL PLAY SOMETHING FOR YOU 7704 (44)
"I'll play something for you, What will you play for me?" 7704 (44)

"I'LL SAIL UPON THE DOG-STAR" 2911 (277)

I'LL SEE YOU AGAIN 722 (345)

"I'll set you aswing" 1541 (276)

"I'll sing of a man who's now dead in his grave" 7732 (115)

"I'll sing the bold Atrides" 3253 (364)

"I'LL SING THEE SONGS OF ARABY" 683* (128, 132, 237)

"I'll sing you a fine ould song made by a fine ould Paddy's pate" 456 (189)

"I'll sing you a song, a good song of the sea" 9426 (279, 343, 366)

"I'll sing you a song, and a very pretty one" 4576 (198)

"I'll sing you a song and it's not very long" 8161 (173, 227)

"I'll sing you a song, though it may be a sad one" 8000 (173)

"I'll sing you a true song of Billy the kid" 7444 (80)

"I'll sing you one-ho! Green grow the rushes-ho" 7640 (35)

"I'll sing you one-o. Green grow the rushes-o" 7640 (44)

"I'll take my gospel trumpet" 8396 (409)

"I'LL TAKE YOU HOME AGAIN, KATHLEEN" 3999 (10, 36, 115, 128, 129, 130, 131, 132, 166, 233, 329, 366)

"I'll tell the tale of a nanny" 3502 (9)

"I'll tell you a story, there is one I know" 7885A (120)

"I'll tell you a story, there's one that I know" 7885A (214)

"I'll tell you how I the Lord" 8362 (409)

"I'll tell you of a wonder that will stiffen up your hair" 5925 (349)

"I'll tell you something, ain't no joke" 8317 (336)

"I'll twine with my ring, made of raven black hair" 7596 (243)

"I'll wander back" 1737 (114)

ILLINOIS 1830 (28)

Illsley (tune) 8944

"Ils vont, les petits canards" 634 (190, 192, 194, 208)

ILTALAULU 4825 (124)

"Ilu hotzi, hotzionu, hotzionu miMitzrayim" 6190 (44)

ILUSIONES PERDIDAS 4498 (73)

I'm. See also Ah'm

"I'm a celebrated lumberman, my duty I never shirk" 7778 (72)

"I'm a dacent young colleen just over from Ireland" 2232 (204)

"I'm a' doun, doun, doun, I'm doun for lack o' Johnnie" 7070 (101, 103, 104)

I'M A' DOUN FOR LACK O' JOHNNIE 7070 (101, 103, 104)

"I'm a farmer's only daughter" 4852 (124)

I'M A FISHER 5653 (164)

"I'm a fisher, in the lowlands I reside" 5653 (164)

"I'm a heartbroken raftsman, from Greenville I came" 7588 (72)

"I'm a lad from Cracow, born in Cracow city" 6754 (159)

"I'm a lad from Krakow, very highly thought of" 2478 (295)

"I'm a light hearted Paddy, a rale Irish laddy" 8061 (189)

"I'm a little prairie flow'r" 7935 (366)

"I'm a lonely soldier sitting here in Korea" 3497 (336)

I'M A PILGRIM 1797 (123, 394)

"I'm a pilgrim, and I'm a stranger" 1797 (123, 394)

"I'm a pilgrim, and I'm a stranger" (Folksongs, United States) 7923 (212)

"I'm a poor countryman from the town of Athlone" 7929 (72)

"I'm a poor lonesome cowboy" 7931A (321), 7931B (120)

I'M A POOR STRANGER 5866 (172)

I'M A POOR STRANGER AND FAR FROM MY HOME 5866 (166, 213)

"I'm a roving gambler" 7968 (170)

I'M A STRANGER HERE 8353 (336)

"I'm a stranger here, just blowed in your town" 8442 (336)

"I'm a thrifty farmer, and my field I plow well" 6685 (295)

I'M A TINKER 4356 (94)

"I'm a tinker, I'm a good one" 4356 (94)

"I'm a tough old salt, and it's never I care" 469 (240)

"I'm a well-known bobby of the stalwart squad" 391 (172)

"I'm a Winin' Boy, don't deny my name" 2540 (336)

"I'm a young married man that is tired of life" 5887 (171)

IM ABENDROTH 3277 (112, 209, 226, 229)

"Im Abendschimmer wallt der Quell" 3289 (141)

"I'm a-goin' to the shuckin' of the corn" 7993 (32, 34)

"I'M A-GOING TO DO ALL I CAN" 8354 (409)

"I'M A-GOING TO JOIN THE BAND" 8355 (409)

"I'm a-going to lay down my sword and shield down by the riverside" 8170 (409)

"I'm a-going to the shucking of the corn" 7993 (44)

I'M A-LOOKING FOR A HOME 8188A (293)

I'M ALWAYS CALLED MIMI 2889 (1)

I'M ALWAYS CHASING RAINBOWS 607 (128, 132, 236)

"I'm always chasing rainbows, watching clouds drifting by" 607 (128, 132, 236)

"I'M AN OLD COWHAND FROM THE RIO GRANDE" 2399 (236)

"I'm an old shoemaker by my trade" 7884 (242)

"I'm a-riding the range" 169 (37)

"Im Arm ein frisches ros'ges Kind" 5518 (31)

I'M A-ROLLIN' 8356 (183)

"I'm a-rollin', I'm a-rollin', I'm a-rollin' through an unfriendly world" 8356 (183)

I'M A-ROLLING 8356 (366)

"I'm a-walkin' down the track, I got tears in my eyes" 7846 (227)

"I'm born of God I know I am" 8438B (409)

"I'M BOUND TO FOLLOW THE LONGHORN COW" 7705 (120)

"I'm broken hearted for tho' we're parted" 2723 (236)

I'M BUTT'NING 5711 (164)

"I'M CALLED LITTLE BUTTERCUP" 3657 (132)

"I'm Captain Jinks of the Horse Marines" 7488 (28, 225, 366)

"I'm coming, I'm coming, for my head is bending low" 1127 (28, 129, 130, 132, 233, 236, 279, 366)

I'M CONSUMED BY A FLAME 1888 (162)

I'M DARK-EYED AND PETITE 8761 (286)

"I'm dark-eyed and petite to hold" 8761 (286)

"I'm dreaming now of Hallie" 4052 (32, 34, 109, 110, 132)

"I'm dreaming now of Hally, sweet Hally" 4052 (128, 129, 130, 184, 279, 366)

"Im Felde schleich' ich still und wild" 3013 (229)

IM FRÜHLINGSANFANG 2578 (226)

"Im Frühlingsschatten fand ich sie" (Strauss) 3630 (250)

"Im Frühlingsschatten fand ich sie" (Zelter) 4139 (229)

IM FRÜHTAU ZU BERGE 7313 (49, 309, 326, 353)

"Im Frühtau zu Berge wir gehn, fallera" 7313 (49, 309, 353)

"Im Frühtau zu Berge wir ziehn, falera" 7313 (326)

"I'm getting old and feeble and I can work no more" 7879 (115)

I'M THE MAN FROM KRAKOW 6733 (37)
"I'm the man from Krakow, all the world may know it"
    6733 (37)
IM TIEFEN KELLER 1077 (31,353)
"IM TIEFEN KELLER SITZ ICH HIER" 1077 (43)
"Im tiefen Keller sitz ich hier" 1077 (353)
"I'm tired of bein' Jim Crowed" 8379 (336)
"I'm Titania, the maid with golden hair" 3732 (292)
I'M TRAMPIN' 8363 (184)
"I'm trampin', trampin' tryin' to make heab'n my home"
    8363 (184)
"Im Verkehr nur Bruder, Schwester" 1030 (256)
"I'm waiting near by the fountain here" 6339A (350)
"Im Wald, im grünen Walde, da steht ein Försterhaus"
    5455 (328)
"IM WALD, IM HELLEN SONNENSCHEIN" 1928 (49,326)
"Im wald, im Wald ist's frisch und grün" 1163 (209)
"IM WALD UND AUF DER HEIDE" 5408 (31,49,99,309,
    326,353)
"I'm 'way down East" 2707 (131)
"I'm wearin' a wa', John, like snaw-wreaths in thaw"
    7087 (100,103)
Im weissen Röss (Granichstaedten) 1348 (257)
Im weissen Rössl 273-274
"I'm with you and you're with me" 7219 (239)
"I'M WORKING ON THE BUILDIN'" 8364 (409)
"IM WUNDERSCHÖNEN MONAT MAI" 3361 (36)
"Imagine a Cuban flower" 1010 (9)
Imandra new (tune) 7582
IMBABURA 4527 (284)
"Imbabura de mi vida, tú serás la preferida" 4527 (284)
IMMACULATE HEART OF MARY 6493 (71)
IMMER NUR LÄCHELN 2095 (254)
IMMERZU SINGT MEIN HERZ DEINEM HERZEN ZU 1990
    (256)
IMMORTAL BABE 3330 (296)
"Immortal Babe Who this dear day" 3330 (296)
IMMORTAL EYES 507 (403)
"Immortal eyes, resplendent, glorious thou art" 507 (403)
IMPATIENCE 3299 (112,327)
IMPOSIBLE 4499 (73)
IMPRESSION 680* (78)
"Imprison'd by love o'er pow'ring" 1365 (292)
"In a cavern, in a canyon excavating for a mine" 2509
    (10,35,128,131,225,233,236,246,366,402)
"In a fact'ry I was brought up, always working" 3463 (162)
"In a little rosewood casket" 7967 (392)
"In a lonely village in Brazil" 4207 (219)
IN A MANGER (Carols, Poland) 9299A (295), 9299B (295)
IN A MANGER (Carols, Russia) 9308 (337)
"IN A MANGER HE IS LYING" 9299A (296)
"In a manger poor sleeps the Christ Child" 9308 (337)
"In a manger sleeps the Infant" 9299A (295), 9299B (295)
IN A PALM GROVE 6318 (322)
"In a palm grove by the sea I met such a lovely maiden"
    6318 (322)
IN A ROSEBUSH 5798 (164)
"In a rosebush I the daylight first did see" 5798 (164)
"In a sea that is blue like the heavens" 4287 (350)
"In a shady nook one moonlight night, a Leprehaun I spied"
    5953 (15)
IN A STRANGE LAND 3709 (275)
"In a wee cot hoose far across the muir" 7083 (100)
"In a wee cot house far across the main" 7083 (235)
"In all our trials, Lord" 1071 (347)

"IN ALLEN GUTEN STUNDEN" 4137 (31)
"In allen guten Stunden, erhöht von Lieb und Wein" 3009
    (99)
"IN AMAR BELLEZZA ALTERA" 43 (253)
"In Amsterdam there liv'd a maid" 9419B (29), 9419G
    (234)
"In Amsterdam there lived a maid" 9419F (173,320)
"In Amsterdam there lives a maid" 9419A (293), 9419C
    (72), 9419D (401)
"In ancient days there dwelt a Turk" 7750 (80)
IN ANCIENT KRAKOW 6849 (295)
"In a-that morning, O my Lord" 8371 (409)
"In August last on one fine day" 1086 (189)
"In bed with my woman just singin' the blues" 8578 (336)
"In Bedleem, in that fair city" 8967 (360)
"In Bedlem that child of life is born of Mary" 8969 (360,
    361)
"In Bedlem this Berd of life is born" 8969 (360)
IN BERLIN, SAGT ER 4184 (99)
"In Berlin, sagt er, musst du fein, sagt er" 4184 (99)
IN BETHLEHEM (Carols, Italy) 9202 (165)
IN BETHLEHEM (Carols, Poland) 9289 (295)
IN BETHLEHEM CITY 8946 (361)
"In Bethlehem city, on Christmas Day morn" 8946 (361)
"In Bethlehem, in Bethlehem, tidings ring triumphant"
    9289 (295)
"In Bethlehem is born, is born the Holy Child" 9202 (165)
"IN BETHLEHEM 'NEATH STARLIT SKIES" 3653 (251)
IN BETHLEHEM, THE LOWLY 9252 (296)
"In Bethlehem, the lowly, Jesus was born this day" 9252
    (296)
"In Bethlehem there is glory" 9366 (314)
IN BETHLEHEM'S MANGER 9309 (244)
"In Bethlehem's manger Jesus Christ is born us" 9309 (244)
"IN BORDEAUX I KNOW NINE LADIES" 4863 (86)
"In Carmel Bay the people say" 7394 (321)
"In Caroline whar I was born" 3564 (109,110)
"In Caroline where I was born" 3564 (185)
"In chains to her doom they dragged her" 3863 (2,300)
IN CIMA AI MONTICELLI 6097 (238)
"In cima ai monticelli ci sta un bel palazzo" 6097 (238)
"In come the duck and drake" 8096 (392)
"IN DARKNESS LET MEE DWELL" 905 (144)
"In days of old, as we've been told" 3544 (189)
"In days of old, when knights were bold" 2337 (28,366)
"In days of winter dreary, when all is gloom and night"
    3636 (277)
"In days of yore, from Britain's shore" 2608 (28,233,279,
    366)
"In days of yore the hero Wolfe" 2608 (294)
"In de ebening by de moonlight" 332
IN DE HEILIGE SCHRIFTURE 6494 (384)
"In de heilige Schrifture vind ik een exempel schoon"
    6494 (384)
"In de valley, I couldn't hear nobody pray" 8332 (183)
"In de vinter, in de vintertime, ven de vin' blows on de
    vindowpane" 7708A (321)
IN DE VINTER TIME 7708A (321)
"In deep distress, O God, I cry to Thee" 1072 (123)
"IN DEEP FOREST MARCHING IS DREARY" 6732 (159)
"In deinen glücklichen" 2765 (218)
IN DEINES VATERS GÄRTELEIN 4826 (49)
"In deines Vaters Gärtelein ein Röslein wuchs all-da"
    4826 (49)
"In dem Dornbusch blüht ein Röslein" 1157 (99,229)

IN DEM SCHATTEN MEINER LOCKEN 4076 (112,220)
"In dem Schatten meiner Locken schlief mir mein Geliebter
      ein" 4076 (112,220)
"IN DEN HEMEL IS EENEN DANS" 6495 (203)
"In Denmark I am born" 3120 (87)
IN DER BARKE 6163 (51)
IN DER FERNE 3482 (31,99)
IN DER FREMDE 3709 (275)
IN DER FRÜHE 4077 (112)
IN DER HEIMAT 1857 (224)
"In der hohen Hall' sass König Siegfried" 2176 (250)
IN DER KUZNYE 6212 (318)
"In der kuznye, bay dem fayer, Shteyt der shmider un er
      shmit" 6212 (318)
IN DER SCHENKE 1676 (31)
"In des Lebens Frühlingstagen" 231 (391)
"IN DIESEN HEIL'GEN HALLEN" 2599 (5,240,390)
"In diesen Wintertagen, nun sich das Licht verhüllt" 3636
      (277)
"In Dombrova a girl is a cherry" 6847 (159)
"In dreams I saw thy face so fair" 3359 (272)
"In Dublin City where the girls, they are so pretty" 5968
      (166)
"In Dublin's fair city, where girls are so pretty" 5968
      (35,249)
"In Dublin's fair city, where the girls are so pretty" 5968
      (172,402)
IN DULCI IUBILO 9159 (334)
"In dulci iubilo, now sing we all Io!" 9159 (334)
IN DULCI JUBILO (Carols, Finland) 9038 (354)
IN DULCI JUBILO (Carols, Germany) 9159 (34,37,199,
      307,319,337,361,375)
"In dulci jubilo let us our homage shew" 9159 (307,319,
      375)
"In dulci jubilo, let us our homage show" 9159 (337,361)
"In dulci jubilo, now sing we all Io" 9159 (199)
"In dulci jubilo, now sing with hearts aglow!" 9159 (34)
"In dulci jubilo, nun singet und seid froh" (Carols, Finland)
      9038 (354)
"IN DULCI JUBILO, NUN SINGET UND SEID FROH" (Carols,
      Germany) 9159 (354)
"In dulci Jubilo, we lift our voice to Thee" 9159 (37)
"IN DUV'ÈLA 'STA RUMAGNÒLA?" 6098 (325)
"IN EACH OF THE KINGDOMS AND COUNTRIES" 1227
      (87)
"In eighteen hundred and forty-one" 7913 (35,110,173,
      227,293,335)
"In eighteen hundred and forty-wan" 7913 (115,225)
"In eighteen hundred and sixty-one" 7913 (145)
"In eighteen hundred forty-one" 7913 (44)
IN EINEM KRIPPLEIN 8871 (354)
"In einem Kripplein lieget das Kindlein" 8871 (354)
IN EINEM KÜHLEN GRUNDE 1281 (42,309,326,353)
"In einem kühlen Grunde, da geht ein Mühlenrad" 1281
      (42,99,309,326,353)
"In einem Tal bei armen Hirten erschien mit jedem jungen
      Jahr" 3284 (141)
"In einem Tal, bei einem Bach, da flog ein bunter
      Schmetterling" 3344 (226)
"In einer Maiennacht" 3644 (222)
IN EVENING'S GLOW 3277 (209)
"In every city on wall and smokestack" 1785 (7)
IN EXCELSIS GLORIA 3445 (334)
"In exchange for these bitter tears" 2766 (253)
"In far-off land, to mortal feet forbidden" 3906 (3)
IN FERNEM LAND 3906 (3,185)

"In fernem Land, unnahbar euren Schritten" 3906 (3,185)
"In fourteen hundred ninety-two, three ships set out to sea"
      7499 (44)
IN FREEDOM WE'RE BORN 386 (44)
"In Galilee high on a hill" 2630 (30)
"In Galilee, in Tel-Chay, Trumpeldor the hero, fell"
      6184 (318)
IN GLENDALOUGH LIVED A YOUNG SAINT 5939 (172)
"In Glendalough lived a young saint, in an odor of sanctity
      dwelling" 5939 (172)
"In gloom of night I stand alone in deep despond" 2949
      (273)
"In glowing Venice no boat is stirring" 1341 (190,192,194)
"IN GOD'S GREAT WISDOM" 2377 (141)
"In good King Charles's golden days" 4791 (14,235,349)
"In good old colony days, when we lived under the King"
      7870 (111)
"In good old colony times, when we were under the King"
      7870 (34,185)
"IN GRÜNEM WALD ICH NEULICH SASS" 3538 (250)
"In grüner Berge Kranze die Silberschnee umsäumt" 5409
      (31)
"In grüner Landschaft Sommerflor, bei kühlem Wasser,
      Schlif und Rohr" 4066 (226)
"In happy moments my love with smiles beaming" 669
      (295)
IN HEAVENLY LOVE ABIDING 2367 (28,366)
IN HEAVEN'S VAULT ABOVE ME 7299 (45)
"In heaven's vault above me the little stars do shine" 7299
      (45)
"In heav'nly love abiding, no change my heart shall fear"
      2367 (28,366)
"In her gilded chamber, the jewel'd Queen lay dreaming"
      8660 (20)
IN HERBSTESNACHT 4058 (356)
"In Herbstesnacht in Sturmesnacht" 4058 (356)
"In het glaasjen of myn Tryntjen, Ik vind weinig onder-
      scheit" 3432 (278)
IN HIS SHALLOP 5724 (92)
"In his shallop on Lake Balaton floats the young fisher lad,
      pale and wan" 5724 (92)
IN HIS STEPS 3331 (347)
"IN HOLLAND STAAT EEN HUIS" 6496 (203)
"IN JEDEM VOLLEN GLASE WEIN" 2165 (31)
"In jeder Stadt gibt es Freude und Schmerz" 674* (396)
IN JESU NAME 9253 (201)
"In Jezu name, broeders eerzame" 9253 (201)
IN JUDAH'S FIELDS 2800 (369)
In Lauterbach hab' ich mein' Strumpf verloren (tune)
      7560
"In Limehouse where yellow chinkies love to play" 395
      (345)
"In Lim'rick city he was brought up" 4545K (34)
"In London City a lady did dwell" 7483 (81)
"In London there lived a mason by trade" 4810C(126)
"In love she fell, my shy Bluebell" 2226 (408)
"In manger bare and lowly lying" 9046 (361)
"In Mantua's dark prison cell, Andreas Hofer lay" 1916
      (7,31)
"In May, in wondrous lovely May" 3361 (36)
"In Maytide, with the bloom on the bramble and the
      broom" 5943 (280)
IN MEINER HEIMAT 3773 (98)
"In meiner Heimat wird es jetzt Frühling" 3773 (98)
IN MIDDLE WINTER THEY SET OUT 8811 (361)

"Io la Musica son, ch'ai dolci accenti" 2507 (179)
IO LA VIDI 3829 (3)
"Io la vidi e il suo sorriso" 3829 (3)
"Io la vidia Piedigrotta" 6160 (51)
"Io l'ho perduta!" 3829 (3)
IO PARTO 6101 (325)
"Io son zitella, Ma sono scaltra" 2777 (218)
"Io ti lascio" 2579 (274)
Io ti lascio, o cara, addio 2579 (274)
"Io vado deh pensa ad Aristea!" 2112 (218)
IORANA 828 (78)
Iphigéne en Tauride 822 (148)
Iphigenie en Tauride 1272
Irby (tune) 1225
"Irene appear! Though all around is darkness!" 574 (146)
"Irene goodnight, Irene goodnight" 2081 (389)
"Iréne, paraissez, malgré les voiles sombres" 574 (146)
Iris 2300 (143)
IRISH CAROL 9195 (337)
IRISH GIRL 5942 (95)
An Irish idyll 3552-3554
THE IRISH JUBILEE 2074 (114, 166, 246)
IRISH LULLABY 5872 (397)
The Irish tune (tune) 6033
IRISH TUNE FROM COUNTY DERRY 5940 (402)
IRISH WAR-SONG 5870 (397)
Irish washerwoman (tune) 8023A
"The Iron Horse draws nigh with its smoke-nostrils high" 8083 (173)
"IS A TASK TOO GREAT FOR ONE?" 6420 (316)
IS AITHNE DÚINN GO LÉIR 5943 (280)
'T IS DE BAZINNE 6498 (203)
"'t Is de bazinne van al de bazinnen" 6498 (203)
"Is dit niet wel een vremde gril?" 6405 (384)
"Is er iemand uit Oost Indiën gekomen" 6582 (384)
"Het is goed pays, goed vrede in alle Vlaamsche landen" 6581 (384)
IS HE THE ONE 3859 (221)
"Is he the one that my sad heart" 3859 (221)
"Is it bitter herb, then?" 3681 (295)
"IS IT BLISS OR IS IT SORROW" 418 (277)
"Is it thou that hast sullied a soul so pure?" 3823 (4)
"IS IT TO THE FIELDS YOU'RE GOING?" 5772 (164)
"Is it true that the women are worse than the men" 4597A (172)
"Is not the life more than meat and body than raiment?" (Fisher) 1080 (398)
"Is not the life more than meat, and the body than raiment?" (Topliff) 3755 (200)
"IS SHE NOT PASSING FAIR" 992 (277)
"'T IS SINT ANNA DIE KOMT AAN" 6499 (203)
IS THAT SO? 6734 (228)
"Is that so? Thank you all" 2318 (1)
I'S THE B'Y 4235 (44)
"I's the b'y that builds the boat" 4235 (44)
"Is the memory erased" 3860 (4)
IS THERE ANY SADNESS? 6669 (86)
"Is there any torment, is there any sadness" 6669 (86)
IS THERE ANYBODY HERE? 8368 (409)
"Is there anybody here who loves my Jesus?" 8368 (409)
IS THERE FOR HONEST POVERTY 7103 (232)
"Is there for honest poverty that hangs his head an' a' that?" 7103 (18)
"Is there for honest poverty that hangs his head and a' that?" 7103 (163, 349)

"Is there for honest poverty that hangs his heid, an' a' that?" 7103 (100, 102)
"Is there for honest poverty that hings his head, an' a' that?" 7103 (232)
ISABEAU S'Y PROMÈNE 5164 (187)
"Isabeau s'y promène le long de son jardin" 5164 (187)
"I'se got a gal an' you got none Li'l Liza Jane" 7779A (128, 129, 130, 131, 236)
"I'se got a little baby but she's out of sight" 1712 (131)
"I'SE GWINE BACK TO DIXIE" 4011 (10, 114, 129, 130, 132)
"I'SE THE B'Y THAT BUILDS THE BOAT" 4235 (186)
IŠLA MARÍNA 4352 (94)
"IŠLA MARÍNA DO CINTORINA" 4352 (86, 94)
THE ISLAND 2944 (121)
THE ISLAND OF JAMAICA 7713 (72)
"Island of rarest splendor, my Puerto Rican land" 94 (291)
ISLAND SONG 5647 (279)
ISLANDS FAIR 4414 (94)
"Islands fair, islands green, oh you fair, green islands!" 4414 (94)
ISLE OF BEAUTY (Bayly) 214 (28, 366)
ISLE OF BEAUTY (Watts) 3954 (241)
THE ISLE OF MULL 7074 (105)
"Isles of Hawaii, verdant in the ocean" 5647 (279)
"IŠLO DIEVČA PRE VODU" 4353 (94)
"Isn't that dandy neat, Mister Banjo" 7828 (331)
ISOLDE'S LIEBESTOD 3922 (1)
Issé 826-827
"Ist denn rechtlos, Undankbarer" 3165 (218)
"IST DER HIMMEL DARUM IM LENZ SO BLAU?" 2806 (98)
IST DER KUTSCHER 5749 (92)
"Ist der Kutscher gross oder klein trinkt er für sein Leben gern Wein" 5749 (92)
"Das ist der Tag des Herrn! Das ist der Tag des Herrn!" 1975 (326)
IST ES DENN NUN 5411 (43)
"Ist es denn nun wirklich wahr" 5411 (43)
"Ist es diese Schwüle oder euer lieblicher Gesang" 1192 (217)
"Ist es ein Traum nur von versunknem Glück?" 2541 (31)
"IST ES NOCH STILL IN DER RUNDE" 9321 (354)
"IST EUCH SCHON DAS LIED BEKANNT" 5434 (309)
ISTEN HOZZÁD SZÜLÖTTEM FÖLD 5730 (23)
"Isten hozzád szülöttem föld, én miattam lehetsz már zöld" 5730 (23)
ISTENEM, ISTENEM 5731 (22)
"Istenem, istenem, áraszd meg a vizet" 5731 (22)
IT AIN'T ALL HONEY AND IT AIN'T ALL JAM 2613 (131)
IT AIN'T GONNA RAIN 7399 (132)
"It ain't gonna rain, it ain't gonna snow" 7399 (132, 321)
"It ain't no mo' cane on dis Brazis" 8169 (227)
"It being on a fine summer's morning, as the birds sweetly tuned on each bough" 5860 (172)
"IT CAME UPON A MIDNIGHT CLEAR" (Willis) 4039 (33, 79, 337)
"IT CAME UPON THE MIDNIGHT CLEAR" (Carols, England) 8949 (305, 307, 319, 363, 410)
"IT CAME UPON THE MIDNIGHT CLEAR" (Willis) 4039 (28, 38, 39, 125, 165, 206, 233, 236, 251, 296, 307, 315, 366, 388, 394)
"It fell on a summers day, while sweet Bessy sleeping lay" 533 (278)
IT HAD TO BE YOU 1811 (345)
"It is all in vain to implore me" 1096 (122, 237, 385)

IT CANNOT BE 7314 (95)

"It is done! And Judea belongs to Tiberius!" 2311 (364)

IT IS ENOUGH 2373 (123, 394)

"It is enough for me by day to walk the same bright earth with him" 703 (358)

"It is enough, O Lord, now take away my life" 2373 (123, 394)

"IT IS FULFILLED" 131 (330)

IT IS HARD TO HIDE LOVE 2625 (164)

"It is hard to hide love that your heart besets" 2625 (164)

IT IS MAY 5036 (95)

"It is May, lovely May, it's the merry month of May" 5036 (95)

"It is night and the stars are brightly shining" 741 (364)

"It is not that I love you less" 342 (36, 273, 397)

IT IS NOT THE TEAR 5944 (349)

"It is not the tear, at this moment shed, when the cold turf has just been laid o'er him" 5944 (349)

"It is of a rich merchant I am going to tell" 8037A (402)

"It is of a wealthy farmer, as you shall hear" 4810B (72)

IT IS SPRING 7714 (44)

"It is spring, the daisies are busting out" 7714 (44)

"It is the sweetest hour for love" 5995 (133)

"It is the truth, then! O heav'n!" 865 (2)

"It is useful no more" 2521 (131, 132)

"IT MAKES A LONG-TIME MAN FEEL BAD" 8369 (336)

"It makes no diff'rence what church you may belong to" 8645 (409)

"It makes no diff'rence where you are" 7611 (321)

"It may be true, but I know too" 860 (292)

"IT MUST BE WONDERFUL INDEED" 2150 (209, 348)

"It now lies on the shelf" 2521 (131, 132)

"It oft-times has been told that the British seamen bold" 7512 (173)

"It rained, it rained, it rained, it rained all over town" 8001 (243)

"It rose upon the sordid street, a cadence sweet and lone" 5970 (133)

"It say in de Bible how Lawd he make man" 1233 (110)

"It seem'd as tho' the heavens had kissed the earth to rest" 3375 (359)

"It seemed as though the heaven so softly kissed the earth" 3375 (112)

"It seemed that heaven had mingled with earth upon a kiss" 3375 (277)

IT SNOWS 270 (191, 193, 195)

"It snows, it snows, large flakes like cotton" 270 (191, 193, 195)

"It takes a long-handled shovel to dig a nine-foot hole" 8407 (336)

"It takes a worried man to sing a worried song" 8636 (293, 336)

It was. See also 'Twas

IT WAS A DREAM 2048 (348)

"It was a fair young shepherdess that fed her lambkins two" 5526 (199)

"IT WAS A LOVER AND HIS LASS" (Morley) 2526 (14, 75, 235, 306, 349, 397, 402)

"It was a lover and his lass" (Parry) 2745 (344)

"IT WAS A LOVER AND HIS LASSE" 2526 (144, 403)

"It was a stately Southern ship and she flew the Stripes and Stars" 9484 (320)

"It was down by the salley gardens my love and I did meet" 5899 (36)

"It was down by the Sally gardens my love and I did meet" 5899 (215)

"It was down in old Joe's barroom" 7603 (109, 110)

"It was early one mornin', Lord" 8498 (336)

"It was good for the prophet Daniel" 8592 (409)

"It was his accents that so sweet to me sounded!" 871 (221)

"It was in a Concert Garden where the fun was at its height" 3887 (131)

"It was in and aboot the Mart'mas time" 4545L (101)

"It was in the merry month of May, when I started for Texas far away" 8069 (331)

"It was in the year of forty-four" 9491 (173)

"It was inch by inch dat I sought the Lord" 8367 (182)

"It was inch by inch that I sought the Lord" 8367 (409)

"It was midnight on the sea, band playin' 'Nearer, my God, to Thee'" 2084 (336)

"It was my last cigar" 1724 (205, 279, 366)

IT WAS NOT TO BE 2644 (132)

IT WAS ON A FINE SUMMER MORNING 5860 (166, 213)

"It was on a fine summer morning, the birds sweetly tun'd on each bough" 5860 (166, 213)

"It was one Sunday mornin', Lawd, Lawd, Lawd" 8297C (216)

"It was po' little Jesus, yes, yes" 9397 (227)

"It was poor little Jesus, yes yes" 9397 (33, 332)

"It was the eve of Christmas, the snow lay deep and white" 2334 (394)

"It was the very noon of night" 183 (244)

IT WAS THOU THE DESTROYER 3823 (310)

"It was thou the destroyer of her I loved" 3823 (310)

"It was upon a Lammas nicht" 7029 (100, 102)

"It was upon a Lammas night" 7029 (285)

"It was when spring was in the air" 651 (341)

L'Italiana in Algeri 3103 (300)

"ITE CALDI SOSPIRI" 1818 (144)

ITISKIT, ITASKIT 7715 (109, 110)

"Itiskit, itaskit, a green and yellow basket" 7715 (109, 110)

"It's a banged-up car I'm driving" 7818 (314)

"It's a long road we have travelled and the end is mighty nigh" 3594 (131)

IT'S A ME, O LORD 8558B (28, 129, 130, 132, 279, 366)

"It's a me, it's a me O lord" 8558B (28, 129, 130, 132, 279, 366)

"It's a sailin' I am at the dawn" 682 (114)

"It's about a fierce highwayman my story I will tell" 5882A (172, 173)

"It's bold Turpin hero is my name" 4783 (198)

"Its clinging, mournful leaves, I said, seem made to thatch a grave" 2227 (408)

"It's gonna take everybody to win this war" 56 (7, 335)

"It's hame, an' it's hame" 7047 (101)

"It's into the city, not far from this spot" 7770 (72)

IT'S ME 8558A (409)

"It's me, it's me, it's me, O Lord" 8558A (183)

"It's me, it's me, O Lord" 8558A (76, 182, 409)

IT'S MY UNION 680 (293)

IT'S NOTHING NEW 844 (164)

"It's nothing new still it is true" 844 (164)

"It's of a brisk young sailor boy, from Dover town he came" 9438 (198)

"It's of a comely young lady fair, was walking out to take the air" 4593 (198)

"It's of a fearless highwayman a story I'll tell" 5882B (35)

"It's of a fierce highwayman a story I will tell" 5882C (72)

"It's of a rich farmer in Cheshire, to market his daughter did go" 4637 (198)

"It's of a rich man's daughter who lived in Maiden Lane" 8137B (72)

"It's of a wealthy farmer, lived on the banks of sweet Dundee" 7425B (72)

"It's on a dark and stormy night, the snow was falling fast" 7984 (72)

IT'S PARTING TIME 6798 (159)

"It's parting time for you, our lady fair" 6798 (159)

"It's pretty well met to my own true love" 7988 (72)

IT'S RAINING, IT'S POURING 7716 (109,110)

"it's raining, it's pouring, the old man is snoring" 7716 (109,110)

IT'S SPRING! 1860 (162)

"It's the hat my dear old father wore upon Saint Patrick's day" 3402 (166)

"It's the last fair deal gone down" 8390 (336)

IT'S THE SYME THE 'OLE WORLD OVER 7717 (225)

"IT'S THE SYME THE WHOLE WORLD OVER" 7717 (34, 109,110)

IT'S VERY TRUE 6083 (36)

IT'S YOUR TIME NOW 455 (336)

IU PARTU 6101 (325)

"Iu partu e su' custrittu di partiri" 6101 (325)

IVAN PETRUSKI SKIVAR 7395 (343)

"I've a crown up in the Kingdom" 8172 (409)

"I've a friend called Michalke, Michalke" 6208 (318)

I'VE A GARDEN 6270 (30)

"I've a garden and a well" 6270 (30)

"I'VE A LONGING IN MY HEART FOR YOU, LOUISE" 1534 (114)

"I've a pair of poodles, poodles" 6207 (318)

I'VE A PURSE 5732 (95)

"I've a purse, but not a penny, can I order wine, then?" 5732 (95)

"I've a secret in my heart" 2516 (131)

"I've been a moonshiner for sev'nteen long years" 7755 (109,110)

"I've been around the world" 2435 (128,131,236)

"I've been a-wandrin' all the night" 9369 (373)

"I've been a-wand'ring all the night" 9369 (312)

"I'VE BEEN ROAMING" 1703 (348)

"I've been to Harlem, I've been to Dover, I've traveled this wide world all over" 4782 (216)

"I've been thro' Carolina" 1019 (28,366)

"I've been working on the levee, all the livelong day" 8370 (44)

I'VE BEEN WORKING ON THE RAILROAD 8370 (114,216)

"I've been working on the railroad, all the livelong day" 8370 (216)

I'VE BEEN WUKKIN' ON DE RAILROAD 8370 (236)

"I've brought you here a bunch of may!" 8960 (334)

"I'VE DANCED AND DANCED THE LIVELONG DAY" 5165 (187)

I'VE DONE WHAT YOU TOLD ME TO DO 8371 (409)

"I'VE FOUND MY BONNY BABE A NEST" 5945 (349)

"I've got a belly full of whiskey and a head full of gin" 8408 (336)

"I've got a home in a-that Rock" 8336 (409)

"I've got a mule an' her name is Sal" 50

"I've got a mule, her name is Sal" 50

"I've got a pal, a reg'lar out an' outer" 1749 (131,132)

"I've got a problem that is bothering me" 3064 (293)

"I've got a robe, you've got a robe, all God's children got a robe" 8177 (129,130,132,233,236)

"I've got a robe, you've got a robe, all of God's children got a robe" 8177 (28,366,409)

"I've got a wife an'-a five li'l chillun'" 8509 (227)

"I've got bricks in my pillow and my head can't rest no more" 8202 (336)

I'VE GOT NO USE FOR WOMEN 7718 (173)

"I've got no use for women, a true one may never be found" 7718 (173)

"I've got ten little fingers" 3400 (128)

"I've got the worried blues, Lord" 8635 (336)

"I've got those Vicksburg blues and I'm singin' it ev'ry-where I go" 8604 (336)

"I've got your picture, and I'm goin' to put it in a frame" 8538 (336)

"I've heard a liltin' at oor yowe milkin'" 7040A (100, 103,104)

"I've heard the lark's cry thrill the sky" 6018 (349)

"I've heard them liltin' at owr ewe milkin'" 7040A (235)

"I've heard them liltin' at the ewe milkin'" 7040A (17)

"I've heard them lilting at our ewe-milking" 7040A (199)

"I've heard them lilting at our yowe-milking" 7040A (349)

"I'VE JUST COME FROM THE FOUNTAIN" 8372 (129, 409)

"I've just got here from Paris" 1250 (114,131)

"I've just got here through Paris" 1250 (204)

"I've oft-times heard of married life and pleasures without equal" 7469 (72)

"I've one memory of across the sea from a balcony" 6967 (132)

"I've rambled and gambled all my money" 7719 (321)

"I've seen some handsome uniforms" 1745 (161)

"I've seen the smiling o' Fortune beguiling" 7040B (100)

"I've seen the smiling of Fortune beguiling" 7040A (163)

"I've sung this song, but I'll sing it again" 1431 (293, 389)

"I've traveled about a bit in my time" 686 (129,130,131)

"I've travelled all over this country" 7882 (227)

"I've tried a hundred diff'rent ways" 1077 (240)

"I've wander'd all over this country" 7882 (293)

"I've wander'd o'er the desert wide" 104 (189)

"I've wandered to the village, Tom" 4038 (212,321)

I'VE WORKED EIGHT HOURS THIS DAY 2234 (114)

"J'ai cru faire un bon coup en changeant de future" 771 (147)

"J'AI CUELLI LA BELLE ROSE" 4997 (187)

"J'ai des poul's à vendre, des roug's et des blanches" 5154 (21)

"J'AI DIT AUX ÉTOILES" 2730 (407)

"J'ai dit aux étoiles: Elle est votre soeur" 2730 (407)

J'AI DU BON TABAC 4998 (88,91)

"J'ai du bon tabac dans ma tabatière" 4998 (88,91)

"J'ai laissé de mon sein de neige" 4023 (140)

J'AI PERDU LE DO 4999 (88)

"J'AI PERDU LE DO DE MA CLARINETTE" 4999 (88,127)

"J'AI PLEURÉ EN RÊVE" 1728 (121,191,193,195)

"J'AI TANT DANSÉ, J'AI TANT SAUTÉ" 5165 (187)

"J'ai un' méchante mère" 5149 (187)

"J'ai vu passer l'hirondelle dans le ciel pur du matin" 25 (237)

"J'aime le son du cor" 1082 (193,240)

J'AIME UN BRUN 5000 (175)

418

THE JENNY LIND MANIA 3998 (189)

JENNY NETTLES 7076 (102)

JENNY PUT YOUR KETTLE ON 7730 (312)

"Jenny, put your kettle on, a little one and big one" 7730 (312)

Jephté 2499-2500

JER AZ ABLAKOMRA, KEDVES 5735 (164)

JER ER SAA GLAD HVER JULEKVELD 9284 (165)

JER ÖLEMBE TUBICÁM 5736 (164)

JERRY 8375 (336)

JERUSALEM (Parker) 2739 (346, 394)

JERUSALEM (Parry) 2744 (306)

JERUSALEM GAUDE 9022 (388)

"Jerusalem gaude gaudio magno" 9022 (388)

"Jerusalem, Jerusalem, thou that killest the prophets" 2391 (123)

JERUSALEM REJOICE 9022 (388)

"Jerusalem rejoice, be glad and joyful" 9022 (388)

JERUSALEM THE GOLDEN 2108 (28, 366)

"Jerusalem the golden! with milk and honey blest" 2108 (28, 366)

JERUSALEM! THOU THAT KILLEST THE PROPHETS 2391 (123)

"Jes wait a little while" 4089 (399)

JESOS AHATONHIA 9193 (165)

JESOUS AHATONHIA 9193 (186, 244)

JESOUS AHATONNIA 9193 (33)

JESS MACFARLANE 7077 (101)

JESSE JAMES 7731A (120, 227) 7731B (34, 109, 110), 7731C (399)

"Jesse James was a lad, he killed many a man" 7731C (399)

"Jesse James was a lad that killed a many a man" 7731A (227)

"Jesse James was a lad who killed many a man" 7731A (120), 7731B (34, 109, 110)

JESSIE THE FLOWER O' DUNBLANE 3522 (100)

"Jest kraina w tej krainie" 2678 (295)

"Jest tu jeden między nami, Cogonazywamy" 6852 (295)

JESTEM SOBIE CHŁOPAK MŁODY 6744 (159)

"Jestem sobie chłopak młody, dy, dy" 6744 (159)

JESU, GEH VORAN 921 (326)

"Jesu, geh voran auf der Lebensbahn!" 921 (326)

"JESU, JOY OF MAN'S DESIRING" 120 (394)

"Jesu neigt sein Haupt und stirbt!" 1144 (250)

JESU REDEMPTOR OMNIUM 9023 (388)

"Jesu, Redemptor omnium, quem lucis ante originem" 9023 (388)

JESU VE'N TREZELON SAI FÉTE 9076 (361)

LA JESUCITA 6359 (35)

JESUKEN EN JANNEKEN 6589 (231)

JESUS AHATONHIA 9193 (154)

"Jesus, and is Thine hour come?" 8830 (361)

JESUS, BABY WONDERFUL 2420 (305)

"Jesus, Baby wonderful, born among the cattle" 2420 (305)

JESUS BORN IN BETHLEA 9361C (331)

"Jesus born in Bethlea, Jesus born in Bethlea" 9361C (331)

JESUS BORN IN BETH'NY 9361B (268)

"Jesus born in Beth'ny, Jesus born in Beth'ny" 9361B (268)

JESUS BORN TO BE A KING 3413 (378)

JESUS BORNED IN BETHLEA 9361A (332)

"Jesus borned in Bethlea, Jesus borned in Bethlea" 9361A (332)

"Jesus Christ, He died for me" 8227 (409)

JESUS CHRIST IS BORN 9290 (388)

"Jesus Christ is born, now unto the world" 9290 (388)

"Jesus Christ lay sweetly sleeping" 9044 (376)

"Jésus Christ s'habille en pauvre" 9044 (88)

"Jesus Christ was born on Christmas" 3721 (251)

"JESUS DRESSED IN GARB SO LOWLY" 9044 (319)

JESÚS ES NAT 8854 (56)

JESUS GOIN' TO MAKE UP MAH DYIN' BED 8376A (80)

JESUS GOIN' TO MAKE UP MY DYING BED 8376B (409)

JESÚS HA NACIDO 8854 (56)

JESUS IN HIS CRADLE 2981 (377)

"Jesus in his cradle sleeping must not be awoken" 2981 (377)

"Jesus in stable! What music may profess" 9055 (334, 361)

JESUS IN THE STALL 8836 (361)

JESUS IS BORN 9193 (33)

JESUS IS RISEN FROM THE DEAD 8377 (409)

JESUS, JESUS, REST YOUR HEAD 9362 (268)

"Jesus, Jesus, rest your head, you has got a manger bed" 9362 (268)

"JESUS, JOY OF MAN'S DESIRING" 120 (50)

JESUS, KING OF THE HOME 2326 (71)

"Jesus lifted up His eyes to heaven, and prayed for His disciples" 1485 (90)

"JESUS, LOVER OF MY SOUL" 2278 (28, 34, 279, 366)

JESUS LOVES ME 388 (28)

"Jesus loves me! this I know" 388 (28)

JESUS, MARIA E JOSÉ 9302 (57)

JESUS, MEINE ZUVERSICHT 735 (326)

"Jesus, meine Zuversicht und mein Heiland" 735 (326)

"Jesus, my all, to heav'n is gone" 7456 (212)

"Jesus, our brother, kind and good" 8908 (79, 165, 214, 249)

"Jesus, our brother, strong and good" 8908 (33)

JESUS, REDEEMER OF THE WORLD 9023 (388)

"Jesus, Redeemer of the world, who, ere the earliest dawn of light" 9023 (388)

"JESUS, SAVIOUR, PILOT ME" 1309 (35)

"JESUS, SHEPHERD, BE THOU NEAR ME" 134 (50)

"Jesus so meek, Jesus so mild" 497 (378)

JESUS SWEET AND MARY 9169 (376)

"JESUS, TENDER SHEPHERD, HEAR ME" 177 (28, 366)

JESUS THE CHRIST IS BORN 9363 (268)

"Jesus the Christ is born, give thanks now ev'ry one" 9363 (268)

"Jesus, the meek and mild, came as a little child" 21 (315)

JESUS WAS BORN TO MARY 9200 (154)

"Jesus was born to Mary, Mary in Bethlehem" 9200 (154)

LA JESUSITA 6359 (247)

JESZCZE JEDEN MAZUR DZISIAJ 6745 (159, 295)

"Jeszcze jeden mazur dzisiaj, choć poranek świta" 6745 (159, 295)

"JESZCZE POLSKA NIE ZGINEŁA" 6746 (7, 159, 295)

"JETZT FÄNGT DAS SCHÖNE FRÜHJAHR AN" 5419 (40, 49, 309, 326)

"JETZT FAHRN WIR ÜBERN SEE" 5420 (49, 309)

"JETZT GANG I ANS BRÜNNELE" 5421 (31, 41, 99, 309, 326, 327, 353)

"JETZT GEHT ES IN DIE WELT" 1630 (49)

"JETZT KOMMEN DIE LUSTIGEN TAGE" 5422 (49, 309, 326, 353)

LA JEUNE FILLE DEMANDE 2343 (224)

JOHNNY RILEY 8137D (72)

JOHNNY SCHMOKER 3070 (189,225)

"Johnny Schmoker, Johnny Schmoker, ich kan spielen" 3070 (225)

"Johnny Schmoker, Johnny Schmoker, ich kann spielen" 3070 (189)

JOHN'S GONE TO HILO 9456 (320)

THE JOHNSON BOYS 7740 (389)

"Johnson Boys was raised in the ashes" 7740 (389)

"Johohoe! Johohohoe!" 3901 (1)

JOIN INTO THE GAME 528 (389)

"Join the chorus, now's the time to start" 820 (128,132)

JOIN THE CIRCLE 4199 (219)

"JOIN WITH US AND HAPPY BE" 6542 (316)

JOLI MOI DE MAI 2088 (297)

JOLI TAMBOUR 5007A (127), 5007B (82,88,91)

JOLICOEUR 6103 (338)

UNE JOLIE BERGÈRE 5006 (66)

"Une jolie bergère, par un de ces matins" 5006 (66)

THE JOLLY BOATSWAIN 7742 (72)

"A jolly fat frog liv'd in the river" 4603 (234)

JOLLY IRISHMEN 599 (189)

THE JOLLY LUMBERMEN 7479 (110)

"Jolly men are we the vet'rans, gay with all our patrons" 6705 (295)

THE JOLLY MILLER (Folksongs, England) 4694 (37,297)

JOLLY MILLER (Folksongs, United States) 7742 (242)

Jolly mortals, fill your glasses (tune) 7165

JOLLY OLD SAINT NICHOLAS 9364 (28,206,296,366)

"Jolly old Saint Nicholas, lean your ear this way!" 9364 (28,206,296,366)

THE JOLLY PLOUGHBOY 5946 (199)

JOLLY SHEPHERD (Melvill) 2360 (144)

JOLLY SHEPHERD (Ravenscroft) 2982 (235)

"Jolly shepherd and up on a hill as he sat" (Melvill) 2360 (144)

"Jolly shepherd and upon a hill he sate" (Ravesncroft) 2982 (235)

THE JOLLY STAGE DRIVER 7743 (72)

THE JOLLY THRASHER 7744 (72)

THE JOLLY WAGGONER 4661A (234), 4661B (145)

THE JOLLY WAGONER 4661C (110)

"Jolting up and down in the little red wagon" 7784 (216)

JONAS 5407 (99)

JONATHAN SMITH 1253 (80)

JONE O' GREENFIELD'S RAMBLE 4662 (198)

"JONGE DOCHTER WILT NIET TREUREN" 6506 (203)

JONTEK'S ARIA 2473 (295)

"Jordan's deep an' Jordan's wide" 8567 (409)

"José con María van a pasear, en la fresca fuente van a descansar" 8855 (53)

JOSÉ Y MARÍA SALEN DE PASEO 8855 (53)

JOSEP I MARÍA VAN A PASSEJAR 8855 (53)

"Josep i Maria van a passejar en una font fresca varen reposar" 8855 (53)

Joseph 2348 (153)

JOSEPH AND GENTLE MARY CAME 8826A (377)

"Joseph and gentle Mary came, unto the town of Bethlehem" 8826A (337), 8826B (370)

JOSEPH AND MARY 8911H (332)

JOSEPH AND THE ANGEL 8911D (361)

JOSEPH DEAREST 9163 (79)

JOSEPH, DEAREST JOSEPH 9163 (33,34)

"Joseph dearest, Joseph mild, help me rock my little child" 9163 (79)

JOSEPH DEAREST, JOSEPH MINE 9163 (307)

"Joseph dearest, Joseph mine, help me cradle the Child divine" 9163 (271,307)

"Joseph dearest Joseph sweet, help me rock my babe to sleep" 9163 (34)

"Joseph dearest, Joseph sweet, help me to rock my child to sleep" 9163 (33)

"Joseph, Joseph, husband mild, help me rock my little child" 9163 (333)

JOSEPH, JOSEPH, HUSBAND MINE 9163 (333)

JOSEPH, LIEBER JOSEPH 9163 (34)

JOSEPH, LIEBER JOSEPH MEIN 9163 (412)

"Joseph, lieber Joseph mein, hilf mir wiegen mein Kindelein" 9163 (34,79,99,412)

JOSEPH, O DEAR JOSEPH MINE 9163 (296)

"Joseph, O dear Joseph mine, help me rock the Child divine" 9163 (296)

JOSEPH WAS AN OLD MAN 8911A (361)

"Joseph was an old man, an old man was he" 8911B (363), 8911H (332)

"Joseph was an old man, and an old man was he" 8911A (334,361)

JOSEPHUS ORANGE BLOSSOM 7745 (225)

JOSÉZITO 6908 (58)

"Josézito já te tenho dito que não é" 6908 (58)

"JOSHUA FIGHT DE BATTLE OB JERICHO" 8383A (76)

JOSHUA FIT DE BATTLE 8383B (110)

"JOSHUA FIT DE BATTLE OB JERICHO" 8383A (35)

"JOSHUA FIT DE BATTLE OF JERICHO" 8383A (185), 8383B (110)

"JOSHUA FIT THE BATTLE O' JERICO" 8383A (183)

"JOSHUA FIT THE BATTLE OF JERICHO" 8383A (145,227,293)

JOU L'POUNT D'O MIRABEL 5008 (65)

"Jou l'pount d'o Mirabel Cotorino lobabo" 5008 (65)

"Jou'l cieu de l'oubernho poulido" 4904 (88)

JOULULAULU 2735 (124)

"Un jour, m'en allant confesser" 4948 (60)

"Un jour que dans les bois fleuris" 4878 (82,91)

"Le jourd' fête, ma mère veut quej' file" 6125 (338)

THE JOURNEY 9407 (165)

JOUTSEN 987 (124)

THE JOVIAL BEGGAR 689 (234)

"Joy and peace and love reign in Heav'n above" 3307 (330)

"Joy divine of Christmas Day, does our very sins away" 8892 (360,361)

JOY IN HEAVEN 7318 (95)

"Joy is fled, sweet hopes are blighted, darkness shrouds me deep as night" 3622 (274)

THE JOY OF LOVE 2282 (348)

"The joy of love may not have long to stay" 2282 (348)

JOY OF MY HEART 1255 (36)

"Joy of my heart, when we're apart" 1255 (36)

JOY TO THE WORLD (Carols, England) 8950 (28,33,35, 79,125,165,206,233,236,251,315,337,343,366)

JOY TO THE WORLD (Hermann) 1636 (49,361)

"Joy to the world! the Lord has come" (Carols, England) 8950 (296)

"JOY TO THE WORLD! THE LORD IS COME" (Carols, England) 8950 (38,39)

"Joy to the world, the Lord is come" (Hermann) 1636 (49,361)

"Joy to thee, my brave canoe" 5190 (86,279,366)

JOYFUL 7746 (212)

A JOYFUL CHRISTMAS SONG 1243 (296)

Lakmé 810-812
Lalla roukh 683* (128,132,237)
LAM', LAM', LAM' 1780 (114,131)
LAMA SUKKU ZU? 6220 (318)
"Lama sukka zu? Aba tov sheli?" 6220 (318)
"A lamb and a kid, a kid and a lamb" 3983 (318)
LAMB OF GOD 315 (123,237,394)
"Lamb of God, thou that takest away the world's guilt" 315 (123,237,394)
"Lamb of God, who takest away the sins of the world" 315 (304)
"Lambert, say, can you sing and can you play?" 4188 (231)
LAMBS HAVE I 7320 (230)
"Lambs have I, both large and small" 7320 (230)
THE LAME DUCK 5180 (21)
LAMENT (Duparc) 943 (408)
LAMENT (Folksongs, Iraq) 5857 (86)
LAMENT (Kratzer) 1967 (295)
THE LAMENT OF FLORA MACDONALD 7039 (100,349)
THE LAMENT OF IAN THE PROUD 1397 (259)
THE LAMENT OF THE IRISH EMIGRANT 818 (212)
LAMENT OF THE OWL 6391A (9)
The lamentation of Aughrim (tune) 5914
LAMENTO 943 (408)
LAMENTO D'ARIANNA 2502 (180,367)
A LAMMAS NIGHT 7029 (285)
LAMMEN HAR JAG 7320 (230)
"Lammen har jag, baa' stora och smaa" 7320 (230)
THE LAMPLIGHTER 6303 (219)
THE LAMPLIT HOUR 2760 (237)
THE LANCER AND THE GIRL 6848 (295)
THE LANCER AND THE MAIDEN 6848 (159)
LANCERS, BONNIE LANCERS 6856 (159)
"Lancers, bonnie lancers from afar are nearing" 6856 (159)
THE LANCERS CAME 6824 (295)
THE LANCER'S FAREWELL 2148 (295)
"LAND DER EWIGEN GEDANKEN" 2290 (49)
Das Land des Lächelns 2094-2095
THE LAND O' THE LEAL 7087 (100,103)
"Land of Borinquen, the fair land where I was born" 6934 (279)
"Land of great plains, fertile country" 2678 (295)
LAND OF MINE 1361 (408)
"Land of mine, dear native land!" 1361 (408)
LAND OF MY FATHERS 1767 (19,234,294,347)
"Land of our fathers, from ocean to ocean" 2421 (236)
"The land of our fathers is in Northern snow" 4849 (124)
"Land of our fathers', sweet home that we adore" 3208 (129,130)
LAND OF THE SILVER BIRCH 4238 (186)
"Land of the silver birch, home of the beaver" 4238 (186)
LAND SO WUNDERBAR! 2408 (391)
"Land so wunderbar! Gärten, reich und schön!" 2408 (391)
LANDESVATER 5442 (31)
THE LANDING OF THE PILGRIMS 459 (129,130)
DIE LANDLUST 1565 (96,209,229)
THE LANE COUNTY BACHELOR 8023A (80)
"Lang in das Birkenlaub rinnt schon der Regen" 2006 (73)
LANG, LANG IST'S HER 215 (326,353)
"LANG ZAL DIE LEVEN" 6524 (316)
Langs ei aa 1383 (121)
LANGSAM FLIESST DER MAROS FLUSS 5763 (92)
"Langsam fliesst der Maros Fluss dahin, Schatz, komm in die Laube von Jasmin" 5763 (92)

LANGSAM IN DEN HOF 5751 (92)
"Langsam in den Hof trägt man den Sarg hinaus" 5751 (92)
LANGSAMER WALZER 1991 (222)
LANGT HØJERE BJERGE 4143 (87)
"Langt højere Bjaerge saa vide paa Jord man har" 4143 (87)
LANGT UDI SKOVEN 4465 (230)
"Langt udi Skoven laa et lille Bjerg" 4465 (230)
LANGUIRAY-JE TOUJOURS? 5012 (61)
LANGUISH AND DISPAIR, MY HEART 4044 (278)
"Languish and dispair my heart, and let thy groans to hills ascend" 4044 (278)
LAPPALAISJOIKU 4839 (124)
LARBOARD WATCH 4037 (205)
LARDY DAH 7767 (225)
"Larger, longer, make the dance-ring stronger" 3950 (318)
LARGO 1485 (28)
LARGO AL FACTOTUM 3098 (4,364)
"LARGO AL FACTOTUM DELLA CITTÀ" 3098 (4,298, 364)
THE LARK (Dvořák) 957 (121)
THE LARK (Lawes) 2066 (107)
THE LARK IN THE CLEAR AIR 5952 (172)
Larry Doolan (tune) 9431
LAS KANT FIND 8728 (11)
LAS KEAN FINE 8728 (252)
LASCIA CH'IO PIANGA 1471 (179,210)
"Lascia ch'io pianga mia cruda sorte" 1471 (179,210)
"Lasciar d'amarti per non penar" 1211 (168)
LASCIATEMI MORIRE 2502 (138,368,404)
"Lasciatemi morire, lasciatemi morire" 2502 (138,167, 180,367,368,404)
"Lass dich nur nichts nicht dauern mit Trauern, sei stille!" 1094 (73)
THE LASS FROM THE COUNTY DOWN 5960A (133)
THE LASS FROM THE LOW COUNTREE 7768 (263)
LASS MICH MIT TRÄNEN 1471 (99)
"Lass mich mit Tränen mein Los beklagen" 1471 (99)
"Lass nur der Jugend, der Jugend, der Jugend ihren Lauf" 5443 (49,326)
LASS NUR DER JUGEND IHREN LAUF! 5443 (49,326)
THE LASS O' GOWRIE 7088 (18,100)
THE LASS O' PATIE'S MILL 7089 (100,102)
"The lass o' Patie's mill sae bonnie, blythe and gay" 7089 (100,102)
"Lass o Welt, o lass mich sein!" 4085 (112,220,359)
THE LASS OF RICHMOND HILL 1692 (14,234,349,402)
THE LASS THAT LOVES A SAILOR 835 (205)
"Lass uns auf die Wiese gehn, Klein-Marei" 2020 (49)
"LASS WITH LIPS LIKE RED BERRIES" 1199 (295)
THE LASS WITH THE DELICATE AIR 77 (122,237,329, 386)
Lasset uns mit Jesu ziehen 125
"Lassie, lassie, little bird mine, since our childhood for you I pine" 4329 (94)
"Lassie, lassie, what have you there?" 4327 (94)
LASSIE, LITTLE BIRD MINE 4329 (94)
LASSIE, WHAT HAVE YOU THERE 4327 (94)
"LASSIE WI' THE LINT-WHITE LOCKS" 7090 (101)
LASSIE, WON'T YOU 4439 (94)
"Lassie, won't you please your door unlock?" 4439 (94)
"LASST AUS DIESEM ENGEN HAUS" 1436 (98)
LASST DOCH DER JUGEND IHREN LAUF 5443 (309,353)
"Lasst doch der Jugend, der Jugend, der Jugend ihren Lauf" 5443 (309,353)

430

433

THE LONESOME GROVE 7796 (109, 110)
LONESOME HOUSE BLUES 8406 (336)
LONESOME ROAD 8410A (35)
LONESOME TRAVELER 1590 (389)
LONESOME VALLEY 7797 (227)
"Long ago a belle and beau with hearts in tune" 2097 (132)
"Long ago at Kazan where I was fighting" 2617 (5)
"LONG AGO, MY LADDY" 4400 (94)
THE LONG DAY CLOSES 3662 (343)
LE LONG DE LA MER JOLIE 5167 (187)
"Le long du quai, les grands vaisseaux" 1044 (140, 210)
LONG-HANDLED SHOVEL 8407 (336)
"Long haired preachers come here every night" 3979 (225)
"Long-haired preachers come out ev'ry night" 3979 (109, 110)
LONG HAVE I WOVEN 6310 (95)
"Long have I woven, woven and woven" 6310 (95)
THE LONG-LINE SKINNER BLUES 8408 (336)
"Long live the merry, merry heart" 1134 (129, 343, 366)
LONG, LONG AGO 215 (28, 128, 136, 233, 236, 260, 279, 366)
"A long, long time and a long time ago" 9461A (29)
"A long, long, time and a very long time" 9461B (320)
"Long may he (she) live" 6524 (316)
A LONG TIME AGO ("A long, long time...") 9461A (29), 9461B (320), 9461C (401)
LONG TIME AGO ("On the lake where droop'd...") 8409 (83)
LONG TIME AGO ("Once there was a little kitty...") 7798 (216)
"Long years ago, as men their flocks were tending" 2800 (369)
"Long years ago in old Madrid" 305 (132)
"LONG YEARS AGO O'ER BETHLEHEM'S HILLS" 1529 (251)
LONGING 1053 (78)
LONGING FOR HOME 4272 (37)
LONGING FOR SPRING 2594 (395)
LONGING HEARTS 3632 (330)
LONTANANZA E GELOSIA 2262 (134)
"Lontananza e gelosia son le pene" 2262 (134)
"LOOK, A NICKEL IN MY HAND" 6507 (316)
"Look-a yonder! Hot boilin' sun comin' over" 8322 (409)
"Look ahead, look astern, look the weather in the lee" 4566 (35)
"LOOK AT THAT LITTLE BROOK" 2266 (134)
"Look at the darkey, Mister Banjo" 7828 (225)
"Look at the stylish man, Monsieur Banjo" 7828 (219)
LOOK AWAY TO BETHLEHEM 9392 (332)
"LOOK DARLING GIRL" 766 (340)
"Look down, look down that lonesome road" 8410A (35, 215), 8410C (242)
LOOK DOWN THAT LONESOME ROAD 8410A (215)
"Look, look away, look away" 9392 (332)
LOOK MY LASSIE 2663 (159)
"Look my lassie have you seen it? troops are coming here this minute, our mounted lancers" 2663 (159)
LOOK, NEIGHBORS, LOOK! 1527 (235)
"Look, neighbors, look! Here lies poor Thomas Day" 1527 (235)
"Look out of thy window, please, ay, ay, ay" 2761 (36)
LOOK OVER YONDER 1234 (109, 110)
"Look over yonder, huh, hot burning sun turning over" 1234 (109, 110)
"Look over yonder on Jerricho's wall" 8467 (409)

LOOK, ST. MARY'S CHURCH 6701 (159)
"Look, St. Mary's Church is standing with a spire so slender" 6701 (159)
LOOK, THE HUSSARS ARE MARCHING 5721 (164)
"Look, the hussars are marching down the street, right here" 5721 (164)
LOOK, THERE IS THE STEAMER 9278 (316)
"Look, there is the steamer arriving from Spain" 9278 (316)
"Look to the East, look to the West" 1001 (189)
"Look up, look down that lonesome road" 8410B (81)
"Look who's a-comin' here, Musieu Banjo" 7828 (77)
LOOKA DAY 9385 (332)
LOOKING-GLASS RIVER 602 (259)
"THE LORD AT FIRST DID ADAM MAKE" 8953A (333, 334, 361), 8953B (154, 334)
"THE LORD AT FIRST DID ADAM MAKE" (The holy well: tune) 8942 (363)
"THE LORD AT FIRST HAD ADAM MADE" 8953B (361)
LORD BATEMAN 4682 (198)
"Lord Bateman was a noble lord, a noble lord of high degree" 4682 (198)
LORD BATESMAN OR THE TURKISH LADY 7799A (393)
"THE LORD BLESS YOU" 119 (50)
"The Lord draws neigh across the fields" 1143 (190, 192, 194)
LORD FOR THY REVEALING GIFTS 4270 (244)
"Lord, grant me what Thou wilt of pleasure or of sorrow" 4074 (408)
"Lord, guard and guide our men who fly" 2743 (344)
"Lord help the po' and the needy" 8366 (409)
"Lord, I couldn' hear nobody pray, Oh, Lord" 8332 (182)
LORD, I WANT TO BE A CHRISTIAN 8411 (409)
"Lord, I want to be a Christian in a my heart" 8411 (409)
"Lord, I want to be a Christian in my heart" 8411 (76)
"Lord I'm bearin' heavy burdens" 8598 (409)
"Lord! in my heart's love deep I hide Thee" 1656 (123)
THE LORD IS MY SHEPHERD (Chaikovskiǐ) 650 (123)
THE LORD IS MY SHEPHERD (Folksongs, United States Negro) 8412 (409)
"THE LORD IS MY SHEPHERD" (Koschat) 1956 (28, 366)
"The Lord is my Shepherd" (Malotte) 2251 (200)
"THE LORD IS MY SHEPHERD" (Schubert) 3323 (90)
"The Lord is my shepherd; I shall not want" 650 (123)
"THE LORD IS MY STRENGTH" 1731 (200)
THE LORD IS RISEN 3661 (398)
"The Lord is risen, He will dwell with men" 3661 (123, 398)
"Lord, it's a bourgeois town" 2078 (336)
"Lord Jesus hath a garden, full of flowers gay" 9243 (271)
"LORD, LET ME LIVE TO-DAY" 2515 (347)
LORD LOVEL 4683 (35, 215)
"Lord Lovel he stood at his castle gate" 4683 (35, 215)
LORD LOVELL 4683 (185, 279, 366)
"Lord Lovell he stood at his castle gate" 4683 (185, 279, 366)
"LORD MAKE ME MORE HOLY" 8413 (409)
"The Lord most High vouchsafed to lie" 9078 (361)
"THE LORD MY SHEPHERD IS" (Helder) 1612 (50)
LORD OF ALL BEING THRONED AFAR 3713 (28, 279, 366)
"Lord of all being, thron'd afar" 3713 (28, 279, 366)
THE LORD OF LOVE 1159 (90)
"The Lord of love my shepherd is" 1159 (90)
"Lord, oh, hear me praying" 8309 (409)
LORD, OUR GOD 2475 (295)

"Lord, our God, Oh Heav'nly Father" 2475 (295)
LORD RANDAL 4684B (185)
LORD RANDALL 4684A (170, 173)
LORD RENDAL 4684A (14, 215)
"LORD, SPEAK TO ME" 3550 (347)
"The Lord, the Lord, the Lord is my shepherd" 8412 (409)
LORD THOMAS 7800D (243)
LORD THOMAS AND FAIR ELINORE. 7800A (173)
LORD THOMAS AND FAIR ELLENDER 7800B (262)
"Lord Thomas rose early one morning in May and dress'd himself in blue" 7800A (173)
"Lord Thomas rose up one merry morning and dressed himself in blue" 7800D (243)
"LORD, WHO AT CANA'S WEDDING FEAST" 484 (50)
LORD WILLOUGHBY 4685 (86)
THE LORD'S BEEN HERE 8414 (409)
"The Lord's been here and blessed my soul" 8414 (409)
"The Lord's my Shepherd, I'll not want" 4557 (199)
"THE LORDS OF CREATION MEN WE CALL" 7801 (225)
THE LORD'S PRAYER (Bach) 127 (89)
THE LORD'S PRAYER (Folksongs, United States Negro) 8415 (76)
THE LORD'S PRAYER (Folksongs, West Indies) 8740 (323)
THE LORD'S PRAYER (Forsyth) 1104 (123)
THE LORD'S PRAYER (Henschel) 1626 (160)
THE LORD'S PRAYER (Mainville) 2244 (71)
THE LORD'S PRAYER (Malotte) 2250 (364)
DIE LORE AM TORE 583 (31, 99, 326, 353)
LORE, DES FÖRSTERS TÖCHTERLEIN 5455 (328)
DIE LORELEI (Liszt) 2151 (276)
DIE LORELEI (Silcher) 3484 (42, 99, 328, 353)
THE LORELFY (Liszt) 2151 (276)
THE LORELEY (Silcher) 3484 (28, 279, 366)
LORENA 3980 (36, 161, 212)
"Lorsque au soleil couchant les rivières sont roses" 790 (122, 237, 408)
"LORSQUE J'AVIONS DES NOISETTES" 5015 (91)
"Lorsque j'étais jeunette, je gardais les moutons" 4974A (47)
LORSQUE J'ÉTAIS PETITE 5091 (66)
"Lorsque j'étais petite, ma mignonne entourée de violettes" 5091 (66)
LORSQUE J'ÉTAIS TANT AMOUREUSE 5016 (68)
"Lorsque j'étais tant amoureuse de mon galant" 5016 (68)
"LORSQUE JE VAIS AU DESSUS DE LA FERME" 4307 (177)
"Lorsque je voyen ordre la brunette" 2979 (121, 362)
"LOS DRUHDY VLAST MNĚ KRÁSNOU PŘÁL" 107 (73)
"Loset, was i euch will sage" 2603 (31)
THE LOSS OF THE ELIZA 9462 (186)
LOST AND CANNOT BE FOUND 8728 (11)
THE LOST CHORD 3663 (28, 122, 132, 237, 329, 346, 348, 394)
"Lost is one stocking at Lauterbach" 5627 (37, 45)
LOST LOVE 6765 (295)
"Lost my partner, what'll I do" 8005 (227)
The Lothian lassie 7091
DIE LOTOSBLUME 3384 (36, 112, 136, 209)
"Die Lotosblume ängstigt sich vor der Sonne Pracht" 3384 (36, 112, 136, 209)
LOTS OF FISH IN BONAVIST' HARBOUR 4239 (186)
THE LOTUS FLOWER 3384 (36, 112, 136, 209, 348)
"The lotus flower bending, turns from the sun's bright light" 3384 (209)
"The lotus flower is anxious, fearing the sun so bright" 3384 (112)

"The lotus flower trembles, fearing the sun so bright" 3384 (36)
"The lotus flow'r doth languish under the sun's fierce light" 3384 (136)
"The lotus flow'r is anxious, when the hot sun shines bright" 3384 (348)
"Lou, Lou, skip to my Lou" 8005 (216)
"Loud rang the challenge through the land" 6027 (280)
"Loud roar'd the dreadful thunder" 785 (14, 234, 366)
"Loud roaring pines, storm swollen flood" 3303 (273)
LOUDER, OH LET ME SING MY SONG 926 (287, 288)
"Loudly I'm calling! Good hot tamales" 6389 (37)
LOUDLY PROCLAIM 8703 (349)
"Loudly proclaim o'er land and sea" 8703 (349)
"Loudly we call, 'Justice for all!'" 8703 (19)
LOUDON'S BONNIE WOODS AND BRAES 7099 (100)
"Loudon's bonnie woods and braes I maun lea' them a', lassie" 7099 (100)
"Lougarias bous un' gardáire, pastrouletto?" 5071 (63)
Lough Sheeling (tune) 5889
"Loughareema! Loughareema lies so high among the heather" 3553 (344)
LOUIS CAMILLE 8741 (286)
"Louis Camille, have you seen Elligon today?" 8741 (286)
"Louis Camille, Où esti Elligon passé?" 8741 (286)
LOUIS KOSSUTH 5752 (7)
LOUISIANA GIRLS 7478D (37)
LOUREIRO, VERDE LOUREIRO 6910 (58)
"Loureiro verde loureiro Não te ponhas triste assim" 6910 (58)
THE LOUSE 4281 (86)
"Lou'siana gals, come and listen to my noise" 8116 (227)
LOUSY DIME 1590 (389)
"LOVE AND MUSIC, THESE HAVE I LIVED FOR" 2903 (143)
A LOVE CALL 486 (237)
"LOVE CAME DOWN AT CHRISTMAS" (Hann) 1521 (307)
"LOVE CAME DOWN AT CHRISTMAS" (Pettman) 2801 (373)
"Love divine, all love excelling" 2880 (50)
"Love, fly on rosy pinions, float in a dream around him" 3864 (1)
"Love for beauty, love and compassion" 2903 (6)
LOVE HAS EYES 310 (348)
"Love I lived by, music I lived for" 2903 (6)
Love in spring-time 3530-3531
LOVE IS A BABLE 1819 (118, 144)
"Love is like any wood-bird wild" 318 (2)
"Love is like dew on lilies at dawn" 3582 (259)
"Love is so sweet to remember" 4193 (9)
LOVE IS TEASIN' 7802 (312)
"Love is very patient, very kind" 376 (37)
LOVE LAMENT FROM TELEMARKEN 6648 (230)
"LOVE LEADS TO BATTLE" 369 (273)
"Love like ours was meant to live forever" 2133 (132)
"Love, love, love, love, love, is a bable" 1819 (118, 144)
LOVE ME AS I LOVE YOU 4252 (9)
LOVE ME LITTLE 4686 (235)
"Love me little, love me long" 4686 (235)
LOVE OF MY HEART 4877 (364)
"Love of my heart is all surrounded" 4877 (364)
"Love, oh, love, oh, careless love" 7490A (35, 109, 110, 173, 215, 293, 331), 7490B (227), 7490D (243)

LULLABY (Folksongs, France) 5017 (95)
LULLABY (Folksongs, Italy) 6108 (95)
LULLABY (Folksongs, Jewish) 6224 (95)
LULLABY (Folksongs, United States Negro) 8416 (409)
LULLABY (Folksongs, Yugoslavia) 8787 (95)
LULLABY (Godard) 1290 (122,132,237)
A LULLABY (Harty) 1541 (276)
LULLABY (Korchmarev) 1953 (162)
A LULLABY (Stanford) 3555 (344)
LULLABY (Surzyński) 3682 (295)
"Lullaby and good night, with roses sleep tight" 436 (385)
"Lullaby, by lullaby, by like a modest flower in the field" 2619 (348)
LULLABY FOR BABY JESUS 8840 (165)
LULLABY FROM THE TATRA MOUNTAINS 2008 (159)
LULLABY JESU 9291A (165)
"Lullaby, Jesu, my pearl and my dear one" 9291A (165)
LULLABY, LILY-BUD 6010 (280)
"Lullaby, lullaby, so I rock, rock my boy" 8787 (95)
"Lullaby, now lullaby dear, Angels watch you from the sky, dear" 6108 (95)
LULLABY OF MARY AND THE ANGELS 9089 (79)
LULLABY, SWEET JESUS 9291A (295)
"Lullaby, sweet Jesus, pearl very precious" 9291A (295)
"Lullaby, to the rest in rose-covered nest" 436 (210)
"Lullaby with a Mexican night above me" 3705 (248)
"Lullay my babe, lie still and sleep" 907 (380)
LULLAY MY LIKING (Carols, England) 8954 (363)
LULLAY MY LIKING (Holst) 1687 (307)
"Lullay my liking, my dear son, my sweeting" (Holst) 1687 (307)
"LULLAY, THOU LITTLE TINY CHILD" 8917A (35,165, 206,296,307,319,333,410)
"Lullay, Thou tiny little child" 8917B (261,268)
LULLE LULLAY (Carols, England) 8917B (261,268)
LULLEE, LULLAY (Bergsma) 286 (358)
"Lullee, lullay, I could not love thee more if thou wast Christ the King" 286 (358)
"Lully, lulla, thou little tiny child" 8917A (38,39,334)
"Lully, lulla you little tiny child" 8917A (361)
LULLY, LULLAY (Carols, England) 8917A (337)
LULLY, LULLAY (Haydn) 1581 (337)
"Lully, lullay, lullay. O sisters too, how may we do" (Haydn) 1581 (337)
"Lully, lullay, thou little tiny child" 8917A (33,337)
"Lully, lulley, lully, lulley" 3444 (334)
LULLY, LULLY, LU 9034 (206)
"LULU IS OUR DARLING PRIDE" 7806 (132)
THE LUMBER CAMP SONG 4241 (186)
THE LUMBERMAN IN TOWN 7807 (227)
LUMBERMAN'S SONG 4835 (36)
Lump mit Herz 608 (258)
"Lundi, au grand matin on bat la générale" 6132 (338)
"Lundi, c'est jour de lavage, frottons, bri bron bron!" 5168 (21)
LUNDI, JOUR DE LAVAGE 5168 (21)
"Lundi matin la branle sonne" 6043 (338)
"La lune blanche luit dans les bois" (Hahn) 1503 (121,140, 191,193,195,237,241)
"La lune blanche luit dans les bois" (Poldowski)
LUNGI DA TE 361 (134)
"Lungi da te, ben mio" 361 (134)
LUNGI DAL CARO BENE 3415 (138)
"Lungi dal caro bene vivere non poss' io" (Sarti) 3166 (353)
"Lungi dal caro bene vivere non poss' io!" (Secchi) 3415 (138)

"Lungi, lungi è amor da me" 1039 (167)
LUSINGHE PIÙ CARE 1446 (211)
"Lusinghe più care, d'amor veri dardi" 1446 (211)
"Die Lust hat mich bezwungen" 42 (49)
EIN LUST'GER MUSIKANTE 5452 (42,353)
"Ein lustger Musikante marschierte einst am Nil" 5452 (31,42,99,353)
LUSTIG, IHR BRÜDER 5456 (309)
"Lustig, ihr Brüder, lasst Grillen und Sorgen sein!" 5456 (309)
LUSTIG IST DAS ZIGEUNERLEBEN 5457 (326,353)
"Lustig ist das Zigeunerleben, faria, faria" 5457 (326, 353)
"Lustig ist's Matrosenleben, haltojo, ist mit lauter Lust umgebn, haltojo" 5458 (49)
LUSTIG IST'S MATROSENLEBN 5458 (309,326,353)
"Lustig ist's Matrosenlebn, haltojo, ist mit lauter Lust umgebn, haltojo" 5458 (309,326,353)
Der lustige Krieg 3614-3615
Die lustige Witwe 2096-2098
Die lustigen Weiber von Windsor 2655-2656
A LUTE LULLABY 907 (380)
LUTHERAN LAD 4427 (94)
"Lutheran lad, I would marry you if I could" 4427 (94)
LUTHER'S CAROL (Hume) 1733 (38,39,125)
LUTHER'S CRADLE HYMN (Herbert) 1631 (28,366)
LUTZOW'S WILD HUNT 3970 (28)
LUULLAHAN 4840 (124)
"Luullahan jotta on lysti olla" 4840 (124)
LUXEMBURG 6317 (86)
"Luxemburg, O sacred homeland, come break the chains that bind" 6317 (86)
"La luz que en tus ojos arde" 4293 (207)
LYDIA 1048 (362)
"Lydia, on your cheeks so glowing" 1048 (362)
LYDIA PINKHAM 7808 (225)
"Lydia, sur tes roses joues" 1048 (362)
LYE STILL MY DEARE 4688 (107)
"Lye still my Deare, why dost thou rise?" 4688 (107)
"Lýry hlas, jenž nitrem mým" 3517 (73)
Lysistrata 2138 (32,34)
"Lyubvi vse vozrasty pokorny" 639 (5)
"Lyulinke mayn feygele Lyulinke mayn kind" 6170 (318)

"M" is for the million things she gave me" 2535 (128,131, 236)
"M...m...my Lord! m...Poor mourner's got a home at last" 8494A (409)
"MA CHÈRE LIBERTÉ" 2208 (411)
"Ma chérie nennt man sein Dirndel" 2992 (257)
MA COMMÈRE QUAND JE DANSE 4942 (127)
"Ma commère quand je danse, mon cotillon va-t-il bien?" 4942 (127)
"MA CULOTTE A DEUX BOUTONS" 5018 (127)
MA FEMME EST PEU TENDRE 4387 (177)
"Ma femme est peu tendre, qu'en feraije, hélas: hei!" 4387 (177)
MA GRAND' MÈRE 5019 (91)
"Ma grand' mère qui n'avait qu'un dent" 5019 (91)
"Ma la selva, il monte intanto van col bel dell' idol" 2859 (179)

Ma mere mariez-moi (tune) 9106
"Ma no! Ma no! Non fuggir" 589 (179)
MA, NO, NON FUGGIR 589 (179)
MA NORMANDIE 282 (86,88,127,383)
"Ma'am dear, and did you ever hear of Molly Brannigan"
    5967 (172)
MAAME 2720 (124)
MAANLJUSET 1523 (355)
MA-ASEH SEH UG'DI 3929 (30)
"MAĆA DIEVČA KONOPE" 4374 (94)
MACARIO ROMERO 6364A (247)
Macbeth 3845-3846
MAC CRIMMON'S LAMENT 7100 (102,105)
MACDONALD'S FARM 7875 (28,233,366)
MACELADA 6911 (57)
THE MACCREGOR'S GATHERING 2086 (101)
"Mach' auf, mach' auf, doch leise, mein Kind" 3633 (112)
MACHADINHA 4201 (219)
MACH'S MIT MIR, GOTT 1862 (50)
"Macht er mir a fayfele" 6208 (318)
MACHT HOCH DIE TÜR 9167 (49)
"Macht hoch die Tür, die Tor macht weit" 9167 (49)
MACIEK 6731 (295)
The Maclean's welcome (tune) 7026 (100,104)
MCPHERSON'S FAREWELL (Folksongs, Scotland) 7101
    (365)
MAC PHERSON'S FAREWELL (Shostakovich) 3460 (342)
McPherson's rant (tune) 7101 (365)
"Mad! Mad! All the world's mad! Where'er enquiry dives"
    3912 (4)
THE MAD SCENE 871 (302)
MADA CANTINNY 8743 (252)
MADAM CSICSO'S DAUGHTERS 5675 (92)
"Madam Csicso's daughters three, oh!" 5675 (92)
"Madam, I have come a-courting, O dear" 4245 (186)
Madama Butterfly 2895-2897
"Madame, I will give to you the keys of Canterbury" 4665
    (44)
MADAME LA MARIÉE 4928 (127)
"Madame la Marquise, votre bras est bien fait" 5028 (88)
Madame Sherry 1709 (237)
"Madame Veto avait promis de faire égorger tout Paris"
    4924 (7,88)
"Madame Veto her promise gave, Madame Veto her promise
    gave, that all of France would be her slave" 4924 (7)
"MADAMINA! IL CATALOGO È QUESTO" 2568 (5,390)
A MADÁRKA A PÁRJÁVAL SZÁLLDOGÁL 5758 (164)
MADEMOISELLE FROM ARMENTIERES 7665 (10,227,233)
"Mademoiselle from Armentieres, parlay-vous?" 7665 (227)
"Mademoiselle from Armentieres, parley voo" 7665 (10,
    225,233)
THE MADONNA MUSES 1073 (244)
"Madre a la puerta hay un niño mas hermosa que el sol bello"
    9305 (154,337)
"Madre, Madre, pietosa Vergine" 3841 (1)
MADRE, PIETOSA VERGINE 3841 (1)
MADRIGAL (Indy) 1748 (191,193,195)
MADRIGALE IN STILE RECITATIVO 1746 (278)
"MAE CROESAWIAD GWRIAG Y TY" 8684 (349)
"Mae hen wlad fy nhadau yn annwyl imi" 1767 (19,234,
    294,347)
"Mae Natur i gyd yn newid ei phyrd" 8671 (20)
"Mae yr Alltud o Gymru yn gwylied y lloer" 8656 (349)
"DER MÄCHTIGSTE KÖNIG IM LUFTREVIER" 5459 (326)

DAS MÄDCHEN AUS DER FREMDE 3284 (141)
EIN MÄDCHEN ODER WEIBCHEN 2600 (4)
"Ein Mädchen oder Weibchen wünscht Papageno sich" 2600
    (4)
DAS MÄDCHEN SPRICHT 405 (330)
MÄDCHENLIED 406 (226)
MÄDCHENPREIS 5460 (99)
"Mädel, schau mir ins Gesicht!" 3341 (99)
"Mädele, ruck, ruck, ruck an meine grüne Seite" 5235
    (99)
MÄDLE RUCK, RUCK, RUCK 5235 (326,353)
"Mädle ruck, ruck, ruck an meine grüne Seite" 5235 (326,
    353)
DER MÄNNER SIPPE 3925 (1)
"Der Männer Sippe sass hier im Saal" 3925 (1)
EIN MÄNNLEIN STEHT IM WALDE 5461 (326)
"Ein Männlein steht im Walde ganz still und stumm" 5461
    (326)
"Mae'r flwyddyn yn marw, ei hamser a ddaeth" 9411 (20)
"Mae'r tŷ ar y bryn, fu'n drystfawr cyn hyn" 8700 (20)
EIN MÄRCHEN 3750 (74)
MÄRCHENTRAUM DER LIEBE 887 (258)
"Maestricht, gij schoone stede" 6522 (384)
"Mag dir, du zartes Frühlingskind" 1385 (209)
MAGASAN REPÜL A DARU 5759 (164)
MAGDALEN 2325 (344)
"Magdalen, at Michael's gate" 2325 (344)
MAGDA'S ARIA 2398 (6)
MAGGIE LAUDER 7102 (100,102)
"The Magi came out of the Orient Land" 9123 (244)
"The magic of my singing will carry you far away" 2368
    (141)
MAGNUM NOMEN DOMINI 2870 (361)
"Magnum nomen domini Emmannuel!" 2870 (361)
MAGOS A RUTAFA 5760 (23)
"Magos a rutafa, ága elágazik, Selyem sárhaja" 5760 (23)
"Magst du mir's, Amarillis" 500 (168)
MAGYAR LAND 3873 (285)
MAGYAR LEADERS 5761 (7)
MAH MAMMY STOLED A COW 8417 (80)
"Mah mule is white, mah charcoal is black" 8216 (110)
MAHNUNG ZUR FREUDE 2404 (31)
DER MAI, DER LUSTIGE MAI 5462 (49)
"DER MAI, DER MAI, DER LUSTIGE MAI" 5462 (49,309)
DER MAI IST GEKOMMEN 2220 (42,326,353)
"Der Mai ist gekommen, die Bäume schlagen aus" 2220
    (31,42,99,326,353)
MAI NON INTESI 2778 (180)
"Mai non intesi per altro sguardo quel dolce stralle" 2778
    (180)
"Mai revient, tout brille aux cieux" 4929 (82)
THE MAID FREED FROM THE GALLOWS 7651 (321)
A MAID, GOING TO A DANCE 7328 (135)
"A maid going to a dance, took red ribbons along" 7328
    (135)
THE MAID OF AMSTERDAM 9419F (173)
MAID OF MY DELIGHT 669 (295)
THE MAID OF SLIEVENAMON 5960A (133), 5960B (172)
THE MAID OF THE SWEET BROWN KNOWE 5961 (172)
Maid of the valley 5919
The Maid of Wicklow (tune) 5927
THE MAID ON THE MOUNTAIN'S BROW 7809 (72)
THE MAID ON THE SHORE 7810A (72), 7810B (186)
"Maid so pretty, maid so little, let me ask you a very hard
    riddle" 6192 (318)

THE MAID WITH THE MOLE ON HER CHEEK 6660 (9)
THE MAIDEN AND I 7294 (135)
"The maiden and I, the maiden and I, strolled where the
    flow'rs were growing" 7294 (135)
THE MAIDEN BLUSH 2937 (344)
"A MAIDEN EMBROIDERED" 7568 (113)
THE MAIDEN FROM AFAR 3284 (141)
"A maiden lay asleep upon a bed of roses" 5145 (187)
"Maiden, pray for thy lover now" 3780 (161)
THE MAIDEN SPEAKS 405 (330)
MAIDEN TELL ME 4375 (209)
"Maiden tell me, maiden tell me! What art thou weaving"
    4375 (209)
"THE MAIDEN TO THE WELL HAS GONE" 7330 (188)
"A MAIDEN WAS ADORING GOD THE LORD" 8814 (244,
    361)
"Maiden young and sweet as springtime, at her door stands
    sighing" 6804 (295)
MAIDENS, REMEMBER 755 (140)
"Maidens, remember, time is on the wing!" 755 (140)
THE MAIDEN'S WISH 674 (37, 295)
"MAIDLE LASS D'R WAS VERZÄHLE" 3485 (326)
"Maids, at morn, grind the good corn" 5998 (349)
THE MAIDS OF CADIZ 809 (208)
DER MAIEN IST KOMMEN 5463 (49, 326)
"Der Maien ist kommen, und das ist ja wahr!" 5463 (49,
    326)
MAIENKÄFER 5674 (92)
"Maienkäfer, Maienkäfer, goldner" 5674 (92)
Die Maienkönigen 1273 (308)
MAIENLIED 2386 (141)
MAIGESANG 239 (97)
THE MAIL BOAT 7811 (216)
MAILIED (Beethoven) 239 (97)
MAILIED (Gabler) 1183 (229)
MAILIED (Lachner) 2011 (31)
MAILIED (Peters) 2787 (31)
MAILIED (Schulz) 3343 (229)
DIE MAINACHT 407 (274)
MAINSAIL HAUL 9464 (320)
Mais il est dans la rivière (tune) 4930
LAS MAJAS DE PARIS 2043 (270)
LAS MAJAS MADRILEÑAS 2044 (270)
"La majas madrileñas son de tal casta" 2044 (270)
MAJERÁN 4376 (94)
"Majerán, majerán, zelený majerán" 4376 (94)
EL MAJO DISCRETO 1347 (245)
Major Graham's Strathspey (tune) 7121B
"Make my living in sandy land" 4702B (214)
"MAKE WE JOY NOW IN THIS FEST" 8956 (360, 361, 374)
LA MAL MARIÉE 5030 (383)
"MAL SOM T'A DIEVČA RAD" 4377 (94)
THE MALAGANIAN 6365 (322)
LA MALAGUEÑA 6365 (322)
MALBROUCK 5020 (34)
"Malbrouck has gone to battle" 5020 (34)
"MALBROUCK S'EN VA-T-EN GUERRE" 5020 (34, 70, 127)
MALBROUGH 5020 (383)
MALBROUGH S'EN VA-T-EN 5020 (91)
"MALBROUGH S'EN VA-T-EN GUERRE" 5020 (7, 82, 88, 91,
    383)
MAŁGORZATKA 6766 (295)
"Malgré la bataille qu'on donne demain" 7355 (155)
"MALHEUREUX QUE A UNE FEMME" 5021 (64)
THE MALLOW FLING 4689 (235)

"MALUROUS QU'O UNO FENNO" 5021 (64)
"Mám často osudné ono tušení" 4144 (73)
MAM CHUSTECZKĘ HAFTOWANĄ 6767 (295)
"Mam chusteczkę haftowaną Co ma cztery rogi" 6767
    295)
MAMA, MAMA 338 (343)
MAMAN, DITES-MOI 5022 (176)
"Maman, dites-moi ce qu'on sent quand on aime" 5022
    (176)
MANAN, FIND ME A HUSBAND 5170 (219)
MAMAN, LES P'TITS BATEAUX 5023 (91)
"Maman, les p'tits bateaux qui vont sur l'eau, ont-ils des
    jambes?" 5023 (91)
"Maman, please find me a husband" 5170 (219)
"Mamaw, mamaw, now I'm married, a single life I wish I'd
    tarried" 8134A (312)
MAMBRÚ 6366 (247)
"MAMBRÚ IS WITH THE ARMY" 6293 (219)
"MAMBRÚ SE FUÉ A LA GUERRA" 6293 (219)
DI MAME IZ GEGANGEN 6225 (318)
"Di mame iz gegangen in mark arayn noch koyln" 6225
    (318)
MAMENYU, LYUBENYU 6226 (318)
"Mamenyu, lyubenyu, kroynele hartsele" 6226 (318)
MAMIE'S BLUES 821 (336)
MAMMA DINAH 8418 (409)
"Mamma Dinah, O ho do mamma Dinah" 8418 (409)
"MAMMA, 'K WIL EEN MAN HE!" 6526 (316)
"Mamma's little baby loves short'nin'" 8534 (225)
"Mammy Logan, she had a daughter" 8251 (336)
"Mammy's baby loves shortn'nin'" 8534 (184)
"Mammy's little baby loves short'nin'" 8534 (37, 128, 236,
    237, 246, 249, 343)
THE MAN BEHIND THE PLOUGH 5072 (297)
"The man behind the plough, he has trouble and to spare"
    5072 (297)
DE MAN, DE SICK WAT MAKEN KUNN 6502 (99)
"Man had his first creation in heevin's guarded place" 7950
    (72)
"Man has a soul of vast defines" 301 (95, 109, 110)
"Man have in mind how here before" 8889 (360)
"A man he left his happy home to go upon the stage" 689*
    (204)
"A man is dead he will arise again" 1349 (123)
"A man is dead yet he'shall rise again" 1349 (346, 400)
"A man is dead yet is He living" 1349 (398)
MAN IS FOR THE WOMAN MADE 2919 (402)
"A man loved a maid with a mole on her cheek" 6660 (9)
"Man, man, man is for woman made" 2919 (402)
"A man named Noah built an Ark" 8478 (185)
THE MAN O' WAR'S MAN 1248 (205)
"THE MAN OF LIFE UPRIGHT" 550 (199)
THE MAN ON THE FLYING TRAPEZE 2702 (34, 115, 128,
    130, 131, 225, 236)
"MAN, REJOICE! YOUR SEARCH IS OVER!" 9170 (165)
MAN SMART, WOMAN SMARTER 8744 (11)
"Man soll hören süsses Singen in den Auen überall" 2386
    (141)
THE MAN THAT BROKE THE BANK AT MONTE CARLO
    1250 (204)
THE MAN WHO BROKE THE BANK AT MONTE CARLO
    1250 (114, 128, 131)
THE MAN WHO FIGHTS THE FIRE 2634 (131)
"The man who loves to serve the Lord" 8392 (409)
"Mañana me voy ¡Caramba! para Veracruz" 6329 (247)
LAS MAÑANITAS 6367 (322)

443

MASSA'S IN DE COLD, COLD GROUND 1118 (233)
MASSA'S IN DE COLD GROUND 1118 (28, 128, 129, 130, 132, 279, 366)
"The master run, hah, hah" 4108 (44)
MASTERS, IN THIS HALL 8957 (35, 165, 337)
"Masters in this hall hear ye news today" 8957 (35, 165, 337)
MATARILE 6294 (219)
Materna (tune) 3944
MATILDA 8747 (11)
"Matilda, Matilda, Matilda she take me money and run Venezuela" 8747 (11)
MATIN 5029 (82)
"Le matin de l'enfance heureuse s'éteint dans lumière nebuleuse" 1858 (224)
MATIN SONG 3759 (241)
LES MATINS DE L'ENFRANCE 1858 (224)
MATRENA AND THE DEACON 1954 (162)
MATROSENLEBEN (Folksongs, Germany) 5458 (49)
MATROZENLIED (Folksongs, Dutch) 6528 (384)
"Matt Casey formed a social club" 3942 (114, 115, 131, 204)
Matthäuspassion 128-129
MATTINATA 3759 (241)
MATTY WALLA-LEF' 8748 (252)
MATUŚ MOJA, MATUŚ 6772 (295)
"Matuś moja matuś, Wydaj mnie za Jasia" 6772 (295)
Maud 3532-3533
LA MAURMARIÉE 5030 (383)
MAUSFALLEN-SPRÜCHLEIN 4079 (250)
"Mavoureen's the flow'r of Kilarney" 5909 (235)
"Maxwellton braes are bonnie, where early fa's the dew" 3405
MAY CAROL ("I've been a-wand'ring...") 9369 (312, 313)
THE MAY CAROL ("This morning is the month of May") 8958 (44)
THE MAY DAY CAROL 8959 (214, 215)
THE MAY-DAY GARLAND 8960 (334)
MAY DAY SONG 1054 (78)
"May dusa payata na lalo ng hapdi" 6669 (86)
MAY FLIGHT 5467 (37)
MAY FORTUNE AYE BE KINDLY 7107 (105)
"May fortune aye be kindly my bonnie lass, to thee" 7107 (105)
MAY IRWIN'S "BULLY" SONG 3767 (114)
MAY IRWIN'S "FROG" SONG 3768 (114)
"May joy come from God above" 8827 (372)
MAY LAURELS CROWN THY BROW 3821 (1, 143)
"May laurels crown thy brow! What! can my lips pronounce language so impious!" 3821 (1, 143)
MAY SONG 2386 (141)
"MAY THE BREWER BE BLESSED" 4312 (324)
"MAY, THE MAIDEN" 603 (241)
"May thou, O tender child of Spring" 1385 (209)
"May you live long and well my lady" 6266 (318)
MAYDAY 5031 (95)
"Mayday is come, now welcome May!" 5031 (95)
Mayfair (tune) 4616
"The Mayflower, on New England's coast, has furl'd her tattered sail" 7924 (189)
MAYN YINGELE 6227 (318)
"Mazanita mojana, beso de fruta" 2186 (245)
THE MAZOVIAN 6886 (295)
MAZUREK 6773 (279, 366)
MAZUREK TRZECIEGO MAJA 6869 (295)
MAZURKA 6719 (295)
MAZURY 3685 (295)

"Me an' my wife an' my wife's gran'pap all raise hell in Cumberland Gap" 7532 (115)
ME AND MY CAPTAIN 8424 (336)
"Me and my captain don't agree" 8424 (336)
"Me and my wife and wife's gran'pap all raise hell in Cumberland Gap" 7532 (225)
"Me and my wife run all over town" 2078 (336)
Me anvez eur goulmik (tune) 8993
I ME DISE CHE IL TEMPO XE BELO 6110 (325)
"I me dise che il tempo xe belo, xela una cana, o xelo un capelo?" 6110 (325)
"Me gusta niña cantarte de la noche en el silencio" 4491 (73)
ME GUSTAN TODAS 7263 (406)
"Me gustan todas, me gustan todas" 7263 (406)
ME JOHNNY MITCHELL MAN 7816 (110)
"Me no wan', me nowan' wa Matty wallalef" 8748 (252)
"ME PLAINDRAI-JE TOUJOURS" 296 (411)
"ME VOICI DANS SON BOUDOIR" 3733 (2, 357)
MEADOW FRESH AND GREEN 6760 (159)
"Meadow, meadow, meadow fresh and green" 6760 (159)
MEADOWLAND 1923 (293)
"Meadowland, meadowland, meadows green and fields in blossom" 1923 (293)
MEADOWLANDS 1923 (288)
"Meadowlands, meadowlands, through you heroes now are treading" 1923 (35)
MEADOW-LARKS 217 (259)
"Meadows are swaying, wild flowers playing" 2994 (176)
"Meanwhile, go seek my darling" 2567 (3)
MECHUTENESTE MAYNE 6228 (318)
"Mechuteneste mayne, mechuteneste getraye, Lomir zayn oyf eybig mechutonim" 6228 (318)
Med en primula veris 1385 (209)
Medea tradita 2257 (134, 179)
Médée 655-656
A MEDLEY OF OLD TIME "SONES" 4291 (207)
MĘDRCY ŚWIATA 9292 (295)
"Mędrcy świata, monarchowie" 9292 (295)
MEDZI HORAMI 4379 (94)
"Medzi horami lipka zelaná" 4379 (94)
"Das Meer erglänzte weit hinaus im letzten Abendscheine" 3302 (99, 240)
"Das Meer glänzt heute so helle" 6144 (51)
MEERES STILLE 3285 (210)
MEERSTERN, ICH DICH GRÜSSE! 5468 (49, 326)
"Meerstern, ich dich grüsse! O Maria, hilf!" 5468 (49, 326)
"MEET ME BY MOONLIGHT" 3896 (129, 130)
"Meet me on the warlock knowe" 7032 (101)
MEETING 4836 (124)
THE MEETING OF THE WATERS 5963 (15, 28, 235, 349, 402)
Mefistofele 354-355
MÉG AZT MONDJÁK PICI KIS BABÁM 5764 (164)
MEG MERRILIES 2427 (199)
"MEGÁLLOK A KERESZTÚTNÁL" 1035 (285)
MEGAN'S FAIR DAUGHTER 8687 (20)
"Megösmerni a kanászt az ö járásáról" 5743 (25)
"Mehefin ddaeth fugeiliaid mwyn" 8692 (349)
MEI MAIDLE 3486 (326)
"Mei Maidle hot e G'sichtle als wie ne Roseblatt" 3486 (326)
MEI' MUATTERL WAR A WIENERIN 1409 (396)
"MEI MUTTER MAG MI NET" 922 (326)
DIE MEI PLEIZANT 6529 (202)
"Die mei pleizant willen wij planten" 6529 (202)
MEI SCHÄTZLE IST FEI 5469 (326)

"Mei Schätzle ist fei, 's könnt feiner net sei" 5469 (326)
MEIN BÜCHSLEIN AM ARM 5470 (49)
"Mein Büchslein am Arm, drei Federn auf dem Hut" 5470 (49)
MEIN CHRISTIAN 5471 (49)
MEIN EIGEN SOLL SIE SEIN 5446 (99)
"Mein einz'ger Schatz ist fern, so fern" 977 (221)
MEIN GLÄUBIGES HERZE, FROLOCKE 114 (122,123,311, 329,394)
"Mein gläubiges Herze, frohlocke, sing scherze" 114 (122, 123,329,394)
"Mein gläubiges Herze, frohlokke, sing' scherze" 114 (311)
"MEIN HANDWERK FÄLLT MIR SCHWER" 5472 (309)
"Mein Handwerk geht durch alle Welt" 3311 (141)
MEIN HERR MARQUIS 3609 (1)
"Mein Herr Marquis, ein Mann wie Sie sollt besser das verstehn" 3609 (1)
MEIN HERR UND GOTT 3907 (5)
"Mein Herr und Gott, nun ruf' ich dich" 3907 (5)
"Mein Herz ist betrübt" 3381 (275)
"MEIN HERZ IST IM HOCHLAND" 1755 (31,326,353)
MEIN HERZ IST SCHWER 3385 (274)
"Mein Herz ist Schwer, auf von der Wand die Laute" 3385 (274)
"Mein Herz ist wie die dunkle Nacht" 2387 (45)
"Mein Herz und mein Sinn schwärmt stets nur für Wien" 3467 (396)
MEIN HUT, DER HAT DREI ECKEN 5473 (353)
"Mein Hut, der hat drei Ecken, drei Ecken hat mein Hut" 5473 (353)
"MEIN LEBENSLAUF IST LIEB UND LUST" 5366 (31,353)
MEIN LIEBESLIED MUSS EIN WALZER SEIN! 3588 (258)
"Mein Lied ist klein, braucht wehig Platz" 717 (229)
"MEIN MÄDEL HAT EINEN ROSENMUND" 4151 (36,210, 229,326,353,357,406)
MEIN MUND, DER SINGT (Carols, Switzerland) 9340 (354)
MEIN MUND, DER SINGT (Regnart) 3008 (41)
"Mein Mund, der singt, mein Herz vor Trauern weint" 3008 (41)
"Mein Mund, der singt, mein Stimm erklingt" 9340 (354)
"Mein Ross so müd' in dem Stalle sich steht" 3281 (273)
"MEIN SCHÄTZLEIN KOMMT VON FERNE" 5474 (309)
"Mein Schatz der ist auf die Wanderschaft hin" 3968 (99, 229)
"Mein Schatz, der ist Postillion" 1406 (223)
"Mein Schatz ist nicht da, ist weit überm See" 424 (229)
"Mein Schatz will Hochzeit halten, ich liege auf den Tod" 1776 (226)
MEIN SCHÖNER STERN 3378 (112)
"Mein Schöner Stern! ich bitte dich" 3378 (112)
"Mein Schwan, mein stiller mit weissem Gefieder" 1391 (137,237)
MEIN SOHN 715 (5)
"Mein Sohn, sei Allahs Frieden hier auf Erden stets bescheiden dir" 715 (5)
MEIN VATER! 3914 (4)
"Mein Vater! Hochgesegneter der Helden" 3914 (4)
MEIN VATERLAND 1907 (31)
MEIN WÜRZBURG 2328 (31)
"MEINE LIEBE IST GRÜN" 408 (112,359)
MEINE LIEDER 409 (45)
"Meine Mus' ist gegangen in des Schenken sein Haus" 2215 (31,99)
MEINE MUSE 2215 (31,99)
"Meine Ruh' ist hin, mein Herz ist schwer" 3273 (276)

"Meine Seele ist nun still geworden" 3572 (98)
"Meine Treue, einer anderen geschworen" 592 (217)
"Meiner Kinderzeit lichte Stunden im Nebel verlöscht und verschwunden" 1858 (224)
MEINES HERZENS BRENNENDE SEHNSUCHT 883 (257)
"Meines Lebens Arbeit warden Pflug zu halten" 5681 (22)
MEISIESFONTEIN 7220 (239)
"EEN MEISJE DAT VAN SCHEVENINGEN KWAM" 6530 (202)
Die Meistersinger von Nürnberg 3909-3913
MEISTERSPRUCH 2291 (49)
MĚLA JSEM MILÉHO HULÁNA 4380 (178)
"Měla jsem milého hulána, hulána" 4380 (178)
MELANCHOLICKÁ PÍSEŇ O LÁSCE 2675 (74)
MELANCHOLISCHES LIED VON DER LIEBE 2675 (74)
MELMILLO 581 (275)
MELODIA 2833 (222)
MELODIA QUE TENÍA 4528 (207)
THE MELODY OF THE HARP 5964 (349)
Melody, piano, op.3, no.1, F major 3118
MÉLY A RIMA ZAVAROS, HA MEGÁRAD 5765 (164)
MEMORARE 1424 (71)
MEMORIES 3792 (233)
"Memories, memories, dreams of love so true" 3792 (233)
A MEMORY 1204 (121)
"Memory, hither come, and tune your merry notes" 2933 (275)
MEMORY LANE 3541 (345)
MEMORY OF POLAND 6872 (295)
"M'en allant promener (relé, relé)" 4883 (187)
"Men are building a tomb for me" 6675 (295)
MEN OF COURAGE, STRENGTH, AND BRAWN 7322 (135)
"Men of courage, strength, and brawn live in Sweden since the dawn" 7322 (135)
THE MEN OF DOVEY'S DELIGHT 8668 (349)
MEN OF HARLECH 8695 (233,234,349,397,402)
"Men of Harlech! honor calls us" 8695 (28,279,366)
"Men of Harlech, in the hollow" 8695 (34,233,397,402)
THE MEN OF THE WEST 7882 (172)
"M'en revanant de la jolie Rochelle" 5150 (186,187,219)
"Men still ask the same old question" 6169 (318)
"Men tell us 'tis fit that wives should submit" 7776 (189)
THE MENAGERIE 7817 (185,225,279,366)
Mens jeg venter 1386
"DER MENSCH HAT NICHTS SO EIGEN" 40 (250)
MENSCHEN, DIE IHR WAR'T VERLOREN 9170 (165)
"Die Menschen sie zanken und streiten" 1968 (396)
MENTRA, GWEN 8686 (349)
"Mentre dormi, Amor fomenti" 2764 (218)
MENUET (Heise) 1608 (87)
MENUET CHANTÉ 204 (269)
MENUET D'EXAUDET 1020 (383)
MENUETT FÜR 2 SOPRANE 362 (217)
MENYBÖL AR ANGYAL 9191 (154)
"Menyböl ar angyal leyött hozzátok" 9191 (154)
"MENYECSKÉNEK NEM JÓ LENNI" 5766 (289)
LA MER' MICHEL 5032 (82,91)
MERCH MEGAN 8687 (20)
MERCH Y MELINYDD 8688 (349)
THE MERCHANT I MARRIED 5169 (187)
MERCY BEAUTY 8788 (95)
"Mercy, beauty, mercy, hear me" 8788 (95)
MERCY POURIN' DOWN 8749 (323)
LA MÈRE MICHEL 5032 (383)
MERENGUE 4502 (86)

"Missionaries us have told, 'tis a story to you old" 9217 (244)

M-I-S-S-I-S-S-I-P-P-I 3747 (128)

"M-i-s-s-i-s-s-i-p-p-i that used to be so hard to spell" 3747 (128)

"Der Missouri rauscht" 1173 (223)

"Missouri she's a mighty river" 9481 (320)

THE MIST-COVERED MOUNTAINS OF HOME 7108 (105)

LA MIST'-EN L'AIRE 5035 (88,127)

THE MIST IT CAME 7822 (242)

"The mist it came, the mist it came, it settled over the town" 7822 (242)

"Mistäs tulet, kustas tulet" 4859 (124)

MISTAH RABBIT 8428 (216)

"Mistah Rabbit, Mistah Rabbit, yo' ears mighty long" 8428 (216)

MR. AND MRS. BROWN 1119 (189)

MISTER BANJO 7828 (331)

MISTER CONGRESSMAN 4048 (293)

MISTER FROGGIE WENT A-COURTIN' 4604A (185)

"Mister Froggie went a-courtin' and he did ride" 4604A (185)

MR. FROGGIE WENT A-COURTING 4604A (173)

"Mister Froggie went a-courting and he did ride" 4604A (173)

MISTER, HERE'S YOUR MULE 281 (225)

MISTER RABBIT 8428 (227)

"Mister Rabbit, Mister Rabbit, your tail's mighty white" 8428 (227)

MR. ROOSTER 6655 (86)

MISTER STORMALONG 9468 (320)

MISTERESSE MINE 2528 (144)

"Misteresse mine well may you fare" 2528 (144)

THE MISTLETOE 8663 (349)

MISTRESS BOND 4695 (249)

MRS. FORD'S RECITATIVE AND ARIA 2656 (6)

MRS. MC GRATH 5966 (172)

MISTRESS MINE 3939 (344)

"Mistress Murphey gave a party, just about a week ago" 1249 (114,131,204,246)

MISTS 3027 (121,408)

"MIT A NODL, ON A NODL" 6231 (318)

Mit deinen blauen Augen 2049

MIT DEM PFEIL, DEM BOGEN 3962 (326,353)

"Mit dem Pfeil, dem Bogen durch Gebirg und Tal" 3962 (326,353)

"Mit der Fiedel auf dem Rukken" 4032 (31)

"Mit der Laute bringt der Traute" 745 (222)

"Mit der Myrthe geschmückt" 3376 (250)

MIT DESEN NIEWEN JARE 9262 (361)

"Mit edeln Purpurröten und hellem Anselschlag" 2804 (31)

MIT EINEM GEMALTEN BAND 242 (330)

MIT EINER PRIMULA VERIS 1385 (209)

MIT LAUTEM JUBEL BRINGEN WIR 5477 (49)

"Mit lautem Jubel brigen wir die schöne Erntekron" 5477 (49)

"Mit Lust tät ich ausreiten durch einen grünen Wald" 2383 (45)

"Mit meinem Blut würde ich erkaufen" 3599 (217)

MIT MEINER MAPPE 2284 (31)

"Mit meiner Mappe unterm Arm, wollt' ins Kolleg ich ziehn" 2284 (31)

MIT MYRTHEN UND ROSEN 3374 (112)

"Mit Myrthen und Rosen, lieblich und hold" 3374 (112)

"Mit welchem Genuss, ihr blühenden Lippen, küsse ich euch und höre euch zu" 2505 (217)

"Mitn hamer a trach, ich halt schojn beim dach" 6189 (230)

"Mitt hjärta längtar till stillhet och ro" 3509 (356)

MITTE CONFITTE 6535 (203)

"Mitte confitte kom t'avond thuis" 6535 (203)

"Die Mitternach zog näher schon" 3358 (272)

"Mmm, baby, Yes, Mama Honey, why don't you change your ways?" 455 (336)

"Mo léan ar an bpíobaire Bearnaí!" 5874 (280)

MO MARY 7109 (111)

"Mo parlé Rémon, Rémon" 7949 (110)

MO RÙN GEAL DÍLEAS 7117 (100,105)

MOANFULLY IN TARJÁN 5734 (164)

"Moanfully in Tarján they the bells do ring" 5734 (164)

THE MOCKING BIRD 7681A (216)

MODERS NAVN 3121 (87)

"Moders navn er en himmelsk Lyd" 3121 (87)

Modersorg 1387 (208)

MODEST HEART 4068 (330)

MODESTA AYALA 6370 (219)

MODLITBA 1094 (73)

"MOE GEWERKT EN MOE GESPEELD" 6536 (384)

"MOEDER, IK WIL HEBBEN EEN MAN" 6537 (202)

"Möge der barmherzige Himmel deinen Leben hinzusetzen" 2245 (218)

MÖGST DU, MEIN KIND 3900 (5)

"Mögst du, mein Kind, den fremden Mann willkommen heissen" 3900 (5)

"Moen c'est un petite brun douxdoux" 8761 (286)

"MÖWE, DU FLIEGST IN DIE HEIMAT" 4047 (223)

LE MOIS DE MAI ("C'est le mai...") 5036 (91)

LE MOIS DE MAI ("Il est de retour...") 5037 (88)

MÓJ WIONECKU Z BARWINECKU 6775 (295)

"Mój wionecku z barwinecku Wiesiałak cie na kołecku" 6775 (295)

MOJA PIESZCZOTKA 669 (295)

"Moja pieszcztoka gdy w wesołej chwili" 669 (295)

MOLAD'TI 669 (295)

MOLAD'TI 6232 (318)

"Molad'ti hi erets K'na-an" 6232 (318)

La molinara 2727

Moll Roe in the morning (tune) 5993

Moll Roone (tune) 5903

MOLLIE DARLING 1592 (129,130)

"Mollie, fairest, sweetest, dearest" 1592 (129,130)

MOLLY! 7110 (102,105)

MOLLY BRANNIGAN 5967 (172)

MOLLY MCALPIN 6002 (349)

Molly Macalpin (tune) 6002

MOLLY MALONE 5968 (166,215,249)

MOLLY, MY DEAR 5869 (349)

MOLLY MY TREASURE 5922 (15,349)

MOLLY O! 3175 (114,131)

UN MOMENTO DI CONTENTO 1443 (181)

"Un momento di contento dolce rende a un fido" 1443 (181)

MOM'S LITTLE OLLE (Tegnér) 3715 (188)

"Mom's little Olle was in the wood" 3715 (188)

"Mon ange, souvent j'ignore quels mots d'amour te dire" 4127 (224)

MON BEAU SAPIN 5038 (88)

"Mon beau sapin, roi des forêts" 5038 (88)

"Mon bien-aimé, mon seul espoir" 977 (221)

"Mon coeur lasse de tout" 1340 (273)

"Mon coeur, souffrez! Mes yeux pleurez!" 1014 (269)

"MON COEUR S'OUVRE À TA VOIX" 3140 (2, 122, 132, 329)
"Mon compère, quand je danse, mon cotillon va-t-il bien?" 4942 (82)
"Mon enfant, ma soeur" 942 (121)
Mon mari s'en est allé (tune) 4925
"Mon oncl', mon oncle a bien mal à sa têt'" 5172 (21)
MON ONCLE, MON ONCLE 5172 (21)
"MON PÈR' M'A DONNÉ UN MARI" 5039 (82)
"Mon per' m'a mariée a la Saint Nicolas" 5030 (383)
"Mon pèr' n'avait fille que moi" 5155 (187)
"Mon père et ma mère, De Lyon ils sont" 4982 (127)
"Mon père m'a mariée avec un vieillard jaloux" 5012 (61)
"Mon père m'a trouvé un' place" 4939 (65)
"Mon père m'y mari avec un marchand de velours" 5169 (187)
MON PETIT OISEAU 5040 (91)
"Mon petit oiseau a pris sa volée" 5040 (91)
MONA 5041 (91)
A MONA LISA 4113 (78)
LA MONACO 5042 (91)
MONARCH OF THE SEA 3658 (205)
DER MOND (Mendelssohn-Bartholdy) 2387 (45)
"Mond an blauen Himmel hing" 1232 (222)
"Der Mond ist aufgegangen" (Schubert) 3247 (141)
"DER MOND IST AUFGEGANGEN" (Schulz) 3334 (31, 49, 99, 229, 309, 326, 353)
"Der Mond steht über dem Berge" 426 (112, 407)
"Monday is the day for washing in the old oak tub" 5168 (21)
"Monday was my wedding day" 7894 (34)
MONDJA MEG ANNAK A KIS LEÁNYNAK 5767 (164)
MONDNACHT (Petrzelka) 2795 (73)
MONDNACHT (Schumann) 3375 (97, 112, 226, 277, 359)
MONEY 7823 (321)
MONEY AM A HARD THING TO BORROW 3782 (189)
MONEY, O! 1598 (273)
MONGOOSE DEAD OH 8751 (11)
"Mongoose gone, mongoose gone; Not my fault he dead" 8751 (11)
"Mongoose stealin' blackbird told me so" 8751 (11)
MONICA PÉREZ 8652 (9)
Monika 885 (255)
THE MONK IN THE MEADOW 4466 (231)
MONKEY DRAW BOW 8752 (252)
MONKEY JAW BONE 8752 (252)
"THE MONKEY MARRIED THE BABOON'S SISTER" 8429 (145, 184)
THE MONKEY SONG 8771 (323)
MONKEY'S WEDDING 8429 (145)
MONOLOG OF TIME 615 (367)
MONOLOGO DEL TEMPO 615 (367)
MONOLOGUE (Musorgskiĭ) 2614 (5)
MONOTONE 716 (348)
MONSIEUR BANJO 7828 (219)
MONSIEUR DE LA PALISSE 5043 (86, 127)
MONSIEUR LE CURÉ 5173 (187)
LES MONTAGNARDS 6112 (238)
"Montagnes de ma vallée, vous êtes mes amours" 6112 (238)
MONTANYAS REGALADAS 4958 (68)
"Montanyas regaladas son las del Canigó" 4958 (68)
MONTE CANINO 6113 (238)
"Monte, écureuil, monte au grand chêne" 3133 (190, 192, 194)

MONTE NERO 6114 (238)
"The months are met with their crownlets on" 1036 (28)
LES MONTS RETENTISSENT 4456 (177)
"Les monts retentissent, les forêts mugissent" 4456 (177)
THE MOON (Mendelssohn-Bartholdy) 2387 (45)
The moon (Purcell) 2920-2921
THE MOON (Schubert) 3251 (199)
MOON AND STARS OF CHRISTMAS EVE 4022 (244)
"The moon-beams whiten boughs all around" 1503 (121)
"The moon had gone down o'er the hills of the west" 8124 (126)
"The moon hangs over the hill" 426 (112)
"The moon is beaming o'er the sparkling rill" 8127 (343)
"The moon is shining on the windowsill" 8127 (132)
THE MOON IS UP 2236 (343)
"The moon is up, the moon is up! the larks begin to fly" 2236 (343)
"Moon of old, striding alone thru the heavens" 1070 (343)
"The moon on the ocean was dimm'd by a ripple" 835 (205)
THE MOON REAPPEARS 2920 (199)
THE MOON SHINES BRIGHT 9000 (333)
"The moon shines bright, and the stars give a light" 9000 (333, 334, 361)
"The moon shines bright, and the stars give light" 9000 (307)
"The moon shines over the mountain" 426 (407)
"Moonless darkness stands between, past O past, no more be seen!" 778 (376)
MOONLIGHT (Debussy) 794 (211)
MOONLIGHT (Folksongs, Italy) 6115 (37)
MOONLIGHT (Saint-Saëns) 3136 (140)
MOONLIGHT (Schumann) 3375 (277, 359)
MOONLIGHT (Szulc) 3707 (191, 193, 195)
MOONLIGHT BAY 3989 (233)
"The moonlight blanches on trees around" 1503 (348)
"Moonlight fullness thy heart illuming" 940 (362)
"The moonlight shimmers thro' the vine" 512 (259)
A MOONLIGHT SONG 512 (259)
"Moonlight's through her window stealing" 6836 (228)
"The moonrays on bayous gleam, ay, ay, ay" 2761 (343)
"The moon's on the lake" 2086 (101)
"Moored by the wharf, the vessels tall" 1044 (140)
MOORSOLDATEN 5478 (7, 293)
MO-OZ TSUR 6233 (37)
MORAVIAN FOLK SONG 4382 (324)
MORAVO! 4382 (324)
"Moravo, Moravo, Moravěnko milá!" 4382 (324)
"The more come in with a free goodwill" 8355 (409)
"More desirable and pretty you will be" 365 (134)
MORE OF CLOYNE 5969 (349)
"More than four thousand years' delay" 9070 (388)
"More than four thousand years, they say" 9070 (33)
The Moreen (tune) 5965
MORENA 4203 (279, 350)
MORENA, MORENA 4203 (9)
"Morena, Morena, O loveliest maiden" 4203 (350)
"Morena, Morena, Oh lady of brown eyes" 4203 (9)
"Morena, Morena, tues olhos castanhos" 4203 (9)
LA MORENA TRINIDAD 4288 (219)
"Morena, when dancing, and with you romancing" 4203 (279)
MORFA RHUDDLAN 8689 (20, 349)
MORVUDD 8690 (20)
MORGEN (Strauss) 3629 (98, 112, 121, 330)

"My bonny cuckoo I tell thee true that through the groves I'll rove with you" 5971 (234)

MY BOY ACROSS THE SEA 1593 (205)

MY BOY BILLY 4549A (44)

MY BOY TAMMIE 7114 (100, 103, 104, 235)

"My brother, I remember when I was a sinner lost" 8403 (409)

"My brother, want to get religion?" 8278 (184)

MY BUDDY 856 (233)

"My calling sounds over the moorland" 6635 (95)

MY CONFESSOR TOLD ME 6756 (159)

"My confessor told me, that hell will enfold me, if I kiss" 6756 (159)

MY CONFESSOR WARNED ME 6756 (295)

"My confessor warned me not to kiss on Sunday" 6756 (295)

"My Constance, my gentle Constance" 4198 (219)

"My coral beads came from a cave" 3764 (121)

"My cottage has a courtyard" 6296 (219)

"MY COUNTRY, 'TIS OF THEE" 7408 (7, 10, 28, 32, 129, 130, 233, 236, 279, 321, 343, 366)

MY COURTYARD 6296 (219)

"My daddy is an engineer, my brother drives a hack" 8607 (293, 321, 336)

"My daddy is dead, and I cannot tell you how" 4602 (249)

"My Daddy was a cowboy and I follow in his footsteps" 1 (293)

MY DAD'S THE ENGINEER 1345 (114)

"My daily work is over" 4825 (124)

MY DAMAGED HEART 4526 (207)

"MY DAME HATH A LAME TAME CRANE" 4012 (235, 349)

MY DARLING (Jimenez) 1789 (291)

MY DARLING (Seismit-Doda) 3421 (245)

"MY DARLING'S LIPS ARE A PETALED ROSE" 4151 (357)

MY DARLING'S LITTLE SHOES 3762 (189)

"MY DAYS HAVE BEEN SO WONDROUS FREE" 1700 (109, 110, 129, 130, 145, 173, 279, 405)

MY DEAR HIELAND LADDIE 7115 (101, 104)

"My dear, I truly love you, and will for all my life" 7314 (95)

"My dear Marquis, it seems to me you should employ more tact" 3609 (1)

"My dear, my darling daughter, will you be a cobbler's wife" 6201 (318)

"MY DEAR ONE'S MOUTH IS LIKE THE ROSE" 4151 (210)

"My dear quail escaped across the water" 6822 (159)

MY DEAR STAR 2198 (159)

"My dear star that hung in heaven" 2198 (159)

"My dear sweetheart came to see me when I left by rail-road train" 2430 (162)

MY DEAREST LOVE 1255 (138)

"My dearest love is far away" 977 (221)

"My dearest love, true will I prove" 1255 (138)

MY DISCREET SWEETHEART 1347 (245)

"My dog did bark and I went to see" 7934 (392)

"My donkey walk, my donkey talk, my donkey eat with a knife and fork" 8717 (77)

"My Dorotka, my maluška, my maluška" 6702 (295)

"My dove with wings so fair, so blue" 8667 (235)

MY DREAM 4171 (207)

"My dream of love that rises with the daybreak" 2153 (329)

"My dream of love will linger on for ever" 2153 (132)

MY DREYDL 6234 (214)

MY DUCKSIE HAS FLED 7830 (72)

MY DWELLING 801 (248)

MY FAITH LOOKS UP TO THEE 2301 (28, 35, 236, 279, 366)

"My faith looks up to Thee Thou Lamb of Calvary" 2301 (28, 35, 236, 279, 366)

MY FAITHU' JOHNNIE 7116 (101)

MY FAITHFUL FAIR ONE 7117 (100, 105)

"My faithful fair one, my own, my rare one" 7117 (100, 105)

"My father bought at great expense a grand high stepping grey" 5926 (349)

"My father gave me an acre of land" 4755 (95)

"My father has no child but me" 5155 (187)

"My father! Highest venerated hero!" 3914 (4)

"My father made me wed a merchant whom he chose for me" 5169 (187)

MY FATHER'S COOK 961 (111)

"My fine lad, why do you come to woo me?" 6844 (228)

"My flock is no longer happy and gay" 3981 (30)

MY FRIEND! MY FRIEND! 5148A (186, 187)

"My friend! My friend! can you play this?" 5148A (186, 187)

MY FRIENDS, DO NOT WORRY 4383 (37)

MY GAL IS A HIGH BORN LADY 1024 (114, 115, 128, 131)

MY GENTLE HARP 5972 (133, 349)

MY GENTLE HARP (Londonderry air tune) 5940 (35)

"My gentle harp! once more I waken" 5972 (133, 349)

"My gentle harp, once more I waken" (Londonderry air tune) 5940 (35)

MY GOOD LORD'S DONE BEEN HERE 8431 (409)

"My good mother often tells me not to be too bold or daring" 6368 (219)

MY GOOD OLD MAN 7831 (216)

"My good steed neighs with impatience" 2148 (295)

MY GOOSE 4699 (214)

"My grandfather had a very fine farm" 700 (189)

MY GRANDFATHER HAD SOME VERY FINE DUCKS 700 (189)

"My Grandfather's clock was too large for the shelf" 4107 (114, 129, 130, 132, 173, 236, 279, 343, 366)

"My grandsire beat the drum complete" 5894 (349)

"MY GRANDSIRE, HE HAD A PEWTER CUP" 3568 (188)

MY GUAJIRITA 1010 (9)

"My Gwendoleen, my heart's delight" 8678 (349)

"My hammer it falls I build roof and walls" 6189 (230)

"My hawk is tired of perch and of hood" 3281 (273)

"MY HEART AT THY SWEET VOICE" 3140 (2, 122, 329)

MY HEART EVER FAITHFUL 114 (329, 394)

MY HEART EVER FAITHFUL SING PRAISES 114 (122, 123)

"My heart ever faithful sing praises, be joyful" 114 (122, 123, 329)

MY HEART HAS A WINDOW 2761 (237)

"My heart has a window, where you can see" 2761 (237)

"My heart hopes and fears" 43 (253)

"MY HEART IS A SILENT VIOLIN" 1139 (387)

"My heart is a-breaking, dear Tittie" 7172A (232, 365)

"My heart is a-breakin', dear tittie" 7172B (101)

"My heart is full of happy tears" 2848 (2)

MY HEART IS IN BLOOM 408 (359)

"My heart is like the gloomy night" 2387 (45)

"My heart is no longer mine" 1056 (134)

"My heart is sad and I am lonely" 8099 (243)

"My heart is sad and I am weeping" 7481 (129, 130, 132)

"My heart is sair" 3381 (275)

MY HEART IS SAIR FOR SOMEBODY 7118 (101, 103)

"My heart is sair, I daurna tell" 7118 (101, 103)

MY HEART IS SORE 6466 (86)

"My heart is wounded sore" 6466 (86)

MY HEART STOOD STILL 3051 (345)

"My heart, the bird of the wilderness" 1707 (259)

"My heart, with inward peace, adores creation" 7324 (231)

MY HEART'S IN THE HIGHLANDS 7119 (102,105)

"My heart's in the Highlands, my heart is not here" 7119 (102,105)

MY HEART'S O'ER THE DEEP BLUE SEA 675* (205)

"My home's in Montana, I wear a bandana" 7523 (120)

"MY HOPE IS IN THE EVERLASTING" 3549 (123)

MY HORSES AIN'T HUNGRY 7719 (267)

"My husband, good-bye" 2978 (121)

"My Jesus, He is sleeping" 9316 (388)

MY JO JANET 7120 (100,105)

"MY JOHNNY WAS A SHOEMAKER" 4700 (86,198)

MY JOYFUL ARDOR 2263 (368)

"My joyful ardor, whether near or far distant" 2263 (368)

MY KING OF ROSES 2295 (132)

"My king of roses! Radiant angels stand in heav'n in thousands" 2295 (132)

"My Laddie, are you not grieving to leave your fair native mountains" 6712 (295)

MY LADY 7832 (132)

MY LADY GREENSLEEVES 4621 (297)

MY LADY'S GARDEN 4877 (297)

MY LAGEN LOVE 1542 (273)

"MY LAND, MY LAND, MY FATHERLAND" 7343 (135)

MY LASS 839 (205)

MY LAST ABODE 3303 (273)

MY LAST CIGAR 1724 (205,279,366)

"My last sun today has risen" 3831 (4)

"My leg is aching worse! Out and saddle, out and saddle" 9082 (361)

MY LITTLE BLACK STAR 8432 (266)

MY LITTLE HEN 4261 (207)

MY LITTLE MOHEE 7787A (267)

MY LITTLE PRETTY ONE 4701 (234)

"My little pretty one, my pretty honey one" 4701 (234)

MY LITTLE QUAIL 6822 (295)

My lodging is on the cold ground (tune) 5876, 7064

"MY LODGING IS THE CELLAR HERE" 1077 (240)

"My lodging is the cellar here" 1077 (273)

"My Lord calls me, He calls me by the thunder" 8560 (10, 28,35,76,129,183,233,279,366,402,409)

"My lord calls me, see can't you jump for joy" 8529 (184)

"My Lord deliver'd Daniel" 8244B (28,366)

MY LORD DELIVERED DANIEL 8244B (28,366)

"My Lord had one hundred sheep" 8271 (332)

"MY LORD, WHAT A MORNIN'" 8433 (182)

"MY LORD, WHAT A MORNING" 8433 (35,76)

"MY LORD WHAT A MOURNING" 8433 (28,366,409)

"My Lord's done just what He said" (MY SINS BEEN TAKEN AWAY) 8436 (409)

"My Lord's done just what he said" (PLENTY GOOD ROOM) 8487 (409)

"MY LORD'S GOIN' MOVE THIS WICKED RACE" 8434 (409)

"My Lords, with your leave an account I will give" 8002 (173)

"My love built me a bonnie bow'r" 7015 (101,103)

"MY LOVE IN GARDEN SPOT IS DWELLING" 4877 (36)

"My love is a flower, all fragrant before me" 2557 (3)

"MY LOVE IS GONE TO SEA" 1701 (36)

MY LOVE IS GREEN 408 (112)

"My love is like a dewdrop" 7833 (72)

"My love is like a dewdrop setting out upon a thorn" 7833 (72)

MY LOVE IS LIKE A RED, RED ROSE 7121A (163,402)

"My love is the flaming sword to fight thro' the world" 52 (237)

"MY LOVE LIKE A DAINTY SHEPHERDESS" 264 (188)

MY LOVE RODE BY 513 (136)

"My love rode by my window" 513 (136)

"MY LOVE, SHE'S BUT A LASSIE YET" 7122 (100,102, 232,235)

"My love was born in Aberdeen" 7203 (232)

"My love was born in Aiberdeen" 7203 (100,103,104)

"My lover did come ere evensong" 4776B (262)

MY LOVELY CELIA 2492 (348)

"My lovely Celia, heav'nly fair, as lilies sweet, as soft as air" 2492 (348)

MY LOVELY STAR 3378 (112)

"My lovely star! I beg of thee" 3378 (112)

MY LOVER IS A FISHERMAN 3646 (137)

MY LOVE'S AN ARBUTUS 5973 (136,166,213,349)

"My love's an arbutus by the borders of Lene" 5973 (136, 166,213,349)

"My lovin' brother when the world's on fire" 8511 (409)

MY LOVIN' GAL LUCILLE 3049 (336)

"MY LUVE IS LIKE A RED, RED ROSE" 7121A (17,36), 7121B (232)

MY LUVE'S IN GERMANIE 7123 (100)

"My luve's in Germanie, send him hame, send him hame" 7123 (100)

"My lytell prety one, my pretie bonie one" 4701 (106)

MY MAGDALINA 2664 (295)

"MY MAIDEN'S LIPS ARE LIKE A ROSE" 4151 (36)

"My mammy's in the cold, cold, ground" 8490C (184)

"My mither ment my auld breeks" 7159 (102)

My moonlight Madonna 1070

MY MOTHER 774 (162)

"MY MOTHER BIDS ME BIND MY HAIR" 1560 (122,275, 329,386)

"My mother gave me a penny to buy some candy" 7578 (293)

"My mother has warned me I never should cry" 4530 (207)

"My mother kept a boarding house" 9451 (173)

"My mother she has an old spinning wheel" 7656 (242)

"My mother was a lady like yours you will allow" 3574 (32,34,246)

"My mother went to market for to buy some coal" 6225 (318)

MY MOTHER'S ADVICE 6368 (219)

MY MOTHER'S BIBLE 3124 (129,130,189)

"My mother's broke the ice and gone" 8193 (409)

MY NAME IS ANNIE CAMPBELL 6636 (231)

"My name is Annie Campbell, my mothers' is the same" 6636 (231)

"My name is Frank Bolar, 'n ol' bach'lor I am" 8023A (80)

"My name is Josephus Orange Blossom" 7745 (225)

"My name is Mick Molloy, in clear and cloudy weather" 5905 (133)

MY NAME IS PADDY LEARY 5974 (166,213)

"My name is Paddy Leary from a place called Tipperary" 5974 (172)

"My name is Paddy Leary, from a shpot call'd Tipperary" 5974 (166,213)

"My name is Peter Amberley" 522 (186)

"My name is Solomon Levi and my store's on Salem Street" 3414 (366)

"My name is Solomon Levi, at my store on Chatham Street" 3414 (402)

"My name is Solomon Levi, at my store on Salem street" 3414 (225)

"My name is Stanford Barnes, I come from Nobleville town" 8024 (110, 227)

"My name is Tom Hight, an old bach'lor I am" 8023A (227)

"My name is William Edwards" 8043 (110)

"My name it is Joe Bowers, and I've got a brother Ike" 7733A (173)

"My name it is Joe Bowers, I have a brother Ike" 7733C (312)

"My name it is Joe Bowers, I've got a brother Ike" 7733A (109, 110)

"My name it is Robert, they call be Bob Pittman" 9483C (186)

MY NAME'S WRITTEN ON HIGH 8435 (409)

MY NANNIE, O 7124 (100)

MY NANNIE'S AWA' 7125 (18, 100, 102)

MY NATIVE LAND (Grechaninov) 1361 (341)

MY NATIVE LAND (Grieg) 1388 (28, 366)

MY NATIVE LAND (Wolf) 4075 (348)

"My native land, again it meets my eye" 2048 (28, 366)

"My native land ne'er more" 3820 (143)

"My native land no more" 3820 (1)

"MY NELLY'S BLUE EYES" 3174 (128, 131, 132)

MY NOBLE KNIGHTS 2409 (176)

"My noble knights, I hail you" 2409 (176)

MY NORMANDY 282 (86)

"My ol' mistiss promise me" 8501 (227)

MY OLD DUTCH 1749 (128, 131, 132)

MY OLD KENTUCKY HOME 1120 (10, 28, 32, 34, 109, 110, 122, 129, 130, 184, 233, 236, 279, 343, 366)

MY OLD KENTUCKY HOME, GOOD NIGHT 1120 (236)

MY OLD MAN 7834 (242)

"My old man, number one, he plays knick-a-knick on the drum" 7834 (242)

"My ole massa promised me" 3240 (109, 110)

My only jo, and dearie O (tune) 7061 (100, 102)

MY OWN DEAR ONE 1255 (329)

"My own dear one, won't you believe" 1255 (329)

MY OWN DEAR ONE'S GONE 7126 (103, 104)

"My own love, Paloma, little dove" 6662 (279)

MY OWN UNITED STATES 985 (233)

MY PARENTS' GRAVE 8658 (20)

"My peace is gone, my heart is sore" 3273 (276)

"My Peggy is a young thing" 7188 (101)

"My place of birth is the land of Canaan" 6232 (318)

MY PRAYER 3526 (347)

MY PRETTY LITTLE MAID 7835 (72)

MY PRETTY LITTLE MISS 4702A (171)

"MY RED CROSS GIRLIE" 2536 (129, 130)

MY REVERIE 798 (236)

MY RIVAL 2037 (248)

MY SABLE FLOWERS 2713 (322)

"My Sarie Marais is so vĕr van my hart" 7223 (239, 384)

"My Saviour spoke these words so sweet" 8640 (409)

MY SHEEP WERE GRAZING 9140 (296)

"My sheep were grazing on a plain" 9140 (296)

MY SHEPHERD, THOU 3647 (347)

MY SHIP COMES IN 2433 (205)

"My ship comes sailing up the sea" 2433 (205)

"My ship is on the ocean" 8557 (409)

MY SINS BEEN TAKEN AWAY 8436 (409)

"My sister, have you got your sword and shield" 8421 (409)

MY SIXTEEN YEAR OLD BROWN-EYED YOUNG MAID" 3698 (285)

"My Son! In all sincerity I wish thee great prosperity" 715 (5)

MY SONG ON WINGS 1505 (329)

"My song to thee would be hieing" 1505 (237)

"My song would fly, all unaided" 1505 (122)

MY SONGS 409 (45)

"My songs to thee would be bringing" 1505 (140)

"MY SOUL IS A WITNESS FOR MY LORD" 8437 (76)

"MY SOUL IS ATHIRST FOR GOD" 1219 (123, 394)

MY SOUL IS DARK 3385 (274)

"My soul is dark Oh quickly, quickly string the harp" 3385 (274)

MY SOUL'S BEEN ANCHORED IN THE LORD 8438A (409), 8438B (409)

"My soul's delight and treasure" 870 (6)

MY SPIRIT BEHOLDETH 9173 (333)

"My spirit beholdeth a wonderful sight" 9173 (333)

MY STAR 2198 (295)

MY SUN 579 (132, 329)

MY SUNSHINE 579 (122)

"My swan, my treasure, with snowy white feather" 1391 (137, 237)

"My swan, so silent with white snowy pinions" 1391 (137, 237)

MY SWEET LITTLE DARLING 494 (319)

"My sweet little darling, my comfort and joy" 494 (319)

MY SWEETEST LESBIA 551 (116)

"My sweetest Lesbia, let us live and love" 551 (116)

"My sweetheart come along, don't you hear the fond song" 4768 (234)

"My sweetheart is a gorgeous gal" 4835 (36)

"MY SWEETHEART'S A MULE IN THE MINES" 7836 (145)

MY SWEETHEART'S THE MAN IN THE MOON 3744 (114, 128, 129, 130, 131, 132)

"My tears now flow unheeded" 3822 (292)

"My tender playmates, my sweet companions now hasten to the woodlands" 645 (357)

"My thought of thoughts, my very inmost being" 1382 (241)

"My thoughts and all my memories belong to thee" 5207 (35)

MY THOUGHTS LIKE HAUNTING MUSIC 437 (112)

"My thoughts like haunting music drift through my mind today" 437 (112)

MY TOMB 6675 (295)

"My Tommy's gone, what shall I do?" 9456 (366)

"My true love is there" 423 (275)

"My true love lives over the mountain" 8014B (225)

MY TRUNDLE BED 152 (189)

MY TRUSTY GUN 2430 (162)

"My verses would flee, sweet and frail" 1505 (191, 193, 195)

"My walking thoughts to thee are ever turning" 1382 (387)

"My wife and I live all alone" 4048 (129, 130, 131, 132)

"My wife and I lived all alone" 4048 (32, 34, 109, 110, 225, 233)

"My wife and I, we lived alone" 4048 (293)

"MY WIFE'S A WINSOME WEE THING" 7127 (101)

MY WILD IRISH ROSE 2705 (166)

"My wild Irish Rose, the sweetest flow'r that grows" 2705 (166)

NIGHTINGALE (Folksongs, Czechoslovakia) 4419 (94)
THE NIGHTINGALE (Folksongs, Denmark) 4467 (231)
NIGHTINGALE (Folksongs, Spain) 7264 (95)
THE NIGHTINGALE (Folksongs, United States) 7845A (81), 7845B (267)
THE NIGHTINGALE (Lawes) 2068 (404)
THE NIGHTINGALE AND THE ROSE (Rimskiĭ-Korsakov) 3037 (348)
THE NIGHTINGALE AND THE ROSE (Saint-Saëns) 3138 (208)
Nightingale canon 1570 (337)
" THE NIGHTINGALE CHARM'D BY THE ROSE" 3037 (407)
"Nightingale, here fold thy wing" 47 (176)
"Nightingale to France you're flying, nightingale" 7264 (95)
"Nightingale who, singing, sets the green grove ringing" 4419 (94)
THE NIGHTINGALES 5104 (174)
"Nightingales in the wood to our voice make reply" 2963 (150)
THE NIGHTINGALE'S SONG 7845C (72)
"Nights are long since you went away" 856 (233)
"NIGHT'S DEW DROPS GLISTEN" 2482 (159)
NIIN SINULLE LAULAN 4843 (124)
NIMM MICH IN DEINE ARME 3562 (257)
NIMMERSATTE LIEBE 4081 (112)
NIMROD 994 (306)
NINA 2769 (311, 368, 386)
NIÑAS HERMOSAS 7269 (219)
"Niñas hermosas ¿para dónde van?" 7269 (219)
NINA'S SONG 1889 (342)
NINCS CSEREPES TANYÁM 2831 (164)
NINCSEN ANNYI TENGERCSILLAG 5777 (164)
NINE FOOT SHOVEL 8444 (77)
900 MILES 7846 (227)
"Nine mo' months an' two mo' days" 8286 (409)
"Nine poun' hammer, Wham!" 8304 (331)
NINETY-FIFTH 7847A (212)
NINNA NANNA (Carols, Italy) 9207 (361)
NINNA-NANNA (Flies) 1085 (199)
"Ninna Nanna Ninna Nanna dormi figlio dormi amore" 9207 (361)
EL NIÑO JESUS 9305 (154, 337)
"Un niño nació en Francia en Dominusté Quéelegancia!" 6366 (247)
NIT DE VETILLA 8856 (55)
"Nita! Juanita! Ask thy soul if we should part" 7261 (28, 34, 70, 132, 233, 236, 279, 343, 366)
"Nita! Juanita! Tu eres mi angel, mi illusión" 7261 (28, 34, 70, 132, 233, 236, 279, 343, 366)
NITRA, DEAREST NITRA 4389 (324)
"Nitra, dearest Nitra, there is glory in your name" 4389 (324)
NITRA, MILÁ NITRA 4389 (86, 94, 324)
"Nitra, milá Nitra, ty vysoká, Nitra" 4389 (86, 94, 324)
NITRA MINE 4389 (94)
"Nitra mine, dear Nitra, noble city Nitra!" 4389 (94)
NITRA, PROUDEST NITRÁ 4387 (86)
"Nitra, proudest Nitra, high above the rivers!" 4387 (86)
NITRA'S BELLS 4436 (95)
"Nitra's bells that ring so sweet" 4436 (95)
"No alientes celos por que te digan lo que no existe en mi corazón" 4505 (73)
"No digas cariño hermosa" 4195 (284)

"No doubt you have heard of the Great Fancy Fair" 2345 (115)
NO EMBERS, NOR A FIRE BRAND 1625 (137)
"No embers, nor a firebrand so fiercely can glow" 1625 (137)
"No gal made has got a shade on sweet Georgia Brown" 293 (345)
"No, good honest people" 2620 (2)
NO GREATER LOVE 636 (263)
"No greater love can I feel than I am feeling" 636 (263)
"No harm have I done you on my knees" 8228 (409)
NO HAY ÁRBOL 6295 (219)
"No hay árbol que no tenga sombra en verano" 6295 (219)
"No hay corazón como el mio para sufrir" 4169 (284)
"No hay rama en el monte, Vidalitá" 4174 (284)
NO HIDING PLACE 8445 (409)
NO HOME, NO HOME 1123 (189)
"No home! no home on my weary way I seek" 1123 (189)
"No I ain't a-shame'" 8280 (409)
"No! I can bear my fate no longer!" 3965 (3)
"No, if my plighted fealty I must betray" 2902 (310)
"NO LE DABA EL SOL" 7266 (282)
"No, let all my tears continue" 2321 (2)
"NO LONGER LET ME LANGUISH" 2502 (368)
"No longer the slave of ambition" 7882 (173)
"No me mates, no me mates, déjame viviren paz" 6287 (219)
"No mo' auction block for me" 8419A (35, 184)
"No more auction block for me" 8419B (186)
NO MORE BOOZE 7848 (109, 110)
"No more entrancing garlands of flowers" 2554 (2)
"No more, no more in Cashel town I'll sell my health a-raking" 6007 (133)
"No more shall I entrust to you my heart" 4526 (207)
NO MORE SHALL SORROW 1367 (211)
"No more shall sorrow displease or vex me" 1367 (211)
"No more weeping and a-wailing" 8553A (409)
"NO! NO! A THOUSAND TIMES NO!" 3451 (128, 131)
"NO, NO, HOPE HAS PERISHED" 593 (138)
"NO, NO, NON SI SPERI" 593 (138, 217)
NO! NOT MORE WELCOME 5979 (166, 213)
"No! not more welcome the fairy numbers of music fall on the sleeper's ear" 5979 (166, 213)
"No one had ever lovelier features" 1748 (191, 193, 195)
"NO ONE KILLS THE COLLEGE SCHOLAR" 5776 (164)
NO ONE LIKE A SOLDIER 6796 (159)
"No one vexes me more than my pretty Kasiu" 6786 (295)
"No one's like a soldier quite so brave and glorious" 6796 (159)
NO, ONLY THOSE WHO KNOW 643 (341)
"No, only those who know love's burning passion" 643 (341)
NO RACE THERE IS TO VIE 7363 (230)
"No race there is to vie, with our mountain herdsman stock" 7363 (230)
NO ROOM IN THE INN 8961 (337)
NO SCHOOL TODAY 5172 (21)
NO SÉ 4507 (73)
"No sé por que te quiere mi corazón herido" 4507 (73)
"No shelter for Mary, who Jesus did carry" 9374 (268)
"No sooner in my bed then I must up again" 6194 (318)
"No star is o'er the lake" 3662 (343)
"No star shone in the heav'nly vault" 3868 (1)
"No te extrañes, mi amada" 1363 (284)

"No te prodigues en dar, porque a quí, como en Cuquío"
6371 (247)
NO, TIRSI, TU NON HAI 3818 (253)
"No, Tirsi, tu non hai quella che sè decaute" 3818 (253)
NO, 'TIS NO SACRIFICE I OFFER! 1268 (362)
NO TREE BUT HAS A SHADOW 6295 (219)
"No tree but has a shadow when June o'ertakes it" 6295
(219)
"No use in guessing how he is dressing" 3826 (292)
"No volverán jamás" 2520 (291)
"Noah built the ark upon dry land açcordin' to command"
8472 (77)
NOAH'S ARK 8478 (28,225,279,366)
"Nobil' donna e tanto onesta" 2409 ·(176)
NOBIS EST NATUS 2871 (361)
"Nobis est natus hodie" 2871 (361)
THE NOBLE DUKE OF YORK 4704 (214)
"Noble Republic! happiest of lands" 2437 (189)
THE NOBLE SKEWBALL 7849 (126)
THE NOBLEMAN'S POLONAISE 1999 (159)
"Nobles alone can bear them with so bold a mien" 1317
(1,6,221)
"NOBLES SEIGNEURS, SALUT!" 2409 (176)
"Noblest of songs for the noblest of gods!" 1686 (358)
NOBODY 7850 (225)
"NOBODY KNOWS DE TROUBLE I SEE" 8446 (35,76,183)
"NOBODY KNOWS DE TROUBLE I'VE SEEN" 8446 (52)
"NOBODY KNOWS THE TROUBLE I SEE" 8446 (10)
"NOBODY KNOWS THE TROUBLE I'VE HAD" 8446 (129,
130,132)
"NOBODY KNOWS THE TROUBLE I'VE SEEN" 8446 (28,
115,236,366)
NOBODY KNOWS WHO I AM 8447 (409)
NOBODY KNOWS YOU WHEN YOU'RE DOWN AND OUT
728 (336)
NOBODY'S BUSINESS 8755 (252)
NOBODY'S BUT MINE 8448 (80)
NOC MAJOWĄ 1957 (295)
LES NOCES DU PAPILLON 5053 (82,383)
NOCH HINTER BERGES RANDE 2022 (49)
"Noch hinter Berges Rande steht braun der Abendschein"
2022 (49)
"Noch ist der Freiheit nicht verloren" 1203 (31)
"Noch ist der Glanz der Frühe nicht erschienen" 1936 (355)
NOCH IST DIE BLÜHENDE, GOLDENE ZEIT 209 (326,353)
"Noch ist die blühende goldene Zeit o du schöne Welt"
209 (31,326,327,353)
"Noch ruh'n die Felder schneebedeckt" 2941 (241)
"Noch schäumen die Becher, noch hallen die Lieder" 3214
(31)
NOCH SIND DIE TAGE DER ROSEN 209 (327)
"Una noche calma, Vidalita, te robe un beso" 4173 (322)
NOCHE DE CARNIVAL 2136 (142)
NOCHE DE PAZ, NOCHE DE AMOR! 1408 (244)
"Noche de paz, noche de amor! Todo duerme en derredor"
1408 (244)
"Noche divina, Sábado de Carnival" 2136 (142)
NOCHE EN VELA 8856 (55)
"Noche pre cursora de La Navidad" 9405 (244)
"La noche silenciosa, fuera del templo Diana" 4516 (73)
Les noches d'Olivette 102-103
NOCTURNE (Curran) 741 (364)
NOCTURNE (Franck) 1142 (190,192,194)
NOCTURNE (Mendelssohn-Bartholdy) 2393 (343)
NODAU 9087 (88)

NOËL ("From o'er the hills...") 9101 (79)
NOEL ("When it was midnight...") 9088 (86)
NOEL! A NEW NOEL! 9091 (361)
"Noel! A new Noel! Here together sing!" 9091 (361)
NÖEL ALSACIEN 9089 (154)
NOËL CHAMPENOIS 9043A (88)
NOËL DES BERGERS 9090 (127)
NOEL, NOEL (Carols, England) 8962 (296,410)
NOEL, NOEL, NOEL (Moorat) 2510 (334)
"'Noel, Noel, Noel', sang the church bell" 2510 (334)
"Noël, Noël, Now sing the Savior giv'n" 8900 (296)
NOËL NOUVELET 9091 (88,383)
"Noël nouvelet, Noël chantons ici" 9091 (88,383)
LA NOËL PASSÉE 9092 (47)
"La Noël passée, povret orphelin" 9092 (47)
NOËL PROVENCAL 9093 (231)
EL NOI DE LA MARE 8857 (55)
"Noi siamoi tre re, noi siamoi tre re" 9343 (155)
NOIE, NOIE, EST VENU 9094 (165)
"NON! CE N'EST PAS UN SACRIFICE" 1268 (362)
"Non dar più peneo caro" 3180 (308)
"NON È VER, CHE ASSISE IN TRONO" 110 (218)
NON FUGGIRAI 488 (180)
"Non fuggirai, no, no, sogno o vaneggio" 488 (180)
"Non ha ragione, ingrato" 3165 (218)
"NON LA SOSPIRI LA NOSTRA CASETTA" 2901 (143)
"Non la volete intendere" 3094 (217)
NON MI DIR 2569 (1,6)
"Non mi dir bell' idol mio" 2569 (1,6)
"Non mi dir di palesar" 2090 (217)
NON NOBIS DOMINE 495 (402)
"Non nobis Domine non nobis sed nomini" 495 (402)
"Non! non! non! j'aime mieux mon bateau" 4984 (383)
NON PIU ANDRAI 2586 (180)
"NON PIU ANDRAI, FARFALLONE AMOROSO" 2586 (5,
299,310)
NON PIÙ DI FIORI 2554 (2)
"Non più di fiori vaghe catene" 2554 (2)
"NON PIÙ FRA SASSI" 2854 (179)
NON PIÙ MESTA 3100 (2)
"Non più mesta accanto al fuoco" 3100 (2,300)
"NON POSSO DISPERAR" 2199 (168,368)
NON POSSO VIVERE 594 (179)
"Non posso vivere, non posso vivere senza il mio ben, no,
no" 594 (179)
"Non sarei si sventurata" 2810 (218)
NON SIATE RITROSI 2560 (4)
"Non siate ritrosi, occhietti vezzosi" 2560 (4)
NON SÒ PIÙ COSA SON 2587 (2)
"NON SÒ PIÙ COSA SON, COSA FACCIO" 2587 (2,301)
"NON SO SE SIA LA SPEME" 1484 (180)
"Non ti ricordi quel mese d'Aprile" 6113 (238)
Non vi piacque; arr. 1488
"NON VOGL'IO SE NON VEDERTI" 3187 (139)
NONE BUT A LOVER KNOWS 643 (36)
"None but a lover knows my lonely yearning" 643 (36)
NONE BUT THE LONELY HEART 643 (132,137,237,329)
"None but the lonely heart can know my anguish" 643
(329)
"None but the lonely heart can know my sadness" 643
(132,137)
"None but the lonely heart knows of my sorrow" 643 (237)
NONE CAN LOVE LIKE AN IRISHMAN 4705 (212)
NONE HE LOVES BUT ME 977 (221)
"None so rare, none so fair" 1089 (3)

460

"Noo in her green mantle blythe Nature arrays" 7125
(100, 102)
NOONDAY ON DE RIBBER 8449 (80)
"Noonday on de ribber, fishin' wid a hook an' line" 8449
(80)
Nora Creina (tune) 5954
Nora Kista (tune) 6041
"Norah, Norah, lemme come in" 8318 (266)
NORAH, THE PRIDE OF KILDARE 2746 (166, 213)
NORDEN 3465 (121)
Norma 254
"A North Country lass up to London did pass" 4712 (14,
235)
"A north-country maid up to London had stray'd" 4712
(349)
NORTH WIND WHISTLES 4386 (94)
"North wind whistles over woods and green wold" 4386 (94)
NORTHBOUN' 681 (78)
NOS GALAN 9408 (19, 349)
NOSSA SENHORA DAS DÔRES 6917 (57)
"Le nostre pene e sentirne pieta!" 2560 (4)
"Not a leaf stirs, all is tranquil" 3631 (112)
NOT A RUSH THIS LAD 5698 (164)
"Not a rush, not a rush, this lad, this lad is worth" 5698
(164)
NOT A SPARROW FALLETH 16 (394)
"Not a sparrow falleth, but its God doth know" 16 (394)
"NOT FOR US IS LOVE AND ROSES" 939 (159)
"NOT FULL TWELVE YEARS" 1099 (119)
"Not in slumber did the dream rise" 3623 (272)
"Not Jerusalem lowly Bethlehem" 9368 (109, 110)
"Not love alone, Nature, too, shares my heart" 2958 (146)
"Not love, nor obedience, nor honor" 3846 (4)
"Not love thee? Ah, ne'er believe it!" 2569 (1)
"Not my brother, but it's me" 8558A (409)
"Not my brother it's a me O Lord" 8558B (129, 130, 132)
"Not my brother (no) it's a-me, O Lord" 8558B (28, 279,
366)
"Not my brother, nor my sister" 8558A (76)
"Not now oh, not now for mushrooms do we go" 6778 (295)
NOT SO LONG AGO 2493 (131)
"Not so quickly, not so quickly" 3356 (112)
"Not that way, my pretty!" 5671 (95)
"Not the soft signs of a cooing dove" 309 (275)
NOT TO YOU MY KATE 6787 (159)
"Not to you my Kate will I be wed" 6787 (159)
"Nothing could be finer than to be in Carolina in the
morning" 853 (345)
"Nothing in the whole world can compare with Russia" 2885
(342)
NOTHING LIKE GROG 7851 (225)
NOTRE ALSACE ADORÉE 5054 (88)
"Notre Alsace adorée, risant et clair séjour" 5054 (88)
NOTRE ÂNE 5055A (127), 5055B (91)
"Notre âne, notre âne a grand mal à sa tête" 5055B (91)
"Notre âne, notre âne, avait grand mal aux pieds" 5055A
(127)
NOTRE BON DUC DE SAVOIE 5059 (91)
"Notre bon duc de Savoie n'est-il pas un bon enfant?" 5056
(91)
NOTTAMUN TOWN 7852 (312)
NOUS ALLONS MA MIE 9095 (361)
"NOUS ÉTIONS TROIS CAPITAINES" 5175 (187)
"NOUS N'IRONS PLUS AU BOIS" 5057 (82, 88, 91, 127, 383)
"Nous somm' venus vous voir" 4928 (91, 127)

"Nous venions de voir le taureau" 809 (93, 191, 193, 195,
208)
NOVA SCOTIA SONG 4243 (186)
NOVELS 8912 (361)
NOVGOROD'S BELLS 6966 (95)
"Novgorod's bells were ringing" 6966 (95)
"Novia del campo amapola, que estas abierta en el trigo"
6321 (248)
THE NOVICE 3278 (276)
"Now after all my hard trav'lin'" 8589 (336)
"Now all the day long on the prairies I ride" 7518 (120)
NOW AND THEN 5773 (285)
"Now beyond the Danube where the Cossack must be riding"
6949 (352)
"Now come all you young fellows that follow the sea" 9426
(72)
"Now didn't ol' Noah build de ark" 8625 (184)
"Now didn't ole Norah build himself an Ark?" 8563 (266)
"Now don't you believe that the Bible ain't true" 8461
(185)
"Now drear and empty dost thou stand" 3355 (273)
"Now farewell, dark days of weeping" 3100 (2)
"Now from the king comes a letter" 6288 (219)
"Now God Almighty down hath sent" 8963 (360, 361)
"NOW GOD BE WITH OLD SIMEON" 2362 (144)
"NOW HAS CHRISTMAS COME AGAIN" 9094 (165)
"Now has come the hour of sad parting" 2133 (233)
"Now here I am a gwine to sing" 8485B (321)
"Now, how I came to get this hat" 3672 (114, 131, 204)
"Now I go to Bethlehem, o'er the cradle hover" 9370 (314)
"Now I know October first will be my marching day, dear"
5725 (95)
"NOW I SEE THY LOOKS WERE FEIGNED" 1100 (118)
"Now I went down to Raleigh" 8596 (266)
"Now if you're white, you're all right" 454 (293, 336)
"Now in her green mantle blythe Nature arrays" 7125
(18)
NOW IN PARIS LIVES A MAIDEN 5158 (187)
"Now in Paris lives a maiden fairer far than day" 5158
(187)
"Now is it not a pity such a pretty girl as I" 7701 (212)
"NOW IS THE MONTH OF MAYING" 2529 (14, 235, 348,
349)
"Now is the time and my heart is afraid" 868 (292)
NOW IT IS CHRISTMAS TIME 9333 (337)
"Now it is Christmastime, vacation will start again" 9333
(337)
"Now, Jacob, get the cows home" 3738 (225)
"Now know ye, now know that the Lord is God" 1763 (90)
NOW LET ME FLY 8450 (35, 183, 184)
"Now let me sing of a secret power" 4843 (124)
"NOW LET US SING, I PRAY THEE" 9051 (361)
"Now listen here what I'se goin' to say" 8474 (185)
NOW MAKE WE MERTHE 8963 (360, 361)
"Now make we merthe all and some" 8963 (360, 361)
"NOW MAY WE SINGEN AS IT IS" 8964 (360, 361)
"Now, my lads, 'tis time to go" 839 (205)
NOW MY SOUL TO BETHLEHEM 2867 (361)
"Now my soul to Bethlehem let our willing way be" 2867
(361)
"Now nature cleads the flow'ry lea" 7090 (101)
"NOW NATURE HANGS HER MANTLE GREEN" 7128 (232)
"Now 'neath the silver moon ocean is glowing" 1303
(28, 35, 233, 236, 279, 343, 366)
"Now, now, soldier, won't you marry me? For o the fife
and drum" 8008C (34)

461

"NOW, O NOW, I NEEDS MUST PART" 908 (197)
"Now old Abe Lincoln, a great giant of a man was he"
    3044 (293)
"Now on the ground there was a tree" 8070B (249)
"Now our golden days are at an end" 2133 (28,279,343,
    366)
"NOW PEEP, BO-PEEP" 2821 (119,144)
"NOW PEEP, BOE PEEP" 2821 (119,144)
"NOW PEEP THEY AT EACH OTHER" 4009 (87)
"Now rest has come unto the weary" 3146 (318)
"NOW, ROBIN, LEND TO ME THY BOW" 4706 (349)
"Now rosy May comes in wi' flow'rs" 7032 (101)
"Now simmer blinks on flow'ry braes" 6999 (100,105)
NOW SING WE, NOW REJOICE 9159 (206)
"Now sing we, now rejoice, now raise to heaven our voice"
    9159 (206)
"Now singing we're bringing our praises before Him" 3790
    (34)
"NOW SLEEPS THE CRIMSON PETAL" 2935 (277)
"Now Spring will come and greet us" 5467 (37)
"Now stop right still Cocky doodle doodle do" 7401 (214)
NOW STRIKE THE HARP GENTLY 8681 (349)
"Now strike the harp gently, let music resound" 8681 (349)
NOW TELL US, GENTLE MARY 9049 (165)
"Now tell us, gentle Mary, what did Gabriel say to Thee?"
    9049 (165)
"NOW THANK WE ALL OUR GOD" (Crüger) 737 (28,366)
NOW THE DANCING SUNBEAMS PLAY 1571 (275)
"Now the dancing sunbeams play on the green and grassy
    sea" 1571 (275)
NOW THE DAY IS OVER 182 (28,132,233,236,279,343,
    366)
"Now the day is over, night is drawing nigh" 182 (28,132,
    233,236,279,343,366)
"Now the day is slowly ending" 1841 (287,288)
NOW THE MOON 1454 (199)
"Now the moon with silver glamour" 1454 (199)
"Now, the same old moon is shining" 3889 (128,131)
"Now the shadows darken, star on stars alight" 1155 (136)
"Now the shadows falling, stars are all alight" 1155 (209)
"Now the sun is shining brightly" 4689 (235)
"NOW THE WEATHER GROWS LESS WAYWARD" 1269 (199)
NOW, THERE ONCE WAS A YOUNG GIRL 5980 (321)
"Now, there once was a young girl diggin' potatoes in her
    father's garden" 5980 (321)
"Now they calls me Hangin' Johnnie" 9444 (401)
"Now thou hast sent the spring anew, arrayed in robes of
    lustrous hue" 3272 (357)
"Now 'twas twenty-five, or thirty years, since Jack first saw
    the light" 9453 (171,186)
NOW WE ARE MET 3960 (235)
"Now we are met let mirth abound" 3960 (235)
NOW WE MUST PART 5490 (95)
NOW WELL MAY WE MERTHIS MAKE 8965 (360,361)
"Now we'll play upon the drum" 9106 (216)
"Now what do you think about dyin' children" 8566 (409)
NOW WHAT IS LOVE 1821 (117,144)
"Now what is love I pray thee, Tell?" 1821 (117,144)
"Now who's the lad for a lass to wed" 2330 (205)
"NOW WINTER NIGHTS ENLARGE" 553 (144)
NOW WITH GLADNESS CAROL WE 9035 (361)
"Now with gladness carol we, with the voice of jubilee"
    9035 (361)
NOW YE SPRINGE IS COME 4707 (107)

"Now ye springe is come, turne to thy love, to thy love"
    4707 (107)
"Now, you get a line and I'll get a pole, honey" 7526A
    (216)
"Now you say good-bye I'm leaving" 745 (132)
"Now, you wake up in the mornin' you hear the ding-dong
    ring" 8426 (389)
"Now you wanna go to heaven, lemme tell you what to do"
    8480 (389)
NOWA MIŁOŚĆ 1951 (295)
"Nowel, nowel, nowel" 8966 (360,361)
"Nowel, Nowel, Nowel, Nowel, Who is this that singeth so"
    8987 (360,361)
"Nowel, Nowel, Nowel, This is salutation of the angel
    Gabriel" 8968 (360,361)
"Nowel, Nowel, Nowel. To us is born Our God Emmanuel"
    8969 (360)
"Nowel, nowel, To us is born" 8969 (360,361)
NOWEL, OUT OF YOUR SLEEP ARISE 8966 (360,361)
"NOWEL, SING WE BOTH ALL AND SOME" 8967 (360,
    361)
"NOWEL SING WE NOW ALL AND SOME" 8967 (360)
NOWEL, THIS IS THE SALUTATION 8968 (360,361)
NOWEL, TO US IS BORN 8969 (360,361)
NOWEL. TO US IS BORN OUR GOD EMANUEL 8969 (360)
"Nowell el el el, now is well" 8901 (334)
NOWELL, NOWELL 8968 (333)
"Nowell, Nowell, Lord, sing a Saviour's birth" (ref) 8900
    (334)
"Nowell, Nowell, now sing a Saviour's birth" 8900 (333,
    337)
"Nowell, Nowell, Nowell, Nowell" (NOWELL, NOWELL:
    TIDINGS TRUE) 8968 (379)
"Nowell, Nowell, Nowell, Nowell, sing all we may" 8912
    (319)
"Nowell, Nowell, Nowell, Nowell! this is the salutation of
    the Angel Gabriel" 8968 (333,334)
"Nowell, Nowell, Nowell, sing we with mirth!" (Ireland)
    1754 (334)
"Nowell, Nowell, O sing a Saviour's birth" 8900 (361)
NOWELL, NOWELL: TIDINGS TRUE 8968 (379)
NOWELL, SING ALL WE MAY 8912 (319)
Le nozze di Figaro 2584-2590
NU ÄR DET JUL IGEN 9333 (79,337,388)
"Nu är det Jul igen, och Nu är det Jul igen" 9333 (79,337,
    388)
NU FALLER NATT ÖFVER HAFVET 1008 (355)
"Nu glider Baaden mod Skaergaards-Ø-en" 1524 (355)
"NU LAAT ONS ALLEN VROLIJK ZIJN" 6542 (316)
"NU RINGER ALLE KLOKKER MOD SKY" 4008 (87)
NU SIJT WILLEKOME JESUS LIEVEN HEER 9263 (361)
Nu ska vi skörda linet i dag (tune) 7310
"NU TÄNDAS TUSEN JULELJUS" 1942 (188)
"NU TITTE TIL HINANDEN" 4009 (87)
"NU TREKT DEN BOER EEN PAAR KLOMPJES AAN" 6544
    (384)
"Nu vilja vi begynna en domaredans" 7302 (135)
"NU WIL IK EEN LIEDEKEN ZINGEN" 6543 (202)
NU ZIJT WELLEKOME 9263 (201,316)
"Nu zijt wellekome, Jesu lieve Heer" 9263 (316)
"Nu zijt wellekome, Jesu lieven Heer" 9263 (201)
"Nün minä neitonen sinulle laulan" 4843 (124)
"La nuit est froide et sombre" 2412 (292)
"La nuit s'approche et mon village s'en dort là-bas silen-
    cieux" 5096 (88)

"Oh a man there lives on the western plain" 7519 (129, 130)

"Oh, a newspaper man meets such interesting people" 2747 (293)

"Oh, a poor man came a-riding by" 9445B (214)

OH, A-ROCK-A MY SOUL 8466 (35)

"Oh, a-rock-a my soul, in de bosom of Abraham" 8466 (35)

"Oh a Shanty man's life is a wearisome life" 7983A (115)

"Oh a shantyman's life is a wearisome life" 7983A (109, 110)

"Oh, a short time ago boys, an Irishman named Doherty" 2074 (114, 166, 246)

O' A' THE AIRTS 7129 (105, 163, 365)

"O'a' the airts the wind can blaw" 7129 (105, 163, 365)

OH! A WAN CLOUD WAS DRAWN 5912 (166, 213)

"Oh! a wan cloud was drawn o'er the dim weeping dawn" 5912 (166, 213)

O ABSALOM 1895 (235, 349)

OH, ABSALOM, MY SON 1895 (173)

"O Absalom, my son, my son" 1895 (173, 235, 349)

"Oh, Adelita, I pray, do not leave me" 6319 (248)

O ADRO TEM QUATRO QUINAS 6889 (58)

"O, ain't I glad I've got out the wilderness" 8171 (409)

"Oh! ain't I glad, Oh! ain't I glad" 8327 (129)

"Oh ain't it a wonderful story" 7749 (392)

O AKADEMIA 1602 (31)

O ALENDROEIRO 6891 (58)

"O alendroeiro, Ond'es tá teu lendroala" 6891 (58)

"Oh all day long I'm lookin' for trees" 3496 (336)

"O, Alouette, gentille Alouette, Alouette, je t'y plumerai" 5141 (186, 187)

O ALTE BURSCHENHERRLICHKEIT 5497 (31, 43, 326, 353)

"O alte Burschenherrlichkeit! Wohin bist du entschwunden" 5497 (43, 326, 353)

"O alte Burschenherrlichkeit! wohin bist du verschwunden?" 5497 (31, 99)

O ANGENIETJE 6545 (384)

"O Angenietje, Mijn honighbietje" 6545 (384)

"O ANGENIETJE, MIJN HONINGBIETJE" 6545 (202)

OH ANSWER ME, MY DORA 7329 (135)

"Oh answer me, my Dora will this year find you wed?" 7329 (135)

O! ARE YE SLEEPIN', MAGGIE? 7130 (100)

O ARRANMORE, LOVED ARRANMORE 5863 (166, 213)

"O, Arranmore, lov'd Arranmore, how oft I dream of thee" 5863 (15, 166, 213)

O ASK ALL THE STARS 6380B (322)

"O ask all the stars if they have not seen me weeping throughout the night" 6380B (322)

O ASK OF THE STARS ABOVE YOU 6380A (142)

"O ask of the stars above you if these my tears did not flow all night" 6380A (142)

"O Babe Divine, now will I sing to Thee" 2796 (359)

"O banner bright with stars and stripes" 746 (343)

"O barber, spare those hairs" 3122 (225)

OH BAY OF DUBLIN! 5921 (349)

"Oh Bay of Dublin! my heart you're troublin'" 5921 (349)

"O beautiful eyes, I do not regret" 2775 (134)

"O beautiful for spacious skies" 3944 (10, 28, 129, 130, 233, 236, 279, 284, 343, 366)

OH BEAUTIFUL MONTH OF MAY 4091 (403)

"OH BEAUTIFUL NORTHLAND, MY MOUNTAINOUS HOME" 7303 (135)

O BEI LUMI 3876 (180)

"O bei lumi, o chiome d'oro" 3876 (180)

O BELLA, VORRESTI VENIRE 6121 (325)

"O belle Marguerite, Reine de mes amours" 4960 (91)

"O BELLISSIMI CAPELLI" 1028 (139)

O BETHLEHEM 8832 (39, 361)

"O BETHLEHEM, DU KLEINE STADT" 8971A (354)

"O Bethlehem! 'Tis not the rosebud's time to open" 8832 (39, 361)

"O Betsy B. was a lady fair that late came from Lancashire" 7438 (72)

"O, BID YOUR FAITHFUL ARIEL FLY" 2146 (276)

O BIENHEUREUSE NUIT 9096 (361)

O BIONDETTA LASCIVETTA 2784 (180)

"O biondetta lascievetta pastorella" 2784 (180)

"OH BIRDS THAT LEAVE EACH YEAR" 2591 (395)

¡OH, BLANCA VIRGEN! 6374 (247)

"¡Oh blanca virgen, a tu ventana asoma el rostro, ven a escuchar" 6374 (247)

"OH, BLESSED FATHERLAND" 1910 (124)

"O blessed Virgin, hear my prayer!" 3916 (1)

O BLESSED YULETIDE 9334 (244)

"O blessed Yuletide, light from the heavens" 9334 (244)

O, BLIJDE NACHT 9264 (384)

"O, blijde nacht! De Christus is geboren" 9264 (384)

"Oh blissful, wondrous, beautiful month of May" 4091 (403)

"Oh, blow the man down, bullies" 9426 (35, 109, 110, 234, 320)

"O blow ye winds westerly, westerly blow" 9430 (145)

"Oh, blow you winds, I long to hear you" 9425A (29)

"O Blütenschnee, sanft fällt du mir auf meines Gartenweges Sand!" 1851 (355)

"Oh, boss man, tell me, what have you done?" 8457 (109)

O BOTHWELL BANK 1060 (103, 104)

"O Bothwell bank, thou bloomest fair" 1060 (103, 104)

"Oh boy! I'm lucky! I'll say, I'm lucky!" 1622 (345)

"Oh, boys, Belle's a beauty" 1019 (28, 366)

OH! BOYS, CARRY ME 'LONG 1124 (129)

OH, BREATHE NOT HIS NAME 5981 (166, 213, 349)

"Oh! breathe not his name, let it sleep in the shade" 5981 (166, 213, 349)

"Oh, breth'ren, do get ready" 8092 (129)

"O bring my terug na die ou Transvaal" 7223 (239, 384)

"Oh bring to me my flute" 4931 (210)

"O brother, you ought t' have been there" 8514 (129, 130, 132)

"O brother you ought to been there" 8514 (233, 409)

"O brother, you'd better believe" 8504 (409)

"O brothers, don't stay away" 8586 (409)

"O brothers, I love Jesus" 8372 (129, 184, 409)

"O brothers let's go down, let's go down, let's go down" 8346 (409)

"O brothers, won't you help, yes, help me" 8356 (366)

"Oh, brothers, you ought t' have been there" 8514 (10, 28, 32, 34, 366)

"O brothers you ought to ha' been there" 8514 (76)

"Oh, brothers you oughter been there" 8514 (183)

"Oh, Buffalo gals, won't you come out tonight" 7478A (185)

"Oh, burry me beneath the willow" 7481 (129, 130, 132)

OH BURY ME NOT 7482F (236)

"O BURY ME NOT ON THE LONE PRAIRIE" 7482A (10, 120, 186, 399), 7482B (115, 227), 7482C (129, 130), 7482D (109, 110), 7482E (132, 279, 366), 7482F (236)

"Oh, by an' by, by an' by, I'm goin' to lay down dis heavy load" 8204 (52, 76)

"O bye and bye, bye and bye, I'm goin' to lay down my heavy load" 8204 (409)

O CAN YE SEW CUSHIONS 7131 (17, 46, 100, 103, 199, 235, 274)

"O can ye sew cushions and can ye sew sheets?" 7131 (17, 44, 46, 100, 103, 199, 235, 274, 402)

O CANADA 2054 (199, 279)

"O Canada! Our home and native land" 2054 (199, 279)

"O Canada! Terre de nos aïeux" 2054 (294)

"Oh, Cape Cod girls are very fine girls, heave away!" 9432 (110)

Oh cara mamma mia (tune) 5473

"Oh, carry me 'long, dere's no more trouble for me" 1124 (129)

O CESSATE 3188 (272)

"O, CESSATE DI PIAGARMI" 3188 (36, 138, 368)

"O cessate di piegarmi" 3188 (272)

O CHARLIE IS MY DARLING 7024 (132, 366)

"O! Charlie is my darling, my darling, my darling!" 7024 (17, 100, 102, 104, 163, 199, 234, 297, 349, 402)

"O charming bird, that swings so lightly upon the branches there" 772 (292)

O, CHE FELICE GIORNO 506 (181)

"O, che felice giorno! O, che lieto ritorno" 506 (181)

"O Christ Jesus! lovest us so dearly" 8812 (361)

"O CHRISTENHEIT, TU AUF DAS OHR" 8976B (354)

"Oh, Christians, Christians, what yer gwineter do" 8521 (184)

"Oh, Christmas come but once a year" 9391 (332)

"O Christmas, O Christmas, O happiest day!" 9285 (165)

O CHRISTMAS PINE 9175A (279, 366)

"O Christmas pine, O Christmas pine, forever true your color!" 9175A (279, 366)

O CHRISTMAS TREE 9175A (33, 79, 165, 206, 216, 251, 296, 315)

"O Christmas Tree, O Christmas Tree, forever true your color" 9175A (206)

"Oh Christmas tree, Oh Christmas tree, how ever green your branches" 9175A (216)

"O Christmas tree, O Christmas tree, how steadfast is thy foliage" 9175 (251)

"O Christmas tree, O Christmas tree, O tree of green, un-changing" 9175A (165)

"O Christmas tree, O Christmas tree! Thou tree most fair and lovely" 9175A (296)

"O Christmas tree! O Christmas tree! Thy leaves are so un-changing" 9175A (315)

"O Christmas tree, O Christmas tree, your brances green delight us!" 9175A (33)

"'O ciao, ciao, Maria Catlina, dumje'" 6100 (338)

O CIELI AZZURI 3820 (143)

"Oh, clear-running brook whose stream hurries by" 7238 (219)

"O Columbia, the gem of the ocean" 221 (28, 233, 236, 279, 366, 10, 129, 130)

"O come, all my young lovers, whomsoever wants to gao" 8079 (109, 110)

O COME, ALL YE FAITHFUL 2996

"O come, all ye faithful, joyful and triumphant" 2996

"Oh come along, boys, and listen to my tale" 7869F (120), 7869G (236)

"O COME, DELIGHTFUL SUMMER NIGHT" 412 (112)

"O come good friends, join our gay throngs" 6870 (295)

"Oh, come, let links eternal bind" 3861 (3)

O COME LITTLE CHILDREN 3339 (33, 79, 165, 251, 296, 388)

"O come, little children, from cot and from hall" 3339 (337)

"O come, little children, O come, one and all!" 3339 (33, 79, 165, 251, 296, 388)

O COME, O COME, EMMANUEL 9036 (33, 38, 39, 125, 337)

"O come, O come, Emmanuel, and ransom captive Israel" 9036 (33, 38, 39, 125, 337)

O COME, O COME, IMMANUEL 9036 (296)

"O come, O come, Immanuel, and ransom captive Israel" 9036 (296)

"Oh, come on, Elder, let's go roun' de wall, dat suits me" 8237 (182)

"Oh, come sit down close to me, my dear" 4232 (186)

"O COME, THE LORD'S ANNOINTED" 9097 (333)

O COME TO HIM! 1051 (400)

O COME TO ME 1328 (89)

"Oh, come to the church in the wildwood" 2830 (32, 34)

"O come to the garden, sweet Morvudd awhile" 8690 (20)

"O come to the window, come, ay, ay, ay" 2761 (322)

OH, COME TO US, SWEET VIRGIN SAINT 1850 (251)

"O come to your window, ay, ay, ay" 2761 (279)

"Oh!, come with me in my little canoe" 151 (110)

"Oh come with me when daylight sinks" 278 (279, 366)

"Oh! comrades fill no glass for me" 1110 (129, 132)

"Oh, cool night, transparent night" 1142 (190, 192, 194)

"Oh, Cordelia Brown What makes your head so red" 8718 (11)

"O could you have in deep Wisła" 2471 (295)

"O Cuba, precious island beneath sunny skies that are blue and serene" 3154 (322)

O CUCO 6902 (57)

"Oh Cudelia Brown, Wa meck yuh head so red?" 8718 (252)

"O curséd be the wars, love, that ever they began" 4635 (198)

"O Dame get up and bake your pies" 8919 (216)

O DANISH MAN 2661 (87)

"O Danish man! with all your might proclaim now your mother's praise" 2661 (87)

"O danke nicht für diese Lieder" 1164

"O Dantzig, halt dich feste" 5218 (31)

"O dass ich dir vom stillen Auge" 226 (210)

"O DASS ICH DOCH DER RÄUBER WÄRE" 2450 (256)

"Oh, de band o' Gideon, band o' Gideon, band o' Gideon over in Jordan" 8190 (183)

"O de blin' man stood on de road an' cried" 8199A (52)

"O de boatman dance, de boatman sing" 7460C (343)

"Oh, de boats on de ribber turn roun' an' roun'" 8174 (80)

"Oh, de boll weevil am a li'l black bug" 8188E (80, 115)

"Oh, de boll weevil am a little black bug" 8188B (109, 110, 335)

"O de bruine, de geurige, zonige hei" 3890 (384)

"Oh, de Lo'd says to Noah, 'It's gwine-a be a little floody'" 8224 (80)

"O de times is very hard" 8547B (409)

"OH! DE' VERD' ANNI MIEI" 3837 (298)

"Oh, de weathah it is balmy" 1805 (78, 184)

"O' de wurl' ain't flat an' de wurl' ain't roun'" 681 (78)

OH! DEAR JESUS 9208 (296)

"Oh, dear star, that glittered brightly" 2198 (295)
"OH, DEAR WHAT CAN THE MATTER BE" 4708 (36, 72,
    114, 128, 234, 279, 366)
"O DEARE, THAT I WITH THEE MIGHT LIVE" 554 (197)
"O dearest name Walter Maldè I love you" 3850 (292)
"OH DEAREST, TELL ME" 205 (253)
O DEATH 7856 (95, 109, 110)
"OH, DEATH IS LIKE THE COOLING NIGHT" 427 (359)
"OH, DEATH IS STILL AND COOL AS NIGHT" 427 (112)
"O death, O death rock me asleep" 66 (107)
"O DEATH PRAY COME AND SAVE ME" 2502 (404)
O DEATH ROCK ME ASLEEP 66 (107)
O DEL MIO DOLCE ARDOR 1276 (274, 368, 404)
"O del mio dolce ardor bramato oggetto" 1276 (274, 368,
    404)
OH! DEM GOLDEN SLIPPERS 333 (10, 32, 34, 129, 130, 184,
    225, 233, 366)
O DERRIÇO 6903 (58)
"Ô des amants deité tutélaire" 2350 (147)
"Oh, dey whupped him up de hill" 8233B (95, 109, 110, 227)
O DI TUA MAN 3880 (181)
"O di tua man mi svena" 3880 (181)
"Oh did you hear a songster's voice at night" 3457 (342)
"O did you hear tell of sweet Betsy from Pike" 8037A (279)
"OH, DID YOU NE'ER HEAR OF THE BLARNEY" 5982 (166,
    213)
"OH! DID YOU NOT HEAR OF KATE KEARNEY?" 5983
    (166, 213)
"O DIEU, S'IL FAUT QU'ON TE CRAIGNE" 5058 (82)
O'DINAH 7857 (243)
"O DINNA THINK, BONNIE LASSIE" 7132 (101)
OH, DIO DEL CIELO 6119 (238)
"Oh, dio del cielo, se fossi una rondinella vorrei volare,
    vorrei volare" 6119 (238)
"Oh! divina Santa Cruz Á vossa porta cheguei" 6922 (58)
O, DIVINE REDEEMER! 1330 (123, 394)
"Oh do my Johnny Boker, come rock and roll me over" 9454
    (320, 366)
"Oh, do not cross the hayfield" 963 (111)
O, DO NOT GRIEVE 2947 (357)
"O, do not grieve for me! For there where ends all sadness"
    2947 (357)
"OH, DO NOT LIGHT THAT LAMP" 71 (341)
"Oh, do you remember Sweet Betsy from Pike" 8037A (170)
"Oh, do you know the muffin man, the muffin man, the
    muffin man" 7826 (216)
O, DOLCISSIMA SPERANZA 3189 (179)
"O, dolcissima speranza, sei il ristoro" 3189 (179)
O DON FATALE 3830 (2, 300)
"O don fatale, o don crudel" 3830 (2, 300)
"Oh, don't you hear that mournful soun'" 8221 (184)
"Oh, don't you remember, sweet Alice, Ben Bolt" 1915
    (36, 114, 129, 130, 132, 173, 212, 279, 366)
"Oh, don't you remember Sweet Betsy from Pike" 8037A
    (80, 110, 185, 215, 331, 335)
"Oh don't you remember the shady old camp" 1915 (173)
"Ô doux printemps d'autrefois" 2308 (122, 329)
"O dreams of youth, so dear, so tender" 3915 (2)
O du Deutschland (tune) 5566
O DU FRÖHLICHE 9025 (326, 353, 412)
"O DU FRÖHLICHE, O DU SELIGE" 9025 (99, 326, 353,
    354, 412)
O DU HEILIGE 9025 (354)
"O du Heilige, Hochgebenedeiete!" 9025 (354)

O, DU HIMMELBLAUER SEE 2453 (255)
O DU LIEBER AUGUSTIN 5498 (42, 326, 353)
"O du lieber Augustin, Augustin, Augustin" 5498 (42,
    132, 326)
"O du lieber Augustin, 's Geld is hin, 's Madl is hin" 5498
    (353)
O, DU LIEBS ÄNGELI 7374 (156)
"O, du liebs Ängeli, Rosmarinstängeli, o du liebs Härzeli,
    tue du nit eso!" 7374 (156)
"O DU MEIN HOLDER ABENDSTERN" 3920 (4, 237, 240,
    364)
O DU SCHÖNER ROSENGARTEN 5499 (309)
"O du schöner Rosengarten, o du schöner Lorienstrauss"
    5499 (309)
"O du schöner Rosengarten, o du schöner Strauss" 5499
    (353)
O DU SCHÖNER WESTERWALD 5500 (326)
"O DU SCHÖNI SÜSSI NACHTIGALL" 4185 (41)
"Oh, Dubrovnik!' Oh Dubrovnik! wake" 8779 (86)
"Oh dulce castellana! cu yo per fil me muestra en luz
    arrebolado" 4517 (73)
O EGUBERRI GAUA 8831 (361)
"O Eitelkeit, du rechte Pest der Jugend" 804 (250)
"O, Elibanks and Elibraes, it was aince I saw ye" 7037
    (365)
"O Eliza, Li'l Liza Jane" 7779A (36, 279, 366, 402)
Ó én édes pintes üvegem" 5666 (26)
OH ENTER DEAR SHEPHERDS 9301 (154)
"Oh enter, enter, dear shepherds" 9301 (154)
"Oh Evening Star, my Evening Star" 3920 (132)
"O Evergreen, O Evergreen! how faithful are your branches"
    9175A (34)
"Oh, ev'ry morning at seven o'clock" 612 (115, 246)
"O, ev'ry time I feel de spirit" 8266 (183)
"O fairest village of Lihue" 5648 (279)
"Oh! faithless vows, never shall ye beguile me!" 2076
    (149)
"O fanciulla dagli occhi celesti perchè a tuti tu neghi
    amor?" 6085 (51)
"Oh, fare thee well, my own true love" 9466 (186)
"Oh fare you well, Old Joe Clark" 7874A (185)
"Oh farmer have you a daughter fair, parlay voo" 7665
    (7, 109, 110)
"Oh, fatal dower, oh cruel gift" 3830 (2)
"O FATHER, ALL CREATING!" 485 (50)
"O father, dear father, come down with the stamps" 4031
    (225)
"Oh, Father put the cow away" 2700 (131)
"O FATHER, SON, AND HOLY GHOST" 1903 (50)
OH, FATHERLAND 7304 (135)
"O festive night, 'tis the eve of Christmas" 9141 (165)
O FICKLE SHEPHERDESS 4902 (36)
"O fleeting shadow upon the meadow" 2412 (292)
"Oh, follow the stream to the clearin'" 7632 (381)
"O for the breath of the briny deep" 2270 (78)
OH FOR THE SWORDS 5984 (349)
"OH FOR THE SWORDS OF FORMER TIME!" 5984 (166,
    213, 349)
OH FOREST COOL 413 (330)
"Ô fortune ennemie! Eh quoi! toujours le Ciel" 1366 (1366)
"O fraîche nuit, nuit transparente" 1142 (190, 192, 194)
O FRED TELL THEM TO STOP 2345 (115)
OH, FREEDOM 8452A (227), 8452B (34, 182), 8452C
    (293)

"O freedom, O freedom, O freedom after awhile" 8452A
(227)
"Oh, freedom! Oh freedom! Oh freedom over me!" 8452B
(34,182), 8452C (293)
O FREUDE ÜBER FREUDE 9174 (49)
"O Freude über Freude ihr Nachbarn kommt und hört" 9174
(49)
"Oh, friendly stars" 1213 (253)
"O Friesche aard, recht edel land" 6546 (201)
"O FRIESLAND, ZOO VOL DEUGDEN" 6546 (201)
"Oh frog went a-courtin' and he did ride" 4604A (110)
"Oh, fy! fain wad I stay at home wi' thee, Molly!" 7100
(102,105)
"Oh, gay are we! Tra la la la, la la!" 5189 (187)
"O Genevieve, I'd give the world" 3774 (10,28,36,129,
130,233,236,366)
"O Genevieve, sweet Genevieve, the days may come, the
days may go" 3774 (10,28,36,129,130,233,236,
366)
"O gentle Shepherd, guide me home" 3647 (347)
"O get around, Jenny" 7729 (312)
"Oh, get right, an' stay right" 8273 (184)
"O GIJ, DIE JEZUS' WIJNGAARD PLANT" 9265 (384)
"O GIN I WERE A BARON'S HEIR" 1681 (100)
"O GIN MY LOVE WERE YON RED ROSE" 7134 (101,102,
105)
O gin ye were dead, Gudeman (tune) 7175A
"Oh, git on boa'd little child'n" 8289 (182)
"OH! GIVE ME A HOME BY THE SEA" 1710 (205)
"Oh, give me a home where the buffalo roam" 7671 (10,
28,35,37,70,115,120,129,130,132,227,233,236,
279,284,329,343,364,366)
"O give me your hand" 8277 (409)
"Oh, glory, glory! Hallelujah! When I lay my burden down"
8620 (182)
"O go and leave me if you want to" 7540 (81)
"O GOD, BENEATH THY GUIDING HAND" 1554 (28,236,
279,366)
"O God of Bethel, by Whose hand Thy people still are fed"
7036 (279,366)
O GOD OF LOVELINESS 5239 (382)
"O God of loveliness, O Lord of Heav'n above" 5239 (382)
"O GOD OUR HELP IN AGES PAST" (Croft) 732 (28,34,
233,366)
O GOLDNE AKADEMIA 2168 (31)
"O, gracious Lord, by whom the morning dawneth" 3464
(343)
OH, GRAVEYARD 8453 (182)
"Oh, graveyard, oh, graveyard, I'm walkin' through de
graveyard" 8453 (182)
"Oh, Great Day! Great Day! de righteous marchin'" 8295
(182)
"O, Guirrim, guirrim hoo" 5935 (172)
O GWIAZDECZKO 2198 (295)
"O GWIAZDECZKO COŚ BŁYSZCZAŁA" 2198 (159,295)
"O gwrandaw! y beraidd fwyalchen" 8674 (349)
"O gwrando! y beraidd fwyalchen" 8674 (19)
OH! HAD WE SOME BRIGHT LITTLE ISLE 5985 (166,213)
"Oh! had we some bright little isle of our own" 5985 (166,
213)
"O hall of song, I give thee greeting" 3919 (1)
"O hallelujah to the lamb!" 8435 (409)
"Oh, han' me down, han' me down" 8307 (184)
"O Hanukkah, O Hanukkah, come light the menorah!"
6187 (33,35)

"Oh, happiness departed, that can never return" 4884
(175)
O, HAPPY DAY! 1295 (385)
"Oh, happy is the farmer's life" 7585 (37)
"Oh, hark to the sound of the music and laughter that fills
the air" 2759 (237)
"Oh, hark to the story of Willie the Weeper" 8138A (80)
"Oh Harp of Erin! what glamour gay" 5964 (349)
OH, HASTEN, YE MAIDENS 616 (138)
"Oh, hasten ye maidens from beauty to flee!" 616 (138)
"O have you heard de lates', de lates' of de songs" 8188
(34,227)
"Oh have you heard de latest de lates' of the songs?" 8188A
(225)
"Oh have you heard the news, my Johnny?" 9470B (35)
"Oh have you heard the tidings? Limerick's aflame" 5924
(349)
"Oh, have you in your village seen him" 1289 (237)
"Oh, have you seen among the village lads" 1289 (348)
"Oh, he flies through the air with the greatest of ease"
2702 (115)
"Oh! he floats thro' the air with the greatest of ease" 2702
(130,131)
"Oh, he was a lord of high degree" 7768 (263)
OH HEAR THE HEAV'NLY ANGELS 8841 (154)
"Oh hear the heav'nly angels in soft and wondrous chorus"
8841 (154)
"O hearken and I will tell you hoo" 7111 (100)
"O Heav'n is so high and I am so low" 8590 (109,110,409)
"O HEER, DIE DAAR DES HEMELS TENTE SPREIDT" 6547
(201)
O HEER DIE DAER 6547 (86)
O HEILIG KIND 8804 (79)
"O HERDERS, LAAT UW BOKSKENS EN SCHAAPKENS"
9266 (384)
"O here are flow'rs and fruit" 1504 (362)
"O, he's a ranting, roving lad" 7203 (100,103,104,232)
"OH, HIGH ON PRESHOV'S TOWER" 4344 (94)
"O HINDS, TUNE UP YOUR PIPES" 9046 (361)
"O holy Infant, small and dear" 3468 (337)
"Oh, Holy Mother Virgin pure, Glorified by Thy son, sweet
Mary" 4130 (159)
O HOLY NIGHT 26
"O holy night, the stars are brightly shining" 26
"O holy Word of truth and wisdom" 1164 (90)
"Oh Hope, thou wilt not let the star" 229 (1)
"Oh hot corn nice hot corn!" 3417 (189)
"O how fair this world of Thine" 3277 (112)
"O, how fair thy beauteous world" 3277 (209)
OH HOW HE SCOLDED 6311 (95)
"Oh how he scolded, oh how he hit me!" 6311 (95)
"Oh! how I love him, if he but knew" 1058 (131)
OH, HOW JOYFULLY 9025 (296)
"Oh, how joyfully, Oh how merrily" 9025 (296)
OH HOW LOFTY 5733 (164)
"Oh how lofty, oh how lofty, lofty is this wayside inn"
5733 (164)
"O, HOW LOVELY IS THE EVENING" 5504 (28,34,37,
114,233,337,366)
"Oh, how lovely is the evening, is the evening, when the
Christmas bells are ringing" 5504 (206)
"O HOW LOVELY IS THE MAIDEN" 3389 (3)
"O HOW LOVELY IS THY WORLD" 3277 (160)
"Oh, how many members gone? Gone, gone" 8324 (182)
"O, I ain't gwine stay no longuh" 8186 (321)

"Oh, I am a bach'lor, I live by myself" 4601A (215)
"Oh, I am a joyful cowboy" 169 (37)
"Oh, I am a poor girl, my fortune's been bad" 8086 (72)
"Oh, I am a widow, the Countess of Laurel" 6300 (219)
"Oh! I am a yankee maid my lot O! tis happy and free" 8151 (189)
"Oh, I been workin' on de levee all de livelong day" 8370 (184)
"'O, I can't stay away'" 8348 (409)
"Oh, I choose John, Matarile" 6294 (219)
"O, I come from ole Virginny wid my head full ob knowledge" 7667 (189)
"O I don' wan' be buried in de stawm, O Lawdy" 8334 (227)
OH, I ENTREAT THEE, SIRE! 2905 (143)
"Oh, I entreat thee, Sire, O Sire, to hear me!" 2905 (143)
"Oh, I had a horse and his name was Bill" 7675 (321)
"Oh, I have got a ship in the North Country" 4617C (198)
"Oh, I have lost her" 3829 (3)
"Oh, I jes' come out before you, to sing a little song" 8574 (184)
"Oh, I just come out afore you" 8574 (212)
"Oh! I know he dreams of loved ones" 1593 (205)
"O I know the Lord, I know the Lord" 8341 (409)
"Oh I lived with my daddy" 5087B (47)
OH, I LOVE A MAIDEN 6820 (159)
"Oh, I love a maiden, my heart's with grief laden" 6820 (159)
"Oh I love the gleaming starlight" 1787 (291)
"Oh, I once loved a boy and a bonny bonny boy" 4698 (198)
"O, I PRAY YOU, DO NOT WOUND ME" 3188 (36)
"Oh, I recall those peaceful, golden hours" 1863 (295)
"Oh! I said it's gay and pretty too" 447 (199)
"OH I SHOULD LIKE TO MARRY" 729 (189)
"O! I think of the days, when but a little child" 1595 (189)
"OH, I WANT TWO WINGS" 8454 (184)
"Oh, I was bo'n in Mobile town" 8370 (28,35,366)
"Oh, I went down South for to see my Sal" 7928 (115,129, 130,132,225,236,279,366,402)
"Oh! I will take you back again" 3999 (128,129,130,131, 132,343)
"Oh! I will take you back, Kathleen" 3999 (10,36,329)
"Oh, I wonder I never got married" 7876A (111)
"Oh, I wrote my love a letter, and I sealed it with a weafer" 7762 (72)
"Oh, if you want a raise in pay" 4090 (293)
O IHR HERREN 3388 (141,330)
"O ihr Herren, o ihr werten, grossen, reichen Herren all'" 3388 (141,330)
"Oh, I'll be ready, I'll be ready" 8351 (184)
O I'M A GOOD OLD REBEL 7858
"O I'm a good old Rebel, now that's just what I am" 7858 (161)
"Oh, I'm a-gwinter sing all de way" 8299 (351)
"Oh, I'm a Texas cowboy" 8051 (120)
"Oh, I'm from Lou'siana as you all know" 8378 (185)
"O image angel like and fair!" 2597 (3)
"Oh, in mah dyin' hour, ah don' want nobody to moan" 8376A (80)
"Oh, in my father's garden" 4888 (34)
OH! INFANT JESUS 9209 (296)
"Oh! Infant Jesus, Thee I love" 9209 (296)
OH! IRISHMEN! NEVER FORGET 5986 (213)
"Oh Irishmen! Never forget! 'tis a foreigner's farm your own little isle" 5986 (213)

"Oh! I'se from Lucianna as you all know" 8378 (212)
O ISIS UND OSIRIS 2601 (5,240,390)
"O Isis and Osiris, favor this noble pair with wisdom's light!" 2601 (5)
"O Isis and Osiris, guide them, send down thy spirit on the pair" 2601 (240)
"O Isis und Osiris, schenket der Weisheit Geist dem neuen Paar!" 2601 (5,240,390)
"Oh, it ain't gonna rain, it ain't gonna snow" 7399B (185)
"OH, IT IS A JOY" 936 (287,288)
"O IT'S GOIN'TO BE A MIGHTY DAY" 8455 (409)
"Oh, it's good-bye, Liza Jane" 7779D (145,214)
"Oh, it's love, oh, love, oh careless love" 7490A (399)
"Oh! Jacob, get the cows home" 3738 (28,279,366)
"O JESU, JOY OF LOVING HEARTS" 5203 (50)
O Jesulein süss 130
O JESULEIN ZART 130 (412)
"O Jesulein zart, dein Kripplein ist hart" 130 (412)
"O Jesus darling of my heart" 9179 (244,296)
O JESUS SOETE AENDACHTICHEIT 9267 (361)
"O JESUS, TRUE AND FERVANT FRIEND" 9267 (361)
"O JESUS, ZOETE AANDACHTIGHEID" 9267 (384)
"Oh, Jimmy, farewell! Your brother fell way down in Alabarmy" 4106 (189)
"Oh, Johnnie's gone, what shall I do? Away to Hilo" 9456 (320)
"Oh Johnny dear I long to hear you" 9425A (109,110)
"Oh, Joseph took Mary up on his right knee" 8911J (186)
"O, Joseph was an old man" 8911C (393)
"O joucat sus lo ribieiro escoundut dins les vernhats" 5046 (88)
O JOUR AFFREUX! 2960 (411)
"O jour affreux! Le ciel met le comble à nos maux! 2960 (411)
OH, JOY UPON THE EARTH 1682 (293)
"Oh, joy upon this earth to live and see the day" 1682 (293)
O JOYFUL SHEPHERDS 9203 (361)
"O joyful shepherds, make haste, with footsteps flying" 9203 (361)
O JUDGES 7651 (243)
"O judges, O judges, just hold your ropes a little little while" 7651B (243)
O JUGENDZEIT 3215 (31)
"O Jugendzeit, wie ist mir bang" 3215 (31)
O JUL MED DIN GLAEDE 9285 (165)
"Oh jump into the sleigh boys" 3416 (189)
OH, KATKA, TELL ME 4337 (94)
"Oh, Katka, tell me, uphill or down" 4337 (94)
"O ken Karanga, Karanga, Karanga day" 8735 (286)
"O KENMURE'S ON AND AWA', WILLIE" 7133 (102,105)
"O KERSTNACHT, SCHOONER DAN DE DAGEN" 9268 (201,384)
"Oh, kind folks, listen to my song" 4050 (44,110)
"O KOMME, HOLDE SOMMERNACHT" 412 (112)
O KÜHLER WALD 413 (330)
"O kühler Wald, wo rauschest du" 413 (330)
"'O la corbleu, la morbleu, Marion" 6133 (338)
"Oh! la vieille, la vieille, la vieille" 5102 (91)
O LAMB, BEAUTIFUL LAMB 8456 (409)
"O Lamb, beautiful Lamb! I'm going to serve God till I die" 8456 (409)
O LAMB OF GOD 315 (346,400)
"O Lamb of God, Thou that takest away our sin" 315 (346, 400)

"O land of my fathers, O land of my love" 1767 (347)

"Oh, land of my fathers, the land of the free" 1767 (234, 294)

"O, láske moře bezdné, lze k tvému dospět dnu?" 2675 (74)

"O lasst, o lasst mich sterben!" 2502 (167)

"O Lawd, I want two wings to hide my face" 8601 (331)

"Oh Lawd! Not a mite not a bite" 8739 (252)

"Oh, Lawd! Oh, mah Lawd! Oh, mah good Lawd! Keep me f'om sinkin' down" 8386 (351)

"O, LAY THY LOOF IN MINE, LASS" 7135 (101, 232)

"O leave your sheep, your lambs that follow after" 9112 (307, 319, 363)

O LEAVE YOUR SHEEP 9112 (307, 363)

"O LÉGÈRE HIRONDELLE" 1326 (292)

"Oh lemon blossom so fair, you have the secret of healing" 6349 (9)

OH! LEMUEL! GO DOWN TO DE COTTON FIELD 1125 (129)

"Oh! Lemuel, my lark," 1125 (129)

O LET ME GROAN 2069 (278)

"O let me groan one word into thine ear" 2069 (278)

"Oh! let sweet sleep my child enfold" 1290 (237)

"Oh, let the Midnight Special shine her light on me" 2426 (389)

O lieb', so Land du lieben kannst 2153

"O, Liebe, Meer ohn' Ende, wer fasste deinen Raum?" 2675 (74)

O LIEBLICHE WANGEN 414 (220, 364)

"O liebliche Wangen, ihr macht mir Verlangen" 414 (220, 364)

"O light of all my being" 870 (292)

"Oh, li'l Liza, li'l Liza Jane" 7779A (185)

Ó LIMÃO 6909 (57)

"Ó limão verde limão" 6909 (57)

"Oh! Limehouse kid, Oh! Oh! Oh! Limehouse kid" 395 (345)

"O, liquor will cause you to murder" 7756 (381)

O LISBONA, ALFIN TI MIRO 861 (298)

"Oh! list, Oh! list, maids that are coy" 572 (150)

"Oh list to the horn that sounds in the morn" 4562 (343)

"O, list to the lay of a poor Irish harper" 5873A (172), 5873B (133)

"O list to the story that never grows old" 22 (315)

O LISTEN, PRETTY DORA 7329 (188)

"O listen, pretty Dora! Wilt thou marry me this year?" 7329 (188)

"O, little did I think He was so nigh" 8229 (409)

O LITTLE ONE 130 (39, 271)

"O Little One sweet, O Little One mild" 130 (39, 271)

"O LITTLE TOWN OF BETHLEHEM" (Carols, England) 8971A (305, 307, 317, 319, 354, 410), 8971B (369)

"O LITTLE TOWN OF BETHLEHEM" (Davies) 776 (307, 376)

"O LITTLE TOWN OF BETHLEHEM" (Noble) 2667 (271)

"O LITTLE TOWN OF BETHLEHEM" (Redner) 2999

OH LITTLE WIZARD, TELL ME 7308 (135)

"Oh little wizard tell me: How long yet must I wait" 7308 (135)

"Oh, Liza, po' gal" 7779B (171)

"Oh Lizer! Sweet Lizer!" 666 (128, 204)

"O, Logie o' Buchan, O Logie the Laird" 7098 (100, 103)

O LOLA 2297 (132)

O LOLA BIANCA 2294 (3)

"O Lola, bianca come fior di spino" 2297 (3)

"O Lola, with thy cheeks rosier than cherries" 2297 (132)

"O Lola, with thy lips like crimson berries" 2297 (3)

"Oh, longtime mo'ner, won't you come out de wilderness" 8393 (182)

O LORD 8457 (109)

O LORD ABOVE 6547 (86)

"O Lord above, who has spread Heaven's blue" 6547 (86)

O LORD, BE MERCIFUL 199 (123)

"Oh Lord, didn't you deliver Daniel from the Lion's den?" 92 (114, 131, 246)

"O Lord, 'gainst Thee alone, Thee only sinning" 227 (8)

O LORD, HAVE MERCY 3602 (368)

"O Lord, have mercy, I call upon Thee" 3602 (368)

"O Lord, I wonder, bye and bye" 9402 (332)

O LORD I'M HUNGRY 8458 (409)

"O Lord I'm hungry I want to be fed" 8458 (409)

"O Lord, I've done what you told me to do" 8371 (409)

"Oh, Lord, Liza poo' gal" 7779B (225)

O LORD, MOST HOLY 1141 (8, 346, 407)

"O Lord, most holy, O Lord, most mighty" 1141 (8, 346, 407)

"O Lord, O my Lord, O my good Lord, keep me from sinking down" 8386 (129, 409)

O LORD OF MERCY 1141 (394)

"O Lord of mercy, O Lord of justice" 1141 (394)

O LORD ON HIGH 2601 (123)

"O Lord on high, we pray Thee to guide us" 2601 (123)

O LORD, OUR GOD 2601 (160)

"O Lord, our God, we seek Thy guidance" 2601 (160)

"O Lord, please lend me now Thine ear" 7525 (80)

"O Lord! Shout for joy!" 8536 (409)

"O Lord, they prophesy against Thee" 2392 (160)

"O Lou'siana girls, won't you come out tonight" 7478D (37)

"O love is teasin' and love is pleasin'" 7802 (312)

"O love, of thy might let me borrow" 3139 (2)

"Oh love, oh love, oh careless love" 7490A (185)

O LOVE THAT CASTS OUT FEAR" 121 (50)

"Oh! Love, what would'st thou with me" 2202 (148)

O LOVE WILL VENTURE IN 7136 (100, 105)

"O love will venture in, where it daurna weel be seen" 7136 (100, 105)

"O lovely dove, you are so beautiful" 6377 (279)

"O LOVELY INFANT, BORN FOR ME" 9041 (361)

"Oh lovely muse, how oft in hours of sadness" 3254 (385)

O LOVELY NIGHT 2688 (122)

"Oh, lovely spring long ago" 2308 (348)

O LOVELY VOICES 8963 (334)

"O LOVELY VOICES OF THE SKY" 8983 (244, 334)

"O LUCE DI QUEST' ANIMA" 870 (6, 292)

"O luce di quest' anima" 870 (6, 292)

"Oh, Lukey's boat is painted green" 4240 (186)

O, LULA! 8459 (227)

"O Lula, O Lord, gal, I want to see you so bad" 8459 (227)

O LUSTY MAY 2363 (144)

"O lusty May with Flora Queen" 2363 (144)

Ô MA BELLE REBELLE 1329 (278)

"Ô ma belle rebelle, Las! que tu m'es cruelle" 1329 (278)

"O MA TANT DOUCE COLOMBELLE" 2496 (175)

"Ô MA TENDRE MUSETTE" 2495 (88, 383)

"O, MADAM, I HAVE COME A-COURTIN'" 7859 (393)

O MÄDCHEN, MEIN MÄDCHEN 2091 (254)

"O Mädchen, mein Mädchen, wie lieb ich dich!" 2091 (254)

"Oh, Magdalina, my Magdalina" 2664 (295)

"O MAGNIFY THE LORD" 1257 (71)

"Oh! Mais on ne voit plus guèrre" 4995 (91)

"O make-a me ho-holy" 8460 (409)

O MAKE ME HOLY 8460 (409)

"Oh! malevolent Fortune! Alas! relentless Fate" 1366 (147)

"Oh! Manias we've had many" 3998 (189)

OH MARIE 578 (128,132)

"Oh Marie, oh Marie, take my heart for it's yours can't you see" 578 (128,132)

O MARIOLIN 6120 (325)

"O Mariolin, la mama te dimanda, la mama me dimanda" 6120 (325)

O MARIOLINA 6120 (325)

"OH, MARY AND THE BABY, SWEET LAMB" 9395 (332)

"O Mary, at thy window be, it is the wish'd, the trysted hour" 7105 (100,102)

"O Mary dear, that you were here" 4016 (277)

O MARY, DON'T YOU WEEP 8461 (28,185,293,366)

"Oh, Mary don't you weep, don't you moan" 8461 (185)

"OH MARY, DON'T YOU WEEP, DON'T YOU MOURN" 8461 (28,184,236,293,366,409)

"O Mary, O Martha, O Mary ring dem bells" 8512 (409)

"Oh Mary Virgin Mother" 2272 (71)

"O MARY, WELL OF PURITY" 9240 (361)

"O Mary what you goin' to name that pretty little baby?" 9388A (244,409)

O MARY, WHERE IS YOUR BABY? 9396 (332)

O MATKO MOJA 2487 (295)

"O matko moja, matko rodzona" 2487 (295)

"Oh maybe it was yesterday, or fifty years ago!" 3552 (344)

O ME! O MY! 7860 (28,366)

"O me! O my! we'll get there by and by" 7860 (28,366)

"Oh, meet me, Jesus, meet me Lord" 8454 (184)

"O mein Theseus! O geliebter Theseus!" 2502 (167)

"Oh, members, rise, oh, rise, an' don't you be ashame'" 8249 (182)

"O MEN FROM THE FIELDS" 1730 (344)

"Oh merry young maiden, come and merrily dance" 6988 (199)

"Oh! Methus'lah was a witness" 8502 (37)

"O meu amor me diexou por outra mais bonitinha" 6900 (58)

"Ó MEU AMORZINHO" 6914 (57)

"O meu amorzinho Eu venho d'arada c'o chapeu" 6914 (57)

"O MEU MENINO E D'OIRO" 6915 (57)

O MIEI GIORNI FUGACI 2774 (180)

"O miei giorni fugaci, o breve vita" 2774 (180)

O MIO BABBINO CARO 2894 (143)

"O mio babino caro, mi piace, e bello bello" 2894 (143)

O, MIO CORE (Cavalli) 621 (181)

"O mio core! Ardi tu?" 621 (181)

O MIO FERNANDO 864 (2,300)

"O mio Fernando! della terra il trono" 864 (2,300)

"Oh, Missie Mouse, I come to see" 4604E (72)

"Oh, Missis McGrath! the sergeant said, 'Would you like to make a soldier out of your son, Ted'" 5966 (172)

"Oh, Mister Rooster, your mother's calling" 6655 (86)

"O Mister we sing-a-ling-a-ling with all our hearts to you" 7998 (343)

O MISTRESS MINE (Byrd) 496 (13,75,215,235)

O MISTRESS MINE (Quilter) 2936 (272)

"O mistress mine, where are you roaming" (Byrd) 496 (13,75,215,235)

"O mistress mine, where are you roaming?" (Quilter) 2936 (272)

"Oh, Mistress, mine, where are you roaming?" (Walthew) 3939 (344)

OH, MISTRESS SHADY 7681 (28,366)

"Oh, Mistress Shady, she is a lady" 7861 (28,366)

"O mode infâme de tant de femmes en ce jour" 952 (269)

O MÓJ ROZMARYNIE 6797 (295)

"O MÓJ ROZMARYNIE ROZWIJAJ SIĘ" 6797 (159,295)

OH, MONAH 8462 (185)

"Oh, mo'ner mo'ner, ain't you tired o' mo'nen?" 8494B (182)

"O money is the meat in the cocoanut" 7823 (321)

"Ô mort! ô mort, affreuse mort! quelle est ta barbarie?" 927 (278)

"O MORTAL MAN, REMEMBER WELL" 8972 (307)

O MOTHER 2487 (295)

"O mother, dear, Jerusalem, Jehovah's throne on high" 4725 (271)

O MOTHER DON'T YOU WEEP 8463 (409)

"O mother Glasco where's yo' lamb?" 8416 (409)

O MOUNT AND GO 7137 (100)

"O mount and go, mount and make ye ready" 7137 (100)

"Oh, Mount Elbrus you are tall!" 2416 (342)

"O mourner, mourner, ain't you tired a mourning" 8494A (409)

"O mourner! O mourner, O mourner look at the people at the bar of God" 8184 (409)

"Oh, mouse in the buttermilk, skip to my Lou" 8005 (212)

"Oh music come and light my heart's dark places" 3254 (199)

"O mutter du ich liebe dich" 1393 (229)

"Oh, my baby is lak' a little black star" 8432 (266)

OH! MY BELOVED DADDY 2894 (143)

"Oh! my beloved daddy, I love him, I love him" 2894 (143)

OH, MY BONNY HIGHLAND LADDIE 7138 (294)

O MY CLARISSA 2072 (107)

"O my Clarissa thou cruell fair" 2072 (107)

OH, MY DARLING CLEMENTINE 2509 (10,128,131,233,236,246,366)

"Oh my darling, well you know me" 3637 (122)

"Oh, my dear old Augustin, Augustin, Augustin" 5498 (70)

O, MY DEIR HERT (Howells) 1720 (274)

"O my deir hert, young Jesus sweit" (Heseltine) 1641 (307)

"O, my deir hert, young Jesus sweit" (Howells) 1720 (274)

"O my dove, dear, I am yearning" 4266 (279)

"Oh, my father has a fine ship a-sailin' on the sea" 4617D (260,263)

"Oh, my father was the keeper of the Eddystone Light" 4664 (111)

"O my Fernando! Earth's enchantments of pleasure" 864 (2)

"Oh, my golden slippers am laid away" 333 (10,32,34,129,130,184,225,233,366)

"O my good Lord, show me the way" 8537 (409)

"Oh, my good Lord's done been here!" 8431 (409)

"Oh, my heart is in bloom" 408 (359)

"Oh, my heart is sad and lonely, where is now the one I love?" 7437 (242)

"Oh, my horses ain't hungry, they won't eat your hay" 7719 (267)

"O, my island! O, my Isle!" 7072 (102,103,104,105)

O MY LASS, O MY LASS 6704 (159)

"O my lass, O my lass, I am in deep despair" 6704 (159)

O MY LITTLE SOUL 8464 (409)

"O my little soul's goin' to shine, shine" 8464 (409)

O MY LOVE 4709A (235, 349), 4709B (36)

"O, MY LOVE IS LIKE A RED, RED ROSE" 7121A (101, 102, 105, 163, 402)

"O my love like the lilac is fresh and green" 408 (112)

"O, my love, lov'st thou me?" 4709A (235, 349), 4709B (36)

"Oh, my lover is a fisherman" 3646 (137)

"O, my luve is like a red, red rose" 7121A (36)

"O my luve's like the red, red rose" 7121B (365)

"Oh, my name it is Jack Hall, chimney sweep, chimney sweep" 4655 (198)

"Oh, my name it is Sam Hall" 7976 (399)

"Oh! My name was Robert Kidd, as I sailed, as I sailed" 7489A (34, 109, 110)

"Oh, my name was William Kidd, as I sailed, as I sailed" 7489C (173)

"O my Nannie! my dear little Nannie!" 6993 (101, 105)

"Oh, my poor Nelly Gray, they have taken you away" 1515 (10, 28, 32, 34, 109, 110, 129, 130, 132, 184, 233, 236, 279, 366)

OH, MY SON! 4298 (86, 324)

"Oh my son, my son, home so soon?" 4298 (324)

"O my son, still be wary!" 3845 (5)

"O, my soul's been anchored in the Lord" 8438A (409)

OH! MY SWEET LITTLE ROSE 6006B (166, 213)

"Oh! my sweet little rose, cease to pine for the past" 6006A (95), 6006B (166, 213)

OH! MY SWETYNGE! 3151 (344)

"Oh! My swetynge! My lyttell prety swetynge" 3151 (344)

"Oh my true native-land, Oh my dear Moravia" 4382 (324)

O NACHT, JALOERSE NACHT! 6548 (384)

"O nacht, jalourse nacht, die tot mijn leet gesworen" 6548 (384)

"Oh, Nancy O, my Nancy O" 8113B (72)

"O NANCY'S HAIR IS YELLOW LIKE GOWD" 7139 (102)

"Oh! Nanny, wilt thou go with me" 3150 (344)

"Oh, native land, how fair you seem" 1388 (28, 366)

OH! NE T'ÉVEILLE PAS 1290 (3, 122, 237, 329)

"Oh! ne t'éveille pas encore" 1290 (3, 122, 237, 329)

O NEDERLAND, LET OP UW ZAAK 6549 (201)

"O Nederland, let op uw zaak, de tijd en stond is daar" 6549 (201)

O NEL FUGGENTE NUVOLO 3822 (292)

"Oh! nel fuggente nuvolo. Non sei tu padre impresso?" 3822 (292)

"Oh, never say that you have reached the very end" 6279 (318)

"O never you mind what Satan say" 8285 (409)

"Oh, New York town is no place for me!" 9473 (401)

"OH! NIGHT AMONG THE THOUSANDS" 9210 (296)

"Oh night divine! come you all to carnival" 2136 (142)

"O NIGHT, RESTFUL AND DEEP" 9096 (361)

O NIGHTINGALE 4965 (406)

"O nightingale awake! And ev'ry songster sing with thee" 9184 (79)

"O nightingale, pray sing that I may hear thy voice" 4965 (406)

"Oh, no harm, no harm, no harm" 8494B (182)

O NO, JOHN 4710 (28, 136, 279, 366)

"O NO LONGER SEEK TO PAIN ME" 3188 (368)

"O NOACH, GOEDE OUDE HEER" 6550 (384)

"O, nobody knows a who I am" 8447 (409)

"Oh, nobody knows the trouble I've seen" 8446 (28, 279, 366)

OH, NOT A CENT 8756 (286)

"Oh, not a cent, not a cent" 8756 (286)

"Oh!, often hae I dress'd my Queen" 7157 (100, 103, 104)

"Oh, oh, lily white, pink carnation, poppy bright" 5828 (92)

"Oh, oh, oh! Run to the ford with the load" 1960 (162)

"O ole Zip Coon he is a larned skoler" 7893 (109, 110)

"Oh, ole Zip Coon he is a learned scholar" 7893 (225)

"Oh, once I courted a pretty little girl way down in Waterloo" 8006 (81)

"Oh, once I knew a pretty girl when pretty girls were but few" 8006 (81)

"O, once I was a waterman and lived at home at ease" 5992 (172)

"Oh, once I was happy, but now I'm forlorn" 2702 (34)

"O once upon a time in Arkansas" 7414 (35)

"Oh, once when lovely spring was young" 651 (277)

OH! OPEN THE DOOR 7140 (100, 105)

"Oh, open the door, some pity to shew" 7140 (100, 105)

"O, our hut is tiny, Father hugs my mother" 6683 (295)

"Oh, our Poland shall not perish" 6746 (295)

OH! PADDY DEAR 6030 (166, 213)

"Oh Paddy dear! an' did ye hear the news that's goin' round?" 6030 (34, 294)

"Oh Paddy dear, and did you hear the news that's going round?" 6030 (7, 15, 28, 37, 172, 233, 279, 366)

"O PANIE, KTÓRYŚ JEST NA NIEBIE" 1963 (159)

"Oh, paper is white, and ink is black or blue" 6241 (318)

"O Paradies das mir zum Ruhme werde" 2408 (391)

"O PARADIS SORTI DE L'ONDE" 2408 (3)

"O Paradise aris'n from ocean" 2408 (3)

"O Paradiso in terra scenso" 2408 (391)

OH PATRIA MIA 3820 (1)

"O patria mia mai più" 3820 (1, 143)

"O patria, o cara patria" 3870 (299)

O pescator dell' onde 2782

"OH, PETER GO RING DEM BELLS" 8465 (28)

"O PETER, GO RING-A DEM BELLS" 8465 (76, 183)

O PIÃO 4206 (219)

"Oh, picket line Priscilla, picket line Priscilla, had a line" 2 (293)

"'O Pierrot, the friendly, by the moon's fair light'" 4885 (210)

"O Pinchossel, dear Pinchossel, O come to me, your loving girl" 6242 (230)

"O pine tree lonely standing" 3144 (45)

"O, Polly, pretty Polly, oh yonder she stands" 7938C (81), 7938E (81)

"Oh! poor Max, there's no use talking" 3978 (189)

"Oh, poor old Reuben Ranzo, Ranzo, boys, Ranzo!" 9472 (29, 320)

O POOR SHEPHERD LAD 5739 (92)

"O poor shepherd lad without a penny" 5739 (92)

"O poor sinner, O now is your time" 8495 (409)

"Oh pore Liza, pore gal" 7779C (80)

"Oh! potatoes they grow small over there!" 5902 (34)

"O praise ye the Lord, praise ye Him!" 3276 (160)

"Oh, pray, have you heard of my Bouchaleen Bawn?" 5881 (133)

"Oh, prayer is de key, bretheren" 8497 (182)

"Oh press this purple flow'r close to thy tender heart" 3941 (387)

"Oh, press thy cheek against mine own" 1775 (137)

"O press your cheek upon my own" 1775 (36)

O PRIMAVERA 3067 (180)
"O Primavera, gioventù dell' anno" 3067 (180)
OH PROMISE ME 808 (32,34)
"Oh promise me that some day you and I" 808 (32,34)
O PUBLISH THE GLAD STORY 9049 (388)
"O publish the glad story nostri salvatoris" 9049 (388)
O PUIRTITH CAULD 7141 (101)
"O puirtith cauld, an' restless love" 7141 (101)
"O pull up your footstool, my fair and sweet one" 6326 (86)
"O quali mi risvegliano Dolcissimi concenti" 390 (329,
     394)
OH! QUAND JE DORS 2154 (190,193,195,211)
"Oh, quand je dors, viens auprés de ma couche" 2154
     (190,193,195,211)
OH! QUE CALMA 6918 (57)
"Oh! que calma vai caindo" 6918 (57)
"O radiant sun I give you greeting!" 3034 (176)
O, RATTLIN', ROARIN' WILLIE 7142 (101)
"O, rattlin', roarin' Willie, O he held to the fair" 7142
     (101)
OH REALM OF LIGHT 1576 (28)
"Oh realm of light! whose morning star" 1576 (28)
"O religion is a fortune, I really do believe" 8503 (182,
     409)
"Oh! remember the poor when your fortune is sure" 6003
     (349)
"O rendetemi la speme" 255 (292)
"O REST IN THE LORD" 2375 (28,122,123,200,346,394)
"Oh, Restitution, Restitution, it's a great doctrine like the
     Constitution" 1678 (76)
O RESTORE TO ME 2886 (139)
"O restore to me shades forbearing" 2886 (139)
"O return again beloved" 255 (292)
"Oh! return, oh! return, sweet loves, oh! return!" 2211
     (150)
OH, RETURN TO ME, MY DARLING 937 (287,288)
"Oh, ride on, Jesus! Ride on, Jesus!" 8505 (182)
"O ridente suol! Vago e bel giardin!" 2408 (391)
"Oh, Rig-a jig-jig and away we go" 7478A (214)
"O rise and come away (Neighbor run!)" 9109 (361)
"O 'rise! shine! for thy light is a-comin'" 8507 (409)
"O Robin is my only jo" 7085 (101)
"O Robin, Robin Redbreast, O Robin, Robin dear" 1986 (28)
OH, ROCK-A MY SOUL 8466 (184)
"Oh, rock-a my soul, in de bosom of Abraham" 8466 (184)
"O, ROCKS DON'T FALL ON ME" 8467 (183,409)
"Oh, roll de cotton, roll it down" 9474 (37)
"Oh! Rowan tree, oh! Rowan tree!" 7161 (100,104,163,
     349)
"O RU-RU-RU, MY LITTLE JESU" 9224 (165)
"O SACRED HEART OF JESUS" 3813 (382)
"Oh sad, so sad! Sad is my fate, indeed!" 6691 (295)
"O säume länger nicht, geliebte Seele" 2584 (311)
"O Sally Brown I love your daughter" 9479 (320)
"Oh Sally Brown's a Creole lady" 9479 (29)
O SALUTARIS HOSTIA 1679 (304)
"O salutaris hostia, Quae caeli pandis ostium" 1679 (304)
O SANCTISSIMA 9025 (35,79,337,354)
"O sanctissima, O piissima" 9025 (35,79,337,354)
"Oh, Santa Anna won the day" 9480A (235), 9480B (320)
"O Santy Anna gained the day" 9480A (35)
"Oh, Santy Anna won the day" 9480A (29)
O SAVIOUR HEAR ME! 1275 (123)
"O Saviour hear me, I implore thee" 1275 (123)
O SAVIOR SWEET 130 (160)

"O Savior sweet, O Savior kind" 130 (160)
O SAW YE BONNIE LESLEY? 7143 (18,101)
"O saw ye bonnie Lesley as she ga'ed o'er the border?"
     7143 (18)
"O saw ye bonnie Lesley as she gaed owre the border?"
     7143 (101)
"Oh, say, can you see, by the dawn's early light" 8021
     (7,10,28,32,34,35,44,129,130,233,236,279,293,
     294,343,366)
"Oh, say can you see, through the gloom and the storm"
     325 (161)
"Oh, say, darling, say, when I'm far away" 1623 (28,
     129,130,131,132,233,366)
"Oh say, little dogies, quit your rovin' around" 7844C
     (80)
"Oh say, little dogies, why don't you slow down?" 7844B
     (120)
"O say, were you ever in Rio Grande" 9473 (29,35,109,
     110,234,335)
O SCHIPMANN 5501 (41)
"O Schipmann, o Schipmann, o Schipmann du" 5501 (41)
"O schitt'rende kleuren van Nederlands vlag" 6597 (384)
"O Schmetterling, sprich, was fliehest du mich?" 3391
     (141)
O SCHÖNE ZEIT 1295 (385)
O SCHÖNE ZEIT, O SELGE ZEIT 1295 (326)
O SCHWARZWALD, O HEIMAT 17 (31)
"O Schwarzwald, o Heimat, wie bist du so schön!" 17
     (31)
OH, SE SAPESTE 2893 (143)
"Oh, se sapeste come il vivere è allegro!" 2893 (143)
"Oh! se una volta sola rivederlo io potessi" 258 (302)
"O see, how dazzling is the glory of the risen sun!" 7392
     (37)
"O Selig, wer liebt!" 3345 (308)
"O send Lewie Gordon hame" 7095 (101)
O SENHOR DO MEIO 6926 (57)
"O senhor do meio cuida que e alguem" 6926 (57)
"O Shannadore, I love your daughter" 9481 (321)
OH! SHE IS NOT LIKE THE ROSE 6016 (166,213)
"Oh! she is not like the rose, that proud in beauty grows"
     6016 (166,213)
O SHENANDOAH 9481 (37)
"O, Shenandoah, I long to hear you" 9481 (35,37,109,
     110,199,223,235,335)
"Oh, Shenandoah! I love your daughter" 9481 (129,279,
     366,401)
"Oh, Shenandoah's my native valley" 9481 (29)
"O shepherdess fickle, your charms I defy" 4902 (36)
O SHEPHERDS SING TOGETHER 9197 (361)
"O shepherds sing together, Sing! O beloved brothers"
     9197 (361)
OH, SHE'S GONE, GONE, GONE 7862 (214)
"Oh, shipmates, come gather and join in my ditty" 9436A
     (145), 9436B (72)
"O sia quest' aura o sia vostro soave canto" 1192 (217)
"O SIADAJ, SIADAJ, KOCHANIE MOJE" 6798 (159)
O, SIGNOR, CHI SARÀ 2264 (181)
"O, Signor, chi sarà mai, chi sarà mai" 2264 (181)
"Oh, sing a song of de city" 8370 (184)
OH SING OF THE LOVE OF JOHN 4933 (36)
"Oh sing, oh sing of the love of Jeanne" 4933 (36)
"Oh! sing the praise of love" 2075 (152)
"O sinner man where are you going" 8540 (230)
"O sinner, sinner, you better pray" 8240 (409)

"Oh the harvest moon is shining on the field of new-mown hay" 6391A (9)

"Oh, the hinges are of leather and the windows have no glass" 7788A (173), 7788B (129), 7788C (186)

"Oh, the little orphan boy, while the tear stood in his eye" 779 (131)

OH! THE MOMENT WAS SAD 5988 (166,213)

"Oh! the moment was sad when my love and I parted" 5988 (166,213)

"Oh, the monkeys have no tails in Zamboanga" 8164 (225)

"Oh, the moon shines tonight on the river" 7550 (225)

"Oh! the night that I struck New York" 1224 (131)

O THE NOBLE DUKE OF YORK 4704 (402)

"O the noble Duke of York, he had five thousand men" 4704 (402)

"Oh, the noble Duke of York, he had ten thousand men" 4704 (214)

"Oh, the nurse pinched the baby" 7853 (321)

O THE OAK AND THE ASH 4712 (235,349)

"Oh, the ol' ark's a-moverin'" 8472A (77)

"O, the old ark's a-movering" 8472A (409)

"Oh, the Old Gray Mare, she ain't what she used to be" 7872 (129,130,131,132,185,233)

"Oh, the praties they are small, over here, over here" 5902 (172)

"Oh, the praties they grow small over here, over here" 5902 (111,173)

"Oh! the pretty, pretty creature!" 3596 (405)

"O the religion that my Lord gave me, Shines like a mornin' star" 8504 (409)

"Oh, the Rio Grande is flowing" 5957 (129,130)

"Oh, the road to home" 3648 (136)

"O, the Rock Island line is a mighty good line" 8510 (216)

"O the rocks and the mountains shall all flee away" 8513 (409)

O the shearin's no for you (tune) 7084

"Oh the sky is growing dark!" 4892 (86)

"Oh, the smartest clipper you can find" 9434 (335)

"Oh, the smartest packet you can find" 9434 (235,320)

"Oh, the times are hard and the wages low" 9458B (366)

"Oh, the toe bone connected to the foot bone" 8260B (216)

"O! the turnpike gate, 'tis the pride of my heart" 1595 (189)

"Oh, the wind blew up an' the wind blew down" 8569 (77)

"O the yelping of hounds, the skelping" 8676 (349)

"Oh, then, Limerick is beautiful as ev'rybody knows" 5957 (172)

"Oh, there was an old soldier and he had a wooden leg" 7893 (110)

"Oh, there was once a little ship" 4994 (187)

"Oh, there's fire in the fore-top, there's fire in the main" 9442D (320)

"Oh, there's Glasgow and Berwick and Penterville" 4177 (86)

"Oh, there's lots of fish in Bonavist' Harbour" 4239 (186)

"Oh they call me Hanging Johnny" 9444 (235,320)

"O, this is a sin-tryin' world" 8590 (109,110)

"O, this is a sin-trying world" 8590 (409)

"Oh, this is de healin' water" 8591 (182)

O THIS IS NO MY AIN LASSIE 7144 (18,100,105)

"O this is no my ain lassie, fair tho' the lassie be" 7144 (18,100,105)

"Oh, this is the place where the fishermen gather" 3173 (186)

"Oh, this kerchief of my brother" 6688 (295)

"O this ol' time religion" 8592 (409)

O THOU BELOV'D 1276 (368)

"O thou belov'd whom long my heart desireth" 1276 (368)

O THOU JOYFUL DAY 9025 (33,35,79,337)

"O thou joyful day, O thou blessed day" 9025 (33,35,79, 337)

"Oh, thou sublime bright evening star" 3920 (364)

"O THOU SUBLIME SWEET EVENING STAR" 3920 (237, 240,329)

OH! 'TIS SWEET TO THINK 5989 (166,213,297)

"Oh! 'tis sweet to think that where e'er we rove" 5989 (166,213,297)

OH, 'TIS THE MELODY 216 (210)

"Oh, 'tis the melody we heard in former years" 216 (210)

OH! TO KISS YOUR LIPS 4276 (322)

"Oh! to kiss your lips alluring" 4276 (322)

O TOI, CHER AUGUSTIN 5498 (88)

"O toi, doux ange, à mes pensers si cher" 1382 (237, 329)

"O toi, mon cher Augustin, tout mon bien, il est tien" 5498 (88)

"Oh! tranquil night, why haste away so soon?" 378 (152)

O TRISTE DI! 2960 (411)

"O triste di! Nel mal or c'immerge il destin" 2960 (411)

"Oh, true believer, oh, looka day" 9385 (332)

"O TRUE LOVE IS A BONNIE FLOWER" 7145 (105)

"O! TU BELL' ASTRO INCANTATOR" 3920 (237,240,298)

"OH, TU CHE IN SENO AGLI ANGELI" 3842 (3)

"O TU, PALERMO, TERRA ADORATA" 3870 (299)

"O Tübingen, du teure Stadt" 3474 (31)

"O turn, turn around, merry wooden steeds" 787 (362)

"O 'twas in the broad Atlantic in an equinoctial gale" 9467B (402)

"Oh, up yonder way Cinch Mountain" 8088 (263)

O VÄRMELAND 7296 (188)

"O Värmeland, O homeland, O fair, happy land" 7296 (95)

"O Värmeland, of Sweden's fair counties the crown" 7296 (188)

OH, VAERMELAND, THE FAIREST 7296 (135)

"Oh, Vaermeland, the fairest, the grandest of all" 7296 (135)

"Oh Vermeland, all praise to the wonderful land" 7296 (279,366)

"Oh! Videira dám' um cacho" 6895 (58)

"O VIN, DISSIPE LA TRISTESSE" 3727 (4)

O VOUS DONT LES TENDRES ANS 9098 (361)

"O wär' ich schon mit dir vereint und dürfte Mann dich nennen!" 230 (311)

"O wäre ich erkoren" 3819 (391)

"Oh, wake her, oh, shake her; Oh, shake that girl with the blue dress on" 9455B (214)

"Oh wake her, Oh shake her, Oh wake dat girl wid de blue dress on" 9445A (234,320)

"Oh! wake not yet from out thy dream" 1290 (3,122)

"O Wales as I leave you the light fades away" 8656 (349)

"O walk together children don't you get weary" 8209 (409)

"Oh, walk together chillun, don' you get weary" 8209 (351)

O WALY, WALY ("O waly, waly, up the bank...") 7146 (100,103)

O WALY, WALY ("The water is wide...") 4714 (48)

"O waly, waly, up the bank, and waly, waly doun the brae" 7146 (100,103)

"OH! WASN'T DAT A WIDE RIBBER" 8468 (129)

"OH, WASN'T THAT A WIDE RIVER" 8468 (28,76, 366)

OH, WATCH THE STARS 7863 (332)

"Oh, watch the stars, see how they run" 7863 (332)

"O water, voice of my heart" 530 (259)

"O we be three poor mariners" 9488 (297)

"Oh, we come on the sloop John B." 7735 (321)

"Oh, we had an old hen and she had a wooden leg" 7893 (109,110)

"Oh, we sailed to Virginia, and thence to Fayal" 4533 (234)

"O weel may the boatie row" 7003 (100,103,104,349)

OH! WEEP FOR THE HOUR 5990 (166,213)

"Oh! weep for the hour when to Eveleen's bow'r the Lord of the valley with false vows came" 5990 (166,213)

"O weint Ach und Weh! Ja weinet! O weint Ach und Weh!" 585 (168)

"Oh, we'll roll back the prices" 7855 (321)

"Oh, well, the Rock Island Line, it is a mighty good road" 8510 (389)

"Oh, we'll wait till Jesus comes" 8254 (28,366)

"Oh we're off Cape Horn with the main sky-sail set" 9424 (320)

"Oh, we're three jolly, jolly, sailor boys" 2293 (28,205)

"Oh, were you ever in Mobile Bay" 9474 (29)

"O were you ever in Rio Grande?" 9473 (37,320)

"O WERT THOU IN THE CAULD BLAST" (Folksongs, Scotland) 7147 (101,105,232,365)

"OH, WERT THOU IN THE CAULD BLAST" (Mendelssohn-Bartholdy) 2388 (28,366)

"OH, WERT THOU IN THE CAULD BLAST" (Shostakovich) 3461 (342)

"O WHA'S AT THE WINDOW" 3523 (101)

"O what a lovely day!" 772 (292)

"OH, WHAT A PAL WAS 'WHOOZIS'" 471 (236)

"O what a parrot! such frivolity!" 6358 (279)

"Oh what is lovelier than this day of sunlight" 579 (279, 366)

"Oh, what is that I see yonder coming" 8081 (293)

"Oh what praises, oh what praises, oh what praises filled the air" 2431 (339)

"Oh, what shall we have for dinner, Mistress Bond?" 4695 (249)

"O what thanks can I render" 3754 (71)

OH, WHAT TIMES 4429 (94)

"Oh, what times are these we live in" 4429 (94)

"Oh what was your name in the States?" 8108 (34,173)

OH WHAT WONDER 6176 (30)

"Oh what wonder, Oh what pleasure! Perfect nights are such a treasure" 6176 (30)

"Oh! what's so fine" 579 (122)

"O, when I come to die" 8276 (76)

"Oh, when I lived in Tennessee" 8516 (184)

OH, WHEN I SLUMBER 2154 (190,193,195)

"Oh, when I slumber, come close to my couch" 2154 (190,193,195)

"Oh, when I was a little boy I lived by myself" 8036B (216)

"Oh, when I was a young horse, all in my youthful prime" 4734 (198)

OH, WHEN I WAS SINGLE 8113A (111)

"Oh, when I was single, oh then, oh then" 8113A (111)

"Oh, when in silent night once more before me" 2943 (237)

O WHEN, O WHEN 4168 (35)

"O when shall I see Jesus" 7468 (212)

"Oh where, and oh where is your Highland laddie gone?" 7000 (17,28,35,366)

"Oh, where are you bound, my pretty fair maid?" 7964 (72)

"Oh, where are you going, my pretty little maid?" 7835 (72)

"Oh, where are you going? 'To Scarb'ro Fair'" 4747A (35)

"O where have you been, Billy boy, Billy boy" 4549B (28,72,114,132,249,279,331,366)

"Oh, where have you been, Jimmy Randal, my son" 4684C (260,263)

"Oh, where have you been, Lord Randal, my son?" 4684B (185)

"Oh, where have you been this livelong day" 7192 (95)

"O where is my boy tonight?" 2197 (34,114,131)

"Oh! where is my lover, tell me I pray?" 1645 (189)

"Oh, where is Pretty Polly? Oh, yonder way she stands" 7938D (264)

"Oh where, oh where is my little dog gone" 7560 (128, 132)

"Oh where, oh where ish mine little dog gone" 7560 (225)

"Oh, where, tell me where, is your Highland laddie gone?" 7000 (100,104,234,349)

OH, WHERE WERE YOU 4361 (94)

"Oh, where were you, Oh, where were you all last night" 4361 (94)

"Oh, whirling around and twirling around" 4206 (219)

"O whiskey is the life of man" 9492B (320)

"O, whistle an' I'll come t' ye, my lad!" 7201 (365)

"O WHISTLE AN' I'LL COME TO YOU, MY LAD" 7201 (101,104)

"Oh, whistle, daughter, whistle, and you shall have a sheep" 8123 (267)

"OH, WHITHER ART ROAMING" 631 (139)

"O whither now, so tired yet swiftly flying" 3427 (322)

O, WHO ARE THEY 9099 (377)

"Oh, who are they, so pure and bright" 9099 (377)

"Oh who is fair as she is fair" 4621 (297)

"O who is like my Johnnie, so leish, so blythe, so bonnie?" 7195 (36)

"O who sits so sadly, and heaves the fond sigh?" 5897 (406)

"Oh! who will shoe your pretty little feet?" 7864C (242)

"O, who will shoe your pretty little foot" 7864B (36)

"Oh, who will shuck my corn" 7773 (381)

"OH, WHO WOULD BE A SHEPHERD BOY" 8973 (361)

"OH, WHO'S GOIN' TO SHOE YOUR PRETTY LITTLE FOOT?" 7864A (262)

"Oh, why don't I work like other men do?" 7649 (35)

"Oh, why don't you work like other men do?" 7649 (109, 110,335)

"OH! WHY LEFT I MY HAME?" 2237 (100,349)

"Oh, why, should any heart be filled with sadness" 820 (128,132)

"OH! WHY SHOULD THE SPIRIT OF MORTAL BE PROUD" 2755 (212)

"Oh why the tears! Pretty cry baby, cry baby, dry your tears lose your sorrow" 6363 (9)

O WIE ÄNGSTLICH 2574 (3)

"O wie ängstlich, o wie feurig" 2574 (3)

OL' TEXAS 7865 (34)

"Olas que el norte arrastra so bre el inmenso mar" 4515 (73)

OLD ABE LINCOLN 7872 (34,44,109,110)

"OLD ABE LINCOLN CAME OUT OF THE WILDERNESS" 7872 (34,109,110,321)

"Old Abe Lincoln, he came out of the wilderness" 7872 (44)

OLD ADAM 7866 (216)

THE OLD ARK A-MOVERIN' ALONG 8472B (28,279,366)

THE OLD ARK'S A MOVERING 8472A (409)

THE OLD ARM CHAIR 3125 (130)

OLD BETTY LARKIN 7867 (312)

OLD BLACK JOE 1127 (28,129,130,132,233,236,279,366)

"The old black monk stood still to hear" 8691 (349)

OLD BLUE 7868A (173), 7868B (169), 7868C (227)

THE OLD CABIN HOME 8473 (184)

THE OLD CHESTNUT TREE 8677 (20)

"The old chestnut tree, which stands on the lea" 8677 (20)

THE OLD CHISHOLM TRAIL 7869A (34,185,227), 7869B (331), 7869C (115), 7869D (227), 7869E (279, 366), 7869G (236)

OLD CHRISTMAS 9371 (332)

OLD COLONY TIMES 7870 (34,185)

OLD CORONATION 1680 (35)

OLD DAN TUCKER 1002

OLD DELSBO WEDDING MARCH 7300 (188)

AN OLD DERRY AIR 5940 (397)

OLD DOG TRAY 1128 (28,129,278,366)

OLD FOLKS AT HOME 1129

OLD GRANDMA 4244 (186)

"Old grandma when the West was new" 4244 (186)

THE 'OLD GRANITE STATE' 7871 (189)

THE OLD GRAY MARE 7872 (129,130,131,132,185,233)

THE OLD GREY GOOSE 7416 (249)

OLD GREYBEARD 7873A (242)

OLD GRUMBLER 7878B (44)

"Old Grumbler swore by the shirt he wore" 7878B (44)

The Old Head of Denis (tune) 5963

The Old Head of Dennis (tune) 5963

The Old Highland laddie (tune) 7005 (365)

OLD HUNDRED 379 (173)

OLD HUNDREDTH 379 (32,34,35)

OLD IRONSIDES 2040 (129,130)

OLD JOE CLARK 7874A (185,227), 7874B (225)

"Old Joe Clark, the preacher's son, preached all over the plain" 7874A (227)

OLD JOE CLARKE 7874A (109,110)

"Old Joe Digger, Sam and Dave" 7643A (227)

OLD JOHN BRADDLEUM 4715 (249)

OLD KING COLE 4716A (44), 4716B (199,234) 4716C (312), 4716D (402)

"Old King Cole was a jolly old soul, and this you may know by his larnin'" 4716C (312)

"Old King Cole was a merry old soul, and a merry old soul was he" 4716A (44), 4716B (199,234), 4716D (402)

OLD KING CROW 8474 (185)

THE OLD LORD BY THE NORTHERN SEA 4718C (260,264)

OLD MACDONALD 7875 (249)

"OLD MACDONALD HAD A FARM" 7875 (28,233,236, 249,366)

THE OLD MAID 7876A (111)

THE OLD MAID SONG ("I wonder I never got married") 7876A (126)

THE OLD MAID'S LAMENT 7877 (72)

THE OLD MAID'S SONG ("I had a sister, Sally...") 4717 (215)

THE OLD MAN 7873B (186)

THE OLD MAN IN THE NORTH COUNTRY 4718A (198)

THE OLD MAN IN THE WOOD 7878A (214)

THE OLD MAN IN THE WOODS 7878A (313)

"Old man Sam Jones he runs and owns a cafe on easy street" 1796 (204)

"Old man Sargent, sittin' at the desk" 8631 (336)

THE OLD MANOR 2673 (159)

"Old Meg she was a gipsy and lived upon the moors" 2429 (199)

THE OLD MINER'S REFRAIN 7879 (115)

"The old Mizzoo, she's a mighty river" 9481 (173)

OLD MOBY DICK 1758 (171)

"Old Nicholas our shepherd (A crazed and simple wight)" 9085 (361)

"Old Noah built himself an ark" 8478 (28,225,279,366)

"Old Noah once he built an ark" 8478 (402)

"Old Noah once he built the Ark" 8478 (35,249)

OLD NORWAY 6645 (279,366)

THE OLD OAKEN BUCKET 1891 (28,32,34,129,130,132, 233,279,366)

OLD PAINT ("Good-by, old Paint...") 7628A (227)

OLD PAINT ("I ride an old paint...") 7695 (169,227)

OLD POLSKA 4858 (124)

"Old Rattler, Rattler, there's a prisoner gone" 7880 (389)

"An old refrain is always haunting me" 1971 (132,236)

THE OLD RIDDLE 6169 (231)

OLD RILEY 7880 (389)

"Old Riley crossed the water" 7880 (389)

OLD RIVER WISŁA 2678 (295)

"The old rocking chair is baby's boat" 1729 (241)

OLD ROGER IS DEAD 7881A (216), 7881B (313)

"Old Roger is dead and gone to his grave" 7881A (216)

"Old Roger is dead and he lies in his grave" 7881B (313)

OLD ROSIN THE BEAU 7882 (173)

"Old Satan's mad and I am glad" 8349 (409)

THE OLD SETTLER'S SONG 7882 (227)

OLD SHIP OF ZION 7883A (32,34)

THE OLD SHOEMAKER 7884 (242)

OLD SISTER PHOEBE 7748B (212)

"Old Sister Phoebe, how happy were we" 7748B (212)

OLD SMOKY 7885A (227), 7885D (243), 7885E (393)

THE OLD SOAP-GOURD 7886 (313)

THE OLD SOLDIERS OF THE KING 7887 (44)

OLD SONG 2513 (358)

"Old songs! New songs! Ev'ry king of song" 1135 (189)

THE OLD SPOTTED COW 4810B (72)

OLD STORMY 9468 (331)

"Old Stormy he is dead and gone" 9468 (235,320,331)

"Old Stormy's dead and gone to rest" 9468 (29)

THE OLD TIMER'S SONG 4229 (186)

OLD TYLER 7888 (312)

"Old Tyler was a good old dog, we thought he'd treed a coon" 7888 (312)

OLD UNCLE NED 1130 (129)

OLD VIRGINNY 7889A (312)

THE OLD WHITE MARE 7890 (185)

AN OLD WOMAN 6819 (159)

The old woman (tune) 6011B

OLD WOMAN ALL SKIN AND BONE 7891 (109,110)

THE OLD WOMAN AND THE PEDLAR 4719A (249)

"On December twenty-five, sing foom, foom, foom!" 8852 (337)

ON DISAIT BIEN 4962 (66)

"On disait bien, que tu animais les filles" 4962 (66)

"L'on dit, que la plus belle c'est toi, c'est toi" 7368 (155)

"On dit que le plus fier c'est moi" 1761 (208)

ON ENTEND PARTOUT 9101 (82)

"On entend partout carillon sur le mont Judée" 9101 (82)

"On ev'ry front and border" 846 (288)

ON FRIDAY EVENING 5787 (164)

"On Friday evening, or Sabbat maybe, when it gets dark I go to my baby" 5787 (164)

ON GEORGIAN HILLS 3038 (340)

"On Georgian hills nocturnal mist has cast its veil" 3038 (340)

"ON GOOD FRIDAY RAVEN GIVES HIS YOUNG ONE A BATH" 5771 (164)

"On her, my treasure, all joy dependeth" 2564 (3)

"On hill and woodland is falling" 1156 (210)

ON ILKLEY MOOR BAHT 'AT 4722 (402)

"On Jordan's stormy banks I stand" 7940 (32, 34, 109, 110, 115)

"On love! On love! Ay, for my heart in his bondage is aching" 1337 (3)

ON MEESH-E-GAN 7895 (109, 110)

"On mules we find two legs behind" 1301 (28, 366)

ON MUSIC 6037 (166, 213, 349)

"On my farm, on my farm I have a pullet" 4261 (207)

ON MY HEAD 5673 (92)

"On my head my new hat so neat" 5673 (92)

"On ne s'avise jamais de tout 2496 (175)

"On one summer's day" 576 (114, 131)

"On Pohjolan hangissa meill' isänmaa" 4849 (124)

"On Richmond Hill there lives a lass" 1692 (14, 234, 349, 402)

ON, ROLL ON 5160 (214)

"On, roll on, my ball, roll on" 5160 (214)

ON SATURDAY, T'WARDS EVENING 4473 (87)

"On Saturday, t'wards evening I was awaiting thee" 4473 (87)

ON SPRINGFIELD MOUNTAIN 7896A (173, 243), 7896B (242)

"On Springfield Mountain, there did dwell" 7896A (34, 80, 109, 110, 173, 243), 7896B (242), 7896C (227)

"On sultry days by river front" 439 (240)

ON THAT CHRISTMAS DAY MORN 436 (307)

"On that Christmas Day morn, when a new world was born" 436 (307)

"On that great getting up morning" 8296B (44)

"ON THE ARCTIC OCEAN" 2882 (342)

"ON THE BANKS OF ALLAN WATER" 7153 (18, 402)

ON THE BANKS OF SWEET LOCH RAE 7897 (126)

"ON THE BANKS OF THAT LONELY RIVER" 7898 (81)

ON THE BANKS OF THE OHIO ("Come all you brisk young fellows") 7991E (331)

ON THE BANKS OF THE OHIO ("I asked my love...") 7899 (243)

"On the banks of the river, near by the village" 6200 (318)

ON THE BATTLE FIELD 6685 (295)

ON THE BEACH AT FONTANA 3433 (85)

ON THE CORNER 9139 (337)

"On the corner, get together" 9139 (337)

"On the deck of Lynch's boat here I sit in woeful plight" 5890 (349)

"ON THE FIRST DAY OF CHRISTMAS" 8998A (33, 35, 215, 249, 268, 337), 8998B (378), 8998D (410)

ON THE FIRST THANKSGIVING DAY 7900 (129, 130)

"On the first Thanksgiving day Pilgrims went to church to pray" 7900 (129, 130)

"On the fourth day of August we sailed from the land" 4551 (198)

ON THE LAKE 3293 (330)

"On the lake where droop'd the willow" 8409 (83)

"On the moonlight turf where the sea-cattle graze" 5862 (280)

"On the mountain the wind bloweth wind" 9168 (388)

"On the mountain where breezes sigh" 9168 (154, 337)

ON THE NIGHT 4368 (94)

"On the night I left my sweetheart" 4368 (94)

ON THE NIGHT WHEN JESUS CAME 9290 (165)

"On the night when Jesus came to earth from heaven" 9290 (165)

"On the ninth day of November, at the dawning in the sky" 8129 (44)

"On the oven, there sits a maiden" 6240 (318)

"On the road to Sevastopol, not too far from Simferopol" 6177 (318)

ON THE ROAD TO VALENCIA 6286 (219)

ON THE ROCKS BY ABERDEEN 1216 (205)

"On the rocks of Aberdeen" 1216 (205)

ON THE ROOF A MAGPIE 5807 (164)

"On the roof a magpie shrieks and not a stork" 5807 (164)

"On the Tom-Big-Bee River one day I was born" 3563 (185)

"ON THE TOP OF THE HILL" 7221 (239)

"On the very night that Marko married" 8786 (86)

ON THE VILLAGE END 5702 (164)

"On the village end quite far, there an old Jew runs a bar" 5702 (164)

ON THIS DAY 8669 (349)

"On this day our King was born" 8669 (349)

ON THIS DAY WAS BORN 9102 (363)

"On this day was born Christ Jesus" 9102 (363)

"On this joyous day we wear the palms" 1052 (132)

ON TOM-BIG-BEE RIVER 3563 (343)

"On Tom-Big-Bee River so bright, I was born" 3563 (343)

ON TOP OF OL' SMOKY 7885B (171)

"On top of Ol' Smoky, all covered with snow" 7885B (171)

ON TOP OF OLD SMOKY 7885A (35, 169, 293), 7885C (242)

"On top of old Smoky, all cover'd with snow" 7887A (35, 293)

"On top of old Smoky, all covered in snow" 7885A (227)

"On top of old Smoky all covered with snow" 7885A (389), 7885C (242), 7885D (243)

ON VINT DE NOUS AIPOUTHA 9103 (361)

"On walking out one summer's morning to take the cool and pleasant air" 8137C (215)

"On wan dark night on Lac San Pierre" 5191 (186)

On Wenlock edge 3802 (277)

ON WINGS OF POLISH SONG 3786 (295)

ON WINGS OF SONG (Mendelssohn-Bartholdy) 2368 (141, 199, 277, 329, 348, 395)

ON WINGS OF SONG (Szopski) 3702 (159)

"On wings of song fly soul of mine" 3702 (159)

"On wings of song I'll bear thee, to those fair Asian lands" 2368 (277)

"On wings of song I'll take you and bear you far away" 2368 (395)

"On wings of song, my treasure, we'll start our voyage from here" 2368 (329)

"On wings of song the skylark his dewy nest forsakes" 2368 (199)

"On wings of song thro' dreamland my love afar I bear" 2368 (348)

"On wrists and fingers these jewels" 2939 (245)

"On yo' knees, down on yo' knees" 8497 (182)

"On yonder dim horizon" 3305 (407)

"On yonder hill there stands a creature" 4710 (28,136,279, 366)

"Once a babulinka from a wealthy family" 6679 (295)

"Once a boy a rose espied" 3274 (136)

"Once a boy a wild-rose spied" 3274 (132,275)

"Once a boy espied a rose" 3274 (112)

ONCE A CANADIAN LAD 5153 (186,187)

"Once a Canadian lad, exiled from hearth and home" 5153 (186,187)

"Once a jolly swagman sat beside the billabong" 4179 (35)

"Once a maid went to confession" 4417 (324)

"Once a mazur gay, young and prosperous" 6886 (295)

"Once again I'll return to my own scentless flowers" 2888 (6)

"Once at dawn, I met the brave array" 9083 (210)

"Once I could laugh and play" 1111 (129)

"Once I crossed the world to find a sweetheart" 6958 (352)

"ONCE I FELL IN LOVE" 4457 (94)

"Once I had an old white mare" 7890 (185)

"Once I lived the life of a millionaire" 728 (336)

"Once I loaded in my wagon" 6508 (316)

"ONCE I LOVED A MAIDEN FAIR" 4723 (36,13)

"ONCE I USED TO LOVE YOU DEARLY" 157 (285)

"Once I was happy but now I'm forlorn" 2702 (115,128, 130,131,225,236)

ONCE I WAS ROWING 4848 (124)

"Once I was rowing with my lover" 4848 (124)

"Once in a blithe greenwood liv'd a hermit wise and good" 4638 (235,349)

ONCE IN MY CHILDHOOD 2300 (143)

"Once in my childhood within a mighty temple" 2300 (143)

"ONCE IN ROYAL DAVID'S CITY" 1225 (38,39,251,307, 315,319,333,337,369,410)

"Once in the dear dead days beyond recall" 2461

"Once in the ev'ning twilight, I dreamt a happy dream" 1356 (394)

"Once, in the long ago, mother rocked my cradle" 3705 (248)

"Once in the village of Labelle" 5178 (21)

"Once, living in our midst we had a comrade" 6247 (318)

ONCE MORE A-LUMB'RING GO 7901 (227)

"Once more, dear home, I with rapture behold thee" 3917 (28)

"Once more I hear the song of India" 3039 (132)

"ONCE MORE THE WINTER'S LEFT US" 6622 (316)

"Once on a time there lived a man, his name was Peter Gray" 7921 (35,170,173)

"Once on a time, there was a man, his name was Peter Gray" 7921 (28,366)

"Once there lived side by side two little maids" 2750 (114, 131,132,204)

ONCE THERE WAS A BABA 6774 (295)

"Once there was a baba who, baba who, baba who" 6774 (295)

"Once there was a Count of Cabra and a widow who wanted to wed" 7291 (219)

"Once there was a little kitty, white as the snow" 7798 (216)

"Once there was a wicked, wicked king" 6206 (318)

"ONCE THERE WERE HAPPY DAYS" 2520 (291)

"Once there were three fishermen" 8055 (28,366)

ONCE UPON A TIME 2033 (87)

"Once upon a time there was. . . is the happy old beginning" 6170 (318)

"Once we sowed seeds with a plough" 1961 (162)

"Once we were sweethearts, not so long ago" 2464 (131)

ONCE WHEN I AWOKE 6631 (86)

"Once when I awoke, there still were stars brilliantly gleaming" 6631 (86)

ONCE YOUNG CHLOE 4901 (175)

"Once young Chloe would when roving, on her shepherd's duties bent" 4901 (175)

L'ONDE 4027 (224)

"Ondina de la fuente de mi vida" 4510 (73)

"One bore a common musket" 1878 (131)

"One bright day in the month of May" 4545F (243)

ONE BUMPER AT PARTING 5993 (166,213)

"One bumper at parting! tho' many have circled the board since we met" 5993 (166,213)

ONE BUTTON, TWO BUTTONS 5711 (37)

"One button, two buttons, and the rest, thirteen on my vest" 5711 (37)

"One calm moon-lit night, away from the light" 8670 (20)

"One Christmas I'm starving, the orphan child said" 9092 (47)

"One dark and stormy night" 4045 (114,131)

"One day as I was strolling, unthinking by the quay" 9489 (234)

"One day as I was walking down by the Clarence Dock" 9489 (320)

"ONE DAY I HAD TO MOW" 4370 (94)

"One day I sat musing alone on the grass" 7787 (331)

"One day I thought I'd have some fun" 8049 (186)

"One day I woke up feelin' weak" 8775 (11)

"One day in a lonesome grove" 7796 (109,110)

"One day in December I'll never forget" 4228 (186)

ONE DAY ISABEL WANDERED 5164 (187)

"One day Isabel wandered down in her garden fair" 5164 (187)

"One day, Marie went to the mill" 5026 (187)

"One day me go dung a Lang-Pan Fe wata" 8752 (252)

"ONE DAY THE LOVELY ROSE COMPLAINED" 1154 (36)

"One day, when I left Havana" 4120 (322)

"One day when out walking I happened to see" 7787D (242)

"One day while walking down Thirty Fifth Street" 7660 (293)

"One duck on a pond, Wibble, wobble" 4585 (28)

"One evening, as I roamed a-shore from my galliant brigantine" 7713 (72)

"One evening, as the sun went down" 7442B (34,227)

"One ev'ning for pleasure I rambled to view the fair fields all alone" 4224 (186)

ONE FINE DAY (Folksongs, Poland) 6671 (159)

ONE FINE DAY (Puccini) 2895 (143)

"One fine day we'll notice" 2895 (143)

"One fine day when flowers are a-blowing" 6671 (159)

ONE FOR THE LITTLE BITTY BABY 9367B (33,389)

"One Friday morn as we set sail" 9467D (249)
"One Friday morn, when we set sail" 9467A (234,349), 9467C (199)
THE ONE-HORSE OPEN SLEIGH 2814
ONE HOUR TONIGHT 1800 (345)
ONE HUNDRED YEARS 6843 (295)
"ONE IS HIGH AND ONE IS LOW" 6969 (95)
"One lovely summer evening while wandering thro' a glade" 4830 (124)
ONE MAN WENT TO MOW 4724 (402)
"One man went to mow, went to mow a meadow" 4724 (402)
ONE MORE DAY 9470A (320), 9470B (35)
ONE MORE DRINK FOR THE FOUR OF US 7902 (225)
ONE MORE RIVER 8478 (35,249,402)
"One more river, and that's the river of Jordan" 8478 (35, 249,402)
ONE MORE RIVER TO CROSS 8478 (185)
"One morning a huntsman all gallant and gay" 2098 (28)
"One morning before the sun mounted" 9178 (37)
"One morning bright I rowed out for fishing" 6637 (37)
"One morning early as I walked forth, by the margin of Lough Leane" 5895 (133)
"One morning early I walked forth, by the margin of Lough Lene" 5895 (16)
ONE MORNING IN MAY 7845B (267)
ONE MORNING IN SPRING TIME 8661 (20)
"One morning in spring-time, when sunlight lay gleaming" 8661 (20)
"One morning in the month of cold December" 9464 (320)
"One morning in the month of May, down by the rolling river" 4663 (234)
"One morning, one morning, one morning in May" 7845A (81), 7845B (267)
"One morning, one morning, the weather being fine" 7694 (109,110)
"One night came on a hurricane, the sea was mountains rolling" 9422 (401)
ONE NIGHT IN SUMMER 4838 (124)
"One night they rowed without a man, papa didn't know, mamma didn't know" 8760 (323)
"ONE NIGHT WHEN SORROW BURDENED" 3520 (394)
"One night while I was a-ramblin' around, met up with that Wild Bill Jones" 8133 (81)
"One o' these mornin's bright an' fair" 8265 (409)
"One pleasant summer morning, when the flowers all were springing, O!" 5910 (133)
"One said it was a lighthouse the second said Nay" 8698 (44)
"ONE SAID TO THE OTHER" 4357 (94)
"One sails away to sea, to sea" 2228 (348)
"One shif me got Ratta cut i'" 8770 (252)
ONE SOLJA MAN 8758 (252)
"One solja man come fe court me" 8758 (252)
ONE STRAW SWIMS 5802 (164)
"One straw swims forsaken in the water forsaken" 5802 (164)
ONE SUMMER EVENING 7903 (37)
ONE SWEETLY SOLEMN THOUGHT 60 (122,123,329,346, 394)
"One sweetly solemn thought comes to me o'er and o'er" 60 (122,123,329,346,394)
"One thousand braves leave their dear Warsaw burning" 6864 (159)
"One, two, three, Caroline" 7491 (219,279,366)

"One, two, three, four, five and six and seven eight!" 5652 (164)
"One, two, three, four, five, six, sev'n" 5540 (37)
"One, two, three, four, paper hat, paper hat" 6452 (316)
ONE WHO HAS YEARNED ALONE 643 (122)
"One who has yearned alone can know my anguish" 643 (122)
ONEGIN'S ARIA 641 (4)
"Ongezunden lichtelach der wekn sich geschlichtelach" 6172 (230)
ONIONS AND POTATOES 7222 (239)
"Onions and potatoes, oh, ev'rybody here knows" 7222 (239)
"Only a Gypsy, I'm knowing, fate bids my love vainly languish" 1378 (176)
"Only a rosebud kissed by the dew" 723 (237)
ONLY FOUR HOURS 4425 (94)
"Only four hours till dawn" 4425 (94)
"Only four of my cornfields are left me of the ranch that was my gloty, Ay!" 1781 (322)
"An only kid, an only kid that father bought for two zuzim" 6168 (318)
ONLY ONE GIRL IN THE WORLD FOR ME 2275 (114,131)
"Only one girl in the world for me" 2275 (114,131)
"Only one more day, my Johnny" 9470A (320)
ONLY TWO GIRLS 5703 (92)
"Only two girls in the village, only two" 5703 (92)
"ONLY YOU CAN TELL ME" 4401 (94)
L'ONORE! LADRI! 3839 (4)
"L'onore! Ladri! Voi state ligi all' onor vostro, voi!" 3839 (4)
"ONS IS GEBOREN EEN KINDEKIJN" 9270 (201)
"ONS IS GHEBOREN EEN KINDEKIJN!" 9270 (154)
"ONS LIESJE ZAT TE TREUREN" 6553 (202)
ONWARD, CHRISTIAN SOLDIERS 3666 (28,233,236,279, 343,366)
"Onward Christian soldiers! Marching as to war" 3666 (28,233,236,279,343,366)
"Onward, ride onward!" 1922 (7)
Oonagh (tune) 6039
"Open, open, open the gates of the temple" 1914 (346, 400)
THE OPEN ROAD 5505 (37)
OPEN THE DOOR 5778 (164)
Open the door (tune) 6012A
"Open the door, baby sweet!" 5778 (164)
OPEN THE DOOR SOFTLY 6012B (349)
OPEN THE GATES OF THE TEMPLE 1914 (346,400)
"OPEN THE WINDOW NOAH" 8479 (409)
"OPEN THY BLUE EYES" 2319 (140,176,237,387)
"OPEN THY LATTICE LOVE" 1131 (348)
"Open wide my lonely dungeon" 3116 (341)
OPEN YOUR HEART 323 (191,193,195)
OPFERLIED 243 (99)
OPHELIA'S SONG 4015 (344)
OPP, AMARYLLIS! 265 (135,188)
"Opp, Amaryllis! Vakna, min lilla!" 265 (135,188)
Or che una nube 2855
"Or ch'io non segno più" 3066 (217)
OR DITESNOUS, MARIE 9049 (165)
L'ORA, O TIRSI 2900 (143)
"L'ora, o Tirsi, è vega e bella" 2900 (143)
ORA PRO NOBIS 2811 (346)

THE PAW PAW PATCH 8120 (216)

PAX VOBISCUM 3291 (229)

PAY DAY AT COAL CREEK 8482 (336)

"Pay day, pay day, oh, pay day, pay day at Coal Creek tomorrow" 8482 (336)

"Pays merveilleux, jardins fortunés" 2408 (3)

PE CAWN I HON 8693 (349)

"Pe cawn i hon yn eiddoi mi" 8693 (349)

PEACE 3260 (275)

"Peace, O world, O grant me peace!" 4085 (112)

PEACEFUL EVENING 790 (348)

"A peaceful monk, who knoweth nought of worldly lore and wisdom" 2616 (5)

PEACEFUL NIGHT, HOLY NIGHT 1408

"Peaceful night! Holy night! All around is calm delight" 1408 (333)

PEACEFUL SLUMBERING 3595 (235)

"Peaceful slumbering on the ocean, seamen fear no danger nigh" 3595 (235)

"THE PEACEFUL WESTERNE WINDE" 556 (197)

THE PEACH 7254 (219)

THE PEACOCKS 2174 (121)

PEANUT-PICKIN' SONG 8483 (37, 129, 130, 279, 366)

THE PEANUT STAND 7919 (44)

THE PEARL 6935 (279)

"A pearl is born in the sea" 6935 (279)

PEARL OF MAZATLAN 6379 (86)

Pearl of the white breast (tune) 6016

PEAS, BEANS, OATS, AND BARLEY 4728 (37)

THE PEASANT'S PILGRIMAGE 9125 (361)

Pease upon a trencher (tune) 6023 (166, 213)

THE PEAT BOG SOLDIERS 5478 (7, 35)

LE PECORELLE 2265 (181)

"Le pecorelle ne' verdi campi il dolce latte" 2265 (181)

PECOS BILL 3412 (331)

"Pecos Bill, he had no garments" 3412 (331)

PEDDLER'S SONG 898 (196)

PEDIDA DE LA POSADA 9222 (165)

PEDIMENTO DE LAS POSADAS 9372 (314)

PEEK-A-BOO! 3176 (114, 131)

The peelers and the goat (tune) 4729

THE PEELERS AND THE PIG 4729 (198)

"Peepin' through the knot-hole of grandpa's wooden leg" 7617 (110)

Peer Gynt 1389

PEGGY BAWN 5865 (213)

PEGGY MINE 3594 (131)

PEGGY O'NEIL 2757 (236)

PENITENCE 227 (364)

THE PENITENT 3793 (398)

THE PENITENTIARY BLUES 7920 (80)

"The pennies of the nation spoke one day" 1147 (293)

"A penny for a spool of thread" 4735 (32, 34)

"Pensan do en el que la quiere" 3429 (245)

PENSIERI 3190 (179)

"Pensieri, pensieri, Ah, Dio qual pena" 3190 (179)

PÉNTEKEN ESTE 5787 (164)

"People all think that I am happy" 4840 (124)

PEOPLE AWAKE! 8789 (7)

"People awake! Hear the earth shake" 8789 (7)

"De people keep a-comin' an' de train done gone" 9393 (332)

"The people keep a-coming and the train done gone" 9393 (332)

PEOPLE, LOOK EAST 9050 (38, 39)

"People, look East. The time is near" 9050 (38, 39)

"People out west heard of John Henry's death" 8382G (77)

"People say, 'Don't take him'" 4438 (95)

"People say that I am happy" 1967 (295)

"The people's flag is deepest red" (O Tannenbaum tune) 9175 (294)

"The people's flag is deepest red" (White Cockade tune) 7203 (294)

EL PEQUEÑO ZAGAL 8861 (53)

"El pequeño zagal soy cansado de tanto andar" 8861 (53)

PER FORMARE LA BETTA 3191 (134)

"Per formare la Betta che adoro" 3191 (134)

"PER LA GLORIA D'ADORARVI" 363 (368)

"Per la più vega e bella" 498 (217)

PER LUI CHE ADORO 3103 (300)

"Per lui che adoro ch'è il mio tesoro" 3103 (300)

PER ME GIUNTO 3831 (4)

"Per me giunto è il dì supremo" 3831 (4)

PER NOUN LANGUI 9108 (361)

PER PIÈTÀ, BEN MIO 2561 (6)

"Per piètà ben mio, perdona all' error" 2561 (6)

"Per pieta, per pieta, deh torna, deh torna a me" 3599 (217)

"PER QUESTE AMARE LACRIME" 2766 (253)

PER SVINAHERDE 7334 (135)

"Per Svinaherde satte sig paa tufvan och sang" 7334 (135)

PERCHÈ MIA BELL' ANNINA 6123 (325)

"Perchè mia bell' Annina abbassi gli occhi lorquando tu m'incontri per la via?" 6123 (325)

UNE PERDRIOLE 5179 (383)

THE PERFECT HOUR 1503 (140, 241)

THE PERFECT ROSE 8885 (279, 366)

"Perfidi! All' Anglo contro me v'unite" 3846 (4)

PERFIDIA 4511 (73)

PERFIDISSIMO VOLTO 508 (253)

"Perfidissimo volto ben l'usata bellezza in te se vede" 508 (253)

PERHAPS WHEN LILIES BLOOM 7335 (95)

LA PERICA 1201 (284)

La Périchole 2692 (362)

PERIWINKLE WREATH, I HAD THEE HUNG 6775 (295)

"Periwinkle wreath, I had thee hung On a wooden peg, I had thee hung" 6775 (295)

PERKÊO 1411 (31)

LA PERLA 6935 (279)

LA PERLA DE MAZATLAN 6379 (86)

La perle du Brésil 772 (292)

Die Perle von Tokay 2991 (258)

PERSONENT HODIE 9030 (361)

"Personent hodie voces puerelae" 9030 (361)

PERSUASIÓN 4512 (73)

PESCATOR, AFFONDA L'ESCA 2847 (4, 298)

THE PESKY SARPENT 7896A (34)

PETER AMBERLEY 522 (186)

PETER, GO RING-A DEM BELLS 8465 (183)

PETER GRAY 7921 (28, 35, 170, 173, 366)

PETER ON DE SEA, SEA, SEA, SEA 8484 (183, 184)

"Peter, Peter, Peter on de sea, sea, sea, sea" 8484 (183, 184)

PETER, THE SWINEHERD 7334 (135)

PETERLE 1908 (223)

"Peterle, du liebes Peterle" 1908 (223)

THE PIOUS JEW BUILDS HIS BOOTH 6189 (230)
"The piper cam' to oor toon" 7155 (163)
"The piper cam' to oor toun" 7155 (18,100,101)
"The piper came to our town" 7155 (234,349)
THE PIPER O' DUNDEE 7155 (18,100,102,163,234)
THE PIPER OF DUNDEE 7155 (349)
"PIPES, OH SO SWEETLY RINGING" 2495 (36)
THE PIPING ON THE HILL 5997 (280)
PIRATE DREAMS 1729 (241)
THE PIRATE SONG 7925 (173)
The pirates 3595-3596
The pirates of Penzance 3669
PIRI-MIRI-DICTUM DOMINI 7926A (264)
Pirithoüs 2548 (149)
PIROS ALMA CSÜNG 5788 (92)
"Piros alma czüng az ágon" 5788 (92)
PIROS, PIROS, PIROS 5789 (92)
"Piros, piros, piros, háromszor is piros" 5789 (92)
Pirro e Demetrio 3192 (404)
PÍSEŇ NA SLOVA SHAKESPEAROVA 1779 (73)
"Pitch boils on the fire" 3147 (318)
EL PITITÍN 7269 (283)
"Pity a father's wounded heart, torn by the pangs of madness" 3857 (5)
"Pity me, pity me! Father pity me!" 5848 (37)
PITY THE DOWNTRODDEN LANDLORD 684 (293)
"Pity the life of a gambler's wife" 2701 (131)
"Più non sia, che m'innamori" 2341 (217)
"Piu non ti voglio credere" 364 (217)
PIÙ VAGA E VEZZOSETTA 365 (134)
"Più vaga e vezzosetta sarai" 365 (134)
"Place here by me the mignonette so fragrant" 3619 (112)
THE PLAGUE OF LOVE 82 (272)
"A plague of those musty old lubbers" 7851 (225)
THE PLAINS OF ILLINOIS 7567B (72)
PLAINTE SUR LA MORT DE MONSIEUR LAMBERT 927 (278)
PLAISIR D'AMOUR 2282 (36,88,405)
"Plaisir d'amour ne dure qu'un moment" 2282 (36,88,405)
The planets. Jupiter 1688 (306)
PLANTATION SONG 7927 (242)
PLANTONIO 7885A (120)
PLANTONIO, THE PRIDE OF THE PLAIN 7885A (214)
PLANTONS LA VIGNE 5078 (82,91)
"Plantons la vigne, la voilà la joli' vigne" 5078 (82,91)
Planxty Kelly (tune) 5911
LA PLATA SONG 4173 (279)
"Plaudern Sie, doch heit're Sachen nur" 882 (257)
"De play begin an' de ball gawn roun'" 8710 (252)
PLAY, GYPSY, PLAY 5727 (92)
"Play, Gypsy, play strains of sorrow and woe" 5727 (92)
"Play, play the latest tune" 6254 (318)
PLAY YOUR MUSIC, GYPSY 3984 (285)
"Play your music, Gypsy, play it" 3984 (285)
"Playing gently o'er the water" 745 (233)
PLEA 1151 (141)
"Pleasant evening, my sweet" 430 (112)
"Please come on board my little ship" 5167 (187)
"Please listen, dearest mother" 3261 (141)
"Please open your hearts and your purses" 684 (293)
PLEASED TO MEET YOU! 5790 (95)
The pleasing melody of Cynnwyd (tune) 8677
THE PLEDGED HORSE 6313 (95)
PLENTY GOOD ROOM 8487 (409)
"PLEUREZ! PLEUREZ, MES YEUX!" 2306 (1)

PŁONIE OGNISKO 6808 (295)
"Płonie ognisko i szumią knieje, Drużynowy siadł wśród nas" 6808 (295)
THE PLOUGHBOY (Pearson) 2756 (293)
THE PLOUGH BOY (Shield) 3455 (48)
PLOW DEEPLY 4351 (324)
"Plow deeply was the cry coming from geese on high" 4351 (324)
PLOWER TO THE SKYLARK 3688 (295)
LA PLUIE 1238 (190,192,194)
"La pluie, la pluie aux doigts verts" 1238 (190,192,194)
PLUME IN THE SUMMER WIND 3852 (237)
"Plume in the summer wind waywardly playing 3852 (237)
"A plump little robin flew down from a tree" 34 (28)
"La plus aimable, à mon gré, je vais vous la présenter" 5095 (91)
"PLUS DE DÉPIT, PLUS DE TRISTESSE" 1367 (211)
"Plus j'observe ces lieux" 2206 (152)
PŁYNIE WISLA 6809 (86)
PŁYNIE WISŁA, PŁYNIE 6809 (159)
"Płynie Wisła płynie, po polskiej krainie" 6809 (159)
PO' BOY 8490A (171), 8490B (109,110), 8490C (184)
PO DOLINE 4395 (94)
"PO DOLINE TICHÝ VETRÍK POVIEVA" 4395 (94,178)
PO' LAZ'US 8488 (227)
PO' LIL JESUS 9397 (227)
PO' MO'NER GOT A HOME AT LAS' 8494B (182)
"PO NOCNEJ ROSIE" 2482 (159,295)
PO' OL' LAZ'RUS 8489 (409)
"Po' ol' Laz'rus layin' in between two mountains" 8489 (409)
POBRE CÉGA 4208 (219)
POBRE CORAZOŃ 4529 (284)
"Pobre corazoń entriste cido, ya no puede más surfrir de olvido" 4529 (284)
EL POBRECILLO ALEGRE 8862 (55)
"¡ Pobrede Lino Zamora! ¡ Ah! que suerte le ha tocada" 6360 (247)
EL POBRET ALEGRE 8862 (55)
"POCHVÁLEN BUD' PÁN JEŽIŠ" 4396 (94)
"POCZEKAJ HANKA TAM U CHRUSTU" 6810 (295)
POD BELEHRADOM 4397 (94)
"Pod Belehradom stojí vrany kôň " 4397 (94)
POD KOPEICZKIEM GRUSZKA ROŚNIE 6811 (159)
POD KRAKOWEM CZARNA ROLA 6799 (159)
"Pod Krakowem czarna rola, ja jej orał nie będę" 6799 (159)
POD NAŠIMA OKNY 4398 (177)
"Pod našima okny teče vodička" 4398 (177)
"POD TÝM NAŠÍM OKIENEČKOM" 4399 (94)
POD ZIELONYM DĘBEM 6812 (159,295)
"Pod zielonym dębem stoi koń siodłany" 6812 (159,295)
PODKÓWECZKI DAJCIE OGNIA 6813 (159,295)
"Podkóweczki, dajcie ognia, Bo dziewczyna tego godna" 6813 (295)
Poeme de l'amour et de la mer 658 (357)
"Poets may sing of their Helicon streams" 2808 (189)
"POGNAŁA WÓŁKI NA BUKOWINE" 6814 (295)
POGNER'S ADDRESS 3911 (5)
POHÁDKA 3750 (74)
POICHÉ L'UMIL CAPANNA 9211 (244,386)
POJADE, MARYSIU, NA BOJE 6815 (159)

"Pojadę Marysiu, na boje nic tu nie pomogą łzy twoje" 6815 (159)

"Pojat kansan urhokkaan" 1972 (124)

"Pojď smrti, pojď již ke mně" 1779 (73)

PÓJDŹMY WSZYSCY 9294 (295)

"Pójdźmy wszyscy do stajenki" 9294 (295)

POJEDZIEMY NA ŁÓW 6816 (295)

"Pojedziemy na łów, na łów, towarzyszu mój" 6816 (295)

PÓKI LWIE SERCA 6817 (295)

"Póki lwie serca sokole poloty" 6817 (295)

POLEĆ PIEŚNI Z MIASTA 2483 (159, 295)

"Poleć pieśni z miasta, choć miasto nie nudzi" 2483 (159, 295)

LA POLICHINELLE 5079 (82, 91)

POLISH BANNERS ON THE KREMLIN 2009 (159)

POLISH LULLABY 9291C (337)

POLISH MAIDENS 2480 (295)

POLISH NATIONAL ANTHEM 6746 (159)

"Pollie gaan mos Pêrel-toe" 6557 (384)

POLLIE, ONS GAAN PÊREL-TOE 6557 (239, 384)

LA POLLITA 4261 (207)

POLLY 2462 (205)

"POLLY, COME WITH ME TO PAARL" 6557 (239)

POLLY OLIVER 4737 (234)

POLLY-WOLLY-DOODLE 7928 (115, 129, 130, 132, 225, 236, 279, 366, 402)

A POMBINHA VOOU 4209 (219)

LE POMMIER D'AOÛT 5080 (91)

Il pomo d'oro 630-631

"'Pon de mountain, childlun call" 8602 (77)

THE POND 3684 (295)

"Pongan atención señores a lo que voy a explicár" 1744 (303)

PONURO JĘCZY WICHER 6818 (295)

"Ponuro jęczy wicher na dworze" 6818 (295)

POOR AND FOREIGN STRANGER 7932B (72)

THE POOR AULD MAIDENS 7156 (103, 104)

THE POOR AUNT 6188 (95)

A POOR BEGGAR'S DAUGHTER 4732 (397)

"A poor beggar's daughter did dwell on a green" 4732 (397)

POOR BOY 8490A (173)

THE POOR COUNTRYMAN 7929 (72)

"Poor drunkards, poor drunkards, take warning by me" 7734 (321)

"Poor Ezra sat on the milking stool" 2700 (131)

POOR HOWARD 7930 (389)

"Poor Howard's dead and gone, left me here to sing this song" 7930 (389)

"Poor Ivan he was a coward" 2246 (342)

POOR LITTLE JESUS 9397 (33, 332)

"Poor little one, tell me why you cry" 5052 (86)

"Poor little turtle dove setting on a pine" 8082 (173)

POOR LONESOME COWBOY 7931A (321), 7931B (120), 7931C (145)

POOR MAN BLUES 8491 (336)

THE POOR MAN'S WISH 4733 (198)

POOR ME 8492 (409)

POOR MISTER MORGAN 3691 (293)

"Poor Mister Morgan cannot pay his income tax" 3691 (293)

POOR MOURNER 8493 (266)

POOR MOURNER'S GOT A HOME 8494A (409)

POOR OLD HORSE 4734 (198)

"A poor old man came riding by and we say so, and we hope so" 9437A (320)

THE POOR OLD WOMAN 6011C (16)

Poor Robin's Maggot 4651

POOR SINNER 8495 (409)

"The poor soul sat pining, alone and lonely" 3849 (1, 6)

"A poor soul sat sighing by a Sycamore tree" (Folksongs, England) 4806 (75, 117, 235, 397)

"A poor soul sat sighing by a sycamore tree" (Sullivan) 3671 (274)

"Poor soul, she sat sighing" 3849 (143)

POOR WAYFARIN' STRANGER 7932D (399)

POOR WAYFARING STRANGER 7932A (321), 7932B (110)

THE POOR WORKING GIRL 7933 (115)

"The poor working girl, may heaven protect her" 7933 (115)

"The poore soule sate sighinge by a sickamoore tree" 4806 (208)

POP! GOES THE WEASEL 4735 (32, 34)

"Pop my whip and I bring the blood" 7910 (171, 173)

"POR COLACIÓN SEIS ABATES" 2046 (270)

"Por la calle van vendiendo" 7464 (113)

"Por qué en el silencio de la callada noche" 4486 (73)

"Por qué te vi para adorarte tanto?" 4484 (73)

"Por ser hoy día de tu santo" 1788 (291)

"Por ti muero de amor, Por ti sola suspiro" 1638 (303)

POR TI SOLA 1638 (303)

"POR UN BESO DE TU BOCA" 4276 (284, 322)

Porcia 1354 (218)

"PORGI AMOR QUALCHE RISTORO" 2588 (1)

Porgy and Bess 1242 (184)

THE PORI MARCH 1972 (124)

PORIN MARSSI 1972 (124)

"Portland, Maine, is just the same as sunny Tennessee" 3048 (336)

"Porzia, verzweifelt belm Anblick des sterbenden Gatten" 1354 (218)

"POSCIA QUANDO IL PASTOR" 2859 (179)

POSSENTI NUMI 2601 (240)

"Possenti Numi I Iside, Osiri, da te a que' petti seno e valor" 2601 (240)

"De 'possum meat am good to eat" 2200 (28, 184, 366)

"Possum settin' on a hick'ry limb" 8316 (225)

'POSSUM TREE 7934 (392)

POSTILLION-LIED 1406 (223)

Le postillon de Longjumeau 27 (391)

"POSTOURO, SÉ TU M'AYMO" 5081 (66)

POSZŁA BABA DO FAROŻA 6819 (159)

"Poszła baba do faroża i pytała się o radę" 6819 (159)

POTPOURRI SONES 4291 (207)

Pots hondert duisent slapperment (tune) 6600 (201)

"Potz marter, Kueri Velti, du hast vil lieder gmacht" 7354 (157)

LE POU ET LA POUCE 6124 (338)

"Le pou et la puce pour Rome sont partis" 6124 (338)

LA POULETTE GRISE 5184 (187)

LES POULETTES 5082 (127)

LA POUPÉE 3784 (356)

Pour aller à la chasse (tune) 4887 (353)

"POUR COLLATION SIX ABBÉS RÉUNIS" 2046 (270)

Pour l'amour de Marie (tune) 8815

POUR L'ENFANT 5083 (65)

"Pour le jour des Hyacinthies" 792 (362)

"Pour moi sa main cueillait des roses" 1140 (140, 210)

"Pour, O love, sweet consolation" 2588 (311)

"Pour savoir si je puis plaire à leurs seigneuries du parterre" 2043 (270)

POUR SE TROUVER SUR LA FOUGÈRE 5084 (174)

"Pour se touver sur la fougère seule avec Colin, la jeune Catin" 5084 (174)

POVEDAL SI 4400 (94)

"Povedal si u farára" 4400 (94)

POVEDZ MI 4401 (94)

"Povedz mi, divčatko" 4401 (94)

Prae-und Postludien, organ, op. 78. Antiphoni mach's mit mir, Gott 1862 (50)

DER PRAGER MUSIKANT 4032 (31)

DER PRAGER STUDENTEN WANDERSCHAFT 5486 (31)

PRAGNĄ OCKI PRAGNĄ 6820 (159)

"Pragną ocki pragną, za dziewczyną ładną" 6820 (159)

PRAIRIE FLOWER 7935 (366)

PRAIRIE WATERS BY NIGHT 1615 (358)

PRAISE BE TO THEE 1458 (160)

"Praise be to Thee, Lord God of Hosts!" 1458 (160)

PRAISE FOR PEACE 1083 (28, 36)

"PRAISE GOD FROM WHOM ALL BLESSINGS FLOW" (Bourgeois) 379 (28, 35, 233, 279, 366)

"Praise God, from whom all blessings flow" (Tallis) 3707 (199)

"PRAISE JESUS CHRIST WHO CAME THIS NIGHT" 8813 (361)

THE PRAISE OF CHRISTMAS 8890 (271, 334)

THE PRAISE OF GOD 228

"PRAISE THE LORD, O MY SOUL" 3997 (160)

"PRAISE THE LORD! YE HEAVENS ADORE HIM" 1563 (199)

"Praise thou me not, I do not sing thee songs" 1164 (329)

"PRAISE TO GOD IN THE HIGHEST!" 9311 (307)

"Praise we the Lord, who made all beauty" 9111 (271)

PRAISE YE THE FATHER 1331 (28)

"Praise ye the Father! Let ev'ry heart give thanks to Him!" 1331 (28)

"Praised and exalted be the Divine Sacrament" 7400 (109, 110)

THE PRATIES THEY GROW SMALL 5902 (111, 173)

"Pray, can you buy me an acre or more" 4747B (186)

"PRAY FOR US THE PRINCE OF PEACE" 8979 (361)

PRAY, LET ME SUFFERING 587 (139)

PRAY, MAIDEN, PRAY! 3780 (161)

"Pray mourner pray may the Lord help you pray" 8402 (409)

PRAY ON 8496 (409)

PRAY PAPA 2519 (225)

"Pray Papa, pray Papa, stay a little longer" 2519 (225)

"Pray, pray, let me, suffering" 587 (139)

PRAYER (Durante) 950 (368)

PRAYER (Fauré) 1046 (89)

PRAYER (Verdi) 3847 (1, 6)

PRAYER (Wolf) 4074 (408)

PRAYER IS DE KEY 8497 (182)

PRAYER OF AMFORTAS 3914 (4)

A PRAYER OF SUPPLICATION 1071 (347)

A PRAYER OF THANKSGIVING 3790 (316)

PRAYER TO THE CHILD JESUS 3468 (337)

PRAYER TO THE GREAT SPIRIT 5851 (279)

THE PREACHER AND THE BEAR 92 (114, 131, 246)

THE PREACHER AND THE SLAVE 3979 (109, 110)

"A preacher went out a hunting" 92 (114, 131, 246)

Preciosa 3973-3974

"Precious Lord, take my hand, lead me on, let me stand" 877 (394)

"PRECZ, PRECZ OD NAS SMUTEK WSZELKI" 2687 (159, 295)

PRECZ, PRECZ, SMUTEK WSZELKI 2687 (295)

PREGHIERA 950 (368)

PREGUNTALE Á LAS ESTRELLAS 6380A (142), 6380B (322)

"Preguntale á las estrellas, si no de noche me ven llorar" 6380A (142)

"Pregúntale a las estrellas si por la noche me ven llorar" 6380B (322)

PREIS DER HIMMELSKÖNIGEN 9176 (99)

"Preisend mit viel schönen Reden ihrer Länder Wert und Zahl" 5510 (31, 326)

PRELET' SOKOL 4402 (94, 178)

"Prelet', sokol, cez náš dvor,. cez háj majránovy" 4402 (178)

"Prelet' sokol cez ten háj, cez háj mariankovy" 4402 (94)

PRELETEL SOKOL 4403 (94)

"Preletel sokol s bučka na topol" 4403 (94)

PRELUDE (Vené) 3815 (382)

Prelude, piano, op. 28, no. 7, A major 671* (295)

Prelude, piano, op. 28, no. 20, C minor 672 (123)

"Le premier jour de mai, que donn'rai-je à ma mie?" 5179 (383)

"Le premier me donna un collier" 3783 (356)

"Le premier qui fut au monde, c'est notre cher Seigneur" 6106 (338)

"PRENDI L'ULTIMO ADDIO" 2271 (134)

"Prendre le dessin d'un bijou" 811 (3)

PREPARE FOR TOMORROW 2837 (7)

"Près de la fontaine, un oiseau chantait" 4867 (88)

"Près de ta mère, clos ta paupière" 9089 (154)

"PRÈS DES REMPARTS DE SÉVILLE 320 (2)

THE PRESIDENTS 8150 (44)

THE PRESIDENT'S HYMN 2607 (212)

President's march 2808

"Press along, cowboy, press along, press along with a cowboy yell" 7440 (214)

"Press along, cowboy, press along with a cowboy yell" 7440 (335)

PRESS THY CHEEK AGAINST MINE OWN 1775 (137)

"PRESTO, PRESTO, IO M'INNAMORO" 2340 (139)

"The prettiest gal that ever I saw" 7795 (109)

"Pretty barberry, her wide leaves nodding" 1950 (295)

"Pretty barmaid, laughing barmaid" 668 (295)

"Pretty barmaid, merry barmaid" 668 (86)

THE PRETTY CREATURE 3596 (405)

PRETTY FAIR MISS 7936 (313)

"A pretty fair miss a-working in the garden" 7936 (313)

THE PRETTY GIRL MILKING HER COW 5860 (280)

The pretty girl of Derby O (tune) 4227 (186, 5990

PRETTY GIRLS AND THE SHOEMAKER 7269 (219)

"Pretty lady! Here's a list I would show you" 2568 (5)

"Pretty lady, pretty gentleman, from mine Vaterland I do bring" 7484 (189)

"Pretty little damsels, how they chat" 2518 (225)

PRETTY MARGARET 1384 (208)

"Pretty Margaret sat in the evening glow" 1384 (208)

PRETTY MARYŠKA 6705 (295)

PRETTY MAUMEE 7787E (81)

PRETTY MILLER'S DAUGHTER 4305 (95)

493

THE ROSES OF ISPAHAN 1050 (208)
"The roses of Ispahan sheathed in soft verdant mosses" 1050 (208)
"Roses picked at twilight from off the hedgerows gray" 422 (329)
"Roses red I gathered beneath the moon's pale ray" 422 (387)
"Roses that I picked in the dusk of ev'ning" 422 (274)
"ROSES, TULIPS, GOLD AND PEARL" 5797 (164)
"Roses white are blooming once again" 1964 (295)
ROSESTOCK, HOLDERBLÜH 5517 (42,353)
"Rosestock, Holderblüh, wann i mein Dirnderl sieh" 5517 (42)
"Rosestock, Holderblüh wenn i mein Dirndel sieh" 5517 (353)
"Rosestock, Holderblüh, wenn i mein Dirnderl sieh" 5517 (99)
ROSESTOCK, HOLDERBLÜT 5517 (31,326,327)
"Rosestock, Holderblüt, wann i mein Dirnderl sieht" 5517 (327)
"Rosestock, Holderblüt, wenn i mei Dirnderl sieh" 5517 (326)
"Rosestock, Holderblüt, wenn i mein Dienderl sieht" 5517 (31)
ROSETTA, SIAMO QUI DA VOI 6135 (325)
THE ROSEWOOD CASKET 7967 (243,392)
LE ROSIER 3113 (82)
"ROSIG, WIE DIE ÄPFEL HANGEN" 5788 (92)
Rosine 1307 (149)
ROSITA (Folksongs, Argentina) 4107 (207)
ROSITA (Folksongs, Brazil) 4211 (350)
"Rosita, a rustic maiden, comely, angelic and pleasing" 4170 (207)
"Rosita, la chacarera, moza lindaz y ladina" 4107 (207)
"Rosita, pretty maid with a laugh like a song" 4294 (350)
"Rosła kalina z liściem szerokiem" 1950 (295)
"Rosmarienhaide zur Maienzeit blüht" 1795 (31)
ROSMARIN UND SALBEIBLÄTTER 6314 (31)
"Rosmarin und Salbeiblätter send ich dir zum Abschiedsgruss" 6314 (31)
ROSSETER'S AYRE 3090 (376)
DU ROSSIGNAL QUE CHANTE 4965 (406)
"Du rossignol qui chant j'ai entendu la voix" 4965 (406)
ROSSIGNOLET DU BOIS 5103 (88,91)
"Rossignolet du bois qui chantes d'une voix douce et plaisante" 5103 (88,91)
ROSSIGNOLET GENTIL, RAMÈNE-MOI MON AMI 7377 (155)
LES ROSSIGNOLS 5104 (174)
ROSSIGNOLS AMOUREUX 2963 (292)
"Rossignols amoureux répondez à nos voix" 2963 (150,292)
"Les rossignols, dans leur tendre ramage" 5104 (174)
ROSY ARE MY APPLES 5788 (92)
"Rosy are my apples growing" 5788 (92)
ROSY, ROSY RED WINE 5789 (92)
"Rosy, rosy, red wine, fill me thrice the red wine" 5789 (92)
ROSY, ROSY, ROSY 5789 (164)
"Rosy, rosy, rosy, rosy, rosy, rosy, glows the red wine in my glass" 5789 (164)
ROTA 2680 (295)
ROTATION BLUES 3497 (336)
ROTE ABENDWOLKEN ZIEH'N 420 (45)
"Rote Abendwolken zieh'n am Firmament" 420 (45)

ROTE HUSAREN 1934 (326)
ROTE LIPPEN UND GOLDNER WEIN 5518 (31)
DER ROTE SARAFAN 3798 (99,353)
"Roten, roten, roten, dreimal just schenkt roten" 5789 (92)
ROTEN, ROTEN, ROTEN, WEIN 5789 (92)
Rothiemurche's rant (tune) 7090 (101)
ROUND AND ROUND HITLER'S GRAVE 7874A (227)
'ROUND AND 'ROUND THE PICKET LINE 7874A (293)
ROUND-DANCE 6971 (95)
"'Round de meadows am a-ringing" 1118 (28,128,129, 130,132,233,279,366)
"'ROUND HER NECK SHE WEARS A YELLER RIBBON" 2672 (129)
A ROUND OF LAUGHTER 4042 (343)
"Round the fence and round the cabin, luli, luli cyt" 6687 (295)
'ROUND THE NORIA 2186 (245)
"Rouse thee, Diamanto! Haste, to the mill you must go!" 5635 (37)
"Rouse thee, now! This I grant thee, to look upon thy son once more" 3823 (310)
"Rouse ye! run apace! to behold His sleeping face" 9109 (361)
THE ROVER (Folksongs, Ireland) 6007 (133)
THE ROVER (Folksongs, Portugal) 6922 (350)
ROVING 9419G (234), 9419H (320)
THE ROVING GAMBLER 7968 (109,110,170)
THE ROVING KIND 623 (389)
THE ROVING PEDLER 7969 (72)
ROW, BURNIE, ROW 4001 (344)
"Row, Burnie, row, through the bracken glen" 4001 (344)
ROW, ROW, ROW YOUR BOAT 7970 (28,114,233,236, 366)
"Row, row, row your boat gently down the stream" 7970 (28,114,233,236,366)
THE ROWAN TREE 7161 (100,104,163,349)
"ROY'S WIFE O' ALDIVALLOCH" 7162 (101)
"Rozkitały pąki białych róż" 1964 (295)
ROŽNOVSKÉ HODINY 4410 (178)
"Rožnovské hodiny smutně bijú" 4410 (178)
RÓZSABIMBÓ TULIPÁN 5797 (164)
RÓZSABOKORBAN JÖTTEM A VILÁGRA 5798 (164)
RUCHOT HAYAM 6245 (318)
"Ruchot hayam m'zamz'mim" 6245 (318)
RUDELSBURG (Allmers) 54 (31,99)
RUDELSBURG (Fesca) 1067 (31)
RÜCKBLICK 5497 (99)
RÜCKKEHR DES ALTEN STUDENTEN 2012 (31)
RUEDE LA BOLA 4283 (279)
The ruffian's rant (tune) 7162
RUGIADOSE, ODOROSE 3193 (138,274,368)
"Rugiadose, odorose, Violette graziose" 3193 (138,274, 368)
RUHE, MEINE SEELE! 3631 (112)
"Ruh'n in Frieden alle Seelen" 3283 (99,274)
"Ruisseau dont le bruit charmant" 383 (152)
RULE BRITANNIA 78 (14,235,279,349,366)
"Rum-de-re-dum, the drums are beating" 5554 (37)
"RUM TADERA RZNIJ GRAJKU" 1200 (159)
"Run away with another man, po' boy" 8490B (109,110)
RUN, MOURNER, RUN 8517 (409)
"Run, my reindeer sure, over dale and hill!" 4827 (124)
RUN, NIGGER, RUN 8518A (80)

"Sail on, sail on, my boat, sail over the deep sea" 6763 (295)

SAILING 2276 (28,366)

SAILING IN THE LOWLANDS LOW 6008 (133)

SAILING ON THE SEA 7973 (44)

SAILING, SAILING 2276 (205,233,236)

"Sailing, sailing, over the bounding main" 2276 (28,205, 233,236,366)

"The sailor at sea, and the soldier on land" 7587 (189)

"A sailor has one pleasure dear" 9457 (37)

THE SAILOR LIKES HIS BOTTLE O 9476 (205)

"The sailor loves the foaming brine, and all the deep-blue sea"" 4842 (124)

THE SAILOR LOVES THE SEA 4842 (124)

The sailor's complaint (tune) 7422

A SAILOR'S DREAM 8034 (113)

THE SAILOR'S FAREWELL 9477 (86)

THE SAILOR'S GRAVE 153 (189)

SAILOR'S HORNPIPE 9478 (205)

A SAILOR'S LIFE FOR ME 4035 (205)

"A sailor's life is a roving life" 9482 (205)

"A sailor's life is merry" 4035 (205)

SAILORS' SONG (Folksongs, Poland) 6726 (295)

A SAILOR'S SONG (Margetson) 2270 (78)

St. Agnes (tune) 965 (315,337)

St. Catherine (tune) 1618 (28,236,279,346,366)

SAINT DISTAFF'S DAY 8699 (235)

St. George's Windsor 998 (28,279,343,366)

ST. JAMES INFIRMARY BLUES 7603 (109,110)

"Saint Joseph and Mary go to Bethlehem" 9405 (244)

SAINT JOSEPH AND THE ANGEL 8911A (363)

ST. JOSEPH SINGS 4082 (112)

St. Joseph was an old man an old man was he" 8911E (126)

Saint Joseph was an old man, an old, old man was he" 8911A (363)

St. Louis (tune) 2999

ST. LOUIS BLUES 1519 (34)

ST. MICHAEL 5523 (49)

SAINT NICOLAS 9080 (127)

"SAINT PATRICK WAS A GENTLEMAN" 6009A (234), 6009B (16,166,213)

SAINT PATRICK'S DAY 4773 (15,166,213)

SAINT STEPHEN 8983 (410)

"SAINT STEPHEN WAS AN HOLY MAN" 8983 (361,410)

SAINT STEPHEN WAS RIDING 9336 (388)

"Saint Stephen was riding and he travel'd afar" 9336 (388)

SAINTE NUIT 1403 (88,383)

"Sainte nuit! a minuit, le hameau dort sans bruit" 1408 (383)

THE SAINT'S DELIGHT 7847B (110)

Saison in Salzburg 2992-2993

Les saisons 696-697

"Sal a bailar, buena moza" 7244 (283)

SALAMANDER 421 (250)

SALANGADOU 7974 (109,110)

"Salangadou, Salangadou, Salangadou, Salangadou, Coté piti fille la yé" 7974 (109,110)

"Salangadou, Salangadou, Salangadou, Salangadou, Oh where is my darling gone?" 7974 (109,110)

SALCE! SALCE! 3849 (1,6,143)

"Salías del Templo un día llorona cuando al pasar yo te vi" 6363 (9)

"S'allontanano alfine! Io sperai rive derlo" 3102 (301)

SALLY BROWN 9479 (29,205,235,320)

"Sally Brown she's a bright mulatter" 9479 (235)

THE SALLY GARDENS 5899 (46)

SALLY IN OUR ALLEY 4744 (13,28,36,132,279,366)

"Sally in the bond, bond-a-larry" 8734 (37)

SALOMÉ! 2311 (364)

"Salomé! Demande au prisonier qui revoit la lumière" 2311 (364)

SALOMÉ! SALOMÉ! 2312 (4)

"Salomé! Salomé! Ah! return! I await" 2312 (4)

"Salomé! Salomé! Ah! reviens! je t'attends" 2312 (4)

"Salome! Then ask the captive freed, who to sunshine returneth" 2311 (364)

SALTARELLA 6136 (95)

SALTEN I BALLEN 9133 (69)

"Salten i ballen els pastorells, dones" 9133 (69)

Les saltimbanques 1202 (35)

"Salto e brinco de contente" 6901 (58)

"Salut à toi, soleil de flamme!" 3034 (176,292)

"SALUT! DEMEURE CHASTE ET PURE" 1321 (3)

THE SALUTATION CAROL 8968 (334)

SALUTE TO FREEDOM 759 (35)

Salvator Rosa 1297

"SALVE REGINA" (Eayrs) 971 (304)

SALVE REGINA (Folksongs, Poland) 6868 (295)

"Salve, salve, feliz año que naces" 4494 (73)

SAM BASS 7975 (227)

"Sam Bass was born in Indiana, it was his native home" 7975 (227)

SAM HALL 7976 (399)

"Sam Johnson he left his happy home" 689* (131)

SAME TRAIN 8522 (37)

"Same train, same train, same train, carry my mother" 8522 (37)

SAMMY DEAD OH! 8765 (252)

Samson 1476 (123)

Samson et Dalila 3139-3141

"Samson, recherchant ma présence" 3139 (2)

SAN JOSÉ Y LA VIRGEN 8864 (54)

"San José y la Vírgen María van en buena compañía, partieron de Nazaret" 8864 (54)

"San José y María van para Belén" 9405 (244)

SAN JUAN DEL RÍO 6383 (247)

"San Juan folk from the mountains" 4165 (207)

"'San mBealtaine breágh buidhe" 5943 (280)

EL SAN PEDRO 8654 (284)

SAN SERENÍ 6298 (219)

"San Serení de la buena, buena vida" 6298 (219)

"San Serení, this is not the time for napping" 6298 (219)

Sancho Pança, gouverneur de l'Île de Barataria 2498 (175)

SANCTUS 3271 (326)

SANDMÄNNCHEN (Zuccalmaglio) 4153 (99)

THE SANDMAN (Molloy) 2463 (129,130)

THE SANDMAN (Zuccalmaglio) 4153 (209)

SANDOVALITO 7977 (314)

"Sandovalito, of all your people you're bereft, you're bereft" 7977 (314)

"Sandovalito toda tu gente ya acabó, ya acabó" 7977 (314)

SANDUNGA DE YERANESA 6384 (247)

"Sanftes Klavier, sanftes Klavier!" 3255 (141)

"Der Sang ist verschollen" 3536 (31,99)

SANKT FLORIAN HILF 2013 (31)

SENHORA VIUVA 4212 (219)
SEÑO GALLOTE 6655 (86)
"Seño Gallote, Seño Gallote, Dice tu mama que venga 6655 (86)
"EL SEÑOR CURA NO BAILA" 7278 (283)
"Señora Monica Pérez, a mi me parece bien" 8652 (9)
SENORITA 7283 (350)
"Senorita, you wear a rose in your hair" 7283 (350)
"Sent my brown jug down-town" 7862 (214)
SENTA'S BALLAD 3901 (1)
SENTO NEL CORE 3196 (139)
"Sento nel core certo dolore" 3196 (139)
SENZA IL MISERO PIACER 2856 (180)
"Senza il misero piacer di veder" 2856 (180)
SEOITHÍN 6010 (280)
SEPARACIÓN 4530 (207)
SEPARATION 4530 (207)
"Separation and jealousy are the punishments" 2262 (134)
SER JAG STJÄRNORNA 3529 (188)
"Ser jag stjärnorna sprida sitt flammande sken" 3529 (188)
"Sera jette, sera jette a la marina" 6154 (34)
The seraglio 836 (348)
EEN SERAPHIJNSCHE TONGE 9271 (384)
"Een seraphijnsche tonge mij nu wel dienst voorwaar" 9271 (384)
SERCE NIE SŁUGA 6829 (159)
"Serce nie sługa, nie wie co to pany" 6829 (159)
"Serce, serce, skąd to bicie" 1951 (295)
SERCH HUDOL 8696 (349)
"Serch hudol swyn, Sy'n llanw'r llwyn" 8696 (349)
Serse 1480-1485
SERDECZNA MATKO 1998 (295)
"Serdeczna Matko, opiekunko ludzi" 1998 (295)
"Sere are the meadows, gray is the sky" 4821 (37)
SERENADE (Brahms) 426 (112, 407)
SERENADE (Donizetti) 859 (3)
SERENADE (Drigo) 925 (132)
SERENADE (Folksongs, Italy) 6161 (51)
SERENADE (Folksongs, Peru) 6664 (350)
SÉRÉNADE (Gounod "Quand tu chantes...") 1332 (237, 274)
SERENADE (Gounod "Vous qui faites...") 1323 (5)
SERENADE (Haydn) 1568 (210)
SERENADE (Kreuder) 1973 (222)
SERENADE (Mozart) 2565 (4)
SÉRÉNADE (Paladilhe) 2730 (407)
SERENADE (Schubert) 3306 (122, 128, 132, 237, 329, 387)
SERENADE (Strauss) 3633 (112)
SERENADE (Tosti) 3760 (386)
SÉRÉNADE DE DON JUAN 637 (240)
SERENADE OF THE LITTLE DUCKS 634 (208)
"Serenaders gaily singing to enchanted maidens" 796 (208)
"The serenading swains and the lovely ladies listening" 946 (190, 192, 194)
LA SERENATA (Braga) 390 (329, 394)
SERENATA (Folksongs, Dominican Republic) 4516 (73)
SERENATA (Folksongs, Uruguay) 8648 (284)
SERENATA (Garcia) 1207 (303)
SERENATA (Mozart) 2565 (298)
LA SERENATA (Tosti) 3760 (386)
SERENE IS THE NIGHT 7980 (279)
"Serían las tres de la tarde" 6369 (247)
"Serments trompeurs, tendre langage" 2076 (149)
"Serve canelas, drink so famous in this hamlet on the mountain" 6290 (219)

SERVING A KING 4855 (124)
"Serving a king in a palace they keep him" 4855 (124)
SET DOWN, SERVANT! 8531 (227, 331)
"Set down servant". 'I cain' set down" 8531 (227)
"'Set down, servant!' 'I can't set down'" 8531 (331)
"Set our wedding day, my Gertjie" 7217 (86)
"SETE ANOS QUE ANDEI NA GUERRA" 6929 (57)
"SETZ' HEUT' FROH DEN NEUEN HUT AUF" 5673 (92)
SEUFZER 3308 (229)
"Seul au milieu de la Nature, je veille hélas, lorsque tout dort" 1764 (278)
"Seuls confidents de mes peines secrètes" 822 (148)
"Seuls, tous deux, ravis, chantants" 1045 (362)
"Seven fancy shirts like moles" 6166 (318)
THE SEVEN JOYS OF CHRISTMAS 8985A (337)
THE SEVEN JOYS OF MARY 8985A (35, 296, 334, 337, 361, 363, 410), 8985C (173), 8985D (261, 268), 8985E (388)
"SEVEN LONG YEARS IN STATE PRISON" 8532 (184)
THE SEVEN REJOICES OF MARY 8985B (361)
SEVEN STEPS 5540 (37)
THE SEVEN VIRGINS 9375 (261)
SEVEN WHITE STARS 5723 (164)
"Seven white stars in the greater bear do shine" 5723 (164)
SEVENTEEN COME SUNDAY 4750A (198), 4750B (72)
SEXTETTE 872 (132)
"SHA, SHTIL, MACHT NISHT KAYN GERUDER!" 6248 (318)
SHABBAT HAMALKA 2456 (318)
SHABES BEYN HASHMOSHES 1004 (318)
SHABES LICHT UN SHABES LOMPN 6249 (318)
"Shabes licht un shabes lompn, O, vi ziz iz ayer shayn!" 6249 (318)
"SHADED WITH OLIVE TREES" 1358 (196)
"Shades of evening close not o'er us" 214 (28, 366)
"Shades of my fathers around me" 2846 (5)
"Shades of night are creeping" 475 (345)
"The shades of night were falling fast" (EXCELSIOR) 1742 (189)
"The shades of night were falling fast" 4789 (402)
"The shadows lie across the dim old room" 1741 (129, 130, 132)
SHADOWS O'ER THE FOREST 5689 (164)
"Shadows o'er the forest spread their thick, dark veil" 5689 (164)
SHADY GROVE 7981 (313)
"Shady Grove my little love" 7981 (313)
SHADY OLD CAMP 1915 (173)
"SHALL A SMILE OR A GUILEFUL GLANCE?" 710 (197)
"Shall I bring beets to thee" 5855 (86)
SHALL I BRING THEE BEETS? 5855 (86)
"SHALL I COME, SWEETE LOVE, TO THEE?" 557 (196)
"Shall I go walk the woods so wild" 4808 (13)
"Shall I show you how the farmer" 4594 (28, 366)
"SHALL I SUE, SHALL I SEEKE FOR GRACE?" 911 (197)
"SHALL WE GATHER AT THE RIVER" 2196 (35)
"Shall we gather by the river" 2196 (84)
"Shall we never more behold thee" 1114 (28, 36, 129, 130, 212, 279, 366)
SHALOM CHAVERIM 6250 (389)
"Shalom Chaverim, Shalom Chaverim, Shalom, Shalom" 6250 (389)
"Shame on the man who pursued her" 2703 (131)
THE SHAMROCK SHORE 4751 (198)
Shamus O'Brien 3557 (344)

"Since my dear one's gone, all the joy of morning" 7126 (103, 104)

"Since my love now loves another" 3698 (285)

"SINCE THE TIME I SAW MY DARLING" 155 (285)

"Since the times have grown harder, I've a mind to leave home" 7965 (72)

"SINCE THOU, O FONDEST" 2127 (344)

"Since times are so hard, I've thought" 8144 (126)

SINCE WE PARTED 51 (45)

"Since we parted yester-eve, I do love thee, Love, believe" 51 (45)

"Since yesterday I vainly seek my master" 1338 (2)

"Since you all must have singing and won't be said 'Nay'" 7887 (44)

"Since you've gone away one thing is clear to me" 1865 (345)

"SIND ES SCHMERZEN, SIND ES FREUDEN" 418 (277)

"SIND WIE VEREINT ZUR GUTEN STUNDE" 1520 (31)

"Sind wir geschieden und leb ich ohne dich" 5447 (229)

"SIND WIR NICHT ZUR HERRLICHKEIT GEBOREN" 5542 (31)

SINDY 7997 (242)

"Sindy is a pretty little girl" 7997 (242)

"Sine musica nulla vita" 2289 (49)

"SING A HO THAT I HAD THE WINGS OF A DOVE" 8539 (409)

SING-A-LAMB 9399 (332)

SING-A-LING-A-LING 7998 (343)

SING A LITTLE 4754 (249)

"Sing a little, and play a little" 4754 (249)

SING A MERRY NEW SONG 2973 (86)

"Sing a merry new song, brother, of a new and happy order" 2973 (86)

"Sing a song of cities, cities great and small" 8031 (28, 366)

SING AGAIN THAT SWEET REFRAIN 781 (114, 129, 130, 131)

SING ALL MEN! 9379 (268)

"Sing all men! 'tis Christmas morning" 9379 (268)

"Sing and heave, and heave and sing, doo da, doo da" 9475 (173)

"Sing cheerilie, couthilie, cantie and free" 7112 (105)

"Sing fare-you-well my bonny young girl" 9452 (320)

"Sing Galileans, ye heroes of battle" 6203 (318)

"Sing, Glory, Hallelujah, over de hills an' ev'rywhere" 9389B (184)

SING HALLELU 9400 (332)

"Sing hey my braw John Highlandman" (O gin ye were dead Gudeman, tune) 7175A (232)

"Sing hey my braw John Highlandman" (The white cockade, tune) 7203 (17, 100, 103, 104, 235)

SING LULLABY! LULLABY BABY 8832 (317)

"Sing lullaby! Lullaby baby, now reclining" 8832 (317, 363, 370)

SING MIR DAS LIED NOCH EINMAL 3644 (222)

"SING', NACHTIGALL, SING'" 1771 (223)

SING NOËL, NOËL 9091 (33)

"Sing Noël, Noël, Noël sing joyfully" 9091 (33)

SING O SING! 9031 (388)

"Sing, o sing! hail the Holy one! Jesus Christ, of God the Son" 9031 (388)

"Sing of love, nightingales, O reply to our song" 2963 (292)

SING OF MAIDEN MARY 9118 (244)

"Sing of Maiden Mary, and of Christ our Lord" 9118 (244)

"Sing of the student's happiest day" 1422 (186)

"Sing on, sing on, amid the leafy branches" 2467 (151)

"SING OUT A SONG OF VICTORY" 9029 (361)

SING OVY, SING IVY 4755 (95)

"Sing ree, sing low, sing fair you well" 7835 (72)

SING RHONDDA 2930 (306)

'SING', SAID THE MOTHER 7999 (216)

SING SANG UND KLING KLANG 5543 (31)

SING, SMILE, SLUMBER 1332 (237)

SING, SWEET HARP 6015 (349)

"Sing, sweet harp, oh sing to me some song of ancient days" 6015 (349)

SING THE UNIVERSAL GLORY 8828 (361)

"Sing the universal glory Lo! the serpent's triple head" 8828 (361)

"SING TO THE STUDENT'S HAPPIEST DAY" 1422 (188)

"Sing unto me, O sing, innocent dove, sing to me of the joy of Yemen" 6273 (318)

SING WE MERRILY (Folksongs, England) 4756 (349)

"Sing we merrily, sing Nowell" (Carols, Basque) 8827 (372)

SING WE NOËL 9119 (125)

"Sing we Noël this holy Christmas morn" 9119 (125)

"SING WE NOW MERRILY" 2364 (144)

"Sing we now merrily, our purses are empty" 4756 (349)

SING WE NOW OF CHRISTMAS 9091 (79)

"Sing we now of Christmas, Noël sing we here!" 9091 (79)

"Sing we Nowell, Nowell, Nowell" 9108 (361)

SING WE THE VIRGIN MARY 9380 (261)

"Sing we the Virgin Mary, sing we that matchless one" 9380 (261)

SING WE, THEN, MERRILY 497 (378)

"SING WE TO THIS MERRY COMPANY" 8986 (360, 361)

"SING, WITH ALL THE SONS OF GLORY" 2802 (371)

"Sing with thy mouth, sing with thy heart" 2983 (235)

SING YOUR SONG 4420 (94)

"Sing your song Marimaba" 2036 (248)

"Sing your song, sing, singer!" 4420 (94)

SINGENDE WANDERSCHAFT 1750 (31)

THE SINGER (Folksongs, Finland) 4840 (124)

THE SINGER (Folksongs, Sweden) 7336 (135)

THE SINGER (Head) 1599 (276)

"A singer in a minstrel show was sitting on the end" 2932 (114)

"SINGET DEM HERRN EIN NEUES LIED" 5544 (326)

SINGIN' IN THE RAIN 458 (236)

SINGING AS I TRAVEL 4860 (124)

"Singing as I travel across the water" 4860 (124)

"Singing, blow ye winds in the morning" 9428 (227)

SINGING IN THE LAND 9401 (332)

SINGING IN THE RAIN 1579 (28)

"Singing twinkeedoodleum, twinkeedoodleum" 7461 (44)

"Singing 'Twinkidoodledum, twinkidoodledum'" 7461 (335)

THE SINGLE GIRL 8113E (109, 110)

"'Sinho-ora do Almurtão Quem vos varreu a capela?" 6930 (57)

'SINHORA' DO ALMURTÃO 6930 (57)

"Die sinkende Sonne weint blutig auf starren Schnee" 3893 (74)

SINNER MAN 8540 (230)

SINNER-MAN SO HARD TO BELIEVE 8541 (182)

"Sinner, O see dat cruel tree" 8542 (76)

513

"Smile! and I'll teach thee" 2570 (6)
"Smile the while you kiss me sad adieu" 4020 (233)
SMILES 3043 (233)
SMILING MAY 223 (188)
"Smiling May, we welcome to our fields today" 223 (188)
"The smiling spring, profusely gay" 8686 (86)
"Smirennyĭ inok vdelakh mirskikh nye mudryĭ sudiya" 2616
     (5)
SMOKY MOUNTAIN BILL 4247 (186)
"Smooth it slides upon its travel" 602 (259)
THE SMUGGLER'S SONG 7280 (37)
SMUTNA DOLA 6691 (295)
"Smutna, smutna, Smutna jest dola ma" 6691 (295)
"Smutno niańki ci śpiewały" 670 (295)
"Snake bake hoe cake" 8347 (242)
Sne 2131 (241)
SNOW (Cimara) 677* (121)
SNOW (Lie) 2131 (241)
SNOW FLAKES 724 (237)
THE SNOW IN THE STREET 3803 (334)
"Snow is melting, oh, my dear, my darling" 5781 (22)
"THE SNOW LAY DEEP UPON THE GROUND" 9215 (244)
"THE SNOW LAY ON THE GROUND" (Carols, England)
     8988 (38,39)
"The snow lay on the ground" (Grimes) 1401 (376)
THE SNOW LIES THICK 3440 (334)
"The snow lies thick upon the earth tonight" 3440 (334)
THE SNOW STORM 1601 (189)
"The snow that yesterday so softly" 3392 (112)
"The snow that yesterday was falling" 3392 (209)
"Snow-white kerchief, dark both field and furrow show"
     5705 (22)
THE SNOW-WHITE STEED 8685 (19)
SNOWBELLS 3392 (112,209)
SNOWDROPS 2883 (121)
"Snowdrops grow on yonder hill" 2883 (121)
SNOWFLAKES 2884 (121)
THE SNOWY BREASTED PEARL 6016 (16,172)
"SO ANCH'IO LA VIRTU MAGICA" 860 (6,302)
"SO BEAUTIE ON THE WATERS STOOD" 1063 (144)
"So beautiful, but so unfaithful" 508 (253)
"SO BEN CHE LA SPERANZA" 2858 (179,218)
"So ben, che mir saettano" 3600 (217)
"SO BEN S'IO PENO" 2753 (180)
"So blow, ye winds, westerly, westerly blow" 9430 (173)
"SO CLEARLY I REMEMBER SEEING" 1263 (340)
"So drowsy and lazy, decrepit this world" 747 (159,295)
"So early in the month of May" 4545A (115)
"SO EARLY IN THE MORNING" 9476 (205,235)
"So favor me, Jesucita" 6359 (35)
"SO GEHT ES IM SCHNÜTZELPUTZ-HÄUSEL" 5546 (309)
"So good-night now once more, with roses roof'd o'er" 436
     (122)
"SO GRÜN ALS IST DIE HEIDEN" 5547 (99)
"So hab' ich doch die ganze Woche mein feines Liebchen
     nicht geseh'n" 425 (229,272)
SO HANDY, MY BOYS, SO HANDY 9443B (320)
"So, I wish him joy where'er he dwell" 4670 (397)
"So ist die Lieb'! So ist die Lieb'! Mit Küssen nicht zu
     stillen" 4081 (112)
"So it seemed. He bade me soon to await him" 3849 (1,6)
"So lassen mir die falschen Zungen" 2977 (250)
"SO LEB DENN WOHL, DU STILLES HAUS" 2604 (99,326,
     353)

SO LONG IT'S BEEN GOOD TO KNOW YUH 1431 (293,
     389)
"So look the mornings when the sun" 2937 (344)
"So many fine white dresses, and so much clatter!" 7281
     (219)
SO MANY WHITE DRESSES 7281 (219)
"So Mister Brown you've come at last" 1119 (189)
"So much pride in one small maiden" 5790 (95)
SO NIMM DENN MEINE HÄNDE 3491 (326)
"So nimm denn meine Hände und führe mich" 3491 (326)
SO PÜNKTLICH ZUR SEKUNDE 5548 (31)
"So pünktlich zur Sekunde trifft keine Uhr wohl ein" 5548
     (31)
"SO QUICKE, SO HOT, SO MAD" 559 (144)
"So ry die trein" 7227 (239)
"SO SCHEIDEN WIR MIT SANG UND KLANG" 5549 (353)
"So sei gegrüsst viel tausendmal" 3366 (96,141)
"So singen wir, so trinken wir" 5541 (31)
SO, SIR PAGE 2586 (310)
"So, Sir Page, now you soon must be going" 2586 (310)
"SO, SO, LEAVE OFF THIS LAST LAMENTING KISS"
     1064 (144)
SO SOON FORGOTTEN 648 (341)
"So soon forgotten, I and you, the the only happiness we
     knew" 648 (341)
"SO STELL ICH MIR DIE LIEBE VOR" 3245 (256)
"So still the lilacs hang" 2147 (85)
"So stolz was ich, so unbeschwert und Liebe war" 888
     (255)
SO SWEET IS THE TORMENT 2508 (404)
"So sweet is the torment, that in my heart lies" 2508
     (404)
SO SWEET IS THY DISCOURSE 560 (276)
"So sweet, so sweet is thy discourse to me" 560 (276)
"So take down your shingle and shut up your shop" 3782
     (189)
"SO TREIBEN WIR DEN WINTER AUS" 5550 (49,309,326)
"So we tap, tap, tap, tap the feet of dancing dollies"
     4951 (214)
"SO WEIT WIE DIE WEISSEN WOLKEN GEHN" 4847 (49)
"So when the Samaritans were come unto Him" 279 (160)
"So, will the Lord!" 644 (2)
"SO WILLST DU DES ARMEN" 419 (276)
"So wollt ihr es haben, so soll es sein" 588 (217)
SOAKING HEMP 4374 (94)
"Soaking hemp a pretty maid" 4374 (94)
"Soaring high, the clouds are proudly borne" 2133 (70)
SOCCORRETE, LUCI AVARE 3649 (180)
"Soccorrete, soccorrete, luci avare" 3649 (180)
SOCCORRETEMI PER PIETA (Anonymous) 6140 (181)
"Soccorretemi per pieta, soccorretemi per pieta, occhi
     belli" (Anonymous) 6140 (181)
"Soccorretemi, soccorretemi, ch'io moro! 591 (217)
THE SODGER'S RETURN 7168 (100)
"Sömnig är jag, my mycket trött" 1852 (355)
"Soffro Lontan lontano" 3027 (121,408)
"Soft and clear a silv'ry toll" 2379 (141)
"Soft as the voice of an angel" 4055 (122,128,129,130,
     132,329,346)
"Soft be thy slumbers, rude cares depart" 1112 (129,132)
"Soft o'er the fountain, ling'ring falls the southern moon"
     7261 (28,34,70,132,233,236,279,343,366)
"Soft the moon o'er field and wood" 3251 (199)

"Soft to the manger stealing, beside the Christ-Child
        kneeling" 9148 (244,361)
SOFT WINDS SIGH 7348 (188)
"Soft winds sigh through the woods in Dalarna, swift-flowing
        rapids join the rivers" 7348 (188)
SOFTLY AND TENDERLY 3741 (398)
"Softly and tenderly, Love is healing" 3741 (398)
"Softly branches are swaying" 3625 (112)
"Softly goes my song's entreaty" 3306 (122,328)
"SOFTLY NOW THE LIGHT OF DAY" 3975 (28,132,233,
        236,366)
SOFTLY -O-HA-HA-SOFTLY! 6836 (228)
"Softly rustling, softly rustling thru the Serbian valley"
        8780 (7)
"Softly sighs the breath of evening" 3966 (28,366)
"Softly through the night is calling, love, my song to thee"
        3306 (387)
Sogno 488 (180)
EN SOIGNANT LE LIN 4363 (177)
"En soignant le lin, je ne savais point, pourquoi mon coeur
        était triste" 4363 (177)
UN SOIR, LORSQU'IL PLEUVAIT 1856 (224)
Soirées musicales 3106-3107
"Sois donc sensible à mes soupirs" 4970 (174)
SOKOŁY 2485 (295)
"Sol per te le pene senze spene di mercè" 362 (217)
"Sola en su aposento con el Hijo amado" 8851 (53)
"SOLCHE HERGELAUFNE LAFFEN" 2575 (5)
DER SOLDAT 3492 (31,99)
LE SOLDAT FRANÇAIS 5112 (82)
DER SOLDAT IM FELDE 3885 (74)
"Un soldat revenant de guerre et coucou!" 7357 (155)
SOLDATEN 5529C (31)
SOLDATENABSCHIED 1067 (99)
DIE SOLDATENBRAUT 3393 (99)
THE SOLDIER 4418 (95)
"A soldier born, 'mid campfires gleaming" 756 (147)
SOLDIER BOY (Folksongs, United States) 8007 (28)
SOLDIER BOY (Morse) 2537 (129,130)
"Soldier boy, one kiss before you go" 2537 (129,130)
"Soldier boy, soldier boy, where are you going" 8007 (28)
"A soldier in the cavalry lay on a canvas bunk" 7421 (225)
"Soldier, O soldier, a-comin' from the plain" 7462A (173)
"Soldier rest, gently pressed" 8047 (343)
SOLDIER, SOLDIER, WILL YOU MARRY ME? 8008A (215),
        8008B (331)
"Soldier, soldier, will you marry me with your musket, fife
        and drum" 8008B (331)
SOLDIER, SOLDIER, WON'T YOU MARRY ME? 8008C (34)
"Soldier, soldier, won't you marry me with your musket,
        fife and drum?" 8008A (215,249)
SOLDIER WON'T YOU MARRY ME 8008A (249)
"Soldiers below layin' cold and dead" 3496 (336)
THE SOLDIER'S FAREWELL (Kinkel) 1898 (28,279,366)
SOLDIER'S FAREWELL (Kücken) 1987 (233)
THE SOLDIER'S FAREWELL, OR THE SOUTH SHALL YET BE
        FREE 1708 (161)
THE SOLDIER'S GRAVE 3125 (161)
SOLDIER'S LAMENT 6831 (295)
THE SOLDIER'S LIFE 4116 (44)
"Soldiers marching down the highway" 6341 (128,132,236)
"Soldiers of underground Poland" 2834 (159)
"Soldier's payment, I must get it" 6673 (295)

THE SOLDIER'S SONG (Heaney) 1600 (172,294)
SOLDIER'S SONG (Moniuszko) 2481 (295)
THE SOLDIERS SUIT OF GREY! 1745 (161)
"IL SOLE DIETRO AI MONTI" 6141 (238)
"Le soleil est droit sur la sente" 633 (190,192,194)
"Soleil qui flambes" 1237 (190,192,194)
SOLEMN MELODY 777 (306)
SOLFA-ING 664 (199)
SOLIDARITY 3565 (293)
"Solidarity forever, solidarity forever" 3565 (293)
THE SOLITARY ONE 3622 (274)
SOLITUDE 4085 (220)
DAS SOLL DER SCHÖNSTE WALZER SEIN! 882 (257)
"SOLL ICH DIR MEIN LIEBSCHEN NENNEN?" 5551 (326)
"Sollt ich die edle Kunst" 2175 (250)
"Sollt ich voller Sorg und Pein um ein schönes Mädchen
        sein?" 1561 (226)
SOLO FOR BASS 340 (278)
"Solomon granpa gawn a Equador" 8755 (252)
SOLOMON LEVI 3414 (225,366,402)
SOLVEIG'S SONG 1389 (276)
SOLVEJGS LIED 1389
SOLVEJG'S SONG 1389 (122,137,329,395)
"SOM ETT SILVERSMYCKE" 1832 (355)
"SOM, SOM, SOM W STAWIE RYBECKI" 6828 (295)
"La sombre nuit sous sa chappe de plomb pesante se traine"
        2359 (224)
EL SOMBRERO ANCHO 6387 (247)
"Some ask'd me where Rubies grew" 3537 (259)
"Some birds can find in wide skies their mates" 6339A
        (343)
SOME DAY 4440 (94)
"SOME DAY I'LL WANDER BACK AGAIN" 1737 (114)
"Some day, some day, though I don't know what day"
        4440 (94)
"Some folk say we should laugh and play" 4835 (199)
SOME FOLKS 1134 (129,343,366)
"Some folks like to sigh" 1134 (129,343,366)
"Some folks say dat a darkey won't steal" 8611 (114)
"Some folks say dat de Dummy don' run" 8261 (80)
"Some for Paul and some for Silas" 8252 (332)
"Some like 'em light, some like 'em brown" 8012 (381)
"Some may sigh, for summer's sky" 8004 (189)
"Some men sing of petticoats" 1222 (240)
"Some o' dese mornin's 'bout ten o'clock" 8461 (184)
SOME OF THESE DAYS 8548 (409)
"Some of these days about four o'clock" 7669 (231)
"Some of these mornings bright and fair" 8461 (236,409)
"Some people have an easy life" 6195 (318)
"Some preachers is out a-preachin'" 8246 (266)
"Some say a ride on the trolley is grand" 2455 (204)
"Some talk of Alexander, and some of Hercules" 4555
        (7,13,35,199,234,349)
"Some think the world is made for fun and frolic" 820 (70)
SOMEBODY (Folksongs, United States) 8009 (321)
SOMEBODY (Schumann) 3381 (275)
"SOMEBODY GOT LOST IN DE STORM" 8549 (184)
"Somebody stole my li'l black dog" 7676 (37)
"SOMEBODY'S BURIED IN THE GRAVEYARD" 8550 (409)
SOMEBODY'S DARLING 1649 (161)
"SOMEBODY'S KNOCKING AT YOUR DOOR" 8551 (76,
        409)
"Somebody's tall and handsome" 8009 (321)

SOMEBODY'S WAITING FOR ME 3887 (128,131)
"Somehow I feel that thou art near" 1204 (121)
SOMERSET CAROL 8915 (334)
SOMETHING IN YOUR EAR 5823 (164)
"Something in your ear I would say, 'Choose me for your
     sweetheart, I pray'!" 5823 (164)
"Sometime a-down a magic stream a little boat comes
     sailing" 3149 (344)
SOMETIMES A MARIGOLD 4172 (322)
"SOMETIMES I FEEL LIKE A MOTHERLESS CHILD" 8552
     (52,183,227,284)
"Sometimes I feel like a motherless chile" 8552 (52)
"Sometimes I feel so lonely" 1677 (76)
"Sometimes I plow my old grey horse" 8629 (227)
"Sometimes I'm up, sometimes I'm down" 8248 (409)
SOMEWHERE 2004 (285)
SOMEWHERE FAR 5668 (164)
"Somewhere far my dearest rose is wandering" 5668 (164)
"Somewhere near the Duna River" 2004 (285)
"Somm' venus dans votre vile" 4935 (91)
LE SOMMEIL DE L'ENFANT JESUS 9064 (296)
"Sommeil, sommeil, viens à l'enfant!" 5083 (65)
"Sommeil, sommeil, viens, viens, viens, sommeil, sommeil,
     viens, viens, viens" 4911 (88)
"Sommeil, vite, vite, vite, sommeil, vite reviens donc"
     4899 (91)
DIE SOMMERNACHT 1279 (99,226)
Ein Sommernachtstraum 2393-2394
SOMMERSEGEN 5552 (49)
"Sommerzeit, wenn am Walle die Rosen blühn" 1859 (31)
"Somos los indios rojos puro Atahualpa" 6659 (207)
SON ANCOR PARGOLETTA 622 (179)
"Son ancor pargoletta, son ancor pargoletta e amor non
     provo" 622 (179)
"Son bella pastorella, che scende ogni mattino" 3106
     (211)
"Son giunta! gazie, o Dio" 3841 (1)
"Son gofran gesa e vengo da Parigge" 721 (132)
SON IO, BARBARA DONNA 949 (181)
"Son io, mio Carlo" 3831 (4)
"Son io, son io, barbara donna" 949 (181)
"SON LO SPIRITO CHE NEGA" 355 (299)
SON LOS OJITOS 6388 (247)
"Son los ojitos de la vida mía los que ando buscando" 6388
     (247)
SON POVERA DONZELLA 2258 (179)
"Son povera donzella, son povera donzella, altro non ho
     che il core" 2258 (179)
SON PRIGIONIERO 2253 (180)
"Son prigioniero del nume arciero" 2253 (180)
SON TRE MESI, CHE FO IL SOLDATO 7383 (155)
"Son tre mesi, son tre mesi che fo il soldato" 7383 (155)
SON VERGIN VEZZOSA 256 (302)
"Son vergin vezzosa in veste di sposa" 256 (302)
Sonata, piano, no.2, op.35, B flat major. Marche funebre
     673 (295)
Sonata, piano, op.27, no.2, C minor. Adagio sostenuto
     246 (123)
SONG (Copland) 705 (85)
"Song bird, song bird, whence came you here?" 2489 (295)
"A song for our banner" (Constance) 702 (129,130)
"A song for our banner?" (Wallace) 3932 (189)
"A song I will sing unto you" 4810A (198)
THE SONG I WON'T FORGET 4528 (207)

"A song I've got my friends for you" 7598 (189)
SONG OF A MEXICAN SARAPE 2469 (9)
SONG OF A THOUSAND YEARS 4110 (129,130,279)
THE SONG OF ALL SONGS 1135 (189)
SONG OF APRIL 322 (191,195)
SONG OF FAREWELL 1890 (339)
SONG OF FATHERLAND 2885 (342)
A SONG OF FELLOWSHIP 1222 (240)
SONG OF FIONNUALA 6014 (166,213)
THE SONG OF FORGETTING 3428 (142,245)
SONG OF FREEDOM 3504 (7)
SONG OF HOPE 6205 (30)
A SONG OF INDIA 3039 (241)
SONG OF JOAN OF ARC 5113 (37)
SONG OF KOŚCIUSZKO 1786 (295)
SONG OF LIFE 3279 (141)
SONG OF LIHUE 5648 (279)
SONG OF OUR COUNTRY 938 (287,288)
SONG OF PENITENCE 227 (8)
SONG OF PRAISE (Folksongs, Finland) 4818 (124)
SONG OF PRAISE (Folksongs, United States) 8010 (242)
SONG OF REVENGE 335 (339)
SONG OF ST. MARY 2283 (330)
A SONG OF SORROW (Duparc) 940 (362)
THE SONG OF SORROW (Folksongs, Ireland) 6031 (166,
     213)
A SONG OF THANKSGIVING 52 (237)
SONG OF THE AIR FORCE (Mîaskovskiĭ) 2418 (162)
SONG OF THE ARMOURER 2650 (240)
SONG OF THE BALTIC FLEET 336 (339)
SONG OF THE CABINET MAKER 3311 (141)
SONG OF THE CRIB 9163 (271,296,307)
SONG OF THE DEW 3639 (341)
THE SONG OF THE DRUMMER 4931 (210)
SONG OF THE FAR EASTERN PARTISANS 100 (7)
SONG OF THE FISHES 9430 (173)
THE SONG OF THE FLEA (Beethoven) 247 (273)
SONG OF THE FRENCH PARTISAN 2277 (293)
SONG OF THE GIRL AT THE WINDOW 3704 (121)
SONG OF THE GOLDEN CALF 1322 (5)
SONG OF THE GOLDEN CORN 6665 (219)
SONG OF THE GREAT WALL 1722 (35)
SONG OF THE HARVESTERS 1049 (408)
SONG OF THE HOMEFRONT 6647 (7)
SONG OF THE INTERNATIONAL BRIGADE 1011 (7)
SONG OF THE LAPPS 4827 (124)
SONG OF THE LARK 2674 (295)
SONG OF THE LUMBERMEN 4854 (124)
SONG OF THE MEADOW LAND 1923 (237)
THE SONG OF THE NAVY 4141 (129,236)
SONG OF THE NIGHT WATCHMAN 5375B (230)
SONG OF THE OPEN 2015 (241)
SONG OF THE PEDLAR 2400 (124)
SONG OF THE PENNIES 1147 (293)
SONG OF THE PORT 303 (30)
SONGS OF THE POSADAS, NO. 1 9222 (251)
SONGS OF THE POSADAS, NO. 2 9221 (251)
SONG OF THE RAFTSMEN 6714 (159)
SONG OF THE REED-BIRDS 5640 (86)
THE SONG OF THE ROOSTER 6304 (37)
THE SONG OF THE SEA (Folksongs, Netherlands) 6582
     (86,316)
SONG OF THE SEA (Indy) 1747 (191,193,195)
SONG OF THE SEA (Kabalevskiĭ) 1843 (339)

"Spring's a pleasant time" 6995 (103,104)
THE SPRING'S ACOMING 4762 (95)
SPRING'S BREEZES PLAYING 7345 (135)
"Spring's breezes playing over the spraying of tiny brooklets all through the land" 7345 (135)
SPRING'S SECRET 400 (275)
"SPRINGT OP EN TOONT UW SCHOEN" 6575 (203)
SPRINGTIME 6866 (295)
"Springtime brings a mem'ry to me" 2308 (132)
"Springtime flaunts his banner blue" 3363 (359)
SPRINGTIME IS HERE 5137 (95)
THE SPRINGTIME OF THE YEAR 4763 (306)
"Spunta l'alba del sedici giugno" 6114 (238)
SQUARIN' UP TIME 8037A (186)
THE SQUID-JIGGIN' GROUND 3176 (186)
THE SQUIRE OF EDINBORO TOWN 8019 (126)
THE SQUIRREL 8020 (214)
"The squirrel is a pretty thing" 8020 (214)
"'STA NOTTE È BELLO LO MARE" 6144 (51)
"Sta sera Nina mia io son mon talo" 820 (70)
Stabat mater 3108-3109
DIE STADT 3305 (407)
DIE STADT DER LIEDER 1674 (396)
STÄNDCHEN (Brahms) 426 (112,407)
STÄNDCHEN (Folksongs, Italy) 6088 (51)
STÄNDCHEN (Mozart) 2582 (99,226,229)
STÄNDCHEN (Schubert "Hark, hark! the lark!") 3309 (75, 132,137,395)
STÄNDCHEN (Schubert "Leise flehen meine Lieder...") 3306 (122,237,328,329,387)
STÄNDCHEN (Strauss, R.) 3633 (112)
STÄNDCHEN (Suppé) 3676 (255)
STÄNDCHEN (Zelter) 4140 (229)
STÄNDCHEN DES DON JUAN 637 (240)
STAFFAN WAR EIN STALLKNECHT 9335 (354)
"Staffan war ein Stallknecht mal" 9335 (354)
STAFFANSVISA 9336 (388)
STAGOLEE DONE KILL DE BULLY 8555 (184)
STAŁA MARYSIA NAD WODA 6838 (159)
"Stała Marysia nad woda, ciesząc sie swoją uroda" 6838 (159)
"The stalwart forests clothe thy rugged mountains" 3464 (343)
STAN' STILL JORDAN 8556 (52,182)
"Stan' still Jordan, stan' still Jordan" 8556 (52,182)
STANCUTZA 6938 (95)
"Stand Navy out to sea, fight our battle cry" 4141 (236)
STAND THE STORM 8557 (409)
"Stand up and rejoice!" 7649 (293)
"Stand up now Saint Simeion, and tell what twelve are" 4472 (230)
"STAND UP, STAND UP, FOR JESUS" 3958 (35)
"THE STANDARD ON THE BRAES O' MAR" 7170 (101)
"Standin' down in New York Town one day" 1429 (336)
STANDIN' IN DE NEED OF PRAYER 8558A (76)
STANDIN' IN THE NEED OF PRAYER 8558A (183)
STANDING ON A HILLOCK 4832 (124)
"Standing on a hillock well above the lake" 4832 (124)
STANDING ON THE MOUNTAIN 5554 (37)
"Standing on the mountain, gaze far down the valley" 5554 (37)
STANDS A DUCK 4359 (94)
"Stands a duck on high hill" 4359 (94)
STANDS A MAPLE 6839 (95)
"Stands a maple tall and fair" 6839 (95)

"Stands a maple tree, deep in the forest" 6258 (95)
STAN'IN' IN DE NEED OF PRAYER 8558A (182)
"Stańmy bracia wraz, Ile jest tu nas" 6840 (295)
STAŃMY, WRAZ 6840 (295)
STAP AN! 6576 (384)
"Stap an, stap an, stap an, recht naar de kroeg" 6576 (384)
A STAR IN HEAVEN 6841 (37)
"A star in heaven shone one night" 9337 (165)
STAR IN THE EAST 9381 (332)
"A star is brightly burning" 2797 (373)
STAR MAIDEN 3569 (188)
"Star maiden, you that I met" 3569 (188)
THE STAR OF BETHLEHEM 2334 (394)
STAR OF COLUMBIA 951 (109,110)
"The Star of Empire poets say, Ho! westward ho!" 851 (189)
STAR OF THE EAST 1762 (410)
"Star of the East! whose beacon light" 1762 (410)
"Star of the mariner! Virgin most holy" 2848 (2)
"Star of the morn, arise" 1337 (3)
STAR OF THE MORNING 3677 (295)
"Star of the morning, God's throne adorning" 3677 (295)
"The star shines above Thee" 1073 (244)
"A star shone up in heaven the night the child was born" 9198 (165)
THE STAR-SPANGLED BANNER 8021 (7,10,28,32,34,35, 44,129,130,233,236,279,293,294,343,366)
THE STAR THAT LED TO BETHLEHEM 9337 (165)
STAR VICINO 3077 (139,275)
"Star vicino al bel' idol che s'ama" 3077 (139,275)
STARA WISŁA 2678 (295)
STARLIGHT AND SUNSHINE 2110 (132)
"Starlight and sunshine will always remind me of you" 2110 (132)
"STARS AND HILLS ARE HOARY" 8833 (361)
"Stars and the sea are smiling" 3856 (1)
"Stars are gleaming, day is o'er" 3541 (345)
STARS ARE SHINING 5660 (164)
"The stars are shining cheerily" 7185 (37,101,102,105, 235)
"Stars are shining to relieve us" 5660 (164)
THE STARS IN HEAVEN ARE BRIGHT 8686 (349)
"Stars in heav'n are shining bright" 810 (292)
STARS IN THE HEAVEN 8022 (332)
"Stars of ice and a wheeling moon" 4022 (244)
"STARS OF THE SUMMER NIGHT" 4097 (28,129,130, 132,233,236,279,366)
"The stars shine above you, yet linger awhile" 3079 (236)
STARS SHINE BRIGHT 5660 (92)
"Stars shine bright their light to give us" 5660 (92)
THE STARS THEY SHINE SO BRIGHTLY 7299 (188)
"The stars they shine so brightly all in the sky above" 7299 (188)
STARS WITH TINY FEET 1160 (407)
"Stars with tiny feet so golden" 1160 (407)
STARVING TO DEATH ON A GOVERNMENT CLAIM 8023A (227)
"Stasera, Nina mia, io son mantato" 820 (128,132)
"Stat op Sankte Simeon og sigmig hvad Tolver" 4472 (230)
STATE OF ARKANSAS 8024 (110,227)
"The stately ships along the quay" 1044 (140)
THE STATELY SOUTHERNER 9484 (320)
THE STATUE AT CZASKOE-SELO 739 (357)

THE STATUE OF TSARSKOYE SELO 739 (340)
STAWAM NA PLACU 6842 (159)
"Stawam na placu, z Boga ordynansu" 6842 (159)
"Stay and I'll sing! What'll you sing?" 9382B (332)
STAY THOU NEAR BY 116 (405)
"Stay thou near by, then go I gladly" 116 (405)
"Stay thou true thy dear to me" 8662 (235)
"STAY TIME, AWHILE, THY FLYING" 915 (197)
"Stay yet awhile, beloved" 2812 (364)
"STEADY, JESUS LISTENIN" 8559 (409)
STEADY NEIGHBORS 9081 (361)
"Steady neighbors give up their labours" 9081 (361)
STEAL AWAY 8560 (10, 28, 35, 76, 129, 233, 279, 366)
"Steal away an' pray, I'm lookin' for my Jesus" 8360 (184)
STEAL AWAY AND PRAY 8360 (409)
"Steal away, steal away, steal away to Jesus!" 8560 (10,
    28, 35, 76, 129, 183, 233, 279, 366, 402, 409)
STEAL AWAY TO JESUS 8560 (183, 402, 409)
"Steal up, young ladies, mah mammy stoled a cow" 8417
    (80)
STEAMBOAT DOWN TO TOWN 8025 (145)
"Steamboat down to town, steamboat down to town" 8025
    (145)
"De steamboats on de Hudson Lawd know what make 'em go"
    7989 (191)
"DER STECHDORN UND DER EFEU" 8941A (354)
DAS STECKENPFERD 1635 (99)
THE STEEL BATTALIONS 2728 (7)
"The steel battalions are marching all singing a fighting
    song" 2728 (7)
STEEL GOT TO BE DROVE 8561 (77)
STEEL-LININ' CHANT 8026 (331)
"Steh ich in finstrer Mitternacht" 5566 (31, 99)
STEH NUR AUF, DU HANDWERKSGESELL 5555 (309)
"Steh nur auf, steh nur auf, du Handwerksgesell" 5555 (309)
"STEHN ZWEI STERN AM HOHEN HIMMEL" 5556 (49,
    309, 326)
"STEIG ICH DEN BERG HINAUF" 5557 (326)
A STEIN SONG 470 (240)
"Stell' auf den Tisch die duftenden Reseden" (Lassen) 2047
    (327)
"Stell' auf den Tisch die duftenden Reseden" (Strauss) 3619
    (112, 122)
STELLA DEL MARINAR 2848 (2)
"Stella del marinar! Virgine Santa" 2848 (2)
La stellidaura vendicata 2886
STEP IT UP AND GO 8562 (336)
STEP TOGETHER 187 (172)
"STERBEN IST EIN HARTE BUSS" 3016 (49)
"STERNE MIT DEN GOLD'NEN FÜSSCHEN" 1160 (407)
"STERNE SIND, DAMIT SIE STRAHLEN" 5660 (92)
Stets in Trauern muss ich leben (tune) 5499 (309)
"STETS IN TRURE MUESS I LEBE" 7385 (158)
STEV FRA TELEMARKEN 6648 (230)
DIE STEWELJIES VAN SANNIE 6577 (384)
DIE STEWELTJES VAN SANNIE 6577 (86)
"Stickorna gaar slamrar och slaar maskorna fogas täta" 2762
    (356)
Stieglitz, Stieglitz, 's Zeiserl is Krank (tune) 5441 (353)
"Still and dark the night about the sheiling" 3161 (307)
STILL AS THE NIGHT 352 (36, 132, 136, 348)
"Still as the night, deep as the sea" 352 (36, 136, 237, 348)
"Still as the night, true constantly" 352 (132)
"Still is the night" 3304 (272)

"Still ist die Nacht" 3304 (98, 250, 272)
"Still, now, and hear my singing" 4231 (186)
"STILL RUHT DER SEE" 2805 (326, 353)
"Still slept the house when I rose this morning" 2682 (124)
STILL, STILL, STILL 9177A (40, 412), 9177B (49)
"STILL, STILL, STILL, WEIL'S KINDLEIN SCHLAFEN WILL"
    9177A (40, 353, 412)
"Still, still, still wer Gott erkennen will" 9177B (49)
"Still, still with Thee, when purple morning breaketh"
    2545 (28, 366)
STILL WIE DIE NACHT 352 (36, 327)
"Still wie die Nacht tief wie das Meer" 352 (36, 327)
STILL, WITH THEE 2545 (28, 366)
"STILL YOU'VE NOT COME" 4322 (94)
STILLE NACHT 1408 (326, 353, 354)
STILLE NACHT! HEILIGE NACHT! 1408 (326, 353, 354)
"Stille Nacht, heilige Nacht! Alles schläft, einsam wacht"
    1408 (326, 353, 354)
STILLE SICHERHEIT 1161 (330)
STILLUNG MARIÄ MIT DEM AUFERSTANDENEN 1666 (98)
"STIMMT AN MIT HELLEM, HOHEM KLANG" 2405 (31,
    326)
STINA DEAR 7321 (135)
"Stina dear, take my arm" 7321 (135)
"Stina här här du mig" 7321 (135)
EN STJÄRNA GICK PAA HIMLEN FRAM 9337 (165)
STJÄRNÖGA 3569 (188)
"Stjärnöga, du som jag mött" 3569 (188)
"Sto crescendo un gentil cardellino" 6068 (51)
STO LAT 6843 (295)
"Sto lat, Sto lat, Niechaj żyje, żyje nam" 6843 (295)
STODOLA PUMPA 4423 (28)
"STÓDUM TVAU Í TÚNI" 5841 (230)
"STÓJÍ JANO PRI POTOCE" 4424 (177)
"EINE STOLZE SCHÖNHEIT LIEBEND" 43 (253)
STOLZENFELS AM RHEIN 2352 (328)
"The stones that built George Ridler's oven" 4610 (198)
"Stop and lemme tell you 'bout the coming of the Savior"
    8296A (227)
"Stop it! boy I angry" 3738 (11)
"Stop po' sinner, don't you run" 8559 (409)
STOP THAT TEASING 6855 (159)
"Stop that teasing, tell me darling, what am I to do"
    6855 (159)
STOR OLA, LILL' OLA 7337 (230)
"Stor Ola, lill' Ola! Nu körer jag vall" 7337 (230)
"Stories are told by prophets of old" 6230 (318)
STORKS IN AUTUMN 5780 (164)
"Storks in autumn on their journey sally forth" 5780 (164)
"The storm o'er the ocean flew furious and fast" 3126
    (189)
"The storm through the forest is roaring amain" 3278
    (276)
STORM WARNING 8768 (11)
STORMALONG 9468 (235)
THE STORMY MORNING 3322 (45)
"THE STORMY SCENES OF WINTER" 9485 (186)
"A story, a story to you I will tell" 7743 (72)
"A story has come down from old Mathusem" 7827 (72)
THE STORY OF NORAH 8563 (266)
THE STORY OF THE SHEPHERD 183 (244)
THE STORY OF TWELVE 9382A (331)
THE STORY THAT NEVER GROWS OLD 22 (315)
"Stosst an! (Jena) soll leben!" 307 (99)

"Stosst an! soll leben!" 307 (31)
STOUT HEARTS 6817 (295)
"Ein Sträusschen am Hute, den Stab in der Hand" 5583 (31)
STRAHLENDER MOND 1994 (255)
"Strahlender Mond, der am Himmelsselt thront" 1994 (255)
"Straight from the dairy, fresh as a fairy" 4973 (95)
"A strain of music is sounding" 6906 (350)
"Strains of Humoresque divine you thrill and fill this heart of mine" 956 (132)
"Lo stral gia non spezzai" 2726 (218)
STRANGE FRUIT 48 (293)
THE STRANGER TOOK THE LAND I HAD 3981 (30)
"The strangest thing I ever heard" 6405 (95)
Straszny dwór 2486-2487
Stratonice 2350 (147)
STRAWBERRIES 4841 (124)
"Strawberries red, and strawberries rare" 59 (189)
STRAWBERRY FAIR 4764 (145)
STRAWBERRY GIRL 8027 (21)
THE STRAWBERRY ROAN 8028 (186)
STREAK O' LEAN 8029 (242)
"Streak o' lean, streak o' fat, a-kill ma dog and kill ye cat" 8029 (242)
"The streamlet swiftly rushing" 3301 (330)
STREET CRIES ("Watermelons...") 8610B (335)
STREET CRY ("Dark the night is...") 6389 (37)
STREET SONG 8564 (409)
STREET URCHINS' MEDLEY 8031 (28,366)
THE STREETS OF LAREDO 8032A (34,171,227)
"Strengthen the hands of our brothers" 6182 (318)
"STRESSO PER ENTRO AL PETTO" 3650 (180)
STRIDE LA VAMPA 3867 (2,300)
"Stride la vampa la folla indomita" 3867 (2,300)
STRIDONO LASSÙ 2115 (1,176)
"Stridono lassù, liberamente lanciati a vol" 2115 (1,176)
THE STRIFE IS O'ER 2734 (346,400)
STRIKE FOR THE SOUTH 2815 (161)
"Strike for the South! let her name be the boast of the true and the brave" 2815 (161)
"Strike, strike, with hammer in your hand" 3147 (318)
"Strömt herbei ihr Völkerscharen" 2788 (31)
"Stroiły mi duszę Brzózki, polne grusze" 3687 (295)
STRONG IS THE OAR 5150 (219)
"Strong is the oar that can hold us in the current" 5150 (219)
"Strongly founded, a marble tower" 2558 (1)
"Stroskany drogiej upadkiem Ojczyny" 6831 (295)
STUDENT SEIN 5558 (31)
"Student sein, wenn die Veilchen blühen, das erste Lied die Lerche singt" 5558 (31)
STUDENTENLEBEN 3026 (31)
STUDENTENLIED 2697 (31)
STUDENTENSINN 5559 (31)
"Studia il passo o mio figlio!" 3845 (5)
STUDIO AUF EINER REIS 3203 (43,353)
"Studio auf einer Reis' juchheidi, juchheida, ganz famos zu leben weiss" 3203 (31,43,353)
STUDY WAR NO MORE 8170 (409)
EIN STÜNDLEIN WOHL VOR TAG 1162 (226)
DER STURMISCHE MORGAN 3322 (45)
"Die Stunden, einst mit dir verbracht" 2649 (223)

"Sturdy, youthful, and handsome" 672* (295)
STYLE ALL THE WHILE 8033 (28,366)
ŠTYRI HODINY 4425 (94)
"Štyri hodiny do dňa" 4425 (94)
SU E GIÒ DEL CORRIDOR 6145 (325)
"Su e giò del corridor per vedé gh'é el pittor su e giò, in ponta de pé" 6145 (325)
SU E GIÙ PER IL CORRIDOIO 6125 (325)
"Su, finiscila coi baci" 2785 (132,223)
SU LA PIÙ ALTA CIMA 6146 (238)
"Su la più alta cima cantava un lugherin" 6146 (238)
"Su, su, su, du Windchen, sing' zur Ruh mein Kindchen" 4067 (308)
"Su su su su su, schlaf, mein liebes Kindelein" 9149 (354)
"Sublime añoranza guarda el alma mía" 146 (284)
SUCH A LI'L' FELLOW 838 (136)
"SUCH A REALLY LOVELY SWEETHEART" 4430 (94)
"Such a really pretty sweetheart" 4430 (95)
"Such' im Wald seit vielen Stunden, Hab' Mädel nicht gefunden" 5720 (25)
SUCKIN' CIDER THROUGH A STRAW 7795 (109)
SUCKING CIDER THRO' A STRAW 7795 (402)
EL SUEÑO 4171 (207)
SUEÑO DE UN MARINO 8034 (113)
SÜRÜ CSILLAG RITKÁN RAGYOG AZ ÉGEN 5801 (164)
"Süsse heilige Natur, lass mich gehn auf deiner Spur" 3336 (96)
SÜSSER DIE GLOCKEN NIE KLINGEN 5539 (353)
"Süsser die Glocken nie klingen als zurder Weihnachtszeit" 5539 (353)
SUFFER THE LITTLE CHILDREN 1556 (123)
SUGAR AND TEA 8035 (242)
SUGAR BABE BLUES 8565 (336)
SUGAR-CANE 8653 (219,322)
SUGARBUSH 7225 (239)
"Sugarbush come dance with me" 7225 (239)
"Sugarcane, sugarbeet, all good children like a treat" 8653 (322)
"ŠUHAJKO BIJÚ MŇA" 4426 (94)
ŠUHAJKO LUTERÁN 4427 (94)
"Šuhajko luterán, a teba vôľu mám" 4427 (94)
SUICIDIO! 2849 (143,301)
"Suicidio! In questi fieri momenti" 2849 (143,301)
"Suikerbos ek wil jou he" 7225 (239)
THE SUITORS 6844 (228)
SUKSIMIESTEN LAULU 695 (124)
SUL CAPPELLO 6147 (238)
"Sul cappello sul cappello che noi portiamo" 6147 (238)
"SUL FIL D'UN SOFFIO ETESTIO" 3840 (143)
"SUL LIMITAR DEL MITE APRIL" 2347 (411)
"Sul mare luccica l'astro d'argento" 1303 (310)
SUL PONTE DI BASSANO 6148 (238)
"Sul ponte di Bassano là ci darem la mano" 6148 (238)
SULEIKA'S SONG 3383 (276)
SULLA CIMA DI QUEL MONTE 6099 (325)
"Sulle, sulle, labbra" 70 (93,329)
"Sullenly raging, wild winds are moaning" 6818 (295)
"SUMER IS ICUMEN IN" 4765 (70,199,235,402)
DER SUMMA IST UMMA 5560 (41)
"Der Summa ist umma, fallen d'Laba vom Baum" 5560 (41)
SUMMER EVENING 4830 (124)

SWEET AND PRECIOUS JESUS 888 (154)
"Sweet and precious Jesus, infant loved and cherished" 8888 (154)
"SWEET BABE, A GOLDEN CRADLE HOLDS THEE" 6019 (199)
SWEET BABY, SLEEP 8989 (271)
"Sweet baby sleep! What ails my dear" 8989 (271)
SWEET BETSY FROM PIKE 8037A (35, 80, 109, 110, 170, 173, 215, 227, 279, 331, 335), 8037C (242)
SWEET BY-AND-BY 3979 (129, 130)
SWEET CHACOUN 8769 (11)
SWEET CHEEKS TO ME TURNING 414 (364)
"Sweet cheeks to me turning, you fill me with yearning" 414 (364)
"Sweet, dreamland faces, passing to and fro" 1741 (129, 130, 132)
"Sweet fa's the eve on Craigie-burn" 7030 (101)
SWEET FERNS 8038 (243)
"Sweet ferns, sweet ferns, they tell me my lover is true" 8038 (243)
SWEET GENEVIEVE 3774 (10, 28, 36, 129, 130, 233, 236, 366)
SWEET GEORGIA BROWN 293 (345)
"SWEET IF YOU LIKE AND LOVE ME STIL" 1822 (144)
SWEET INNISFALLEN 6020 (349)
"Sweet Innisfallen, fare thee well" 6020 (349)
SWEET JANE 8039 (262)
SWEET KATE 1823 (196, 199)
"Sweet Kate of late ran away and left me 'plaining" 1823 (196, 199)
SWEET KITTY CLOVER 4767 (402)
"Sweet Kitty Clover, she bothers me so, O, O!" 4767 (402)
SWEET MARIE 2516 (114, 131, 132)
"SWEET MARY THROUGH A THORN-GROVE DID GO" 9169 (230)
SWEET NIGHTINGALE (Folksongs, England) 4768 (234)
SWEET NIGHTINGALE (Folksongs, France) 5117 (95)
"Sweet nightingale, awake, awake, come forth fair warbler now" 9184 (388)
"Sweet nightingale, forever faithful" 5117 (95)
"Sweet nightingales, with their accents entrancing" 5104 (174)
"SWEET NYMPH, COME TO THY LOVER" 2530 (196)
SWEET ORANGES 8568 (184)
"Sweet oranges, sweeter than de honey" 8568 (184)
"Sweet our legends and our stories" 6960 (352)
SWEET POLLY OLIVER 4737 (48)
SWEET ROSIE O'GRADY 2681 (166)
"Sweet Rosie O'Grady, my dear little rose" 2681 (166)
"Sweet sings the soaring lark" 3286 (141)
"Sweet sir, for your courtesie, when ye come by the Bass" 7120 (100, 105)
"Sweet sounds the woodland horn" 1082 (240)
"Sweet, sweet, sweet! O happy I am" 217 (259)
"Sweet, sweet, sweet, sweet, sweet tea" 3743 (85)
SWEET THING 7526C (227)
SWEET TRINITY 4617A (111)
"A sweet Tuxedo girl you see" 3172 (32, 34)
SWEET VIOLETS 8040 (321)
"Sweet violets, covered all over with shnow" 8040 (321)
SWEET WAS THE SONG (Attey) 99 (144, 197)
"Sweet was the song the Virgin sang" (Attey) 99 (197)
"SWEET WAS THE SONG THE VIRGIN SANG" (Ballet) 166 (307, 333, 361)

"Sweet was the song the Virgin sung" (Attey) 99 (144)
SWEET WILLIE 8041 (243)
"SWEETE CUPID, RIPEN HER DESIRE" 711 (196)
SWEETE KATE 1823 (144)
"Sweete Kate of late ran away and left me playning" 1823 (144)
"Sweeter sounds the song of birds" 410 (137)
"The sweetest girl I ever saw, sat sucking cider thro' a straw" 7795 (402)
"Sweetheart, I have grown so lonely" 842 (114, 131)
"Sweetheart mine, good night, dearest love, good night!" 5353 (95)
"Sweetly play and sweetly laugh" 2776 (134)
"SWEETLY SANG A GENTLE NIGHTINGALE" 1260 (341)
"SWEETLY SING THE GLORIOUS ANGELS" 9410 (315)
"Sweetly sing when the hour of daylight fades away" 1332 (237)
"Sweetly sings the donkey at the break of day" 7552 (28, 343)
"The swift gazelle has enchanted me" 5856 (86)
"SWIFT MY HEART SURRENDERS" 2340 (139)
"Swift through the yielding air I glide" 2066 (107)
"Swiftly flies life's moment brief of happiness" 7546 (113)
"The swineherd Peter, sitting on the grass, sang this song:" 7334 (135)
THE SWING 1835 (199)
SWING ALONG, SUE 8569 (77)
SWING LOW 8570 (409)
SWING LOW SWEET CHARIOT 8570 (10, 28, 35, 76, 78, 129, 130, 182, 183, 233, 236, 279, 343, 366, 402)
"Swing low, sweet chariot, comin' fo' to carry me home" 8570 (28, 279, 343, 366)
"Swing low, sweet chariot, comin' for to carry me home" 8570 (10, 35, 76, 129, 130, 132, 233, 236)
"Swing low, sweet chariot, coming for to carry me home" 8570 (78, 402, 409)
SWING ON THE CORNER 8042 (110)
"Swing your partner, hold her tight" 8005 (399)
"Swing'n turn, Jubilee" 7747 (313)
SWORD BLADE MARCH 2242 (7)
THE SWORD OF ROBERT LEE 327 (161)
"Sydämestäni rakastan sua elinaikani" 4853 (124)
"Sylva, Sylva, one day, one day" 4599 (198)
SYLVELIN 3505 (122, 137)
"Sylvelin, God's own blessing be on you the whole day through" 3505 (122)
"Sylvelin, may God's blessing rest ever upon your head" 3505 (137)
"Sylvelin, segne Gott Dich auf Erden zu jeder Stund'!" 3505 (122, 137)
SYMPHONY FROM THE CHRISTMAS ORATORIO 139 (307)
Symphony, no. 5, op. 64, E minor. Andante cantabile 650 (123)
Symphony, no. 5, op. 95, New World 958 (343)
Symphony, no. 9, op. 125, D minor. Presto; arr. 248 (99)
SYNTYMISTÄÄN SUREVA 4850 (124)
SYR HARRI DDU 8697 (349)
SYSEL A KRTEK 1977 (74)
"SZAGOS MÁLYVA, GYÖNGYVIRÁG" 1879 (285)
SZALMASZÁL A VIZBE 5802 (164)
"SZÁNT A BABÁM CSIREG, CSÖRÖG" 5803 (23)
"A szántói hires utca, Cimbalommal van kirakva" 5804 (289)
A SZÁNTÓI UTCA 5804 (289)

TELL, O TELL HER 1958 (121)

"Tell, O tell her, forget the compulsion of fate" 1958 (121)

"Tell us true, where are you going, Limpy low, limpy lee?" 5146 (21)

"Temerari, sortite fuori di questo loco!" 2558 (1)

TEMETŐBE LÁTTALAK MEG 5817 (92)

"Temetőbe láttalak meg legelébb, mikor az édesanyádat temették" 5817 (92)

TEMETŐBEN LÁTTALAK MEG LEGELÉBB 5817 (164)

The tempest 2924-2926

"Il tempo, il tempo, fugge" 615 (367)

LE TEMPS DES LILAS 658 (357)

"Le temps des lilas et le temps des roses" 658 (357)

"Tempt me not, O world, again" 4085 (220,359)

Tempus adest floridum (tune) 8935 (28,33,35,38,39,79, 125,154,199,206,296,305,315,319,334,349,361, 363,366,388)

"Ten fingers, ten toesies, as sweet as the posies" 1901 (128)

TEN GREEN BOTTLES 4770 (402)

TEN LITTLE FINGERS AND TEN LITTLE TOES 3400 (128)

Ten little Indians (tune) 8120 (170)

TEN THOUSAND MILES 7661 (215)

"A TENDER CHILD WAS BORN THIS DAY" 9328 (154)

A TENDER EMOTION 2583 (211)

"A tender emotion I feel in my bosom" 2583 (211)

"A tender flow'r thou seemest, so pure so fair thou art" 3117 (385)

"The tender moon beam bathes in the wood" 1503 (237)

THE TENDERFOOT 8049 (186)

TENDRESSES 3785 (356)

"Teneste la promessa...La disfida ebbe luogo" 3858 (301)

"Tengo mi carro paseado" 7818 (314)

TENGO 'NU CHIUOVO 'MPIETTO 6151 (325)

"Tengo 'nu chiuovo 'mpietto e nun ce pare" 6151 (325)

TENGO UNA NOVIA 6392 (247)

"Tengo una novia muy alta muy delgadita" 6392 (247)

"TENHO BARCOS, TENHO REMOS" 6932 (58)

TENKRATE BUDE VICTORIA 4435 (231)

TENTING ON THE OLD CAMP GROUND 1904 (10,28,279, 366)

TENTING TONIGHT 1904 (32,34,109,110)

TERESINA, VA, TI VESTI 6152 (325)

"Teresina, va, ti vesti, ché al bal te vol menar" 6152 (325)

"The term is past, and once again are ended the seven years" 3899 (4)

IL TESTAMENTO DEL CAPITANO 6153 (238)

"Teures Bändchen, süsse Schlinge" 1212 (167)

TEUTOBURGER SCHLACHT 5562• (31)

THE TEUTON'S TRIBULATION 8050 (189,225)

TEUTS SÖHNE 5563 (31)

TEXAS COWBOY 8051 (120)

THE TEXIAN BOYS 8116 (227)

Tha tighin fodham Eirigh! (tune) 7169 (101,102)

Thady, you gander (tune) 5989 (166,213,297)

Thamama Hulla (tune) 5956 (166,213)

THANK GOD I'M ON MY WAY TO HEAVEN 8582 (409)

THANK YOU, NO! 6649 (95)

THANKS 2696 (123)

"Thar' is gwine to be a festival this evenin'" 1024 (114, 115,131)

"Thar was a man, and he lived in England" 7799B (331)

That. See also Dat

"That big husky brute from the cattle chute" 7440 (214)

"That chuck wagon brute from the cattle chute" 7440 (335)

"That Gospel Train is comin'" (THE GOSPEL TRAIN) 8289 (110)

"That gospel train is coming" (KING JESUS IS A-LIS'ENIN') 8389 (366)

THAT GREAT GETTING-UP MORNING 8296B (44)

THAT LAD IS NOTHING WORTH 5698 (92)

"That lad is nothing worth who shyness can't o'ercome" 5698 (92)

THAT LONESOME ROAD 8410B (81)

"That nice little window, the cute little window" 7012 (170,173)

"That seat of science, Athens, and earth's proud mistress, Rome" 4555 (115)

"THAT YOUR MOTHER SHOULD TAKE YOU" 2896 (143)

"That's George that I hear" 423 (199)

THAT'S HOW I LOVE YOU, MAME 2610 (204)

THAT'S MY GIRL 5818 (95)

"That's my girl, what a girl!" 5818 (95)

"That's why I'm singin'" 8215 (336)

LE THÉ 1941 (190,192,194)

THEE, O LORD 6689 (295)

"Thee, O Lord, we humbly praise, Lord, our God, Creator eternal" 6689 (295)

THEE WITH TENDER CARE 137 (319)

"Thee with tender care I'll cherish" 137 (319)

"Their's was no dream, Oh! monarch hill, with Heavn's own azure crown'd" 8673 (20,349)

Them. See also Dem

THEM LONESOME MOANIN' BLUES 1807 (184)

Then. See also Den

"Then away, you Santy, my dear Annie" (ref) 9431 (35)

"Then blame me not for weeping" 7898 (81)

"Then blow, ye winds, heigh ho! A-roving I will go!" 9433 (28,205,225,233,366)

"Then blow ye winds westerly, westerly blow" 9430 (35, 109,110,214)

"Then, cheer them on" 7587 (189)

"Then cherish her with care" 3508 (114,131)

"Then dance, the boatmen, dance!" 7460A (335)

"Then drill, ye tarriers, drill" 612 (246)

"Then drink, boys, drink!" 4626 (37)

"Then fancy not, dearest, that wine can steal" 5975 (166, 213)

"Then hear, and observe me well!" 3911 (5)

"Then how can I merry be, now my love is gone" 6265 (318)

THEN I'D BE SATISFIED WITH LIFE 691 (114)

"Then lay down the shovel and the hoe" 1130 (28,279, 366)

"Then love your neighbor as yourself" 686 (129,130,131)

"Then Mary took her young Son and set Him on her knee" 8911G (361)

THEN MY LITTLE SOUL'S GONNA SHINE 8583 (185)

"Then praise the Lord, both high and low" 9008 (334,361)

"Then remember where-ever your goblet is crown'd" 5916 (15,166,213)

THEN RISE TO VICTORY 4435 (231)

"Then shall the eyes of the blind be opened" 1466 (123, 200)

"Then shall the King say, Come, come, come ye blessed" 1217 (394)

"THEN SHALL THE RIGHTEOUS SHINE FORTH" 2376 (160)
"Then, then shall the King say unto them upon His right hand"
3410 (200)
"Then weep! O grief-worn eyes" 2306 (1)
THEN YOU'LL REMEMBER ME 159, (36,122,128,132)
Theodora 1496 (275,394)
There. See also Dar, Dere
"There among the Swiss free people" 1786 (295)
"THERE ARE MANY FLAGS IN MANY LANDS" 8052 (28,
366)
"There are no lice on us" 7408 (321)
"There are no more men who force the fates" 5857 (86)
THERE ARE PITS 5657 (164)
"There are pits and there are ditches" 5657 (164)
"There are smiles that make us happy" 3043 (233)
THERE ARE THREE BOYS 6884 (159)
"There are three boys, I meet them with pleasure" 6884
(159)
THERE ARE THREE BROTHERS 3693 (293)
"There are three brothers named Dupont" 3693 (293)
THERE ARE TWA BONNIE MAIDENS 7174 (101,102)
"There are twa bonnie maidens, and three bonnie maidens"
7174 (101,102)
THERE BEHIND THAT LAKE AWAY 6724 (159)
"There behind that lake away, dark the woods at end of day"
6724 (159)
"There blooms a bonnie flower up the heather glen" 5924
(133)
"There breathes no charming flow'r so fair that cannot fairer
be" 1092 (71)
THERE BY KRIVAN 4345 (94)
"There by Krivan, the world is very bright" 4345 (94)
"THERE CAME A SHY INTRUDER" 8831 (361)
THERE CAME THREE KINGS 9121 (369)
"There came three kings, at break of day" 9121 (369)
THERE COMES A GALLEY SAILING 9153 (206)
"There comes a galley sailing with angels flying fast" 9153
(206)
"There comes a stillness in the heart" 981 (123)
THERE COMES A VESSEL LADEN 9153 (296)
"There comes a vessel laden with full sail flying fast" 9153
(296)
"There goes Maciek through town" 6731 (295)
"There grows a bonnie briar bush in our kailyard" 7007 (234)
"There grows a bonnie brier bush in oor kailyaird" 7007
(101,103)
"There grows a bonnie brier-bush in our kailyard" 7007
(163,349)
"There I sat on Buttermilk Hill" 7739 (35)
"There I shall sleep in royal state alone" 3828 (5)
"There I shall visit the place of my birth" 7108 (105)
"There in shining moonlight, Peirrot, hear my plea" 4885
(362)
"THERE IN THE FIELD WE PARTED" 5841 (230)
"There in the king's golden palace they keep him" 4855
(95)
THERE IS A BALM IN GILEAD 8189 (182)
"There is a Balm in Gilead to make the wounded whole"
8189 (182,409)
"There is a burning in my heart and in my head" 6196
(318)
"There is a charm I can't explain about a girl I've seen"
2651 (34,115)
"There is a flower within my heart" 749 (32,34,114,131)

"There is a gal in our town, she wears a yaller striped gown"
8223 (80)
"There is a garden, a wonderful garden" 6339A (132)
"THERE IS A GARDEN IN HER FACE" 561 (116,196)
"There is a garden that all sweets encloses" 4877 (297)
"THERE IS A GREEN HILL FAR AWAY" 1313 (123,394)
"There is a house in New Orleans they call the Rising Sun"
8323 (336,389)
THERE IS A LADIE SWEET AND KIND 1102 (144)
"There is a lady sweet and kind" (Cockram) 687* (36,122,
132,236,348)
"THERE IS A LADY SWEET AND KIND" (Dello Joio) 815
(358)
"There is a ladye sweet and kind" (Cockram) 687* (136,
209)
THERE IS A LAND 4005 (87)
"There is a land, far north in gleaming ocean" 4005 (87)
"There is a road from the coast to the coast" 1430 (336)
"THERE IS A TAVERN IN THE TOWN" 8053 (10,114,128,
129,131,233,402)
"THERE IS A TAVERN IN THE TOWN" (Hill) 1655 (36,
236,366)
"There is fire in the galley, there is fire down below" 9442B
(205)
"There is fire up aloft, there's fire down below" 9442C
(216)
"There is no land upon the earth contains the same amount
of worth" 7459A (173)
"THERE IS NO ROSE OF SUCH VIRTUE" 8990 (360,361)
THERE IS NOT IN THE WIDE WORLD 5963 (166,213)
"There is not in the wide world a valley so sweet" 5963
(15,28,166,213,235,349,402)
"THERE IS NOTHING THAT CAN CONJURE" 3129 (87)
"There is nought on earth so still as the snow" 2131 (241)
"There is one class of men in this country" 4222 (186)
"There is one for whom I'm sighing" 1877 (131)
"There is one here at the party, to whom we give cheers
most hearty" 6852 (295)
"There is one more step to climb" 2897 (143)
"There is three jolly boochers, three jolly boochers, three"
8057 (126)
"There lived an old lord by the northern sea, bow down"
4718C((215,260,264)
"There on high they cry, in freedom flying" 2115 (1,176)
"There once was a man named Michael Finnigin" 4693 (72)
"There once was a miller who lived by his mill" 7742 (242)
"There once was a union maid" 8080 (293)
"There once was old Abram, lived out in the West" 8037A
(321)
"There sat two lovers side by side" 4592 (198)
"There sits the man that plows up the land" 4728 (37)
"There stands the maiden of stone" 739 (357)
"There was a bee-i-ee-i-ee" 7433 (28,366)
"There was a bold fisherman who sailed out from Pimbeco"
7461 (214,335)
"There was a bold fisherman who sailed out from Pimlico"
7461 (44)
"There was a bold soldier that lately came from war" 7462B
(72)
"There was a bonny blade, had married a country maid"
4587A (37,234)
"There was a bridal in the toun" 7053 (103,104)
"There was a charro a-sitting on the fence of a wide corral"
6336 (219)

THERE WAS AN OLD SOLDIER 7893 (110)

"There was an old sow who had three little pigs" 8059
(249)

THERE WAS AN OLD WOMAN ("There was an old woman
and she had a little pig") 7892B (264)

THERE WAS AN OLD WOMAN ("There was an old woman
as I've heard tell") 4719A (234)

"There was an old woman all skin and bones" 7891A (109,
110), 7891B (312, 313)

"There was an old woman and she had a little pig" 7892A
(216, 313), 7892B (264)

"There was an old woman as I've heard tell" 4719A (234)

"There was an old woman in our town" 7566 (111)

"There was an orphan female whose fortune was not told"
7425A (81)

"There was birch rine, tar twine, cherry wine, and turpentine" 4237 (186)

"There was blood on the saddle" 7457 (186)

"There was bul-lud on the saddle" 7457 (80)

"There was Gormac O'Con, of the great Con grandson"
5994 (86)

"There was music on the hillside and singing in the glen"
9327 (412)

"There was old Bob Cloy, that could out-roar a buffalo
bull, you bet" 7538 (126)

"There was once a farmer who had a son" 7584 (126)

THERE WAS ONCE A LITTLE SHIP 4994 (187)

"There was once a simple maiden came to New York" 2231
(129, 130, 131)

"There was one, there was two, there was three little angels"
7411 (332)

"There was one, there were two, there were three little
angels" 7411 (216)

"There were nine lambs in our little park!" 4866 (86)

"There were nine to guard the British ranks and five to guard
the town about" 7576 (111)

"There were seven sons, and two of them twins" 7545 (72)

"There were ten green bottles hanging on the wall" 4770
(402)

"There were three brothers in Merry Scotland" 4631A (173)

"There were three crows sat on a tree, O Billy Magee Magar"
7528 (28, 366)

"There were three gypsies a-come to my door" 7212 (35,
70)

"There were three jolly hunters a-hunting one fine day"
8698 (44)

"There were three ra'ens sat on a tree" 4776A (111)

"There were three ravens sat on a tree" 4776A (14, 35,
235, 397)

"There were three young and gallant chafers" 3772 (28,
366)

"There were twa sisters sat in a bou'r" 4718E (101)

"There were two doves flew over the water" 6261 (318)

"There were two lofty ships from old England came" 9447A
(169, 173, 235, 401)

"There were two sisters sat in a bow'r, Binnorie, oh Binnorie"
4718D (111)

"There were two sisters sat in a bow'r, Hey ho, my Nannie,
oh" 4718B (198)

"There were two wild stallions on the mountain" 7423
(170)

THERE'LL BE A HOT TIME 2406 (32, 34)

"There'll be a hot time in the old town tonight" 2406
(32, 34)

"There'll be a new world beginnin' from t'night" 446 (305,
307)

"There's a beech tree grove by the riverside" 5976 (16)

"There's a bend of the river" 344 (205)

"THERE'S A BIG CRY BABY IN THE MOON" 463 (129, 130,
131)

"Ther's a bird whose mellow note in early spring is heard"
5879 (15)

THERE'S A BOWER OF ROSES (Stanford) 3559 (344)

"There's a bower of roses by Bendemeer's stream" (Folksongs, Ireland) 5878 (35, 166)

"There's a bower of roses by Bendemeer's stream" (Stanford)
3559 (344)

"There's a brand new wind a-blowin'" 3470 (110)

THERE'S A CAPE-CART 7226 (239)

"There's a Cape-cart! The cart has a load" 7226 (239)

"There's a charming little yallar gal, yallar gal she nearly
drives me wild" 1017 (246)

"There's a church in the valley by the wildwood" 2830
(28, 32, 34, 233, 236, 279, 343, 366)

"There's a cliff climbing high to a place in the sky" 6946
(86)

"There's a colleen fair as May, for a year and for a day"
6016 (16, 172)

THERE'S A DEAR LITTLE PLANT 661 (166, 213)

"There's a dear little plant that grows in our isle" 661 (15,
166, 172, 213)

"THERE'S A DOVE WITHIN THE FOREST" 2002 (285)

"There's a dusky husky maiden in the Arctic" 4249 (186)

"There's a famous fabled country never seen by mortal eyes"
7420 (189)

"There's a farmer in the country and a worker in the town"
8093 (293)

THERE'S A GOOD TIME COMING 1136 (129)

"There's a good time coming, boys, a good time coming"
1136 (129)

THERE'S A GREAT CAMP MEETING 8209 (409)

"THERE'S A HOLE IN MY BUCKET" 4771 (402)

THERE'S A HOUSE 5701 (164)

"There's a house far out of town, 'what do'th thou my maid-
en brown?" 5701 (164)

"There's a hut on the edge of town and its roof is green"
6179 (318)

"There's a land that is fairer than day" 3979 (32, 34, 129,
130)

"There's a little rosewood casket" 7967 (243)

"There's a little side street" 441 (114, 131)

"THERE'S A LITTLE WHEEL A-TURNIN' IN MY HEART"
8054 (216)

THERE'S A LONG, LONG TRAIL 996 (233)

"There's a long, long trail a-winding" 996 (233)

"There's a low green valley on the old Kentucky shore"
1515 (10, 28, 32, 34, 109, 110, 129, 130, 132, 184,
233, 236, 279, 366)

THERE'S A MEETING HERE TONIGHT 8585 (409)

"There's a name that's never spoken" 1346 (114, 204)

"There's a place in Vancouver the loggers know well"
8037A (186)

"THERE'S A PRETTY GIRL IN THE RING" 4217 (279)

"There's a pretty little dwelling" 801 (248)

"There's a rose that grows on "No Man's Land" 510 (129)

"There's a saucy wild packet, and a packet of fame" 9439A
(173)

"There's a silver moon shining brightly" 6347 (350)

THEY WOULD FAIN KNOW WHO I AM 2725 (367)
THIJSKEN VAN DEN SCHILDE 6581 (384)
THINE EYES SO BLUE 2049 (387)
"THINE EYES SO BLUE AND TENDER" 2049 (132)
"Thine eyes so soft and tender" 2049 (387)
THINE IS ALL GLORY 6853 (295)
"Thine is all glory, O God Almighty!" 6853 (295)
THINGS ABOUT COMIN' MY WAY 8589 (336)
"Think of the spider, a man so false" 3888 (131)
THINK OF YOUR HEAD IN THE MORNING 3943 (161)
THINK ON ME 3407 (100,102,103,105)
THINKING OF YOU 3119 (345)
"THINK'ST THOU TO SEDUCE ME THEN" 562 (144)
THIRD OF MAY MAZURKA 6869 (295)
This. See also Dis
"This at last is the moment" 2584 (1)
"This be our task on life's long rugged way" 3331 (347)
"This beautiful young maiden, carrabi" 7249 (219)
"This book is all that's left me now" 3124 (129,130,189)
"This cotton want a-pickin' so bad" 8483 (335)
"THIS DAY IS BORN EMMANUEL" 2868 (361)
"This day to you is born a Child of Mary meek, the Virgin
        mild" 9314 (337)
THIS ENDERS NIGHT 8992 (360,361)
"This enders night I saw a sight" 8992 (360,361)
THIS ENDERS NYZGT 8992 (296)
THIS ENDRIS NIGHT 8992 (333,334)
"This endris night I saw a sight" 8992 (333,334)
THIS ENDRIS NYZGT 8992 (206)
THIS FIGHT I TOOK UP 6842 (159)
"This fight I took up at our Lord's pleasure" 6842 (159)
"This flower that you threw to me" 317 (3)
THIS GARDEN NOW 8679 (349)
THIS GIRL 5696 (164)
"This girl took it in her head, that she'll by her love be wed"
        5696 (164)
THIS HAPPY MORN 2871 (361)
"This happy morn, to day is born" 2871 (361)
THIS IS A SIN-TRYIN' WORLD 8590 (109,110)
THIS IS A SIN-TRYING WORLD 8590 (409)
"This is a story of passive resistance" 962 (111)
"This is a tedious road we're in" 9108 (361)
THIS IS DE HEALIN' WATER 8591 (182)
"THIS IS MY BROWN-EYED GIRL" 3501 (164)
"This is my native land" 4075 (348)
This is no my ain house (tune) 7144 (18,100,105)
THIS IS NO MY PLAID 7179 (101,103)
"This is no my plaid, my plaid, my plaid, this is no my
        plaid" 7179 (101,103)
"This is the hammer that killed John Henry" 8382C (409)
"This is the last night she'll spend in grandfather's old place"
        6747 (295)
"This is the secret place where the smugglers are hiding"
        319 (93)
"This is the song that ye shall hear" 8939 (360,361)
"This is the time for planting" 6216 (318)
"This is the way the ploughboy goes" 2756 (293)
"This is the world's old riddle" 6169 (231)
"This is the year of Jubilee" 8507 (409)
"THIS JOYFUL EASTERTIDE" 9274 (319)
"This joyful Eastertide, away with sin and sorrow!" 9274
        (319)
"This life's a play from the start" 473 (345)
"This morning is the month of May" 8958 (44)

"This morning when I came awake" 686* (136,241)
THIS NEW CHRISTMAS CAROL 8993 (334,361,410)
"This new Christmas carol let us bravely sing" 8993 (361)
"This new Christmas Carol let us cheerfully sing" 8993
        (334,410)
"This ol' hammer killed John Henry!" 8382D (409)
THIS OL' TIME RELIGION 8592 (409)
THIS OLD MAN 4772 (402)
"This old man, he played one, he played nick nack on my
        drum" 4772 (216,249,402)
"This pretty little flow'r which I take from my breast" 3177
        (129,130,131)
"This pretty widow will marry" 4212 (219)
"This song of mine all unaided" 1505 (329)
"This strange new world fills the soul of me" 2317 (6)
"This, the song of David's making" 6367 (322)
"THIS THE TRUTH SENT FROM ABOVE" 8994 (307)
"THIS WAY, THIS WAY, LET IT BE" 4129 (30)
"This way, you willowbee, you willowbee, you willowbee"
        8139 (216)
"This world's a wilderness of woe" 8368 (409)
THO' DARK ARE OUR SORROWS 4773 (166,213)
"Tho' dark are our sorrows, today we'll forget them" 4773
        15,166,213)
THO' NOT DESERVING 518 (368)
"Tho' not deserving thy cruel scorn" 517 (368)
THO' THE LAST GLIMPSE OF ERIN 6021 (166,213)
"Tho' the last glimpse of Erin with sorrow I see" 6021
        (166,213)
"Tho' to care we are born" 4638 (235,349)
"Those cruel people! Hammering!" 8305 (409)
THOSE EVENING BELLS 6022 (28,279,366)
"Those evening bells! those evening bells! How many a
        tale their music tells" 6022 (28,279,366)
THOU, ALL MY BLISS 1255 (368)
"Thou, all my bliss, believe but this" 1255 (348)
THOU ANCIENT, THOU FREE-BORN 7303 (188)
"Thou ancient, thou free-born, thou mountainous North"
        7303 (188)
THOU ART, MY DEAR BELOVED 1276 (404)
"Thou art, my dear beloved of all the most desir'd" 1276
        (404)
"Thou art my life, my soul and heart" 3387 (359)
"Thou art my thoughts, my present and my future" 1382
        (122,176)
"THOU ART REPOSE" 3260 (36)
THOU ART SO LIKE A FLOWER 3379 (122,176)
"Thou art so like a flower, so gentle, pure and fair" 3379
        (122,176)
"Thou art so like a flower, so pure, and fair, and kind"
        3117 (241)
"Thou art standing by the wall" 4176 (37)
"Thou art sweet Peace" 3260 (275)
"THOU ART THE NIGHT WIND" 1223 (241)
THOU BELIEVEST THAT IT IS LOVE 3159 (164)
"Thou believest that it is love if your cheeks are glowing"
        3159 (164)
"THOU BONNIE WOOD O' CRAIGIELEA" 185 (100)
"THOU BONNIE WOOD OF CRAIGIELEA" 185 (349)
"Thou camest from heav'n we are told" 9208 (296)
"THOU DIDST LEAVE THY THRONE" 8995 (39)
"Thou enchanted land, gardens of delight" 2408 (3)
"THOU HAST LEFT ME EVER, JAMIE" 7180 (101,104)
"Thou holy art, how oft in hours of sadness" 3254 (274)

TINKERMAN TRUE 4367 (94)
"Tinkerman true, starting to roam far and wide" 4367 (94)
THE TINKER'S SONG 8062 (335)
"Tiny leaflets, tiny flowers" 242 (330)
"A tiny little man stands in forest dim" 5461 (28,366)
"TINY STAR, WHERE ART THOU?" 2624 (407)
EL TÍO BABÚ 7284 (281)
TIP-TOE THRU' THE TULIPS WITH ME 475 (345)
"Tip-toe to window, by the window, that is where I'll be"
    475 (345)
TIRANA (Ferrer) 1066 (270)
TIRANA (Laserna) 2045 (270)
TIRITOMBA 6154 (34,37)
TIROL, TIROL, DU BIST MEIN HEIMATLAND 1013 (326)
"Tirol, Tirol, Tirol, du bist mein Heimatland" 1013 (326)
TIROLER CHRISTKINDL WIEGENLIED 8798 (40)
EIN TIROLER WOLLTE JAGEN 5564 (326)
"Ein Tiroler wollte jagen einen Gensbock, Gemsbock
    silbergrau" 5564 (326)
Tirsi chiamare a nome 2858 (179,218)
TIRSIS 2547 (108)
"Tirsis au bord des eaux" 2547 (108)
"'Tis a long time that I have been waiting" 7946 (186)
"'Tis advertised in Boston, New York and Buffalo" 9428
    (145,173,227)
'TIS BELIEVED THAT THIS HARP 6024 (166,213)
"'Tis believed that this harp, which I wake now for thee"
    6024 (166,213)
"'TIS BUT A LITTLE FADED FLOWER" 3737 (129,130)
'TIS CHRISTMAS TIME 1583 (319)
"'Tis Christmas time, the gladsome chime" 1583 (319)
"'Tis done, the edict past, by Heaven decreed" 1210 (109,
    110)
"'Tis fair and good the beauty of this head was" 5940 (16)
'TIS GONE, AND FOR EVER 5988 (349)
"'Tis gone, and for ever, the light we saw breaking like
    Heaven's first dawn" 5988 (349)
"'Tis here we are pledging with heart and with hand" 5616
    (28,366)
"'Tis humdrum, 'tis mum" 1526 (349)
"'Tis I! all gone to smash" 3733 (2)
"'Tis I! all is now broken - no matter! here I am!" 3733
    (357)
"'Tis I, dear Carlos" 3831 (4)
"'Tis miserable out of doors" 6214 (318)
"'Tis moonlight on the sea, boys" 3164 (28,366)
"'Tis of a counselor I write" 8160 (126)
"'Tis of a gallant Yankee ship that flew the stripes and
    stars" 8152 (173)
"'Tis of a lady so gay and possessed of beauty bright"
    7785 (72)
"'Tis of a rich merchant I am going to tell" 8037A (185)
"'Tis old Stonewall the Rebel that leans on his sword" 7008
    (161)
"'TIS PRETTY TO BE IN BALLINDERRY" 6025 (133,166,
    213)
'TIS SPRING 3363 (359)
'TIS SPRINGTIME 3655 (28,366)
"'Tis spring time, 'tis spring time, cold winter is past"
    3655 (28,366)
"'Tis the cartman, 'tis the cartman, 'tis the cartman from
    the marsh" 4167 (207)
"'Tis the day for the fiesta!" 6385 (37)

"'Tis the day, the blessed day, on which our Lord was born"
    8962 (296,410)
"'TIS THE ECSTASY OF LANGUOR" 786 (121)
'TIS THE EVE OF CHRISTMAS 9141 (165)
"'Tis the gift to be simple" 7995 (83)
'TIS THE LAST ROSE OF SUMMER 5921 (166,213,329)
"'Tis the last rose of summer, left blooming alone" 5921
    (15,28,36,93,122,128,132,166,213,279,292,
    329,366,402)
"'Tis the moment, O Vitellia" 2554 (2)
"'Tis the old ship of Zion" 7883A (32,34)
"'Tis the Old Ship Zion, Hallelujah!" 7883B (72)
"'Tis three long days, that Nina" 2769 (138)
'TIS TIME 3447 (342)
"'Tis time, my friend, 'tis time" 3447 (342)
"'Tis true, alas, that love is not with just a kiss abated"
    4081 (112)
"'Tis well! my way lies yonder" 613 (143)
TIS WOMEN 2927 (173)
"'Tis women makes us love" 2927 (173)
"'Tis years since last we met" 4118 (129,130)
TISCHLERLIED 3311 (141)
LES TISSERANDS 5121 (91)
"Les tisserands sont plus que les évêques" 5121 (91)
TIT WILLOW 3665 (132)
TITANIC 2084 (336)
Titon et l'Aurore 2467-2468 (147,151)
"Tiyalti baemek b'makel nod" 1021 (30)
TIZENHAT ESZTENDÖS BARNA KIS LÁNY 3698 (285)
"TO A LITTLE CASTLE THERE CAME A KNIGHT" 7364
    (230)
"TO A MAN OF MY IMPORTANCE" 3096 (5)
"To a mansion in the city" 3593 (131)
"To a virgin meek and mild, came an angel holy" 8848
    (244)
"TO ALL MEN A CHILD IS COME" 2873 (33,361)
TO ALL THE EARTH 9417 (165)
"To all the earth comes the song of angels" 9417 (165)
TO ALL YOU LADIES 4777 (235,397)
"To all you ladies now at land" 4777 (235)
"To all you ladies now on land" 4777 (397)
"To an underground hideout, came the mountain brigands
    stout" 6862 (295)
TO ANNE, WHO THREW SNOW 2980 (362)
TO ANTHEA 1555 (272)
TO ATOCHA GOES A GIRL 7249 (219)
"To Babet's door, Philint came near" 1577 (405)
"To battle! To Battle! The dark earth is gaping, in anguish
    is riven" 2706 (7)
"TO BE NEAR THE FAIR IDOL" 3077 (139)
"To beautiful Sunday! I wish it would never come Monday!"
    1344 (131)
"To begin with, if you please, sing a scale for me" 722
    (345)
TO BETHLEHEM 8826B (370)
"TO BETHL'EM I WOULD GO" 8880 (337)
To brune öjne 1394 (45,229)
TO CARMENCITA 8773 (350)
"To Castle Hyde to market I was going out one morning"
    5996 (172)
"To create Betta whom I adore" 3191 (134)
"TO DEPART WE ARE NOW READY" 6738 (159)
"To die, appalling fortune" 3844 (4)

"To earth I bid a last fare-well" 875 (3)
TO FOLD, YE LAMBKINS 6650 (406)
"To fold, ye lambkins, come, the day is done" 6650 (406)
"To France there journey'd two Grenadiers" 3357 (273)
"To France were returning two Grenadiers" 3357 (137, 240)
TO FRIENDSHIP 1559 (210)
"To Gitchi Manitou praises be" 5851 (279)
"To go on! When my head's whirling with madness" 2116 (3)
"To her daughter t'other day" 7805 (189)
"To her I go, to my dearest Colette!" 3111 (153)
TO HER SON 1845 (342)
TO HIS SWEET LUTE 565 (144)
"To his sweet lute Apollo sung the motions of the Spheares" 565 (144)
"TO JESUS, FROM THE ENDS OF EARTH" 9193 (165)
To Julia 2937-2938 (344)
"To kiss my Celia's fairer breast" 806 (259)
TO LADIES EYES 6026 (166, 213)
"To ladies' eyes around, boy, we can't refuse, we can't refuse" 6026 (166, 213)
TO LAUTERBACH 5627 (37)
TÔ LES AN QUAN NOEI S'EPRÔCHE 9124 (361)
"To love and love as no one has ever loved before" 7406 (113)
TO MARY 4016 (277)
"To me, way! and we'll furl, and we'll pay Paddy Doyle for his boots!" 9471A (29)
"To me way, hay, hay, hay, yah, We'll pay Paddy Doyle for his boots" 9471A (320)
TO MONTELIMAR 4947 (86)
TO MUSIC 3254 (199, 220, 274, 385)
TO MY CLAVIER 3255 (141)
"To my land a thousand nights I've gladly given" 1040 (30)
"To my little one's cradle in the night" 6243 (214)
"To my native home I'm near" 3101 (6)
"To other shores across the sea we speed with swelling sail" 5907 (349)
"To our fair Provence come home" 3860 (310)
"To our Father dear, sing a song of praise" 8010 (242)
TO PORTSMOUTH 2365 (144, 349)
"To Portsmouth, to Portsmouth, it is a gallant town" 2365 (144, 349)
TO REST, TO REST 4088 (359)
"To rest, to rest, the toil is over" 4088 (359)
"To say that I love you, O dear one is not enough" 2252 (134)
TO SONG 1894 (124)
"To such a love, Leonora" 863 (5)
TO TARNOCA I WENT 5664 (164)
"To Tarnóca I went as a farmer's hand" 5664 (164)
TO THE BELOVED 226 (210)
TO THE BIRDS 1726 (191, 211)
TO THE CHILD JESUS 9043A (244)
TO THE CHILDREN 2940 (237, 275)
TO THE DISTANT BELOVED 3263 (141)
TO THE DOOR I STROLLED 5663 (37)
"To the door of my girl I strolled" 5663 (37)
TO THE EVENING STAR 3920 (364)
TO THE FAITHLESS ONE 225 (272)
TO THE FOREST 647 (273)
TO THE GRAVEYARD 4352 (94)

"To the graveyard goes Mary tripping" 4352 (94)
"To the heart of youth the world is a highway side" 3804 (272, 344)
TO THE HOME THAT SHE LEFT 2888 (143)
"To the home that she left at the voice of her lover" 2888 (143)
TO THE INFINITE GOD 3259 (160)
"To the knights in the days of old" 889 (343)
"To the lark's sweet singing" 2674 (295)
"To the Lords of Convention 'twas Claverhouse spoke" 7008 (17, 28, 163, 235, 349)
TO THE LYRE 3253 (364)
"To the manger, this day O hasten away" 9214 (361)
TO THE MAYPOLE HASTE AWAY 4778 (349)
TO THE PINES 8410C (242)
TO THE RADIANT BEAUTY OF YOUR FACE 3881 (367)
TO THE SOUL 3558 (344)
TO THE SPRING 3250 (141)
"To the stable hasten yonder" 9294 (295)
TO THE SUNSHINE 3354 (209)
"TO THE WELL A MAIDEN WENT" 4353 (94)
TO THE WEST 1433 (189)
"To the west! to the land of the free" 1433 (189)
"To Thee, dear Jesus, now we raise our song of praise" 9193 (279)
TO THEE FOREVER 1874 (37)
"To Thee now Christès dere derling" 8979 (361)
TO THEE, O COUNTRY! 988 (28)
"To thee O country great and free" 988 (28)
"TO THINK I THOUGHT SO MUCH OF YOU" 1146 (9)
"To this asylum led, by some protecting pow'r" 1290 (237)
TO THIS WE'VE COME 2398 (6)
"To this we've come: that men withhold the world from men" 2398 (6)
TO THY FAIR CHARM 697 (209)
"To thy fair charm all yield" 697 (209)
TO TSOBANOPOULO 5638 (36)
"To turn back Pharaoh's army" 8599 (28)
TO US A LITTLE CHILD IS BORN 2872 (361)
"To us a little Child is born of mother maid before the morn" 2872 (361)
"To us a Son is given" 9260 (361)
"To us in Bethlem city was born a little Son" 9150 (337)
"TO US IS BORN A LITTLE CHILD" 9179 (244, 296)
"TO WAR HAS GONE DUKE MARLBOROUGH" 5020 (279, 366)
TO WAWEL 6780A (295)
"To Wawel, to Wawel, little lad of Krakow" 6780A (295)
TO WEARY SHEPHERDS SLEEPING 9211 (244, 386)
"To weary shepherds sleeping, a blinding light appeared" 9211 (244, 386)
TO YOU 3637 (122)
"To you, beloved comrade" 1870 (293)
"To you who set me aflame" 2775 (134)
"To your soul is it wine" 2015 (241)
TOAST ("Jest tu jeden...) 6852 (295)
THE TOAST ("Przyszedł dzisia j czas...") 6840 (295)
TOBACCO (Folksongs, England) 4779A (198)
TOBACCO (Hume) 1735 (273)
"Tobacco is an Indian weed" 4779A (198)
TOBACCO IS LIKE LOVE 1735 (144)
"Tobacco, tobacco, sing sweetly for tobacco" 1735 (273)
"TOBACCO'S BUT AN INDIAN WEED" 4779B (173)

"Turn to me, dark eye so tender" 1151 (137, 210)
"TURN, TURN, MY BUSY WHEEL" 1270 (199)
"Turn, turn, turn, my mill" 2813 (191, 193, 195)
"Turn, turn, turn your eyes" 2920 (199)
TURN YE TO ME 7185 (37, 101, 102, 105, 235)
TURNER, AUF ZUM STREITE! 3651 (353)
"Turner, auf zum Streite! Tretet in die Bahn!" 3651 (353)
TURNIE, NASZE, TURNIA 2679 (295)
"Turnie nasze, turnie, Hale nasze hale" 2679 (295)
THE TURNPIKE GATE 1595 (189)
TUROLURETO, VOI LAN LA! 5126 (86)
TURPIN HERO 4783 (198)
EL TURRONERO 6395 (247)
THE TURTLE DOVE (Folksongs, England "Fare you well, my
    dear...") 4784 (36)
THE TURTLE DOVE (Folksongs, United States "Poor little
    turtle dove") 8082 (173)
TUS CABELLOS 4520 (73)
TUS OJILLOS NEGROS 1033 (121)
"Tuším, tuším, tuším, Že já umřít musím" 4435 (231)
TUSSCHEN KEULEN EN PARIJS 6585 (384)
"Tusschen Keulen en Parijs leit de weg naar Rome" 6585 (384)
"TUTTI QUI, LESTI A VOL" 571 (411)
"Tutto e deserto, ne per l'aure" 3862 (4, 298)
TUTU MARAMBÁ 4215A (284), 4215B (279)
"Tutu marambá, não venhas mais cá" 4215A (284)
"Tutu Marmaba shall never harm my child" 4215B (279)
THE TWA CORBIES 4776B (262)
THE TWA SISTERS O' BINNORIE 4718E (101)
'Twas. See also It was
"'Twas a bright and sunny day" (Rosenfeld) 3085 (114,
    131, 204)
"'Twas a brilliant star in the sky" 9286 (154)
"'Twas a sad, sad hour of parting" 1593 (205)
"'Twas a sunny day in June" 2534 (131)
'TWAS A WONDER IN HEAVEN 9402 (332)
"'Twas an orphan boy one day" 779 (131)
'TWAS APRIL 651 (277)
"'Twas at the river of Jordan" 8253 (409)
"'Twas down at Dan McDevitt's at the corner of this street"
    1884 (114, 115, 131)
"'TWAS EARLY, EARLY ALL IN THE SPRING" 4785 (198)
"'Twas for luck, as I thought, that I chang'd my betrothed"
    771 (147)
"'Twas Friday morn when we set sail!" 9467E (205)
"'Twas in eighty-eight on a winter's night 2332 (205)
"'Twas in 'fifty-five, on a winter's night" 2332 (28, 366)
"'Twas in the cold month of December, when all of my
    money was spent" 9460 (29)
"'TWAS IN THE LOVELY MONTH OF MAY" 3361 (137)
"'Twas in the merry month of May" 4545G (109, 110, 399)
"'Twas in the merry month of May, the Easter time was
    near" 9365 (261)
'TWAS IN THE MOON OF WINTER TIME 9193 (154, 173,
    186, 244, 251)
"'Twas in the town of Jacksboro in the spring of seventy
    three" 7479 (129)
"'Twas in the town of Jacksboro in the year of seventy
    three" 7479 (227)
"'Twas Jack, the jolly ploughboy, was ploughing in his land"
    5946 (199)
"'Twas jolly old Roger, the tinmaker man" 8062 (335)
"'Twas just as dawn rose o'er the North Sea" 4617G (80)
"'Twas late one Sunday evening as you can plainly see"
    7725 (126)

'TWAS MAY DAY IN THE MORNING 8073 (44)
"'Twas midnight! and the silent moon shone on the dimpled
    sea" 153 (189)
"'TWAS NIGHT AND ALL AROUND WAS STILL" 3868 (143)
'Twas off the blue Canaries, or my last cigar 1724 (205,
    279, 366)
"'Twas off the blue Canary Isles" 1724 (205, 279, 366)
"'Twas on a Monday morning" 7024 (17, 100, 102, 104, 163,
    199, 297, 349)
"'Twas on a pleasant morning all in the bloom of spring"
    8137B (72)
"'Twas on a simmer's afternoon" 7088 (18, 100)
"'Twas on a Sunday bright and clear" 1295 (385)
"'Twas on a Sunday morning" 7024 (132, 234, 366)
"'Twas on a Sunday night when I went for a walk" 5192
    (186, 187)
"'TWAS ON ONE SUNDAY MORNING" 8600 (409)
"'Twas on the morn of sweet Mayday, when nature painted
    all things gay" 4807 (234)
'TWAS ONE OF THOSE DREAMS 6028 (349)
"'Twas one of those dreams that by music are brought"
    6028 (349)
'TWAS ONLY AN IRISHMAN'S DREAM 713 (166)
"'TWAS PRETTY TO BE IN BALLINDERRY" 6025 (349)
"'Twas summer and softly the breezes were blowing" 4544
    (37)
"'Twas three pretty maids walk'd out one afternoon" 4775
    (198)
"'Twas twenty five or thirty years since Jack first saw the
    light" 9453 (249)
'TWAS WINTER AND BLUE TORY NOSES 4544 (225)
"'Twas winter and blue Tory noses were freezing" 4544
    (225)
"'TWAS WITHIN A MILE O' EDINBURGH TOWN" 1693
    (163)
TWEE VOERLUI 6586 (384)
TWELFTH NIGHT COMES 5695 (164)
"Twelfth night comes again, when once the year is round"
    5695 (164)
THE TWELVE APOSTLES 9382B (332)
THE TWELVE DAYS OF CHRISTMAS 8998A (33, 35, 215,
    249, 337), 8998B (378), 8998C (332), 8998D
    (333, 410)
THE TWELVE HOLY THINGS 4472 (230)
THE TWENTY-THIRD PSALM 2251 (200)
TWENTY YEARS AGO 4038 (212, 321)
TWICE BLOOM THE ACACIA TREES 5746 (164)
"Twice bloom the acacia trees along the lane" 5746 (164)
TWICKENHAM FERRY 2294 (132)
TWILIGHT 2307 (191, 193, 195)
"Twilight is drawing near, bright stars will soon appear"
    1303 (132)
"'Twill soon be midnight now" 646 (6)
Twine the Plaiden (tune) 7145 (105)
"'Twinkidoodledum, twinkidoodledum'" 7461 (214)
TWINKLE, LITTLE STAR 4874 (28, 366)
"TWINKLE, TWINKLE, LITTLE STAR" 4874 (28, 132, 366)
The twisting of the rope (tune) 5928 (213)
"'TWIXT GENTLE OX AND ASS SO GRAY" 9064 (79)
TWO BROWN EYES 1394 (45, 229)
"Two children play'd on the sandy shore" 2436 (205)
"Two drummers sat at dinner in a grand hotel one day"
    3574 (32, 34, 246)
TWO DUKES 8074 (126)
TWO DUKES A'RIDING 8075 (313)

UND IN DEM SCHNEEGEBIRGE 5571* (41,49,309,326,353)
"Und in dem Schneegebirge da fliesst ein Brünnlein kalt" 5571* (41,49,309,326,353)
"Und jetzo kommt die Nacht herbei" 5196 (49)
"UND JETZT GANG I ANS PETERSBRÜNNELE" 5572 (41, 49,309,326)
UND JETZT ISTS AUS 5570* (309)
"Und jetzt ists aus und nichts mehr" 5570* (309)
"Und Morgen wird die Sonne wieder scheinen" 3629 (98, 112,121,330)
UND OB DIE WOLKE 3967 (1)
"Und ob die Wolke sie verhülle" 3967 (1,311)
"UND WENN DAS GLÖCKLEIN FÜNFMAL SCHLÄGT" 5572* (49,309)
"Und wieder sass beim Weine" 1423 (31)
"UND WILLST DU DEINEN LIEBSTEN STERBEN SEHEN" 4084 (112)
UNDAUNTED MARY 7425A (81)
"Under a tree in Paree ev'ry night you'll see a harlequin" 925 (132)
"Under baby's cradle here there's an all-white nanny, dear" 6264 (318)
"UNDER BETHLEM'S STAR SO BRIGHT" 8878 (319)
UNDER EAVES 5690 (164)
"Under eaves their nest the swallows made" 5690 (164)
"Under my window a cowboy" 6339A (322)
"Under my window, hark to the voice of the plowman" 7235 (219)
UNDER THE BAMBOO TREE 1808 (32,34)
UNDER THE GREENWOOD TREE (Arne) 83 (75,277)
UNDER THE GREENWOOD TREE (Folksongs, England) 4786 (235,349)
UNDER THE GREENWOOD TREE (Moore) 2514 (358)
"Under the greenwood tree who loves to lie with me" (Arne) 83 (75,277)
"Under the greenwood tree who loves to lie with me" (Moore) 2514 (358)
UNDER THE ROSE 1081 (136)
"Under the setting sun waters blush like roses" 790 (348)
UNDER THE SILVER STAR 4294 (350)
"Under the wide and starry sky" 1690 (45)
"Under the wreck of passion and love's illusion" 2713 (322)
UNDER THIS STONE 2928 (349)
"Under this stone lies Gabriel John" 2928 (349)
Under yonder oaken tree (tune) 8684 (349)
"UNDERNEATH A CYPRESS TREE" 2823 (196)
UNDERNEATH AN APPLE BOWER 6823 (295)
"Underneath an apple bower, I begged Zosia by the hour" 6823 (295)
"UNDERNEATH OUR COTTAGE WINDOW" 4399 (94)
UNDERNEATH THE EAVES 5690 (92)
"Underneath the eaves the swallows dwell" 5690 (92)
UNDERNEATH THE GREEN OAK 6812 (159,295)
"Underneath the green oak a saddled horse is standing" 6812 (159)
"Underneath the green oak stands a saddled brown steed" 6812 (295)
"Underneath the lantern by the barrack gate" 3333 (35)
THE UNDISCOVERED COUNTRY 290 (275)
"Undzer lid is ful mit troyer" 3114 (318)
DER UNERBITTLICHE HAUPTMANN 5502A (99)
"Unfold, unfold, unfold ye portals everlasting" 1334 (28)
UNFOLD, YE PORTALS 1334 (28)
UNFORTUNATE MISS BAILEY 4787 (72,186)

THE UNFORTUNATE TROUBADOUR 964 (111)
Die ungarische Hochzeit 887 (258)
UNGEDULD 3299 (112,327)
Ungetreuer du (tune) 5405 (353)
DER UNGLÜCKLICHE 3315 (97,220,240,272,359)
Unglückselige 2395 (276)
UNHAPPY JEREMIAH 7469 (72)
"Unhappy men find life infernal" 3842 (3)
"The Union forever, Hurrah! boys, Hurrah!" 3068 (28,115, 129,130,279,366)
UNION MAID 8080 (293)
THE UNION MAN 1909 (293)
UNION TRAIN 8081 (293)
THE UNION WAY 4048 (293)
UNITED FRONT 991 (293)
UNITED NATIONS 8387 (293)
"United Nations make a chain" 8387 (227,293)
UNIVERSI POPULI 2874 (361)
"Universi populi omnes jam gaudete" 2874 (361)
"Unkind, love? Ah! no, Ottavio!" 2569 (6)
"Unnumber'd diamonds lie within the caverns" 3039 (241)
UNO JIONTO POSTOURO 5006 (66)
"Uno jionto postouro, un d'oquèć motis" 5006 (66)
THE UNPRETENTIOUS LOVER 4068 (112)
UNSER HANS 5573 (41)
"Unser Hans hat Hosen an, und die sind zu klein" 5573 (41)
UNSER HEILAND IST GEBOREN 9312 (354)
"Unser Heiland ist geboren, Halleluja" 9312 (354)
"Unser Leben gleicht der Reise eines Wanders in der Nacht" 5242 (43)
UNSER LIEBE FRAUE 5573* (49)
"Unser liebe Fraue vom kalten Brunnen" 5573* (49)
UNTER DEM KIND'S VIGELE 6264 (318)
"Unter dem kind's vigele Shteyt a klorvays tsigele" 6264 (318)
UNTER DEM LINDENBAUM 975 (327)
UNTER DEM STERNENZELT 3061 (222)
"Unter dem Sternenzelt reich' mir die Hand" 3061 (222)
UNTERLÄNDERS HEIMWEH 5281 (31,99)
"Until now each hour was dreary" 3871 (9)
"UNTO US A BOY IS BORN" (Carols, Germany) 9181* (38,39,307)
"UNTO US A BOY WAS BORN" (Carols, Germany) 9181 (337)
"UNTO US A CHILD IS BORN" (Carols, Germany) 9181 (363,377)
"UNTO US IS BORN A SON" (Carols, Germany) 9181 (319,334)
"UNTO US IS BORN A SON" (Praetorius) 2873 (33)
"Untouched whiteness, bearers of milk" 3186 (134)
UNTREU 717 (229)
UNTREUE 5574 (99,326,353)
"Unüberwindlich starker Held St. Michael" 5523 (49)
"An un-used string in mem'ry's harp" 3145 (45)
"Up aloft, amid the rigging swiftly blows the fav'ring gale" 5947 (173)
"Up and down the city streets at fall of night" 6303 (219)
"Up and get us gone, to help the world along" 9047 (271)
"UP AND SHAKE THEE PETERKIN" 9120 (361)
"Up Czechs! War is here!" 3518 (7)
UP IN A BALLOON 1039 (189,214)
"Up in a balloon, boys" 1037 (189,214)
"Up in Horse-pasture we used to go fishin'" 7495 (381)
UP IN THE MORNING EARLY 7186 (101,102)

"Way down in Rio once there lived a jealous lover" 3872 (132)

"Way down in the meadow where the lily first blows" 7541 (129,130,343)

"Way down South where bananas grow" 7569 (110)

WAY DOWN THE OHIO 8089 (110)

"Way down the Ohio my little boat I steered" 8089 (110)

"'Way down upon de Swanee Ribber" 1129 (10,128,184, 199,233,402)

"Way down upon de Swanee River" 1129 (129,130,236)

"'Way down upon the Swanee River" 1129 (35,115,132, 284)

"'Way down upon the Wabash, Sich land was never known" 7567A (34,110,145,279)

"Way down yonder in de middle o' de fiel'" 8450 (35,183, 184)

WAY DOWN YONDER IN THE CORNFIELD 8611 (114)

"'Way down yonder in the grave-yard walk" 8272 (409)

"Way down yonder on Beaver Creek" 8385A (343)

"Way, haul away, haul away, my rosies" 9445A (331)

"Way, haul away, Oh haul and sing together" 9445A (214)

"Way, haul away, we'll haul away the bowlin'" 9445A (35, 199)

"Way, hay, and away we go, Highland laddie" 9448A (320)

"Way, hay, up she rises" 9440A (173,320)

"Way hey and up she rises" 9440A (331)

"Way, hey, there she rises" 9440A (29)

"The way of evil doing is a-wide and fair" 8461 (28,366)

"Way out in Western Texas where the clear Forkwaters flow" 7520 (80)

"'Way over in Egypt's land, you shall gain the victory!" 8420 (409)

'WAY OVER IN THE PROMISED LAND 8612 (80)

"'Way up high in the Mogollons, among the mountain tops" 7616 (80)

WAY UP ON CLINCH MOUNTAIN 8090A (321), 8090B (321)

"Way up on Clinch Mountain I wander alone" 8090A (321) 8090C (109,110)

"Way up on Clinch Mountain where the wild geese fly high" 8090B (321)

WAY UP ON OLD SMOKY 7885A (110)

"Way up on old Smoky, all covered with snow" 7885A (110)

"Way up yonder above the moon, a jaybird lived in a silver spoon" 7477A (34)

"'Way up yonder above the sky, a bluebird lived in a jay- bird's eye" 7477B (227)

THE WAY-WORN TRAVELLER 90 (279)

THE WAYFARER'S SONG OF HOPE 3578 (398)

WAYFARING STRANGER 7932A (44,173,227)

"The ways of my girl are charming" 4253 (219)

WE ALL LOVE THOSE VETERANS PARTIES 6705 (159)

"We all love those Vet'rans parties, best place for your leisure" 6705 (159)

"We all went down to New Orleans" 1253 (161)

"We are a band of brothers" 2222 (34,129,130,161)

WE ARE ALL NODDIN' 8091 (343)

"We are all noddin' nid, nid, noddin'" 8091 (343)

"We are alone here; even in the air I hear not the usual singing" 3862 (4)

"WE ARE CLIMBING JACOB'S LADDER" 8373 (32,34,233, 409)

"WE ARE CLIMBING THE HILLS OF ZION" 8092 (129)

WE ARE COMING, FATHER ABRA'AM 7677B (279,366)

"We are coming, Father Abra'am, three hundred thousand more" 7677B (279,366)

WE ARE JOLLY FELLOWS THAT FOLLOW THE PLOUGH 4794 (198)

"We are just plain folks" 3593 (129,130,131)

"We are marching to Pretoria" 7219 (239)

WE ARE POOR 4399 (95)

WE ARE SMART, OUR DRESS IS PRETTY 6677 (159)

"We are smart, our dress is pretty, yes it's pretty, yes it's pretty" 6677 (159)

"We are tenting on the old Camp Ground" 1904 (10)

"WE ARE THREE YOUNG CAPTAINS JOLLY" 5175 (187)

"We are trav'ling in the footsteps of those who've gone before" 8114 (389)

"We ask not that the slave should lie" 379 (109,110,173)

WE BE THREE MARINERS 9488 (37)

"WE BE THREE POOR MARINERS" 9488 (37,235,349,397)

"We bid Thee welcome, Thou Saviour of all" 8802 (388)

"We came here for our country yearning" 2248 (159)

"We children, we gambol, we dance in a ring" 2580 (199)

"We chip the scuppers and paint the hull, and scrub the decks and then" 4035 (205)

"We come on the sloop, 'John B'" 7735 (389)

"We crave your condescension, we'll tell you what we know" 392 (115,225)

WE DO WORSHIP THEE 2732 (296)

"We do worship Thee, Jesus, we praise and bless Thy most holy name" 2732 (296)

"We Eastern Kings from afar" 9077 (373)

"We from childhood play'd together" 2233 (114,131,132)

"We gather together to ask the Lord's blessing" 3790 (44, 236,279,316,343,366)

"We give thee thanks, thy name we sing" 1684 (28,366)

"WE GOT A LOT FOR CHRISTMAS" 9186 (337)

"We got deacons in de church" 8283 (409)

WE GOT TO ALL GET TOGETHER 8093 (293)

"We greet Thee, blessed heavenly dove" 8804 (79)

WE GREET THEE, HEAVENLY DOVE 8804 (79)

"WE HAIL THEE WITH REJOICING" 3346 (296)

"We have come from the mountains" 7871 (189)

"We have come to the land, our home" 6171 (318)

"We have forests, many fields and rivers" 938 (287,288)

"We have just seen the bullfight" 809 (191,193,195)

"WE HAVE LIVED AND LOVED TOGETHER" 1757 (129, 130)

"We legionnaires - fight's our aim only" 6769 (159)

"We legionnaires, the army's music" 6769 (295)

WE LOVE OUR LAND 2034 (188)

"We love our land when the blessed Yuletide" 2034 (188)

WE MAY ROAM THRO' THIS WORLD 5916 (15)

"We may roam thro' this world, like a child at a feast" 5916 (15,166,213)

"We mean to make things over" 1812 (34)

"We meet today in freedom's cause and raise our voices" 7670 (293)

WE MUST GO TO DEBRECEN 5677 (164)

"We must go to Debrecen fair, we must buy a turkey hen there" 5677 (164)

WE MUST PART 6939 (95)

"We must up and haste away" 7038 (103,105)

"We never miss the sunshine, until the shadows fall" 161 (237)

"WE NEVER SPEAK AS WE PASS BY" (Egerton) 986 (204)

WE NEVER SPEAK AS WE PASS BY (Milford) 2428 (114, 128, 131)

"WE PARTED BY THE RIVER SIDE" 1596 (129, 130, 205)

"WE ROAM OVER HILLS DRENCHED WITH DEW" 7346 (188)

"WE SAIL THE OCEAN BLUE" 3659 (205)

"We sailed the sloop John B." 9469 (11)

"We sat by the river, you and I" 179 (129, 130, 131)

"WE SAW A LIGHT SHINE OUT AFAR" (Carols, England) 9003 (361)

"We saw a light shine out afar" (Carols, France) 9051 (244, 296, 379)

"We shall go a hunting, hunting, friend of mine we'll go!" 6816 (295)

"WE SHALL HAVE PEACE!" 2951 (341)

"We shall meet, but we shall miss him" 3075 (28, 114, 366)

WE SHALL NOT BE MOVED 8613 (293)

"We shall not, we shall not be moved" 8613 (293)

"We shall not yield our sacred soil" 2680 (159)

"We shall see, audacious old man" 3836 (4)

"WE SHALL WALK THROUGH THE VALLEY" 8614 (409)

"We shoulder'd guns and march'd and march'd away" 392 (115)

"We shouldered guns and marched and marched away" 392 (225)

"We sing a song to you, a song to you" 6275 (318)

"We sing how Guerilla Veljko sent word" 8781 (86)

"WE SING OF DAVID'S DAUGHTER" 8829 (361)

"We stand before the Christmas tree, a symbol for the faithful" 9175A (337)

"We start with a lay lo lay" 1790 (291)

WE THANK OUR GREAT LEADER 2841 (162)

"We thank Thee for our daily bread" 4041 (343)

WE THANK THEE, GOD 124 (199)

"We thank Thee God, that they who in Thy faith abided" 124 (199)

WE THREE KINGS 1696 (34)

"WE THREE KINGS OF ORIENT ARE" 1696 (28, 33, 34, 38, 39, 79, 125, 165, 206, 251, 271, 296, 305, 307, 315, 333, 334, 337, 349, 366, 388, 410)

WE WANDERED 438 (36)

"We wandered, we two together" 438 (36)

"We want a land that by right is free" 3504 (7)

"We was camped on the plains at the head of the Cimarron" 8165 (120, 225)

"We were forty miles from Albany, forget it, I never shall" 7574A (32, 34, 227), 7574B (173)

"We were none of us thinking of danger" 1345 (114)

"We were sailing along on Moonlight Bay" 3989 (233)

"We were wand'ring 'neath the shadow of the pines" 7711 (393)

WE WHOOPED AND WE HOLLERED 8094 (214)

"We whooped and we hollered and the first thing we did find" 8094 (214)

"WE WILL TAKE THE GOOD OLD WAY" 7189 (102)

"WE WISH YOU A MERRY CHRISTMAS" (Carols, England) 9004 (33, 44, 165, 214, 249, 249, 296, 319)

"WE WISH YOU A MERRY CHRISTMAS" (Kent) 1886 (337)

"A wealth of diamonds lie within the caverns" 3039 (329)

THE WEALTHY FARMER'S SON 4795 (198)

THE WEALTHY OLD MAID 8095 (171)

"A wealthy young squire of Tamworth, we hear" 4615 (198)

WEARIN' O' THE GREEN 6030 (294)

WEARIN' OF THE GREEN 6030 (34)

"Weariness, so tormentingly green" 797 (362)

WEARING OF THE GREEN 6030 (7, 15, 28, 37, 166, 172, 213, 233, 279, 366)

"Weary fa' you, Duncan Gray" 7035 (365)

THE WEATHER CAROL 9104 (361)

WEBERLIED 5590 (49)

WECHSELGESANG 5783 (26)

THE WEDDING ARRAY 7301 (230)

WEDDING HYMN TO OUR LADY 3424 (382)

THE WEDDING IN HÄRMÄ 4823 (124)

WEDDING MARCH FROM A COUNTRY WEDDING 3527 (188)

WEDDING MARCH FROM THE WEDDING AT ULFÅSA 3528 (188)

THE WEDDING OF MISS DUCK 8096 (392)

THE WEDDING OF THE BIRDS 5578 (230)

A WEDDING SONG (Bartlett) 200 (123)

WEDDING SONG (Folksongs, Poland) 6747 (295)

A WEDDING SONG (Folksongs, United States) 8097 (243)

WĘDROWNA PTASZYNA 2489 (295)

"A wee bird cam' to oor ha' door" 7187 (100, 104)

"A wee bird cam' to our ha' door" 7187 (163, 349)

WEE COCK SPARRA' 7190 (249)

"A wee cock sparra sat on a tree" 7190 (249)

THE WEE COOPER O' FIFE 7191 (101, 102, 163, 171, 173, 249)

THE WEE CROODIN' DOO 7192 (95)

Wee Totum Fogg (tune) 7194 (104)

THE WEE, WEE GERMAN LAIRDIE 7193 (18, 101, 102)

WEE WILLIE GRAY 7194 (104)

"Wee Willie Gray and his leather wallet" 7194 (104)

"Wee Willie has climbed our apple tree" 5171 (21)

"Weel about and turn about and do jis' so" 3030 (115, 185)

WEEL MAY THE KEEL ROW 7195 (36, 402)

WEEP ALL YE LITTLE RAINS 8098 (215)

"Weep all ye little rains" 7505A (321), 7505B (321, 389)

"Weep all ye little rains, wail, wind, wail" 8098 (215)

WEEP NO MORE 5536 (95)

WEEP NO MORE (Folksongs, Finland) 4816 (124)

"Weep no more, my lady" 1120 (10, 28, 32, 34, 109, 110, 122, 129, 130, 184, 233, 236, 279, 343, 366)

WEEP NOT FOR ME, BUT WEEP FOR YOURSELVES 1616 (8)

WEEP NOT, I PRAY 8696 (349)

"Weep not I pray, though on this day" 8696 (349)

WEEP ON, WEEP ON 6031 (166, 213)

"Weep on, weep on, your hour is past" 6031 (166, 213)

THE WEEP-WILLOW TREE 4617D (260, 263)

"WEEP YOU NO MORE, SAD FOUNTAINS" 916 (118, 144, 197)

WEEPIN' MARY 8615 (52)

WEEPING, SAD AND LONELY 3775 (109, 110, 189)

WEEPING WILLOW 8099 (243)

WEEST NU VERBLIJD 6609 (201)

"Weest nu verblijd, te dezer tijd" 6609 (201)

WEEVILY WHEAT 8100A (109, 110), 8100B (185)

"WEG MIT BÜCHERN UND PAPIEREN" 3046 (31)

"Wege schüttet man im Walde" 5819 (22)

WEGELIED ZUM SCHWEIZERFEST 3221 (31)

WEH, ICH HAB GEDACHT 4062 (226)

"Weh, ich hab gedacht all diese Nacht an mein so gross Beschwere" 4062 (226)

551

552

"When cold in the earth lies the friend thou hast lov'd" 6033 (213)

"When Constantine was five years old" 5639 (86)

"WHEN CUCKOOS SANG IN MAYTIME" 3716 (188)

WHEN DAISIES PIED 84 (75,235,275)

"When daisies pied and violets blue" 84 (75,235,275)

WHEN DAVID'S DAUGHTER 8822 (361)

"When David's daughter to David's city bore Christ the strong to save" 8822 (361)

WHEN DAY IS DONE 1865 (345)

"When day is done and shadows fall" 1865 (345)

"When day puts out its tapers and silence basks the vale" 3683 (295)

"When December's winds were stilled, past the month snowing" 8848 (244)

WHEN E'ER TO THE CLERGYMAN'S HOUSE 5716 (164)

"When e'er to the clergyman's house I myself betake" 5716 (164)

WHEN EYES ARE GLEAMING 803 (248)

WHEN FAR FROM MY DEAR TREASURE 3415 (138)

"When far from my dear treasure life seems a heavy burden" 3415 (138)

WHEN FERGUS SMOTE THE SHIELD 6027 (280)

"When first his standard caught the eye" 7024 (132,366)

"When first I came to Louisville" 7780 (321)

"When first I came to the county Limrick" 5942 (95)

"When first I deserted I thought myself free" 4579 (198)

"WHEN FIRST I EVER SAW YOU" 3506 (188)

WHEN FIRST I SAW SWEET PEGGY 5946 (28,166,213,279, 366)

"When first I saw sweet Peggy, 'twas on a market day" 5946 (28,166,172,213,279,366)

"When first I saw Voreema combing out her locks" 8085 (37)

"When first I went a-waggoning, a-waggoning did go" 4661A (234), 4661B (145), 4661C (110)

"When first I went a-wagoning, a-wagoning did go" 4661C (110)

"When first she cam' to toun" 7077 (101)

"When forc'd to bid farewell to Loo" 2335 (205)

"WHEN FRANCIS DANCES WITH ME" 1254 (128)

"When freedom from her mountain height" 3777 (129,130)

"When freedom raised her glowing form" 172 (86)

"WHEN FROM MY LOVE I LOOKTE" 196 (197)

"When from out the darkness of the night" 6116 (343)

"WHEN GAZING IN THINE EYES SO DEAR" 3362 (387)

"When God entrusted you, dear Rachel, to my keeping" 1507 (3)

WHEN GOOD FELLOWS GET TOGETHER 470 (240)

"WHEN GRANNIE GOES UP TO TOWN" 167 (21)

WHEN HE WHO ADORES THEE 6034 (166,172,213)

"When he who adores thee, has left but the name" 6034 (166,172,213)

"When I am laid, am laid in earth" 2908 (2)

WHEN I AM LAID IN EARTH 2908 (2)

"When I blow from the frozen north" 1353 (136)

"When I can read my title clear to mansions in the skies" 7847B (110)

"When I can read my title clear to mansions in the sky" 7847 (212)

"When I cast an eye on this world" 2000 (295)

WHEN I FIRST CAME TO THIS LAND 8111 (44)

"When I first came to this land, I was not a wealthy man" 8111 (44)

"When I first came to town, the boys strove to be near me" 4580B (72)

"When I first was drafted, only last fall, then I did not care for music at all" 4326 (95)

"When I from Havana sever'd so long ago" 4120 (142)

"When I get up in Heaven and a my work is done" 8431 (409)

"When I go a-courtin', I go on the train" 7779B (171)

"When I go a-courtin', I'll go on the train" 7779 (225)

"When I go at the break of day to see my garden grow" 3395 (385)

"WHEN I GROW TOO OLD TO DREAM" 3063 (236)

"When I had money, money, O!" 1598 (273)

"When I hae a saxpence under my thumb" 7163 (104)

"WHEN I HEAR THE BAGPIPES PLAYING" 4350 (324)

"WHEN I KNEEL DOWN TO PRAY" 4145 (347)

WHEN I LAY DOWN 8619 (336)

"When I lay down and die on my old tired hunkers" 8619 (336)

WHEN I LAY MY BURDEN DOWN 8620 (182)

"WHEN I LAYS DOWN AND I DO DIE" 8112 (265)

"When I no more behold thee, think on me" 3407 (100, 102,103,105)

"When I once make up my mind to wed, boy" 6649 (95)

WHEN I PASS BEFORE YOUR WINDOW 1166 (285)

"When I pass before your window, I must turn 'way from it" 1166 (285)

"When I pretend I'm gay I never feel that way" 473 (345)

WHEN I RAISE MY EYES 6164 (95)

"When I raise my eyes and see you" 6164 (95)

WHEN I SAID GOOD-BYE 6750 (295)

WHEN I SAID GOOD-BYE AND PARTED 6750 (159)

"When I said good-bye and parted, and my horses' hoofs had started" 6750 (295)

"When I said good-bye and parted, and my horse's shoes had started" 6750 (159)

"When I saw her smile in greeting" 3829 (3)

WHEN I SAW SWEET NELLY HOME 1084 (28,32,34,129, 130,233,236,279,366)

"When I survey the world" around" 4670 (397)

WHEN I TEACH SINGING 6282 (219)

"When I think of the last great round up" 7637 (10)

"When I walk dat levee 'round" 3767 (114,115,128,131)

"When I walked out one day (relay, relay)" 4883 (187)

"When I was a bachelor I lived all alone" 4601A (48)

"When I was a bach'lor I lived all alone" 4601A (35,173)

"When I was a bach'lor, I lived by myself" 4601A (331)

WHEN I WAS A LADY 5498 (28,366)

"When I was a lady, a lady, a lady" 5498 (28,366)

"When I was a learner, I sought both night and day" 9389A (296)

"When I was a little boy" 7647 (44,214)

"When I was a little boy, I lived by myself" 8036A (145, 313)

"When I was a little lad and so my mother told me" 9445A (173)

"When I was a seeker, I sought both night an' day" 9389A (154)

"When I was a seeker, I sought both night and day" 9389A (337)

"When I was a sinner, I prayed both night and day" 9389A (33)

"When I was a tiny baby" 4814 (37)

"When I was a young lad we had a fine cook" 961 (111)

"When I was a young man I lived all alone" 4601A (366)
"When I was a youngster I sail'd with the rest" 9459 (29)
WHEN I WAS A-MARCHING 6739 (295)
"When I was a-marching to the music clear" 6739 (295)
"When I was a-walking one morning for pleasure" 7614A (145)
"When I was blind and could not see" 8515 (366,409)
"When I was bound apprentice in famous Lincolnshire" 4674 (13,111,234,249,402)
"WHEN I WAS HOME WITH FATHER" 5087C (187)
"When I was on my feet, I couldn't walk down the street" 8571 (336)
"When I was seeking Jesus" 8274 (409)
WHEN I WAS SEVENTEEN 7325 (135,137)
WHEN I WAS SINGLE 8113A (170,173)
WHEN I WAS SINGLE (I) (WOMAN'S STORY) 8113D (227)
WHEN I WAS SINGLE (II) (MAN'S COMPLAINT) 8113A (227)
"When I was single, marrying was my crave" 8113D (72)
"When I was single, oh then, oh then" 8113A (170,173), 8113C (185)
"When I was single, went dressed all so fine" 8113D (227), 8113E (109,110)
"When I was walking by down where the grass is growing" 5166 (187)
"When I was young and pretty, I watched over my flock" 4974A (47)
"When I was young and scarce eighteen" 4721 (198)
"When I was young I us'd to wait on Massa and hand him de plate" 7459B (35)
"When I was young I use' to wait on Massa an' hand him his plate" 7459B (35)
"When I was young, I used to wait on master and give him his plate" 7459A (293)
"When I was young I used to wait on master and hand him his plate" 7459B (216)
"When I was young I used to wait on master and hand him the plate" 7459A (44)
"When I was young I used to wait on my master and give him his plate" 7459A (173)
"When I was young I used to wait on old massa and hand him his plate" 7459D (331)
"When I was young, I used to wait on my old Massa and hand his plate" 7459C (185)
"When I was young I used to wait, on my ole Massa, him de plate" 7459B (399)
"When I went down in de valley to pray" 8466 (184)
"When I went down in the valley to pray" 8466 (35)
"WHEN ICICLES HANG BY THE WALL" 85 (75)
"When I'll give you my love?" 318 (357)
WHEN I'M DEAD 8621 (409)
"WHEN I'M DEAD, DON'T YOU GRIEVE AFTER ME" 8621 (184,409)
"When I'm gone, when I'm gone" 8463 (409)
WHEN IN DEATH I SHALL CALM RECLINE 6035 (16,213)
"When in death I shall calm recline, oh, bear my heart to my mistress dear" 6035 (16,212,213)
WHEN IN MY DREAMS 2154 (211)
"When in the east the mighty sun no more did tarry" 9353 (314)
WHEN IN THE EAST THE SUN ARISES 9353 (314)
"When in the setting sun" 790 (122)
"WHEN IRISH EYES ARE SMILING" 163 (233)
"When Israel was in Egyp' Lan'" 8279 (35)
"When Israel was in Egypt land" 8279 (227,293)

"When Israel was in Egypt's land" 8279 (28,76,109,110, 183,233,366,409)
"When it was midnight on Noel" 9088 (86)
WHEN IT'S RAINY 6690 (159)
"When it's rainy, when it's mournful, left, right, left" 6690 (159)
WHEN I'VE DONE MY BEST 878 (394)
"When I've done the best I can, if my friends don't understand" 878 (394)
"When January days are here" 5416 (28,366)
"WHEN JESUS CHRIST WAS TWELVE YEARS OLD" 9008 (334,361)
"WHEN JESUS CHRIST WAS YET A CHILD" 649 (319,334)
WHEN JESUS WALKED ON GALILEE 981 (123)
WHEN JESUS WEPT 302 (109,110)
"When Jesus wept the falling tear" 302 (109,110)
WHEN JOAN'S ALE WAS NEW 4796 (198)
"When John Henry was a baby" 8382B (331)
"When John Henry was about three days old" 8382A (264, 293)
WHEN JOHNNY COMES DOWN 9445A (234)
WHEN JOHNNY COMES DOWN TO HILO 9445A (320)
"WHEN JOHNNY COMES MARCHING HOME" 1253 (7,10, 28,35,44,109,110,115,128,129,130,214,233, 236,279,366)
"When Joseph war an olden man" 8911K (265)
"When Joseph was an old man, an old man was he" 8911A (154)
"When Joseph was an olden man" 8911I (261,268)
WHEN JUDAH'S LOYAL SOUL ALONE 9257C (361)
"When Judah's loyal soul alone kept covenant before the throne" 9257C (361)
"When Judgment Day is drawing nigh, where shall I be?" 8121 (321)
WHEN LAURA SMILES 3092 (36,116,144,196,199)
"When Laura smiles her sight revives both night and day" 3092 (36,116,144,196,199)
"When, like the early rose, Eileen Aroon" 5901 (210)
"When little children close their eyes" 3371 (141)
"WHEN LO! BY BREAKE OF MORNING" 2532 (196)
WHEN LOVE IS KIND 4797 (132,136,237,329)
"When love is kind, cheerful and free" 4797 (132,136, 237,329)
"WHEN LOVE ON TIME AND MEASURE MAKES HIS GROUND" 1827 (144)
WHEN MCGUINNESS GETS A JOB 7769 (72)
"When Mary Ann walks in the woods" 8746 (11)
"When mighty roast beef was the Englishman's food" 2121 (14,235,349)
"When Moses an' his soldiers from Egypt's land did flee" 8314 (76)
"When music is most gay" 3686 (295)
WHEN MY BLOOD RUNS CHILLY AND COLD 8622 (227)
"When my heart begins a-rhyming, to the music of its chiming" 409 (45)
"When my stepfather sent me away from home" 4972 (86)
"When Nature, kind Goddess, first form'd this big ball" 8154 (145)
"When 'neath the setting sun" 790 (237)
WHEN NIGHT HAS FALLEN 356 (143)
"When night has fallen, when in the caverns deep below the earth" 356 (143)
"When night's falling, those two guitars are calling" 6980 (132,236)
"When o'er the hill the evening star" 7092 (95)

"When on Ramilies' bloody field the baffled French were
forced to yield" 5886 (349)
"When on Ramillies bloody field the baffled French were
forced to yield" 5886 (235)
"When on the fair shore of your dear country" 6872 (295)
"When once again the land is hoping" 282 (86)
"WHEN OTHER FRIENDS ARE ROUND THEE" 3894 (129)
"When other lips and other hearts their tales of love shall tell"
159 (36, 122, 128, 132)
"When our battle flag is flying" 8777 (293)
"When our dear old mother's voice train'd us all in singing"
960 (348)
"When our Polish dance's measure" 1999 (159)
"When owre the hill the eastern star" 7092 (100, 105)
WHEN RIGHTEOUS JOSEPH 8894A (334)
"WHEN RIGHTEOUS JOSEPH WEDDED WAS" 8894A (334,
361), 8894B (361)
"WHEN SHALL WE BE MARRIED JOHN?" 4798 (249)
"When shaws are sheen and shrubs full fair" 4740 (86)
"WHEN SHE ANSWERED ME HER VOICE WAS LOW" 6036
(166, 213, 349)
When she came ben, she bobbed (tune) 7086 (100, 104)
"When she smiles, the starlight gleaming" 3862 (4)
"When she takes her way" 410 (277)
"When slumber light in its arms doth enfold me" 2154 (211)
"When soft asleep I held thee, sweet" 3624 (330)
WHEN SOFT THE BREEZES 1171 (138)
"When soft the breezes sweetly are blowing" 1171 (138)
"When sounds the thrilling bugle blast" 7948 (145)
WHEN SPRING WAS IN THE AIR 651 (341)
"When Sunday vespers end, we all then have our chance"
5143 (186, 187)
"When swallows dart from cottage eaves, and farmers dream
of barley sheaves" 4807 (349)
"When tears becloud your eyes with sadness" 1889 (342)
"When that band of darkies began to play" 2454 (114, 115,
128, 131)
WHEN THAT I WAS (Arne) 86 (235)
"WHEN THAT I WAS AND A LITTLE TINY BOY" (Arne)
86 (75, 235)
"When that I was and a little tiny boy" (Stanford) 3556
(344)
"When that I was and a tiny boy" 2655 (5)
"When that my dark-haired Anne I see" 2979 (121, 362)
"When the big brass band began to play" 2454 (32, 34)
"When the birds begin their singing" 2690 (6)
"WHEN THE BOYS SHALL COME A-WOOING" 6672 (159)
WHEN THE BRIGHT GOD OF DAY 4799 (397)
"When the bright god of day drove to westward his ray" 4799
(397)
"When the Christ Child came to us on earth" 3399 (141)
WHEN THE COCK CROWS 6051 (36)
"When the cock crows at break of day" 6051 (36)
"WHEN THE CORN IS WAVING" 329 (28, 129, 130, 132, 366)
"WHEN THE CORN IS WAVING, ANNIE DEAR" 329 (36)
WHEN THE CRIMSON SUN 9187A (333)
"When the crimson sun descended" 9187A((333)
"WHEN THE CRIMSON SUN HAD SET" 9187B (373)
"WHEN THE CURTAINS OF NIGHT ARE PINNED BACK" 7533
(321)
"When the curtains of night are pinned back by the stars"
7533 (132, 321, 343)
"When the dawn comes again, Adelita" 6319 (350)

"When the dawn from sleep is winging all the earth of Thee
is singing" 2458 (295)
"When the drums do beat" 7137 (100)
"When the farmer comes to town with his wagon broken
down" 7583 (109, 110, 293, 335)
"When the gen'l roll is called" 8352 (409)
WHEN THE ICE WORMS NEST AGAIN 4249 (186)
WHEN THE KING ENJOYS HIS OWN AGAIN 4800 (294)
WHEN THE KYE COMES HAME 7199 (100, 105)
WHEN THE LIGHTS ARE LOW 2031 (132)
"When the little bluebird, who has never said a word" 2860
(345)
WHEN THE LORD OF LOVE WAS BORN 23 (315)
"When the lumberman comes down, ev'ry pocket bears a
crown" 7807 (227)
"WHEN THE MOON COMES OVER THE MOUNTAIN" 4100
(132, 326)
"When the moon rises over Marechiare" 3758 (310)
"When the Navy floats its battleboats to rule the rolling sea"
440 (44)
"When the new season will come" 291 (190, 192, 194)
"When the night falls silently" 2138 (32, 34)
"When the night is fair, music fills the air" 802 (9)
"When the night sinks over all" 8662 (19)
"When the nights grow cold" 5335 (28, 366)
"When the old farmer was sowing his good grain" 5142
(21)
"When the papers run by tories" 680 (293)
WHEN THE ROBINS NEST AGAIN 1711 (114, 129, 130, 131,
132, 204)
WHEN THE ROSES BLOOM 3020 (122)
"When the route is proclaim'd thro' the old barrack yard"
5871 (349)
WHEN THE SAINTS GO MARCHING IN 8114 (389)
"When the shades of night are falling, my love" 3306 (128,
132)
"When the ship is trim and ready" 2336 (28, 205, 366)
"When the signs of spring can first be seen" 218 (348)
"When the silvery moon gleams" 407 (274)
"When the Slovak started away" 4367 (95)
"When the stars over forest and glimmering lake" 3529
(188)
WHEN THE STARS SHED THEIR LIGHT 3529 (188)
"When the storm warning posted in St. Croix" 8768 (11)
"When the sun comes back and the first quail calls" 529
(389)
"When the sun rose this morning I was feelin' mighty bad"
8264 (336)
"WHEN THE SWALLOWS HOMEWARD FLY" 20 (28, 114,
132, 366)
WHEN THE TIME ARRIVED 4299 (324)
"When the time arrived and the army called John" 4299
(324)
"When the toys are growing weary and the twilight gathers
in" 2463 (129, 130)
"WHEN THE TRAIN COMES ALONG" 8623 (409)
"When the two sisters go to fetch water" 1499 (91, 93, 121)
"When the wind blows free 'cross the key from the sea"
6582 (86)
"When the winter comes at last" 5157 (186, 187)
"When the winter is gone and the summer is come" 4738
(198)
WHEN THE WORK'S ALL DONE 8115 (44)

"When the work's all done at last" 5162 (187)
WHEN THE WORK'S ALL DONE THIS FALL 8115 (10,129, 130)
WHEN THEY LAID THE BODY 5751 (164)
"When they laid the body on the courtyard floor" 5751 (164)
"When they poured across the border" 2277 (293)
WHEN THIS CRUEL WAR IS OVER 3775 (109,110,189)
"When thou comest, when thou comest to the judgment" 3109 (394)
WHEN THOU MUST HOME 568 (144)
"When thou must home to shades of underground" 568 (144)
"When thou singest when nestling at eve close by my side" 1332 (348)
"When Thou wouldst pour the living stream" 8923 (244)
"When thoughts, like bees, come buzzing" 3262 (330)
"When thou'rt cradled at eve on my breast, breathing forth song" 1332 (274)
WHEN THRO' LIFE UNBLEST WE ROVE" 6037 (166,213,349)
"When thro' life unblest we rove, losing all that made life dear" 6037 (166,213,349)
"When through love's garden at nightfall I glide" 5003 (45)
"When to an eager maiden music I'm teaching" 6282 (219)
"WHEN TO HER LUTE CORINNA SINGS" 569 (117,348)
"When trees did bud, and fields were green" 1691 (100,103)
"When twilight falls on the dim old walls" 2031 (132)
"WHEN UPON THE FIELD OF GLORY" 3241 (161)
"WHEN WE COME HAND IN HAND" 7305 (135)
"When we first came on this campus" 7503 (225)
"When we were little childer we had a quare wee house" 1546 (344)
"When whippoorwills call and ev'ning is nigh" 855 (236)
"When wild war's deadly blast was blawn" 7168 (100)
"When will come the happy morning, sweetest flow'rs the day adorning" 4168 (35)
WHEN WILL YOU COME AGAIN? (Folksongs, Germany) 5605 (95)
"When will you come again" (Folksongs, Scotland) 7116 (101)
"When wilt Thou save the people?" 7622 (321)
"When with my trusty walking-stick" 4072 (121)
"WHEN YESTERDAY WE MET" 2945 (272)
WHEN YOU AND I WERE YOUNG, MAGGIE 483 (28,32, 34,132,233,236,279,343,366)
"When you are dressed in green" 8742 (11)
WHEN YOU GO A-COURTIN' 8116 (227)
"When you go a-courtin', I'll tell you where to go" 8116 (227)
"When you go from Sevastopol on the way to Simferopol" 6177 (293)
WHEN YOU GO TO A BATTLE 5871 (349)
"When you hear dem a bells go ding, ling, ling" 2406 (246)
"When you look into your mailbox" 8258 (336)
WHEN YOU WORE A TULIP 3991 (128,129,130,236)
"When you wore a tulip, a sweet yellow tulip" 3991 (128, 129,130,131,236)
WHEN YOU WORE A TULIP AND I WORE A BIG RED ROSE" 3991 (131)
"When youth was at the spring-time" 511 (136,241)
"When-a my blood runs chilly an' col'" 8622 (227)
WHENAS THE ROSE OF JERICHO 9235 (361)
"Whenas the Rose of Jericho was fainting for the springtime's breath" 9235 (361)
WHENCE COME YOU, SHEPHERD MAIDEN? 9059A (186, 187)

WHENCE COMES ALL OUR LIGHT 2055 (285)
"Whence comes all our light, whence the falling dusk" 2055 (285)
WHENCE COMES THIS RUSH OF WINGS? 8817 (296,337)
"Whence comes this rush of wings afar" 8817 (165,206, 296,337)
"Whence comes this unwonted oppression?" 1321 (3)
"Whence dost thou fly thou tireless little swallow?" 3427 (132)
"WHENCE IS THAT GOODLY FRAGRANCE" 9111 (307)
"WHENCE, O SHEPHERD MAIDEN?" 9059A (388)
"Whence, O shepherd maiden, whence come you?" 9059A (186,187)
"Whene'er a snow flake leaves the sky" 724 (237)
"Whene'er I long to sit and sing" 6648 (230)
WHENE'ER I SEE THOSE SMILING EYES 6038 (166,213)
"Whene'er I see those smiling eyes, so full of hope and joy, and light" 6038 (166,213)
WHENE'ER THOU ART IN NEED OF ME 8923 (244)
"Whenever we happen to meet, time has wings" 2038 (248)
"Where am I?" 1268 (362)
WHERE ARE THE JOYS? 7200 (100,105)
"Where are the joys I have met in the morning" 7200 (100, 105)
WHERE ARE THE MEN 8689 (235)
"Where are the men who went forth in the morning" 8689 (235)
"WHERE ARE YOU BOUND, JOHNNY DEAR" 8872 (324)
"Where are you going, my good old man?" 7831 (216)
"Where are you going, pretty maids" 7265 (219)
"WHERE ARE YOU GOING TO MY PRETTY MAID?" (Folksongs, England) 4801 (249)
"WHERE ARE YOU GOING TO, MY PRETTY MAID?" (Folksongs, United States) 8117 (214)
"'Where away?' said a stranger to a lad of eighteen" 8118 (145)
WHERE AWAY, STRANGER 8118 (145)
"Where be ye goin', sweet little maid" 7819 (263)
"Where Cart rins rowin' to the sea" 7042 (100,104)
WHERE CORALS LIE 993 (274)
"Where did you come from, where did you go?" 7516 (214)
WHERE DID YOU GET THAT HAT? 3672 (114,131,204)
"Where did you get that hat, folks ask me ev'ry day" 3402 (166)
"WHERE DO WE GO FROM HERE?" 3992 (129,130,236)
WHERE DO YOU GO 7253 (219)
"Where do you think I foun' my soul" 8398 (409)
"Where dost thou wave, oh forest cool" 413 (330)
WHERE GO YE NOW? 9113 (165)
"Where go ye now, my friend, my neighbor" 9113 (165)
"Where ha' ye been, John Bramble, my son?" 4684A (331)
"Where ha'e ye been a' the day" 7011 (17,235)
"Where have you been all the day" 9448A (320)
"Where have you been all the day, Billy Boy" 4549C (173)
"Where have you been all the day, my boy Billy?" 4549A (44)
"Where have you been all the day, my boy Willie?" 4549A (173)
"Where have you been all the day, Randall, my son?" 4684A (170,173)
"Where have you been all the day, Rendal, my son?" 4684A (14,215)

"Widow Machree, 'tis no wonder you frown" 2194 (166, 213)
Wie bin ich doch so herzlich froh 141 (337)
"WIE BIST DU, MEINE KÖNIGIN" 435 (220, 277)
"Wie blüht es im Tale, wie grünt's auf den Höhn!" 3368 (141)
"Wie braust durch die Wipfel der heulende Sturm" 3278 (276)
"WIE CHRISTUS, DER HERR, AM OELIBERG GING" 7390 (157)
WIE DER MOND 1069 (73)
"Wie der Mond sich leuchtend dränget durch den dunklen Wolkenflor" 1069 (73)
WIE DIE BLÜMLEIN DRAUSSEN ZITTERN 5607 (326)
"Wie die Blümlein draussen zittern in der Abendlüfte wehn!" 5607 (326)
"Wie die hohen Sterne kreisen" 1284 (49)
"Wie eine Rosenknospe im Maienlicht erblüht" 2096 (256)
"Wie fremd und todt ist Alles umher" 3516 (2)
"Wie freundlich glühte ihres Fensters Schimmer!" 6086 (51)
"Wie gaat mee, gaat mee over zie!" 6582 (316)
"Wie glänzt das Meer so blau" 6048 (51)
"Wie glüht er im Glase" 2052 (31)
"WIE GROSS IST DES ALLMÄCHTGEN GÜTE" 1917 (326)
"Wie hat der Sturm zerrisen des Himmels graues Kleid" 3322 (45)
"Wie herrlich leuchtet mir die Natur" (Beethoven) 239 (97)
"Wie herrlich leuchtet mir die Natur!" (Gabler) 1183 (229)
WIE IM MÄRCHEN 1997 (74)
"WIE KÖNNT ICH DEIN VERGESSEN" 1985 (31)
"WIE KOMM ICH DENN ZUR TÜR HEREIN" 5608 (226)
"Wie lange zog sich die bleiern träge verdammte Nacht!" 2359 (224)
WIE LIEBLICH SCHALLT 3494 (326)
"Wie lieblich schallt durch Busch und Wald des Waldhorns süsser Klang" 3494 (326)
"Wie lieblich und fröhlich" 3314 (330)
"WIE MACHEN'S DENN DIE SCHNEIDER" 5609 (40)
"WIE MEIN AHNERL ZWANZIG JAHR" 4134 (258)
"WIE MEIN AHNL ZWANZIG JAHR" 4134 (258)
WIE MELODIEN ZIEHT ES MIR 437 (112)
"Wie Melodien zieht es mir leise durch den Sinn" 437 (112)
"Wie mit innigstem Behagen" 3383 (276)
"WIE NAHTE MIR DER SCHLUMMER" 3966 (1, 311, 326)
"Wie nahte mir der Schlummer, bevor ich ihn geseh'n?" 3966 (1, 311, 326)
"WIE SCHÖN BLÜHT UNS DER MAIEN" 5610 (31, 49, 309, 326)
"Wie schön ist mein Geliebter" 3 (217)
"WIE SCHÖN LEUCHTET DER MORGENSTERN" (Bach) 141 (337)
"WIE SCHÖN LEUCHTET DER MORGENSTERN" (Nicolai) 2658 (326)
"WIE SIND MIR MEINE STIEFEL GESCHWOLLN" 5611 (49, 309)
"WIE SOLL ICH DICH EMPFANGEN?" 140 (337)
"Wie soll ich nicht tanzen?" 3295 (112)
"Wie strahlt die Sonne hell in volem Glanze" 579 (223)
"Wie süss, o teurer Gatte" 1354 (218)
"Wie Todesahnung, Damm'rung deckt die Lande" 3920 (4, 237, 240, 364)
"Wie töricht ist doch der Verliebte" 2752 (217)
"Wie wil hooren een nieu liet?" 6465 (384)
"Wie wilt hooren een historie" 6588 (384)
"WIECZOR MGLISTY, WIECZÓR BLADY" 4157 (159)

"Wieder einmal ausgeflogen" 1943 (49)
"Wieder hinaus ins strahlende Licht" 1855 (256)
WIEGENLIED (Brahms) 436 (96, 99, 122, 132, 136, 141, 210, 226, 229, 276, 327, 329, 385)
WIEGENLIED (Carols, Russia) 9313 (354)
WIEGENLIED (Dvorak) 959 (74)
WIEGENLIED (Flies) 1085 (99, 209, 229, 326, 328)
WIEGENLIED (Folksongs, Germany) 5612 (231)
WIEGENLIED (Reger) 3007 (229)
WIEGENLIED (Schubert) 3318 (96, 226, 229, 275)
WIEGENLIED (Schulz) 3348 (229)
WIEGENLIED (Weber) 3977 (99)
WIEGENLIED (Wolf) 4067 (308)
WIEGENLIED FÜR MEINEN JUNGEN 3228 (226)
WIEGENLIED IM MAI 3348 (226, 229)
WIEJSKA SERENADE 2488 (295)
THE WIELEWAAL 6518 (316)
WIEN, DU STADT MEINER TRÄUME 3467 (396)
WIEN NEERLANDSCH BLOED 6614 (384)
"Wien Neerlandsch bloed in d'andren vloeit" 6614 (384)
WIEN, WIEN, NUR DU ALLEIN 3467 (396)
WIEN WIRD BEI NACHT ERST SCHÖN! 3592 (396)
EIN WIENER WALZER 275 (222)
WIENERLIED (Gruber) 1409 (396)
WIENERLIED (Stolz "Kinder schaut's zum Fenster...") 3587 (396)
WIENER-LIED (Stolz "Wenn bekrittelt wird...") 3592 (396)
WIENIEC MELODJI NARODOWYCH 3786 (295)
WIE'S DAHEIM WAR 4063 (326)
"Wie's daheim war, wo die Wiege stand" 4063 (326)
"Wife beloved, thou whom I cherish" 1470 (2)
"Wife", I said, "you'll never find me into tempers flying" 6307 (95)
THE WIFE OF USHER'S WELL 8130 (260, 262)
THE WIFE WHO WAS DUMB 4587B (72)
THE WIFE'S LAMENT 8131 (381)
WIJ BOEREN EN BOERINNEN 6615 (203, 384)
"Wij boeren en boerinnen wij werken dag en nacht" 6615 (203, 384)
"Wij Geuskens willen nu singhen" 6587 (384)
"WIJ KLOMMEN OP HOOGE BERGEN" 6616 (202)
WIJ KOMEN VAN OOSTEN 9276 (203)
"Wij komen van Oosten, wij komen van ver" 9276 (203)
WIJ LEVEN VRIJ 6617 (384)
"Wij leven vrij, wij leven blij Op Neerlands dierb'ren grond" 6617 (384)
WIJ ZIJN AL BIJEEN 6618 (203)
"Wij zijn al bijeen, al goe kadulletjes" 6618 (203)
"EEN WIJF HAD EEN KABAAS" 6619 (203)
WILD AMERICAY 8132 (72)
WILD BILL JONES 8133 (81)
"Wild flow'rs in the dell, soft green on the hill!" 3368 (141)
THE WILD ROSE 3274 (275)
"Wild roved an Indian maid" 3673 (185, 279, 366)
"Wild was the day when he came with greeting" 1153 (137)
DAS WILDE HEER 3227 (31)
DIE WILDEN SCHWÄNE 1936 (355)
WILDROSEN 1377 (31)
Wildwood flower (tune) 7951 (293)
WILDWOOD FLOWERS 2304 (279, 366)
WILDWOOD ROSE 3390 (407)
"Wildwood rose, growing free" 3390 (407)

Wilhelm, komm an meine Seite (tune) 5471 (49)

HET WILHELMUS 6620 (316)

WILHELMUS OF NASSAU 6620 (7)

"Wilhelmus, Prince of Nassau, of old Dutch blood am I" 6620 (7)

WILHELMUS VAN NASSOUWE 6620 (201)

"Wilhelmus van Nassouwe ben ick van duytschen bloet" 6620 (7)

"Wilhelmus van Nassouwe ben ick van duytschen bloet" 6620 (316)

"Wilhelmus van Nassouwe ben ik van Duitschen bloed" 6620 (201)

WILL DER HERR GRAF 2589 (390)

"Will der Herr Graf ein Tänzchen nun wagen" 2589 (390)

"WILL I GET A CHRISTMAS PRESENT?" 1573 (337)

"WILL ICH IN MEIN GÄRTLEIN GEHN" 5613 (40)

"WILL SAIDE TO HIS MAMMY" 1828 (144)

WILL, THE WEAVER 8134A (312)

"Will ye gang down the waterside" 7020 (17)

"Will ye gang o'er the learig" 7092 (18)

"Will ye gang to the Hielands, Leezie Landsay?" 7093 (18, 28,37,45,101,104,199,235,366)

"Will ye gang to the Hielans, Leezie Lindsay?" 7093 (36, 163,349)

"Will ye go, lassie go to the braes o' Balquidder" 7016 (235)

"WILL YE GO TO THE EWE-BUCHTS, MARION?" 7205 (101, 105)

WILL YE NO COME BACK AGAIN? 7206 (100,104,163,349)

"Will you buy my fresh eggs? White or brown, they're fresh eggs!" 5154 (21)

"Will you come and skate today with me?" 7382 (343)

"Will you come with me, my Phyllis dear" 465 (10,28,128, 129,130,131,132,215,236,279,366)

WILL YOU GO OUT WEST? 8135 (72)

Will you go to Flanders (tune) 5922 (128,132,166,213)

"Will you join in the gay camarrita" 4197 (350)

"Will you love me, pretty one as I love thee?" 2088 (297)

WILL YOU LOVE ME THEN AS NOW? 8136 (132)

"Will you wear white, O my dear, O my dear?" 7728 (216, 227)

WILLEN WIJ 'T HAASKEN JAGEN? 6471 (202)

"Willen wij, willen wij 't Haasken jagen door de hei?" 6471 (202)

"Willen wij, willen wij t'Haesken jagen door de hei?" 6471 (384)

WILLIAM AND DINAH 8037D (81)

WILLIAM OF NASSAU 6620 (316)

WILLIAM REILLY AND HIS COLLEEN BAWN 8137B (72)

WILLIAM RILEY 8137A (212)

"Willie Fitzgibbons who used to sell ribbons" 3456 (246)

WILLIE, TAKE YOUR DRUM 9106 (165)

"Willie, take your little drum" 9106 (33,165,307,337)

WILLIE THE WEAVER 8134B (72)

WILLIE THE WEEPER 8138A (80,109,110)

WILLIE'S GANE TO MELVILLE CASTLE 7207 (100,102)

"WILLIE'S RARE AND WILLIE'S FAIR"' 7208 (100,103,104)

"WILLINGLY WOULD I DIE" 46 (253)

"Willkommen im Grünen!" 3340 (308)

"Willkommen, o silberner Mond" 1271 (250)

"Willkommen, schöner Jüngling!" 3250 (141)

THE WILLOW SONG (Folksongs, England) 4806 (75,117)

The willow song (tune) (Folksongs, Wales) 8658 (20)

THE WILLOW SONG (Sullivan) 3671 (274)

THE WILLOW SONG (Verdi) 3849 (1,143)

WILLOWBEE 8139 (216)

"WILLST DU DEIN HERZ MIR SCHENKEN" 115 (311,313)

WILLY, THE WEEPER 8138B (35)

WILT HEDEN NU TREDEN 3790 (34,201,316)

"Wilt heden nu treden voor God den Heere" 3790 (34, 201,316)

"WILT THOU BE MY DEARIE?" 7209 (18,101,105)

WILT THOU LEND ME 2632 (349)

"Wilt thou lend me thy mare to go a mile" 2632 (349)

"Wilt thou, my child, give kindly welcome to a stranger" 3900 (5)

"Wilt thou then indeed forsake me" 417 (275)

WIMOWEH 7229 (389)

"The win' blows East, an' the win' blows West" 8257 (409)

"THE WIND BLEW UP, THE WIND BLEW DOWN" 8140 (264)

"The wind blows off yon rocky shore" 3087 (189)

"Der Wind, der Wind, der weht!" 1946 (49)

WIND, GENTLE EVERGREEN 1588 (235,349)

"Wind, gentle evergreen, to form a shade" 1588 (235, 349)

"The wind is fair, the day is fine and swiftly, swiftly runs the time" 7038 (103,105)

WIND OF NIGHT 6761 (95)

"Wind of night, rover, come bend the grass over" 6761 (95)

THE WIND SPEAKS 1353 (136)

"De wind waait uit den Oosten" 6568 (384)

"Wind whines and whines the shingle" 3433 (85)

WINDE WEHN, SCHIFFE GEHN 4862 (49,309)

"Winde wehn, Schiffe gehn weit in fremde Land" 4862 (49,309)

"WINDEKEN, DAAR HET BOSCH AF DRILT" 6621 (202)

"The winds chant across the sea" 6245 (318)

WINDSOR 8141 (34)

WINDY BILL 8142 (120)

WINE I DRINK 5830 (95)

"Wine I drink, despite your warning, lovely star, darling dove, beauty mine!" 5830 (95)

"Wine, O wine, O wine so ruby-red" 4445 (94)

WINE SO RUBY-RED 4445 (94)

WINGS OF NIGHT 3955 (259)

WININ' BOY BLUES 2540 (336)

"A winning way, a pleasant smile" 2669 (131,166)

WINNSBORO COTTON MILL BLUES 8631 (336)

THE WINTER 1939 (192,194)

WINTER, ADE! 5198 (326,353)

"Winter, ade! Scheiden tut weh" 5198 (99,326,353)

THE WINTER CAMP 5157 (186,187)

A WINTER DEDICATION 3636 (277)

"DER WINTER, DER IST MIR NET Z'WIDER" 5614 (326)

WINTER HAS COME 8143 (44)

"Winter has come upon our loved ones" 8143 (44)

"The winter has gone and the leaves turn green" 7508 (243)

WINTER IS NEAR 8671 (20)

"DE WINTER IS VERGANGEN" 6622 (202,316)

"DE WINTER IS VERGANGHEN" 6622 (384)

"DER WINTER IST VERGANGEN" 6622 (31,41,49,309,326)

"THE WINTER IT IS PAST" 7210 (101)

"Der Winter mag scheiden, der Frühling vergeh'n" 1389 (122,137,329)

"The winter may go, and the spring may die" 1389 (122)

YA SOY FELÍZ 4524 (73)

"Ya viene el alba" 7682 (113)

"Yachne-Dvoshe fort in mark, Zi halt zich in eyn pakn, bakn" 6209 (318)

"Yachne-Dvoshe's in a dither, packing for the market-place" 6209 (318)

THE YACHT AND THE BRIG 103 (205)

"YAFIM HALEYLOT BI-CHNA-AN" 6269 (318)

"Yah-nah, ha-way-ee, yah-nah-nee-nah!" 5852 (321)

YAH-NAH-NEE 5852 (321)

YALE BOOLA 1667 (128,236)

YANKEE DOODLE 8150 (7,10,28,32,34,109,110,115,129, 130,173,233,236,279,294,366)

YANKEE MAID 8151 (189)

THE YANKEE MAN-OF-WAR 8152 (173)

YANKEE MANUFACTURES 8153 (189)

"A YANKEE SHIP, AND A YANKEE CREW" 1896 (205)

"A YANKEE SHIP CAME DOWN THE RIVER" 9425A (109, 110), 9425C (401), 9425D (145)

YANKEE TARS 8154 (145)

"The Yankees boast that they can make clocks" 4049 (225)

YANKELE 1229 (318)

YANKO 8792 (95)

YANKO GRAZED HIS OXEN 4394 (94)

"Yanko grazed his oxen through green meadows" 4394 (94)

"YANO DANS L'EAU RUISSELANTE" 4424 (177)

YARAVI 4266 (279)

YASHA AND KASHA 6877 (95)

"Yasha fed his horses, Kasha pumped the water" 6877 (95)

YE BANKS AN' BRAES 7213 (17)

"Ye banks an' braes o' bonnie Doon, how can ye bloom sae fresh an' fair" 7213 (17)

YE BANKS AND BRAES 7213 (34,100,103,104,235,297)

"Ye banks, and braes, and streams around" 7055 (101)

YE BANKS AND BRAES O' BONNIE DOON 7213 (163,349, 402)

"Ye banks and braes o' bonnie Doon, how can ye bloom sae fresh and fair" 7213 (34,100,103,104,163, 232,235,297,349,365,402)

"Ye country maidens, gather dew, while yet the morning breezes blow" 8916 (70)

"Ye Demo's attend and ye Federals, too" 7674 (109,173)

"Ye galliants and nobles, I pray listen all" 7849 (126)

"Ye gentlemen and ladies fair, who grace this famous city" 4787 (173)

"Ye Gods forsaken! grant, grant me your vengeance" 3904 (2)

"Ye gods of endless night, ye gods of endless nights that wait on death below" 1267 (1)

"Ye Heilands and ye Lawlands, o whare hae ye been?" (Gurney) 1417 (272)

"Ye Hielands, and ye Lowlands, O whaur ha'e ye been?" 7009 (101)

"Ye Hielands, and ye Lowlands, O where hae ye been?" (Folksongs, Scotland) 7009 (46)

"Ye jovial boys who love the joys" 7041 (365)

YE MAIDENS OF ONTARIO 4251 (186)

"Ye maidens of Ontario, give ear to what I write" 4251 (186)

YE MARINERS OF ENGLAND 525 (349,397)

"Ye mariners of England that guard our native seas" 525 (349,397)

"Ye men of earth in God rejoice" 8158 (32,34)

"Ye nations all, on you I call" 9347 (332)

YE PARLIAMENT OF ENGLAND 8155 (34)

"Ye Parliament of England, Ye Lords and Commons too" 8155 (34)

YE PARLIAMENTS OF ENGLAND 8155 (173)

"Ye parliaments of England, ye Lords and Commons too" 8155 (173)

"Ye people, rend your hearts" 2372 (123,200)

"Ye rambling boys of Erin" 4223 (186)

"Ye saints who dwell on Europe's shore" 7650 (173)

YE SHEPHERDS, LEAVE YOUR FLOCKS 9112 (317)

"Ye shepherds, leave your flocks upon the mountains" 9112 (317)

"Ye sons of Columbia your attention I do crave" 7601 (129)

"Ye sons of France, awake to glory" 3110 (7,28,35,233, 279,366)

"Ye sons of Freedom, wake to glory!" 3110 (161)

"YE TWICE TEN HUNDRED DEITIES" 2914 (272)

YE VERDANT HILLS 1491 (277)

"Ye verdant hills, ye balmy vales" 1491 (277)

"Ye wand'ring breezes heard me, when grief was all I knew" 3905 (1)

"YE WATCHERS AND YE HOLY ONES" 9189 (38,39)

"YEA, THE HEAVENLY CHILD IS BORN" 9070 (154)

A YEAR BEGINS OF JOY AND GRACE 9262 (361)

"A year begins of joy and grace, like ev'ry year that sees His face" 9262 (361)

YEAR OF JUBILO 4108 (109,110)

YEARNING 4857 (124)

"Years are coming, speed them onward!" 9025 (28,366)

"The years creep slowly by, Lorena" 3980 (36,161,212)

YEARS OF PEACE 9025 (28,366)

YELENKA 4219 (95)

"Yelenka, Yelenka, sick your love is lying" 4219 (95)

THE YELLOW BOREEN 5859 (280)

THE YELLOW-HAIRED LADDIE 7214 (100,104)

"The yellow-haired laddie sat on yon burn brae" 7214 (100, 104)

THE YELLOW ROSE OF TEXAS 8156 (161,236)

YENITCHKU 4454 (95)

"Yenitchku, poor fellow, had you then heard Mother, now you'd wear no saber" 4454 (95)

YEO, HEAVE HO! 9493 (35)

"Yeo, heave ho! 'Round the capstan go" 9493 (35)

"Yeo, ho, and we'll haul, aye, we'll hang Paddy Doyle for his boots" 9471B ·(366)

A YEOMAN'S CAROL 9013 (334)

"Yes, beloved, well thou knowest" 3637 (408)

"Yes, ev'ry time I feel the spirit" 8266 (366)

"Yes for this eve I am queen" 3732 (221)

"Yess, for this evening I am queen" 3732 (6)

"Yes, her doom is to die!" 2846 (5)

"Yes, I will, draw nearer unto me" 3865 (5)

"Yes, I'm always called Mimi, but my name is Lucia" 2889 (1)

"Yes, I'm in love" 82 (272)

"Yes, Mimi is what I'm called but my name is Lucia" 2889 (1)

"Yes, my boy, will you tanz' mit mir?" 2992 (257)

"Yes, she's my daughter" 3851 (4)

"Yes, she's the girl that they call Adelita" 6319 (322)

"Yes the book of Revelations to be brought forth on that day" 8455 (409)

"Yes, the candidate's a dodger" 7548 (83,293)

"Yes, they shall not be spared" 656 (148)

YES, THEY TELL ME 5764 (164)
"Yes, they tell me, oh my sweetheart dear" 5764 (164)
"Yes time with fate e'er striving" 258 (6)
"Yes, we'll rally round the flag, boys" 3068 (28,115,129, 130,279,366)
"Yes, yes, my Lord, I'm going to join the heav'nly choir" 8617 (28)
"YESH BANU KAOCH" 1022 (30)
YESH LI GAN 6270 (30)
"Yesh li gan uv'er yesh li" 6270 (30)
"Yesterday while out a-walkin', I met a dear little girl" 854 (166)
"Yesterday Yanko fell upon our village" 8792 (95)
"Yestreen the Queen had four Maries" 7157 (100,103,104)
"Y'heave ho! my lads, the wind blows free" 2276 (28, 366)
YIPPY TI-YI-YO, GIT ALONG, LITTLE DOGIES 7614D (185)
YIS'M'CHU ADIRIM 6271 (318)
"Yis'm'chu adirim, adirim, B'simchat matan Tora" 6271 (318)
"Yksi ruusu on kasvanut laaksossa" 4837 (124)
"Ylös Suomen pojat nuoret" 695 (124)
"Ym Mhalas Llwyn Onn gynt" 8683 (19)
YMADAWIAD Y BRENIN 8703 (349)
Y'MEY HANOAR 6268 (318)
"Y'mey hanoar Chalfu avaru" 6268 (318)
"Yn iach i ti Gymru" 8682 (349)
"Yn Mhalas Llwyn On gynt" 8683 (349,402)
YN NYFFRYN CLWYD 8704 (349)
"Yn Nyffryn Clwyd nid oes" 8704 (349)
YN NYFFRYN LLANGOLLEN 8705 (349)
"Yn Nyffryn Llangollen ac ochor y Glyn" 8705 (349)
"Yn y dyddiau gynt, pan chwareuai'r gwynt" 8663 (349)
"Yn ymyl y dre' o ddiffyg gwell lle" 8670 (20)
DEN YNDIGSTE ROSE 8886 (206)
"Yo heave ho! yo heave ho! Pull once more, lads, pull once more!" 6974 (122)
"Yo ho and up she rises" 9440A (111)
"Yo jabla con ño Fransico" 3502 (9)
"YO' LOW DOWN WAYS" 8637 (409)
"Yo me deleito al con templar tu talle" 4504 (73)
YO ME ENCELERÉ 1208 (303)
"YO NO QUIERO MÁS PREMIO" 7293 (283)
YO NO SE POR QUE TE QUIERO 58 (303)
"Yo no sé qué tienen tus ojillos negros" 1033 (121)
"YO NO SE SI ME QUIERES" 6401 (142)
"Yo perdí mis ilusiones" 4498 (73)
"Yo quie ro mucho a la luna" 1787 (291)
YO QUISIERA QUERERTE 4267 (207)
"Yo quisiera quererte pero tu me has de olvidar" 4267 (207)
"Yo quisiera ser mishito" 5641 (322)
"Yo soc el petit bailet cansadet de molt cami" 8861 (53)
"Yo soy el mejor torero Naciodo en Andalucia" 1298 (245)
"Yo soy el muchacho alegre que me divierto cantando" 7825 (314)
YO SOY FAROLERO 6303 (219)
"Yo soy farolero de la Puerta' el Sol" 6303 (219)
"Yo soy la Viudita del Conde Laurel" 6300 (219)
"Yo soy pajarillo errante lejos del nido, lejos del nido" 6376 (247)
"Yo soy Valentín Mancera, borrega nixtamalera" 6396 (247)

"Yo te podré olvidar cuando las flores" 4499 (73)
"Yo te vi que bailabas un dia" 3421 (245)
"Yo tengo, yo tengo, para hacer cria" 4261 (207)
"Yo vi volar una blanca paloma" 4509 (73)
YO, YEA 837 (235)
Yo yea, or the friendly tars 837 (235)
"Yohohoey! Yohohohoey!" 3901 (1)
YOM L'YABASHA (SHIR HAG'ULA) 6272 (318)
"Yom l'yabasha nehefchu m'tsulim" 6272 (318)
"Yon assassin is my equal; he stabs in darkness" 3853 (4)
"YON MAIDEN'S LIPS ARE ROSY RED" 4151 (406)
"Yonder comes my dearest Billie" 7542 (392)
"Yonder comes Roberta! Tell me how do you know?" 8486 (184)
YONDER COMES SISTER MARY 9404 (332)
"Yonder comes Sister Mary, How do you know it is her?" 9404 (332)
"YONDER COMES THE HIGH SHERIFF" 8638 (184)
"Yonder, from swamplands lowly" 3027 (408)
"Yonder in the crib sleeps a baby holy" 1243 (296)
YONDERS TREE 8157A (28,44,366)
"Yoodahyah noh hetsoo jee woe" 9218 (244)
YORK 8158 (32,34)
Yorkshire (tune) 3928 (333,337,410)
THE YORKSHIRE BITE 4810B (72), 4810C (126)
THE YORKSHIRE FARMER 4810A (198)
The Yorkshire lasses (tune) 5991 (166,213)
THE YORKSHIRE TYKE 582 (235)
YOU 4162 (219)
YOU AND I 179 (129,130,131)
YOU ARE A BRIDE 6984 (95)
"You are a bride, girl, yet you look woeful" 6984 (95)
"You are caught! Now I see the way clearly" 3513 (3)
"YOU ARE GOING TO THE WARS, WILLIE BOY" 1650 (161)
"You are gone and all is gone, and through each weary day" 1621 (345)
YOU ARE JUST LIKE A FLOWER 3379 (112)
"You are just like a flower, so sweet, so pure, so fair" 3379 (112)
"You are leaving me behind, my own true love" 6198 (318)
"YOU ARE MY LOVE, FOR I LOVE YOU" 6390 (322)
"You are my sugar and tea" 8035 (242)
"You are my thoughts, my end and my beginning" 1382 (36)
YOU ARE SO LIKE A FLOWER 3379 (36)
"You are so like a flower so fair and pure and kind" 3379 (36)
YOU ARE TEASING ME, MY DARLING 6855 (295)
"You are teasing me, my darling, stop it, will you please!" 6855 (295)
"You are the plowmen and you sow" 6263 (318)
"You ask me why so oft, father" 2741 (189)
"You bad leetle boy, not moche you care" 2695 (240)
"You can never win us back" 326 (161)
"You can't look it down" 8561 (77)
YOU COULD SEE MY FAITH 6878 (95)
"You could see my faith, you could see my faith" 6878 (95)
"You desire to be divorce' from dat man Crown?" 1242 (184)
YOU DO SOMETHING TO ME 2861 (345)
"You do something to me, Something that simply mysti- fies me" 2861 (345)

"You don't have to pay for a beautiful day" 1798 (129, 130)

YOU DON'T KNOW MY MIND 8639 (336)

"You don't know, you don't know, you don't know my mind" 8639 (336)

"You dwell with angel hosts on high" 3842 (3)

"You fooled me, dear, now for a year" 3162 (345)

"You gentle birds of Erin's Isle who crossed the Atlantic sea" 8132 (72)

"You gentle spirit, heart so true" 3387 (112)

YOU GENTLEMEN OF ENGLAND 4811 (349)

"You gentlemen of England that live at home at ease" 4811 (349)

"You get a line and I'll get a pole, baby" 7526A (145)

"You get a line and I'll get a pole, honey" 7526A (44)

"You go aboard of a leaky boat" (A RIPPING TRIP) 4735 (173)

"You got a gal an' I got none" 7779A (279, 366)

"You got a gal and I got none, Li'l Liza Jane" 7779A (185)

"You got to jump down, turn around" 8486 (34, 227)

"You got to walk that lonesome valley" 7797 (227)

YOU GOTTA GO DOWN 1432 (293)

"You gotta go down and join the union" 1432 (293)

"You had a dream, dear, I had one too" 760 (233)

"You had a dream, well, I had one too" 760 (131, 246)

YOU HAVE FORGOTTEN ME 6748 (295)

"You have loved lots of girls" 1713 (34)

YOU HAVE NO LOOKS 2692 (362)

"You have no looks nor have you wealth" 2692 (362)

"You have told me that you love me" 8136 (132)

"YOU HEAR THE LAMBS A-CRYING" 8640 (409)

"You kin do jes'-a what you please" 8483 (37, 129, 130, 279, 366)

"You know how much I have loved you" 3756 (134)

"You know I love you madly" 6118 (95)

"You know I'm lonesome and the blues is in my way" 8405 (336)

"You know the answer, you hold the key" 2590 (2)

"You made me what I am today" 2809 (128, 129)

"YOU MAY BURY ME IN THE EAST" 8641 (366, 409)

"You may bury my body" 8556 (52)

"You may talk about good eating" 1538 (225)

"You may talk about me jes as much as you please" 8582 (409)

"You may talk of Clara Nolan's Ball" 4237 (186)

"You must answer me questions nine" 7547B (171, 173)

"You must know that my uncle is a farmer" 2995 (205)

"You needn't min' my dyin'" 8376B (409)

"You never come back; I say good bye when I see you going in the doors" 814 (358)

YOU NEVER MISS THE WATER TILL THE WELL RUNS DRY 1715 (114, 131, 204)

"You ought to see my Cindy, she lives way down south" 7501 (293)

"You ought-a see my Cindy, she lives away down South" 7501 (293)

"You read in de Bible, an' you understan'" 8437 (76)

"You read in the Bible and you understand" 8437 (409)

"You say you're aiming for the skies" 8277 (409)

"You shall be a clipper built yacht" 103 (205)

YOU SHALL NEVER HAVE THE RING 4453 (95)

YOU SHALL NOT WALK 6193 (231)

"You shall not walk anywhere with another girl" 6193 (231)

YOU SHALL REAP 8642 (409)

"You shall reap jes what you sow" 8642 (409)

YOU SIMPLE BOSTONIANS 8106 (109, 110)

"You simple Bostonians, I'd have you beware" 8106 (110)

YOU SPOTTED SNAKES 2394 (75)

"You spotted snakes, with double tongue" 2394 (75)

"You sweet little star, how tiny you are" 3352 (141)

"You talk about yo' elder when he's tryin' to preach the word" 8637 (409)

YOU TELL ME YOUR DREAM, I'LL TELL YOU MINE 760 (131, 233, 246)

"You that in merriment delight, pray listen unto what I recite" 7752 (72)

"YOU THAT MAKE A TOIL OF PLEASURE" 9126 (361)

"You think! oh! Strephon that your piping" 2961 (152)

"You told me to pray and I done that too" 8288 (409)

"YOU WERE ONCE THAT WHICH YOU ARE NO MORE" 1370 (362)

"YOU WHO ARE KNOWING" 2590 (36)

"You who believe in the tears" 1549 (134)

YOU WHO DON'T BELIEVE IT 7459A (173)

"You who knew worldly pride" 3832 (1)

"YOU, YOU, IN MY HEART LIVING" 5283 (36)

YOU'D BETTER MIN' 8643 (409)

"You'd better min' how you talk" 8643 (409)

YOU'D BETTER RUN 8644 (409)

"You'd better run, run, run-a-run" 8644 (409)

"You'd fain be hearing what dress he's wearing" 3826 (6)

"You'll be rich one day, my Zhamele" 6276 (318)

"YOU'LL CLIMB THE MOUNTAIN" 6854 (295)

"You'll rue it my boy, now mind what I say" 2171 (189)

"You'll visit that old dame?" 4947 (86)

YOUNG CHARLOTTE 8159A (242)

"Young Charlotte lived in her father's home" 8159A (242)

"Young Charlotte lived on a mountain top, in a bleak and lonely spot" 8159B (44)

YOUNG CONSTANTINE 5639 (86)

THE YOUNG COUNSELOR 8160 (126)

THE YOUNG COWHERD 2682 (124)

"Young folks, old folks, ev'rybody come" 7439 (72)

"Young Jamie lo'ed me weel, and socht me for his bride" 2087 (100, 103)

"YOUNG LOVE LIES SLEEPING" 3531 (344)

YOUNG MAIDEN 6804 (295)

"Young man in the carriage driving like he's mad" 7942 (72)

THE YOUNG MAN WHO WOULDN'T HOE CORN 8161 (173, 227)

The young man's dream (tune) 5864 (213)

THE YOUNG MAY MOON 6042 (166, 213)

"The young May moon is beaming, love" 6042 (166, 213)

"Young men and maids, pray tell your age" 7793 (109, 110)

"Young Molly who lived at the foot of the hill" 77 (122, 237, 329, 386)

YOUNG RILEY THE FISHERMAN 4812 (198)

"Young Roger the miller he courted of late" 4622 (198)

YOUNG ROGER THE PLOUGHBOY 4813 (198)

"Young Roger the ploughboy a crafty young swain" 4813 (198)

YOUNG RORY O'MORE 2195 (166, 213)

"Young Rory O'More courted Kathaleen bawn" 2195 (166, 213)

THE YOUNG SHEPHERD 5638 (36)

YOUNG SOPHIE 6781 (159)

571

INDEX OF AUTHORS

Chazot, Paul de 1049
Checínski, J. 2486-2487,2488
Cheetham, Everett 7457
Chekhov, Anton 2951
Chemnitz, Matthäus F. 268
Chenier, Joseph 2346
Cherry, Andrew 785
Cherryman, Myrtle Koon 15,784
Chesterton, Frances 1719,8943
Chesterton, G. K. 9012,9164
Chezy, Helmine von 1987
Chorley, Henry F. 1552,3662
Christie, W. 7110
Chrystabel, (pseud) 1239
Cicognini, Giacinto Andrea 621,629,3650
Cini, Francesco 504
Civinini, Guelfo 2892-2893
Claiborne, Adrienne 7781
Claiborne, Bob 7781
Clairville 2832
Clark, Badger 7616
Clarke, Grant 30,36
Clarke, H. A. 181
Claudius, Hermann 841,1925,2285,2288,2290,4093
Claudius, Matthias 63,2405,3246,3247,3310,3312,3334,
        3342
Cobb, James 3595-3596
Cobb, Will D. 3456
Cobos, Maria Teresa de 6985
Coburn, Richard 3080
Cockburn, Mrs. 7040
Cöster, F. B. 738
Cole, Bob 1803,1808
Coleridge, Samuel Taylor 953,8794
Collin, Matthäus, Edler von 3287
Collins 3499
Colman, George 5988
Colum, Padraic 1730
Congreve, William 1477-1479
Connell, J. M. 7203
Constable, Henry 2819,3148
Cook, Eliza 1739
Cook Joseph Simpson 8935
Coolbrith, Ina 217
Cooper, George 313,675*,1119,2434,2435,2715,3734,
        3774,7630
Corancez, M. de 3112
Corneille, Pierre 655-656,2731
Cornelius, Peter 4063
Cowan, Samuel K. 2183
Craigher, J. N. 3278
Crawford, Annie (Barry) 13,173,734
Crawford, R. 1691,7019
Creamer, Henry 1800
Croly, George 2641
Croo, Robert 1581,8917A
Crosy, F. 1914
Crowell, Grace Noll 1671
Cullen, Countee 692
Cummings, E. E. 339,705
Cuney, Waring 1501,1502
Cunningham, Agnes 4048
Cunningham, Allan 7047,7878C

Currie, Edward C. 2272
Czeczott, J. 2484

Dach, Simon 39,40,41,42
Dahlgren, F. A. 2969
Dahn, Felix 3618,3621
Dana, Mary S. B. 1797
Danchet, Antoine 571-574,822
The dancing music 4574
Dancourt, L. H. 1277
Dandridge, Raymond Garfield 2696
Daniel, Samuel 758
Danziger, U. 334
Da Ponte, Lorenzo 2557-2561, 2563-2570, 2584-2590
Daumer, G. F. 397,404,411,435
Davies, Thomas 5908,6032
Davies, W. H. 1598
Davis, Benny 37,203
Davis, Christine K. 2385
Davis, H. C. 7814
Davis, Henry W. 9201
Davis, Katherine Kennicott 3257
Davis, Robert 8908
Davis, Thomas 5886
Davison, Francis 1822
Dawson, E. M. 8867
Dawson, Ernest 3409
Dearmer, Percy 8933,8935,9061
De Burgh, Hubert 2851
DeCaen, Leo 803
Dehmel, Richard 3228,3237,3635
Dehmel, Willy 1405-1406,1913
Dehn, Christian 4969
Dekker, Thomas 3555
Dekner, Hanns 1403
De la Coste, Marie Ravenel 1649
De La Mare, Walter 581
Deland, Margaret 2226,2227
Delâtre, Louis 323
Delavigne, Germain 101
Della Luna, Carlo 596
Dempsey, J. E. 472
Dennery, Adolphe Philippe 2306
Dennet, F. J. 1837
Dercy, 2119
Deschamps, J. M. 2119
Desriaux, Philippe 614
De Sylva, George Gard 1619,1621,1622,1865,3078,3541
De Vere, Stephen Edward 6016
Devine, John V. 4222
Devlin, Edward 2793
Dewing, E. B. 3978
Diack, J. Michael 7107,7126
Dibdin, Charles 310,5894
Dickinson, Dorothy 2192
Dickinson, Emily 1168
Dickinson, John 386
Didiée, Julien 1349
Dingelstedt, Franz 2877
Dippel, Heinrich 1654
Dirnböck, Jacob 3434
Disselhoff, August 5491

Dix, William 3566
Dixon, Mort 2838,4099
Djordjevic, Jovan 1774
Doane, George W. 523
Dobbyn, Dermot 3424
Dobrovolsky, I. 2841
Doddridge, Philip 1557,7036
Dodge, Mary Mapes 724
Doehler, Gottfried 5409
Doelitz, Martin 3005
Dörmann, Felix 3605
Doleva, D. 334
Dolmatovsky, E. 1842
Donne, John 1064
Donop, F. Teo von 1232
Dorset, Baron 4777
Doud, Mabel C. 2436
Douglas, William 3405
Downey, Laura 3524
Drachmann, Holger 2661
Drake, Joseph Rodman 3777
Dreckschmidt, Hermann 5293
Dreves, Lebrecht 3545
Drimhorn, Franz Gabriel 350
Droste-Hülshoff, Annette von 720
Drummond, William Henry 2695,5191
Dryden, John 2915-2917
Dubin, Al 473,475
Duché, Joseph François 822
Du Commun du Locle, Camille 3828-3832
Düringer, Philipp Jacob 5268
Dufferin, Lady Helen Selina 3142,5921
Duffield, George 3958
Dufft, Christian Timotheus 3327
Duffy, Charles Gavan 5941
Dunbar, Paul Laurence 604,1511,1512,1805,2270
D'Urfey, Thomas 2909,2911,4587A,4627,8890
Duval, Alexsandre 2348
Duveyrier, Charles 3870
Dwight, Dr. 951
Dybeck, R. 7303
Dyer, Sir Edward 906
Dyk, Viktor 2717

Earle, Giles Song-book, 1615: 4759,4804
Eastman, C. G. 3072
Egan, Raymond B. 4018,4019,4020
Eichendorff, Joseph von 1148,1156,1174,2021,2218,2219,
    2367,2382,3373,3375,3482,4087,5486
Ekelund, Vilhelm 1007,1179
Elder, Mrs. C. D. 1236
Elizondo, J. F. 1781
Elliot, Ebenezer 7622
Elliot, Jane 7040
Elliott, C. W. 3735
Elmenhorst, Hinrich 1144
Elst, F. van der 25
Ely, Lois Anna 4022
Engel, Carl 2736,9308
Enoch, Frederick 2827
Enslin, Karl 3004
Ephelia, (pseud) 1246
Eschenburg, Johann Joachim 1561

Eskew, Garnett Laidlaw 7989
Esrom, D. A. 2537
Estic 3791
Étienne, Charles Guillaume 754
Ewald, Carl 1624
Ewen, John 7003

Faber, Fr. 3814
Faber, Frederick W. 733,1618
Fahy, F. A. 5905,5958
Falbaire, C. G. Fenouillot de 1367
Falconer, E. (pseud) See O'Rourke, Edmund
Falke, Gustav 3571
Fallersleben, Heinrich Hoffmann von 1563,1907,1985,2216,
    3366,3368,3391,3396,3397,3709,5198,5209,
    5237,5441,5461,5541,5549,5567*,9172
Farnie, H. B. 748
Farrell, Joseph C. 2455
Favart, Charles 1020
Fawcett, John 2626
Feist, Felix F. 707,2634
Felderer, Karl 5624
Felinzki, Ks. Alojzy 1998
Feltz, Kurt, 852,2991-2993
Ferguson, Sir Samuel 5952
Ferretti, Jacopo 3100
Fet, 3036
Feuchtersleben, Ernst von 2377
Fiallo, Fabio 832,2268
Field, Eugene 3621
Fielding, Henry 4536
Fink, E. 2431
Fionn's Celtic Lyre 7060
Flaccus, Quintus Horatius 1083
Fléchier 9055
Fleming, Carroll 1016,1878
Flemming, Paul 414,1094
Fletcher, Curley W. 8028
Fletcher, John 1420,2907
Flex, Walter 3937
Florian, J. P. Claris de 1289,4916
Foner, Henry 1147
Fontaine, Lamarr 1644
Fontenelle, Bernard Le Bovier de 698
Ford, Walter H. 441
Forzano, Giovacchino 2894
Fosdick, W. W. 2862
Fourcaud, Louis de Boussés de 1142
Fouser, Sarah C. 1137
Frande, Peter 3061
Frank, Hans 1933
Franzén, Frans Mikael 4827
Fredrik, Oscar 7348
Freed, Arthur 457,458
Freese, Myron V. 3994
Freiligrath, Ferdinand 2180
Freise, Hermann 2167
Frenkel, I. 2418
Freudenthal, August 1295
Frey, Adolf, 409,1373,1377
Friend, Cliff 3162
Furber, Douglas 395

Gabet, C. 2832

Gabriel, J. J. 772

Gabriel, Wilhelm 5334

Gagg, Robert Ferdinand 3211

Gale, Norman 2129

Gall, Richard 6996

Gannett, William C. 1231

Ganzhorn, Wilhelm 5275

Gardner, W. H. 2229

Gardner, William H. 3062

Garnett, Louise Ayres 1729

Garnett, Richard 993

Garrick, David 76

Gascoigne, George 193

Gaszynski, K. 6872

Gautier, Théophile 289-291, 657, 773, 943, 1032, 2027, 4023

Gawalewicz, M. 1199

Gay, John 1440, 2120

Geddes, Alex. 7095

Geibel, Emanuel 208, 1155, 1906, 1928, 2024, 2220, 3389

Geijer, E. G. 3507

Gellert, Christian Fürchtegott 109, 111, 227, 228, 235, 1917

Genée, Richard 2443-2446, 2447-2450, 3607-3609, 3612, 3614-3615, 3616-3617, 3675-3676

George, Daniel 1210

Gérard, Rosemonde 633-634, 652

Gerhard, Wilhelm 3381, 5458

Gerhardt, Paul 118, 122, 136, 736, 974, 1550, 1629, 3229, 5579*

Gérin-Lajoie, M. A. 5153

Gershwin, Ira 1242

Gersin, N. 1307

Gherardini, Giovanni 3101

Ghislanzoni, A. 1297, 3819-3821

Giacomo, S. di 3758

Giacosa, Giuseppe 2887-2891, 2895-2897, 2901-2903

Gibson, Wilfred Wilson 1718

Gilbert, Mereedes 1518

Gilbert, Robert 273-274, 1348, 3588

Gilbert, Sir William Schwenck 3656-3659, 3664-3665, 3668, 3669

Gilfillan, R. 2237

Gille, Phillippe Émile François 810-812, 2314-2318

Gillespie, Arthur 842

Gilm, Hermann von 3619, 3637

Girling, Mabel Elizabeth 3988

Giustiniani, Girolamo Ascanio 2260, 2264, 2265

Glaser, Ray 4048, 4090, 7578

Glazer, Tom 1550, 7551

Gleim, Johann Wilhelm Ludwig 1566, 2562

Glen, William 7187

Glik, Hirsh 1261, 6279

Glinski, K. 3684

Globa, A. 6951, 6972

Goethe, Johann Wolfgang von 239-241, 244, 247, 249, 643, 976, 1183, 1872, 1892, 2152, 2595, 3009, 3011, 3012, 3013, 3014, 3017, 3219, 3235, 3251, 3264, 3270, 3274, 3280, 3285, 3292, 3316, 3317, 3380, 3383, 3543, 3560, 3993, 4080, 4083, 4137, 4138, 5404, 5527, 5528

Goldoni, Carlo 3290

Golenistchev-Kutuzov 2622, 2623

Goltz, Eric von der 1139

Gondinet, Pierre Edmond Julien 810-812

Gongora, Luis 2186

Gorodetsky, S. 3639

Goslawski, Maurycy 6710

Gotter, Friedrich Wilhelm 1085

Graff, George, Jr. 163

Graham of Gartmore 3660

Grant, Mrs. 7000, 7162

Grant, Robert 1572

Grattan, J. P. 729

Graves, Alfred Perceval 4618, 4624, 4737, 4790, 5867, 5871, 5890, 5893, 5907, 5912, 5924, 5925, 5945, 5952, 5959, 5962, 5964, 5969, 5973, 5987, 5991, 5998, 6000, 6003, 6013, 6018, 6025, 6036, 7211

Graves, John Woodcock 4660

Graves, Robert 9164

Gray, Charles 7145

Gray, John 8973, 9277

Greenbank, Harry 1829

Grémont, H. (pseud) See Hartmann, Georges

Grenier, Edouard 2730

Greville, Fulkes 891, 918

Gribitz, Jo 3643

Griffin, Gerald 5901, 5932

Grimke, A. 4113

Grohe, Melchior 412

Groth, Klaus 415, 437

Grübel, J. C. 3024

Grünbaum, Fritz 1030, 3585

Grünwald, A. 4, 5, 6, 7,

Grundtvig, Nicolai F. S. 164, 284-285, 3121, 4143

Grundtvig, Ved Svend 4473

Gruppe 405

Gspandl, Julius Rudolf 2160

Guarini, Giovanni Batt 500, 3067, 6069

Güll, Friedrich Wilhelm 3710

Günther, Johann Christian 3210, 3239

Guerrero, Manuel Ortiz 1088

Guichard, H. 2997

Guillard, Nicolas François 1272

Guinand, E. 2812-2813

Gullberg, Hjalmar 2130, 3987

Gussev, V. 1923

Guthrie, Woody 8066, 8080, 8575, 8576, 8577, 8578, 8579

Guy, Jean Henry 1365, 1366

Haas, Walther 349

Haas, Rudolf 1887

Häring, Georg Wilhelm 2178

Haffner, Karl 3607-3609

Hagedorn, Friedrich von 1293, 1294, 1355

Hagedorn, Hermann 3058

Hahn, Carl F. 1635, 2281

Helévy, Ludovic 316-321, 2692

Halket, George 7098

Hall, Joseph 3330

Hall, Norman H. 1300

Hall, Owen 1829

Halley, W. 7179

Halm 3367

Halpern, I 1005

Halphin, Earnest 995

Halvorsen, M. 3562

Hamilton, Anthony 4925,4930
Hamilton, John 7129,7186
Hamilton, Mary C. D. 2743
Hamilton, N. 1476
Hammerstein, Oscar, II 3063
Hanlon, Bert 3747
Hannes, Hans 2351
Haraucourt, Edouard 1065
Hardt-Warden, Bruno 1866-1867,3591,3640-3641
Harrell, Mack 125,1458,3259,3276
Hart, Heinrich 3620
Hart, Lorenz 3051,3052
Hartman, S. 3752
Hartmann, Georges 2309-2313,2321
Hasentödter, Hans 5218
Hatton, Christopher 1245
Hatzfeld, Adolf von 1931
Hauerbach, Otto A. 1709
Hauff, Wilhelm 2637,5512,5566*
Hausmann, Julie von 3491
Hawkes, R. S. 4760
Hausmann, Otto 337
Havergal, Frances R. 3550
Hayden, Joe 2406
Hayes, Alfred 3045
Hayes, Xavier M. 3813
Haym, N. F. 1441
Hayne, William H. 1353
Hays, Lee 7963
Hebel, Johann Peter 2603,3233,5362
Heber, Reginald 968,1525,3746,3995
Heiberg, J. L. 1996
Heidenstam, Werner von 1523,3568
Heine, Heinrich 427,1149,1150,1160,1775,2151,2368,
        2379,3117,3302,3304,3305,3357,3358,3359,
        3360-3362,3374,3379,3384,3484,3622
Heiseler, Bernt von 2287
Heiser, L. W. 752
Held, Ludwig 4131,4132-4134
Hele, Thomas d' 1368
Hellén, Immi 2682
Heller, H. 1993,1994
Hemans, Felicia 459,8702
Hemmer, Jarl 1832
Henckell, Karl 3627,3628,3631,3636
Henderson, Daniel 2249
Henley, William 845,1398
Henry, Fortuné 5099
Herbert, A. P. 5878
Herbert, William, Earl of Pembroke 2069
Herder, Johann Gottfried 2177
Herman, Nikolaus 3891,3892
Hermanns, Rudolf 2164,2165
Hermannsthal, H. von 460
Hermecke, Hermann 882-883,885,887
Herrick, Robert 416,1555,2059,2060,2061,2070,2071,
        2937-2938,3537,3931,8906,8910
Herrnschmidt, Johann Daniel 5454
Herrossee 250,1582
Hertz, Wilhelm 1776
Herwegh, Georg 2217,2221
Herzer, Ludwig 2091,2092,2094,2095
Hettisch, A. L. 1769
Hewitt, J. H. 3241

Hey, Wilhelm 3476,3493,5566
Heyck, Eduard 2106,2157,2161
Heyck, Hans 2544
Heydt, H. A. 4156
Heyse, Paul 406,4065,4076,4082,4084
Heyward, Du Bose 1242
Hichens, Robert S. 1706
Hiemer, Franz Carl 3977
Hill, Joe 3979
Hill, Patti S. 1653
Hiller, 1355
Hinkson, Katharine Tynan 5940
Hinrichs, Hinrich 3572
Höfling, E. 5497
Hölty, Ludwig Heinrich Christof 407,410,3265,3286,
        3307,3308
Hoffman, François Benoît 2350
Hofmannswaldau 1738
Hofshstein, D. 3463
Hogg, James 1343,6993,7026,7039,7096,7174,7195,7199,
        7204
Hohman, M. L. 659,1243,8877
Hoier, Thomas 2522
Holland, Josiah Gilbert 1530
Hollingsworth, Thekla 980
Holmes, Oliver Wendell 64,2040,3713
Holtei, Carl von 4192,5346
Hooft, P.C. 6621
Hooft, W. D. 6602
Hopkins, Gerard Manley 778
Hopkinson, Francis 8150
Hopkinson, Joseph 2808
Hopper, Edward 1309
Horey, Annette 3149
Hornfeck, Friedrich 2010
Hornig, Josef 1410,1705
Hough, Will M. 1713
Housman, A. E. 3534-3535,3802
Housman, Laurence 2510,2511
Hovey, Richard 470
Howard, Katherine 686*
Howard, Sir Robert H. 2913-2914
Howarth, Ellen C. 3737
Howe, Julia Ward 3565
Howells, William Dean 2228
Howliston, M. H. 8052
Howse, Marguerite 2653
Hoyt, Charles H. 1224
Hubbard, Frances V. 2650
Hübner, Ernst 346
Hückstadt, Friedrich 2718
Huggenberger, Alfred 3216,3222
Hughes, Henry 2064
Hughes, Langston 3470,3582
Hughes, William 5646,5647,5648
Hugo, Victor 1042,1045,1332,1506,2149,2154,3133
Hunter, Eleanor A. 694
Hussein, Tahir 3450

Illica, Luigi 2300,2887-2891,2895-2897,2898-2900,
        2901-2903
Image, Selwyn 3440,3441,3446
Imber, Nephtali Herz 6205

Scott, Sir Walter 2086,3156,3281,3411,3412,7001,7008,
    7078,7154
Scribe, Augustin Eugène 101,861,863-865,1507-1508,2408,
    2409-2411,2413-2414,3870
Scull, Florence 3413
Sears, Edmund Hamilton 965,4039,8949
Sedaine, J. M. 1369,2496,2497
Sedley, Sir Charles 1668,2918
Seidel, Gabriel 2182
Seidel, Heinrich 5273
Selinger, Emily 730
Semp, A. 2714
Semple, Francis 7102
Sequinault 2548
Shadwell, Thomas 2922
Shakespeare, William 311,496,1105,1876,2146,2514,2936,
    4013
    As you like it: 81,83,2526,2745
    Cymbeline: 3309
    Hamlet: 4015,4537,4641
    Henry VIII: 3667
    Love's Labour lost: 84,85
    A midsummer-night's dream: 2394
    Much ado about nothing: 3576
    Othello: 3671
    The Tempest: 87,2924-2926,3670
    Twelfth Night: 86,1578,3556,3939
    Two gentlemen of Verona: 3256
Shaw, David T. 221
Shaw, G. Fernandez 3428
Shelley, Percy Bysshe 1038,2934,3422,3765,4016
Sheridan, William 4632
Shestalov, N. 1841
Shields, Ren 1018
Shlonsky, A. 375
The shoemaker's holiday 4568
Sidney, Sir Philip 909
Siegel, Ralph Maria 4046
Sienkiewicz, Karol 2001
Sigerson, Dr. 5924
Silcher, Mel. von 5432
Silesius, Angelus 1286
Silvestre, Armand 1043,2307,2320
Silvestre, P. A. 1290
Simmonds, James 3417
Simon, Henry W. 2864
Simoni, R. 2904-2906
Simpson, K. W. 8807,9050,9148
Simrock, Karl 2835,5489
Sinclair, Carrie Bell 1745,2222,2815
Sirl, Otto 5614
Sissle, Noble 328
Skinner, John 7184
Sköld, Hannes 1061
Słowaczynski, Jędrzej 6784
Smith, Harry B. 808,1853-1854
Smith, John 7587
Smith, Samuel Francis 2280,7408
Smith, Seba 1601
Smith, Walter C. 4001
Soane, George 1703
Sografi, A. S. 678*
Sola, Wäinö 3464

Solera, Temistocle 3822
Somma, Antonio 3823-3827
Sonnleithner, J. 230,231,232,233
Southey, Robert 4630
Southwell, Robert 1754
Sova, Ant 2006
Spencer, C. Mordaunt 1265
Spitta, C. J. Ph. 1616
Splittegarb, K. F. 9171
Spring-Rice, Cecil 1688
Šrámek, Fráňa 3750,3885
Stall, Lucile Isbell 1416
Stange, Stanislaus 985
Stanley, Ralph 2708
Stchipatchev, S. 2415,2416
Stein, Gertrude 3743
"Stella" of Washington 2742
Stephens, James 168
Stephens, Riccardo 1544
Sterbini, Cesare 3096-3099
Sterk, Wilhelm 3585,3592
Sterling, Andrew 3887,3889
Sterling, George 7394
Sternau, C. O. 5607
Stevenson, Robert Louis 602,1690,1835,3804,3805
Stieler, Karl 3215
Stiles, Lelia C. 2863
Stoddard, Richard Henry 1081
Stöcklein, Erich 2833
Stolberg, Friedrich Leopold Graf 3336
Stoll, Jos. Ludwig 226
Stone, Alfred 3542
Stone, Samuel J. 3996
Stoppe, Daniel 3718,3720
Storck, P. A. 3281
Storey, Violet Alleyn 491
Storm, Theodore 1372,1943,1944,4115
Stowe, Harriet Beecher 2545
Strachwitz, Moritz, Graf von 3213
Strandberg, C. V. A. 2142
Stratton, Mike 1,2
Straub, Celestia 1138
Striggio, A. 2507
Sturm, Chr. 2578
Suchodolski, R. 171
Suckling, Sir John 2063,3959
Sugar, Maurice 7829
Suonio 695
Sventsitski 6859
Svetloff, M. 2882
Sylvester, Joshua 1636
Symons, Arthur 530
Szelestey, 3501
Szenes, Andor 3158,3159

Tagore, Sir Rabindranath 601,1499-1500,1707
Tannahill, Robert 185,3522,7016,7044,7099,7115,7130,
    7149
Tapia, Louis de 2728
Targioni-Tozzetti, G. 2295-2299
Tate, Nahum 126,1488,2339,2908,9009
Taylor, Bayard 2824

Wette, Adelheid (Humperdinck) 1736, 4067
Wetzel, Karl Friedrich Gottlob 4002
White, Johnny 3400
White-Melville, G. J. 3757
Whitehill, Michel 3611
Whiting, George 855
Whiting, William 966
Whitman, Walt 4095
Whymark, H. J. 2085
Wickenburg, Albrecht, Graf von 2166
Wilde, Oscar 680*
Wildgans, Anton 1145
Wilken, H. 701
Willard, Emma 1919
Williams, Charles 2920-2921
Williams, Claude 7963
Williams, Lucy Ariel 681
Williams, William 189
Willner, Alfred Maria 1030
Wilpert, Richard von 2459
Wilson, Fred 447, 1639
Wilson, Steuart 9047, 9111
Wingate, Philip 2790
Winkworth, C. 8947
Winner, Septimus 7560
Winther, Christian 1539, 1905
Wither, George 8989
Witwicki, Stefan 668, 670, 670*, 673*, 6827
Wolff, W. A. P. 3973-3974
Wollheim, Hermann 5542
Wolski, Włodzimierz 2473-2476
Wood, Frances B. 1584, 3895
Wood, J. T. 1182
Woods, Fannie Carter 2879
Woodward, G. R. 68, 8946
Woodward, Samuel 4787
Woodworth, Samuel 1891
Wooler, J. P. 2968
Woolf, B. 684
Wrede, Princess Gabriele 2014
Wybicki, Jozef 6746
Wylie, Elinor 929, 1716
Wyspianski, S. 6885
Wyttenbach, A. 2515

Yang Ching Chin 2126
Yang Lin-Liu 4270
Yazykov, N. 2957
Yeames, James 3435
Yeats, William Butler 5899
Young, Joseph 1076, 1620
Young, Rida Johnson 2704

Zacharjasiewicz, J. 2490
Zaleski, B. 672*
Zamacois, Niceton de 3427
Zanardini, A. 2844
Zangarini, Carlo 2892-2893
Zell, F. (pseud) See Walzel, Camillo
Zeno, Apostolo 72, 1548
Zesen, Phillip von 31
Zhitlowsky, Chaim 6263

Zielinski, G. 2198
Ziganoff, N. G. 3798
Zinzendorf, N. L., Graf von 921
Zuccalmaglio, Anton Wilhelm Florentin von 430, 5414
Zwick, Johannes 3935